Microsoft® Office® XP

Volume I

Microsoft® Office® XP

Volume I

Sarah E. **Hutchinson**

Glen J. **Coulthard**

Boston Burr Ridge, IL Dubuque, IA Madison, WI New York
San Francisco St. Louis Bangkok Bogotá Caracas Kuala Lumpur
Lisbon London Madrid Mexico City Milan Montreal New Delhi
Santiago Seoul Singapore Sydney Taipei Toronto

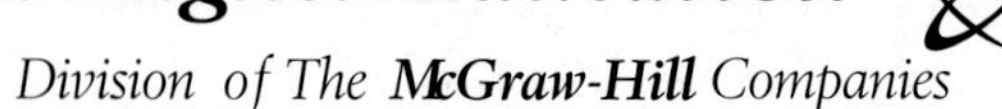

ADVANTAGE SERIES MICROSOFT® OFFICE XP 2002, VOLUME I

Published by McGraw-Hill/Irwin, an imprint of The McGraw-Hill Companies, Inc. 1221 Avenue of the Americas, New York, NY, 10020.

This book is printed on acid-free paper.

4 5 6 7 8 9 0 WEB/WEB 0 9 8 7 6 5 4 3 2

ISBN 0-07-247262-6

Publisher: *George Werthman*
Associate editor: *Steve Schuetz*
Developmental editor: *Craig S. Leonard*
Senior marketing manager: *Jeff Parr*
Senior project manager: *Christine A. Vaughan*
Lead production supervisor: *Heather D. Burbridge*
Senior producer, media technology: *David Barrick*
Freelance design coordinator: *Laurie J. Entringer*
Lead supplement producer: *Marc Mattson*
Cover design: Asylum Studios
Interior design: Asylum Studios
Typeface: *11/13 Garamond 3*
Compositor: *GTS Graphics, Inc.*
Printer: *Webcrafters, Inc.*

Library of Congress Cataloging-in-Publication Data
Hutchinson, Sarah E.
Microsoft Office XP, Volume I / Sarah E. Hutchinson, Glen J. Coulthard.
p. cm. – (Advantage series)
ISBN 0-07-247262-6 (alk paper)
1. Microsoft Office XP, Volume I 2. Business–Computer programs. I. Coulthard, Glen J. II. Title.
III. Series.

HF5548.4.M525 H886 2001
005.369–dc21

2001044377

Information Technology
At McGraw - Hill/Irwin

McGRAW-HILL HIGHER EDUCATION publishes instructional materials for the higher education market. To expand the tools of higher learning, we publish everything you need: texts, lab manuals, study guides, testing materials, software, and multimedia products.

Technology has created and will continue to create new media for professors and students to use in managing resources and communicating with one another. McGraw-Hill/Irwin provides the most flexible and complete teaching and learning tools available as well as solutions to the changing world of teaching and learning. McGraw-Hill/Irwin is dedicated to providing tools for today's instructors and students that will enable them to navigate the world of information technology.

- **Seminar series and focus groups**—McGraw-Hill/Irwin's seminar series and focus groups are offered across the country every year. At the seminar series we provide the latest technology products and encourage collaboration among teaching professionals. We conduct focus groups year round so we can hear from you what we need to publish.
- **Information Technology Advisory Panel (ITAP)**—This is a focus group where we gather top IT educators for three days to tell us how to publish the best IT texts possible. ITAPs are instrumental in driving our publishing plans.
- **McGraw-Hill/Osborne**—This trade division company in the family of the McGraw-Hill Companies is known for its best-selling Internet titles *Harley Hahn's Internet & Web Yellow Pages* and the *Internet Complete Reference.* If what you're looking for isn't in McGraw-Hill/Irwin's CIT/MIS catalogs, visit Osborne at **www.osborne.com**.
- **Digital solutions**—Whether you want to teach a class online or just post your "bricks-and-mortar" class syllabus, McGraw-Hill/Irwin can help. Taking your course online doesn't have to be a solitary adventure, nor does it have to be difficult. We have ways to help you enjoy the benefits of having your course material online.
- **Packaging options**—For more information about our discount options, contact your McGraw-Hill/Irwin sales representative at 1-800-338-3987 or visit our Web site at **www.mhhe.com/it**.

Preface
The Advantage Series

Goals/Philosophy

The @dvantage Series presents the **what, why, and how** of computer application skills to today's students. Each lab manual is built upon an efficient learning model that provides students and faculty with complete coverage of the most powerful software packages available today.

Approach

The @dvantage Series uses an efficient learning model that provides students and faculty with complete coverage and enhances critical thinking skills. This **case-based, problem-solving approach** teaches the what, why, and how of computer application skills.

The @dvantage Series introduces the **Feature-Method-Practice** layered approach. The **Feature** describes the command and tells the importance of that command. The **Method** shows students how to perform the feature. The **Practice** allows students to apply the feature in a keystroke exercise.

About the Series

The @dvantage Series: Offers three levels of instruction. Each level builds upon the previous level. The following are the three levels of instruction:

Brief: Covers the basics of the application, contains two to four chapters, and is typically 120–190 pages long.

Introductory: Includes the Brief lab manuals plus four additional chapters. The Introductory lab manuals are approximately 300 pages long and prepare students for the *Microsoft Office User Specialist Proficient Exam (MOUS Certification).*

Complete: Includes the Introductory lab manuals plus an additional four chapters at an advanced level. The Complete lab manuals are approximately 600–800 pages long and prepare students to take the *Microsoft Office User Specialist Expert Exam (MOUS Certification).*

The lab manuals for the four Office applications are also offered as a set:

Office XP, Volume I: Includes the Brief lab manuals for Word, Excel, Access, and PowerPoint, plus three chapters of Integrating and Extending Microsoft Office XP.

Office XP, Volume II: Includes the additional chapters for the Introductory lab manuals for Word, Excel, Access, and PowerPoint.

Approved Microsoft Courseware

Use of the Microsoft Office User Specialist Approved Courseware logo on this product signifies that it has been independently reviewed and approved as complying with the following standards: acceptable coverage of all content related to the Microsoft Office Exam entitled *Microsoft Office XP, Volume I* and sufficient performance-based exercises that relate closely to all required content, based on sampling of text. For further information on Microsoft's MOUS certification program please visit Microsoft's Web site at **http://www.mous.net/**.

preface

Features of This Book

New and Improved Features

- The new design makes it easier for students to follow the material and succeed with it.
- Twice the number of screenshots from previous editions enhances the visual appeal and helps students successfully complete the hands-on steps.
- 50% more review and exercise material is available on the Web site.
- Updated cases and hands-on exercises provide valuable practice.
- Better implementation of design elements and shading increase usability of the Feature, Method, Practice sections.
- New! Prerequisites for each chapter ensure that students are prepared.

Elements

Each lab manual features the following elements:

- **Learning Objectives:** At the beginning of each chapter, a list of action-oriented objectives is presented to detail what is expected of the students.
- **Prerequisites:** Each chapter begins with a list of prerequisites that identify the skills necessary to complete the modules in that chapter.
- **Chapters:** Each lab manual is divided into chapters.
- **Modules:** Each chapter contains three to five independent modules, requiring appoximately 30–45. minutes each to complete. Although we recommend you complete an entire chapter before proceeding, you may skip or rearrange the order of these modules to best suit your learning needs.
- **Case Studies:** Each chapter begins with a case study. The student is introduced to a fictitious person or company and their immediate problem or opportunity. Throughout the chapter, students obtain the knowledge and skills necessary to meet the challenges presented in the case study. At the end of each chapter, students are asked to solve problems directly related to the case study.
- **Feature-Method-Practice:** Each chapter highlights our unique Feature-Method-Practice layered approach. The *Feature* layer describes the command or technique and persuades students of its importance and relevance. The *Method* layer shows them how to perform the procedure, and the *Practice* layer lets them apply the feature in a hands-on, step-by-step exercise.
- **Instructions:** The numbered step-by-step progression for hands-on examples and exercises is clearly identified. Students will find it easy to follow the logical sequence of keystrokes and mouse clicks with no need to worry about missing a step.
- **In Addition Features:** Placed strategically throughout the chapter, these features provide information on advanced topics that are beyond the scope of the current discussion.
- **Self-Check Questions:** At the end of each module, a brief self-check question appears for students to test their comprehension of the material. Answers to these questions appear at the end of the learning guide.
- **Chapter Summary:** Including a *Command Summary* and *Key Terms,* the summary provides an excellent review of the chapter content and prepares

students for the short-answer, true/false, and multiple-choice questions at the end of each chapter.

- **Hands-On Exercises:** Each chapter includes six hands-on exercises rated according to difficulty level. The easy and moderate projects use a running-case approach, whereby the same person or company appears at the end of each chapter in a particular tutorial. The two *difficult* or *on your own* projects provide greater latitude in applying the software to a variety of creative problem-solving situations.
- **Appendix: Preparing to Use Office XP:** Each lab manual contains this quick reference for Microsoft Windows and Office. This appendix teaches students the fundamentals of using a mouse and a keyboard, illustrates how to interact with a dialog box, and describes the fundamentals of how to use the Office XP Help system.

preface

Features of This Lab Manual

Case Studies

Each chapter begins with a case study. Throughout the chapter, students obtain the knowledge and skills necessary to meet the challenges presented in the case study. At the end of each chapter, students are asked to solve problems directly related to the case study.

Feature-Method-Practice

Each chapter highlights our unique Feature-Method-Practice layered approach. The Feature layer describes the command or technique and persuades students of its importance and relevance. The Method layer shows them how to perform the procedure, and the Practice layer lets them apply the feature in a hands-on, step-by-step exercise.

New Design

The new @dvantage Series design offers a shaded area to maintain the focus in each Feature-Method-Practice section with its numbered step-by-step instructions.

CaseStudy STUDENT TUTORING SERVICES Alex Federov is helping to pay his university tuition by tutoring high school and university students. Over the last two years, he developed an excellent reputation for making complex topics simple and easy to remember.

Although he is an excellent tutor, last year he didn't earn as much as he had expected. Alex thinks his lackluster earnings can be attributed to poor advertising and inadequate record keeping. This year, he plans to operate his tutoring services more like a real business. His first priority is to learn how to use Microsoft Word so that he can prepare advertising materials, send faxes and memos, and organize his student notes.

In this chapter, you and Alex create simple documents from scratch and from built-in document templates. You will save, open, and print your work and create file folders for keeping your work organized. You will also perform basic editing procedures including using the Undo command, correcting mistakes as you type, and selecting and changing text.

1.1 Getting Started with Word

Microsoft Word is a **word processing** application program that enables you to create, edit, format, and print many types of documents including résumés and cover letters, reports and proposals, World Wide Web pages, and more. By the time you complete this learning guide, you will be skilled in creating all types of documents and in getting them to look the way you want. In this module, you load Microsoft Word and proceed through a guided tour of its primary components.

1.1.1 Loading and Exiting Word

feature → You load Word from the Windows Start menu, accessed by clicking the Start button (Start) on the taskbar. Because Word requires a significant amount of memory, you should always exit the application when you are finished doing your work. Most Windows applications allow you to close their windows by clicking the Close button (☒) appearing in the top right-hand corner.

method → To load Word:

- CLICK: Start button (Start)
- CHOOSE: Programs, Microsoft Word

To exit Word:

- CLICK: Close button (☒) appearing in the top right-hand corner, or
- CHOOSE: File, Exit from Word's Menu bar

practice → You will now launch Microsoft Word using the Windows Start menu.

1. Position the mouse pointer over the top of the Start button (Start) and then click the left mouse button once. The Start pop-up menu appears.

preface

Features of This Lab Manual

Chapter 4 Printing and Web Publishing WD 153
5. Since it is our intention to keep the first page header and footer blank, let's close the Header and Footer toolbar.
CLICK: Close button on the Header and Footer toolbar
6. Save and then close the "Web Business" document.
In Addition CHANGING PAGE ORIENTATION WITH SECTION BREAKS
To change the page orientation for a portion of a document, you can use section breaks. This procedure is useful when your document or report includes a table that is wider than the default page width. To change the orientation of a portion of a document from portrait to landscape, or vice versa, position the insertion point in the section you want to change and then choose File, Page Setup. Then, click the Margins tab and select a button in the Orientation area. To complete the procedure, select "This section" from the Apply to drop-down list and click the OK command button.
Word

4.4 What are sections used for?
4.5 Publishing to the Web
For those of you new to the online world, the Internet is a vast collection of computer networks that spans the entire planet, made up of many smaller networks connected by standard telephone lines, fiber optics, and satellites. The term intranet refers to a private and usually secure local or wide area network that uses Internet technologies to share information. To access the Internet, you need a network or modem connection that links your computer to your account on the university's network or an independent service provider (ISP).
Hands-On exercises

1. Laura Howard: Customizing a Resume
Laura is still in the job hunt. In this exercise, you assume the role of Laura and practice changing margins and inserting and modifying a header.
1. Open the WD04HE01 data file. This document provides a model for a sample résumé.
2. Save the document as "LH Resume" to your personal storage location.
3. To set the left and right margins to 0.5":
CHOOSE: File, Page Setup
CLICK: Margins tab
CLICK: down arrow beside the Left margin text box until the value decreases to 0.5"
CLICK: down arrow beside the Right margin text box until the value decreases to 0.5"
CLICK: OK command button

In Addition Features

Placed strategically throughout the chapter, these features provide information on topics that are beyond the scope of the current discussion.

Self-Check Questions

At the end of each module, a brief self-check question appears for students to test their comprehension of the material. Answers to these questions appear at the end of the learning guide.

Instruction

The numbered step-by-step progression for hands-on examples and exercises is clearly identified. Students will find it easy to follow the logical sequence of keystrokes and mouse clicks, and not worry about missing a step.

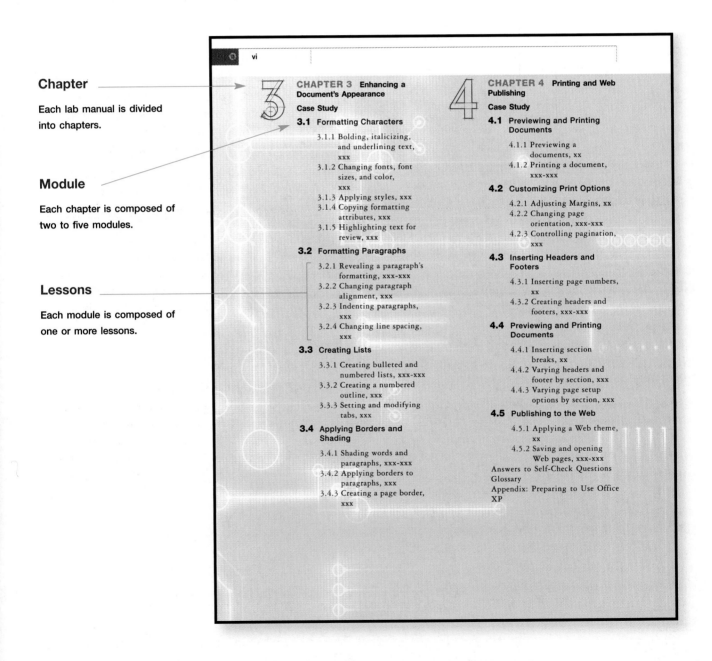

preface

Features of This Lab Manual

Chapter

Each lab manual is divided into chapters.

Module

Each chapter is composed of two to five modules.

Lessons

Each module is composed of one or more lessons.

vi

CHAPTER 3 Enhancing a Document's Appearance

Case Study

3.1 Formatting Characters

3.1.1 Bolding, italicizing, and underlining text, xxx
3.1.2 Changing fonts, font sizes, and color, xxx
3.1.3 Applying styles, xxx
3.1.4 Copying formatting attributes, xxx
3.1.5 Highlighting text for review, xxx

3.2 Formatting Paragraphs

3.2.1 Revealing a paragraph's formatting, xxx-xxx
3.2.2 Changing paragraph alignment, xxx
3.2.3 Indenting paragraphs, xxx
3.2.4 Changing line spacing, xxx

3.3 Creating Lists

3.3.1 Creating bulleted and numbered lists, xxx-xxx
3.3.2 Creating a numbered outline, xxx
3.3.3 Setting and modifying tabs, xxx

3.4 Applying Borders and Shading

3.4.1 Shading words and paragraphs, xxx-xxx
3.4.2 Applying borders to paragraphs, xxx
3.4.3 Creating a page border, xxx

CHAPTER 4 Printing and Web Publishing

Case Study

4.1 Previewing and Printing Documents

4.1.1 Previewing a documents, xx
4.1.2 Printing a document, xxx-xxx

4.2 Customizing Print Options

4.2.1 Adjusting Margins, xx
4.2.2 Changing page orientation, xxx-xxx
4.2.3 Controlling pagination, xxx

4.3 Inserting Headers and Footers

4.3.1 Inserting page numbers, xx
4.3.2 Creating headers and footers, xxx-xxx

4.4 Previewing and Printing Documents

4.4.1 Inserting section breaks, xx
4.4.2 Varying headers and footer by section, xxx
4.4.3 Varying page setup options by section, xxx

4.5 Publishing to the Web

4.5.1 Applying a Web theme, xx
4.5.2 Saving and opening Web pages, xxx-xxx

Answers to Self-Check Questions
Glossary
Appendix: Preparing to Use Office XP

preface

Teaching Resources

We understand that in today's teaching environment, offering a textbook alone is not sufficient to meet the needs of the many instructors who use our books. To teach effectively, instructors must have a full complement of supplemental resources to assist them in every facet of teaching from preparing for class, to conducting a lecture, to assessing students' comprehension. ***The @dvantage Series*** offers a fully integrated supplements package and Web site, as described below.

Instructor's Resource Kit

The Instructor's Resource Kit contains an Instructor's Manual, a computerized Test Bank, and PowerPoint presentation slides:

- **Instructor's Manual:** The Instructor's Manual contains a chapter overview, lecture outlines, teaching tips, teaching strategies, pre-tests, post-tests, and additional case problems. Also included are answers to all end-of chapter material.
- **Computerized test bank:** The test bank contains over 1,200 multiple-choice, true/false, fill-in-the-blank, short-answer, and essay questions. Each question is accompanied by the correct answer, the level of learning difficulty, section number reference, corresponding page references, and mouse objective reference. Our flexible Diploma software allows you to easily generate custom exams.
- **PowerPoint presentation slides:** The presentation slides include lecture outlines, text figures, and speaker's notes. Also included are bullets to illustrate key terms and answers to frequently asked questions.

Online Learning Center (OLC) Web Site

Found at **www.mhhe.com/cit/advantage2002**, this site provides additional learning and instructional tools to enhance the comprehension of the text. The OLC Web site is divided into these three areas:

- **Information Center:** Contains core information about the text, supplements, and the authors.
- **Instructor Center:** Offers instructional materials, downloads, additional exercises, and other relevant links for professors.
- **Student Center:** Consists of 50% more end-of-chapter questions, hands-on projects, matching exercises, Internet exercises, learning objectives, prerequisites, chapter outlines, and more!

Skills Assessment

SimNet eXPert (Simulated Network Assessment Product)—SimNet provides a way for you to test students' software skills in a simulated environment. SimNet is available for Microsoft Office 97, Microsoft Office 2000, and Microsoft Office XP. SimNet provides flexibility for you in your course by offering:

- Pre-testing options
- Post-testing options
- Course placement testing
- Diagnostic capabilities to reinforce skills
- Proficiency testing to measure skills
- Web or LAN delivery of tests
- Computer-based training tutorials (new for Office XP)

- MOUS preparation exams
- Learning verification reports
- Spanish version

For more information on skills assessment software, please contact your local sales representative, or visit us at **www.mhhe.com/it**.

Digital Solutions to Help You Manage Your Course

- **PageOut** PageOut is our Course Web Site Development Center that offers a syllabus page, URL, McGraw-Hill Online Learning Center content, online exercises and quizzes, grade book, discussion board, and an area for student Web pages.

  Available free with any McGraw-Hill/Irwin product, PageOut requires no prior knowledge of HTML, no long hours of coding, and a way for course coordinators and professors to provide a full-course Web site. PageOut offers a series of templates—simply fill them with your course information and click on one of 16 designs. The process takes under an hour and leaves you with a *professionally designed Web site.* We'll even get you started with sample Web sites, or enter your syllabus for you! PageOut is so straightforward and intuitive, it's little wonder that over 12,000 college professors are using it.

  For more information, visit the PageOut Web site at **www.pageout.net**.

- **Online Courses Available** Online Learning Centers (OLCs) are your perfect solutions for Internet-based content. Simply put, these centers are "digital cartridges" that contain a book's pedagogy and supplements. As students read the book, they can go online and take self-grading quizzes or work through interactive exercises. The centers also provide students appropriate access to lecture materials and other key supplements.

  Online Learning Centers can be delivered through any of these platforms:

  - McGraw-Hill Learning Architecture (TopClass)
  - Blackboard.com
  - eCollege.com (formerly Real Education)
  - WebCT (a product of Universal Learning Technology)

  McGraw-Hill has partnerships with **WebCT** and **Blackboard** to make it even easier to take your course online. Now you can have McGraw-Hill content delivered through the leading Internet-based learning tool for higher education.

  McGraw-Hill has the following service agreements with WebCT and Blackboard:

  - **Instructor Advantage:** Instructor Advantage is a special level of service McGraw-Hill offers in conjunction with WebCT to help you get up and running with your new course. A *team of specialists* will be immediately available to ensure everything runs smoothly through the life of your adoption.
  - **Instructor Advantage Plus:** Qualified McGraw-Hill adopters will be eligible for an even higher level of service. A certified WebCT or Blackboard specialist will provide a full day of on-site training for you and your staff. You will then have unlimited e-mail and phone support through the life of your adoption. Please contact your local McGraw-Hill representative for more details.

- **PowerWeb** PowerWeb is an exciting new online product available from McGraw-Hill. A nominally priced token grants students access through our Web site to a wealth of resources—all contributing to computer literacy. Features include an interactive glossary; current events with quizzing, assessment, and measurement options; a Web survey; links to related text content; and Web-searching capability via Northern Lights, an academic search engine. Visit the PowerWeb site at **www.dushkin.com/powerweb**.

preface

Acknowledgments

This series of tutorials is the direct result of the teamwork and heart of many people. We sincerely thank the reviewers, instructors, and students who have shared their comments and suggestions with us over the past few years. We do read them! With their valuable feedback, our tutorials have evolved into the product you see before you.

Many thanks go to Steve Schuetz and Craig Leonard, whose management helped to get this book produced in a timely and efficient manner. Special recognition goes to all of the individuals mentioned in the credits on the copyright page. And finally, to the many others who weren't directly involved in this project but who have stood by us the whole way, we appreciate your encouragement and support.

Special Thanks to the Advantage Team

We would like to thank the following technical editors, who worked so hard to make sure every book is accurate:

Ric Blamer, John Carroll University

Joan Blumeyer, Palomar College

Tony Bower, St. Philip's College

George Dollar, Clearwater Christian College

Joanne Fitzpatrick, Merrimack College

Shelley Gaskin, Pasadena City College

Donna Guillot, Quinebaug Valley College

Rhonda Henderson, North Carolina A&T State University

Michelle Hulett, Southwest Missouri State University

Thelma King, North Carolina A&T State University

Harry Knight, Franklin University

Mary Alys Lillard, Southern Methodist University

Marilyn Meyer, Fresno City College

Laura Nicholson, Northern Oklahoma College

Judy Novakowski, Oakland Community College

Vic Picinich, Heald College

Krystal Scott, Oklahoma Baptist University

Mike Scroggins, Southwest Missouri State University

Thanks also to our supplement authors, Ed Blevins of DeVry Institute of Technology—Dallas, and Pete DePasquale of Virginia Tech.

We also thank Lori Becker and her Graphics team at GTS Publishing Services for shepherding the book through production, Verlaine Murphy for her work on the Microsoft Office XP 2002, Volume II manual and Anita Wagner for her professional advice and skillful copyediting.

Write to Us

We welcome your response to this tutorial, for we are trying to make it as useful a learning tool as possible. Please contact us at

Sarah E. Hutchinson—sclifford@home.com

Glen J. Coulthard—glen@coulthard.com

APPROVED COURSEWARE

What Does This Logo Mean?

It means this courseware has been approved by the Microsoft® Office User Specialist Program to be among the finest available for learning Microsoft Office XP, Microsoft Word 2002, Microsoft Excel 2002, Microsoft PowerPoint 2002 and Microsoft Access 2002. It also means that upon completion of this courseware, you may be prepared to become a Microsoft Office User Specialist.

What Is a Microsoft Office User Specialist?

A Microsoft Office User Specialist is an individual who has certified his or her skills in one or more of the Microsoft Office desktop applications of Microsoft Word, Microsoft Excel, Microsoft PowerPoint® or Microsoft Access. The Microsoft Office User Specialist Program typically offers certification exams at the "Core" and "Expert" skill levels.* The Microsoft Office User Specialist Program is the only Microsoft-approved program in the world for certifying proficiency in Microsoft Office desktop applications. This certification can be a valuable asset in any job search or career advancement.

More Information

To learn more about becoming a Microsoft Office User Specialist, visit **www.mous.net**

To purchase a Microsoft Office User Specialist certification exam, visit **www.DesktopIQ.com**

To learn about other Microsoft Office User Specialist approved courseware from McGraw Hill/Irwin, visit **http://www.mhhe.com/catalogs/irwin/cit/mous/index.mhtml.**

*The availability of Microsoft Office User Specialist certification exams varies by application, application version, and language. Visit www.mous.net for exam availability.

Who benefits from Microsoft® Office User Specialist certifications?

Employers Microsoft Office User Specialist ("MOUS") certification helps satisfy employers' needs for qualitative assessments of employees' skills. Training, coupled with MOUS certification, offers organizations of every size the ability to enhance productivity and efficiency by enabling their employees to unlock many advanced and labor-saving features in Microsoft Office applications. MOUS certification can ultimately improve the bottom line.

Employees MOUS certification demonstrates employees' productivity and competence in Microsoft Office applications, the most popular business applications in the world. Achieving MOUS certification verifies that employees have the confidence and ability to use Microsoft Office applications in meeting and exceeding their work challenges.

Instructors MOUS certification validates instructors' knowledge and skill in using Microsoft Office applications. It serves as a valuable credential, demonstrating their potential to teach students these essential applications. The MOUS Authorized Instructor program is also available to those who wish to further demonstrate their instructional capabilities.

Students MOUS certification distinguishes students from their peers. It demonstrates their efficiency in completing assignments and projects, leaving more time for other studies. Improved confidence in meeting new challenges and obstacles is yet another benefit. Achieving MOUS certification gives students the marketable skills necessary to set them apart in the competitive job market.

Contents Word

PART 1 WORD

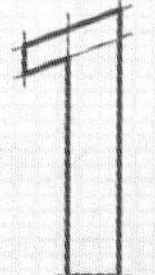

CHAPTER 1 Creating a Document

Case Study

1.1 Getting Started with Word

1.1.1 Loading and exiting Word, 2
1.1.2 Touring Word, 3
1.1.3 Customizing menus and toolbars, 6

1.2 Creating Your First Document

1.2.1 Inserting and deleting text, 10
1.2.2 Inserting the date and time, 14
1.2.3 Putting "word wrap" to work, 15
1.2.4 Using smart tags, 16

1.3 Managing Files

1.3.1 Beginning a new document, 19
1.3.2 Saving and closing a document, 22
1.3.3 Opening and printing a document, 25
1.3.4 Creating a new file folder, 28

1.4 Customizing Your Work Area

1.4.1 Selecting a view, 31
1.4.2 Zooming the display, 33

CHAPTER 2 Modifying a Document

Case Study

2.1 Editing a Document

2.1.1 Positioning the insertion point, 49
2.1.2 Using Undo and Redo, 52
2.1.3 Correcting mistakes as you go, 53
2.1.4 Selecting and changing text, 54

2.2 Finding and Replacing Text

2.2.1 Finding text, 57
2.2.2 Replacing text, 59

2.3 Copying and Moving Information

2.3.1 Using the Clipboard, 61
2.3.2 Using drag and drop, 64

2.4 Proofing a Document

2.4.1 Using the spelling and grammar checker, 66
2.4.2 Using the Thesaurus, 69

CHAPTER 3 Enhancing a Document's Appearance

Case Study

3.1 Formatting Characters

3.1.1 Bolding, italicizing, and underlining text, 83
3.1.2 Changing fonts, font sizes, and colors, 85
3.1.3 Applying styles, 87
3.1.4 Copying formatting attributes, 90
3.1.5 Highlighting text for review, 92

3.2 Formatting Paragraphs

3.2.1 Revealing a paragraph's formatting, 93
3.2.2 Changing paragraph alignment, 95
3.2.3 Indenting paragraphs, 97
3.2.4 Changing line spacing, 100

3.3 Creating Lists

3.3.1 Creating bulleted and numbered lists, 102
3.3.2 Creating a numbered outline, 105
3.3.3 Setting and modifying tabs, 108

3.4 Applying Borders and Shading

3.4.1 Shading words and paragraphs, 111
3.4.2 Applying borders to paragraphs, 113
3.4.3 Creating a page border, 116

CHAPTER 4 Printing and Web Publishing

Case Study

4.1 Previewing and Printing Documents

4.1.1 Previewing a document, 130
4.1.2 Printing a document, 132

4.2 Customizing Print Options

4.2.1 Adjusting margins, 134
4.2.2 Changing page orientation, 136
4.2.3 Controlling pagination, 137

4.3 Inserting Headers and Footers

4.3.1 Inserting page numbers, 141
4.3.2 Creating headers and footers, 142

4.4 Using Sections to Apply Varied Formatting

4.4.1 Inserting section breaks, 145
4.4.2 Varying headers and footer by section, 148
4.4.3 Varying page setup options by section, 151

4.5 Publishing to the Web

4.5.1 Applying a Web theme, 154
4.5.2 Saving and opening Web pages, 156

Answers to Self-Check Questions
Glossary
Appendix: Preparing to Use Office XP

Contents Excel

PART 1 EXCEL

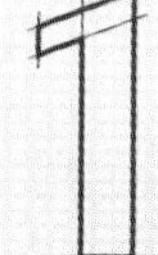

CHAPTER 1 Creating a Worksheet

Case Study

1.1 Getting Started with Excel

1.1.1 Loading and Exiting Excel, 4
1.1.2 Touring Excel, 5
1.1.3 Customizing Menus and Toolbars, 8

1.2 Creating Your First Worksheet

1.2.1 Moving the Cell Pointer, 11
1.2.2 Entering Text, 13
1.2.3 Entering Dates, 15
1.2.4 Entering Numbers, 16
1.2.5 Entering Formulas, 17

1.3 Editing Your Work

1.3.1 Editing a Cell's Contents, 21
1.3.2 Selecting and Erasing Cell Contents, 24
1.3.3 Using Undo and Redo, 26

1.4 Managing Files

1.4.1 Beginning a New Workbook, 28
1.4.2 Saving and Closing, 30
1.4.3 Opening an Existing Workbook, 34
1.4.4 Creating a Workbook Folder, 36

CHAPTER 2 Modifying a Worksheet

Case Study

2.1 Entering and Reviewing Data

2.1.1 Selecting Cells and Ranges, 56
2.1.2 Entering Data Using AutoComplete, 60
2.1.3 Using AutoCalculate and AutoSum, 62
2.1.4 Inserting and Deleting Cells, 66

2.2 Copying and Moving Data

2.2.1 Using the Windows Clipboard, 69
2.2.2 Using the Office Clipboard, 72
2.2.3 Using Drag and Drop, 75
2.2.4 Creating a Series Using AutoFill, 77
2.2.5 Extending a Cell's Contents, 80

2.3 Modifying Rows and Columns

2.3.1 Changing Column Widths, 83
2.3.2 Changing Row Heights, 86
2.3.3 Inserting and Deleting Rows and Columns, 88
2.3.4 Hiding and Unhiding Rows and Columns, 91

CHAPTER 3 Formatting and Printing

Case Study

3.1 Enhancing a Worksheet's Appearance

3.1.1 Applying Fonts, Font Styles, and Colors, 110
3.1.2 Formatting Numbers and Dates, 114
3.1.3 Aligning, Merging, and Rotating Cells, 117
3.1.4 Adding Borders and Shading, 120

3.2 Applying and Removing Formatting

3.2.1 Using Format Painter, 124
3.2.2 Removing Formatting Attributes, 127
3.2.3 Using the Paste Special Command, 129
3.2.4 Using the AutoFormat Command, 131

3.3 Printing and Web Publishing

3.3.1 Previewing and Printing a Worksheet, 133
3.3.2 Previewing and Publishing to the Web, 136

3.4 Customizing Print Options

3.4.1 Adjusting Page and Margin Settings, 139
3.4.2 Inserting Headers and Footers, 141
3.4.3 Selecting Worksheet Content to Print, 143

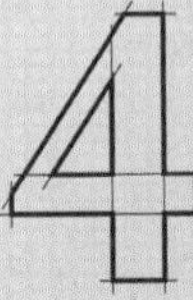

CHAPTER 4 Analyzing Your Data

Case Study

4.1 Working with Named Ranges

4.1.1 Naming Cell Ranges, 162
4.1.2 Managing Range Names, 165
4.1.3 Using References in Formulas, 167
4.1.4 Entering Natural Language Formulas, 169

4.2 Using Built-In Functions

4.2.1 Adding Values (SUM), 172
4.2.2 Calculating Averages (AVERAGE), 174
4.2.3 Counting Values (COUNT), 175
4.2.4 Analyzing Values (MIN and MAX), 176
4.2.5 Calculating Dates (NOW and TODAY), 179

4.3 Creating an Embedded Chart

4.3.1 Creating a Chart Using the Chart Wizard, 185
4.3.2 Previewing and Printing an Embedded Chart, 189

Answers to Self-Check Questions
Glossary
Appendix: Preparing to Use Office XP

Contents PowerPoint

PART 1 POWERPOINT

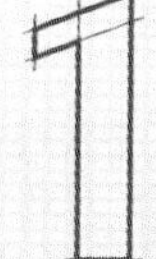

CHAPTER 1 Creating a Presentation

Case Study

1.1 Getting Started with PowerPoint

1.1.1 Loading and Exiting PowerPoint, 2
1.1.2 Touring PowerPoint, 4
1.1.3 Customizing Toolbars, 6

1.2 Starting a New Presentation

1.2.1 Starting with the AutoContent Wizard, 9
1.2.2 Starting with a Design Template, 13

1.3 Creating a Textual Presentation

1.3.1 Starting with a Blank Presentation, 16
1.3.2 Creating a Title Slide, 18
1.3.3 Inserting New Slides and Using the Outline Tab, 20
1.3.4 Formatting Text on Slides, 23

1.4 Managing Files

1.4.1 Saving and Closing a Presentation, 26
1.4.2 Opening an Existing Presentation, 29
1.4.3 Printing a Presentation, 30
1.4.4 Creating a New File Folder, 31

CHAPTER 2 Modifying and Running Presentations

Case Study

2.1 Editing Slides

2.1.1 Applying an Alternate Layout, 48
2.1.2 Customizing Placeholders, 51
2.1.3 Changing Slide Order, 53
2.1.4 Adding Footer Text, 54

2.2 Changing a Presentation's Design

2.2.1 Applying an Alternate Design Template, 57
2.2.2 Applying Multiple Design Templates, 58
2.2.3 Editing a Design Template, 59

2.3 Running a Slide Show

2.3.1 Starting Slide Shows, 62
2.3.2 Navigating Slide Shows, 64

CHAPTER 3 Adding Graphics

Case Study

3.1 Inserting Clip Art, Pictures, and More

3.1.1 Inserting Clip Art, 82
3.1.2 Inserting Pictures, 88
3.1.3 Inserting Graphs, 90
3.1.4 Inserting Organization Charts, 95

3.2 Inserting Draw Objects

3.2.1 Inserting Objects on the Draw Layer, 99
3.2.2 Manipulating and Formatting Draw Objects, 102
3.2.3 Ordering and Grouping Objects, 107

3.3 Inserting Text Labels

3.3.1 Labeling Draw Objects, 109
3.3.2 Inserting Text Outside Placeholders, 111

Answers to Self-Check Questions
Glossary
Appendix: Preparing to Use Office XP

Contents Access

PART 1 ACCESS

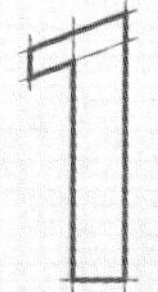

CHAPTER 1 Working with Access

Case Study

1.1 Getting Started with Access

1.1.1 Loading and Exiting Access, 3
1.1.2 Opening a Database File at Startup, 4
1.1.3 Touring Access, 7
1.1.4 Working in the Database Window, 10

1.2 Viewing and Printing Your Data

1.2.1 Moving Around a Datasheet, 14
1.2.2 Adjusting Column Widths and Row Heights, 18
1.2.3 Previewing and Printing, 20

1.3 Manipulating Table Data

1.3.1 Selecting and Editing Data, 23
1.3.2 Using the Undo Command, 26
1.3.3 Adding Records, 27
1.3.4 Deleting Records, 30

CHAPTER 2 Creating a Database

Case Study

2.1 Designing Your First Database

2.1.1 Planning a Database, 50
2.1.2 Starting a New Database, 51
2.1.3 Employing the Database Wizard, 54

2.2 Creating a Simple Table

2.2.1 Creating a Table Using the Table Wizard, 60
2.2.2 Creating a Table in Datasheet View, 63

2.3 Using the Table Design View

2.3.1 Creating a Table in Design View, 65
2.3.2 Assigning a Primary Key, 68
2.3.3 Defining and Removing Indexes, 70

2.4 Modifying a Table

2.4.1 Inserting and Deleting Fields, 72
2.4.2 Renaming and Moving Fields, 75
2.4.3 Printing a Table's Design Structure, 77

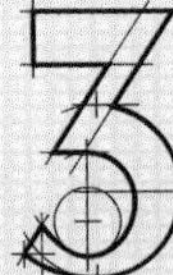

CHAPTER 3 Organizing and Retrieving Data

Case Study

3.1 Customizing Datasheet View

3.1.1 Formatting a Datasheet, 98
3.1.2 Changing the Field Column Order, 101
3.1.3 Hiding and Unhiding Columns, 103
3.1.4 Freezing and Unfreezing Columns, 106

3.2 Sorting, Finding, and Maintaining Data

3.2.1 Sorting Records in a Datasheet, 107
3.2.2 Performing a Simple Search, 110
3.2.3 Specifying Search Patterns, 111
3.2.4 Performing a Find and Replace, 113
3.2.5 Spell-Checking a Datasheet, 114

3.3 Using Filters

3.3.1 Filtering for Input, 116
3.3.2 Filtering by Selection, 118
3.3.3 Filtering by Form, 120

3.4 Creating a Simple Query

3.4.1 Creating a Query Using the Query Wizard, 124
3.4.2 Displaying the Query Window, 127

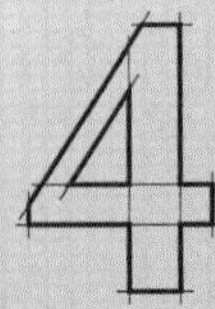

CHAPTER 4 Presenting and Managing Data

Case Study

4.1 Creating a Simple Form

4.1.1 Creating a Form Using the AutoForm Wizards, 147
4.1.2 Creating a Form Using the Form Wizard, 151
4.1.3 Navigating Data Using a Form, 155
4.1.4 Working with a Form, 158

4.2 Creating a Simple Report

4.2.1 Creating a Report Using the AutoReport Wizards, 161
4.2.2 Creating a Report Using the Report Wizard, 163
4.2.3 Previewing and Printing a Report, 167
4.2.4 Publishing a Static Report to the Web, 170

4.3 Generating a Mailing Labels Report

4.3.1 Creating a Report Using the Label Wizard, 174

4.4 Managing Database Objects

4.4.1 Renaming, Copying, and Deleting Objects, 180
4.4.2 Compacting, Repairing, and Converting a Database, 183

Answers to Self-Check Questions
Glossary
Appendix: Preparing to Use Office XP

Contents Integrating

PART 1 INTEGRATING

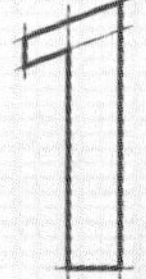

CHAPTER 1 Integrating Word and Excel

Case Study

1.1 Using the Office Clipboard

1.1.1 Activating the Office Clipboard, 2
1.1.2 Pasting and Clearing Clipboard Items, 6

1.2 Pasting, Linking, and Embedding

1.2.1 Pasting Data from Word to Excel, 10
1.2.2 Linking Excel Data to a Word Document, 12
1.2.3 Embedding Excel Data in a Word Document, 15

1.3 Manipulating Shared Objects

1.3.1 Moving, Resizing, and Deleting Shared Objects, 17
1.3.2 Editing Shared Objects, 19

1.4 Inserting New Worksheets and Charts in Word

1.4.1 Inserting a New Worksheet in Word, 21
1.4.2 Inserting a New Chart in Word, 22

CHAPTER 2 Performing More Integration Tasks

Case Study

2.1 Creating a Presentation from a Word Document

2.1.1 Creating an Outline in Word, 42
2.1.2 Converting a Word Outline to PowerPoint, 44

2.2 Integrating PowerPoint with Word and Excel

2.2.1 Copying PowerPoint Slides to Word, 46
2.2.2 Copying an Excel Chart to PowerPoint, 49

2.3 Integrating Access with Word and Excel

2.3.1 Exporting Access Reports to Word, 51
2.3.2 Exporting a Worksheet List to Access, 54

CHAPTER 3 Extending Microsoft Office to the Web

Case Study

3.1 Using Hyperlinks

3.1.1 Inserting Hyperlinks in Office Documents, 72
3.1.2 Browsing with the Web Toolbar, 76

3.2 Saving Existing Documents to HTML

3.2.1 Saving Word, Excel, and PowerPoint Documents to HTML, 78
3.2.2 Displaying an Access Table on the Web, 82

3.3 Preparing Web Pages Using Office

3.3.1 Applying Web Themes to Word Documents, 87
3.3.2 Creating a Framed Table of Contents in Word, 89
3.3.3 Creating an Interactive Worksheet Page, 90
3.3.4 Customizing a Web Presentation, 94

Answers to Self-Check Questions
Glossary
Appendix: Preparing to Use Office XP

Contents End Matter

Word

Answers to Self Check, **EM/WD-1**

Glossary, **EM/WD-3**

Index, **EM/WD-6**

Excel

Answers to Self Check, **EM/EX-10**

Glossary, **EM/EX-12**

Index, **EM/EX-16**

PowerPoint

Answers to Self Check, **EM/PP-19**

Glossary, **EM/PP-20**

Index, **EM/PP-22**

Access

Answers to Self Check, **EM/AC-26**

Glossary, **EM/AC-28**

Index, **EM/AC-32**

Integrating

Answers to Self Check, **EM/IMO-35**

Glossary, **EM/IMO-36**

Index, **EM/AP-22**

@dvantage series

Microsoft® Office® XP

Volume I

Microsoft® **Word**®

2002

CHAPTER 1

Creating a Document

CHAPTER OUTLINE

Case Study

1.1 Getting Started with Word

1.2 Creating Your First Document

1.3 Managing Files

1.4 Customizing Your Work Area

Chapter Summary

Chapter Quiz

Hands-On Exercises

Case Problems

PREREQUISITES

Although this chapter assumes no previous experience using Microsoft Word, you should be comfortable using a keyboard. You should know how to use a mouse in the Microsoft Windows environment. You should be able to launch and exit programs and perform basic Windows file management operations, such as opening and closing documents.

LEARNING OBJECTIVES

After completing this chapter, you will be able to:

- Identify different components of the application window
- Select commands and options using the Menu bar and right-click menus
- Create, save, open, and print a document
- Correct mistakes

CaseStudy STUDENT TUTORING SERVICES

Alex Federov is helping to pay his university tuition by tutoring high school and university students. Over the last two years, he developed an excellent reputation for making complex topics simple and easy to remember.

Although he is an excellent tutor, last year he didn't earn as much as he had expected. Alex thinks his lackluster earnings can be attributed to poor advertising and inadequate record keeping. This year, he plans to operate his tutoring services more like a real business. His first priority is to learn how to use Microsoft Word so that he can prepare advertising materials, send faxes and memos, and organize his student notes.

In this chapter, you and Alex create simple documents from scratch and from built-in document templates. You will save, open, and print your work and create file folders for keeping your work organized. You will also perform basic editing procedures including using the Undo command, correcting mistakes as you type, and selecting and changing text.

1.1 Getting Started with Word

Microsoft Word is a **word processing** application program that enables you to create, edit, format, and print many types of documents including résumés and cover letters, reports and proposals, World Wide Web pages, and more. By the time you complete this learning guide, you will be skilled in creating all types of documents and in getting them to look the way you want. In this module, you load Microsoft Word and proceed through a guided tour of its primary components.

1.1.1 Loading and Exiting Word

feature

You load Word from the Windows Start menu, accessed by clicking the Start button (Start) on the taskbar. Because Word requires a significant amount of memory, you should always exit the application when you are finished doing your work. Most Windows applications allow you to close their windows by clicking the Close button (✕) appearing in the top right-hand corner.

method

To load Word:

- CLICK: Start button (Start) on the Windows taskbar
- CHOOSE: Programs, Microsoft Word

To exit Word:

- CLICK: Close button (✕) appearing in the top right-hand corner

or

- CHOOSE: File, Exit from Word's Menu bar

practice

You will now launch Microsoft Word using the Windows Start menu.

1. Position the mouse pointer over the top of the Start button (Start) and then click the left mouse button once. The Start pop-up menu appears.

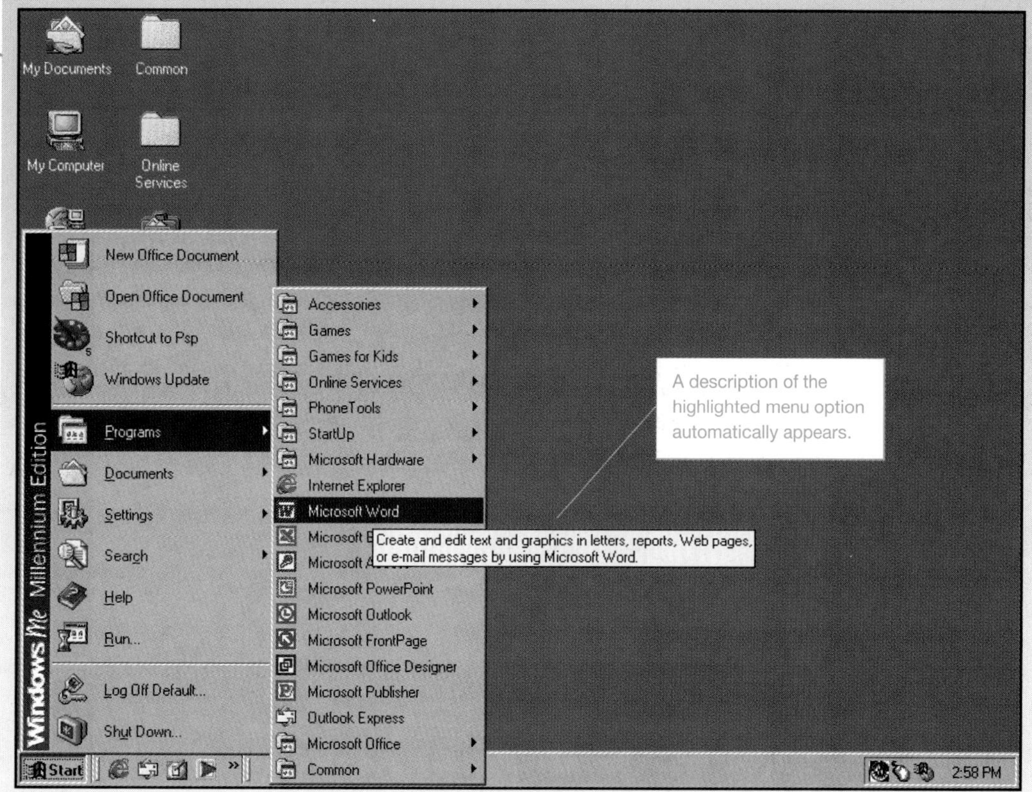

Figure 1.1

The Programs menu

2. Point to the Programs cascading command using the mouse. Note that you do not need to click the left mouse button to display the list of programs in the fly-out or cascading menu.
3. Move the mouse pointer horizontally to the right until it highlights an option in the Programs menu. You can now move the mouse pointer vertically within the menu to select an option. Your screen may now appear similar, but not identical, to Figure 1.1.
4. Point to the Microsoft Word menu item and then click the left mouse button once to execute the command. After a few seconds, the Microsoft Word screen appears.
5. After a few more seconds, an Office Assistant character, like "Clippit" (shown at the right), may appear. You learn how to hide this character in lesson 1.1.2.

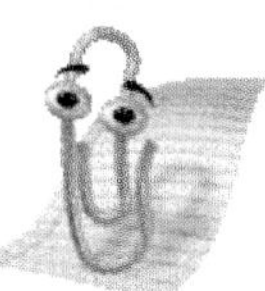

1.1.2 Touring Word

The Word **application window** acts as a container for your document. It contains the primary interface components for working in Word including the *Windows icons, Menu bar, toolbars, task pane,* and *status bar.* It also includes several tools that you will use when creating and editing documents including the *ruler, scroll bars,* and *View buttons.* Figure 1.2 identifies several of these components. The Word application window may also contain an Office Assistant.

In a guided tour, you explore the features of Word's application window. Ensure that you've loaded Word.

1. Word's application window is best kept maximized to fill the entire screen, as shown in Figure 1.2. As with most Windows applications, you use the Title bar icons—Minimize (▭), Maximize (□), Restore (▣), and Close (☒)—to control the display of a window using the mouse. Familiarize yourself with the components labeled in Figure 1.2.

Figure 1.2

Word's application window

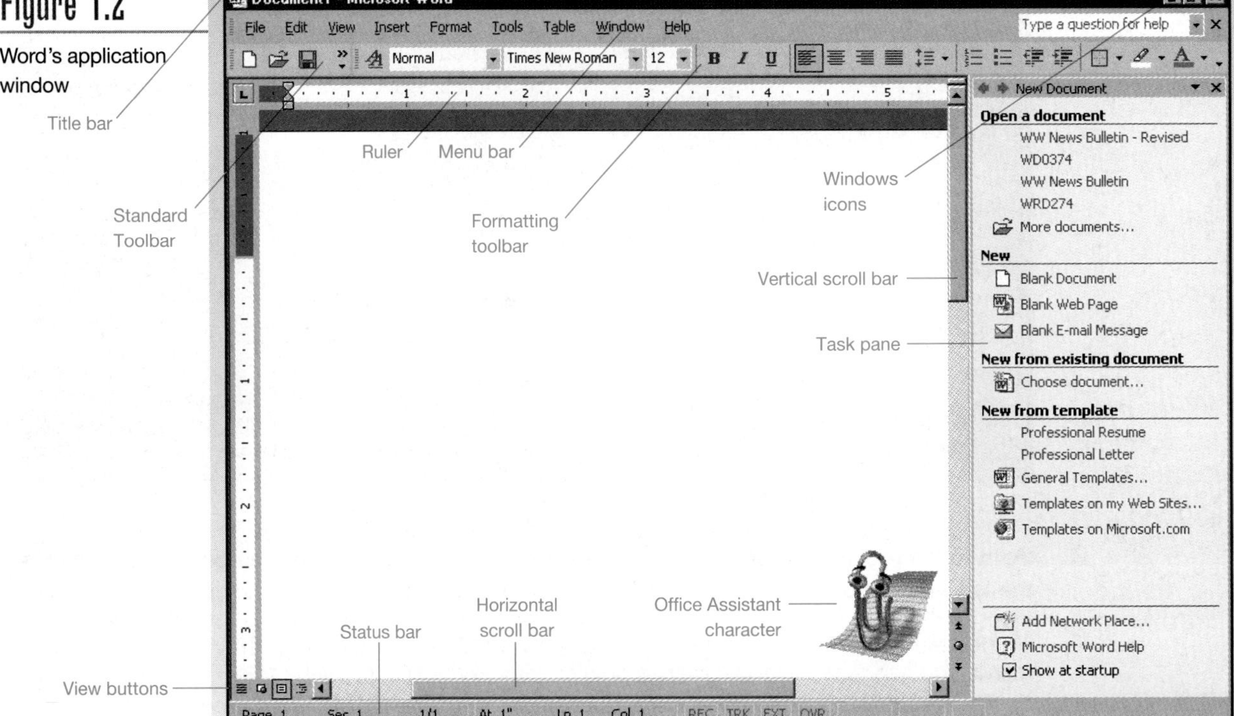

2. The Menu bar contains the Word menu commands. To execute a command, you click once on the desired Menu bar option and then click again on the command. Commands that appear dimmed are not available for selection. Commands that are followed by an ellipsis (...) will display a dialog box.

3. To practice working with the Word Menu bar:
CHOOSE: Help
This instruction tells you to click the left mouse button once on the Help option appearing in the Menu bar.

4. To display other pull-down menus, move the mouse to the left over other options in the Menu bar. As each option is highlighted, a pull-down menu appears with its associated commands.

5. Highlight the View pull-down menu. The options in this menu let you customize the look of your document to your preferred way of working. We describe the options on this menu in module 1.4. Your screen should now appear similar to Figure 1.3. (*Note:* Some options may be grayed out.)

Figure 1.3

Word's View Menu

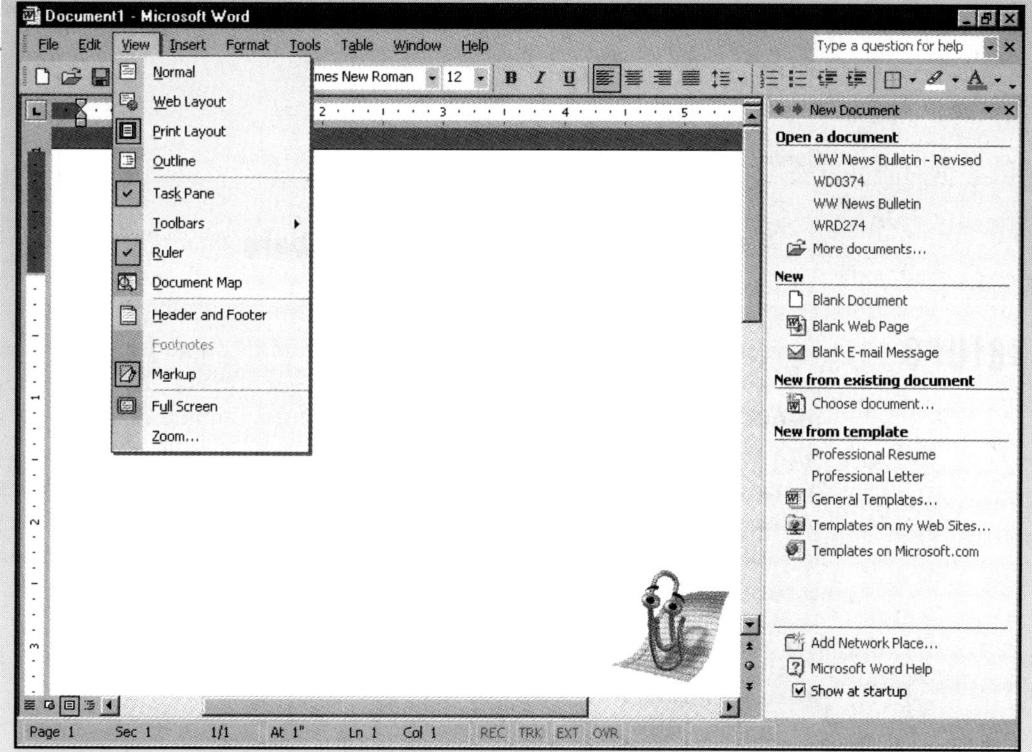

6. For now, do the following to ensure that your screen looks the same as ours:
   CHOOSE: Print Layout

7. Word provides context-sensitive right-click menus for quick access to menu commands. Rather than searching for the appropriate command in the Menu bar, you can position the mouse pointer on any object, such as a graphic or toolbar button, and right-click the mouse to display a list of commonly selected commands.

   To display a document's right-click menu:
   RIGHT-CLICK: in the blank document area
   The menu in Figure 1.4 should now appear.

Figure 1.4

Right-click menu

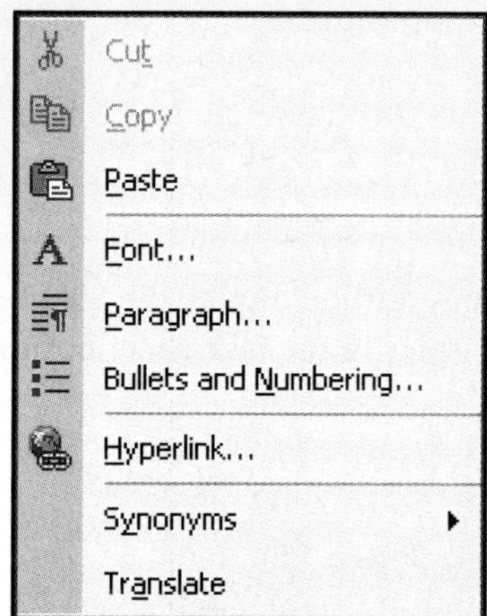

8. To remove the right-click menu from the screen:
   CLICK: in the blank document area

9. If an Office Assistant character currently appears on your screen, do the following to hide it from view:
RIGHT-CLICK: the character
CHOOSE: Hide

10. Continue to the next lesson.

1.1.3 Customizing Menus and Toolbars

feature

Some people argue that software becomes more difficult to learn with the addition of each new command or feature. In response to this sentiment, Microsoft developed **adaptive menus** that display only the most commonly used commands. By default, Office XP ships with the adaptive menus feature enabled. However, you may find this dynamic feature confusing and choose to turn off the adaptive menus. Likewise, the Standard and Formatting toolbars are positioned side-by-side in a single row by default. Again, you may find it easier to locate buttons when these toolbars are positioned on separate rows. Finally, the **task pane** is positioned on the right side of your screen, providing convenient access to relevant commands and options. Some new users find that the task pane is distracting and consumes too much of their workspace. Fortunately, you can hide and display the task pane using a simple menu command.

method

To disable the adaptive menus feature and display the Standard and Formatting toolbars on separate rows:

- CHOOSE: Tools, Customize
- CLICK: *Options* tab
- SELECT: *Show Standard and Formatting toolbars on two rows* check box
- SELECT: *Always show full menus* check box
- CLICK: Close command button

To display or hide a toolbar:

- CHOOSE: View, Toolbars
- CHOOSE: a toolbar from the menu

To display and hide the task pane:

- CHOOSE: View, Task Pane

or

- CLICK: its Close button (☒)

practice

In this lesson, you disable the adaptive menus feature, display the Standard and Formatting toolbars on separate rows, and toggle the display of the task pane. Ensure that you've completed the previous lesson.

1. To begin, display the Tools menu.
CHOOSE: Tools
You should now see the Tools pull-down menu (Figure 1.5).

Figure 1.5

Tools pull-down menu

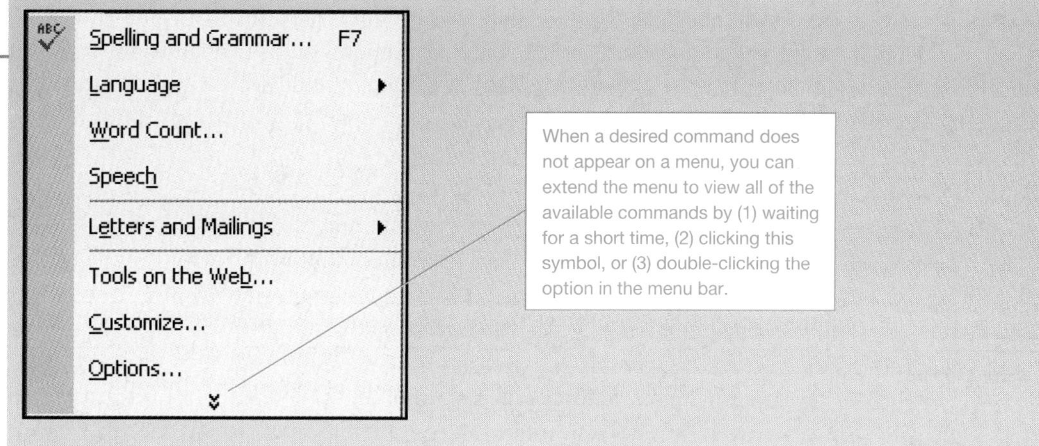

2. To turn off the adaptive menus feature and customize the Standard and Formatting toolbars, do the following:
CHOOSE: Customize from the Tools pull-down menu
CLICK: *Options* tab
The Customize dialog box should now appear (Figure 1.6).

Figure 1.6

Customize dialog box: *Options* tab

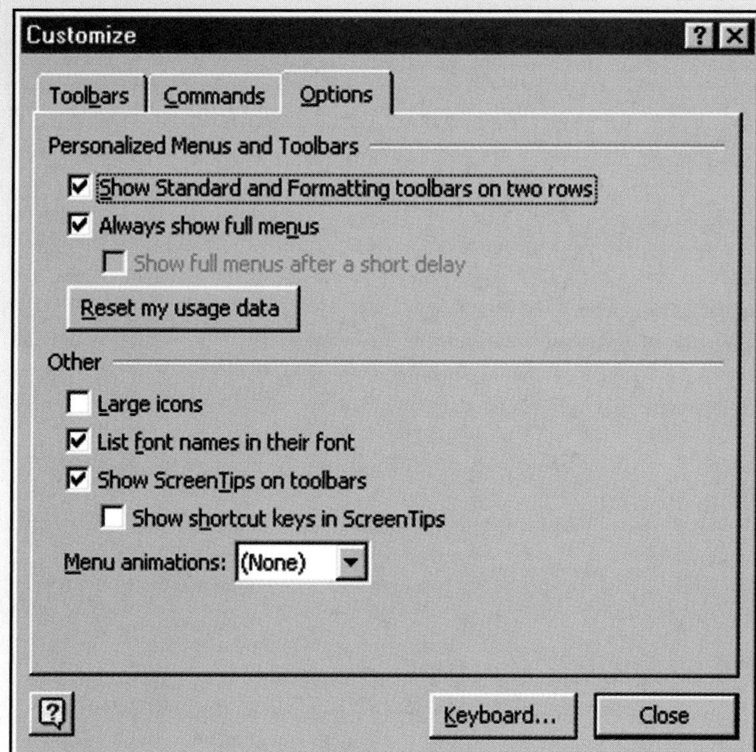

3. On the *Options* tab of the Customize dialog box:
SELECT: *Show Standard and Formatting toolbars on two rows* check box
SELECT: *Always show full menus* check box
(*Note:* When a check box is empty, selecting it displays a check mark (✓). If a check mark already appears, selecting the check box removes the check mark.)

4. To proceed:
CLICK: Close command button

Word

Figure 1.7 displays the Standard and Formatting toolbars as they should now appear on your screen. The Standard toolbar provides access to file management and editing commands, in addition to special features. The Formatting toolbar lets you access formatting commands.

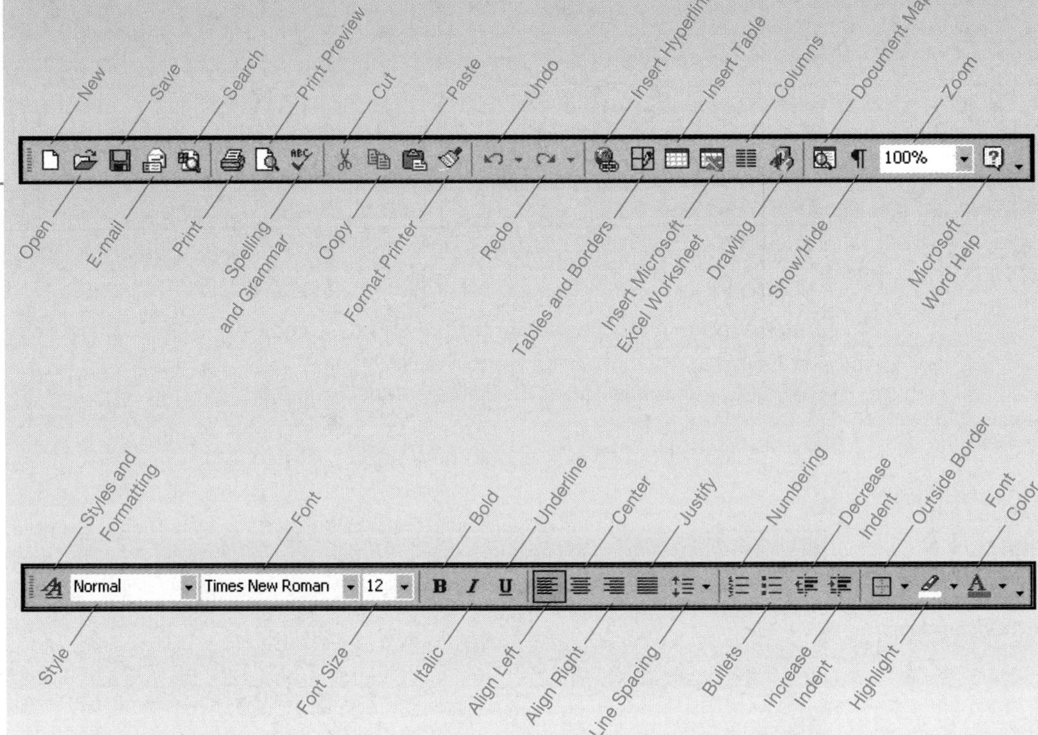

Figure 1.7

Standard toolbar

Formatting toolbar

5. To hide the task pane:
   CHOOSE: View, Task Pane
   (*Note:* When a toolbar or the task pane is displayed, a check mark appears beside the option in the pull-down menu.)

6. To display the task pane:
   CHOOSE: View, Task Pane
   Your screen should now appear similar to Figure 1.8.

IMPORTANT: For the remainder of this learning guide, we assume that the adaptive menus feature has been disabled and that the Standard and Formatting toolbars are positioned on separate rows.

In Addition MOVING TOOLBARS

You can move toolbars around the Word application window using the mouse. A docked toolbar appears attached to one of the window's borders. An undocked or floating toolbar appears in its own window, complete with a Title bar and Close button. To float a docked toolbar, drag the Move bar ( ) at the left-hand side toward the center of the window. To redock the toolbar, drag its Title bar toward a border until it attaches itself automatically.

1.1 How do you remove a right-click menu from view?

Figure 1.8

Customizing the application window

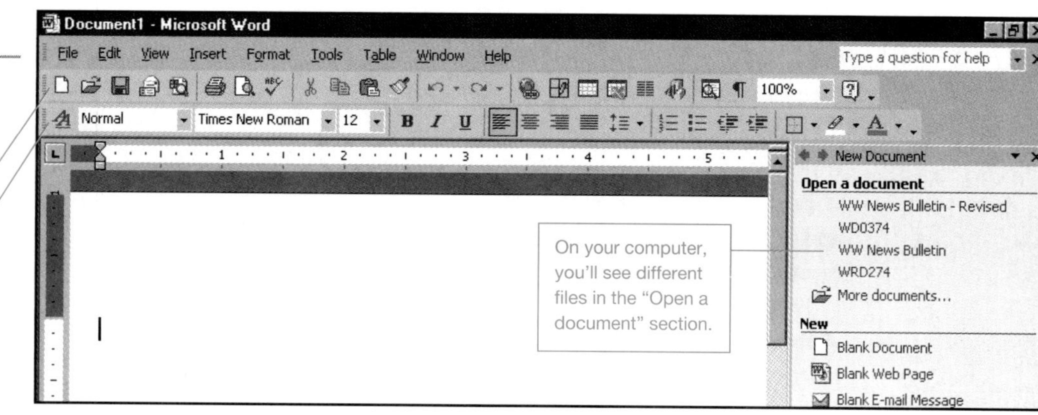

1.2 Creating Your First Document

Creating a document in Word is easy. You type information onto the screen, save the document to the disk, and, if desired, send it to the printer. In the next few lessons, you create the letter appearing in Figure 1.9.

Figure 1.9

Sample document

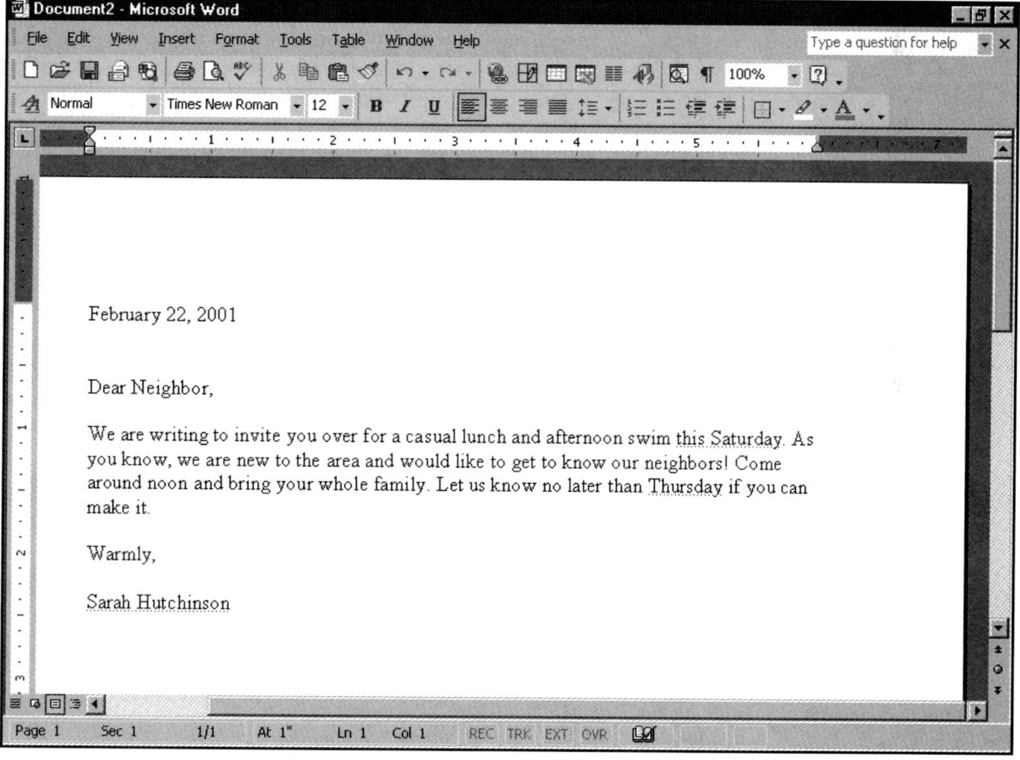

1.2.1 Inserting and Deleting Text

feature

You create and edit documents by inserting and deleting text. As you type, Word employs three separate features to help you get your work done. Word's **AutoText feature** makes it easy to insert frequently used text, such as the current date and the words "Sincerely" and "Thank you." Word's **AutoCorrect feature** works on your behalf to correct common capitalization, spelling, and grammatical errors. For example, AutoCorrect will automatically replace "teh" with "the", "firts" with "first", and "sPorting" with "Sporting". Word's **AutoFormat feature** enhances your text's appearance as you type, applying special formatting to headings, bulleted and numbered lists, borders, and numbers.

method

- To insert text, begin typing. Insert spaces by pressing the Space Bar. Insert blank lines by pressing ENTER.
- To toggle between Insert and Overtype modes, double-click the OVR indicator in the Status bar.
- Press DELETE to delete text to the right of the insertion point. Press BACKSPACE to delete text to the left of the insertion point.

practice

Next, you begin a letter in order to practice the basics of inserting and deleting text. You will also see Word's AutoText and AutoCorrect features in action. Ensure that you've completed the previous lesson and that a blank document appears.

1. Let's begin by inserting a date at the top of your letter. Before you begin typing, make sure that you have a blinking **insertion point** in the upper left-hand corner of the document window. This marks the location where text is inserted. Although you can type the current date directly, let's take advantage of Word's AutoText feature. Assuming the current date is February 22, 2001, do the following:
   TYPE: **Febr**
   Word now displays the complete month name in a yellow suggestion box above your typed letters. Your screen should now appear similar to Figure 1.10. (*Note:* If "February" isn't displaying, you may need to activate the AutoText feature. To do this, choose Insert, AutoText from the Menu bar. Then, choose AutoText from the submenu and select the *Show AutoComplete suggestions* check box so that a check mark appears. After clicking the OK command button, finish typing in the current date and then skip to step 3.)

Figure 1.10

An AutoText suggestion appears

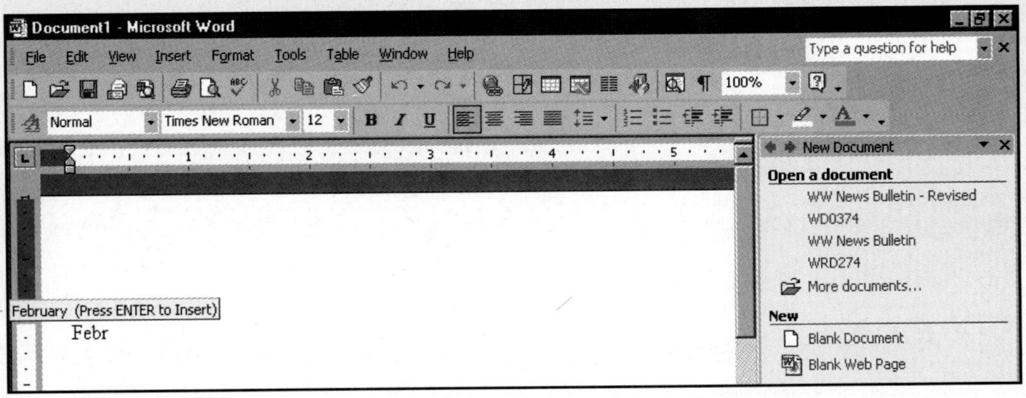

AutoText suggestion

Document1 - Microsoft Word

File Edit View Insert Format Tools Table Window Help

Type a question for help

Normal | Times New Roman | 12 | 100%

New Document

Open a document

WW News Bulletin - Revised
WD0374
WW News Bulletin
WRD274
More documents...

New

Blank Document
Blank Web Page

February (Press ENTER to Insert)

Febr

2. As indicated in the suggestion box, you must press **ENTER** to insert the current month in your document.
   PRESS: **ENTER**
   Word automatically inserted the rest of the characters in the current month.

3. To proceed with typing in the date:
   PRESS: Space Bar
   If "February 22, 2001" were the actual current date, your screen would now look like Figure 1.11. Continue with step 4.

Figure 1.11

Another AutoText suggestion appears when you type the current date

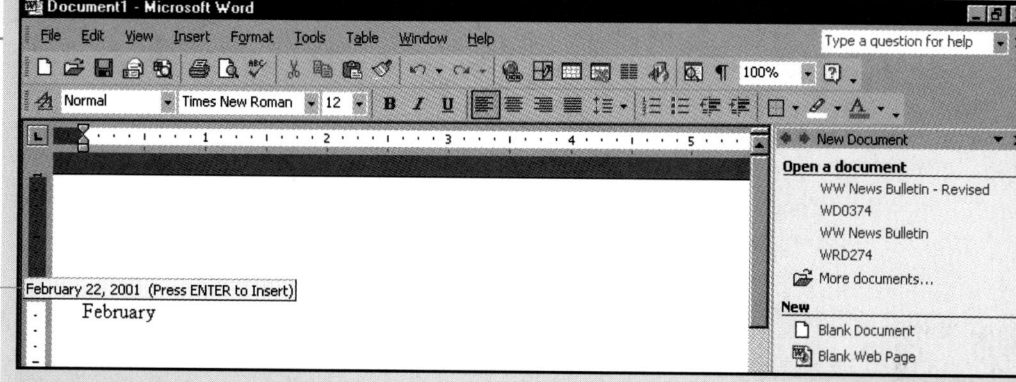

Another AutoText suggestion

4. TYPE: 22
   TYPE: ,
   PRESS: Space Bar
   TYPE: 2001
   The date of February 22, 2001, in its entirety, should now appear at the top of your document. The insertion point appears one character to the right of the date.

5. To move the insertion point back to the beginning of the date line:
   PRESS: **HOME**
   The insertion point should now appear to the left of the date (Figure 1.12). Note that purple dots now appear beneath the date. (*Note:* If the dots don't appear yet, they will in step 6, when you press the **ENTER** key.) These dots indicate that the date is a *smart tag*. When you move the mouse pointer over a smart tag, Word displays the Smart Tag Actions button (ⓘ). We describe smart tags in more detail in lesson 1.2.4. For now, ignore each smart tag in your document and its associated Smart Tag Actions button (ⓘ).

Figure 1.12

The date has been entered

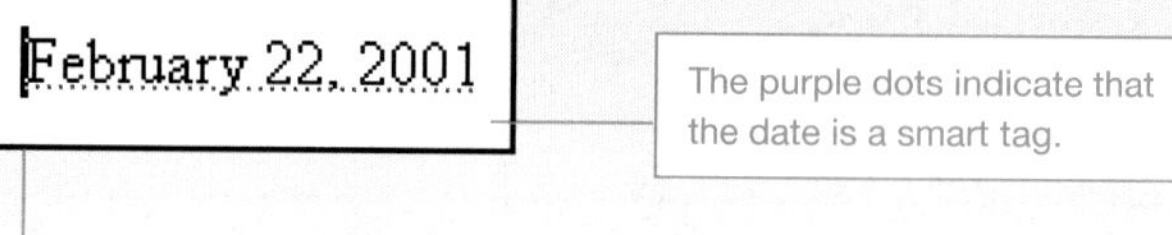

The purple dots indicate that the date is a smart tag.

Note the location of the insertion point.

6. The **ENTER** key inserts blank lines into a document and signifies the end of a paragraph. To illustrate:
   PRESS: **ENTER** three times
   Note that the date moves down with the insertion point and blank lines are inserted into the document.

7. To get the date back to its original location, you must delete the blank lines. To move the insertion point to the top of the document:
PRESS: CTRL + HOME
This instruction tells you to press and hold down the CTRL key and tap HOME once. You then release both keys. The insertion point jumps to the left side of the first line in the document.

8. To delete the blank lines:
PRESS: DELETE three times

9. To move the insertion point down three lines without moving the date, you must first position the insertion point at the end of the line. To illustrate:
PRESS: END to move the insertion point to the end of the line
PRESS: ENTER three times
The insertion point is now in the correct position for you to type your salutation. (*Note:* A salutation is a greeting, such as "Dear Mr. Jones," that appears at the beginning of a letter.)

10. Type the following, exactly as it appears:
TYPE: **NEighbor,**
Conveniently, Word's AutoCorrect feature automatically corrected your capitalization error at the beginning of the word. Your document should now appear similar to Figure 1.13.

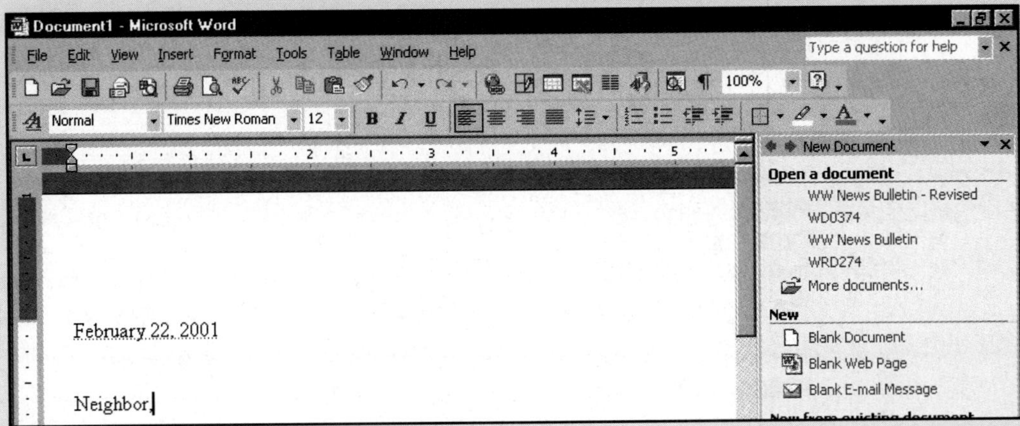

Figure 1.13

Word's application window

11. Note that the letters OVR in the Status bar appear dimmed. This tells you that Word's current mode is Insert mode and not Overtype mode. To move the insertion point back to the beginning of the line so you can insert the word "Dear," do the following:
PRESS: HOME
A hollow blue bar (▭), the AutoCorrect Options button, should now appear beneath the "N" of "Neighbor." For now, ignore this button.

12. TYPE: **Dear**
PRESS: Space Bar
The Insert mode lets you insert text and spaces at the current position by simply typing the characters and pressing the Space Bar. The existing information was pushed to the right.

13. Locate OVR, the abbreviation for Overtype mode, on the Status bar (Figure 1.14).
DOUBLE-CLICK: OVR
The letters OVR appear highlighted (not dimmed) in the Status bar.

14. TYPE: **My**
PRESS: Space Bar
The letters and following space overwrote the first three characters of "Neighbor,". Your screen should now appear similar to Figure 1.14.

Figure 1.14

Overtype mode

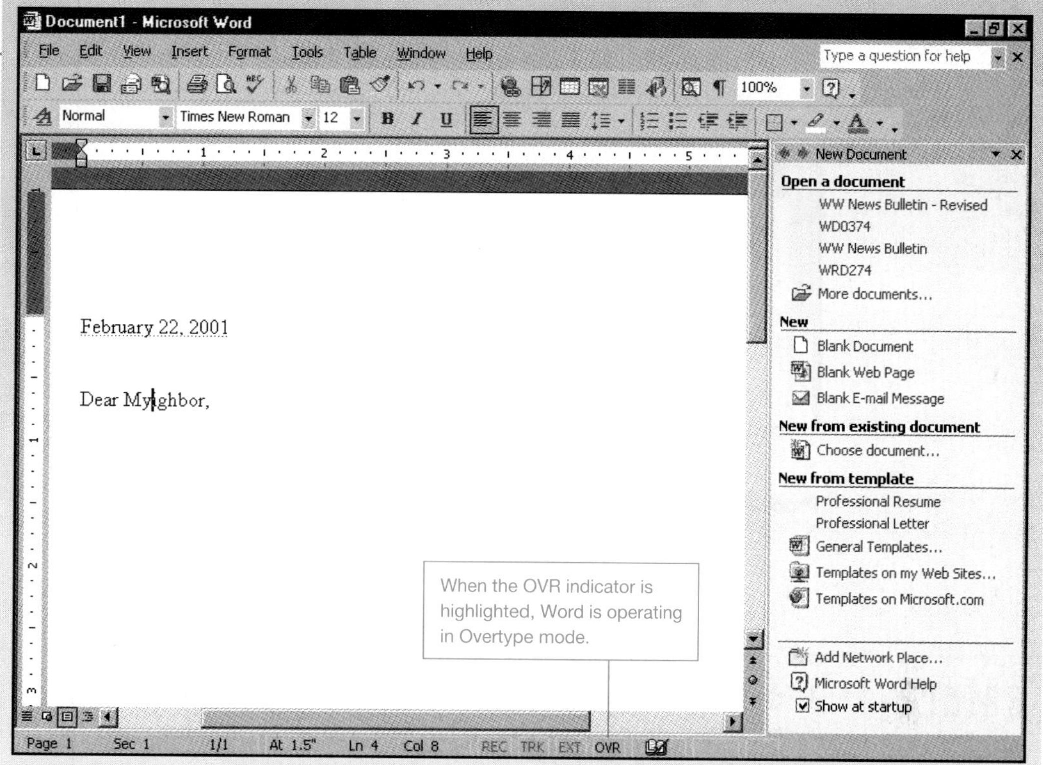

15. To toggle back to Insert mode:
DOUBLE-CLICK: OVR in the Status bar
The letters OVR should now appear dimmed.

16. To complete the phrase:
TYPE: **Nei**

17. To illustrate the use of the BACKSPACE key, position the insertion point to the left of the word "Neighbor,".

18. PRESS: BACKSPACE three times
The word "My" and the space are deleted. The text now reads "Dear Neighbor,".

19. To prepare for the next lesson, let's delete the date from the top of your document.
PRESS: CTRL + HOME
PRESS: DELETE until the month information is deleted

20. While being careful to not delete any blank lines:
PRESS: DELETE a few more times to delete the day and year information
The insertion point should now be positioned on a blank line at the top of your document (Figure 1.15).

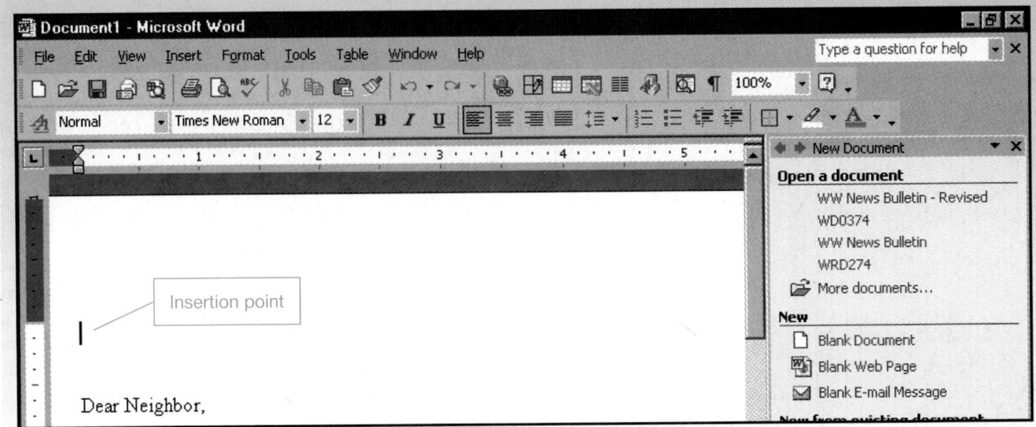

Figure 1.15

The insertion point is positioned on a blank line

21. Proceed to the next lesson.

1.2.2 Inserting the Date and Time

feature

In the last lesson, Word assisted you when typing the current date. You can also insert the current date in its entirety using a command from the Menu bar. Optionally, you can insert the current date as a field that causes Word to update the date whenever you open or print the document.

method

- CHOOSE: Insert, Date and Time
- SELECT: a format in the *Available formats* list box
- CLICK: OK command button

practice

You will now insert the current date at the top of your document. Ensure that you've completed the previous lesson. The insertion point should be positioned on a blank line at the top of your document, as shown in Figure 1.15.

1. CHOOSE: Insert, Date and Time
The Date and Time dialog box appears, as shown in Figure 1.16.

Figure 1.16

Date and Time dialog box

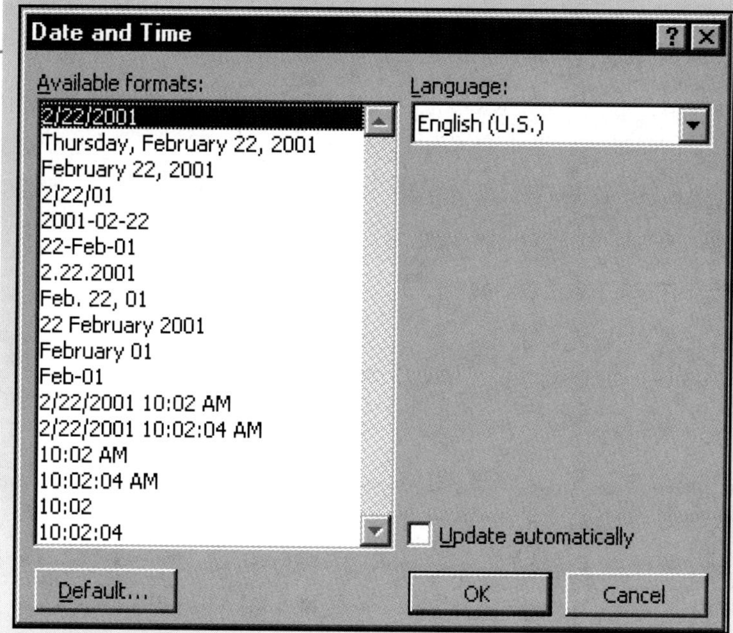

2. SELECT: the "Month ##, 200#" format (depicted as "February 22, 2001" in Figure 1.16)
   CLICK: OK command button
   The date was inserted at the top of the document.
3. To position the insertion point in the correct position so you can begin typing your letter:
   PRESS: CTRL + END to move to the end of your document
   PRESS: ENTER twice
4. If the Office Assistant appears:
   RIGHT-CLICK: the Office Assistant character
   CHOOSE: Hide
5. Proceed to the next lesson.

1.2.3 Putting "Word Wrap" to Work

feature → The **word wrap** feature of Word allows you to continuously type without having to press the ENTER key at the end of each line. This feature is designed to help you type faster.

method → When typing a paragraph, do not press the ENTER key at the end of each line. The ENTER key is used only to end a paragraph or to insert a blank line in a document.

practice → You will now complete the sample document. Ensure that you've completed the previous lesson. The insertion point should be positioned two lines below the salutation. Do not press ENTER unless we tell you to do so.

1. TYPE: **We are writing to invite you over for a casual lunch and afternoon swim this Saturday. As you know, we are new to the area and would like to get to know our neighbors!**

Come around noon and bring your whole family. Let us know no later than Thursday if you can make it.
PRESS: ENTER twice

2. To complete the note:
TYPE: **Warmly,**
PRESS: ENTER twice
TYPE: **your name**
(*Note:* Be sure to type your own name here.)

3. Because the task pane may be obscuring a portion of your document, let's hide it from view.
CHOOSE: View, Task Pane
Your screen should now appear similar to Figure 1.17. (*Note:* If your screen's resolution is different from ours, words may wrap in a different place.)

Figure 1.17

Sample document

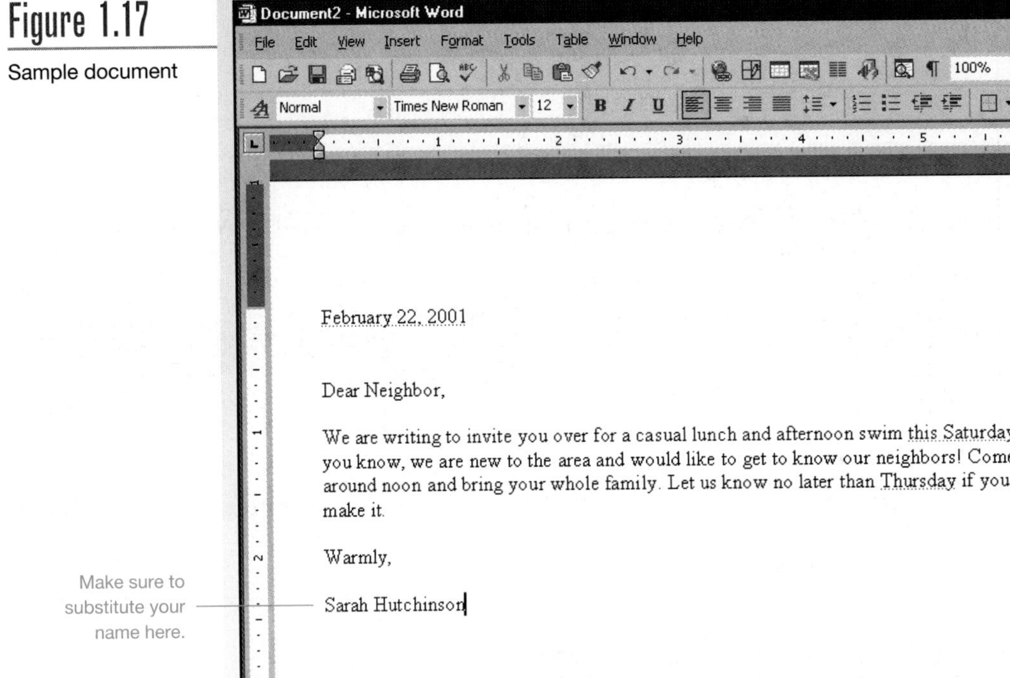

4. With your document still displaying, proceed to the next lesson.

1.2.4 Using Smart Tags

feature

As you already know, Word includes many features that work in the background to save you time. For example, Word automatically corrects common capitalization, spelling, and grammatical errors. Word even tags some data, such as a person's name or the current date, so that you can more easily use the data elsewhere, such as in your address book or e-mail message. Once Word recognizes a piece of data, it labels it with a purple dotted underline. Information that has been marked in this way is called a **smart tag.** When you move the mouse pointer over a smart tag, a **Smart Tag Actions button** appears (ⓘ) that you can click to display a list of possible actions. Since smart tags won't appear in your printed documents it's also fine to ignore them.

method

To perform an action on a smart tag:

- CLICK: Smart Tag Actions button (ⓘ)
- CHOOSE: an option from the menu

practice

You will now see what actions you can perform on the four smart tags displaying in your sample document.

1. Position the mouse pointer over the current-date smart tag at the top of the document. The Smart Tag Actions button (ⓘ) should now appear.

2. To see what actions you can perform on this smart tag:
   CLICK: Smart Tag Actions button (ⓘ)
   Your screen should now appear similar to Figure 1.18. Note that Word identified the smart tag as a Date field, as indicated at the top of the smart tag menu.

Figure 1.18

Smart Tag Actions menu

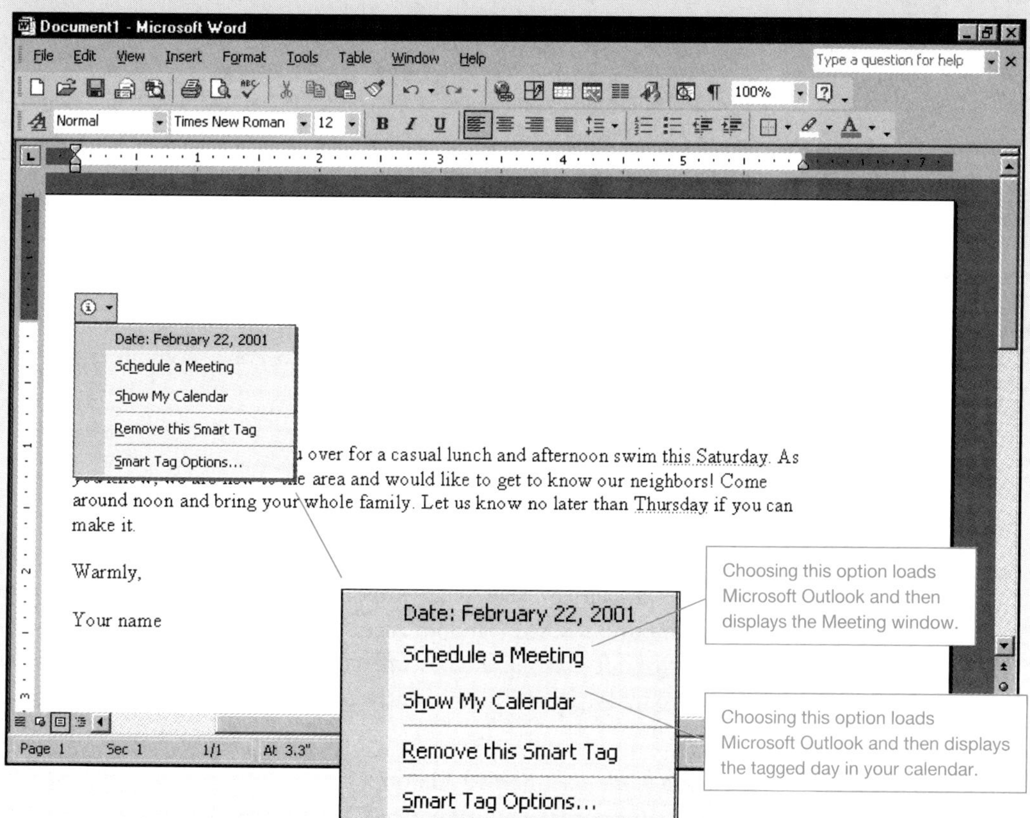

3. To remove the smart tag:
   CHOOSE: Remove this Smart Tag
   The date should no longer be marked as a smart tag.

4. In the body of your letter, "this Saturday" and "Thursday" may be marked as smart tags. Your name should also be marked as a smart tag at the end of the letter. Move the mouse pointer over your name.
CLICK: Smart Tag Actions button () associated with your name.
The menu in Figure 1.19 should now appear. Note that the menu contains different options than before.

Figure 1.19

Smart Tag Actions menu

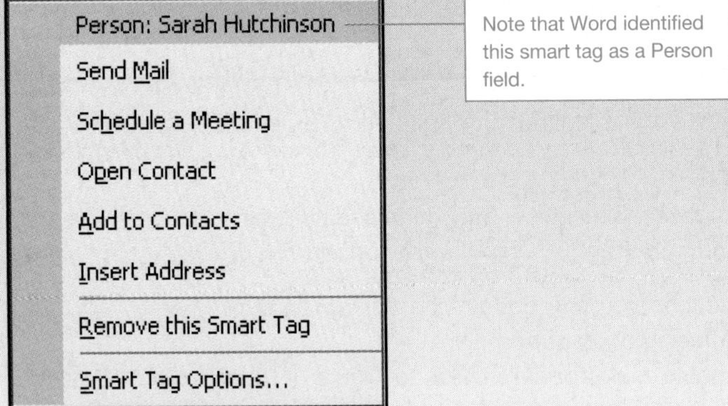

5. To ignore the displayed menu and return to your document:
CLICK: in the document area

6. To conclude this module, you will close the document without saving changes. From the Menu bar:
CHOOSE: File, Close

7. In the dialog box that appears:
CLICK: No command button
There should be no documents open in the application window.

1.2 How would you insert a word in the middle of a sentence?

1.3 Managing Files

Managing your document files is an important skill. When you create a document, it exists only in the computer's RAM (random access memory), which is highly volatile. In other words, if the power to your computer goes off, your document is lost. For safety and security, you need to save your document permanently to the local hard disk, a network drive, or a floppy diskette.

Saving your work to a named file on a disk is like placing it into a filing cabinet. Important documents (ones that you cannot risk losing) should be saved every 15 minutes, or whenever you're interrupted, to protect against an unexpected power outage or other catastrophe.

Saving a file without closing it is like placing a current copy in a filing cabinet. When naming your document files, you can use up to 255 characters, including spaces, but it's wise to keep the length under 20 characters. Furthermore, you cannot use the following characters in naming your documents:

\ / : ; * ? " < > |

In the following lessons, you practice several file management procedures, including creating a new document, saving and closing documents, and opening existing documents.

IMPORTANT: In this guide, we refer to the files that have been created for you as the ***student data files.*** *Depending on your computer or lab setup, these files may be located on a floppy diskette, in a folder on your hard disk, or on a network server. If necessary, ask your instructor or lab assistant where to find these data files. To download the Advantage Series' student data files from the Internet, visit our Web sites at:*

http://www.mhhe.com/it
http://www.advantageseries.com

You will also need to identify a personal storage location for the files that you create, modify, and save.

1.3.1 Beginning a New Document

feature

There are three ways to start creating a new document. One is to start with a blank document and then create the document from scratch. Another is to select a document **template** that provides preexisting data and design elements. Or you can employ a **wizard** to lead you step-by-step through creating a particular type of document.

method

To display a new blank document:

- CLICK: New button (□) on the Standard toolbar

To begin a document using a template or wizard:

- CHOOSE: File, New

practice

In this example, you use one of Word's prebuilt templates to create a résumé. Ensure that no documents are open in the application window.

1. A document template is a model that you can use to create new documents. By its very nature, a template is a time-saver that promotes consistency in both design and function. To view the templates that are available to you, do the following:
CHOOSE: File, New
The New Document task pane should now appear, as shown in Figure 1.20. Task panes contain textual links, called **hyperlinks,** for performing Word procedures. When you move the mouse pointer over a link, the mouse pointer changes to a hand (☝). You select a link by clicking.

Figure 1.20

New Document task pane

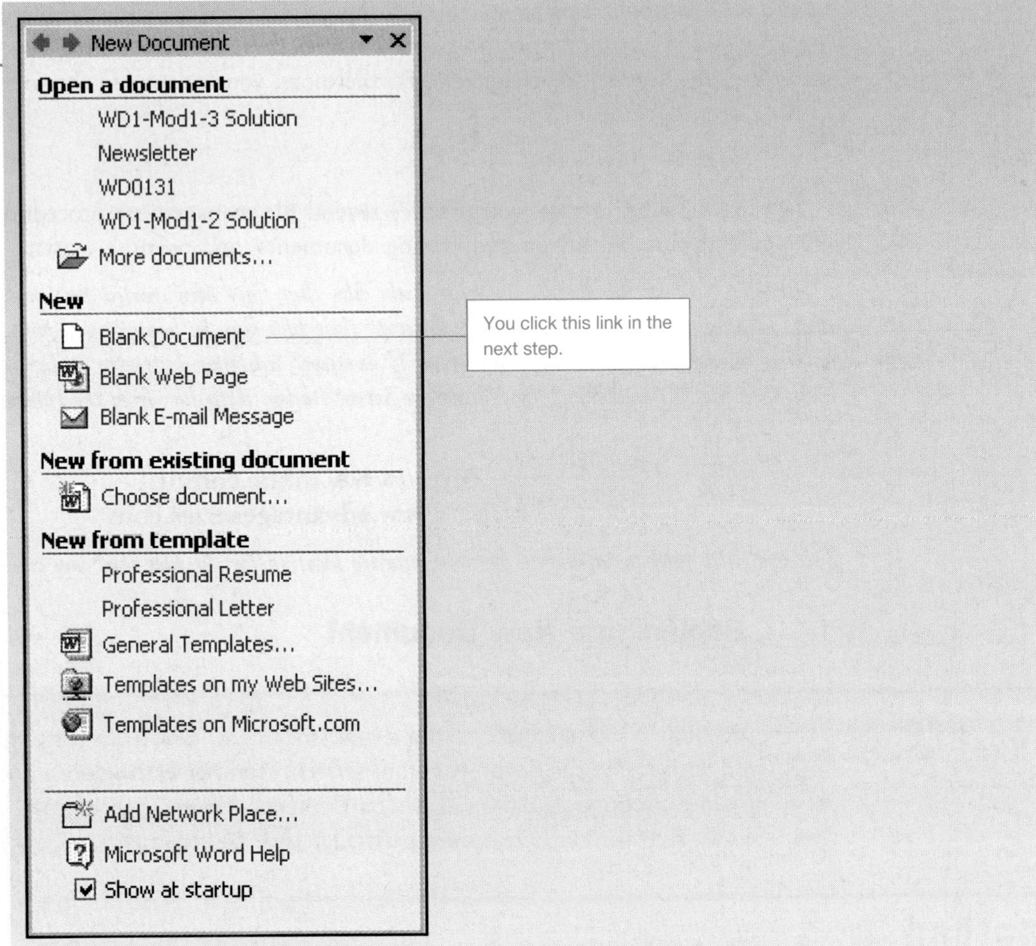

2. Move the mouse pointer over the "Blank Document" hyperlink. Note that a hand (☝) appears indicating that you're pointing to a hyperlink. To select the link:
   CLICK: "Blank Document" link
   A blank document appears. The task pane should no longer appear. You can also start a new document by clicking the New button (🗋) on the Standard toolbar.

3. Word includes many custom templates that simplify the process of starting common documents such as résumés and letters. For example, to display a selection of templates for creating résumés:
   CHOOSE: File, New
   CLICK: "General Templates" link
   CLICK: *Other Documents* tab
   The Templates dialog box should look like Figure 1.21. (*Note:* Different tabs may be displaying on your computer.)

Figure 1.21

Displaying custom document templates

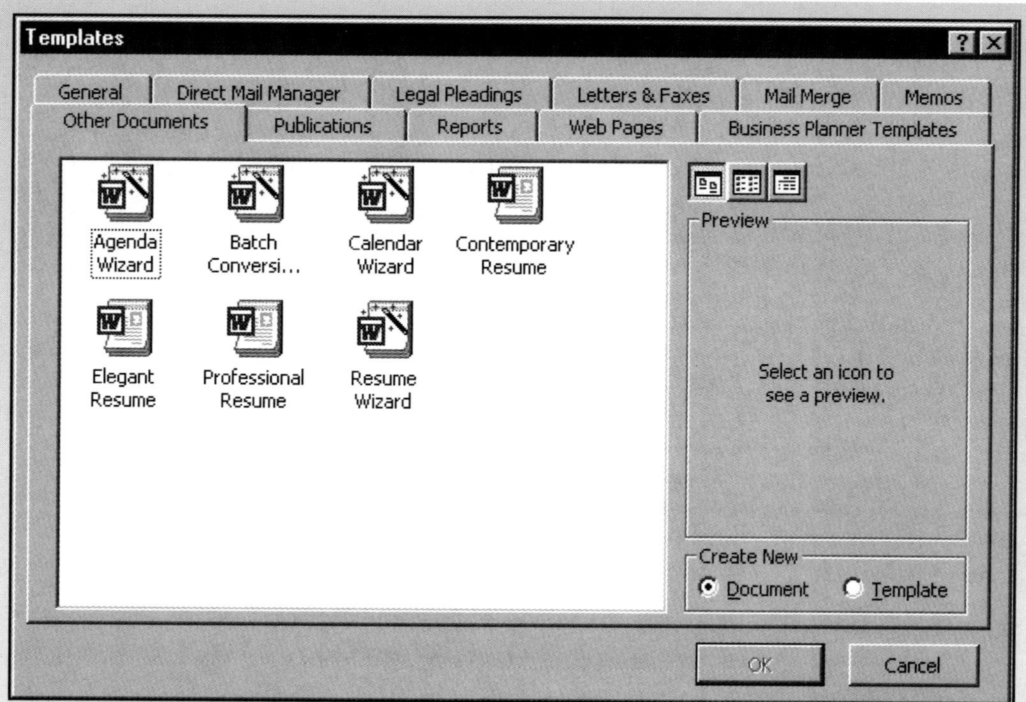

4. To create a new document based on the "Professional Resume" template:
DOUBLE-CLICK: Professional Resume template icon
(*Note:* If your lab administrator has not installed the document templates, skip to step 6.) You should now see the Professional Resume template, as shown in Figure 1.22. If you were creating your resume right now, you would proceed by editing this document to include your information.

Figure 1.22

New document based on the Professional Resume template

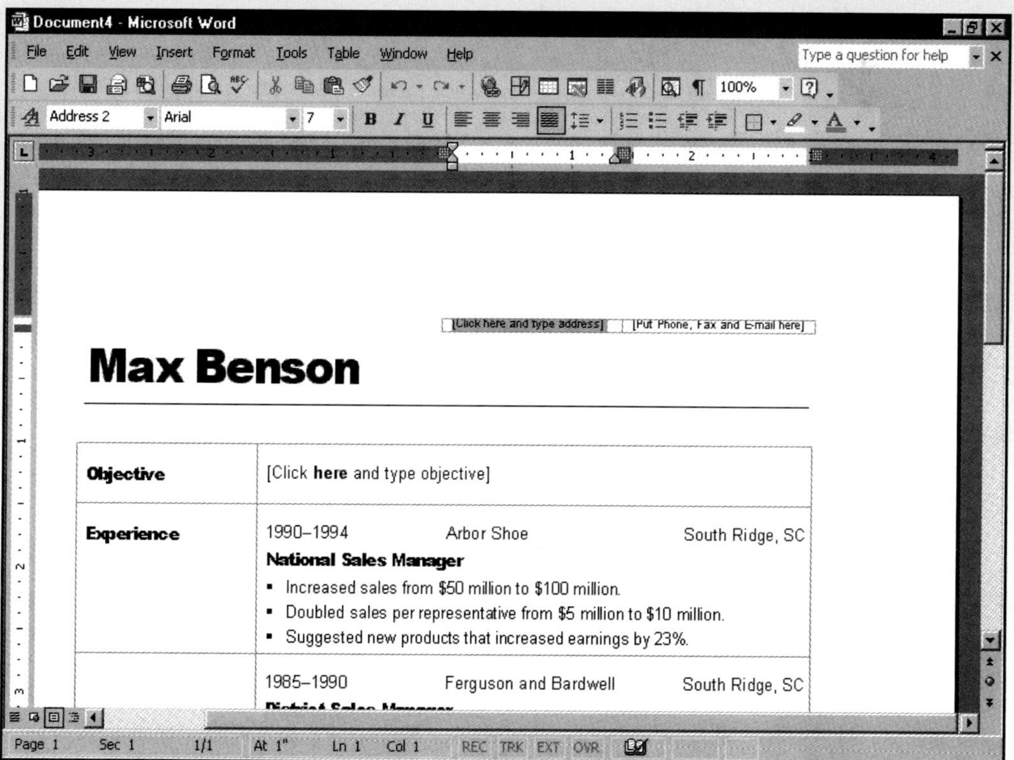

5. Rather than editing this document now, let's close the document and continue our discussion of file management.
CHOOSE: File, Close
CLICK: No command button, if asked to save the changes

6. The blank document should be displaying. Do the following:
TYPE: **Saving Files**
PRESS: ENTER twice
(*Note:* Depending on what settings are in effect on your computer, Word may have automatically formatted your title using a heading style.)

7. Again, let word wrap happen naturally. Don't press ENTER after each sentence.
TYPE: **Saving your work to a named file on a disk is like placing it into a filing cabinet. Important documents (ones that you cannot risk losing) should be saved every 15 minutes, or whenever you're interrupted, to protect against an unexpected power outage or other catastrophe.**
Your screen should now appear similar to Figure 1.23. In the next lesson, you learn how to save this document.

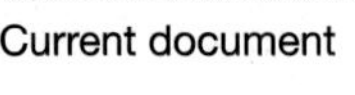

Current document

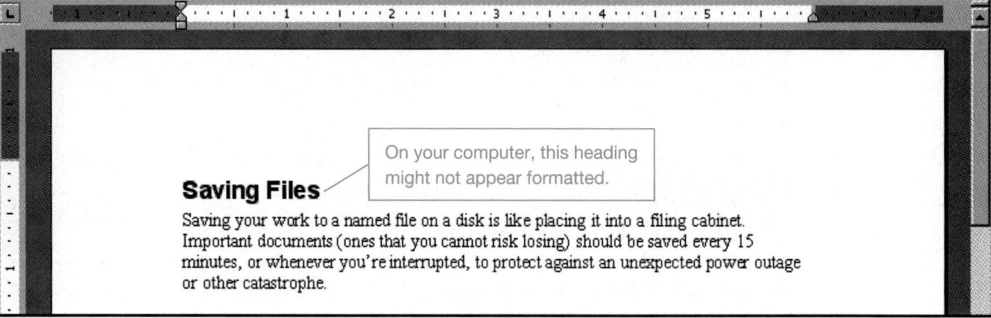
On your computer, this heading might not appear formatted.
Saving Files
Saving your work to a named file on a disk is like placing it into a filing cabinet. Important documents (ones that you cannot risk losing) should be saved every 15 minutes, or whenever you're interrupted, to protect against an unexpected power outage or other catastrophe.

1.3.2 Saving and Closing a Document

feature →

You can save the currently displayed document by updating an existing file on the disk, by creating a new file, or by selecting a new storage location. The File, Save command and the Save button (💾) on the toolbar allow you to overwrite a disk file with the latest version of a document. The File, Save As command enables you to save a document to a new filename or storage location. When you are finished working with a document, ensure that you close the file to free up valuable RAM.

method →

To save a document:

- CLICK: Save button (💾) on the Standard toolbar,

or

- CHOOSE: File, Save,

or

- CHOOSE: File, Save As

To close a document:

- CHOOSE: File, Close

practice

You now practice saving and closing a document. Ensure that you have completed the previous lesson. You also need to identify a storage location for your personal document files. If you want to use a diskette, place it into the diskette drive now. Also, always write your name on the diskette label in pen.

1. If you are working in a new document that has not yet been saved, Word displays the Save As dialog box (Figure 1.24), regardless of the method you choose to save the file. To demonstrate:
   CLICK: Save button (💾) on the Standard toolbar
   (*Note:* The filenames and directories that appear in your Save As dialog box may differ from those shown in Figure 1.24.) The **Places bar,** located along the left border of the dialog box, provides convenient access to commonly used storage locations.

Figure 1.24

Save As dialog box

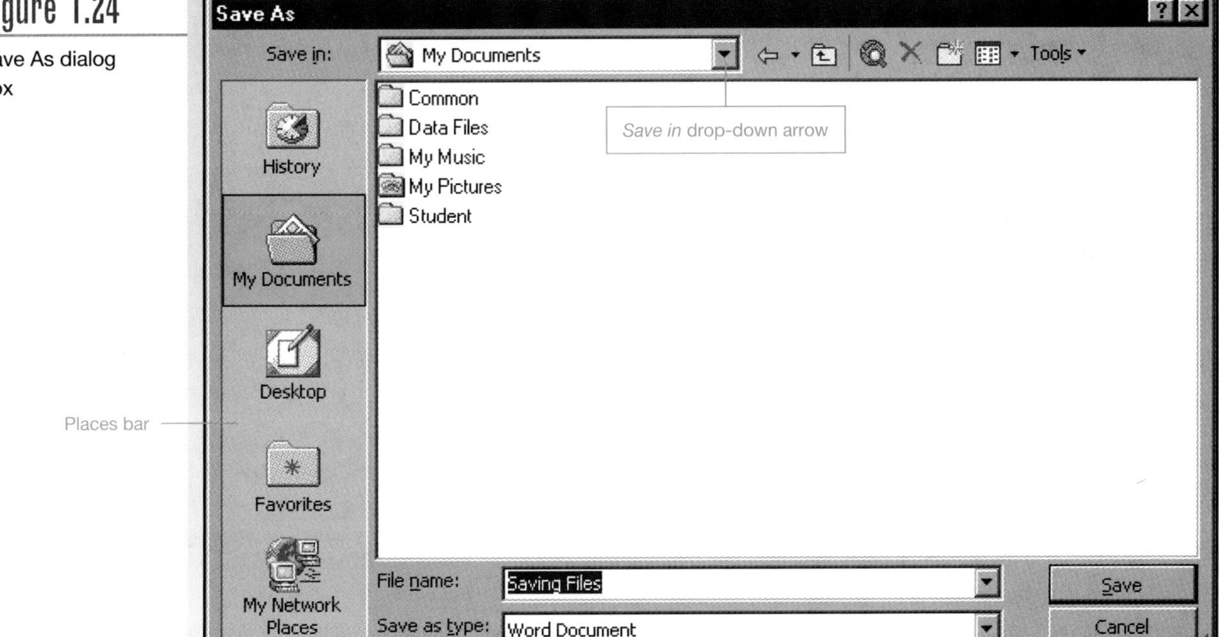

2. In the next few steps, you practice navigating your computer's disks. To begin, let's view a list of the files that you've worked with recently:
   CLICK: History button in the Places bar

3. To browse the files in your folder called My Documents:
   CLICK: My Documents button

4. To browse the local hard disk:
   CLICK: down arrow attached to the *Save in* drop-down list box
   SELECT: Local Disk C:
   (*Note:* Your hard drive may have a different name.) The list area displays the folders and files stored in the root directory of your local hard disk.

5. To drill down into one of the folders:
DOUBLE-CLICK: Program Files folder
(*Note:* If the Program Files folder isn't located on your local hard disk, select an alternate folder to open.) This folder contains the program files for several applications.

6. Let's drill down one step further:
DOUBLE-CLICK: Microsoft Office folder
This folder contains the Microsoft Office program files. Your screen may now appear similar, but not identical, to Figure 1.25.

Figure 1.25

Displaying the contents of the Microsoft Office folder

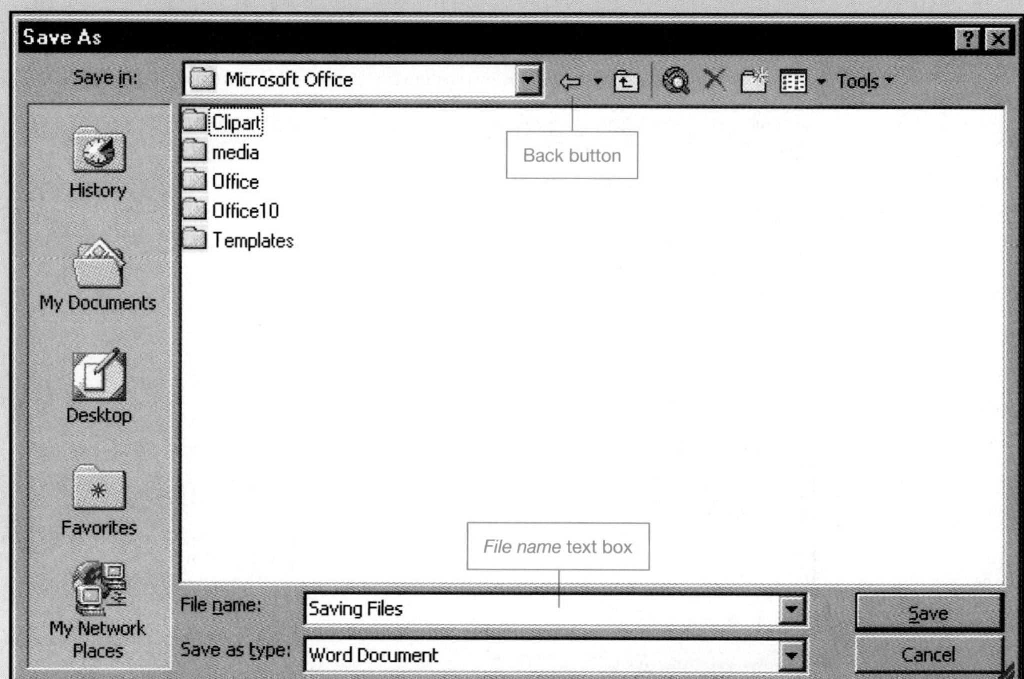

7. To return to the previous display:
CLICK: Back button (⇦) in the dialog box
(*Note:* The button is renamed Program Files, since that is where you will end up once the button is clicked.)

8. To return to the My Documents display:
CLICK: Back button (⇦) twice
(*Hint:* You could also have clicked the My Documents button in the Places bar.)

9. Now, using either the Places bar or the *Save in* drop-down list box:
SELECT: *a storage location for your personal files*
(*Note:* In this guide, we save files to the Data Files folder, located in the My Documents folder.)

10. Next, you need to give the document file a unique name. Let's stick with the name of "Saving Files" that already appears in the *File name* text box.

11. To save your work:
CLICK: Save command button
Note that the document's name now appears in the Title bar (Figure 1.26).

Figure 1.26

The file name now appears in the Title bar

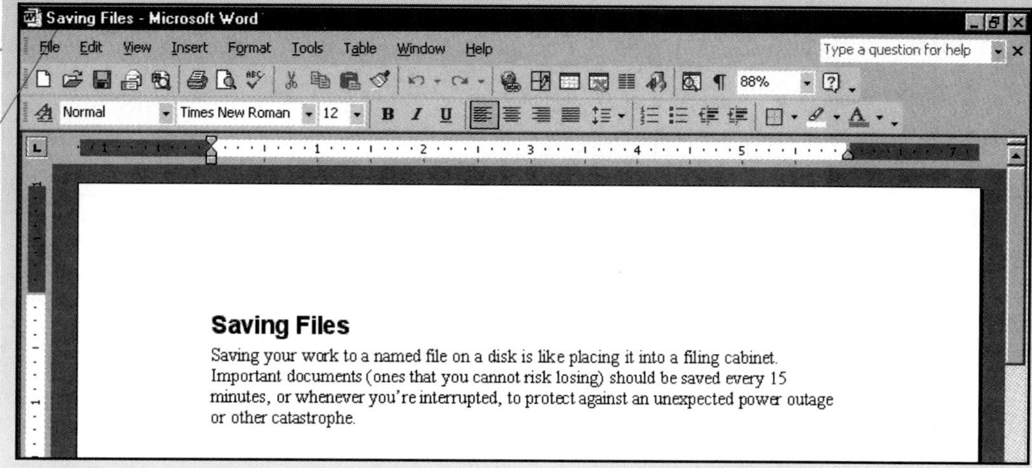
The document's name
Saving Files - Microsoft Word
File Edit View Insert Format Tools Table Window Help
Type a question for help
Normal
Times New Roman
12
88%
Saving Files
Saving your work to a named file on a disk is like placing it into a filing cabinet. Important documents (ones that you cannot risk losing) should be saved every 15 minutes, or whenever you're interrupted, to protect against an unexpected power outage or other catastrophe.

Word

12. Move the insertion point to the bottom of the document.

13. To insert a blank line and then type your name:
PRESS: ENTER
TYPE: **your name** *(for example, Joey Smith)*

14. To save the updated document:
CLICK: Save button
Sometimes you want to save an existing document under a different filename. For example, you may want to keep different versions of the same document on your disk. Or, you may want to use one document as a template for future documents that are similar in style and format. To do this, save the document under a different name using the File, Save As command.

15. Let's save a copy of the "Saving Files" document to your personal storage location and name the copy "Backup Document".
CHOOSE: File, Save As
TYPE: **Backup Document** to replace the existing filename
CLICK: Save command button
The document was saved as "Backup Document" to your personal storage location.

16. To close the document:
CHOOSE: File, Close

1.3.3 Opening and Printing a Document

feature

You use the Open dialog box to search for and retrieve existing documents that are stored on your local hard disk, a floppy diskette, a network server, or on the Web. To load Word and an existing document at the same time, you can use the Open Office Document command on the Start menu. Or, if you have recently used the document, you can use the Documents command on the Start menu. This menu lists the 15 most recently used files. Once you've opened a document, especially a long document that you haven't worked with before, you may choose to send a copy of it to the printer and then review the printed copy.

method

To open a document:

- CLICK: Open button ( ) on the Standard toolbar,

or

- CHOOSE: File, Open

To print a document:

- CLICK: Print button ( )

practice

In this lesson, you open and print a document that announces an upcoming snowboard vacation. Ensure that you have completed the previous lesson. No documents should be displaying in the application window. You will also need to know the storage location for the student data files.

1. To display the Open dialog box:
   CLICK: Open button ( ) on the Standard toolbar

2. Using the Places bar or the *Look in* drop-down list box, display the contents of the folder containing the student data files. These are the files we've provided. (*Note:* In this guide, we retrieve the student data files from a folder named "Student".)

3. To view additional information about each file:
   CLICK: down arrow beside the Views button (see Figure 1.27)
   CHOOSE: Details
   Each document is presented on a single line with additional file information, such as its size, type, and date it was last modified, as shown in Figure 1.27.

Figure 1.27

Open dialog box

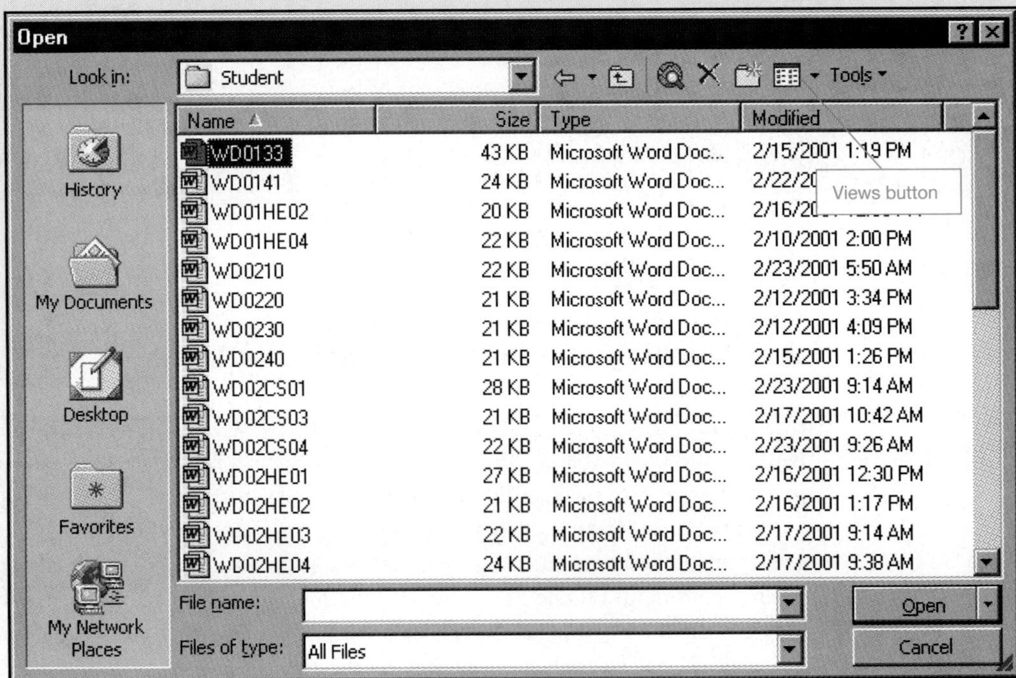

4. To alphabetically sort the list of files displayed in the Open dialog box:
CLICK: Name button in the column heading area

5. When you click the same column heading a second time, the order of the listing is reversed. To illustrate:
CLICK: Name button

6. To sort the list by size:
CLICK: Size button in the column heading area

7. To chronologically sort the file list by the date of modification:
CLICK: Modified button
Your file list should now appear similar to Figure 1.28.

Figure 1.28

Sorted file list

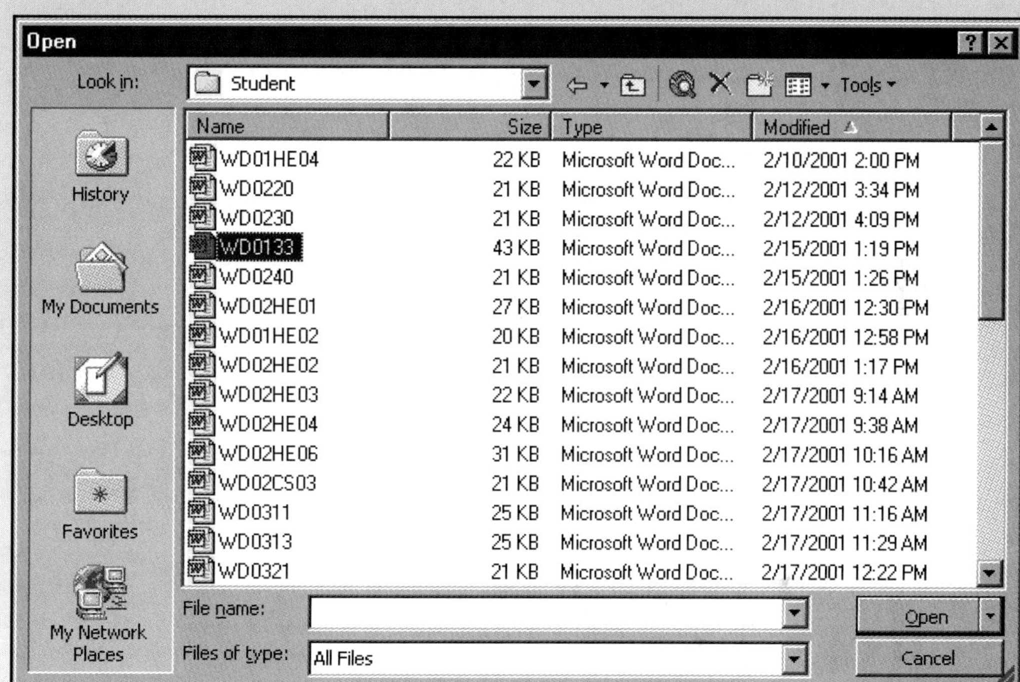

8. To re-sort the list in order by the Name field and then return to a list format:
CLICK: Name button
CLICK: down arrow beside the Views button
CHOOSE: List

9. Let's open one of the documents in the list area:
DOUBLE-CLICK: WD0133
The dialog box disappears and the document is loaded into the application window. (*Note:* The "WD0133" filename reflects that this document is used in lesson 1.3.3 of the Word learning guide.)

10. To print the current document:
CLICK: Print button ()
(*Note:* We describe printing in more detail in Chapter 4.)

11. Keep this file open for use in the next lesson.

1.3.4 Creating a New File Folder

feature

As more and more files accumulate on your computer, you may want to create folders to help you better organize your work. For example, you may have one folder for your faxes and memos and individual folders for each course you are taking at school. In Word, you create folders directly within the Open and Save As dialog boxes. Microsoft Word uses the Folder icon ( ) to identify folders.

method

To create a new folder:

- In the Open or Save As dialog box, navigate to the disk or folder where you want to create the new folder.
- RIGHT-CLICK: *an empty part of the dialog box*
- CHOOSE: New, Folder from the right-click menu
- TYPE: **a folder name**

To delete a folder:

- In the Open or Save As dialog box, navigate to the folder you want to delete.
- RIGHT-CLICK: a folder
- CHOOSE: Delete from the right-click menu

practice

In this lesson, you create a folder named "My Homework" in the "My Documents" folder. You then save the open file into the new folder. As a final step, you delete the folder and file.

1. To display the Save As dialog box:
   CHOOSE: File, Save As

2. To open the My Documents folder:
   CLICK: My Documents button in the Places bar

3. To create a new folder called "My Homework" in the My Documents folder:
   RIGHT-CLICK: *an empty part of the window*
   CHOOSE: New from the right-click menu
   The New menu is shown in Figure 1.29. (*Note:* Your screen may differ slightly.)

Figure 1.29

Creating a new folder

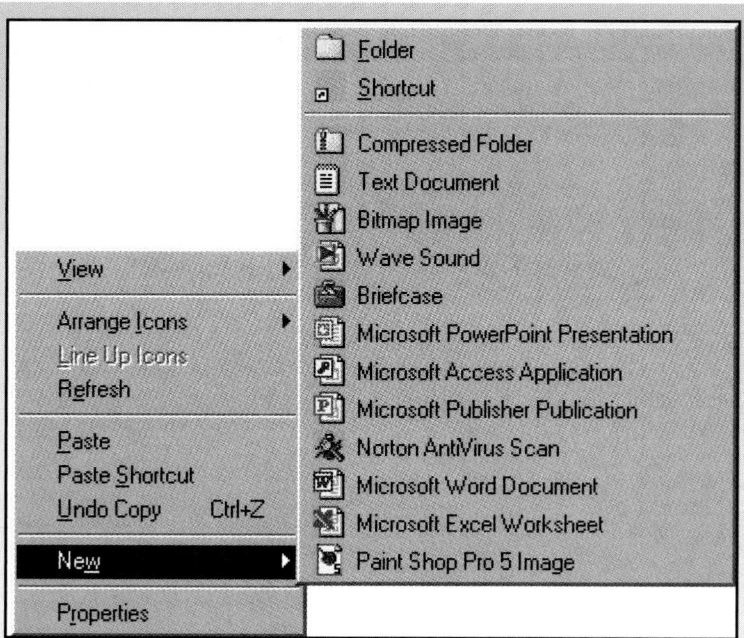

4. To proceed with creating the new folder:
   CHOOSE: Folder
   A folder entitled New Folder should appear, as shown below:

   New Folder

5. Since the folder's title is already highlighted, you can simply type over the name to name your new folder. Do the following:
   TYPE: **My Homework**
   PRESS: ENTER
   A new folder named My Homework should appear in the file listing. The Folder icon identifies the new item as a folder.

6. To open the new folder:
   DOUBLE-CLICK: My Homework folder
   The Save As dialog box should now appear similar to Figure 1.30. Note that the folder is empty.

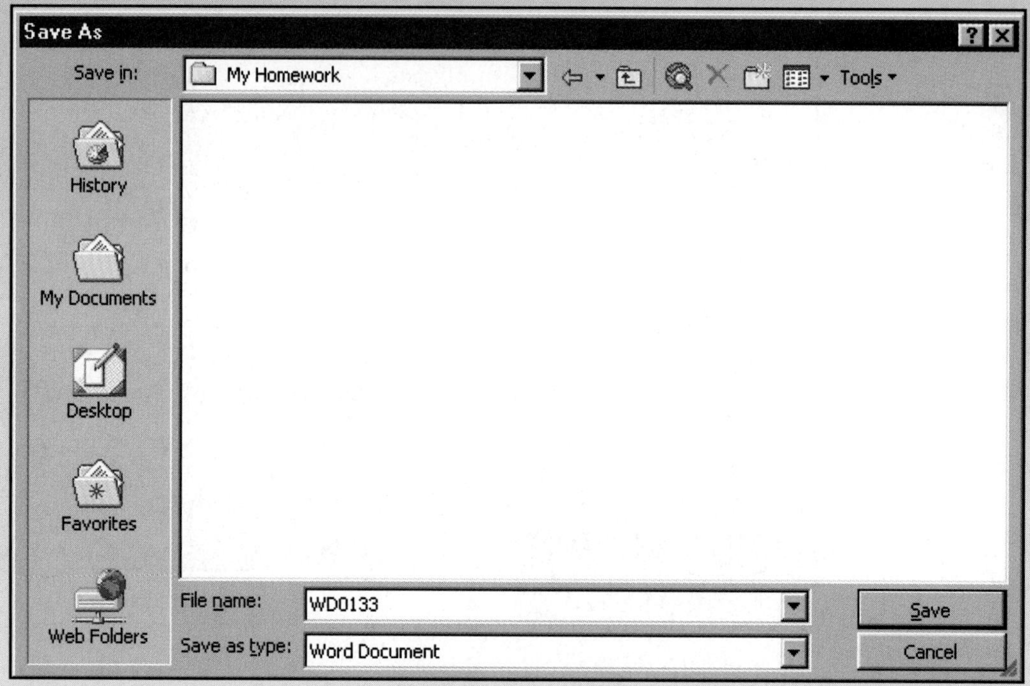

Figure 1.30
"My Homework" folder

7. To save the open file to the new folder, using the same filename:
   CLICK: Save command button
   This is a great way to keep your files organized!
8. Close the document.
9. As a final housekeeping task, let's delete the My Homework folder and its contents. Let's use the Open dialog box this time.
   CLICK: Open button ( )
   The My Homework folder is open and its contents appear.
10. Before you can delete a folder, you must close it and display its name in your file list. To do this:
    CLICK: My Documents button in the Places bar
    The My Homework folder appears in the file list.
11. To delete the folder:
    RIGHT-CLICK: the folder
    CHOOSE: Delete from the right-click menu
    CLICK: Yes command button to delete the folder and its contents
    The My Homework folder and its contents have been moved to the Recycle Bin.
12. To leave the Open dialog box:
    CLICK: Cancel command button
13. Close any documents that remain open.

1.3 Under what circumstances might you want to save a file under a different filename?

1.4 Customizing Your Work Area

Word provides four primary views for working with documents: Normal, Web Layout, Print Layout, and Outline. While each view has its own advantages, it is their combination that gives you the best overall working environment. In addition, for optimal viewing Word lets you zoom in and out on a document, increasing and decreasing its display size.

1.4.1 Selecting a View

feature →

Your selection of a view depends on the type of work you are performing. You will want to perform most of your work in **Normal view.** In this view mode, your document displays without headers, footers, and columns. To view how text and graphics will appear on the printed page, use **Print Layout view. Web Layout view** enables you to see how a document will look in a Web browser, and **Outline view** provides a convenient environment for organizing a document.

method →

To change the display view of an open document, do one of the following:

- CHOOSE: View, Normal (or click [icon])
- CHOOSE: View, Web Layout (or click [icon])
- CHOOSE: View, Print Layout (or click [icon])
- CHOOSE: View, Outline (or click [icon])

practice →

You will now practice switching views using a two-page newsletter. Ensure that no documents are open in the application window.

1. Open the WD0141 data file. If you completed the last module, the task pane should not be displaying.
2. Save a copy as "Newsletter" to your personal storage location. The "Newsletter" document should be displaying in Print Layout view (Figure 1.31). The blank space at the top of the document corresponds to the top margin.

Figure 1.31

Print Layout view

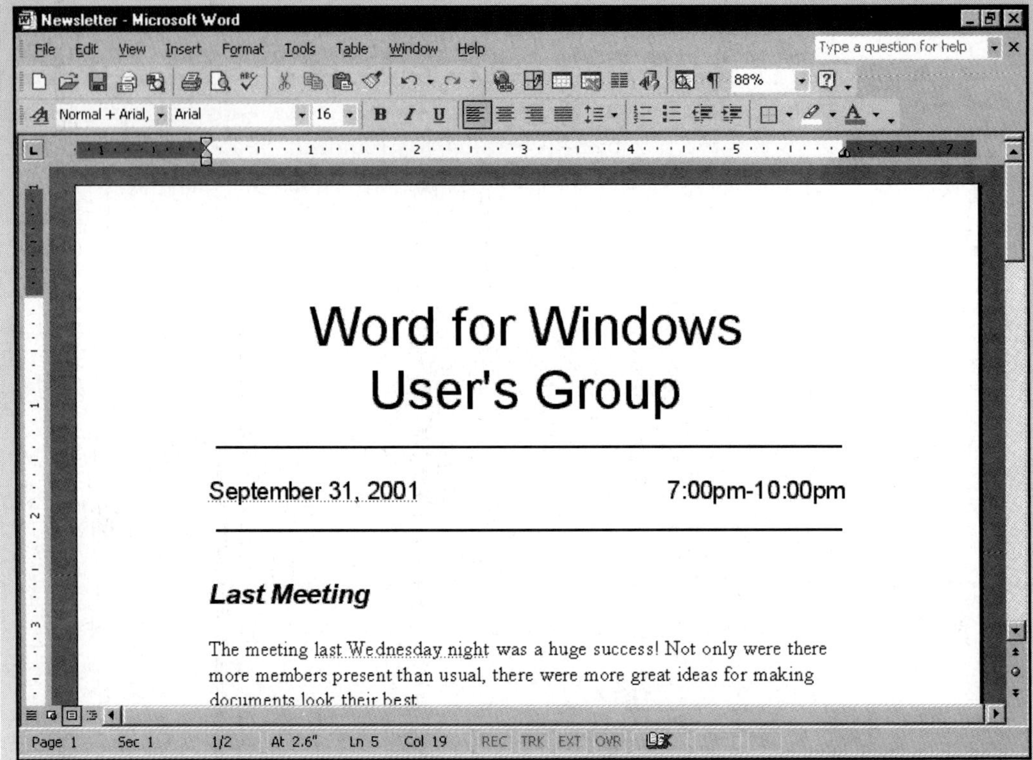

3. To switch to Normal view:
CHOOSE: View, Normal
(*Note:* You can also click the Normal View button (), located to the left of the horizontal scroll bar.) Your screen should now appear similar to Figure 1.32.

Figure 1.32

Normal view

Note that you no longer see the space allotted for the top margin.

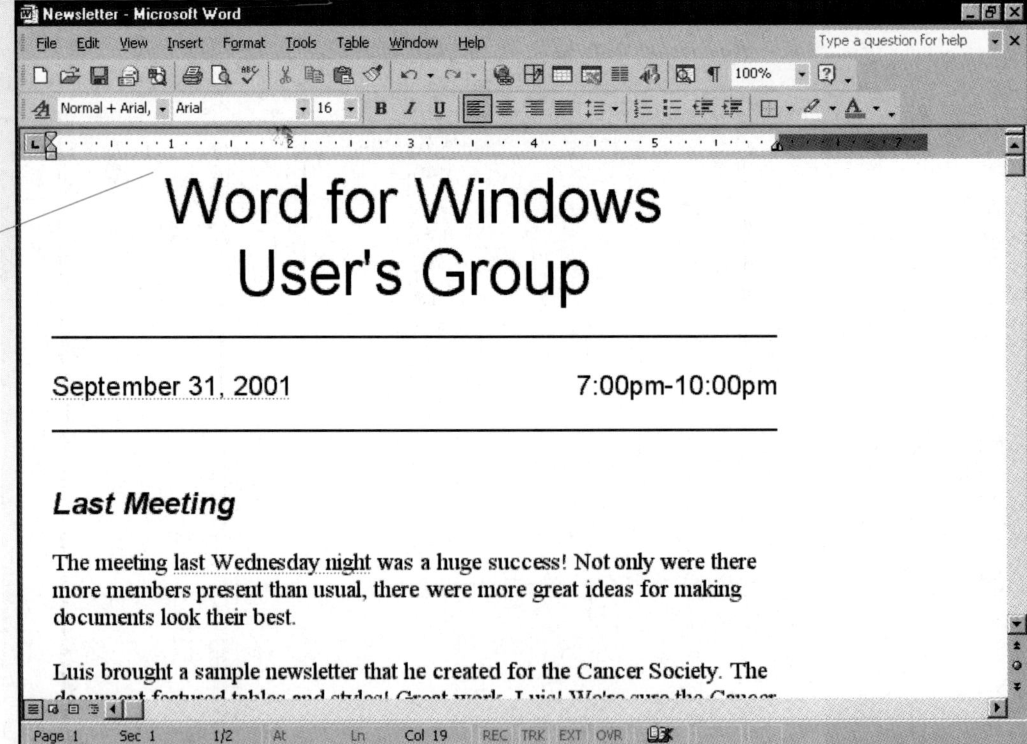

4. To switch to Web Layout view:
CHOOSE: View, Web Layout
In this mode, you see how your document will look when viewed in a Web browser.

5. Let's view the document in Outline view.
CHOOSE: View, Outline
The Outlining toolbar is now positioned above the Formatting toolbar.

6. To view just the main headings in the document:
CLICK: Show Level drop-down arrow (Show All Levels)
CHOOSE: Show Level 1 from the drop-down list
Your screen should now appear similar to Figure 1.33. In this view mode, it's easy to organize the different parts of your document.

Figure 1.33

Outline view

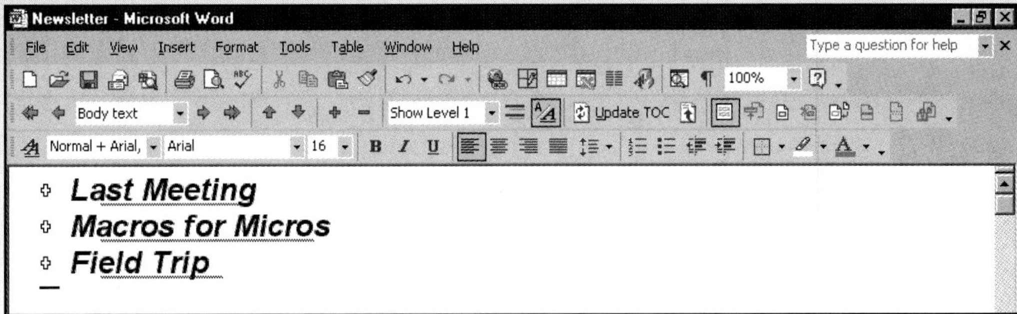

7. To redisplay the document in Print Layout view:
CHOOSE: View, Print Layout

8. Continue to the next lesson.

1.4.2 Zooming the Display

feature

Regardless of the view you select, Word lets you zoom in and out on a document, increasing and decreasing its display size. For example, you may want to enlarge Word's Normal view to 200% of its original size when working with detailed graphics.

method

- CLICK: Zoom drop-down arrow (100%),

or

- CHOOSE: View, Zoom

practice

You will now practice zooming the display. Ensure that you've completed the previous lesson and that the "Newsletter" document is displaying.

88%
500%
200%
150%
100%
75%
50%
25%
10%
Page Width
Text Width
Whole Page
Two Pages

1. To zoom the document to 200% of its original size:
   CLICK: Zoom drop-down arrow (100%) on the Standard toolbar
   The drop-down menu, shown on the right, should now appear.

2. From the drop-down list:
   CHOOSE: 200%
   Your screen should now appear similar to Figure 1.34. The document is immediately magnified to twice its original size.

Figure 1.34

Increasing the zoom factor

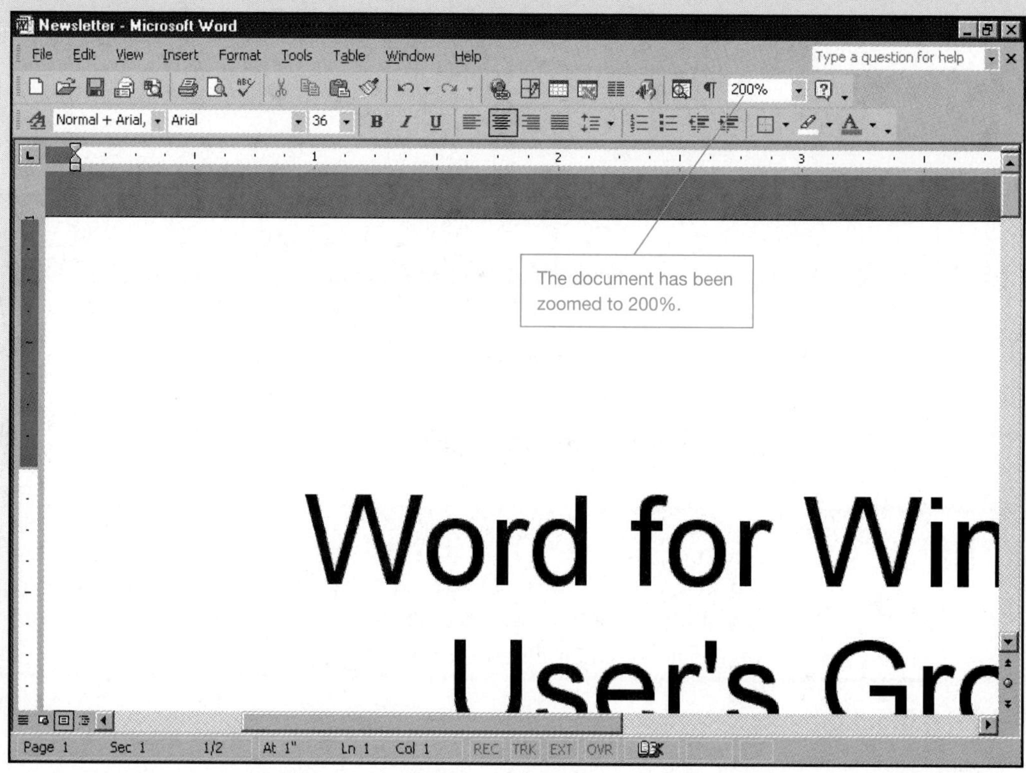

3. To find the best-fit magnification:
CLICK: Zoom drop-down arrow (100%)
SELECT: Page Width from the drop-down list
The view is zoomed to the best fit for your screen's resolution.

4. To conclude this lesson, close the "Newsletter" document.
CHOOSE: File, Close
There should be no documents open in the application window.

In Addition USING CLICK AND TYPE

In Print Layout and Web Layout views, consider trying out Word's Click and Type feature. This feature enables you to insert text just about anywhere in your document. Simply double-click where you want to begin typing and the Click and Type feature will align the insertion point depending on where you clicked. If you double-click near the center of your page, Click and Type will center-align the insertion point. Likewise, if you double-click near the right side of your page, Click and Type will right-align the insertion point.

1.4 What is the difference between Normal and Print Layout view?

Chapter Summary

To create a basic document in Word, simply begin typing after loading the application. Keep in mind that when the end of the current line is reached, the feature called *word wrap* automatically moves the insertion point to the beginning of the next line. You can easily remove characters from a document using DELETE and BACKSPACE, and insert blank lines using ENTER. Word also employs the AutoText and AutoCorrect features to correct certain errors automatically. Besides creating documents, it is important to know how to execute common file management procedures including saving, opening, closing, and printing documents.

Command Summary

Many of the commands and procedures appearing in this chapter are summarized in the following table.

Skill Set	To Perform This Task	Do the Following
Starting and Exiting Word	Launch Microsoft Word	CLICK: Start button (Start) CHOOSE: Programs, Microsoft Word
	Exit Microsoft Word	CLICK: its Close button (X), or CHOOSE: File, Exit
Inserting and Modifying Text	Insert the date and time	CHOOSE: Insert, Date and Time
	Insert blank lines	PRESS: ENTER
	Toggle between Insert and Overtype modes	DOUBLE-CLICK: OVR in the Status bar
	Delete text to the right of the insertion point	PRESS: DELETE
	Delete text to the left of the insertion point	PRESS: BACKSPACE
	Perform an action on a smart tag	CLICK: Smart Tag Actions button () CHOOSE: an option from the menu
Managing Documents	Browse through files	CLICK: buttons on the Places bar, located in the Save As or Open dialog boxes CLICK: *Save in* or *Look in* drop-down list and select a disk location CLICK: Back button () to return to the previous location
	Save a document with the same name	CLICK: Save button ()
	Save a document with a different name	CHOOSE: File, Save As
	Close a document	CLICK: Close button (X) of the document window; or CHOOSE: File, Close
	Begin a new blank document	CLICK: New button ()
	Begin a new document from a wizard or template	CHOOSE: File, New
	Open a document	CLICK: Open button (); or CHOOSE: File, Open
	Print a document	CLICK: Print button (); or CHOOSE: File, Print
	Create a new file folder	RIGHT-CLICK: an empty part of the Open or Save As dialog box CHOOSE: New, Folder TYPE: a folder name
Customizing Your Work Area	Switching views	CHOOSE: View, Normal, or CHOOSE: View, Web Layout, or CHOOSE: View, Print Layout, or CHOOSE: View, Outline
	Zooming the display	CLICK: Zoom drop-down arrow (100%), or CHOOSE: View, Zoom

Key Terms

This section specifies page references for the key terms identified in this chapter. For a complete list of definitions, refer to the Glossary at the back of this learning guide.

adaptive menus, *p. WD 6*
application window, *p. WD 3*
AutoCorrect feature, *p. WD 10*
AutoFormat feature, *p. WD 10*
AutoText feature, *p. WD 10*
hyperlinks, *p. WD 19*
insertion point, *p. WD 10*
Normal view, *p. WD 31*
Outline view, *p. WD 31*
Places bar, *p. WD 23*
Print Layout view, *p. WD 31*
smart tag, *p. WD 16*
Smart Tag Actions button, *p. WD 17*
task pane, *p. WD 6*
template, *p. WD 19*
Web Layout view, *p. WD 31*
wizard, *p. WD 19*
word processing, *p. WD 2*
word wrap, *p. WD 15*

Chapter quiz

Short Answer

1. What is the purpose of Word's AutoCorrect feature?
2. What is the difference between clicking the New button () and choosing File, New?
3. How can you leave a menu without making a command selection?
4. How do you delete the character to the right of the insertion point?
5. What happens if you press ENTER when the insertion point is in the middle of a paragraph?
6. How do you delete a single character to the left of the insertion point?
7. What do purple dots beneath a word or phrase signify?
8. What is *word wrap?*
9. Without leaving Word, how can you create a new folder for organizing your work?
10. How do you close a document without saving it?

True/False

1. ____ You can remove a smart tag from a document.
2. ____ To permanently save your work, you must save it to a disk.
3. ____ Using the Open dialog box, you can sort a file listing.
4. ____ To exit Word, you must choose File, Close.
5. ____ The insertion point marks the location where text is inserted.
6. ____ Outline view describes in outline form how your document will appear in your Web browser.

7. ____ To move to the top of the document, press CTRL + HOME.

8. ____ To switch between Insert and Overtype modes, double-click the OVR indicator on the Status bar.

9. ____ To delete the character to the left of the insertion point, press DELETE.

10. ____ In Print Layout view, you see how your document will look when viewed in a Web browser.

Multiple Choice

1. Which of the following procedures is the most like placing your work in a filing cabinet?
   a. opening
   b. closing
   c. saving
   d. printing

2. When you create a document, it exists:
   a. in the Clipboard
   b. in the Open dialog box
   c. on disk
   d. in the computer's RAM

3. To display an option in the Menu bar, you must ____________ the option.
   a. click
   b. right-click
   c. Both a. and b.
   d. None of the above

4. Which of the following keys deletes the character to the right of the insertion point?
   a. DELETE
   b. BACKSPACE
   c. HOME
   d. END

5. Which of the following can you use to close the application window?
   a. [Minimize button]
   b. [Maximize button]
   c. [Close button]
   d. [Restore button]

6. To save a document using a different name, choose ____________.
   a. File, Save
   b. File, Save As
   c. File, Print
   d. All of the above

7. To leave the Menu bar without making a selection, click:
   a. any option in the pull-down menu
   b. Office Assistant character
   c. Title bar
   d. All of the above

8. The ____________ feature enables you to type continuously without having to press ENTER at the end of each line.
   a. Office Assistant
   b. Undo
   c. AutoCorrect
   d. word wrap

9. In ____________, you can view just the main headings in your document.
   a. Normal view
   b. Web Layout view
   c. Print Layout view
   d. Outline view

10. In ____________, you can see how text and graphics will appear on the printed page.
    a. Normal view
    b. Web Layout view
    c. Print Layout view
    d. Outline view

Hands-On exercises

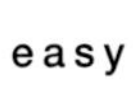

easy

1. Laura Howard: Creating a Document

Laura Howard has just graduated from college and is looking for a job. In this exercise, you assume the role of Laura and create the letter pictured in Figure 1.35. This exercise practices creating and saving a document.

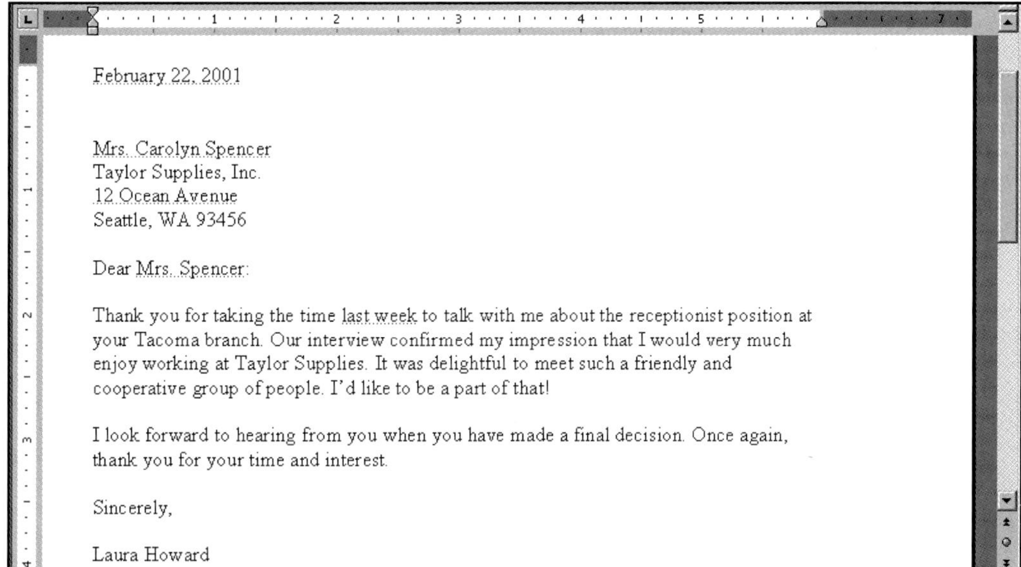

February 22, 2001

Mrs. Carolyn Spencer
Taylor Supplies, Inc.
12 Ocean Avenue
Seattle, WA 93456

Dear Mrs. Spencer:

Thank you for taking the time last week to talk with me about the receptionist position at your Tacoma branch. Our interview confirmed my impression that I would very much enjoy working at Taylor Supplies. It was delightful to meet such a friendly and cooperative group of people. I'd like to be a part of that!

I look forward to hearing from you when you have made a final decision. Once again, thank you for your time and interest.

Sincerely,

Laura Howard

Figure 1.35

"LH Thanks" document

1. Start a new blank document.
2. To insert the date at the top of the blank document:
   CHOOSE: Insert, Date and Time
   SELECT: the appropriate format in the *Available formats* list box
   CLICK: OK command button
3. To position the insertion point before typing the name and address information:
   PRESS: ENTER three times
4. TYPE: **Mrs. Carolyn Spencer**
   PRESS: ENTER
   TYPE: **Taylor Supplies, Inc.**
   PRESS: ENTER
   TYPE: **12 Ocean Avenue**
   PRESS: ENTER
   TYPE: **Seattle, WA 93456**
5. To position the insertion point before typing the salutation:
   PRESS: ENTER twice
   TYPE: **Dear Mrs. Spencer:**
   PRESS: ENTER twice

6. If the Office Assistant character appears:
RIGHT-CLICK: the character
CHOOSE: Hide

7. TYPE: **Thank you for taking the time last week to talk with me about the receptionist position at your Tacoma branch. Our interview confirmed my impression that I would very much enjoy working at Taylor Supplies. It was delightful to meet such a friendly and cooperative group of people. I'd like to be a part of that!**
PRESS: ENTER twice

8. TYPE: **I look forward to hearing from you when you have made a final decision. Once again, thank you for your time and interest.**
PRESS: ENTER twice

9. To complete the letter:
TYPE: **Sincerely,**
PRESS: ENTER twice
TYPE: **Laura Howard**

10. Save the letter as "LH Thanks" to your personal storage location.

11. Print and then close the document. Your printout should look like the document in Figure 1.35.

2. DigiTech Services: Editing an Existing Document

DigiTech Services is a privately owned company that specializes in providing computer networking support to individuals and companies. In this exercise, you assume the role of Joanne, a DigiTech Services account manager. This exercise practices editing and saving an existing document.

1. Open the WD01HE02 data file.

2. Save the document as "DS Account Letter" to your personal storage location.

3. Let's change the payment amount in the main paragraph from $2,345.32 to $50. To begin, position the insertion point to the left of dollar sign ($).

4. To delete the current number and then type in the new number:
PRESS: DELETE nine times
TYPE: **$50**

5. Let's add the following paragraph to the document. Before typing, position the insertion point at the end of the main paragraph (to the right of "agreement").

6. PRESS: ENTER twice

7. TYPE: **Our products are under a full warranty for a period of one year from the date of installation. Problems caused by staff members adjusting the internal settings are not covered by this warranty and will be billed in the future at our regular rates.**

   Your document should appear similar to Figure 1.36.

Figure 1.36

Completed "DS Account Letter" document

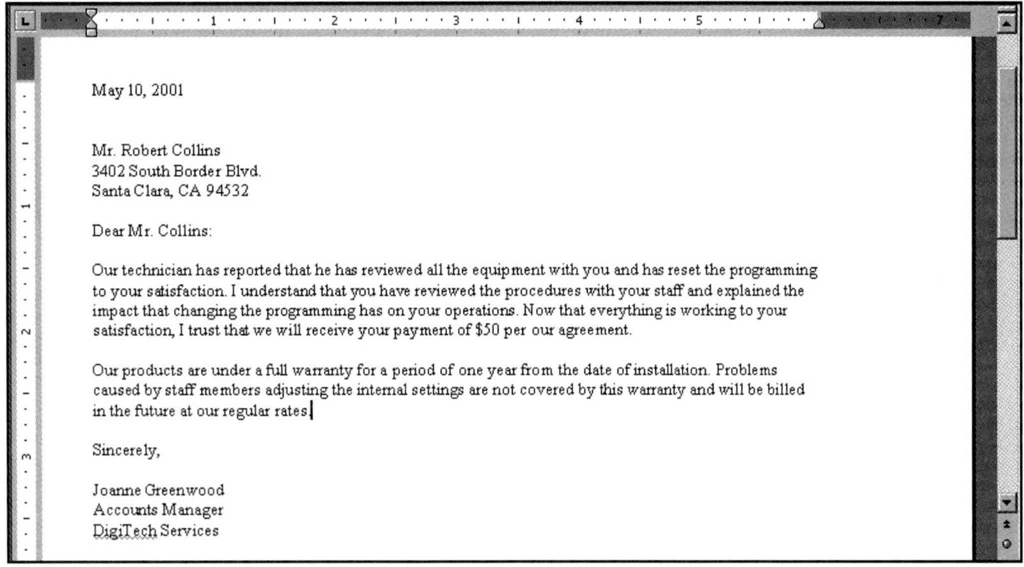

May 10, 2001

Mr. Robert Collins
3402 South Border Blvd.
Santa Clara, CA 94532

Dear Mr. Collins:

Our technician has reported that he has reviewed all the equipment with you and has reset the programming to your satisfaction. I understand that you have reviewed the procedures with your staff and explained the impact that changing the programming has on your operations. Now that everything is working to your satisfaction, I trust that we will receive your payment of $50 per our agreement.

Our products are under a full warranty for a period of one year from the date of installation. Problems caused by staff members adjusting the internal settings are not covered by this warranty and will be billed in the future at our regular rates.

Sincerely,

Joanne Greenwood
Accounts Manager
DigiTech Services

8. Print, save, and then close the document.

moderate 

3. Celsius Gear, USA: Creating a Fax from a Template

If you need some warm clothing, try the Celsius Gear, USA brand. In this exercise, you assume the role of Dennis, a Celsius employee, and create a fax using the "Contemporary Fax" template.

1. To launch the template:
   CHOOSE: File, New
   CLICK: "General Templates" hyperlink in the task pane
   CLICK: *Letters & Faxes* tab
   DOUBLE-CLICK: Contemporary Fax
2. Click in the upper-left corner of the document where it says "Click here and type address."
3. Type the following name and address:
   Celsius Gear, USA
   9090 Seascape Blvd.
   Fort Worth, TX 98720
4. Complete the fax by clicking in the appropriate areas so that it includes the details shown below:

   To: James Wiggins
   From: Dennis Tuma
   Fax: 314-893-5446
   Re: Conference Call

5. In the area below the fill-in lines, delete the paragraph that begins with the word "Notes" and then type the following text (it's all right if the text appears with bold letters):

   The conference call on our upcoming product line is scheduled for April 3rd at 9am Pacific Standard Time and is expected to last 2 hours. Please notify Regional Headquarters whether your office will participate in the call. Standard conference protocol will be in effect.

   Thanks.

6. Save the document as "Celsius Fax" to your personal storage location. At this point, the fax document should appear similar to Figure 1.37. Note that Word automatically formatted "3rd" as "3rd".

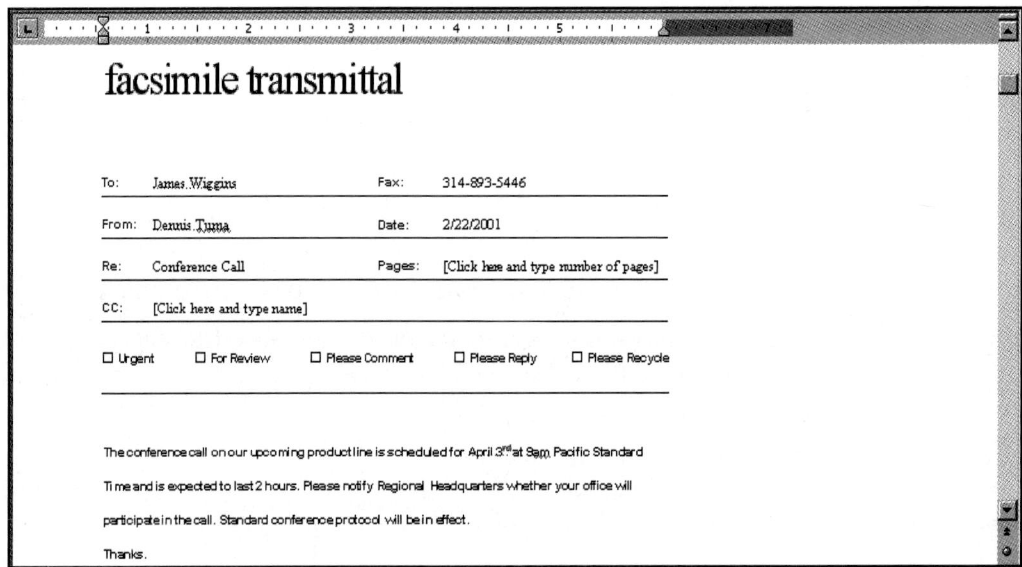

Figure 1.37

"Celsius Fax" document

7. Print and then close the document.

moderate 

4. Worldwide Conventions, Inc.: Editing a Memo

Worldwide Conventions, Inc. acts as the coordinator of all types of business conventions throughout the world. In this exercise, you assume the role of Albert to edit and then save an existing document.

1. Open the WD01HE04 data file.
2. Save the document as "WW Memo" to your personal storage location.
3. Albert typically customizes his display before beginning work. To suit his preferences, change the document's display view to Normal view and then zoom the display to 150%.
4. Delete the text "Administrators" and then type "District Coordinators".
5. Add the following sentence to the paragraph that ends with "commitments."
   Please specify how much space you will need and whether you want to be located on the main aisle of the convention floor or on an exterior row.

   Your completed document should appear similar to Figure 1.38.

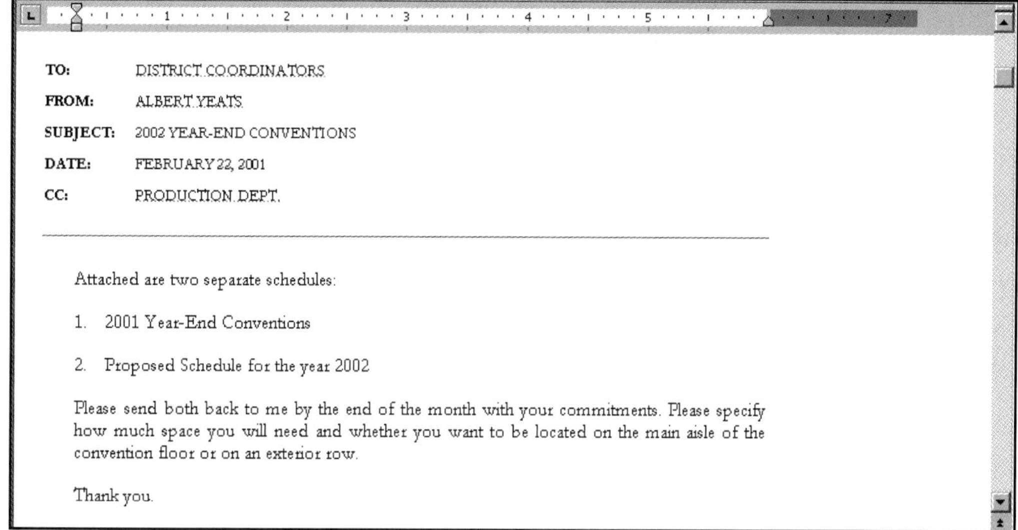

TO: DISTRICT COORDINATORS
FROM: ALBERT YEATS
SUBJECT: 2002 YEAR-END CONVENTIONS
DATE: FEBRUARY 22, 2001
CC: PRODUCTION DEPT.

Attached are two separate schedules:

1. 2001 Year-End Conventions

2. Proposed Schedule for the year 2002

Please send both back to me by the end of the month with your commitments. Please specify how much space you will need and whether you want to be located on the main aisle of the convention floor or on an exterior row.

Thank you.

Figure 1.38

Completed "WW Memo" document

6. Save, print, and then close the revised memo.

difficult 

5. On Your Own: Creating a Letter to a Friend

To practice creating and editing a new document, use Word to write a letter to a friend. This document should begin with the current date and include at least three paragraphs. In the first paragraph, share your excitement about the courses you're taking. In the second paragraph, describe some of the extracurricular activities you're currently involved in, if any. Insert a few closing remarks in the final paragraph. The letter should end with your name in the closing. Review the document for spelling errors before saving it as "Letter to a Friend" to your personal storage location. Print and then close the document.

difficult 

6. On Your Own: Customizing Your Work Area

Customize your work area to your preferred way of working by changing the current view and zooming the display. Then, write a letter to your instructor that describes your optimal work environment and the commands that you issued. Save this document as "Optimal Work Environment" to your personal storage location. Print and then close the document.

Case Problems

Student Tutoring Services

Now that Alex has completed the first chapter of this learning guide, he decides that he can start using Word to organize his business. He realizes that he still has minimal skills, but decides to begin preparing the documents that he needs. He'll format them later, once he masters some basic formatting skills.

In the following case problems, assume the role of Alex and perform the same steps that he identifies. You may want to re-read the chapter opening before proceeding.

1. Alex has decided to prepare notices to be posted on bulletin boards around the college. He found an old copy of the notice that he used last year (shown below), and decides that he will use Word to create the same notice for this term.

   Student Tutoring Services

   Personal tutoring, lab prep, and review services available in the following subjects:

   Computer Science 101, 102, and 201
   Biology 101, 104
   Chemistry 102, 103, 201, and 204
   Physics 101

   Reasonable rates (both individuals and groups)

   For more information, call:
   Alex Federov
   Phone: 319-4234
   E-mail: afederov@sts.com

   He then saves his work as "STS Notice." The completed document is shown in Figure 1.39.

Figure 1.39

Completed "STS Notice" document

Word automatically applied formatting to the title.

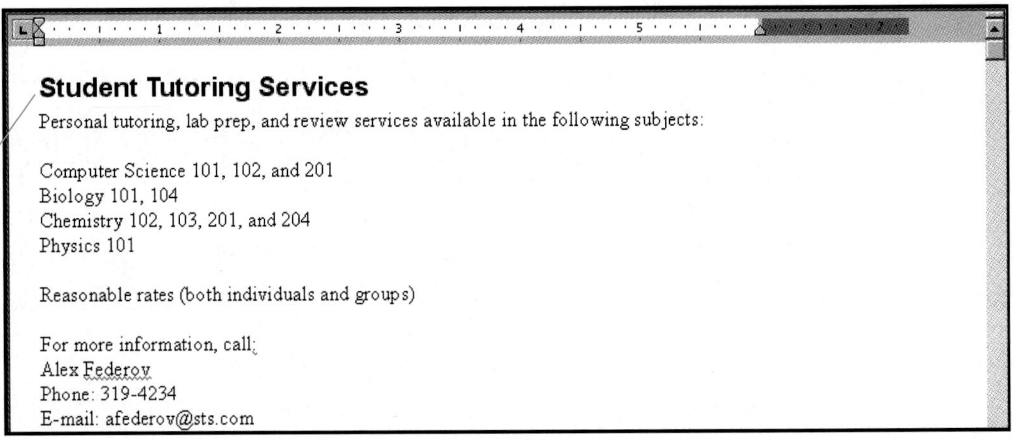

Student Tutoring Services
Personal tutoring, lab prep, and review services available in the following subjects:

Computer Science 101, 102, and 201
Biology 101, 104
Chemistry 102, 103, 201, and 204
Physics 101

Reasonable rates (both individuals and groups)

For more information, call:
Alex Federov
Phone: 319-4234
E-mail: afederov@sts.com

2. After completing the notice for the college bulletin boards, Alex shows the notice to his friend Seth for feedback. Seth reminds him that before a notice can be posted in the Student Union building, it must be submitted to the Student Union office for review. Alex decides to use a Word template to create a memo to accompany the notice. He starts a new document based on the "Contemporary Memo" template.

   Next, he switches to Normal view and zooms the display to 150% so that he doesn't have to strain his eyes when looking at the screen. He now modifies the memo to reflect the information shown below. He also takes time to delete any information from the memo template that he doesn't need.

To: South Western Student Union Association
From: Alex Federov
Re: Tutoring Advertisement

Attached is a copy of the posting that will be placed on campus bulletin boards on September 10th. I request that a copy of this posting be placed on the Student Union bulletin boards.

After saving the memo as "STS Memo," he prints and then closes the document. The completed document appears in Figure 1.40.

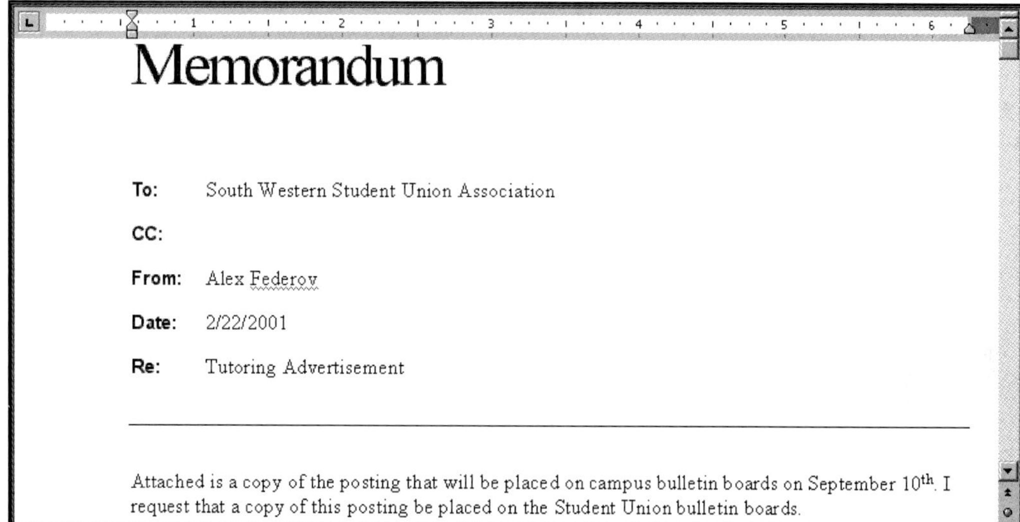

Figure 1.40

Completed "STS Memo" document

3. Alex decides that he should also place an advertisement in the SouthWestern Banner, the student newspaper. After phoning to determine the rates and get a price for his ad, he arranges to fax a copy by tomorrow morning. Alex opens the original notice file saved earlier as "STS Notice" and edits the document to resemble the following:

   Personal tutoring, lab prep, and review services available.
   Computer Science 101,102,201
   Biology 101,104
   Chemistry 102,103,201,204
   Physics 101
   Reasonable rates
   For info call Alex Federov 319-4234
   E-mail: afederov@sts.com

   He then saves the document again and assigns the new name of "STS Notice (Short)". Finally, he prints and then closes the revised document. The completed document appears in Figure 1.41.

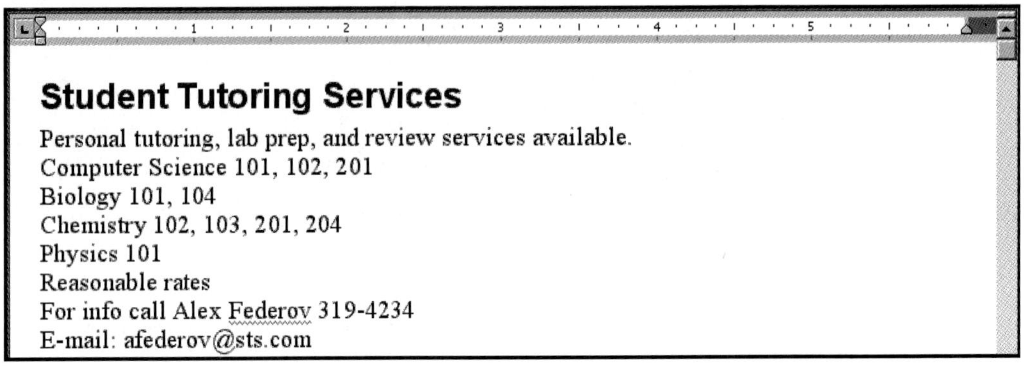

Figure 1.41

Completed "STS Notice (Short)" document

Student Tutoring Services
Personal tutoring, lab prep, and review services available.
Computer Science 101, 102, 201
Biology 101, 104
Chemistry 102, 103, 201, 204
Physics 101
Reasonable rates
For info call Alex Federov 319-4234
E-mail: afederov@sts.com

4. Alex decides to fax the advertisement to the newspaper in order to meet tomorrow morning's deadline. He creates a new fax document based on the "Contemporary Fax" template and modifies the template to reflect the information shown below.

   Student Tutoring Services
   302-1011 College Circle
   Dayton, Ohio 53345

   To: Melody Baker
   From: Alex Federov
   Fax: 319-1234
   Re: Advertisement
   Pages: 1

   Attached is a copy of the advertisement to be posted in the September 12th edition of the Banner and repeated again in the September 26th edition. I have already given you my charge card information and agree to be billed immediately in the amount of $13.57.

   He now saves the document as "STS Fax". Then he prints and finally closes the document. The completed document is shown in Figure 1.42.

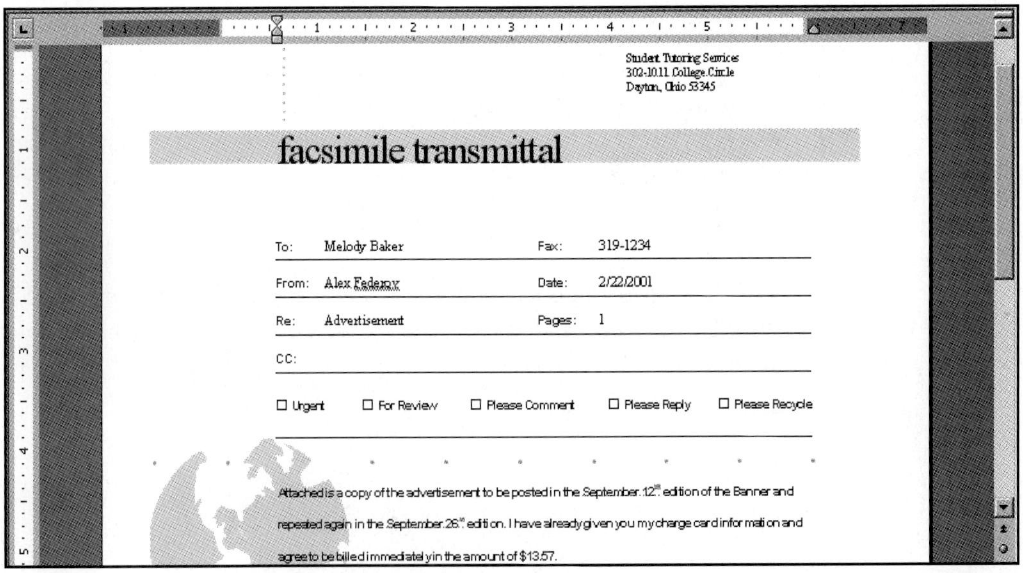

Figure 1.42

Completed "STS Fax" document

Student Tutoring Services
302-1011 College Circle
Dayton, Ohio 53345

facsimile transmittal

To:	Melody Baker	Fax:	319-1234
From:	Alex Federov	Date:	2/22/2001
Re:	Advertisement	Pages:	1
CC:			

☐ Urgent ☐ For Review ☐ Please Comment ☐ Please Reply ☐ Please Recycle

Attached is a copy of the advertisement to be posted in the September 12th edition of the Banner and repeated again in the September 26th edition. I have already given you my charge card information and agree to be billed immediately in the amount of $13.57.

Microsoft® **Word®** 2002

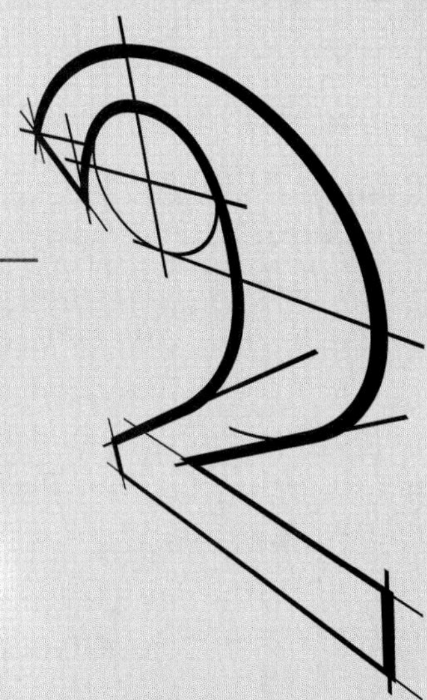

CHAPTER 2

Modifying a Document

CHAPTER OUTLINE

Case Study

2.1 Editing a Document

2.2 Finding and Replacing Text

2.3 Copying and Moving Information

2.4 Proofing a Document

Chapter Summary

Chapter Quiz

Hands-On Exercises

Case Problems

PREREQUISITES

To successfully complete this chapter, you must be able to insert and delete text in Word. You will also be asked to open, save, and close documents, and use Word's toolbars, Menu bar, and right-click menus.

LEARNING OBJECTIVES

After completing this chapter, you will be able to:

- Use fundamental editing procedures
- Search for and replace words and phrases
- Copy and move information within the same document and among documents
- Check for spelling and grammar errors

CaseStudy **MAIN STREET ANTIQUES** Bryan Mion is the owner of Main Street Antiques, a crafts and antiques store on Main Street in Opelousas, Louisiana. Bryan's store is divided into sections that he rents to talented folk who sell their wares. For example, Freda Morris rents the corner space, where she displays antique kitchen items such as cooking utensils and pots and pans. Angel Harris's nook is covered with picture frames that she hand-paints. Other tenants include Abel, the rock painter; Roger, the furniture refinisher; and Dorris, the doll-maker. In addition to collecting rent from these people, Bryan takes a small percentage off the top of any sales made in the store.

Bryan recently purchased a computer that came with a preinstalled copy of Microsoft Word. For the last few months he has been using any slow hours at the store to learn more about Word and has even posted several promotional documents on the store's bulletin board. One of his tenants pointed out several improvements that Bryan could make in the posted documents. Bryan agrees, but is unsure of how to proceed.

In this chapter, you and Bryan practice modifying documents. You learn how to position the insertion point, use the Undo command, correct mistakes as you type, and select and change text. You also learn how to find and replace text, copy and move information, and proof your work.

2.1 Editing a Document

What if you type a word into a document and then decide it needs to be changed? Novices and experts alike make data entry errors when creating documents. Fortunately, Word provides several features for editing information that has already been entered. One of Word's most popular commands is the Undo command, because it lets you correct mistakes by undoing your most recent actions. Another popular feature is the spelling and grammar checker, which scans your documents for errors as you type. This module covers both of these features.

You will find that many editing procedures require that you first position the insertion point in a certain location, or select one or more characters of text. Word provides an invisible column in the extreme left margin of the document window called the **Selection bar.** When the mouse is moved into this area, the pointer changes from an I-beam to a right-pointing diagonal arrow (↗). The Selection bar provides shortcut methods for using the mouse to select text, as summarized in Table 2.1, along with other selection methods.

Word

Table 2.1

Selecting text using the mouse

To select this ...	Do this ...
Single letter	Position the I-beam pointer to the left of the letter you want to select. Press down and hold the left mouse button as you drag the mouse pointer to the right.
Single word	Position the I-beam pointer on the word and double-click the left mouse button.
Single sentence	Hold down CTRL and click once with the I-beam pointer positioned on any word in the sentence.
Block of text	Move the insertion point to the beginning of the block of text and then position the I-beam pointer at the end of the block. Hold down SHIFT and click once.
Single line	Move the mouse pointer into the Selection bar, beside the line to be selected. Wait until the pointer changes to a right-pointing arrow and then click once.
Single paragraph	Move the mouse pointer into the Selection bar, beside the paragraph to be selected. Wait until the pointer changes to a right-pointing arrow and then double-click.
Entire document	Move the mouse pointer into the Selection bar. Wait until the pointer changes to a right-pointing arrow and then hold down CTRL and click once. (*Note:* You can also press CTRL+A to select the entire document.)

We describe each of these features in the following lessons.

2.1.1 Positioning the Insertion Point

feature

Like many procedures in Word, the mouse provides the easiest method for moving through a document. To position the insertion point, you scroll the document window until the desired text appears and then click the I-beam mouse pointer in the text. Contrary to what you might think, scrolling the document window does not automatically move the insertion point. If you forget to click the mouse and start typing or press an arrow key, Word takes you back to the original location of the insertion point before you started scrolling.

method

Some common methods for positioning the insertion point using the keyboard include:

- ↑ or ↓ to move up or down one line
- ← or → to move to the previous or next character
- END to move to the end of the current line
- HOME to move to the beginning of the current line
- PgUp or PgDn to move up or down one screen
- CTRL+HOME to move to the beginning of the document
- CTRL+END to move to the end of the document

To access the Go To dialog box:

- CHOOSE: Edit, Go To

practice

You will now open an existing two-page document and then practice positioning the insertion point. Ensure that you've loaded Word and that you've disabled the adaptive menus feature as described in Chapter 1. Also, ensure that the Standard and Formatting toolbars are positioned on separate rows.

1. Open the WD0210 data file. This document discusses how computers are used in the field of manufacturing.

2. If the task pane is displaying:
CHOOSE: View, Task Pane to hide it from view

3. Save the file as "Manufacturing" to your personal storage location. (*Hint:* Choose File, Save As.) Your screen should now appear similar to Figure 2.1. Note that the insertion point is positioned at the beginning of the document.

Figure 2.1

"Manufacturing" document

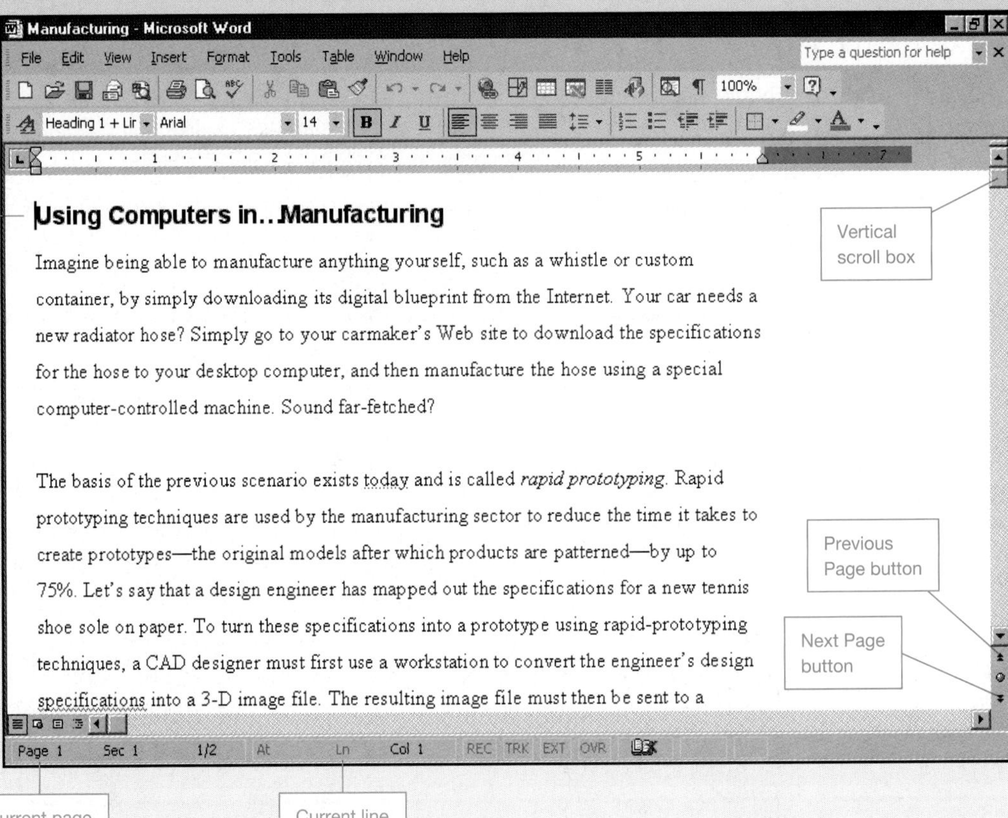

4. To move down through the document one screen at a time:
CLICK: below the vertical scroll box on the vertical scroll bar repeatedly

5. To move to the top of the document:
DRAG: the scroll box to the top of the vertical scroll bar
(*Note:* The term "drag" means to press and hold down the mouse button as you move the mouse pointer from one location to another.) As you drag the scroll box along the scroll bar, Word displays the current page number. You can also see the current page number in the bottom-left corner of the screen.

6. To move the insertion point directly to the bottom of the document using the keyboard:
PRESS: CTRL + END

7. To move back to the top of the document using the keyboard:
PRESS: CTRL + HOME

8. To move to the end of the current line:
PRESS: END

9. To move to the beginning of the current line:
PRESS: HOME

10. To move to the top of the second page in the document:
CLICK: Next Page button (▼) on the vertical scroll bar
The insertion point automatically moves to the first line of page 2 (Figure 2.2).

Figure 2.2

The insertion point is on the top of page 2

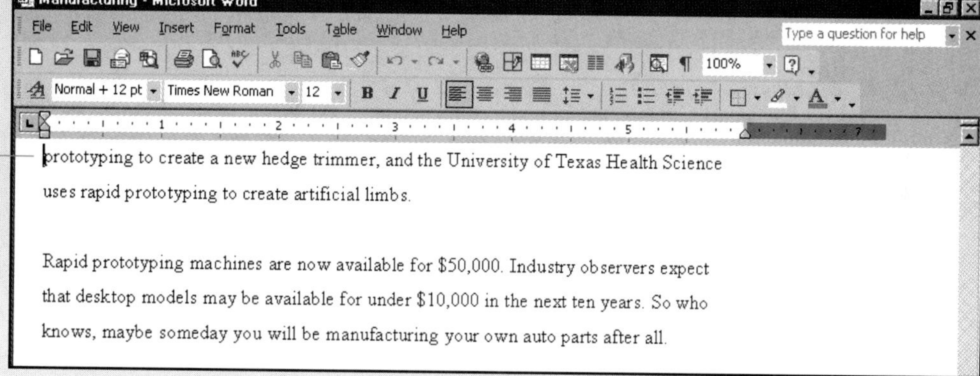

11. To practice using the Go To dialog box:
CHOOSE: Edit, Go To
Other methods for displaying the Go To dialog box include double-clicking the page area—"Page 2"—in the Status bar or pressing F5. Your screen should now appear similar to Figure 2.3.

Figure 2.3

Find and Replace dialog box: Go To tab

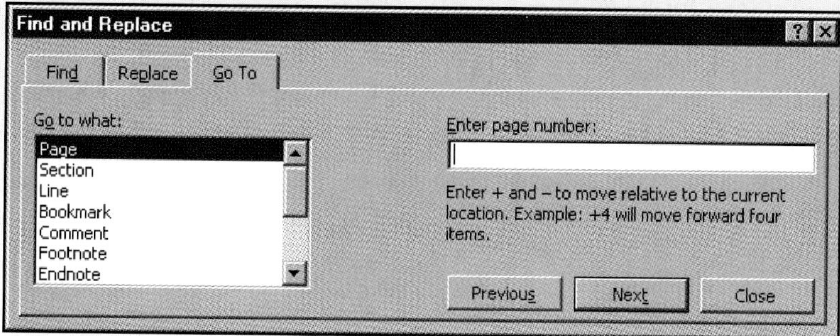

12. TYPE: **P1L8**
CLICK: Go To command button
The "P" tells Word that the following number is a page number, and the "L" tells Word that the next number is a line number. The letters can be typed in either uppercase or lowercase characters. In this step, the insertion point is moved to line 8 on page 1.

13. In the Go To dialog box:
CLICK: Close command button

14. To move to the top of the document:
PRESS: CTRL + HOME

15. Close the "Manufacturing" document.

2.1.2 Using Undo and Repeat

feature

The **Undo** command enables you to cancel the last several commands you performed in a document. The **Repeat** command repeats the last action you performed in the document, such as inserting or deleting text, or using a menu command.

method

To undo the last action:

- CLICK: Undo button (↶) on the Standard toolbar,

or

- CHOOSE: Edit, Undo,

or

- PRESS: CTRL+z

To undo the last several actions:

- CLICK: down arrow next to the Undo button (↶)
- CLICK: an action in the drop-down list to execute that action and all the actions above

To repeat the last command:

- CHOOSE: Edit, Repeat

practice

You will now practice using the Undo and Repeat commands. Ensure that no documents are open in the application window.

1. To display a new document:
CLICK: New button (□) on the Standard toolbar
A new document, entitled Document#, appears in the document area. (*Note:* The name "Document#" is provided as a temporary name until you name the document yourself.)

2. TYPE: **Your First Document**

3. To undo the typing you just performed:
CLICK: Undo button (↶) on the Standard toolbar
(*CAUTION:* Place the tip of the mouse pointer over the curved arrow on the left side of the button, as opposed to the downward pointing arrow, before clicking the left mouse button.) The title should have disappeared.

4. In this step, you retype the title and perform several actions.
TYPE: **Your First Document**
PRESS: ENTER twice
PRESS: ↑ twice to move to the top of the document
PRESS: DELETE four times to delete the characters "Your"
TYPE: **My**

Your document should now appear similar to Figure 2.4. Depending on the settings of your computer, Word may have applied automatic formatting to the text.

Figure 2.4

Using the Undo command

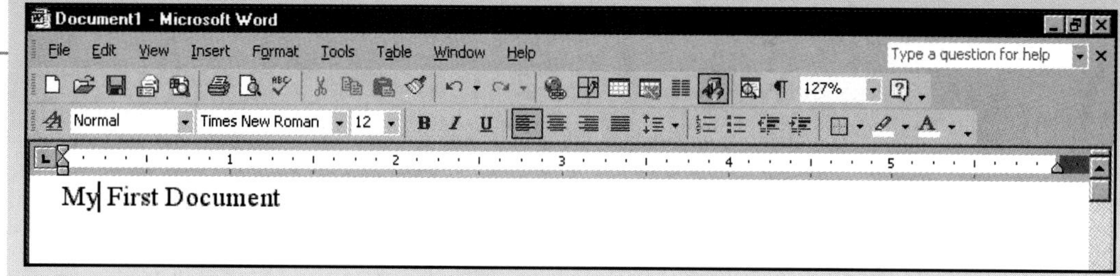

5. To view all the actions that you can undo:
   CLICK: down arrow beside the Undo button
   Your screen should now appear similar to Figure 2.5.

Figure 2.5

Using the Undo command

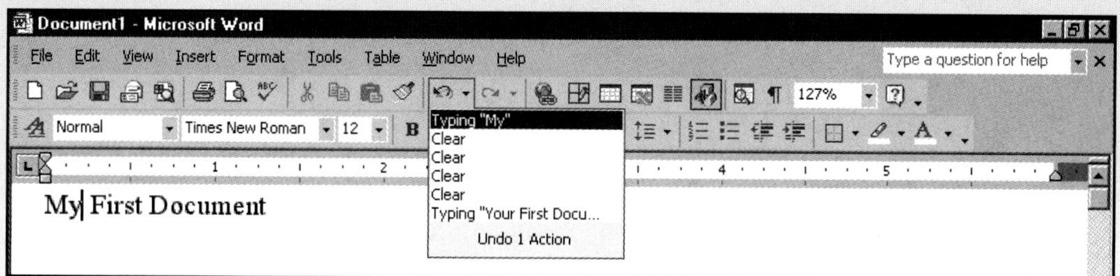

6. To exit the drop-down list without selecting an item:
   CLICK: in the Title bar
7. To illustrate the use of the Repeat command:
   CHOOSE: Edit, Repeat from the Menu bar
   Because the last action you performed was to type the word "My" in your document, "My" appears at the insertion point.
8. To remove the duplicate "My" from the document:
   CLICK: Undo button

2.1.3 Correcting Mistakes as You Go

feature

By default, Word checks your documents for spelling and grammar errors as you type. Word marks spelling errors with a red wavy underline and grammar errors with a green wavy underline. You have the choice of accepting or ignoring Word's suggestions.

method

To correct spelling and grammar errors:

- Point to a word with a wavy red or green underline and then right-click with the mouse.
- Choose Word's suggestion from the right-click menu, or choose the Ignore All or Ignore Sentence command if no error has been made, or edit the error yourself.

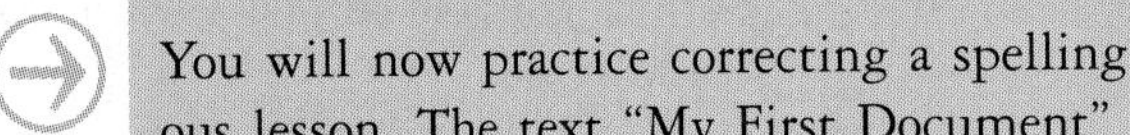

practice

You will now practice correcting a spelling error. Ensure that you've completed the previous lesson. The text "My First Document" should now appear in the document window.

1. In this step, force an intentional spelling error by deleting the "o" of "Document" on your screen.
2. To register the error with Word, you must move the insertion point.
   PRESS: ⬇
   Note that a red wavy underline appears beneath the misspelled word.
3. To correct the word, point to the word and then right-click using the mouse. Your screen should now appear similar to Figure 2.6.

Figure 2.6

The Spelling right-click menu

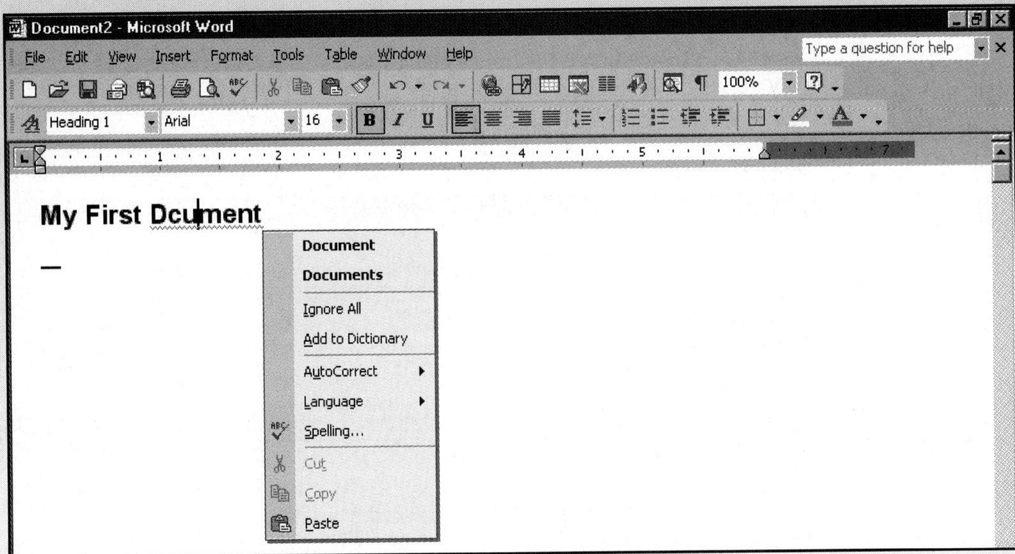

4. Using the mouse, choose the word "Document" in the menu. The word "Document" should have replaced "Dcument" in the document.
5. To conclude this lesson, close the document without saving changes.
   CHOOSE: File, Close
   CLICK: No command button

2.1.4 Selecting and Changing Text

feature

A selection of text may include letters, words, lines, paragraphs, or even the entire document. Many Word procedures require that you begin by making a text selection.

method

The methods for selecting text are summarized in Table 2.1, shown earlier. To deselect text, click once in the text area.

practice

You will now open the "Manufacturing" document you saved in lesson 2.1.1 and practice selecting text. You also practice changing selected text.

1. Open the "Manufacturing" data file.
2. To select the word "Manufacturing" in the title, first position the I-beam mouse pointer anywhere on the word.
3. DOUBLE-CLICK: Manufacturing
   The word should be highlighted in reverse video. Your screen should now appear similar to Figure 2.7. (*Note:* Unless a font color has been applied to text, selected text always appears in reverse video, with white text on a black background.)

Figure 2.7

Selecting a word

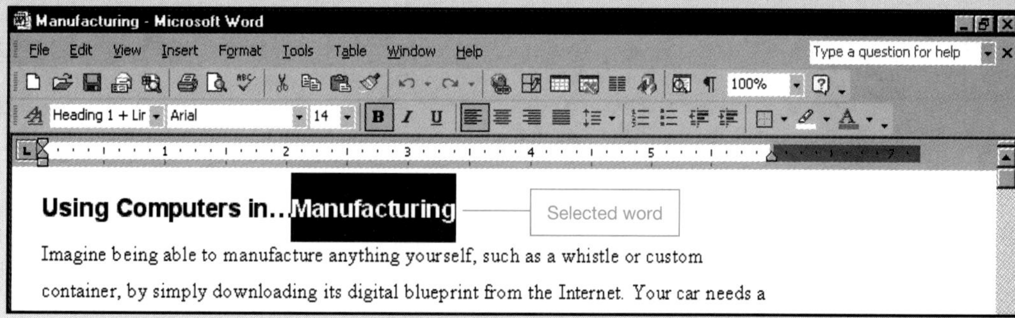

4. In the title, let's select the letters "Computer" in the word "Computers". To do this, first position the I-beam pointer to the left of the "C" in "Computers."
5. PRESS: left mouse button and hold it down
   DRAG: I-beam to the right until "Computer" is highlighted
6. To select the first sentence in the first paragraph, first position the I-beam pointer over any word in the sentence.
7. PRESS: CTRL and hold it down
   CLICK: left mouse button once
   The first sentence, including the period and following space, is highlighted (Figure 2.8).

Figure 2.8

Selecting a sentence

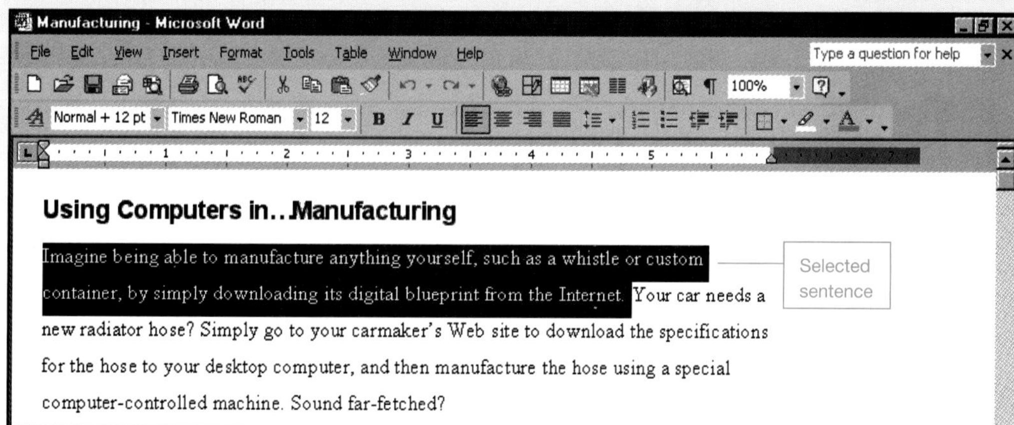

8. To select only the second line in the first paragraph, position the mouse pointer to the left of the line in the Selection bar. The mouse pointer should change from an I-beam to a right-pointing diagonal arrow.

9. CLICK: the Selection bar beside the first word in the second line

10. To select the entire first paragraph:
DOUBLE-CLICK: the Selection bar beside the first paragraph
(*Note:* You can also position the I-beam pointer on any word in the paragraph and triple-click the left mouse button to select the entire paragraph.) Your screen should now appear similar to Figure 2.9.

Figure 2.9

Selecting a paragraph

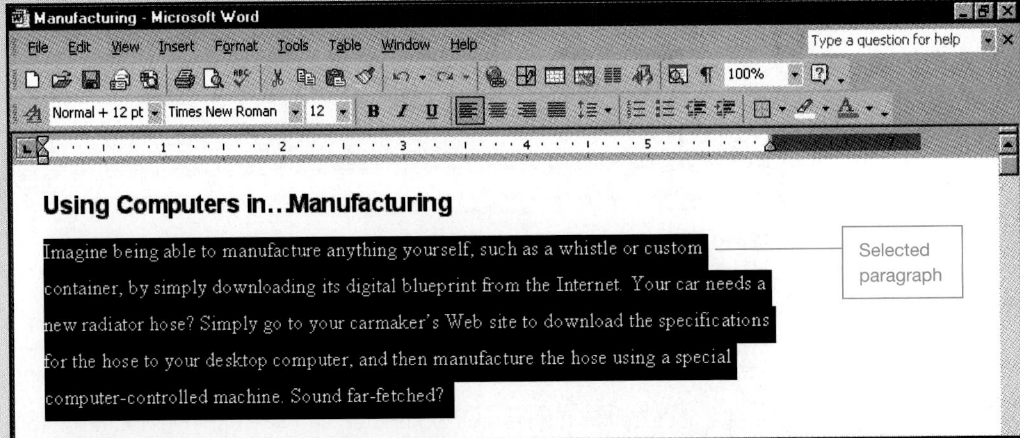

11. To delete the selected paragraph:
PRESS: DELETE
The entire paragraph was removed from the document.

12. To undo the previous action:
CLICK: Undo button ( )

13. To practice changing selected text, do the following:
SELECT: the word "manufacture" in the first sentence

14. TYPE: **create**
Note that your typed words replaced the current selection (Figure 2.10).

Figure 2.10

Changing selected text

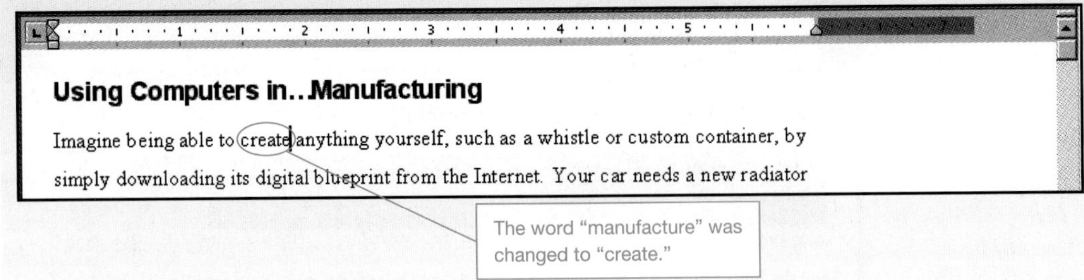

15. To select the entire document:
PRESS: CTRL and hold it down
CLICK: once anywhere in the Selection bar
(*Note:* You can also position the mouse pointer in the Selection bar and triple-click the left mouse button to select the entire document.)

16. To remove highlighting from the text:
CLICK: once anywhere in the text area

17. Save and then close the document.

2.1 What is the difference between the Undo and Repeat commands?

2.2 Finding and Replacing Text

Imagine that you have just completed a 200-page proposal supporting the importation of llamas as household pets in North America. As you are printing the final pages, a colleague points out that you spelled *llama* with one l throughout the document. The spell checker didn't catch the error since both *llama,* the animal, and *lama,* the Tibetan monk, appear in Word's dictionary. Therefore, you must use another of Word's editing features—the Find and Replace utility—to correct your mistake.

2.2.1 Finding Text

feature

The Find command enables you to search for text (like "hello"), nonprinting characters (like the paragraph symbol ¶), and formatting characteristics (like boldface). This tool is also useful for quickly finding your place in a document.

method

To use the Find command:

- CHOOSE: Edit, Find
- TYPE: **the text you're looking for** in the *Find what* text box
- CLICK: More button to refine your search (optional)
- CLICK: Find Next command button

practice

You will now open a document that describes how computers are used in dentistry and then practice finding text. Ensure that Word is loaded and that the application window is maximized.

1. Open the WD0220 data file.

2. Save the file as "Dentistry" to your personal storage location.

3. To begin a search for a word or phrase in a document:
CHOOSE: Edit, Find
The Find and Replace dialog box should now appear (Figure 2.11).

Figure 2.11

Find and Replace dialog box: *Find* tab

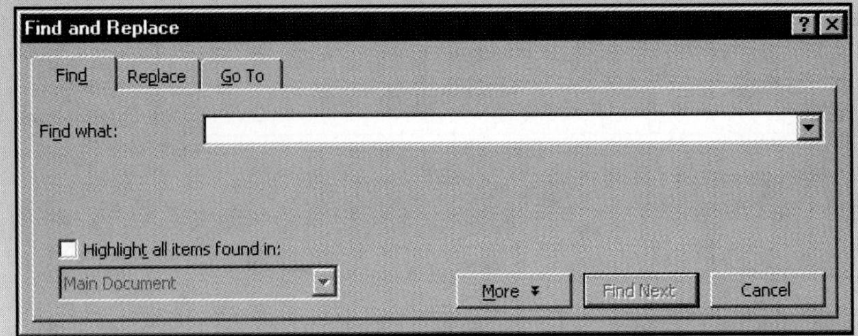

4. With the insertion point in the *Find what* text box:
   TYPE: **monitor**

5. Let's see what options are available when you click the More button.
   CLICK: More command button in the Find and Replace dialog box
   The Find and Replace dialog box should appear similar to Figure 2.12. Note the *Find whole words only* option. In our example, this option would be useful for bypassing those words containing the letters "monitor," such as *monitoring* or *monitors.*

Figure 2.12

Find and Replace dialog box: Displaying additional options

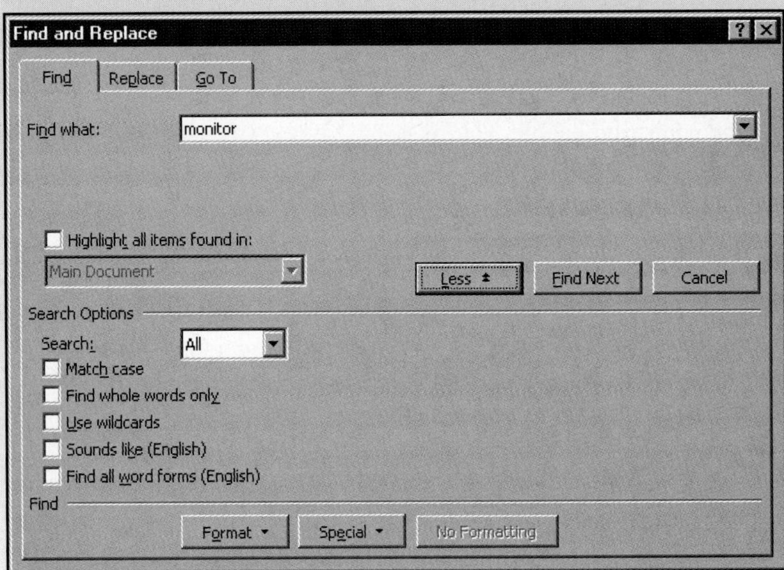

6. To display less information in the Find and Replace dialog box:
   CLICK: Less command button

7. To tell Word to begin the search:
   CLICK: Find Next command button

8. Word stops at the first occurrence of "monitor." (*Note:* You may have to drag the dialog box downward or to the side to see that "monitor" is now selected in your document.) To continue the search:
   CLICK: Find Next command button
   Word stops at the second occurrence of "monitor".

9. To continue the search:
CLICK: Find Next command button
The dialog box in Figure 2.13 should now appear.

Figure 2.13

The search is complete

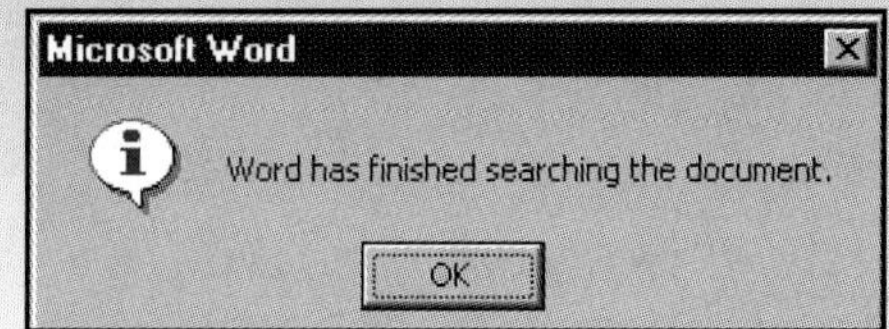

10. To continue:
CLICK: OK command button

11. To close the Find and Replace dialog box:
CLICK: Cancel command button

2.2.2 Replacing Text

feature

The Replace command enables you to search for and replace text, nonprinting characters, and formatting characteristics. This command is extremely useful when you've made the same error repeatedly throughout a document.

method

To Replace text:

- CHOOSE: Edit, Replace
- TYPE: ***the text you're looking for*** in the *Find what* text box
- TYPE: ***the replacement text*** in the *Replace with* text box
- CLICK: More command button to refine your search (optional)
- CLICK: Replace, Replace All, or Find Next command button

practice

You will now replace the word "monitor" with "screen" throughout the "Dentistry" document. Ensure that the insertion point is positioned at the beginning of the "Dentistry" document.

1. CHOOSE: Edit, Replace
Notice that the word "monitor" already appears in the *Find what* text box from the last time you performed the Edit, Find command.

2. To enter the replacement text, click the I-beam mouse pointer in the *Replace with* text box to position the insertion point.

3. TYPE: **screen**
The Find and Replace dialog box should now appear similar to Figure 2.14.

Figure 2.14

Find and Replace dialog box: *Replace* tab

4. To execute the replacement throughout the document:
   CLICK: Replace All command button
   A dialog box appears informing you that two replacements were made in the document.
5. To close the dialog boxes:
   CLICK: OK command button
   CLICK: Close command button
6. To make all occurrences of the word "screen" appear in bold letters:
   CHOOSE: Edit, Replace
7. In the *Find what* text box:
   TYPE: **screen**
8. Position the insertion point in the *Replace with* text box by clicking the I-beam mouse pointer in the text box.
9. Since the word "screen" already appears in this text box, you need only specify the bold formatting option. To do this, you can use the keyboard shortcut for applying bold formatting. (*Note:* You learn how to apply many types of formatting in Chapter 3.)
   PRESS: CTRL+**b**
   Notice that the text "Format: Font: Bold" appears below the text box (Figure 2.15).

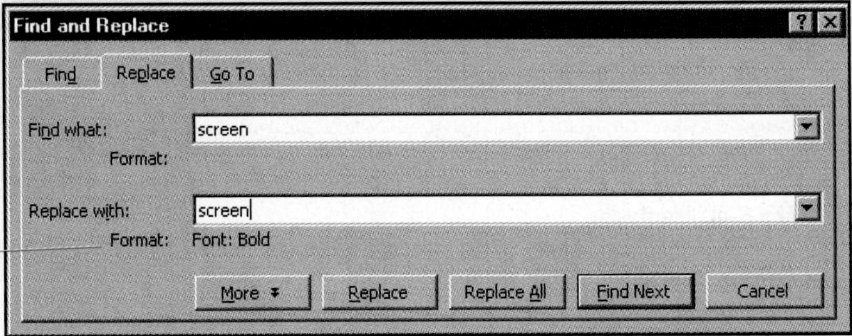

Figure 2.15

Using the Replace command to apply bold formatting

Bold formatting specification

10. To perform the replacement:
    CLICK: Replace All command button
    Similar to last time, two replacements are made in the document.

11. To close the dialog boxes:
CLICK: OK command button
CLICK: Close command button
If you browse through the document, you will notice that both occurrences of the word "screen" are now bold.

12. Save and then close the "Dentistry" document.

2.2 What is the procedure for replacing text in a document?

2.3 Copying and Moving Information

In Word, it's easy to copy and move information within the same document and among documents. Like all Microsoft Office applications, Word provides several methods for copying and moving information. First, you can cut or copy a single piece of data from any application and store it on the **Windows Clipboard.** Then, you can paste the data into any other application. Second, you can use the new **Office Clipboard** to collect up to 24 items, and then paste the stored data singularly or as a group into any one of the Office XP applications. You can also use **drag and drop** to copy and move information using the mouse.

2.3.1 Using the Clipboard

feature →

You use the Windows and Office Clipboards to copy and move information within Word and among other applications. The Windows Clipboard can store a single item of data from any application, and the Office Clipboard can store up to 24 items. (*Note:* The last item that you cut or copy to the Office Clipboard will appear as the one item stored on the Windows Clipboard.) When working in any one of the Office 2002 applications, such as Word, you can display the Office Clipboard toolbar for use in copying, managing, and pasting information.

method →

To view and manage data stored on the Office Clipboard:

- CHOOSE: Edit, Office Clipboard

To move selected information to the Windows Clipboard:

- CLICK: Cut button (✂), or press CTRL+x

To copy selected information to the Windows Clipboard:

- CLICK: Copy button, or press CTRL+c

To paste information from the Windows Clipboard into your document:

- CLICK: Paste button, or press CTRL+v

practice

You will now open a document that warns about the effects of extreme temperatures on computer systems. You will then practice using the Windows Clipboard. Ensure that you have completed the previous lesson and that no documents are open in the application window.

1. Open the WD0230 data file.
2. Save the file as "Hardware" to your personal storage location.
3. To copy the phrase "Computer systems" from the first sentence to the top of the document, first you must select the text:
   SELECT: Computer systems
   Your document should now appear similar to Figure 2.16.

Figure 2.16

Text has been selected

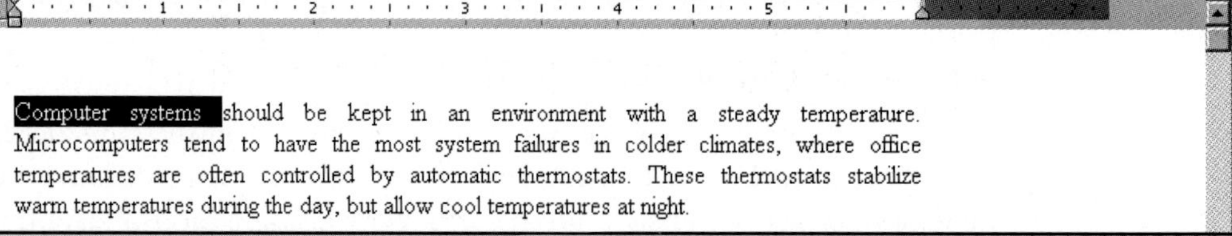

4. To copy the selection to the Clipboard:
   CLICK: Copy button ( ) on the Standard toolbar
5. PRESS: ⇧ twice
6. To paste the contents of the Clipboard at the insertion point of the document:
   CLICK: Paste button ( ) on the Standard toolbar
   Your document should now appear similar to Figure 2.17. Note the appearance of the Paste Options button ( ).

Figure 2.17

Text has been copied

Paste Options button

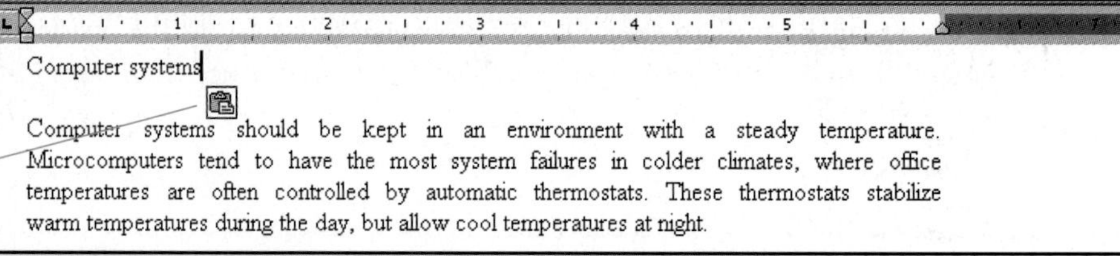

7. Let's see what happens when we click the Paste Options button.
   CLICK: Paste Options button ( )
   Your screen should now appear similar to Figure 2.18. You will learn more about paste options in Chapter 6 of our Introductory and Complete editions. For now, let's not change the current selection.

Figure 2.18

Paste Options menu

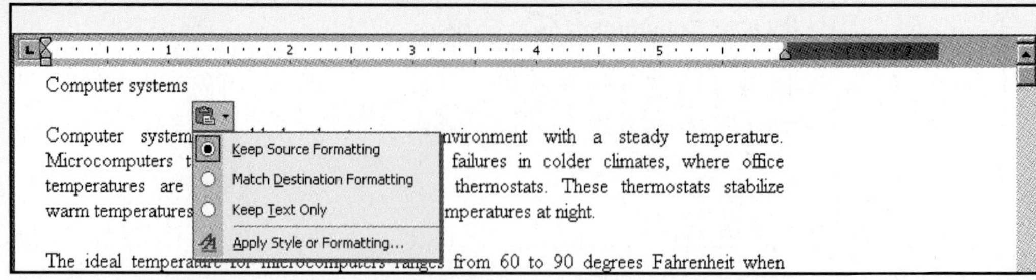

8. To remove the Paste Options menu:
   CLICK: in the blank document area
   Note that the Paste Options button (📋) remains visible.
9. To change the copied text to uppercase:
   SELECT: "Computer systems" appearing at the top of the document
   PRESS: SHIFT + F3 once
   The title should now read "COMPUTER SYSTEMS".
10. Let's move the entire second paragraph (beginning with the words "The ideal temperature") to the end of the document:
    SELECT: the second paragraph
11. To move (not copy) the selected paragraph to the Clipboard:
    CLICK: Cut button (✂) on the Standard toolbar
    Note that the paragraph is removed from the document.
12. To move to the bottom of the document and add a blank line:
    PRESS: CTRL + END
    PRESS: ENTER
13. To paste the contents of the Clipboard at the insertion point of the document:
    CLICK: Paste button (📋)
    The paragraph is inserted at the bottom of the document. (*Note:* It may be necessary for you to delete an extra blank line.)
14. When information is placed in the Clipboard, it can be pasted multiple times. To illustrate:
    PRESS: ENTER
    CLICK: Paste button (📋)
    Note that the same paragraph has been pasted twice (Figure 2.19).

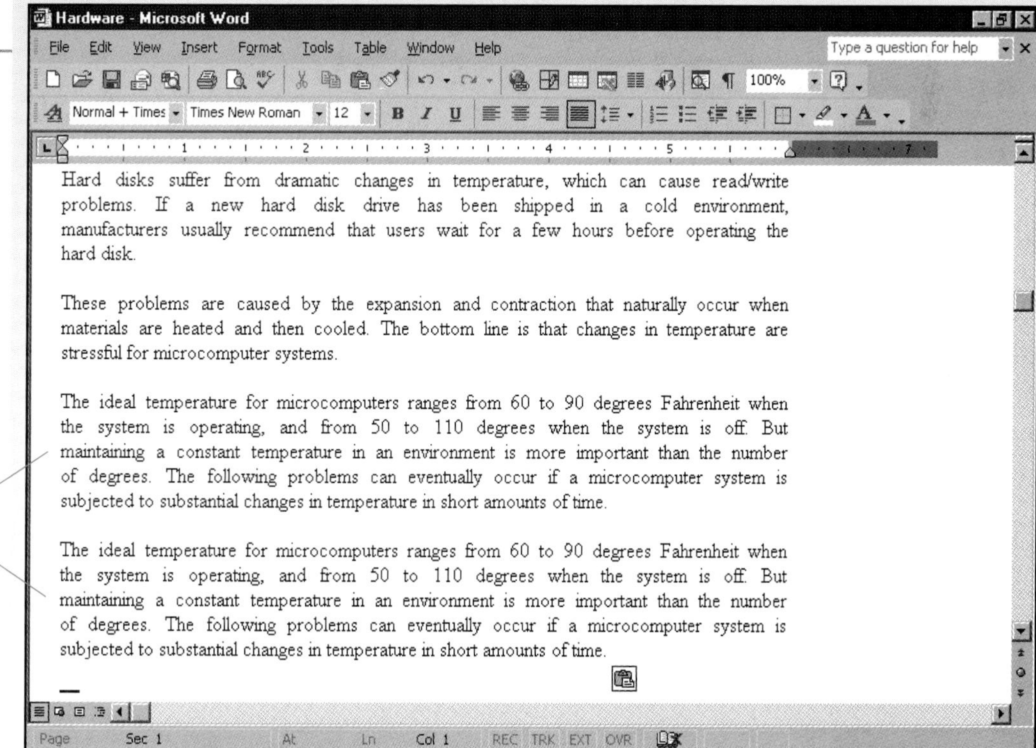

Figure 2.19

Pasting a selection multiple times

15. Let's view the contents of the Office Clipboard:
CHOOSE: Edit, Office Clipboard
The Clipboard task pane shows the contents of the Office Clipboard (Figure 2.20). The Office Clipboard contains the most recent item you copied to the Clipboard.

Figure 2.20

Office Clipboard

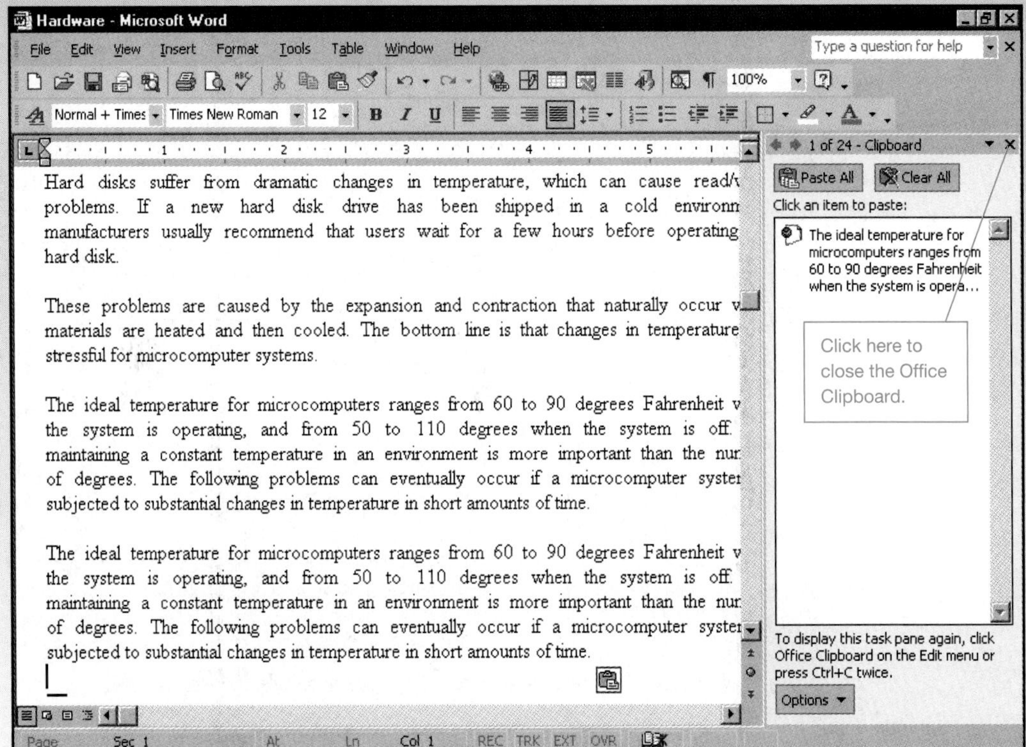

16. To close the Office Clipboard:
CLICK: the Clipboard's Close button, as indicated in Figure 2.20

17. Proceed to the next lesson.

2.3.2 Using Drag and Drop

feature

You can use the mouse (and bypass the Clipboards altogether) to drag and drop information from one location in your document to another. Although you cannot perform multiple pastes, the drag and drop method provides the easiest and fastest way to copy and move selected text and graphics short distances.

method

To copy or move text using the drag and drop method:

- SELECT: the text that you want to copy or move
- If you want to perform a copy operation, hold down the CTRL key.

- DRAG: the selection to the target destination
- Release the mouse button. (*Note:* If you're performing a copy operation, release the CTRL key also.)

practice

You will now practice using drag and drop. Ensure that you have completed the previous lesson and that the "Hardware" document is displaying.

1. Select the first sentence of the first paragraph.
2. Position the mouse pointer over the selected text. Note that the pointer shape is a left-pointing diagonal arrow and not an I-beam. To move this sentence using drag and drop:
   CLICK: left mouse button and hold it down
   The mouse pointer changes shape to include a phantom insertion point at the end of the diagonal arrow. This dotted insertion point indicates where the selected text will be inserted.
3. Drag the phantom insertion point to the beginning of the second paragraph and position it immediately to the left of the word "The". At this point, your document should appear similar to Figure 2.21.

Figure 2.21

Positioning the phantom insertion point

COMPUTER SYSTEMS

Computer systems should be kept in an environment with a steady temperature. Microcomputers tend to have the most system failures in colder climates, where office temperatures are often controlled by automatic thermostats. These thermostats stabilize warm temperatures during the day, but allow cool temperatures at night.

The chips inside the system unit can work their way out from their sockets in the system boards. In addition the chip connectors can corrode more quickly so that they become brittle and crack.

Phantom insertion point

4. Release the left mouse button. Note that the sentence is inserted at the mouse pointer, causing the existing text to wrap to the next line. Your document should now appear similar to Figure 2.22.

Figure 2.22

The selected sentence was moved using drag and drop

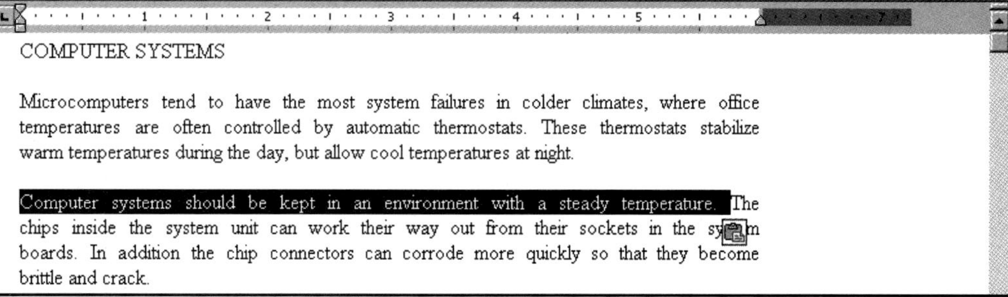

5. To deselect the text and move the insertion point to the top of the document:
   PRESS: CTRL + HOME
6. The drag and drop method can also be used to copy text. To illustrate:
   SELECT: the words "system failures" in the first paragraph

7. To copy these words into the title area:
PRESS: CTRL and hold it down

8. Position the mouse pointer over the selected text and then drag the selection to the blank line below the title.

9. Release the left mouse button and then the CTRL key.

10. The copied text is currently selected. To change the copied text to uppercase:
PRESS: SHIFT + F3
PRESS: SHIFT + F3 again
PRESS: END
PRESS: ENTER
Your document should now appear similar to Figure 2.23. (*Note:* You may have to insert a blank line between the subtitle and following paragraph.)

Figure 2.23

Using drag and drop to copy text

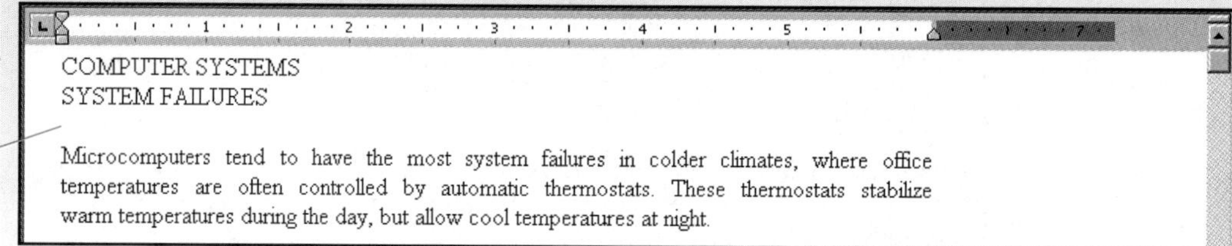

If necessary, insert a blank line so that space separates the title from the first paragraph.

11. Save and then close the document.

2.3 How would you go about moving text to the Clipboard?

2.4 Proofing a Document

Although Word checks your document for spelling and grammar errors as you type, you might want to wait to proof your work until after you've finished typing what you want to say. The **Spelling and Grammar** command analyzes your document all at once for spelling and grammar errors and reports the results. Word's **Thesaurus** feature is useful for pinpointing the most effective words for getting your message across. We describe both of these proofing tools in this module.

2.4.1 Using the Spelling and Grammar Checker

feature→

Although there's no substitute for reading a document carefully, Word's spelling and grammar checker can help you locate some of the more obvious errors quickly. When Word performs a spelling check, it begins by comparing each word to entries in Word's main dictionary, which contains well over 100,000 words. If a word cannot be found, the spell checker attempts to find a match in a custom dictionary that you may have created. Custom dictionaries usually contain proper names, abbreviations, and technical terms. Word's grammar checker contains grammatical rules and style considerations for different occasions. Word offers the following styles of grammar checking: Casual, Standard (the default setting), Formal, Technical, and Custom. You can also customize Word to check only for specific rules and wording styles.

method

- CLICK: Spelling and Grammar button () on the Standard toolbar

or

- CHOOSE: Tools, Spelling and Grammar
- When a misspelled word is found, you can: accept Word's suggestion, change the entry, ignore the word and the suggested alternatives provided by Word, or add the term to the AutoCorrect feature or custom dictionary. When a grammar error is detected, you can accept Word's suggestion, change the entry, or ignore the sentence.

practice

After opening an existing document, you will perform a spelling and grammar check and display some statistics about your document. Ensure that Word is loaded and that the application window is maximized.

1. Open the WD0240 data file.
2. Save the document as "Legal" to your personal storage location.
3. To start the spelling check:
   CLICK: Spelling and Grammar button () on the Standard toolbar
   When Word finds the first misspelled word, it displays a dialog box (Figure 2.24) and waits for further instructions. In the dialog box, Word applies red to spelling selections and green to grammar selections.

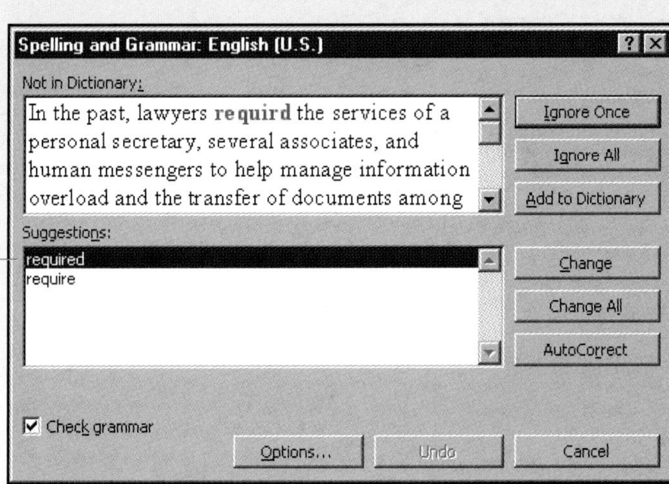

Figure 2.24

Spelling and Grammar dialog box

4. To correct the misspelled word "requird", ensure that the correct spelling of the word appears in the *Suggestions* list box and then:
   CLICK: Change command button

5. Word has now detected a grammar error (Figure 2.25). The dialog box shows the offending phrase, and the title of the first text box suggests why it was flagged. In this case, Word suggests that the sentence's subject and verb don't agree. Word also provides two suggestions for how the sentence might be reworded. To accept the selected suggestion:
CLICK: Change command button

Figure 2.25

Checking for grammar

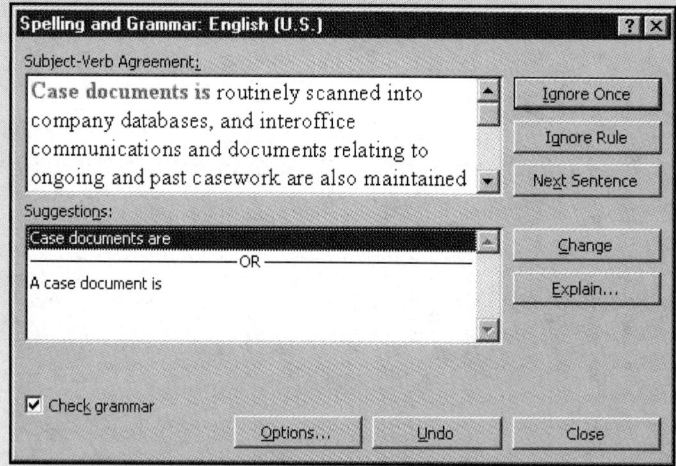

6. On your own, continue the spelling and grammar check for the rest of the document. A message dialog box will appear when it is finished. To clear this dialog box:
CLICK: OK command button

7. The Word Count command is another useful tool that provides some basic document statistics. To display the Word Count dialog box:
CHOOSE: Tools, Word Count
The dialog box in Figure 2.26 should now appear.

Figure 2.26

Word Count dialog box

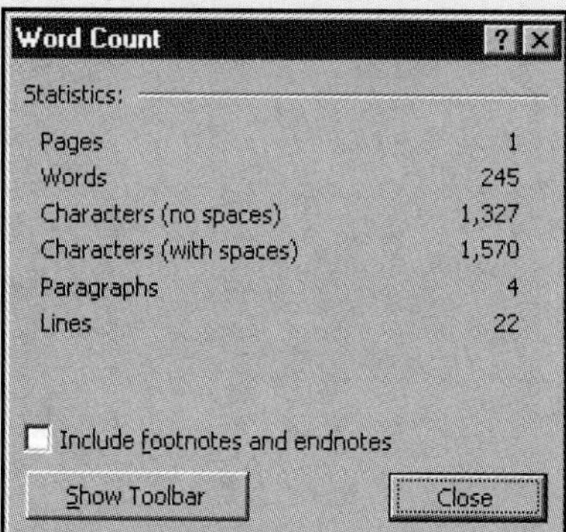

8. To close the Word Count dialog box:
CLICK: Close command button

9. Save the document and then keep the document open for use in the next lesson.

2.4.2 Using the Thesaurus

feature

A thesaurus provides quick access to synonyms (words with similar meanings) and antonyms (words with opposite meanings) for a given word or phrase. Word provides a built-in thesaurus for those times when you've found yourself with the "perfect" word at the tip of your tongue—only to have it stay there!

method

To look up a word in the Thesaurus and replace it:

- SELECT: a word
- CHOOSE: Tools, Language, Thesaurus (or press SHIFT + F7)
- SELECT: the desired word in the *Replace with Synonym* list box
- CLICK: Replace command button

practice

You will now practice using the Thesaurus. Ensure that you've completed the previous lesson and that the "Legal" document is displaying.

1. Using the mouse, select the word "massive" in the first sentence.
2. CHOOSE: Tools, Language, Thesaurus
   The Thesaurus dialog box should now appear, as shown in Figure 2.27.

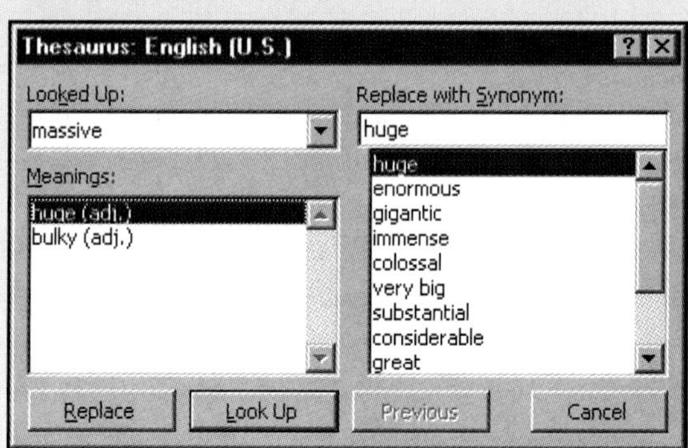

Figure 2.27

Thesaurus dialog box

3. To replace the word "massive" with "enormous":
   SELECT: "enormous" in the *Replace with Synonym* list box
   CLICK: Replace command button
4. Let's find a synonym for the word "big", appearing at the beginning of the first sentence in the second paragraph. To begin:
   SELECT: "big"
5. To start the thesaurus using the keyboard method:
   PRESS: SHIFT + F7
6. In the *Replace with Synonym* list box:
   SELECT: "large"

7. To look up synonyms for "large":
CLICK: Look Up command button
The Thesaurus dialog box should now appear similar to Figure 2.28.

Figure 2.28

Displaying synonyms for "large"

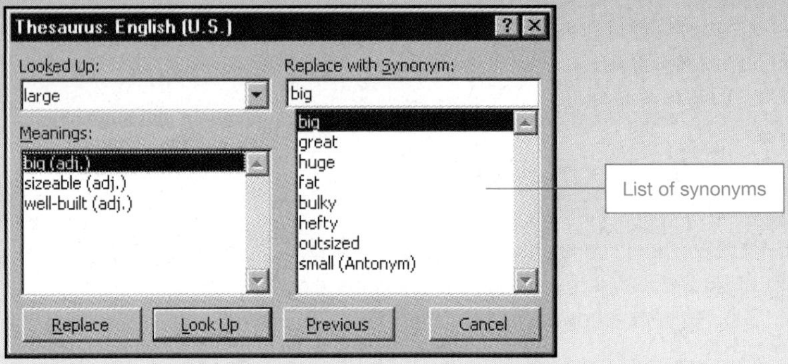

Thesaurus: English (U.S.)
Looked Up: large
Replace with Synonym: big
Meanings: big (adj.), sizeable (adj.), well-built (adj.)
big, great, huge, fat, bulky, hefty, outsized, small (Antonym)
Replace | Look Up | Previous | Cancel
List of synonyms

8. To display the previous list of synonyms:
CLICK: Previous command button

9. To replace the word "big" with "large":
SELECT: "large" in the *Replace with Synonym* list box
CLICK: Replace command button

10. Save and then close the "Legal" document.

2.4 What is the procedure for adding a word to Word's custom dictionary?

Chapter Summary

Two procedures that you should know about before modifying text are positioning the insertion point and selecting text. As with most Windows applications, Word is based upon a Select and then Do approach to editing. Therefore, the proper selection of text is extremely important for executing many commands and working effectively with Word.

Word includes a powerful set of features for modifying your work. The Find and Replace commands simplify the process of locating the information you need and making multiple changes at once throughout a document. You can easily reorganize a document using the Cut, Copy, and Paste commands. You can even drag and drop information short distances. Before sending your document out to others, you should always check it for spelling errors. You can either perform this check as you type or all at once. You can also use the Thesaurus to find just the right word to convey your message.

Command Summary

Many of the commands and procedures appearing in this chapter are summarized in the following table.

Skill Set	To Perform This Task	Do the Following
Modifying Text	Undo your last action	CLICK: Undo button ( ), or CHOOSE: Edit, Undo, or PRESS: CTRL +z
	Undo the last several actions	CLICK: down arrow next to the Undo button ( ) CLICK: an action in the drop-down list to execute that action and all actions above
	Repeat the last action	CHOOSE: Edit, Repeat
	Find text	CHOOSE: Edit, Find
	Replace text	CHOOSE: Edit, Replace
	Copy text to the Clipboard	CLICK: Copy button ( )
	Move text to the Clipboard	CLICK: Cut button ( )
	Paste text from the Clipboard	CLICK: Paste button ( )
	Drag and drop text (copy)	PRESS: CTRL and then drag the selected text to a new location
	Drag and drop text (move)	DRAG: the selected text to a new location
Proofing a Document	Correct spelling and grammar errors as you type	RIGHT-CLICK: any word or phrase with a wavy red or green underline CHOOSE: an option from the right-click menu
	Check a document for spelling and grammar errors all at once	CLICK: Spelling and Grammar button ( )
	Use the Thesaurus	CHOOSE: Tools, Language, Thesaurus

Key Terms

This section specifies page references for the key terms identified in this chapter. For a complete list of definitions, refer to the Glossary at the back of this learning guide.

drag and drop, *p. WD 61*

Office Clipboard, *p. WD 61*

Repeat command, *p. WD 52*

Selection bar, *p. WD 48*

Spelling and Grammar command, *p. WD 66*

Thesaurus, *p. WD 66*

Undo command, *p. WD 52*

Windows Clipboard, *p. WD 61*

Chapter quiz

Short Answer

1. What are the two methods for copying and moving information?
2. What can you do to remove a red wavy underline from a document?
3. What procedure would you use to move the insertion point efficiently to page 2, line 16?
4. Besides a word count, what other statistics appear in the Word Count dialog box?
5. What procedure selects a single sentence?
6. What procedure selects an entire document?
7. In Word, when might you want to use the Thesaurus?
8. What procedure would you use to delete a selected block of text?
9. What menu command enables you to replace text in a document?
10. What happens when you type over a selection of text?

True/False

1. ____ When replacing text in Word, you can instruct Word to retrieve whole words.
2. ____ To move to the end of a document, press END.
3. ____ To move a selection of text using drag and drop, hold down CTRL before dragging.
4. ____ You can select a single word by double-clicking it.
5. ____ Scrolling moves the insertion point.
6. ____ Drag and drop is used for moving text between documents.
7. ____ In Word, you can search for words, but not phrases.
8. ____ Word's grammar checker offers several styles of grammar checking.
9. ____ The Thesaurus provides quick access to synonyms.
10. ____ Once information is placed in the Clipboard, it can be pasted multiple times.

Multiple Choice

1. In relation to a document, where is the Selection bar located?
   a. top
   b. bottom
   c. left
   d. right

2. You can select a word by ______________.
   a. single-clicking
   b. double-clicking
   c. Both a. and b.
   d. None of the above

3. Which of the following is best for quick "from-here-to-there" copy operations?
   a. the Clipboard
   b. cut, copy, and paste
   c. drag and drop
   d. AutoText

4. Which of the following operations moves text from the Clipboard?
   a. cut
   b. copy
   c. paste
   d. drag and drop

5. Which of the following provides a list of synonyms?
   a. Find command
   b. Replace command
   c. Thesaurus
   d. Spelling and Grammar command

6. Which of the following enables you to paste data multiple times?
   a. Windows Clipboard
   b. Office Clipboard
   c. drag and drop
   d. Both a. and b.

7. To display statistics about a document:
   a. CHOOSE: Insert, Statistics
   b. CHOOSE: Tools, Spelling and Grammar
   c. CHOOSE: Tools, Statistics
   d. CHOOSE: Tools, Word Count

8. Which of the following can't be selected?
   a. letter
   b. word
   c. line
   d. Selection bar

9. Which of the following enables you to make multiple changes in a document at once?
   a. Find command
   b. Replace command
   c. drag and drop
   d. Copy command

10. What should you always do before submitting a document to others?
    a. use the Undo command
    b. use the Replace command
    c. spell check the document
    d. launch the Thesaurus

Hands-On exercises

1. Laura Howard: Proofing a Letter

In this exercise, Laura continues her job search. Assume the role of Laura to modify an existing document. You will use the Find and Replace command and Word's proofing tools.

1. Open the WD02HE01 data file.
2. Save the document as "LH Interview Request" to your personal storage location.
3. To replace every occurrence of "Manager" with "Sales Manager", do the following:
   CHOOSE: Edit, Replace
   TYPE: **Manager** in the *Find what* text box
   TYPE: **Sales Manager** in the *Replace with* text box

4. Perform this step if you see "Font: Bold" beneath the *Replace with* text box. (*Note:* This code will display if you completed lesson 2.2.2 in this chapter.)
   PRESS: CTRL+**b** twice to remove the formatting command
   No text should be displaying beneath the *Replace with* text box.

5. CLICK: Replace All command button
   Word should have made two replacements.

6. To proceed:
   CLICK: OK command button
   CLICK: Close command button to leave the Find and Replace dialog box

7. After moving the insertion point to the top of the document, if it is not there already, let's check the document for spelling and grammar errors.
   CLICK: Spelling and Grammar button ( )

8. During the spelling and grammar check, do the following:
   - Change "intrest" to "interest"
   - Change "apealing" to "appealing"
   - Delete the second occurrence of "you"

9. At the completion of the spelling and grammar check:
   CLICK: OK command button

10. Find a different word for the word "appealing" in the first paragraph. It is up to you to use the Thesaurus command and choose a word. Your document should appear similar to Figure 2.29.

Figure 2.29

Printed "LH Interview Request" document

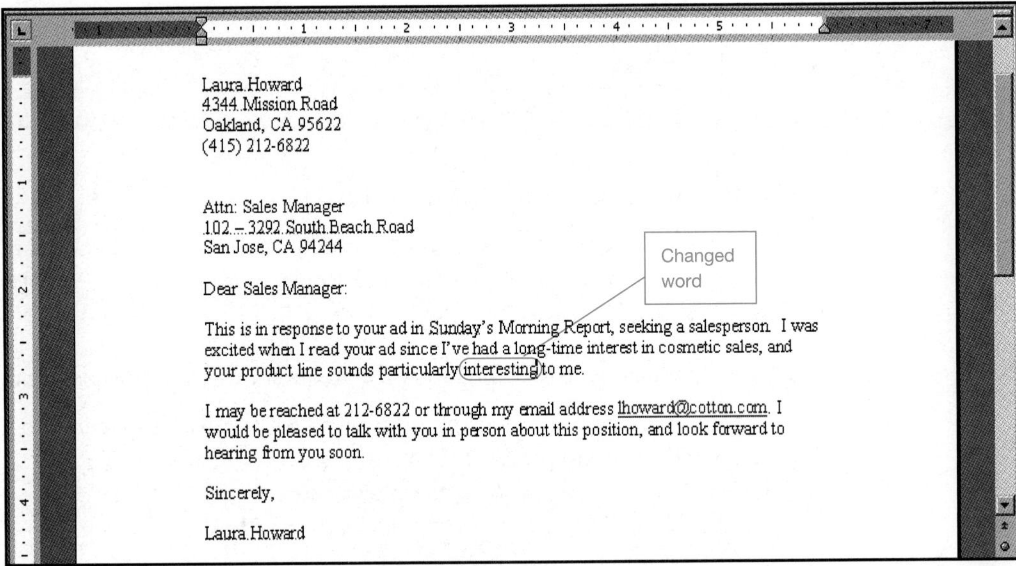

Laura Howard
4344 Mission Road
Oakland, CA 95622
(415) 212-6822

Attn: Sales Manager
102 – 3292 South Beach Road
San Jose, CA 94244

Dear Sales Manager:

This is in response to your ad in Sunday's Morning Report, seeking a salesperson. I was excited when I read your ad since I've had a long-time interest in cosmetic sales, and your product line sounds particularly interesting to me.

I may be reached at 212-6822 or through my email address lhoward@cotton.com. I would be pleased to talk with you in person about this position, and look forward to hearing from you soon.

Sincerely,

Laura Howard

11. Print the document.

12. To display statistics about this document:
    CHOOSE: Tools, Word Count

13. Write the statistics that relate to Words, Characters (no spaces), and Paragraphs near the bottom of your printout. When you're finished, click the Close command button to leave the Word Count dialog box.
14. Save and then close the document.

2. DigiTech Services: Editing a Report

Victor, a DigiTech Services employee, is working on a short report about a popular Internet technology. Assume the role of Victor in editing the report. You will practice several useful techniques including positioning the insertion point, selecting and changing text, and spell checking.

1. Open the WD02HE02 data file.
2. Save a copy of the file as "DS Report" to your personal storage location. You should see the new filename in the Title bar.
3. To move the insertion point to the end of the document and then insert some text:
   PRESS: CTRL + END
   PRESS: ENTER once
   TYPE: **For more information or to establish service, contact your local sales representative.**
4. To move the insertion point back to the beginning of the document:
   PRESS: CTRL + HOME
5. SELECT: the existing title (DSL) at the top of the document
6. To replace the selected text:
   TYPE: **About Digital Subscriber Lines (DSL)**
7. To delete the first main paragraph of the document:
   SELECT: the first main paragraph of the document by clicking the paragraph three times
   PRESS: DELETE
8. To undo the last action you performed:
   CHOOSE: Edit, Undo Clear from the Menu bar
9. Proof the document for spelling and grammar errors. You decide what changes, if any, should be made.
10. Save, print, and then close the document.

moderate 

3. Celsius Gear, USA: Copying and Moving Information

Dennis, a Celsius Gear, USA employee, has decided to improve the organization of an existing memo document. In this exercise, you assume the role of Dennis and practice using drag and drop, and the Cut, Copy, and Paste commands. You will also practice using Word's AutoFormat command, which we described in lesson 1.2.1.

1. Open the WD02HE03 data file.
2. Save the document as "Celsius Memo" to your personal storage location.
3. Using drag and drop, change the order of the information lines to reflect the following: Date, RE, To, From, Cc, and Priority.

4. Insert a blank line between the Date, RE, To, From, Cc, and Priority lines.

5. In this step, you will add some formatting to the document using Word's AutoFormat command. Position the insertion point one line beneath the "Memorandum" heading.

6. To insert an automatic borderline at the insertion point:
   TYPE: *three equal signs (=)*
   PRESS: ENTER
   A double borderline should now appear beneath the Memorandum heading. (*Note:* If you had typed in dashes, a single borderline would have appeared.) The AutoCorrect Options button () should also appear. You can use its associated menu to undo the inserted borderline or to turn off the borderline feature.

7. Position the insertion point two lines beneath the Priority line.

8. To insert an automatic borderline at the insertion point:
   TYPE: *three equal signs (=)*
   PRESS: ENTER
   Your memo should now appear similar to Figure 2.30.

Figure 2.30

"Celsius Memo" document with borders

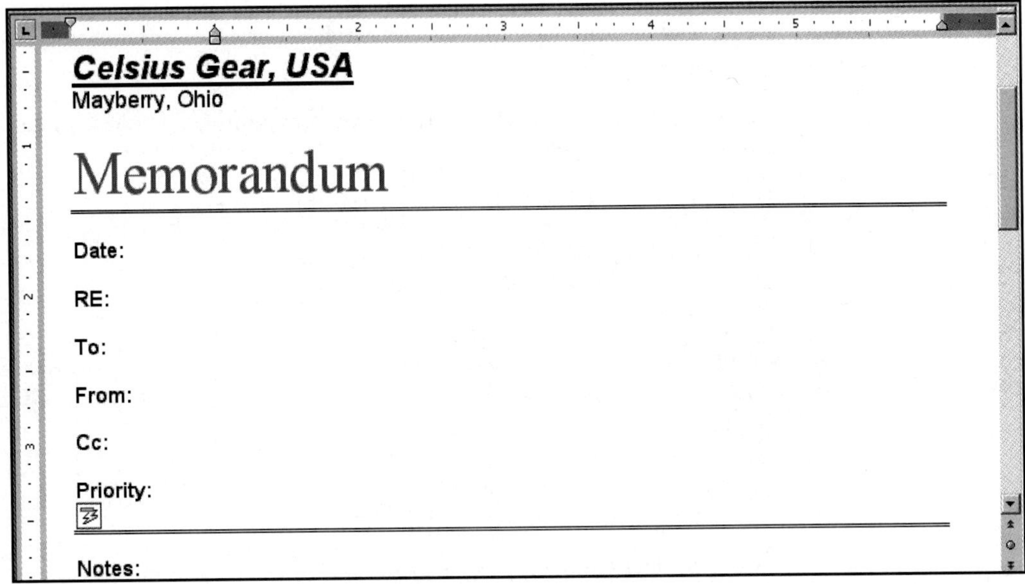

9. Select the entire memo and then copy it to the Clipboard.

10. Paste the contents of the Clipboard below the existing memo to create two memos on a single page. Once printed, this document can be cut in half to create two memos.

11. Save the revised document.

12. Print and then close the document.

moderate 

4. Worldwide Conventions, Inc.: Modifying a Document

Jason McGonigle, the president of Worldwide Conventions, Inc., must inform his employees of the company's new employee stock purchase plan. In this exercise, you assume the role of Jason and use the Clipboard, Thesaurus, and spelling and grammar checker to finalize an existing document.

1. Open the WD02HE04 data file.
2. Save the document as "WW News Bulletin" to your personal storage location.
3. Use the Clipboard to rearrange the order of the information sessions (the items with dates) so that they are arranged in chronological order.
4. Use the Clipboard to move the last sentence of the document (beginning with "Purchase arrangements . . .") to the beginning of the second paragraph (before "To ensure . . .").
5. Use the Thesaurus to find alternative words for "council" and "attitude" in the first paragraph.
6. Check the document for spelling and grammar errors.
7. Save, print, and then close the document. The completed document appears in Figure 2.31.

Figure 2.31

Completed "WW News Bulletin" document

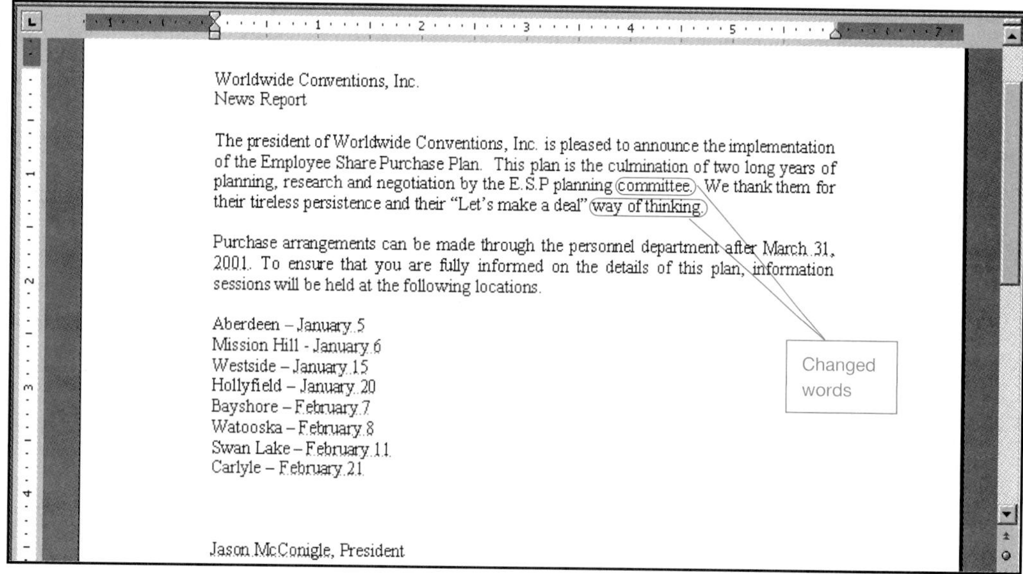

Worldwide Conventions, Inc.
News Report

The president of Worldwide Conventions, Inc. is pleased to announce the implementation of the Employee Share Purchase Plan. This plan is the culmination of two long years of planning, research and negotiation by the E.S.P planning committee. We thank them for their tireless persistence and their "Let's make a deal" way of thinking.

Purchase arrangements can be made through the personnel department after March 31, 2001. To ensure that you are fully informed on the details of this plan, information sessions will be held at the following locations.

Aberdeen – January 5
Mission Hill - January 6
Westside – January 15
Hollyfield – January 20
Bayshore – February 7
Watooska – February 8
Swan Lake – February 11
Carlyle – February 21

Jason McConigle, President

difficult 

5. On Your Own: Describing Your Hobby

In a 1- to 2-page document, describe your hobby or favorite pursuit. Be sure to insert a title at the top of your document, with your name appearing one line below. Check the document for spelling and grammar errors before saving it to your personal storage location as "Hobby Description". Print and then close the document.

difficult 

6. On Your Own: Finalizing a Document

Open the WD02HE06 data file and then save it to your personal storage location as "Leopard". Perform the following steps:

- Change your document's display view to Normal view and change the zoom level to 75%. Your document should appear similar to Figure 2.32.

Figure 2.32

"Leopard" document

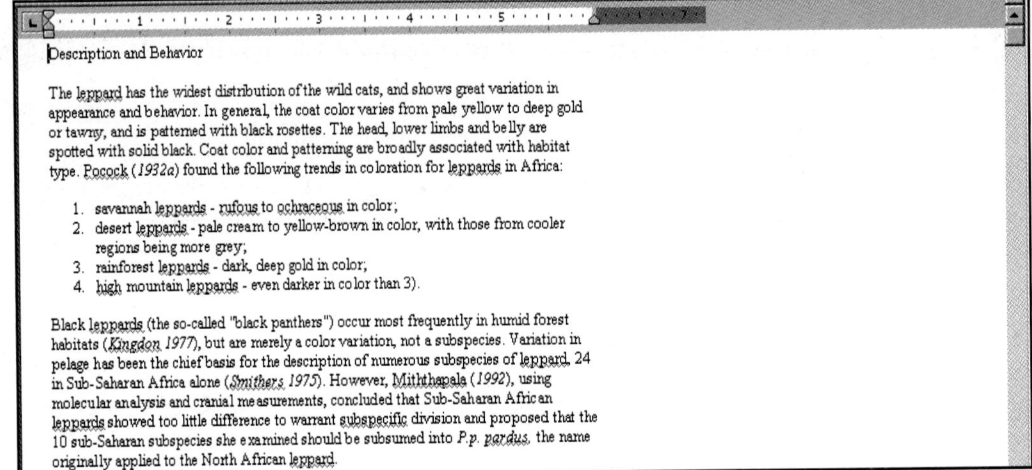
Description and Behavior

The leppard has the widest distribution of the wild cats, and shows great variation in appearance and behavior. In general, the coat color varies from pale yellow to deep gold or tawny, and is patterned with black rosettes. The head, lower limbs and belly are spotted with solid black. Coat color and patterning are broadly associated with habitat type. Pocock (*1932a*) found the following trends in coloration for leppards in Africa:

1. savannah leppards - rufous to ochraceous in color;
2. desert leppards - pale cream to yellow-brown in color, with those from cooler regions being more grey;
3. rainforest leppards - dark, deep gold in color;
4. high mountain leppards - even darker in color than 3).

Black leppards (the so-called "black panthers") occur most frequently in humid forest habitats (*Kingdon 1977*), but are merely a color variation, not a subspecies. Variation in pelage has been the chief basis for the description of numerous subspecies of leppard, 24 in Sub-Saharan Africa alone (*Smithers 1975*). However, Miththapala (*1992*), using molecular analysis and cranial measurements, concluded that Sub-Saharan African leppards showed too little difference to warrant subspecific division and proposed that the 10 sub-Saharan subspecies she examined should be subsumed into *P.p. pardus*, the name originally applied to the North African leppard.

- Search for the word "leppard" and replace it throughout with the word "leopard". There should be 47 replacements.
- Near the top of the document, use the Clipboard to change the order of the list to match the following: rainforest leopards, high mountain leopards, desert leopards, savannah leopards. (*Note:* Close the Office Clipboard if it appears.)
- In the second bulleted item, manually change the number "3" to "1".
- Move the second to last paragraph (beginning with "Leopards are generally . . .") to the end of the document.
- Insert two blank lines after the final paragraph and then type the following: **(c) Copyright 1996 IUCN - The World Conservation Union. Modified for classroom use by your name.** Note that Word automatically formatted "(c)" as ©. (*Note:* Make sure to substitute your name for the words "your name.")
- Spell check the document, but disregard any suggested changes.
- Save the revised document. Print and then close the document.

Case Problems

Main Street Antiques

Now that Bryan, the owner of Main Street Antiques, has learned several techniques for modifying documents, he decides to update the documents he posted previously on his store's bulletin board. In the following case problems, assume the role of Bryan and perform the same steps he would perform to complete these tasks.

1. Bryan begins by opening the WD02CS01 data file and saving it as "Intro to Antiques" to his personal storage location. The document appears in Figure 2.33.

Figure 2.33

"Intro to Antiques" document

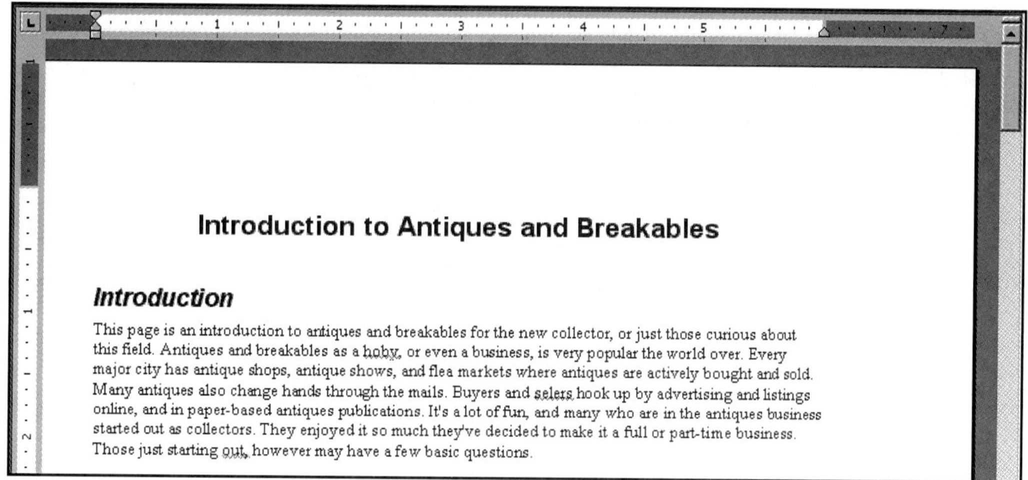
Introduction to Antiques and Breakables

Introduction

This page is an introduction to antiques and breakables for the new collector, or just those curious about this field. Antiques and breakables as a hoby, or even a business, is very popular the world over. Every major city has antique shops, antique shows, and flea markets where antiques are actively bought and sold. Many antiques also change hands through the mails. Buyers and selers hook up by advertising and listings online, and in paper-based antiques publications. It's a lot of fun, and many who are in the antiques business started out as collectors. They enjoyed it so much they've decided to make it a full or part-time business. Those just starting out, however may have a few basic questions.

He begins by replacing every occurrence of the word "breakable" with the word "collectible". There should have been 11 replacements. Proof the document using the spelling and grammar checker. You decide which suggested changes to accept. Save and print the document. Keep the document open for use in the next exercise.

2. One of Bryan's tenants pointed out to him that the "Intro to Antiques" document should be rearranged. The tenant thinks that the sections should be arranged in the following order: Introduction, Getting Started, Who Are the Collectors, What Are Antiques, What Are Collectibles. Bryan implements these changes using the Clipboard. He then saves the revised document as "Intro to Antiques (revised)" to his personal storage location and then closes the document. (*Hint:* It is always best to insert blank lines to give you a "landing area" for your rearrangements. This prevents any formatting from adversely affecting your changes. Then remember to delete any extra blank rows.)

3. Bryan wants to update another of his bulletin board documents. He opens the WD02CS03 document and saves it to his personal storage location as "Appraisal". He starts by inserting a border beneath the heading. He does this by positioning the insertion on the blank line beneath the heading, typing 3 dashes (-), and then pressing ENTER. (*Note:* If the border doesn't appear, choose Tools, AutoCorrect Options from the menu, click the *AutoFormat As You Type* tab, and then select the *Border lines* check box so that a check appears. Then, retype the dashes.) He ignores the AutoCorrect Options button displaying in his document, as this won't appear in the printed version.

   Next, he inserts a dash followed by a space at the beginning of each of the remaining lines of the document. After moving the last item in the list to the beginning, he performs a spelling and grammar check. The completed document appears in Figure 2.34. As a final step, he prints and then closes all documents.

Figure 2.34

Completed "Appraisal" document

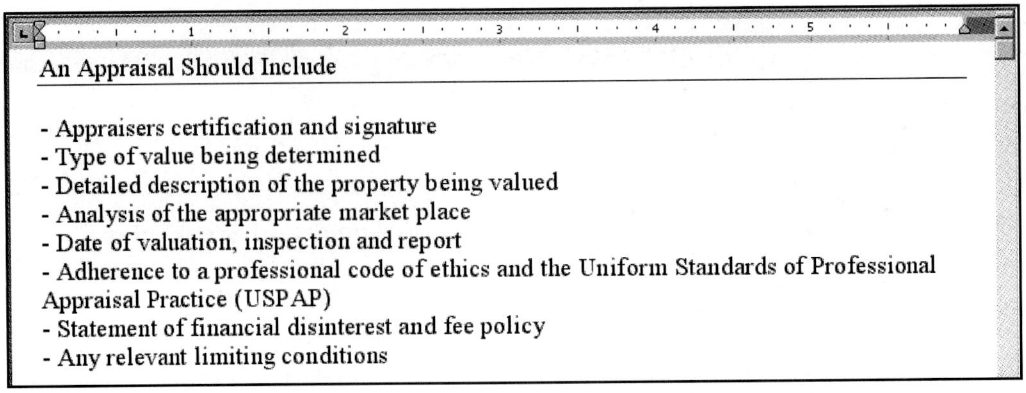

An Appraisal Should Include

- Appraisers certification and signature
- Type of value being determined
- Detailed description of the property being valued
- Analysis of the appropriate market place
- Date of valuation, inspection and report
- Adherence to a professional code of ethics and the Uniform Standards of Professional Appraisal Practice (USPAP)
- Statement of financial disinterest and fee policy
- Any relevant limiting conditions

4. Bryan opens an existing document, named WD02CS04, and then saves it to his personal storage location as "Our Credo". Bryan replaces the word "paper" with "document" throughout the document. There should only have been two replacements. He then moves the "Our credo" section to the beginning of the document. Next, he rearranges the "Who and Why" section so that the Estates/Estate Planning bullet appears first in the list. A portion of the completed document appears in Figure 2.35. After proofing it for errors, he prints and then closes the document.

Figure 2.35

Completed "Our Credo" document

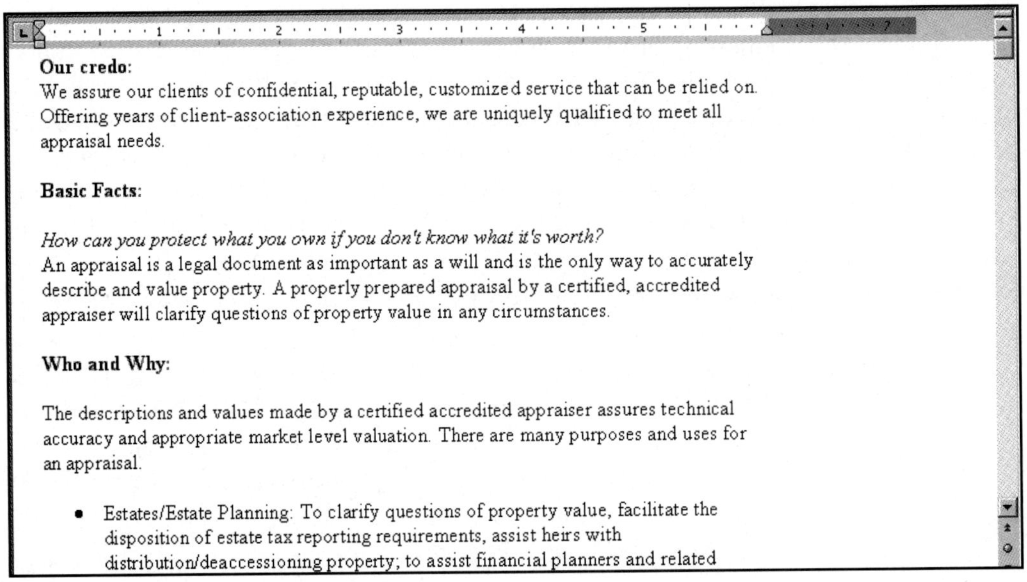

Our credo:
We assure our clients of confidential, reputable, customized service that can be relied on. Offering years of client-association experience, we are uniquely qualified to meet all appraisal needs.

Basic Facts:

How can you protect what you own if you don't know what it's worth?
An appraisal is a legal document as important as a will and is the only way to accurately describe and value property. A properly prepared appraisal by a certified, accredited appraiser will clarify questions of property value in any circumstances.

Who and Why:

The descriptions and values made by a certified accredited appraiser assures technical accuracy and appropriate market level valuation. There are many purposes and uses for an appraisal.

- Estates/Estate Planning: To clarify questions of property value, facilitate the disposition of estate tax reporting requirements, assist heirs with distribution/deaccessioning property; to assist financial planners and related

Microsoft® **Word®** 2002

CHAPTER 3

Enhancing a Document's Appearance

CHAPTER OUTLINE

Case Study

3.1 Formatting Characters

3.2 Formatting Paragraphs

3.3 Creating Lists

3.4 Applying Borders and Shading

Chapter Summary

Chapter Quiz

Hands-On Exercises

Case Problems

PREREQUISITES

To successfully complete this chapter, you must be able to position the insertion point, make text selections, and change text. We also assume you know how to use toolbars, the Menu bar, and right-click menus, and how to manage your files.

LEARNING OBJECTIVES

After completing this chapter, you will be able to:

- Change the look of text using character-formatting commands
- Indent and align paragraphs, and vary line spacing
- Create bulleted and numbered lists, and set tabs
- Incorporate shading and borders in your documents

CaseStudy ANIMAL CARE LEAGUE The Animal Care League in Willow Tree, Kansas, has recently purchased a computer system and software for their office. Natalia Federov, a volunteer with the league, has offered to use her recently acquired word processing skills to convert many of the current typewritten letters and printed forms to Microsoft Word documents. Natalia has used Word before to prepare several documents for the league; however, they have looked rather plain. She is looking forward to learning how to use Word's formatting features to add impact to her work and to make more efficient use of her time.

In this chapter, you and Natalia improve the look of your documents using a variety of formatting commands. You will use several commands for controlling the look of characters, paragraphs, and lists, and learn how to apply borders and shading.

3.1 Formatting Characters

In word processing, enhancing the appearance of text is called *character formatting* and involves selecting typefaces, font sizes, and attributes for text. Word's character formatting commands are accessed through the Font dialog box (Figure 3.1), the Formatting toolbar, or by using shortcut keyboard combinations. Since many of the features are accessible from the Formatting toolbar and shortcut keys, you may never need to use the Format, Font menu command except to select a special character attribute in the dialog box. Table 3.1 summarizes some common mouse and keyboard methods for choosing character formatting commands.

Figure 3.1

Font dialog box

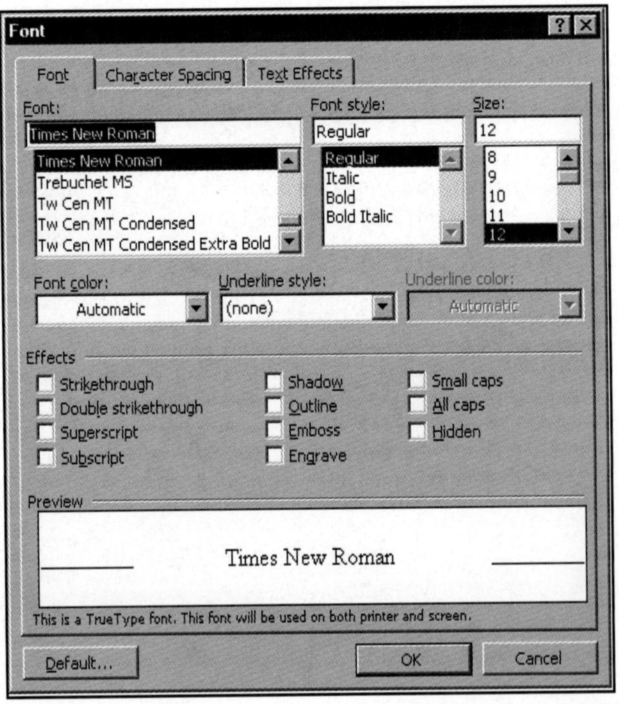

Table 3.1

Character Formatting Summary

Toolbar button	Keyboard shortcut	Description
B	CTRL+b	Makes the selected text bold
I	CTRL+i	*Italicizes* the selected text
U	CTRL+u	Applies a single underline
A		Changes the font color
Times New Roman	CTRL+SHIFT+f	Specifies a font or typeface
10	CTRL+SHIFT+p	Specifies a point size for the font
	CTRL+[	Decreases the point size by 1 point
	CTRL+]	Increases the point size by 1 point
	CTRL+SHIFT+a	CAPITALIZES the selection
	SHIFT+F3	Changes the case of the selection
	CTRL+Space Bar	Removes all character formatting

3.1.1 Bolding, Italicizing, and Underlining Text

feature

The bold, italic, and underline attributes help to emphasize important text.

method

- To make selected text bold, click the Bold button (B) or press CTRL+b
- To italicize selected text, click the Italic button (I) or press CTRL+i
- To underline selected text, click the Underline button (U) or press CTRL+u

practice

You will now open an existing document and apply bold, italic, and underline effects. No documents should be open in the application window.

1. Open the WD0311 student file.
2. Save the file as "Computers" to your personal storage location. Your document should appear similar to Figure 3.2.

Figure 3.2

"Computers" document before formatting

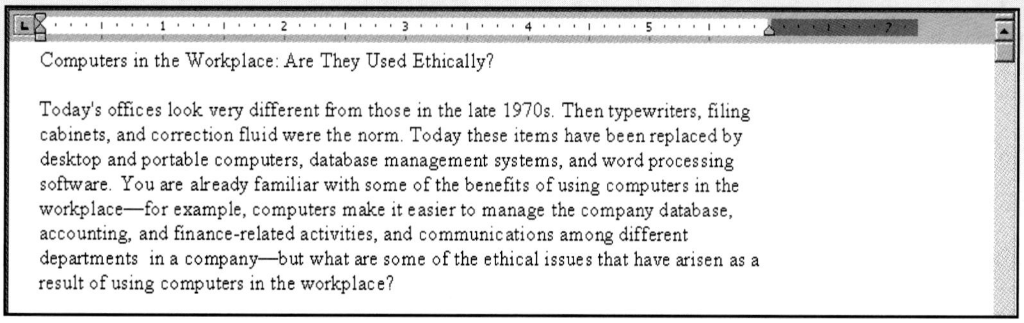

Computers in the Workplace: Are They Used Ethically?

Today's offices look very different from those in the late 1970s. Then typewriters, filing cabinets, and correction fluid were the norm. Today these items have been replaced by desktop and portable computers, database management systems, and word processing software. You are already familiar with some of the benefits of using computers in the workplace—for example, computers make it easier to manage the company database, accounting, and finance-related activities, and communications among different departments in a company—but what are some of the ethical issues that have arisen as a result of using computers in the workplace?

3. To insert a new line between the title and the first paragraph:
PRESS: END
PRESS: ENTER

4. To add an italicized subtitle for this document:
CLICK: Italic button (I) on the Formatting toolbar
TYPE: **The Information Age and the Age of Humanity**

5. To stop typing in italic:
CLICK: Italic button (I)

6. To select this subtitle, position the mouse pointer in the Selection bar to the left of the line and click the left mouse button once.

7. To make the subtitle bold and underlined using the buttons on the Formatting toolbar:
CLICK: Bold button (B)
CLICK: Underline button (U)

8. To deselect the text to better see the changes you've made:
CLICK: anywhere in the text area below
Your document should now appear similar to Figure 3.3.

Figure 3.3

Inserting a formatted subtitle

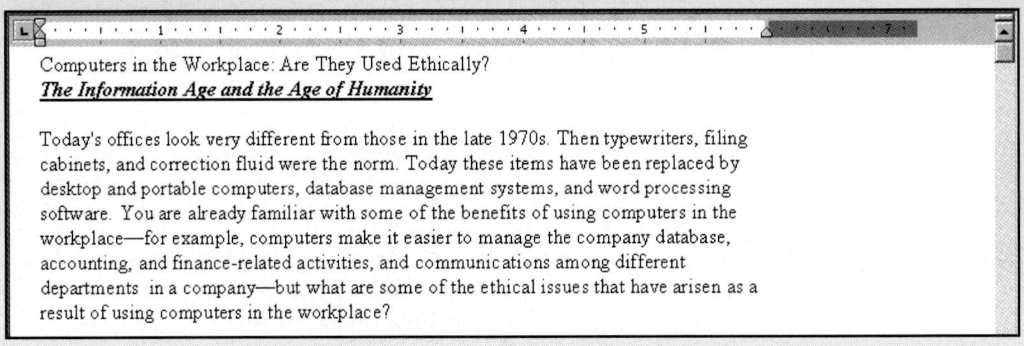

Computers in the Workplace: Are They Used Ethically?
The Information Age and the Age of Humanity

Today's offices look very different from those in the late 1970s. Then typewriters, filing cabinets, and correction fluid were the norm. Today these items have been replaced by desktop and portable computers, database management systems, and word processing software. You are already familiar with some of the benefits of using computers in the workplace—for example, computers make it easier to manage the company database, accounting, and finance-related activities, and communications among different departments in a company—but what are some of the ethical issues that have arisen as a result of using computers in the workplace?

9. Make the following formatting changes in the first paragraph using either the Formatting toolbar buttons or the keyboard shortcuts.

Text to be formatted	*Formatting to apply*
computers	italic and bold
database management systems	italic
word processing software	italic

Your document should now appear similar to Figure 3.4.

Figure 3.4

Bolding, italicizing, and underlining text

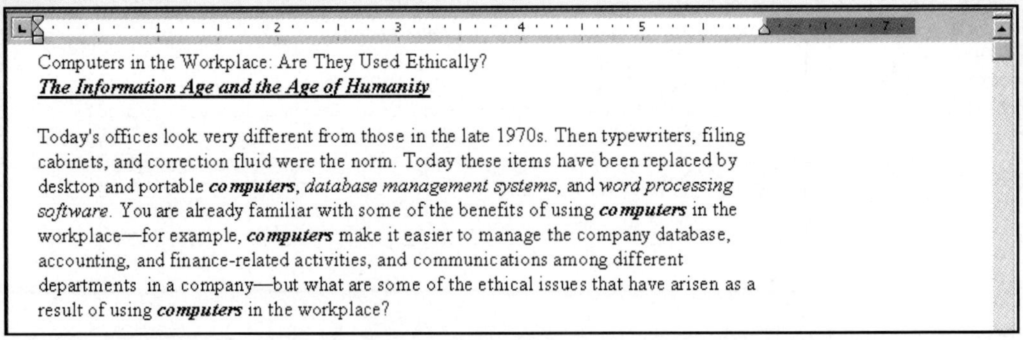

Computers in the Workplace: Are They Used Ethically?
The Information Age and the Age of Humanity

Today's offices look very different from those in the late 1970s. Then typewriters, filing cabinets, and correction fluid were the norm. Today these items have been replaced by desktop and portable ***computers***, *database management systems*, and *word processing software*. You are already familiar with some of the benefits of using ***computers*** in the workplace—for example, ***computers*** make it easier to manage the company database, accounting, and finance-related activities, and communications among different departments in a company—but what are some of the ethical issues that have arisen as a result of using ***computers*** in the workplace?

10. Save the "Computers" document and keep it open for use in the next lesson.

3.1.2 Changing Fonts, Font Sizes, and Colors

feature

A font is defined as all the symbols and characters of a particular style of print. Font size is measured in *points*. By selecting fonts and font sizes, you provide your document with the right tone for your message. Also, by selecting colors other than black for typed text, you visually enhance your documents. Remember, it is best to select text first, then apply any formatting changes to it.

method

To select a typeface:

- CLICK: Font drop-down arrow (Times Roman)
- SELECT: the desired font

To change the font size:

- CLICK: Font Size drop-down arrow (10)
- SELECT: the desired point size

To change the font color:

- CLICK: Font Color button (A) to select the most recently used color
- CLICK: Font Color drop-down arrow (A) to display a palette of colors that you can choose from

practice

You will now change some of the fonts, point sizes, and font colors in the "Computers" document.

1. SELECT: the main title on the very first line
2. To display a list of the available fonts:
   CLICK: Font drop-down arrow (Times New Roman)
   Figure 3.5 provides an example of the Font drop-down list. The list on your computer may be different.

Figure 3.5

Font drop-down list

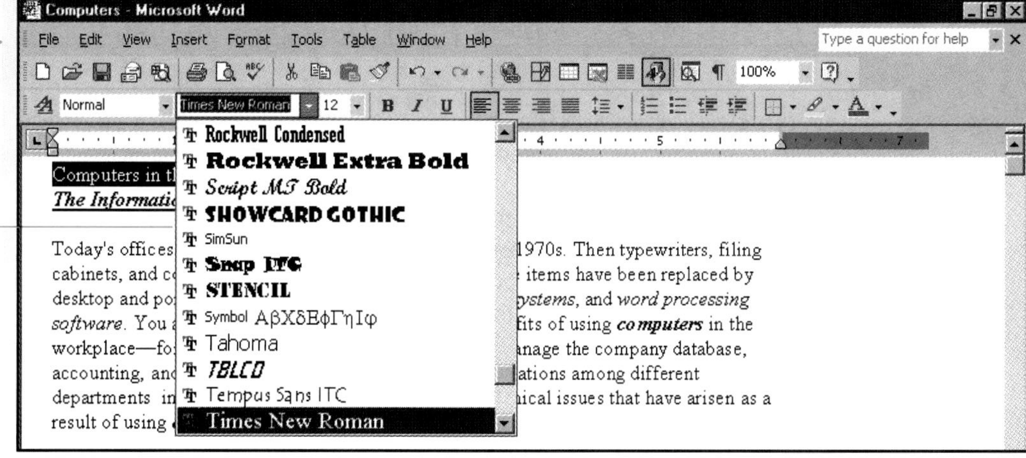

3. Scroll through the font choices by clicking the up and down arrows on the drop-down list's scroll bar or by dragging the scroll box.

4. SELECT: Arial (or a font that is available on your computer)
(*Hint:* You select a font from the drop-down list by clicking on it.)

5. To display the range of available font sizes:
CLICK: Font Size drop-down arrow (10)

6. SELECT: 16-point font size
CLICK: Bold button (B)
CLICK: in the document to deselect the text
The title and formatted subtitle should appear similar to Figure 3.6.

Figure 3.6

Formatted headings

Computers in the Workplace: Are They Used Ethically?

The Information Age and the Age of Humanity

7. Let's apply a different font color to the title and subtitle.
SELECT: the title and subtitle
CLICK: Font Color drop-down arrow (A)
A palette of colors should now appear (Figure 3.7).

Figure 3.7

Color palette

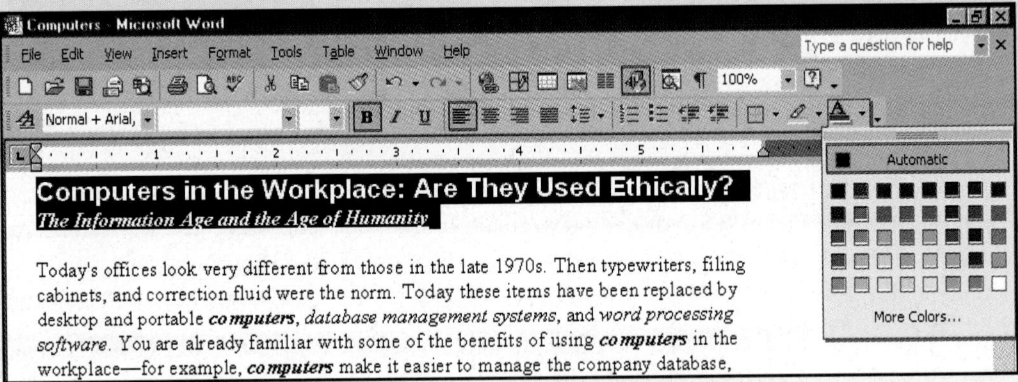

8. In this step you will pick the color blue from the color palette. If you hover for a moment over a color, a ScreenTip will appear identifying the current color. Use this procedure to identify the color blue, and then:
CLICK: Blue in the color palette
CLICK: in the document to deselect the text
The title and subtitle should now appear similar to Figure 3.8. The Font Color button now displays blue because this was the most recently applied color.

Figure 3.8

Changing Font Color

Computers in the Workplace: Are They Used Ethically?
The Information Age and the Age of Humanity

9. Save and then close the document.

3.1.3 Applying Styles

feature

Styles are collections of character and paragraph formatting commands that make it unnecessary to perform repetitive formatting procedures, reducing the amount of time it takes to create documents. Styles also help ensure that your documents are formatted consistently. Word comes with a number of built-in styles that you can use in your documents. Each of these styles includes several formatting instructions that you can apply to document paragraphs with a few clicks of the mouse.

method

To apply styles:

- CLICK: in a paragraph or select multiple paragraphs
- To display a complete list of styles, press SHIFT and hold it down.
- CLICK: down arrow on the Style button (Normal)
- CHOOSE: a style from the Style drop-down list

To clear formatting attributes:

- CHOOSE: Clear Formatting from the Style drop-down list

practice

This lesson practices applying styles. You will also see how to clear formatting attributes from a selection of text. Ensure that no documents are open in the application window.

1. Open the WD0313 data file. This document is unformatted and describes an upcoming tour to Russia.

2. Save a copy of the file as "Schedule" to your personal storage location. Your screen should now appear similar to Figure 3.9. At this point, all the text in this document is formatted according to the Normal style.

Figure 3.9

"Schedule" document

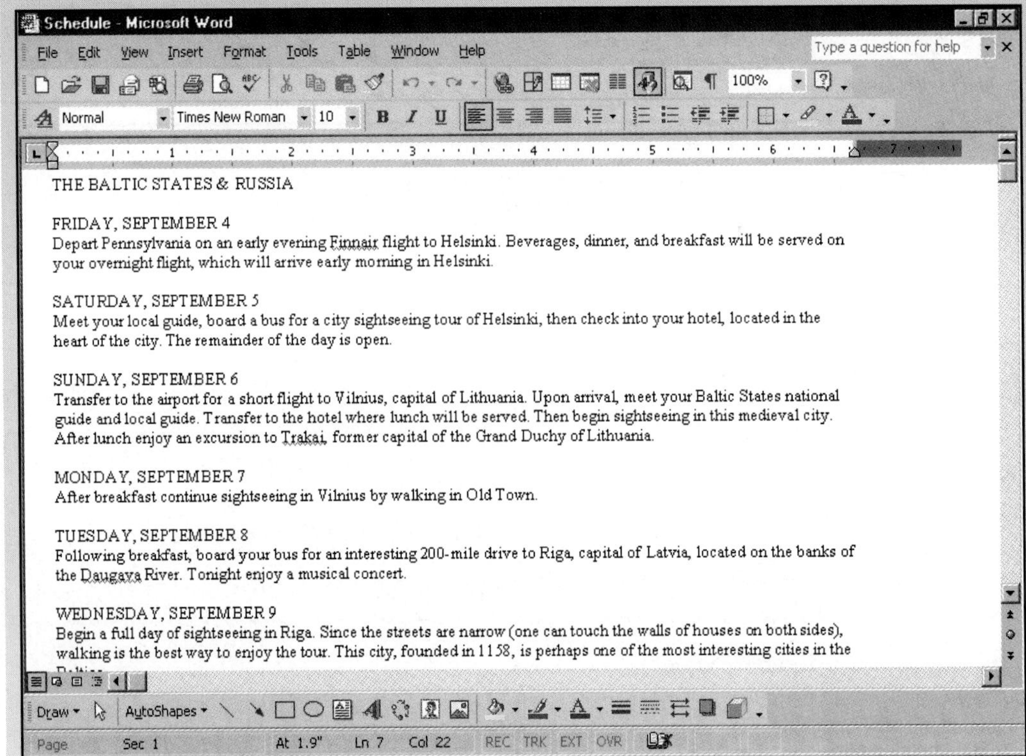

3. Let's begin by applying the Heading 1 style to the main heading of the document:
CLICK: in the "The Baltic States & Russia" heading
Because the Heading 1 style is a paragraph style, you don't need to select the entire heading before applying the style.

4. CLICK: down arrow on the Style button (Normal)
Your screen should now appear similar to Figure 3.10.

Figure 3.10

Style menu

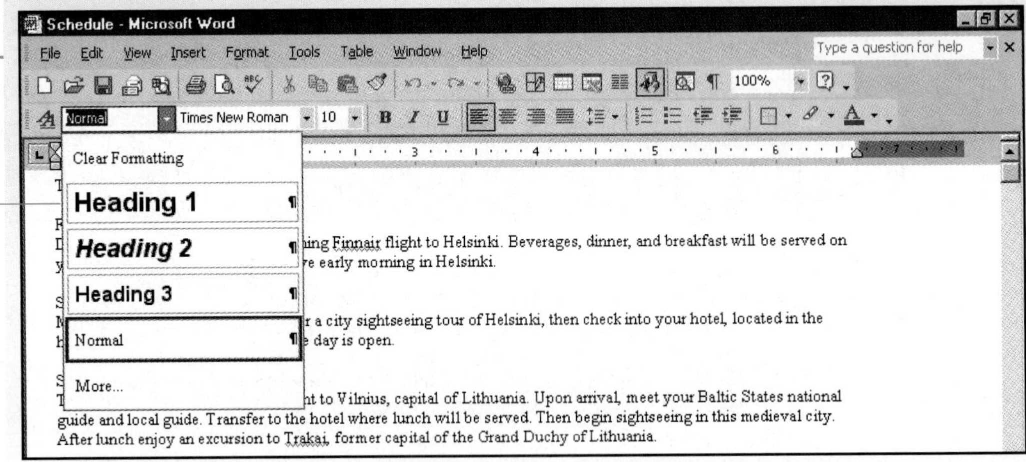

5. To apply the Heading 1 style:
CHOOSE: Heading 1

6. To illustrate how you can clear the formatting from a paragraph, do the following:
CLICK: down arrow on the Style button (Normal)
CHOOSE: Clear Formatting from the *Style* drop-down list
The formatting should have been removed from the heading.

7. To undo the previous command:
CHOOSE: Edit, Undo Clear Formatting

8. To format the first subheading using a style:
CLICK: in the "FRIDAY, SEPTEMBER 4" heading

9. This time, let's display the complete list of styles that are available in the Normal template. To do so, you must hold the SHIFT key down while clicking the Style button.
PRESS: SHIFT and hold it down
CLICK: down arrow on the Style button (Normal)
A greater selection of styles appears in the style list (Figure 3.11).

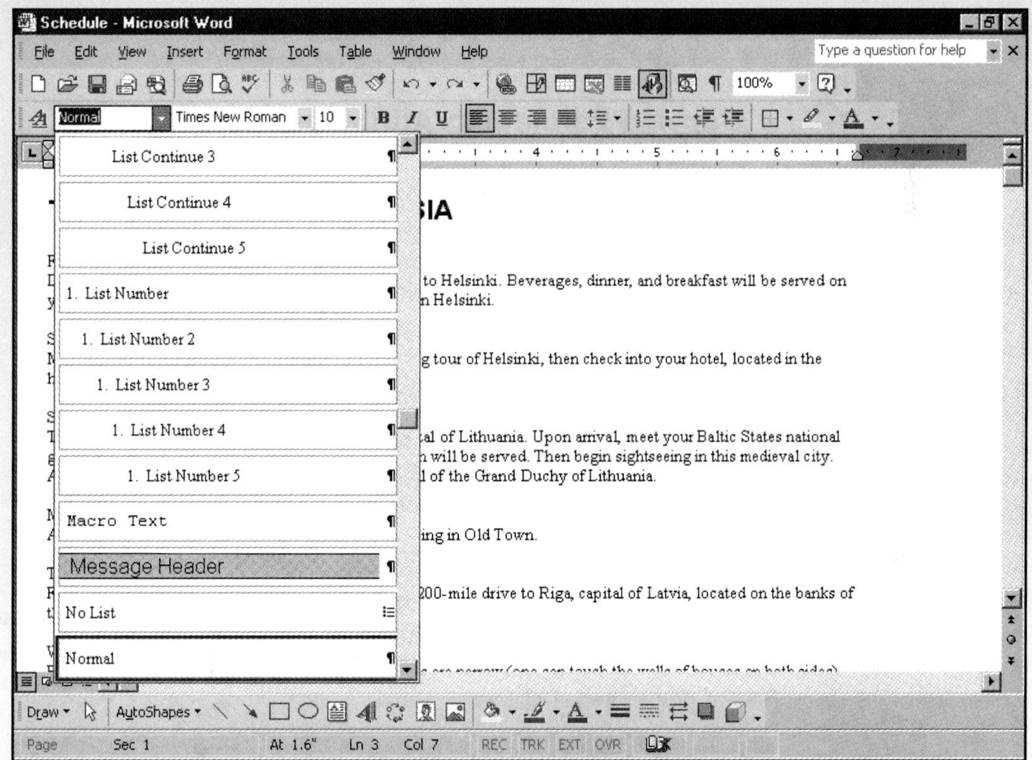

Figure 3.11

Displaying a complete list of styles

10. To remove the style list without making a selection:
CLICK: in your document, away from the style menu

11. In this step, you format the heading using the Heading 2 style. Ensure that the insertion point is still positioned in the "FRIDAY, SEPTEMBER 4" heading.
CLICK: down arrow on the Style button (Normal)
CHOOSE: Heading 2

12. On your own, format all the itinerary dates in the Heading 2 style. (*Hint:* It may be easier to click a line and then press CTRL+Y, or F4, to repeat the style formatting you applied in the previous step.) With the insertion point at the top of the document, your document should now appear similar to Figure 3.12. At this point, the document is formatted with three different styles: Heading 1, Heading 2, and Normal.

Figure 3.12

"Schedule" document after applying styles

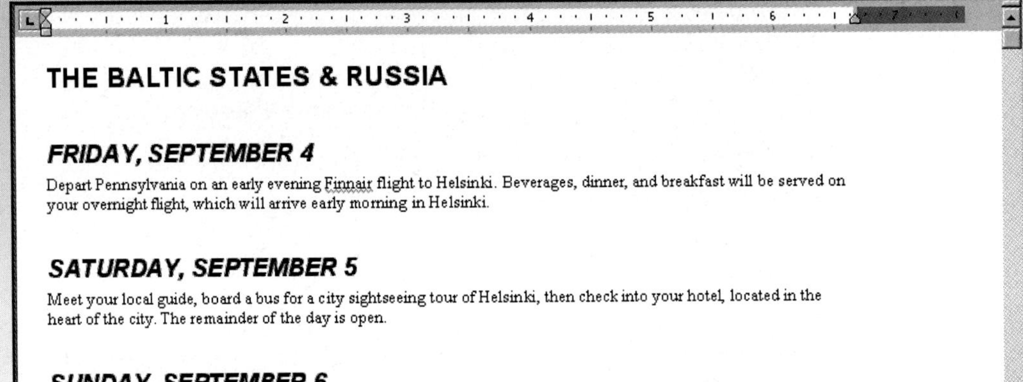
THE BALTIC STATES & RUSSIA

FRIDAY, SEPTEMBER 4

Depart Pennsylvania on an early evening Finnair flight to Helsinki. Beverages, dinner, and breakfast will be served on your overnight flight, which will arrive early morning in Helsinki.

SATURDAY, SEPTEMBER 5

Meet your local guide, board a bus for a city sightseeing tour of Helsinki, then check into your hotel, located in the heart of the city. The remainder of the day is open.

SUNDAY, SEPTEMBER 6

Transfer to the airport for a short flight to Vilnius, capital of Lithuania. Upon arrival, meet your Baltic States national guide and local guide. Transfer to the hotel where lunch will be served. Then begin sightseeing in this medieval city. After lunch enjoy an excursion to Trakai, former capital of the Grand Duchy of Lithuania.

13. Save the "Schedule" document and keep it open for use in the next lesson.

3.1.4 Copying Formatting Attributes

feature

The **Format Painter** enables you to copy the formatting styles and attributes from one area in your document to another. Not only does this feature help speed up formatting operations, it ensures consistency among the different areas in your document.

method

To copy formatting to another area in your document:

- SELECT: the text with the desired formatting characteristics
- CLICK: Format Painter button () on the Standard toolbar
- SELECT: the text that you want to format

To copy formatting to several areas in your document:

- SELECT: the text with the desired formatting characteristics
- DOUBLE-CLICK: Format Painter button () on the Standard toolbar
- SELECT: the text that you want to format
- Repeat procedure, as desired.
- CLICK: Format Painter button () to deselect it

practice

You will now practice using the Format Painter on the "Schedule" document.

1. Move the insertion point to the top of the document and then:
SELECT: the heading entitled "FRIDAY, SEPTEMBER 4"

2. To change the formatting of this heading:
CLICK: Bold button () to remove the bold effect
CLICK: Italic button () to remove the italic effect

CLICK: Underline button (U) to apply the underline effect.
Your document should now appear similar to Figure 3.13.

Figure 3.13

"Schedule" document

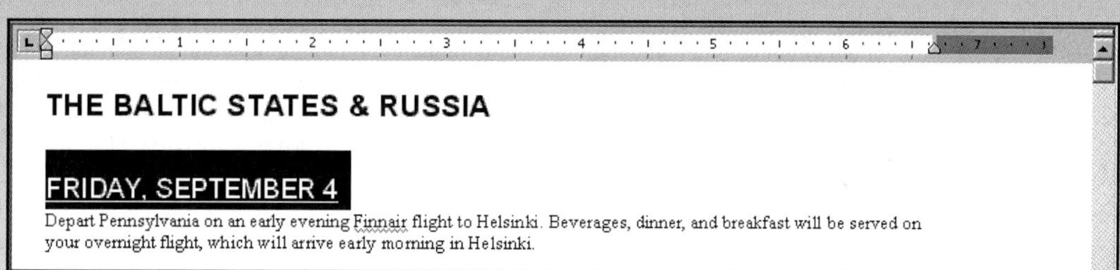
THE BALTIC STATES & RUSSIA
FRIDAY, SEPTEMBER 4
Depart Pennsylvania on an early evening Finnair flight to Helsinki. Beverages, dinner, and breakfast will be served on your overnight flight, which will arrive early morning in Helsinki.

3. To copy the formatting characteristics of the selected text "FRIDAY, SEPTEMBER 4":
   CLICK: Format Painter button on the Standard toolbar
4. Move the mouse pointer into the document area. Notice that it becomes an I-beam attached to a paintbrush.
5. To copy the formatting to the second heading (SATURDAY, SEPTEMBER 5):
   DRAG: mouse pointer over the heading
   When you release the mouse button, the second heading is formatted with the same characteristics as the first heading. Note that the mouse pointer has returned to its normal state.
6. To copy this formatting to several areas in the document:
   DOUBLE-CLICK: Format Painter button
7. Using the I-beam paintbrush mouse pointer, select all the remaining headings in the document.
8. To finish using the paintbrush mouse pointer:
   CLICK: Format Painter button
9. To deselect the current text and move the insertion point to the beginning of the document:
   PRESS: CTRL + HOME
   Your screen should now appear similar to Figure 3.14.

Figure 3.14

The Format Painter was used to apply formatting to this document

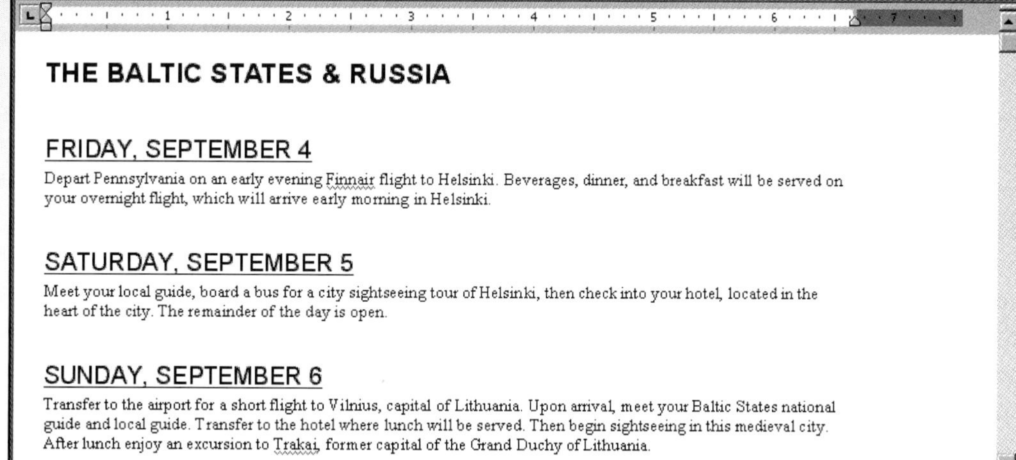
THE BALTIC STATES & RUSSIA
FRIDAY, SEPTEMBER 4
Depart Pennsylvania on an early evening Finnair flight to Helsinki. Beverages, dinner, and breakfast will be served on your overnight flight, which will arrive early morning in Helsinki.
SATURDAY, SEPTEMBER 5
Meet your local guide, board a bus for a city sightseeing tour of Helsinki, then check into your hotel, located in the heart of the city. The remainder of the day is open.
SUNDAY, SEPTEMBER 6
Transfer to the airport for a short flight to Vilnius, capital of Lithuania. Upon arrival, meet your Baltic States national guide and local guide. Transfer to the hotel where lunch will be served. Then begin sightseeing in this medieval city. After lunch enjoy an excursion to Trakai, former capital of the Grand Duchy of Lithuania.

10. Save the revised document and keep it open for use in the next lesson.

3.1.5 Highlighting Text for Review

feature

When others will be reviewing your document online, you may want to highlight those elements that deserve special attention. You can access Word's Highlight tool from the Formatting toolbar and select an alternate highlight color using the Highlight drop-down arrow. Keep in mind that if your intention is to print your document, you should stick with lighter highlight colors so that your text isn't obscured.

method

To activate the highlighter:

- CLICK: Highlight button on the Formatting toolbar

To change the highlight color:

- CLICK: Highlight drop-down arrow on the Formatting toolbar
- CHOOSE: None (no color) or an alternate highlight color

practice

You will now practice highlighting text in the "Schedule" document.

1. Let's begin by selecting a color for the highlighter:
   CLICK: Highlight drop-down arrow on the Formatting toolbar
   SELECT: red
   Word's Highlight tool is now activated, as indicated by the highlighter mouse pointer.
2. With the Highlight tool activated, you simply select the text you want to highlight.
   SELECT: the first sentence beneath FRIDAY, SEPTEMBER 4
   The sentence now appears highlighted in red.
3. SELECT: the first sentence beneath SATURDAY, SEPTEMBER 5
   Your screen should now appear similar to Figure 3.15.

Figure 3.15

Highlighting text

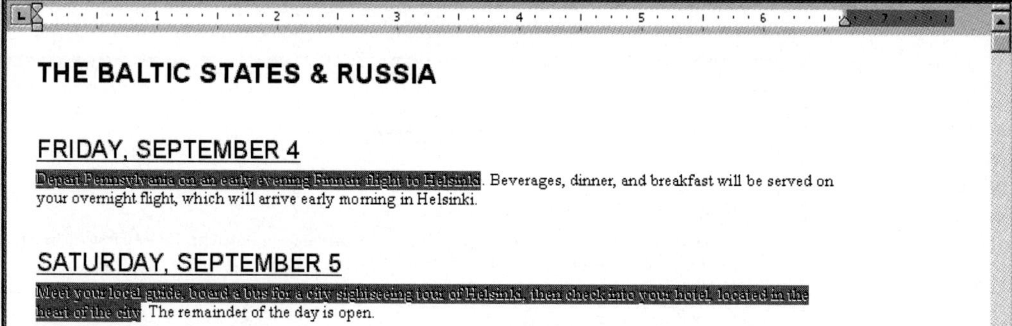
THE BALTIC STATES & RUSSIA
FRIDAY, SEPTEMBER 4
Depart Pennsylvania on an early evening Finnair flight to Helsinki. Beverages, dinner, and breakfast will be served on your overnight flight, which will arrive early morning in Helsinki.
SATURDAY, SEPTEMBER 5
Meet your local guide, board a bus for a city sightseeing tour of Helsinki, then check into your hotel, located in the heart of the city. The remainder of the day is open.

4. To deactivate the Highlight tool:
   CLICK: Highlight button on the Formatting toolbar
5. To remove highlighting from the first paragraph:
   SELECT: the first sentence of the first paragraph
   CLICK: Highlight drop-down arrow on the Formatting toolbar
   CHOOSE: None

6. On your own, remove the highlighting from the "Saturday, September 5" section.
7. Save and then close the "Schedule" document.

3.1 How would you boldface and underline existing text?

3.2 Formatting Paragraphs

Paragraph formatting involves changing alignment, line spacing, indentation, and tab settings for a paragraph. To apply paragraph formatting commands to a paragraph, position the insertion point anywhere in the paragraph—you do not need to select any text—and then issue the desired command.

Paragraph formatting commands are accessed through the Paragraph dialog box, from the Formatting toolbar, using the mouse, and using keyboard shortcut combinations. The Paragraph dialog box (Figure 3.16) is useful for entering specific measurements and accessing the full range of paragraph formatting options.

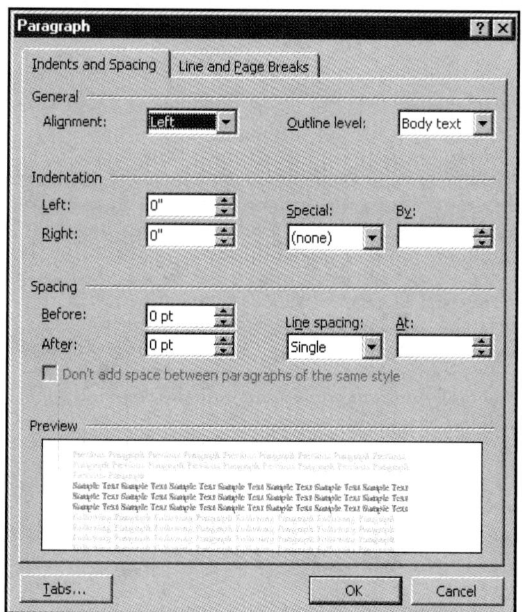

Figure 3.16

Paragraph dialog box

3.2.1 Revealing a Paragraph's Formatting

feature

If someone has given you an existing document to work with, you may want to inspect it first to see how it has been formatted. In Word, you can do this with a simple command. Also, Word stores paragraph formatting information in the paragraph mark (¶), which is inserted at the end of a paragraph when you press ENTER. By default, paragraph marks and other nonprinting characters are hidden from view. By revealing these codes, you can more thoroughly check a document for errors.

method

To display a paragraph's formatting:

- CHOOSE: Help, What's This?
- CLICK: in the paragraph

To display paragraph marks and all other nonprinting characters:

- CLICK: Show/Hide button (¶) on the Formatting toolbar

practice

You will now open a document that discusses how to use the Web to sell products and services. You will then practice displaying a paragraph's marks and formatting. Ensure that no documents appear in the application window.

1. Open the WD0321 data file.
2. Save the document as "Commerce" to your personal storage location.
3. If they are not already displayed, show the document's nonprinting characters by doing the following:
   CLICK: Show/Hide button (¶) on the Formatting toolbar
   Your screen should now appear similar to Figure 3.17.

Figure 3.17

Displaying paragraph marks and other nonprinting characters

Paragraph
marks

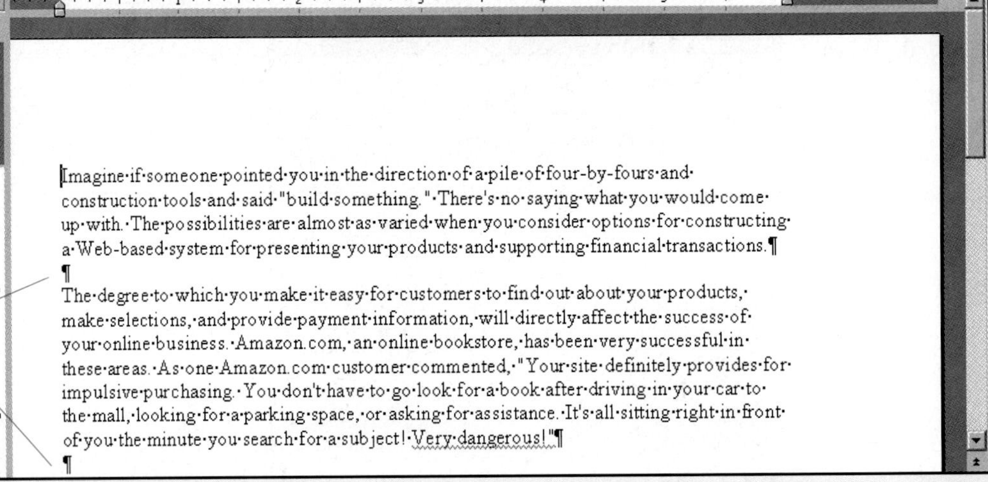
Imagine·if·someone·pointed·you·in·the·direction·of·a·pile·of·four-by-fours·and·
construction·tools·and·said·"build·something."·There's·no·saying·what·you·would·come·
up·with.·The·possibilities·are·almost·as·varied·when·you·consider·options·for·constructing·
a·Web-based·system·for·presenting·your·products·and·supporting·financial·transactions.¶
¶
The·degree·to·which·you·make·it·easy·for·customers·to·find·out·about·your·products,·
make·selections,·and·provide·payment·information,·will·directly·affect·the·success·of·
your·online·business.·Amazon.com,·an·online·bookstore,·has·been·very·successful·in·
these·areas.·As·one·Amazon.com·customer·commented,·"Your·site·definitely·provides·for·
impulsive·purchasing.·You·don't·have·to·go·look·for·a·book·after·driving·in·your·car·to·
the·mall,·looking·for·a·parking·space,·or·asking·for·assistance.·It's·all·sitting·right·in·front·
of·you·the·minute·you·search·for·a·subject!·Very·dangerous!"¶
¶

4. Before proceeding, let's hide the symbols:
   CLICK: Show/Hide button (¶)
5. A useful procedure for reviewing a document's formatting involves choosing Help, What's This? from the Menu bar. To illustrate:
   CHOOSE: Help, What's This?
6. Position the question mark mouse pointer over any letter in the second paragraph:
   CLICK: left mouse button once
   The Reveal Formatting task pane is now displaying showing the paragraph's formatting characteristics (Figure 3.18).

Figure 3.18

Displaying a paragraph's formatting characteristics

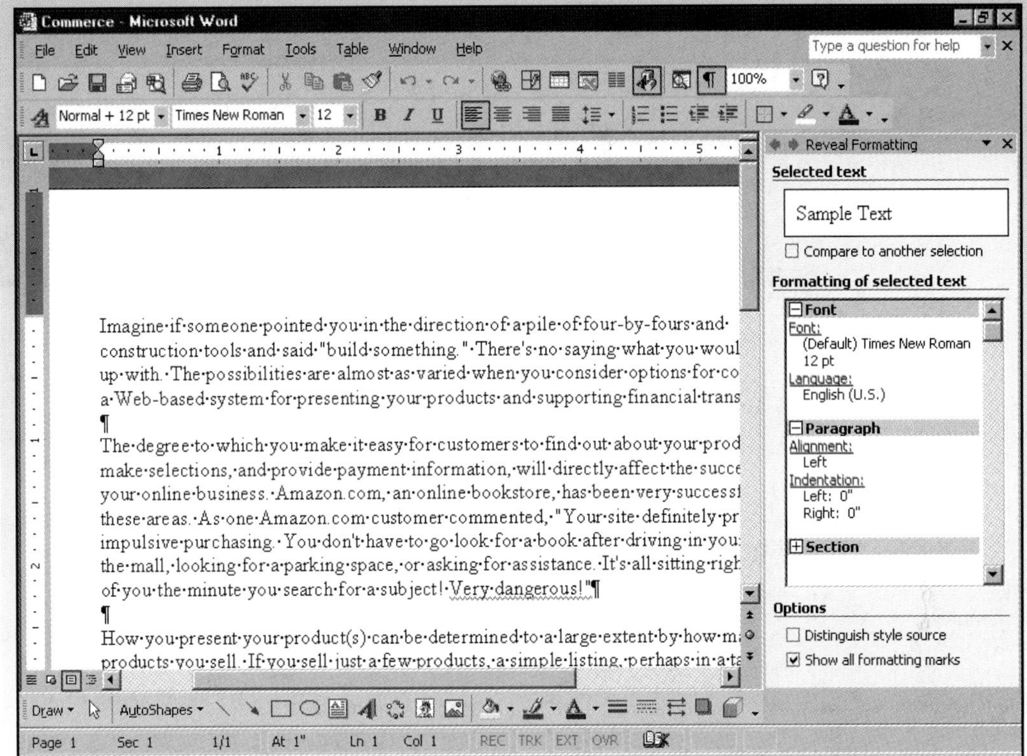

7. To close the task pane:
   CHOOSE: View, Task Pane

3.2.2 Changing Paragraph Alignment

feature

Justification refers to how text aligns within the margins. *Left justification* aligns text on the left but leaves jagged right edges as a typewriter does. A new document in Word is left-justified by default. *Center justification* centers the line or paragraph between the left and right margins. *Right justification* positions text flush against the right margin. *Full justification* provides even text columns at the left and right by automatically spacing words on the line.

method

To apply left justification:

- CLICK: Align Left button (), or press CTRL+l

To apply center justification:

- CLICK: Center button (), or press CTRL+e

To align text against the right margin:

- CLICK: Align Right button (), or press CTRL+r

To justify text between the margins:

- CLICK: Justify button (), or press CTRL+j

practice

You will now practice changing justification in the "Commerce" document.

1. Position the insertion point anywhere in the first paragraph.
2. CLICK: Center button (≡) on the Formatting toolbar
   The paragraph is immediately centered between the left and right margins.
3. CLICK: Align Right button (≡) on the Formatting toolbar
   The paragraph is positioned flush against the right margin.
4. CLICK: Justify button (≡) on the Formatting toolbar
   The paragraph is positioned flush against both the left and right margins.
5. To move the paragraph back to its original position:
   CLICK: Align Left button (≡) on the Formatting toolbar
   Figure 3.19 provides an example of each alignment option.

Figure 3.19

Aligning paragraphs

Align Left

Imagine if someone pointed you in the direction of a pile of four-by-fours and construction tools and said "build something." There's no saying what you would come up with. The possibilities are almost as varied when you consider options for constructing a Web-based system for presenting your products and supporting financial transactions.

Center

Imagine if someone pointed you in the direction of a pile of four-by-fours and construction tools and said "build something." There's no saying what you would come up with. The possibilities are almost as varied when you consider options for constructing a Web-based system for presenting your products and supporting financial transactions.

Align Right

Imagine if someone pointed you in the direction of a pile of four-by-fours and construction tools and said "build something." There's no saying what you would come up with. The possibilities are almost as varied when you consider options for constructing a Web-based system for presenting your products and supporting financial transactions.

Justify

Imagine if someone pointed you in the direction of a pile of four-by-fours and construction tools and said "build something." There's no saying what you would come up with. The possibilities are almost as varied when you consider options for constructing a Web-based system for presenting your products and supporting financial transactions.

6. Proceed to the next lesson.

3.2.3 Indenting Paragraphs

feature

Indenting a paragraph means to move a body of text in from the normal page margins. When you indent a paragraph, you temporarily change the text's positioning relative to the left and right margins. You can indent a paragraph on the left side only, right side only, or on both sides.

method

To increase or decrease the left indent of an entire paragraph:

- CLICK: Increase Indent button on the Formatting toolbar,

or

- CLICK: Decrease Indent button on the Formatting toolbar

To customize the left and right indents:

- DRAG: the indent markers on the Ruler

practice

You will now practice indenting text in the "Commerce" document.

1. To begin, position the insertion point anywhere in the second paragraph.
2. To add a left indent to this paragraph:
   CLICK: Increase Indent button on the Formatting toolbar
   The paragraph moves to the right 0.5 inches to the next tab stop (Figure 3.20).

Figure 3.20

Indenting a paragraph 0.5 inch

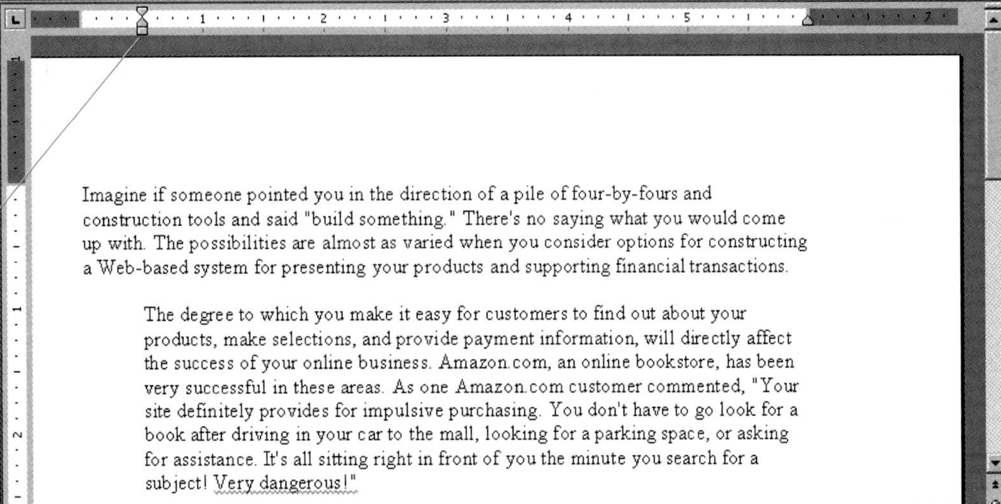
Imagine if someone pointed you in the direction of a pile of four-by-fours and construction tools and said "build something." There's no saying what you would come up with. The possibilities are almost as varied when you consider options for constructing a Web-based system for presenting your products and supporting financial transactions.
The degree to which you make it easy for customers to find out about your products, make selections, and provide payment information, will directly affect the success of your online business. Amazon.com, an online bookstore, has been very successful in these areas. As one Amazon.com customer commented, "Your site definitely provides for impulsive purchasing. You don't have to go look for a book after driving in your car to the mall, looking for a parking space, or asking for assistance. It's all sitting right in front of you the minute you search for a subject! Very dangerous!"

Note that the indent markers on the ruler have moved.

3. You can also customize your indents by dragging the indent markers on the Ruler. We label these markers in Figure 3.21 and describe them in Table 3.2.

Figure 3.21

Indent markers on Ruler

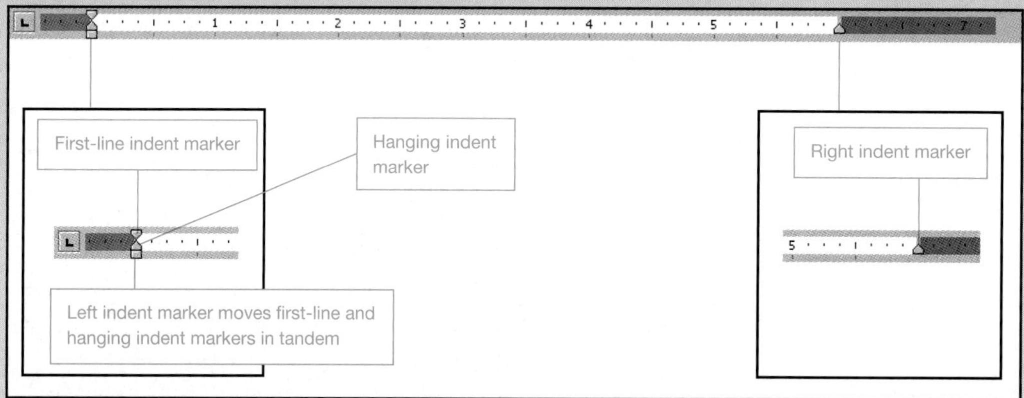
First-line indent marker
Hanging indent marker
Right indent marker
Left indent marker moves first-line and hanging indent markers in tandem

To indent the paragraph 1 inch from the right margin:
DRAG: right indent marker to the left by 1 inch (to 5 inches on the Ruler)
Your screen should now appear similar to Figure 3.22.

Figure 3.22

Indenting paragraphs

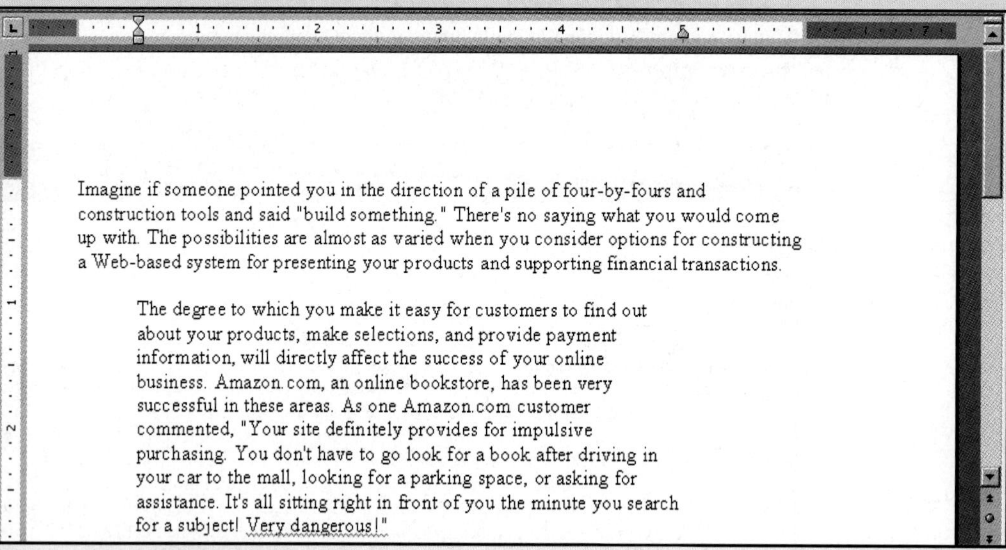
Imagine if someone pointed you in the direction of a pile of four-by-fours and construction tools and said "build something." There's no saying what you would come up with. The possibilities are almost as varied when you consider options for constructing a Web-based system for presenting your products and supporting financial transactions.
The degree to which you make it easy for customers to find out about your products, make selections, and provide payment information, will directly affect the success of your online business. Amazon.com, an online bookstore, has been very successful in these areas. As one Amazon.com customer commented, "Your site definitely provides for impulsive purchasing. You don't have to go look for a book after driving in your car to the mall, looking for a parking space, or asking for assistance. It's all sitting right in front of you the minute you search for a subject! Very dangerous!"

4. To remove the left indent:
CLICK: Decrease Indent button ( )
Notice that this button has no effect on the right indent marker.

5. To remove the right indent:
DRAG: right indent marker back to the right margin (at 6 inches on the Ruler)

6. Move the insertion point to the end of the "Commerce" document.

7. Insert a new blank line at the end of the document.

8. In this next step, you insert a hanging indent, which means that the first line of the paragraph lines up with the left margin and the remainder of the paragraph is indented. To begin:
DRAG: hanging indent marker to 1 inch on the Ruler

Table 3.2

Indent Markers

Type	Description
First-line indent marker	This indent marker moves only the first line of a paragraph in from the left margin. This paragraph format is often used in documents to avoid having to press the TAB key at the start of each new paragraph.
Hanging indent marker	This indent marker moves all but the first line of a paragraph in from the left margin, leaving the first-line indent marker in its current position.
Left indent marker	The left indent marker moves the first-line and hanging indent markers in tandem.
Right indent marker	The right indent marker moves the body of the entire paragraph in from the right margin. Left and right indents are often used together to set quotations apart from normal body text in a document.

(*Caution:* Make sure that the tip of your mouse pointer points to the triangle and not to the bottom rectangle when dragging.) If performed correctly, the Ruler should now appear similar to Figure 3.23.

Figure 3.23

Creating a hanging indent

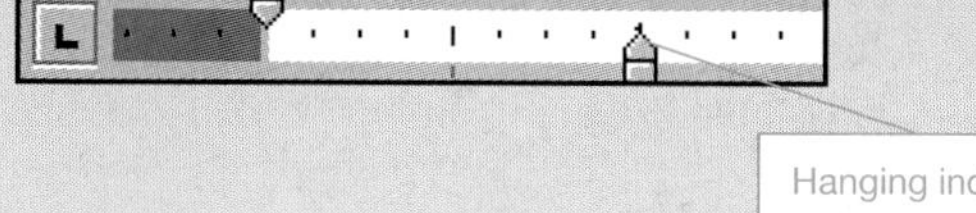
Hanging indent marker

9. TYPE: **Summary**
PRESS: TAB

10. TYPE: **For your online business to be successful, your Web site must be easy to use for first-time visitors.**
Your document should now appear similar to Figure 3.24.

Figure 3.24

Creating a hanging indent in the "Commerce" document

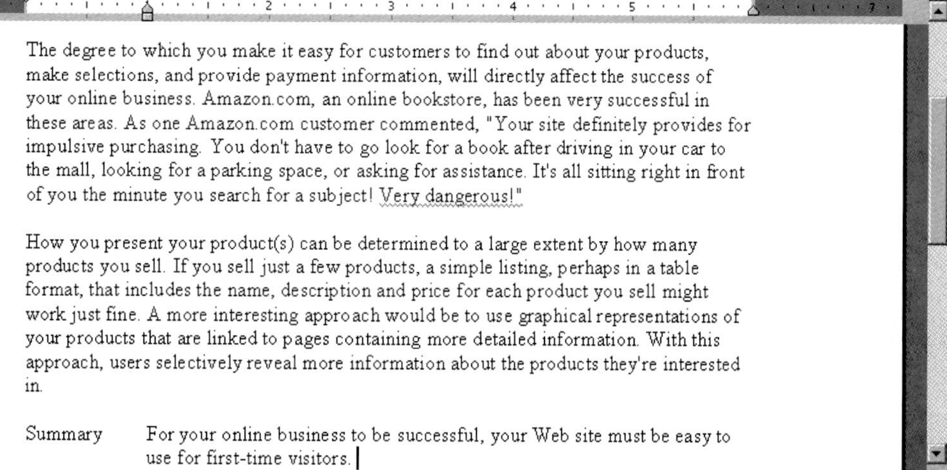
The degree to which you make it easy for customers to find out about your products, make selections, and provide payment information, will directly affect the success of your online business. Amazon.com, an online bookstore, has been very successful in these areas. As one Amazon.com customer commented, "Your site definitely provides for impulsive purchasing. You don't have to go look for a book after driving in your car to the mall, looking for a parking space, or asking for assistance. It's all sitting right in front of you the minute you search for a subject! Very dangerous!"
How you present your product(s) can be determined to a large extent by how many products you sell. If you sell just a few products, a simple listing, perhaps in a table format, that includes the name, description and price for each product you sell might work just fine. A more interesting approach would be to use graphical representations of your products that are linked to pages containing more detailed information. With this approach, users selectively reveal more information about the products they're interested in.
Summary For your online business to be successful, your Web site must be easy to use for first-time visitors.

11. Save the "Commerce" document and keep it open for use in the next lesson.

3.2.4 Changing Line Spacing

feature

Sometimes changing the line spacing in a document makes the document easier to read. The standard options for line spacing are 1.0, 1.5, 2.0, 2.5, and 3.0 spacing, but your choices aren't limited to these.

method

To change line spacing using the toolbar:

- CLICK: Line Spacing drop-down arrow ( ) on the Formatting toolbar
- CHOOSE: an option from the drop-down menu

To select a specific line spacing option:

- CHOOSE: Format, Paragraph
- CLICK: down arrow beside the *Line spacing* drop-down list box
- SELECT: *the desired spacing*
- CLICK: OK command button

practice

You will now practice changing the line spacing in the "Commerce" document.

1. Move the insertion point into the first paragraph.

2. To double-space this paragraph:
CLICK: Line Spacing drop-down arrow ( )
Your screen should now appear similar to Figure 3.25.

Figure 3.25

Changing line spacing

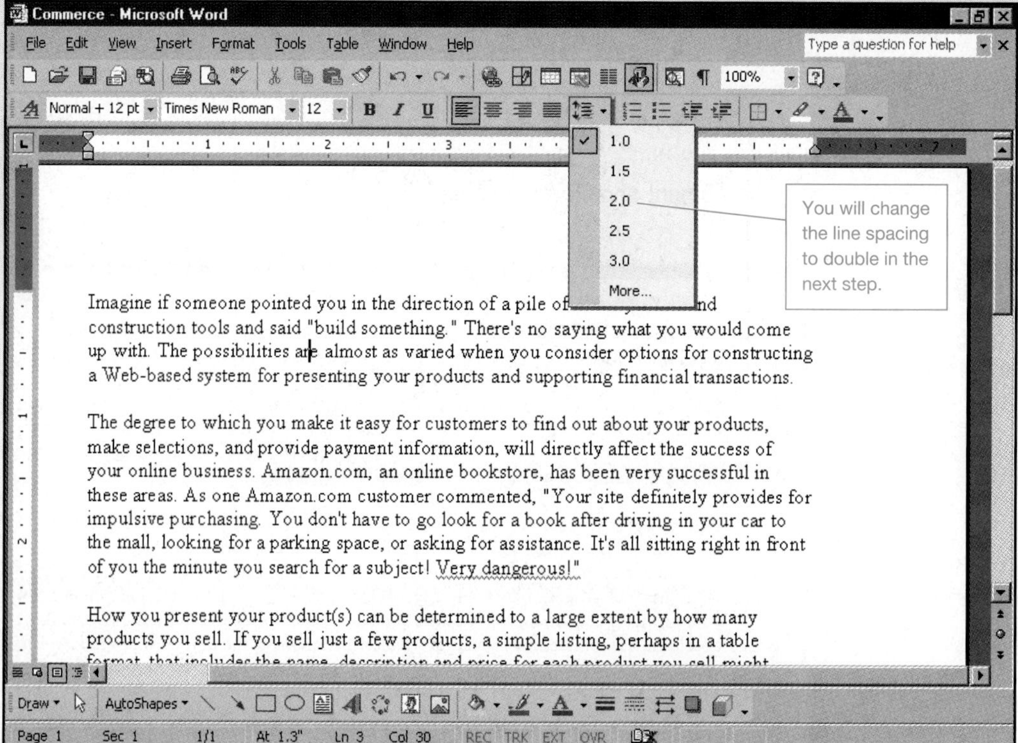
Commerce - Microsoft Word
File Edit View Insert Format Tools Table Window Help
Type a question for help
Normal + 12 pt
Times New Roman
12
100%
1.0
1.5
2.0
2.5
3.0
More...
You will change the line spacing to double in the next step.
Imagine if someone pointed you in the direction of a pile of nd construction tools and said "build something." There's no saying what you would come up with. The possibilities are almost as varied when you consider options for constructing a Web-based system for presenting your products and supporting financial transactions.
The degree to which you make it easy for customers to find out about your products, make selections, and provide payment information, will directly affect the success of your online business. Amazon.com, an online bookstore, has been very successful in these areas. As one Amazon.com customer commented, "Your site definitely provides for impulsive purchasing. You don't have to go look for a book after driving in your car to the mall, looking for a parking space, or asking for assistance. It's all sitting right in front of you the minute you search for a subject! Very dangerous!"
How you present your product(s) can be determined to a large extent by how many products you sell. If you sell just a few products, a simple listing, perhaps in a table
Draw AutoShapes
Page 1 Sec 1 1/1 At 1.3" Ln 3 Col 30 REC TRK EXT OVR

3. CHOOSE: 2.0 from the drop-down menu
Note that only the first paragraph is double-spaced (Figure 3.26).

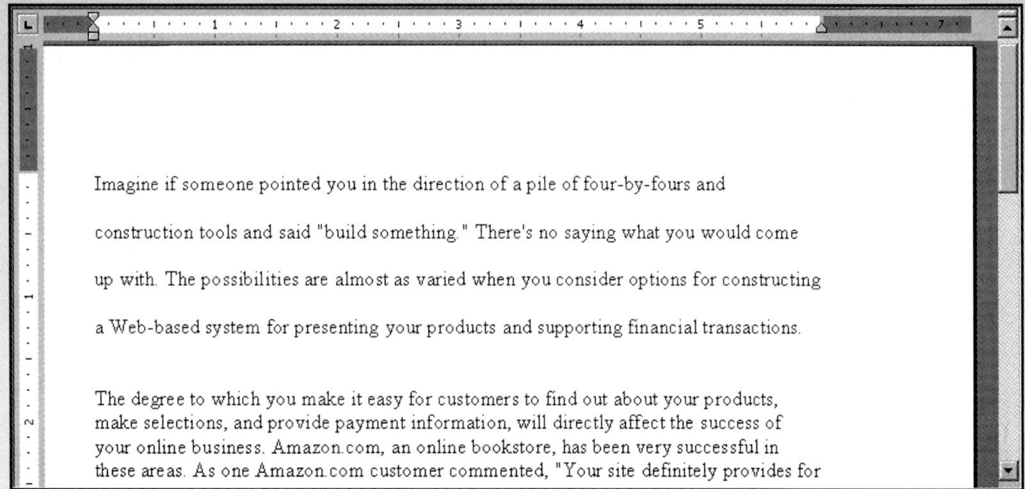
Imagine if someone pointed you in the direction of a pile of four-by-fours and
construction tools and said "build something." There's no saying what you would come
up with. The possibilities are almost as varied when you consider options for constructing
a Web-based system for presenting your products and supporting financial transactions.
The degree to which you make it easy for customers to find out about your products,
make selections, and provide payment information, will directly affect the success of
your online business. Amazon.com, an online bookstore, has been very successful in
these areas. As one Amazon.com customer commented, "Your site definitely provides for

Figure 3.26

Double-spacing the first paragraph

4. To apply 1.5-line spacing:
CLICK: Line Spacing drop-down arrow ( )
CHOOSE: 1.5 from the drop-down menu
5. To return the paragraph to single spacing:
CLICK: Line Spacing drop-down arrow ( )
CHOOSE: 1.0 from the drop-down menu
6. To double-space the entire document, you need to first select the document. Move the mouse pointer into the Selection bar and triple-click the left mouse button. The entire document should be highlighted in reverse video (white on black) before you proceed.
7. CLICK: Line Spacing drop-down arrow ( )
CHOOSE: 2.0 from the drop-down menu
The entire "Commerce" document is now double-spaced.
8. With the document still selected, let's use the Paragraph dialog box to return the document to single spacing.
CHOOSE: Format, Paragraph
The Paragraph dialog box should now appear, as shown in Figure 3.27.

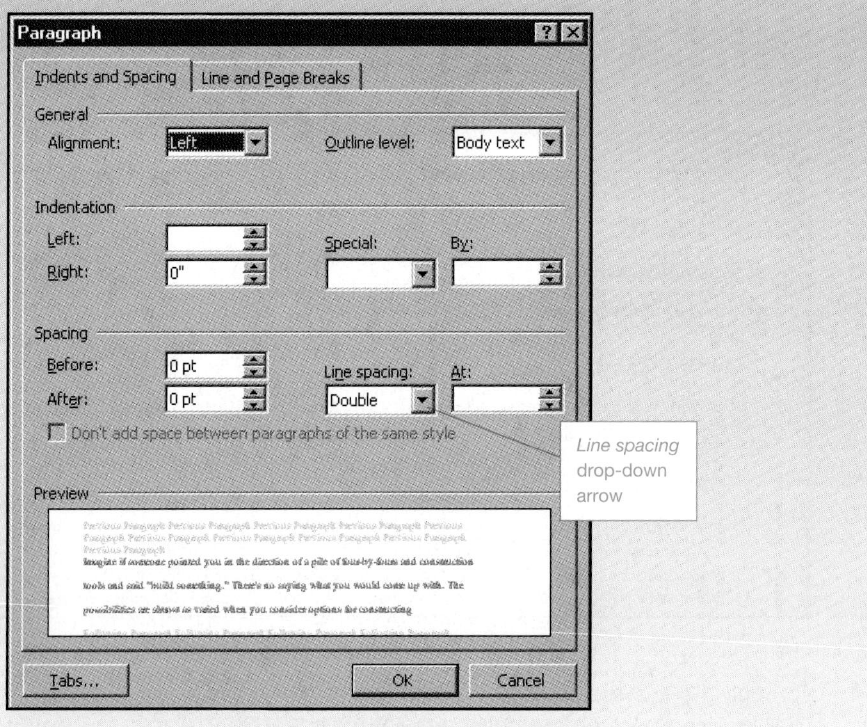

Figure 3.27

Using the Paragraph dialog box to change line spacing

9. CLICK: *Line spacing* drop-down arrow
   CHOOSE: Single from the drop-down list
   CLICK: OK command button
10. CLICK: anywhere in the document to remove the current selection
11. Save and then close the "Commerce" document.

3.2 How do you display a document's hidden symbols?

3.3 Creating Lists

Word provides several features for managing lists of items. In this module we describe how to create bulleted and numbered lists and numbered outlines. We also discuss how to arrange lists of information by changing your document's tab settings.

3.3.1 Creating Bulleted and Numbered Lists

Word provides a utility for automatically creating lists with leading **bullets** or numbers. Although round circles are the standard shape for bullets, you can select from a variety of shapes and symbols. Numbered lists can use numbers, Roman numerals, or letters.

method

To create a bulleted list

- CLICK: Bullets button (☰) on the Formatting toolbar

To create a numbered list

- CLICK: Numbering button (☰) on the Formatting toolbar

To modify the bullet symbols or numbering scheme:

- CHOOSE: Format, Bullets and Numbering

practice

You will now begin a new document and create bulleted and numbered lists.

1. To begin a blank document:
   CLICK: New button (🗋) on the Standard toolbar
2. TYPE: **To Do List**
   PRESS: ENTER twice
   (*Note:* Depending on your AutoCorrect settings, Word may have applied a heading style to the title.)
3. To create a bulleted list:
   CLICK: Bullets button (☰) on the Formatting toolbar
   A bullet appears and the indent markers are moved on the Ruler.
4. Enter the following text, pressing ENTER at the end of each line:
   Pick up dry cleaning
   Meet Jesse at the gym
   Go grocery shopping
   Mail letter to Mom
5. You will notice that Word automatically starts each new line with a bullet when you press ENTER. To turn off the bullets, ensure that your insertion point is on the line below "Mail letter to Mom" and then:
   PRESS: ENTER
   Because the previous line was empty, Word automatically turned off bullet formatting. You could also have clicked the Bullets button (☰) to turn off bullet formatting. Your document should now appear similar to Figure 3.28.

Figure 3.28

Bulleted list

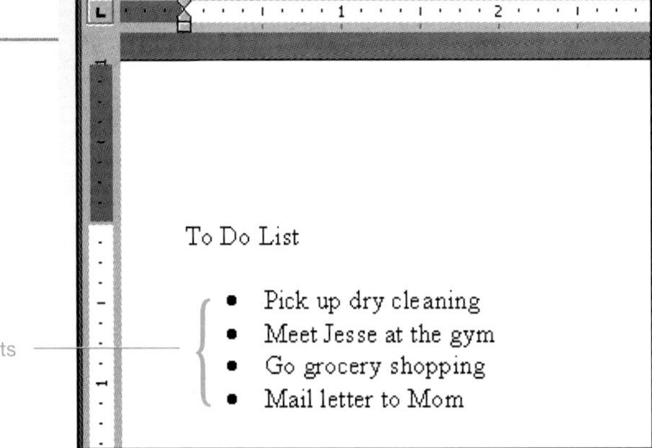

6. In this next example, you create a numbered list after you've already entered information into your document. To begin:
TYPE: **Travel Itinerary**
PRESS: ENTER twice

7. Enter the following lines of text, as before:
Aug 12: Flight 455 to Sydney.
Aug 28: Flight 87 to Auckland.
Aug 29: Flight A101 to Christchurch.
Sep 11: Flight 110 to Vancouver.

8. Using the mouse pointer in the Selection bar, select the text that you entered in step 7.

9. CLICK: Numbering button (☰)
The selected text is automatically numbered and indented.

10. To use letters rather than numbers for the list:
CHOOSE: Format, Bullets and Numbering
Your screen should now appear similar to Figure 3.29.

Figure 3.29

Bullets and Numbering dialog box: *Numbered* tab

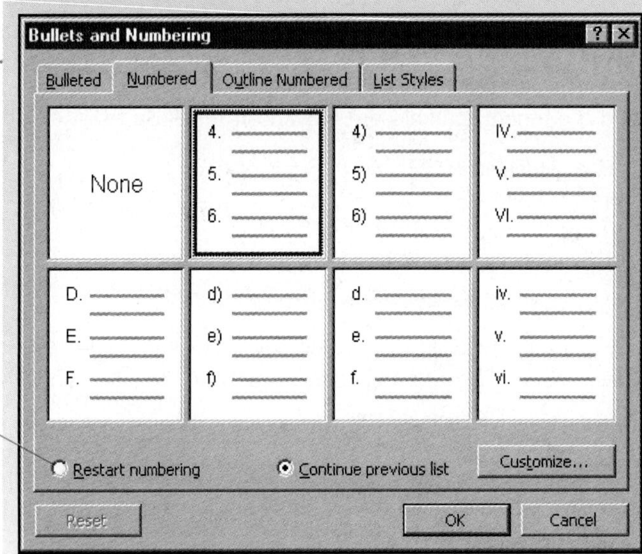

11. Ensure that the *Numbered* tab is selected in the dialog box.

12. If needed, so that the lettering in this list begins with "a" rather than "d", do the following:
SELECT: *Restart numbering* option button
SELECT: the option located in the bottom row, second from the left

13. CLICK: OK command button
CLICK: anywhere in the document to remove the highlighting
Your document should now appear similar to Figure 3.30.

Figure 3.30

Numbered and bulleted lists

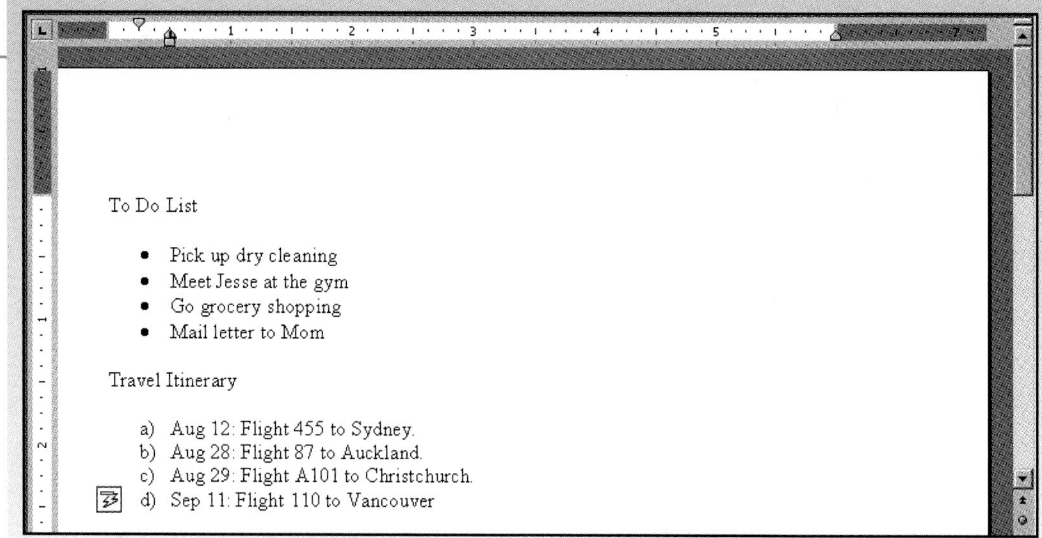

14. To add an item to your travel itinerary between Christchurch and Vancouver, position the insertion point at the end of the Christchurch line, item c, and press ENTER.
15. TYPE: **Sep 10: Flight 904 to Seattle.**
    Notice that Word automatically renumbers, or in this case reletters, the list for you when you insert new entries.
16. Save the document as "To Do List" to your personal storage location. (*Note:* The filename "To Do List" may already appear as a suggested filename.)
17. Close the document.

3.3.2 Creating a Numbered Outline

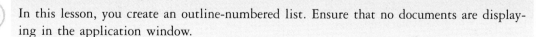

feature

Have you ever created an outline for a document and then had to retype the outline numbers when your outline changed? If so, you'll appreciate Word's ability to manage numbered outlines.

method

- CHOOSE: Format, Bullets and Numbering
- CLICK: *Outline Numbered* tab
- SELECT: an outline style
- CLICK: OK command button

practice

In this lesson, you create an outline-numbered list. Ensure that no documents are displaying in the application window.

1. Open the WD0332 data file.
2. Save the file as "Montelleron" to your personal storage location. In the next few lessons, you will prepare this document (Figure 3.31) for use at one of Montelleron, Inc.'s company meetings.

Figure 3.31

"Montelleron" document

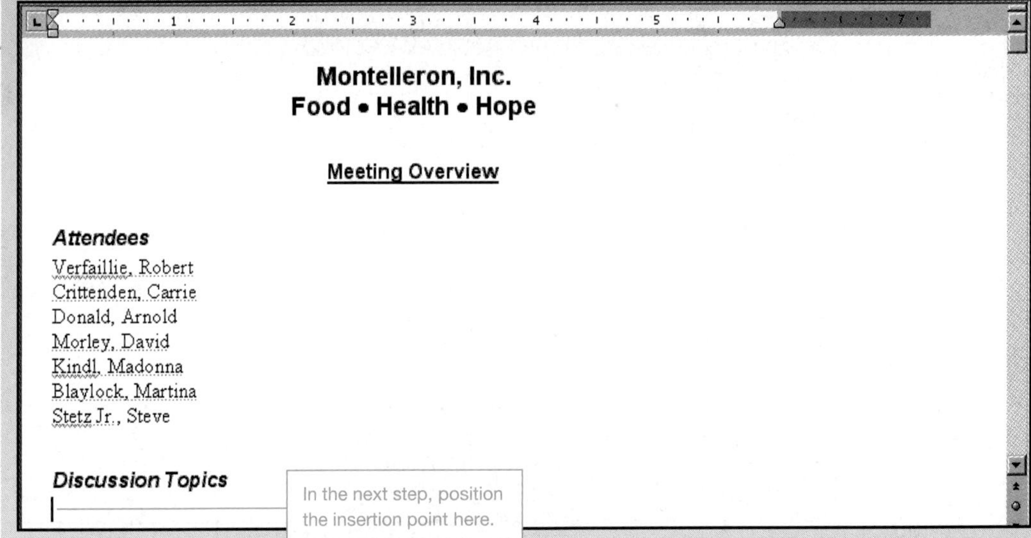

3. Scroll downward through the document to review its contents. Then:
CLICK: one line below the Discussion Topics heading
At this location, you're going to prepare an outline of the meeting's discussion topics.

4. Let's type the outline using Word's outline-numbering capabilities. To begin:
CHOOSE: Format, Bullets and Numbering
CLICK: *Outline Numbered* tab
The Bullets and Numbering dialog box should now appear similar to Figure 3.32. Word provides seven outline styles from which you can choose.

Figure 3.32

Bullets and Numbering dialog box: *Outline Numbered* tab

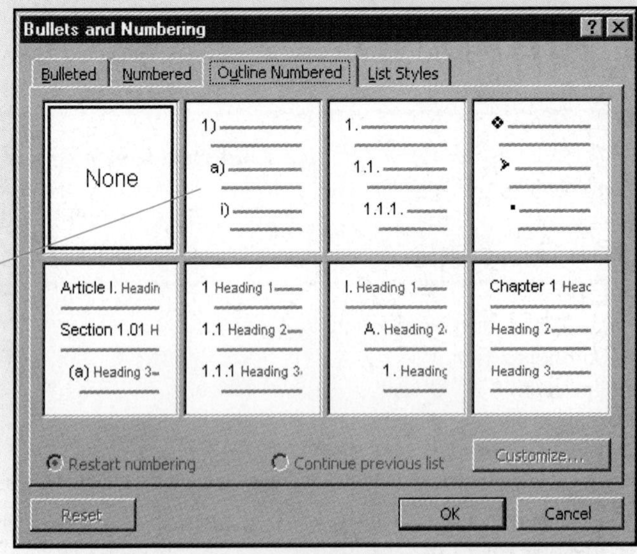

5. Let's select the first style (located to the right of the "None" box) in the dialog box. This style will use numbers for level-one headings, letters for level-two headings, and Roman numerals for level-three headings.
SELECT: 1) a) i) style (located in the first row, second column)
CLICK: OK command button

6. The insertion point should be blinking to the right of the number 1.
TYPE: **Delivering on the life sciences strategy**
PRESS: ENTER

7. To insert three demoted headings:
PRESS: TAB
TYPE: **The strong performance of our base businesses**
PRESS: ENTER
TYPE: **The continued increase in spending for growth**
PRESS: ENTER
TYPE: **A series of acquisitions and alliances**
PRESS: ENTER

8. To type heading at a promoted level:
PRESS: SHIFT + TAB
Your document should now appear similar to Figure 3.33.

Figure 3.33

Typing in a numbered outline

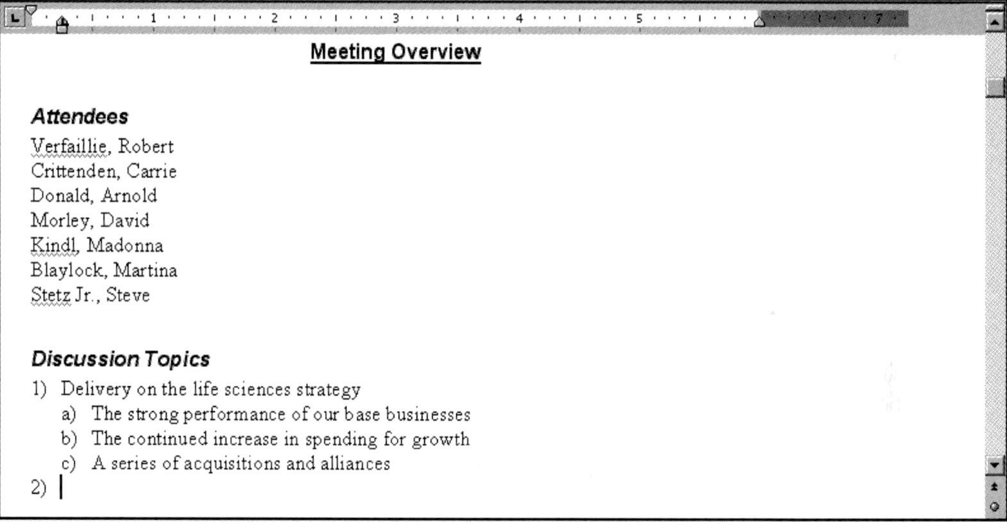

Meeting Overview

Attendees
Verfaillie, Robert
Crittenden, Carrie
Donald, Arnold
Morley, David
Kindl, Madonna
Blaylock, Martina
Stetz Jr., Steve

Discussion Topics
1) Delivery on the life sciences strategy
   a) The strong performance of our base businesses
   b) The continued increase in spending for growth
   c) A series of acquisitions and alliances
2)

9. Complete the outline by referring to Figure 3.34.

Figure 3.34

Completing the outline

2) Review of cash flow
   a) Cash flow remains strong
   b) Divided policy is unchanged
3) Additional financial information
   a) Risk management
   b) Company prepares for year 2002
      i) Internal systems
      ii) Suppliers
      iii) Contingency plans
4) Net sales

10. Save and then close the revised document.

3.3.3 Setting and Modifying Tabs

feature

Tabs enable you to neatly arrange text and numbers on a page. The four basic types of tabs are left, center, right, and decimal. (By default, Word supplies left-aligned tabs every half inch.) You can also create tab **leaders,** which are dotted, dashed, or solid lines that fill the space between text and tab stops. Leaders are commonly used in tables of contents to visually join the section headings with the page numbers.

method

To select a tab:

- CLICK: the Tab Alignment button (L), located on the left side of the Ruler, until the tab symbol you want appears
- CLICK: the desired location on the Ruler to set the tab stop

To remove a tab:

- DRAG: the tab stop down and off the Ruler

To create a custom tab that includes a tab leader:

- CHOOSE: Format, Tabs to display the Tabs dialog box

practice

This exercise practices setting tabs. Ensure that you've completed the previous lessons in this module. The application window should be empty.

1. To begin a new document:
   CLICK: New button (□)
   In the next few steps, you create an itinerary for a trip to the Baltic States and Russia.
2. TYPE: **Dear Friends,**
   PRESS: ENTER twice
   (*Note:* If the Office Assistant appears, hide it from view.)
3. TYPE: **We are pleased to offer this long-anticipated tour to the Baltic States and Russia. Once hidden together behind the Iron Curtain, the Baltic nations of Lithuania, Latvia, and Estonia now stand independently in sharp cultural contrast to the former Soviet Union and to each other. This in-depth tour enables you to learn how these distinct countries, while in the lingering shadow of Russia, have embraced their new freedom. The tour involves visits to the following cities:**
   PRESS: ENTER twice

In the next few steps, you set tabs and type text so that your document resembles Figure 3.35 when completed.

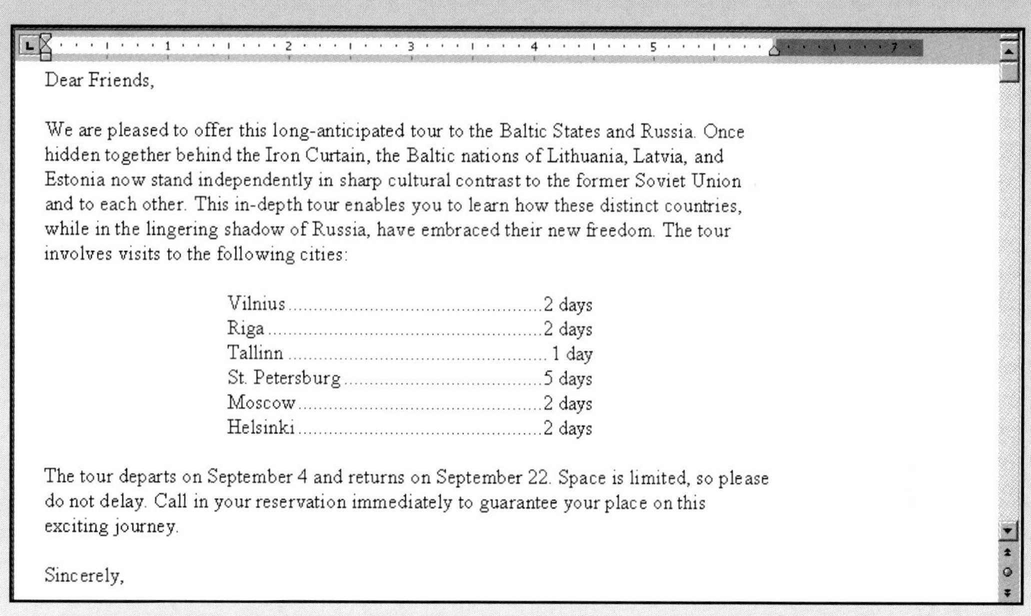

Dear Friends,
We are pleased to offer this long-anticipated tour to the Baltic States and Russia. Once hidden together behind the Iron Curtain, the Baltic nations of Lithuania, Latvia, and Estonia now stand independently in sharp cultural contrast to the former Soviet Union and to each other. This in-depth tour enables you to learn how these distinct countries, while in the lingering shadow of Russia, have embraced their new freedom. The tour involves visits to the following cities:
Vilnius ..... 2 days
Riga ..... 2 days
Tallinn ..... 1 day
St. Petersburg ..... 5 days
Moscow ..... 2 days
Helsinki ..... 2 days
The tour departs on September 4 and returns on September 22. Space is limited, so please do not delay. Call in your reservation immediately to guarantee your place on this exciting journey.
Sincerely,

Figure 3.35

"Baltic" document

4. To specify a tab position for the City names:
   CLICK: Tab Alignment button until the left-aligned tab symbol (L) appears
   (*Note:* This left-aligned symbol may already be displaying.)

5. To specify a tab position for the city names:
   CLICK: 1.5 inches on the Ruler
   (*Hint:* If the tab stop is not correctly positioned, drag it along the Ruler using the mouse. You can also fully remove a tab by dragging it down and off the Ruler.)

6. To specify a tab type and position for the number of days:
   CLICK: Tab Alignment button until the right-aligned tab symbol (┘) appears
   CLICK: 4.5 inches on the Ruler
   The Ruler should now appear similar to Figure 3.36.

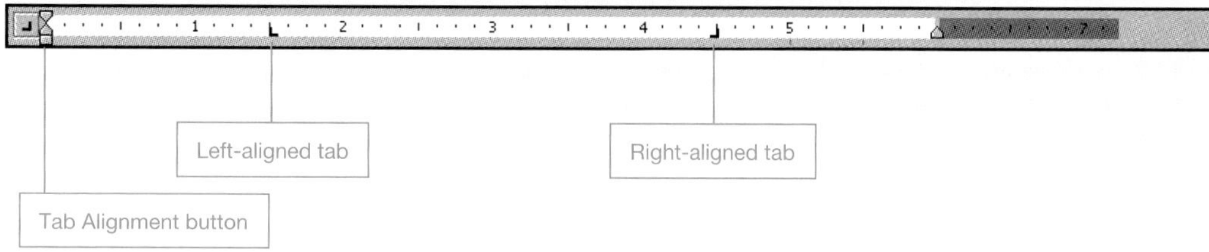

Left-aligned tab
Right-aligned tab
Tab Alignment button

Figure 3.36

Changing tab settings on the Ruler

7. To edit the right-aligned tab to be a dot leader:
CHOOSE: Format, Tabs
SELECT: 4.5″ in the *Tab stop position* list box
SELECT: 2 in the *Leader* area
The dialog box should now appear similar to Figure 3.37.

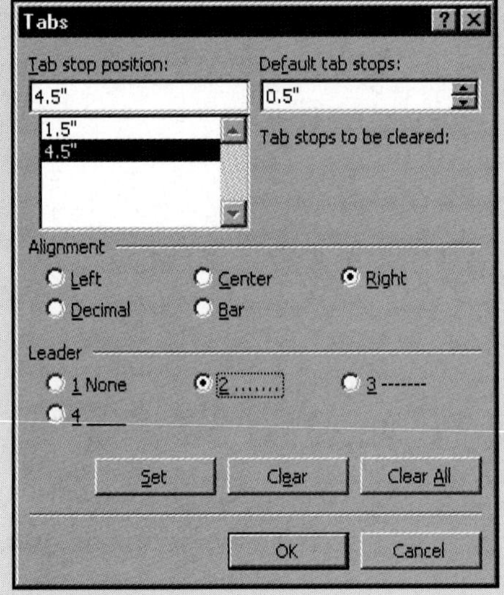

Figure 3.37
Tabs dialog box

8. CLICK: OK command button

9. To keep track of your keystrokes:
CLICK: Show/Hide button (¶)

10. Now let's enter the first row of information.
PRESS: TAB to move the insertion point to the first tab stop on the Ruler
TYPE: **Vilnius**
PRESS: TAB to move the insertion point to the next tab stop on the Ruler
TYPE: **2 days**
PRESS: ENTER
Note that each press of the TAB key results in the tab symbol (→) (Figure 3.38).

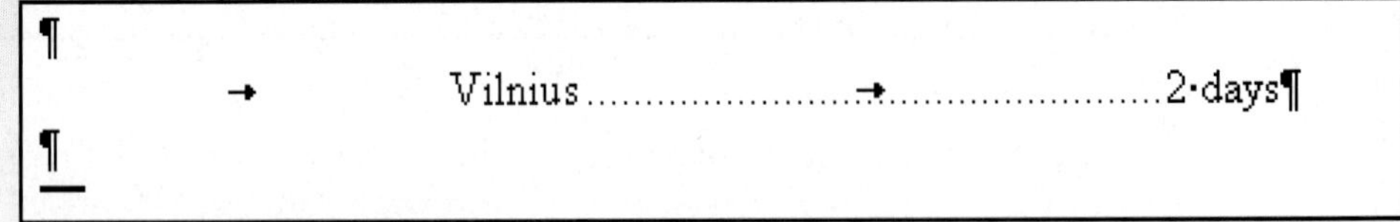

Figure 3.38
Pressing the Tab key

11. Enter the following information in the city and number of days columns, using the TAB key to position the insertion point:

Riga	**2 days**
Tallinn	**1 day**
St. Petersburg	**5 days**
Moscow	**2 days**
Helsinki	**2 days**

12. To continue:
PRESS: ENTER twice

13. Before typing the rest of the letter, remove the two tabs you inserted in steps 5 and 6 by dragging them down and off the Ruler.

14. TYPE: **The tour departs on September 4 and returns on September 22. Space is limited, so please do not delay. Call in your reservation immediately to guarantee your place on this exciting journey.**
PRESS: ENTER twice
TYPE: **Sincerely,**
PRESS: ENTER three times
TYPE: **your name**
PRESS: ENTER
TYPE: **Director of Travel**

15. Let's remove the hidden codes from view.
CLICK: Show/Hide button (¶)
Your document should appear similar to Figure 3.35, shown earlier.

16. Save the document as "Baltic" to your personal storage location.

17. Close the document.

3.3 What dialog box enables you to create an outline-numbered list?

3.4 Applying Borders and Shading

Documents that incorporate interesting visual effects do a better job of engaging readers than those that use plain formatting. You already know how to use character and paragraph formatting commands to add visual emphasis to words and paragraphs. Shading and page borders can make your documents even more visually engaging.

3.4.1 Shading Words and Paragraphs

feature →

Shading provides another means for emphasizing text. Just make sure that your shading color doesn't match your text color too closely. Otherwise, your text will be difficult to read.

method →

- CHOOSE: Format, Borders and Shading
- CLICK: *Shading* tab
- CLICK: a color in the *Fill* palette or choose an option from the *Style* drop-down list
- SELECT: Text or Paragraph in the *Apply to* drop-down list
- CLICK: OK command button

practice

You will now open an existing flier and then apply shading to words and paragraphs. Ensure that no documents are open in the application window.

1. Open the WD0340 student file.
2. Save the document as "Sleepy Hollow" to your personal storage location.
3. Drag the vertical scroll bar downward until you see the three days and times (Figure 3.39). In the next few steps, you shade this information so that it will stand out on the printed flier.

Figure 3.39

Portion of the "Sleepy Hollow" document

Saturday, 8am-noon

Tuesday-Thursday, 8am-7pm

Monday and Friday, 8am-5pm

4. Position the insertion point anywhere in the "Saturday, 8am-noon" line.
5. To shade the text selection:
   CHOOSE: Format, Borders and Shading
   SELECT: *Shading* tab
   Your screen should now appear similar to Figure 3.40.

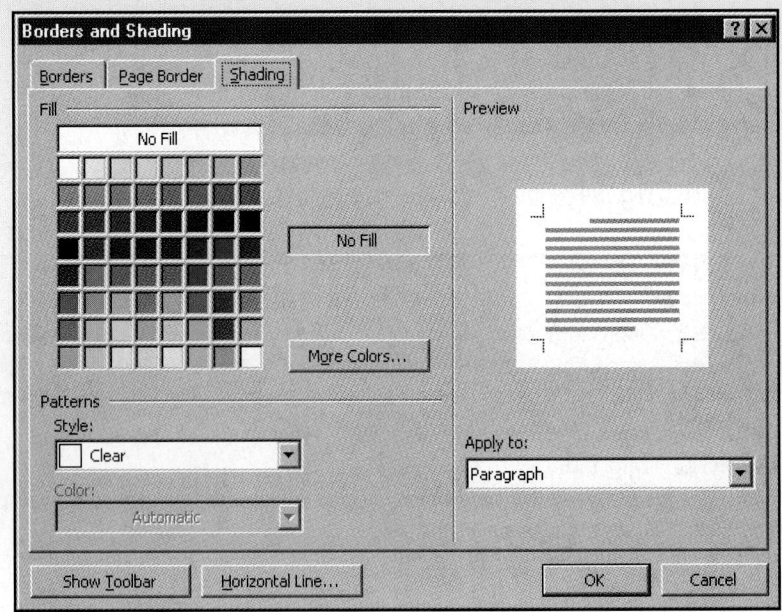

Figure 3.40

Borders and Shading dialog box: *Shading* tab

6. In the *Fill* palette:
CLICK: Yellow

7. Next, take a look at the setting in the *Apply to* drop-down list. When "Text" is selected, the shading only covers the selected letters. When "Paragraph" is selected, the shading will extend from the left to the right margin of the page. If "Paragraph" isn't currently selected:
SELECT: Paragraph from the *Apply to* drop-down list
CLICK: OK command button
The date and time, as well as a line that extends from the left to the right margin, should now appear shaded.

8. To repeat the same shading for the next date:
SELECT: Tuesday-Thursday, 8am-7pm
CHOOSE: Edit, Repeat Borders and Shading
(*Note:* You could have also pressed CTRL+y.)

9. Using the same procedure as in step 8, repeat the shading for the "Monday and Friday, 8am-5pm" date.

10. CLICK: away from the shaded text so that no text is selected
Your screen should now appear similar to Figure 3.41.

Figure 3.41

Shading document text

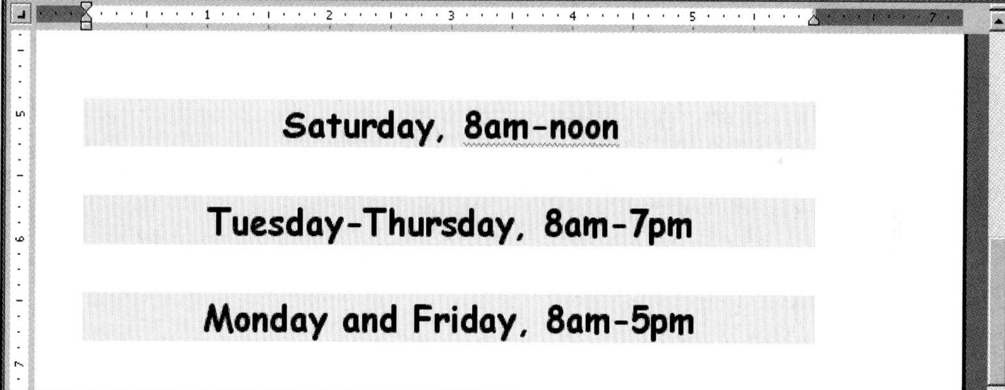

11. Save the revised document and keep it open for use in the next lesson.

3.4.2 Applying Borders to Paragraphs

feature

Borders allow you to emphasize important text and divide a document into separate areas. You can control the position of borders so that they appear on the top, bottom, left, right, or all sides of the current paragraph. You can also customize a border's style, color, and width. Borders are often used in conjunction with shading.

method

To apply a border to an entire paragraph:

- CLICK: in the paragraph you want to affect
- CHOOSE: Format, Borders and Shading
- CLICK: *Borders* tab

To position the border:

- CLICK: an image in the *Setting* area, or
- CLICK: on the diagram in the *Preview* area

To customize the border, perform one or more of the following procedures:

- SELECT: a style in the *Style* list box
- SELECT: a color from the *Color* drop-down list
- SELECT: a rule width from the *Width* drop-down list
- CLICK: OK command button

practice

In this lesson, you insert borders and apply 5% shading. Ensure that the "Sleepy Hollow" document is displaying.

1. Near the top of your document:
CLICK: in the "Extended Hours" line

2. To apply borders to this text:
CHOOSE: Format, Borders and Shading
CLICK: *Borders* tab
Your screen should now appear similar to Figure 3.42. To insert borders around a paragraph, select an image in the *Setting* area. To apply customized borders, click on the image in the *Preview* area.

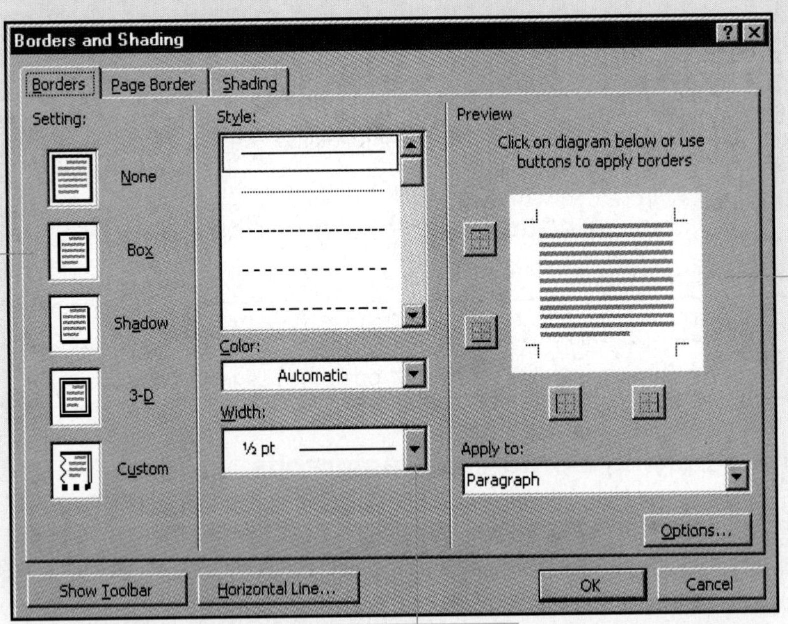

Figure 3.42
Borders and Shading dialog box: *Borders* tab

3. To increase the width of the borders to 2 points:
SELECT: "2 ¼ pt" from the *Width* drop-down list

4. To apply a border to the top of the text:
CLICK: near the top of the Preview diagram *(refer to Figure 3.43)* until a border appears in the diagram
A border should now appear near the top of the Preview diagram.

5. To apply a border to the bottom of the title:
CLICK: near the bottom of the Preview diagram *(refer to Figure 3.43)*

Figure 3.43
Using the Preview diagram to apply borders

6. Since we're already displaying the Borders and Shading dialog box, let's apply 5% gray shading to the title.
CLICK: *Shading* tab
CLICK: 5% from the *Style* drop-down list
CLICK: OK command button
Your screen should now appear similar to Figure 3.44.

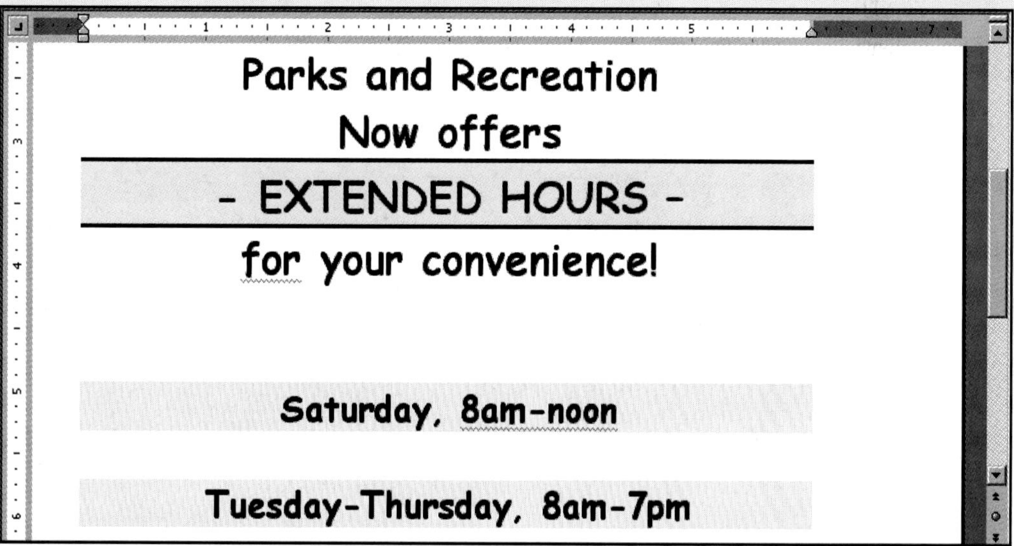

Figure 3.44
Applying borders and shading to the title

7. Save the revised document and keep it open for the next lesson.

3.4.3 Creating a Page Border

feature

Page borders are very effective when used on title pages, flyers, and newsletters. Your borders can consist of a solid line or a graphic that is repeated around the page.

method

To add a page border:

- CHOOSE: Format, Borders and Shading
- CLICK: *Page Border* tab
- CLICK: an option in the *Setting* area, or
- CHOOSE: a graphic from the *Art* drop-down list
- SELECT: a color from the *Color* drop-down list (optional)
- SELECT: a rule width from the *Width* drop-down list (optional)
- CLICK: OK command button

practice

You will now add a page border to the "Sleepy Hollow" flier.

1. To insert a page border:
   CHOOSE: Format, Borders and Shading
   SELECT: *Page Border* tab

2. Let's see what happens when we click the *Box* graphic in the *Setting* area.
   CLICK: *Box* graphic in the *Setting* area
   Your screen should now appear similar to Figure 3.45. The result of your selection displays in the *Preview* area to the right.

Figure 3.45

Borders and Shading dialog box: *Page Border* tab

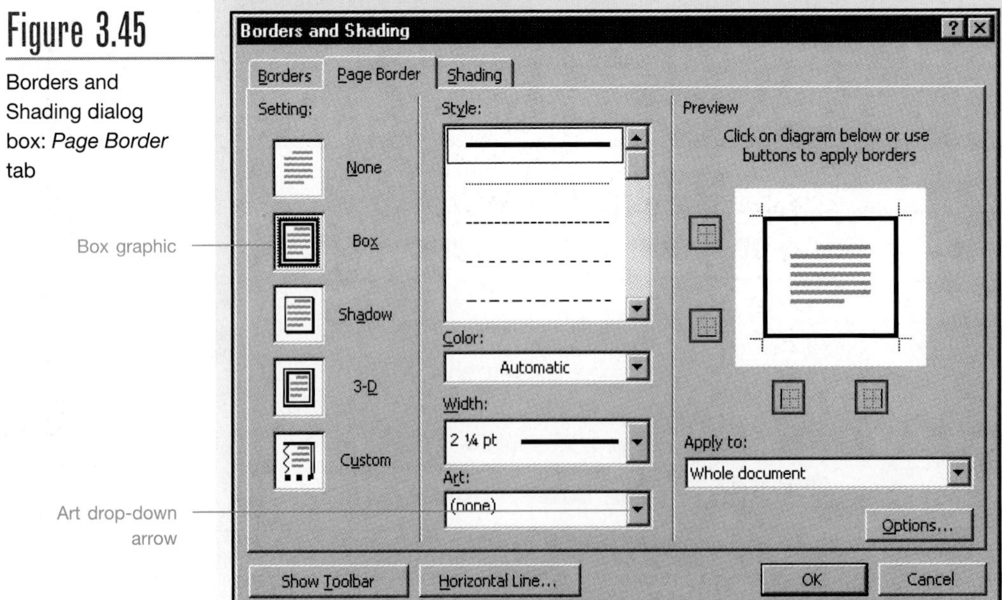

3. Let's increase the width of the line.

CLICK: *Width* drop-down arrow
CHOOSE: 3 pt from the drop-down list

4. To experiment with changing the border style:
CLICK: *Shadow* graphic in the *Setting* area

5. Let's select a graphic for the border.
CLICK: *Art* drop-down arrow
DRAG: the menu's vertical scroll box down until you see a row of green trees
CHOOSE: tree graphic

6. To continue:
CLICK: OK command button

7. If you drag the document's vertical scroll bar up and down, you'll see that the border surrounds the page (Figure 3.46).

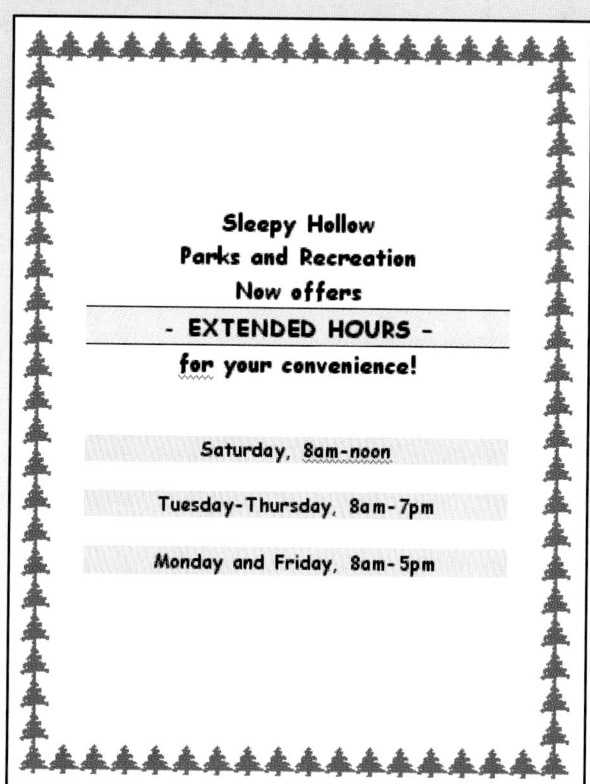

Figure 3.46

Creating a graphic page border

8. Save and then close the "Sleepy Hollow" document.

3.4 What are page borders used for?

Chapter Summary

Word's formatting commands can be used to your advantage to create compelling documents. Character formatting such as bold, italic, and underlines are useful for emphasizing important text, and your selection of fonts, font sizes, and colors contribute to the overall tone for your message. You can further enhance your documents using paragraph-formatting commands and engage the attention of your audience using borders and shading.

Command Summary

Many of the commands and procedures appearing in this chapter are summarized in the following table.

Skill Set	To Perform This Task . . .	Do the Following . . .
Modifying Text	Bold text	CLICK: Bold button (B)
	Italicize text	CLICK: Italic button (I)
	Underline text	CLICK: Underline button (U)
	Select a font	CLICK: Font drop-down arrow (Times New Roman)
	Change the font size	CLICK: Font Size drop-down arrow (10)
	Change the font color	CLICK: Font Color button (A) to apply the most recently selected color, or CLICK: Font Color drop-down arrow (A) to choose from a palette of colors
	Highlight text	CLICK: Highlight button
	Clear formatting	CHOOSE: Clear Formatting from the Style drop-down list (Normal)
	Copy formatting options to another area	CLICK: Format Painter button
	Copy formatting options to several areas	DOUBLE-CLICK: Format Painter button
Modifying Paragraphs	Show/Hide paragraph marks	CLICK: Show/Hide button (¶)
	Reveal a paragraph's formatting	CHOOSE: Help, What's This? CLICK: in the paragraph
	Left-align a paragraph	CLICK: Align Left button
	Center-align a paragraph	CLICK: Center button
	Right-align a paragraph	CLICK: Align Right button
	Justify a paragraph	CLICK: Justify button
	Increase indentation	CLICK: Increase Indent button
	Decrease indentation	CLICK: Decrease Indent button

Skill Set	To Perform This Task . . .	Do the Following . . .
	Customize the left and right indents	DRAG: the indent markers on the Ruler
	Create a first-line or hanging indent	DRAG: First-line indent or hanging indent marker on the Ruler to the right
	Create a bulleted list	CLICK: Bullets button ( )
	Create a numbered list	CLICK: Numbering button ( )
	Specify bullet symbols or numbering schemes	CHOOSE: Format, Bullets and Numbering
	Create a numbered outline	CHOOSE: Format, Bullets and Numbering CLICK: *Outline Numbered* tab
	Change line spacing	CLICK: Line Spacing drop-down arrow ( ) CHOOSE: an option from the drop-down menu
	Set tabs	SELECT: a tab type using the Tab Alignment button ( ) CLICK: the desired location on the Ruler to set the tab stop
	Create a tab leader	CHOOSE: Format, Tabs
	Remove tabs	DRAG: tab stop down and off the Ruler
	Apply styles	CHOOSE: a style from the Style drop-down list (Normal)
	Shade selected words and paragraphs	CHOOSE: Format, Borders and Shading CLICK: *Shading* tab
	Apply borders	CHOOSE: Format, Borders and Shading CLICK: *Borders* tab
	Create a page border	CHOOSE: Format, Borders and Shading CLICK: *Page Border* tab

Key Terms

This section specifies page references for the key terms identified in this chapter. For a complete list of definitions, refer to the Glossary at the back of this learning guide.

bullets, *p. WD 102*

font, *p. WD 85*

Format Painter, *p. WD 90*

justification, *p. WD 95*

leaders, *p. WD 108*

paragraph mark, *p. WD 93*

style, *p. WD 87*

Chapter quiz

Short Answer

1. Describe four types of tabs you can include in a document.
2. How would you set line spacing to 1.5 lines?
3. What is the procedure for right-aligning a paragraph?
4. What is the significance of the paragraph symbol?
5. How do you create a page border?
6. What does the phrase *character formatting* refer to?
7. What is a tab leader?
8. What is a style?
9. How would you go about changing the font and point size of a selection of text?
10. What procedure would you use to change the color of a selection of text to red?

True/False

1. ____ A style is a collection of character and paragraph formatting commands.
2. ____ The left indent marker moves the first-line and hanging indent markers in tandem.
3. ____ To double-space a document, click the Double Space button on the Formatting toolbar.
4. ____ You can preview your font selections in the Font dialog box.
5. ____ It's possible to control the width and color of page borders.
6. ____ To number text after it has been typed, you must select it and then click the Numbering button ( ).
7. ____ To customize a numbering scheme, you must use the Bullets and Numbering dialog box.
8. ____ One method to create a hanging indent involves dragging the hanging indent marker on the ruler.
9. ____ It's possible to clear character and paragraph formatting using the Style drop-down list on the Formatting toolbar.
10. ____ By default, tabs display with a dot leader.

Multiple Choice

1. Character formatting involves choosing:
   a. typefaces
   b. font sizes
   c. text attributes
   d. All of the above

2. To increase a paragraph's indentation level, click:
   a.
   b.
   c.
   d. None of the above

3. Which of the following line spaces can you apply to a document?
   a. 1.0
   b. 1.5
   c. 3.0
   d. All of the above

4. Which of the following enables you to copy formatting styles and attributes?
   a. styles
   b. Format Painter
   c. tabs
   d. Font dialog box

5. To remove a tab stop from the Ruler:
   a. Drag the tab stop down and off the Ruler
   b. Select the tab stop and press DELETE
   c. Position the insertion point to the right of the tab stop and press BACKSPACE
   d. All of the above

6. To create a tab leader, you must use the:
   a. Tabs dialog box
   b. Ruler
   c. period (.) key
   d. All of the above

7. Which of the following is a collection of character and paragraph formatting commands?
   a. style
   b. Format Painter
   c. tab
   d. Font dialog box

8. Which of the following moves all but the first line of a paragraph in from the left margin, leaving the first-line indent marker in its current position?
   a. Hanging indent marker
   b. Left indent marker
   c. Right indent marker
   d. None of the above

9. To display a document's paragraph marks:
   a. CHOOSE: File, Marks
   b. CLICK: Show/Hide button
   c. Both a. and b.
   d. None of the above

10. To align text so that it is even on both the left and right margins, you must click the ______________.
    a. Center button
    b. Justify button
    c. Align Right button
    d. Both a. and b.

Hands-On exercises

1. Laura Howard: Formatting a Letter

In this exercise, Laura applies a more professional look to an existing document. Assume the role of Laura to practice changing fonts and sizes.

1. Open the WD03HE01 data file.
2. Save a copy of the document as "LH Letter" to your personal storage location. This is the same letter you edited in the first hands-on exercise in Chapter 2.
3. Let's select the entire document and then set the font formatting for the entire document to 11 point, Times New Roman.
   PRESS: CTRL and hold it down
   CLICK: once anywhere in the Selection bar
   SELECT: Times New Roman from the Font drop-down list (Times New Roman)
   SELECT: 11 from the Font Size drop-down list (10)

4. Laura decides to format the beginning of her letter to look more like letterhead stationery. Do the following:
   SELECT: Laura Howard
   SELECT: Arial from the Font drop-down list (Times New Roman)
   SELECT: 16 from the Font Size drop-down list (10)
   CLICK: Bold button (B)
   CLICK: Underline button (U)
5. To format Laura's address using an Arial, 9-point font:
   SELECT: the three address and phone number lines
   SELECT: Arial from the Font drop-down list (Times New Roman)
   SELECT: 9 from the Font Size drop-down list (10)
6. With the three address lines still selected:
   CLICK: Font Color drop-down arrow (A)
   SELECT: a shade of green
   The formatted document should now appear similar to Figure 3.47.

Figure 3.47

"LH Letter" document

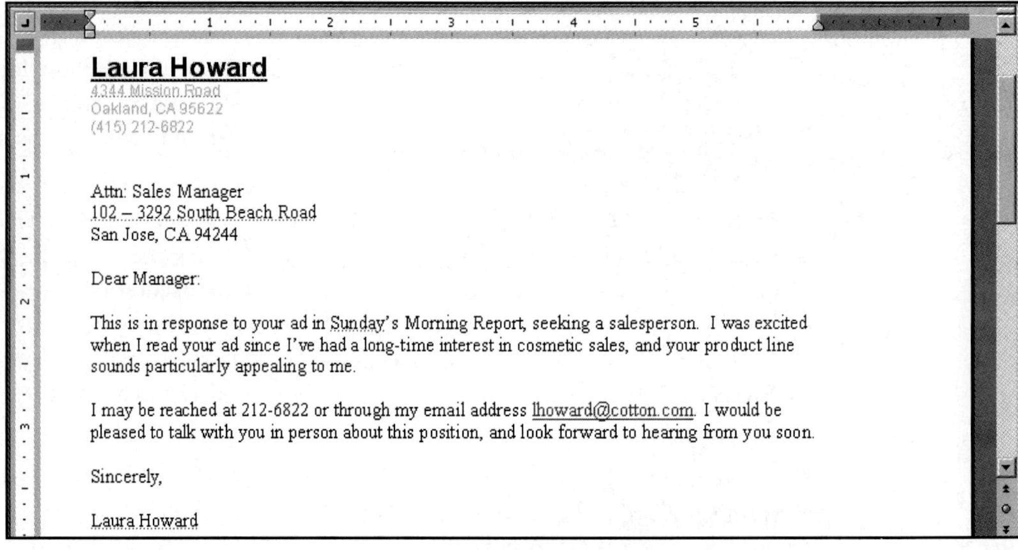

7. Preview and print the letter.
8. Save and then close the revised document.

easy

2. DigiTech Services: Designing a Memo

In this exercise, Joanne designs a memo form like the one pictured in Figure 3.48. Assume the role of Joanne and practice setting tabs and applying paragraph formatting. DigiTech Services employees will use this memo in printed form.

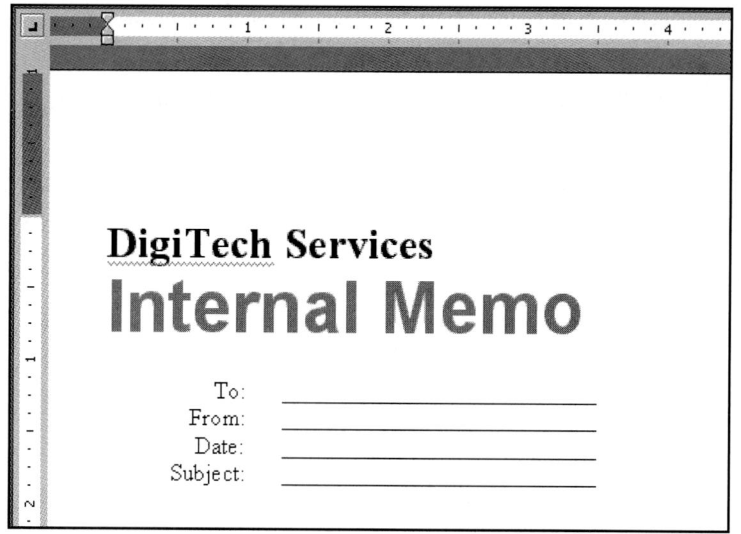

Figure 3.48

"DS Memo" document

1. Create a new blank document.
2. TYPE: **DigiTech Services**
   PRESS: ENTER
3. TYPE: **Internal Memo**
   PRESS: ENTER twice
4. Format the company name using Times New Roman, 22 points, and the bold attribute.
5. Format the words "Internal Memo" using Arial, 36 points, and the bold attribute.
6. Change the color of the text "Internal Memo" to red.
7. To move to the end of the document:
   PRESS: CTRL + END
   The insertion point is now positioned two lines below the text "Internal Memo".
8. To insert a right tab at position 1″ and left tabs at positions 1.25″ and 3.5″:
   SELECT: Right-aligned tab (⌋) using the Tab Alignment button
   CLICK: 1 inch on the Ruler
   SELECT: Left-aligned tab (L) using the Tab Alignment button
   CLICK: 1.25 inches on the Ruler
   CLICK: 3.5 inches on the Ruler
9. Let's format the tab at 3.5″ to include a line leader.
   CHOOSE: Format, Tabs
   SELECT: 3.5″ in the *Tab stop position* list box
   SELECT: 4 in the *Leader* area
   CLICK: OK command button
10. To begin typing the "To:" line of the memo, do the following:
    PRESS: TAB to move the insertion point to the next tab stop
    TYPE: **To:**
    PRESS: TAB twice to move the insertion point to the last tab stop on the Ruler
    PRESS: ENTER

11. Using the same method as in the previous step, proceed by typing in the "From", "Date", and "Subject" lines.
12. Save the document as "DS Memo" to your personal storage location.
13. Print and then close the document.

3. Celsius Gear, USA: Reformatting a Memo

In the last chapter, Dennis improved the organization of an existing memo. In this exercise, you and Dennis improve its formatting.

1. Open the WD03HE03 data file. This is the memo you edited in the third hands-on exercise in Chapter 2.
2. Save the document as "Celsius Memo—Revised" to your personal storage location.
3. Format the business name using the Tahoma font, if available.
4. Format the business name using a 20-point font size and remove the italic formatting.
5. Format the word "Memorandum" to include a 36-point font size.
6. Change the color of the text "Memorandum" to orange.
7. Format the remaining lines in the document using a Tahoma, 10-point font, keeping the bold effect intact.
8. Change the color of the lines you formatted in the previous step to orange. The revised document should now appear similar to Figure 3.49.

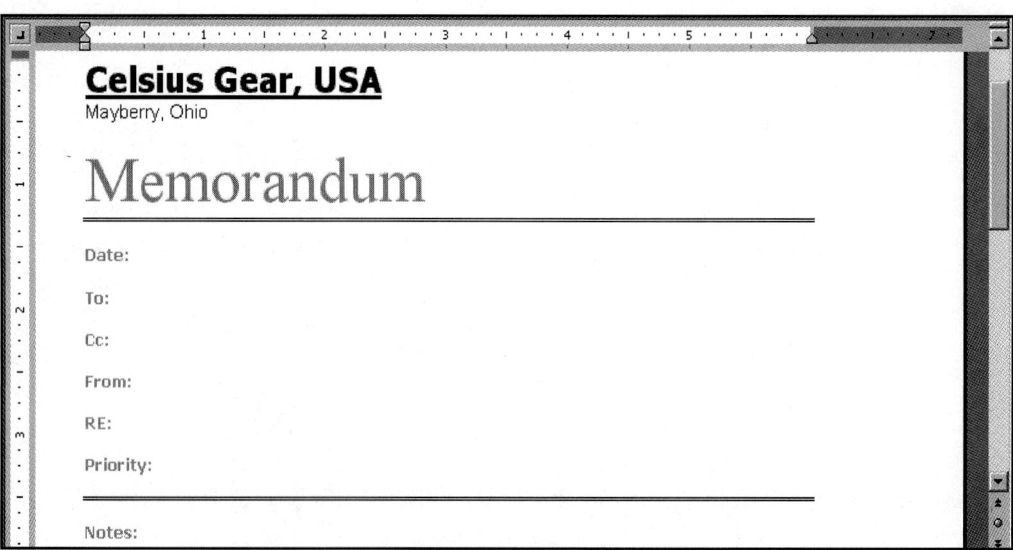

Figure 3.49

"Celsius Memo—Revised" document

9. Save, print, and then close the revised document.

moderate 

4. Worldwide Conventions, Inc.: Bulletin

In the last chapter, Jason McGonigle, the president of Worldwide Conventions, Inc., modified an existing document and proofed it for errors. In this exercise, you and Jason apply character and paragraph formatting commands to give the document a more professional look.

1. Open the WD03HE04 data file.
2. Save a copy of the document as "WW News Bulletin - Revised" to your personal storage location.
3. Change the formatting of the entire document to a 12-point Arial font.
4. Format the words "News Report" to include a 20-point font size.
5. Format the business name to include the bold and underline attributes.
6. Change the color of the business name to a shade of green.
7. Format the first two paragraphs of the document so they are left-aligned.
8. Apply bullets to the city and date lines.
9. Change the spacing of the city and date lines to 1.5 lines.
10. Left-align the final paragraph of the document.
11. Insert a page border in the document that is 6 points wide. Use the 3-D style and apply the same shade of green you used in step 6. A portion of your document appears in Figure 3.50.

Figure 3.50

"WW News Bulletin—Revised" document

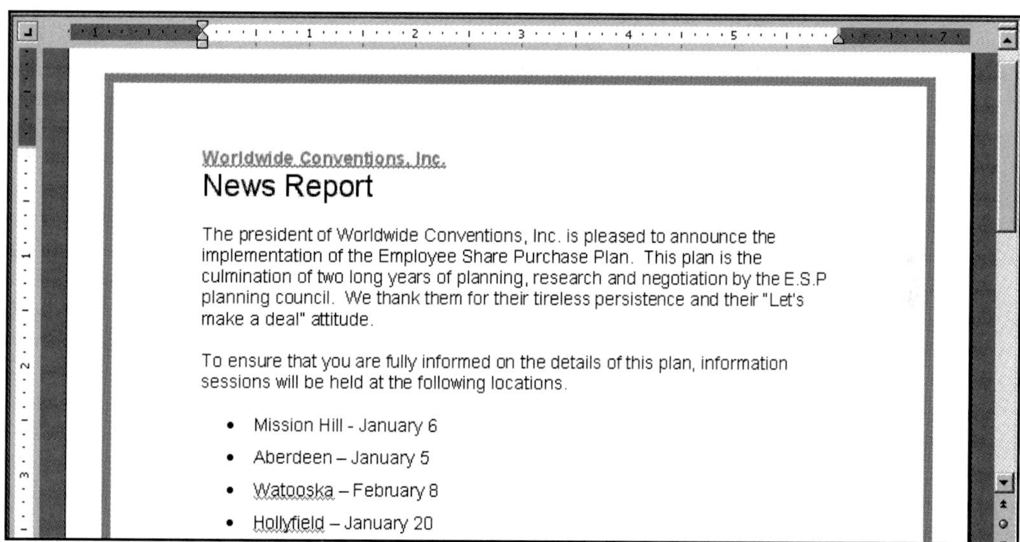

12. Save, print, and then close the revised document.

difficult 

5. On Your Own: Garage Sale Notice

In this exercise, you must use your formatting skills to create a garage sale notice to be posted on notice boards throughout your neighborhood. Your notice should detail the time and location of the sale and include a list of some of the key items you hope to sell quickly. After preparing your notice, apply attention-grabbing formatting including borders and shading. Save your work as "Garage Sale" to your personal storage location. Print and close the document.

ffficult 

6. On Your Own: Applying Styles

To practice applying character and paragraph formatting, create an itinerary describing a vacation in a city you have never been to but would like to visit. For each day in your week-long vacation, detail the types of activities that you will be doing, such as taking a tour or visiting a monument. Give the itinerary a professional look using styles, borders, and shading. Save the document as "Itinerary" and then print and close the document.

Case Problems

Animal Care League

Now that Natalia has learned some techniques for creating professional-looking documents, she decides to tackle those documents in her office that will benefit the most from her newly attained skills. Among the documents she creates are a letter to the general membership, a notice about upcoming society events, and a thank you note.

In the following case problems, assume the role of Natalia and perform the same steps as she would perform to complete these tasks.

1. Natalia begins her work by preparing a letter to the general membership about this year's fund-raising campaign. She creates and formats the letter pictured in Figure 3.51. She uses a green, Times New Roman font for the main title in the letterhead and a green, Arial font for the letterhead's subheading. The remainder of the letter uses an Arial font. Natalia tries to get her letter to look as much as possible like the letter in Figure 3.51. (*Note:* Text will wrap in different locations on your computer.) Once finished, she saves the document as "League Letter" and then prints and closes the document.

Figure 3.51

"League Letter" document

Animal Care League
75 Heron Lane, Willow Tree, Kansas 72434

Dear Fellow Animal Lovers:

This summer marks the tenth anniversary of the league's first permanent animal shelter. Through our cruelty and neglect investigations and our education programs, we are working hard to promote the humane treatment of animals and responsible pet ownership.

> This year's campaign goal of $25,000 will enable us to continue working for the needy animals of the county. We know you care, please give generously!

Thanks to your generous support, since May 1989 <u>over 10,000 unwanted and abandoned pets have found loving homes</u>, and have been able to lead the happy, healthy lives they deserve. On behalf of the animals, thank you!

Yours truly,

Jason Peters, President

2. Natalia decides to prepare the notice pictured in Figure 3.52 listing the upcoming events organized by league members. The heading and subheading are centered between the margins. Natalia must insert bullets and indent text in order to achieve the desired results. Natalia tries to get her notice to look as much as possible like the notice in Figure 3.52. (*Note:* Text will wrap in different locations on your computer.) Once finished, she saves the document as "League Notice" and then prints and closes the document.

Figure 3.52

"League Notice" document

Animal Care League
We speak for those who cannot speak for themselves

UPCOMING EVENTS AT A GLANCE

- May 3: 10th Anniversary of the shelter construction and launch of annual fundraising appeal
- May 24: Second Annual Book Sale at Baker Place
- June 5: Coldstream Pet Walk-a-Thon
- June 20: Farmer's Market Bake Sale
- July 8: Taylor Park Pet Look-Alike Contest

Volunteers needed for all events. Please call 948-3728.

3. Jason Peters, the league's president, has asked Natalia to create a document that can be used as an advertisement in the local newspaper. The purpose of the advertisement is to give thanks to several companies for contributing to the league. To create the document, Natalia must set a dot-leader tab in position 3.5 inches and create a hanging indent in position 3.5 inches. Natalia saves the document as "League Thanks" and then prints and closes the document. The completed document is pictured in Figure 3.53.

Figure 3.53

"League Thanks" document

Animal Care League
We speak for those who cannot speak for themselves

We thank you!!

Amigos Pet Food & Feed Store	for your donation of Science Diet food
Betterson Elementary School Students	for your donation of fundraising proceeds to the league's shelter
Kalamalka Business Students	for donating your profits to the league
Intra Travel	for sponsoring our booth during the DVA Sunshine Festival
Landscaping Volunteers	for sowing grass, weeding, nurturing trees, and transforming our former landfill site
Mae's Meats	for holding a barbeque benefiting the league
The Hanson Family	for providing entertainment for the league's open house

4. Natalia needs to prepare a list of the Board of Directors for posting on the league's bulletin board. She starts by creating a document with the information shown below. After formatting the first three lines similar to other league documents, she uses a line-leader tab to separate each director's name from his/her corresponding title. Natalia applies 1.5-line spacing to the list of directors and uses character-formatting commands to give the listing a more professional look. After saving the document as "League Board," she prints the document.

Animal Care League
Willow Tree, Kansas
2001-2002 Board of Directors

Alfred Baker President
Claire Daingerfield Vice-President
Eldon Frank Treasurer
Gloria Holdings Secretary
Ivan Jackson Past President
Kelly Lindgren Director-at-Large Area E
Mark Neilson Director-at-Large Area D
Olivia Peters Regional District Representative

Natalia saves the document as "League Board" and then prints and closes the document.

Microsoft® Word® 2002

CHAPTER 4

Printing and Web Publishing

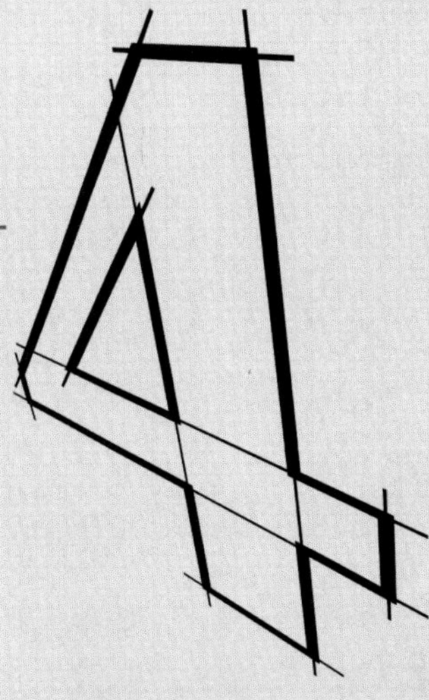

CHAPTER OUTLINE

Case Study

4.1 Previewing and Printing Documents

4.2 Customizing Print Options

4.3 Inserting Headers and Footers

4.4 Using Sections to Apply Varied Formatting

4.5 Publishing to the Web

Chapter Summary

Chapter Quiz

Hands-On Exercises

Case Problems

PREREQUISITES

To successfully complete this chapter, you must be able to format characters and paragraphs, create lists, and apply borders. We also assume you know how to save, open, close, and print your files.

LEARNING OBJECTIVES

After completing this chapter, you will be able to:

- Adjust page and margin settings, and control pagination
- Insert page numbers and create headers and footers
- Insert section breaks
- Prepare a document for posting on a Web server

CaseStudy YARD SMART DESIGNS Mark and Christine Anderson of Florence, North Dakota, operate a small landscaping business called Yard Smart Designs. Christine is widely recognized for her creativity and innovative use of materials. Mark laughingly admits that he provides the labor behind their efforts and that his creative bent is best applied to managing the paperwork and administration needed to run a successful enterprise.

Mark is enthusiastic about computers and is currently enrolled in a Microsoft Word course. His objective is to use his word processing skills to create professional-looking documents that can be published in print form and on his company's Web site.

In this chapter, you and Mark learn how to preview and print documents, change a document's margins and page orientation, and insert headers and footers. You also learn how to vary formatting within a document and prepare documents for display on the World Wide Web.

4.1 Previewing and Printing Documents

This module focuses on outputting your document creations. Most commonly, you will print a document for inclusion in a report or other document.

4.1.1 Previewing a Document

feature

Before sending a document to the printer, you can preview it using a full-page display that closely resembles the printed version. In this Preview display mode, you can move through the document pages, and zoom in and out on desired areas.

method

- CLICK: Print Preview button ( ) on the Standard toolbar,

or

- CHOOSE: File, Print Preview

practice

You will now open a relatively large document and then preview it on the screen. Ensure that no documents are displayed in the application window.

1. Open the WD0410 data file.
2. Before continuing, save the file as "For Printing" to your personal storage location.
3. To preview how the document will appear when printed:
   CLICK: Print Preview button ( ) on the Standard toolbar
   Your screen should now appear similar to Figure 4.1.

Figure 4.1

Previewing a document

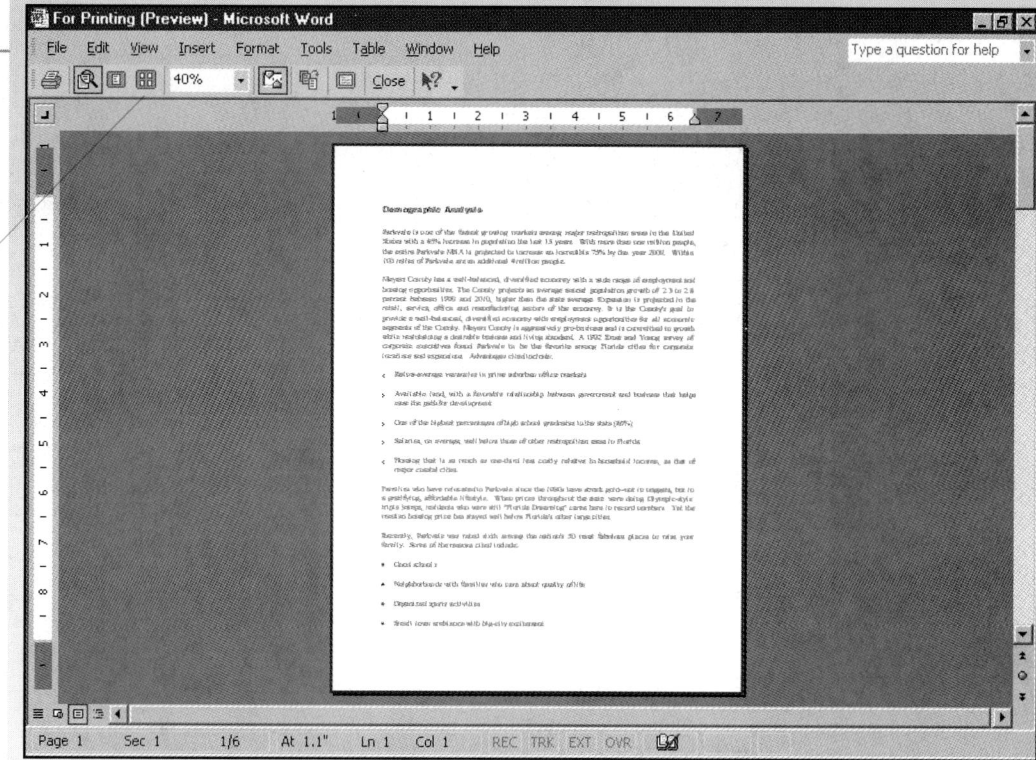

4. To display multiple pages at once:
   CLICK: Multiple Pages button (⊞) in the toolbar

5. In the drop-down menu, point with the mouse to the icon located on the second row, in the middle position. If you click this icon, you will be able to preview four pages (2 × 2) of your document at once.
   CLICK: the icon located in the second row, in the middle position
   Small representations (called *thumbnails*) of the first four pages now appear in the Preview window. Your screen should now appear similar to Figure 4.2.

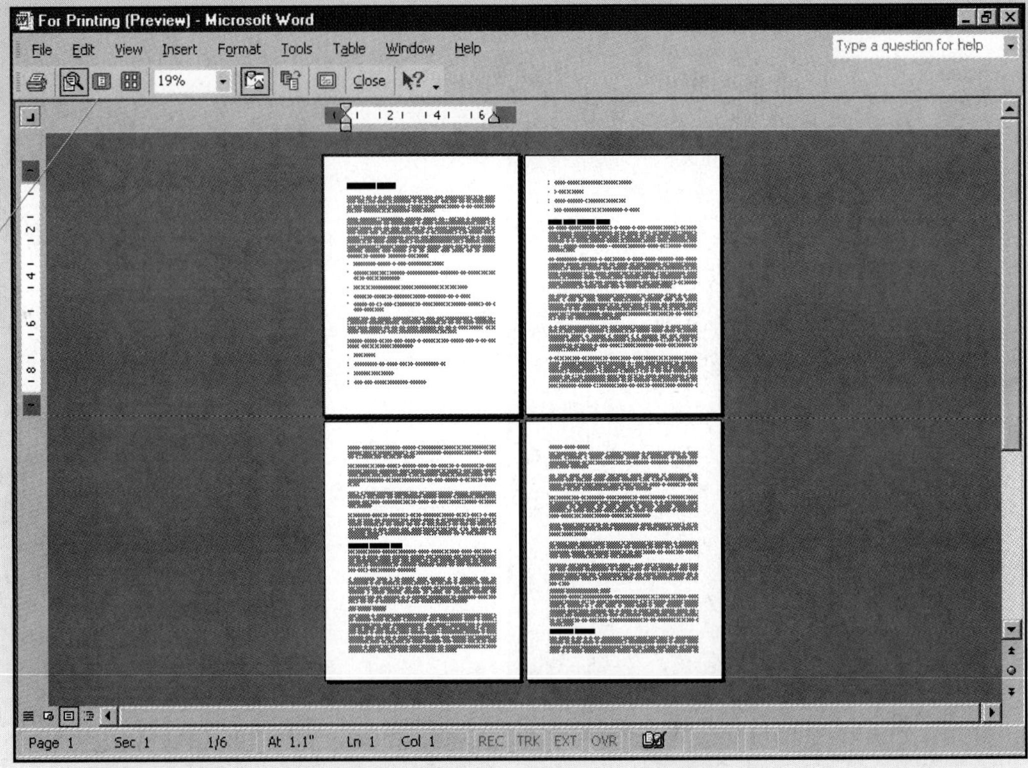

Figure 4.2

Previewing four pages at once

6. To redisplay a single page:
   CLICK: One Page button (▣) in the toolbar
7. To zoom in on the document, move the magnifying glass mouse pointer over the document area and then click once.
8. To zoom out on the display, click the mouse pointer once again.
9. To exit Preview mode:
   CLICK: Close button on the Print Preview toolbar
10. Continue to the next lesson.

4.1.2 Printing a Document

feature → When you are satisfied with a document's appearance, it is time to send it to the printer.

method →

- CLICK: Print button (🖶) on the Standard toolbar,

or

- CHOOSE: File, Print

practice → You will now send the "For Printing" document to the printer.

1. Assuming that you are satisfied with the layout of the document, let's send it to the printer. Do the following:

CHOOSE: File, Print

The dialog box displayed in Figure 4.3 appears. You can use this dialog box to specify what to print and how many copies to produce. (*Note:* As you know from previous lessons, the quickest method for sending the current document to the printer is to click the Print button (🖨) on the Standard toolbar.)

Figure 4.3

Print dialog box

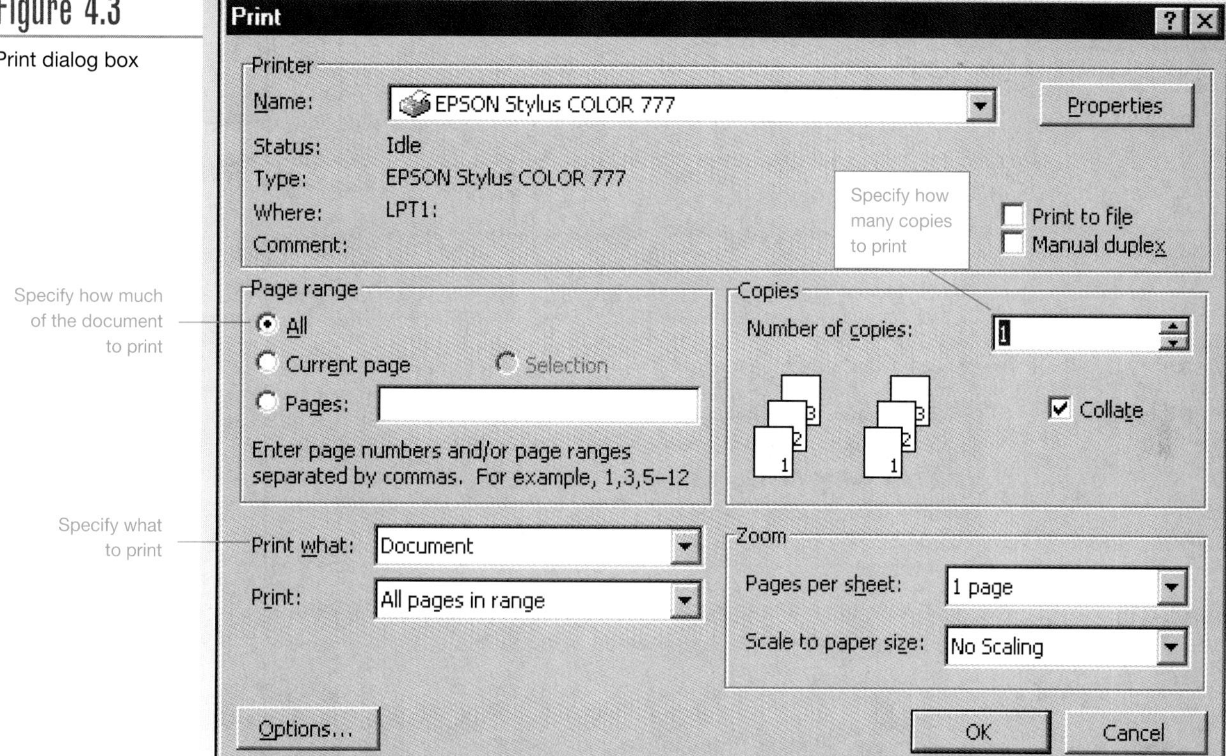

2. If you do not have access to a printer, click the Cancel button. If you have a printer connected to your computer and want to print the document, do the following:
   CLICK: OK command button
   After a few moments, the document will appear at the printer.

3. Close the "For Printing" document.

4.1 What is the procedure for printing your work?

4.2 Customizing Print Options

Now that you know how to create a document, edit, and apply character and paragraph formatting commands, it's time to think about finalizing your work for others to see. To present your work in the most flattering way, you may want to change the layout of your document before printing.

Your document's page layout is affected by many factors, including the margins or white space desired around the edges of the page, the size of paper you are using, and the page orientation. Fortunately for us, Word provides a single dialog box, called the Page Setup dialog box, for controlling all of these factors. This module includes lessons on setting margins, changing page orientation, and controlling pagination.

4.2.1 Adjusting Margins

feature

Word allows you to set the top, bottom, left, and right margins for a page. In addition, you can set a gutter margin to reserve space for binding a document. The **gutter** is where pages are joined in the center of the binding or hole-punched for a ring binder. Word provides default settings of 1.25 inches for the left and right margins and 1 inch for the top and bottom margins. The gutter margin is initially set at 0 inches, as most documents are not bound.

method

To change a document's margins:

- CHOOSE: File, Page Setup
- CLICK: *Margins* tab to display the settings page for margins
- Specify a gutter margin if binding the document, as well as the top, bottom, left, and right margins.

practice

You will now open a long document and then practice changing margins. Ensure that no documents are open in the application window.

1. Open the WD0420 student file.
2. Save a copy as "Printing Practice" to your personal storage location.
3. To change the margins from the default settings to an even 1 inch around the entire page:
   CHOOSE: File, Page Setup
   CLICK: *Margins* tab
   The Page Setup dialog box should now appear, as shown in Figure 4.4.

Figure 4.4

Page Setup dialog box: *Margins* tab

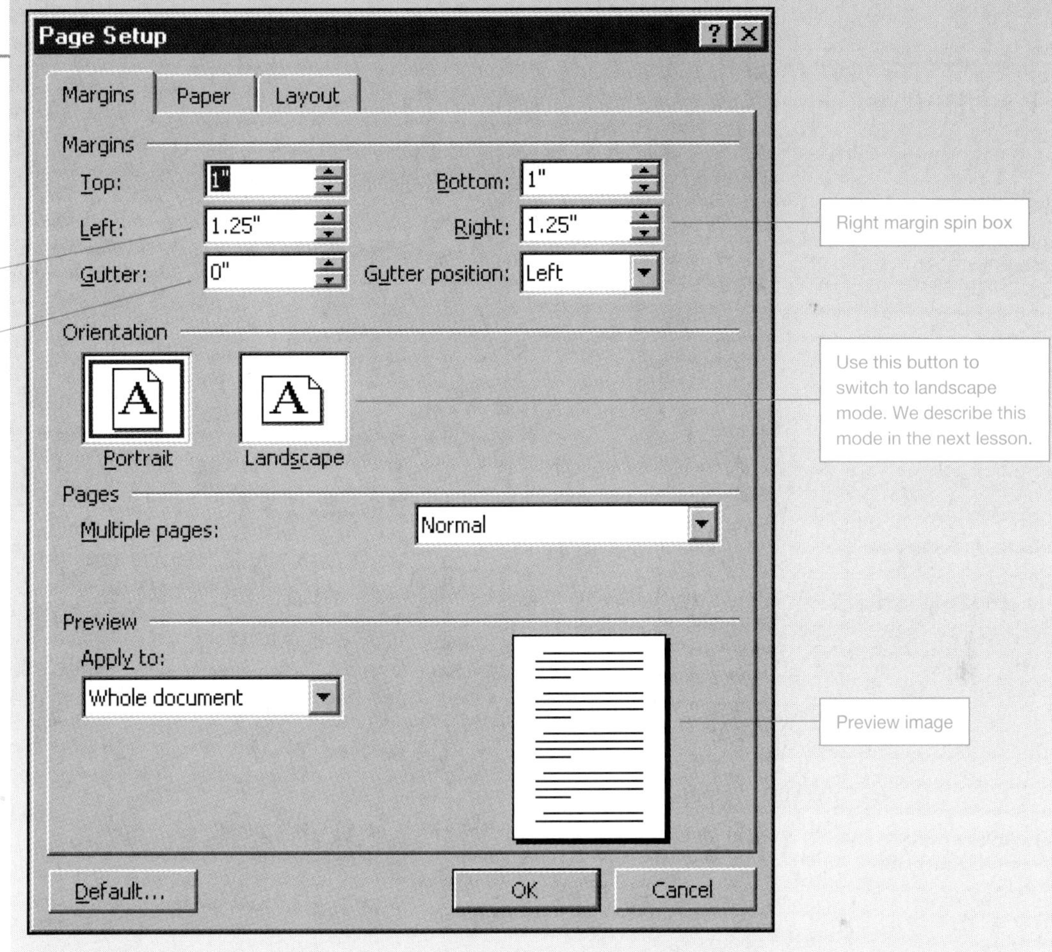

4. To change the left and right margins to 1 inch:
CLICK: down arrow beside the *Left* margin spin box repeatedly, until the value decreases to 1 inch
CLICK: down arrow beside the *Right* margin spin box repeatedly, until the value decreases to 1 inch
(*Note:* As you click the symbols, the *Preview* area below shows the effect of the change on your document.)

5. To illustrate the use of a gutter, increase the counter in the *Gutter* text box to 0.5 inches:
CLICK: up arrow beside the *Gutter* spin box repeatedly, until the value increases to 0.5 inches
Note that the gutter is represented in the *Preview* area.

6. Reset the gutter margin to 0 inches.

7. To leave the Page Setup dialog box:
CLICK: OK command button

8. Save the document, keeping it open for use in the next lesson.

4.2.2 Changing Page Orientation

feature

If you consider a typical document printed on an 8.5-inch by 11-inch piece of paper, text usually flows across the 8.5-inch width of the page. In this case, your document is said to have a **portrait orientation** (8.5 inches wide and 11 inches tall). When text flows across the 11-inch dimension of the page, the document is said to have a **landscape orientation** (11 inches wide and 8.5 inches tall). In Word, it's easy to switch between portrait and landscape orientation.

method

To change a document's orientation:

- CHOOSE: File, Page Setup
- CLICK: *Margins* tab
- CLICK: *Portrait* or *Landscape* option button in the *Orientation* area

practice

You will now practice displaying your document using a landscape orientation. The "Printing Practice" document should be open in the application window.

1. To specify a landscape orientation:
   CHOOSE: File, Page Setup
   CLICK: *Margins* tab, if it isn't displaying already
2. SELECT: *Landscape* button in the *Orientation* area
   Note that the *Preview* area changes with your selection.
3. To proceed:
   CLICK: OK command button
4. At this point, the page may be too wide to fit in the current view. To remedy this problem:
   CLICK: Zoom drop-down arrow (100% ▾) on the Standard toolbar
   CHOOSE: Page Width
   Your screen should now appear similar to Figure 4.5.

Figure 4.5

Page Width or Normal view with a landscape orientation

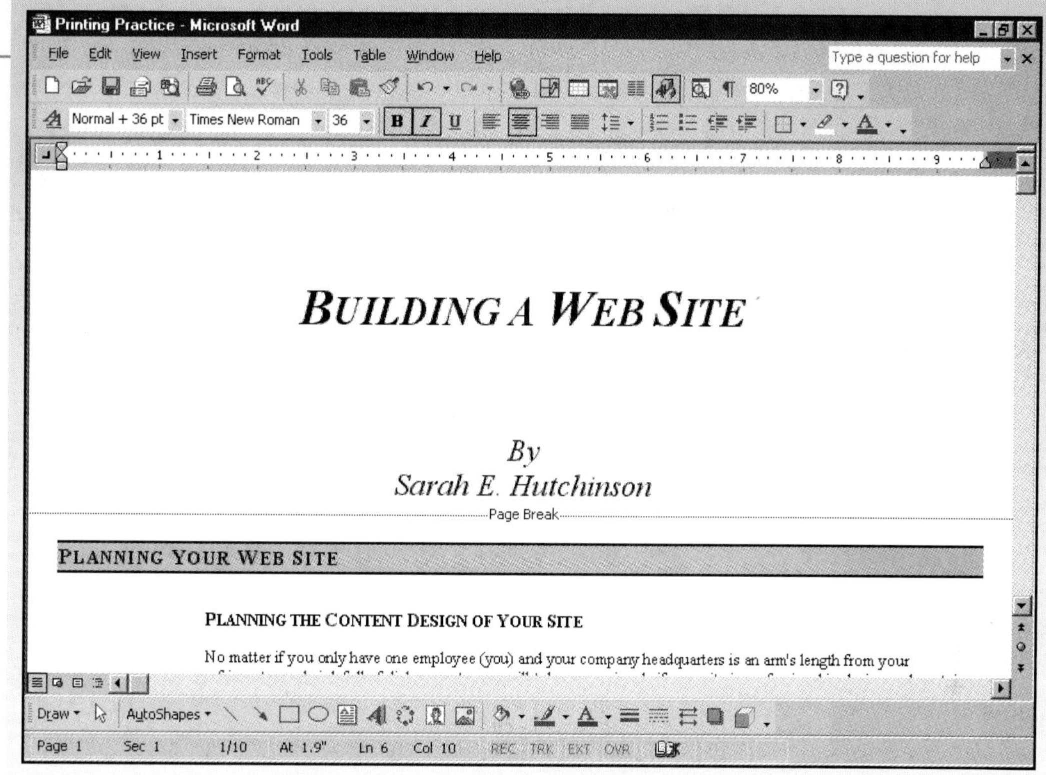

5. To return your document to a portrait orientation:
   CHOOSE: File, Page Setup
   SELECT: *Portrait* button in the *Orientation* area
   CLICK: OK command button
6. Proceed to the next lesson.

4.2.3 Controlling Pagination

feature

Word automatically repaginates a document as you insert and delete text. In Word's Normal view, a dotted line appears wherever Word begins a new page, sometimes splitting an important paragraph or a list of items. Rather than leaving the text on separate pages, you can either insert a hard page break before the text or instruct Word to keep certain lines together. To prevent sentences from being separated from their paragraphs by page breaks, you will want to protect against widows and orphans. A **widow** is created when the last sentence in a paragraph flows to the top of the next page. An **orphan** is created when the first sentence of a paragraph begins on the last line of a page. Widows and orphans make the reader work harder to keep up with the flow of the text.

method

To force a hard page break:

- Position the insertion point at the beginning of the line that you want moved to the top of the next page.
- PRESS: CTRL + ENTER

or

- CHOOSE: Insert, Break and select the *Page Break* option button

To control text flow:

- CHOOSE: Format, Paragraph
- CLICK: *Line and Page Breaks* tab

To prevent widows and orphans:

- SELECT: *Widow/Orphan control* check box so that a check appears (a check may already appear by default)

To prevent a page break from occurring within the selected paragraph:

- SELECT: *Keep lines together* check box so that a check appears

To prevent a page break from occurring within the current selection, ensure that you performed the previous step and then:

- SELECT: *Keep with next* check box so that a check appears
- CLICK: OK command button

practice

In this lesson, you customize the current pagination settings in the "Printing Practice" document.

1. To make it easier to view page breaks and the flow of text, switch to Normal view.
2. Position the insertion point one line beneath the name "Sarah E. Hutchinson". In the next step, you force a page break at the insertion point in order to create a title page for the document. The text above the page break will display alone on a single page.
3. To insert a page break at this location:
   PRESS: CTRL + ENTER
   Your document should now appear similar to Figure 4.6. Note that a dotted line, containing the words "Page Break," now appears above the insertion point. Note also that the insertion point is now positioned at the top of page 2.

Figure 4.6

Inserting a page break

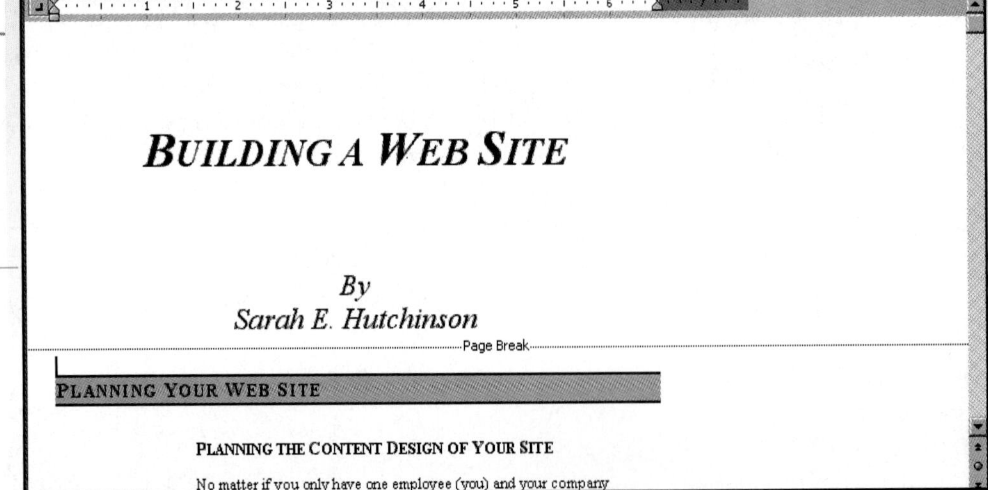

4. Let's practice deleting the page break. Position the insertion point on the line containing the words "Page Break" by clicking on the line once.
5. PRESS: DELETE to delete the page break
6. To restore the page break to the document:
   CHOOSE: Edit, Undo Clear
7. Move the insertion point to the bottom of page 4. Note that the "Planning for Commerce at Your Site" heading and the "Creating an Online Catalog" subheading are currently separated by a page break from the rest of the text in the section.
8. To use the Paragraph dialog box to instruct Word to display the headings currently located on the bottom of page 4 with the following paragraph:
   SELECT: the two headings located on the bottom of page 4 and the first paragraph on the top of page 5
   Your document should now appear similar to Figure 4.7.

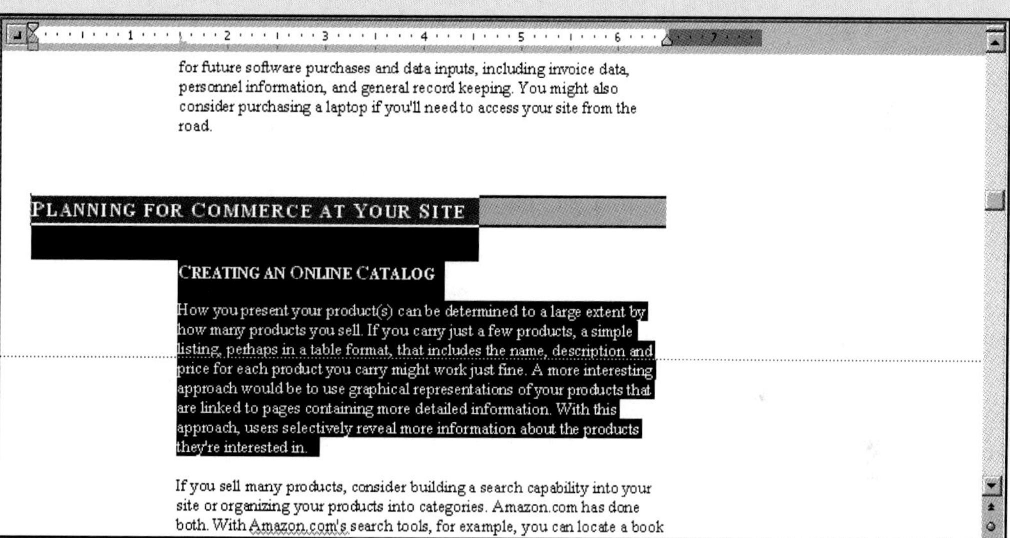

Figure 4.7

Selecting paragraphs that you want to display together

9. CHOOSE: Format, Paragraph
   CLICK: *Line and Page Breaks* tab
   The Paragraph dialog box should appear similar to Figure 4.8. Note that the *Widow/Orphan control* check box is already selected.

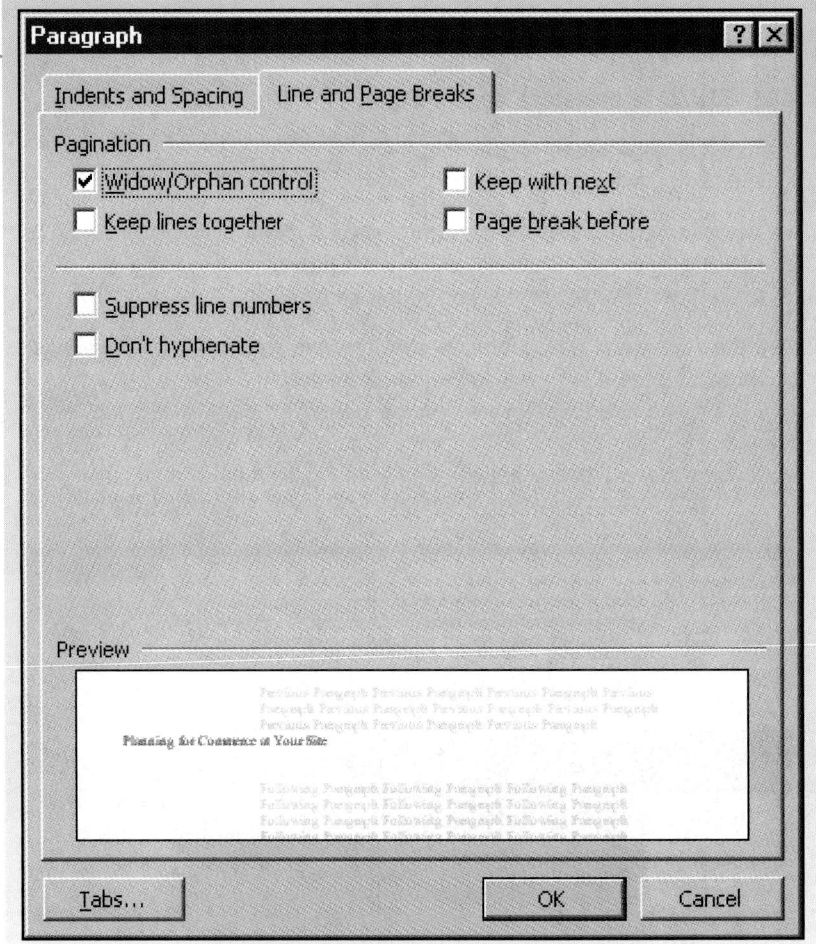

Figure 4.8

Paragraph dialog box: *Line and Page Breaks* tab

10. To keep the selected paragraphs together:
SELECT: *Keep with next* check box
SELECT: *Keep lines together* check box
CLICK: OK command button
Note that the page break has now moved to above the "Planning for Commerce at Your Site" heading.

11. Save and then close the revised document.

4.2 In inches, how wide are the left and right margins by default?

4.3 Inserting Headers and Footers

A document **header** and **footer** appear at the top and bottom of each page respectively. The header often contains the title or section headings for a document, and the footer might show the page numbers or copyright information. Adding a header or footer produces a more professional-looking document and makes longer documents easier to read.

4.3.1 Inserting Page Numbers

feature →

In Word, you position page numbers in a document's header or footer. You can align the page number with the left, center, or right margins. To view inserted page numbers, you must preview or print the document or switch to Print Layout view.

method →

To insert page numbers:

- CHOOSE: Insert, Page Numbers
- SELECT: an option from the *Position* drop-down list box
- SELECT: an option from the *Alignment* drop-down list box
- CLICK: OK command button

practice →

You will now insert page numbers in an existing three-page document. No documents should be open in the application window.

1. Open the WD0430 student file.
2. Save the file as "Consumer Confidence" to your personal storage location.
3. CHOOSE: Insert, Page Numbers
   The dialog box in Figure 4.9 should appear on your screen.

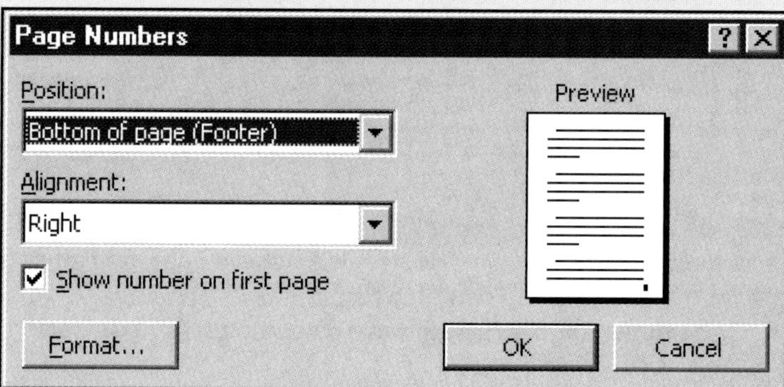

Figure 4.9
Page Numbers dialog box

4. Note that "Bottom of page (Footer)" is selected in the *Position* box and "Right" is selected in the *Alignment* box. To insert the page number with these default settings:
   CLICK: OK command button
5. You can only view inserted page numbers in Print Layout view, the current view mode. To view the page number on the bottom of page 1, do the following:

DRAG: the horizontal scroll box to the bottom of page 1
If you look closely, you'll see the page number in the bottom-right corner of the page (Figure 4.10). The page number only appears dimmed on screen; it won't appear dimmed in the printed document.

Figure 4.10

Viewing the inserted page number

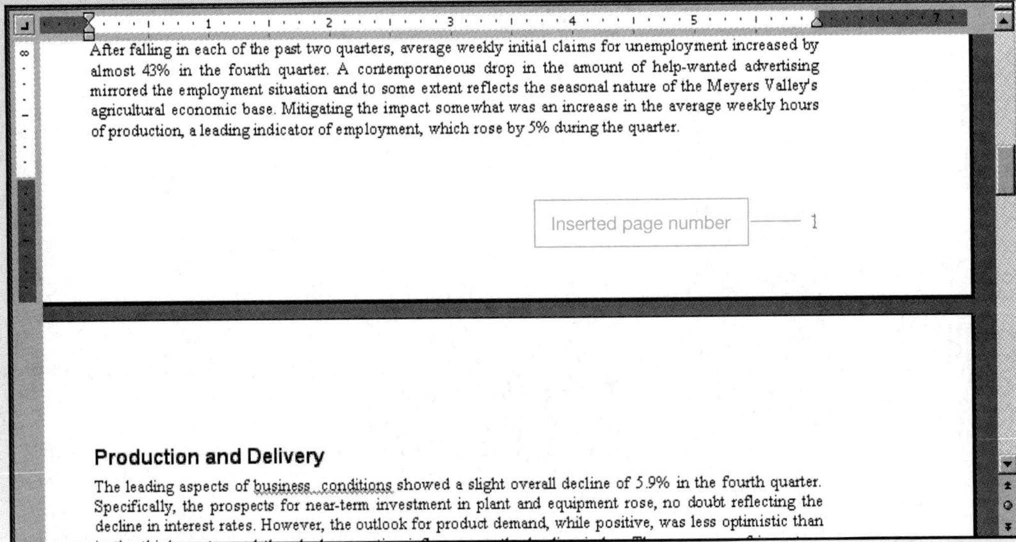

After falling in each of the past two quarters, average weekly initial claims for unemployment increased by almost 43% in the fourth quarter. A contemporaneous drop in the amount of help-wanted advertising mirrored the employment situation and to some extent reflects the seasonal nature of the Meyers Valley's agricultural economic base. Mitigating the impact somewhat was an increase in the average weekly hours of production, a leading indicator of employment, which rose by 5% during the quarter.
Inserted page number
1
Production and Delivery
The leading aspects of business conditions showed a slight overall decline of 5.9% in the fourth quarter. Specifically, the prospects for near-term investment in plant and equipment rose, no doubt reflecting the decline in interest rates. However, the outlook for product demand, while positive, was less optimistic than

6. Save the revised document.
7. To prepare for the next lesson:
PRESS: CTRL + HOME to move the insertion point to the top of the document

4.3.2 Creating Headers and Footers

feature

By default, the information that you include in a header or footer prints on every page in your document.

method

To insert a header and footer:

- CHOOSE: View, Header and Footer
- Edit and format the header and footer using the regular formatting commands and the buttons on the Header and Footer toolbar.
- CLICK: Close button on the Header and Footer toolbar

practice

You will now create a header in the "Consumer Confidence" document. You will also edit the existing footer to include additional information.

1. To edit the document's header:
CHOOSE: View, Header and Footer
Word now displays the Header and Footer toolbar, creates a framed editable text area for the header and footer, and dims the document's body text. Your screen should appear similar to Figure 4.11. Figure 4.12 identifies the buttons in the Header and Footer toolbar.

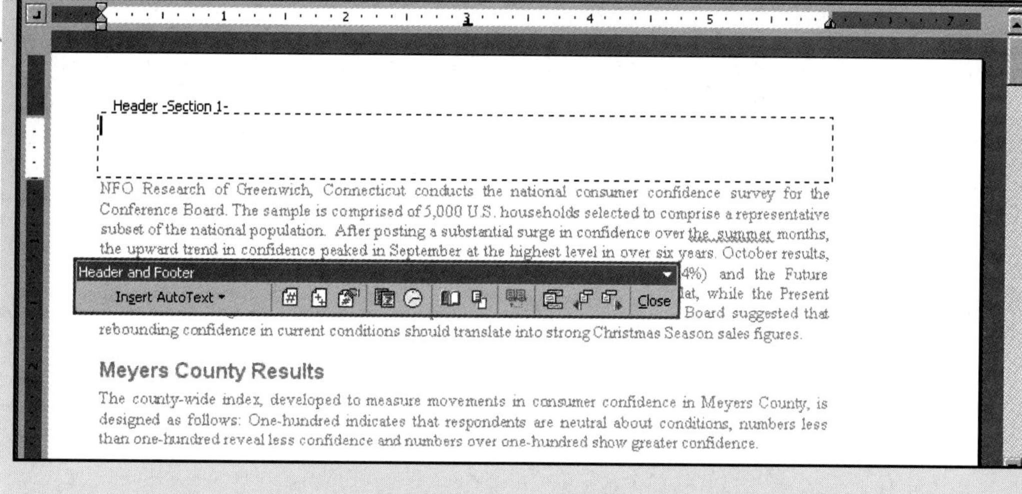

Figure 4.11

Viewing a document's header

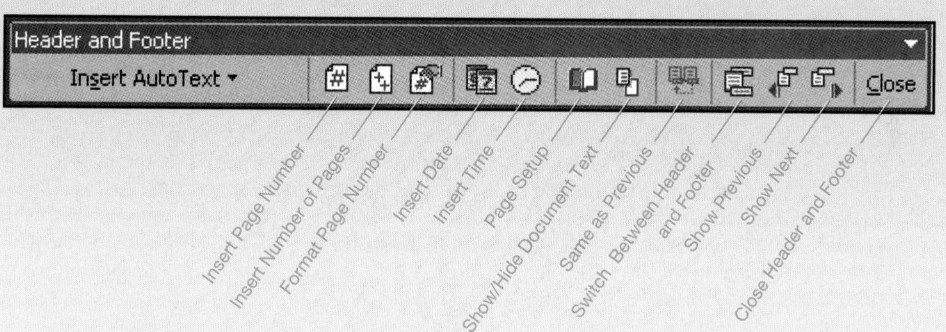

Figure 4.12

Header and Footer toolbar

2. The insertion point is blinking in the document's header area.
   TYPE: **Annual Consumer Confidence Survey**

3. To format the header, do the following:
   SELECT: header text
   CHOOSE: Arial from the Font drop-down list
   CHOOSE: 14 from the Font Size drop-down list
   CLICK: Bold button (B)
   CLICK: Center button (≡)

4. To view the footer:
   CLICK: Switch Between Header and Footer button (▤) on the Header and Footer toolbar

5. The page number, inserted in the last lesson, appears at the far right-hand side of the first line in the footer area (Figure 4.13). Your insertion point should appear flashing at the left edge.

Figure 4.13

Viewing a document's footer

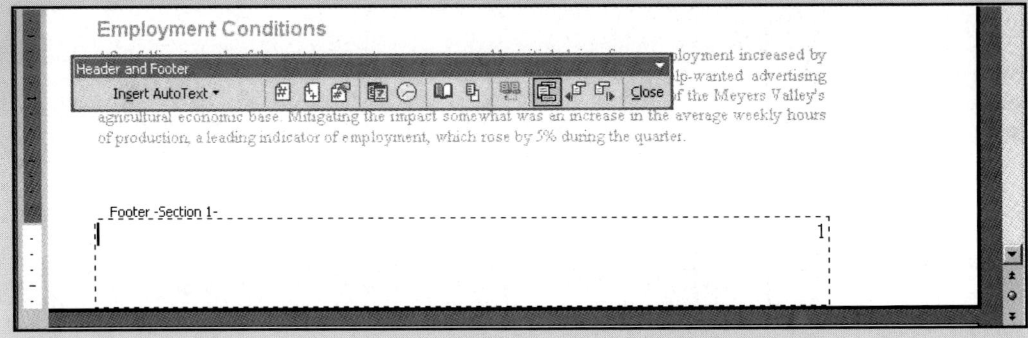

Let's now enter information about when the document was last printed.
TYPE: **Printed on**
PRESS: Space Bar

6. To place the date and time in the footer and have them automatically updated when you print the document:
CLICK: Insert Date button () on the Header and Footer toolbar
PRESS: Space Bar
TYPE: **at**
PRESS: Space Bar
CLICK: Insert Time button () on the Header and Footer toolbar

7. To format the footer, you must first select the text in the footer. Because the footer includes inserted fields, the easiest way to do this is to use the Edit, Select All command.
CHOOSE: Edit, Select All to select the footer text

8. Issue the following character formatting commands:
SELECT: Arial from the Font drop-down list (Times New Roman)
CLICK: Bold button (B)
Your screen should now appear similar to Figure 4.14 (with a different date and time in the footer, of course). Congratulations, you've finished creating and formatting a header and footer.

Figure 4.14

Formatting the footer

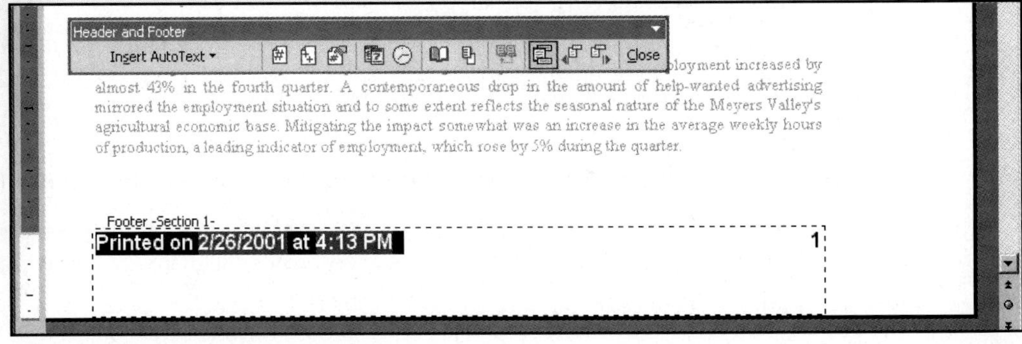

9. To return to your document:
CLICK: Close button on the Header and Footer toolbar

10. Scroll through the document to view the headers and footers.

11. Save and then close the document.

4.3 How do you insert page numbers in a document?

Word

4.4 Using Sections to Apply Varied Formatting

Simple documents contain the same formatting—headers, footers, page numbers, margins, and so on—throughout the document. As your documents become more complex, you will need to use additional and varied formatting. Word enables you to divide a document into *sections,* which can then be formatted as individual documents within a larger document. This ability is especially useful in documents that include major topics or chapters because you can format each topic with its own header and footer. Sections are also useful in desktop-published documents to incorporate varied column formatting.

4.4.1 Inserting Section Breaks

feature

By default, a document contains one section as referenced by the "Sec 1" indicator on the Status bar. A **section break** marks the beginning of a new section. To vary document formatting, such as headers and footers within a document, you must divide it into sections.

method

- Position the insertion point where you want the break to occur.
- CHOOSE: Insert, Break
- SELECT: an option in the *Section breaks* area
- CLICK: OK command button

practice

This exercise involves opening a long document and then dividing it into four sections. Ensure that Word is loaded and that no documents are open in the application window.

1. Open the WD0440 data file. This is a copy of a file you used earlier in this chapter.

2. Save the document as "Web Business" to your personal storage location.

3. To prepare for inserting section break codes, switch to Normal view. In this view mode, it's easier to see inserted section break codes and to position the insertion point.

4. Scroll through the document to become familiar with its contents. The document contains a title page and four major topics. In the following steps, you will divide the document as follows, with each section beginning on a new page:

Section	*Contents*
1	Title page, Getting Started topic
2	Planning Your Web Site topic
3	Planning for Commerce at Your Site topic
4	Promoting Traffic to Your Site topic

5. Let's begin by inserting a section break just before the "Planning Your Web Site" main heading. Position the insertion point one line above the "Planning Your Web Site" main heading, located on page 3.

6. To insert a section break at this location:
CHOOSE: Insert, Break
Your screen should now appear similar to Figure 4.15.

Figure 4.15

Inserting a section break

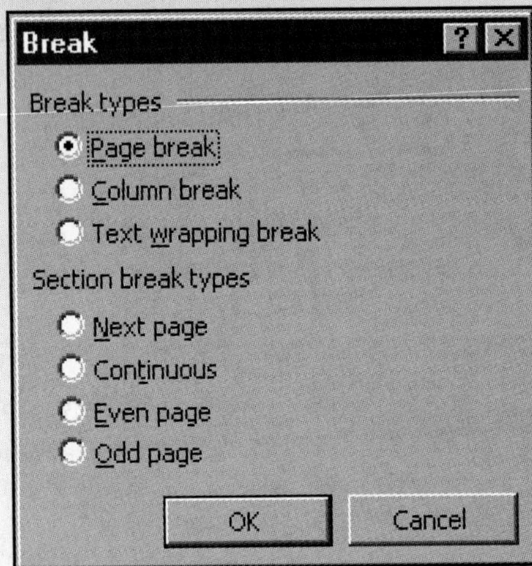

7. Let's insert a section break that begins on a new page.
SELECT: *Next page* option
CLICK: OK command button
Your document should now appear similar to Figure 4.16. At this point, the entire document below the section break is part of Section 2.

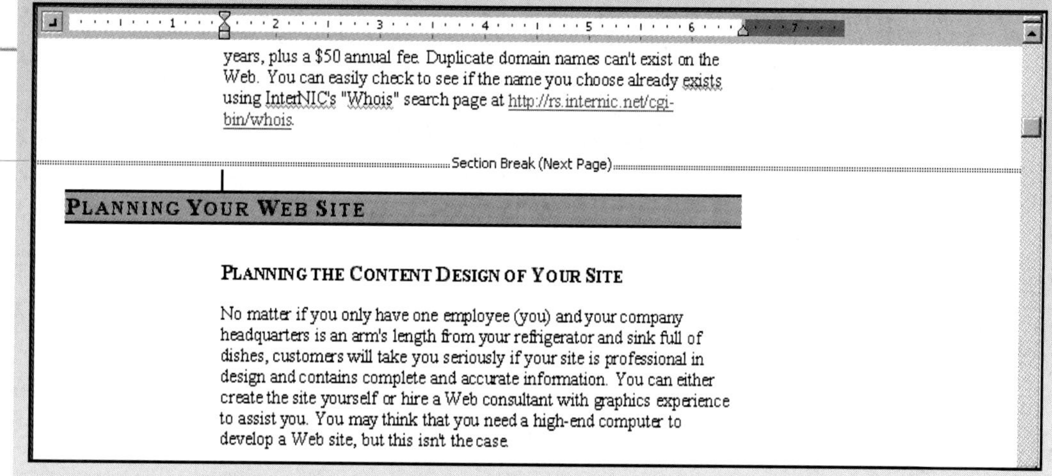

years, plus a $50 annual fee. Duplicate domain names can't exist on the Web. You can easily check to see if the name you choose already exists using InterNIC's "Whois" search page at http://rs.internic.net/cgi-bin/whois.
Section Break (Next Page)
PLANNING YOUR WEB SITE
PLANNING THE CONTENT DESIGN OF YOUR SITE
No matter if you only have one employee (you) and your company headquarters is an arm's length from your refrigerator and sink full of dishes, customers will take you seriously if your site is professional in design and contains complete and accurate information. You can either create the site yourself or hire a Web consultant with graphics experience to assist you. You may think that you need a high-end computer to develop a Web site, but this isn't the case.

Figure 4.16

Inserting a section break

Section break

8. The insertion point is blinking on the blank line located below the section break. To delete the blank line:
PRESS: DELETE

9. To prepare for inserting the next section break, position the insertion point one line above the "Planning for Commerce at Your Site" main heading.

10. To insert a section break at this location:
CHOOSE: Insert, Break
SELECT: *Next page* option
CLICK: OK command button

11. To delete the blank line below the section break:
PRESS: DELETE

12. To prepare for inserting the final section break, position the insertion point one line above the "Promoting Traffic to Your Site" main heading.

13. To insert a section break at this location:
CHOOSE: Insert, Break
SELECT: *Next page* option
CLICK: OK command button

14. To delete the blank line below the section break:
PRESS: DELETE
Note that "Sec 4" now appears in the Status bar.

15. Save the revised document and keep it open for use in the next lesson.

16. In preparation for the next exercise, move the insertion point to the top of the document. The insertion point is now positioned in Section 1.

4.4.2 Varying Headers and Footers by Section

feature

Once you've divided a document into sections, you can embellish the document with varied headers and footers. By default, the headers and footers in a multisection document are linked. This means that if you type your name into the header for section 1, all remaining sections will also include your name. To create a unique header or footer, you must break the link to the previous section.

method

To create a unique header or footer in the current section:

- Position the insertion point in the header or footer for the current section.
- CLICK: Same as Previous button () to deselect it
- Proceed by typing text into the header or footer.

practice

The following exercise involves creating headers for the "Web Business" document that include the current topic and page number. You will also create a footer with the following text: Prepared by: *your name.* The footer will remain the same for each of the four sections. The insertion point should be positioned at the top of the "Web Business" document in Section 1.

1. Let's begin by creating the header for the first section.
   CHOOSE: View, Header and Footer
   The insertion point should be blinking inside the Section 1 header.
2. Let's type the topic heading "Getting Started" and the current page number in the right-aligned position.
   CLICK: Align Right button () on the Standard toolbar
   TYPE: **Getting Started,**
   PRESS: Space Bar
   TYPE: **Page**
   PRESS: Space Bar
   CLICK: Insert Page Number button () on the Header and Footer toolbar
3. On your own, format the text in the header using Arial, 10 point, and the bold attribute. With no text selected, the Section 1 header should appear similar to Figure 4.17.

Figure 4.17

Viewing the Section 1 header

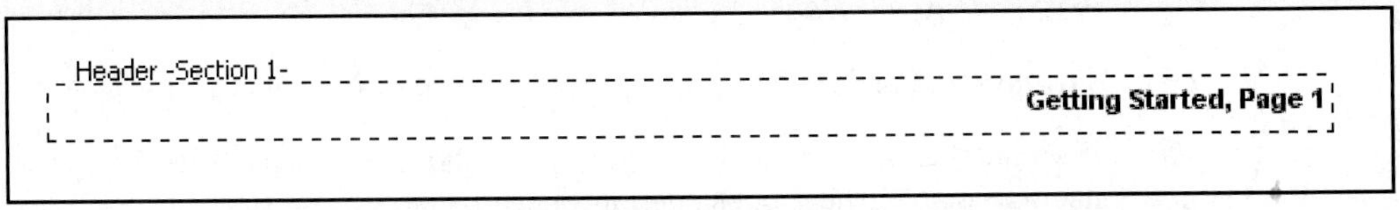

Header -Section 1-

Getting Started, Page 1

4. To define the header for Section 2:
CLICK: Show Next button (icon) on the Header and Footer toolbar
Note the "Same as Previous" setting in the header identifier area (Figure 4.18). Because this setting is in effect, the Section 2 header is currently identical to the Section 1 header.

Figure 4.18

Viewing the Section 2 header

Note the "Section 2" designation

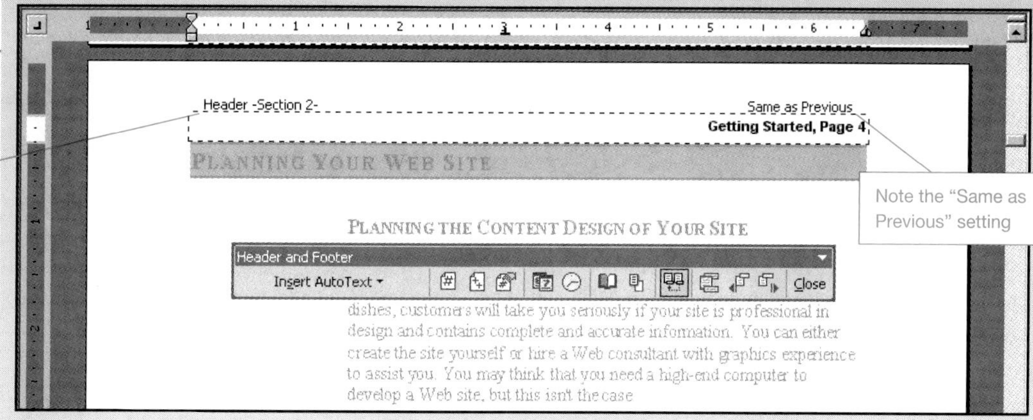

5. To create a unique header for Section 2, you must click the Same as Previous button (icon) on the Header and Footer toolbar to toggle off the Same as Previous setting.
CLICK: Same as Previous button (icon) to deselect this setting
Note that the "Same as Previous" designation no longer appears in the header identifier area.

6. SELECT: "Getting Started" in the header area
TYPE: **Planning Your Web Site**
The Section 2 header should appear similar to Figure 4.19.

Figure 4.19

Viewing the Section 2 header

Header -Section 2-

Planning Your Web Site, Page 4

Note the "Same as Previous" setting no longer appears

7. Now, let's edit the Section 3 header.
CLICK: Show Next button (icon)

8. Remember, before you edit the header to reflect the current topic, you must detach it from the previous header.
CLICK: Same as Previous button (icon) to deselect this setting
SELECT: "Planning Your Web Site" in the header area
TYPE: **Planning for Commerce at Your Site**

9. To edit the Section 4 header:
CLICK: Show Next button (icon)
CLICK: Same as Previous button (icon) to deselect this setting
SELECT: "Planning for Commerce at Your Site" in the header area
TYPE: **Promoting Traffic to Your Site**
The headers are complete! Now let's define the footer. Since the same footer will appear throughout the document, you only have to create the footer once, in Section 1.

10. To prepare to create the footer:
DRAG: the vertical scroll box to the top of the vertical scroll bar
CLICK: in the Section 1 header area

11. To view the Section 1 footer:
CLICK: Switch Between Header and Footer button () on the Header and Footer toolbar
The insertion point should be blinking in the Section 1 footer area (Figure 4.20).

Figure 4.20

Viewing the Section 1 footer

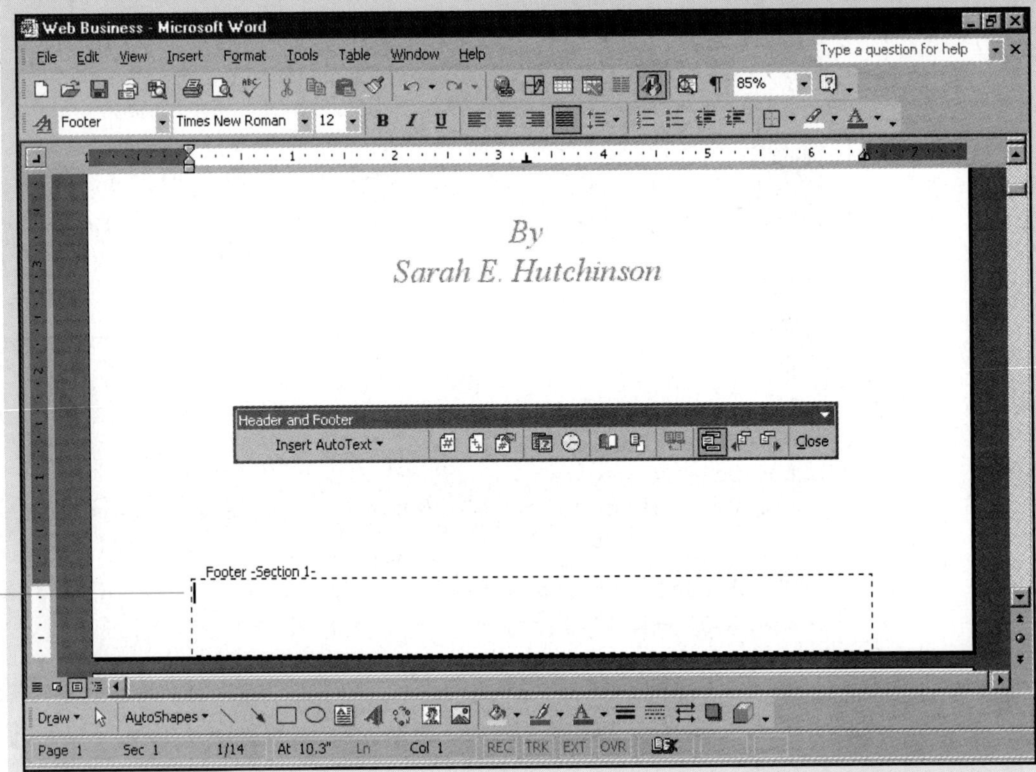

The insertion point is positioned in the Section 1 footer.

12. You will begin creating the footer by pressing ENTER. This will force extra space to appear between the body text and the footer text.
PRESS: ENTER
TYPE: **Prepared by: Your Name**
(*Note:* Be sure to substitute your name in place of the words "Your Name.")

13. On your own, format the footer using Arial, 10 point. With no text selected, the footer should appear similar to Figure 4.21.

Figure 4.21

Completed Section 1 footer

Footer -Section 1-

Prepared by: Your Name

14. Now that you're done defining the headers and footers for this document:
CLICK: Close button on the Header and Footer toolbar

15. Switch to Print Layout view so that you can view the document's headers and footers. Note that the Section 1 header and footer appear on the title page. Because title pages don't typically include a header or footer, in the next lesson we show you how to change the format of the first page of the document.

16. Move the insertion point to the top of page 2. Your screen should appear similar to Figure 4.22.

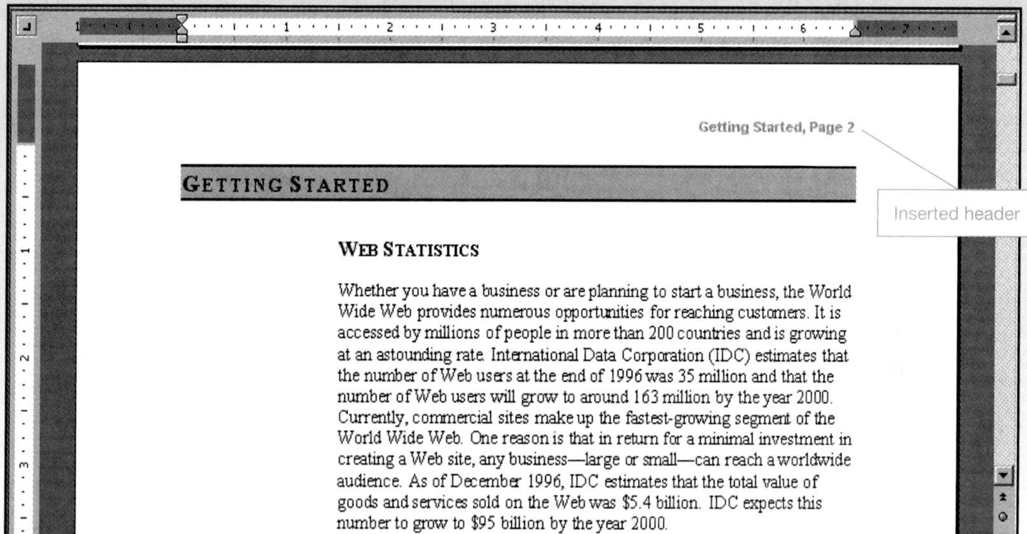

Getting Started, Page 2
GETTING STARTED
Inserted header
WEB STATISTICS
Whether you have a business or are planning to start a business, the World Wide Web provides numerous opportunities for reaching customers. It is accessed by millions of people in more than 200 countries and is growing at an astounding rate. International Data Corporation (IDC) estimates that the number of Web users at the end of 1996 was 35 million and that the number of Web users will grow to around 163 million by the year 2000. Currently, commercial sites make up the fastest-growing segment of the World Wide Web. One reason is that in return for a minimal investment in creating a Web site, any business—large or small—can reach a worldwide audience. As of December 1996, IDC estimates that the total value of goods and services sold on the Web was $5.4 billion. IDC expects this number to grow to $95 billion by the year 2000.

Figure 4.22
Viewing the inserted header using Print Layout view

17. Save the revised document.

18. To prepare for the next lesson, move the insertion point to the beginning of the "Web Business" document.

4.4.3 Varying Page Setup Options by Section

feature →

In Word, you can format document sections uniquely using the Page Setup dialog box. For example, you may want to change an individual section's margins or orientation, or further customize the section's header and footer.

method →

To apply a different page setup to a section:

- Position the insertion point in the section you want to change.
- CHOOSE: File, Page Setup
- CLICK: *desired tab* and then make your changes
- Ensure that "This section" is selected in the *Apply to* drop-down list.
- CLICK: OK command button

In this lesson, you use the Page Setup dialog box to remove the header and footer from the first page of Section 1. Ensure that you've completed the previous lesson and that the insertion point is positioned at the top of the "Web Business" document.

1. To prevent the header and footer from printing on the first page of Section 1, the document's title page, you must begin by displaying the *Layout* tab of the Page Setup dialog box.
CHOOSE: File, Page Setup
CLICK: *Layout* tab
The Page Setup dialog box should now appear similar to Figure 4.23.

Figure 4.23

Page Setup dialog box: *Layout* tab

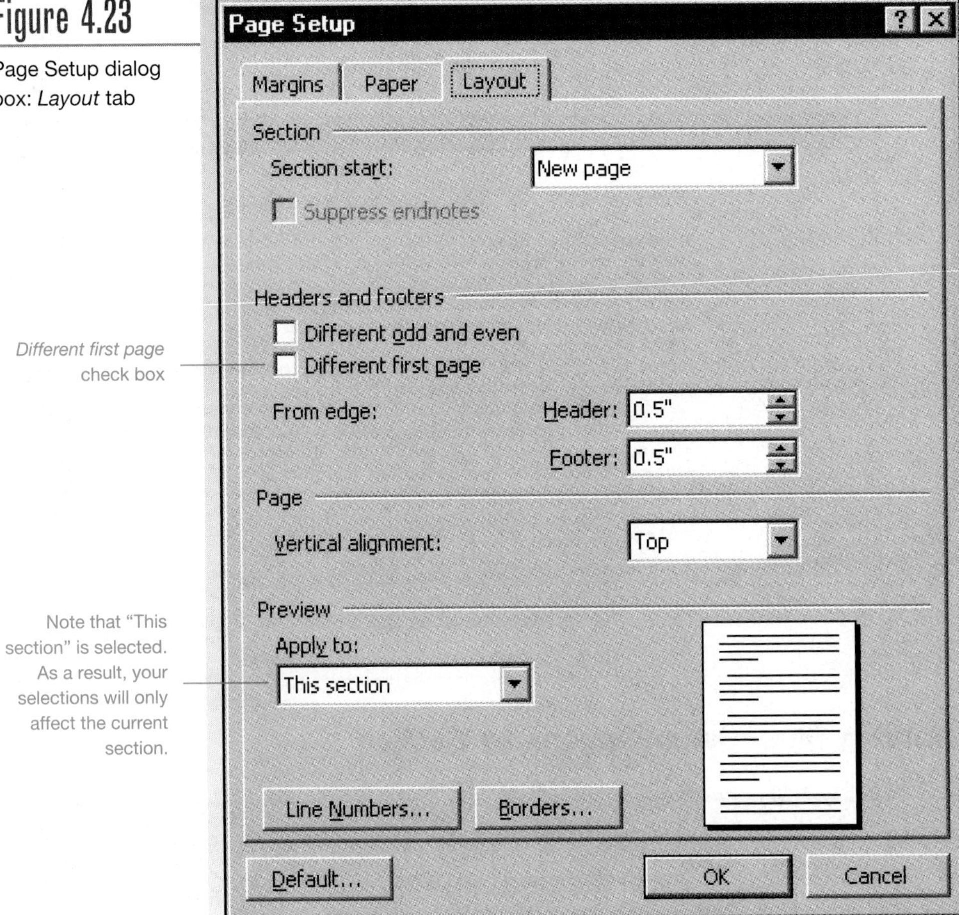

2. SELECT: *Different first page* check box

3. To proceed:
CLICK: OK command button
Note that the header and footer no longer appear on the first page.

4. To look at the header identifier for the first page of Section 1:
CHOOSE: View, Header and Footer
Note that the header identifier now reads "First Page Header-Section 1-," as shown in Figure 4.24.

Figure 4.24

First page header

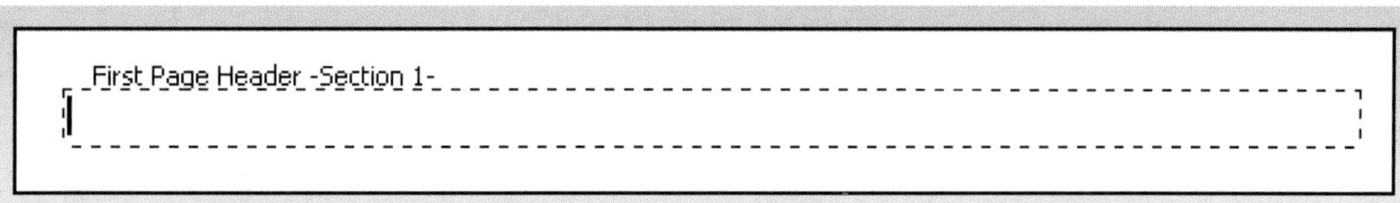

First Page Header -Section 1-

5. Since it is our intention to keep the first page header and footer blank, let's close the Header and Footer toolbar.
CLICK: Close button on the Header and Footer toolbar

6. Save and then close the "Web Business" document.

In Addition CHANGING PAGE ORIENTATION WITH SECTION BREAKS

To change the page orientation for a portion of a document, you can use section breaks. This procedure is useful when your document or report includes a table that is wider than the default page width. To change the orientation of a portion of a document from portrait to landscape, or vice versa, position the insertion point in the section you want to change and then choose File, Page Setup. Then, click the *Margins* tab and select a button in the *Orientation* area. To complete the procedure, select "This section" from the *Apply to* drop-down list and click the OK command button.

4.4 What are sections used for?

4.5 Publishing to the Web

For those of you new to the online world, the **Internet** spans the entire planet utilizing a vast collection of computer networks connected by standard telephone lines, fiber optics, and satellites. The term **intranet** refers to a private and usually secure local or wide area network that uses Internet technologies to share information. To access the Internet, you need a network or modem connection that links your computer to your account on the university's network or an independent service provider (ISP).

Once you are connected to the Internet, you can use Web browser software, such as Microsoft Internet Explorer or Netscape Navigator, to access the **World Wide Web.** The Web provides a visual interface for the Internet and lets you search for information by simply clicking on highlighted words and images, known as **hyperlinks.** When you click a link, you are telling your computer's Web browser to retrieve a page from a Web site and display it on your screen. Not only can you publish your documents on the Web, you can incorporate hyperlinks directly within a document to facilitate navigating between documents.

4.5.1 Applying a Web Theme

feature

Office XP includes more than 60 themes for optimizing the look of your documents in Word and on the Web. A theme determines what colors and text fonts are used in a document, as well as the appearance of other graphical elements such as bullets and horizontal lines.

method

- CHOOSE: Format, Theme from Word's Menu bar
- SELECT: a theme in the *Choose a Theme* list box
- CLICK: OK command button

practice

You will now apply a Web theme to an existing document. Ensure that Word is loaded and that no documents are displaying.

1. Open the WD0450 data file.
2. Save the document as "Office and the Web" to your personal storage location. Your document should appear similar to Figure 4.25.

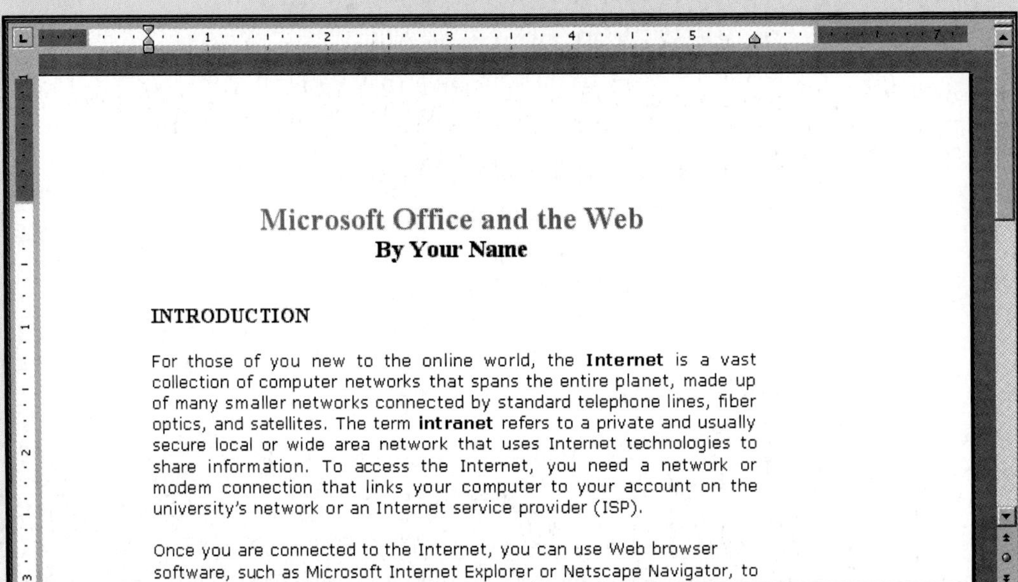

Figure 4.25

"Office and the Web" document

3. Let's apply a Web theme to this document.
   CHOOSE: Format, Theme from Word's Menu bar
4. To view some of the different themes, click their names in the *Choose a Theme* list box.
5. Before continuing:
   CLICK: Artsy in the *Choose a Theme* list box
   The Theme dialog box should now appear similar to Figure 4.26.

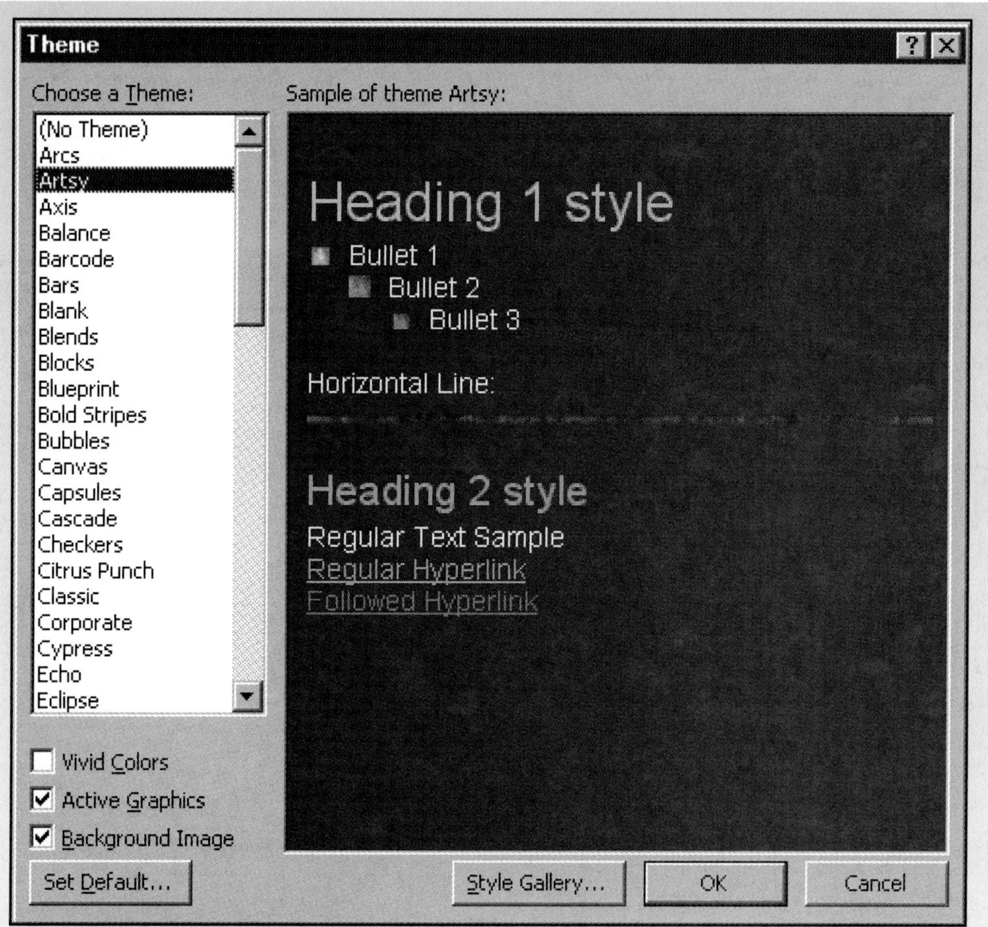

Figure 4.26

Theme dialog box

6. To apply this theme to the document:
CLICK: OK command button
With the insertion point at the top of the document, your document should now appear similar to Figure 4.27.

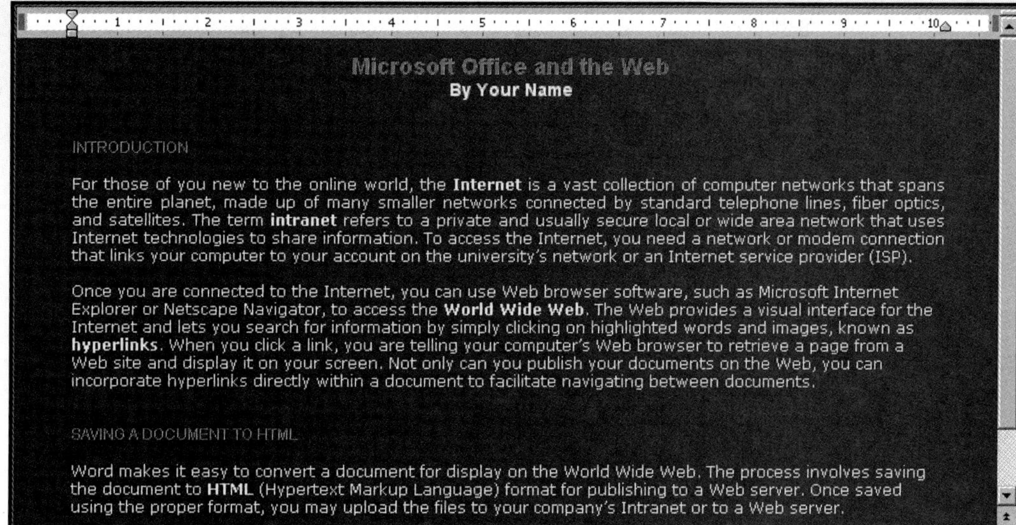

Microsoft Office and the Web
By Your Name

INTRODUCTION

For those of you new to the online world, the **Internet** is a vast collection of computer networks that spans the entire planet, made up of many smaller networks connected by standard telephone lines, fiber optics, and satellites. The term **intranet** refers to a private and usually secure local or wide area network that uses Internet technologies to share information. To access the Internet, you need a network or modem connection that links your computer to your account on the university's network or an Internet service provider (ISP).

Once you are connected to the Internet, you can use Web browser software, such as Microsoft Internet Explorer or Netscape Navigator, to access the **World Wide Web**. The Web provides a visual interface for the Internet and lets you search for information by simply clicking on highlighted words and images, known as **hyperlinks**. When you click a link, you are telling your computer's Web browser to retrieve a page from a Web site and display it on your screen. Not only can you publish your documents on the Web, you can incorporate hyperlinks directly within a document to facilitate navigating between documents.

SAVING A DOCUMENT TO HTML

Word makes it easy to convert a document for display on the World Wide Web. The process involves saving the document to **HTML** (Hypertext Markup Language) format for publishing to a Web server. Once saved using the proper format, you may upload the files to your company's Intranet or to a Web server.

Figure 4.27

Applying the "Artsy" theme

7. Save the revised document.
8. To prepare for the next lesson, ensure that the insertion point is positioned at the top of the document.

4.5.2 Saving and Opening Web Pages

feature

Word makes it easy to convert a document for display on the World Wide Web. The process involves saving the document to **HTML** (Hypertext Markup Language) format for publishing to a Web server. Once files are saved using the proper format, you may upload them to your company's intranet or to a Web server.

method

To preview a document as a Web page:

- CHOOSE: File, Web Page Preview

To save a document into HTML format for Web publishing:

- CHOOSE: File, Save as Web Page

To open a Web page in Word:

- CHOOSE: File, Open

practice

You will now save the "Office and the Web" document to HTML for publishing on the Web.

1. To preview the "Office and the Web" document as a Web page:
   CHOOSE: File, Web Page Preview
   The document should be displaying in your browser, such as Internet Explorer, and look similar to Figure 4.27, shown in the last lesson. You may need to maximize the browser window (□).
2. To close your browser:
   CLICK: its Close button (☒)
3. To save the current document as a Web page:
   CHOOSE: File, Save as Web Page
   The Save As dialog box appears with some additional options (Figure 4.28). Note that "Web Page" appears as the file type in the *Save as type* drop-down list box.

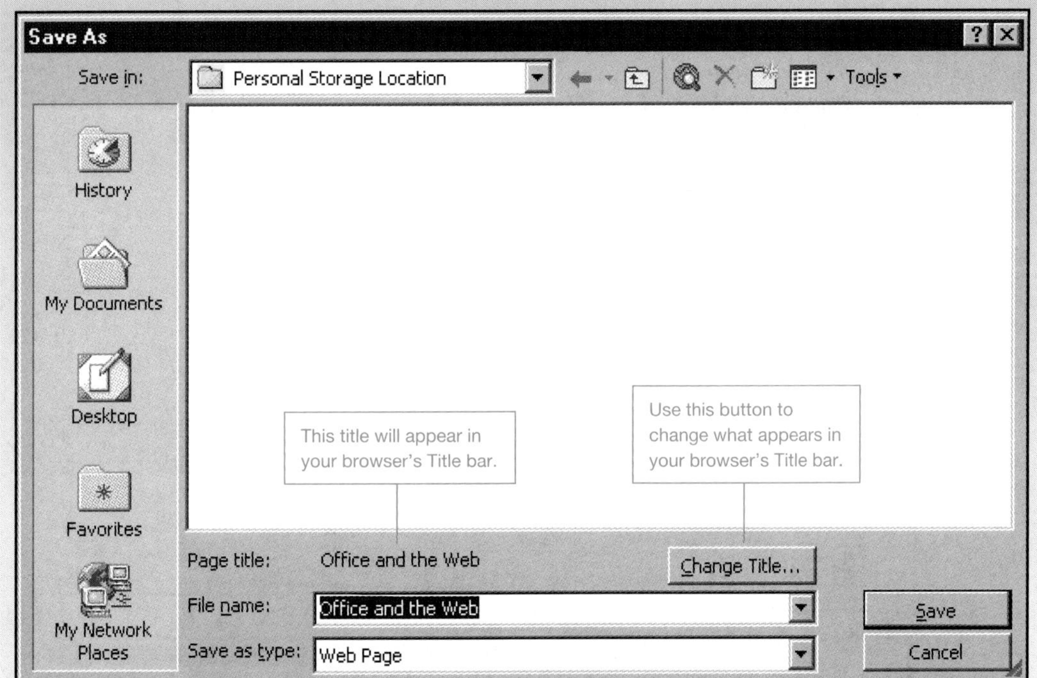

Figure 4.28

Saving a file as a Web page

4. Using the *Save in* drop-down list box or the Places bar:
   SELECT: *your storage location,* if not already selected
5. To proceed with the conversion to HTML:
   CLICK: Save command button
6. Close the "Office and the Web" document, saving any changes.
7. CHOOSE: File, Open
8. Using the *Look in* drop-down list box or the Places bar:
   SELECT: *your storage location,* if not already selected
9. SELECT: Web Pages and Web Archives from the *Files of type* drop-down list
   The Open dialog box should now appear similar to Figure 4.29. As you can see from the file listing, Word automatically created a file named "Office and the Web.htm" in your storage location. Word also created a folder named "Office and the Web_files" and stored two additional files Word needs to display your document on the Web.

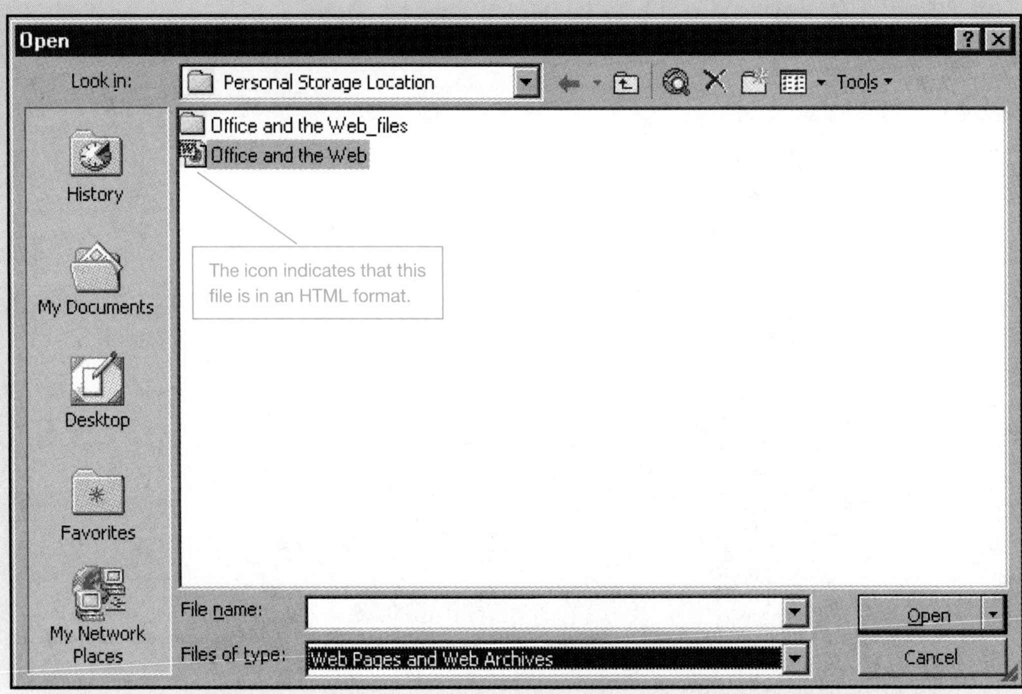

Figure 4.29

Displaying Web pages in the file list

10. To open the Web page:
    DOUBLE-CLICK: "Office and the Web" Web document
    The Web page should appear in Word.

11. Close the current document.

4.5 Why might you want to convert a Word document to HTML?

Chapter summary

Depending on your output requirements, you may want to change one or more page layout settings before printing. Using the Page Setup dialog box, you can improve the layout of your document by changing margins and switching between portrait and landscape modes. You can further improve a document using headers, footers, and page numbers; these elements help provide a structure for your document in order to keep your audience focused. You may even choose to divide a document into sections in order to vary these settings within a document. Once your document looks the way you want, you can print it or even publish it on your personal or company Web site. Before publishing a document to a Web site, you must save it to HTML.

Command Summary

Many of the commands and procedures appearing in this chapter are summarized in the following table.

Skill Set	To Perform This Task	Do the Following
Printing Documents	Preview a document	CLICK: Print Preview button (); or CHOOSE: File, Print Preview
	Print a document	CLICK: Print button (); or CHOOSE: File, Print
Formatting Documents	Change margins	CHOOSE: File, Page Setup CLICK: *Margins* tab and then adjust the settings in the *Margins* area
	Change page orientation	CHOOSE: File, Page Setup CLICK: *Margins* tab CLICK: *Portrait* or *Landscape* button
	Insert page numbers	CHOOSE: Insert, Page Numbers
	Create a header or footer	CHOOSE: View, Header and Footer
	Insert a section break	CHOOSE: Insert, Break SELECT: an option in the *Section breaks* area
	Format first-page headers and footers differently	CHOOSE: File, Page Setup CLICK: *Layout* tab SELECT: *Different first page* check box
	Varying Page Setup options by section	CHOOSE: File, Page Setup CLICK: *desired tab* CHOOSE: "This section" from the *Apply to* drop-down list
Customizing Paragraphs	Insert a page break	PRESS: CTRL+ENTER, or CHOOSE: Insert, Break
	Control pagination	CHOOSE: Format, Paragraph CLICK: *Line and Page Breaks* tab
Collaborating in Workgroups	Save a document as a Web page	CHOOSE: File, Save as Web Page
	Open a Web Page in Word	CHOOSE: File, Open and then navigate to your storage location SELECT: Web Pages and Web Archives from the *Files of type* drop-down list DOUBLE-CLICK: the file you want to open
	Preview a Web page	CHOOSE: File, Web Page Preview
	Apply a theme	CHOOSE: Format, Theme

Key Terms

This section specifies page references for the key terms identified in this chapter. For a complete list of definitions, refer to the Glossary at the back of this learning guide.

footer, *p. WD 141*
gutter, *p. WD 134*
header, *p. WD 141*
HTML, *p. WD 156*
hyperlink, *p. WD 153*
Internet, *p. WD 153*
intranet, *p. WD 153*
landscape orientation, *p. WD 136*
orphan, *p. WD 137*
portrait orientation, *p. WD 136*
section break, *p. WD 145*
widow, *p. WD 137*
World Wide Web, *p. WD 153*

Chapter quiz

Short Answer

1. How do you create a Web document from a standard Word document?
2. What is the difference between a document that prints with a portrait orientation versus one that prints with a landscape orientation?
3. What is a Web theme?
4. What is a page break?
5. In Word, what is a widow?
6. How is the term *gutter* used in Word?
7. What is the difference between the Internet and an intranet?
8. What is the procedure for viewing headers and footers on the screen?
9. In Word, how do you insert a hard page break?
10. How wide are a document's top and bottom margins by default?

True/False

1. ____ Using the Insert, Page Numbers command, page numbers are inserted in the header or footer area.
2. ____ The Header and Footer toolbar automatically appears when you create a header or footer.
3. ____ Section breaks always mark the beginning of a new page.
4. ____ Once a page number is inserted, it's not possible to apply character formatting to it.
5. ____ By default, a footer appears at the top of the page.
6. ____ It's not possible to vary margins within a document.
7. ____ Page breaks are always used when printing documents in a landscape orientation.

8. ____ You can delete a page break by positioning the insertion point on the break and pressing DELETE.

9. ____ You can align page numbers with the left or right margin or center them.

10. ____ In Word, you can format headers and footers using regular formatting commands.

Multiple Choice

1. Which of the following are commonly found on Web pages?

a. hyperlinks
b. Internet
c. intranet
d. All of the above

2. Which of the following do you use to change margins?

a. Standard toolbar
b. Formatting toolbar
c. Page Setup dialog box
d. Paragraph dialog box

3. To force a page break, press:

a. CTRL + BREAK
b. CTRL + ALT
c. CTRL + ENTER
d. None of the above

4. To create a footer, choose:

a. View, Footer
b. View, Header and Footer
c. Insert, Header and Footer
d. Both a. and b.

5. To enable varied formatting within a document, Word allows you to divide a document into ___________.

a. master documents
b. outline views
c. multiple documents
d. sections

6. To view headers and footers, you must switch to:

a. Normal view
b. Print Layout view
c. Print Preview mode
d. Both b. and c.

7. Which of the following can you change using the Page Setup dialog box?

a. margins
b. page orientation
c. first-page headers and footers
d. All of the above

8. By default, your documents print with:

a. 1-inch top and bottom margins
b. 1.25-inch left and right margins
c. a portrait orientation
d. All of the above

9. Switching between portrait and landscape modes involves the:

a. Print Layout view
b. Page Setup dialog box
c. Header and Footer toolbar
d. None of the above

10. By default, the information you store in a header or footer prints:

a. on just the first page
b. on every other page
c. on every page
d. None of the above

Hands-On exercises

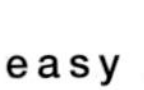

1. Laura Howard: Customizing a Resume

Laura is still in the job hunt. In this exercise, you assume the role of Laura and practice changing margins and inserting and modifying a header.

1. Open the WD04HE01 data file. This document provides a model for a sample résumé.
2. Save the document as "LH Resume" to your personal storage location.
3. To set the left and right margins to 0.5″:
   CHOOSE: File, Page Setup
   CLICK: *Margins* tab
   CLICK: down arrow beside the *Left* margin spin box until the value decreases to 0.5″
   CLICK: down arrow beside the *Right* margin spin box until the value decreases to 0.5″
   CLICK: OK command button
4. In this step, you insert a header that includes Laura's name and address.
   CHOOSE: View, Header and Footer
   TYPE: **Laura Howard** in the Header area
   PRESS: ENTER
   TYPE: **4344 Mission Road**
   PRESS: ENTER
   TYPE: **Oakland, CA 95622**
   PRESS: ENTER
5. To apply a larger point size and right-align the name and address lines:
   SELECT: the name and address lines
   SELECT: 14 from the Font Size drop-down list
   CLICK: Align Right button ( ) on the Formatting toolbar
   CLICK: Close on the Header and Footer toolbar
6. Let's edit the header so that it is centered between the margins.
   CHOOSE: View, Header and Footer
   SELECT: the name and address lines
   CLICK: Center button ( ) on the Formatting toolbar
   CLICK: Close on the Header and Footer toolbar
7. Let's increase the left margin to 0.75 inches.
   CHOOSE: File, Page Setup
   CLICK: *Margins* tab
   SELECT: the value in the *Left* margin text box
   TYPE: **0.75**
   CLICK: OK command button

8. Save the revised document. A portion of the completed document appears in Figure 4.30.

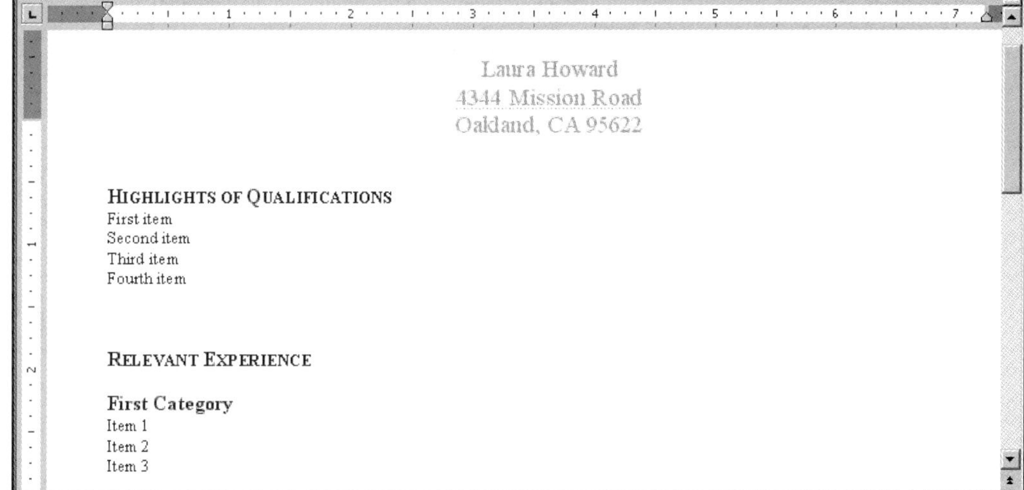

Figure 4.30
"LH Resume" document

9. Preview, print, and then close the document.

easy 

2. DigiTech Services: Creating Letterhead Stationery

Joanne, the DigiTech Services account representative you were introduced to in Chapter 1, is taking the initiative to create letterhead stationery that can be used by company personnel. In this exercise, you assume the role of Joanne and practice creating a header and applying shading. You will create the letterhead stationery shown in Figure 4.31.

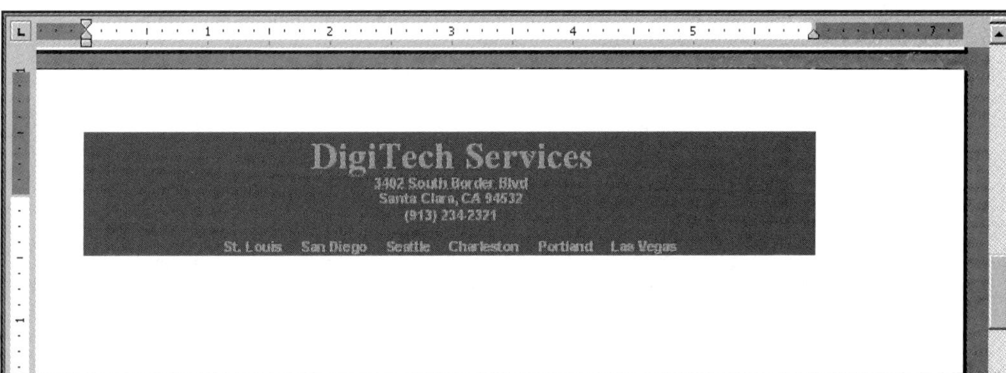

Figure 4.31
"DS Letterhead" document

1. Create a new blank document.
2. To open the header section of the document:
   CHOOSE: View, Header and Footer

3. Do the following to begin creating the header:
   PRESS: TAB to move to the center tab position
   TYPE: **DigiTech Services**
   PRESS: ENTER
   PRESS: TAB to move to the center tab position
   TYPE: **3402 South Border Blvd**
   PRESS: ENTER
   PRESS: TAB to move to the center tab position
   TYPE: **Santa Clara, CA 94532**
   PRESS: ENTER
   PRESS: TAB to move to the center tab position
   TYPE: **(913) 234-2321**
   PRESS: ENTER twice
4. To complete the header text:
   PRESS: TAB to move to the center tab position
   TYPE: **St. Louis**
   PRESS: Space bar five times
   TYPE: **San Diego**
   PRESS: Space bar five times
5. Continue typing the remaining city names (Seattle, Charleston, Portland, Las Vegas) using the same procedure as in the previous step. Don't press the Space Bar after typing the final city (Las Vegas).
6. Format the company name using Times New Roman, 22 points, and the bold attribute.
7. Format the address and business locations using Arial, 8 points, and the bold attribute.
8. To apply blue shading to the entire header:
   CHOOSE: Edit, Select All
   CHOOSE: Format, Borders and Shading
   CLICK: *Shading* tab
   CLICK: a shade of blue in the *Fill* color palette
   CLICK: OK command button
9. With the contents of the header still selected, apply white as the font color.
10. Close the Header and Footer toolbar.
11. Save the document as "DS Letterhead" before printing and closing.

3. Celsius Gear, USA: Varying a Report's Formatting

Dennis, a Celsius Gear employee, has ideas for one of his existing reports. By dividing it into sections and applying unique formatting to the sections, he's sure the report will take on a more professional look. In this exercise, assume the role of Dennis in modifying the report.

1. Open the WD04HE03 data file.
2. Save the document as "Celsius Report" to your personal storage location.
3. Insert a "Next page" section break at the beginning of the first main paragraph of the document. (*Note:* Position the insertion point to the left of "In the past . . .".)
4. On your own, apply formatting to the text in Section 1 so that the page resembles a report's title page.
5. Position the insertion point in Section 2 of the document and then display the Page Setup dialog box.
6. Using the Page Setup dialog box, specify a 1″ gutter and then make sure that "This section" is selected in the *Apply to* drop-down list. Click the OK command button when you're finished.
7. Insert a header that displays in Section 2 only that displays the words "Buyer's Guide: Tape Backup" in the right-aligned position. (*Hint:* Make sure to deselect the "Same as Previous" button on the Header and Footer toolbar.) Format the header using an Arial, 8-point font, and then apply the bold attribute to the header text.
8. Add a footer that displays in Section 2 only that includes a page number centered between the margins. (*Hint:* Make sure to deselect the "Same as Previous" button on the Header and Footer toolbar.) Format the footer using an Arial, 8-point font.
9. Format the "Size Matters" heading using an Arial, 10-point bold font. Using the Format Painter, apply this same formatting to the remaining headings in the report.
10. Ensure that Widow/Orphan protection is enabled.
11. After closing the Header and Footer toolbar, save the revised document.
12. Save, print, and then close the revised report.

moderate 

4. Worldwide Conventions, Inc.: Formatting a Document for the Web

Albert must prepare an existing document for the Web. Assume the role of Albert and practice changing margins and page orientation, and applying a Web theme.

1. Open the WD04HE04 data file.
2. Save the document as "WW Advertisement" to your personal storage location.
3. Set the top and bottom margins to 1″ and the left and right margins to 1″.
4. Change the orientation of the document from portrait to landscape.
5. Using the *Layout* tab of the Page Setup dialog box, use the *Vertical Alignment* drop-down list to align all the text in this document between the top and bottom margins.
6. Save the document as a Web page named "WW Advertisement" to your personal storage location and then close the document.
7. Open the "WW Advertisement" Web page into Word.

8. Apply the Axis theme to the document and then preview the document in your browser. Your screen should now appear similar to Figure 4.32.

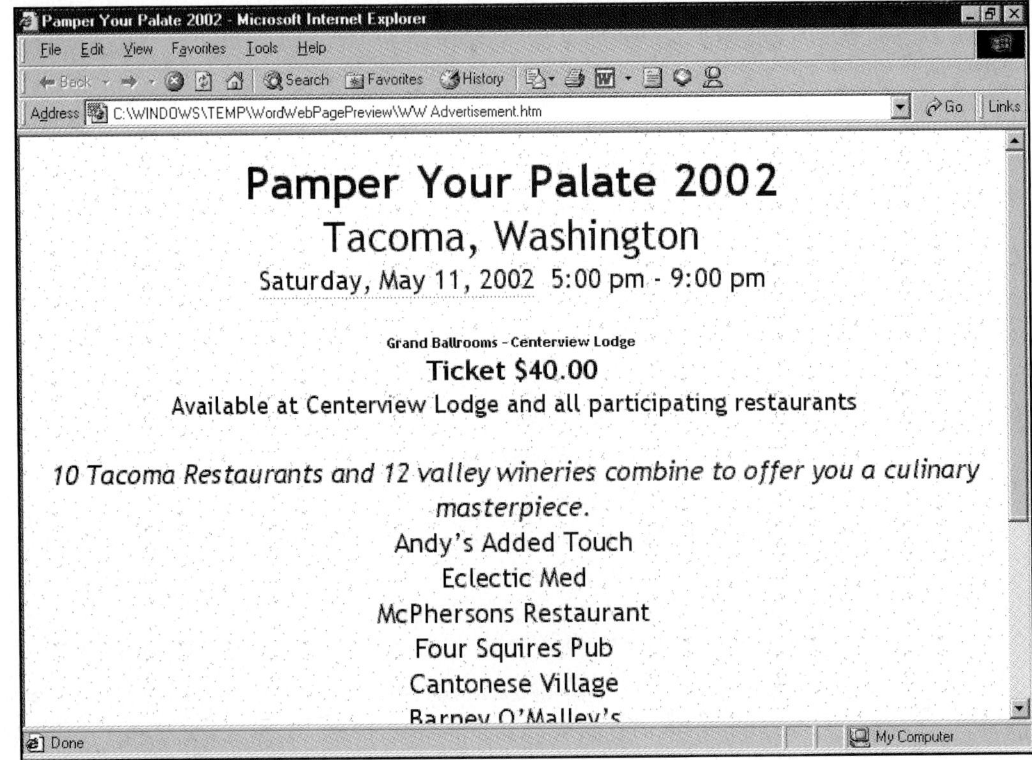

Figure 4.32

"WW Advertisement" Web page

9. Close your browser window.
10. After saving the revised Web page in Word, print and then close the document.

difficult 

5. On Your Own: Designing a Budget Document

This exercise practices using some commands from previous chapters as well as several page layout commands.

1. Start a new document and then switch to Normal view.
2. Set the following page dimensions:

Paper Orientation:	Portrait
Top Margin:	1 inch
Bottom Margin:	1 inch
Left Margin:	1 inch
Right Margin:	1 inch

3. Enter the information in Figure 4.33. (*Hint:* Use tabs.)

Figure 4.33

Budget information

ABC REALTY INC.

	2000
Revenue	
Commercial Properties	$125,500,000
Residential Properties	35,000,000
Leased Properties	875,000
Total Revenue	**$161,375,000**
Expenses	
Insurance	$50,000
Salaries	750,000
Commissions	15,500,000
Office Supplies	25,000
Office Equipment	20,000
Utilities	15,000
Leased Automobiles	50,000
Travel	250,000
Advertising & Promotion	25,000,000
Total Expenses	**41,660,000**
Net Income	**$119,715,000**

4. Apply the shading and borders of your choice to the title "ABC Realty Inc.".

5. Save the document as "Company Budget" to your personal storage location. Figure 4.34 shows a portion of the completed document.

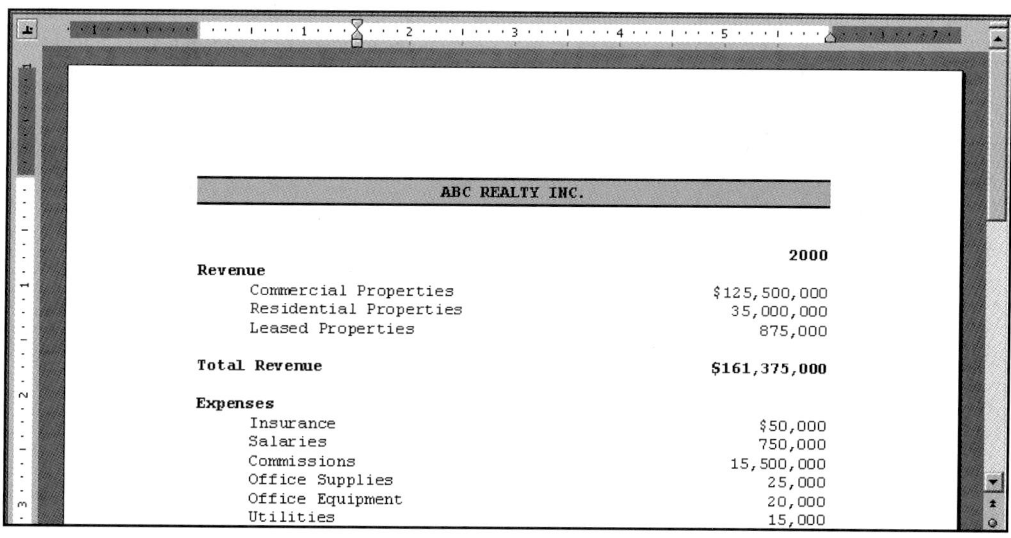

ABC REALTY INC.

	2000
Revenue	
Commercial Properties	$125,500,000
Residential Properties	35,000,000
Leased Properties	875,000
Total Revenue	**$161,375,000**
Expenses	
Insurance	$50,000
Salaries	750,000
Commissions	15,500,000
Office Supplies	25,000
Office Equipment	20,000
Utilities	15,000

Figure 4.34

"Company Budget" document

6. Preview and print the document.

difficult 

6. On Your Own: Formatting a Newsletter

In this exercise, you open the WD04HE06 student file and format it to create a presentable newsletter. Change the orientation of the newsletter to landscape. It should include the text "Twin Valley Banner" in the header and the header text should appear in a large, bold font with 15% shading. The footer should include the current date in the left-aligned position and the current page number in the right-aligned position. The "Twin Valley Brewery" heading currently appears alone on the bottom of page 1. Issue a command to keep the heading with its following paragraph.

Finally, format all the headings in the newsletter with yellow shading that spans from the left to the right margin. The first page of the newsletter should appear similar to Figure 4.35. Save the document as "Twin Valley Banner" and then preview and print your work. Close the document.

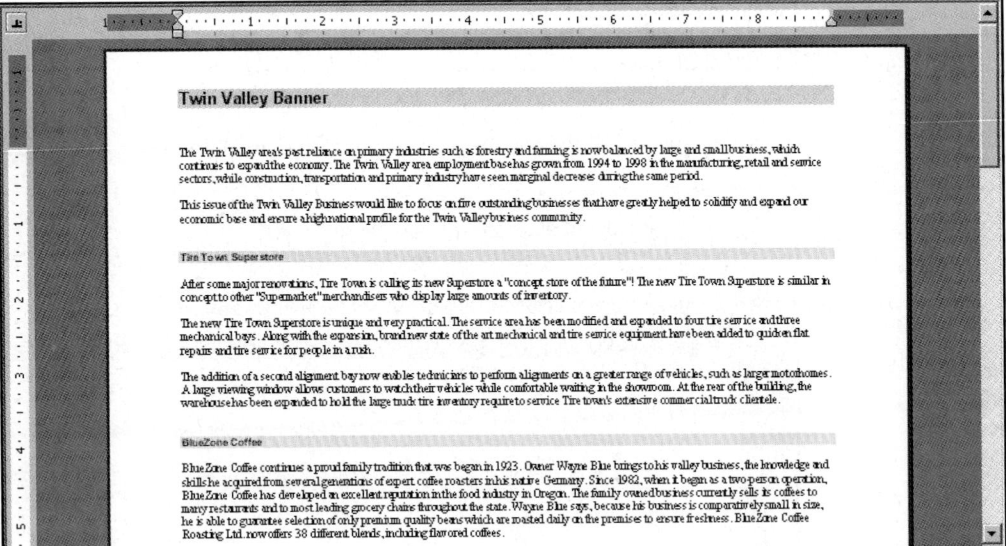

Twin Valley Banner

The Twin Valley area's past reliance on primary industries such as forestry and farming is now balanced by large and small business, which continues to expand the economy. The Twin Valley area employment base has grown from 1994 to 1998 in the manufacturing, retail and service sectors, while construction, transportation and primary industry have seen marginal decreases during the same period.

This issue of the Twin Valley Business would like to focus on five outstanding businesses that have greatly helped to solidify and expand our economic base and ensure a high national profile for the Twin Valley business community.

Tire Town Superstore

After some major renovations, Tire Town is calling its new Superstore a "concept store of the future"! The new Tire Town Superstore is similar in concept to other "Supermarket" merchandisers who display large amounts of inventory.

The new Tire Town Superstore is unique and very practical. The service area has been modified and expanded to four tire service and three mechanical bays. Along with the expansion, brand new state of the art mechanical and tire service equipment have been added to quicken flat repairs and tire service for people in a rush.

The addition of a second alignment bay now enables technicians to perform alignments on a greater range of vehicles, such as larger motorhomes. A large viewing window allows customers to watch their vehicles while comfortable waiting in the showroom. At the rear of the building, the warehouse has been expanded to hold the large truck tire inventory require to service Tire town's extensive commercial truck clientele.

BlueZone Coffee

BlueZone Coffee continues a proud family tradition that was began in 1923. Owner Wayne Blue brings to his valley business, the knowledge and skills he acquired from several generations of expert coffee roasters in his native Germany. Since 1982, when it began as a two-person operation, BlueZone Coffee has developed an excellent reputation in the food industry in Oregon. The family owned business currently sells its coffees to many restaurants and to most leading grocery chains throughout the state. Wayne Blue says, because his business is comparatively small in size, he is able to guarantee selection of only premium quality beans which are roasted daily on the premises to ensure freshness. BlueZone Coffee Roasting Ltd. now offers 38 different blends, including flavored coffees.

Figure 4.35

"Twin Valley Banner" document

Case Problems: Yard Smart Designs

Now that Mark has learned how to change page layout, create headers and footers, and vary print options within a document, he is ready to finalize some of the draft documents that he had prepared previously.

In the following case problems, assume the role of Mark and perform the same steps he would perform to complete these tasks.

1. Mark decides to add some finishing touches to a document he likes to send out to new customers about maintaining a healthy lawn. After opening the WD04CS01 data file, he saves it as "Yard Smart Lawn" to his personal storage location. He begins by creating a centered footer that reads "Article courtesy of the Toro Company" and applies the bold attribute. Next, he inserts a page break before the "What does fertilizer do for my

lawn?" heading. After saving the revised document, he previews the document as a Web page. Satisfied with its appearance in his Web browser, he then saves it to HTML for later posting on his company's Web site.

2. Mark decides that the company letterhead stationery should include a listing of some of the services that Yard Smart provides. He drafts several designs to discuss with Christine, then develops and prints a copy of his favorite design (Figure 4.36). (*Hint:* He inserts the letterhead information in a header and sets center tabs in positions 1.75, 3, and 4.5 inches. He also sets a right tab in the 6-inch position.) He saves this file as "Yard Smart Letterhead."

Figure 4.36

"Yard Smart Letterhead"

Yard Smart Designs
12348 Main St., Florence, ND 88345
Phone: 542-3457 Fax: 542-2358

Cutting & Raking	Weed Control	Fertilizing	Pest Control	Aerating
De-Thatching	Landscaping	Pruning	Planting	Seeding

3. Yard Smart could use a more professional-looking invoice. Mark determines what information should be included and drafts a design that looks clean and readable (Figure 4.37). He includes all the text at the top of the document in the header, down to and including the word "INVOICE". He then changes the margins of the invoice to 1 inch on all sides. He prepares, previews and prints his new document, then saves it as "Yard Smart Invoice."

Figure 4.37

"Yard Smart Invoice"

Yard Smart Designs

Landscaping
Garden Watering
Free Estimates

INVOICE

DATE: ____________
INVOICE NO: ____________

CLIENT: ____________
STREET: ____________
CITY/STATE: ____________
ZIP CODE: ____________

The following work was completed on ____________.

Description: ____________

AMOUNT DUE: ____________
(Payable upon request)

4. Mark wants to begin distributing a newsletter to his customers. He opens the document named WD04CS04 that he prepared previously and then makes some changes to his work. He includes his bulletin name **Yard Smart Designs** centered on the first line of the header, his slogan **Growing in Excellence** centered on the second line, the text **Issue #1** aligned to the left on the third line, and the date aligned to the right on the third line. He then applies green shading to the entire header, changes the font color of the header text to white, applies the bold attribute, and enlarges the font size of the bulletin name to 16 points. He adds a footer that displays the business name, address, and phone numbers on separate lines, centered between the left and right margins.

Next, Mark inserts a page break before the "FALL" heading and inserts an extra line at the top of page 2 so that there is space between the heading and the header information. After previewing and printing the bulletin, he saves it as "Yard Smart Bulletin." Figure 4.38 shows a portion of the document's first page.

Figure 4.38

"Yard Smart Bulletin"

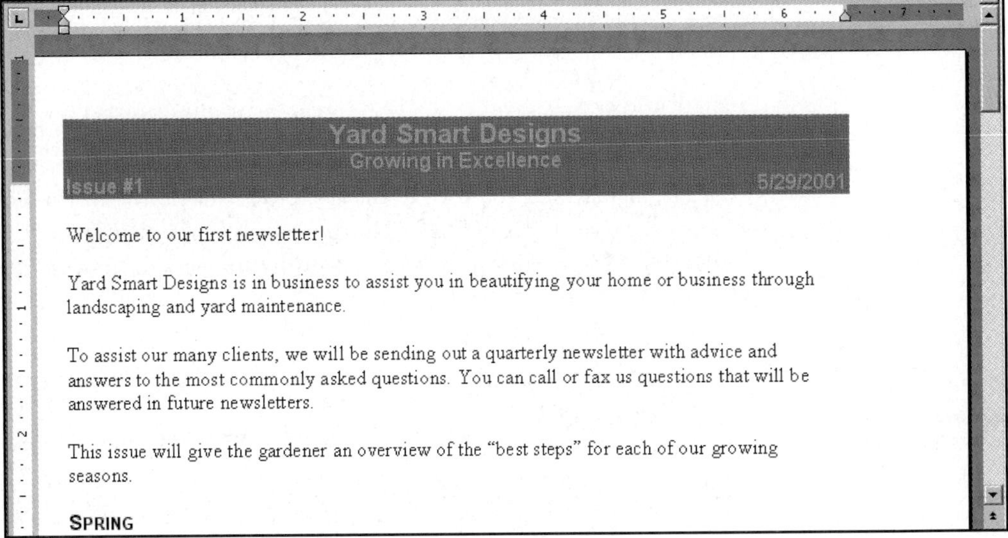

NOTES

NOTES

NOTES

NOTES

NOTES

NOTES

Microsoft® **Excel®** 2002

CHAPTER 1

Creating a Worksheet

CHAPTER OUTLINE

Case Study

1.1 Getting Started with Excel

1.2 Creating Your First Worksheet

1.3 Editing Your Work

1.4 Managing Files

Chapter Summary

Chapter Quiz

Hands-On Exercises

Case Problems

PREREQUISITES

Although this chapter assumes no previous experience using Microsoft Excel, you should be comfortable working with the mouse in the Microsoft Windows environment. You should also be able to launch and exit programs and perform basic Windows file management operations, such as opening and closing documents.

LEARNING OBJECTIVES

After completing this chapter, you will be able to:

- Describe the different components of the Excel application and workbook windows
- Select commands using the Menu bar and right-click menus
- Enter text, dates, numbers, and simple formulas in a worksheet
- Edit and erase cell data
- Use the Undo and Redo commands
- Start a new workbook
- Save, open, and close a workbook

CaseStudy **H. F. CHARTERS** H. F. Charters is a small, privately owned airline charter company operating in the Pacific Northwest. The company's business consists of flying tourists to remote fishing lodges and transporting geological and forestry survey crews. Earlier this year, H. F. Charters added a third aircraft to their fleet of floatplanes and retained two full-time and three part-time pilots. Along with the pilots, H. F. Charters employs a dockhand and a mechanic. Hank Frobisher, the general manager, started the company and oversees all aspects of its operation.

To date, H. F. Charters has been operating with a bare minimum of paperwork and manual record-keeping. All bookings are handwritten into a scheduling chart and the pilots fill out trip logs at the end of each flight. Invoices and receipts are simply turned over to a bookkeeping service, as Hank cannot afford a staff accountant. Just lately, however, Hank is finding it increasingly difficult to obtain the information he needs to make key decisions. To remedy this, he hired Jennifer Duvall, the daughter of one of his pilots, as an office assistant. Jennifer is enrolled in a Microsoft Excel course at the local college and has expressed some interest in creating worksheets for the company.

In this chapter, you and Jennifer learn how to work with Microsoft Excel. Specifically, you create new worksheets from scratch and enter text, numbers, dates, and formulas. Then you learn how to edit and modify cell entries and even practice using the Undo command. To complete the chapter, you practice saving and opening workbooks.

1.1 Getting Started with Excel

Microsoft Excel is an electronic spreadsheet program that enables you to store, manipulate, and chart numeric data. Researchers, statisticians, and businesspeople use spreadsheets to analyze and summarize mathematical, statistical, and financial data. Closer to home, you can use Excel to create a budget for your monthly living expenses, analyze returns in the stock market, develop a business plan, or calculate your student loan payments.

Excel enables you to create and modify worksheets—the electronic version of an accountant's ledger pad—and chart sheets. A **worksheet** (Figure 1.1) is divided into vertical columns and horizontal rows. The rows are numbered and the columns are labeled from A to Z, then AA to AZ, and so on to column IV. The intersection of a column and a row is called a **cell.** Each cell is given a **cell address** (also called a **cell reference**), like a post office box number, consisting of its column letter followed by its row number (for example, B4 or FX400). Excel allows you to open multiple worksheets and chart sheets within its application window.

Figure 1.1

An electronic worksheet

Book1

	A	B	C	D	E	F	G
1	Mutual Fund Manager						
2							
3	Date	Close	Shares	Value	Volume	High	Low
4	30-Jun	$9.78	511.274	$5,000.26			
5	31-Jul	$9.74	511.274	$4,979.81			
6	31-Aug	$9.95	511.274	$5,087.18			
7	30-Sep	$10.15	1,420.123	$14,414.25			
8	31-Oct	$10.62	1,420.123	$15,081.71			
9	30-Nov	$10.52	1,420.123	$14,939.69			
10	31-Dec	$9.98	1,420.123	$14,172.83			
11							
12							

Sheet1 / Sheet2 / Sheet3

Excel

A **chart sheet** (Figure 1.2) displays a chart graphic that is typically linked to data stored in a worksheet. When the data are changed, the chart is updated automatically to reflect the new information. Charts may also appear alongside their data in a worksheet.

Figure 1.2

A chart sheet

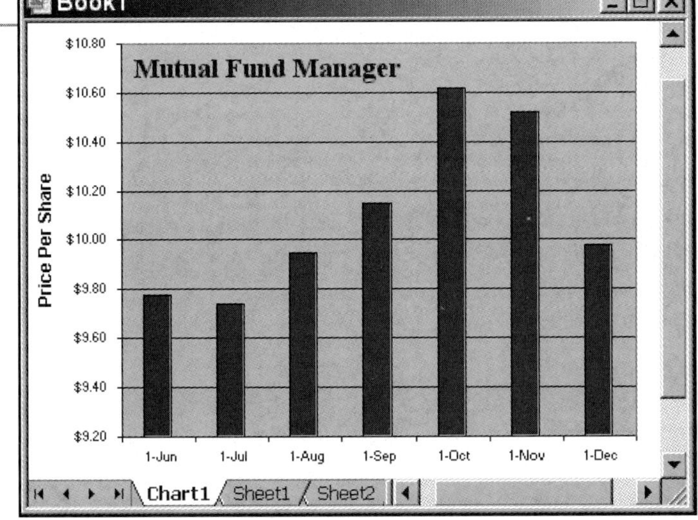

Related worksheets and chart sheets are stored together in a single disk file called a **workbook**. You can think of an Excel workbook as a three-ring binder with tabs at the beginning of each new page or sheet. In this module, you learn to load Microsoft Excel and then proceed through a guided tour of its primary components.

1.1.1 Loading and Exiting Excel

feature

To launch Excel, begin at the Windows Start menu and click the Start button (Start) on the taskbar. Then, choose the Programs menu option and, finally, click Microsoft Excel. After a few moments, the Excel application window appears.

When you are finished doing your work, you should exit Excel so that the system's memory is freed for use by other Windows applications. To do so, choose the File, Exit command or click on the Close button (X) appearing in the top right-hand corner. These methods are used to close most Microsoft Windows applications.

method

To launch Excel:

- CLICK: Start button (Start)
- CHOOSE: Programs, Microsoft Excel

To exit Excel:

- CHOOSE: File, Exit from Excel's Menu bar,

or

- CLICK: its Close button (X)

practice

You will now launch Microsoft Excel using the Windows Start menu and then practice closing the application. Ensure that you have turned on your computer and that the Windows desktop appears.

1. Position the mouse pointer over the Start button (Start) appearing in the bottom left-hand corner of the Windows taskbar and then click the left mouse button once. The Start pop-up menu appears as shown here.

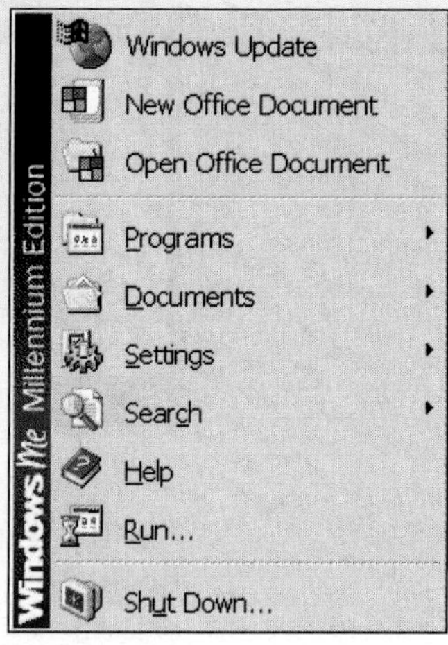

2. Position the mouse pointer over the Programs menu option. Notice that you do not need to click the left mouse button to display the list of programs in the fly-out or cascading menu.
3. Move the mouse pointer horizontally to the right until it highlights an option in the Programs menu. You can now move the mouse pointer vertically within the menu to select an application.
4. Position the mouse pointer over the Microsoft Excel menu option and then click the left mouse button once. After a few seconds, the Excel application window appears (Figure 1.3).

Figure 1.3

Microsoft Excel application window

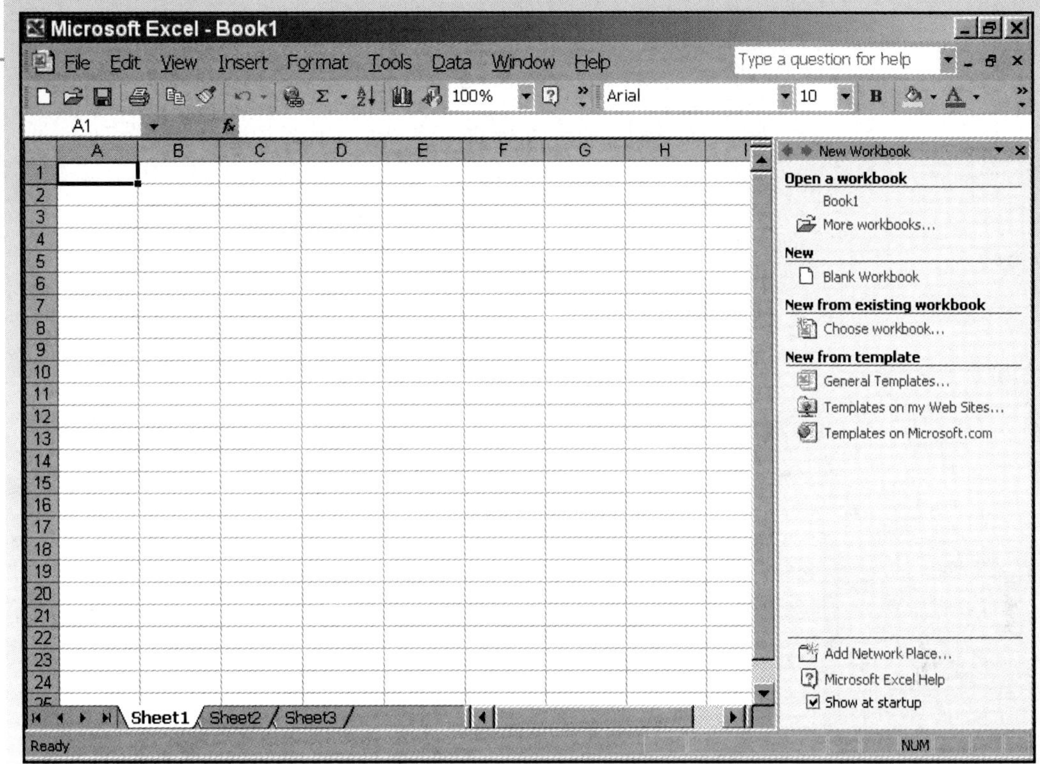

5. Depending on your system's configuration, an Office Assistant character, like "Clippit" (shown at the right), may appear. You will learn how to hide this character in lesson 1.1.2.

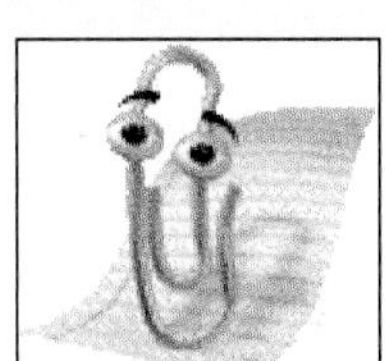

6. To exit Excel:
   CLICK: its Close button (☒) in the top right-hand corner
   Assuming that no other applications are running and displayed, you are returned to the Windows desktop.

In Addition SWITCHING AMONG APPLICATIONS

A button appears on the Windows taskbar for each "running" application or open document. Switching among open applications is as easy as clicking the appropriate taskbar button, like switching channels on a television set.

1.1.2 Touring Excel

feature→

The Excel **application window** acts as a container for the worksheet and chart windows. It also contains the primary components for working in Excel, including the *Windows icons, Menu bar, toolbars, task pane, Name box, Formula bar,* and *Status bar.* The components of a worksheet **document window** include *scroll bars, sheet tabs, Tab Split box,* and *Tab Scrolling arrows.* Figures 1.4 and 1.5 identify several of these components.

practice 

In a guided tour, you now explore the features of the Excel application and document windows. Ensure that the Windows desktop appears.

1. Launch Microsoft Excel, referring to the previous lesson if necessary.
2. Excel's application window is best kept maximized to fill the entire screen, as shown in Figure 1.4. As with most Microsoft Windows applications, you use the Windows Title bar icons—Minimize (▭), Maximize (▢), Restore (▣), and Close (☒)—to control the display of a window using the mouse. Figure 1.4 labels some of the components of Excel's application window.

Figure 1.4

Components of Excel's application window

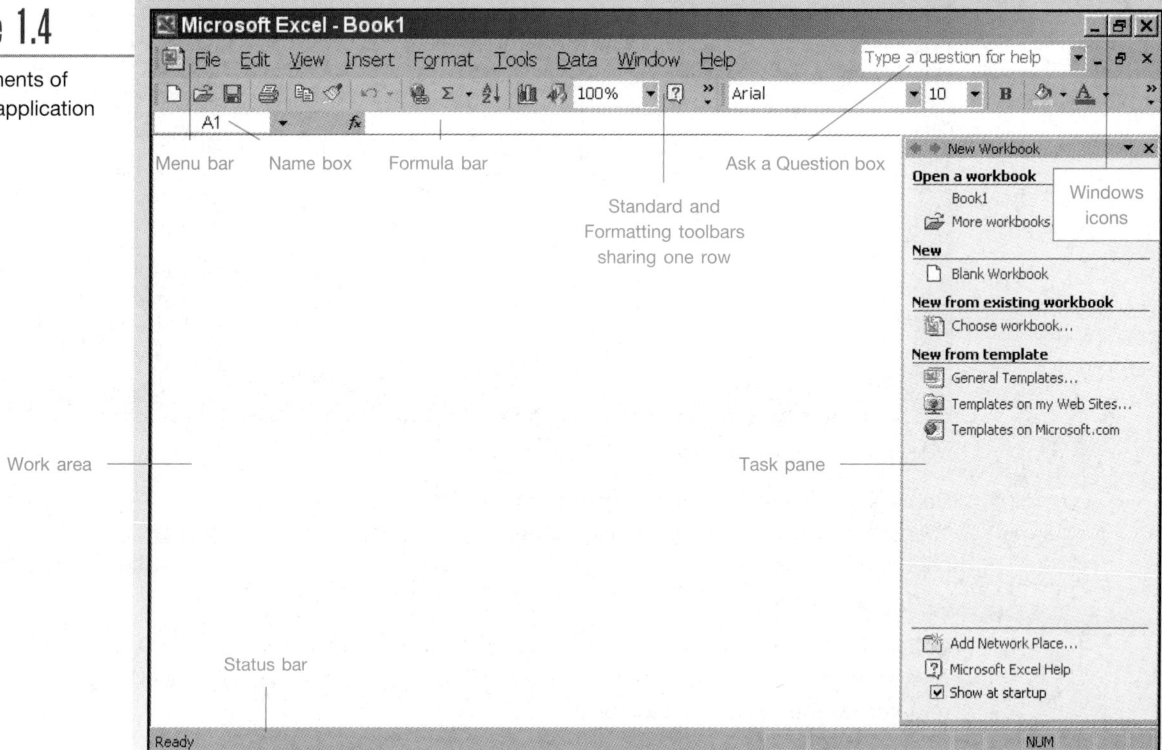

3. Below the Windows icons for the Excel application window, there are additional icons for minimizing, restoring, and closing the worksheet window. To restore the worksheet to a window within the work area:
   CLICK: its Restore button (▣)
   A worksheet window should now appear in the work area. Figure 1.5 labels the components found in a typical worksheet window.

Figure 1.5

Components of Excel's worksheet window

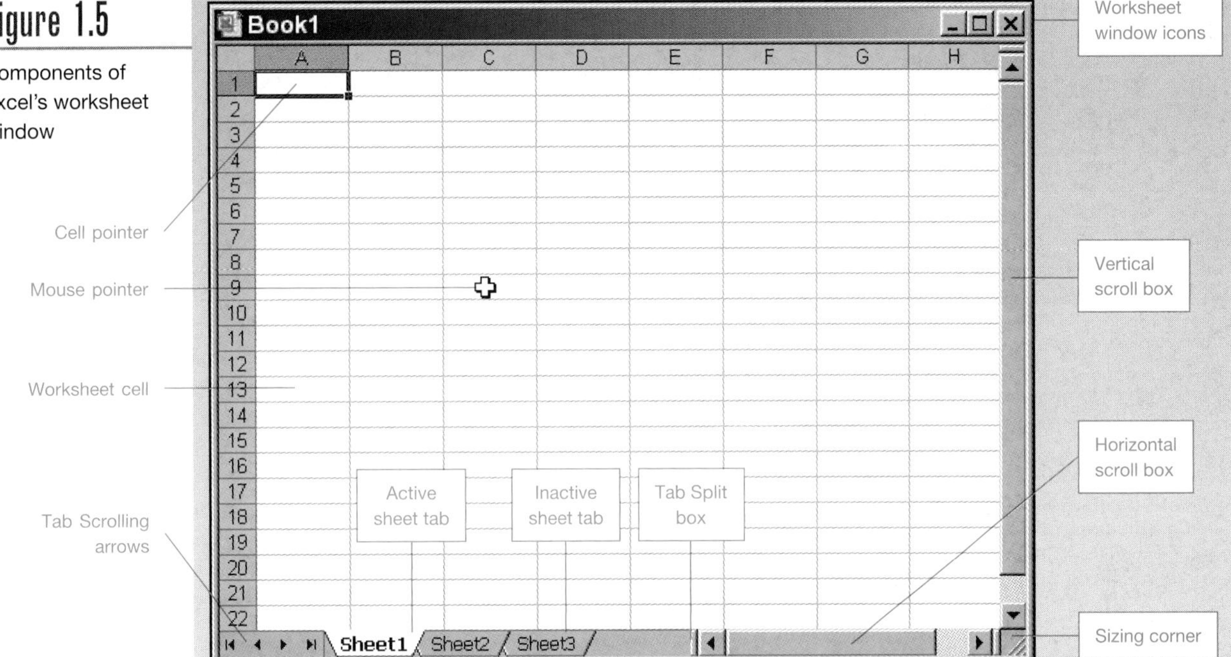

4. Let's return the worksheet window to its maximized state:
CLICK: its Maximize button (□)
Your screen should now appear similar to Figure 1.3.

5. The Menu bar contains the Excel menu commands. To execute a command, click once on the desired Menu bar option and then click again on the command. Commands that appear dimmed are not available for selection. Commands that are followed by an ellipsis (...) will display a dialog box. Pull-down menus that display a chevron (☐) at the bottom contain additional menu options.

To practice working with the Menu bar:
CHOOSE: Help
This instruction tells you to click the left mouse button once on the Help option appearing in the Menu bar. The Help menu appears, as shown here. (*Note:* All menu commands that you execute in this guide begin with the instruction "CHOOSE.")

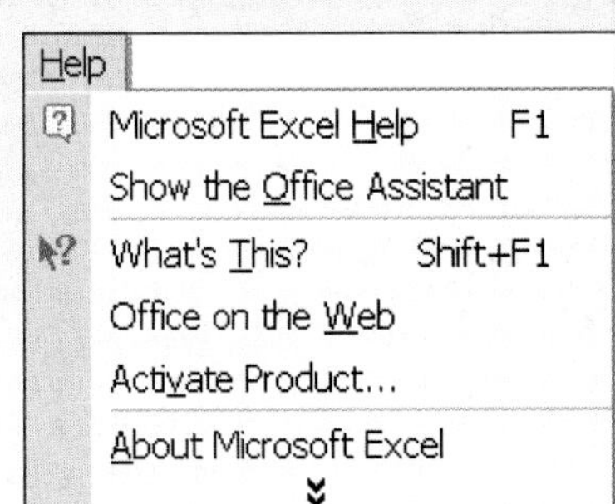

6. To display other pull-down menus, move the mouse to the left over other options in the Menu bar. As each option is highlighted, a pull-down menu appears with its associated commands.

7. To leave the Menu bar without making a command selection:
CLICK: in a blank area of the Title bar

8. Excel provides context-sensitive *right-click menus* for quick access to menu commands. Rather than searching for the appropriate command in the Menu bar, you can position the mouse pointer on any object, such as a cell, graphic, or toolbar button, and right-click the mouse to display a list of commonly selected commands.

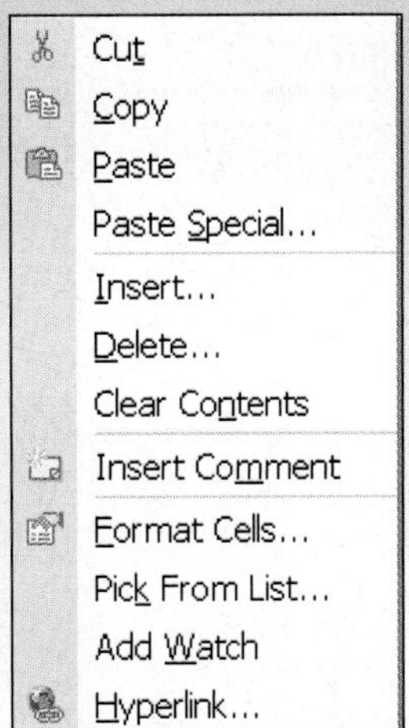

To display a cell's right-click menu:
RIGHT-CLICK: cell A1
The pop-up menu at the right should appear.

9. To remove the cell's right-click menu from the screen:
PRESS: ESC

10. If an Office Assistant character appears on your screen, do the following to hide it from view:
RIGHT-CLICK: *the character*
CHOOSE: Hide from the right-click menu
(*Note:* The character's name may appear in the command, such as "Hide Clippit.")

1.1.3 Customizing Menus and Toolbars

feature

Some people argue that software becomes more difficult to learn with the addition of each new command or feature. In response to this sentiment, Microsoft developed adaptive menus that display only the most commonly used commands. By default, Microsoft Office XP ships with the **adaptive menus** feature enabled. However, you may find this dynamic feature confusing and choose to turn off the adaptive menus. Likewise, the Standard and Formatting toolbars are positioned side-by-side in a single row by default. Again, you may find it easier to locate buttons when these toolbars are positioned on separate rows. Finally, the **task pane** is positioned on the right side of your screen, providing convenient access to relevant commands and options. The New Workbook task pane is displayed automatically when you first start Microsoft Excel and when you choose the File, New command from the Menu bar. Fortunately, you can hide (and redisplay) the task pane using the View menu command.

method

To disable the adaptive menus feature and display the Standard and Formatting toolbars on separate rows:

- CHOOSE: Tools, Customize
- CLICK: *Options* tab
- SELECT: *Show Standard and Formatting toolbars on two rows* check box
- SELECT: *Always show full menus* check box
- CLICK: Close command button

To display or hide a toolbar:

- CHOOSE: View, Toolbars
- CHOOSE: a toolbar from the menu

To display and hide the task pane:

- CHOOSE: View, task pane

or

- CLICK: its Close button (☒)

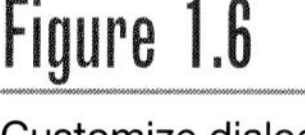

In this lesson, you disable the adaptive menus feature, display the Standard and Formatting toolbars on separate rows, and toggle the display of the task pane. Ensure that you've completed the previous lesson.

1. To begin, display the Tools menu:
   CHOOSE: Tools
   You should now see the Tools pull-down menu. (*Hint:* When a desired command does not appear on a menu, you can extend the menu to view all of the available commands by waiting for a short period, by clicking on the chevron (¥) at the bottom of the pull-down menu, or by double-clicking the option in the Menu bar.)

2. Let's turn off the adaptive menus feature and customize the Standard and Formatting toolbars. Do the following:
   CHOOSE: Customize from the Tools pull-down menu
   CLICK: *Options* tab
   The Customize dialog box should now appear (Figure 1.6).

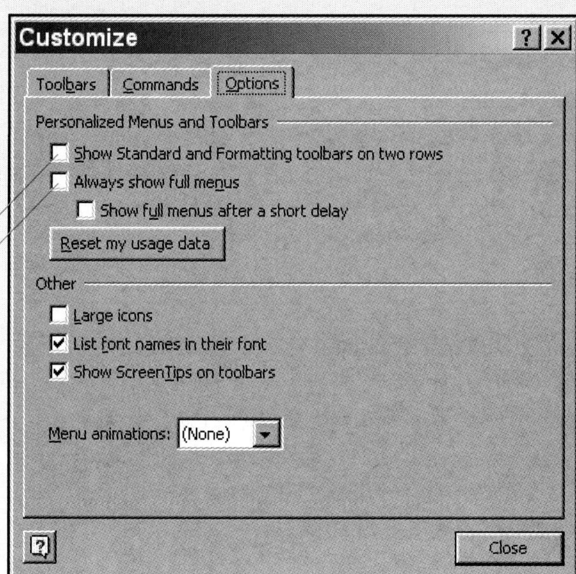

Figure 1.6

Customize dialog box: *Options* tab

3. On the *Options* tab of the Customize dialog box:
   SELECT: *Show Standard and Formatting toolbars on two rows* check box
   SELECT: *Always show full menus* check box
   (*Note:* When you select a check box, a check mark (✓) appears.)

4. To proceed:
CLICK: Close command button
Figure 1.7 displays the Standard and Formatting toolbars as they should now appear on your screen. The Standard toolbar provides access to file management and editing commands, in addition to special features such as wizards. The Formatting toolbar lets you access cell formatting commands.

Figure 1.7

Standard toolbar

New, Open, Save, E-mail, Search, Print, Print Preview, Spelling, Cut, Copy, Paste, Format Painter, Undo, Redo, Insert Hyperlink, AutoSum, Sort Ascending, Sort Descending, Chart Wizard, Drawing, Zoom, Microsoft Excel Help

Formatting toolbar

5. To hide the task pane:
CHOOSE: View, Task Pane
(*Note:* When a toolbar or the task pane is displayed, a check mark appears beside the option in the pull-down menu.)

6. To display the task pane:
CHOOSE: View, Task Pane
Your screen should now appear similar to Figure 1.8.

Figure 1.8

Customizing the application window

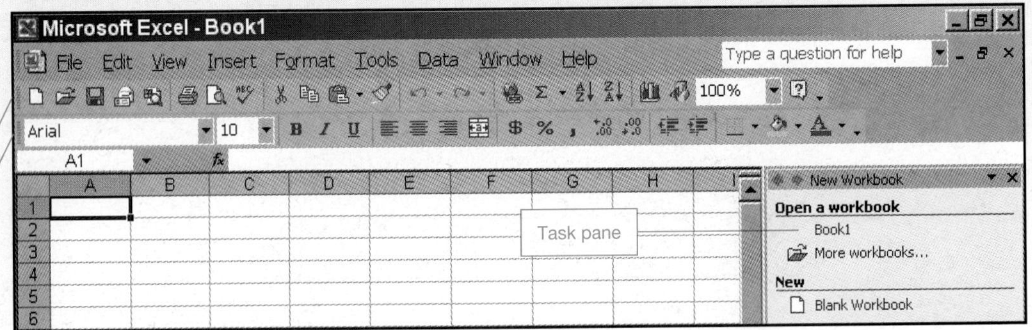

IMPORTANT: For the remainder of this learning guide, we assume that the adaptive menus feature has been disabled and that the Standard and Formatting toolbars are positioned on separate rows.

In Addition MOVING TOOLBARS

You can move toolbars around the Excel application window using the mouse. A *docked* toolbar appears attached to one of the window's borders. An *undocked* or *floating* toolbar appears in its own window, complete with a Title bar and Close button (☒). To float a docked toolbar, drag the Move bar ( ) at the left-hand side toward the center of the window. To redock the toolbar, drag its Title bar toward a border until it attaches itself automatically.

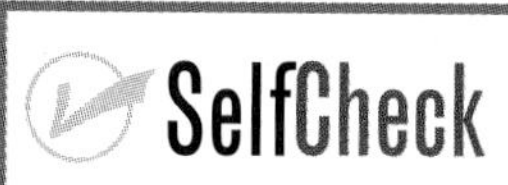

1.1. How do you turn the adaptive menus feature on or off?

1.2 Creating Your First Worksheet

You create a worksheet by entering text labels, numbers, dates, and formulas into the individual cells. To begin entering data, first move the cell pointer to the desired cell in the worksheet. Then type the information that you want to appear in the cell. Complete the entry by pressing ENTER or by moving the cell pointer to another cell. In this module, you learn how to navigate a worksheet, enter several types of data, and construct a simple formula expression.

1.2.1 Moving the Cell Pointer

feature

The **cell pointer** is the cursor used to select a cell in the worksheet using either the mouse or keyboard. When you first open a new workbook, the *Sheet1* worksheet tab is active and the cell pointer is positioned in cell A1. As you move the cell pointer around the worksheet, Excel displays the current cell address in the **Name box,** as shown here.

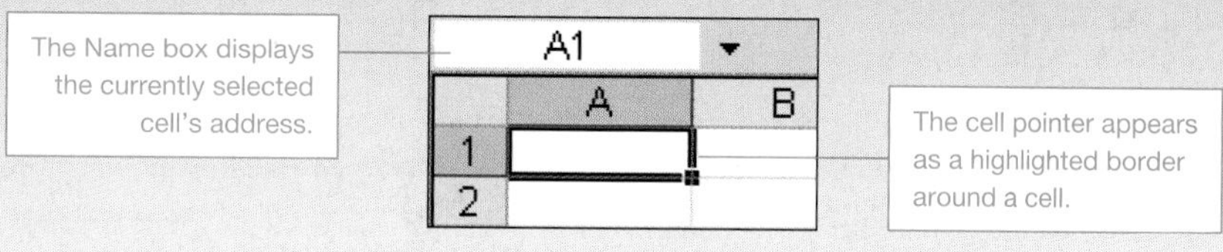

The Name box displays the currently selected cell's address.
A1
A
B
1
2
The cell pointer appears as a highlighted border around a cell.

method

Some common keystrokes for navigating a worksheet include:

- ↑, ↓, ←, and →
- HOME, END, PgUp, and PgDn
- CTRL + HOME to move to cell A1
- CTRL + END to move to the last cell in the active worksheet area
- F5 (GoTo) key for moving to a specific cell address

Excel

practice

You will now practice moving around an empty worksheet. Ensure that Excel is loaded and a blank worksheet appears.

1. With the cell pointer in cell A1, move to cell D4 using the following keystrokes:
   PRESS: → three times
   PRESS: ↓ three times
   Notice that the cell address, D4, is displayed in the Name box and that the column (D) and row (4) headings in the frame area appear highlighted.
2. To move to cell E12 using the mouse:
   CLICK: cell E12
   (*Hint:* Position the cross mouse pointer over cell E12 and click the left mouse button once.)
3. To move to cell E124 using the keyboard:
   PRESS: PgDn until row 124 is in view
   PRESS: ↑ or ↓ to select cell E124
   (*Hint:* The PgUp and PgDn keys are used to move up and down a worksheet by as many rows as fit in the current document window.)
4. To move to cell E24 using the mouse, position the mouse pointer on the vertical scroll box and then drag the scroll box upward to row 24, as shown in Figure 1.9. Then click cell E24 to select the cell.

Figure 1.9

Dragging the vertical scroll box

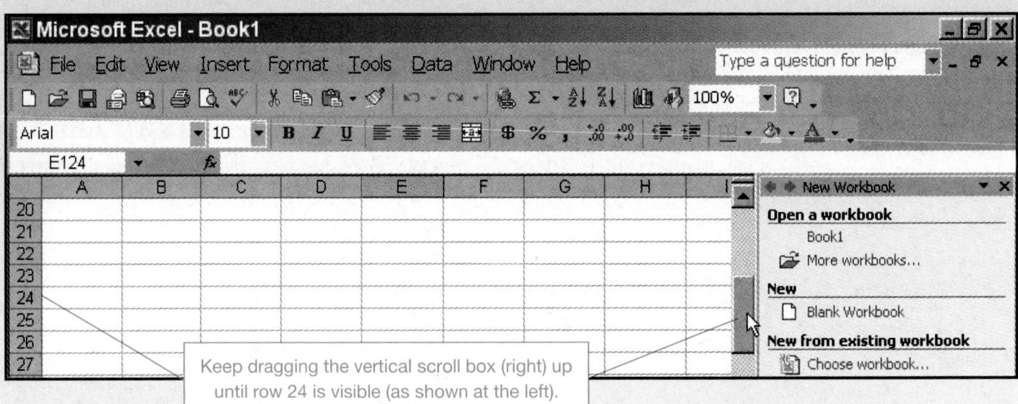

5. To move quickly to a specific cell address, such as cell AE24:
   CLICK: once in the Name box
   TYPE: **ae24**
   PRESS: ENTER
   The cell pointer scoots over to cell AE24. (*Hint:* Because cell addresses are not case sensitive, you need not use capital letters when typing a cell address.)
6. To move the cell pointer in any direction until the cell contents change from empty to filled (with data), filled to empty, or until a border is encountered, press CTRL with an arrow key. For example:
   PRESS: CTRL + → to move to column IV
   PRESS: CTRL + ↓ to move to row 65536
   The cell pointer now appears in the bottom right-hand corner of the worksheet. Also notice that "IV65536" appears in the Name box.
7. To move back to cell A1:
   PRESS: CTRL + HOME

1.2.2 Entering Text

feature

Text labels are the headings, instructions, and other descriptive information that you place in a worksheet to enhance its readability. Although a typical worksheet column is only eight or nine characters wide, a single cell can store thousands of characters. With longer entries, the text simply spills over the column border into the next cell, if it is empty. If the adjacent cell is not empty, the text will be truncated at its right border.

method

To enter text:

- TYPE: **text**
- PRESS: ENTER

practice

In this example, you begin a simple worksheet by specifying text labels for the row and column headings. Ensure that the cell pointer is positioned in cell A1 of the *Sheet1* worksheet.

1. Let's begin the worksheet by entering a title. As you type the following entry, watch the Formula bar:
   TYPE: **Income Statement**
   Your screen should appear similar to Figure 1.10.

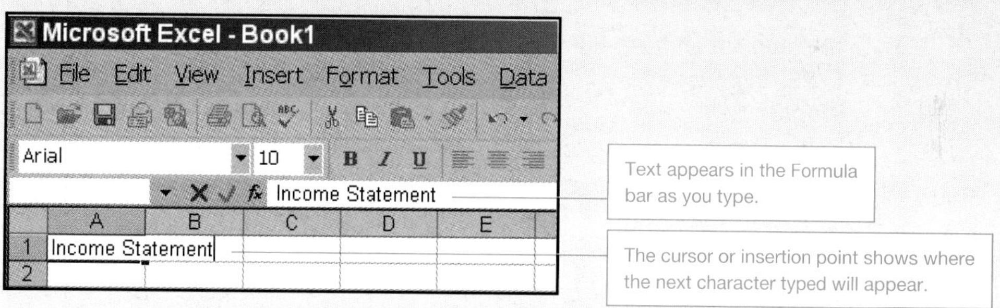

Figure 1.10
Typing text into the Formula bar

2. To enter the text into the cell, you press ENTER or click the Enter button (✓) in the Formula bar. To cancel an entry, you press ESC or click the Cancel (✗) button. Let's accept the entry:
   PRESS: ENTER
   Notice that the entry does not fit in a single column and must spill over into column B. This is acceptable as long as you don't place anything in cell B1. Otherwise, you need to increase the width of column A.
   After you press ENTER, the cell pointer will move to the next row. (*Note:* If your cell pointer remains in cell A1, choose Tools, Options from the Menu bar and click the *Edit* tab in the Options dialog box. Ensure that there is a check mark in the *Move selection after Enter* check box, as shown in Figure 1.11.)

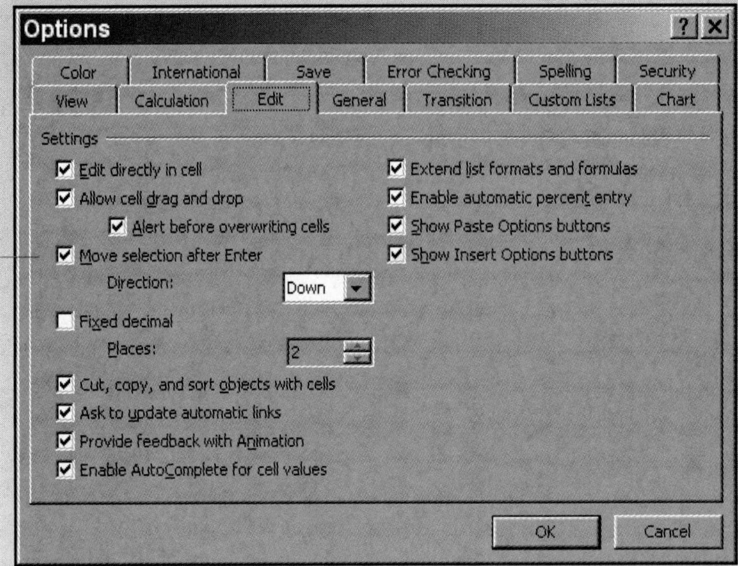

Figure 1.11

Options dialog box: *Edit* tab

Ensure that this check box is selected and that the *Direction* drop-down list box displays "Down."

3. Move the cell pointer to cell B3.

4. Enter the following text label:
TYPE: **Revenue**
PRESS: ⬇
Notice that pressing ⬇ has the same result as pressing ENTER.

5. To complete entering the row labels:
TYPE: **Expenses**
PRESS: ⬇
TYPE: **Profit**
PRESS: ENTER
All of the text data have now been entered into the worksheet, as shown in Figure 1.12.

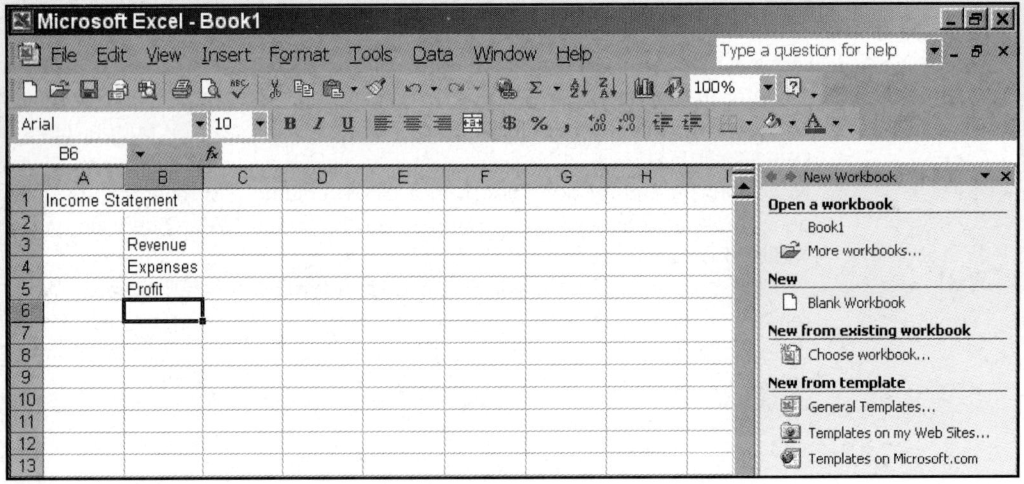

Figure 1.12

Entering text into a worksheet

1.2.3 Entering Dates

feature

You enter dates into a cell using one of the common date formats recognized by Excel, such as mm/dd/yy (12/25/02) or dd-mmm-yy (25-Dec-02). Excel treats a date (or time) as a formatted number or value. Consequently, you can use date values to perform arithmetic calculations, such as finding out how many days have elapsed between two calendar dates.

method

To enter a date value:

- TYPE: **a date**, such as **2/25/02**
- PRESS: ENTER

practice

You will now add date values as column headings. Ensure that you have completed the previous lesson.

1. Move to cell C2.
2. To enter a month and year combination as a date value, you can use the format mmm-yyyy. For example:
   TYPE: **Sep-2002**
   PRESS: →
   Excel reformats the value to appear as "Sep-02." So why wouldn't you type "Sep-02" in the first place? The answer is that Excel watches your entries and makes certain assumptions. If you enter "Sep-02," Excel assumes that you want September 2nd of the current year, which may or may not be 2002. By entering a four-digit year value, you avoid having Excel misinterpret your entry.
3. Starting in cell D2, do the following:
   TYPE: **Oct-2002**
   PRESS: →
   TYPE: **Nov-2002**
   PRESS: →
   TYPE: **Dec-2002**
   PRESS: ENTER
4. Move the cell pointer to cell C2 and compare your work with Figure 1.13. Looking in the Formula bar, notice that the date entry reads "9/1/2002" and not "Sep-02." As illustrated by this example, a cell's appearance on the worksheet can differ from its actual contents.

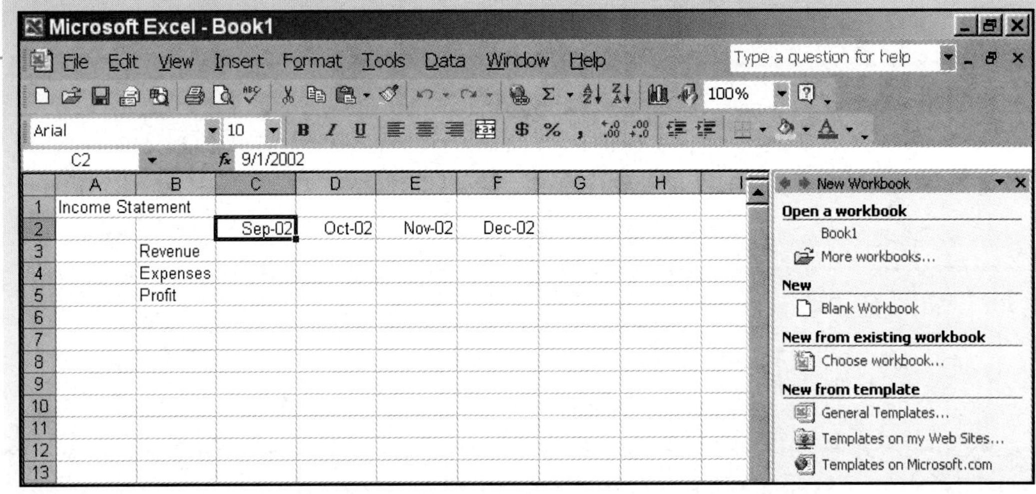

Figure 1.13
Entering date values into a worksheet

1.2.4 Entering Numbers

feature

Numbers are entered into a worksheet for use in performing calculations, preparing reports, and creating charts. You can enter a raw or unformatted number, like 3.141593, or a formatted number, such as 37.5% or $24,732.33. It is important to note that phone numbers, Social Security numbers, and zip codes are not treated as numeric values, since they are never used in performing mathematical calculations. Numbers and dates are right-aligned when entered as opposed to text, which aligns with the left border of a cell.

method

To enter numbers:

- TYPE: **a number**, such as **$9,987.65** or **12.345%**
- PRESS: ENTER

practice

You will now add some numbers to the worksheet. Ensure that you have completed the previous lesson.

1. Move to cell C3.
2. To enter a value for September's revenue, do the following:
   TYPE: **112,500**
   PRESS: →
   Notice that you placed a comma (,) in the entry to separate the thousands from the hundreds. Excel recognizes symbols such as commas, dollar signs, and percentage symbols as numeric formatting.
3. Starting in cell D3, do the following:
   TYPE: **115,800**
   PRESS: →
   TYPE: **98,750**

PRESS: →
TYPE: **112,830**
PRESS: ENTER

4. Move the cell pointer to cell C3 and compare your work with Figure 1.14. Notice that the Formula bar reads "112500" without a comma separating the thousands. Similar to date values, numeric values may be formatted to display differently than the actual value stored.

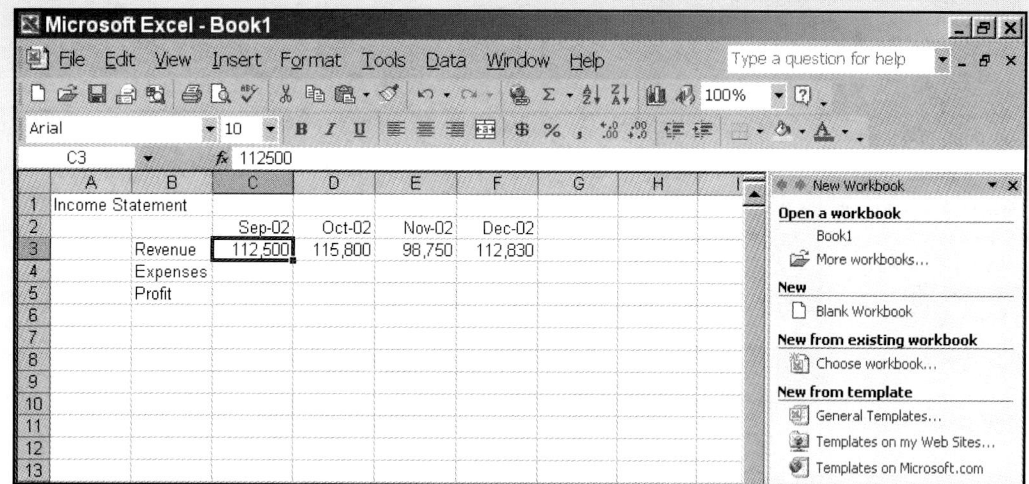

Figure 1.14

Entering numbers into a worksheet

1.2.5 Entering Formulas

feature

You use formulas to perform calculations, such as adding a column of numbers. A **formula** is an expression, containing numbers, cell references, and/or mathematical operators, that is entered into a cell in order to display a result. The basic mathematical operators ("+" for addition, "−" for subtraction, "/" for division, and "*" for multiplication) and rules of precedence from your high school algebra textbooks apply to an Excel formula. In other words, Excel calculates what appears in parentheses first, exponents second, multiplication and division operations (from left to right) third, and addition and subtraction (again from left to right) last.

method

To enter a formula:

- SELECT: the cell where you want the result to appear
- TYPE: = (an equal sign)
- TYPE: **a formula**, such as **a4+b4**
- PRESS: ENTER

practice

You will now enter formulas into the Income Statement worksheet. Ensure that you have completed the previous lesson.

Excel

1. Move to cell C4. Notice that the first step in entering a formula is to move to the cell where you want the result to display.

2. To tell Excel that you want to enter a formula, use an equal sign:
TYPE: =

3. In order to calculate September's expenses, multiply the cell containing the monthly revenue (cell C3) by 60%. Do the following:
TYPE: **c3*60%**
Your screen should appear similar to Figure 1.15. Notice that the formula's cell address is color-coded and that this coding corresponds to the cell borders highlighted in the worksheet. This feature, called **Range Finder,** is especially useful when you need to identify whether a calculation is drawing data from the correct cells.

Figure 1.15

Typing a formula expression into the Formula bar

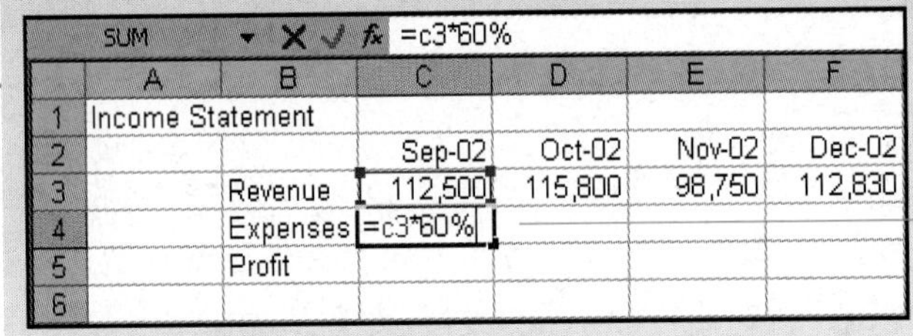

SUM =c3*60%

	A	B	C	D	E	F
1	Income Statement					
2			Sep-02	Oct-02	Nov-02	Dec-02
3		Revenue	112,500	115,800	98,750	112,830
4		Expenses	=c3*60%			
5		Profit				
6						

Notice that the blue-highlighted cell address in the formula expression corresponds with the cell outline immediately above.

4. To complete the entry and move to the next cell:
PRESS: →
The result, 67500, appears in the cell.

5. Let's use a method called *pointing* to enter the required formula into cell D4. With pointing, you use the mouse or keyboard to point to the cell reference that you want to include in an expression. To illustrate:
TYPE: =
PRESS: ↑
Notice that a dashed marquee appears around cell D3 and that the value "D3" appears in the Formula bar.

6. To finish entering the formula:
TYPE: ***60%**
PRESS: →
The result, 69480, appears in the cell.

7. For November's calculation, use the mouse to point to the desired cell reference. Do the following:
TYPE: =
CLICK: cell E3
Notice that cell E3 displays a dashed marquee to denote its selection.

8. To complete the row:
TYPE: ***60%**
PRESS: ➔
The result, 59250, appears.

9. Last, enter the formula for December by typing:
TYPE: **=f3*.6**
PRESS: ENTER
The result, 67698, appears in cell F4. Notice that you used the value .6 instead of 60% to yield this result. Your worksheet should now appear similar to Figure 1.16.

Figure 1.16

Entering formulas into a worksheet

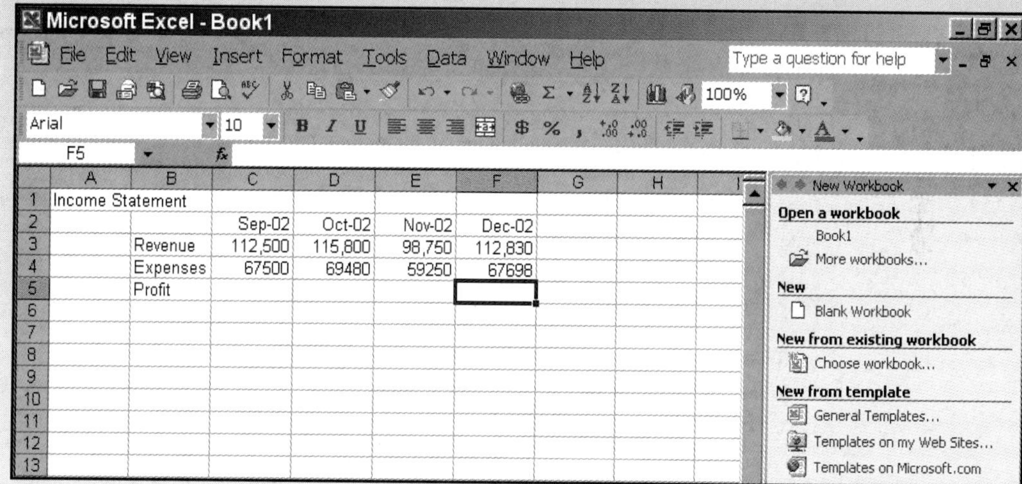

10. To finish the worksheet:
SELECT: cell C5

11. You will now enter a formula to calculate the profit by subtracting expenses from revenues for each month. Do the following:
TYPE: **=c3-c4**
Notice that "c3" appears in blue and "c4" appears in green, as shown below.

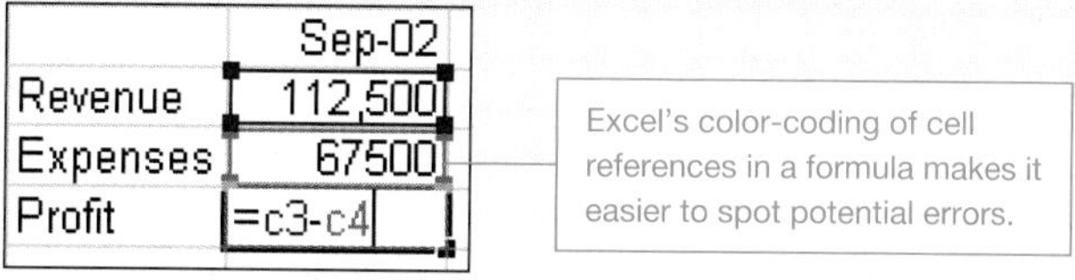

Excel's color-coding of cell references in a formula makes it easier to spot potential errors.

12. On your own, enter formulas into cells D5, E5, and F5 to complete the worksheet. Your screen should now appear similar to Figure 1.17.

Figure 1.17

Completing the worksheet

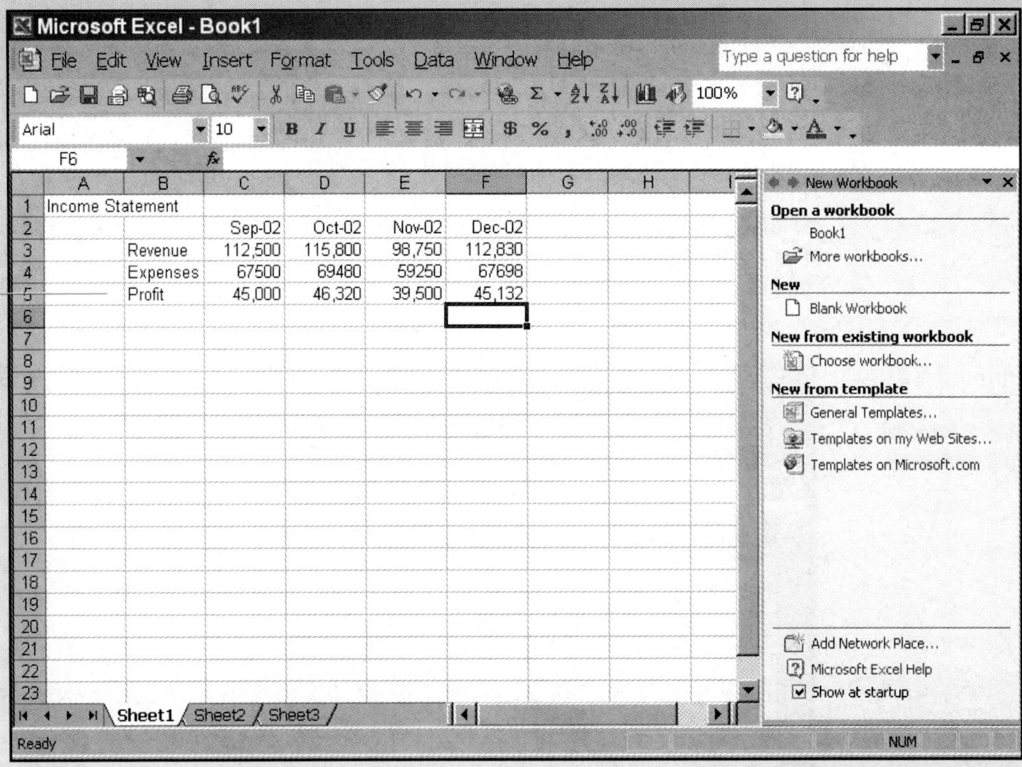

13. To illustrate the true power of an electronic worksheet, you will now change a single cell's value and watch all the formulas that reference that cell update automatically. Do the following:
SELECT: cell F3
TYPE: **100,000**
PRESS: ENTER
Notice that the Expense calculation for Dec-02 (cell F4) is immediately updated to 60000 and the Profit cell now displays 40,000.

14. To conclude the module, you will close the worksheet without saving the changes. From the Menu bar:
CHOOSE: File, Close
The following dialog box appears.

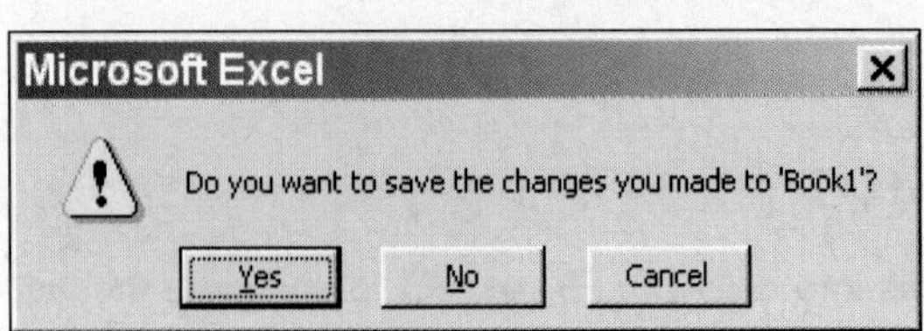

15. CLICK: No command button
There should be no workbooks open in the application window.

In Addition REFERENCING CELLS IN A FORMULA

Two types of cell addresses (also called *cell references*) can be entered into formulas: *relative* and *absolute.* A relative cell address, such as B4, is one that is relative in position to other cells on the worksheet. When copied within a formula to the next column, for example, the relative cell address "B4" adjusts automatically to become "C4." An absolute cell address, on the other hand, refers to a specific cell in the worksheet and does not adjust when copied. Absolute cell addresses contain dollar signs, such as $B$4. It is important to note that Excel defaults to using relative cell addresses in your formulas. Relative and absolute cell referencing are covered further in Chapter 4.

1.2 Explain why a phone number is not considered a numeric value in an Excel worksheet.

1.3 Editing Your Work

What if you type a label, a number, or a formula into a cell and then decide it needs to be changed? Novices and experts alike make data entry errors when creating a worksheet. Fortunately, Excel provides several features for editing information that has already been entered. In this module, you learn how to modify existing cell entries, erase the contents of a cell, and undo a command or typing error.

1.3.1 Editing a Cell's Contents

feature

You can edit information either as you type or after you have entered data into a cell. Effective editing of a worksheet is an extremely valuable skill. Few worksheets are created from scratch anymore. In fact, most worksheets are prepared by revising existing or template-generated worksheets. As a relatively new user of Excel, you will typically find yourself modifying and maintaining worksheets created by other people.

method

To edit cell contents:

- To edit data as you type, press BACKSPACE and then correct the typographical error or spelling mistake.
- To replace a cell's contents entirely, select the cell and then type over the original data. When you press ENTER or select another cell, the new information overwrites the existing data.
- To edit a cell in which the text is too long or complicated to retype, double-click the cell to perform **in-cell editing.** In this mode, the flashing insertion point appears ready for editing inside the cell. Alternatively, you can press the F2 (Edit) key or click in the Formula bar to enter Edit mode, in which case you edit the cell's contents in the Formula bar. Regardless, once the insertion point appears, you perform your edits using the arrow keys, DELETE, and BACKSPACE.

practice

In this lesson, you create a simple inventory worksheet and then practice modifying the data stored in the worksheet cells. Ensure that no workbooks are open in the application window.

1. To display a new workbook and worksheet:
CLICK: New button ( ) on the Standard toolbar
A new workbook, entitled Book2, appears in the document area and the task pane is hidden. (*Note:* As an alternative to using the toolbar, you can start a new workbook by clicking the "Blank Workbook" option under the *New* heading in the New Workbook task pane.)

2. SELECT: cell A1
(*Note:* For the remainder of this guide, you may use either the keyboard or mouse to move the cell pointer.)

3. Let's enter a title for this worksheet:
TYPE: **Staples Food Supplies**
PRESS: ↓
TYPE: **Inventory List**
PRESS: ENTER

4. SELECT: cell A4

5. Now let's add some column headings:
TYPE: **Code**
PRESS: →
TYPE: **Product**
PRESS: →
TYPE: **Quantity**
PRESS: →
TYPE: **Price**
PRESS: ENTER

6. On your own, complete the worksheet as displayed in Figure 1.18. If you make a typing error, use BACKSPACE to correct your mistake prior to pressing ENTER or an arrow key.

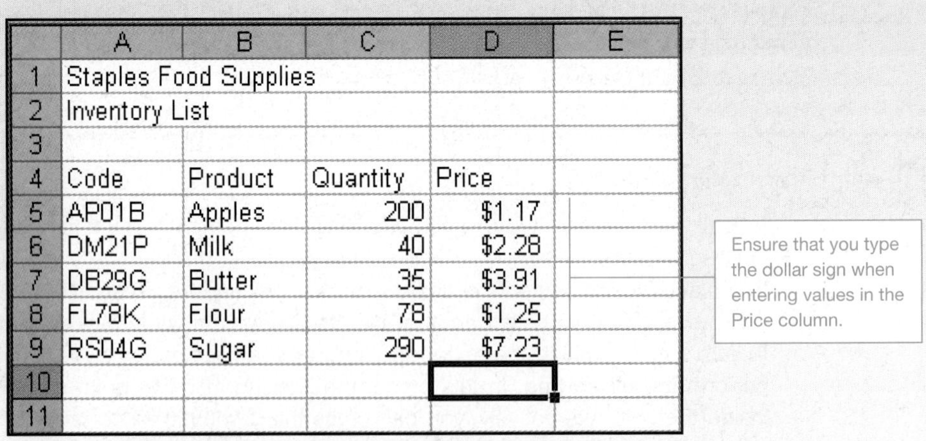

Figure 1.18

Creating an inventory worksheet

	A	B	C	D	E
1	Staples Food Supplies				
2	Inventory List				
3					
4	Code	Product	Quantity	Price	
5	AP01B	Apples	200	$1.17	
6	DM21P	Milk	40	$2.28	
7	DB29G	Butter	35	$3.91	
8	FL78K	Flour	78	$1.25	
9	RS04G	Sugar	290	$7.23	
10					
11					

Ensure that you type the dollar sign when entering values in the Price column.

7. As the editor for this worksheet, you would like to change the column heading in cell D4 to read "Cost" and not "Price." To replace this entry:
SELECT: cell D4

8. TYPE: **Cost**
PRESS: ENTER
Notice that the new entry overwrites the existing cell contents. (*Hint:* If you start typing an entry in the wrong cell, you can press ESC to exit Edit mode and restore the previous value.)

9. You activate in-cell editing by double-clicking a cell. To practice, let's change the quantity of butter from 35 to 350 packages:
DOUBLE-CLICK: cell C7
Notice that the Status bar now reads "Edit" in the bottom left-hand corner, instead of the word "Ready." A flashing insertion point also appears inside the cell, as shown here.

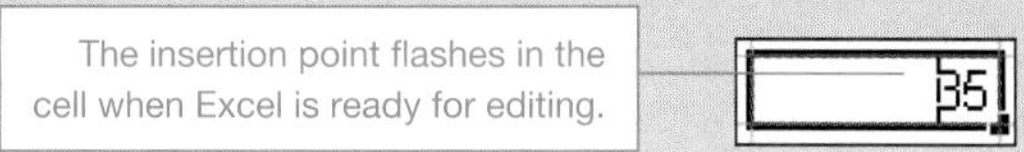

The insertion point flashes in the cell when Excel is ready for editing.
35

10. To add a "0" to the end of the cell's contents:
PRESS: END to move the insertion point to the far right
TYPE: **0**
PRESS: ENTER
Notice that the Status bar once again reads "Ready" in the bottom left-hand corner.

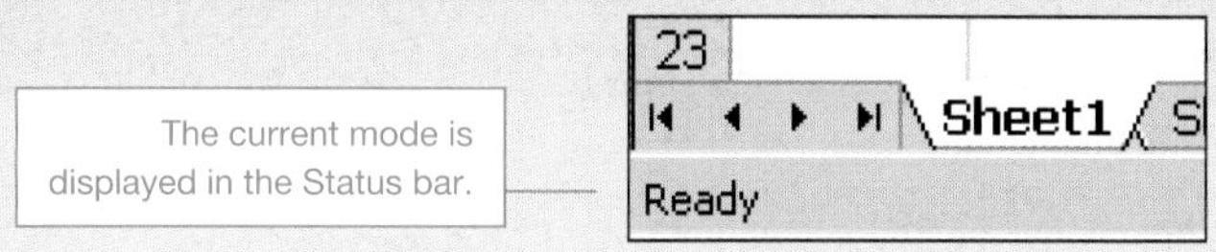

The current mode is displayed in the Status bar.
23
Sheet1
Ready

11. You can also activate Edit mode by pressing the F2 (Edit) key or by clicking the I-beam mouse pointer inside the Formula bar. In this step, you edit one of the product codes. Do the following:
SELECT: cell A6
Notice that the text "DM21P" appears in the Formula bar.

12. To modify "DM" to read "DN," position the I-beam mouse pointer over the Formula bar entry, immediately to the left of the letter "M." Click the left mouse button and drag the mouse pointer to the right until the "M" is highlighted, as shown below.

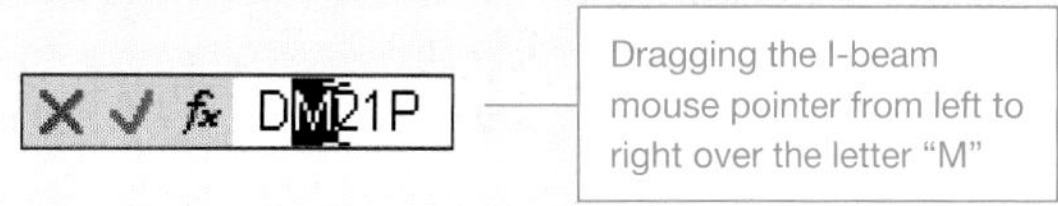

13. Now that the desired letter is selected:
TYPE: **N**
PRESS: ENTER
The letter "N" replaces the selected letter in the Formula bar. Your screen should now appear similar to Figure 1.19.

Excel

Figure 1.19

Editing a worksheet

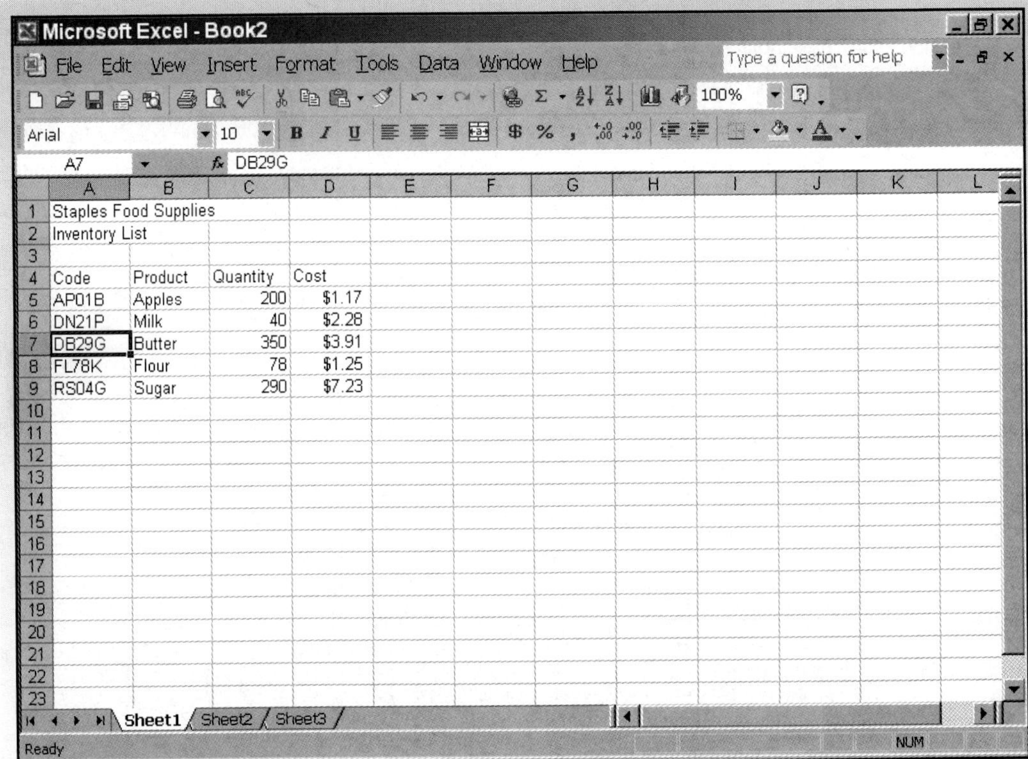

1.3.2 Selecting and Erasing Cell Contents

feature

You can quickly erase a single cell, a group of cells, or the entire worksheet with a few simple keystrokes. To erase a cell's contents, select the cell and then press DELETE. You can also use the mouse to drag over a range of cells prior to pressing DELETE. If you would like to delete other characteristics of a cell, such as formatting attributes or attached comments, choose the Edit, Clear command from the Menu bar.

method

To erase the contents of a cell or group of cells:

- SELECT: the cell or cell range
- PRESS: DELETE

To remove other attributes of a cell or cell range:

- CHOOSE: Edit, Clear
- SELECT: *one of the command options*

All	Removes the cell contents and other attributes
Formats	Removes the cell formatting only
Contents	Removes the cell contents only (DELETE)
Comments	Removes the cell comments only

practice

You will now practice erasing information that is stored in the inventory worksheet. Ensure that you have completed the previous lesson.

1. SELECT: cell A2
2. To delete the subtitle:
PRESS: DELETE
Notice that you need not press ENTER or any other confirmation key. Pressing DELETE removes the contents of the cell immediately.
3. SELECT: cell A9
4. In order to delete more than one cell at a time, you first select the desired range of cells. In this step, you will select the cells from A9 to D9. Do the following:
PRESS: SHIFT and hold it down
CLICK: cell D9
RELEASE: SHIFT
The four cells should now appear highlighted, as shown in Figure 1.20.

Figure 1.20

Selecting a group of cells to erase

	A	B	C	D	E
1	Staples Food Supplies				
2					
3					
4	Code	Product	Quantity	Cost	
5	AP01B	Apples	200	$1.17	
6	DN21P	Milk	40	$2.28	
7	DB29G	Butter	350	$3.91	
8	FL78K	Flour	78	$1.25	
9	RS04G	Sugar	290	$7.23	
10					
11					

Cell A9 is the active cell in this cell range, as noted by the white background.

5. To erase all of the cell information, including contents and formatting:
CHOOSE: Edit, Clear from the Menu bar
CHOOSE: All from the cascading menu
6. To erase the dollar values in the Cost column:
CLICK: cell D5 and keep the mouse button pressed down
DRAG: the mouse pointer downward to cell D8
Your screen should now appear similar to Figure 1.21.

Figure 1.21

Selecting cells using the mouse

	A	B	C	D	E
1	Staples Food Supplies				
2					
3					
4	Code	Product	Quantity	Cost	
5	AP01B	Apples	200	$1.17	
6	DN21P	Milk	40	$2.28	
7	DB29G	Butter	350	$3.91	
8	FL78K	Flour	78	$1.25	
9					
10					
11					

After clicking cell D5, keep the mouse button depressed and drag the mouse pointer down to cell D8. Once the desired cells are highlighted, you may release the mouse button.

Excel

7. Release the mouse button when the cells are highlighted.
8. PRESS: DELETE to remove the contents of the cell range
9. PRESS: CTRL + HOME to move the cell pointer to cell A1

1.3.3 Using Undo and Redo

feature

The **Undo command** allows you to cancel up to your last 16 actions. The command is most useful for immediately reversing a command or modification that was mistakenly performed. If an error occurred several steps before, you can continue "undoing" commands until you return the worksheet to its original state prior to the mistake. Although it sounds somewhat confusing, you can use the Redo command to undo an Undo command. The **Redo command** allows you to reverse an Undo command that you performed accidentally.

method

To reverse an action or command:

- CLICK: Undo button ( )

or

- CHOOSE: Edit, Undo

or

- PRESS: CTRL +z

To reverse an Undo command:

- CLICK: Redo button ( )

practice

Let's practice reversing some editing mistakes using the Undo command. Ensure that you have completed the previous lesson.

1. SELECT: cell A5
2. In order to practice using the Undo command, let's delete the contents of the cell:
   PRESS: DELETE
3. To undo the last command or action performed:
   CLICK: Undo button ( ) on the Standard toolbar
   (*CAUTION:* The tip of the mouse pointer should be placed over the curved arrow and not on the attached down arrow.)
4. SELECT: cell C5
5. To modify the quantity of apples:
   TYPE: **175**
   PRESS: ENTER
6. To undo the last entry using a keyboard shortcut:
   PRESS: CTRL +z
   The value 175 is replaced with 200 in cell C5. (*Hint:* This shortcut keystroke is useful for quickly undoing a command or incorrect entry.)

7. Now let's see how Excel tracks commands for the Undo command. Do the following:
SELECT: cell B5
TYPE: **Oranges**
PRESS: ⬇
TYPE: **Juice**
PRESS: ENTER

8. Let's view the commands that Excel has been tracking for the Undo command. To begin, position the mouse pointer over the down arrow attached to the Undo button (↶ ▾) on the Standard toolbar. Then click the down arrow once to display the drop-down list of "undoable" or reversible commands.

9. Move the mouse pointer slowly downward to select the two entries. Your screen should appear similar to Figure 1.22.

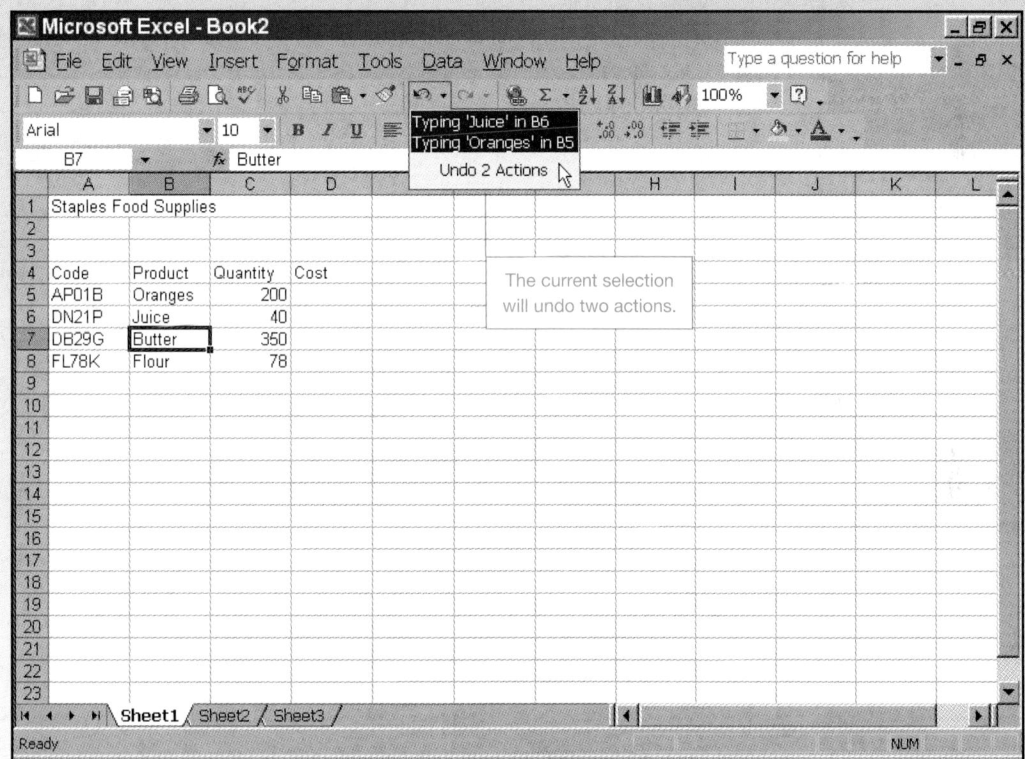

Figure 1.22
Displaying reversible commands

10. To perform the Undo operation, ensure that the items are highlighted as shown in Figure 1.22 and then do the following:
CLICK: "Typing 'Oranges' in B5" Undo option
(*Hint:* To remove the Undo drop-down menu, click the Title bar or the button's attached down arrow again.)

11. To conclude this module, close the worksheet without saving the changes. Do the following:
CHOOSE: File, Close

12. When the dialog box appears:
CLICK: No command button

1.3 Why is worksheet editing such a valuable skill?

1.4 Managing Files

Managing the workbook files that you create is an important skill. When you are creating a workbook, it exists only in the computer's RAM (random access memory), which is highly volatile. If the power to your computer goes off, your workbook is lost. For this reason, you need to save your workbook permanently to the local hard disk, a network drive, or a removable disk. Creating, saving, opening, and closing workbooks are considered file management operations.

Saving your work to a named file on a disk is similar to placing it into a filing cabinet. For important workbooks (ones that you cannot risk losing), you should save your work at least every 15 minutes, or whenever you're interrupted, to protect against an unexpected power outage or other catastrophe. Saving a file without closing it is like placing a current copy in a filing cabinet. When naming workbook files, you can use up to 255 characters, including spaces, but it's wise to keep the length under 20 characters. You cannot, however, use the following characters:

\ / : ; * ? " < > |

In this module, you practice creating a new workbook, saving and closing workbooks, creating workbook folders, and opening existing workbooks.

Important: *In this guide, we refer to the files that have been created for you as the student data files. Depending on your computer or lab setup, these files may be located on a floppy diskette, in a folder on your hard disk, or on a network server. If necessary, ask your instructor or lab assistant where to find these data files. You will also need to identify a storage location for the files that you create, modify, and save. To download the Advantage Series' student data files from the Internet, visit our Web sites at:*

http://www.mhhe.com/it

http://www.advantageseries.com

1.4.1 Beginning a New Workbook

feature →

There are three ways to start creating a new workbook. First, you can start with a blank workbook and enter all of the data from scratch. This is the method that you've used to this point in the chapter. Next, you can select a workbook **template** that provides preexisting data and design elements. A template is a timesaving utility that promotes consistency in both design and function. And last, you can employ a **wizard** to lead you step-by-step through creating a particular type of workbook.

method →

To display a new blank workbook:

- CLICK: New button ()

To begin a workbook using a template or wizard:

- CHOOSE: File, New

practice

In this example, you use a workbook template to create a new workbook for an invoicing application. Ensure that no workbooks are displayed in the application window.

1. To view the templates that are available:
CHOOSE: File, New
The New Workbook task pane appears in the work area, as shown here.

2. Using the hand mouse pointer ():
CLICK: General Templates, located under the *New from template* heading

3. The blank "Workbook" template icon appears selected on the *General* tab of the Templates dialog box. Excel accesses this template when you click the New button () on the Standard toolbar. To view the custom templates that are shipped with Excel, do the following:
CLICK: *Spreadsheet Solutions tab*
Your screen should now appear similar to Figure 1.23.
(*Note:* Depending on how Excel was installed and configured on your system, different template options may appear in your dialog box.)

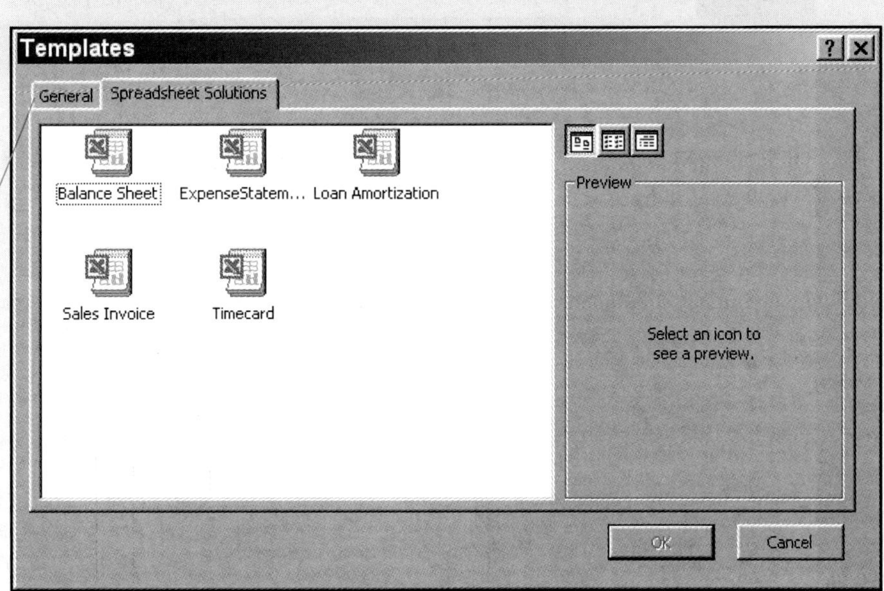

Figure 1.23

Displaying custom workbook templates

By default, Excel provides the *General* and *Spreadsheet Solutions* tabs for organizing workbook templates.

4. To create a new workbook based on the "Sales Invoice" template:
DOUBLE-CLICK: Sales Invoice template icon ()
(*Note:* If you or your lab administrator has not installed the workbook templates, you must skip to step 5.)

5. If the selected template has not been installed, Excel attempts to find and install it. Assuming that it is available, Excel loads the template and displays the workbook shown in Figure 1.24. (*Note:* A warning dialog box may appear stating that the template may contain a **macro virus.** A virus is a hostile program that is secretly stored and shipped inside another program or document. As this template is from Microsoft and not an unknown source, you can safely enable the macros.)

Figure 1.24

New workbook based on the Invoice template

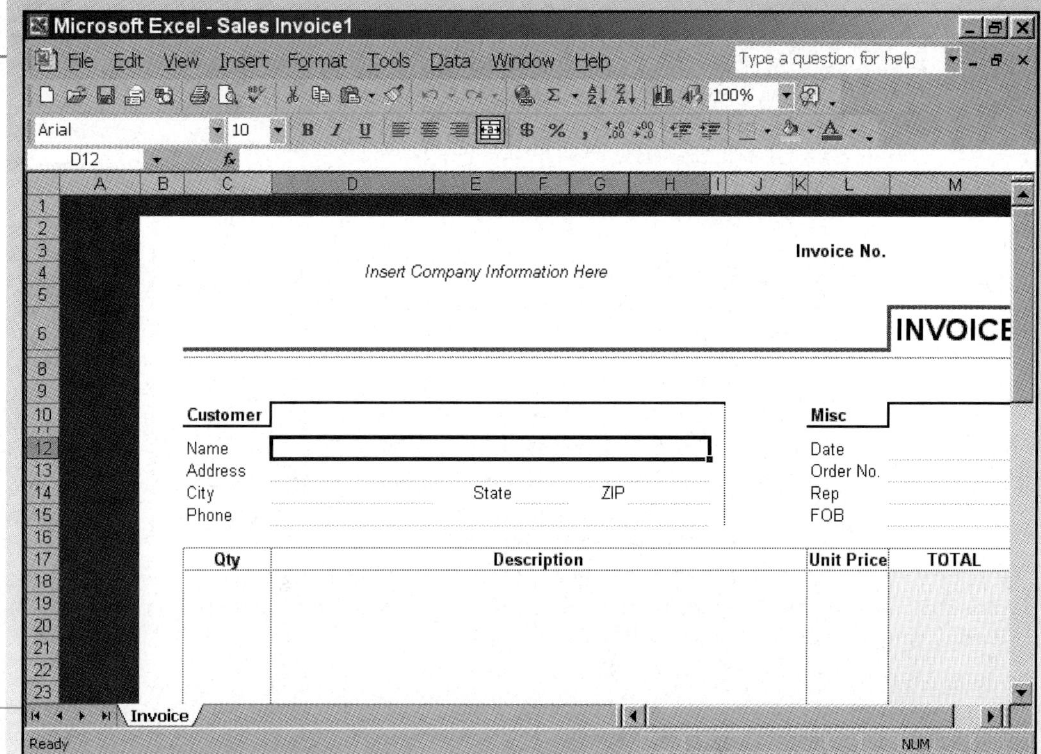

The Sales Invoice1 workbook contains a single worksheet tab named "Invoice."

6. The workbook templates provided by Excel contain many advanced features. Rather than introducing these features now, let's close the workbook and continue our discussion of file management.
CHOOSE: File, Close
CLICK: No command button, if asked whether to save the changes

In Addition ACCESSING OTHER WORKBOOK TEMPLATES

Besides the templates that ship with Microsoft Office XP, additional templates are available for free on the Internet. In the New Workbook task pane are two options that you may use to download such templates. First, the Templates on my Web Sites option lets you retrieve workbook templates stored on Web servers from around the world. This option is especially useful for a company using an *intranet* to share files. Second, the Templates on Microsoft.com option launches a Microsoft Web page in your default browser. Before creating a new workbook from scratch, you can peruse these templates to search for a possible starting point.

1.4.2 Saving and Closing

Many options are available for saving a workbook to a permanent storage location. The File, Save command and the Save button (💾) on the toolbar allow you to overwrite an existing disk file with the latest version of a workbook. The File, Save As command enables you to save a workbook to a new filename or storage location. You can also specify a different file format, such as an earlier version of Excel, for the workbook using the Save As command. This is especially handy when you need to share a workbook with associates who haven't upgraded to the latest version of Excel. Once you have finished working with a workbook, make sure you close the file to free up valuable system resources (RAM).

Excel

method

To save a workbook:

- CLICK: Save button
or
- CHOOSE: File, Save
or
- CHOOSE: File, Save As

To close a workbook:

- CLICK: its Close button
or
- CHOOSE: File, Close

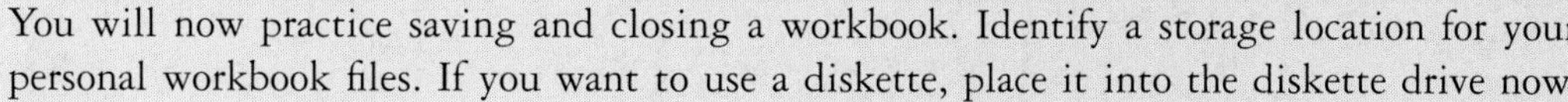

practice

You will now practice saving and closing a workbook. Identify a storage location for your personal workbook files. If you want to use a diskette, place it into the diskette drive now.

1. To create a new workbook from scratch:
CLICK: New button
TYPE: **My First Workbook** into cell A1
PRESS: ENTER

2. To save the new workbook:
CLICK: Save button
(*Note:* If the current workbook has not yet been saved, Excel displays the Save As dialog box regardless of the method you chose to save the file. The filenames and folder directories that appear in your Save As dialog box may differ from those shown in Figure 1.25.)

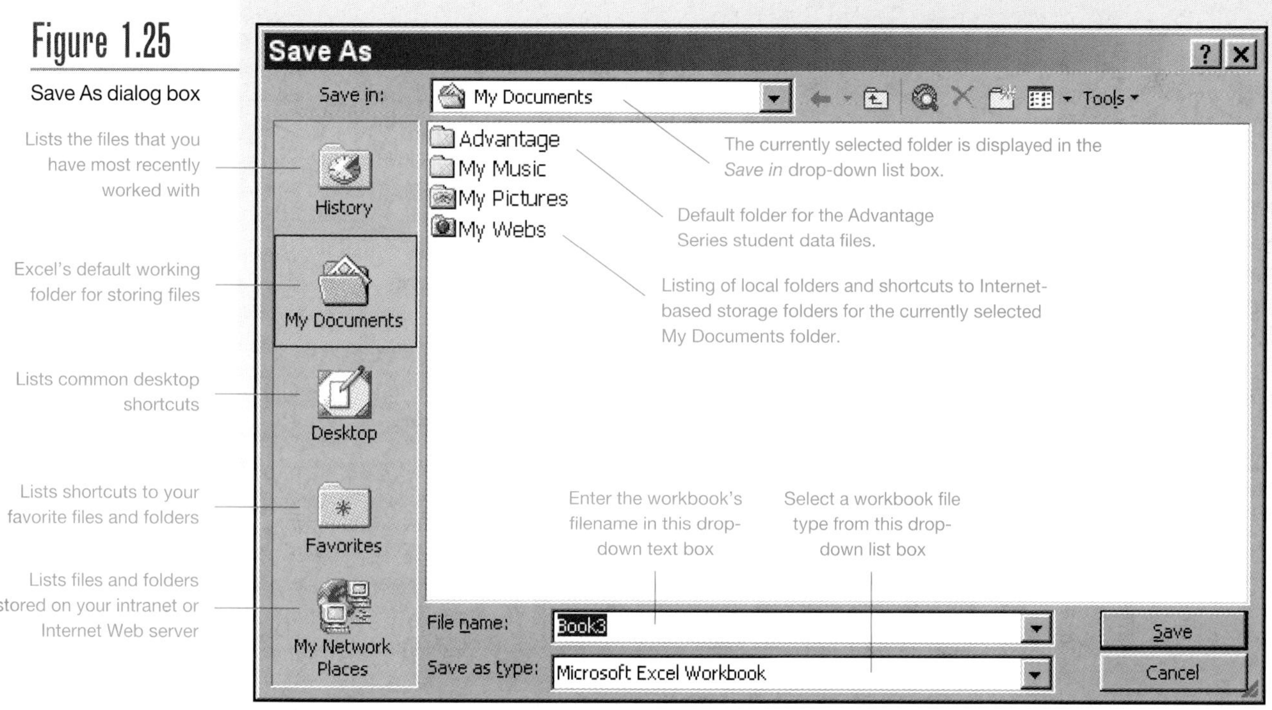

Figure 1.25

Save As dialog box

3. The **Places bar,** located along the left border of the dialog box, provides convenient access to commonly used storage locations. To illustrate, let's view the files in your My Documents folder:
CLICK: My Documents folder button, as shown here

4. Let's navigate through the storage areas:
CLICK: down arrow attached to the Save in drop-down list box
Your screen will appear similar, but not identical, to Figure 1.26.

Figure 1.26

Navigating the storage areas

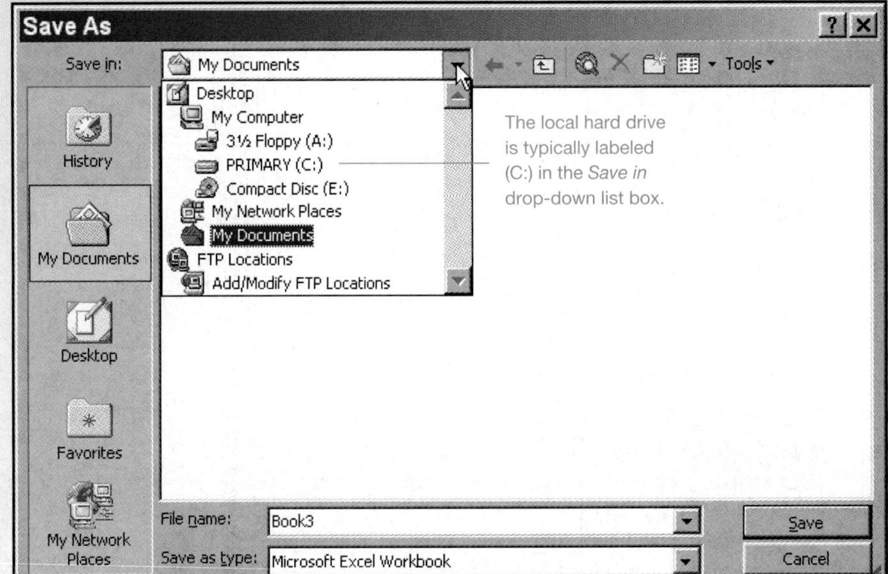

5. To browse the local hard drive:
SELECT: your local hard disk, usually labeled (C:)
The list area displays the folders and files stored in the root directory of your local hard disk. (*Note:* Your instructor may provide an alternate storage location if drive C: is not accessible.)

6. To drill down into one of the folders:
DOUBLE-CLICK: Program Files folder
This folder contains the program files for several applications. Figure 1.27 shows how full of applications this folder can become.

Figure 1.27

The Program Files folder of the author's local hard drive (C:)

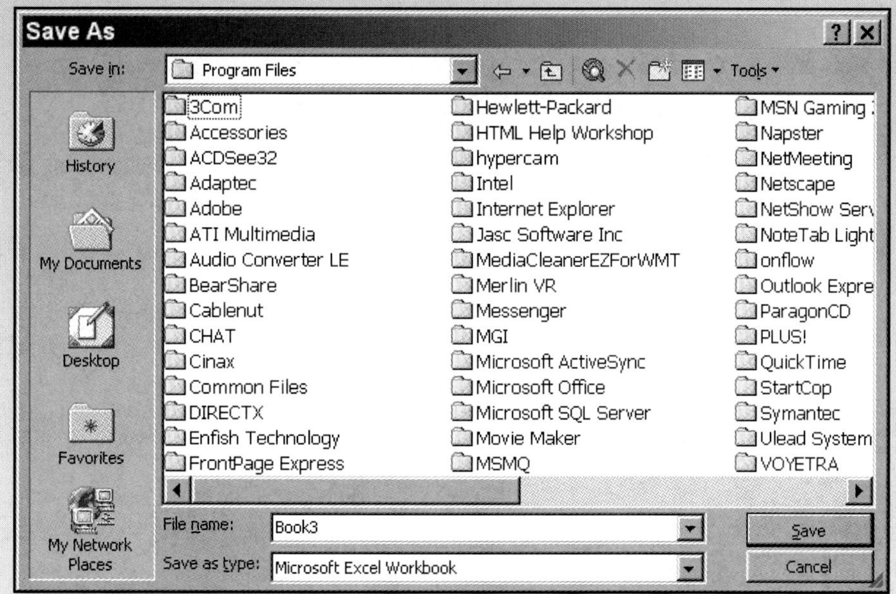

7. To return to the previous display:
   CLICK: Back button (⇦) in the dialog box

8. Now, using either the Places bar or the Save in drop-down list box:
   SELECT: *a storage location for your personal files*
   (*Note:* In this guide, we save files to either the My Documents folder or to a new folder you create in lesson 1.4.4.)

9. Let's give the workbook file a unique name. Position the I-beam mouse pointer over the workbook name in the *File name* text box and then:
   DOUBLE-CLICK: the *workbook name,* "Book3" in this example
   The entire workbook name should appear highlighted.

10. To replace the existing workbook name:
    TYPE: **My First Workbook** as shown below

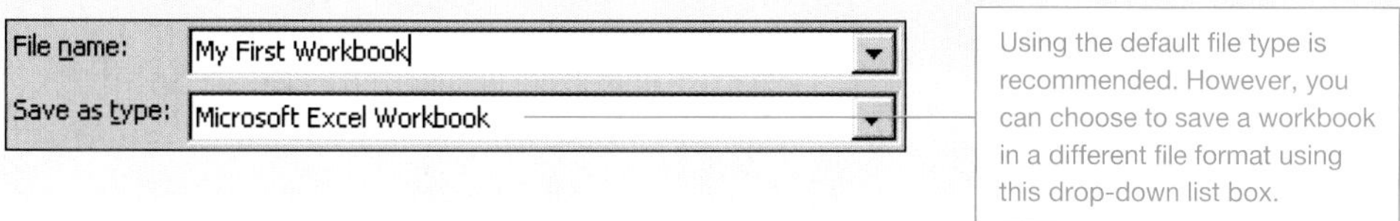

Using the default file type is recommended. However, you can choose to save a workbook in a different file format using this drop-down list box.

11. To complete the procedure:
    CLICK: Save command button
    When you are returned to the worksheet, notice that the workbook's name now appears in the Title bar.

12. Let's close the workbook:
CHOOSE: File, Close

Sometimes you'll want to save an existing workbook under a different filename. For example, you may want to keep different versions of the same workbook on your disk. Or, you may want to use one workbook as a template for future workbooks that are similar in style and format. Rather than retyping an entirely new workbook, you can retrieve an old workbook file, edit the information, and then save it under a different name using the File, Save As command. Furthermore, in the New Workbook task pane, the "Choose workbook" option in the New from existing workbook area allows you to create a new workbook based on the contents of an existing file.

1.4.3 Opening an Existing Workbook

feature →

You use the Open dialog box to search for and retrieve existing workbooks that are stored on your local hard disk, a floppy diskette, a network server, or on the Web. If you want to load an existing workbook when you start Excel, use the Open Office Document command on the Start menu. Or, if you have recently used the workbook, you can try the Start, Documents command, which lists the most recently used files.

method →

To open an existing workbook:

- CLICK: Open button ( )

or

- CHOOSE: File, Open

practice →

You will now retrieve a student data file named EX0140 that displays the market penetration for snowboard sales by Canadian province. Ensure that you have completed the previous lesson. There should be no workbooks displayed in the application window. You will also need to know the storage location for the student data files.

1. To display the Open dialog box:
CLICK: Open button ( )

2. Using the Places bar and the *Look in* drop-down list box, locate the folder containing the student data files. (*Note:* In this guide, we retrieve the student data files from a folder named "Advantage.") Your screen should appear similar to Figure 1.28 before proceeding.

Figure 1.28

Viewing the student data files for the Microsoft Excel Brief Edition tutorial

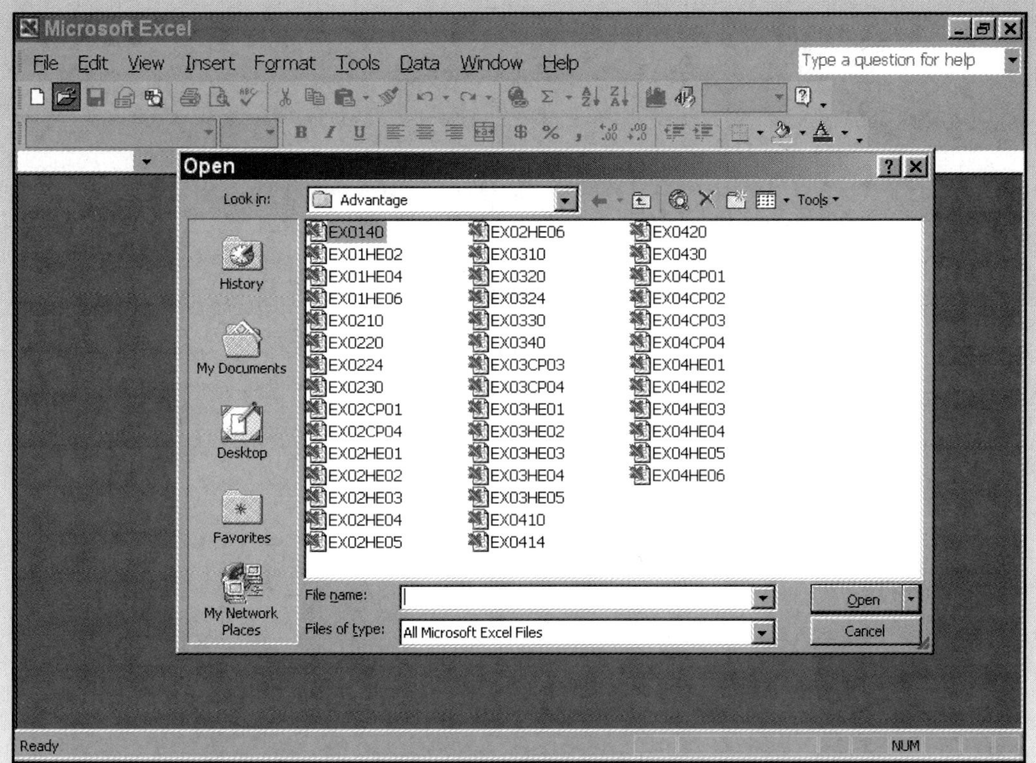

3. To view additional information about each file:
CLICK: down arrow beside the Views button
The drop-down list shown at right appears.

4. CHOOSE: Details
Each workbook is presented on a single line with additional file information, such as its size, type, and date. (*Hint:* You can sort the filenames in this list area by clicking on one of the column heading buttons.)

5. To return to a multicolumn list format:
CLICK: down arrow beside the Views button
CHOOSE: List
Your screen should look like Figure 1.28 once again.

6. Let's open one of the workbooks:
DOUBLE-CLICK: EX0140
The dialog box disappears and the workbook is loaded into the application window, as shown in Figure 1.29. (*Note:* The "EX0140" filename reflects that this workbook is used in module 1.4 of the Microsoft Excel learning guide.)

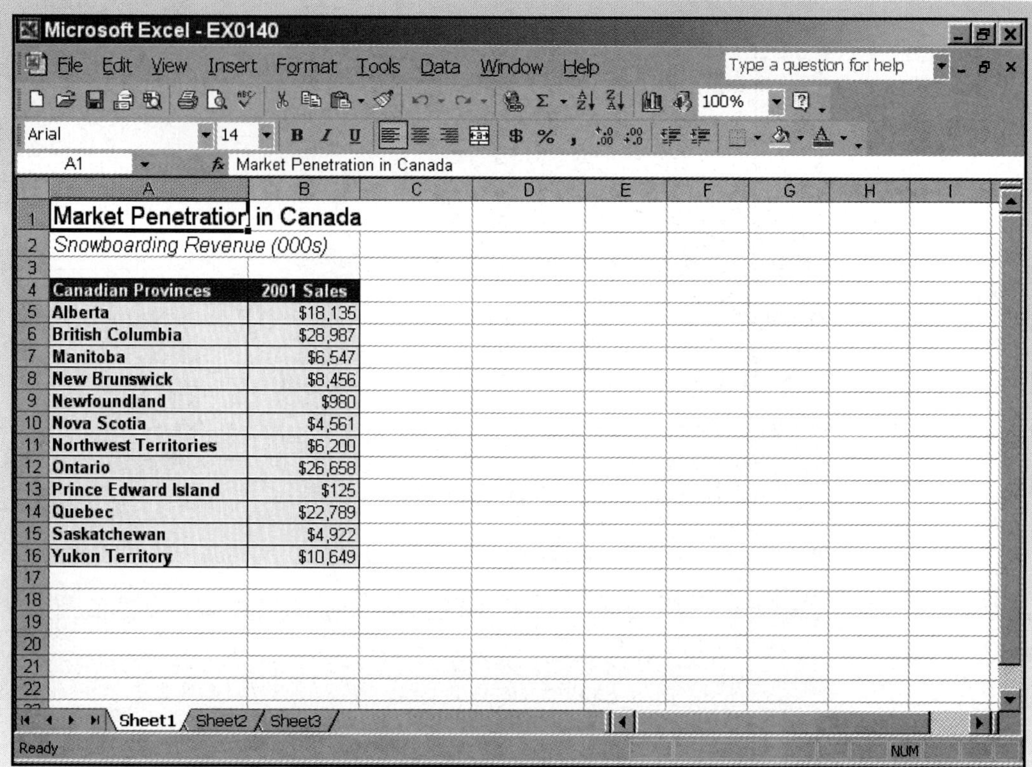

Figure 1.29

Opening the EX0140 workbook

7. Let's make a small change to the workbook. Do the following:
   SELECT: cell B5
   TYPE: **18500**
   PRESS: ENTER
   Notice that you need not type the dollar sign and comma, since the cell already contains the formatting information required to display the value as "$18,500."

8. Now proceed to the next lesson to learn how to create a new folder for saving and storing the modified workbook.

In Addition OPENING AND SAVING FILES OF DIFFERENT FORMATS

In the Open and Save As dialog boxes, you will notice a drop-down list box named *Files of type* and *Save as type* respectively. These list boxes allow you to select different file formats for opening and saving your files. For instance, you can save a workbook so that users with an earlier version of Excel are able to open and edit its contents. You can also open a file that was created using another spreadsheet software program, such as Lotus or Quattro Pro.

1.4.4 Creating a Workbook Folder

Folders can help you organize your work. They also make it easier to find documents and back up your data. For example, you can use a folder to collect all of the workbooks related to a single fiscal period. You can also specify a folder to hold all of your personal documents, such as resumes and expense reports. Although Windows Explorer should be used for most folder management tasks, Excel allows you to create a new folder from the Save As dialog box. After you navigate to where you want the folder to appear, click the Create New Folder button ( ) and then complete the steps presented below.

method

To create a new workbook folder:

- CLICK: Create New Folder button (📁) in the Save As dialog box
- TYPE: **a name** for the new folder
- CLICK: OK command button

practice

You now create a folder for storing the workbooks that you will create in the remaining pages of this tutorial. Ensure that you have completed the previous lesson.

1. You create a new folder for your workbooks using the File, Save As command. To begin:
CHOOSE: File, Save As

2. This exercise assumes that you are able to create folders on your computer's local hard disk. If this is not the case, you may substitute a removable diskette drive for the My Documents folder. To begin, use the Places bar to select the desired location for the new folder:
CLICK: My Documents folder button (shown here)

3. To create a subfolder in the My Documents folder:
CLICK: Create New Folder button (📁)
Your screen should now appear similar to Figure 1.30.

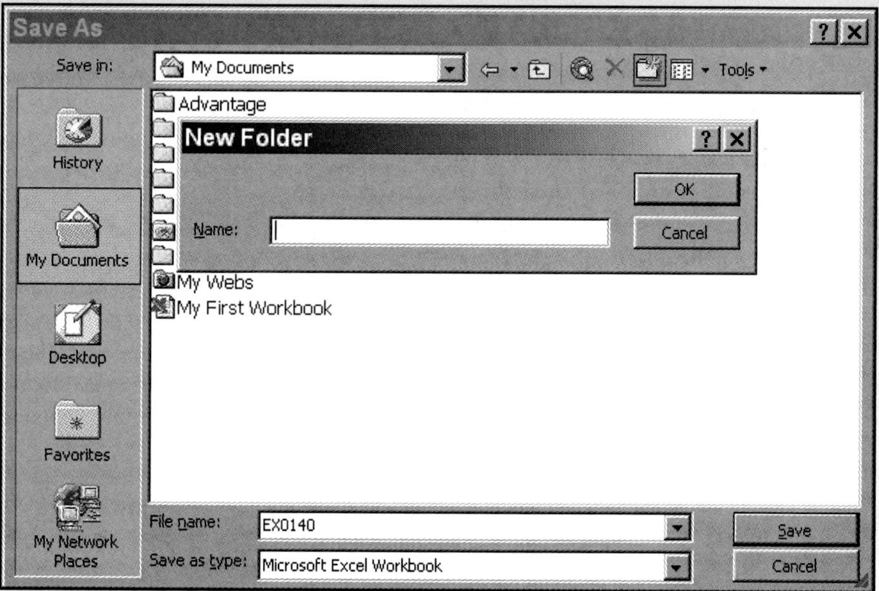

Figure 1.30

Creating a new folder in the Save As dialog box

4. In the New Folder dialog box:
TYPE: **My Workbooks**
CLICK: OK command button
You are immediately transferred into the new folder, as shown in the *Save in* drop-down list box.

5. Now you can save the workbook in the new folder. Let's choose a different filename for the workbook:
DOUBLE-CLICK: "EX0140" in the *File name* text box
The filename should appear highlighted before you proceed.

6. To replace the existing workbook name:
TYPE: **Snowboarding** as shown below

7. To complete the procedure:
CLICK: Save command button

8. Let's close the workbook:
CHOOSE: File, Close

9. To exit Microsoft Excel:
CHOOSE: File, Exit

In Addition RENAMING AND DELETING A WORKBOOK FOLDER

Besides creating a workbook folder using the Open or Save As dialog boxes, you can rename and delete folders displayed in the list area. To rename a folder, right-click the folder and then choose Rename from the shortcut menu that appears. The folder's name will appear in Edit mode within the list area. Type the new name and press ENTER. (*Hint:* You can also click on a folder twice slowly in order to edit a folder's name.) To delete a folder, right-click the desired folder and choose the Delete command. You will be asked to confirm the folder deletion in a dialog box. Make sure that you do not accidentally delete a folder containing files that you want to keep! To avoid this, you should open a folder and view its contents before performing the Delete command.

1.4 In the Open and Save As dialog boxes, how do the List and Details views differ? Name two other views that are accessible from the Views button.

Chapter summary

Microsoft Excel is an electronic spreadsheet program. Spreadsheet software is used extensively in business and other areas for performing statistical analyses, summarizing numerical data, and publishing reports. To create a worksheet in Excel, you enter text, numbers, dates, and formulas in cells. Editing worksheets is an important skill because many worksheets are regularly updated for long-term use. File management—creating, saving, and opening workbook files, and creating a workbook folder for storing your work—is also an important skill.

Command Summary

Many of the commands and procedures appearing in this chapter are summarized in the following table.

Skill Set	To Perform This Task	Do the Following
Using Excel	Launch Microsoft Excel	CLICK: Start button (Start) CHOOSE: Programs, Microsoft Excel
	Exit Microsoft Excel	CLICK: its Close button (×), or CHOOSE: File, Exit
	Close a workbook	CLICK: its Close button (×), or CHOOSE: File, Close
	Customize menus and toolbars	CHOOSE: Tools, Customize
Managing Workbooks	Create a new workbook	CLICK: New button, or CHOOSE: File, New and make a selection from the New Workbook task pane
	Use a template to create a new workbook	CHOOSE: File, New CLICK: General Templates under the *New from template* area of the New Workbook task pane CLICK: *Spreadsheet Solutions* tab in the Templates dialog box DOUBLE-CLICK: *a template*
	Locate and open an existing workbook	CLICK: Open button, or CHOOSE: File, Open
	Open files of different formats	SELECT: a format from the *Files of type* drop-down list box in the Open dialog box
	Save a workbook	CLICK: Save button, or CHOOSE: File, Save
	Save a workbook using a different filename, location, or format	CHOOSE: File, Save As
	Create a new folder while displaying the Save As dialog box	CLICK: Create New Folder button
Working with Cells and Cell Data	Navigate to a specific cell	CLICK: in the Name box TYPE: **a cell address**
	Enter text labels, numbers, and dates	TYPE: **"the desired" entry**
	Enter a formula	TYPE: =**expression**
	Replace a cell's contents with new data	TYPE: **a new entry**
	Activate Edit mode to revise a cell's contents	DOUBLE-CLICK: the desired cell, or CLICK: in the Formula bar, or PRESS: F2 (Edit) key
	Delete cell contents	PRESS: DELETE
	Delete all information associated with a cell	CHOOSE: Edit, Clear, All
	Reverse or undo a command or series of commands	CLICK: Undo button, or CHOOSE: Edit, Undo, or PRESS: CTRL+z
	Reverse or undo an Undo command	CLICK: Redo button

Excel

Key Terms

This section specifies page references for the key terms identified in this chapter. For a complete list of definitions, refer to the Glossary at the back of this learning guide.

adaptive menus, *p. EX 9*
application window, *p. EX 5*
cell, *p. EX 2*
cell address, *p. EX 2*
cell pointer, *p. EX 11*
chart sheet, *p. EX 3*
document window, *p. EX 5*
formula, *p. EX 17*
in-cell editing, *p. EX 21*
macro virus, *p. EX 29*
Name box, *p. EX 11*
Places bar, *p. EX 32*
Range Finder, *p. EX 18*
Redo command, *p. EX 26*
task pane, *p. EX 9*
template, *p. EX 28*
Undo command, *p. EX 26*
wizard, *p. EX 28*
workbook, *p. EX 3*
worksheet, *p. EX 2*

Chapter quiz

Short Answer

1. Explain the difference between an application window and a document or workbook window.
2. What is the difference between a toolbar and the Menu bar?
3. What is the fastest method for moving to cell DF8192?
4. What is significant about how dates are entered into a worksheet?
5. How do you enter a formula into a cell? Provide an example.
6. With respect to entering a formula, explain the term *pointing*.
7. How would you reverse the last three commands executed?
8. How do you create a new workbook based on a template?
9. How would you save a copy of the currently displayed workbook onto a diskette?
10. How would you save a workbook so that a person with Microsoft Excel 95 is able to open and edit the file?

True/False

1. ____ The cell reference "100AX" is an acceptable cell address.
2. ____ Pressing CTRL + HOME moves the cell pointer to cell A1.
3. ____ An Excel worksheet contains over 64,000 rows.

4. ____ Once a formula has been entered into a cell, you cannot edit the expression.

5. ____ A formula may contain both numbers and cell references, such as =A1*B7-500.

6. ____ Pressing DELETE erases the contents of a cell.

7. ____ Pressing CTRL+x will undo the last command executed.

8. ____ You can create a new folder from within the Save As dialog box.

9. ____ You access Excel's workbook templates using the File, Open command.

10. ____ You can open workbook files that have been created using earlier versions of Excel.

Multiple Choice

1. Which mouse shape is used to select cells in a worksheet?
   a. arrow
   b. cross
   c. hand
   d. hourglass

2. Excel displays the current cell address in the:
   a. Name box
   b. Status bar
   c. Title bar
   d. Standard toolbar

3. Using a mouse, you move around a worksheet quickly using the:
   a. Status bar
   b. Tab Scrolling arrows
   c. Tab Split bar
   d. scroll bars

4. When you enter a text label, Excel justifies the entry automatically between the cell borders as:
   a. left-aligned
   b. centered
   c. right-aligned
   d. fully justified

5. When you enter a date, Excel justifies the entry automatically between the cell borders as:
   a. left-aligned
   b. centered
   c. right-aligned
   d. fully justified

6. Which keyboard shortcut lets you modify the contents of a cell?
   a. CTRL
   b. SHIFT
   c. F2
   d. F5

7. Which is the correct formula for adding cells B4 and F7?
   a. =B4*F7
   b. @B4+F7
   c. $B4:F7
   d. =B4+F7

8. To save the current workbook using a different filename:
   a. CHOOSE: File, Save
   b. CHOOSE: File, Save As
   c. CLICK: Save button
   d. CLICK: File, Rename

9. To open a new blank workbook:
   a. CLICK: New button
   b. CHOOSE: File, Open
   c. CHOOSE: File, Blank
   d. CHOOSE: File, Template

10. To reverse an Undo command:
    a. CHOOSE: Edit, Go Back
    b. CHOOSE: File, Reverse Undo
    c. CLICK: Reverse button
    d. CLICK: Redo button

Excel

Hands-On exercises

easy 

1. Brentwood Academy: Semester Information

This exercise lets you practice fundamental worksheet skills, such as moving around a worksheet and entering text labels.

1. Load Microsoft Excel and ensure that a blank worksheet is displayed.
2. Now enter a title label for the worksheet:
   SELECT: cell A1
   TYPE: **Brentwood Academy**
   PRESS: ENTER
3. In cell A2:
   TYPE: **Enrollment Statistics**
   PRESS: ↓ twice
   The cell pointer should now appear in cell A4.
4. Let's add some row heading labels:
   TYPE: **Courses**
   CLICK: cell A7
   Notice that when you click a new cell location, the contents are moved from the Formula bar into the previous cell as if you had pressed ENTER.
5. TYPE: **Instructors**
   CLICK: cell A10
6. TYPE: **Students**
   PRESS: ENTER
   Your worksheet should appear similar to Figure 1.31.

Figure 1.31

Creating a new worksheet for Brentwood Academy

	A	B	C	D	E
1	Brentwood Academy				
2	Enrollment Statistics				
3					
4	Courses				
5					
6					
7	Instructors				
8					
9					
10	Students				
11					
12					
13					

7. On your own, enter the following text labels:

Move to cell	*TYPE:*
B5	**credit**
B6	**non-credit**
B8	**salaried**
B9	**contract**
B11	**full-time**
B12	**part-time**

8. To quickly move the cell pointer to the first column heading:
CLICK: the Name box
TYPE: **c4**
PRESS: ENTER

9. In cells C4 and D4, enter the following column headings:
TYPE: **Fall-01**
PRESS: →
TYPE: **Spring-02**
PRESS: ENTER

10. To move the cell pointer to cell A1:
PRESS: CTRL + HOME
Your worksheet should appear similar to Figure 1.32.

Figure 1.32

Completing the Brentwood Stats worksheet

	A	B	C	D	E
1	Brentwood	Academy			
2	Enrollment	Statistics			
3					
4	Courses		Fall-01	Spring-02	
5		credit			
6		non-credit			
7	Instructors				
8		salaried			
9		contract			
10	Students				
11		full-time			
12		part-time			
13					

11. Save the workbook as "Brentwood Stats" to your personal storage location. (*Hint:* If you are unsure where to store your personal files, select the My Documents folder.)

12. Close the workbook before proceeding.

2. Top Picks Video: Store Summary

In this exercise, you will edit text labels in an existing worksheet, enter numbers and dates, and practice using the Undo command.

1. Open the data file named EX01HE02 to display the workbook shown in Figure 1.33.

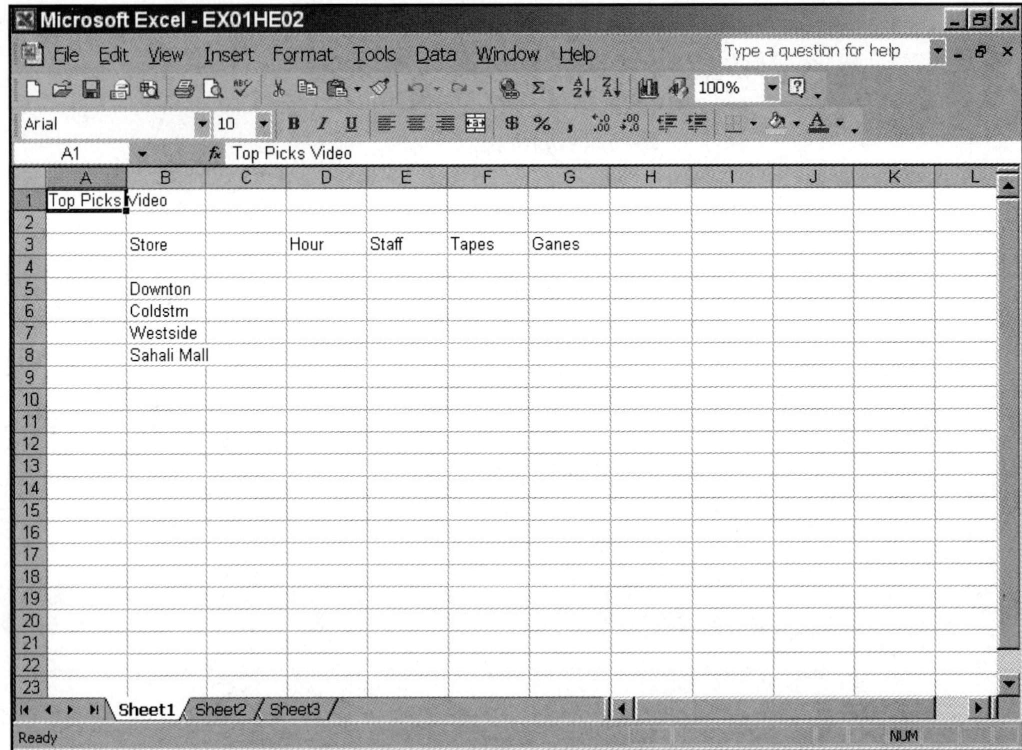

Figure 1.33

Opening the EX01HE02 workbook

2. Save the workbook as "Video Stores" to your personal storage location.

3. To change the "Store" column heading to read "Location":
   SELECT: cell B3
   TYPE: **Location**
   PRESS: ENTER

4. To correct a spelling mistake that occurs in the first location's name:
   DOUBLE-CLICK: cell B5
   PRESS: END
   PRESS: ←
   TYPE: **w**
   PRESS: ENTER
   The entry should now read "Downtown."

5. To expand upon the abbreviation used for the second location's name, ensure that cell B6 is selected and then:
   PRESS: F2
   PRESS: BACKSPACE to remove the last letter
   TYPE: **ream**
   PRESS: ENTER
   The location name should now read "Coldstream."

6. To correct an error appearing in the second column heading:
   SELECT: cell D3

7. Position the I-beam mouse pointer to the right of the text in the formula bar, as shown below.

8. CLICK: the left mouse button once
   The flashing insertion point should appear at the end of the word "Hour."
9. You can now complete the entry:
   TYPE: **s**
   CLICK: Enter button (✓)
   The entry now reads "Hours." Notice that the cell pointer remains in cell D3.
10. On your own, change the column heading "Tapes" to "Videos" and then correct the last heading so that it reads "Games."
11. Now let's put a date on the worksheet:
    SELECT: cell D1
    TYPE: **15-Jan-2001**
    Notice that the date is displayed as "15-Jan-01" in the worksheet.
12. Complete the worksheet as shown in Figure 1.34.

Figure 1.34

Entering values into the Video Stores worksheet

	A	B	C	D	E	F	G	H
1	Top Picks Video			15-Jan-01				
2								
3		Location		Hours	Staff	Videos	Games	
4								
5		Downtown		68	7	2,325		
6		Coldstream		68	5	1,790		
7		Westside		62	3	857		
8		Sahali Mall		74	9	2,114		
9								
10								
11								
12								

13. To delete the heading in the last column:
    SELECT: cell G3
    PRESS: DELETE
14. Now let's select the information for the Sahali Mall location:
    SELECT: cell D8
    PRESS: SHIFT and hold it down
    CLICK: cell F8
15. To erase all of the information in the selected cells:
    CHOOSE: Edit, Clear from the Menu bar
    CHOOSE: All from the cascading menu
16. To undo the deletion of the previous step:
    CLICK: Undo button (↶) on the Standard toolbar
17. Return to cell A1. Your worksheet should appear similar to Figure 1.35.

18. Save and then close the workbook.

Figure 1.35

Completing the Video Stores worksheet

	A	B	C	D	E	F	G	H
1	Top Picks	Video		15-Jan-01				
2								
3		Location		Hours	Staff	Videos		
4								
5		Downtown		68	7	2,325		
6		Coldstream		68	5	1,790		
7		Westside		62	3	857		
8		Sahali Mall		74	9	2,114		
9								
10								
11								
12								

moderate 

3. Staples Foods: Variance Analysis

You will now practice creating a worksheet from scratch that includes text, values, and formulas.

1. To display a new workbook and a blank worksheet:
   CLICK: New button ( )
2. Enter the company name in cell A1:
   TYPE: **Staples Foods**
   PRESS: ⬇
   TYPE: **Today is:**
   PRESS: ➡
3. Enter today's date in cell B2:
   TYPE: **your date** using the format dd-mmm-yy
   (*Hint:* The date 9/24/2001 would be entered as 24-Sep-2001.)
4. Complete the worksheet as shown in Figure 1.36.

Figure 1.36

Entering data into a blank worksheet

Microsoft Excel - Book2

File Edit View Insert Format Tools Data Window Help — Type a question for help

Arial 10 — 100% — E5

	A	B	C	D	E	F	G	H	I	J	K	L
1	Staples Foods											
2	Today is:	24-Sep-01										
3			Budget	Actual	Variance							
4	Income											
5		Sales	43,000	41,380								
6		Services	17,500	19,620								
7		Total										
8												
9	Expenses											
10		Materials	11,500	12,340								
11		Overhead	6,700	6,700								
12		Supplies	12,500	12,975								
13		Total										
14												
15												
16												
17												
18												
19												
20												
21												
22												
23												

Sheet1 / Sheet2 / Sheet3

Ready — NUM

5. To calculate the Sales variance:
   SELECT: cell E5
   TYPE: **=d5-c5**
   PRESS: ENTER
   The value –1620 appears in the worksheet.
6. Using the same method, calculate the remaining variances for cells E6, E10, E11, and E12.
7. To sum the Budget Income column:
   SELECT: cell C7
   TYPE: =
   CLICK: cell C5
   TYPE: +
   CLICK: cell C6
   CLICK: Enter button (☑)
8. On your own, complete the entries for cells D7 and E7.
9. To sum the Budget Expenses column:
   SELECT: cell C13
   TYPE: **=c10+c11+c12**
   PRESS: ENTER
10. On your own, complete the entries for cells D13 and E13. Your screen should now appear similar to Figure 1.37.
11. Save the workbook as "Staples Variance" to your personal storage location.
12. Close the workbook.

Figure 1.37

Completing the Staples Variance workbook

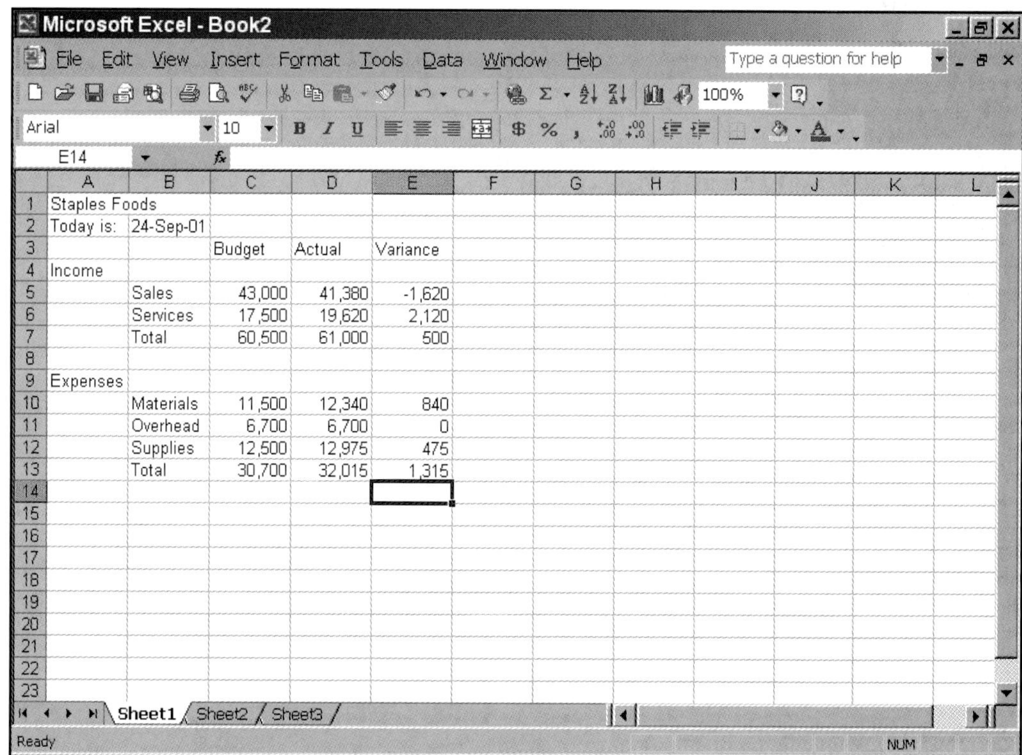

moderate 

4. Sutton House Realty: Current Listings Report

This exercise lets you practice adding and modifying text, numbers, and formulas in an existing workbook.

1. Open the data file named EX01HE04 to display the workbook shown in Figure 1.38.

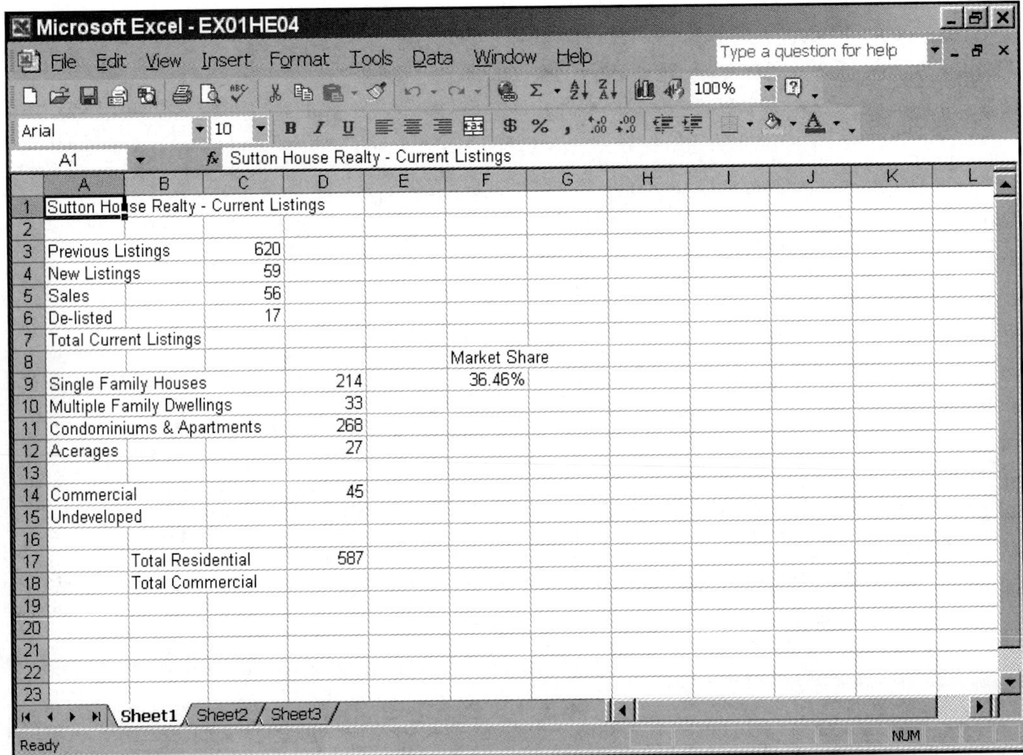

Figure 1.38

Opening the EX01HE04 workbook

2. Save the workbook as "Sutton House Listings" to your personal storage location.
3. In cell C7, you will now construct a formula to calculate the "Total Current Listings." You will add the previous and new listings together and then subtract the listings sold and delisted. Do the following:
   SELECT: cell C7
   TYPE: = **c3+c4-c5-c6**
   PRESS: ENTER
   The value 606 should appear.
4. In cell A15, change the label from "Undeveloped" to read "Undeveloped Commercial."
5. In cell D15, you will enter the number of Undeveloped Commercial listings. As you do so, watch the formula in cell D17 recalculate after you press ENTER. Do the following:
   TYPE: **19**
   PRESS: ENTER
6. Unfortunately, the formula in cell D17 for "Total Residential" is incorrect. To edit the formula and remove references to the "Commercial" and "Undeveloped Commercial" listings, do the following:
   SELECT: cell D17

7. Position the I-beam mouse pointer to the right of the formula in the Formula bar. Then, do the following:
CLICK: the left mouse button and hold it down
DRAG: the I-beam mouse pointer to the left to select "+D14+D15"
Notice how the cells in the worksheet and the cell references in the Formula bar are color-coded, as shown in Figure 1.39.

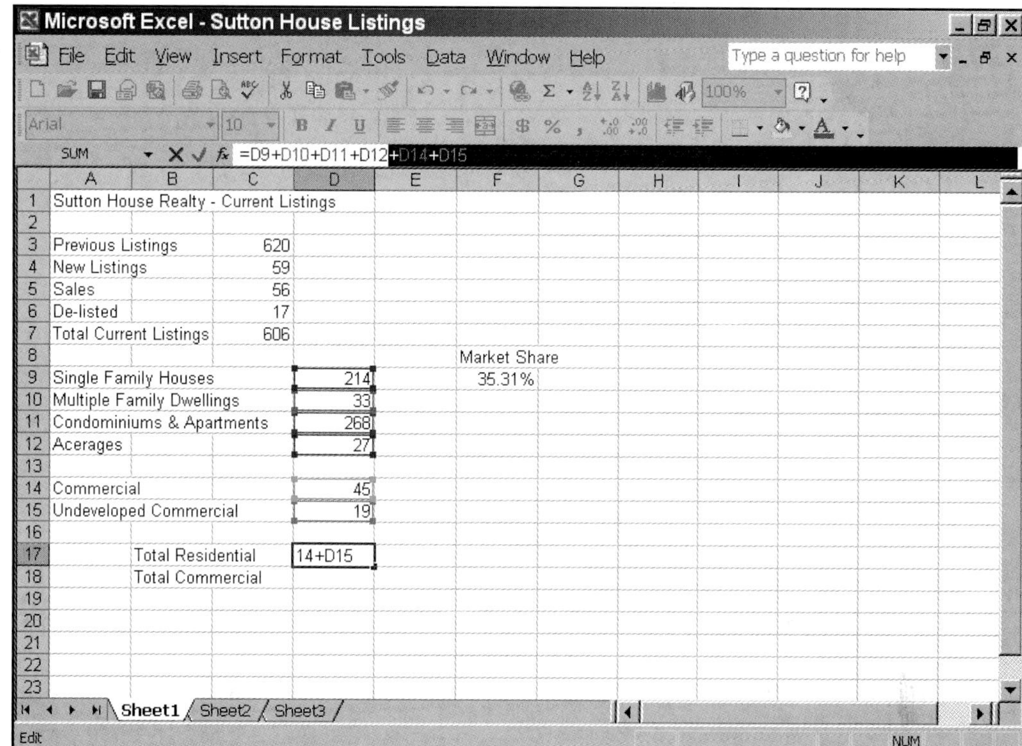

Figure 1.39

Selecting cell references in the Formula bar

8. Once the selection is made, release the mouse button. Then:
PRESS: DELETE

9. To complete the entry:
PRESS: ENTER
The value 542 appears in cell D17.

10. In cell D18, enter a formula that adds up the Commercial (cell D14) and Undeveloped Commercial (cell D15) listings.

11. The Market Share column shows the proportional value of a particular row category as compared to either the Total Residential or Total Commercial results. To examine the formula used to calculate the Market Share for Single Family Houses, do the following:
SELECT: cell F9
The expression "=D9/D17" appears in the Formula bar.

12. Enter formulas in cells F10, F11, and F12 that calculate their respective market shares of the residential listings. (*Hint:* Divide each row value in column D by the Total Residential value in cell D17.)

13. Enter formulas in cells F14 and F15 that calculate their respective market shares of the commercial listings. (*Hint:* Divide each row value in column D by the Total Commercial value in cell D18.) Your screen should appear similar to Figure 1.40.

14. Save and then close the workbook.

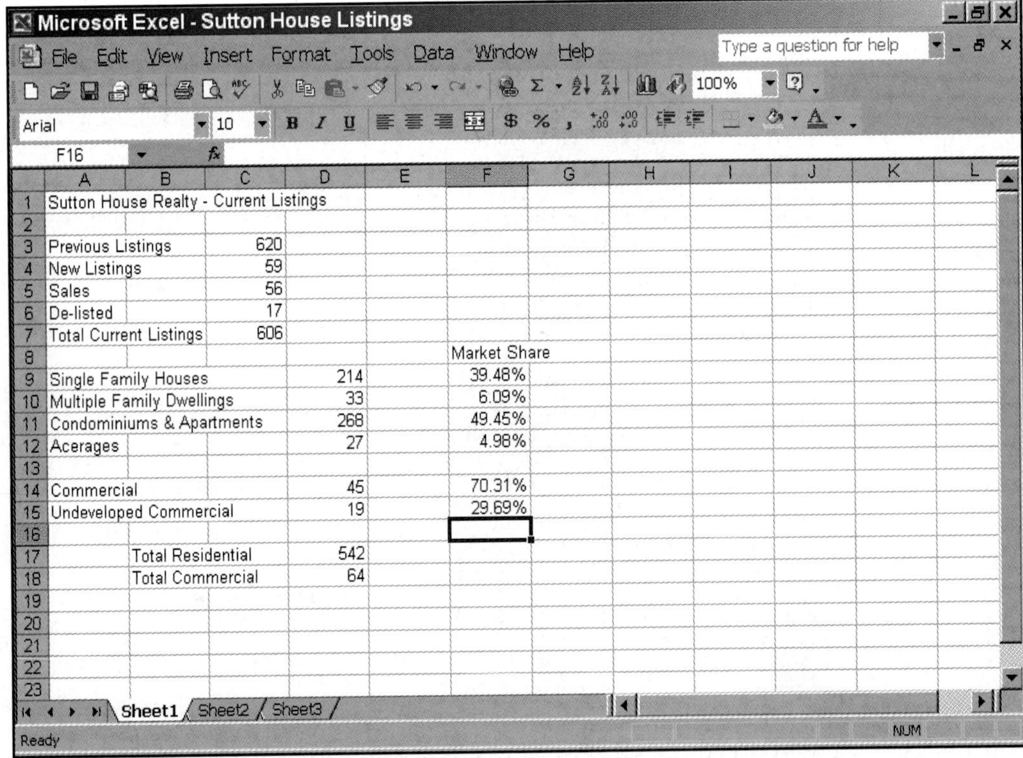

Figure 1.40

Completing the Sutton House Listings workbook

difficult

5. On Your Own: Personal Monthly Budget

To practice working with text, values, and formulas, ensure that Excel is loaded and then display a blank workbook. You will now begin creating a personal budget. Enter a title that contains the words "My Monthly Budget." Under this title include your name and the current month. Now enter the following expense categories and a reasonable amount for each:

- Rent/Mortgage
- Food
- Clothing
- Car expenses
- Utilities
- Education
- Entertainment

In the same column as the labels, enter the words "Total Expenses." Then, beneath the column of numbers, enter a formula that sums the column. Now add a new column next to these budget figures that displays the percentage share for each budget category of the total expenses. For example, you would divide the value for Food by the Total Expenses value to calculate its share of the budget. Don't worry about formatting the results as percentages. Figure 1.41 provides an example of a completed worksheet. Experiment with increasing and decreasing the budget expense figures to see their effect on the percentage share calculations. When completed, save the workbook as "My Budget" to your personal storage location and then close the workbook.

Figure 1.41

Completing the My Budget workbook

	A	B	C	D	E
1	My Monthly Budget				
2	John Smith				
3	Month:	January			
4			Budget	Share	
5	Rent/Mortgage		$600	0.421053	
6	Food		$300	0.210526	
7	Clothing		$75	0.052632	
8	Car expenses		$100	0.070175	
9	Utilities		$50	0.035088	
10	Education		$200	0.140351	
11	Entertainment		$100	0.070175	
12	Total Expenses		$1,425		
13					

6. On Your Own: My Grade Book

To practice working with data and formulas, open the EX01HE06 workbook (Figure 1.42). Before continuing, save the workbook as "My Grades" to your personal storage location. Enter sample marks into column D of the worksheet.

Figure 1.42

Opening the EX01HE06 workbook

	A	B	C	D	E	F	G
1	My Grade Book						
2							
3	Business Computer Systems			MARK	OUT OF	%	
4		assigment #1			30		
5		mid-term test			120		
6		assignment #2			45		
7		final exam			100		
8		TERM PERCENTAGE:					
9							
10	Pacific Rim Studies			MARK	OUT OF	%	
11		assigment #1			50		
12		mid-term test			30		
13		assignment #2			50		
14		final exam			80		
15		TERM PERCENTAGE:					
16							
17	AVERAGE OF BOTH COURSES:						
18							
19							
20							

Enter formulas that calculate the percentage grade for each test or assignment by dividing the "MARK" column by the "OUT OF" column. Then, enter formulas that calculate the Term Percentages for each course. The results should display in cells F8 and F15. (*Hint:* You will need to use parentheses to group data in your formula equation. Specifically, you must divide the total course marks achieved by the total marks possible.) Finally, enter a formula that calculates the average percentage of both courses for display in cell F17. Adjust some of the sample marks to check that the formulas are working correctly.

Save the workbook to your personal storage location. Close the workbook and exit Microsoft Excel.

Case Problems

H. F. Charters

H. F. Charters, a small airline charter business in the Pacific Northwest, is in the process of modernizing how it tracks and analyzes its business data. As an initial step, the new office assistant, Jennifer Duvall, is learning how to use Microsoft Excel. Her boss, Hank Frobisher, wants Jennifer to create a worksheet that will enable him to compare the monthly efficiency of each of his three planes. You see, Hank has an opportunity to purchase an additional floatplane for well below market value. And, as a cost-conscious businessman, Hank wants to have a clear understanding of how his current equipment is performing before deciding to spend any money.

In the following case problems, assume the role of Jennifer and perform the same steps that she identifies. You may want to re-read the chapter opening before proceeding.

1. Jennifer decides to create a new worksheet that she can use as a template for each month's report. She begins by loading Microsoft Excel and displaying a blank workbook. Her first step will be to enter the title and the row and column headings. Then, the workbook needs to be saved to disk so that it can be later retrieved as a starting point for the monthly reports.

   Jennifer creates the worksheet shown in Figure 1.43 and then saves it as "Aircraft Stats" to her personal storage location.

Figure 1.43

The Aircraft Stats workbook

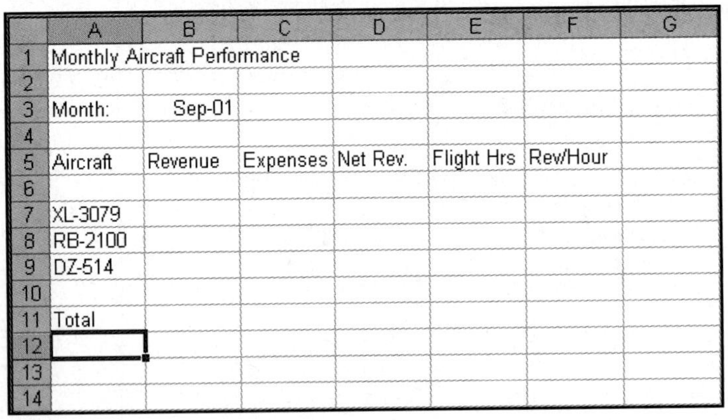

	A	B	C	D	E	F	G
1	Monthly Aircraft Performance						
2							
3	Month:	Sep-01					
4							
5	Aircraft	Revenue	Expenses	Net Rev.	Flight Hrs	Rev/Hour	
6							
7	XL-3079						
8	RB-2100						
9	DZ-514						
10							
11	Total						
12							
13							
14							

2. Satisfied that this format will provide Hank with the information he needs, Jennifer begins to fill in the first month's figures. Most of the data she uses is taken directly from the monthly revenue and expense summaries prepared by the bookkeeping service. The pilots' trip logs provide the rest of the data. After entering the data in Figure 1.44, Jennifer saves the workbook as "September Stats" to her personal storage location.

Figure 1.44

September's aircraft performance report

	A	B	C	D	E	F	G
1	Monthly Aircraft Performance						
2							
3	Month:	Sep-01					
4							
5	Aircraft	Revenue	Expenses	Net Rev.	Flight Hrs	Rev/Hour	
6							
7	XL-3079	15,326	4,259		87		
8	RB-2100	17,210	3,876		95		
9	DZ-514	9,845	2,633		53		
10							
11	Total						
12							
13							
14							

3. Now, Jennifer tackles entering the formulas for the worksheet:
   - She constructs formulas for display in row 11 that add the values appearing in the Revenue, Expenses, and Flight Hrs columns. The three formulas are entered into cells B11, C11, and E11.
   - She enters formulas in cells D7, D8, and D9 that calculate the Net Revenue by subtracting the Expenses for an aircraft from the Revenue it generated. She then enters a sum formula for the column in cell D11.
   - She calculates and displays the Net Revenue per Hour in cells F7, F8, F9, and F11. The calculation she uses is simply the Net Revenue from column D divided by the Flight Hours in column E.

   Unfortunately, Hank has already gone home. Jennifer decides to call it a day; she saves the workbook as "September Calcs" and then closes it. She is already looking forward to showing off her new creation to Hank in the morning.

4. The next morning, Jennifer opens the "September Calcs" workbook and asks Hank to take a look at it. He is very pleased with the report and amazed at how quickly Excel can perform the calculations. Hank asks Jennifer what it would take to produce this report for another month. She explains that all she needs to do is enter the month's revenues, expenses, and flight hours into the appropriate cells; Excel then recalculates the worksheet automatically. Hank is impressed, realizing that he will finally have some decent information on which to base business decisions.

   After mulling over the worksheet, Hank decides it would be prudent to purchase the fourth aircraft. With some minor modifications to the worksheet, he realizes that this information would come in handy during his meeting with the bank's loan officer. Hank calls Jennifer over to his desk and explains the revisions he wants her to make. First, the title of the report, explains Hank, should read "H. F. Charters." The "Monthly Aircraft Performance" title should be moved down to row 2. Furthermore, the aircraft should be identified by their names instead of their registration numbers. For example, the aircraft names are Eagle (XL-3079), Wanderer (RB-2100), and Sky Spirit (DZ-514). The worksheet should now appear as shown in Figure 1.45.

Figure 1.45

Completing the September Summary workbook

	A	B	C	D	E	F	G
1	H. F. Charters						
2	Monthly Aircraft Performance						
3	Month:	Sep-01					
4							
5	Aircraft	Revenue	Expenses	Net Rev.	Flight Hrs	Rev/Hour	
6							
7	Eagle	15,326	4,259	11,067	87	127.2069	
8	Wanderer	17,210	3,876	13,334	95	140.3579	
9	Sky Spirit	9,845	2,633	7,212	53	136.0755	
10							
11	Total	42,381	10,768	31,613	235	135	
12							
13							
14							

Jennifer makes the requested changes. She then saves the workbook as "September Summary" and closes the workbook. As a last step, she exits Microsoft Excel.

Microsoft® **Excel®** 2002

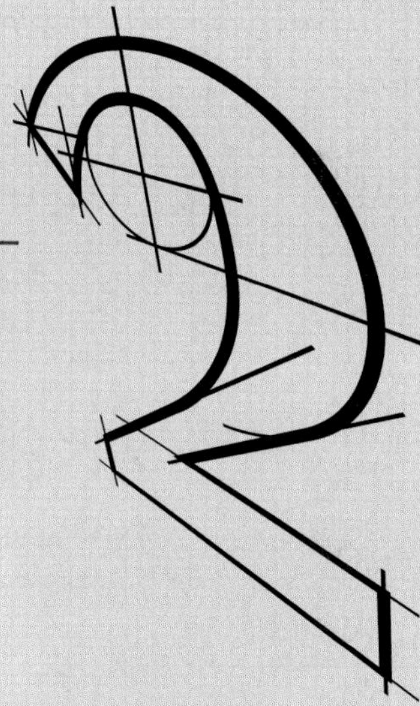

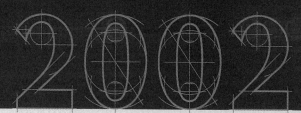

CHAPTER 2

Modifying a Worksheet

CHAPTER OUTLINE

Case Study

2.1 Entering and Reviewing Data

2.2 Copying and Moving Data

2.3 Modifying Rows and Columns

Chapter Summary

Chapter Quiz

Hands-On Exercises

Case Problems

PREREQUISITES

To successfully complete this chapter, you must be able to perform basic data entry and file management operations in Excel. Besides entering text, numbers, dates, and formulas into a worksheet, you will be asked to open, save, and close workbooks. You must also know how to use the toolbar, Menu bar, and right-click shortcut menus in Excel.

LEARNING OBJECTIVES

After completing this chapter, you will be able to:

- Use several "Auto" features provided by Excel for entering and editing data and formulas
- Copy and move information with the Windows and Office Clipboards, and by using drag and drop
- Use the AutoFill feature and Fill commands to duplicate and extend data and formulas
- Insert and delete cells, rows, and columns
- Hide, unhide, and adjust rows and columns

CaseStudy CITYWIDE INSURANCE AGENCY The Citywide Insurance Agency, located at the corner of 43rd and Main in Middleton's business district, is the city's largest private insurance company. Citywide Insurance has always maintained a high profile in the community by sponsoring youth programs and providing assistance to local charities. This sense of community was one of the main attractions for Scott Allenby, who recently joined the agency as their internal business manager.

Just last week, one of the agency partners purchased a new computer for Scott and made him personally responsible for generating the company's monthly profitability reports. With an increased workload, Scott knows that he must streamline operations and find a more efficient method for summarizing the data he receives. Fortunately, the computer came with Microsoft Excel installed and, after only a few days, Scott is now creating his own worksheets. Far from being comfortable with Excel's vast number of features, Scott has asked a knowledgeable friend to help construct a few simple workbooks for him to use.

In this chapter, you and Scott learn to modify and manipulate worksheet data. In addition to copying and moving information, you are introduced to inserting and deleting cells, rows, and columns. You also learn how to hide specific columns before generating reports.

2.1 Entering and Reviewing Data

Even novice users find it easy to build and use simple worksheets. In this module, you are introduced to some popular tools that can help speed your learning and improve your efficiency. Specifically, Excel provides three "Auto" features that may be used to enter repetitive data and perform calculations. Once you've practiced selecting ranges, you learn to use these three "Auto" features, called *AutoComplete, AutoCalculate,* and *AutoSum.*

2.1.1 Selecting Cells and Ranges

feature

A **cell range** is a single cell or rectangular block of cells. Each cell range has a beginning cell address in the top left-hand corner and an ending cell address in the bottom right-hand corner. To use a cell range in a formula, you separate the two cell addresses using a colon. For example, the cell range B4:C6 references the six cells shown shaded below. Notice that the current or active cell, B4, does not appear shaded in this graphic.

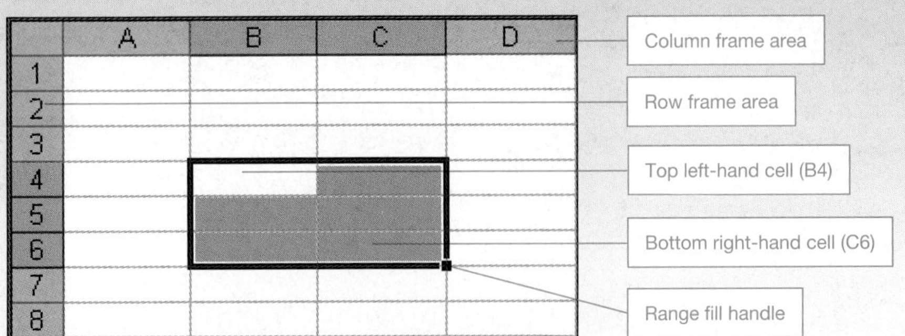

method

To select a cell range using the mouse:

- CLICK: the cell in the top left-hand corner
- DRAG: the mouse pointer to the cell in the bottom right-hand corner

To select a cell range using the keyboard:

- SELECT: cell in the top left-hand corner
- PRESS: SHIFT and hold it down
- PRESS: *an arrow key* to extend the range highlighting
- RELEASE: SHIFT

practice

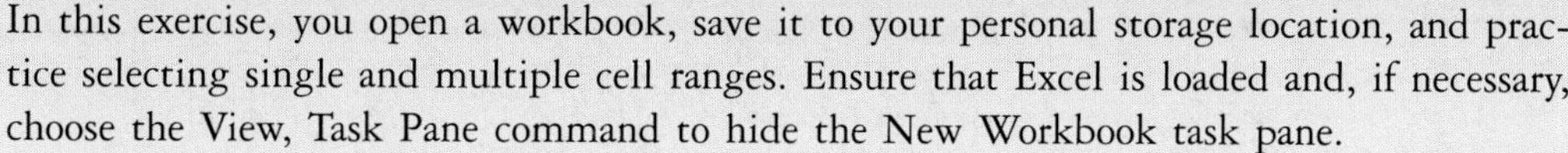

In this exercise, you open a workbook, save it to your personal storage location, and practice selecting single and multiple cell ranges. Ensure that Excel is loaded and, if necessary, choose the View, Task Pane command to hide the New Workbook task pane.

1. Open the data file named EX0210.
2. In the next two steps, you will save the file as "My Gift List" to your personal storage location. Do the following:
   CHOOSE: File, Save As
   TYPE: **My Gift List** (but do not press ENTER)
3. Using the *Save in* drop-down list box or the Places bar:
   SELECT: *your storage location* (for example, the My Documents or My Workbooks folder)
   CLICK: Save command button
   (*Note:* Most lessons in this guide begin by opening a student data file and then saving it immediately using a new filename.)
4. Let's practice selecting cell ranges. To begin:
   SELECT: cell A3
   (*Hint:* The word SELECT tells you to place the cell pointer at the identified cell address using either the keyboard or the mouse.)
5. To select the range from cell A3 to E3 using the keyboard:
   PRESS: SHIFT and hold it down
   PRESS: → four times
   Although it is not explicitly stated in the above instruction, you release the SHIFT key once the range is selected. Your screen should appear similar to Figure 2.1.

Figure 2.1

Selecting the cell range A3:E3

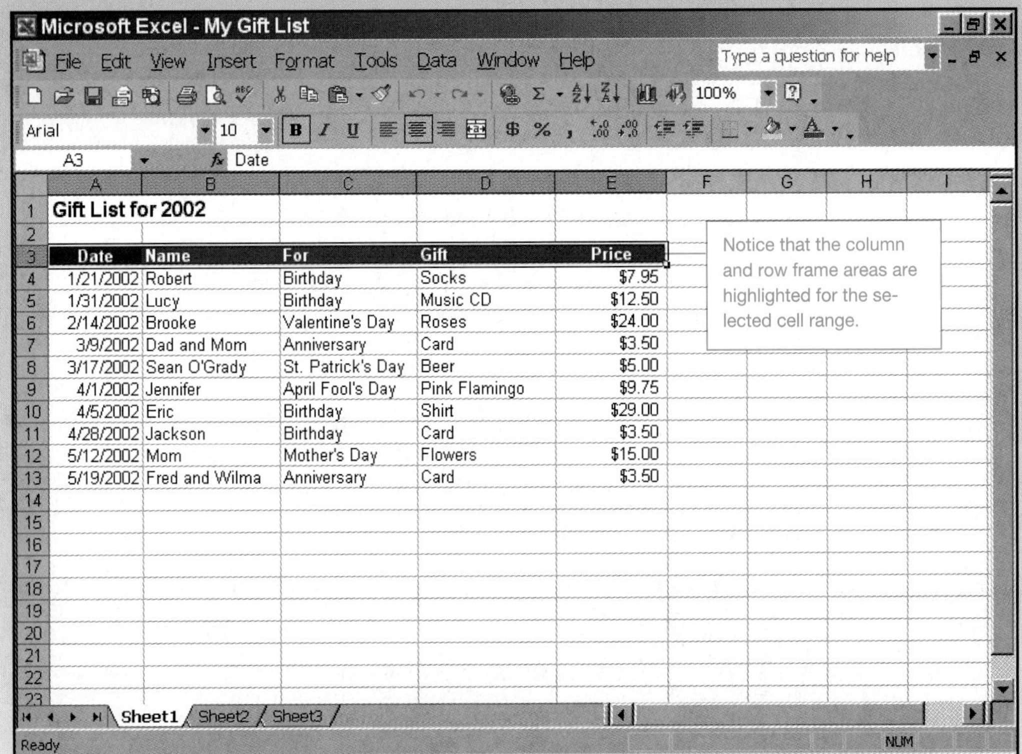

6. You learned in the previous chapter that the CTRL+HOME combination moves the cell pointer to cell A1. You will now press the HOME key by itself in order to move the cell pointer to column A within the same row. To move the cell pointer back to cell A3:
   PRESS: HOME

7. To select the same cell range, but faster and more efficiently:
   PRESS: SHIFT and hold it down
   PRESS: CTRL+→ together
   Notice that the entire range is selected. You may remember from the last chapter that the CTRL+arrow combination moves the cell pointer until the cell contents change from empty to filled or filled to empty.

8. To select a cell range using the mouse:
   CLICK: cell C6 and hold down the left mouse button
   DRAG: the mouse pointer to E8 (and then release the button)
   Notice that the column letters and row numbers in the frame area appear bold for the selected cell range, as shown in Figure 2.2.

Figure 2.2

Selecting a cell range using the mouse

	A	B	C	D	E	F
1	Gift List for 2002					
2						
3	Date	Name	For	Gift	Price	
4	1/21/2002	Robert	Birthday	Socks	$7.95	
5	1/31/2002	Lucy	Birthday	Music CD	$12.50	
6	2/14/2002	Brooke	Valentine's Day	Roses	$24.00	
7	3/9/2002	Dad and Mom	Anniversary	Card	$3.50	
8	3/17/2002	Sean O'Grady	St. Patrick's Day	Beer	$5.00	
9	4/1/2002	Jennifer	April Fool's Day	Pink Flamingo	$9.75	
10	4/5/2002	Eric	Birthday	Shirt	$29.00	
11	4/28/2002	Jackson	Birthday	Card	$3.50	
12	5/12/2002	Mom	Mother's Day	Flowers	$15.00	
13	5/19/2002	Fred and Wilma	Anniversary	Card	$3.50	
14						
15						

Use the cross mouse pointer to select a cell range.

9. There is an easier method for selecting cell ranges for novice mouse users. To demonstrate, let's select the cell range from B10 to D13:
CLICK: cell B10
PRESS: SHIFT and hold it down
CLICK: cell D13
The range between the two cells should now appear highlighted. (*Note:* Remember to release the SHIFT key after the last selection is made.)

10. You can also select multiple cell ranges on a worksheet. To begin:
DRAG: from cell A6 to cell E6
PRESS: CTRL and hold it down
DRAG: from cell A9 to cell E9
You should see two separate cell ranges highlighted on the worksheet.

11. To select a third cell range:
PRESS: CTRL and hold it down
DRAG: from cell A12 to cell E12
(*Note:* Release the CTRL key after the last selection is made.) Your screen should now look similar to Figure 2.3.

12. To move the cell pointer to cell A1:
PRESS: CTRL + HOME

Figure 2.3

Selecting multiple cell ranges using CTRL

	A	B	C	D	E	F
1	Gift List for 2002					
2						
3	Date	Name	For	Gift	Price	
4	1/21/2002	Robert	Birthday	Socks	$7.95	
5	1/31/2002	Lucy	Birthday	Music CD	$12.50	
6	2/14/2002	Brooke	Valentine's Day	Roses	$24.00	
7	3/9/2002	Dad and Mom	Anniversary	Card	$3.50	
8	3/17/2002	Sean O'Grady	St. Patrick's Day	Beer	$5.00	
9	4/1/2002	Jennifer	April Fool's Day	Pink Flamingo	$9.75	
10	4/5/2002	Eric	Birthday	Shirt	$29.00	
11	4/28/2002	Jackson	Birthday	Card	$3.50	
12	5/12/2002	Mom	Mother's Day	Flowers	$15.00	
13	5/19/2002	Fred and Wilma	Anniversary	Card	$3.50	
14						

The active cell is the top left-hand cell in the final cell range selected.

2.1.2 Entering Data Using AutoComplete

feature

The **AutoComplete** feature second-guesses what you are typing into a worksheet cell and suggests how to complete the entry. After analyzing your first few keystrokes and scanning the same column for similar entries, AutoComplete tacks on the remaining letters when it thinks it has found a match. You can accept the AutoComplete entry, or you can ignore its suggestion and continue typing. This feature can greatly reduce the number of repetitive entries you make in a worksheet.

method

By default, the AutoComplete feature is turned on. If, however, you view its helpfulness as an intrusion, you can turn it off. To do so:

- CHOOSE: Tools, Options
- CLICK: *Edit* tab in the dialog box
- SELECT: *Enable AutoComplete for cell values* check box to toggle AutoComplete on and off

practice

You will now practice using Excel's AutoComplete feature to enter data. Ensure that the "My Gift List" workbook is displayed.

1. SELECT: cell A14
2. To add a new entry to the worksheet:
   TYPE: **6/2/2002**
   PRESS: →
   TYPE: **Anda**
   PRESS: →
3. You will now enter the word "Birthday" into cell C14. After typing the first letter, Excel notices that there is only one other entry in the column that begins with the letter "B" and makes the assumption that this is the word you want to enter. To demonstrate:
   TYPE: **B**
   Notice that Excel completes the word "Birthday" automatically, as shown in Figure 2.4.

Figure 2.4

The AutoComplete feature completes an entry for "Birthday"

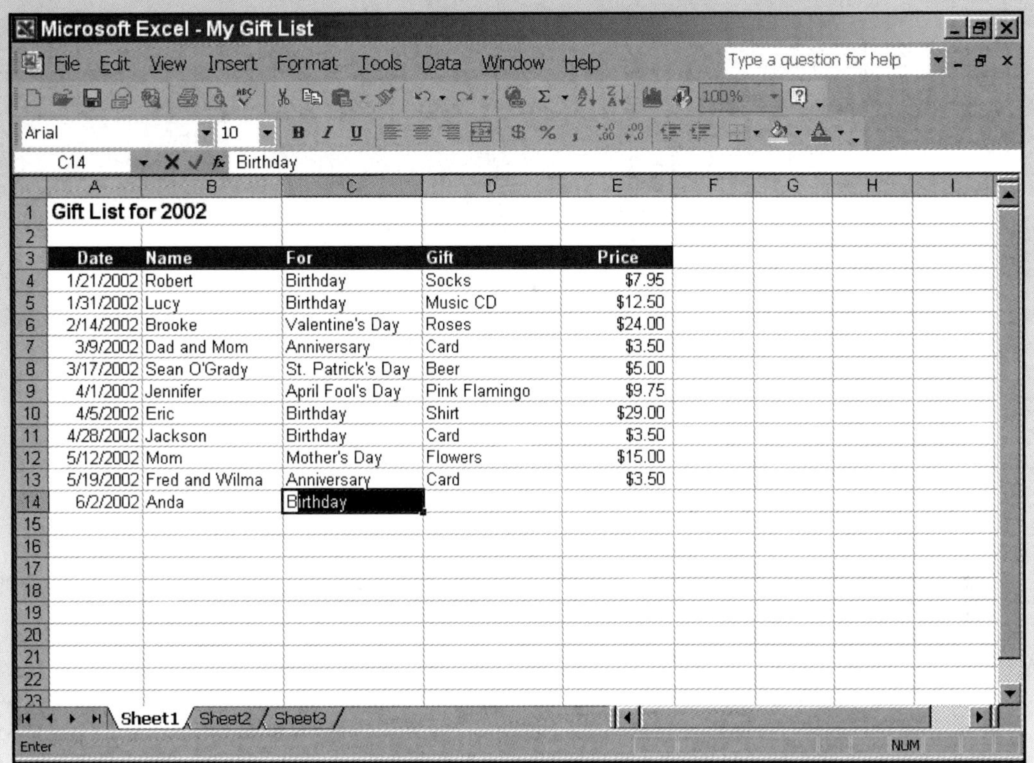

4. To accept the completed word:
   PRESS: ➡

5. For the remaining cells in the row:
   TYPE: **Shoes**
   PRESS: ➡
   TYPE: **$19.95**
   PRESS: ENTER
   PRESS: HOME
   Your cell pointer should now appear in cell A15.

6. Let's add another entry to the worksheet. Do the following:
   TYPE: **6/5/2002**
   PRESS: ➡
   TYPE: **Trevor and Ann**
   PRESS: ➡

7. You can also use Excel's AutoComplete feature to display a sorted list of all the unique entries in a column. To illustrate:
   RIGHT-CLICK: cell C15 to display its shortcut menu
   CHOOSE: Pick From List
   AutoComplete generates the list and then displays its results in a pop-up list box, as shown in Figure 2.5.

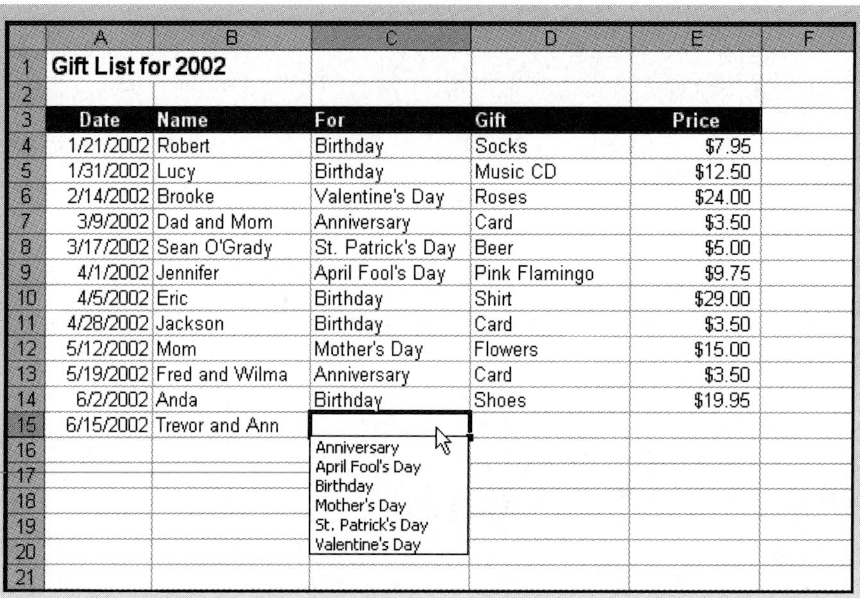

	A	B	C	D	E	F
1	Gift List for 2002					
2						
3	Date	Name	For	Gift	Price	
4	1/21/2002	Robert	Birthday	Socks	$7.95	
5	1/31/2002	Lucy	Birthday	Music CD	$12.50	
6	2/14/2002	Brooke	Valentine's Day	Roses	$24.00	
7	3/9/2002	Dad and Mom	Anniversary	Card	$3.50	
8	3/17/2002	Sean O'Grady	St. Patrick's Day	Beer	$5.00	
9	4/1/2002	Jennifer	April Fool's Day	Pink Flamingo	$9.75	
10	4/5/2002	Eric	Birthday	Shirt	$29.00	
11	4/28/2002	Jackson	Birthday	Card	$3.50	
12	5/12/2002	Mom	Mother's Day	Flowers	$15.00	
13	5/19/2002	Fred and Wilma	Anniversary	Card	$3.50	
14	6/2/2002	Anda	Birthday	Shoes	$19.95	
15	6/15/2002	Trevor and Ann				
16			Anniversary			
17			April Fool's Day			
18			Birthday			
19			Mother's Day			
20			St. Patrick's Day Valentine's Day			
21						

Displaying the AutoComplete pick list

Figure 2.5

Entering data using the AutoComplete pick list

8. To make a selection:
CLICK: Anniversary in the pick list
(*Hint:* As an alternative to choosing the Pick From List command in the right-click menu, you can press ALT+⬇ in a cell to display the column's pick list.)

9. To complete the row:
CLICK: cell D15
TYPE: **Picture Frame**
PRESS: ➡
TYPE: **$15.00**
PRESS: ENTER

10. Save the workbook and keep it open for use in the next lesson. (*Hint:* The fastest methods for saving a workbook include clicking the Save button (💾) or pressing CTRL+s.)

2.1.3 Using AutoCalculate and AutoSum

feature→

The **AutoCalculate** feature allows you to select a range of values and view their sum in the Status bar. This feature is useful for checking the result of a calculation without having to store its value in the worksheet. If, on the other hand, you need to store a result, click the **AutoSum** button (Σ▾) on the Standard toolbar. Excel reviews the surrounding cells, guesses at the range you want to sum, and then places a SUM function (described later in this book) into the current or active cell.

method→

To use the AutoCalculate feature:

- SELECT: the range of values that you want to sum

To use the AutoSum feature:

- SELECT: the cell where you want the result to appear
- CLICK: AutoSum button (Σ▾)

practice

Using the same worksheet, you will now practice viewing AutoCalculate results and entering an addition formula using AutoSum. Ensure that you have completed the previous lessons in this module and that the "My Gift List" workbook is displayed.

1. Let's say you want to know how much money to set aside for gifts in April. To find the answer, do the following:
   SELECT: cell range from E9 to E11
   Notice that only the April values are selected in the "Price" column.

2. Review the Status bar information. Notice that "Sum=$42.25" now appears near the right-hand side of the Status bar, as shown in Figure 2.6.

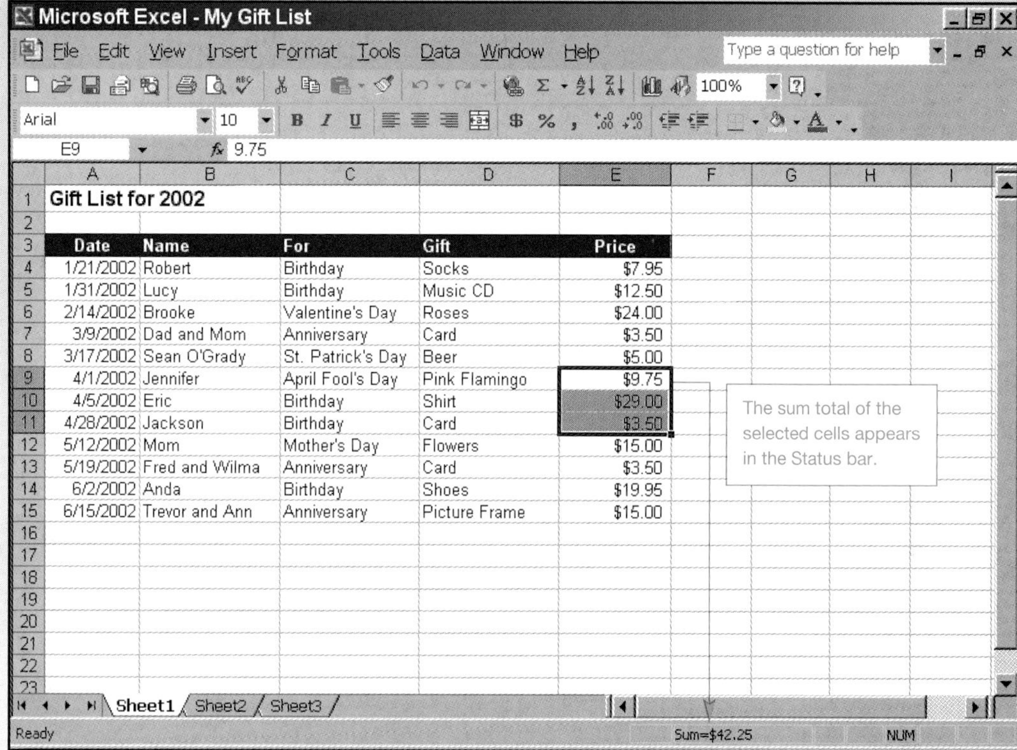

Figure 2.6

Using the AutoCalculate feature

3. Let's perform another calculation:
   SELECT: cell E4
   PRESS: SHIFT and hold it down
   PRESS: CTRL+↓
   All of the cells under the "Price" column heading should now appear selected. Assuming that you completed the previous lessons, the Status bar will now display "Sum=$148.65."

4. Using the AutoCalculate feature, you can also view the result of other calculations in the Status bar. To demonstrate, let's calculate the average value of gifts in the selected cell range:
   RIGHT-CLICK: "Sum=$148.65" in the Status bar
   Your screen should now appear similar to Figure 2.7.

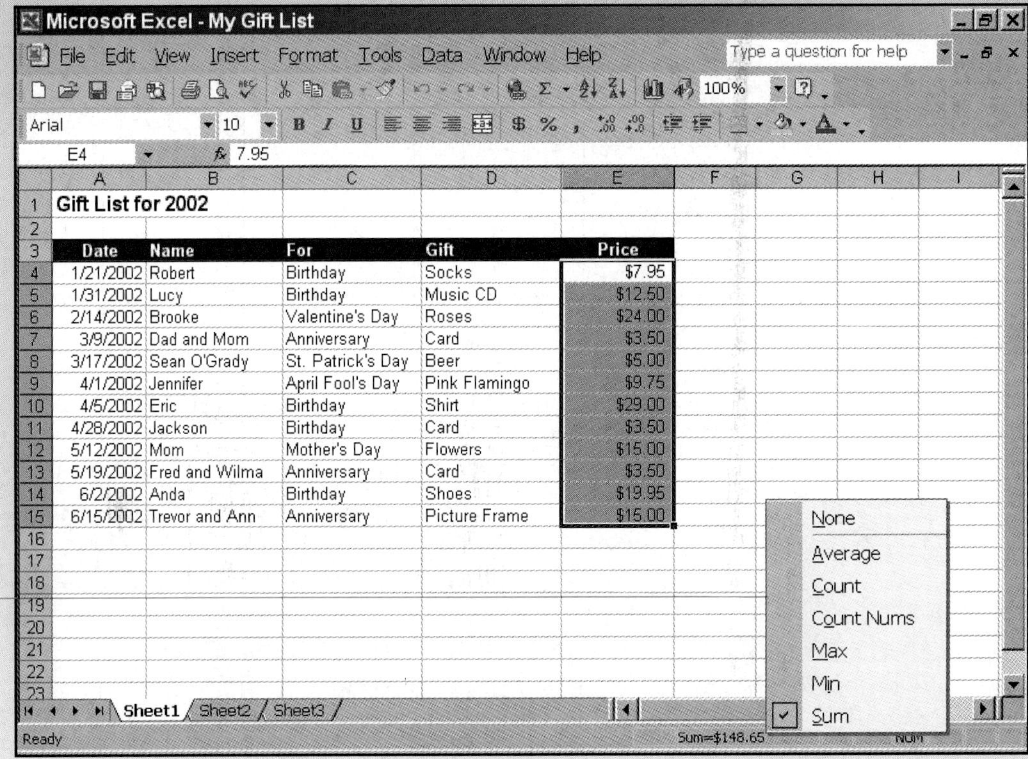

Date	Name	For	Gift	Price
1/21/2002	Robert	Birthday	Socks	$7.95
1/31/2002	Lucy	Birthday	Music CD	$12.50
2/14/2002	Brooke	Valentine's Day	Roses	$24.00
3/9/2002	Dad and Mom	Anniversary	Card	$3.50
3/17/2002	Sean O'Grady	St. Patrick's Day	Beer	$5.00
4/1/2002	Jennifer	April Fool's Day	Pink Flamingo	$9.75
4/5/2002	Eric	Birthday	Shirt	$29.00
4/28/2002	Jackson	Birthday	Card	$3.50
5/12/2002	Mom	Mother's Day	Flowers	$15.00
5/19/2002	Fred and Wilma	Anniversary	Card	$3.50
6/2/2002	Anda	Birthday	Shoes	$19.95
6/15/2002	Trevor and Ann	Anniversary	Picture Frame	$15.00

Figure 2.7

Displaying the right-click menu for the AutoCalculate feature

Displaying the AutoCalculate right-click menu for choosing calculation methods.

5. In the AutoCalculate right-click menu that appears:
   CHOOSE: Average
   The Status bar now displays "Average=$12.39."

6. Now return the Status bar display to showing the sum of the selected cell range. Do the following:
   RIGHT-CLICK: "Average=$12.39" in the Status bar
   CHOOSE: Sum

7. SELECT: cell D16

8. Let's enter a text label for the next calculation:
   TYPE: **Total Cost**
   PRESS: [Enter]

9. The quickest way to sum a row or column of values is using the AutoSum button (Σ ▾) on the Standard toolbar. Make sure that you click the sigma (Σ) portion of the button, rather than the down arrow. To demonstrate:
   CLICK: AutoSum button (Σ ▾) once
   A built-in function called SUM is entered into the cell, along with the range that Excel assumes you want to sum (Figure 2.8).

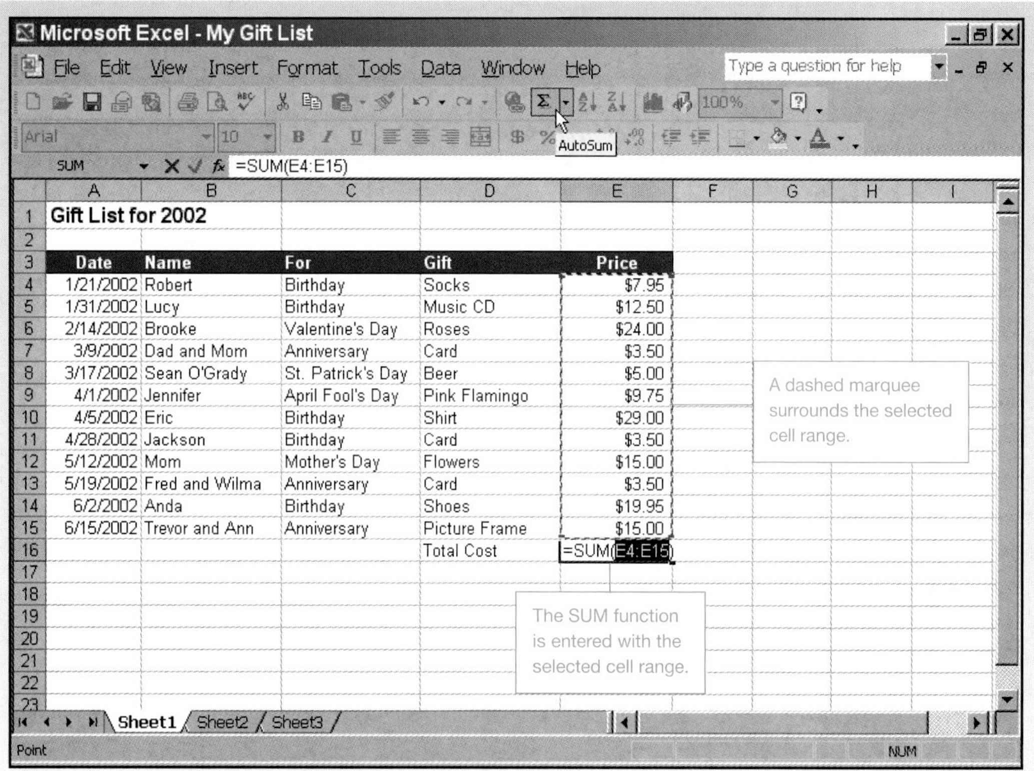

Figure 2.8

Using the AutoSum button (Σ ▾) to sum a cell range

Excel

10. To accept the highlighted cells as the desired range:
CLICK: AutoSum button (Σ ▾) again
The result, $148.65, now appears in cell E16. (*Note:* You can also press ENTER or click the Enter button (✓) to accept the AutoSum entry.)

11. Let's change one of the column entries. Do the following:
SELECT: cell E14
TYPE: **$119.95**
PRESS: ENTER
Notice that the AutoSum result in cell E16 now reads $248.65.

12. Save the workbook by clicking the Save button (💾).

In Addition USING THE AUTOSUM BUTTON (Σ ▾)

Similar to AutoCalculate's right-click menu that allowed you to display an average value, AutoSum provides alternative calculations from the drop-down arrow next to its button (Σ ▾). Click the down arrow to display a list of possible functions. When you click a function command, Excel inserts the function into the cell with the appropriate range parameters.

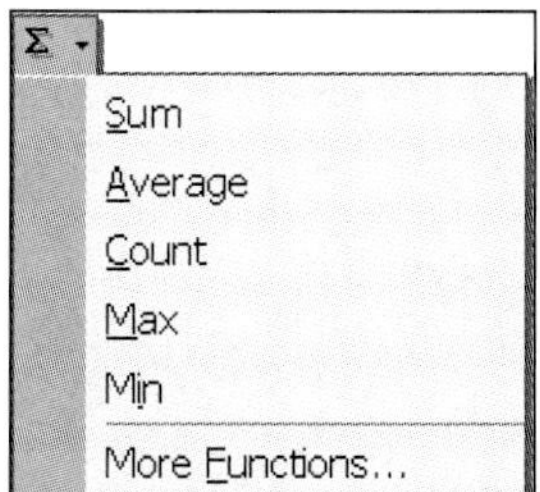

2.1.4 Inserting and Deleting Cells

feature

You can insert a new, empty cell or cell range in the middle of existing data by shifting the data that is in the current selection into the cells immediately below or to the right. Likewise, you can delete a cell or cell range and close the gap that is normally left when you clear the contents of a range.

method

To insert a cell or cell range:

- SELECT: the desired cell or cell range
- CHOOSE: Insert, Cells
- SELECT: *Shift cells right* or *Shift cells down* option button
- CLICK: OK command button

To delete a cell or cell range:

- SELECT: the desired cell or cell range
- CHOOSE: Edit, Delete
- SELECT: *Shift cells left* or *Shift cells up* option button
- CLICK: OK command button

practice

You will now practice inserting and deleting cells. *Setup:* Ensure that the "My Gift List" workbook is displayed.

1. Let's insert a new item into the worksheet list in the proper ascending date order. To begin:
SELECT: cell range from A9 to E9

2. To insert a new range of cells:
CHOOSE: Insert, Cells
The Insert dialog box appears, as shown in Figure 2.9.

Figure 2.9

Inserting a range of cells

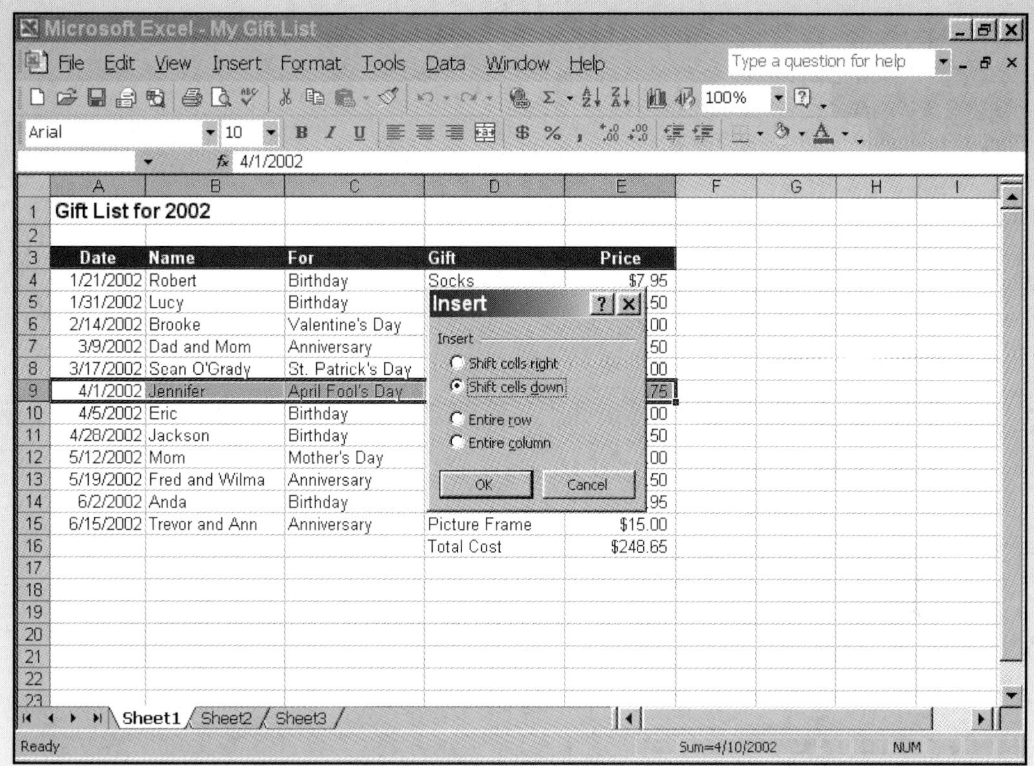

3. To complete the procedure, ensure that the *Shift cells down* option is selected and then do the following:
   CLICK: OK command button
   The existing data is pushed down to make space for the new cells. Notice that the Insert Options icon ( ) appears attached to the right side of the cell range, as shown here. You can use this icon to choose formatting options for the newly inserted cells. Since we want to keep the default formatting for the new row, you can ignore the Insert Options icon ( ) for now.

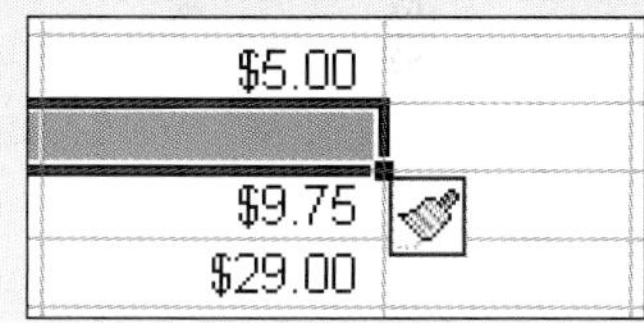

4. With the cell range from A9 to E9 still selected, let's enter a new item:
   TYPE: **3/31/2002**
   PRESS: ENTER
   Notice that the cell pointer moves to the next cell in the selected range, even though you pressed ENTER and not →.

5. To complete the row item with an Anniversary entry:
   TYPE: **Tim and Starr**
   PRESS: ENTER
   TYPE: **An**
   PRESS: ENTER
   TYPE: **Mirror**
   PRESS: ENTER
   TYPE: **$37.00**
   PRESS: ENTER
   Notice that the cell pointer wraps around to the beginning of the selected range and that the "Total Cost" value in cell E17 is updated.

6. Now let's remove Jackson's Birthday from the list:
SELECT: cell range from A12 to E12

7. To delete the selected cells:
CHOOSE: Edit, Delete
The Delete dialog box, similar to the Insert dialog box, is displayed, as shown in Figure 2.10.

Figure 2.10

Deleting a range of cells

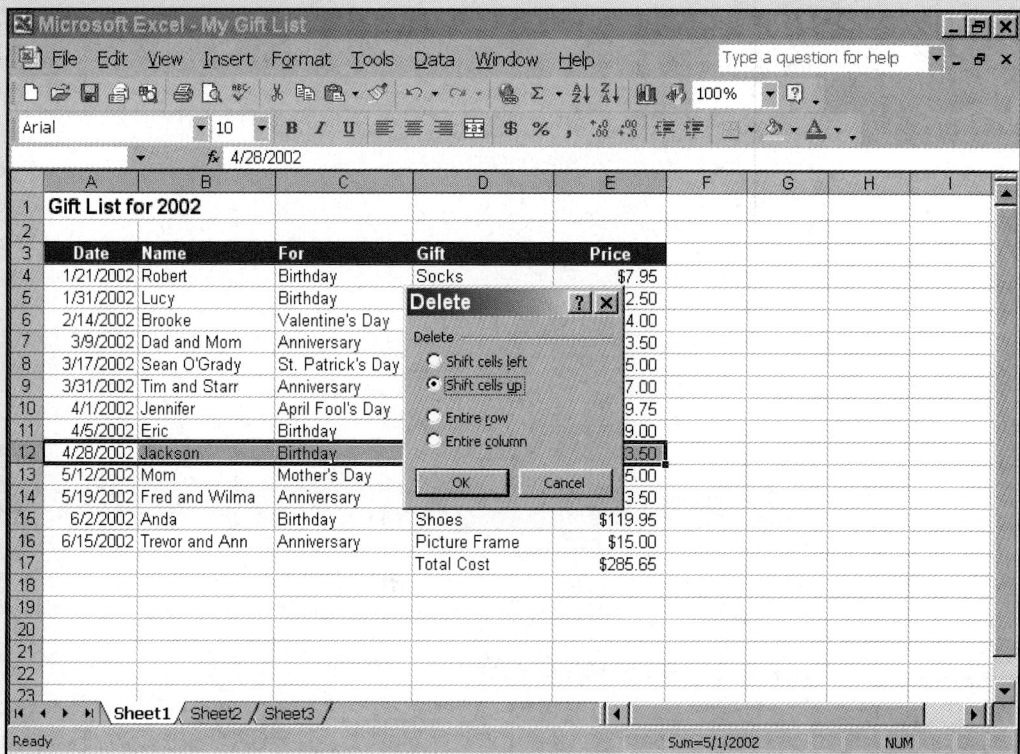

8. To complete the procedure, ensure that the *Shift cells up* option is selected and then do the following:
CLICK: OK command button
The remaining cells slide up one row to close the gap and the "Total Cost" value in cell E16 is updated to $282.15.

9. PRESS: CTRL+HOME to move to cell A1

10. Save and then close the workbook.

2.1. Which of the "Auto" features enables you to sum a range of values and display the result in the Status bar?

Excel

2.2 Copying and Moving Data

Excel provides several tools for copying, moving, and pasting data. Like the "Auto" features, these tools can help you reduce the number of repetitive entries you are required to make. For example, once you enter a formula to sum one column of values, you can duplicate that formula to sum the adjacent columns. There are three primary methods for copying and moving data. First, you can cut or copy a single piece of data from any application and store it on the **Windows Clipboard.** Then, you can paste the data into any other worksheet, workbook, or application. Second, you can choose the **Office Clipboard** to collect up to 24 items and then paste the stored data singularly or as a group into any other Office XP application. Last, you can use **drag and drop** to copy and move cell information short distances using the mouse. In this module, you practice duplicating cell contents and extending data and formulas in a worksheet cell range.

2.2.1 Using the Windows Clipboard

feature

The Windows Clipboard is a software feature provided by the Windows operating system and is shared by the applications running on your computer. A limitation of this Clipboard is that it can hold only a single piece of data at any given time. Its advantage is that you can use it to copy and move data among a variety of software programs. Once data exists on the Clipboard, it may be pasted multiple times and into multiple applications. The contents of the Clipboard are wiped clean, however, when the computer is turned off. When you perform a simple cut, copy, and paste operation in Microsoft Excel, you are using the Windows Clipboard. Your alternatives are to use the Office Clipboard (discussed in the next lesson) for copying multiple items at once or the mouse for quick drag and drop editing.

method

Task description	Menu command	Toolbar button	Keyboard shortcut
Move data from the worksheet to the Clipboard	Edit, Cut		CTRL+x
Place a copy of the selected data on the Clipboard	Edit, Copy		CTRL+c
Insert data stored on the Clipboard into the worksheet	Edit, Paste		CTRL+v

practice

Using the Windows Clipboard, you now practice copying and pasting data in a worksheet. The steps for moving data are identical to copying, except you use the Cut command instead of Copy. Ensure that no workbooks are displayed in the application window.

1. Open the data file named EX0220 to display the workbook shown in Figure 2.11.

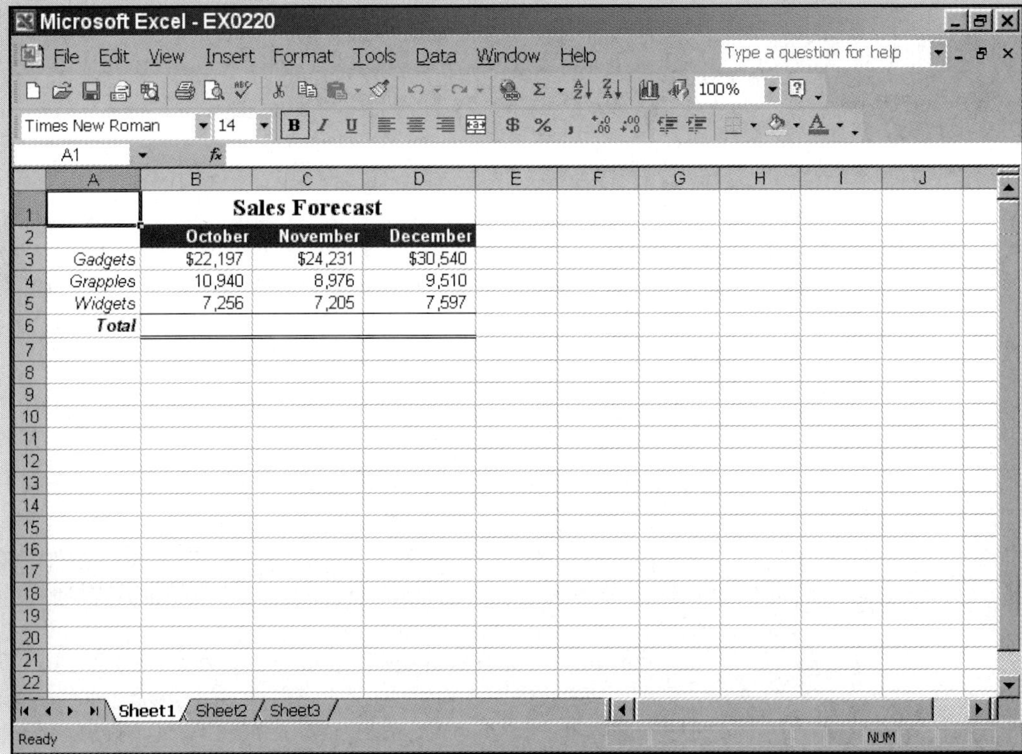

Figure 2.11

Opening the EX0220 workbook

2. Save the file as "Sales Forecast" to your personal storage location.

3. To calculate totals for row 6 in the worksheet:
   SELECT: cell range from B6 to D6
   CLICK: AutoSum button (Σ)
   The results appear immediately in the selected range (Figure 2.12). Notice that you can fill an entire cell range using the AutoSum feature.

Figure 2.12

Entering totals using the AutoSum button (Σ)

	A	B	C	D	E
1		Sales Forecast			
2		October	November	December	
3	*Gadgets*	$22,197	$24,231	$30,540	
4	*Grapples*	10,940	8,976	9,510	
5	*Widgets*	7,256	7,205	7,597	
6	***Total***	$40,393	$40,412	$47,647	
7					
8					

4. You will now use the Copy command to duplicate some cells in the worksheet. To begin:
   SELECT: cell range from A2 to D6
   Notice that all the data is selected, except for the title in row 1.

5. To copy the range selection to the Windows Clipboard:
   CLICK: Copy button (📋) on the Standard toolbar
   The range that you want to copy appears surrounded by a dashed marquee or moving border, as shown in Figure 2.13.

Figure 2.13

Selecting and copying a range to the Clipboard

	A	B	C	D	E
1		Sales Forecast			
2		October	November	December	
3	Gadgets	$22,197	$24,231	$30,540	
4	Grapples	10,940	8,976	9,510	
5	Widgets	7,256	7,205	7,597	
6	Total	$40,393	$40,412	$47,647	
7					
8					

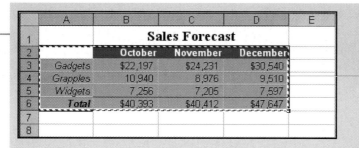

The dashed marquee or moving border is used to signify that the data has been placed onto the Clipboard.

6. You now select the top left-hand corner of the worksheet location where you want to place the copied data. Do the following:
   SELECT: cell A9

7. To paste the data from the Clipboard into the worksheet:
   CLICK: Paste button ( )
   Make sure that you click the clipboard portion of the Paste button ( ) and not the down arrow. Once the data is pasted, notice that the Paste Options icon ( ) is displayed at the bottom right-hand corner of the new cell range. This icon allows you to select advanced formatting and paste options. For our purposes, you can ignore this icon and proceed to the next step.

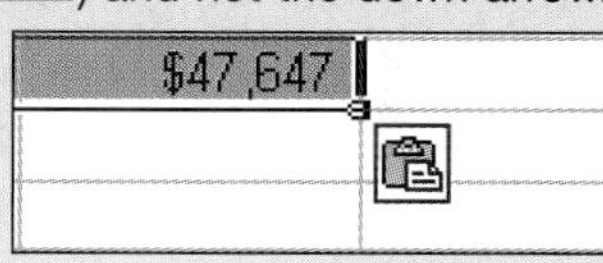

8. While the dashed marquee moves around the original cell range (A2:D6), the data on the Windows Clipboard remains available for pasting. Let's continue pasting the copied data into the worksheet using a shortcut keystroke:
   SELECT: cell A16
   PRESS: CTRL+v to paste the data
   Your screen should now appear similar to Figure 2.14.

Figure 2.14

Copying and pasting data in a worksheet

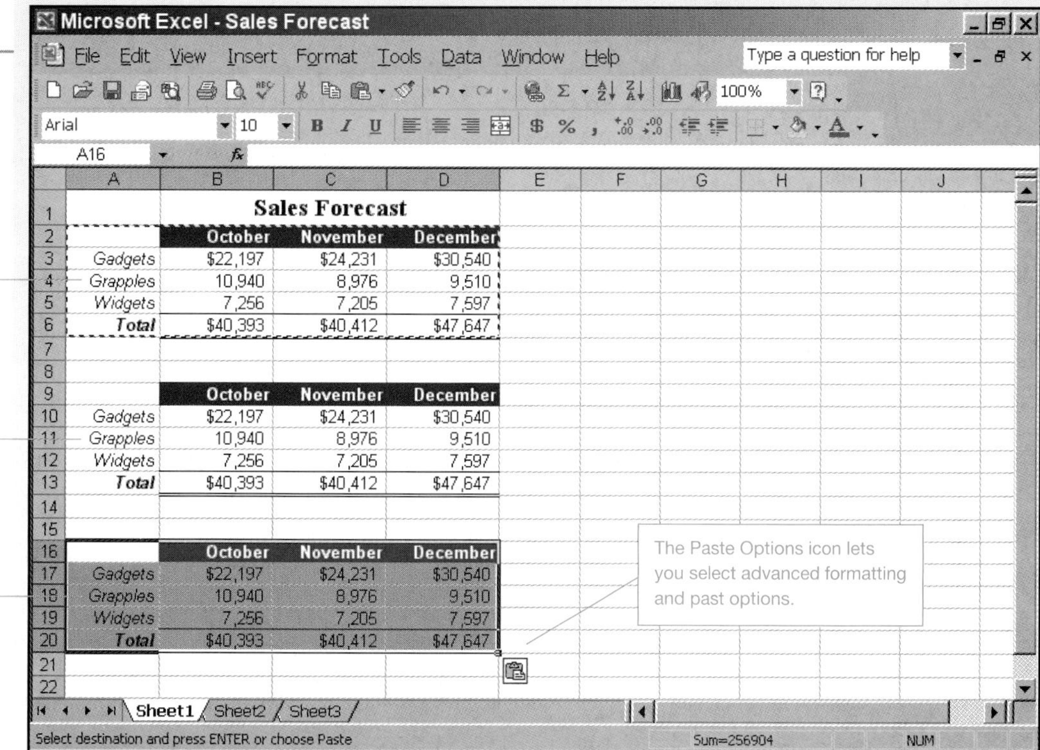

9. To remove the dashed marquee:
PRESS: ESC
Notice that the Paste button on the toolbar is now dimmed. In other words, the data is no longer available for pasting into the worksheet.

10. To return to cell A1:
PRESS: CTRL + HOME

2.2.2 Using the Office Clipboard

feature

The Office Clipboard allows you to collect up to 24 data items and then paste them into Office XP applications like Word, Excel, Access, and PowerPoint. For all intents and purposes, you work with the Office Clipboard in the same manner as you would the system or Windows Clipboard. (*Note:* The last item that you cut or copy to the Office Clipboard will appear as the one item stored on the Windows Clipboard.) However, to copy an item to the Office Clipboard, you must first display the Clipboard task pane using the Edit, Office Clipboard command. Depending on your system's configuration, the Clipboard task pane may open automatically when you perform certain operations.

method

To use the Office Clipboard:

- CHOOSE: Edit, Office Clipboard

practice

You will now practice using the Office Clipboard. Ensure that you have completed the previous lesson and that the "Sales Forecast" workbook is displayed.

1. To demonstrate using the Office Clipboard:
CHOOSE: Edit, Office Clipboard
The Clipboard task pane appears docked at the right side of the application window, as shown in Figure 2.15. (*Hint:* Remember that, unlike the Windows Clipboard, the Office Clipboard can store up to 24 items and then paste them all at the same time.)

Figure 2.15

Displaying the Clipboard task pane

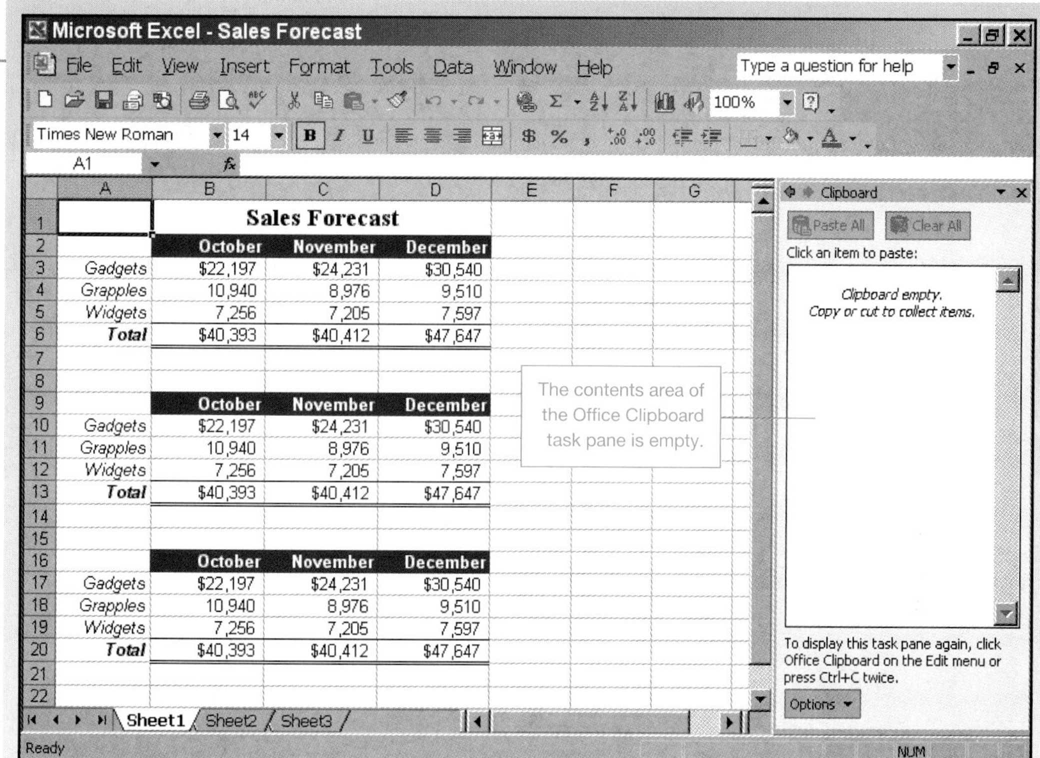

2. If the contents area of the Clipboard task pane is not empty:
   CLICK: Clear All button (Clear All) in the task pane

3. Now let's add data items to the Office Clipboard:
   SELECT: cell A3
   CLICK: Copy button ( )
   Notice that the contents area of the Clipboard task pane now shows "Gadgets" and its title bar reads "1 of 24 – Clipboard."

4. To continue adding items:
   SELECT: cell B3
   CLICK: Copy button ( )
   SELECT: cell C3
   CLICK: Copy button ( )
   SELECT: cell D3
   CLICK: Copy button ( )
   Your Office Clipboard should now appear similar to Figure 2.16. (*Note:* The title bar now reads "4 of 24." If you were to continue adding items, the first item ["Gadgets," in our example] would be overwritten by the 25th item collected.)

Figure 2.16

Clipboard task pane after collecting items

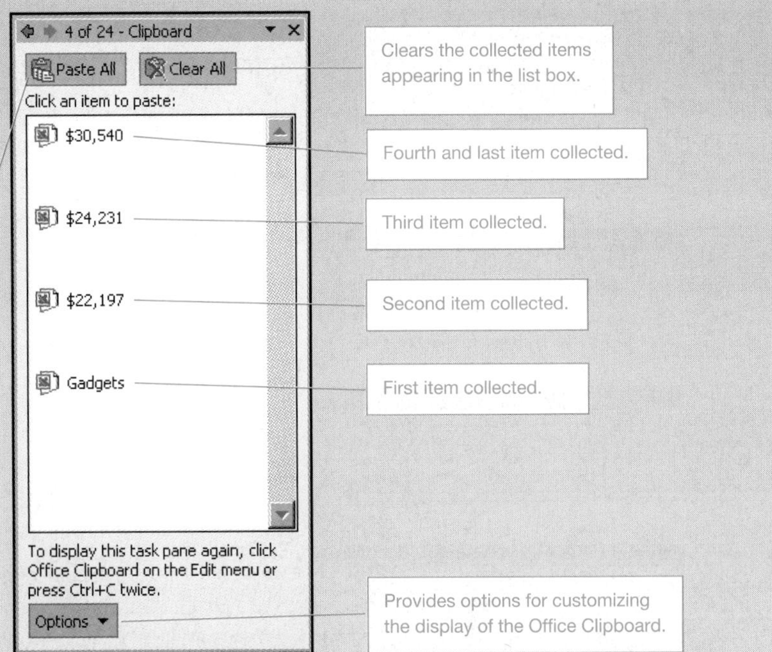

5. Position the mouse pointer over one of the data items in the Clipboard task pane. The item will appear highlighted with a border and an attached down arrow at the right-hand side. On your own, click the down arrow to display the pop-up menu shown here. You use this menu to paste a single item from the list or to remove an item that you no longer need. To remove the pop-up menu, click the attached down arrow a second time.

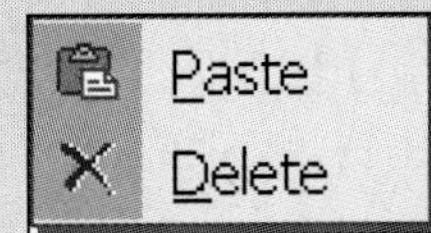

6. Now let's use the Paste All button to insert all of the collected data items into the worksheet. Do the following:
SELECT: cell F2
CLICK: Paste All button (Paste All) in the Clipboard task pane
The contents of the Office Clipboard are pasted vertically into a single column in the worksheet; each data item is placed into its own row, as shown here.

7. Let's prepare for another copy operation:
CLICK: Clear All button (Clear All) in the Clipboard task pane

8. In this step, you want to collect, reorder, and then paste information from rows 3 through 5. The key to this step is to collect the data in the order that you want to paste it later. For example:
SELECT: cell range A5 through D5
PRESS: CTRL+c
SELECT: cell range A3 through D3
PRESS: CTRL+c
SELECT: cell range A4 through D4
PRESS: CTRL+c
You should now see three items listed in the Clipboard task pane.

9. Now let's paste the results on top of an existing data area in the worksheet. Do the following:
SELECT: A10
CLICK: Paste All button (Paste All)
Notice that you need only select the top left-hand corner of the desired target range. Your screen should now appear similar to Figure 2.17.

Figure 2.17

Pasting multiple items into the worksheet

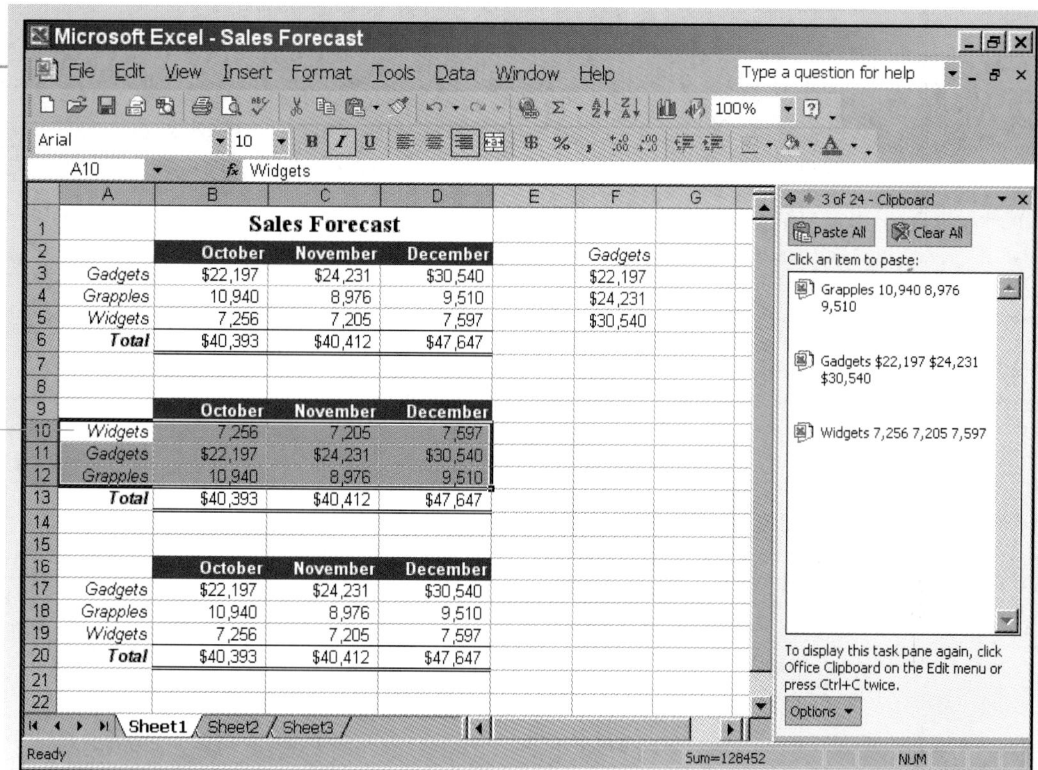

Notice that the rows are ordered differently than the original cell range in rows 3 through 5.

Excel

10. To clear the Office Clipboard and close the Clipboard task pane:
CLICK: Clear All button (Clear All)
CLICK: its Close button (☒)

11. Move the cell pointer to cell A1.

12. Save the workbook and keep it open for use in the next lesson.

In Addition USING THE OFFICE CLIPBOARD TO EXCHANGE DATA IN OFFICE XP

The Office Clipboard is an excellent tool for sharing data among the Microsoft Office XP applications. You can copy worksheet data to the Office Clipboard and then paste the contents into a Word document or a PowerPoint presentation. You can also collect rows of data from an Access database and place them into your worksheet for analysis. When you need to transfer data, consider using the Office Clipboard instead of performing more complex linking and importing routines.

2.2.3 Using Drag and Drop

You can use the mouse (and bypass the Clipboards altogether) to drag and drop data from one location in your worksheet to another. Although you cannot perform multiple pastes, the drag and drop method provides the easiest and fastest way to copy and move cell information short distances.

method

To use drag and drop:

- SELECT: the cell range that you want to copy or move
- Position the mouse pointer over the border of the cell range, until a white arrow pointer appears.
- If you want to perform a copy operation, hold down the CTRL key.
- DRAG: the cell range by the border to the target destination
- Release the mouse button and, if necessary, the CTRL key.

practice

Using a mouse, you will now practice dragging and dropping a cell range in the worksheet. Ensure that you have completed the previous lesson and that the "Sales Forecast" workbook is displayed.

1. Let's practice moving the data that was copied to column F in the previous lesson. Do the following:
   SELECT: cell range from F2 to F5
2. Position the mouse pointer over a border of the selected cell range until a white diagonal arrow over a four-pronged cross appears, as shown here.

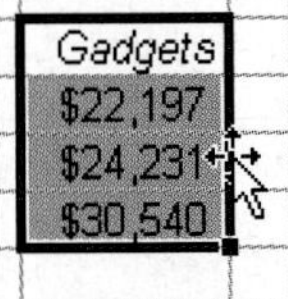

3. CLICK: left mouse button and hold it down
   DRAG: mouse pointer downward until the ToolTip displays "F9:F12"
   Your screen should now appear similar to Figure 2.18.

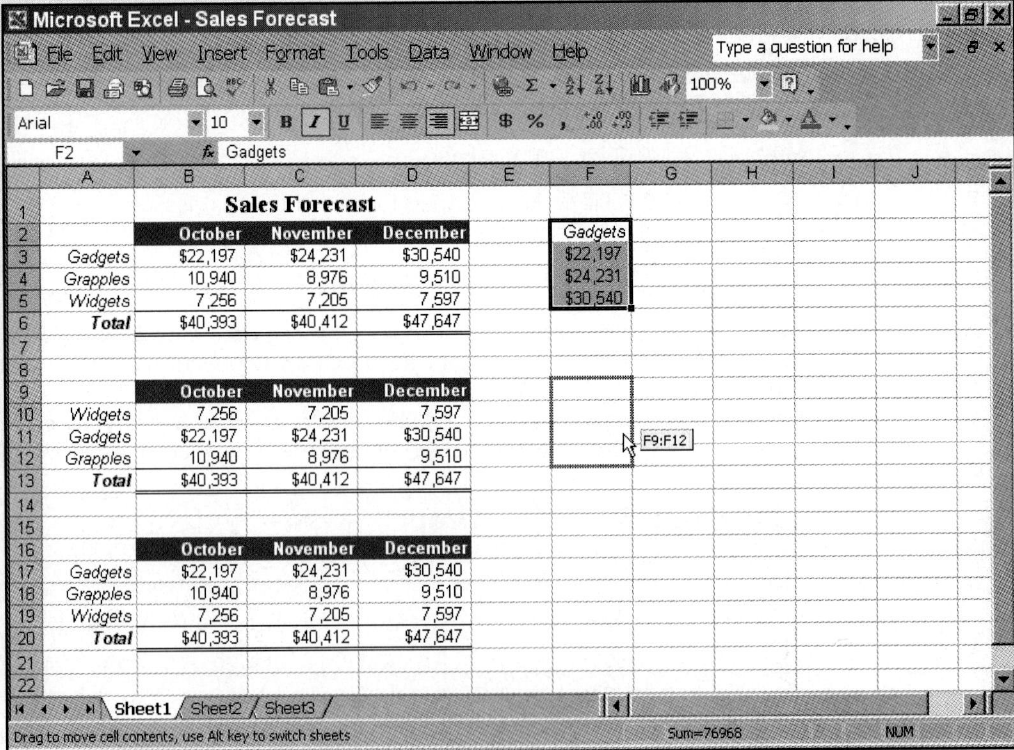

Figure 2.18

Using drag and drop to move cell data

4. Release the mouse button to complete the drag and drop operation.
5. You will now copy the selected cell range back to its original location. To begin, ensure that the cell range from F9 to F12 is highlighted.
6. Position the mouse pointer over a border of the cell range until a white diagonal arrow over a four-pronged cross appears. Then, do the following:
   PRESS: CTRL and hold it down
   You should notice a plus sign added to the diagonal arrow mouse pointer.
7. CLICK: left mouse button and hold it down
   DRAG: mouse pointer upward to F2:F5
   The target cell range should appear as shown here.

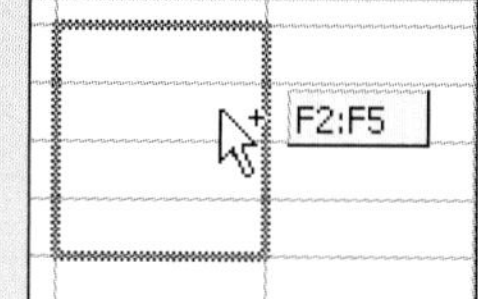

8. Release the mouse button and CTRL key to complete the copy operation. Your screen should appear similar to Figure 2.19.
9. Save and then close the workbook.

Figure 2.19

Completing the Sales Forecast worksheet

Microsoft Excel - Sales Forecast

	A	B	C	D	E	F
1			Sales Forecast			
2		October	November	December		Gadgets
3	Gadgets	$22,197	$24,231	$30,540		$22,197
4	Grapples	10,940	8,976	9,510		$24,231
5	Widgets	7,256	7,205	7,597		$30,540
6	Total	$40,393	$40,412	$47,647		
7						
8						
9		October	November	December		Gadgets
10	Widgets	7,256	7,205	7,597		$22,197
11	Gadgets	$22,197	$24,231	$30,540		$24,231
12	Grapples	10,940	8,976	9,510		$30,540
13	Total	$40,393	$40,412	$47,647		
14						
15						
16		October	November	December		
17	Gadgets	$22,197	$24,231	$30,540		
18	Grapples	10,940	8,976	9,510		
19	Widgets	7,256	7,205	7,597		
20	Total	$40,393	$40,412	$47,647		

Sheet1 / Sheet2 / Sheet3 — Ready — Sum=76968 — NUM

2.2.4 Creating a Series Using AutoFill

Excel's **AutoFill** feature allows you to enter a data series into a worksheet. Whether a mathematical progression of values (1, 2, 3, . . .) or a row of date headings (Jan, Feb, Mar, . . .), a **series** is a sequence of data that follows a pattern. This feature is a real time-saver and reduces the potential for making data entry errors.

method

To use AutoFill:

- SELECT: the cell range containing the data you want to extend
- DRAG: the **fill handle,** which is a black square that appears in the lower right-hand corner of the cell range, to extrapolate the series
- Release the mouse button to complete the operation.

practice

In this exercise, you create a new workbook and then extend the contents of cells using the fill handle and the AutoFill feature. Ensure that no workbooks appear in the application window.

1. To display a new workbook:
   CLICK: New button (□)
2. Let's enter some source data from which you will create a series:
   SELECT: cell A3
   TYPE: **Jan**
   PRESS: ↓
   TYPE: **Period 1**
   PRESS: ↓
   TYPE: **Quarter 1**
   PRESS: ENTER
   Each of these entries will become the starting point for creating a series that extends across their respective rows.
3. To extend the first entry in row 3:
   SELECT: cell A3
4. Position the mouse pointer over the small black square (the fill handle) in the bottom right-hand corner of the cell pointer. The mouse pointer will change to a black cross when positioned correctly. (*Hint:* Figure 2.20 identifies the fill handle and mouse pointer.)

Figure 2.20

Using a cell's fill handle

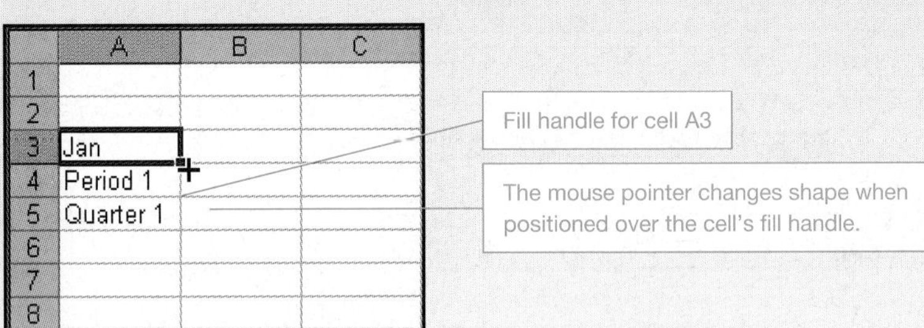

5. CLICK: left mouse button and hold it down
   DRAG: the mouse pointer to column F, until the ToolTip displays "Jun"
6. Release the mouse button to complete the AutoFill operation. The AutoFill Options icon (▦) appears in the bottom right-hand corner of the range (shown here) to provide additional fill options. For our purposes, you can ignore this icon and proceed to the next step.

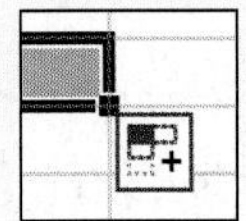

7. Let's extend the next two rows:

SELECT: cell A4
DRAG: fill handle for cell A4 to column F
SELECT: cell A5
DRAG: fill handle for cell A5 to column F
(*Note:* Always release the mouse button after dragging to the desired location.) Notice that Excel recognizes the word "quarter"; it resumes at Quarter 1 after entering Quarter 4, as shown in Figure 2.21.

Figure 2.21

Using AutoFill to complete cell ranges

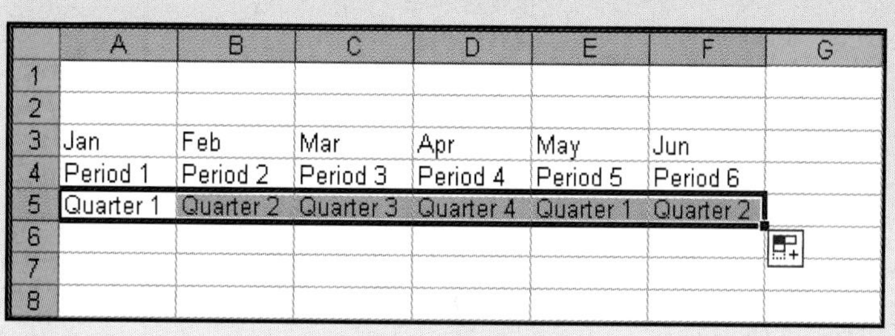

	A	B	C	D	E	F	G
1							
2							
3	Jan	Feb	Mar	Apr	May	Jun	
4	Period 1	Period 2	Period 3	Period 4	Period 5	Period 6	
5	Quarter 1	Quarter 2	Quarter 3	Quarter 4	Quarter 1	Quarter 2	
6							
7							
8							

8. You can also extend a date series using the fill handle:
SELECT: cell A7
TYPE: **Sep-2001**
PRESS: →
TYPE: **Dec-2001**
PRESS: ENTER

9. To extend the range using the same increment, select both cells and then drag the range's fill handle. Do the following:
SELECT: cell range from A7 to B7
DRAG: fill handle for the range to column F
The quarterly dates to Dec-2002 appear.

10. You can also extract a nonlinear series from a range of values:
SELECT: cell A9
TYPE: **12**
PRESS: →
TYPE: **15**
PRESS: →
TYPE: **17**
PRESS: ENTER
Notice that there isn't a static incrementing value in this example.

11. To continue this range of values:
SELECT: cell range from A9 to C9
DRAG: fill handle for the range to column F
Excel calculates a "best guess" for the next few values. Your worksheet should now appear similar to Figure 2.22.

12. Save the workbook as "My Series" and then close the workbook.

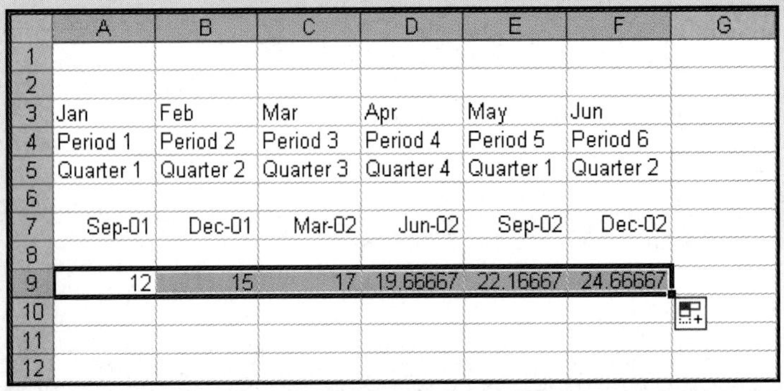

	A	B	C	D	E	F	G
1							
2							
3	Jan	Feb	Mar	Apr	May	Jun	
4	Period 1	Period 2	Period 3	Period 4	Period 5	Period 6	
5	Quarter 1	Quarter 2	Quarter 3	Quarter 4	Quarter 1	Quarter 2	
6							
7	Sep-01	Dec-01	Mar-02	Jun-02	Sep-02	Dec-02	
8							
9	12	15	17	19.66667	22.16667	24.66667	
10							
11							
12							

Figure 2.22

Completing the My Series workbook

2.2.5 Extending a Cell's Contents

feature

Another method for extending the contents of a cell is to use the Edit, Fill commands. These commands are especially useful for extending a formula across a row or down a column in a single step, saving you time. If you prefer using the mouse, you can use a cell's fill handle to perform the same function, as covered in the previous lesson.

method

To extend cell contents:

- SELECT: the desired cell range, ensuring that the data you want to copy is located in the top left-hand corner
- CHOOSE: Edit, Fill, Right (or Left) to copy across a row

or

- CHOOSE: Edit, Fill, Down (or Up) to copy down (or up) a column

practice

In this exercise, you open a cash flow worksheet and then copy and extend the formulas stored in it. Ensure that no workbooks appear in the application window.

1. Open the data file named EX0225 to display the workbook shown in Figure 2.23.

Figure 2.23

Opening the EX0225 workbook

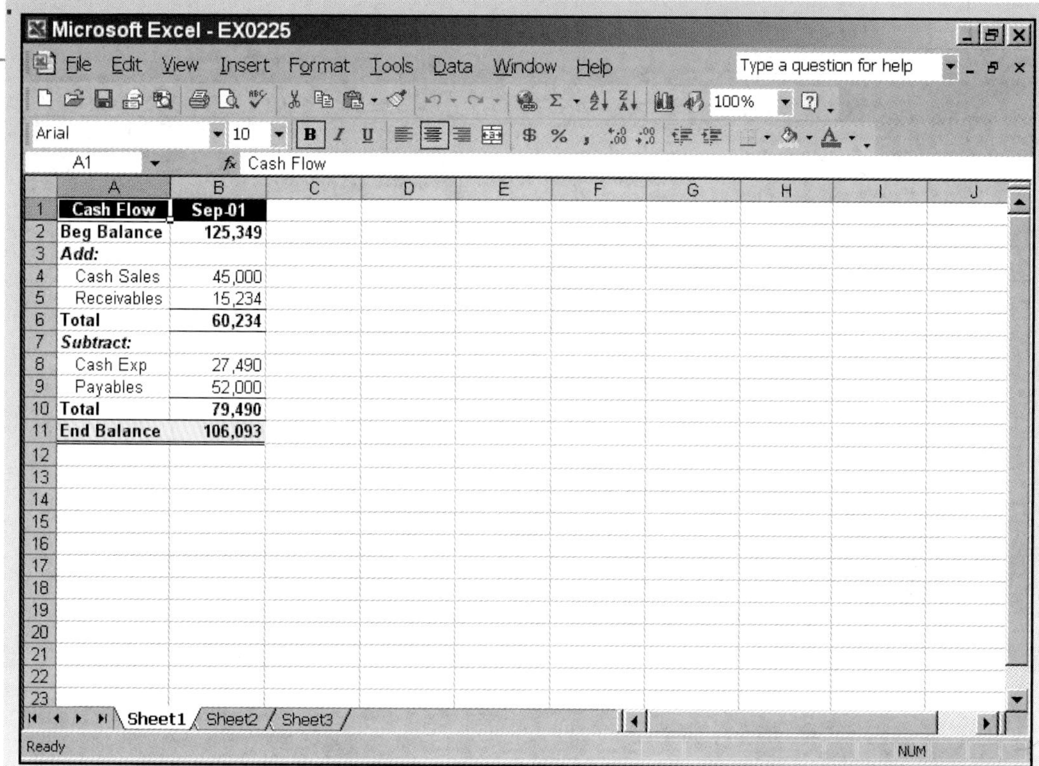

2. Save the file as "Filling Cells" to your personal storage location.

3. To extend the date headings using the AutoFill feature:
SELECT: cell B1
DRAG: fill handle for cell B1 to column E
When you release the mouse button, the formatted date headings are entered into the columns up to Dec-01.

4. In this worksheet, the beginning balance for a new month is the ending balance from the previous month. To enter this formula into column C:
SELECT: cell C2
CLICK: Bold button (**B**) to apply boldface to the cell
TYPE: =**b11**
PRESS: ENTER

5. To copy and extend this formula to the right:
SELECT: cell range from C2 to E2
Notice that the top left-hand cell in the selected range contains the formula (and formatting) that you want to copy.

6. CHOOSE: Edit, Fill, Right
For the moment, only zeroes will appear in the remaining cells, as shown in Figure 2.24.

Figure 2.24

Extending cells using the Edit, Fill, Right command

	A	B	C	D	E	F
1	**Cash Flow**	**Sep-01**	**Oct-01**	**Nov-01**	**Dec-01**	
2	**Beg Balance**	**125,349**	**106,093**	**0**	**0**	
3	***Add:***					
4	Cash Sales	45,000				
5	Receivables	15,234				
6	**Total**	**60,234**				
7	***Subtract:***					
8	Cash Exp	27,490				
9	Payables	52,000				
10	**Total**	**79,490**				
11	**End Balance**	**106,093**				
12						
13						

The top left-hand cell in the cell range contains the data that you want extended to the otehr cells.

7. To extend the formulas for multiple ranges:
SELECT: cell range from B6 to E6
PRESS: CTRL and hold it down
SELECT: cell range from B10 to E10
SELECT: cell range from B11 to E11
When all the ranges are highlighted, release the CTRL key.

8. To fill each row with formulas from column B:
CHOOSE: Edit, Fill, Right
Your worksheet should now appear similar to Figure 2.25.

Figure 2.25

Filling multiple ranges with formulas stored in the leftmost column

	A	B	C	D	E	F
1	**Cash Flow**	**Sep-01**	**Oct-01**	**Nov-01**	**Dec-01**	
2	**Beg Balance**	**125,349**	**106,093**	**106,093**	**106,093**	
3	***Add:***					
4	Cash Sales	45,000				
5	Receivables	15,234				
6	**Total**	**60,234**	**0**	**0**	**0**	
7	***Subtract:***					
8	Cash Exp	27,490				
9	Payables	52,000				
10	**Total**	**79,490**	**0**	**0**	**0**	
11	**End Balance**	**106,093**	**106,093**	**106,093**	**106,093**	
12						
13						

9. On your own, enter sample values into the worksheet and observe how the formulas recalculate the totals.

10. Save and then close the workbook.

2.2. Which method would you use to copy several nonadjacent worksheet values for placement into a single column?

2.3 Modifying Rows and Columns

By adjusting the row heights and column widths in a worksheet, you can enhance its appearance for both viewing and printing—similarly to how a textbook employs white space or a document uses double-spacing to make the text easier to read. You can also reorganize or modify the structure of a worksheet by inserting and deleting rows and columns. This module shows you how to manipulate the appearance and structure of a worksheet.

2.3.1 Changing Column Widths

feature

You can increase and decrease the width of your worksheet columns to allow for varying lengths of text labels, numbers, and dates. To speed the process, you can select and change more than one column width at a time. Excel can even calculate the best or **AutoFit** width for a column based on its existing entries. The maximum width for a column is 255 characters.

method

To change a column's width using the mouse:

- DRAG: its right borderline in the frame area

To change a column's width using the menu:

- SELECT: a cell in the column that you want to format
- CHOOSE: Format, Column, Width
- TYPE: a value, such as 12, for the desired width

To change a column's width to its best fit:

- DOUBLE-CLICK: its right borderline in the frame area,

or

- CHOOSE: Format, Column, AutoFit Selection

practice

In this lesson, you open a workbook used to summarize the income earned by organizers of a craft fair. Then you practice changing the worksheet's column widths to better view the data stored therein. Ensure that no workbooks are open in the application window.

1. Open the data file named EX0230 to display the workbook shown in Figure 2.26.

Excel

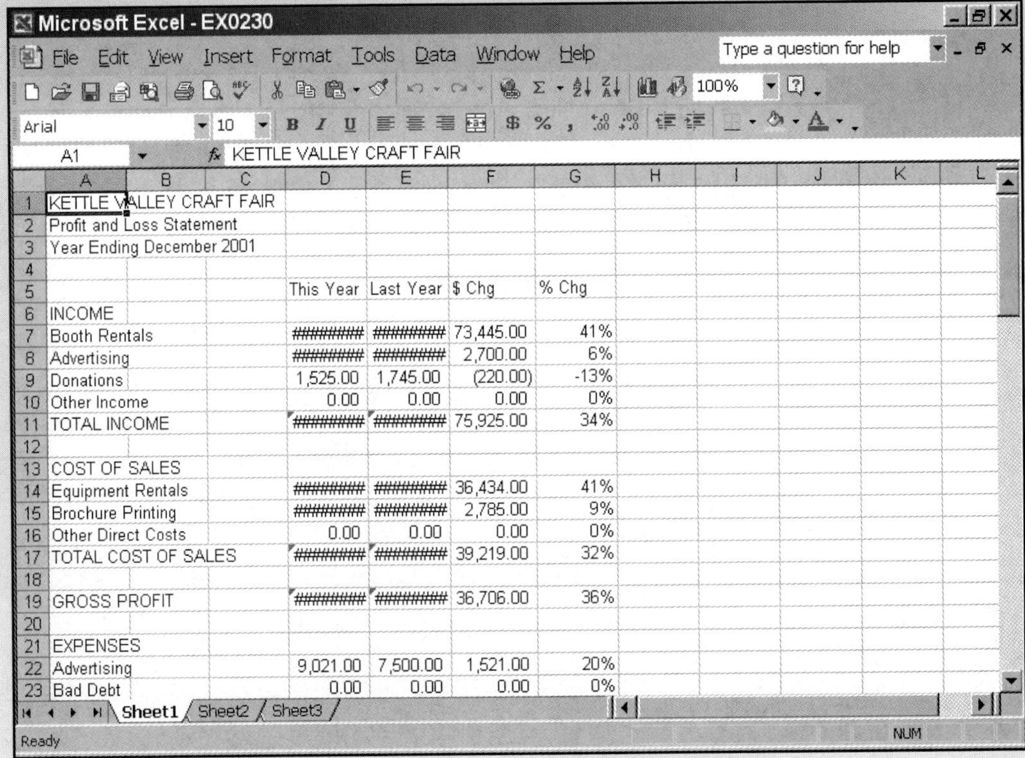

Figure 2.26

Opening the EX0230 workbook

2. Save the file as "Craft Fair" to your personal storage location.

3. In columns D and E of the worksheet, notice that some cells contain a series of "#" symbols. These symbols inform you that the columns are not wide enough to display the contents. To adjust the width of column D using a command from the Menu bar, first:
   SELECT: cell D1
   Notice that you need not select the entire column to change its width; in fact, you can choose any cell within the column.

4. CHOOSE: Format, Column, Width
   The Column Width dialog box appears, as shown here. Notice that 8.43 characters is the default column width.

5. Enter the desired width as measured in characters:
   TYPE: **12**
   PRESS: ENTER or CLICK: OK
   All of the values stored in column D should now be visible.

6. Now let's adjust the width for column E using the mouse. In the frame area, position the mouse pointer over the borderline between columns E and F. The mouse pointer changes shape when positioned correctly, as shown in Figure 2.27.

7. CLICK: the borderline and hold down the mouse button
DRAG: the mouse pointer to the right to increase the width to 12.00
Notice that the width (in characters and pixels) is displayed in a ToolTip. Your screen should now appear similar to Figure 2.27.

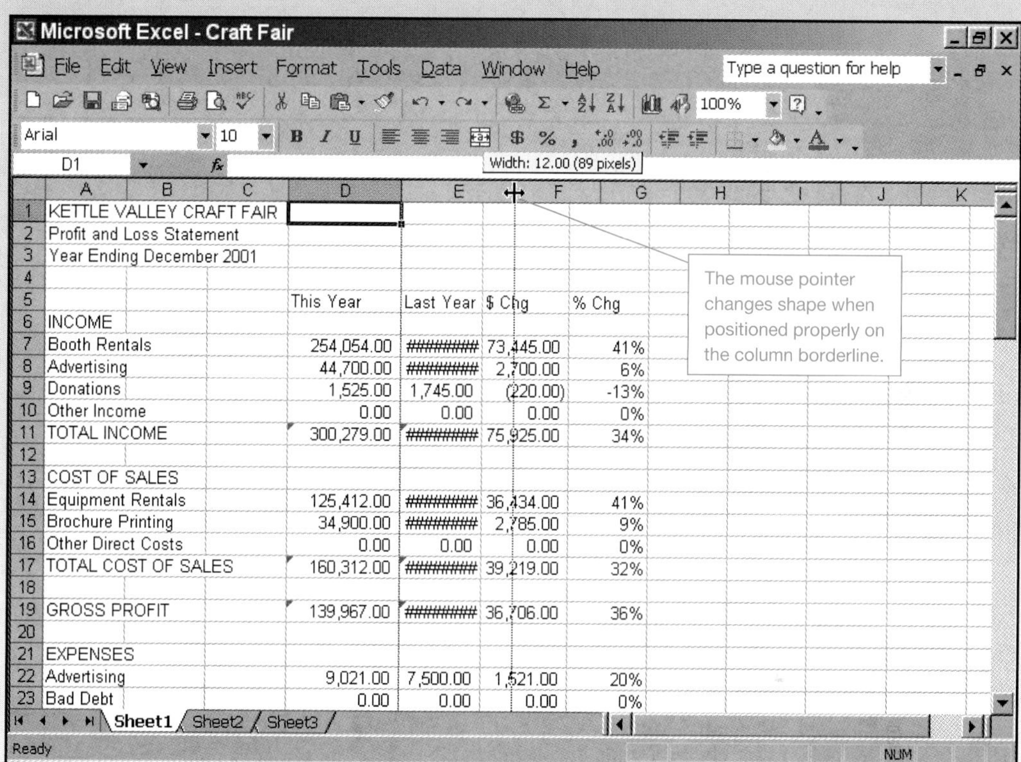

Figure 2.27

Changing a column's width

8. Remember to release the mouse button to finalize the new column width setting.

9. The AutoFit feature enables you to find the best width for a column based on its existing entries. To adjust column A, let's select the entire column as the basis for the width calculation. Do the following:
SELECT: column A
(*Hint:* This instruction tells you to move the mouse pointer over the "A" in the column frame area and click once. When this is done properly, the entire column will appear highlighted, as shown here.)

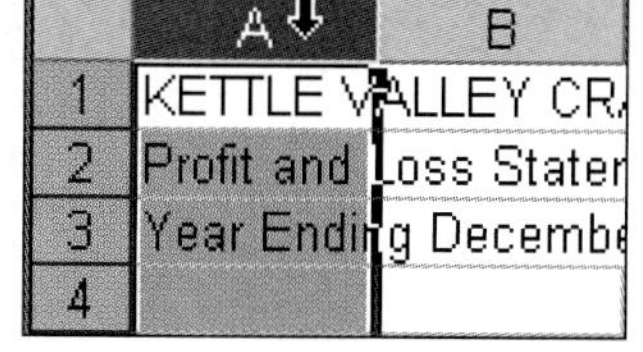

10. CHOOSE: Format, Column, AutoFit Selection
Notice that the width has been adjusted so that it can comfortably hold the longest entry in the column.

In Addition DOUBLE-CLICKING TO AUTOFIT A COLUMN OR ROW

When you become comfortable using the mouse to select the frame borderlines, try double-clicking the right frame borderline of a column or the bottom frame borderline of a row to AutoFit its width or height.

2.3.2 Changing Row Heights

feature →

You can change the height of any worksheet row to customize the borders and line spacing in a worksheet. What's more, a row's height is adjusted automatically when you increase or decrease the font size of information appearing in the row. A row's height is measured in points, where 72 points is equal to one inch. The larger the font size that you select for a given cell, the larger its row height.

method →

To change a row's height using the mouse:

- DRAG: its bottom borderline in the frame area

To change a row's height using the menu:

- SELECT: a cell in the row that you want to format
- CHOOSE: Format, Row, Height
- TYPE: **a value,** such as 20, for the desired height in points

To change a row's height to its best fit:

- DOUBLE-CLICK: its bottom borderline in the frame area,

or

- CHOOSE: Format, Row, AutoFit

practice →

You will now change some row heights in a worksheet to improve the spacing between data. Ensure that you have completed the previous lesson and that the "Craft Fair" workbook is displayed.

1. SELECT: cell A1
2. In the next two steps, you will change the line spacing for the entire worksheet. As with most formatting commands, you must first select the object for which you want to apply formatting. In this case, you need to select the entire worksheet. To begin:
   CLICK: Select All button ( ), as shown below

Click here to select all of the cells in the entire worksheet.

	A	B
1	KETTLE VALLEY CRAFT FAIR	
2	Profit and Loss Statement	
3	Year Ending December 2001	
4		

3. With the entire worksheet highlighted:
   CHOOSE: Format, Row, Height
   The dialog box on the following page appears.

4. In the *Row height* text box, enter the desired height as measured in points:
   TYPE: **20**
   PRESS: ENTER or CLICK: OK
   Notice that the rows are enlarged, providing more white space, as shown in Figure 2.28.

Figure 2.28

Changing the row height of all cells in the worksheet

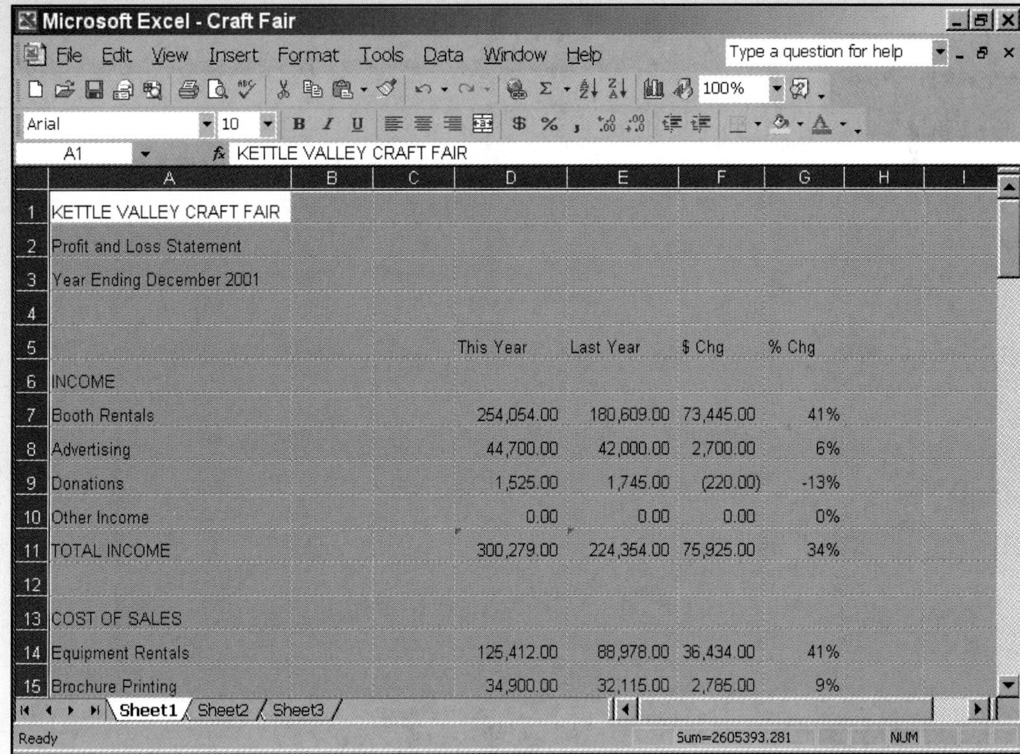

5. To remove the selection highlighting:
   CLICK: cell A1

6. Let's change the height of row 4 using the mouse. To do so, position the mouse pointer over the borderline between rows 4 and 5. Then:
   CLICK: the borderline and hold down the mouse button
   DRAG: the mouse pointer up to decrease the height to 9.00 points
   As when you changed the column width, the mouse pointer changes and a yellow ToolTip appears with the current measurement, as shown here.

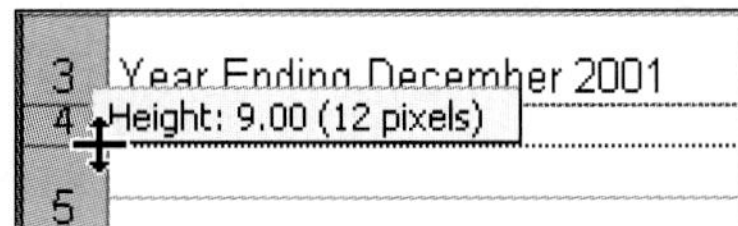

7. Release the mouse button to finalize the new setting.

8. Let's practice adjusting a row to its best height:
SELECT: row 5
(*Hint:* This instruction tells you to move the mouse pointer over the "5" in the row frame area and click once. When this is done properly, the entire row will appear highlighted.)

9. CHOOSE: Format, Row, AutoFit
The row height is adjusted automatically, as shown in Figure 2.29.

10. Save the workbook and keep it open for use in the next lesson.

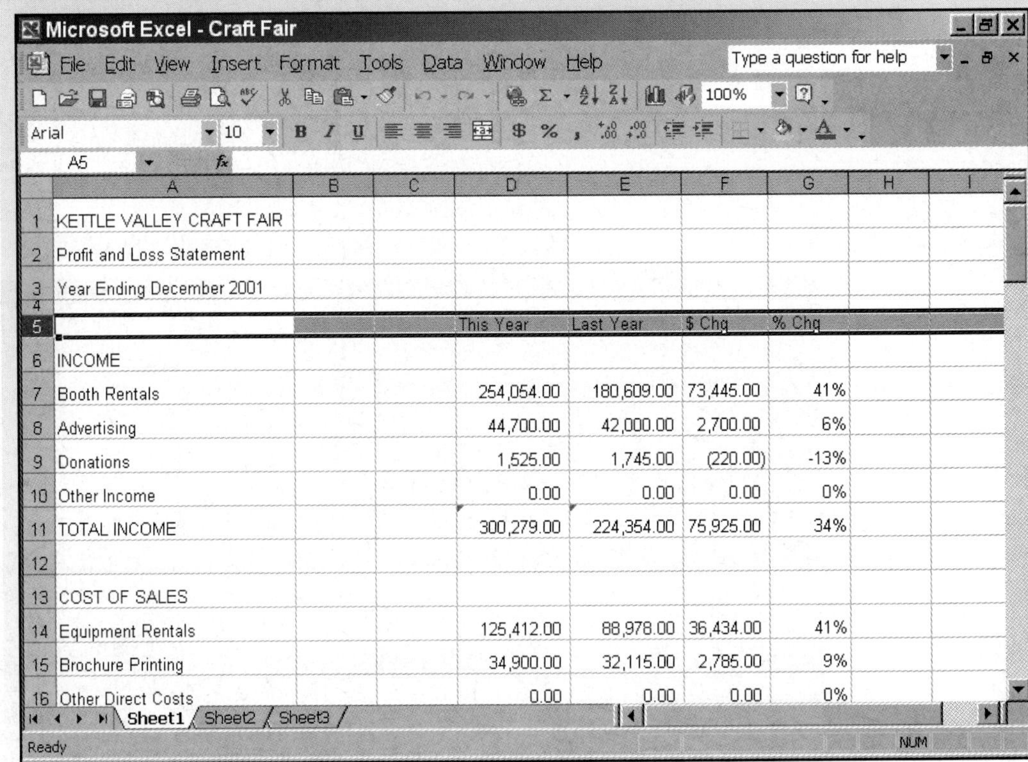

Figure 2.29

Using AutoFit to change a row's height

2.3.3 Inserting and Deleting Rows and Columns

feature

You insert and delete rows and columns to affect the structure of a worksheet. But in doing so, you must be careful not to change other areas in your worksheet unintentionally. Deleting column B, for example, removes all of the data in the entire column, not just the cells that are currently visible on your screen.

method

To insert or delete a row:

- RIGHT-CLICK: a *row number* in the frame area
- CHOOSE: Insert or Delete

To insert or delete a column:

- RIGHT-CLICK: a *column letter* in the frame area
- CHOOSE: Insert or Delete

practice

In this lesson, you will practice inserting and deleting rows and columns. Ensure that you have completed the previous lessons and that the "Craft Fair" workbook is displayed.

1. After adjusting the width for column A earlier in the module, you may have noticed that columns B and C do not contain any data. Before deleting rows or columns, however, it is always wise to check your assumptions. To do so:
   CLICK: cell B1
   PRESS: CTRL+↓
   The cell pointer scoots down to row 65536. If there were data in the column, the cell pointer would have stopped at the cell containing the data.

2. To check whether there is any data in column C:
   PRESS: →
   PRESS: CTRL+↑
   The cell pointer scoots back up to row 1, not stopped by any cells containing data.

3. Now that you are sure that these columns are indeed empty, let's delete them from the worksheet. To begin, select both of the columns:
   CLICK: column B in the frame area
   DRAG: the mouse pointer right to also highlight column C, as shown here
   Release the mouse button after the two columns appear highlighted.

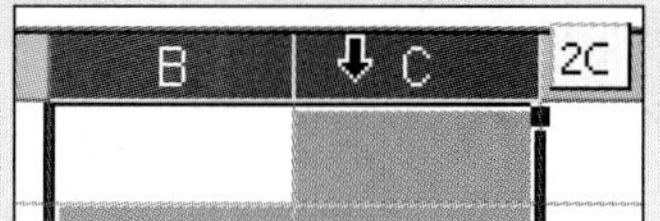

4. To delete these two columns:
   RIGHT-CLICK: column C in the frame area
   Notice that you need only right-click one of the selected column letters. Your screen should now appear similar to Figure 2.30.

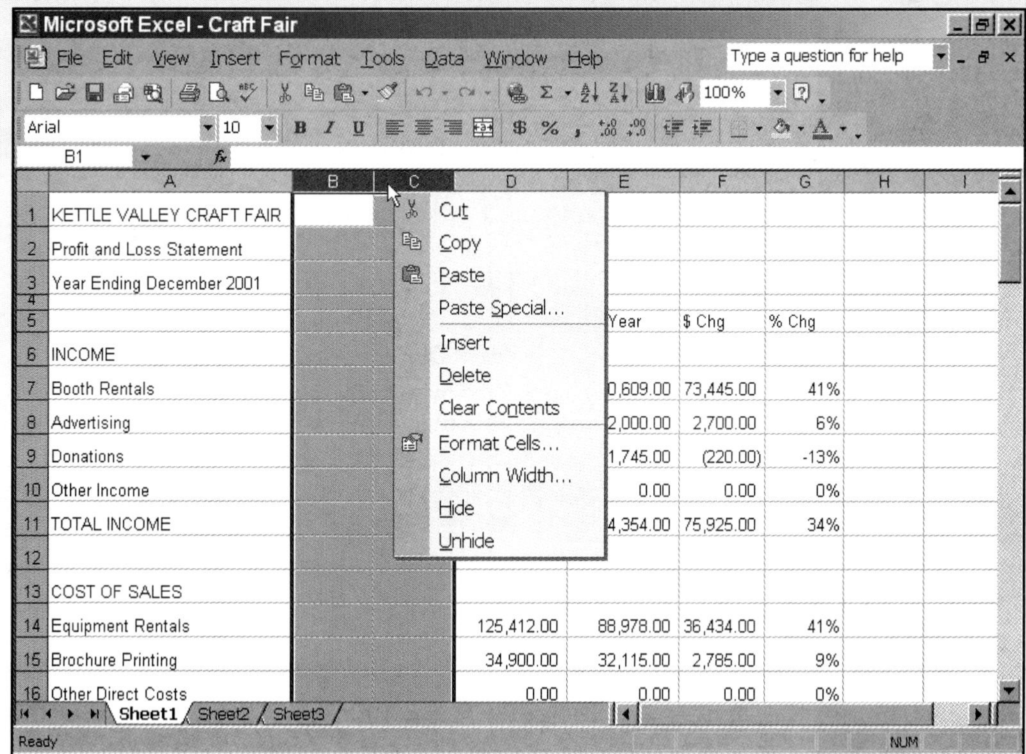

Figure 2.30

Displaying the right-click menu for selected columns

Excel

5. From the right-click menu:
CHOOSE: Delete
The blank columns are removed, but the column selection remains highlighted in case you want to apply additional formatting commands.

6. To insert a row:
RIGHT-CLICK: row 8 in the frame area
CHOOSE: Insert
A new row is inserted at row 8, pushing down the existing rows. The Insert Options icon () also appears below the newly inserted row.

7. To enter some new information:
SELECT: cell A8
TYPE: **Food Pavilion**
PRESS: →
TYPE: **55800**
PRESS: →
TYPE: **43750**
PRESS: ENTER

8. To copy the formulas for calculating the annual increase:
SELECT: cell range D7 to E8
CHOOSE: Edit, Fill, Down
The results, 12,050.00 and 28%, now appear in row 8.

9. Move to cell A1. Your screen should appear similar to Figure 2.31.

10. Save the workbook and keep it open for use in the next lesson.

Figure 2.31

Inserting and deleting rows in the Craft Fair workbook

Microsoft Excel - Craft Fair

File Edit View Insert Format Tools Data Window Help — Type a question for help

A1 — KETTLE VALLEY CRAFT FAIR

	A	B	C	D	E
1	KETTLE VALLEY CRAFT FAIR				
2	Profit and Loss Statement				
3	Year Ending December 2001				
4					
5		This Year	Last Year	$ Chg	% Chg
6	INCOME				
7	Booth Rentals	254,054.00	180,609.00	73,445.00	41%
8	Food Pavilion	55,800.00	43,750.00	12,050.00	28%
9	Advertising	44,700.00	42,000.00	2,700.00	6%
10	Donations	1,525.00	1,745.00	(220.00)	-13%
11	Other Income	0.00	0.00	0.00	0%
12	TOTAL INCOME	356,079.00	268,104.00	87,975.00	33%
13					
14	COST OF SALES				
15	Equipment Rentals	125,412.00	88,978.00	36,434.00	41%
16	Brochure Printing	34,900.00	32,115.00	2,785.00	9%

Sheet1 / Sheet2 / Sheet3

Ready NUM

Newly inserted row with information entered

2.3.4 Hiding and Unhiding Rows and Columns

feature

Rather than deleting a row or column, you can modify a worksheet so that not all of the data are displayed. For example, you may want to hide rows and columns that contain sensitive data, such as salaries or commissions. You can also hide detailed information temporarily if you do not want it included in a particular report.

method

To hide a row or column:

- RIGHT-CLICK: the frame area of the desired row or column
- CHOOSE: Hide

To unhide a row or column:

- SELECT: the rows or columns on both sides of the hidden row or column
- RIGHT-CLICK: the frame area of the selected rows or columns
- CHOOSE: Unhide

practice

In this lesson, you practice hiding and unhiding worksheet information. Ensure that you have completed the previous lessons and that the "Craft Fair" workbook is displayed.

1. Let's hide columns D and E from displaying. Do the following:
   CLICK: column D in the frame area
   DRAG: the mouse pointer right to also highlight column E
2. To hide the selected columns:
   RIGHT-CLICK: column E in the frame area
   CHOOSE: Hide
   Notice that the column frame area now shows A, B, C, and then F.
3. To hide several rows in the worksheet:
   SELECT: rows 6 through 11 in the frame area
   RIGHT-CLICK: row 6 in the frame area
   CHOOSE: Hide
   PRESS: CTRL+HOME to move the cell pointer
   The row frame area, as shown in Figure 2.32, now displays a gap between row 5 and row 12.

Figure 2.32

Hiding columns and rows

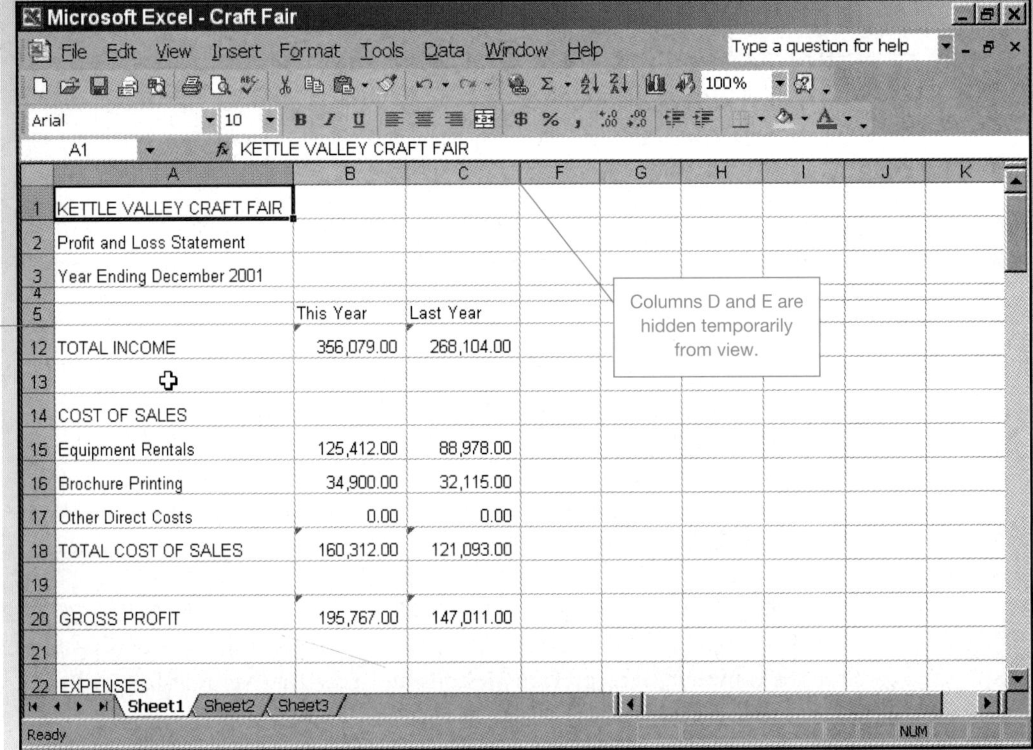

4. To unhide columns D and E, you must select the columns on either side. For example:
   CLICK: column C in the frame area
   DRAG: the mouse pointer right to also highlight column F
5. Let's use the Menu bar to unhide the columns:
   CHOOSE: Format, Column, Unhide
   The columns reappear on the worksheet.
6. To unhide the rows:
   SELECT: rows 5 through 12
   CHOOSE: Format, Row, Unhide
   The rows reappear on the worksheet.
7. Move to cell A1. Your screen should now appear similar to Figure 2.31 at the end of the last lesson.
8. Save and then close the workbook.
9. Exit Microsoft Excel.

2.3. Why must you be careful when deleting rows or columns?

Chapter summary

Excel provides tools that make it easier to modify the contents and structure of a worksheet. The "Auto" features include AutoComplete to finish typing an entry that matches other entries, and AutoSum and AutoCalculate for entering formulas. AutoFill completes a series of data when a cell range's fill handle is dragged. The Windows and Office Clipboards and Excel's drag and drop feature make it easy to move or copy data. To modify the structure of a worksheet, cells, rows, and columns can be inserted and deleted. Rows and columns can also be hidden or unhidden for use in various reports, and row height and column widths can be adjusted for a better appearance.

Command Summary

Many of the commands and procedures appearing in this chapter are summarized in the following table.

Skill Set	To Perform This Task	Do the Following
Creating and Revising Formulas	Enter the SUM function using the AutoSum button	SELECT: a cell to place the result CLICK: AutoSum button (Σ)
	Display the sum result of a calculation using AutoCalculate	SELECT: a cell range and view the result in the Status bar
Working with Cells and Cell Data	Insert a cell or cell range	SELECT: the desired cell range CHOOSE: Insert, Cells
	Delete a cell or cell range	SELECT: the desired cell range CHOOSE: Edit, Delete
	Insert data using AutoComplete	RIGHT-CLICK: the desired cell CHOOSE: Pick From List SELECT: the desired data
	Copy or move data using the toolbar	SELECT: the desired cell or range CLICK: Copy ( ) or Cut ( ) SELECT: the target cell or range CLICK: Paste button ( )
	Move data using drag and drop	SELECT: the desired cell or range DRAG: the selection by its border
	Copy data using drag and drop	SELECT: the desired cell or range PRESS: CTRL and hold it down DRAG: the selection by its border
	Display the Clipboard task pane	CHOOSE: Edit, Office Clipboard
	Clear the Office Clipboard	CLICK: Clear All button (Clear All)
	Paste all of the contents from the Office Clipboard into the worksheet	CLICK: Paste All button (Paste All)
	Create a data series using the fill handle	SELECT: the desired range DRAG: the fill handle
	Copy a formula across a row or down a column	SELECT: the range to fill, with the formula in the top left-hand corner CHOOSE: Edit, Fill, Right (or Down)

Skill Set	To Perform This Task	Do the Following
Formatting and Printing Worksheets	Change a cell's column width	CHOOSE: Format, Column, Width TYPE: width in characters
	Change a cell's row height	CHOOSE: Format, Row, Height TYPE: height in points
	Insert and delete columns	RIGHT-CLICK: a column's frame area CHOOSE: Insert or Delete
	Insert and delete rows	RIGHT-CLICK: a row's frame area CHOOSE: Insert or Delete
	Hide a row or column	RIGHT-CLICK: in the frame area CHOOSE: Hide
	Unhide a row or column	SELECT: rows or columns on either side of the hidden row or column RIGHT-CLICK: the frame selection CHOOSE: Unhide

Key Terms

This section specifies page references for the key terms identified in this chapter. For a complete list of definitions, refer to the Glossary at the back of this learning guide.

AutoCalculate, *p. EX 62*
AutoComplete, *p. EX 60*
AutoFill, *p. EX 77*
AutoFit, *p. EX 83*
AutoSum, *p. EX 62*
cell range, *p. EX 56*
cell reference, *p. EX 2*
drag and drop, *p. EX 69*
fill handle, *p. EX 78*
Office Clipboard, *p. EX 69*
series, *p. EX 77*
Windows Clipboard, *p. EX 69*

Chapter quiz

Short Answer

1. What visible feature differentiates the active cell in a selected cell range?
2. How do you select more than one cell range at a time?
3. Where does Excel's AutoComplete feature get the values to display in a pick list?
4. What are the two choices for shifting existing data when you insert a new cell or cell range?
5. Name the two types of Clipboards and explain how they differ.

6. What is the primary difference between using the Clipboards and using the drag and drop method to copy information?
7. What is the fastest way to place five years' worth of quarterly headings at the top of your worksheet (that is, Jan-02, Mar-02, Jun-02, . . .)?
8. What does "########" in a cell indicate?
9. What is meant by a "best fit" or "AutoFit" column width?
10. In what circumstances might you want to hide a row or column?

True/False

1. ____ You use ALT to select a range of cells using the keyboard.
2. ____ Excel's AutoComplete feature allows you to sum a range of values and place the result into a worksheet cell.
3. ____ You use the Edit, Clear command to delete the contents of a cell and the Edit, Delete command to delete the actual cell.
4. ____ You can collect up to 24 items for pasting using the Office Clipboard.
5. ____ You can collect up to four items for pasting using the Windows Clipboard.
6. ____ When you drag and drop using the CTRL key, a plus sign appears indicating that you are using the copy feature.
7. ____ To copy and extend a formula to adjacent cells, you can use either the fill handle or the Edit, Fill, Right command.
8. ____ When you insert a column, the existing column is pushed left.
9. ____ When you insert a row, the existing row is pushed down.
10. ____ You unhide rows and columns using the Window, Unhide command.

Multiple Choice

1. You hold down the following key to select multiple cell ranges using the mouse.
   a. ALT
   b. CTRL
   c. SHIFT
   d. PRTSCR
2. This feature allows you to view the sum of a range of values without entering a formula into a worksheet cell.
   a. AutoCalculate
   b. AutoComplete
   c. AutoTotal
   d. AutoValue
3. The AutoSum feature enters this function into a cell to sum a range of values:
   a. ADD
   b. SUM
   c. TOTAL
   d. VALUE
4. If you want to delete cells from the worksheet, you select the desired range and then choose the following command:
   a. Edit, Clear, All
   b. Edit, Clear, Cells
   c. Edit, Cells, Delete
   d. Edit, Delete

5. To perform a drag and drop operation, you position the mouse pointer over the selected cell or cell range until it changes to this shape.
   a. ‡
   b. ✥
   c. ✣
   d. ✛

6. What menu command allows you to copy a formula in the active cell to a range of adjacent cells in a row?
   a. Edit, Fill, Down
   b. Edit, Fill, Right
   c. Edit, Copy, Right
   d. Edit, Extend, Fill

7. To select an entire column for editing, inserting, or deleting:
   a. PRESS: ALT + ↓ with the cell pointer in the column
   b. DOUBLE-CLICK: a cell within the column
   c. CLICK: the column letter in the frame area
   d. CHOOSE: Edit, Select Column

8. The height of a row is typically measured using these units.
   a. characters
   b. fonts
   c. picas
   d. points

9. To change a column's width using the mouse, you position the mouse pointer into the column frame area until it changes to this shape.
   a. ╋
   b. ✥
   c. ↖
   d. ✛

10. Row 5 is hidden on your worksheet. To unhide the row, you must make this selection before issuing the appropriate menu command.
   a. rows 4 and 6
   b. rows 1 through 4
   c. row 4
   d. row 6

Hands-On exercises

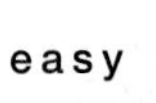

1. Brentwood Academy: Course List

In this exercise, you practice using Excel's "Auto" features to enter information and calculate results.

1. Load Microsoft Excel.
2. Open the data file named EX02HE01 to display the workbook shown in Figure 2.33.

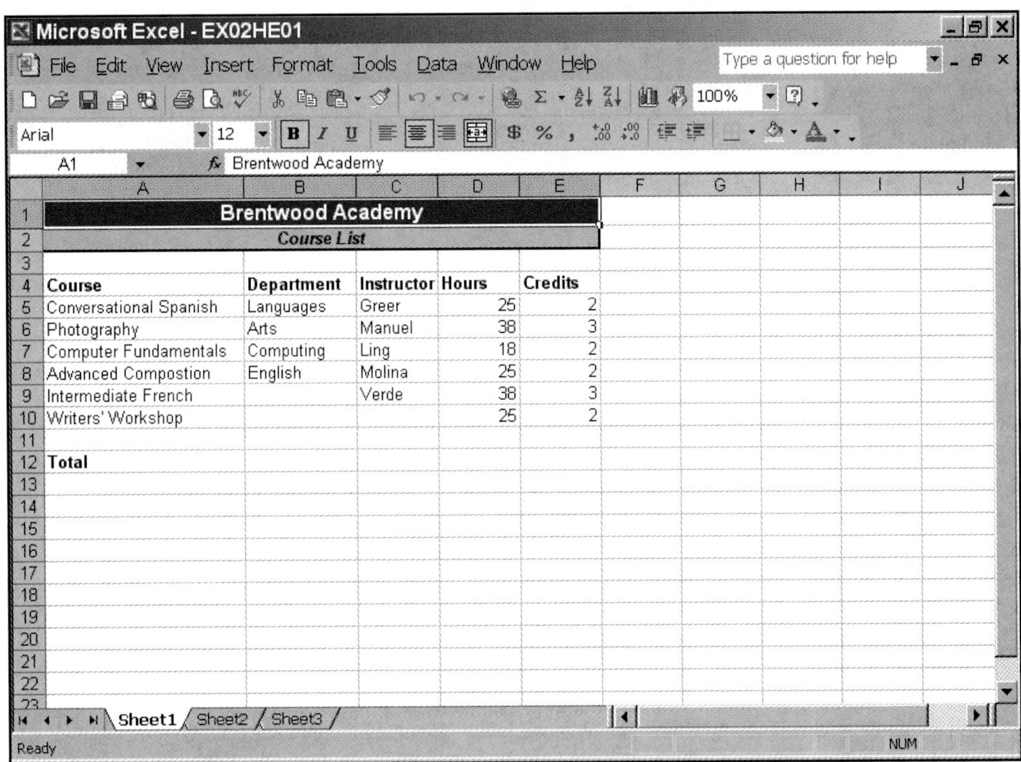

Figure 2.33

Opening the EX02HE01 workbook

3. Save the workbook as "Course List" to your personal storage location.
4. To complete this worksheet, you must enter some additional information for "Intermediate French." To begin:
   SELECT: cell B9
   TYPE: **L**
   PRESS: ENTER
   Notice that the word "Languages" is inserted automatically.
5. To enter some data for the "Writer's Workshop," do the following:
   RIGHT-CLICK: cell B10
   CHOOSE: Pick From List
   A pick list appears with four options, as shown here.

6. CLICK: English in the pick list
7. To access a column's AutoComplete pick list using the keyboard:
   SELECT: cell C10
   PRESS: ALT + ↓
   PRESS: ↓ four more times to highlight "Molina"
   PRESS: ENTER

8. Now let's use the AutoCalculate feature to sum the total number of hours without placing an entry into the worksheet. Do the following:
   SELECT: cell range from D5 to D10
   Notice that the Status bar now displays "Sum=169."

9. To enter a formula to total the Hours column:
   SELECT: cell D12
   CLICK: AutoSum button (Σ)
   Excel reviews the worksheet and highlights its best guess of the range you want to sum, as shown in Figure 2.34.

Figure 2.34

Summing a column of values using the AutoSum button (Σ)

	A	B	C	D	E	F
1	Brentwood Academy					
2	*Course List*					
3						
4	**Course**	**Department**	**Instructor**	**Hours**	**Credits**	
5	Conversational Spanish	Languages	Greer	25	2	
6	Photography	Arts	Manuel	38	3	
7	Computer Fundamentals	Computing	Ling	18	2	
8	Advanced Compostion	English	Molina	25	2	
9	Intermediate French	Languages	Verde	38	3	
10	Writers' Workshop	English	Molina	25	2	
11						
12	**Total**			=SUM(D5:D11)		
13						
14						

10. To accept the cell range:
    CLICK: AutoSum button (Σ) again
    The answer, 169, now appears in the cell.

11. On your own, total the values in column E and place the result in cell E12 using the AutoSum button (Σ).

12. Save and then close the workbook.

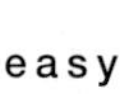 

2. Top Picks Video: Top Five Rentals

You will now practice copying and moving data using Excel's AutoFill feature, drag and drop, and the Windows and Office Clipboards.

1. Open the data file named EX02HE02 to display the workbook shown in Figure 2.35.

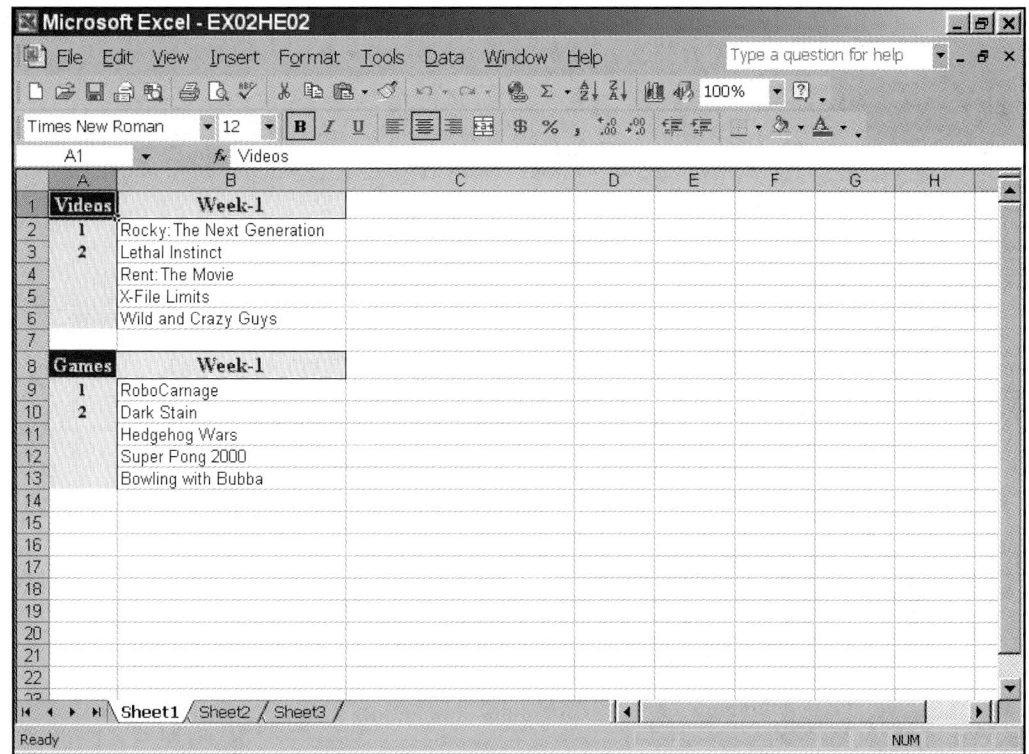

Figure 2.35

Opening the EX02HE02 workbook

2. Save the workbook as "Top Five" to your personal storage location.
3. Let's use the AutoFill feature to extend the heading to column C:
   SELECT: cell B1
   DRAG: fill handle for cell B1 to column C
   Notice that the text entry becomes "Week-2" and that the formatting is also copied.
4. On your own, extend the column heading in cell B8 to column C.
5. You will now extend the numeric row labels for "Videos" in column A. Do the following:
   SELECT: cell range from A2 to A3
   DRAG: fill handle for the selected cell range to row 6
6. On your own, extend the numeric row labels for "Games" in column A.
7. Using the Windows Clipboard, you will now copy the first two videos from Week-1 (*Rocky: The Next Generation* and *Lethal Instinct*) to the same positions in Week-2:
   SELECT: cell range from B2 to B3
   CLICK: Copy button ( ) on the Standard toolbar
   SELECT: cell C2
   CLICK: Paste button ( )
   PRESS: ESC to remove the dashed marquee

8. Using drag and drop, you will now copy the number 3 video of Week-1 (*Rent: The Movie*) to the number 5 position of Week-2:
   SELECT: cell B4

9. Position the mouse pointer over the border of the selected cell. Then, do the following:
   PRESS: CTRL and hold it down
   DRAG: mouse pointer to cell C6
   Your screen should now appear similar to Figure 2.36.

Figure 2.36

Using drag and drop to copy a video title

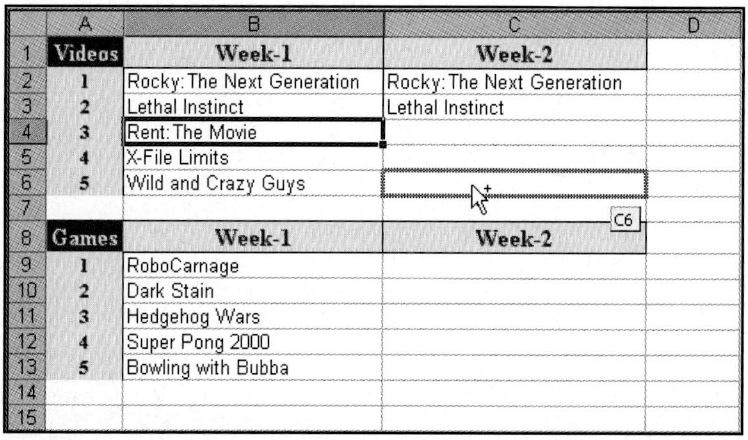

	A	B	C	D
1	Videos	Week-1	Week-2	
2	1	Rocky: The Next Generation	Rocky: The Next Generation	
3	2	Lethal Instinct	Lethal Instinct	
4	3	Rent: The Movie		
5	4	X-File Limits		
6	5	Wild and Crazy Guys		
7			C6	
8	Games	Week-1	Week-2	
9	1	RoboCarnage		
10	2	Dark Stain		
11	3	Hedgehog Wars		
12	4	Super Pong 2000		
13	5	Bowling with Bubba		
14				
15				

10. Release the mouse button and then the CTRL key to complete the copy operation.

11. Using drag and drop, copy the cell range B5:B6 (*X-File Limits* and *Wild and Crazy Guys*) to cells C4:C5.

12. You will now use the Office Clipboard to modify the Games order from Week-1 to Week-2. First, display the Clipboard task pane:
    CHOOSE: Edit, Office Clipboard
    (*Note:* If the Clipboard task pane contains data items, click the Clear All button (Clear All) to remove the items from the list area.)

13. Now, let's add the Games to the Office Clipboard:
    SELECT: cell B12
    CLICK: Copy button ()
    SELECT: cell B9
    CLICK: Copy button ()
    SELECT: cell B10
    CLICK: Copy button ()
    SELECT: cell B13
    CLICK: Copy button ()
    SELECT: cell B11
    CLICK: Copy button ()

14. Now paste all of the data elements into the Week-2 column:
    SELECT: cell C9
    CLICK: Paste All button (Paste All)

15. Move to cell A1 in order to remove the selection highlighting. Your screen should now appear similar to Figure 2.37.

Figure 2.37

Completing the Top Five workbook

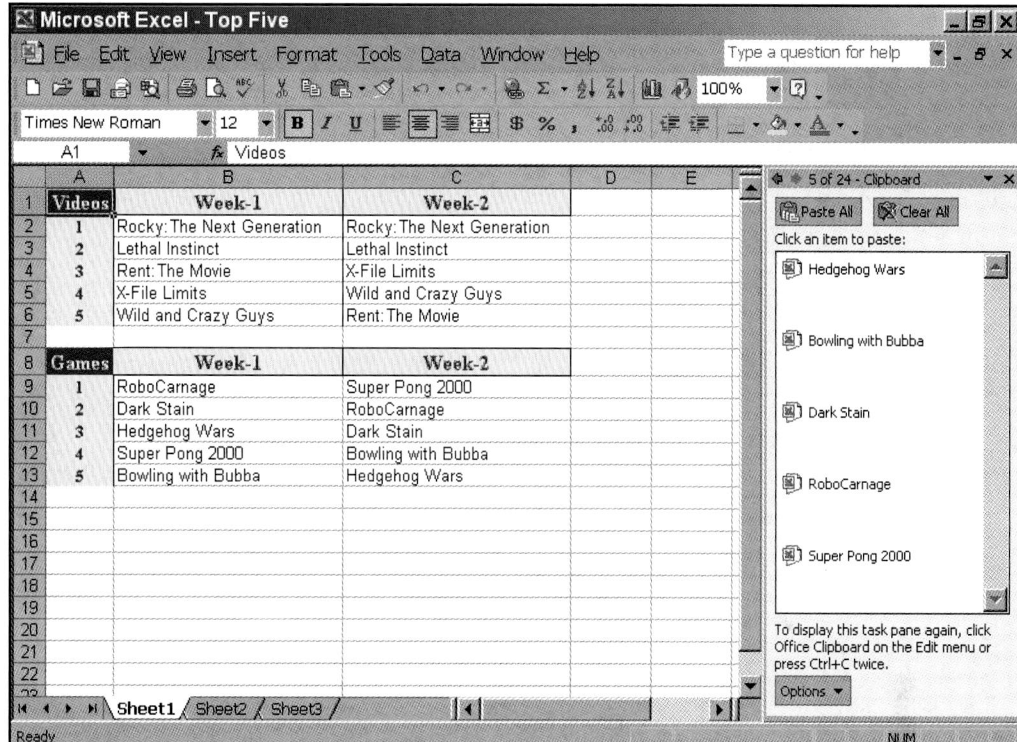

16. To clear the contents of the Office Clipboard:
    CLICK: Clear All button (Clear All)

17. Hide the Clipboard task pane:
    CLICK: its Close button (☒)

18. Save and then close the "Top Five" workbook.

moderate 

3. Staples Foods: Sales Force

In this exercise, you practice modifying an existing worksheet that is used to track sales representatives for Staples Foods.

1. Open the data file named EX02HE03 to display the workbook shown in Figure 2.38.

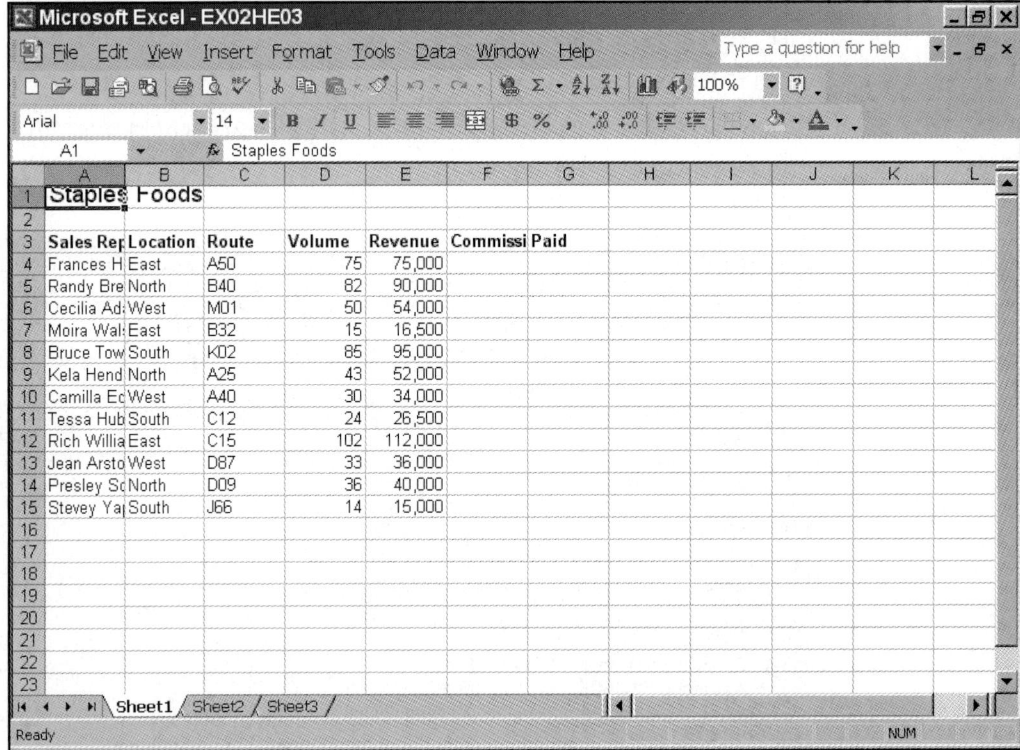

	A	B	C	D	E	F	G
1	Staples Foods						
2							
3	Sales Rep	Location	Route	Volume	Revenue	Commissi	Paid
4	Frances H	East	A50	75	75,000		
5	Randy Bre	North	B40	82	90,000		
6	Cecilia Ad	West	M01	50	54,000		
7	Moira Wal	East	B32	15	16,500		
8	Bruce Tow	South	K02	85	95,000		
9	Kela Hend	North	A25	43	52,000		
10	Camilla Ec	West	A40	30	34,000		
11	Tessa Hub	South	C12	24	26,500		
12	Rich Willia	East	C15	102	112,000		
13	Jean Arsto	West	D87	33	36,000		
14	Presley Sc	North	D09	36	40,000		
15	Stevey Ya	South	J66	14	15,000		

Figure 2.38

Opening the EX02HE03 workbook

2. Save the workbook as "Sales Force" to your personal storage location.
3. You may have noticed that the title in cell A1 is difficult to read. Adjust the height for row 1 to its "best fit" or "AutoFit" height.
4. The sales representatives' names are truncated by the "Location" entries in column B. Therefore, adjust the width of column A to ensure that all the names are visible.
5. Change the column width for columns B through D to 8 characters.
6. Change the column width for columns E through G to 10 characters.
7. Change the height of rows 2 through 15 to 15.00.
8. In cell F4, enter a commission rate of 5%.
9. In cell G4, multiply the commission rate (F) by the Revenue (E).
10. Using the Edit, Fill, Down command, copy the entries in cells F4 and G4 down the column to row 15. Your worksheet should now look similar to Figure 2.39.

Figure 2.39

Adjusting rows and columns and copying formulas

	A	B	C	D	E	F	G	H
1	Staples Foods							
2								
3	**Sales Rep**	**Location**	**Route**	**Volume**	**Revenue**	**Commission**	**Paid**	
4	Frances Hillman	East	A50	75	75,000	5%	3750	
5	Randy Brewski	North	B40	82	90,000	5%	4500	
6	Cecilia Adams	West	M01	50	54,000	5%	2700	
7	Moira Walsh	East	B32	15	16,500	5%	825	
8	Bruce Towne	South	K02	85	95,000	5%	4750	
9	Kela Henderson	North	A25	43	52,000	5%	2600	
10	Camilla Edsell	West	A40	30	34,000	5%	1700	
11	Tessa Huberty	South	C12	24	26,500	5%	1325	
12	Rich Williams	East	C15	102	112,000	5%	5600	
13	Jean Arston	West	D87	33	36,000	5%	1800	
14	Presley Schuler	North	D09	36	40,000	5%	2000	
15	Stevey Yap	South	J66	14	15,000	5%	750	
16								
17								

Excel

11. Remove the Route information by deleting column C.
12. Remove the information for Bruce Towne by deleting the cell range A8 to F8 and then closing up the gap.
13. Hide the two end columns used in calculating and displaying a sales rep's commission.
14. Without placing a formula on the worksheet, calculate the total revenue collected by these sales reps. What is this value?
15. Save and then close the workbook.

moderate 

4. Sutton House Realty: Sales Projections

In this exercise, you practice copying data and modifying a worksheet.

1. Open the data file named EX02HE04 to display the workbook shown in Figure 2.40.

Figure 2.40

Opening the EX02HE04 workbook

	A	B	C	D	E
1	**Sutton House Realty**				
2					
3	*RESIDENTIAL (000's)*				
4	**District**	**Y2000**	**Y2001**	**Y2002**	
5	Brookview	1,200	1,377	1,408	
6	Cedar Hill	856	1,234	1,498	
7	Newton	875	754	699	
8	Westside	623	500	432	
9	**TOTAL**				
10					
11					

2. Save the workbook as "Sales Volume" to your personal storage location.
3. Increase the width of column A to 12 characters.
4. Use the AutoSum button (Σ ▾) to sum the values for columns B through D and display the results in row 9.
5. To extend the table to project values for the years 2003, 2004, and 2005, first select the cell range from B4 to D9.
6. Drag the fill handle of the selected range to column G. When you release the mouse button, the range is filled with projected results (Figure 2.41). These results are based on the trends calculated from the selected columns of data. Notice that you did not enter any formulas into the worksheet, other than using AutoSum to provide a row for totals.

Figure 2.41

Using the fill handle to make projections

	A	B	C	D	E	F	G	H
1	**Sutton House Realty**							
2								
3	*RESIDENTIAL (000's)*							
4	**District**	**Y2000**	**Y2001**	**Y2002**	**Y2003**	**Y2004**	**Y2005**	
5	Brookview	1,200	1,377	1,408	1,536	1,640	1,744	
6	Cedar Hill	856	1,234	1,498	1838	2,159	2,480	
7	Newton	875	754	699	600	512	424	
8	Westside	623	500	432	327.3333	231.8333	136.3333	
9	**TOTAL**	3,554	3,865	4,037	4,302	4,543	4,785	
10								
11								

7. Hide the District values in rows 5 through 8.
8. Move the cell pointer to cell A1.
9. Save and then close the workbook.

difficult 

5. On Your Own: Magic Lights Personnel

A friend of yours has just accepted a position at Magic Lights Personnel. In addition to her general administrative duties, she must help the accountant prepare monthly income statements. Since she seemed quite nervous about the new position, you offered to help her develop an Excel worksheet. You open the EX02HE05 workbook that she has been using and save it as "Magic Lights" to her personal storage location.

After adjusting the column widths, you review the structure of the worksheet. To begin, you insert a row above EXPENSES and label it "Total Revenue." Then, you use the AutoSum feature to sum the revenues for September and October. Continuing in this manner, you adjust and insert rows, data, and formulas so that the worksheet appears similar to Figure 2.42. Then, you save and close the workbook.

Figure 2.42

Modifying a worksheet's structure and appearance

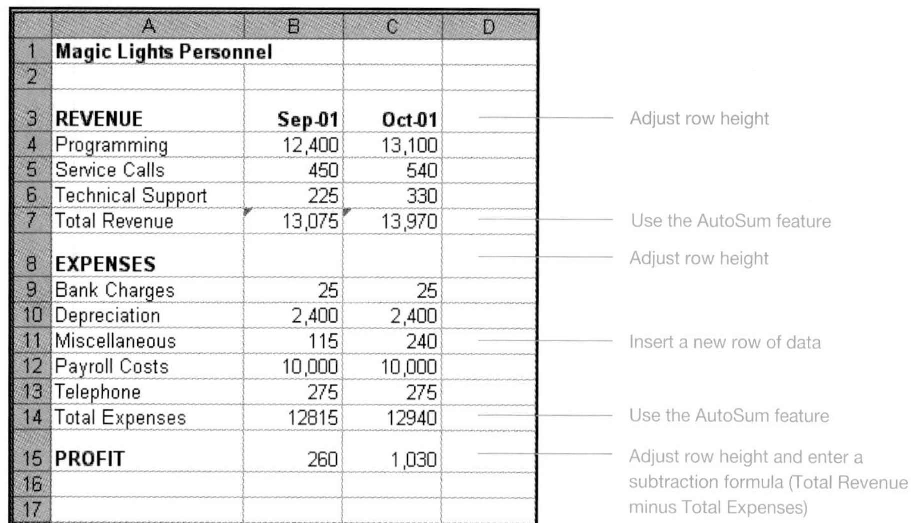

	A	B	C	D
1	**Magic Lights Personnel**			
2				
3	**REVENUE**	**Sep-01**	**Oct-01**	
4	Programming	12,400	13,100	
5	Service Calls	450	540	
6	Technical Support	225	330	
7	Total Revenue	13,075	13,970	
8	**EXPENSES**			
9	Bank Charges	25	25	
10	Depreciation	2,400	2,400	
11	Miscellaneous	115	240	
12	Payroll Costs	10,000	10,000	
13	Telephone	275	275	
14	Total Expenses	12815	12940	
15	**PROFIT**	260	1,030	
16				
17				

6. On Your Own: Running Diary

It's May and you're finally getting around to that New Year's resolution of getting into shape. To motivate yourself, you decide to create a running diary using Microsoft Excel. Open the data file named EX02HE06 (Figure 2.43) and then save it as "My Running Diary" to your personal storage location.

Figure 2.43

Opening the EX02HE06 workbook

	A	B	C	D	E	F
1	**Running Diary**					
2						
3	**Date**	**Miles**	**Time**	**Max Rate**	**Cool Down**	
4	5-May	3	18:00.0	152	80	
5	7-May	3	17:55.0	140	84	
6	9-May	3	18:23.0	148	82	
7	12-May	4	26:10.0	155	86	
8	14-May	4	25:43.0	160	82	
9	16-May	4	24:58.0	154	80	
10	18-May	4	25:18.0	155	79	
11	21-May	5	36:40.0	154	87	
12	23-May	5	34:12.0	152	85	
13						
14						

Given your current statistics, you'd like to project how long it will take you to reach 10 miles. To do so, select the cell range from B4 through B12. Then drag the fill handle for the range downward until the ToolTip displays a value over 10. Press CTRL+HOME to return to the top of the worksheet. To make it easier to count the number of runs, insert a new column A with the column heading "Run" and then move the title "Running Diary" back into cell A1 using drag and drop. You then number each run in the column, using the fill handle to make the process faster. *How many runs will it take you to reach 10 miles?* Using Excel's Auto-Calculate feature, you find out how many miles you've run as of May 23rd. *How many miles have you run thus far?*

Impressed with your computer knowledge, your running partner asks you to track her running statistics also. Rather than create a new worksheet, you copy and paste the column headings beside your own, so that they begin in column H. Save and close the workbook and then exit Excel.

Case Problems

Citywide Insurance Agency

Scott Allenby, the business manager for the Citywide Insurance Agency, is responsible for generating monthly profitability reports. One of the key business areas for Citywide involves a long-standing agreement with a local car dealer to manage the dealer's financing, insurance, and after-market sales. Upon reviewing some of the past data for the dealership, Scott identifies an opportunity to use Microsoft Excel for generating their reports.

In the following case problems, assume the role of Scott and perform the same steps that he identifies. You may want to re-read the chapter opening before proceeding.

1. Scott decides to focus his attention on one report that is generated for the car dealership at the end of each month. He calls a good friend, whom he knows has several months' experience using Excel, and describes what he needs over the phone. He then sends him a fax of the actual report to help clarify the discussion. The next day, Scott receives a diskette from his friend that contains a workbook called EX02CP01. He opens the workbook (Figure 2.44) and then saves it as "PROFIT" to his personal storage location.

Figure 2.44

Opening the EX02CP01 workbook

	A	B	C	D	E	F	G
1	**Performance Review of Finance and Insurance Totals**						
2							
3	**Product Category**		**New Cars**	**Revenue**	**Used Cars**	**Revenue**	
4							
5	Retail Sales		20	492,000	15	138,000	
6	Life Ins. Policies		4	1,250	2	2,500	
7	Option Packages		5	2,150	0	0	
8	Rust Protection		3	1,800	0	0	
9	Ext. Warranties		1	375	1	340	
10	**Totals**						
11							
12							

The "PROFIT" report, which is the car dealer's own abbreviation for a "Profitability Review of Finance and Insurance Totals," summarizes the number of new and used cars that are sold in a given month, including the number of financing, insurance, warranty, and rust protection packages. After reviewing the worksheet, Scott decides to make a few additions and modifications.

- In cell A1, edit the title to read "Profitability Review of Finance and Insurance Totals."
- In cells G3 and H3, enter the headings "Total Cars" and "Revenue," respectively.
- In cell G5, enter a formula that adds the number of new car sales to the number of used car sales.
- In cell H5, enter a formula that adds the revenue for new car sales to the revenue for used car sales.
- Using the fill handle, copy the formulas in cells G5 and H5 down their respective columns to row 9.

- Using the AutoSum feature, sum the values in columns C through H and place the results in row 10.

Save the workbook and keep it open for use in the next problem.

2. Wednesday morning does not start out well for Scott. The owner of the dealership calls to request that Citywide Insurance no longer track the sale of "Rust Protection" packages. He also asks Scott to hide the "Used Cars" columns in the report. Fortunately, Scott remembers how to remove and hide cells, rows, and columns. He also feels that this is a great opportunity to adjust some of the worksheet's column widths and row heights. Specifically, Scott performs the following steps:

   - Select the "best fit" or "AutoFit" width for column A. Notice that the width is adjusted to handle the length of the title in cell A1.
   - Specify a column width of 18 characters for column A.
   - Specify a column width of 10 characters for columns C through H.
   - Specify a row height of 7.50 points for row 4.
   - Ensure that column B is empty. Then delete the entire column.
   - Select the cell range (A8:G8) for Rust Protection. Then choose the Edit, Delete command to remove the cells from the worksheet and shift the remaining cells upward.
   - Select columns D and E for the Used Cars data. Then hide the columns (keep them from displaying).

   Move the cell pointer to cell A1. Your screen should appear similar to Figure 2.45. Save the workbook and keep it open for use in the next problem.

Excel

Figure 2.45

Manipulating columns and rows in a worksheet

	A	B	C	F	G	H
1	Profitability Review of Finance and Insurance Totals					
2						
3	Product Category	New Cars	Revenue	Total Cars	Revenue	
4						
5	Retail Sales	20	492,000	35	630,000	
6	Life Ins. Policies	4	1,250	6	3,750	
7	Option Packages	5	2,150	5	2,150	
8	Ext. Warranties	1	375	2	715	
9	Totals	30	495775	48	636615	
10						
11						

3. Scott decides that it would be helpful to develop a projection for next month's PROFIT report. Rather than create a new worksheet, he unhides columns D and E and then copies the data from cells A3 through G9 to the Windows Clipboard. He moves the cell pointer to cell A12, pastes the data, and then presses ESC to remove the dashed marquee. To complete the operation, Scott adjusts row 13 to match the height of row 4.

   In order to start with a clean slate, Scott selects cells B14 through E17 and erases the cell contents in the range. Then he selects cell B14 and enters a formula that shows an increase of 20% over the value stored in cell B5. In other words, he multiplies the value in cell B5 by 1.2. Next, Scott copies the formula to the remaining cells in the range, as shown in Figure 2.46. To ensure that the projection area works properly, Scott changes some of the values in the original table area. Satisfied that the bottom projection table updates automatically, he saves and closes the workbook.

Figure 2.46

Creating a projection based on an existing range of cells

	A	B	C	D	E	F	G	H
1	**Profitability Review of Finance and Insurance Totals**							
2								
3	**Product Category**	**New Cars**	**Revenue**	**Used Cars**	**Revenue**	**Total Cars**	**Revenue**	
4								
5	Retail Sales	20	492,000	15	138,000	35	630,000	
6	Life Ins. Policies	4	1,250	2	2,500	6	3,750	
7	Option Packages	5	2,150	0	0	5	2,150	
8	Ext. Warranties	1	375	1	340	2	715	
9	**Totals**	30	495775	18	140840	48	636615	
10								
11								
12	**Product Category**	**New Cars**	**Revenue**	**Used Cars**	**Revenue**	**Total Cars**	**Revenue**	
13								
14	Retail Sales	24	590400	18	165600	42	756,000	
15	Life Ins. Policies	4.8	1500	2.4	3000	7.2	4,500	
16	Option Packages	6	2580	0	0	6	2,580	
17	Ext. Warranties	1.2	450	1.2	408	2.4	858	
18	**Totals**	36	594930	21.6	169008	57.6	763938	
19								
20								

4. Scott opens a second workbook, EX02CP04, that he received from his friend. He saves the workbook, shown in Figure 2.47, as "Car Buyers" to his personal storage location. This particular workbook stores customer information from each sale made in the month.

Figure 2.47

Opening the EX02CP04 workbook

	A	B	C	D	E	F	G
1	**Report of New Customers**						
2							
3	**Name**		**Bought**	**Make**	**Model**	**Price**	
4	Frank Chihowski		5-Jan-02	GMC	Sierra	$37,492	
5	Rosalie Spears		13-Jan-02	Dodge	Dakota	$28,340	
6	Joellen Baldwin		17-Jan-02	Ford	Taurus	$18,500	
7	Veronica Cattermole		18-Jan-02	Ford	Explorer	$29,990	
8	Charles Visentin		18-Jan-02	GMC	Silverado	$42,050	
9	Lynne Morrow		23-Jan-02	Honda	Accord	$14,975	
10	Sean Hussey		26-Jan-02	Ford	Windstar	$22,450	
11	Heidi Buehre		30-Jan-02	GMC	Astro Van	$19,109	
12							
13							

Scott reviews the worksheet and decides to make a few changes. First, he inserts a new column A and moves the title back into cell A1. He then enters 1 into cell A4 and 2 into cell A5. Using the mouse, Scott selects both cells and then drags the range's fill handle downward to continue numbering the customers. *What is the number of the last customer, Heidi Buehre?* He then moves to cell E12 and displays the AutoComplete pick list. *What vehicles are listed in the pick list and in what order do they appear?* To remove the pick list, Scott presses the ESC key. Finally, Scott uses Excel's AutoCalculate feature to sum the purchase price of all vehicles sold in January without having to enter a formula into the worksheet. *What is the total value of vehicles purchased?*

Ready to go home for the day, Scott saves and then closes the workbook. Then he exits Microsoft Excel.

Microsoft® **Excel®** 2002

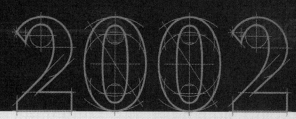

CHAPTER 3

Formatting and Printing

CHAPTER OUTLINE

Case Study

3.1 Enhancing a Worksheet's Appearance

3.2 Applying and Removing Formatting

3.3 Printing and Web Publishing

3.4 Customizing Print Options

Chapter Summary

Chapter Quiz

Hands-On Exercises

Case Problems

PREREQUISITES

To successfully complete this chapter, you must be comfortable performing basic data entry and editing tasks. You will be asked to modify worksheet information using toolbar buttons, Menu commands, and right-click shortcut menus. Although printing and Web publishing are introduced in this chapter, you should already know how to set up your printer in Windows and how to launch your Web browser software for viewing Web pages.

LEARNING OBJECTIVES

After completing this chapter, you will be able to:

- Format cell entries to appear boldface or italic and with different typefaces and font sizes
- Format numeric and date values
- Format cells to appear with borders, shading, and color
- Preview and print a worksheet
- Publish a worksheet to the World Wide Web
- Define page layout options, such as margins, headers and footers, and paper orientation, for printing your worksheets

CaseStudy **HIP HOP HITS** Hip Hop Hits is an independently owned sidewalk store that is located in the downtown core of Randall, Virginia. Established in 1974, Hip Hop Hits has successfully sold record albums, eight-track tapes, cassettes, and audio CDs. Just recently, they began stocking movie videos and DVDs. For the past 25 years, Hip Hop Hits' most prominent business strategy has been a commitment to stocking a large selection of music that appeals to a broad audience. They have always taken pride in their large inventory and in providing personalized customer service.

Stacey Marvin, the store's owner and general manager, is concerned for her business. She recently read in the newspaper that a large discount superstore is planning to move into the area. In a meeting with Justin Lee, her senior sales associate, she discussed some possible advertising ideas for combating the new competitor. For the past 18 months, Justin has been acting as Stacey's right hand. He handles much of the purchasing and receiving duties and is the primary contact person for Hip Hop Hits' suppliers. Justin is also familiar with using the custom accounting software and Microsoft Excel, both of which are loaded on the office's personal computer.

In this chapter, you and Justin learn more about working with Excel worksheets. First, you learn how to format a worksheet to make it appear more attractive and easier to read. After previewing and printing a worksheet, you learn to save it as an HTML document for publishing to a Web site. You also customize several layout options, such as margins and headers, for more effective printing.

3.1 Enhancing a Worksheet's Appearance

Most people realize how important it is to create worksheets that are easy to read and pleasing to the eye. Clearly, a visually attractive worksheet will convey information better than an unformatted one. With Excel's formatting capabilities, you can enhance your worksheets for publishing online or to print. In addition to choosing from a variety of fonts, styles, and cell alignments, you can specify decimal places and add currency and percentage symbols to values. The combination of these features enables you to produce professional-looking spreadsheet reports and presentations.

3.1.1 Applying Fonts, Font Styles, and Colors

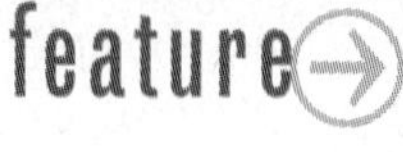

Applying **fonts** to titles, headings, and other worksheet cells is often the most effective means for drawing a reader's attention to specific areas in your worksheet. You can also specify font styles, like boldface and italic, adjust font sizes, and select colors. Do not feel obliged, however, to use every font that is available to you in a single worksheet. Above all, your worksheets must be easy to read—too many fonts, styles, and colors are distracting. As a rule, limit your font selection for a single worksheet to two or three common **typefaces**, such as Times New Roman and Arial.

To apply character formatting, you select the desired cell range and then do any of the following:

- CLICK: Font list box (Arial)
- CLICK: Font Size list box (10)
- CLICK: Bold button (B)
- CLICK: Italic button (I)
- CLICK: Underline button (U)
- CLICK: Font Color button (A)

To display the *Font* formatting options:

- SELECT: cell range to format
- CHOOSE: Format, Cells
- CLICK: *Font* tab in the Format Cells dialog box
- SELECT: the desired font, font style, size, color, and effects

practice

In this lesson, you open and format a workbook that tracks a mutual fund portfolio. Ensure that Excel is loaded.

1. Open the data file named EX0310 to display the workbook shown in Figure 3.1.

Figure 3.1

Opening the EX0310 workbook

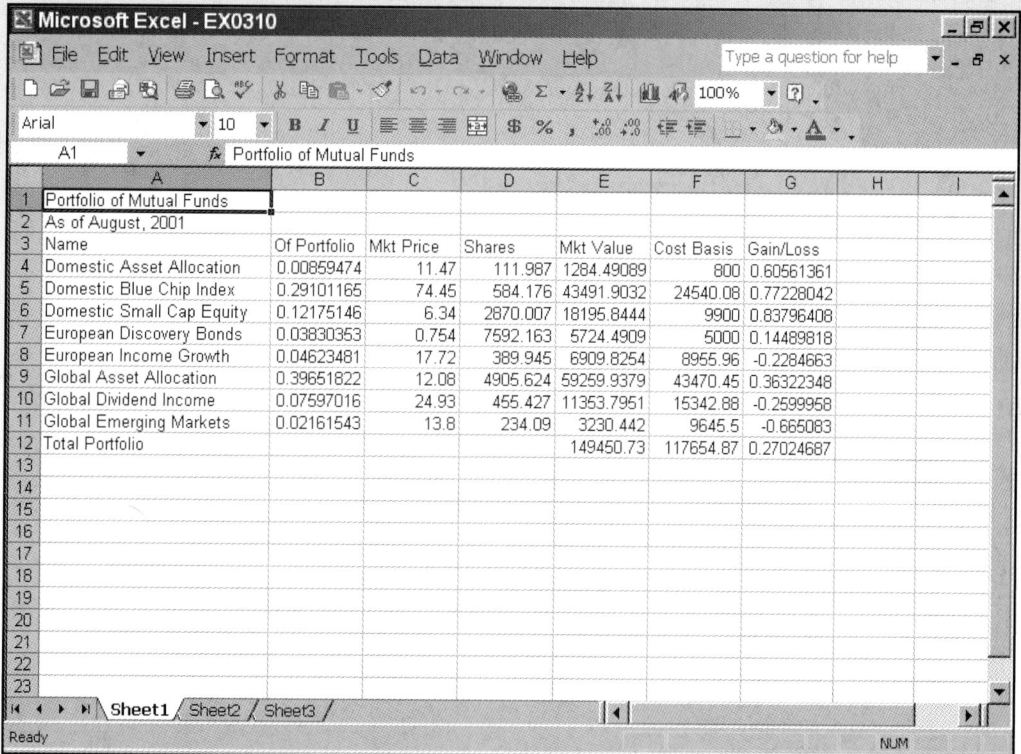

	A	B	C	D	E	F	G
1	Portfolio of Mutual Funds						
2	As of August, 2001						
3	Name	Of Portfolio	Mkt Price	Shares	Mkt Value	Cost Basis	Gain/Loss
4	Domestic Asset Allocation	0.00859474	11.47	111.987	1284.49089	800	0.60561361
5	Domestic Blue Chip Index	0.29101165	74.45	584.176	43491.9032	24540.08	0.77228042
6	Domestic Small Cap Equity	0.12175146	6.34	2870.007	18195.8444	9900	0.83796408
7	European Discovery Bonds	0.03830353	0.754	7592.163	5724.4909	5000	0.14489818
8	European Income Growth	0.04623481	17.72	389.945	6909.8254	8955.96	-0.2284663
9	Global Asset Allocation	0.39651822	12.08	4905.624	59259.9379	43470.45	0.36322348
10	Global Dividend Income	0.07597016	24.93	455.427	11353.7951	15342.88	-0.2599958
11	Global Emerging Markets	0.02161543	13.8	234.09	3230.442	9645.5	-0.665083
12	Total Portfolio				149450.73	117654.87	0.27024687

2. Save the file as "My Portfolio" to your personal storage location.

3. Your first step is to select the cell range to format. Do the following to begin formatting the column labels:
SELECT: cell range from A3 to G3

4. Let's make these labels bold and underlined:
CLICK: Bold button (B)
CLICK: Underline button (U)

5. Now you will format the title labels in cells A1 and A2. To begin:
SELECT: cell range from A1 to A2

6. To change the typeface used in the cells:
CLICK: down arrow attached to the Font list box (Arial)
(*Note:* The fonts that appear in the list box are available for your use in Excel. Some fonts are loaded with Windows and Microsoft Office, and a variety of other fonts may appear in the list from other application programs that you've installed.) Your screen should appear similar but not identical to Figure 3.2.

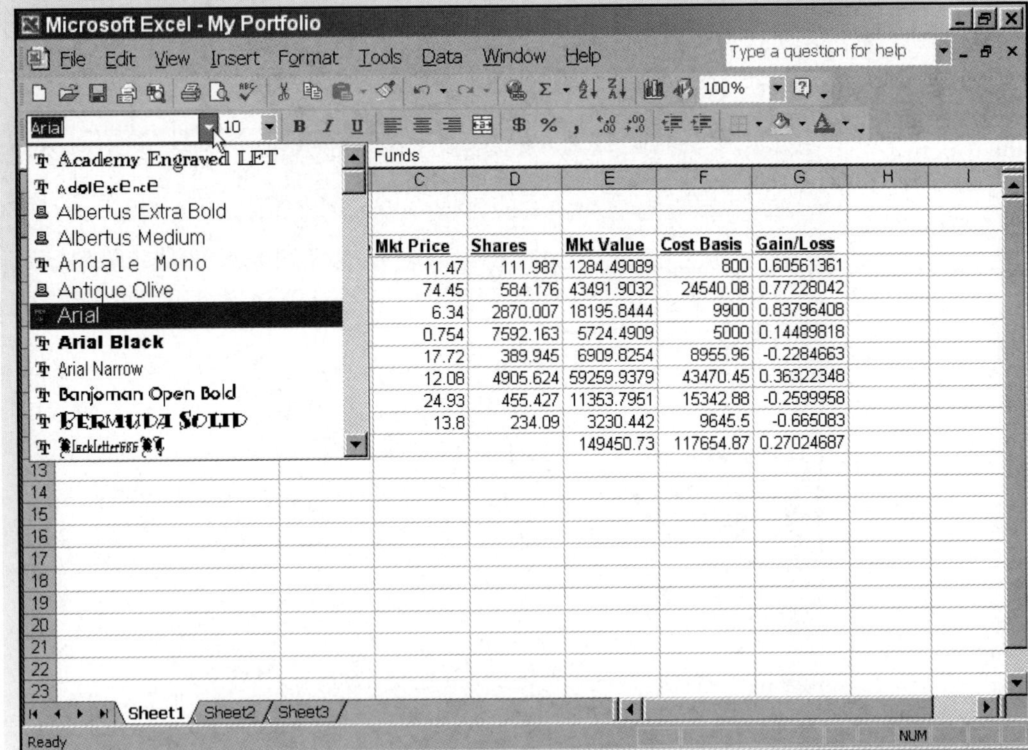

Figure 3.2

Selecting a typeface from the Font list box

7. Using the scroll bar attached to the drop-down list box:
SELECT: Times New Roman

8. To increase the font size:
CLICK: down arrow attached to the Font Size list box (10)
SELECT: 14
The cells now appear formatted using a 14-point, Times New Roman typeface; the row heights have also been adjusted automatically.

9. You can also use the Format Cells dialog box to apply formatting to the selected cell range. Do the following:
SELECT: cell A1
CHOOSE: Format, Cells
CLICK: *Font* tab
The Format Cells dialog box (Figure 3.3) displays the current formatting options for the active cell.

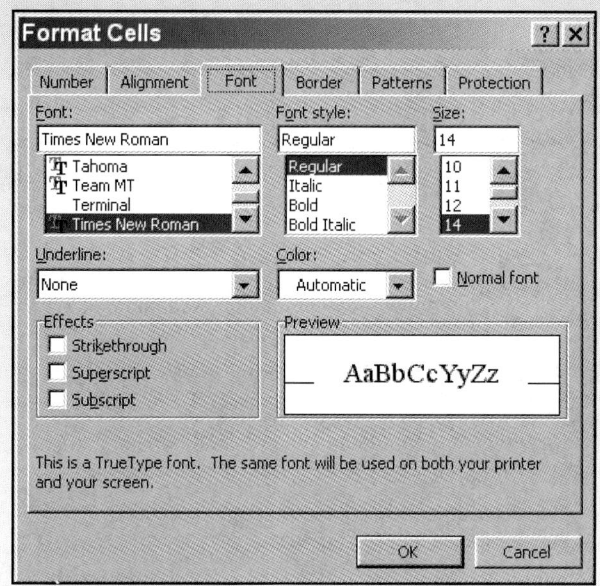

Figure 3.3

Format Cells dialog box: *Font* tab

10. To add some additional flare to the title:
SELECT: *any typeface* from the *Font* list box
SELECT: Bold in the *Font style* list box
SELECT: 16 in the *Size* list box
SELECT: Blue from the *Color* drop-down list box
CLICK: OK command button
The title in cell A1 should now stand out from the rest of the data.

11. You can also use shortcut keys to apply formatting. To demonstrate:
SELECT: cell range from A12 to G12
PRESS: CTRL+**b** to apply boldface

12. Save the workbook and keep it open for use in the next lesson.

In Addition COMMON FORMATTING SHORTCUT KEYS

To help speed up formatting operations, select the desired cell range and then use the following key combinations:

- CTRL+**b** to apply boldface
- CTRL+**i** to apply italic
- CTRL+**u** to apply underlining
- CTRL+SHIFT+**f** to select a font typeface
- CTRL+SHIFT+**p** to select a font point size

Excel

3.1.2 Formatting Numbers and Dates

feature→

Numeric formats improve the appearance and readability of numbers in a worksheet by inserting dollar signs, commas, percentage symbols, and decimal places. Although a formatted number or date appears differently on the worksheet, the value that is stored and displayed in the Formula bar does not change. Excel stores date and time entries as values and, therefore, allows you to customize their display as you do numbers.

method→

To apply number formatting, you select the desired cell range and then do one of the following:

- CLICK: Currency Style button ($)
- CLICK: Percent Style button (%)
- CLICK: Comma Style button (,)
- CLICK: Increase Decimal button (.00)
- CLICK: Decrease Decimal button (.00)

To display the *Number* formatting options:

- SELECT: cell range to format
- CHOOSE: Format, Cells
- CLICK: *Number* tab
- SELECT: a number or date format from the *Category* list box
- SELECT: formatting options for the selected category

practice→

You will now apply number, currency, percentage, decimal place, and date formatting to the worksheet. Ensure that you have completed the previous lesson and that the "My Portfolio" workbook is displayed.

1. Columns B and G in the worksheet contain data that is best represented using a percent number format. First, column B displays the proportional share of an investment compared to the total portfolio. Column G calculates the gain or loss performance. To display these calculated results as percentages, do the following:
SELECT: cell range from B4 to B11
PRESS: CTRL and hold it down
SELECT: cell range from G4 to G12

2. Release the CTRL key after the last range is selected. Notice that these two ranges are highlighted independently—ready for formatting. (*Note:* You will no longer be reminded to release the CTRL key when dragging the cell pointer over a range.)

3. To apply a percent style:
CLICK: Percent Style button (%)

4. To display the percentages with two decimal places:
CLICK: Increase Decimal button (.00) twice
Your worksheet should now appear similar to Figure 3.4.

Figure 3.4

Applying percent formatting to multiple cell ranges

	A	B	C	D	E	F	G	H
1	Portfolio of Mutual Funds							
2	As of August, 2001							
3	Name	Of Portfolio	Mkt Price	Shares	Mkt Value	Cost Basis	Gain/Loss	
4	Domestic Asset Allocation	0.86%	11.47	111.987	1284.49089	800	60.56%	
5	Domestic Blue Chip Index	29.10%	74.45	584.176	43491.9032	24540.08	77.23%	
6	Domestic Small Cap Equity	12.18%	6.34	2870.007	18195.8444	9900	83.80%	
7	European Discovery Bonds	3.83%	0.754	7592.163	5724.4909	5000	14.49%	
8	European Income Growth	4.62%	17.72	389.945	6909.8254	8955.96	-22.85%	
9	Global Asset Allocation	39.65%	12.08	4905.624	59259.9379	43470.45	36.32%	
10	Global Dividend Income	7.60%	24.93	455.427	11353.7951	15342.88	-26.00%	
11	Global Emerging Markets	2.16%	13.8	234.09	3230.442	9645.5	-66.51%	
12	Total Portfolio				149450.73	117654.87	27.02%	
13								
14								

5. Let's apply some further number formatting:
   SELECT: cell range from C4 to C11
   CHOOSE: Format, Cells
   CLICK: *Number* tab

6. In the Format Cells dialog box that appears:
   SELECT: Currency in the *Category* list box
   SELECT: 4 in the *Decimal places* spin box
   SELECT: Black ($1,234.3210) in the *Negative numbers* list box
   Your screen should now appear similar to Figure 3.5.

Figure 3.5

Format Cells dialog box: *Number* tab

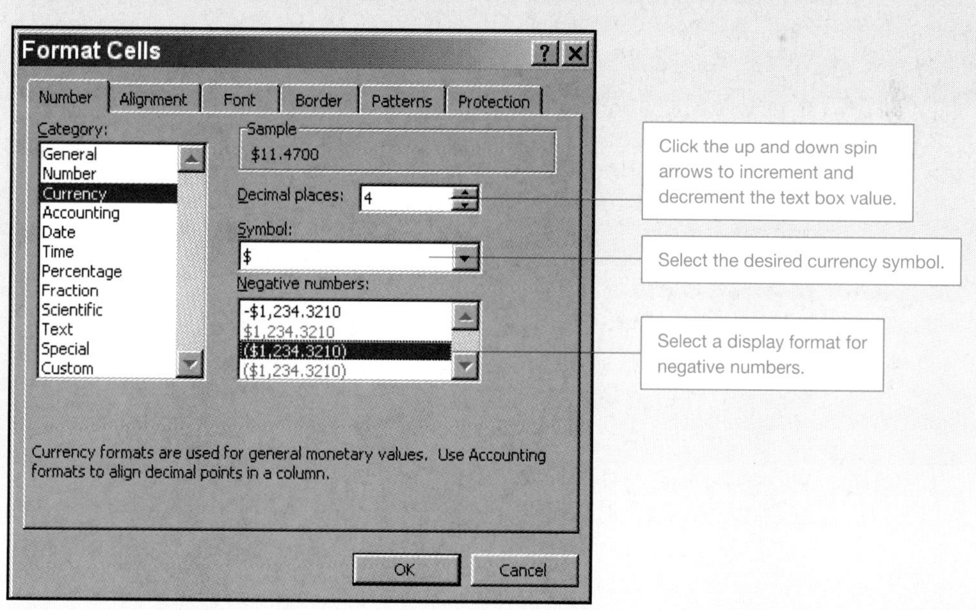

7. To apply the formatting options:
   CLICK: OK command button

8. To increase the decimal places in the Shares column:
   SELECT: cell range from D4 to D11
   CLICK: Increase Decimal button ( )

9. To format the remaining values using the Currency style:
SELECT: cell range from E4 to F12
CLICK: Currency Style button ($)

10. Depending on your system, the columns may not be wide enough to display the formatted values. With the cell range still selected:
CHOOSE: Format, Column, AutoFit Selection
You should now see all the data contained in the column, as shown in Figure 3.6.

Figure 3.6

Formatting values in the worksheet

	A	B	C	D	E	F	G	H
1	Portfolio of Mutual Funds							
2	As of August, 2001							
3	Name	Of Portfolio	Mkt Price	Shares	Mkt Value	Cost Basis	Gain/Loss	
4	Domestic Asset Allocation	0.86%	$11.4700	111.9870	$ 1,284.49	$ 800.00	60.56%	
5	Domestic Blue Chip Index	29.10%	$74.4500	584.1760	$ 43,491.90	$ 24,540.08	77.23%	
6	Domestic Small Cap Equity	12.18%	$6.3400	2870.0070	$ 18,195.84	$ 9,900.00	83.80%	
7	European Discovery Bonds	3.83%	$0.7540	7592.1630	$ 5,724.49	$ 5,000.00	14.49%	
8	European Income Growth	4.62%	$17.7200	389.9450	$ 6,909.83	$ 8,955.96	-22.85%	
9	Global Asset Allocation	39.65%	$12.0800	4905.6240	$ 59,259.94	$ 43,470.45	36.32%	
10	Global Dividend Income	7.60%	$24.9300	455.4270	$ 11,353.80	$ 15,342.88	-26.00%	
11	Global Emerging Markets	2.16%	$13.8000	234.0900	$ 3,230.44	$ 9,645.50	-66.51%	
12	Total Portfolio				$ 149,450.73	$ 117,654.87	27.02%	
13								
14								

11. Now let's create a notes area:
SELECT: cell A14
TYPE: **Notes**
PRESS: ↓

12. To enter the first note or comment:
TYPE: **31-Aug-2001**
PRESS: →
TYPE: **The market rebounded from a low of 9,200 in June.**
PRESS: ENTER

13. SELECT: cell A15
In the Formula bar, notice that the date reads 8/31/2001.

14. To format the date to appear differently on the worksheet:
CHOOSE: Format, Cells
SELECT: Date in the *Category* list box, if it is not already selected

15. To apply a new format, select one of the listed versions:
SELECT: "March 14, 2001" in the *Type* list box
CLICK: OK command button
(*Note:* The *Type* list box displays the date formats for March 14, 2001. Keep in mind that you are selecting a display format and not a date value to insert into the worksheet.) Your screen should now appear similar to Figure 3.7.

Figure 3.7

Applying number and date formats

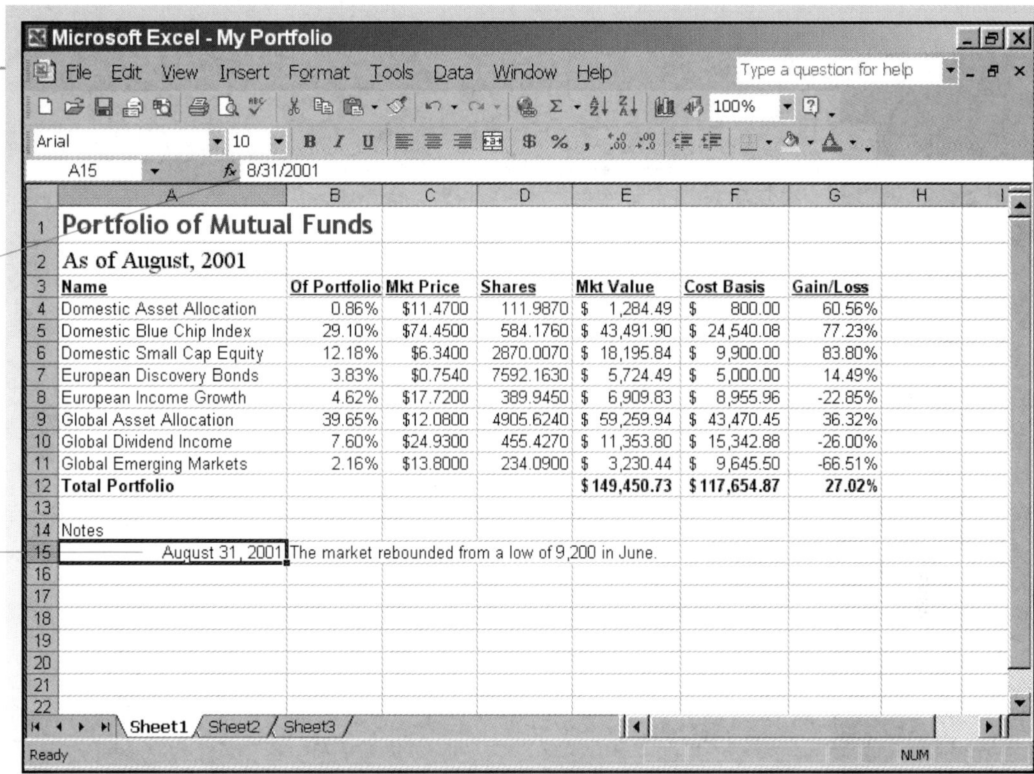

16. Save the workbook and keep it open for use in the next lesson.

3.1.3 Aligning, Merging, and Rotating Cells

feature

You can change the **cell alignment** for any type of data entered into a worksheet. By default, Excel aligns text against the left edge of a cell and values against the right edge. Not only can you change these default alignments, you can also merge or combine data across cells. Rotating text within a cell allows you to fit longer text entries into a narrow column.

method

To align and merge data, you select the desired cell range and then do one of the following:

- CLICK: Align Left button
- CLICK: Center button
- CLICK: Align Right button
- CLICK: Merge and Center button

To display the *Alignment* formatting options:

- SELECT: cell range to format
- CHOOSE: Format, Cells
- CLICK: *Alignment* tab
- SELECT: to align, merge, or rotate cells

Excel

practice

You will now practice aligning, merging, and rotating text in cells. Ensure that you have completed the previous lessons in the module and that the "My Portfolio" workbook is displayed.

1. You align the contents of a cell using buttons on the Formatting toolbar. Let's manipulate the "Notes" title in cell A14:
   SELECT: cell A14
   CLICK: Bold button ( )
   CLICK: Underline button ( )

2. To practice changing a cell's alignment:
   CLICK: Align Right button ( )
   CLICK: Align Left button ( )
   CLICK: Center button ( )
   Notice the change in alignment that takes place with each mouse click.

3. You can change the cell alignment for number and date values also:
   SELECT: cell A15
   CLICK: Center button ( )
   The date appears centered under the column heading for "Notes."

4. More interesting is the ability to merge cells together and center the contents. Do the following:
   SELECT: cell range from A1 to G1
   CLICK: Merge and Center button ( )
   Notice that the title is now centered over the table area, as shown in Figure 3.8. (*Note:* The merged cell is still considered to be cell A1. The next cell in the row is cell H1.)

Figure 3.8

Aligning and merging cells

Text is centered in cell A1, which is a merged cell over the range A1:G1.

Text is centered in cell A14

Value is centered in cell A15

	A	B	C	D	E	F	G	H
1	Portfolio of Mutual Funds							
2	As of August, 2001							
3	**Name**	**Of Portfolio**	**Mkt Price**	**Shares**	**Mkt Value**	**Cost Basis**	**Gain/Loss**	
4	Domestic Asset Allocation	0.86%	$11.4700	111.9870	$ 1,284.49	$ 800.00	60.56%	
5	Domestic Blue Chip Index	29.10%	$74.4500	584.1760	$ 43,491.90	$ 24,540.08	77.23%	
6	Domestic Small Cap Equity	12.18%	$6.3400	2870.0070	$ 18,195.84	$ 9,900.00	83.80%	
7	European Discovery Bonds	3.83%	$0.7540	7592.1630	$ 5,724.49	$ 5,000.00	14.49%	
8	European Income Growth	4.62%	$17.7200	389.9450	$ 6,909.83	$ 8,955.96	-22.85%	
9	Global Asset Allocation	39.65%	$12.0800	4905.6240	$ 59,259.94	$ 43,470.45	36.32%	
10	Global Dividend Income	7.60%	$24.9300	455.4270	$ 11,353.80	$ 15,342.88	-26.00%	
11	Global Emerging Markets	2.16%	$13.8000	234.0900	$ 3,230.44	$ 9,645.50	-66.51%	
12	**Total Portfolio**				**$ 149,450.73**	**$ 117,654.87**	**27.02%**	
13								
14	**Notes**							
15	August 31, 2001	The market rebounded from a low of 9,200 in June.						
16								
17								

5. Let's merge and center the subtitle in cell A2 using the dialog box:
   SELECT: cell range from A2 to G2
   CHOOSE: Format, Cells
   CLICK: *Alignment* tab
   The Format Cells dialog box appears, as shown in Figure 3.9.

Figure 3.9

Format Cells dialog box: *Alignment* tab

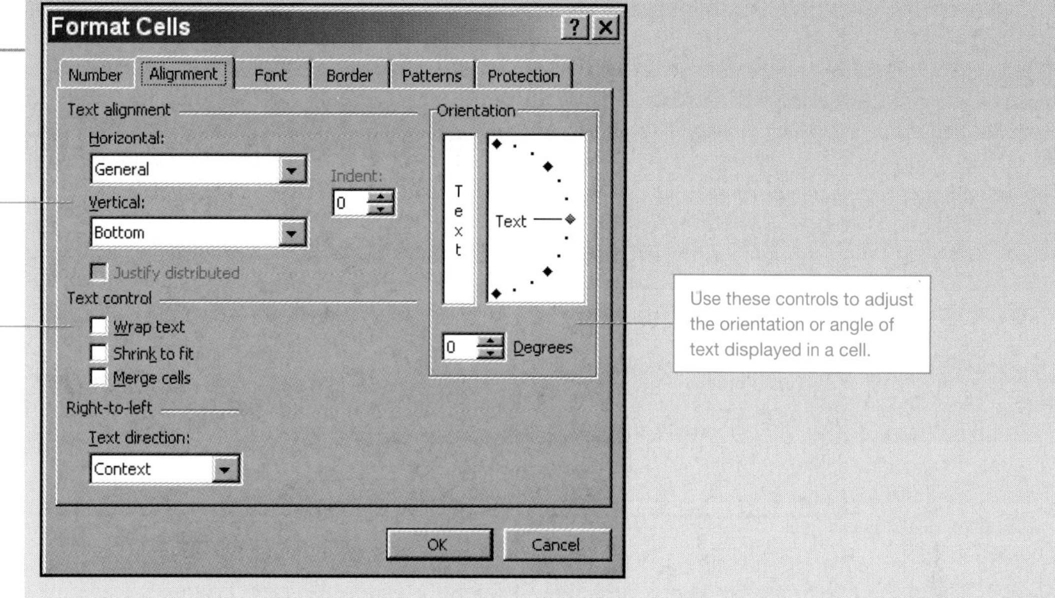

6. In the Format Cells dialog box:
   SELECT: Center from the *Horizontal* drop-down list box
   SELECT: *Merge cells* check box
   CLICK: OK command button

7. Let's practice splitting up a merged cell without using the Undo command. Ensure that cell A2 (which now covers the area to G2) is still selected and then do the following:
   CHOOSE: Format, Cells
   The last tab that was selected in the dialog box (*Alignment*) is displayed automatically.

8. To split the merged cell:
   SELECT: *Merge cells* check box so that no ✓ appears
   CLICK: OK command button
   The entry remains centered, but only between column A's borders.

9. Now let's practice rotating text. Do the following:
   SELECT: cell range from B3 to G3
   CHOOSE: Format, Cells

10. You set the rotation for text by clicking and dragging in the *Orientation* area of the dialog box. You can also specify a positive value in the *Degrees* spin box to angle text from bottom left to upper right. In this step, use the mouse to select an angle of 30 degrees:
    DRAG: the "Text" line in the *Orientation* area to 30 degrees, as shown here

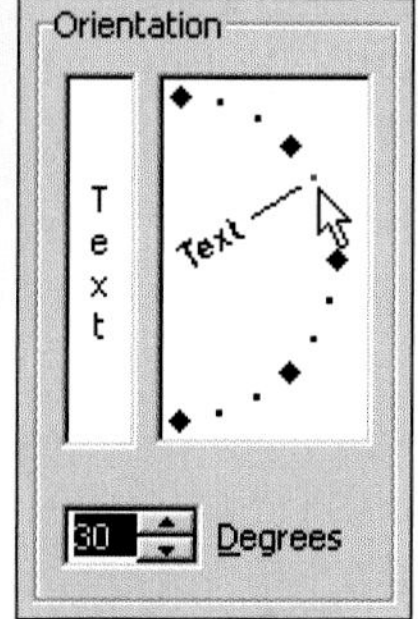

11. To apply the formatting change:
    CLICK: OK command button
    Your screen should now appear similar to Figure 3.10.

Figure 3.10

Changing the orientation or angle of text

	A	B	C	D	E	F	G	H
1	Portfolio of Mutual Funds							
2	As of August, 2001							
3	Name	Of Portfolio	Mkt Price	Shares	Mkt Value	Cost Basis	Gain/Loss	
4	Domestic Asset Allocation	0.86%	$11.4700	111.9870	$ 1,284.49	$ 800.00	60.56%	
5	Domestic Blue Chip Index	29.10%	$74.4500	584.1760	$ 43,491.90	$ 24,540.08	77.23%	
6	Domestic Small Cap Equity	12.18%	$6.3400	2870.0070	$ 18,195.84	$ 9,900.00	83.80%	
7	European Discovery Bonds	3.83%	$0.7540	7592.1630	$ 5,724.49	$ 5,000.00	14.49%	
8	European Income Growth	4.62%	$17.7200	389.9450	$ 6,909.83	$ 8,955.96	-22.85%	
9	Global Asset Allocation	39.65%	$12.0800	4905.6240	$ 59,259.94	$ 43,470.45	36.32%	
10	Global Dividend Income	7.6[illegible]%	$24.9300	455.4270	$ 11,353.80	$ 15,342.88	-26.00%	
11	Global Emerging Markets	2.16%	$13.8000	234.0900	$ 3,230.44	$ 9,645.50	-66.51%	
12	**Total Portfolio**				**$ 149,450.73**	**$ 117,654.87**	**27.02%**	
13								
14	**Notes**							
15	August 31, 2001	The market rebounded from a low of 9,200 in June.						
16								
17								

12. Save the workbook and keep it open for use in the next lesson.

In Addition DISPLAYING LONG TEXT ENTRIES IN A CELL

Excel provides several tools for working with long text entries. First, you can increase the row height of a cell and align its contents vertically between the top and bottom borders. You can then wrap the text to display in a single cell. Second, you can use the ALT + ENTER key combination to place a hard carriage return or line feed within a cell. Third, you can shrink an entry to fit between a column's borders.

3.1.4 Adding Borders and Shading

As with the other formatting options, you use borders, patterns, shading, and colors to enhance a worksheet's readability. The gridlines that appear in the worksheet window are nonprinting lines, provided only to help you line up information. Borders are used to place printed gridlines on a worksheet and to separate data into logical sections. These formatting options also enable you to create professional-looking invoice forms, memos, and tables.

method→

To apply borders or coloring, you select the desired cell range and then:

- CLICK: Borders button ( )

and/or

- CLICK: Fill Color button ( )

To display the *Border* and *Patterns* formatting options:

- SELECT: cell range to format
- CHOOSE: Format, Cells
- CLICK: *Border* or *Patterns* tab
- SELECT: borders or pattern, shading, and fill color options

practice

In this exercise, you format a worksheet by applying borders and fill coloring to selected cell ranges. Ensure that you have completed the previous lessons in the module and that the "My Portfolio" workbook is displayed.

1. Move to cell A1.
2. In order to better see the borders that you will apply in this lesson, let's remove the **gridlines** from the worksheet display. To do so:
   CHOOSE: Tools, Options
   CLICK: *View* tab
   SELECT: *Gridlines* check box, so that no check ✓ appears
   CLICK: OK command button
   Your worksheet should now appear similar to Figure 3.11.

Figure 3.11

Removing the gridlines from displaying

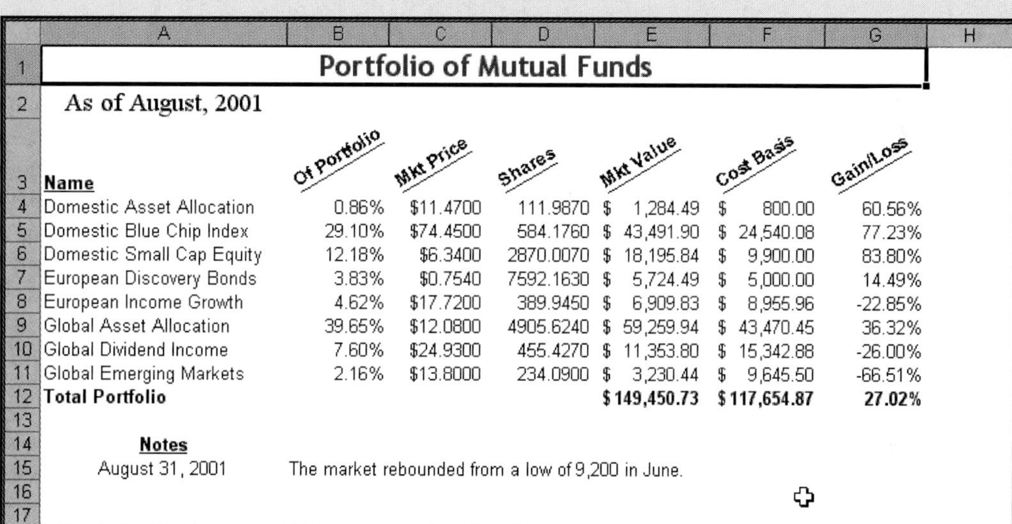

	A	B	C	D	E	F	G
1	Portfolio of Mutual Funds						
2	As of August, 2001						
3	**Name**	Of Portfolio	Mkt Price	Shares	Mkt Value	Cost Basis	Gain/Loss
4	Domestic Asset Allocation	0.86%	$11.4700	111.9870	$ 1,284.49	$ 800.00	60.56%
5	Domestic Blue Chip Index	29.10%	$74.4500	584.1760	$ 43,491.90	$ 24,540.08	77.23%
6	Domestic Small Cap Equity	12.18%	$6.3400	2870.0070	$ 18,195.84	$ 9,900.00	83.80%
7	European Discovery Bonds	3.83%	$0.7540	7592.1630	$ 5,724.49	$ 5,000.00	14.49%
8	European Income Growth	4.62%	$17.7200	389.9450	$ 6,909.83	$ 8,955.96	-22.85%
9	Global Asset Allocation	39.65%	$12.0800	4905.6240	$ 59,259.94	$ 43,470.45	36.32%
10	Global Dividend Income	7.60%	$24.9300	455.4270	$ 11,353.80	$ 15,342.88	-26.00%
11	Global Emerging Markets	2.16%	$13.8000	234.0900	$ 3,230.44	$ 9,645.50	-66.51%
12	**Total Portfolio**				**$ 149,450.73**	**$ 117,654.87**	**27.02%**
13							
14	**Notes**						
15	August 31, 2001	The market rebounded from a low of 9,200 in June.					
16							
17							

3. Now let's apply some borders:
   SELECT: cell range from A12 to G12
   (*Hint:* Use the column and row frame highlighting to help you line up the cell range.)
4. To display the border options available:
   CLICK: down arrow attached to the Borders button
   A drop-down list of border options appears, as shown below.

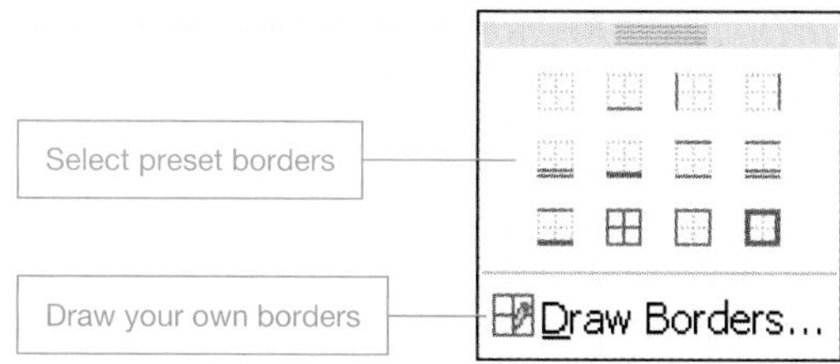

5. You can choose from a variety of preset border options or choose to draw your own borders. For this step, let's use the preset borders:
SELECT: Top and Double Bottom Border ( ) in the drop-down list
CLICK: cell A1 to remove the highlighting
A nice border now separates the data from the summary information. (*Note:* Clicking the Underline button ( ) underlines only the words in a cell, whereas applying borders underlines the entire cell.)

6. To outline the "Notes" area:
SELECT: cell range from A14 to G18
CLICK: down arrow attached to the Borders button ( )
SELECT: Outside Borders button ( )

7. Now let's apply a new fill color (sometimes called *shading*) to the "Notes" area. Ensure that the cell range from A14 to G18 is still selected and then do the following:
CLICK: down arrow attached to the Fill Color button ( )
A drop-down list of colors appears, as shown below.

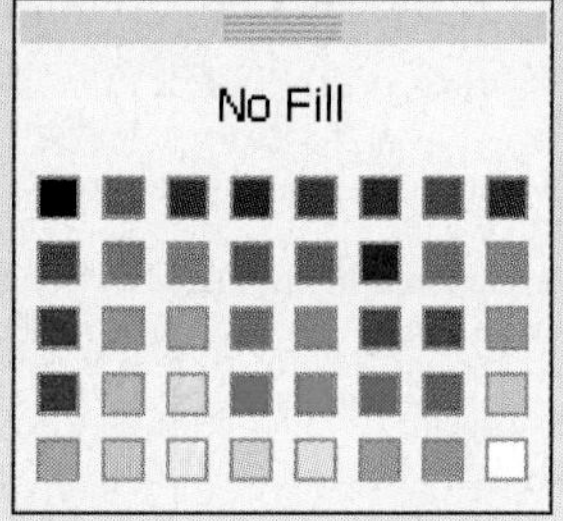

8. SELECT: a pale yellow color from the drop-down list
CLICK: cell A1 to remove the highlighting
The "Notes" area should now appear on a colored background.

9. To enhance the title in cell A1:
CLICK: down arrow attached to the Fill Color button ( )
SELECT: a dark blue color from the drop-down list

10. To better see the title, you will need to adjust the text color:
CLICK: down arrow attached to the Font Color button ( )
SELECT: white from the drop-down list
Your screen should now appear similar to Figure 3.12.

Figure 3.12

Applying borders and colors to a worksheet

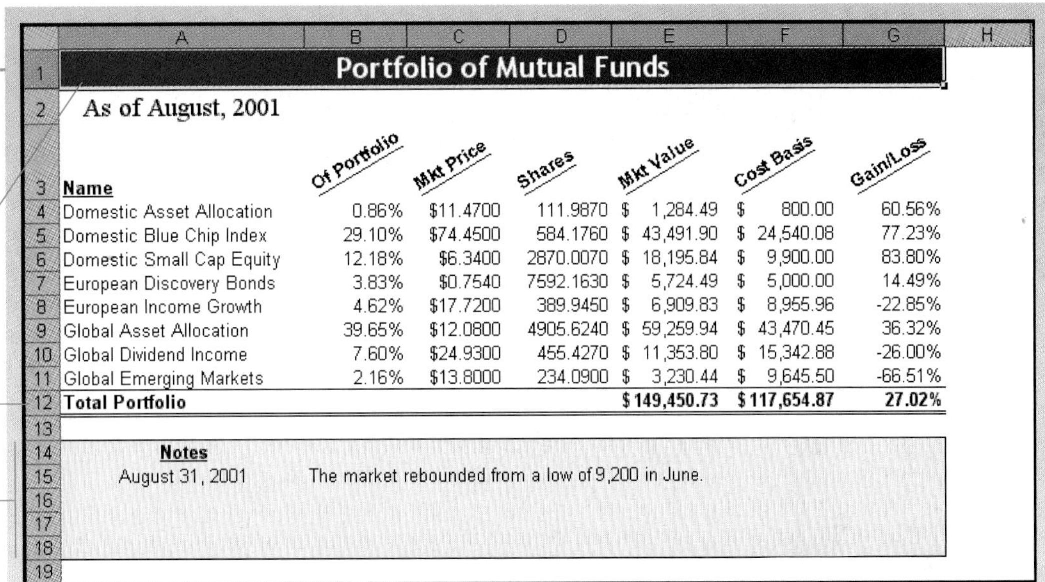

	A	B	C	D	E	F	G
1	Portfolio of Mutual Funds						
2	As of August, 2001						
3	Name	Of Portfolio	Mkt Price	Shares	Mkt Value	Cost Basis	Gain/Loss
4	Domestic Asset Allocation	0.86%	$11.4700	111.9870	$ 1,284.49	$ 800.00	60.56%
5	Domestic Blue Chip Index	29.10%	$74.4500	584.1760	$ 43,491.90	$ 24,540.08	77.23%
6	Domestic Small Cap Equity	12.18%	$6.3400	2870.0070	$ 18,195.84	$ 9,900.00	83.80%
7	European Discovery Bonds	3.83%	$0.7540	7592.1630	$ 5,724.49	$ 5,000.00	14.49%
8	European Income Growth	4.62%	$17.7200	389.9450	$ 6,909.83	$ 8,955.96	-22.85%
9	Global Asset Allocation	39.65%	$12.0800	4905.6240	$ 59,259.94	$ 43,470.45	36.32%
10	Global Dividend Income	7.60%	$24.9300	455.4270	$ 11,353.80	$ 15,342.88	-26.00%
11	Global Emerging Markets	2.16%	$13.8000	234.0900	$ 3,230.44	$ 9,645.50	-66.51%
12	Total Portfolio				$149,450.73	$117,654.87	27.02%
13							
14	Notes						
15	August 31, 2001	The market rebounded from a low of 9,200 in June.					
16							
17							
18							
19							

11. To turn the worksheet gridlines back on:
CHOOSE: Tools, Options
CLICK: *View* tab
SELECT: *Gridlines* check box, so that a check ✓ appears
CLICK: OK command button
Notice that the gridlines do not show through the cells that have been colored.

12. You will now practice drawing a border using the Borders toolbar. Do the following:
CLICK: down arrow attached to the Borders button ( )
CHOOSE: Draw Borders
The Borders toolbar appears, as shown with labels below.

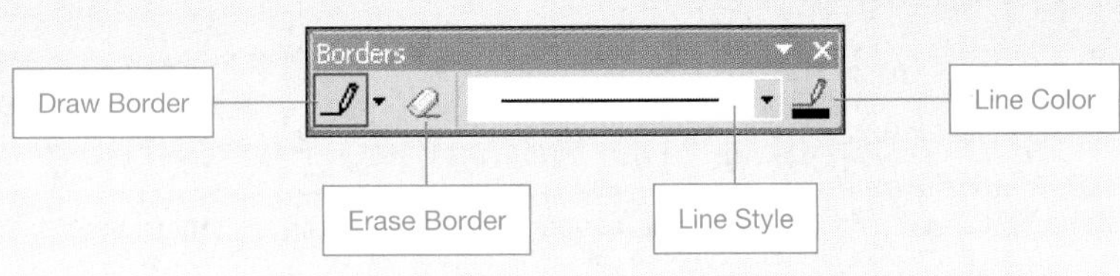

13. DRAG: the Borders toolbar by its Title bar so that cells E3 to E12 are visible (see Figure 3.13)

14. The Draw Borders button ( ) is set for "Draw Border," by default, which places an outline border around a cell range. Alternatively, you can choose the "Draw Border Grid" option to place a border around each cell in a range. Let's accept the default selection and use the pencil mouse pointer ( ) to draw an outline border:
CLICK: in the middle of cell E3
DRAG: downward to the middle of cell E11
The border extends as you move the mouse pointer down. Your screen should appear similar to Figure 3.13.

Excel

Figure 3.13

Drawing a border around a cell range

	A	B	C	D	E	F	G	H
1	Portfolio of Mutual Funds							
2	As of August, 2001							
3	Name			...ares	Mkt Value	Cost Basis	Gain/Loss	
4	Domestic Asset Allocation	0.86%	$11.4700	111.9870	$ 1,284.49	$ 800.00	60.56%	
5	Domestic Blue Chip Index	29.10%	$74.4500	584.1760	$ 43,491.90	$ 24,540.08	77.23%	
6	Domestic Small Cap Equity	12.18%	$6.3400	2870.0070	$ 18,195.84	$ 9,900.00	83.80%	
7	European Discovery Bonds	3.83%	$0.7540	7592.1630	$ 5,724.49	$ 5,000.00	14.49%	
8	European Income Growth	4.62%	$17.7200	389.9450	$ 6,909.83	$ 8,955.96	-22.85%	
9	Global Asset Allocation	39.65%	$12.0800	4905.6240	$ 59,259.94	$ 43,470.45	36.32%	
10	Global Dividend Income	7.60%	$24.9300	455.4270	$ 14,353.80	$ 15,342.88	-26.00%	
11	Global Emerging Markets	2.16%	$13.8000	234.0900	$ 3,230.44	$ 9,645.50	-66.51%	
12	Total Portfolio				$ 149,450.73	$ 117,654.87	27.02%	
13								
14	Notes							
15	August 31, 2001	The market rebounded from a low of 9,200 in June.						
16								
17								
18								
19								

15. Release the mouse button to finish drawing the line. In addition to outlining the cell range, the border extends on an angle to follow the rotated text in cell E3.

16. To close the Borders toolbar:
CLICK: its Close button (☒)

17. Save and then close the workbook.

SelfCheck

3.1. What is the basic difference between using the Underline button (U) and the Borders button (▭▾)?

3.2 Applying and Removing Formatting

Microsoft Excel provides a wealth of formatting commands for improving the appearance of a worksheet, its individual cells, and the contents within those cells. In addition to selecting formatting options individually, you can use the Format Painter button (🖌) and the Edit, Paste Special command to copy formatting characteristics. These tools, along with Excel's AutoFormat feature, can help you apply formatting commands to a worksheet consistently and more efficiently. In this module, you work with these tools as well as learn how to remove formatting characteristics from a worksheet.

3.2.1 Using Format Painter

feature→

You use the **Format Painter** feature to copy formatting styles and attributes from one area in your worksheet to another. Not only does this feature help speed up formatting procedures, it ensures formatting consistency among cells in your worksheet.

To copy formatting from one cell range to another:

- SELECT: the cell range whose formatting you want to copy
- CLICK: Format Painter button (🖌) on the Standard toolbar
- SELECT: the cell range that you want to format

practice

You will now use Format Painter to copy formatting from one area of a worksheet to another. Ensure that no workbooks are open in the application window.

1. Open the data file named EX0320 to display the workbook shown in Figure 3.14.

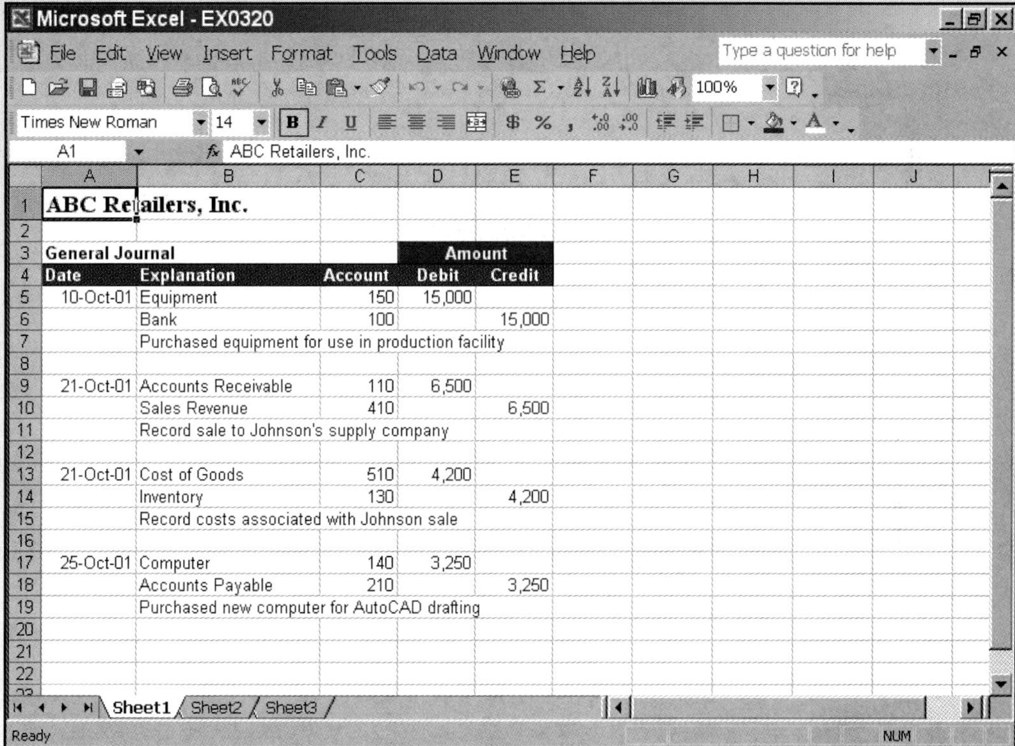

Figure 3.14

Opening the EX0320 workbook

2. Save the file as "ABC Retailers" to your personal storage location.

3. You will now apply formatting commands to the first journal entry in the worksheet. Once the formatting is completed, you will copy the set of formatting options to the other journal entries. To begin: SELECT: cell A5

4. To change the date formatting:
CHOOSE: Format, Cells
CLICK: *Number* tab
SELECT: Date in the *Category* list box
SELECT: 3/14/2001 in the *Type* list box
CLICK: OK command button
(*Hint:* You may have to scroll down the list to find the option.) The cell entry now appears as 10/10/2001.

Excel

5. To emphasize the account numbers and explanation:
SELECT: cell range from C5 to C6
CLICK: Bold button (B)
SELECT: cell B7
CLICK: Italic button (I)
SELECT: Green from the Font Color button (A)

6. To show the values in the Amount column as currency:
SELECT: cell range from D5 to E6
CLICK: Currency Style button ($)

7. To change the width of columns D and E, ensure that the cell range from D5 to E6 remains selected. Then, do the following:
CHOOSE: Format, Column, AutoFit Selection
The journal entry now appears formatted, as shown in Figure 3.15.

Figure 3.15

Formatting the first journal entry

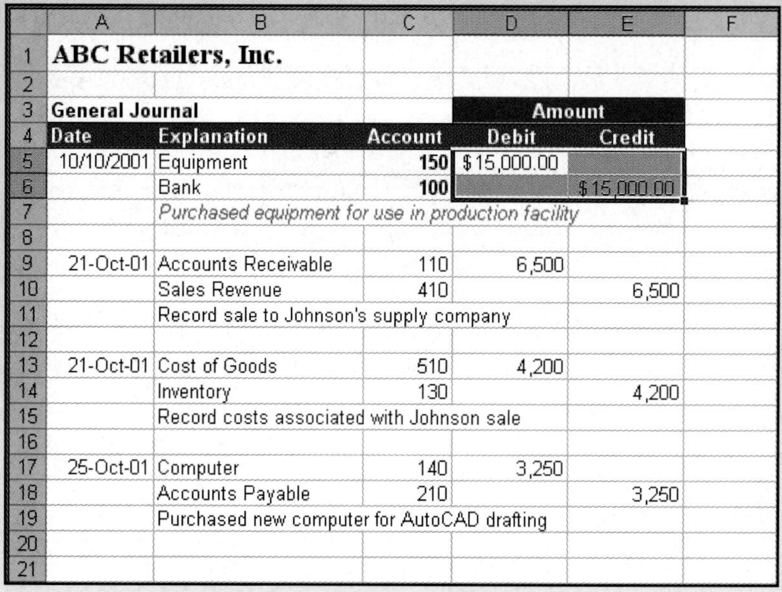

	A	B	C	D	E	F
1	**ABC Retailers, Inc.**					
2						
3	**General Journal**			**Amount**		
4	**Date**	**Explanation**	**Account**	**Debit**	**Credit**	
5	10/10/2001	Equipment	**150**	$15,000.00		
6		Bank	**100**		$15,000.00	
7		*Purchased equipment for use in production facility*				
8						
9	21-Oct-01	Accounts Receivable	110	6,500		
10		Sales Revenue	410		6,500	
11		Record sale to Johnson's supply company				
12						
13	21-Oct-01	Cost of Goods	510	4,200		
14		Inventory	130		4,200	
15		Record costs associated with Johnson sale				
16						
17	25-Oct-01	Computer	140	3,250		
18		Accounts Payable	210		3,250	
19		Purchased new computer for AutoCAD drafting				
20						
21						

8. Using Format Painter, you will copy the formatting from this journal entry to another journal entry in the worksheet. Do the following:
SELECT: cell range from A5 to E7

9. To copy the formatting attributes:
CLICK: Format Painter button ( ) on the Standard toolbar
Notice that a dashed marquee, sometimes referred to as a moving border, appears around the selected range.

10. To apply the formatting to the next journal entry:
CLICK: cell A9 using the Format Painter mouse pointer ( )
(*Note:* You need only click the top left-hand cell in the target range.)

11. You can apply more than one coat using Format Painter. To demonstrate, ensure that the cell range A9 through E11 remains highlighted and then do the following:
DOUBLE-CLICK: Format Painter button ( )
Double-clicking the toolbar button will make the button stay active even after you apply the first coat to a target cell range.

12. With the Format Painter button (🖌) toggled on, you can apply multiple formatting coats. Do the following:
CLICK: cell A13
CLICK: cell A17
The remaining journal entries have been formatted. Your screen should now appear similar to Figure 3.16.

Figure 3.16

Applying a formatting coat using Format Painter

Cell range containing the formatting information to be copied

Last cell range to have formatting applied

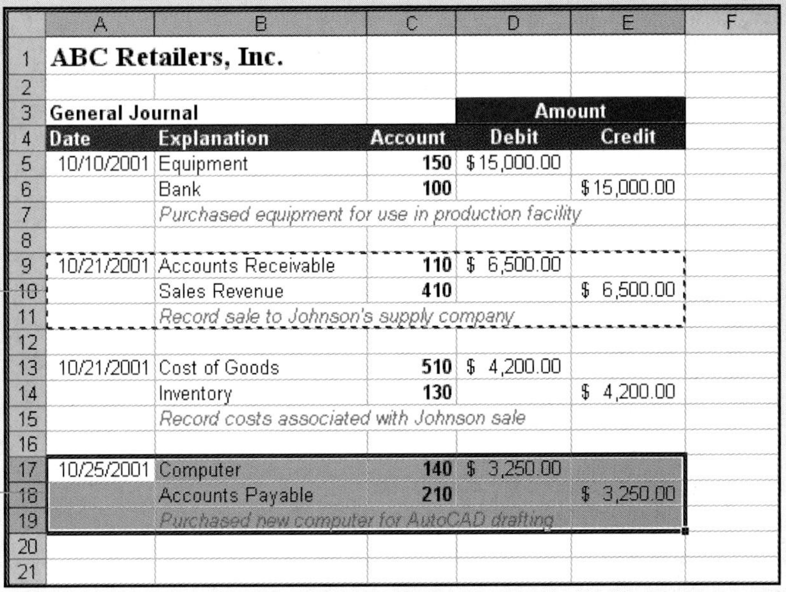

	A	B	C	D	E	F
1	ABC Retailers, Inc.					
2						
3	General Journal			Amount		
4	Date	Explanation	Account	Debit	Credit	
5	10/10/2001	Equipment	150	$15,000.00		
6		Bank	100		$15,000.00	
7		*Purchased equipment for use in production facility*				
8						
9	10/21/2001	Accounts Receivable	110	$ 6,500.00		
10		Sales Revenue	410		$ 6,500.00	
11		*Record sale to Johnson's supply company*				
12						
13	10/21/2001	Cost of Goods	510	$ 4,200.00		
14		Inventory	130		$ 4,200.00	
15		*Record costs associated with Johnson sale*				
16						
17	10/25/2001	Computer	140	$ 3,250.00		
18		Accounts Payable	210		$ 3,250.00	
19		*Purchased new computer for AutoCAD drafting*				
20						
21						

13. To toggle this feature off:
CLICK: Format Painter button (🖌)

14. To better view your handiwork, do the following:
PRESS: CTRL + HOME

15. Save the workbook and keep it open for use in the next lesson.

3.2.2 Removing Formatting Attributes

feature

You can safely remove a cell's formatting without affecting the contents of the cell. The easiest method, of course, is to click the Undo button (↶) immediately after choosing a formatting command. You can also remove formatting characteristics by choosing the Edit, Clear, Formats command.

method

To remove all formatting from a cell range:

- SELECT: the desired cell range
- CHOOSE: Edit, Clear, Formats

practice

You will now practice removing formatting characteristics from a cell range. Ensure that you have completed the previous lessons in the module and that the "ABC Retailers" workbook is displayed.

1. Let's demonstrate the effects of entering data into a formatted cell. In this example, you will attempt to enter a value into a cell that is formatted to display a date. Do the following:
SELECT: cell A17
TYPE: **1000**
PRESS: ENTER
The cell displays 9/26/1902.

2. You will now remove the formatting from this cell:
SELECT: cell A17
CHOOSE: Edit, Clear, Formats
The cell now displays the correct value, 1000.

3. The Edit, Clear, Formats command removes all formatting from a cell or cell range. To remove a single formatting characteristic, you can simply modify that characteristic. You will now remove the green color from the journal entry's explanatory note. To do so:
SELECT: cell B19
CLICK: down arrow attached to the Font Color button ( )
SELECT: Automatic from the drop-down list
The text retains the italic formatting but changes to the default black color.

4. To remove the italic formatting:
CLICK: Italic button ( ) once
(*Note:* Several formatting commands are toggled on and off by clicking their respective toolbar buttons.)

5. To remove all of the formatting characteristics for the last two journal entries, do the following:
SELECT: cell range from A13 to E19
CHOOSE: Edit, Clear, Formats
Notice that the date in cell A13 is stored as a value, 37185, as shown in Figure 3.17. In the next lesson, you will use a new method to reapply formatting to the journal entries.

Figure 3.17

Removing formatting using the Edit, Clear, Formats command

	A	B	C	D	E	F
1	**ABC Retailers, Inc.**					
2						
3	**General Journal**			**Amount**		
4	**Date**	**Explanation**	**Account**	**Debit**	**Credit**	
5	10/10/2001	Equipment	**150**	$15,000.00		
6		Bank	**100**		$15,000.00	
7		*Purchased equipment for use in production facility*				
8						
9	10/21/2001	Accounts Receivable	**110**	$ 6,500.00		
10		Sales Revenue	**410**		$ 6,500.00	
11		*Record sale to Johnson's supply company*				
12						
13	37185	Cost of Goods	510	4200		
14		Inventory	130		4200	
15		Record costs associated with Johnson sale				
16						
17	1000	Computer	140	3250		
18		Accounts Payable	210		3250	
19		Purchased new computer for AutoCAD drafting				
20						
21						

3.2.3 Using the Paste Special Command

feature

The Edit, Paste Special command allows you to copy portions or characteristics of a cell or cell range to another area. Some of these characteristics include cell values, formulas, comments, and formats. Like the Format Painter feature, this command is useful for copying formatting options from one cell range to another.

method

To copy and paste formatting characteristics:

- SELECT: the cell or range whose formatting you want to copy
- CLICK: Copy button
- SELECT: the cells where you want to apply the formatting
- CHOOSE: Edit, Paste Special
- SELECT: *Formats* option button
- CLICK: OK command button

practice

In this exercise, you practice copying and pasting formatting characteristics using the Edit, Paste Special command. Ensure that you have completed the previous lessons in the module and that the "ABC Retailers" workbook is displayed.

1. In order to paste formatting characteristics, you must first copy them to the Clipboard. Do the following:
SELECT: cell range from A9 to E11
CLICK: Copy button
A dashed marquee or moving border appears around the selected range.

2. To display the Paste Special dialog box:
SELECT: cell A13
CHOOSE: Edit, Paste Special
The Paste Special dialog box, shown in Figure 3.18, provides several intermediate and advanced features. (*Hint:* You can also display this dialog box by clicking the down arrow attached to the Paste button and choosing Paste Special from the drop-down menu.)

Figure 3.18

The Paste Special dialog box

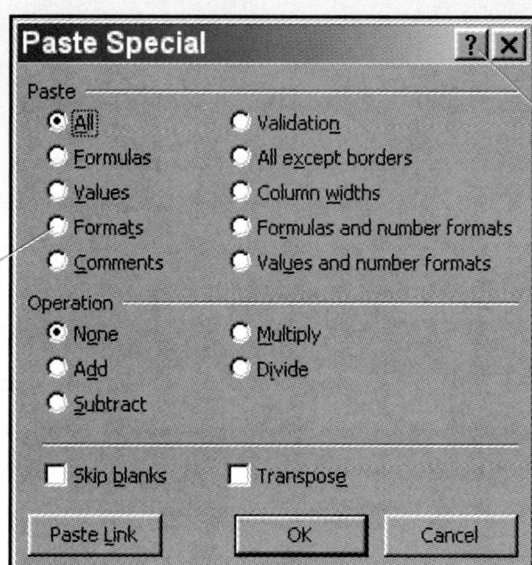

This option button allows you to paste only the formatting characteristics from a cell or cell range.

To find out more about the featurers of this dialog box, click the question mark button and then click on one of the option buttons. A brief ToolTip window will appear. Click again to remove the ToolTip.

Excel

3. To paste the formatting:
SELECT: *Formats* option button
CLICK: OK command button
The formatting is applied.

4. To format the last journal entry:
SELECT: cell A17
CHOOSE: Edit, Paste Special
SELECT: *Formats* option button
CLICK: OK command button

5. To complete the copy and paste operation:
PRESS: ESC

6. SELECT: cell A17
TYPE: **10/25/2001**
PRESS: ENTER
Your worksheet should now appear similar to Figure 3.19.

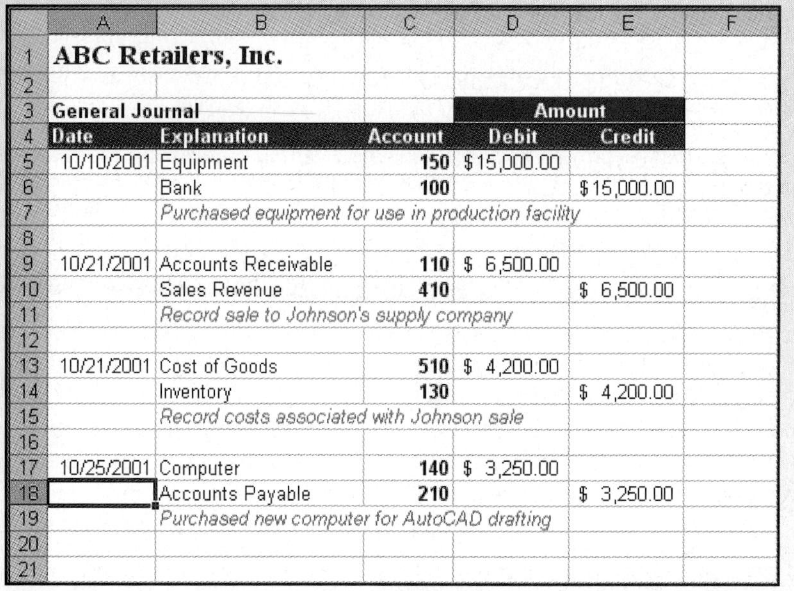

Figure 3.19

Completing the ABC Retailers workbook

	A	B	C	D	E	F
1	**ABC Retailers, Inc.**					
2						
3	**General Journal**			**Amount**		
4	**Date**	**Explanation**	**Account**	**Debit**	**Credit**	
5	10/10/2001	Equipment	**150**	$15,000.00		
6		Bank	**100**		$15,000.00	
7		*Purchased equipment for use in production facility*				
8						
9	10/21/2001	Accounts Receivable	**110**	$ 6,500.00		
10		Sales Revenue	**410**		$ 6,500.00	
11		*Record sale to Johnson's supply company*				
12						
13	10/21/2001	Cost of Goods	**510**	$ 4,200.00		
14		Inventory	**130**		$ 4,200.00	
15		*Record costs associated with Johnson sale*				
16						
17	10/25/2001	Computer	**140**	$ 3,250.00		
18		Accounts Payable	**210**		$ 3,250.00	
19		*Purchased new computer for AutoCAD drafting*				
20						
21						

7. Save and then close the workbook.

In Addition PASTING FORMATS USING THE PASTE OPTIONS ICON ( )

When you complete a copy and paste operation using the Copy ( ) and Paste ( ) buttons on the toolbar, you may notice a small Paste Options icon ( ) appear near the bottom right-hand corner of the pasted range. By clicking the down arrow attached to this icon, you display a pop-up menu with the options shown here. Notice that you may select the Formatting Only option button to paste only the formatting of the copied cell range.

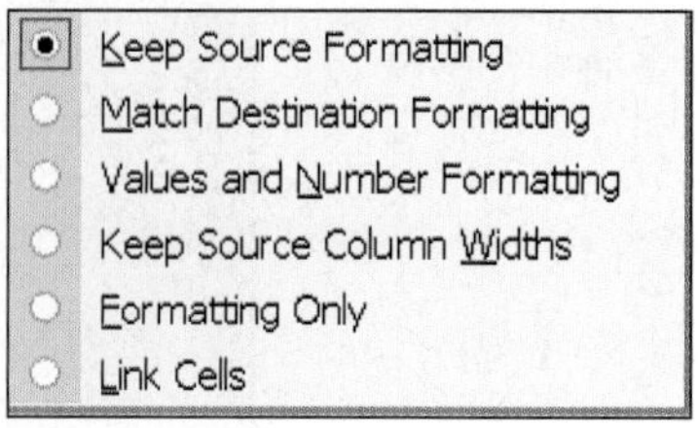

- (•) Keep Source Formatting
- ( ) Match Destination Formatting
- ( ) Values and Number Formatting
- ( ) Keep Source Column Widths
- ( ) Formatting Only
- ( ) Link Cells

3.2.4 Using the AutoFormat Command

feature

Rather than spend time selecting formatting options, you can use the **AutoFormat** feature to quickly apply an entire group of formatting commands to a cell range. The AutoFormat command works best when your worksheet data is organized using a table layout, with labels running down the left column and across the top row. After you specify one of the predefined table formats, Excel proceeds to apply fonts, number formats, alignments, borders, shading, and colors to the selected range. It is an excellent way to ensure consistent formatting across worksheets.

method

- SELECT: cell range to format
- CHOOSE: Format, AutoFormat
- SELECT: an option from the list of samples

practice

You now apply a predefined table format to an appliance sales worksheet. Ensure that no workbooks are open in the application window.

1. Open the data file named EX0324 to display the worksheet shown in Figure 3.20.

Figure 3.20

Opening the EX0324 workbook

	A	B	C	D	E	F	G
1	**Sandy's Appliance Department**						
2							
3		Qtr 1	Qtr 2	Qtr 3	Qtr 4	Total	
4	Dishwasher	5,764	6,409	6,390	7,255	25,818	
5	Dryer	8,331	12,259	10,668	10,871	42,129	
6	Microwave	2,980	3,310	1,872	2,390	10,552	
7	Refrigerator	35,400	42,810	46,230	35,788	160,228	
8	Stove/Range	24,767	28,105	27,492	21,560	101,924	
9	Washer	12,890	16,881	12,452	13,700	55,923	
10	Total	90,132	109,774	105,104	91,564	396,574	
11							
12							

2. Save the workbook as "Sandy's Appliances" to your personal storage location.
3. To apply an AutoFormat style to specific cells in a worksheet, you select the cell range that you want to format. Do the following:
   SELECT: cell range from A3 to F10
   (*Hint:* As long as the table layout does not contain blank rows or columns, you can place the cell pointer anywhere within the table.)
4. To display the AutoFormat options:
   CHOOSE: Format, AutoFormat
   The AutoFormat dialog box appears as shown in Figure 3.21.

Figure 3.21

AutoFormat dialog box

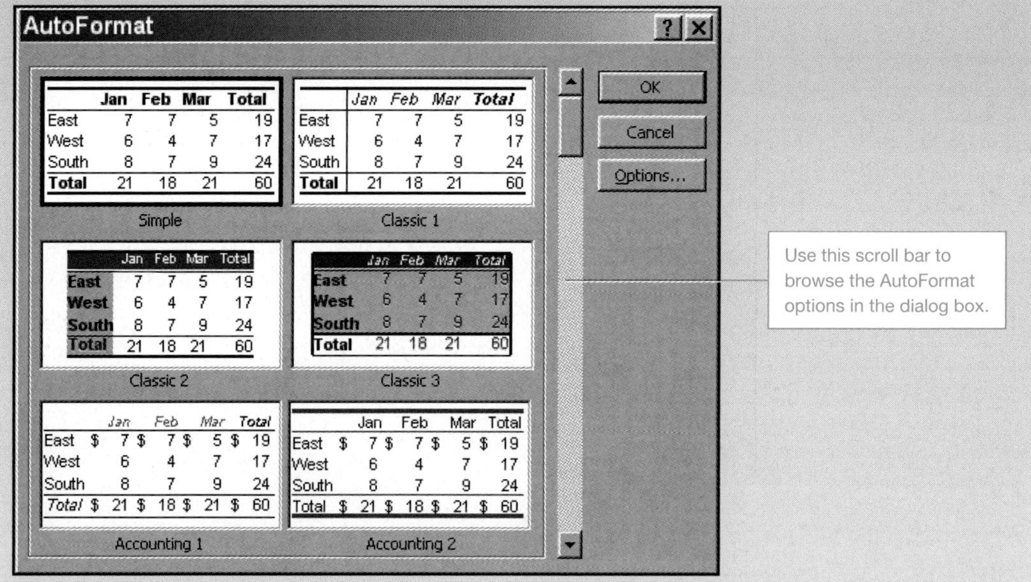

5. After scrolling the list in the AutoFormat dialog box, do the following:
   SELECT: Colorful 2 option
   CLICK: OK command button

6. To remove the highlighting from the cell range:
   CLICK: cell A1
   Your worksheet should now appear similar to Figure 3.22.

Figure 3.22

Applying an AutoFormat

	A	B	C	D	E	F	G
1	Sandy's Appliance Department						
2							
3		*Qtr 1*	*Qtr 2*	*Qtr 3*	*Qtr 4*	*Total*	
4	***Dishwasher***	5,764	6,409	6,390	7,255	25,818	
5	***Dryer***	8,331	12,259	10,668	10,871	42,129	
6	***Microwave***	2,980	3,310	1,872	2,390	10,552	
7	***Refrigerator***	35,400	42,810	46,230	35,788	160,228	
8	***Stove/Range***	24,767	28,105	27,492	21,560	101,924	
9	***Washer***	12,890	16,881	12,452	13,700	55,923	
10	**Total**	90,132	109,774	105,104	91,564	396,574	
11							
12							

7. On your own, place the cell pointer within the table area and then apply some of the other AutoFormat options, such as Classic 2.

8. Save and then close the workbook.

In Addition SPECIFYING FORMATTING OPTIONS USING AUTOFORMAT

Using the AutoFormat dialog box, you can specify which formatting options to apply to a range. Click the Options command button to expand the dialog box. You can then select or unselect a variety of format check boxes, including *Number, Border, Font, Patterns, Alignment,* and *Width/Height.* Only those formatting options that are selected will be applied to the range.

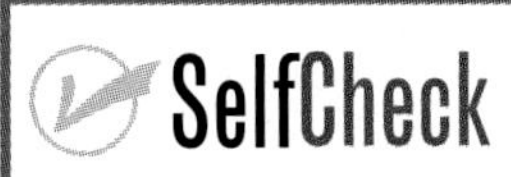

3.2. How might you ensure that related worksheets and workbooks are formatted consistently?

3.3 Printing and Web Publishing

This module focuses on outputting your worksheet creations. Most commonly, you will print a worksheet for inclusion into a report or other such document. However, the Internet is a strong publishing medium unto itself. With the proper access, anyone can become an author and publisher. This lesson introduces you to previewing and printing workbooks using traditional tools, as well as to publishing workbooks electronically on the World Wide Web.

For those of you new to the online world, the **Internet** is a vast collection of computer networks that spans the entire planet. This worldwide infrastructure is made up of many smaller networks connected by standard telephone lines, fiber optics, cable, and satellites. The term **intranet** refers to a private and usually secure local or wide area network that uses Internet technologies to share information. To access the Internet, you need a network or modem connection that links your computer to your account on the university's network or an independent service provider (ISP).

Once you are connected to the Internet, you can use Web browser software, such as Microsoft Internet Explorer or Netscape Navigator, to access the **World Wide Web.** The Web provides a visual interface for the Internet and lets you search for information by clicking on highlighted words and images, known as **hyperlinks.** When you click a link, you are telling your computer's Web browser to retrieve a page from a Web site and display it on your screen. Not only can you publish your workbooks on the Web, you can incorporate hyperlinks directly within a worksheet to facilitate navigating between documents.

3.3.1 Previewing and Printing a Worksheet

feature

Besides the **Normal view** that you've used thus far, Excel provides two additional views for adjusting how your worksheet will appear when printed. In **Print Preview** mode, the worksheet is displayed in a full-page WYSIWYG (What You See Is What You Get) window with margins, page breaks, and headers and footers. You can use this view to move through the workbook pages, zoom in and out on desired areas, and modify layout options, such as print margins and column widths. When satisfied with its appearance, you can send the workbook to the printer directly from this window. Similar to Print Preview, **Page Break Preview** lets you view and adjust the layout of information on particular pages. In Page Break Preview mode, you set the print area and page breaks for a workbook. In this lesson, you use Print Preview and the Print command.

method

To preview a workbook:

- CLICK: Print Preview button ()

or

- CHOOSE: File, Print Preview

To print a workbook:

- CLICK: Print button
or
- CHOOSE: File, Print

practice

You will now open a relatively large workbook, preview it on the screen, and then send it to the printer. Ensure that no workbooks are displayed in the application window.

1. Open the data file named EX0330.
2. Save the workbook as "Published Titles" to your personal storage location.
3. To preview how the workbook will appear when printed:
   CLICK: Print Preview button
   Your screen should now appear similar to Figure 3.23.

Figure 3.23

Previewing a workbook

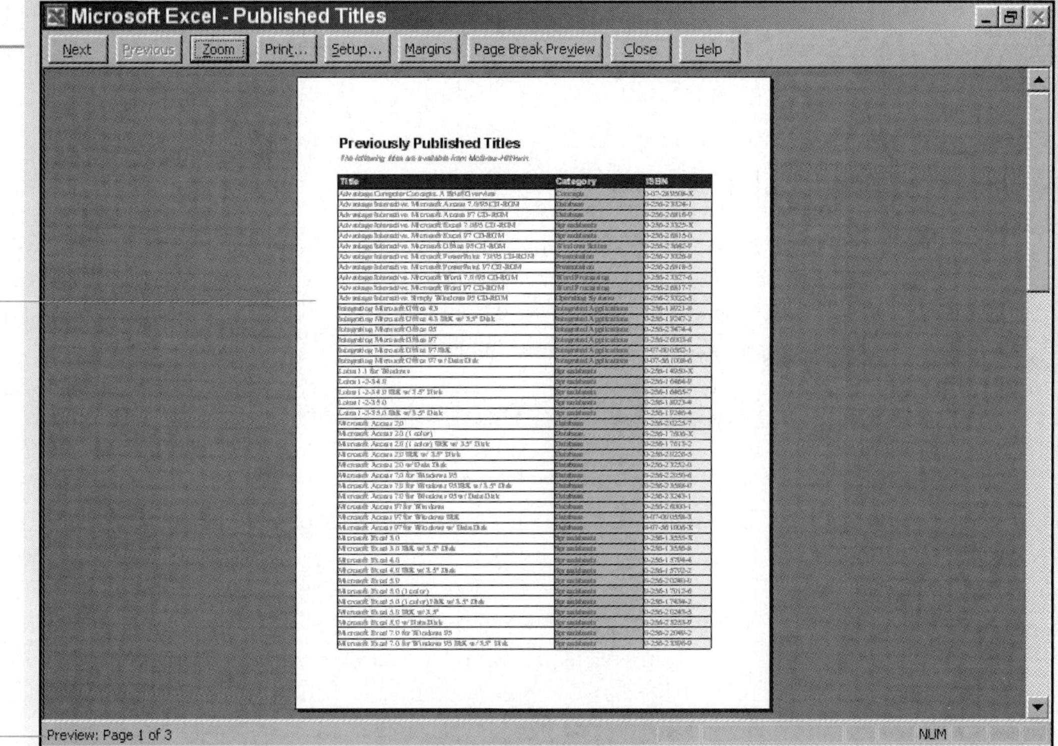
Microsoft Excel - Published Titles
Next
Previous
Zoom
Print...
Setup...
Margins
Page Break Preview
Close
Help
Previously Published Titles
Title
Category
ISBN
Preview: Page 1 of 3
NUM
Print Preview mode displays the page as it will appear when printed. If your printer does not support color, the page appears with shades of gray as shown here.
Identifies that you are in Preview mode and viewing "Page 1 of 3" total pages

4. At the top of the Print Preview window, Excel provides a row of buttons for performing various functions. To display the next page:
   CLICK: Next button in the toolbar

5. To return to the first page:
CLICK: Previous button

6. To zoom in on the worksheet, move the magnifying glass mouse pointer (🔍) over the worksheet area and then click once. Your screen should appear similar to Figure 3.24.

Figure 3.24

Zooming in on the worksheet

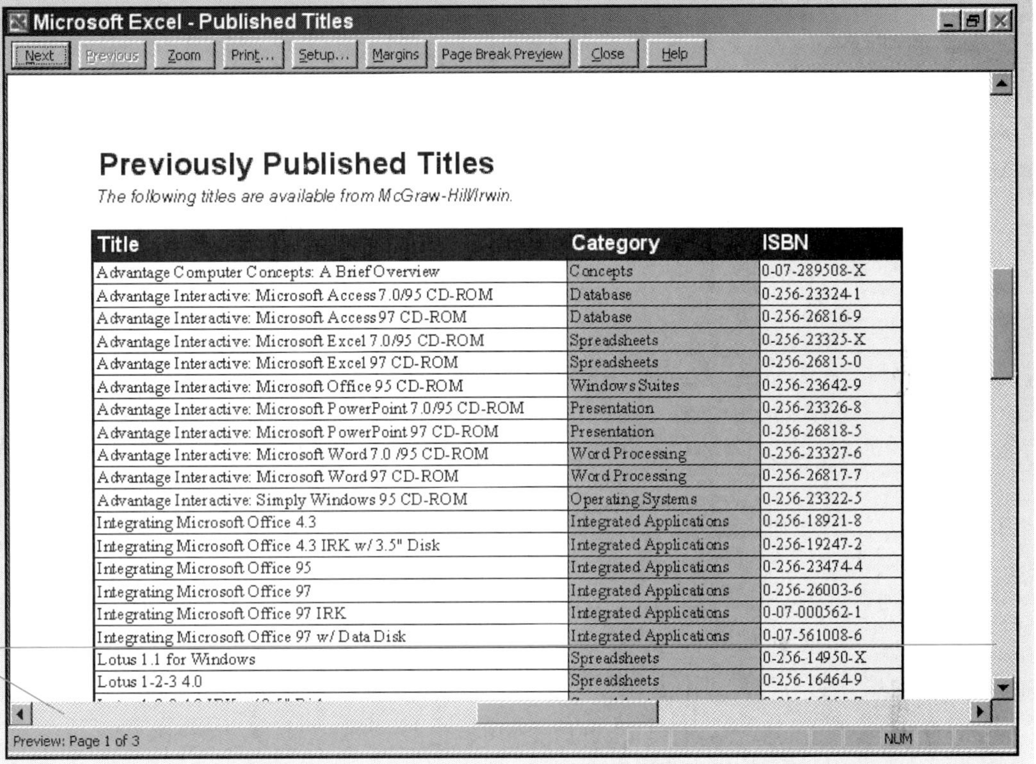

Microsoft Excel - Published Titles

Next | Previous | Zoom | Print... | Setup... | Margins | Page Break Preview | Close | Help

Previously Published Titles

The following titles are available from McGraw-Hill/Irwin.

Title	Category	ISBN
Advantage Computer Concepts: A Brief Overview	Concepts	0-07-289508-X
Advantage Interactive: Microsoft Access 7.0/95 CD-ROM	Database	0-256-23324-1
Advantage Interactive: Microsoft Access 97 CD-ROM	Database	0-256-26816-9
Advantage Interactive: Microsoft Excel 7.0/95 CD-ROM	Spreadsheets	0-256-23325-X
Advantage Interactive: Microsoft Excel 97 CD-ROM	Spreadsheets	0-256-26815-0
Advantage Interactive: Microsoft Office 95 CD-ROM	Windows Suites	0-256-23642-9
Advantage Interactive: Microsoft PowerPoint 7.0/95 CD-ROM	Presentation	0-256-23326-8
Advantage Interactive: Microsoft PowerPoint 97 CD-ROM	Presentation	0-256-26818-5
Advantage Interactive: Microsoft Word 7.0 /95 CD-ROM	Word Processing	0-256-23327-6
Advantage Interactive: Microsoft Word 97 CD-ROM	Word Processing	0-256-26817-7
Advantage Interactive: Simply Windows 95 CD-ROM	Operating Systems	0-256-23322-5
Integrating Microsoft Office 4.3	Integrated Applications	0-256-18921-8
Integrating Microsoft Office 4.3 IRK w/ 3.5" Disk	Integrated Applications	0-256-19247-2
Integrating Microsoft Office 95	Integrated Applications	0-256-23474-4
Integrating Microsoft Office 97	Integrated Applications	0-256-26003-6
Integrating Microsoft Office 97 IRK	Integrated Applications	0-07-000562-1
Integrating Microsoft Office 97 w/ Data Disk	Integrated Applications	0-07-561008-6
Lotus 1.1 for Windows	Spreadsheets	0-256-14950-X
Lotus 1-2-3 4.0	Spreadsheets	0-256-16464-9

Preview: Page 1 of 3 NUM

Use the horizontal and vertical scroll bars to adjust the window once you zoom in on an area.

7. To zoom out on the display, click the mouse pointer once again.

8. On your own, practice zooming in and out on different areas of the page and using the scroll bars to position the window.

9. Assuming that you are satisfied with how the workbook appears, you can send it to the printer from Print Preview. To demonstrate:
CLICK: Print button
You are returned immediately to Normal view and the Print dialog box appears, as shown in Figure 3.25. You can use this dialog box to specify what to print and how many copies to produce. (*Note:* The quickest method for sending the current worksheet to the printer is to click the Print button (🖨) in Normal view.)

Excel

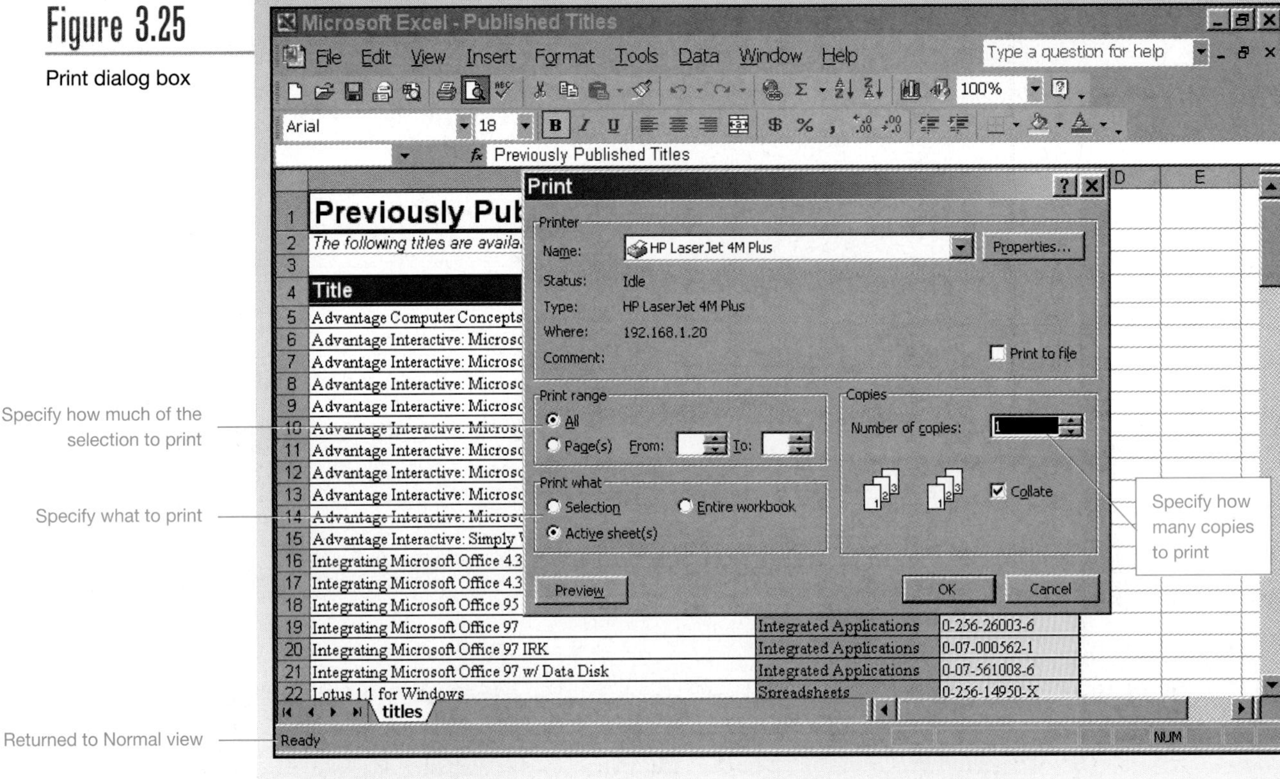

Figure 3.25

Print dialog box

10. If you do not have access to a printer, click the Cancel command button and proceed to the next lesson. If you have a printer connected to your computer and want to print the worksheet, do the following:
CLICK: OK command button
After a few moments, the worksheet will appear at the printer.

3.3.2 Previewing and Publishing to the Web

feature

Excel makes it easy to convert a workbook for display on the World Wide Web. The process involves saving the workbook in **HTML** (Hypertext Markup Language) format for publishing to a Web server. You can choose to publish a single worksheet or an entire workbook, complete with graphics and hyperlink objects. Once files are saved using the proper format, you may upload them to your company's intranet or to a Web server.

method

To save a worksheet as a Web page:

- CHOOSE: File, Save as Web Page

To view a worksheet as a Web page:

- CHOOSE: File, Web Page Preview

practice

You will now practice saving and viewing a worksheet as an HTML Web document. Ensure that you have completed the previous lesson and that the "Published Titles" workbook is displayed.

1. To save the current worksheet as a Web page:
   CHOOSE: File, Save as Web Page
   The Save As dialog box appears with some additional options, as shown in Figure 3.26. Notice that "Web Page" appears as the file type in the *Save as type* drop-down list box.

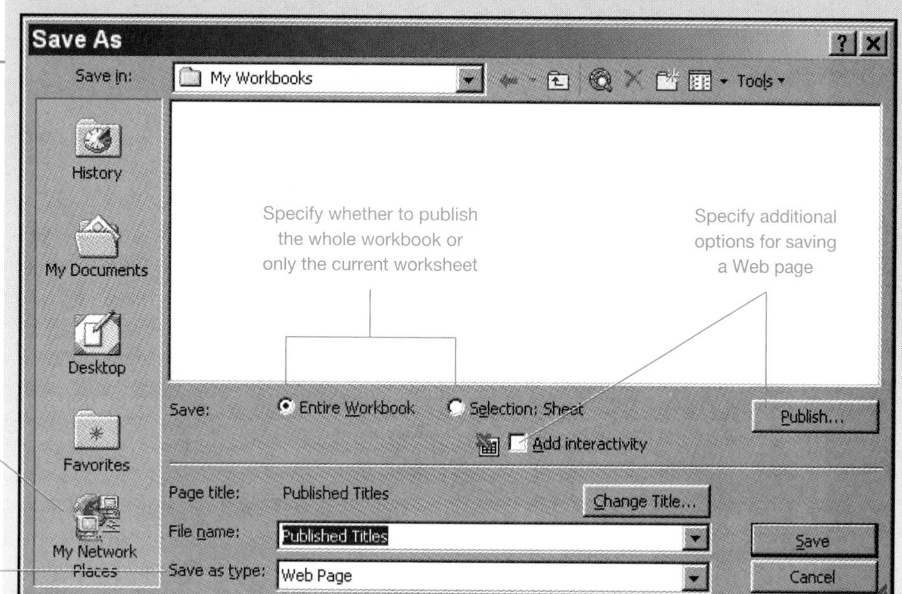

Figure 3.26

Save As dialog box for a Web page

2. Using the *Save in* drop-down list box or the Places bar:
   SELECT: *your personal storage location,* if not already selected
   (*Note:* To publish or post your workbook Web page directly to an intranet or to the Internet, click the My Network Places button shown here and then select a server location.)

3. To proceed with saving the workbook as a Web page:
   CLICK: Save command button
   The workbook document is saved as "Published Titles.htm" to your personal storage location.
4. To preview how the workbook will appear in a Web browser:
   CHOOSE: File, Web Page Preview
   After a few moments, the workbook appears displayed in a Web browser window. Figure 3.27 shows the worksheet Web page displayed using Internet Explorer.

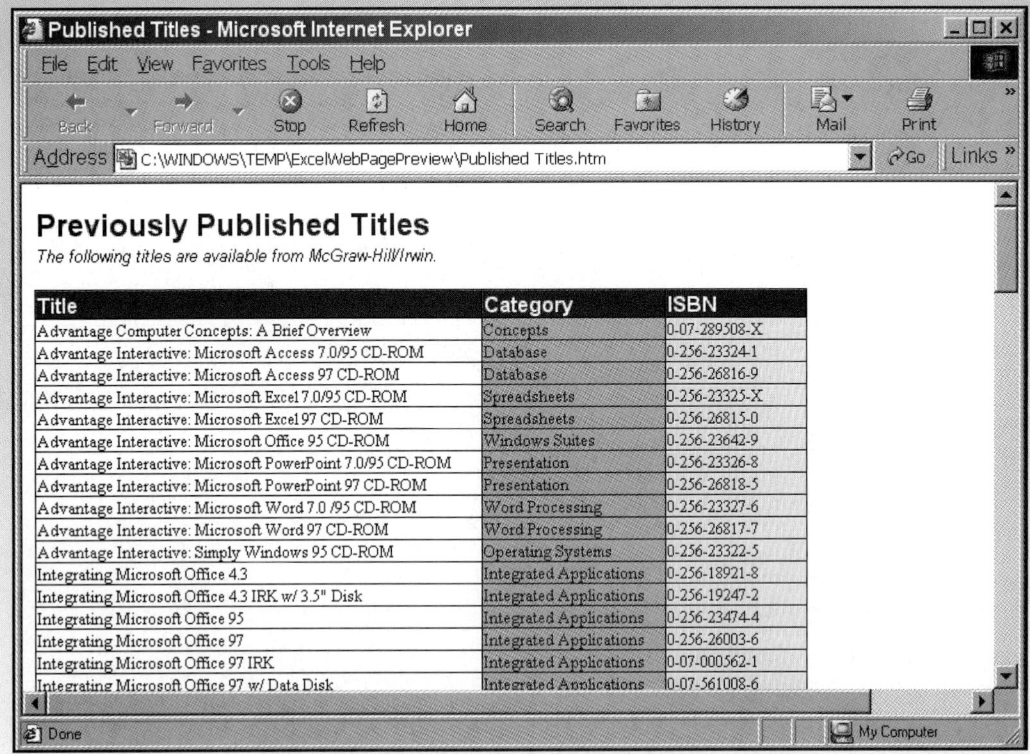

Figure 3.27

Viewing a worksheet as a Web page

5. To close the Web browser window:
   CLICK: its Close button (☒)
6. Close the "Published Titles" workbook without saving the changes.

In Addition PUBLISHING AN INTERACTIVE WEB PAGE

With Microsoft Internet Explorer and the Office Web Components, you can save a workbook as an interactive Web page, allowing users to enter, edit, and format data in your worksheet using their Web browser. To create an interactive worksheet Web page, select the *Add interactivity* check box option in the Save As dialog box (Figure 3.26) and then click the Publish command button to specify further options.

3.3. How does the Print Preview display mode differ from the Web Page Preview display mode?

3.4 Customizing Print Options

To ensure the appearance of your workbooks when printed, it is important to define page layout settings using the File, Page Setup command. In the dialog box that appears, you may specify *margins, headers, footers,* and whether gridlines or row and column headings should appear on the final printed output. To make the process more manageable, Excel organizes the page layout settings under four tabs (*Page, Margins, Header/Footer,* and *Sheet*) in the Page Setup dialog box. The features and settings accessible from these tabs are discussed in the following lessons.

3.4.1 Adjusting Page and Margin Settings

feature

You use the *Page* tab in the Page Setup dialog box to specify the paper size, print scale, and print orientation (for example, portrait or landscape) for a workbook. The *Margins* tab allows you to select the top, bottom, left, and right page **margins,** and to center the worksheet both horizontally and vertically on a page. You can also manipulate the page margins while viewing a worksheet in Print Preview mode.

method

- CHOOSE: File, Page Setup
- CLICK: *Page* and *Margins* tabs
- SELECT: the desired page layout options

practice

In this lesson, you open and print a workbook that summarizes a company's amortization expense. Ensure that no workbooks are open in the application window.

1. Open the data file named EX0340 to display the workbook in Figure 3.28.

Figure 3.28

Opening the EX0340 workbook

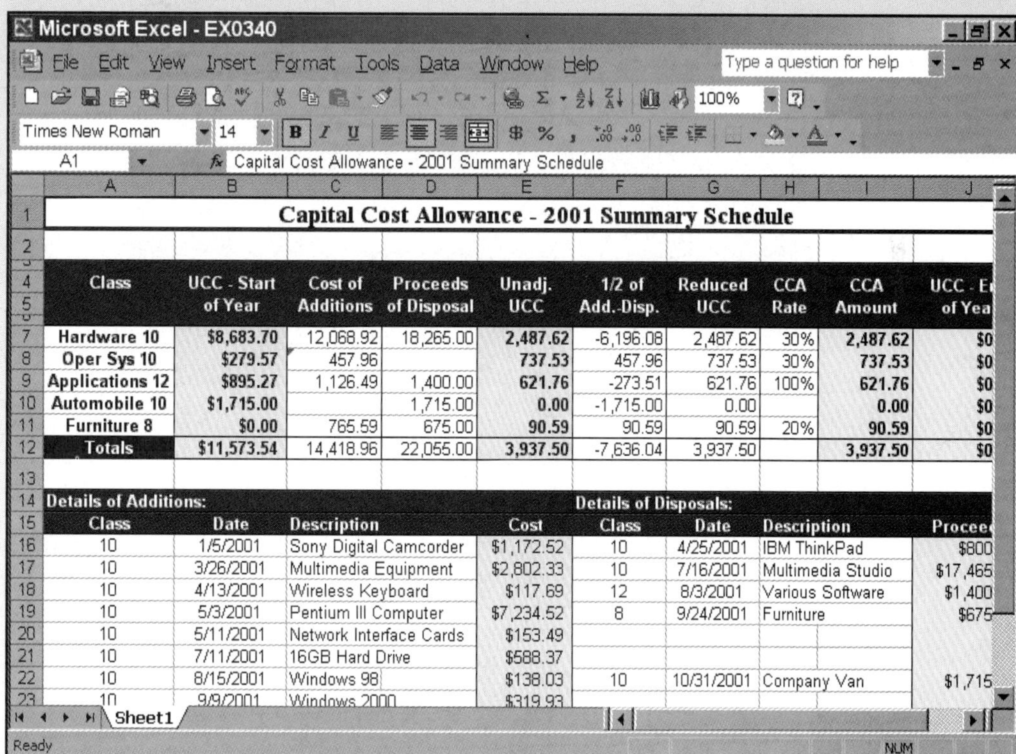

2. Save the file as "CCA Schedule" to your personal storage location.

3. To begin, let's display the worksheet using Print Preview mode:
CLICK: Print Preview button ()

Excel

4. Practice zooming in and out on the worksheet using the Zoom command button and the magnifying glass mouse pointer (🔍).

5. To view the second page of the printout:
CLICK: Next command button
Notice that the worksheet does not fit on a single page for printing.

6. To exit from Print Preview mode:
CLICK: Close button

7. To make the worksheet fit on a single page, we will adjust some page layout settings. Do the following:
CHOOSE: File, Page Setup
CLICK: *Page* tab, if it is not already selected
Your screen should now appear similar to Figure 3.29.

Figure 3.29

Page Setup dialog box: *Page* tab

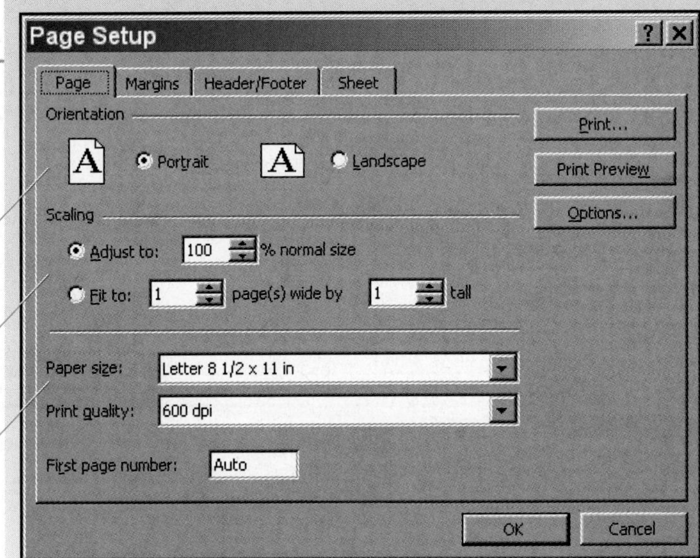

Specify a portrait (tall) or landscape (wide) page orientation

Specify whether to scale or shrink down the contents to fit the page

Specify printer settings, such as paper size and print quality

8. In the *Orientation* area:
SELECT: *Landscape* option button

9. To ensure that a worksheet prints on a single page, you specify scaling options in the Page Setup dialog box. In the *Scaling* area:
SELECT: *Fit to* option button

10. Now specify "1" for *pages(s) wide by* and then clear the *tall* spin box using DELETE. (*Hint:* You clear the *tall* option in order to let Excel calculate the best height for the page.) The *Scaling* area now appears as shown here.

11. For narrower worksheets, you can center the printout between the left and right page margins. To do so, you make a check box selection on the *Margins* tab:
CLICK: *Margins* tab
SELECT: *Horizontally* check box in the *Center on page* area

12. CLICK: Print Preview command button
As shown in Figure 3.30, the entire worksheet now appears centered between the margins on a single printed page.

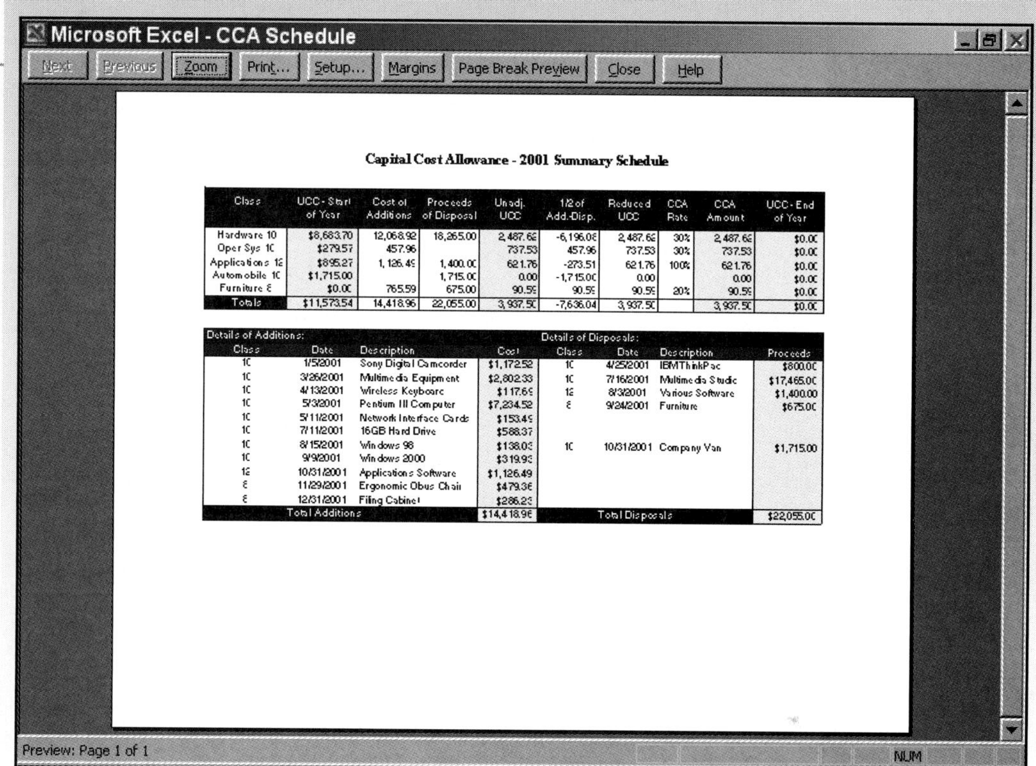

Figure 3.30
Previewing a worksheet after setting page options

3.4.2 Inserting Headers and Footers

feature

Descriptive information, such as the current date at the top or bottom of a page, can add a lot to your worksheet's presentation. The contents of a **header** (at the top of a page) or **footer** (at the bottom of a page) repeat automatically for each page that is printed. Some suggestions include using these areas for displaying your name, copyright information, the words "confidential" or "first draft," or page numbering. You may simply want to place the workbook's filename in the header so that you can easily find it again on your hard disk.

method

- CHOOSE: File, Page Setup
- CLICK: *Header/Footer* tab
- SELECT: a predefined header or footer

or

- CLICK: Custom Header button to design a new header

or

- CLICK: Custom Footer button to design a new footer

practice

You will now add a custom header and footer to the worksheet. Ensure that you have completed the previous lesson and that the "CCA Schedule" workbook is displayed in Print Preview mode.

1. To return to the Page Setup dialog box from Print Preview mode:
   CLICK: Setup command button
   The dialog box appears, displaying the last tab that was selected.

2. To add headers and footers to the page:
   CLICK: *Header/Footer* tab

3. The first step is to select a footer for printing at the bottom of each page. Do the following:
   CLICK: down arrow attached to the *Footer* drop-down list
   SELECT: "CCA Schedule, Page 1" option
   Once you make the selection, you should see the workbook's filename "CCA Schedule" appear centered in the footer preview area, and the words "Page 1" appear right-aligned, as shown below.

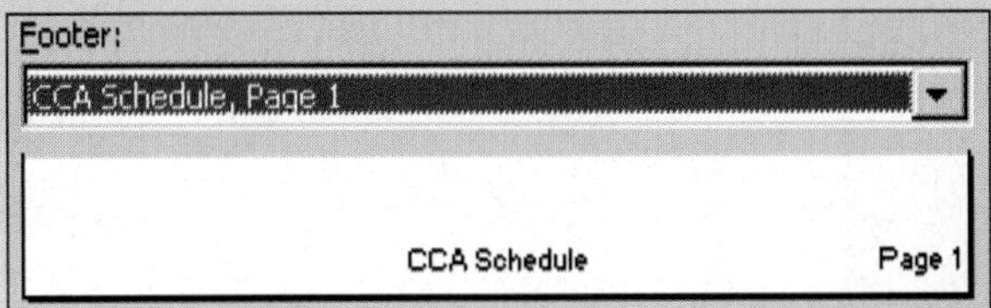

4. Now let's create a custom header:
   CLICK: Custom Header command button
   Figure 3.31 shows the Header dialog box and labels the buttons used for inserting information into the different sections.

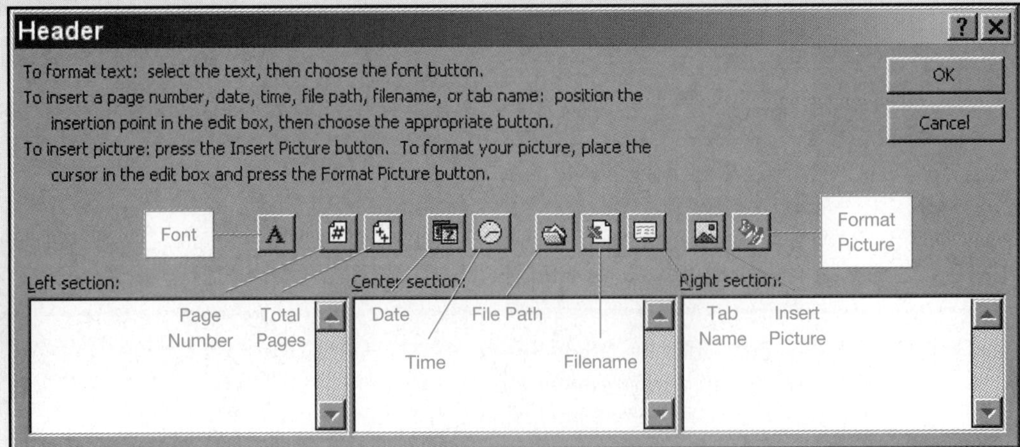

Figure 3.31
Custom Header dialog box

5. To create a header that prints your name at the left margin:
   CLICK: the mouse pointer in the *Left section* area
   TYPE: **Created by: your name**
   (*Hint:* Enter your name rather than the text "your name.")

6. Now place the date against the right margin:
CLICK: the mouse pointer in the *Right section* area
TYPE: **Printed on:**
PRESS: Space Bar once
CLICK: Date button (📅) as labeled in Figure 3.31
CLICK: OK command button
You will see the custom header appear in the preview area, as shown in Figure 3.32. (*Note:* Your name and the current date will appear in the *Header* preview area.)

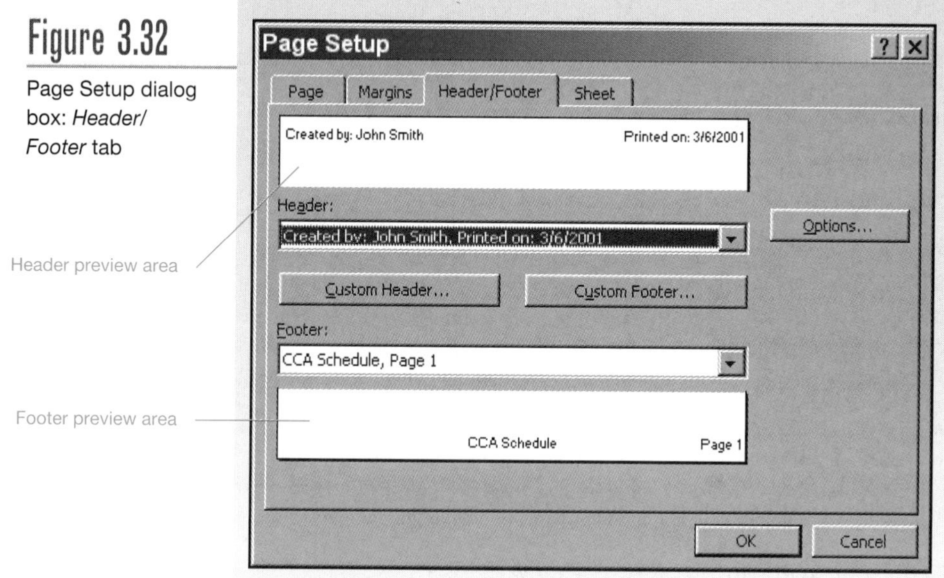

Figure 3.32

Page Setup dialog box: *Header/ Footer* tab

7. To return to Print Preview mode:
CLICK: OK command button
Notice the newly inserted header and footer in the Print Preview window.

8. To exit from Print Preview mode:
CLICK: Close button

3.4.3 Selecting Worksheet Content to Print

feature

From the Print dialog box, you can choose to print an entire workbook, a single worksheet, or a specified cell range. Alternatively, you can preselect a cell range to print by first specifying the print area. Other print options are available from the Page Setup dialog box, where you can choose to print the worksheet gridlines or row and column headings.

method

To specify a print area:

- SELECT: a cell range
- CHOOSE: File, Print Area, Set Print Area

To clear a selected print area:

- CHOOSE: File, Print Area, Clear Print Area

To select from the general print options:

- CHOOSE: File, Print
- SELECT: one of the following *Print what* option buttons—*Selection, Active sheet(s),* or *Entire workbook*
- SELECT: *Number of copies* to print

To specify whether to print gridlines or row and column headings:

- CHOOSE: File, Page Setup
- CLICK: *Sheet* tab
- SELECT: *Gridlines* check box to toggle the printing of gridlines
- SELECT: *Row and column headings* check box to print the frame area

practice

In this lesson, you practice selecting print options and setting print areas. Finally, you have the opportunity to print the worksheet. Ensure that you have completed the previous lesson and that the "CCA Schedule" workbook is displayed.

1. You will often find the need to print specific ranges in a worksheet, rather than the entire workbook. This need is solved by first setting a print area. To practice selecting a cell range for printing:
   SELECT: cell range from A1 (a merged cell) to J12
   CHOOSE: File, Print Area, Set Print Area

2. Now that you have defined a specific cell range as the print area:
   CLICK: Print Preview button ( )
   Notice that only the selected range is previewed for printing, as shown in Figure 3.33.

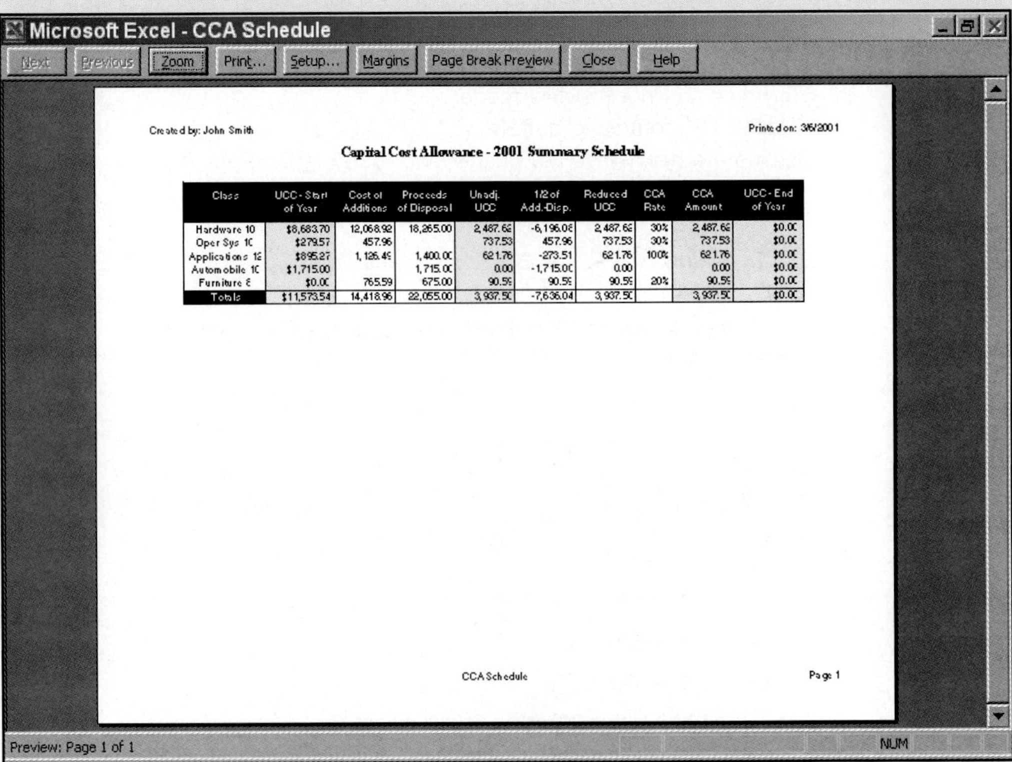

Class	UCC - Start of Year	Cost of Additions	Proceeds of Disposal	Unadj. UCC	1/2 of Add.-Disp.	Reduced UCC	CCA Rate	CCA Amount	UCC - End of Year
Hardware 10	$8,683.70	12,068.92	18,265.00	2,487.6	-6,196.0	2,487.6	30%	2,487.6	$0.0
Oper Sys 1	$279.57	457.96		737.53	457.96	737.53	30%	737.53	$0.0
Applications 1	$895.27	1,126.4	1,400.0	621.76	-273.51	621.76	100%	621.76	$0.0
Automobile 1	$1,715.00		1,715.0	0.00	-1,715.0	0.00		0.00	$0.0
Furniture	$0.0	765.59	675.00	90.5	90.5	90.5	20%	90.5	$0.0
Totals	$11,573.54	14,418.96	22,055.00	3,937.5	-7,636.04	3,937.5		3,937.5	$0.0

Figure 3.33

Previewing a selected print area

3. To return to the worksheet:
CLICK: Close button

4. To return to printing the entire worksheet:
CHOOSE: File, Print Area, Clear Print Area
This command removes the print area definition.

5. Let's view some other print options:
CHOOSE: File, Page Setup
CLICK: *Sheet* tab
Your screen should now appear similar to Figure 3.34.

Page Setup dialog box: *Sheet* tab

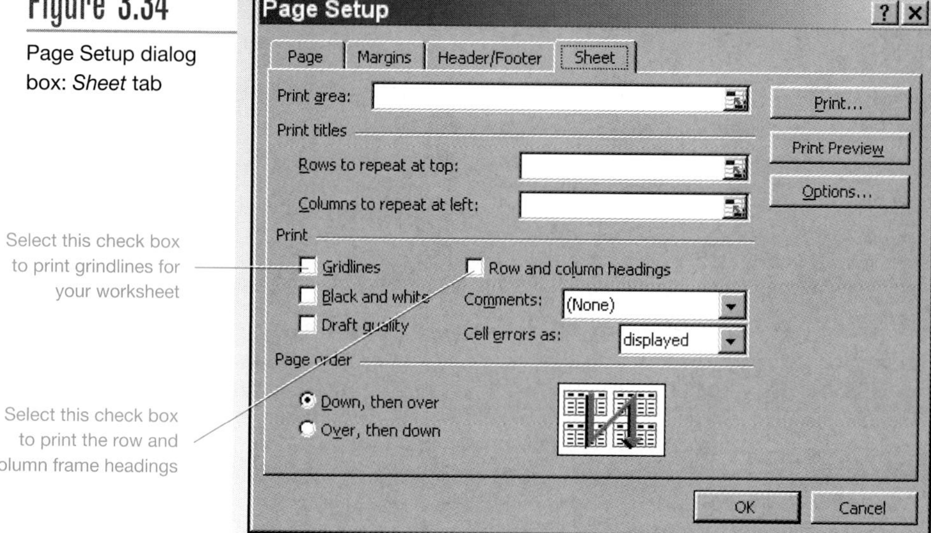

6. Sometimes printing the gridlines or row and column headings is useful for reviewing a worksheet for errors. To demonstrate:
SELECT: *Gridlines* check box in the *Print* area
SELECT: *Row* and *column headings* check box
CLICK: Print Preview command button
Figure 3.35 shows that the printed worksheet now looks similar to the screen display, with the exception of the header and footer. (*Note:* All page setup options are saved along with the workbook file.)

Figure 3.35

Print previewing with gridlines and row and column headings

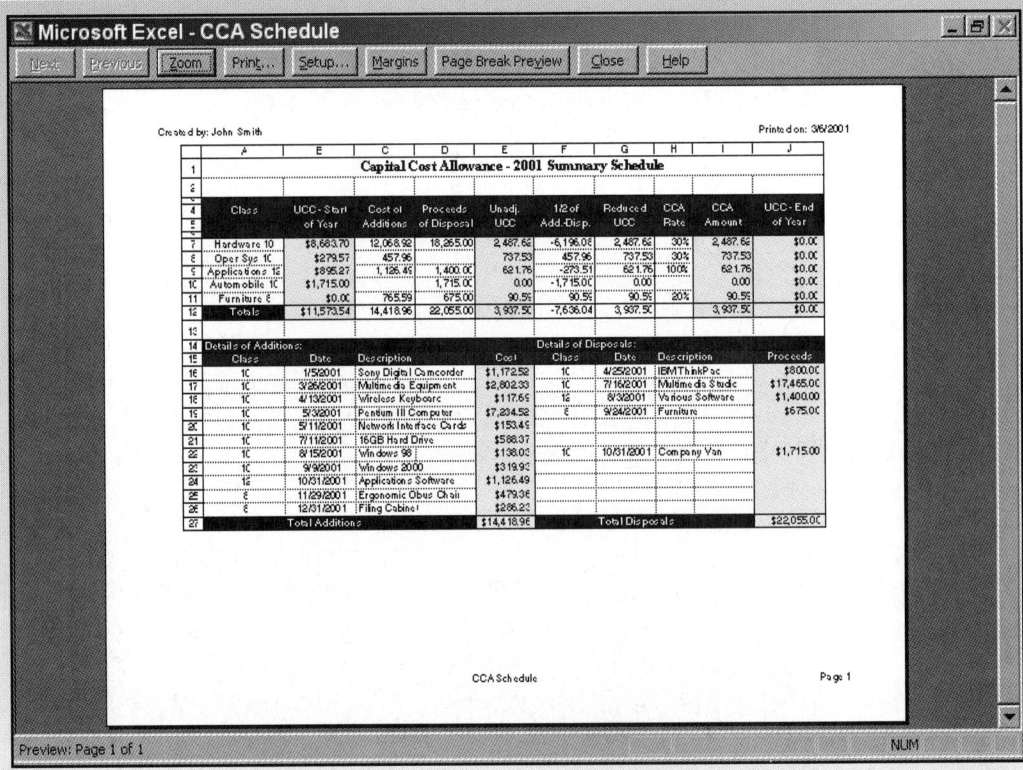

7. If you have a printer connected to your computer, perform the following steps. Otherwise, proceed to the next step.
   CLICK: Print command button
   CLICK: OK, when the Print dialog box appears
8. If necessary, close the Print Preview window. Then save and close the "CCA Schedule" workbook.
9. Exit Microsoft Excel.

In Addition SENDING THE SCREEN TO THE PRINTER

Did you know that you can capture a screen image using the Print Screen key on your keyboard? When you press the Print Screen key, the current screen image is copied to the Windows Clipboard. You can then paste this image into a document or workbook for printing.

3.4. How would you create a custom footer that displayed your name against the left page border and your company's name against the right page border?

Chapter summary

To enhance the appearance of worksheets, Excel offers many formatting capabilities and shortcuts that speed up formatting and help keep style consistent. Specific formats include fonts, number formats, cell alignment, borders, colors, and predefined table formats. Excel also provides options to control and customize page layout. Once the worksheet is formatted, it can be printed or displayed on the World Wide Web.

Command Summary

Many of the commands and procedures appearing in this chapter are summarized in the following table.

Skill Set	To Perform This Task	Do the Following
Formatting and Printing Worksheets	Apply font typefaces, font sizes, and font styles	CHOOSE: Format, Cells CLICK: *Font* tab
	Apply number formats	CHOOSE: Format, Cells CLICK: *Number* tab
	Increase and decrease decimal places	CLICK: Increase Decimal button () CLICK: Decrease Decimal button ()
	Modify a cell's alignment	CHOOSE: Format, Cells CLICK: *Alignment* tab
	Merge a range of cells	CHOOSE: Format, Cells CLICK: *Alignment* tab SELECT: *Merge cells* check box
	Add borders, patterns, and shading using the menu	CHOOSE: Format, Cells CLICK: *Border* or *Patterns* tab
	Add borders and fill colors using the Formatting toolbar	CLICK: Borders button () CLICK: Fill Color button ()
	Copy formatting from one range to another using the toolbar	SELECT: the desired range CLICK: Format Painter button () SELECT: the target range
	Copy formatting from one range to another using the Clipboard	SELECT: the desired range CLICK: Copy button () SELECT: the target range CHOOSE: Edit, Paste Special SELECT: *Formats* option button
	Clear formatting that appears in a range	SELECT: the desired range CHOOSE: Edit, Clear, Formats
	Use AutoFormat	CHOOSE: Format, AutoFormat SELECT: *a predefined format*
	Preview a worksheet	CLICK: Print Preview button (), or CHOOSE: File, Print Preview
	Print a worksheet	CLICK: Print button (), or CHOOSE: File, Print
	Print the selected cell range, active worksheet, or the entire workbook	CHOOSE: File, Print SELECT: *the desired option button*
	Set the worksheet area to print	SELECT: the desired range CHOOSE: File, Print Area, Set Print Area
	Clear the selected print area	CHOOSE: File, Print Area, Clear Print Area
	Specify worksheet orientation and paper size	CHOOSE: File, Page Setup CLICK: *Page* tab
	Specify print margins and placement on a page	CHOOSE: File, Page Setup CLICK: *Margins* tab

Excel

Skill Set	To Perform This Task	Do the Following
	Define headers and footers for printing	CHOOSE: File, Page Setup CLICK: *Header/Footer* tab
	Take a snapshot of the screen and store it on the Clipboard	PRESS: Print Screen key
Workgroup Collaboration	Save worksheet as an HTML document	CHOOSE: File, Save as Web Page
	Preview worksheet as a Web page	CHOOSE: File, Web Page Preview

Key Terms

This section specifies page references for the key terms identified in this chapter. For a complete list of definitions, refer to the Glossary at the back of this learning guide.

AutoFormat, *p. EX 131*
cell alignment, *p. EX 117*
fonts, *p. EX 110*
footers, *p. EX 141*
Format Painter, *p. EX 124*
gridlines, *p. EX 121*
headers, *p. EX 141*
HTML, *p. EX 136*
hyperlinks, *p. EX 133*
Internet, *p. EX 133*
intranet, *p. EX 133*
margins, *p. EX 139*
Normal view, *p. EX 133*
Print Preview, *p. EX 133*
Page Break Preview, *p. EX 133*
typefaces, *p. EX 110*
World Wide Web, *p. EX 133*

Chapter quiz

Short Answer

1. Why should you limit the number of typefaces used in a worksheet?
2. Name two methods for specifying decimal places in a worksheet.
3. How do you split a merged cell?
4. How do you apply multiple coats using the Format Painter tool?
5. Name two color settings that you can change in a worksheet.
6. How do you keep gridlines from displaying in a worksheet?
7. How do you make gridlines print in a worksheet?
8. What should you do prior to sending a worksheet to the printer?
9. Name the tabs in the Page Setup dialog box.
10. How do you create a Web page from a standard Excel worksheet?

True/False

1. ____ The **B** button stands for bold. The **U** button stands for underline. The *I* button stands for incline.
2. ____ You use the *Number* tab in the Format Cells dialog box to select date and time formatting options.
3. ____ Whenever you merge cells, the contents must also be centered.
4. ____ You can remove formatting from a cell range by choosing the Edit, Clear, Special command.
5. ____ The AutoFormat command works best when your data is organized using a table layout.
6. ____ You can zoom in and out on a worksheet using Print Preview mode.
7. ____ You can view a worksheet as it would appear in a Web browser, prior to saving it as a Web page.
8. ____ The two options for page orientation are *Picture* and *Landscape.*
9. ____ You can access the Page Setup dialog box directly from Print Preview mode.
10. ____ To convert a worksheet for display on the World Wide Web, you save the workbook into HTML format.

Multiple Choice

1. To change the text color of a cell entry:
   a. CLICK: Fill Color button ( )
   b. CLICK: Font Color button ( )
   c. CLICK: Text Color button ( )
   d. You cannot change the text color of a cell entry.

2. Excel stores date and time entries as:
   a. formats
   b. formulas
   c. labels
   d. values

3. To merge a range of cells, you select the *Merge cells* check box on this tab of the Format Cells dialog box:
   a. *Number* tab
   b. *Alignment* tab
   c. *Margins* tab
   d. *Merge* tab

4. To remove a cell's formatting, you can:
   a. CHOOSE: Edit, Clear, Formats
   b. CHOOSE: Edit, Formats, Clear
   c. CHOOSE: Format, Cells, Clear
   d. CHOOSE: Format, Clear

5. To copy a cell's formatting characteristics to another cell, you can:
   a. Use the AutoFormat feature
   b. Use the AutoPainter feature
   c. Use the Format Painter feature
   d. Use the Edit, Paste Formats command

6. To select one of Excel's prebuilt table formats:
   a. CHOOSE: Format, AutoTable
   b. CHOOSE: Format, TableFormat
   c. CHOOSE: Format, AutoFormat
   d. CHOOSE: Format, Table

7. To produce gridlines on your printed worksheet:
   a. SELECT: *Gridlines* check box in the Page Setup dialog box
   b. CHOOSE: File, Print, Gridlines
   c. CLICK: Underline button ( ) on the Formatting toolbar
   d. Both a and b above

8. To identify a specific cell range on the worksheet for printing:
   a. CHOOSE: File, Print Range
   b. CHOOSE: File, Print Area, Set Print Area
   c. CHOOSE: File, Set Print Area
   d. CHOOSE: File, Set Print Range

9. To print data at the top of each page, you create the following:
   a. footer
   b. footnote
   c. headline
   d. header

10. To save the current worksheet as a Web page:
   a. CLICK: Save button ( )
   b. CHOOSE: File, Save as Web Page
   c. CHOOSE: File, Save as HTML
   d. CHOOSE: File, Publish to Web

Hands-On exercises

1. Brentwood Academy: Bookstore Inventory

In this exercise, you practice using Excel's formatting commands to enhance the appearance of a monthly bookstore report.

1. Load Microsoft Excel.
2. Open the data file named EX03HE01 to display the worksheet shown in Figure 3.36.

Figure 3.36

Opening the EX03HE01 workbook

	A	B	C	D	E	F	G	H
1	Brentwood Academy							
2								
3	ISBN	Title	Cost	Markup	Price	On Hand	Value	
4	0-201-06672-6	Algorithms	34	0.38	46.92	42	1970.64	
5	0-02-395540-6	Fiction 100 Anthology	42.4	0.4	59.36	1039	61675.04	
6	0-256-03331-5	Intermediate Accounting	44.95	0.4	62.93	430	27059.9	
7	0-13-526293-3	Law and Business Admin	56.2	0.5	84.3	110	9273	
8	0-201-40931-3	Legal Guide to Multimedia	44.95	0.63	73.2685	78	5714.943	
9	0-07-034745-X	Marketing Research	35.99	0.475	53.08525	339	17995.9	
10	Total Value					2038	123689.4	
11								
12								

3. Save the workbook as "Bookstore" to your personal storage location.
4. Let's start by formatting the worksheet's title:
   SELECT: cell A1
   CHOOSE: Format, Cells
   CLICK: *Font* tab in the dialog box
5. In the Format Cells dialog box, make the following selections:
   SELECT: Times New Roman in the *Font* list box
   SELECT: Bold Italic in the *Font style* list box
   SELECT: 16 in the *Size* list box
   SELECT: Dark Red in the *Color* drop-down list box
   Notice that the *Preview* area in the dialog box displays all of your choices.

6. To accept the dialog box selections:
CLICK: OK command button

7. Let's center the title across the width of the worksheet:
SELECT: cell range from A1 to G1
CLICK: Merge and Center button ()

8. To apply percentage formatting:
SELECT: cell range from D4 to D9
CLICK: Percent Style button ()
CLICK: Increase Decimal button () twice

9. To apply currency formatting:
SELECT: cell range from C4 to C10
CLICK: Currency Style button ()
(*Hint:* You include cell C10 in the range so that you can later copy this column's formatting to other ranges in the worksheet.)

10. Let's copy this column's formatting to the other columns. With the range still selected, do the following:
DOUBLE-CLICK: Format Painter button ()
CLICK: cell E4 to apply one formatting coat
CLICK: cell G4 to apply another formatting coat
CLICK: Format Painter button () to toggle the feature off

11. Now change the width of column G:
CHOOSE: Format, Column, AutoFit Selection
Your screen should now appear similar to Figure 3.37.

Figure 3.37

Formatting the Bookstore worksheet

	A	B	C	D	E	F	G	H
1	***Brentwood Academy***							
2								
3	ISBN	Title	Cost	Markup	Price	On Hand	Value	
4	0-201-06672-6	Algorithms	$ 34.00	38.00%	$ 46.92	42	$ 1,970.64	
5	0-02-395540-6	Fiction 100 Anthology	$ 42.40	40.00%	$ 59.36	1039	$ 61,675.04	
6	0-256-03331-5	Intermediate Accounting	$ 44.95	40.00%	$ 62.93	430	$ 27,059.90	
7	0-13-526293-3	Law and Business Admin	$ 56.20	50.00%	$ 84.30	110	$ 9,273.00	
8	0-201-40931-3	Legal Guide to Multimedia	$ 44.95	63.00%	$ 73.27	78	$ 5,714.94	
9	0-07-034745-X	Marketing Research	$ 35.99	47.50%	$ 53.09	339	$ 17,995.90	
10	Total Value					2038	$123,689.42	
11								
12								

12. To apply an AutoFormat to the data area:
SELECT: cell range from A3 to G10
CHOOSE: Format, AutoFormat

13. In the AutoFormat dialog box:
SELECT: Classic 2
CLICK: OK command button

14. To better see the results of the formatting:
CLICK: cell A1
A much nicer looking report!

15. Save and then close the workbook.

easy 

2. Top Picks Video: Sales Analysis

You now practice enhancing the layout of an existing worksheet by adjusting rows and columns and by formatting its text labels, numbers, and headings.

1. Open the data file named EX03HE02 to display the workbook shown in Figure 3.38.

Figure 3.38

Opening the EX03HE02 workbook

	A	B	C	D	E	F
1	Top Picks Video					
2	Sales Analysis					
3						
4				Amount	Pct of Total	
5	Rentals					
6		New Releases		1071.35	0.4379203	
7		Weekly Movies		826	0.3376321	
8		Games		549.1	0.2244477	
9		Total Rentals		2446.45	0.8463468	
10	Retail Sales					
11		Videos		132.5	0.2983226	
12		Snacks		311.65	0.7016774	
13		Total Retail		444.15	0.1536532	
14						
15	Total Sales			2890.6		
16						
17						

2. Save the workbook as "Video Sales" to your personal storage location.
3. To begin, let's adjust the width of column C to 5 characters:
   SELECT: cell C1
   CHOOSE: Format, Column, Width
   TYPE: **5**
   CLICK: OK command button
4. Now, delete row 3 using the following steps:
   RIGHT-CLICK: row 3 in the frame area
   CHOOSE: Delete
5. To format the headings:
   SELECT: cell A4
   PRESS: CTRL and hold it down
   CLICK: cell A9
   CLICK: Bold button (B)
   Remember to release the CTRL key when you are finished.
6. To format the "Total Sales" label with boldface and italic:
   SELECT: cell A14
   CLICK: Bold button (B)
   CLICK: Italic button (I)
7. To format the two column headings:
   SELECT: cell range from D3 to E3
   PRESS: CTRL+**b** to apply boldface
   PRESS: CTRL+**u** to underline the contents

8. To format the values in the Amount column:
   CLICK: cell D5
   PRESS: SHIFT and hold it down
   CLICK: cell D14
   All of the cells between these two should now appear highlighted.

9. To apply currency formatting:
   CLICK: Currency Style button ($)

10. To apply percent formatting to the values in the adjacent column:
    SELECT: cell range from E5 to E12
    CLICK: Percent Style button (%)
    CLICK: Increase Decimal button (.00) twice

11. To format all of the category labels at the same time:
    SELECT: cell range from B5 to B8
    PRESS: CTRL and hold it down
    SELECT: cell range from B10 to B12 by dragging with the mouse
    There should be two highlighted ranges on the worksheet, as shown in Figure 3.39.

Figure 3.39

Formatting multiple ranges on a worksheet

	A	B	C	D	E	F
1	Top Picks Video					
2	Sales Analysis					
3				Amount	Pct of Total	
4	**Rentals**					
5		New Releases		$1,071.35	43.79%	
6		Weekly Movies		$ 826.00	33.76%	
7		Games		$ 549.10	22.44%	
8		Total Rentals		$2,446.45	84.63%	
9	**Retail Sales**					
10		Videos		$ 132.50	29.83%	
11		Snacks		$ 311.65	70.17%	
12		Total Retail		$ 444.15	15.37%	
13						
14	***Total Sales***			$2,890.60		
15						
16						

12. To italicize the data and align it to the right:
    CLICK: Italic button (I)
    CLICK: Align Right button

13. Finally, let's format the titles in rows 1 and 2. Do the following:
    SELECT: cell range from A1 to A2
    CLICK: Bold button (B)
    CLICK: down arrow attached to the Font list box (Arial)
    SELECT: Times New Roman
    CLICK: down arrow attached to the Font Size list box (10)
    SELECT: 14

14. To center the titles across the active area:
    SELECT: cell range from A1 to E1
    CLICK: Merge and Center button
    SELECT: cell range from A2 to E2
    CLICK: Merge and Center button

15. Save and then close the workbook.

moderate 

3. Staples Foods: Inventory Projections

Incorporating some skills learned in Chapter 2, you now practice modifying a worksheet and applying formatting commands.

1. Open the workbook named EX03HE03. This workbook contains quarterly inventory information.
2. Save the workbook as "Staples Seasonal" to your personal storage location.
3. Adjust the width of column A to 18 characters.
4. Delete column B.
5. Adjust columns B through E to their best-fit widths.
6. Format the headings in row 1 to appear boldface and centered in their respective columns.
7. Format the "Total" label in cell A7 to appear boldface and italic. Your worksheet should now appear similar to Figure 3.40.

Figure 3.40

Formatting the Staples Seasonal workbook

	A	B	C	D	E	F
1		**Qtr1**	**Qtr2**	**Qtr3**	**Qtr4**	
2	Raw Materials	157,000	96,250	211,000	182,500	
3	Packaging	256,750	202,500	128,600	96,350	
4	Work-in-process	39,600	35,100	51,000	75,480	
5	Finished Products	82,360	48,300	76,500	106,900	
6						
7	***Total***	535,710	382,150	467,100	461,230	
8						
9						

8. Insert two rows at the top of the worksheet for entering a title. (*Hint:* Rather than performing the Insert command twice to insert two rows, you can select rows 1 and 2 first and then perform the command once.)
9. Enter a title for the worksheet:
   SELECT: cell A1
   TYPE: **Seasonal Inventory Projections**
   PRESS: ENTER
10. Merge and center the title in cell A1 between columns A and E.
11. Format the title to appear with a larger and more unique font. Also, apply a dark blue color to the font text on a light yellow background fill. Then, surround the merged cell with a Thick Box border.
12. To bring out the Total row, apply a Top and Double Bottom border to cells A9 through E9. With the cell range highlighted, assign a light gray background fill color.
13. To remove the highlighting:
    CLICK: cell A1
14. Save and then close the workbook.

Figure 3.41

Completing the Staples Seasonal workbook

Seasonal Inventory Projections

	Qtr1	Qtr2	Qtr3	Qtr4
Raw Materials	157,000	96,250	211,000	182,500
Packaging	256,750	202,500	128,600	96,350
Work-in-process	39,600	35,100	51,000	75,480
Finished Products	82,360	48,300	76,500	106,900
Total	535,710	382,150	467,100	461,230

moderate 

4. Sutton House Realty: Listing Summary

In this exercise, you use the AutoFormat command and modify the page layout in an existing workbook.

1. Open the workbook named EX03HE04.
2. Save the workbook as "Listing Summary" to your personal storage location.
3. Apply the "Classic 3" AutoFormat style to the cell range from A3 to K10.
4. Rotate the column headings in row 3 to appear similar to Figure 3.42 and then decrease the width of columns B through K.
5. Format the worksheet title in cell A1 to make it stand out from the table information. Your screen should appear similar to Figure 3.42.

Figure 3.42

Applying an AutoFormat to the Listing Summary workbook

Listings by Region – Sept '01

Agent	Downtown	Mission	Middledale	Westside	Cedar Hill	Kent	Brookview	Fintry	Newton	Total
Alvarez	3	5		1	2	11	3	2	1	28
Carlisle		2	15			13		1		31
DaCosta	5	6		8		7	4		5	35
Fulton	1	7	1	4		1	9	5		28
Low	12		3	2	1	5		4		27
Patel	2	4	5	9	1	4	3	1	2	31
Total	23	24	24	24	4	41	19	10	8	177

6. Display the Page Setup dialog box. Use the *Page* tab to change the page orientation to *Landscape* and to fit by "1" page wide.
7. Use the *Margins* tab in the Page Setup dialog box to center the worksheet horizontally on the page.
8. Use the *Header/Footer* tab to add a custom footer that prints the workbook's filename aligned left and the page number aligned right.
9. Add a custom header that shows the company name, "Sutton House Realty," aligned left and the current date aligned right.

Excel

10. Preview the worksheet. Your screen should now appear similar to Figure 3.43.

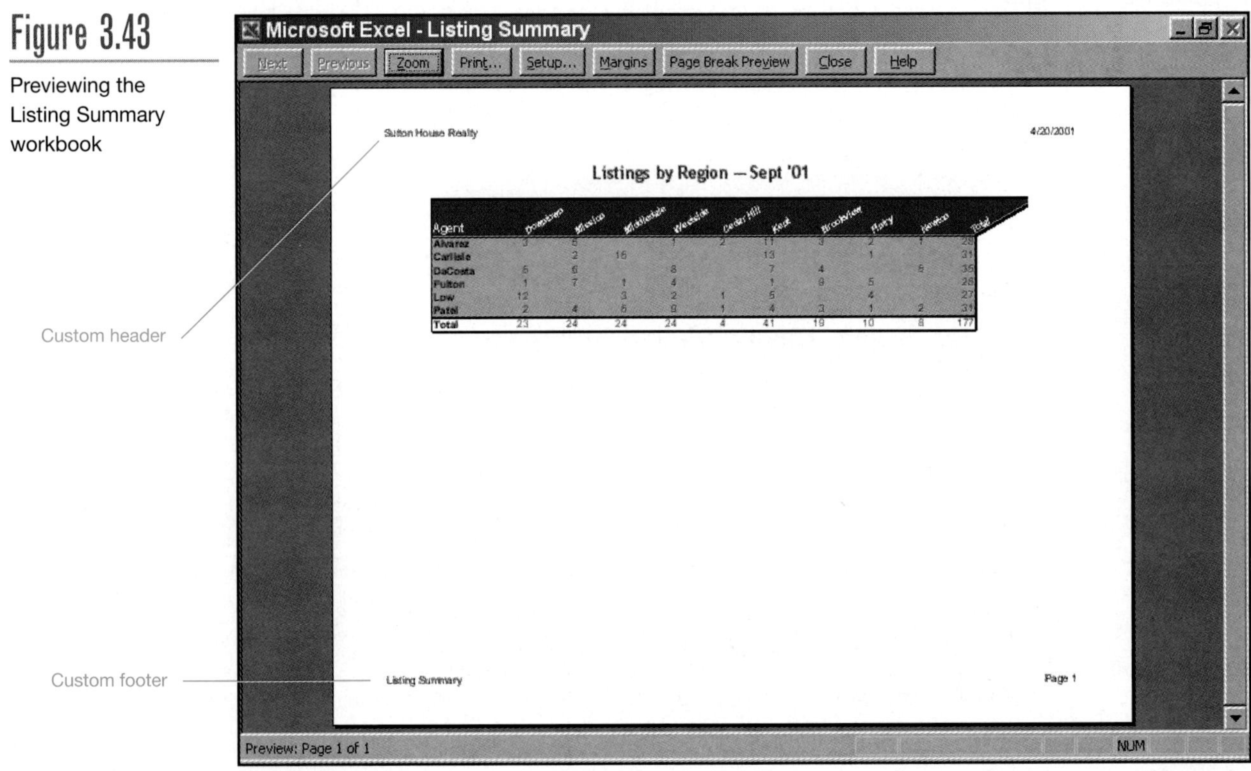

Figure 3.43

Previewing the Listing Summary workbook

11. Print a copy of the worksheet.
12. Save and then close the workbook.

difficult 

5. On Your Own: Financial Data Table

To practice formatting and manipulating data, open the workbook named EX03HE05. Then make a copy of the file by saving the workbook as "Financial Data" to your personal storage location. On your own, resize all of the columns to ensure that the data is visible. Insert a new row at the beginning of the worksheet and enter the worksheet title "United Consolidated Group." Using fonts, colors, alignment, borders, and background fills, format the titles in rows 1 and 2 to stand out from the rest of the data. Figure 3.44 shows one possible solution.

Figure 3.44

Formatting the title rows in a worksheet

	A	B	C	D	E	F
1	United Consolidated Group					
2	Selected Financial Data					
3		2000	2001	Difference	% Change	
4	Revenue	45259	52344	7085	0.15654345	
5	Income from Operations	2416	4196	1780	0.736754967	
6	Net Income	1742	3978	2236	1.28358209	
7	Income per Common Share	0.16	0.3	0.14	0.875	
8	Short-term Investments	39451	30877	-8574	-0.217332894	
9	Common Share High Bid	19.08	22.5	3.42	0.179245283	
10						
11						

Format the data in columns B through D with currency formatting and two decimal places, except for the date headings. Format the data in column E with percent formatting and two decimal places. Center and apply boldface to the column headings in row 3. Then apply boldface and italics to the cell range from A4 to A9. Before proceeding, adjust the column widths and row heights as required. When satisfied, preview and print the worksheet. Save and then close the workbook.

difficult 

6. On Your Own: Personal Expense Comparison

To practice working with formatting and page layout options, use Excel to create a monthly expense comparison worksheet. After displaying a blank workbook, enter the following column headings in a single row: **Expense, January, February,** and **Change.** Then enter the following expense categories in a single column under the "Expense" heading.

- Rent/Mortgage
- Food
- Clothing
- Transportation
- Utilities
- Education
- Entertainment

For both the January and February columns, enter some reasonable data. Add the label "Total" below the last expense category and then use AutoSum to calculate totals for the monthly columns. Create formulas to calculate the difference for each expense category. Use the AutoFormat "Accounting 2" option to format the worksheet. Your worksheet should appear similar, but not identical, to Figure 3.45.

Figure 3.45

Creating an expense worksheet

	A	B	C	D	E
1	**Expense**	January	February	Change	
2	Rent/Mortgage	$ 600.00	$ 600.00	$ -	
3	Food	200.00	250.00	50.00	
4	Clothing	75.00	100.00	25.00	
5	Transportation	50.00	60.00	10.00	
6	Utilities	50.00	50.00	-	
7	Education	200.00	200.00	-	
8	Entertainment	100.00	75.00	(25.00)	
9	Total	$1,275.00	$1,335.00	$60.00	
10					
11					

For printing purposes, add a custom footer that prints the current date, your name, and the page number at the bottom of each page. When you are finished, save the workbook as "My Expenses" to your personal storage location. Preview and print the worksheet, and then close the workbook and exit Excel.

Excel

Case Problems

Hip Hop Hits

The Hip Hop Hits music store is facing increased competitive pressures with the recent announcement that a discount superstore chain is moving into the area. Stacy Marvin realizes that in order to stay competitive, she needs to be able to track and analyze her inventory costs, stock levels, and sales trends quickly and accurately. Fortunately, her senior sales associate, Justin Lee, has explained how he can use Excel to create worksheets that will make these tasks easier.

In the following case problems, assume the role of Justin and perform the same steps that he identifies. You may want to re-read the chapter opening before proceeding.

1. Stacey asks Justin to prepare a worksheet that will summarize Hip Hop Hits' current stock levels. He begins by launching Microsoft Excel so that a new blank workbook is displayed. As shown in Figure 3.46, he enters the worksheet title, row and column labels, and inventory values for each category. (*Note*: Column A's width has been adjusted slightly so that you can see the text label entries.)

Figure 3.46

Creating an inventory worksheet

	A	B	C	D	E
1	Inventory by Category				
2		CDs	Tapes	Total	
3	Pop	18500	6500		
4	Rock	23600	15350		
5	Dance	19000	9200		
6	Country	15420	8670		
7	Easy Listening	11330	3200		
8	Classical	5680	1340		
9	Soundtracks	4200	1030		
10	Total				
11					
12					

Using the AutoSum feature, Justin has Excel calculate totals for both the row and column values. He then selects the cell range from A2 to D10 and applies the "Classic 2" AutoFormat style. Not yet satisfied, he merges and centers the title between columns A and D, and then applies formatting to make it appear consistent with the rest of the worksheet. Justin saves the workbook as "HHH Inventory1" to his *personal storage location* and then prints a copy to show to Stacey.

2. After reviewing the worksheet, Stacey asks Justin to make the following adjustments:
   - Insert a new row for "World Music" at row 9, enter 4100 for CDs and 3500 for Tapes, and ensure the totals are updated.
   - Adjust the width of column A to 15 characters and then change the height of row 1 to 24 points. Increase the title's font size to fit snugly within the new row height.
   - Make the values appear with dollar signs and commas, but with no decimal places.
   - Adjust the width of columns B, C, and D to at least 10 characters wide.

   When Justin finishes customizing the worksheet (Figure 3.47), he saves the workbook as "HHH Inventory2" and then closes it.

Figure 3.47

Customizing the inventory worksheet

	A	B	C	D	E
1	Inventory by Category				
2		CDs	Tapes	Total	
3	Pop	$ 18,500	$ 6,500	$ 25,000	
4	Rock	$ 23,600	$ 15,350	$ 38,950	
5	Dance	$ 19,000	$ 9,200	$ 28,200	
6	Country	$ 15,420	$ 8,670	$ 24,090	
7	Easy Listening	$ 11,330	$ 3,200	$ 14,530	
8	Classical	$ 5,680	$ 1,340	$ 7,020	
9	World Music	$ 4,100	$ 3,500	$ 7,600	
10	Soundtracks	$ 4,200	$ 1,030	$ 5,230	
11	Total	$ 101,830	$ 48,790	$ 150,620	
12					
13					

3. The next day, Stacey assigns Justin the task of completing the company's Advertising Schedule worksheet that she started a few days earlier. Justin opens the workbook named EX03CP03 and then saves it as "HHH Advertising" to his *personal storage location.* According to the sticky notes attached to Stacey's printout of the worksheet, Justin needs to enter the following three new promotions:

   - Back-to-School: 1 newspaper ad on August 27th for $500
   - Rocktober Blitz: 6 radio spots on October 11th for $2900
   - Christmas: 3 TV ads starting December 1st for $9000

   After entering the new data, Justin formats the worksheet by applying the Currency style to the "Cost" column and increasing the width of the column. He then decreases the decimal places shown to 0. Using the Format Cells dialog box, Justin changes the date values in column C to appear in a "dd-mmm-yy" format and then adjusts the column's width to 10 characters.

   Noticing that Stacey placed an extra column between the "Theme" and "Date" columns, Justin deletes column B and then resizes column A to display using its best-fit width. He also selects a new typeface, font size, and alignment for the column headings and title, as shown in Figure 3.48. Justin prints, saves, and then closes the workbook.

Figure 3.48

Formatting the HHH Advertising workbook

	A	B	C	D	E	F
1	*Advertising Schedule*					
2						
3	Theme	Date	Quantity	Type	Cost	
4	Winter Warm-up	15-Jan-02	1	Flyer	$ 450	
5	Valentine Special	10-Feb-02	5	Radio	$ 2,135	
6	Inventory Blow-out	26-Mar-02	2	Newspaper	$ 750	
7	Midnight Madness	2-May-02	1	TV	$ 3,800	
8	Downtown Promotion	12-Jun-02	1	Magazine	$ 1,200	
9	Summertime Blues	1-Jul-02	1	Newspaper	$ 495	
10	Hot Hits	14-Aug-02	1	Flyer	$ 450	
11	Back-to-School	27-Aug-02	1	Newspaper	$ 500	
12	Rocktober Blitz	11-Oct-02	6	Radio	$ 2,900	
13	Christmas	1-Dec-02	3	TV	$ 9,000	
14						
15						

4. Having completed his work for Stacey, Justin opens one of his pet worksheet projects named EX03CP04. This workbook contains a sales transaction analysis that summarizes information from the store's point-of-sale equipment. He immediately saves the workbook as "HHH Daily Sales" to his *personal storage location.*

   To speed the formatting process, Justin uses the AutoFormat feature to apply a combination of table formatting attributes to the worksheet. Then, to distinguish the cells containing the times of day from the rest of the worksheet area, Justin applies a dark red fill color to the background of Row 1 and makes the font color white. Next he increases the width for all of the columns to give the worksheet a roomier look. At the top of the worksheet, Justin inserts a new row and then enters the title "Sales Transactions by Time Period." He merges and centers the title over the columns and then applies formatting to make the title stand out from the data.

   To prepare for printing, Justin adds a custom header that places the company name at the center of the page. He then adds a custom footer that contains the words "Prepared by *your name*" on the left, the date in the center, and the page number on the right-hand side. Next, he adjusts the page setup so the worksheet is centered horizontally on the page. After printing the worksheet, Justin saves it as a Web page and views it using his Web browser. He closes the Web browser when he is ready to proceed. Satisfied that he's put in a full day, Justin saves and closes the workbook. Then he exits Microsoft Excel.

Microsoft® **Excel®**

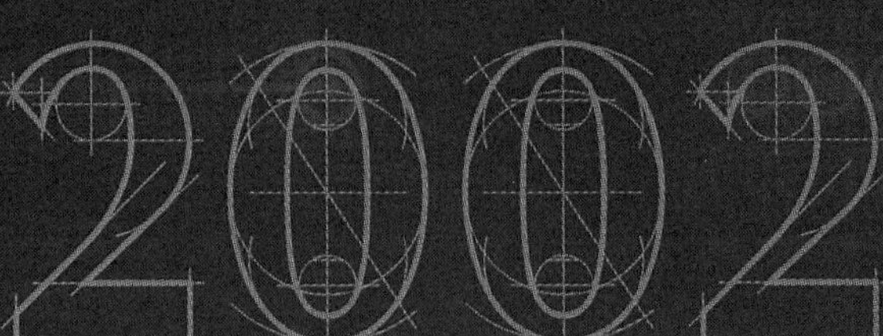

CHAPTER 4

Analyzing Your Data

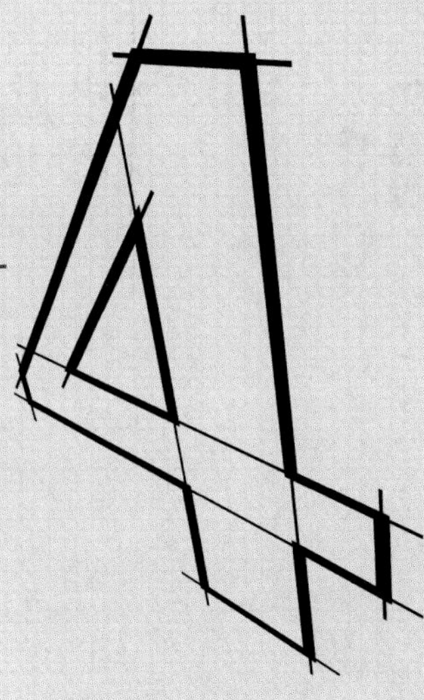

CHAPTER OUTLINE

Case Study

4.1 Working with Named Ranges

4.2 Using Built-In Functions

4.3 Creating an Embedded Chart

Chapter Summary

Chapter Quiz

Hands-On Exercises

Case Problems

PREREQUISITES

To successfully complete this chapter, you must be able to enter values, dates, and simple formulas into a worksheet. You will be asked to select multiple cell ranges, modify worksheet information, and access Excel features using the toolbar and menus. The final module on creating and printing embedded charts assumes no prior charting knowledge, but you need to know how to preview and print a worksheet.

LEARNING OBJECTIVES

After completing this chapter, you will be able to:

- Create, modify, remove, and apply range names
- Understand absolute and relative cell addresses
- Use natural language formulas in a worksheet
- Use mathematical and statistical functions, such as SUM, AVERAGE, COUNT, MIN, and MAX
- Use date functions, such as NOW and TODAY
- Embed, move, and size a chart on a worksheet
- Preview and print a chart

CaseStudy PRAIRIE SOCCER ASSOCIATION

The Prairie Soccer Association consists of eight elite soccer teams in as many communities. The PSA is run by a small group of dedicated volunteers who handle everything from coaching to administration. An ex-player himself, Brad Stafford has volunteered for the organization for the past four years. In addition to fundraising, Brad is responsible for keeping records and tracking results for all of the teams in the league.

Shortly after the end of the season, the PSA publishes a newsletter that provides various statistics and other pertinent information about the season. In the past, this newsletter required weeks of performing manual calculations, followed by days of typing results into a word processor. Having enrolled in an Excel course last month, Brad now realizes that worksheets and charts can help him to complete his upcoming tasks.

In this chapter, you and Brad learn about using ranges and functions in Excel worksheets. First, you use named ranges to create formula expressions that are easier to understand. Then you practice using Excel's built-in functions to perform calculations. Last, you learn how to plot and print your worksheet data in a chart.

4.1 Working with Named Ranges

In its simplest form, a cell range is a single cell, such as B4. Still, the term *cell range* is more commonly used to describe a "from here to there" area on a worksheet. A range can also cover a three-dimensional area, crossing more than one worksheet within a workbook. In a new workbook, Excel provides three worksheets named *Sheet1, Sheet2,* and *Sheet3.* It may help you to think of a worksheet as a tear-off page on a notepad—the notepad representing the workbook. You access the worksheets in a workbook by clicking on the tabs appearing along the bottom of the document window.

A **range name** is a nickname given to a group of cells that can later be used in constructing formulas. For example, the formula expression **=Revenue–Expenses** is far easier to understand than **=C5–C6**. Working with cell references from more than one worksheet adds another level of complexity. For example, if the value for Revenue is stored on Sheet1 and the value for Expenses is stored on Sheet2, the formula would read **=Sheet1!C5–Sheet2!C6**. Notice that the worksheet name is separated from the cell address using an exclamation point (!). By default, range names already contain this information, making them far easier to remember than these cryptic expressions. In this module, you learn how to name ranges and how to work with different types of cell references.

4.1.1 Naming Cell Ranges

By naming parts of a worksheet, you make it (and the formulas contained therein) much easier to read and construct. There are two ways to name cell ranges. One way is to click in the Name box, located at the far left of the Formula bar, and then type a unique name with no spaces. Or you can use a menu command to create names automatically from the row and column headings appearing in a worksheet.

Excel

method

To name a cell range using the Name box:

- SELECT: the desired range
- CLICK: in the Name box
- TYPE: **a range name**, such as "Profit," without spaces

To name a cell range using the Menu bar:

- SELECT: the desired range, including the row and column headings
- CHOOSE: Insert, Name, Create

practice

You will now name cell ranges appearing in an existing worksheet using the two methods described above. Ensure that Excel is loaded.

1. Open the data file named EX0410 to display the worksheet shown in Figure 4.1.

Figure 4.1

Opening the EX0410 workbook

	A	B	C	D	E
1	**Salary Schedule**				
2					
3	**Factor**	3.50%			
4					
5	**Salaries**	**F-2001**	**F-2002**	**F-2003**	
6	**Matthew**	$40,000			
7	**Jennifer**	$52,000			
8	**Carlos**	$23,500			
9	**Samantha**	$37,800			
10					
11					

2. Save the workbook as "Salaries" to your personal storage location.
3. To increase Matthew's salary by the growth factor appearing in cell B3, perform the following steps:
   SELECT: cell C6
   TYPE =**b6*(1+b3)**
   PRESS: ENTER
   The answer, 41400, appears in cell C6.
4. Now put yourself in the place of another user who needed to understand this calculation. That person would first have to track down each cell address in the formula. A better approach is to name the cells that you will often refer to in formulas. Let's name the cell containing the growth factor before entering a formula to increase Jennifer's salary:
   SELECT: cell B3
   CLICK: in the Name box with the I-beam mouse pointer
   TYPE: **Growth** (as shown below)

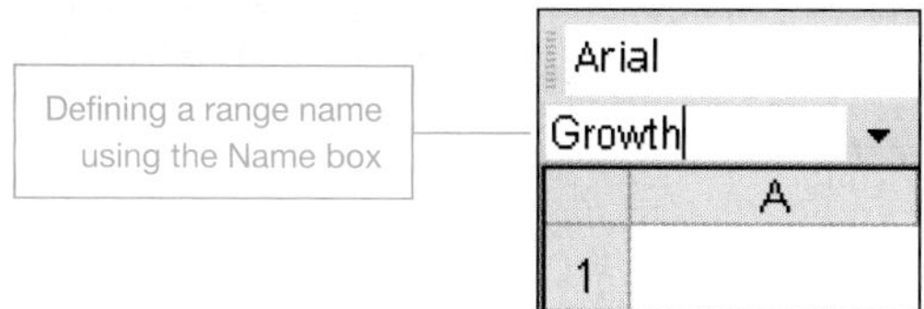

Defining a range name using the Name box

5. PRESS: ENTER
You have now created a named range called "Growth" that you can use in place of the cell address when entering formulas.

6. To use the range name:
SELECT: cell C7
TYPE: **=b7*(1+Growth)**
PRESS: ENTER
The answer, 53820, appears. A new user reading this formula would be better able to decipher its objective.

7. You can also use range names to navigate within your worksheet:
CLICK: down arrow attached to the Name box
SELECT: Growth in the drop-down list that appears
The cell pointer moves immediately to cell B3.

8. Now update the growth factor:
TYPE: **5%**
PRESS: ENTER
The worksheet cells containing formulas are updated.

9. Another method for creating range names uses the existing heading labels in your worksheet. You can use this method effectively when the data is organized in a table layout. To demonstrate:
SELECT: cell range from A5 to D9
Notice that the selected range includes the fiscal years across the top row and the employee names down the leftmost column.

10. To specify that the heading labels be used in naming the ranges:
CHOOSE: Insert, Name, Create

11. In the Create Name dialog box, ensure that the *Top row* and *Left column* check boxes appear selected as shown in Figure 4.2.

Figure 4.2

Creating range names from worksheet values

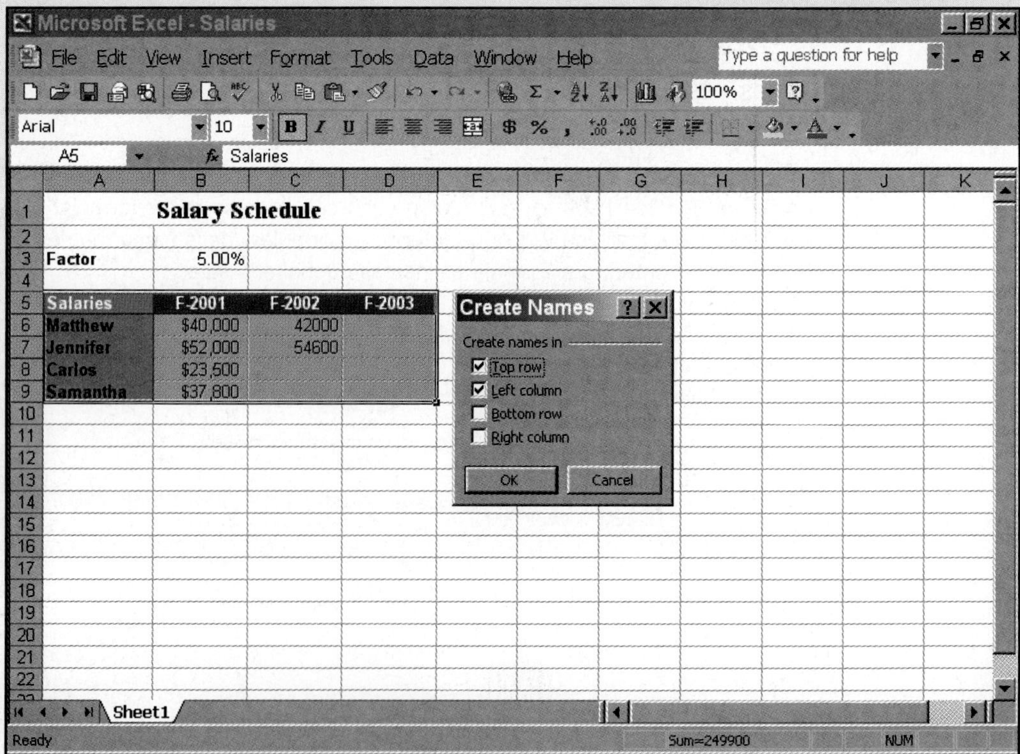

12. To complete the operation:
CLICK: OK command button

13. Now let's practice selecting named ranges:
CLICK: down arrow attached to the Name box
Many range names now appear in the drop-down list, as shown in Figure 4.3.

Figure 4.3

Displaying range names in the Name box

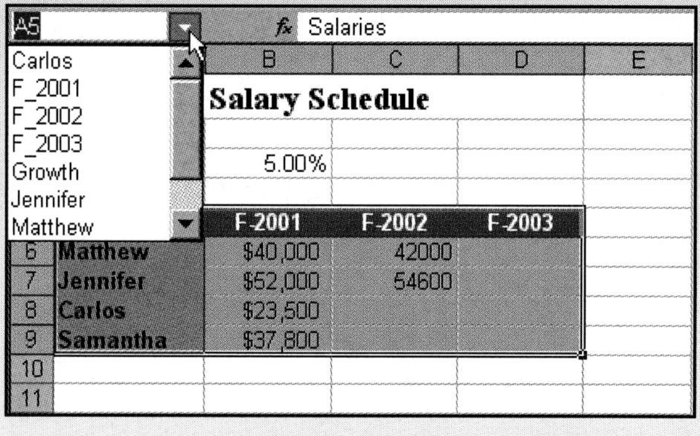

14. To move the cell pointer to one of the row ranges:
CLICK: Jennifer in the drop-down list
The cell range from B7 to D7 appears selected.

15. To display one of the column ranges:
CLICK: down arrow attached to the Name box
CLICK: F_2003 in the drop-down list
(*Note:* The label "F-2003" is used as the column heading instead of the value 2003, since Excel can create range names only from labels, not values. You must also beware of conflicts with cell addresses. For example, the range name F2003 is unacceptable because it refers to an actual cell address on the worksheet.)

16. Finally, let's select the entire data area in the table:
CLICK: down arrow attached to the Name box
CLICK: Salaries in the drop-down list
The range from cell B6 to D9 is highlighted.

17. PRESS: CTRL + HOME to remove the highlighting

18. Save the workbook and keep it open for use in the next lesson.

4.1.2 Managing Range Names

feature

Once you have created range names, you can easily modify and delete them using the Define Name dialog box. Another useful Excel feature is the ability to paste a list of the existing range names into your worksheet. You can then refer to this list when you are building formula expressions or when you need to jump to a particular spot in the worksheet.

method

To display the Define Name dialog box:

- CHOOSE: Insert, Name, Define

To paste range names into the worksheet:

- CHOOSE: Insert, Name, Paste

Excel

practice

You will now practice deleting and pasting range names. Ensure that you have completed the previous lesson and that the "Salaries" workbook is displayed.

1. You manipulate range names using the Define Name dialog box. To illustrate, let's delete the yearly range names that were created in the last lesson. Do the following:
CHOOSE: Insert, Name, Define
The dialog box in Figure 4.4 should now appear on the screen.

Figure 4.4

The Define Name dialog box

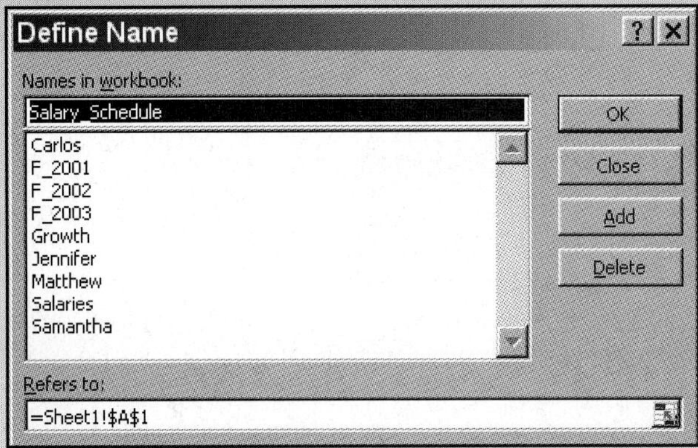

2. To remove the "F_2001" range name:
SELECT: F_2001 in the *Names in workbook* list box
Notice that the range address "=Sheet1!$B$6:$B$9" appears in the *Refer to* text box. (*Note:* If necessary, you can edit the cell references appearing in this text box. The significance of dollar signs in the range address is discussed in the next lesson.)
3. CLICK: Delete command button
4. To remove the remaining yearly range names:
SELECT: F_2002 from the list box
CLICK: Delete command button
SELECT: F_2003 from the list box
CLICK: Delete command button
5. To dismiss the dialog box:
CLICK: Close command button
6. To help you document and double-check the cell references in a worksheet, Excel enables you to paste a list of all named ranges into the worksheet. To demonstrate this technique:
SELECT: cell A12
CHOOSE: Insert, Name, Paste
CLICK: Paste List command button
7. To remove the highlighting:
PRESS: CTRL + HOME
Your screen should now appear similar to Figure 4.5.

Figure 4.5

Pasting a list of range names into the worksheet

	A	B	C	D	E
1	Salary Schedule				
2					
3	Factor	5.00%			
4					
5	Salaries	F-2001	F-2002	F-2003	
6	Matthew	$40,000	42000		
7	Jennifer	$52,000	54600		
8	Carlos	$23,500			
9	Samantha	$37,800			
10					
11					
12	Carlos	=Sheet1!$B$8:$D$8			
13	Growth	=Sheet1!$B$3			
14	Jennifer	=Sheet1!$B$7:$D$7			
15	Matthew	=Sheet1!$B$6:$D$6			
16	Salaries	=Sheet1!$B$6:$D$9			
17	Samantha	=Sheet1!$B$9:$D$9			
18					
19					

Range names and their cell references can be pasted into the worksheet for reference.

8. Save the workbook and keep it open for use in the next lesson.

In Addition MAKING EFFICIENT USE OF RANGE NAMES

Range names facilitate the entry of formulas and functions in a worksheet. By using range names in place of cell references, you are less likely to make data entry errors when constructing complex formulas. For those cells that you must refer to frequently on a worksheet, consider naming the cell ranges immediately. You can always delete, rename, or redefine these range names at a later date.

4.1.3 Using References in Formulas

feature

There are two types of cell references that you can enter into formulas: *relative* and *absolute.* The difference between the two types becomes especially important when you start copying and moving formulas in your worksheet. A **relative cell address** in a formula adjusts itself automatically when copied, since the cell reference is relative to where it sits in the worksheet. An **absolute cell address** always refers to an exact cell location in the worksheet.

method

The formulas that you have entered so far have all used relative cell references—Excel's default method. To specify an absolute reference, you precede each column letter and row number in a cell address with a dollar sign. For example, to make cell B5 an absolute cell reference, you type $B$5. A **mixed cell address,** on the other hand, locks only a portion of a cell address by placing the dollar sign ($) before either the address's column letter or row number, such as B$5. Sometimes it helps to vocalize the word "absolutely" as you read a cell address, so that $B$5 would be read as "absolutely column B and absolutely row 5."

In this lesson, you practice using relative and absolute cell addressing in performing simple copy and paste operations. Ensure that you have completed the previous lesson and that the "Salaries" workbook is displayed.

1. Let's begin by reviewing the formula in cell C6:
SELECT: cell C6
Review the expression "=B6*(1+B3)" in the Formula bar. You can vocalize the formula in cell C6 as "take the value appearing one cell to my left and then multiply it by 1 plus the value appearing three rows up and one column to the left." Notice that you need to use cell C6 as a point of reference for this formula to make any sense. This is an example of using relative cell references.

2. Let's copy the formula in cell C6 to cell D6:
CLICK: Copy button on the Standard toolbar
SELECT: cell D6
CLICK: Paste button
PRESS: ESC to remove the dashed marquee
The result, 42000, appears in cell D6. This, however, is not the desired result. The value has not been incremented by the growth factor.

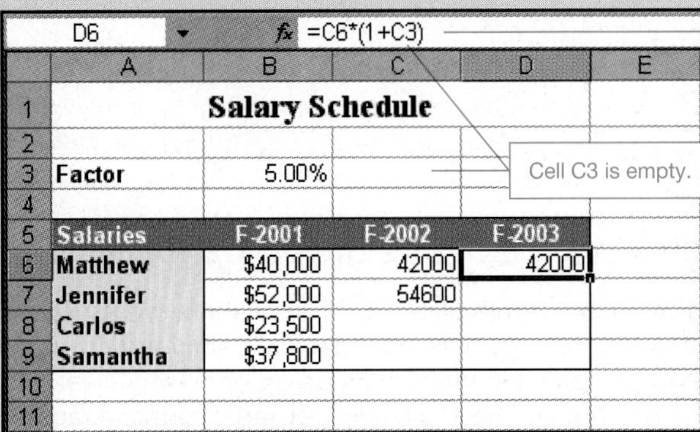
D6
=C6*(1+C3)
Salary Schedule
Factor 5.00%
Salaries F-2001 F-2002 F-2003
Matthew $40,000 42000 42000
Jennifer $52,000 54600
Carlos $23,500
Samantha $37,800
Cell C3 is empty.
When the formula in cell B6 is copied to cell C6, the cell references in the formula also change to reflect their relative positions on the worksheet. Unfortunately, this was not the intention for this copy and paste operation.

Figure 4.6
Copying a formula with relative cell addresses

3. In the Formula bar, notice that the formula "=C6*(1+C3)" no longer performs the correct calculation. Copying and pasting has modified the cell addresses by automatically adjusting the column letters. To ensure that Excel does not change a cell address during a copy operation, you need to make it absolute:
PRESS: DELETE to remove the formula in cell D6
SELECT: cell C6

4. Position the I-beam mouse pointer over the cell address B3 in the Formula bar and then click the left mouse button once.

5. To change the growth factor reference into an absolute address, you type dollar signs in front of the column letter and row number. Or, you can do the following:
PRESS: F4 (ABS key; ABS stands for absolute)
Notice that B3 now appears as $B$3, as shown below.

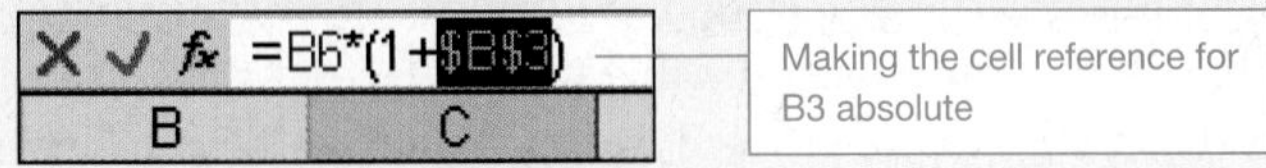
=B6*(1+$B$3)
B
C
Making the cell reference for B3 absolute

6. Continue pressing F4 to see how Excel cycles through possible combinations of relative, absolute, and mixed cell addressing.

7. Before proceeding, ensure that $B$3 appears in the Formula bar and then press ENTER.

8. Copy and paste the formula stored in cell C6 into cell D6 again. The correct result, 44100, now appears in the cell.

9. Remember that you used a range name in constructing the formula for cell C7. On your own, copy the formula in cell C7 to cell D7, as shown in Figure 4.7. The formula calculates correctly because range names, such as Growth, are defined using absolute cell addresses.

Figure 4.7

Copying and pasting a formula with a range name

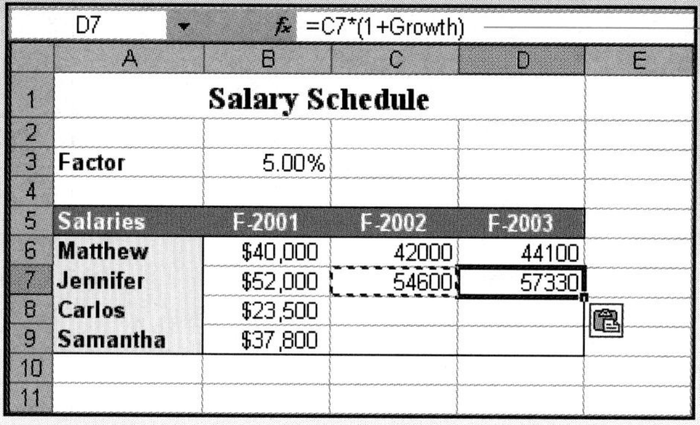

D7 =C7*(1+Growth)

	A	B	C	D	E
1	Salary Schedule				
2					
3	Factor	5.00%			
4					
5	Salaries	F-2001	F-2002	F-2003	
6	Matthew	$40,000	42000	44100	
7	Jennifer	$52,000	54600	57330	
8	Carlos	$23,500			
9	Samantha	$37,800			
10					
11					

A range name is defined using an absolute cell reference. Therefore, using a range name in a formula ensures that its cell addresses refer to the correct location.

10. To continue:
PRESS: ESC to remove the marquee

11. PRESS: CTRL + HOME to move to cell A1

12. Save and then close the worksheet.

4.1.4 Entering Natural Language Formulas

feature

Another alternative to using cell references is to enter a special type of expression called a **natural language formula.** Similar to using range names, a natural language formula allows you to build a formula using the row and column labels from the active worksheet. In effect, a natural language formula uses implicit range names. In order for natural language formulas to work effectively, however, the worksheet must be organized in a table format with distinctly labeled rows and columns.

method

- SELECT: the cell where you want the result to appear
- TYPE: = (an equal sign)
- TYPE: **an expression**, such as **Revenue-Expenses**, using the actual row and column labels
- PRESS: ENTER

practice

You will now use natural language formulas to calculate an expression in a worksheet. Ensure that no workbooks are open in the application window.

1. Open the data file named EX0414.

2. Save the workbook as "Natural" to your personal storage location.

3. Before you begin, you'll need to review some configuration settings:
CHOOSE: Tools, Options
CLICK: *Calculation* tab
This tab, as shown in Figure 4.8, enables you to specify calculation options and dictate whether Excel recognizes labels in formulas.

Figure 4.8

Options dialog box: *Calculation* tab

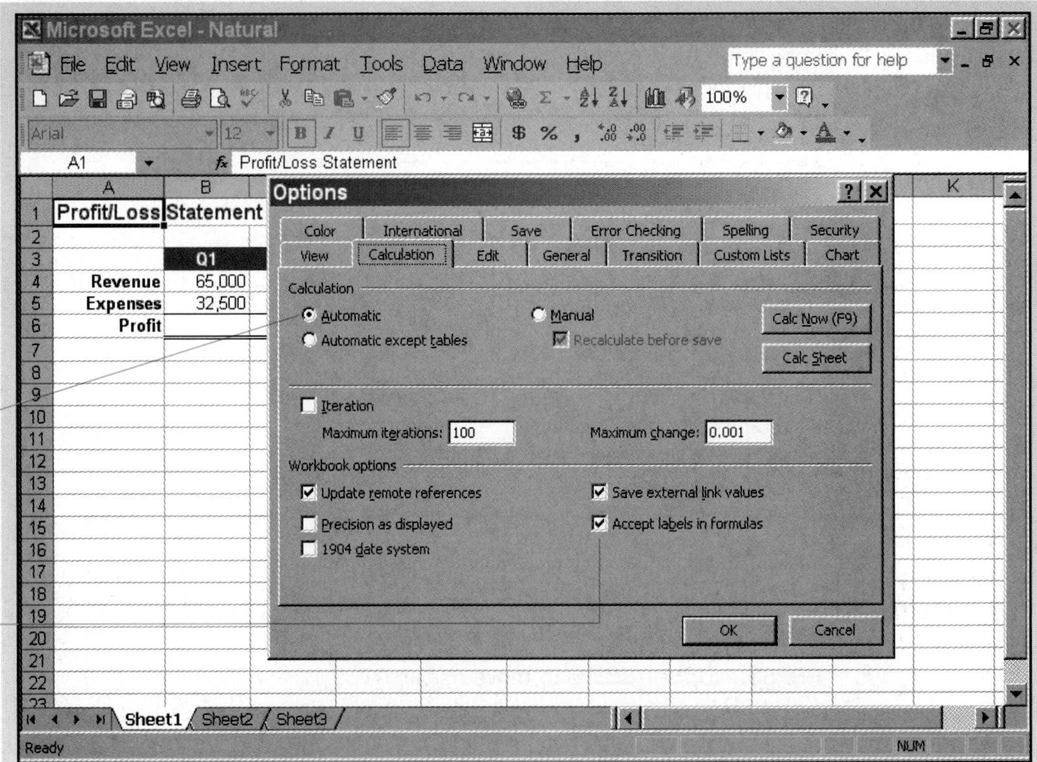

Select this option to have Excel recalculate the formulas in your worksheet whenever you change a value.

Ensure that this check box is selected before attempting to enter a natural language formula.

4. On the *Calculation* tab of the Options dialog box:
   SELECT: *Automatic* option button, if not already selected
   SELECT: *Accept labels in formulas* check box so that a ✓ appears
   CLICK: OK command button

5. To calculate the profit for Q1 using a natural language formula:
   SELECT: cell B6
   TYPE: **=Revenue-Expenses**
   PRESS: ➔
   The result, 32500, appears in the cell. (*CAUTION:* You cannot mix labels with cell references in a natural language formula. For example, the formula **=Revenue-B5** does not compute.)

6. To proceed, enter the same natural language formula into cell C6. Notice that Excel calculates the results correctly.

7. Now try copying the formula in cell C6 to cells D6 and E6. As illustrated, you can copy and paste natural language formulas as well. Your worksheet should now appear similar to Figure 4.9.

Figure 4.9

Entering and copying natural language formulas

E6 =Revenue-Expenses

	A	B	C	D	E	F
1	**Profit/Loss Statement**					
2						
3		**Q1**	**Q2**	**Q3**	**Q4**	
4	**Revenue**	65,000	90,000	86,800	110,000	
5	**Expenses**	32,500	42,300	40,500	63,400	
6	**Profit**	32500	47700	46300	46600	
7						
8						

A natural language formula uses row and column labels.

8. Let's ensure that "Revenue" and "Expenses" are not range names:
CHOOSE: Insert, Name, Define
Notice that there are no range names defined in the dialog box.

9. CLICK: Close command button

10. Save and then close the workbook.

4.1. Why is "AD2002" an unacceptable name for a cell range?

4.2 Using Built-In Functions

This module introduces you to Excel's built-in **functions.** Don't let the word *function* conjure up visions of your last calculus class; functions are shortcuts that you use in place of entering lengthy and complicated formulas. Functions are incredible time-savers that can increase your productivity in creating worksheets.

There are several methods for entering a function into a worksheet cell. To begin with, you can type a function name, preceded by an equal sign (=), and then enter its **arguments** (labels, values, or cell references). Many functions are quite complex, however, and all require that you remember the precise order, called **syntax,** in which to enter arguments. An easier method is to search for and select a function from the Insert Function dialog box shown in Figure 4.10. You access this dialog box by choosing the Insert, Function command or by clicking the Insert Function button (fx). In addition to organizing Excel's functions into tidy categories (further described in Table 4.1), the Insert Function dialog box lets you view a function's syntax, along with a brief description.

Figure 4.10

Insert Function dialog box

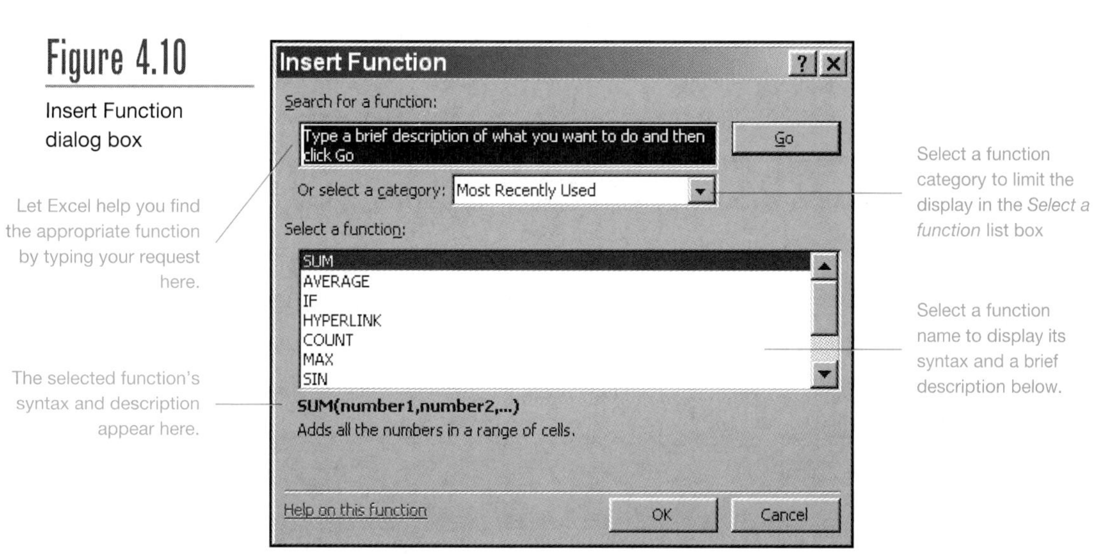

Table 4.1

Function Categories

Category	Description
Financial	Determine loan payments, present and future values, depreciation schedules, and rates of return
Date & Time	Perform date and time calculations; input the current date and/or time into a cell
Math & Trig	Sum a range of values; perform trigonometric calculations; determine absolute and rounded values
Statistical	Determine the average, median, minimum, and maximum values for a range; calculate statistical measures, like variance and standard deviation
Lookup & Reference	Look up and select values from a range; return the active cell's column letter and row number
Database	Perform mathematical and statistical calculations on worksheet values in a table or list format
Text	Manipulate, compare, format, and extract textual information; convert values to text (and vice versa)
Logical	Perform conditional calculations using IF statements; compare and evaluate values
Information	Return information about the current environment; perform error-checking and troubleshooting

4.2.1 Adding Values (SUM)

You use the SUM function to add the values appearing in a range of cells. SUM is the most frequently used function in Excel, saving you from having to enter long addition formulas such as =A1+A2+A3+ . . . +A99. The AutoSum button (Σ) inserts the SUM function into a worksheet cell automatically, guessing at the range argument to use.

method

- **=SUM(range)**

practice

You will now practice entering the SUM function. Ensure that no workbooks appear in the application window.

1. Open the data file named EX0420 to display the worksheet shown in Figure 4.11.

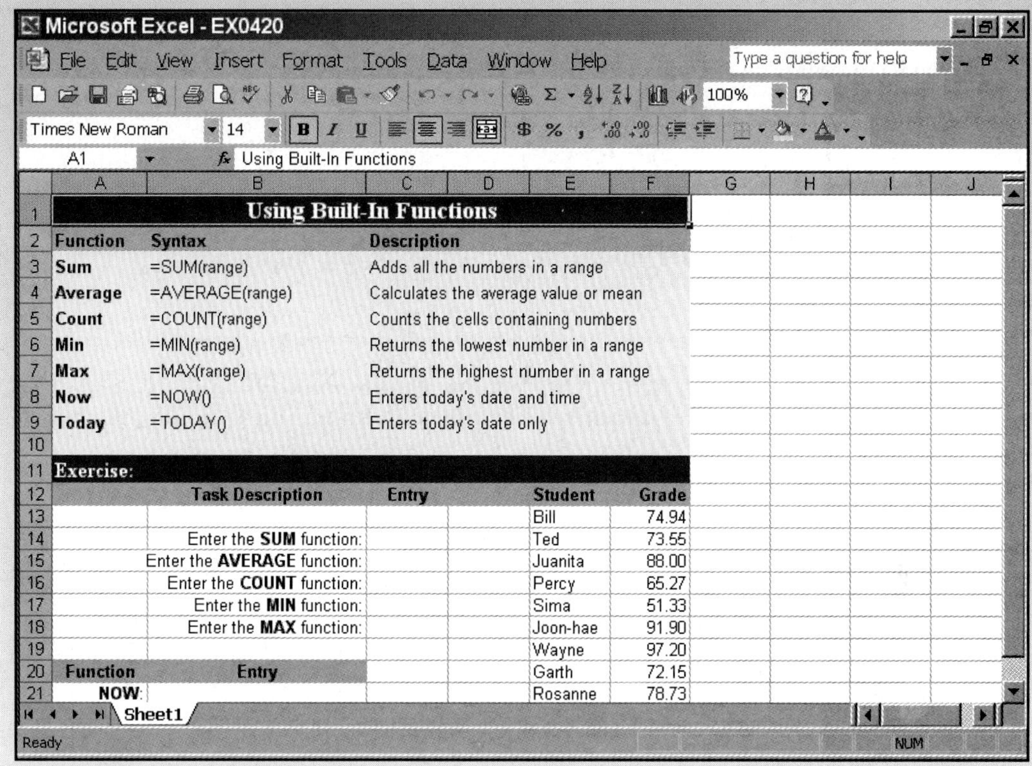

Figure 4.11

Opening the EX0420 workbook

2. Save the workbook as "Functions" to your personal storage location.

3. Let's total the grade values in column F. Do the following:
SELECT: cell C14

4. To enter the SUM function:
TYPE: **=sum(f13:f22)**
Notice that the cell range is highlighted with Excel's Range Finder feature (shown below) as you enter the function arguments.

Entering the SUM function.

=sum(f13:f22)	Bill	74.94
	Ted	73.55
	Juanita	88.00

Excel's Range Finder feature outlines the cell range.

5. PRESS: ENTER
The result, 761.51, appears in the cell. (*Note:* You can enter a function's name and arguments using either lowercase or uppercase letters. Ensure that no blank spaces have been entered mistakenly.)

6. Let's change Percy's grade from 65.27:
SELECT: cell F16

7. To enter the revised grade:
TYPE: **75.27**
PRESS: ENTER
The new SUM result displays 771.51 in cell C14.

8. Save the workbook and keep it open for use in the next lesson.

4.2.2 Calculating Averages (AVERAGE)

feature You use the AVERAGE function to compute the average value (sometimes called the arithmetic mean) for a range of cells. This function adds together all of the numeric values in a range and then divides the sum by the number of cells used in the calculation.

method

- =AVERAGE(range)

practice In this exercise, you calculate the average value for a named range in a worksheet. Ensure that you have completed the previous lesson and that the "Functions" workbook is displayed.

1. To make it easier to enter functions, let's name the cell ranges on your worksheet. First, name the range that contains the grade values:
   SELECT: cell range from E12 to F22
   Notice that you include the column headings, Student and Grade, in the selection.
2. CHOOSE: Insert, Name, Create
   Your screen should now appear similar to Figure 4.12.

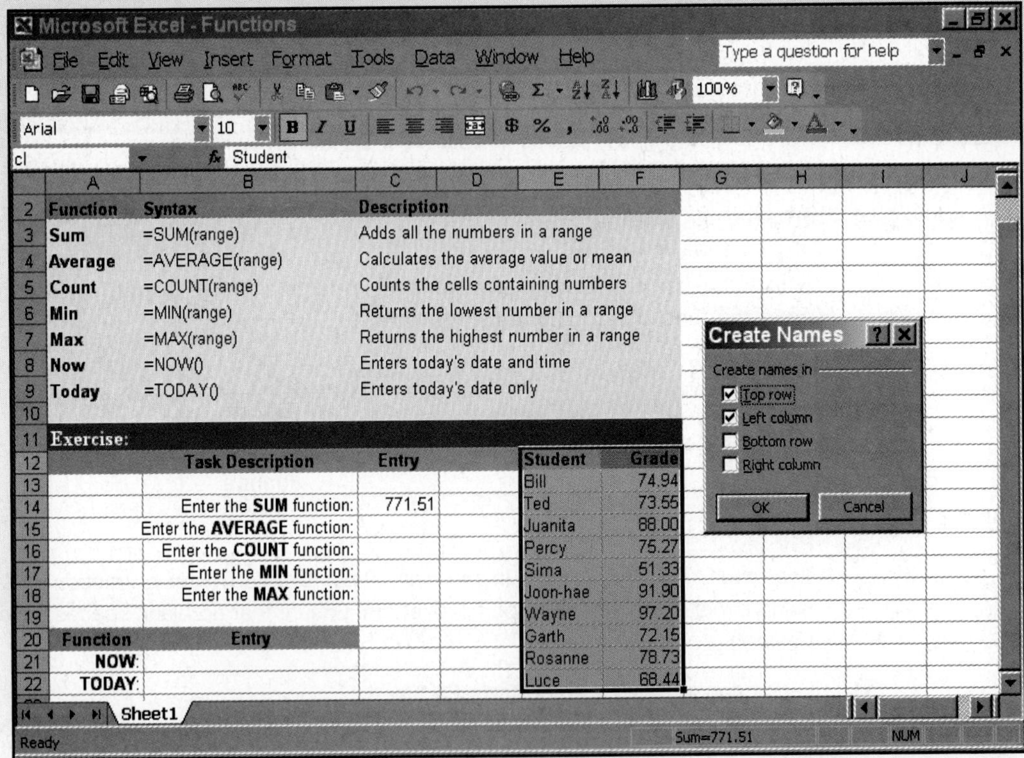

Figure 4.12 Naming a cell range on the worksheet

3. In the Create Name dialog box:
   SELECT: *Top row* check box, if not already selected
   SELECT: *Left column* check box, if not already selected
   CLICK: OK command button

4. To view the range names that have been created:
CLICK: down arrow attached to the Name box
The Name box should appear as shown here.

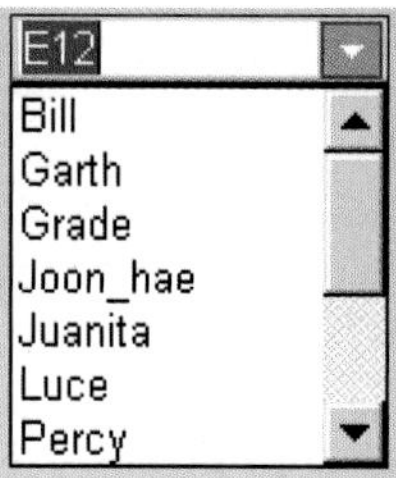

E12
Bill
Garth
Grade
Joon_hae
Juanita
Luce
Percy

5. In the drop-down list box that appears:
CLICK: Garth
Your cell pointer should now be positioned in cell F20. Notice also that the Name box displays the name "Garth."

6. To select the entire "Grade" range:
CLICK: down arrow attached to the Name box
CLICK: Grade in the drop-down list
The cell range from F13 to F22 is selected.

7. Let's use the range name to calculate the average grade:
SELECT: cell C15
TYPE: =**average(grade)**
Notice again how the Range Finder feature highlights the cell range.

8. PRESS: ENTER
The result, 77.151, appears in the cell.

9. To determine the average of a list of nonadjacent values, separate the items in the list using commas. To illustrate:
SELECT: cell D15
TYPE: =**average(Bill,Ted,Sima,Rosanne)**
Your worksheet should appear similar to Figure 4.13.

Figure 4.13

Averaging a list of nonadjacent cells

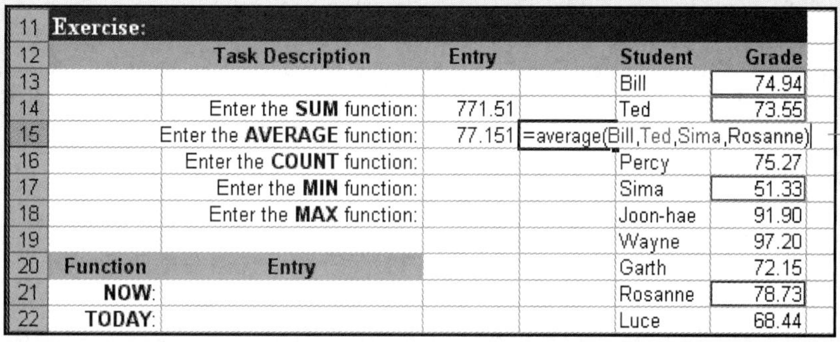

11	Exercise:					
12		Task Description	Entry		Student	Grade
13					Bill	74.94
14		Enter the **SUM** function:	771.51		Ted	73.55
15		Enter the **AVERAGE** function:	77.151	=average(Bill,Ted,Sima,Rosanne)		
16		Enter the **COUNT** function:			Percy	75.27
17		Enter the **MIN** function:			Sima	51.33
18		Enter the **MAX** function:			Joon-hae	91.90
19					Wayne	97.20
20	Function	Entry			Garth	72.15
21	NOW:				Rosanne	78.73
22	TODAY:				Luce	68.44

Notice that Excel's Range Finder color-codes each range name to its cell.

10. PRESS: ENTER
The result, 69.6375, appears as the average of only these students' grades.

4.2.3 Counting Values (COUNT)

feature

The COUNT function counts the number of cells in a range that contain numeric or date values. This function ignores cells containing text labels.

method

- =**COUNT(range)**

Excel

practice

You will now enter the COUNT function in the "Functions" workbook. Ensure that you have completed the previous lessons and that the "Functions" workbook is displayed.

1. Move the cell pointer to where you want the result to appear:
   SELECT: cell C16
2. You will now use the mouse to help you count the number of entries in a range. To begin:
   TYPE: **=count(**
3. Using the mouse, position the cell pointer over cell F13. Then:
   CLICK: cell F13 and hold down the left mouse button
   DRAG: mouse pointer to cell F22
   Notice that as you drag the mouse pointer, the range is entered into the function as an argument. When you reach cell F22, the argument displays the range name "Grade," as shown in Figure 4.14.

Figure 4.14

Using the mouse to select a cell range

11	**Exercise:**					
12		**Task Description**	**Entry**		**Student**	**Grade**
13					Bill	74.94
14		Enter the **SUM** function:	771.51		Ted	73.55
15		Enter the **AVERAGE** function:	77.151	69.6375	Juanita	88.00
16		Enter the **COUNT** function:	=count(Grade		Percy	75.27
17		Enter the **MIN** function:	COUNT(**value1**, [value2], ...)			51.33
18		Enter the **MAX** function:			Joon-hae	91.90
19					Wayne	97.20
20	**Function**	**Entry**			Garth	72.15
21	**NOW**:				Rosanne	78.73
22	**TODAY**:				Luce	68.44

When the cell range is fully selected, its range name appears.

Function ToolTip

Mouse pointer

4. Release the mouse button.
5. To complete the function entry:
   TYPE: **)**
   PRESS: ENTER
   The result, 10, appears in cell C16.
6. Save the workbook and keep it open for use in the next lesson.

In Addition THE DIFFERENCE BETWEEN COUNT AND COUNTA

The COUNT function has a second cousin named the COUNTA function. Whereas COUNT tallies the cells containing numbers and dates, COUNTA counts all nonblank cells. The primary difference, therefore, is that the COUNTA function includes text labels in its calculations.

4.2.4 Analyzing Values (MIN and MAX)

You use the MIN and MAX functions to determine the minimum (lowest) and maximum (highest) values in a range of cells.

- =MIN(range)
- =MAX(range)

practice

In this lesson, you use the Function Arguments dialog box to calculate the minimum and maximum grades in a range. Ensure that you have completed the previous lessons in this module and that the "Functions" workbook is displayed.

1. To calculate the lowest grade achieved:
   SELECT: cell C17
   TYPE: **=min(grade)**
   PRESS: ➔
   The result, 51.33, appears.

2. To find the lowest grade achieved among three students:
   TYPE: **=min(Wayne,Garth,Luce)**
   Your worksheet should appear similar to Figure 4.15.

Figure 4.15

Using the MIN function

11	**Exercise:**					
12		**Task Description**	**Entry**		**Student**	**Grade**
13					Bill	74.94
14		Enter the **SUM** function:	771.51		Ted	73.55
15		Enter the **AVERAGE** function:	77.151	69.6375	Juanita	88.00
16		Enter the **COUNT** function:	10		Percy	75.27
17		Enter the **MIN** function:	51.33	=min(Wayne,Garth,Luce)		
18		Enter the **MAX** function:			Joon-hae	91.90
19					Wayne	97.20
20	**Function**	**Entry**			Garth	72.15
21	**NOW:**				Rosanne	78.73
22	**TODAY:**				Luce	68.44

3. PRESS: ENTER
   The result, 68.44, appears.

4. Now let's use Excel's Function Arguments dialog box to calculate the maximum value in a range. Do the following:
   SELECT: cell C18
   TYPE: **=max(**
   Ensure that you include the open parentheses, (, at the end of the function name.

5. To display the Function Arguments dialog box:
   CLICK: Insert Function button (fx) in the Formula bar
   The Function Arguments dialog box appears, as shown in Figure 4.16.

Excel

Figure 4.16

Function Arguments dialog box

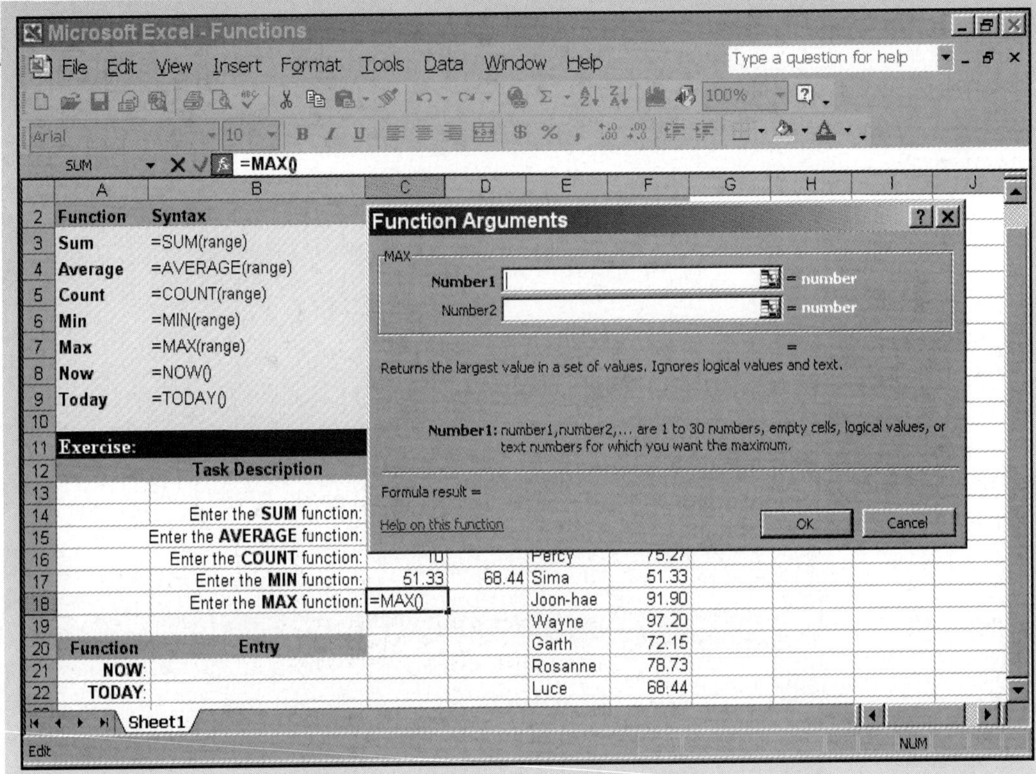

6. In the *Number1* argument text box:
   TYPE: **grade**
   Notice that the actual cell contents appear at the right of the text box and that the result is calculated immediately, as shown in Figure 4.17.

Figure 4.17

Entering arguments for the MAX function

Function Arguments
MAX
Number1 grade = {74.94;73.55;88;75
Number2 = number
= 97.2
Returns the largest value in a set of values. Ignores logical values and text.
Number1: number1,number2,... are 1 to 30 numbers, empty cells, logical values, or text numbers for which you want the maximum.
Formula result = 97.2
Help on this function
OK Cancel

Actual values from the cell range appear here.

Calculated result

The calculated formula result appears here.

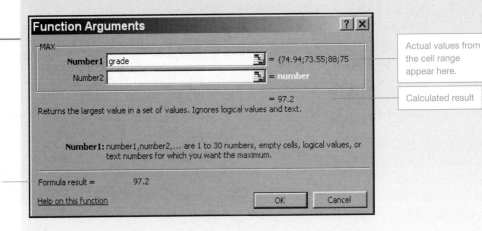

7. To complete the entry:
   CLICK: OK command button
   The result, 97.2, is placed into the cell.
8. To find the maximum grade achieved among three students:
   SELECT: cell D18
   TYPE: **=max(**
   CLICK: Insert Function button (fx)

9. In the Function Arguments dialog box:
TYPE: **Juanita**
PRESS: TAB
TYPE: **Ted**
PRESS: TAB
TYPE: **Luce**
Notice that the Formula bar displays the function as you build it in the Function Arguments dialog box (Figure 4.18).

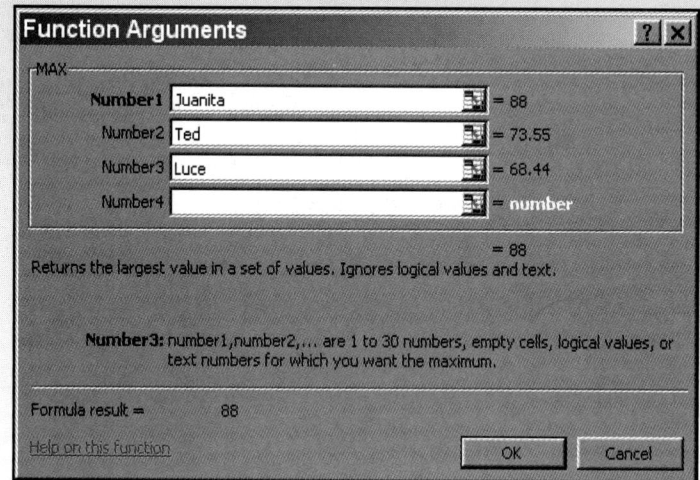

Figure 4.18

Entering arguments into the Function Arguments dialog box

10. To complete the entry:
CLICK: OK command button
The result, 88, appears in the cell.

4.2.5 Calculating Dates (NOW and TODAY)

feature

You can use the NOW and TODAY functions to display the date and time in your worksheets. The NOW function returns the current date and time as provided by your computer's internal clock. The TODAY function provides the current date only. Neither of these functions require any arguments.

method

- **=NOW( )**
- **=TODAY( )**

practice

In this exercise, you insert the NOW and TODAY functions into the workshseet. Ensure that you have completed the previous lessons in this module and that the "Functions" workbook is displayed.

1. To start this lesson, let's practice using the Insert Function dialog box to search for a function. First, position the cell pointer where you want the result to appear:
SELECT: cell B21

2. Now display the Insert Function dialog box:
CLICK: Insert Function button (fx)
(*Hint:* You can also choose the Insert, Function command on the menu.)

3. In the *Search for a function* text box:
TYPE: **to display the current time**
CLICK: Go command button
The dialog box should now appear similar to Figure 4.19.

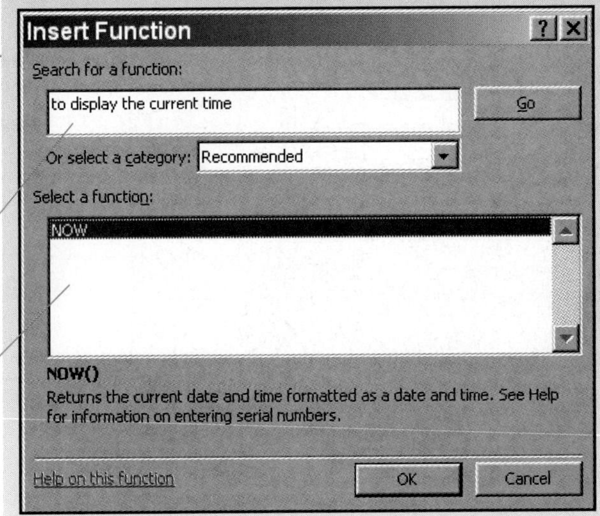

Figure 4.19

Searching for a function "to display the current time"

Type your request for a function here and then click the Go command button.

The results of the function search appear in the list box.

4. With the NOW function selected in the *Select a function* list box, read the description that starts with "Returns the current date and time."

5. To insert the NOW function into cell B21:
CLICK: OK command button

6. The Function Arguments dialog box appears, as shown in Figure 4.20, asking for confirmation:
CLICK: OK command button
The date is displayed in cell B21 using the "mm/dd/yyyy" format (depending on your default settings), and the time is typically displayed using the "hh:mm" 24-hour clock format.

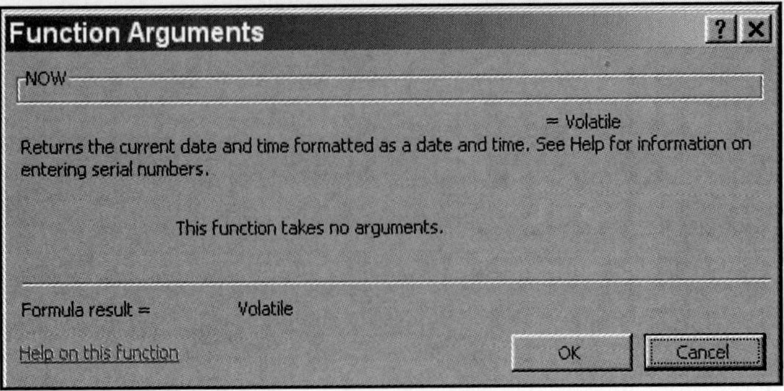

Figure 4.20

Function Arguments dialog box for the NOW function

7. To display only the time in the cell, you must format the entry:
SELECT: cell B21, if it is not already selected
CHOOSE: Format, Cells
CLICK: *Number* tab

8. You must now select a time format:
SELECT: Time in the *Category* list box
SELECT: 1:30:55 PM in the *Type* list box
Figure 4.21 shows the selections in the Format Cells dialog box.

Figure 4.21

Formatting the display of the current time

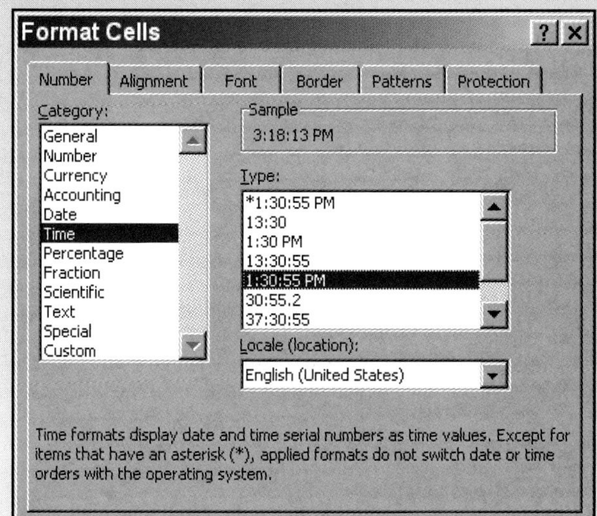

9. CLICK: OK command button

10. To recalculate the NOW function:
PRESS: F9 (CALC key)
You should see the cell value change to the current time. (*Hint:* You can use F9 to recalculate all formulas and functions in a worksheet.)

11. To select a function for entering the current date:
SELECT: B22
CLICK: Insert Function button (fx)

12. To display a list of the available function categories, as shown here:
CLICK: down arrow attached to the *Or select a category* drop-down list box
SELECT: Date & Time

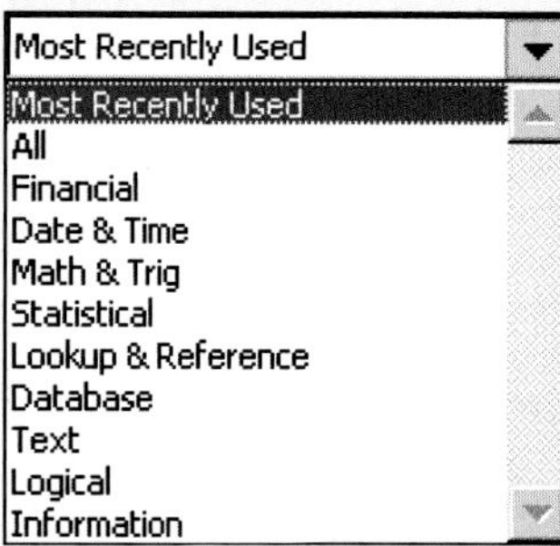

13. In the *Select a function* list box:
SELECT: TODAY
CLICK: OK command button

14. The Function Arguments dialog box asks for confirmation:
CLICK: OK command button
The current date now appears in cell B22. Your worksheet should now appear similar to Figure 4.22.

Excel

Figure 4.22

Completing the Functions workbook

11	**Exercise:**					
12		**Task Description**	**Entry**		**Student**	**Grade**
13					Bill	74.94
14		Enter the **SUM** function:	771.51		Ted	73.55
15		Enter the **AVERAGE** function:	77.151	69.6375	Juanita	88.00
16		Enter the **COUNT** function:	10		Percy	75.27
17		Enter the **MIN** function:	51.33	68.44	Sima	51.33
18		Enter the **MAX** function:	97.2	88	Joon-hae	91.90
19					Wayne	97.20
20	**Function**	**Entry**			Garth	72.15
21	**NOW:**	3:28:39 PM			Rosanne	78.73
22	**TODAY:**	3/7/2001			Luce	68.44

15. Save and then close the workbook.

In Addition THE IF FUNCTION

Arguably the most useful of Excel's functions, the IF function allows you to employ conditional logic in your worksheets. Specifically, the IF function lets you test for a condition and then, depending on the result, perform one of two calculations. The IF function is covered in Chapter 6 of our Introductory and Complete editions.

4.2. When might you use the Function Arguments dialog box or Insert Function dialog box to enter a function into the worksheet?

4.3 Creating an Embedded Chart

Since the earliest versions of spreadsheet software, users have been able to display their numerical data using graphs and charts. Although these graphics were acceptable for in-house business presentations and school projects, they often lacked the depth and quality required by professional users. Until now! You can confidently use Excel to produce visually stunning worksheets and charts that are suitable for electronic business presentations, color print masters, Internet Web pages, and 35mm slide shows.

Many types of charts are available for presenting your worksheet data to engineers, statisticians, business professionals, and other audiences. Some popular business charts—line chart, column chart, pie chart, and XY scatter plot diagram—are described below.

- ***Line Charts*** When you need to plot trends or show changes over a period of time, the **line chart** is the perfect tool. The angles of the line reflect the degree of variation, and the distance of the line from the horizontal axis represents the amount of the variation. An example of a line chart appears in Figure 4.23, along with some basic terminology.

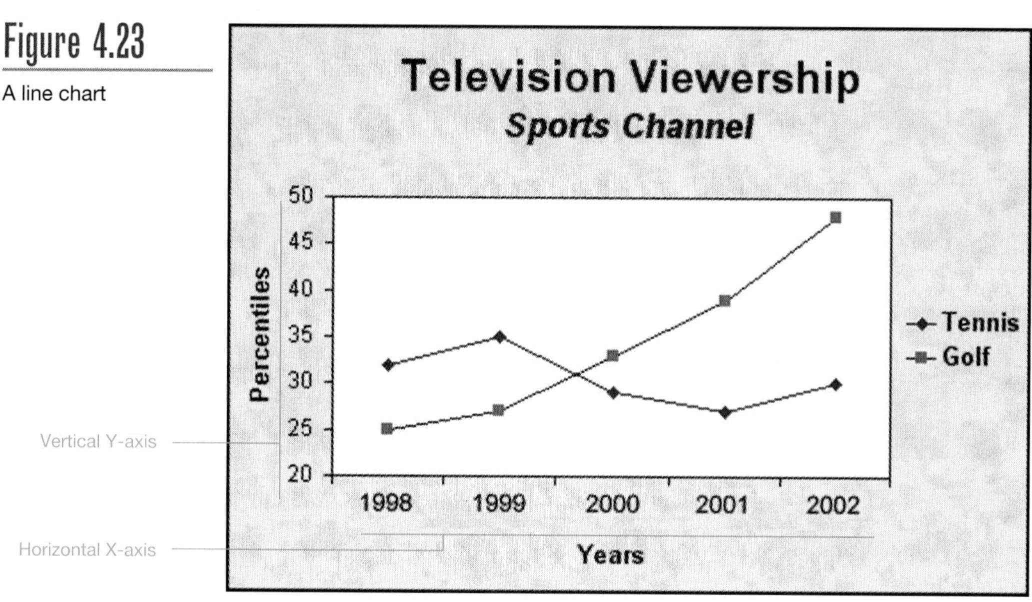

Figure 4.23

A line chart

- ***Bar or Column Charts*** When the purpose of the chart is to compare one data element with another data element, a **column chart** is the appropriate form to use. A column chart (Figure 4.24) shows variations over a period of time, similarly to a line chart. A **bar chart** also uses rectangular images, but they run horizontally rather than vertically.

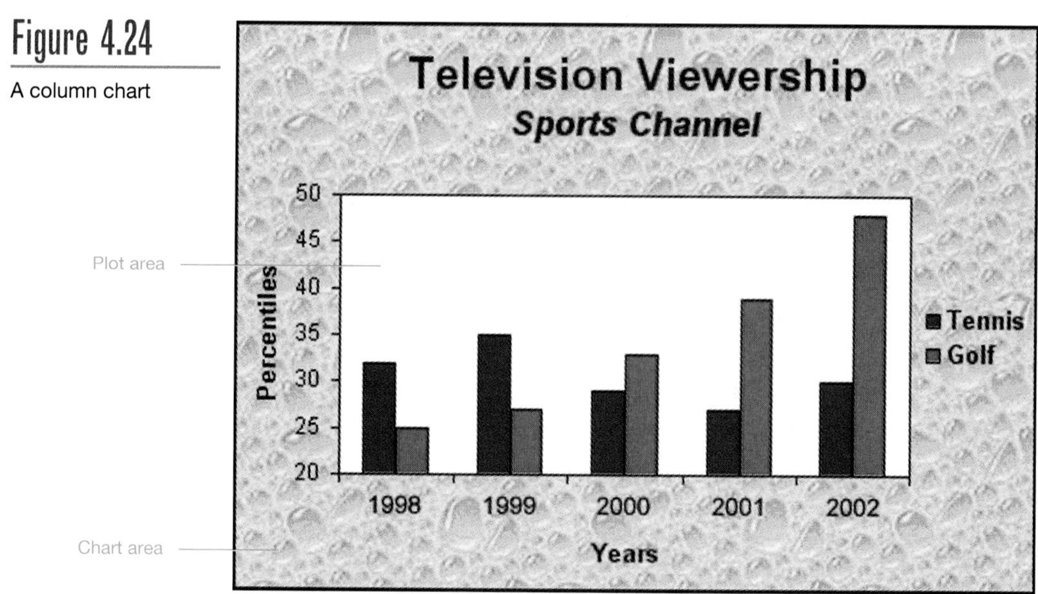

Figure 4.24

A column chart

- ***Pie Charts*** A **pie chart** shows the proportions of individual components compared to the total. Similar to a real pie (the baked variety), a pie chart is divided into slices or wedges. (In Excel, you can even pull out the slices from the rest of the pie.) An example of a pie chart appears in Figure 4.25.

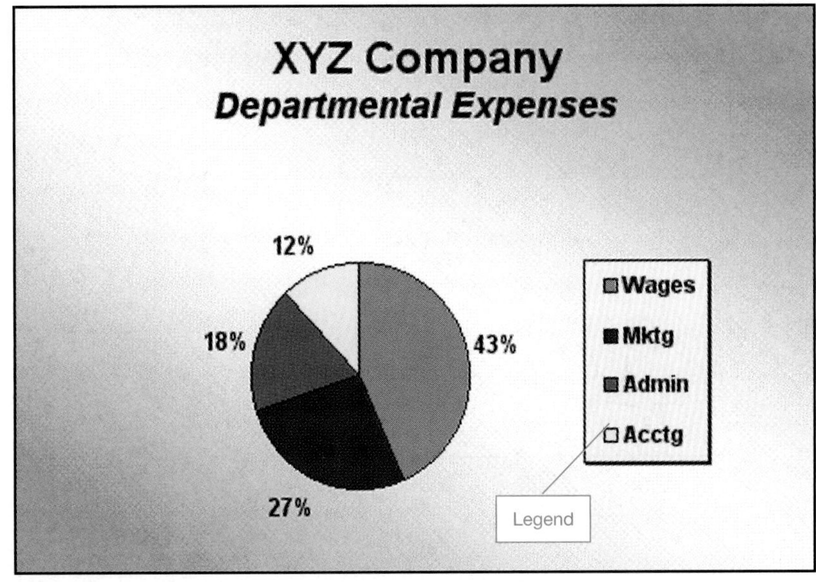

Figure 4.25
A pie chart

- ***Scatter Plot Charts*** **XY charts,** which are commonly referred to as **scatter plot diagrams,** show how one or more data elements relate to another data element. Although they look much like line charts, XY charts show the correlation between elements and include a numeric scale along both the X and Y axes. The XY chart in Figure 4.26 shows that worker productivity diminishes as stress levels increase.

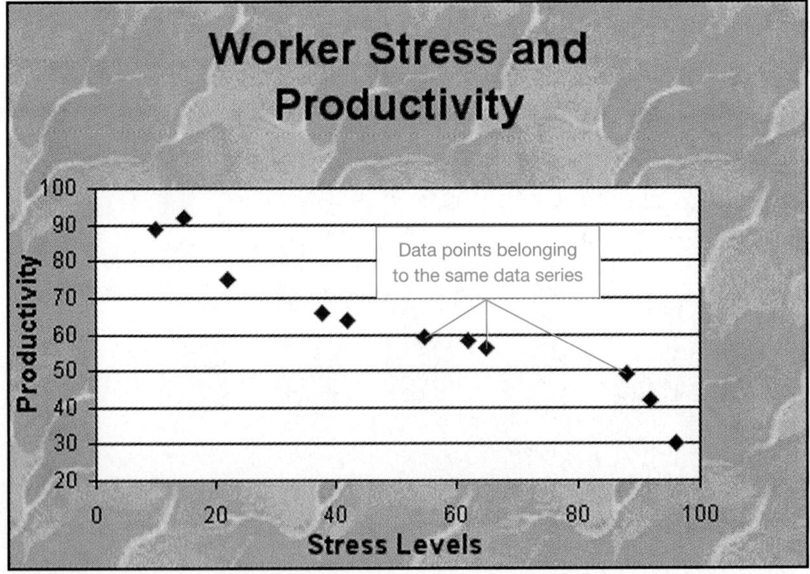

Figure 4.26
An XY chart

There are two methods for creating a chart in Excel, differing primarily in the way the chart is stored and printed. First, you can create a new chart as a separate sheet in a workbook. This method works well for printing full-page charts and for creating computer-based presentations or electronic slide shows. Second, you can create an **embedded chart** that is stored on the worksheet. Embed a chart when you want to view or print the chart alongside the worksheet data. Whichever method you choose, you can use the step-by-step features in Excel's **Chart Wizard** to construct the chart from existing worksheet data.

In this module, you learn how to create and print an embedded chart.

4.3.1 Creating a Chart Using the Chart Wizard

feature

Creating a chart in Excel is surprisingly easy. To begin, select a range of cells that you want to plot and then launch the Chart Wizard. The wizard examines the selected range and then displays its dialog box. Make your selections, such as choosing a chart type, and proceed through the steps to embed the chart on the worksheet. An embedded chart is actually placed over—not entered into—a cell range. Once it is embedded, you can move, size, and delete the chart.

method

- SELECT: the cell range to plot in a chart
- CLICK: Chart Wizard button ( )
- Complete the steps in the Chart Wizard.

practice

You will now create and embed a new chart onto a worksheet.

1. Open the data file named EX0430 to display the worksheet in Figure 4.27.

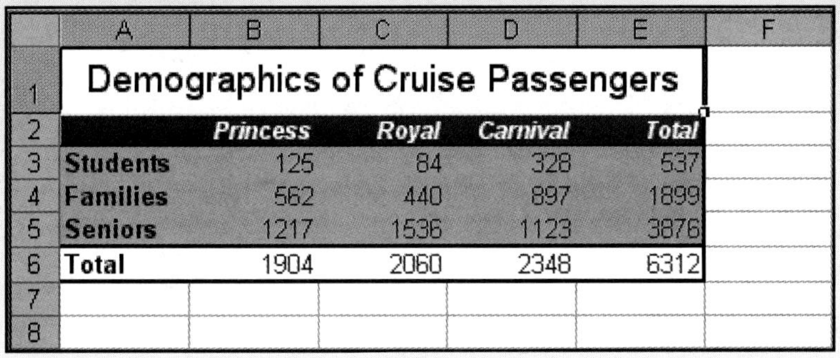

Figure 4.27

Opening the EX0430 workbook

	A	B	C	D	E	F
1	Demographics of Cruise Passengers					
2		Princess	Royal	Carnival	Total	
3	Students	125	84	328	537	
4	Families	562	440	897	1899	
5	Seniors	1217	1536	1123	3876	
6	Total	1904	2060	2348	6312	
7						
8						

2. Save the workbook as "Cruising" to your personal storage location.
3. Let's plot the worksheet's demographic data. To begin, select both the column headings and the data area:
   SELECT: cell range from A2 to D5
   (*Caution:* Do not include the title in cell A1 or the "Total" cells in row 6 or column E in the range selection.)
4. To start the Chart Wizard:
   CLICK: Chart Wizard button ( ) on the Standard toolbar
   The Chart Wizard dialog appears, as shown in Figure 4.28.

Excel

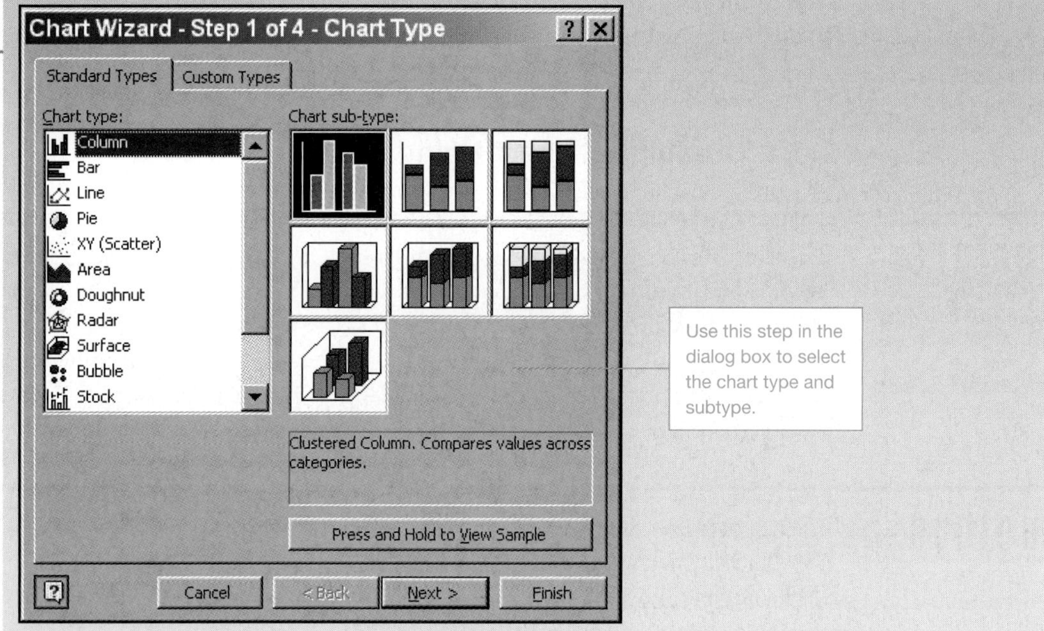

Figure 4.28

Chart Wizard: Step 1 of 4

5. To see a sample of how Excel will plot this data:
CLICK: "Press and Hold to View Sample" command button
(*Note:* You must hold down the left mouse button to see the chart inside the *Sample* preview window. When finished viewing, release the mouse button.)

6. Let's select a different chart subtype that amalgamates (adds together) the data series in a column. Do the following:
SELECT: Stacked Column in the *Chart sub-type* area
When you click on a chart subtype, the chart's name and description appear above the "Press and Hold to View Sample" command button.)

7. Once again, preview a sample of the chart:
CLICK: "Press and Hold to View Sample" command button

8. To continue creating the chart:
CLICK: Next > to proceed to Step 2 of 4
Your screen should now appear similar to Figure 4.29.

Chart Wizard: Step 2 of 4

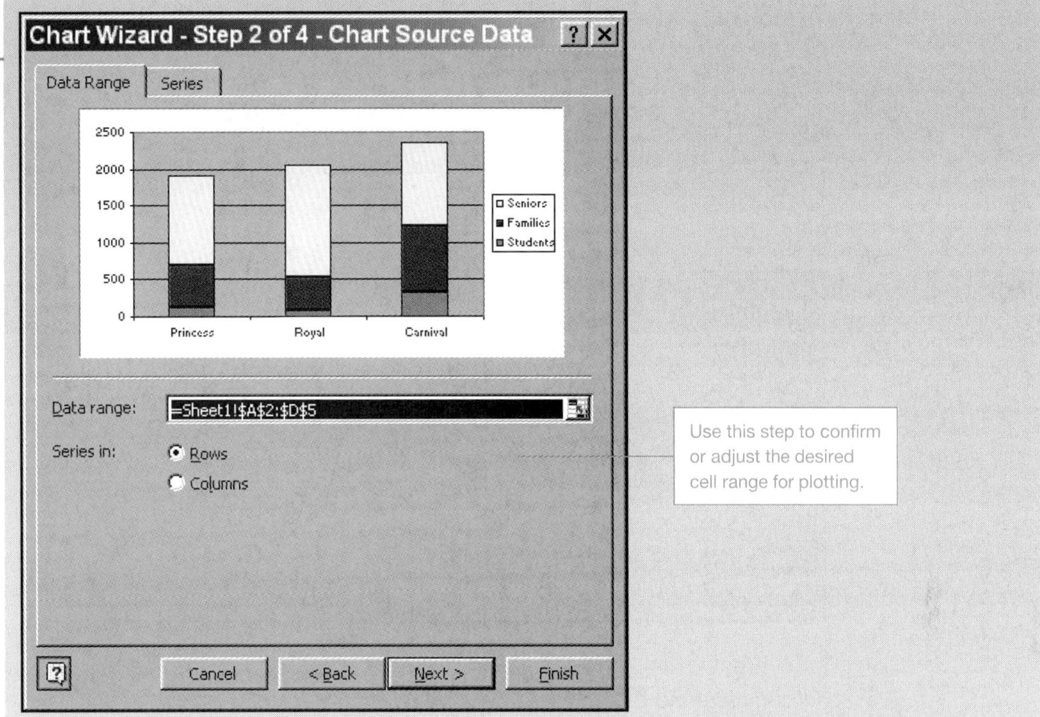

9. Because you selected the data range prior to launching the Chart Wizard, you can accept the default entry in Step 2 and proceed:
   CLICK: Next > to proceed to Step 3 of 4

10. In Step 3 of 4 of the Chart Wizard:
    TYPE: **Cruise Lines** into the *Category (X)* axis text box
    TYPE: **Passengers** into the *Value (Y)* axis text box
    (*Hint:* Click the I-beam mouse pointer into a text box and then type the appropriate text. You can also press TAB to move forward through the text boxes.) Notice that the preview area is immediately updated to display the new titles, as shown in Figure 4.30.

Figure 4.30

Chart Wizard: Step 3 of 4

Use this step of the Chart Wizard to add and customize titles, gridlines, legends, and other chart elements.

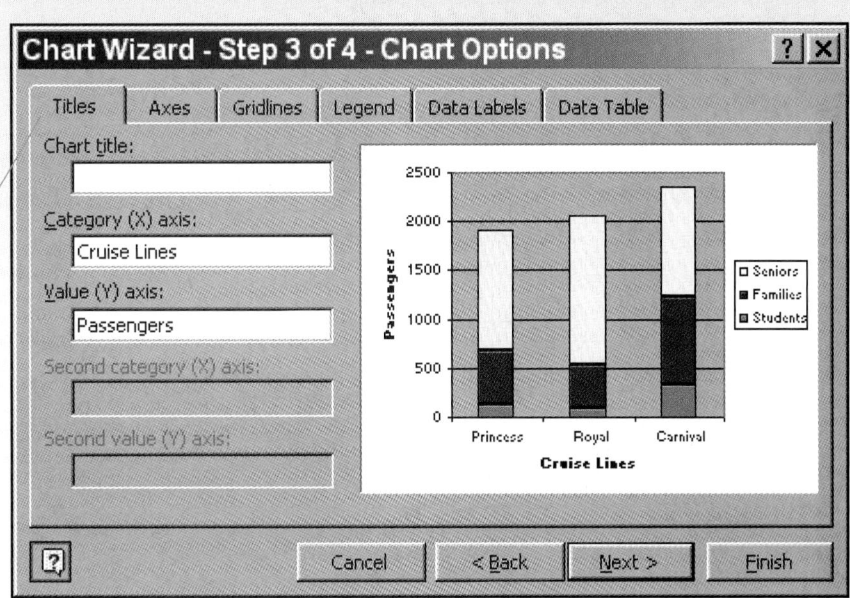

11. To proceed to the final step:
CLICK: Next >

12. In Step 4 of 4, you specify where you want to store the chart. To create an embedded chart:
SELECT: *As object in* option button, as shown in Figure 4.31
Notice that the current worksheet's name, Sheet1, already appears in the drop-down list box next to the option button.

Figure 4.31

Chart Wizard: Step 4 of 4

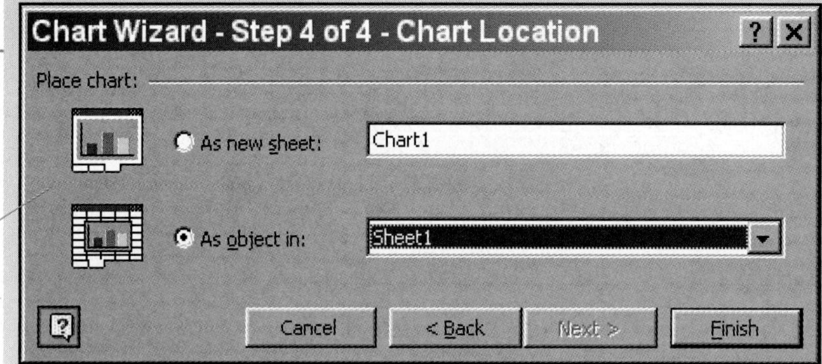

Use this step to specify the target location for the new chart.

13. To complete the Chart Wizard:
CLICK: Finish
The embedded chart appears in the application window, as shown in Figure 4.32. (*Note:* You may also see Excel's Chart toolbar appear.)

Figure 4.32

Adding a chart as an embedded object to the worksheet

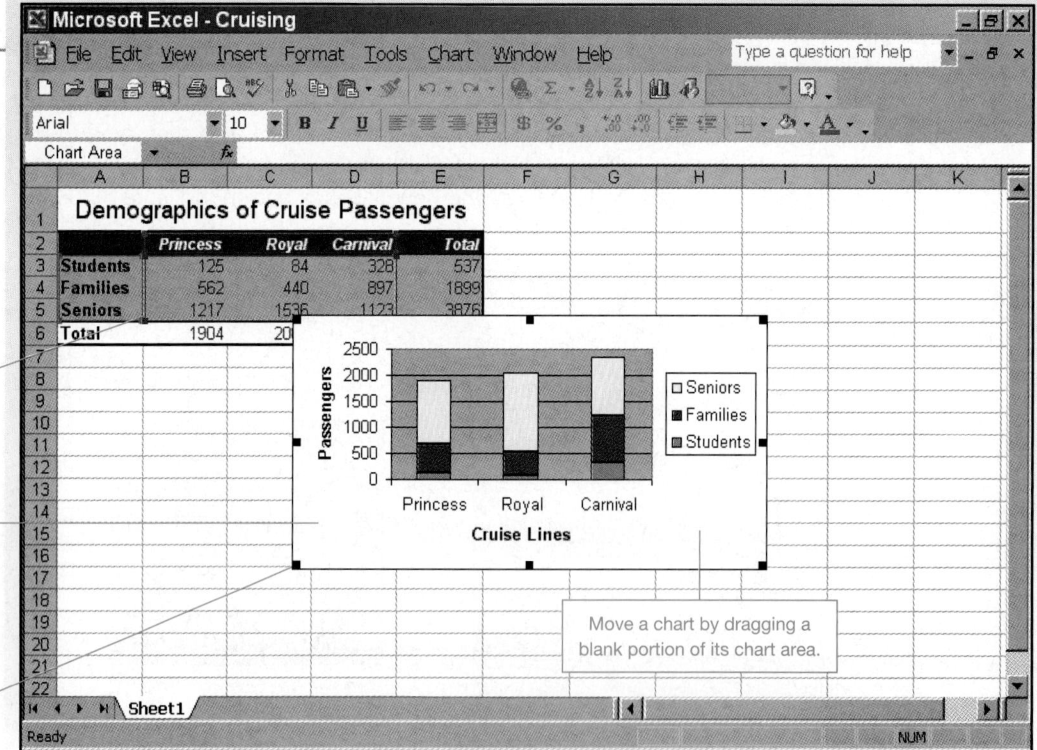

Excel's Range Finder displays the range plotted in the selected chart.

Embedded chart object floats above the cells in the worksheet.

Sizing handles appear when the chart object is selected.

14. The black selection handles that surround the chart indicate that it is currently selected. Using the mouse, you can size the embedded chart by dragging these handles. On your own, practice sizing the chart.

15. You can also move the chart by dragging the object using the mouse. Position the white mouse arrow over a blank portion of the chart's background area. Then, drag the chart into position. Practice moving and sizing the chart to cover the range from cell A8 to E20, immediately beneath the data area.

16. To return focus to the worksheet:
CLICK: any visible cell in the worksheet area, such as cell A1
Notice that the selection boxes around the chart disappear.

17. The embedded chart is dynamically linked to the information stored in the worksheet. To demonstrate, let's update the "Carnival" column in the embedded chart:
SELECT: cell D5
TYPE: **400**
PRESS: ENTER
The chart is updated immediately to reflect the new data, as shown in Figure 4.33.

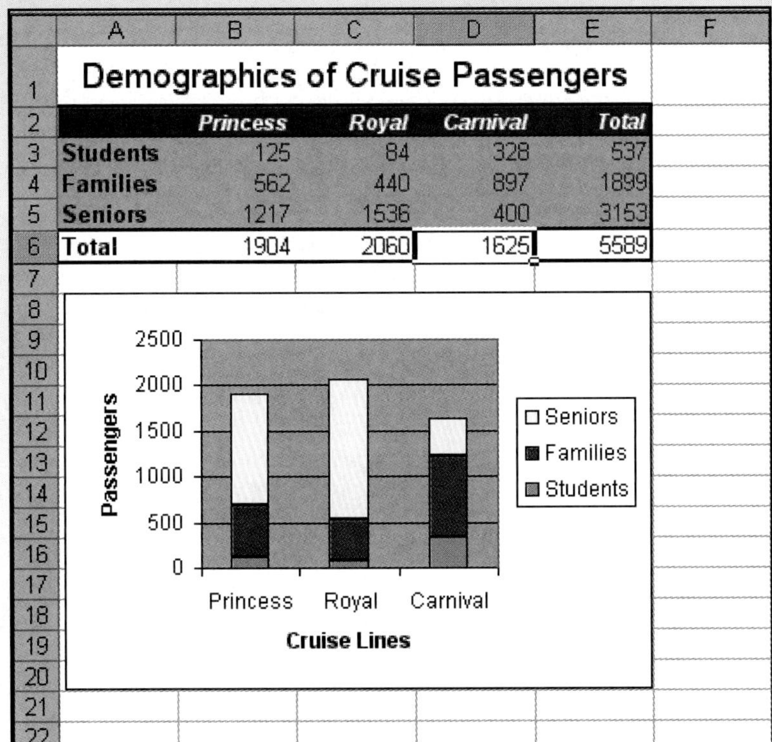

Figure 4.33
Manipulating an embedded chart on a worksheet

18. Save the workbook and keep it open for use in the next lesson.

4.3.2 Previewing and Printing an Embedded Chart

feature

The primary reason for embedding a chart on a worksheet is to view and print it alongside its worksheet data. You must ensure, however, that the print area (or range) includes the entire chart object. As before, remember to preview your worksheet and chart prior to printing.

method

- SELECT: a cell range that includes the chart
- CHOOSE: File, Print Area, Set Print Area
- CHOOSE: File, Print Preview

or

- CHOOSE: File, Print

practice

You now preview and print an embedded chart along with its worksheet data. Ensure that you have completed the previous lesson and that the "Cruising" workbook is displayed.

1. To print the worksheet and embedded chart on the same page:
   SELECT: cell range from A1 to F21
   (*Note:* Depending on the size and placement of your chart object, you may need to increase or decrease this print range. Make sure that the entire object is covered in the highlighted range.)
2. CHOOSE: File, Print Area, Set Print Area
3. To preview the worksheet and chart:
   CLICK: Print Preview button
4. To zoom in on the preview window:
   CLICK: Zoom command button
5. On your own, scroll the preview window so it appears similar to Figure 4.34. Notice that the chart is printed immediately and seamlessly below the worksheet data. (*Note:* If you have specified a color printer as your default, the worksheet and chart will appear in color in Print Preview.)

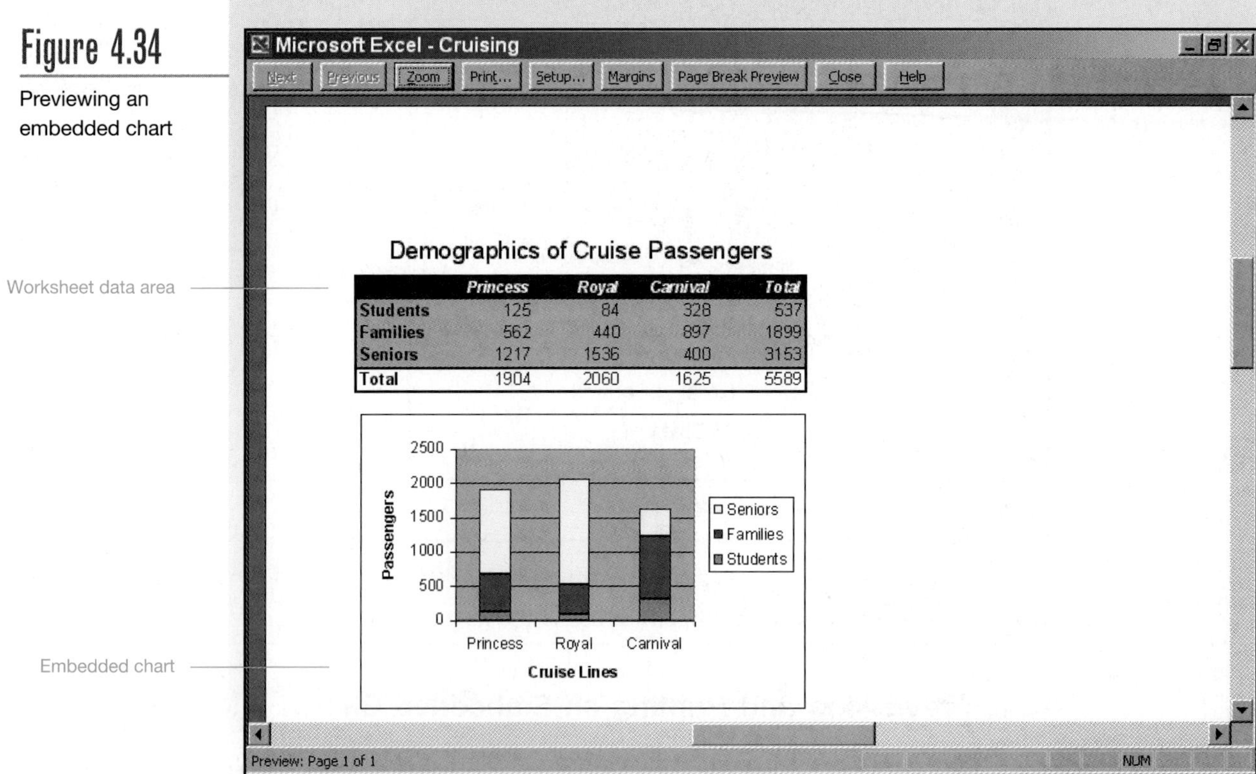

Figure 4.34

Previewing an embedded chart

6. To print the chart from the Preview window:
CLICK: Print command button

7. If you don't have access to a printer, click the Cancel command button and proceed to the next step. If you have a printer attached to your computer and want to print this chart, do the following:
CLICK: OK command button

8. To remove the highlighting from the worksheet area:
CLICK: cell A1
(*Hint:* You may have noticed that we often select cell A1 prior to saving the workbook. The reason is that Excel saves and restores the cell pointer's position for the next time you open the workbook.)

9. Save and then close the workbook.

10. Exit Microsoft Excel.

4.3. What must you do when selecting the print range for a worksheet that contains an embedded chart?

Chapter summary

Excel provides powerful tools for analyzing and summarizing data. The ability to name cells and ranges for use in constructing expressions and navigating the worksheet increases accuracy and efficiency. Formula expressions may contain relative or absolute cell references. Specifying an absolute cell address by adding dollar signs ($) serves to anchor a cell reference to an exact location on the worksheet. The default is a relative cell address, which Excel can adjust when copied to new locations in the worksheet.

Built-in functions, such as SUM and AVERAGE, are used as shortcuts to perform complex or lengthy calculations. Use the Insert Function dialog box to locate and select a function. Assistance in entering the arguments for a function is available in the Function Arguments dialog box.

The Chart Wizard makes it easy to create a chart and embed it in a worksheet, where the chart can print alongside its data.

Command Summary

Many of the commands and procedures appearing in this chapter are summarized in the following table.

Skill Set	To Perform This Task	Do the Following
Working with Cells and Cell Data	Name a cell range	SELECT: the desired range CLICK: in the Name box TYPE: **range name**
	Create range names from labels appearing on the worksheet	SELECT: the desired range CHOOSE: Insert, Name, Create

Skill Set	To Perform This Task	Do the Following
	Modify and delete range names	CHOOSE: Insert, Name, Define
	Paste a list of range names onto the worksheet	CHOOSE: Insert, Name, Paste
Creating and Revising Formulas	Modify and use cell references (absolute, relative, and mixed)	SELECT: the desired cell CLICK: in the cell address in the Formula bar PRESS: F4 to apply reference type
	Recalculate formulas in a worksheet	PRESS: F9 (CALC key)
	Use the Insert Function dialog box to enter a function and its arguments	CLICK: Insert Function button (fx) SELECT: a category and function
	Use basic functions: • Sum a range of values • Average a range of values • Count the numeric and date values in a range • Find the lowest value in a range • Find the highest value in a range	 =**SUM(range)** =**AVERAGE(range)** =**COUNT(range)** =**MIN(range)** =**MAX(range)**
	Use date functions: • Enter the current date and time • Enter today's date	 =**NOW()** =**TODAY()**
Creating and Modifying Graphics	Use the Chart Wizard to create a chart	SELECT: the cell range to plot CLICK: Chart Wizard button
	Preview and print an embedded chart	SELECT: the desired range CHOOSE: File, Print Area, Set Print Area CLICK: Print Preview or Print

Key Terms

This section specifies page references for the key terms identified in this chapter. For a complete list of definitions, refer to the Glossary at the back of this learning guide.

absolute cell address, *p. EX 167*
arguments, *p. EX 171*
bar chart, *p. EX 183*
Chart Wizard, *p. EX 185*
column chart, *p. EX 183*
embedded chart, *p. EX 184*
functions, *p. EX 171*
line chart, *p. EX 182*
mixed cell address, *p. EX 167*
natural language formula, *p. EX 169*
pie chart, *p. EX 183*
range name, *p. EX 162*
relative cell address, *p. EX 167*
scatter plot diagram, *p. EX 184*
syntax, *p. EX 171*
XY charts, *p. EX 184*

Chapter quiz

Short Answer

1. Why would you want to name a range of cells?
2. How do you place a list of range names into the worksheet?
3. Name the two primary types of cell references and explain how they differ.
4. In order for natural language formulas to work effectively, how should the worksheet be organized?
5. Which function would you use to extract the highest value from a range named "salary"? How would you enter the function?
6. Which function would you use to place only the current time in your worksheet? What else might you want to do?
7. What is the name of the dialog box that you can use to select functions from categories? How do you access this dialog box?
8. What is the name of the dialog box that can help you to enter a function's arguments correctly? How do you access this dialog box?
9. Describe the four steps in creating a chart using the Chart Wizard dialog boxes.
10. What are the black boxes called that surround an embedded chart? What are they used for?

True/False

1. ____ Range names that you create use absolute cell references.
2. ____ Cell addresses that you enter into formulas use, by default, relative cell references.
3. ____ The "&s" in the cell reference &D&5 indicate an absolute cell reference.
4. ____ You cannot mix labels, such as "Revenue," with cell references in a natural language formula.
5. ____ You enter a function using parentheses instead of the equal sign.
6. ____ The SUM function appears in the Statistical function category of the Insert Function dialog box.
7. ____ You must use the Function Arguments dialog box to enter the COUNT function.
8. ____ The TODAY function updates the computer's internal clock to the current date and time.
9. ____ A pie chart shows the proportions of individual components compared to the total.
10. ____ You can move and size an embedded chart once it is placed on the worksheet.

Multiple Choice

1. What menu command allows you to create range names using the labels that already appear in the worksheet?

a. Edit, Name, Create
b. Range, Name, Create
c. Insert, Name, Create
d. Insert, Name, Define

2. Which of the following symbols precedes an absolute cell reference?

a. $
b. @
c. &
d. #

3. In Edit mode, which key do you press to change a cell address to being absolute, relative, or mixed?

a. F2
b. F3
c. F4
d. F9

4. Which key do you press to recalculate or update a worksheet?

a. F2
b. F3
c. F4
d. F9

5. Which is the correct expression for adding the values stored in the cell range from A1 to A20?

a. **=ADD(A1+A20)**
b. **=SUM(A1:A20)**
c. **=SUM(A1+A20)**
d. **=AutoSUM(A1,A20)**

6. Which is the correct expression for determining the average of a range named "Units"?

a. **=AVG(Units)**
b. **=UNITS(Average)**
c. **=AVERAGE(Units)**
d. **=SUM(Units/Average)**

7. What does the COUNT function actually count?

a. All of the cells in a range.
b. All of the cells containing data in a range.
c. Only those cells containing text and numbers.
d. Only those cells containing numeric or date values.

8. Which button do you click to display the Insert Function dialog box?

a. fx
b.
c.
d. Σ

9. What is the name of the step-by-step charting tool provided by Excel?

a. Chart Master
b. Chart Wizard
c. Plot Master
d. Plot Wizard

10. A chart may be created as a separate chart sheet or as an embedded object. In which step of the Chart Wizard do you specify how a chart is created and stored?

a. Step 1
b. Step 2
c. Step 3
d. Step 4

Hands-On exercises

easy

1. Brentwood Academy: Enrollment Statistics

In this exercise, you practice creating and working with named cell ranges in constructing formulas.

1. Open the data file named EX04HE01.
2. Save the workbook as "Enrollment" to your personal storage location.
3. To begin, let's name a cell range on the worksheet:
   SELECT: cell B8
   CLICK: in the Name box
   TYPE: **Total**
   PRESS: ENTER
   You have successfully named this cell "Total."
4. To create a set of range names using existing worksheet labels:
   SELECT: cell range from A2 to B7
   CHOOSE: Insert, Name, Create
   Your worksheet should now appear similar to Figure 4.35.

Figure 4.35

Naming a cell range

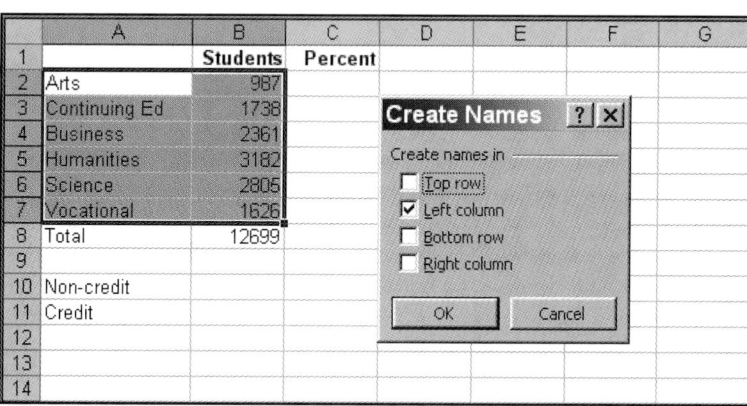

5. To accept the default selection of the *Left column* check box:
   CLICK: OK command button
6. To view the list of range names that you just created:
   SELECT: cell E2
   CHOOSE: Insert, Name, Paste
   CLICK: Paste List command button
   SELECT: cell A1 to remove the highlighting
   (*Note:* The list is pasted in alphabetical order.)
7. Now let's enter a formula using the named cell ranges:
   SELECT: cell B10
   TYPE: =
   CLICK: cell B3
   Notice that "Continuing_Ed" appears in the Formula bar in place of the cell B3 reference.

8. To continue the formula:
   TYPE: +
   CLICK: cell B7

9. To complete the formula entry:
   CLICK: Enter button (✓)
   The expression now reads "=Continuing_Ed+Vocational" in the Formula bar.

10. Now let's type an expression into cell B11 that totals the rest of the departments not included in the previous formula:
    SELECT: cell B11
    TYPE: **=Arts+Business+Humanities+Science**
    Your screen should now appear similar to Figure 4.36.

Figure 4.36

Entering a formula using named ranges

TODAY ▾ X ✓ fx =Arts+Business+Humanities+Science

	A	B	C	D	E	F	G
1		**Students**	**Percent**				
2	Arts	987			Arts	=Sheet1!$B$2	
3	Continuing Ed	1738			Business	=Sheet1!$B$4	
4	Business	2361			Continuing	=Sheet1!$B$3	
5	Humanities	3182			Humanitie:	=Sheet1!$B$5	
6	Science	2805			Science	=Sheet1!$B$6	
7	Vocational	1626			Total	=Sheet1!$B$8	
8	Total	12699			Vocational	=Sheet1!$B$7	
9							
10	Non-credit	3364					
11	Credit	=Arts+Business+Humanities+Science					
12							
13							

11. To complete the formula entry:
    PRESS: ENTER

12. Let's calculate the enrollment percentage for each department. Starting in cell C2, you will enter a formula that can be later used for copying. To do so, you need to specify an absolute cell reference for the Total value and a relative cell reference for the Arts value. To illustrate:
    SELECT: cell C2
    TYPE: **=b2/Total**
    PRESS: ENTER
    (*Note:* A range name provides an absolute cell reference. Therefore, you cannot use the range name "Arts" in the formula expression.)

13. To copy the formula to the remaining departments:
    SELECT: cell C2
    DRAG: the fill handle for cell C2 to cell C8
    (*Hint:* The fill handle for a cell or cell range is the small black box in the bottom right-hand corner of the range selection.)

14. On your own, select the cells in the range C2:C8 and view the contents in the Formula bar. Notice that the relative cell references (B2, B3,... B8) adjust automatically. The range name "Total" remained absolute.

15. Save and then close the "Enrollment" workbook.

2. Top Picks Video: Rental Category Chart

You will now practice creating a chart using Excel's Chart Wizard.

1. Open the data file named EX04HE02.
2. Save the workbook as "Video Chart" to your personal storage location.
3. To begin, select the cell range that contains the data for plotting:
   SELECT: cell range A3 to G5
   Notice that you did not include the "Total" row or "Total" column.
4. Launch the Chart Wizard:
   CLICK: Chart Wizard button (icon) on the Standard toolbar
5. To display the two categories, New Release and Weekly, side by side:
   SELECT: Column as the *Chart type*
   SELECT: Clustered Column as the *Chart sub-type*
   CLICK: Next > to proceed to Step 2 of 4
6. To accept the default range selection and continue:
   CLICK: Next > to proceed to Step 3 of 4
7. On the *Titles* tab of Step 3 in the Chart Wizard:
   TYPE: **Income by Category** into the *Chart title* text box
   TYPE: **Movie Category** into the *Category (X)* axis text box
   TYPE: **Rental Income** into the *Value (Y)* axis text box
   Your screen should now appear similar to Figure 4.37.

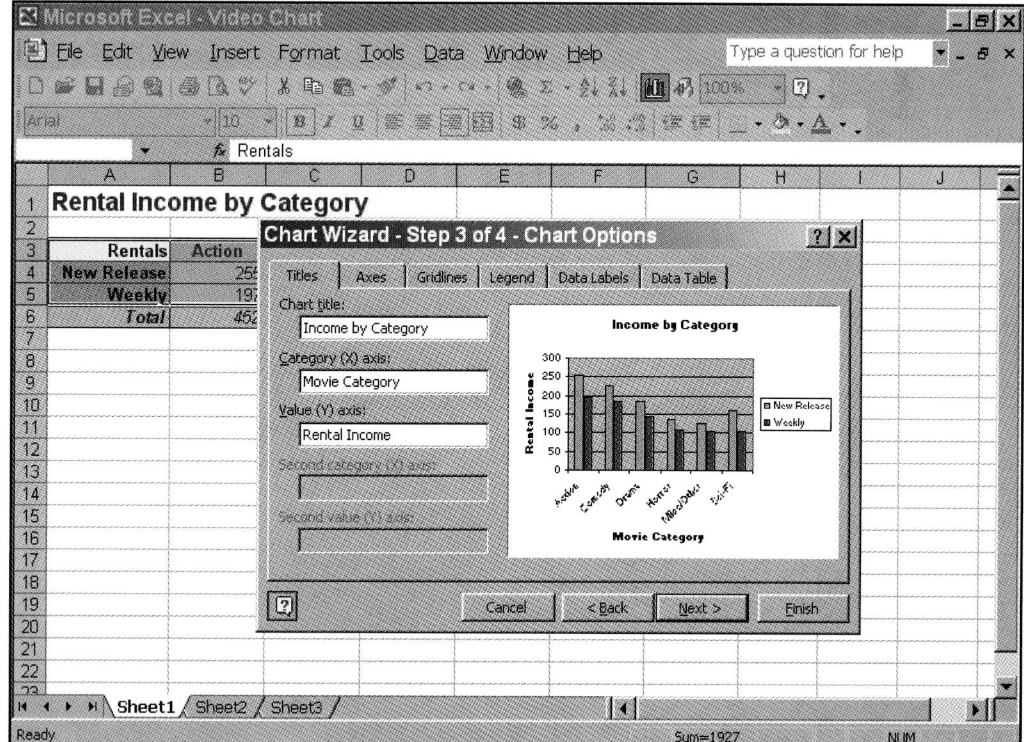

Figure 4.37

Completing Step 3 of the Chart Wizard dialog box

8. To proceed to the last step:
   CLICK: Next >

9. You can now specify the target location for the chart. To do so:
   SELECT: *As object in* option button, if it is not already selected
   CLICK: Finish
   The chart object appears in the middle of the application window.

10. To move the embedded chart, position the mouse pointer on an empty portion of the chart's background. Then do the following:
    DRAG: the chart below the data area

11. To size the embedded chart, position the mouse pointer over the selection handle in the bottom right-hand corner. Then:
    DRAG: the selection handle down and to the right to enlarge the chart

12. On your own, finalize the size and placement of the embedded chart so that it appears similar to Figure 4.38.

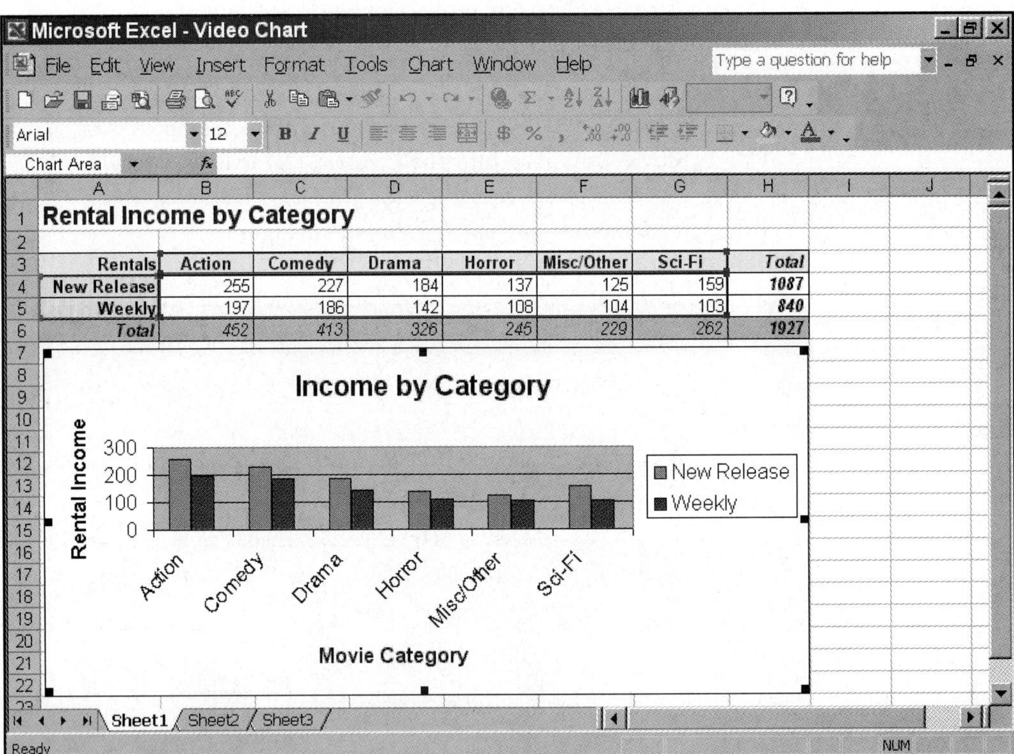

Figure 4.38

Sizing and moving an embedded chart

13. You've just received word that some information in the worksheet has been entered incorrectly. Study the Misc/Other category columns on the chart. Now, update the worksheet:
    SELECT: cell F4
    TYPE: **104**
    PRESS: ⬇
    TYPE: **175**
    PRESS: ENTER
    Notice that the chart has been updated to reflect the new values.

14. Save and then close the "Video Chart" workbook.

3. Staples Foods: Daily Production

You will now practice using some of Excel's built-in functions in an existing worksheet. You will also use the AutoFill feature to create a series and then the Fill command to copy formulas.

1. Open the data file named EX04HE03 to display the worksheet in Figure 4.39.

Figure 4.39

Opening the EX04HE03 workbook

	A	B	C	D	E	F
1	Daily Production					
2		Corn	Peas	Beans	Other	
3	Monday	4500	1580	2600	3300	
4		4750	1725	2350	3150	
5		3800	1565	2975	2590	
6		2600	1520	2845	2810	
7		3375	1635	2100	3050	
8						
9	Minimum					
10	Maximum					
11	Average					
12						
13	Total					
14						
15						

2. Save the workbook as "Staples Daily" in your personal storage location.
3. Use the fill handle to complete a series listing the days of the week (Monday through Friday) in cells A3 to A7.
4. In cell B9, enter the following function to calculate the minimum production amount for corn:
   TYPE: **=min(b3:b7)**
   PRESS: ENTER
5. Using the same approach as before, enter formulas in cells B10 and B11 to calculate the maximum and average production for corn.
6. Select the cell range from B9 to E11 and then use the Edit, Fill, Right command to copy the formulas to columns C, D, and E.
7. Select the cell range from A2 to E7 and then use the Insert, Name, Create command to assign range names using the existing row and column labels.
8. To calculate the total production for Corn:
   SELECT: cell B13
   TYPE: **=sum(corn)**
   PRESS: ENTER
9. Using the same technique, calculate the totals for the Peas, Beans, and Other columns. (*Note:* You cannot use the Edit, Fill, Right command since the named range "Corn" uses an absolute cell reference.)
10. Figure 4.40 shows the completed worksheet. Save and then close the workbook.

Excel

Figure 4.40

Completing the Staples Daily workbook

	A	B	C	D	E	F
1	Daily Production					
2		Corn	Peas	Beans	Other	
3	Monday	4500	1580	2600	3300	
4	Tuesday	4750	1725	2350	3150	
5	Wednesday	3800	1565	2975	2590	
6	Thursday	2600	1520	2845	2810	
7	Friday	3375	1635	2100	3050	
8						
9	Minimum	2600	1520	2100	2590	
10	Maximum	4750	1725	2975	3300	
11	Average	3805	1605	2574	2980	
12						
13	Total	19025	8025	12870	14900	
14						
15						

moderate 

4. Sutton House Realty: Mortgage Rate Chart

In this exercise, you create an embedded chart and then print it alongside the worksheet data.

1. Open the data file named EX04HE04.
2. Save the workbook as "Mortgage Chart" to your personal storage location.
3. Select the cell range from A2 to G8.
4. Launch the Chart Wizard.
5. In the *Chart type* and *Chart sub-type* list boxes, select a line chart with markers displayed at each data value, as shown in Figure 4.41. Then proceed to the next step.

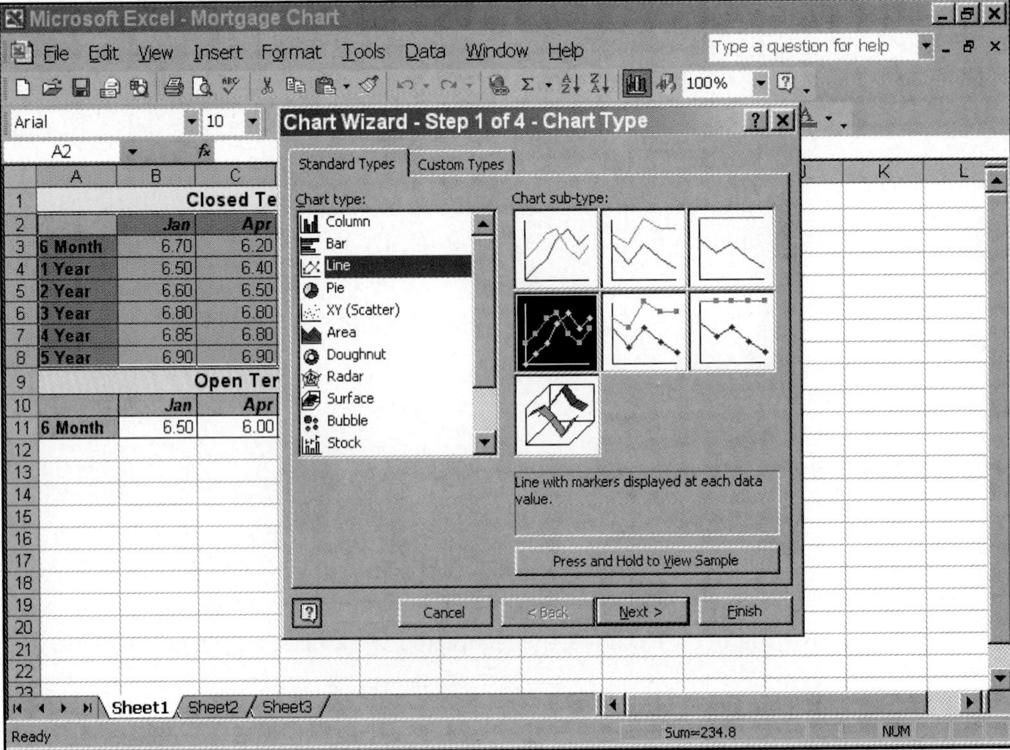

Figure 4.41

Selecting a type and sub-type for the chart

6. Accept the selected cell range for plotting and proceed to the third step.
7. In Step 3 of the Chart Wizard, add the title "Average Mortgage Rates" to appear at the top of the chart. Then proceed to the next step.
8. Save the chart as an object in Sheet1 and then click the Finish command button.
9. Size and move the embedded chart so that it covers the range from cell A13 to G27, as shown in Figure 4.42.

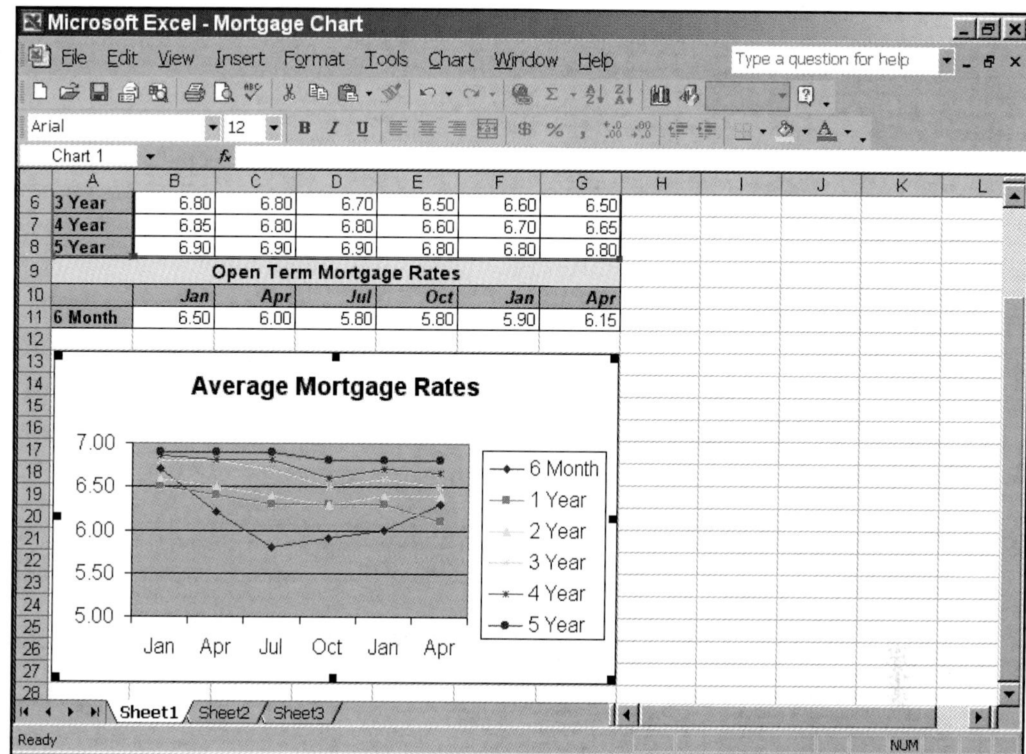

Figure 4.42

Sizing and positioning an embedded chart

10. Set the print area to cover the range from A1 to H28.
11. Preview and then print the selected print area.
12. Save and then close the "Mortgage Chart" workbook.

difficult 

5. On Your Own: Auto Fuel Comparison

This exercise lets you practice naming ranges and entering functions. To begin, open the EX04HE05 workbook and then save it as "Auto Fuel" to your personal storage location.

To begin, let's create some range names. Assign the name "Capacity" to the cell range B2:B7. Assign the name "City" to the cell range C2:C7. Assign the name "Hwy" to the cell range D2:D7. Paste a list of the range names in column F. In row 8, calculate the average for each column using their respective range names and the AVERAGE function. For more practice, enter a function in cell B10 that returns a count of the number of numerical entries in the "Capacity" range. In cell C10, display the minimum miles per gallon city rating. In cell D10, display the maximum miles per gallon highway rating. Then, put descriptive labels above each calculation in row 9. Your worksheet should appear similar to Figure 4.43.

When you are finished, save and then close the "Auto Fuel" workbook.

Figure 4.43

Completing the Auto Fuel workbook

	A	B	C	D	E	F	G	H
1	Make and Model	Fuel Capacity	MPG (City)	MPG (Hwy)				
2	Aston Martin DB7	23.5	14	20		Capacity	=Sheet1!$B$2:$B$7	
3	Chevrolet Corvette	19.1	18	27		City	=Sheet1!$C$2:$C$7	
4	Ferrari F50	27.7	8	11		Hwy	=Sheet1!$D$2:$D$7	
5	Jaguar XJR	21.4	16	21				
6	Lamborghini Diablo	26.0	9	14				
7	Porsche 911 Carrera	17.2	19	32				
8	Average	22.48333333	14	20.83333333				
9		Count	Min Result	Max Result				
10		6	8	32				
11								

difficult 

6. On Your Own: Personal Expense Chart

For additional practice creating charts, open the EX04HE06 data file. Before continuing, save the workbook as "Expense Chart" to your personal storage location. Then complete the worksheet by inputting your monthly expenses into the appropriate cells.

Using the Chart Wizard, create a pie chart of these expenses. Do not add a title to the chart and save it as an embedded object in the worksheet. Once it appears on the worksheet, size the chart so that the information is easily read. Position the chart to the right of the worksheet data. Print the worksheet data and the chart on the same page. Remember to use the Set Print Area command and Print Preview to ensure that your settings are correct. When you are satisfied with the results, send the worksheet and embedded chart to the printer.

Save and then close the "Expense Chart" workbook. Then, exit Excel.

Case Problems

Prairie Soccer Association

The Prairie Soccer Association is an elite soccer league that is just finishing its current season. As one of the many volunteers that keep the PSA going, Brad Stafford has the task of summarizing various statistics for inclusion into the season-end newsletter. Brad has recently learned how to use ranges and functions in Excel and now wants to use them to produce worksheets that can be incorporated into the newsletter.

In the following case problems, assume the role of Brad and perform the same steps that he identifies. You may want to re-read the chapter opening before proceeding.

1. It's 8:00 P.M. on a Sunday evening when Brad decides to sit down at his home computer and spend some time working on the PSA newsletter. After loading Excel, he opens the EX04CP01 workbook that he has been using to project next year's attendance levels. Brad wants to communicate the fine growth in attendance that the PSA has been experiencing. Before continuing, he saves the workbook as "PSA Attendance" to his

personal storage location.

Having learned about range names, Brad's first step is to use the Name box and apply a range name of "Factor" to cell C12. Then, he selects the cell range A2:B10 and uses the Insert, Name, Create command to create range names from the selection's row and column labels. To verify that the range names are correct, Brad selects cell E1 in the worksheet and then pastes a list of all existing named ranges. After returning to cell A1, Brad's worksheet appears similar to Figure 4.44.

Figure 4.44

Pasting range names into the worksheet

	A	B	C	D	E	F	G	H
1		Attendance			Bristol	=Sheet1!$B$3		
2		*Current*	*Projected*		Creston	=Sheet1!$B$10		
3	Bristol	39,526			Current	=Sheet1!$B$3:$B$10		
4	Riverbend	32,895			Dupont	=Sheet1!$B$5		
5	Dupont	28,691			Factor	=Sheet1!$C$12		
6	Midlands	30,254			Midlands	=Sheet1!$B$6		
7	Pinegrove	33,672			Pinegrove	=Sheet1!$B$7		
8	Silverdale	25,637			Riverbend	=Sheet1!$B$4		
9	Steele	23,516			Silverdale	=Sheet1!$B$8		
10	Creston	24,583			Steele	=Sheet1!$B$9		
11								
12		Growth Factor:	7%					
13								
14								

Brad remembers that to calculate next year's attendance using a growth factor formula, he will have to use both relative and absolute cell addresses. Otherwise, when he performs a copy operation, the formula's cell addresses won't be adjusted automatically. Brad wants to ensure that the formulas always use the value in cell C12 as the growth factor. Fortunately, Brad also remembers that a named range is, by default, an absolute reference. Therefore, using a relative cell address and the "Factor" range name, he can complete his task. To begin, he enters the formula **=b3*(1+Factor)** into cell C3. Notice that Brad typed "b3" and not "Bristol" into the cell. (*Hint:* The range name "Bristol" refers to the absolute cell address $B$3 and not the relative cell address that is required for this calculation.) This formula calculates next year's projected attendance for Bristol.

Brad uses Excel's AutoFill feature to extend the formula in cell C3 for the rest of the teams. Finally, he uses the Format Painter to copy the numbering formats from column B to the new results in column C. Brad saves and then closes the workbook.

2. Brad Stafford is constructing a worksheet that shows the team standings at the end of the PSA's regular season play. To review the worksheet, he opens the EX04CP02 file and then saves it as "PSA Standings" to his personal storage location.

With the teams already in the proper order, Brad wants to chart their results. He selects the cell range B2:C10 and then launches the Chart Wizard. In the first step, Brad selects a "Clustered bar with a 3-D visual effect" chart. Then he clicks the Finish command button. When the embedded chart appears in the application window, Brad sizes it so that all the team names are visible on the vertical axis. He then moves the chart below row 13, as shown in Figure 4.45.

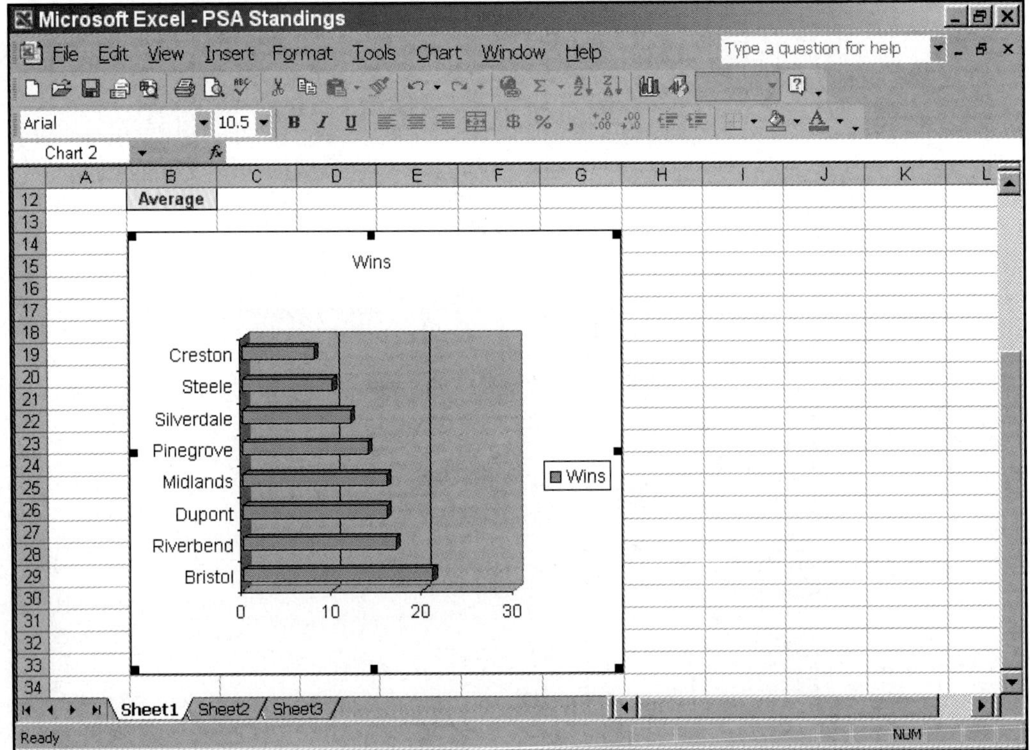

Figure 4.45

Analyzing data using an embedded chart

Continuing his work, Brad enters a formula into cell C12 that averages the values in that column. He uses the Edit, Fill, Right command to extend the formula across to column F. Finally, Brad saves, prints, and then closes the workbook.

3. With the deadline for the season-end newsletter fast approaching, Brad is determined to finish the Team Statistics worksheet. He opens the EX04CP03 data file and then saves it as "PSA Team Stats" to his personal storage location.

   After double-checking to make sure that the formulas in column D are correct, Brad copies the formula from cell D3 to the cell range D14:D21. He then uses the AutoSum button (Σ) to enter SUM functions into cells C11 and C22 that sum the goals for Offense and Defense, respectively. In column G, Brad uses Excel's built-in functions to find the highest, lowest, and average number of goals for both Offense and Defense. He names the two data ranges in column C (C3:C10 and C14:C21) and then enters the functions into the appropriate cells, as shown in Figure 4.46. When he is finished, Brad saves and then closes the workbook.

Figure 4.46

Completing the PSA Team Stats workbook

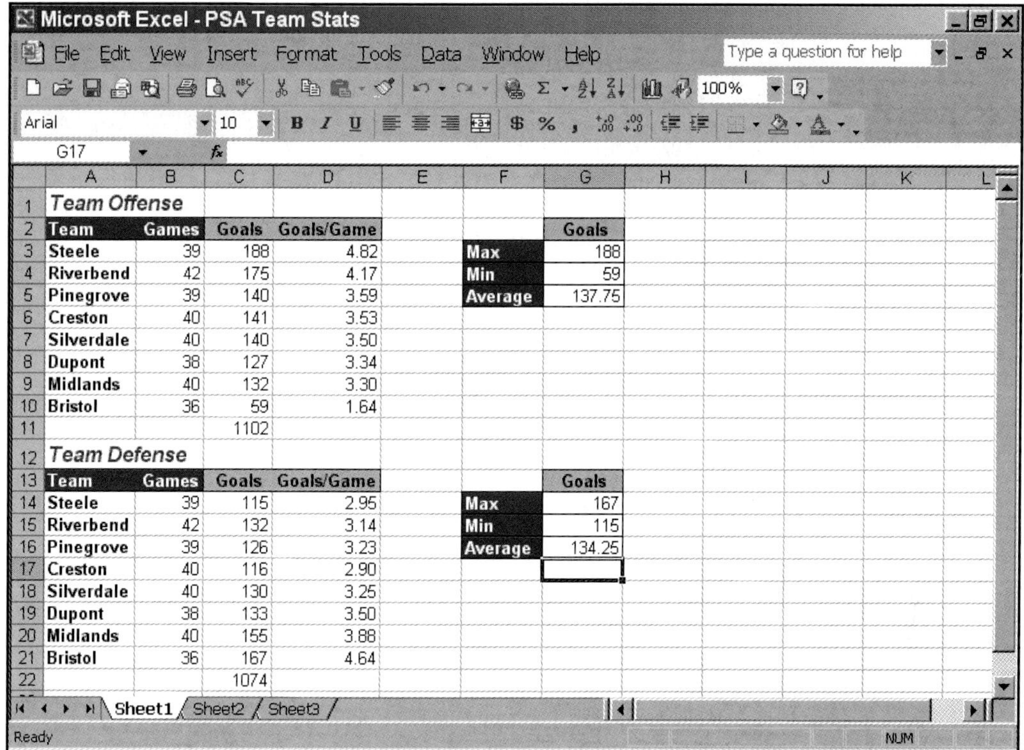

	A	B	C	D	E	F	G
1	*Team Offense*						
2	Team	Games	Goals	Goals/Game			Goals
3	Steele	39	188	4.82		Max	188
4	Riverbend	42	175	4.17		Min	59
5	Pinegrove	39	140	3.59		Average	137.75
6	Creston	40	141	3.53			
7	Silverdale	40	140	3.50			
8	Dupont	38	127	3.34			
9	Midlands	40	132	3.30			
10	Bristol	36	59	1.64			
11			1102				
12	*Team Defense*						
13	Team	Games	Goals	Goals/Game			Goals
14	Steele	39	115	2.95		Max	167
15	Riverbend	42	132	3.14		Min	115
16	Pinegrove	39	126	3.23		Average	134.25
17	Creston	40	116	2.90			
18	Silverdale	40	130	3.25			
19	Dupont	38	133	3.50			
20	Midlands	40	155	3.88			
21	Bristol	36	167	4.64			
22			1074				

4. The final worksheet that Brad needs to compile is for the "Scoring Per Half" statistics. He opens the EX04CP04 data file and saves it as "PSA Scoring" in his personal storage location.

Using one of Excel's built-in functions, Brad calculates and displays the total goals scored by the first team in column E. After entering the function, he uses the cell's fill handle to extend the formula to the rest of the teams. Next, he uses the appropriate function in row 11 to calculate the average for the first half. He formats the result to display with no decimal places and then extends the formula to cover columns C through E. Brad completes the worksheet using the MIN and MAX functions to calculate the high and low scores for each period. As before, he extends these functions to cover the remaining columns.

Satisfied with the results thus far, Brad decides to place an embedded stacked column chart under the data table. He sizes and positions the chart to appear similar to Figure 4.47, as shown on the next page.

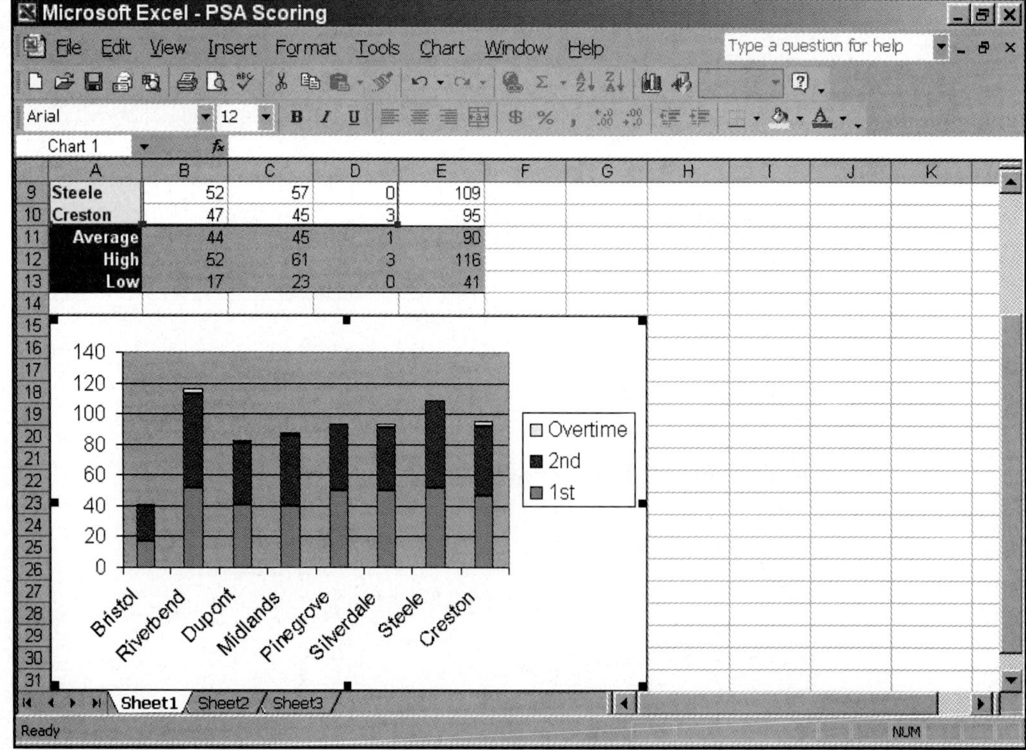

Figure 4.47

Completing the PSA Scoring workbook

Brad then previews and prints the worksheet and chart on the same page. Then he saves and closes the workbook and then exits Excel.

NOTES

NOTES

Microsoft® PowerPoint® 2002

CHAPTER 1

Creating a Presentation

CHAPTER OUTLINE

Case Study

1.1 Getting Started with PowerPoint

1.2 Starting a New Presentation

1.3 Creating a Textual Presentation

1.4 Managing Files

Chapter Summary

Chapter Quiz

Hands-On Exercises

Case Problems

PREREQUISITES

Although this chapter assumes no previous experience using Microsoft PowerPoint, you should be comfortable working with the mouse in the Microsoft Windows environment. You should be able to launch and exit programs. You should also be able to perform basic Windows file management operations, such as opening and closing documents.

LEARNING OBJECTIVES

After completing this chapter, you will be able to:

- Describe the different components of the application window
- Select commands and options using the Menu bar and right-click menus
- Begin new presentations and add slides
- Insert and format slide text
- Create, save, open, and print a presentation

CaseStudy CUSHMAN COMMUNICATIONS Zach Reynolds is the public relations coordinator for Cushman Communications, a large firm in New York. Earlier this morning Zach received a request from an important client to create a Microsoft PowerPoint presentation summarizing the status of one of his projects. Then, during his coffee break, he received an e-mail message with a PowerPoint attachment from Matthew, his sixth-grade nephew in Canada. Frustrated that he doesn't yet know how to use PowerPoint, Zach decides to roll up his sleeves and learn how to use this clearly useful tool.

In this chapter, you and Zach load Microsoft PowerPoint and create new presentations. Specific tasks include creating a Title slide, adding new slides, and using basic file-management procedures.

1.1 Getting Started with PowerPoint

Microsoft PowerPoint is a presentation graphics program that enables you to create on-screen presentations, Web presentations, overhead transparencies, and 35mm slides. Even if you don't consider yourself a graphics designer, you can still create informative and attractive presentations using PowerPoint. In this module, you start Microsoft PowerPoint and proceed through a guided tour of its primary components.

1.1.1 Loading and Exiting PowerPoint

feature

You load PowerPoint from the Windows Start menu, accessed by clicking the Start button (Start) on the taskbar. Because PowerPoint requires a significant amount of memory, you should always exit the application when you are finished doing your work. Most Windows applications allow you to close their windows by clicking the Close button (×) appearing in the top right-hand corner.

method

To load PowerPoint:

- CLICK: Start button (Start)
- CHOOSE: Programs, Microsoft PowerPoint

To exit PowerPoint:

- CLICK: Close button (×) appearing in the top right-hand corner

or

- CHOOSE: File, Exit from PowerPoint's Menu bar

You will now launch Microsoft PowerPoint using the Windows Start menu.

1. Position the mouse pointer over the top of the Start button (Start) and then click the left mouse button once. The Start pop-up menu appears.
2. Point to the Programs command using the mouse. Note that you do not need to click the left mouse button to display the list of programs in the cascading menu.
3. Move the mouse pointer horizontally to the right until it highlights an option in the Programs menu. You can now move the mouse pointer vertically within the menu to select an option. Your screen may now appear similar, but not identical, to Figure 1.1.

Figure 1.1

The Programs menu

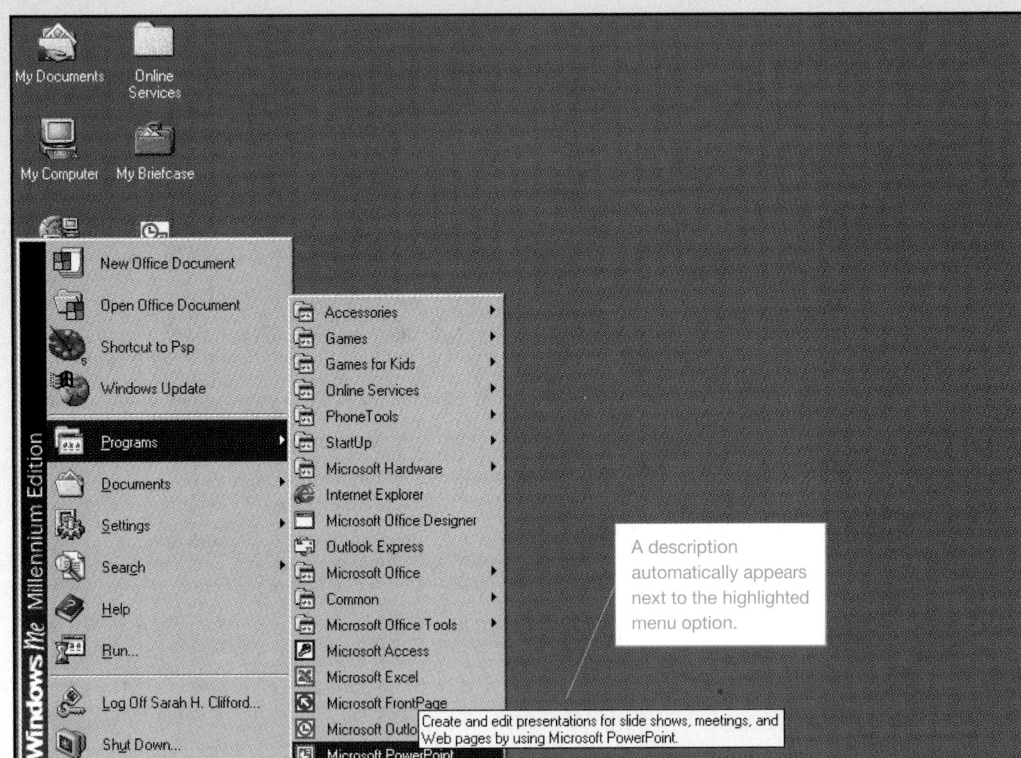

4. Highlight the Microsoft PowerPoint menu item, as shown, and then click the left mouse button once to execute the command. After a few seconds, the Microsoft PowerPoint screen appears (Figure 1.2).

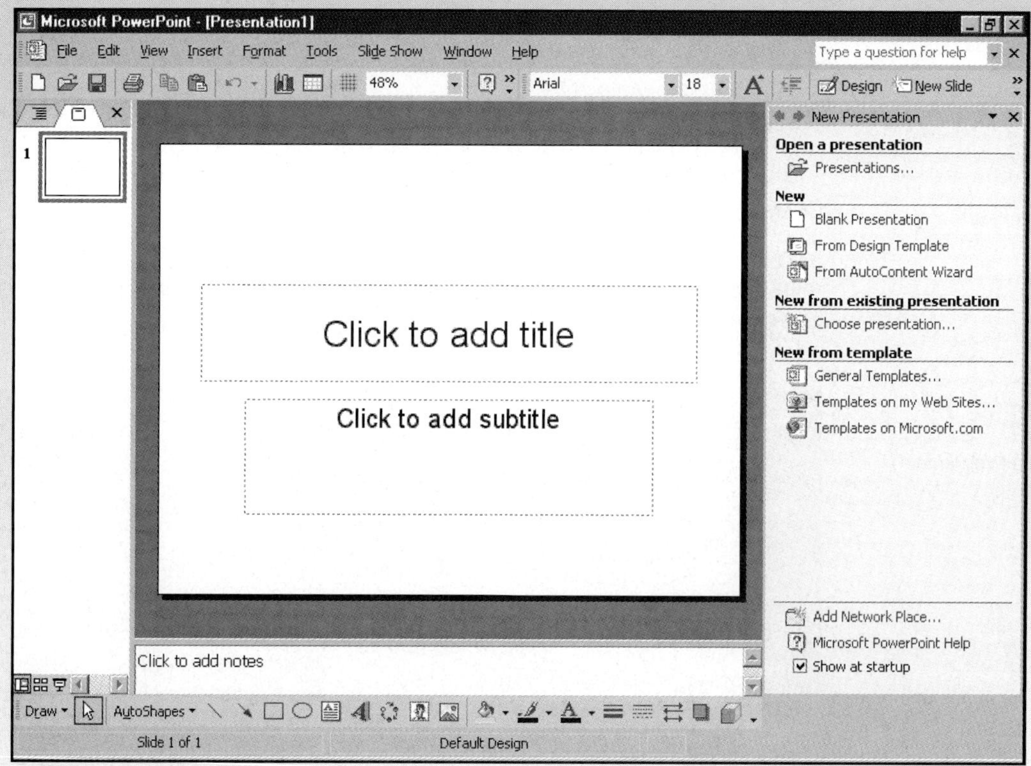

Figure 1.2
Opening PowerPoint screen

5. The Office Assistant, the animated paper clip, may be displaying. To hide it from view, do the following:
RIGHT-CLICK: the character
CHOOSE: Hide from the right-click menu

1.1.2 Touring PowerPoint

feature →

The PowerPoint **application window** acts as a container for your presentation. It also contains the primary interface components for working in PowerPoint, including the *Windows icons, Menu bar, toolbars, task pane, View buttons,* and *Status bar.* Figure 1.3 identifies several of these components.

practice →

In a guided tour, you explore the features of PowerPoint's application window. Ensure that you have already loaded PowerPoint.

1. PowerPoint's application window is best kept maximized (to fill the entire screen), as shown in Figure 1.3. As with most Windows applications, you use the Title bar icons—Minimize (▁), Maximize (□), Restore (🗗), and Close (✕)—to control the display of a window using the mouse. Familiarize yourself with the components labeled in Figure 1.3.

Figure 1.3

PowerPoint's application window

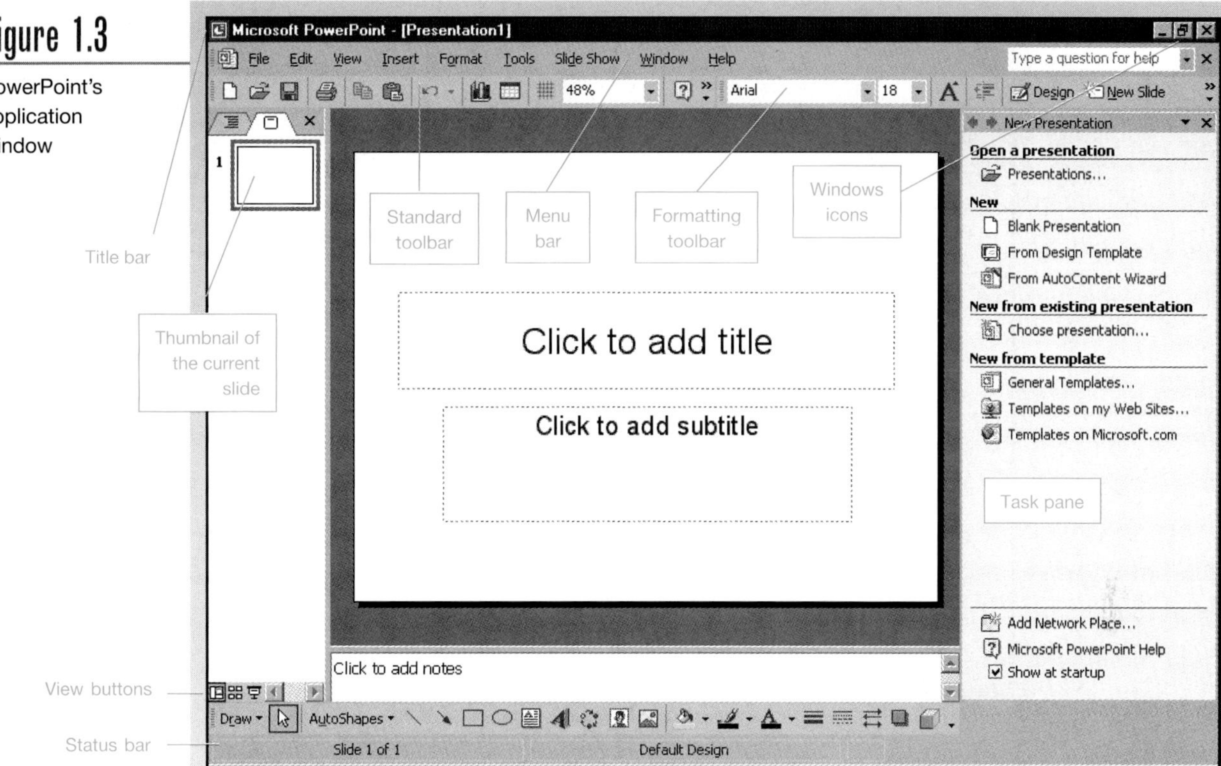

2. The Menu bar contains the PowerPoint menu commands. To execute a command, you click once on the desired Menu bar option and then click again on the command. Commands that appear dimmed are not available for selection. Commands that are followed by an ellipsis (…) will display a dialog box. To practice working with the PowerPoint Menu bar:
CHOOSE: Help
This instruction tells you to click the left mouse button once on the Help option appearing in the Menu bar.

3. To display other pull-down menus, move the mouse to the left over other options in the Menu bar. As each option is highlighted, a pull-down menu appears with its associated commands.

4. To leave the Menu bar without making a command selection:
CLICK: in a blank area of the Title bar at the top of the screen

5. PowerPoint provides *context-sensitive right-click menus* for quick access to menu commands. Rather than searching for the appropriate command in the Menu bar, you can position the mouse pointer on any object, such as a graphic or toolbar button, and right-click the mouse to display a list of commonly selected commands. To display a slide's right-click menu:
RIGHT-CLICK: near the top of the large slide that appears centered on your screen (refer to Figure 1.4)
Your screen should now appear similar to Figure 1.4.

Figure 1.4

Right-click menu

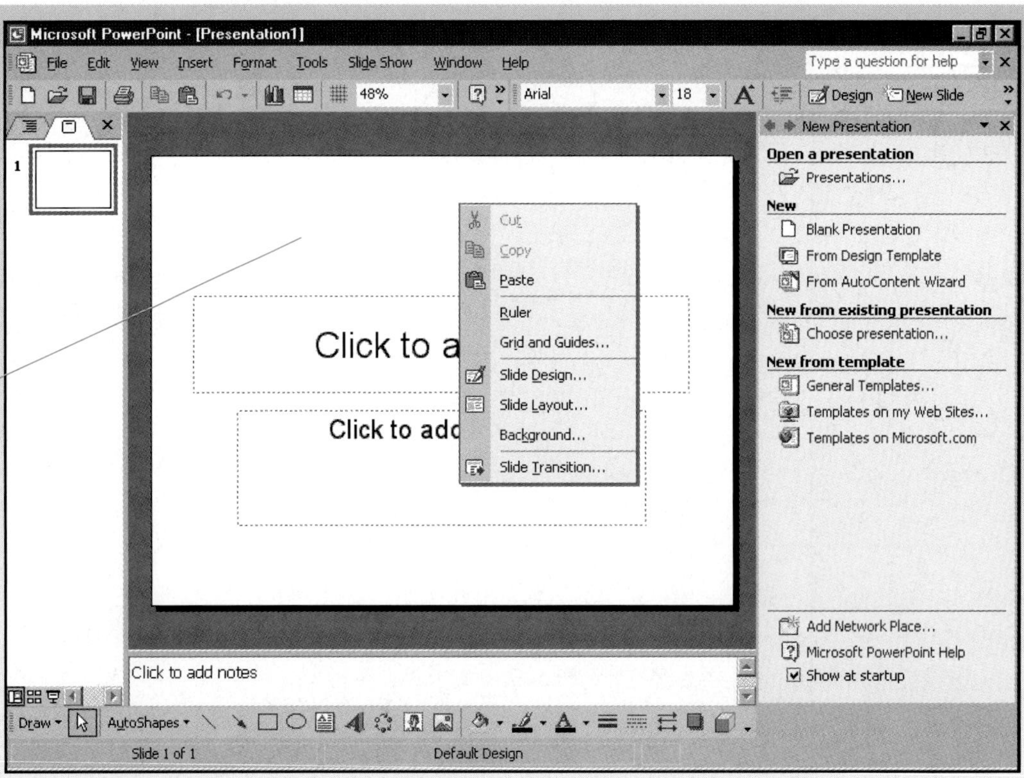

Right-click in this area of the slide

6. To remove the right-click menu from the screen:
   CLICK: in the same area of the slide you clicked in step 5
7. Continue to the next lesson.

1.1.3 Customizing Toolbars

feature →

By default, Office XP ships with the Standard and Formatting toolbars positioned side-by-side in a single row. You may find it easier to locate buttons when these toolbars are positioned on separate rows. Also, the **task pane** is positioned on the right side of your screen, providing convenient access to relevant commands and options. Some new users find that the task pane is distracting and consumes too much of their workspace. Fortunately, you can hide and display the task pane using a simple menu command.

method →

To display the Standard and Formatting toolbars on separate rows:

- CHOOSE: Tools, Customize
- CLICK: *Options* tab
- SELECT: *Show Standard and Formatting toolbars on two rows* check box
- CLICK: Close command button

To display or hide a toolbar:

- CHOOSE: View, Toolbars
- CHOOSE: a toolbar from the menu

To display or hide the task pane:

- CHOOSE: View, task pane

or

- CLICK: its Close button (☒)

practice

In this lesson, you display the Standard and Formatting toolbars on separate rows, and toggle the display of the task pane. Ensure that you've completed the previous lesson.

1. To customize the Standard and Formatting toolbars so they display on separate rows:
CHOOSE: Tools, Customize
CLICK: *Options* tab
The Customize dialog box should now appear (Figure 1.5).

Figure 1.5

Customize dialog box: *Options* tab

If you select this option, the Standard and Formatting toolbars will display on separate rows.

With this option selected, PowerPoint disables its adaptive menus feature and always displays completed menus.

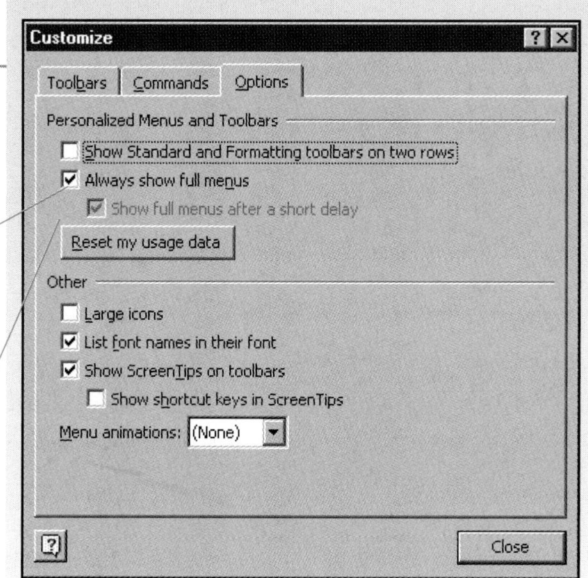

2. On the *Options* tab of the Customize dialog box:
SELECT: *Show Standard and Formatting toolbars on two rows* check box
(*Note:* When you select a check box, a check mark (✓) appears. If you click on the check box again, the check mark disappears.)

3. If the *Always show full menus* check box isn't selected on your computer, select it now.
SELECT: *Always show full menus* check box (refer to Figure 1.5)
A check mark (✓) should be displaying next to the option, as in Figure 1.5.

4. To proceed:
CLICK: Close button
Figure 1.6 displays the Standard and Formatting toolbars as they should now appear on your screen. The Standard toolbar provides access to file management and editing commands, in addition to special features. The Formatting toolbar lets you access formatting commands.

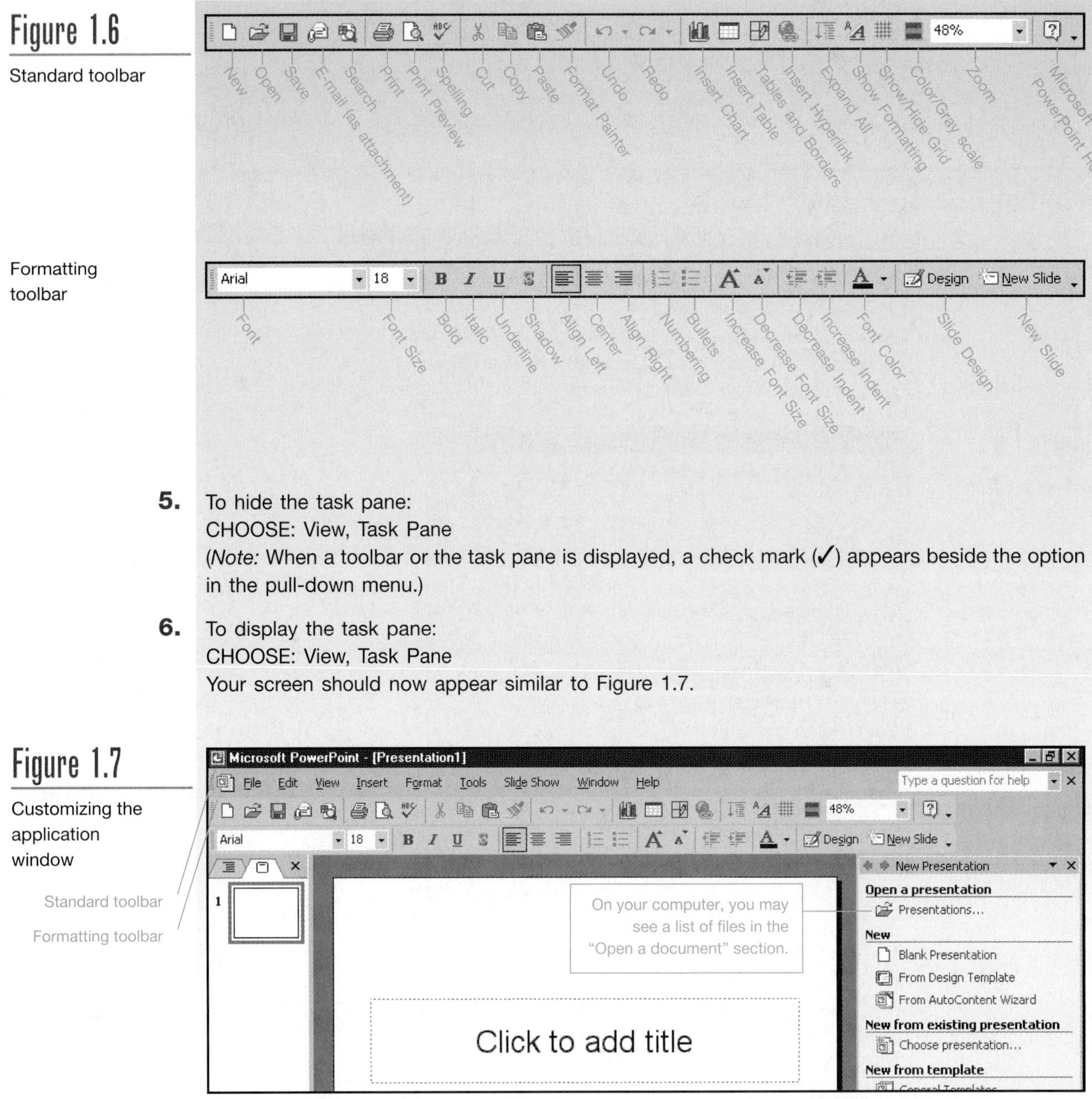

Figure 1.6

Standard toolbar

Formatting toolbar

5. To hide the task pane:
   CHOOSE: View, Task Pane
   (*Note:* When a toolbar or the task pane is displayed, a check mark (✓) appears beside the option in the pull-down menu.)
6. To display the task pane:
   CHOOSE: View, Task Pane
   Your screen should now appear similar to Figure 1.7.

Figure 1.7

Customizing the application window

Important: For the remainder of this learning guide, we assume that the Standard and Formatting toolbars are positioned on separate rows.

In Addition MOVING TOOLBARS

You can move toolbars around the PowerPoint application window using the mouse. A *docked* toolbar appears attached to one of the window's borders. An *undocked* or *floating* toolbar appears in its own window, complete with a Title bar and Close button. To float a docked toolbar, drag the Move bar ( ) at the left-hand side toward the center of the window. To redock the toolbar, drag its Title bar toward a border until it attaches itself automatically.

1.1. How do you remove a right-click menu from view?

1.2 Starting a New Presentation

PowerPoint provides several ways to start a new presentation. If you are looking for design and content suggestions, start with the **AutoContent Wizard.** This wizard provides the quickest and easiest method for starting a new presentation. AutoContent presentations, consisting of 5 to 10 slides each, are available on a range of topics. Once the slides are created, you simply customize the presentation to meet your needs.

For design (not content) suggestions, consider starting a new presentation from a design template. A **design template** determines the look of your presentation by defining its color scheme, background, and use of fonts. If neither the AutoContent Wizard nor a design template sounds tempting, you can start a presentation from scratch by clicking the New button (). You will use that procedure later in module 1.3.

1.2.1 Starting with the AutoContent Wizard

feature

If you are finding it difficult to organize and write down your thoughts, consider letting the AutoContent Wizard be your guide. After progressing through the Wizard's dialog boxes, you'll have the basic framework for building a complete presentation.

method

If the task pane is not displaying:

- CHOOSE: File, New
- CLICK: "From AutoContent Wizard" link in the New Presentation task pane

practice

You will now practice launching the AutoContent Wizard. Ensure that PowerPoint is loaded.

1. The New Presentation task pane should already be displaying on your screen. If not, choose File, New to display the New Presentation task pane. Figure 1.8 shows the New Presentation task pane. Task panes contain textual links, called **hyperlinks,** for performing PowerPoint procedures. When you move the mouse pointer over a link, the mouse pointer changes to a hand (). You select a link by clicking on it.

PowerPoint

Figure 1.8

New Presentation task pane

2. Move the mouse pointer over the hyperlinks in the task pane and note that a hand (☝) appears. You can always tell you are pointing to a hyperlink when a hand appears.

3. To select a link:
CLICK: "From AutoContent Wizard" link
The initial AutoContent Wizard screen should now appear (Figure 1.9). Note that the New Presentation task pane no longer appears.

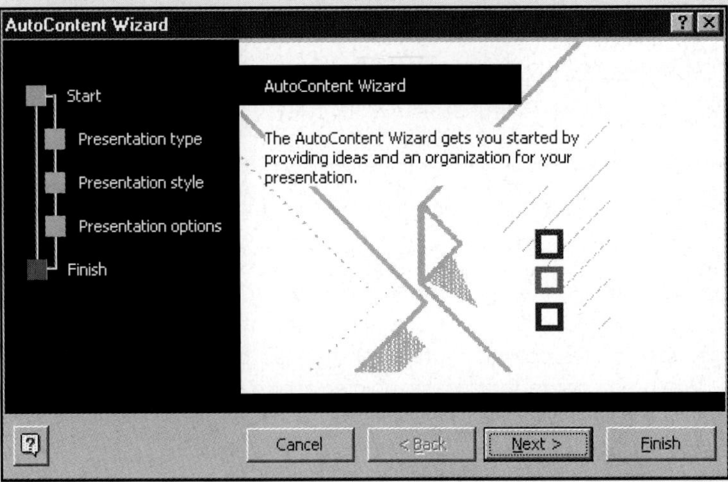

Figure 1.9

Initial AutoContent Wizard screen

4. The left side of the dialog box shows the steps the wizard will go through in order to format the final presentation. To proceed to the next step, do the following:
CLICK: Next command button

5. In this step, you select the type of presentation you are going to give (Figure 1.10). When you click a category option button, a list of related presentations appears in the list box to the right.

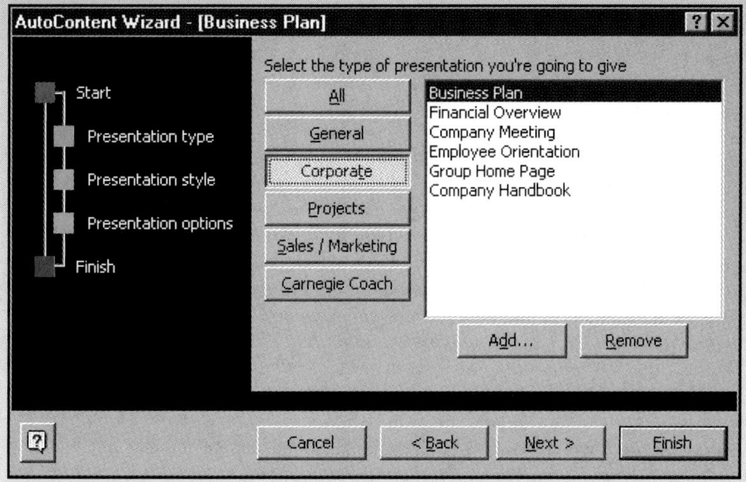

Figure 1.10
Selecting a presentation type

Do the following:
CLICK: Corporate button
SELECT: Company Meeting in the list box
CLICK: Next command button
You must now select an output option for the presentation (Figure 1.11).

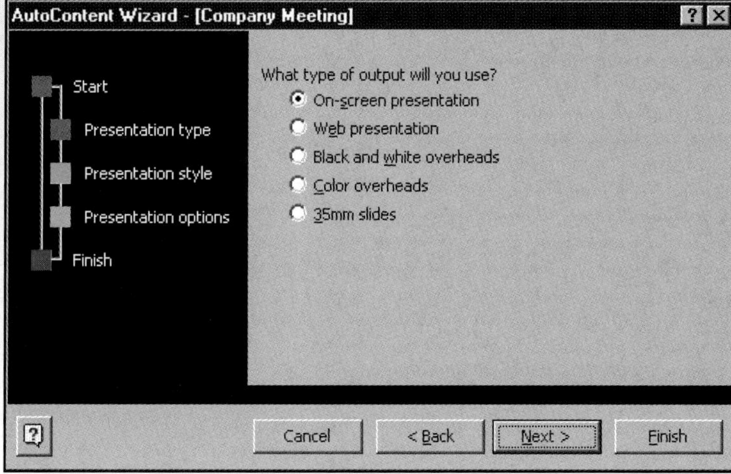

Figure 1.11
Selecting an output type

6. SELECT: *On-screen presentation* option
CLICK: Next command button
Your screen should now appear similar to Figure 1.12.

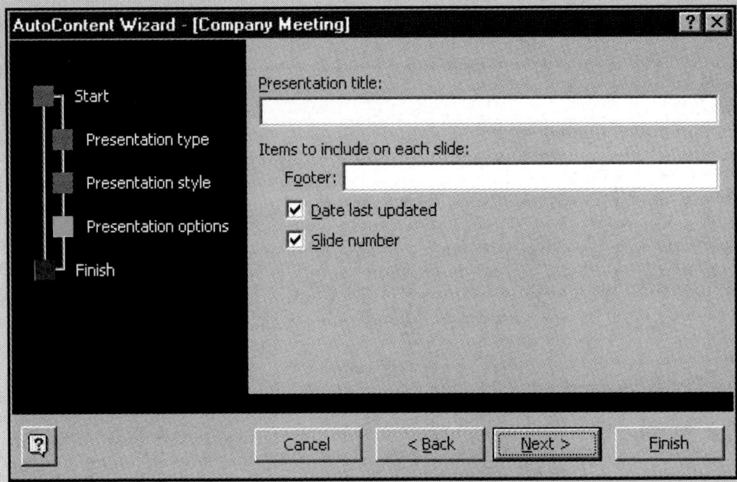

Figure 1.12

Defining the opening slide

7. In this step, you enter the information you want to appear on the opening slide of your presentation.
CLICK: in the *Presentation title* text box
TYPE: **Effective Communication Skills**
(*Note:* Leave the footer information blank for now.)

8. Do the following to proceed:
CLICK: Next command button
CLICK: Finish command button
At this point, as shown in Figure 1.13, the presentation is compiled with some content suggestions that you can edit to meet your needs. This view of your presentation is called **Normal view** and provides one place for building the different parts of your presentation. In Figure 1.13, we label and describe the different areas you see in Normal view.

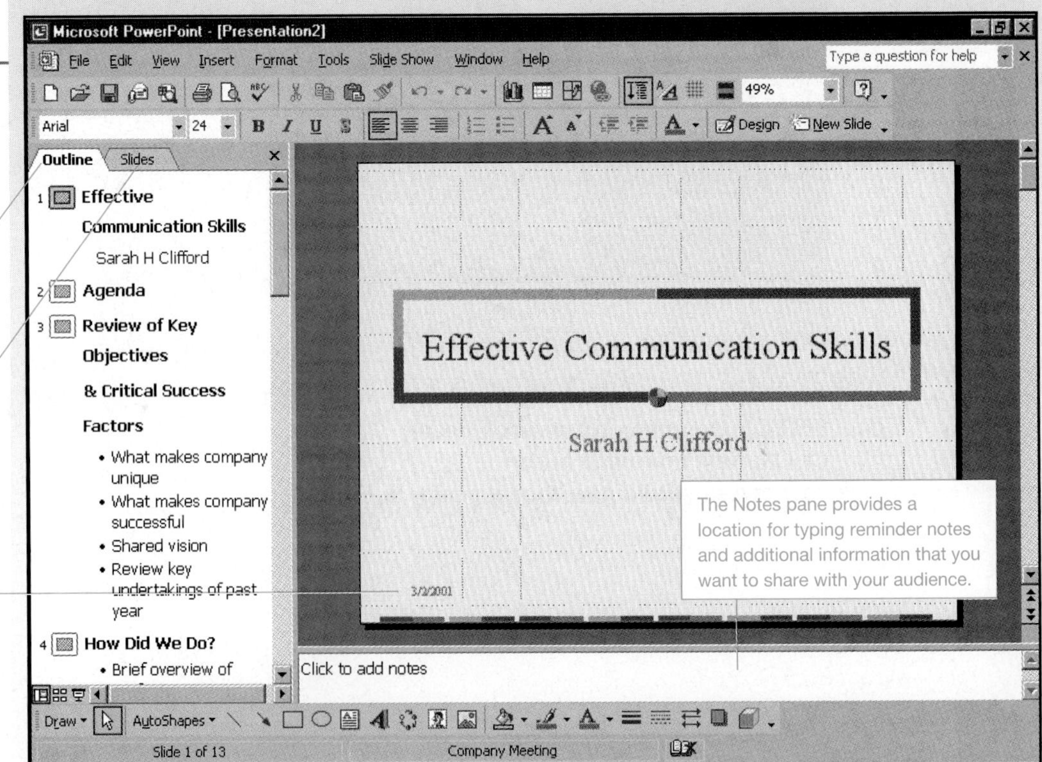

Figure 1.13

Displaying a presentation in Normal view

The *Outline* tab is used for typing and rearranging the text or your presentation.

The *Slides* tab is used for displaying the slides in your presentation using thumbnails.

The Slide pane is used for displaying an enlarged view of the current slide.

9. The Next Slide (⯆) and Previous Slide (⯅) buttons on the vertical scroll bar enable you to navigate through your presentation. To illustrate:
CLICK: Next Slide button (⯆) to view the second slide
CLICK: Previous Slide button (⯅) to view the first slide

10. Advance through the entire presentation by pressing the Next Slide button (⯆) 12 times.

11. When slide 13 is displaying in the Slide pane, do the following:
CLICK: *Slides* tab
Your screen should now appear similar to Figure 1.14. Note how your screen displays small "thumbnail" images of your slide presentation along the left side of your screen.

Figure 1.14

Displaying the contents of the *Slides* tab

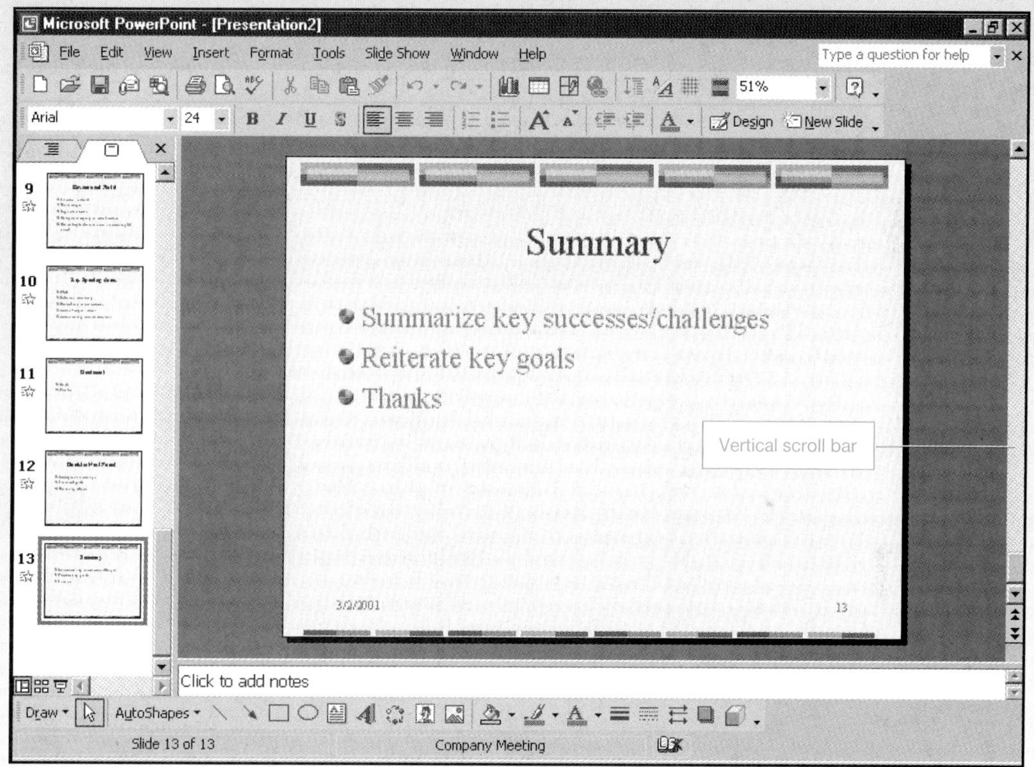

12. To conclude this lesson, you will close the document without saving changes. From the Menu bar:
CHOOSE: File, Close

13. In the dialog box that appears asking "Do you want to save the changes . . .":
CLICK: No command button
There should be no presentations open in the application window.

1.2.2 Starting with a Design Template

Some people who are skilled writers and content researchers may find it difficult to work with graphics. Fortunately, PowerPoint provides a selection of design templates that you can use to start new presentations.

PowerPoint

method

- CHOOSE: File, New to display the New Presentation task pane
- CLICK: "From Design Template" hyperlink
- DOUBLE-CLICK: a design thumbnail in the Slide Design task pane

practice

You will now practice applying design templates. Ensure that PowerPoint is loaded and that no presentations are open.

1. Your first step is to display the New Presentation task pane.
CHOOSE: File, New

2. To select a design template:
CLICK: "From Design Template" hyperlink
The Slide Design task pane should appear with a selection of thumbnail designs (Figure 1.15).

Figure 1.15

Slide Design task pane

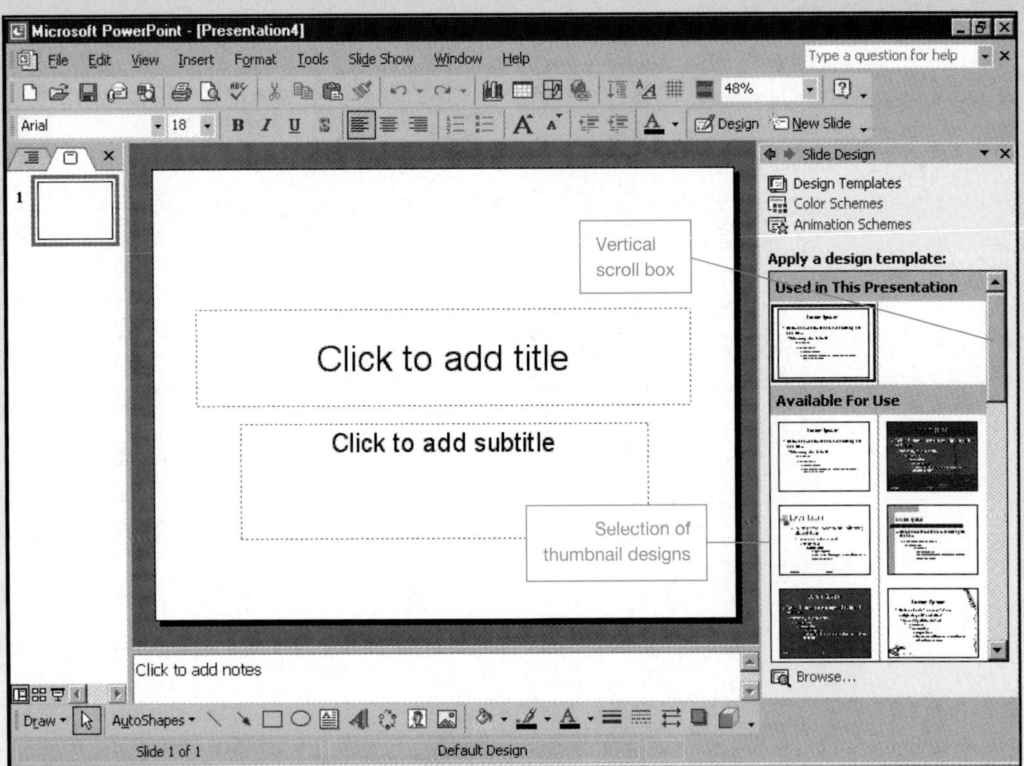

3. When you move the mouse pointer over a thumbnail, its name appears. On your own, move the mouse pointer over the different displayed thumbnails to view their names.

4. To view additional thumbnail designs:
DRAG: the vertical scroll box on the lower right side of your screen to the bottom of the scroll bar

5. Before continuing, drag the vertical scroll box back to the top of the vertical scroll bar.

6. You may have noticed that when you point to a thumbnail, a drop-down arrow appears on the right side of the thumbnail. You can click the drop-down arrow to display a selection of commands. To illustrate, point to a design template in the task pane.

7. CLICK: the thumbnail's drop-down arrow
The thumbnail should now appear similar to Figure 1.16.

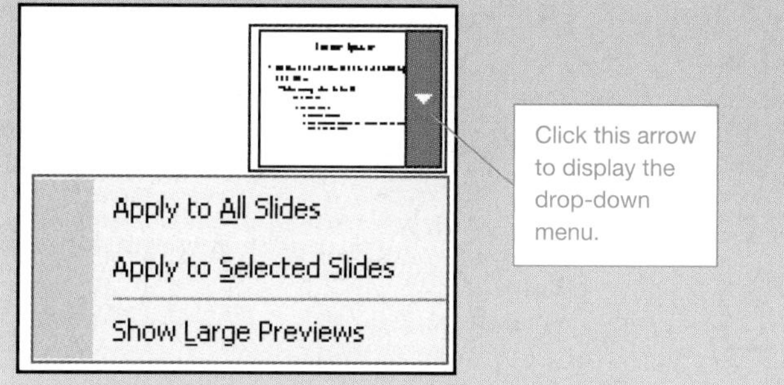

Figure 1.16
Thumbnail with associated menu

8. To view large thumbnails, do the following:
CHOOSE: Show Large Previews from the drop-down menu

9. To redisplay small thumbnails:
CLICK: a thumbnail's drop-down list
CHOOSE: Show Large Previews to deselect the option

10. Open the "Balance" design template. This template is mostly brown in color and should appear near the top of the thumbnails list. Locate the "Balance" design template and then:
CLICK: its drop-down arrow
CHOOSE: Apply to All Slides from the drop-down list
(*Note:* You can also double-click a thumbnail to apply its design to all slides.) Your screen should now appear similar to Figure 1.17.

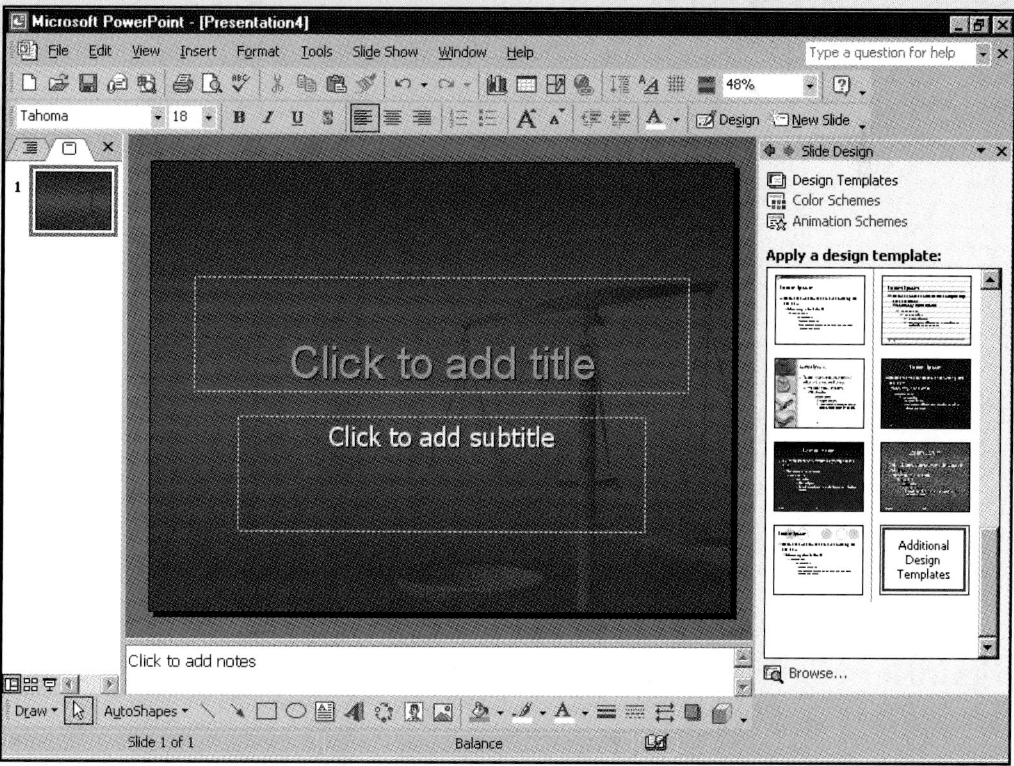

Figure 1.17
Applying the "Balance" design template

11. At this point, you could proceed with creating the presentation. However, to conclude this lesson, you will close the document without saving changes. From the Menu bar:
CHOOSE: File, Close

PowerPoint

12. In the dialog box:
CLICK: No command button
There should be no presentations open in the application window.

1.2. How does an AutoContent presentation differ from a design template?

1.3 Creating a Textual Presentation

When building a presentation, you will naturally need to add new slides. Part of the process of adding a new slide to a presentation involves selecting a layout for the slide. PowerPoint categorizes its selection of layouts according to whether they include text only, graphics only, or both text and graphics. PowerPoint uses **placeholders** to mark the location of text and graphics objects and to provide instructions for editing them. This module concentrates on editing text-only slides. PowerPoint provides four text-only slide layouts, each of which appears labeled in Figure 1.18.

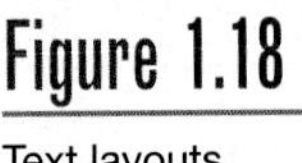

Figure 1.18

Text layouts

Title Slide layout

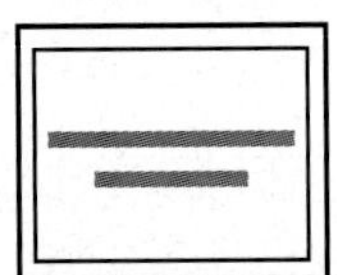

Title only layout

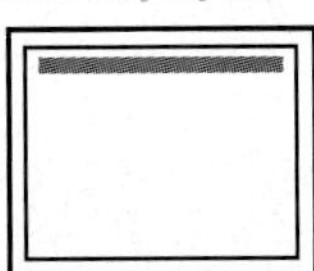

Title and text layout

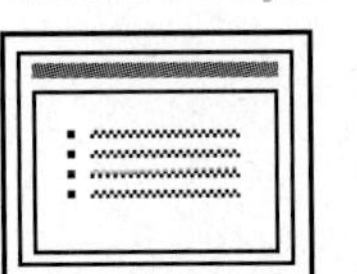

Title and 2-column Text layout

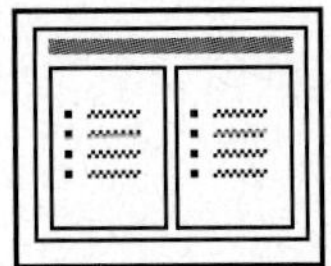

1.3.1 Starting with a Blank Presentation

feature

Rather than use the AutoContent Wizard or a design template to start a new presentation, you may prefer to start from scratch. Blank presentations are just that—blank. They do not contain any content or design suggestions. By default, the first slide of a blank presentation uses the Title Slide layout.

method

- CLICK: New button ( )

practice

You will now start a blank presentation and practice selecting alternate layouts.

1. CLICK: New button ( )
A new, blank presentation appears. Note that the Title Slide layout is selected in the task pane (Figure 1.19), as indicated by the darker border. (*Hint:* Move the mouse pointer over a particular layout to see its name.)

Figure 1.19

Blank presentation: Title Slide layout

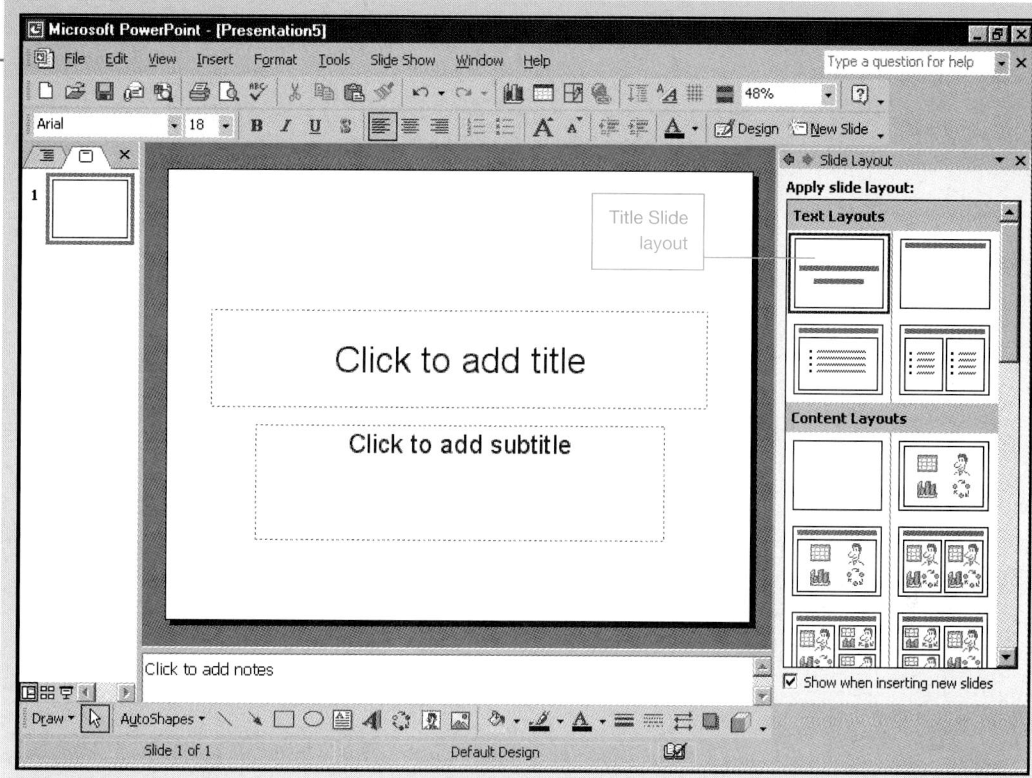

2. You can see what the other text layouts look like. To do this, you click their associated thumbnails in the Slide Layout task pane.
CLICK: Title Only layout (located adjacent to the Title Slide layout)
Note that the Title Only layout now appears in the Slide pane, as shown in Figure 1.20.

Figure 1.20

Blank presentation: Title Only layout

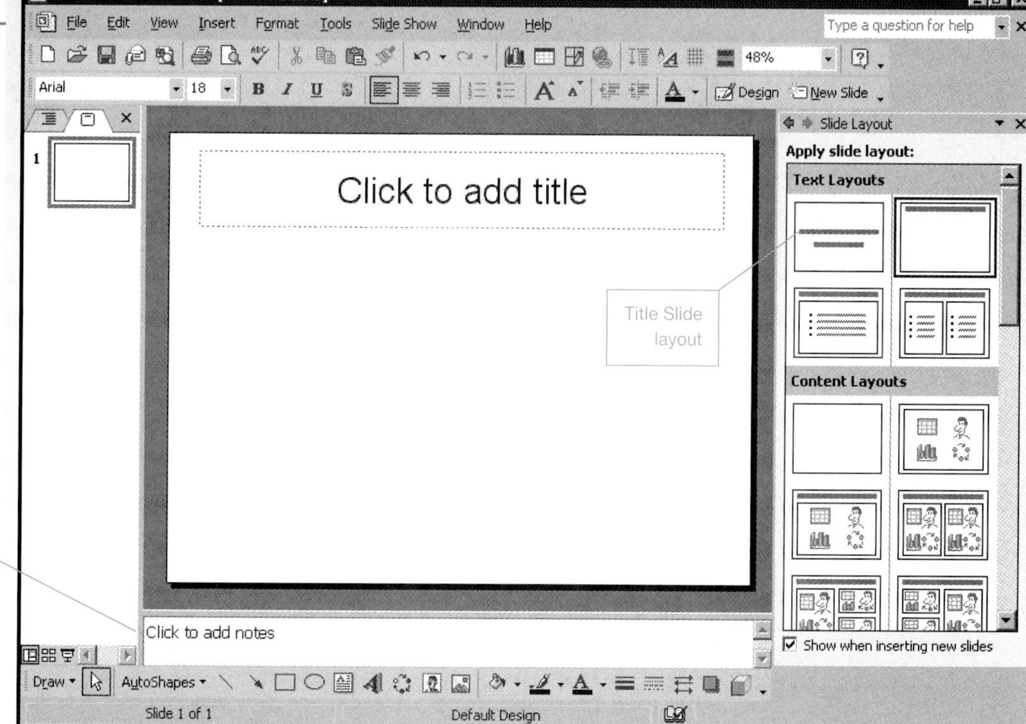

PowerPoint

3. On your own, click the Title and Text layout, and then the Title and 2-Column Text layout in the task pane.
4. Before proceeding:
CLICK: Title Slide layout in the task pane
5. Proceed to the next lesson.

1.3.2 Creating a Title Slide

feature

In most cases, the easiest way to add text to slides is to type it directly into a text placeholder in the Slide pane. If you type more text than can fit in the placeholder, PowerPoint's **AutoFit feature** will automatically resize the placeholder to accommodate the text. You can also insert text by typing in the *Outline* tab.

method

To add text to the Slide pane:

- CLICK: in a text placeholder and then begin typing

practice

You will now add text using the Slide pane and *Outline* tab.

1. To type text into the title placeholder:
CLICK: in the title placeholder, marked by the text "Click to add title"
The insertion point should be blinking in the center of the title placeholder.
2. Ensure that the *Outline* tab is displaying. If it isn't, do the following:
CLICK: *Outline* tab by referring to Figure 1.21
3. TYPE: **Getting Started with PowerPoint**
Note that the title text also appears on the *Outline* tab (Figure 1.21).

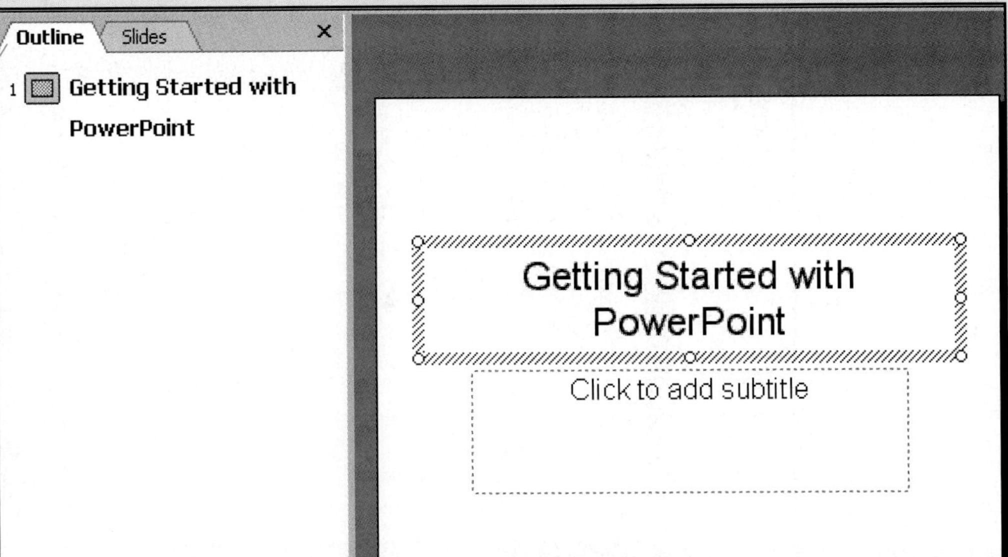

Figure 1.21
Filling in the Title placeholder

Click here to select the *Outline* tab.

4. To type text into the subtitle placeholder:
   CLICK: in the subtitle placeholder, marked by "Click to add subtitle"
5. TYPE: **By your name**
   (*Note:* Be sure to substitute your actual name in place of words "your name.") Your screen should now appear similar to Figure 1.22. Although the message "Click to add notes" also appears on the bottom of the PowerPoint window, we're not going to enter them now.

Figure 1.22

Filling in the Subtitle placeholder

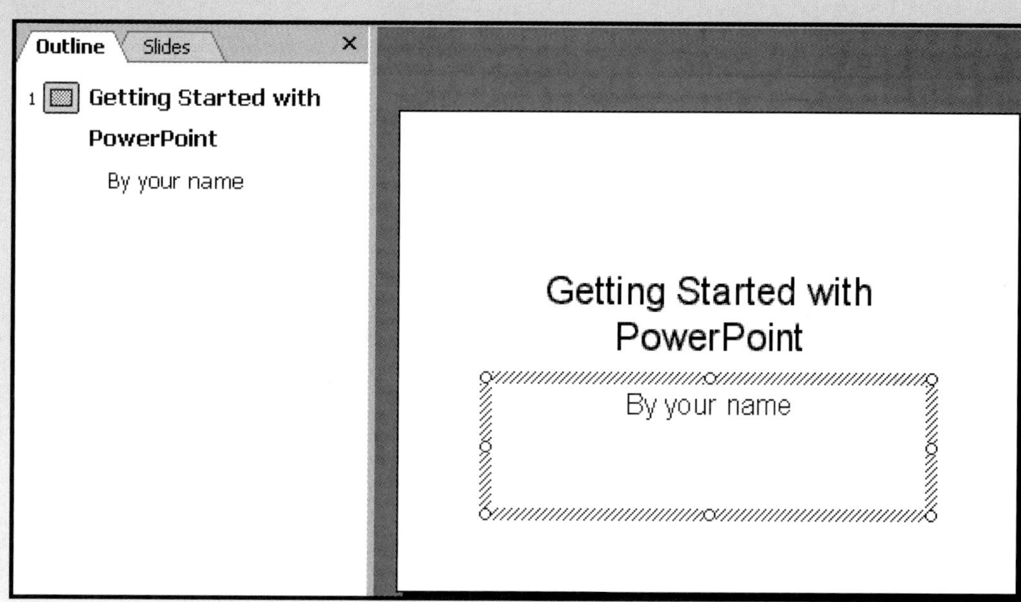

6. Edit the text in the title placeholder. But this time, use the *Outline* tab.
   SELECT: the text "Getting Started with" by dragging the mouse over the text
   The selected text should be highlighted in reverse video.
7. TYPE: **Introducing**
   The title should now read "Introducing PowerPoint" in both the *Outline* tab and Slide pane.
8. CLICK: to the right of the subtitle text in the *Outline* tab
9. PRESS: ENTER
   The insertion point was moved down to the next line.
10. TYPE: **the name of your school/business**
    (*Note:* Be sure to substitute your actual school or business name in the subtitle, or just make one up.) The subtitle now contains two lines of text. Your screen should now appear similar to Figure 1.23.

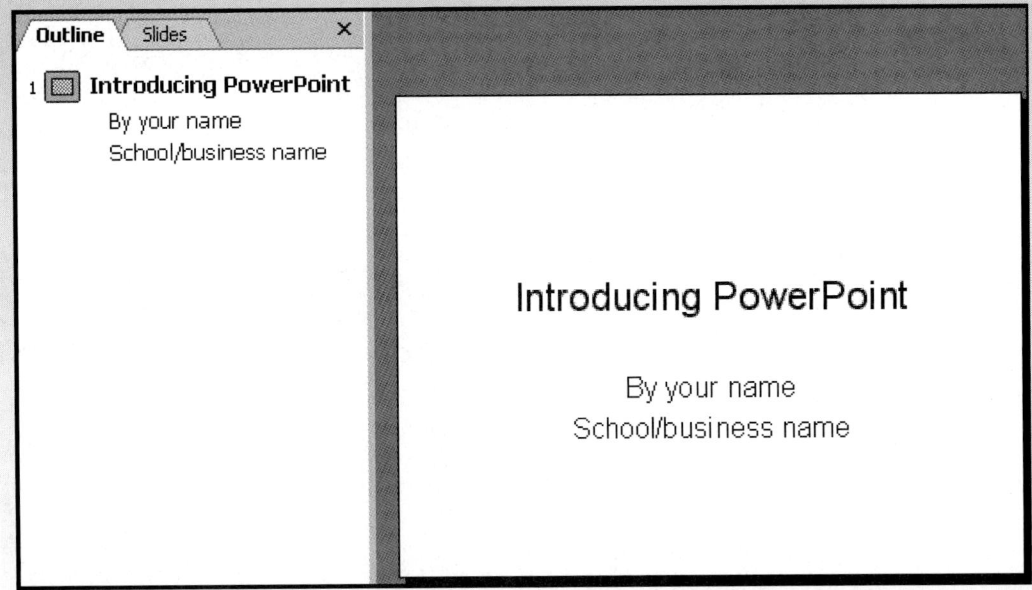

Figure 1.23
Editing text

11. Proceed to the next lesson.

1.3.3 Inserting New Slides and Using the Outline Tab

feature

New slides are inserted after the current, or displayed, slide. Once inserted, select a layout for the slide and edit any text placeholders using the Slide pane or *Outline* tab.

method

To insert or delete a slide:

- CLICK: New Slide button ( ) to add a new slide
- CHOOSE: Edit, Delete Slide to delete a slide,

or

- SELECT: the slide in the *Outline* tab and press DELETE

To create a bulleted list in the *Outline* tab, use the following options:

- CLICK: to begin typing at the current level
- PRESS: TAB to begin typing at a demoted (lower) outline level
- PRESS: SHIFT + TAB to begin typing at a promoted (higher) outline level

practice

You will now practice inserting and deleting slides and typing text in the *Outline* tab. Ensure that you have completed the previous lessons in this module and that the "Introducing PowerPoint" slide is displaying in the Slide pane.

1. To insert a new slide after the current slide:
   CLICK: New Slide button ( ) on the Formatting toolbar near the top right of your screen
   Your screen should now appear similar to Figure 1.24. PowerPoint automatically applied the Title and Text layout to the new slide.

Figure 1.24

A new slide was added

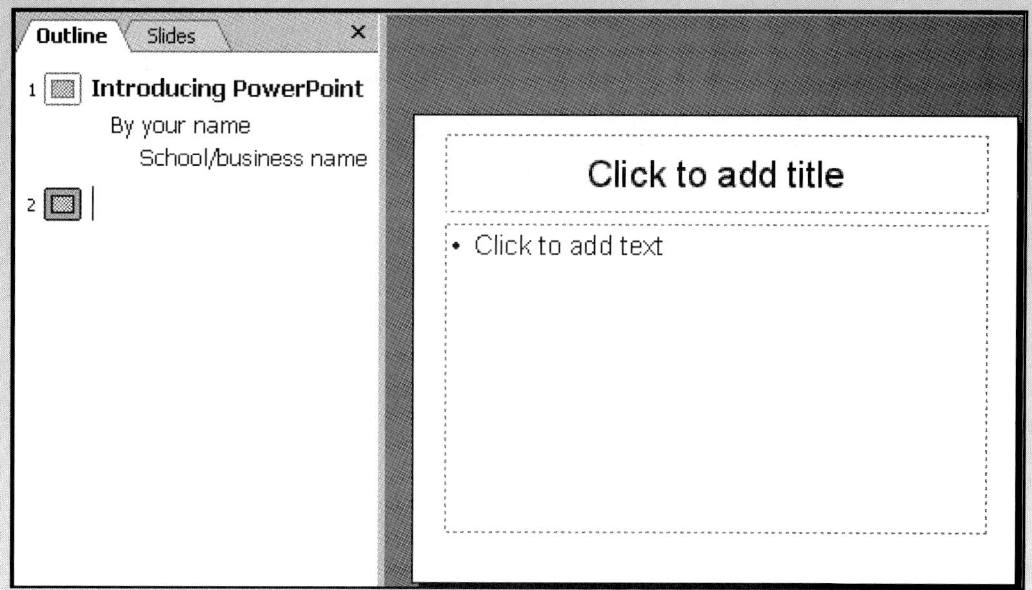

2. Note that the insertion point is blinking to the right of the slide number and icon in the *Outline* tab.
   TYPE: **PowerPoint lets you create:**
   PRESS: ENTER
   Note that when you pressed ENTER, PowerPoint automatically inserted another slide (slide 3). We correct this in the next step.

3. To demote the current outline level so that you can type a bulleted list on slide 2 (not slide 3), do the following:
   PRESS: TAB to demote the current outline level
   Your screen should now appear similar to Figure 1.25.

Figure 1.25

A new slide was added

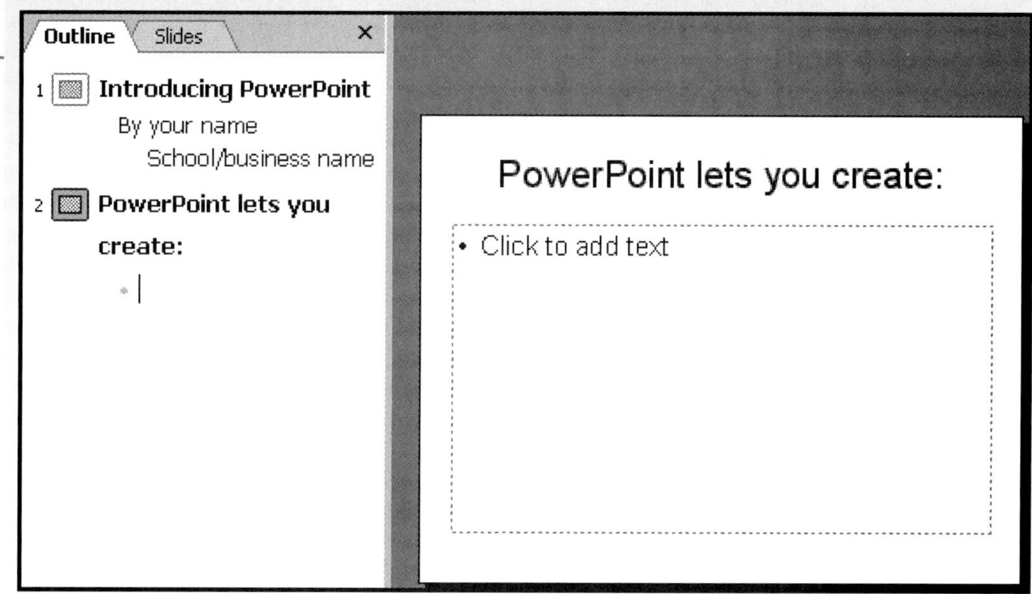

4. To create the bulleted list:
TYPE: **On-screen presentations**
PRESS: ENTER
TYPE: **Web presentations**
PRESS: ENTER
TYPE: **Overhead transparencies**
PRESS: ENTER
TYPE: **35mm slides**
Your screen should now appear similar to Figure 1.26.

Figure 1.26

Typing a bulleted list in the Outline pane

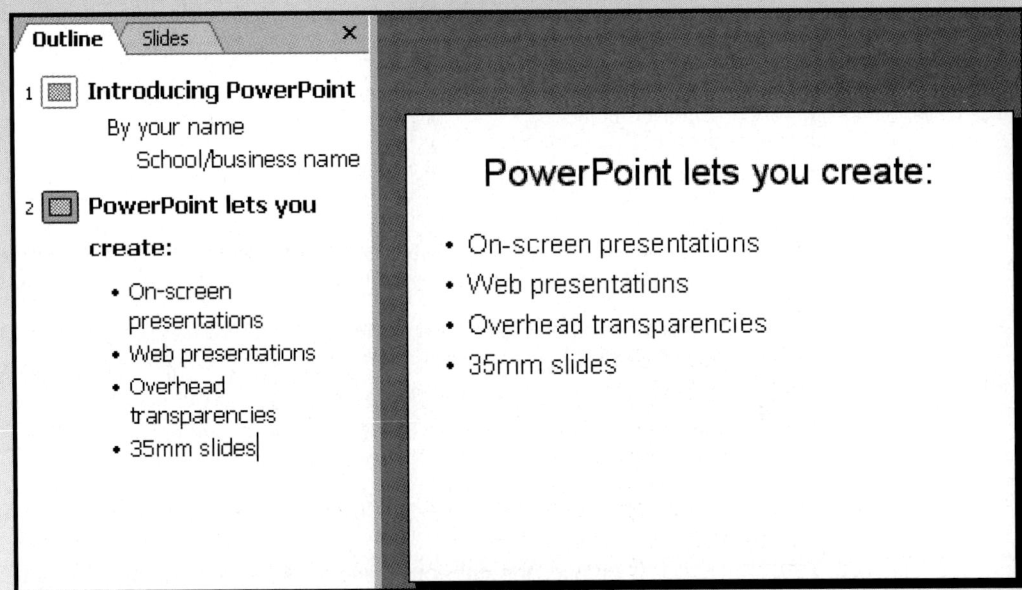
Outline
Slides
1 Introducing PowerPoint
By your name
School/business name
2 PowerPoint lets you create:
• On-screen presentations
• Web presentations
• Overhead transparencies
• 35mm slides
PowerPoint lets you create:
• On-screen presentations
• Web presentations
• Overhead transparencies
• 35mm slides

5. As one final step, let's use the Slide pane to add an additional item to the bulleted list.
CLICK: to the right of the last bulleted item in the Slide pane
PRESS: ENTER
TYPE: **Audience handouts**
The *Outline* tab and the Slide pane can be used interchangeably for entering and editing text.

6. To insert a new slide after the current slide:
CLICK: New Slide button (▤) on the Formatting toolbar
CLICK: Title and 2-Column Text layout (its thumbnail appears in the Slide Layout task pane)
The presentation now includes three slides. Note that the *Outline* tab also includes three slide icons (Figure 1.27).

Figure 1.27

Inserting a third slide

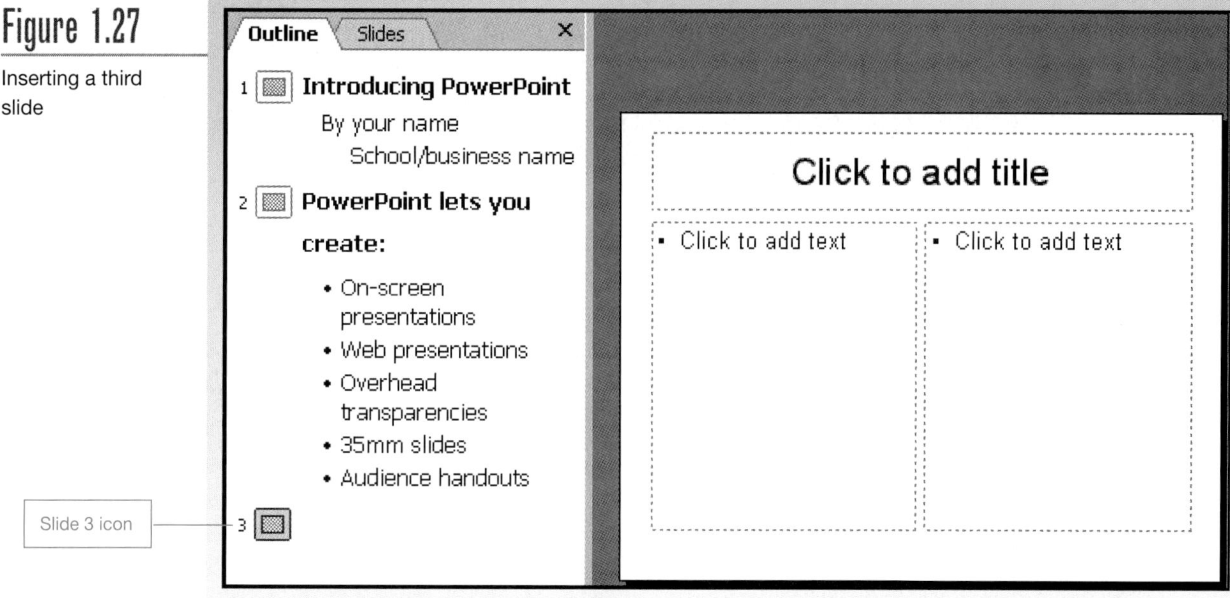

7. To delete the newly inserted third slide using the *Outline* tab:
   CLICK: slide 3 icon located on the lower left of your screen
   PRESS: DELETE
   The slide 3 icon should no longer appear.
8. Continue to the next lesson.

1.3.4 Formatting Text on Slides

feature

PowerPoint's Formatting toolbar provides many commands for getting text to look the way you want. For example, you can select typefaces, font sizes, and attributes for text. You can also change a paragraph's **justification,** which refers to how text is aligned within its placeholder.

method

- To make text bold, italicized, or underlined, click the Bold button (B), Italic button (I), or Underline button (U) on the Formatting toolbar
- To select an alternate typeface, use the Font drop-down list (Times Roman) on the Formatting toolbar
- To change the current font size, use the Font Size drop-down list (10) on the Formatting toolbar
- To change paragraph alignment, click the Align Left (), Center (), or Align Right () button on the Formatting toolbar

practice

This lesson practices formatting text using the Formatting toolbar. Ensure that slide 2 ("PowerPoint lets you create") is displaying in the Slide pane.

1. Apply the bold and underline attributes to the title:
SELECT: the title by dragging over the text with the mouse
CLICK: Bold button (B)
CLICK: Underline button (U)
CLICK: outside the selected text to better view your modifications
The Slide pane should appear similar to Figure 1.28.

Figure 1.28

Applying character attributes to the title

PowerPoint lets you create:
• On-screen presentations
• Web presentations
• Overhead transparencies
• 35mm slides
• Audience handouts

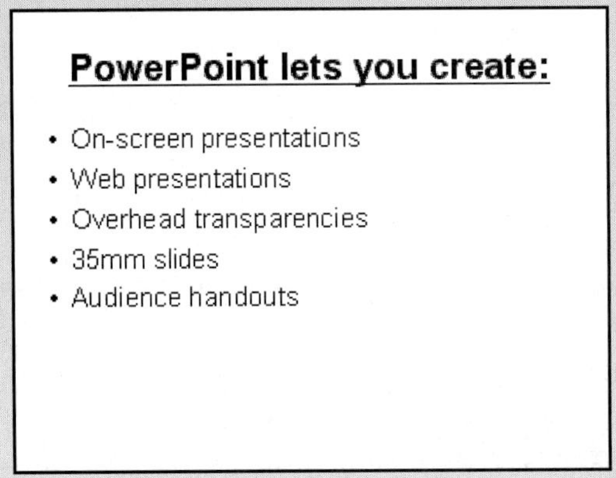

2. To change the font in the title placeholder:
SELECT: the text in the title placeholder
CLICK: down arrow beside the Font drop-down list (Times New Roman)
SELECT: Arial Unicode MS (or another font that is available on your computer if you cannot find Arial Unicode MS)

3. To change the title's font size:
CLICK: down arrow beside the Font Size drop-down list (10)
SELECT: 54-point font size
Note that the enlarged text is too big to fit in the placeholder and that a button, called the AutoFit Options button, is displaying on the slide (Figure 1.29).

Figure 1.29

Changing font size

AutoFit Options button
PowerPoint lets you create:
-screen presentations
• Web presentations
• Overhead transparencies
• 35mm slides
• Audience handouts

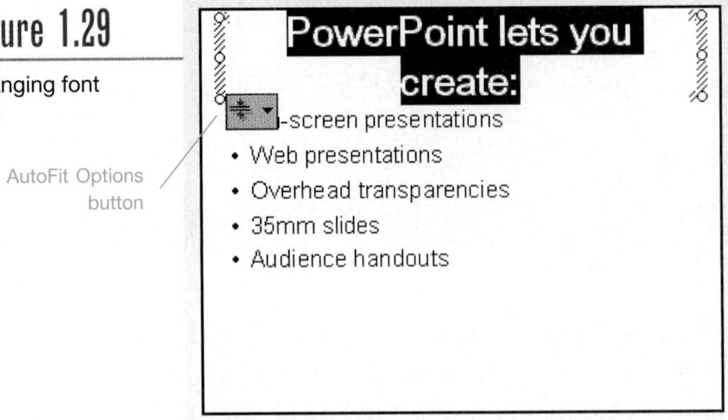

4. CLICK: AutoFit Options button
SELECT: *AutoFit Text to Placeholder* option
Note that the title text now fits within the placeholder.

5. To practice changing paragraph alignment:
   CLICK: in the first bulleted item
   This item is currently aligned to the left in its placeholder.

6. CLICK: Align Right button (≡) on the Formatting toolbar
   The item is positioned on the right side of the placeholder, as shown in Figure 1.30.

Figure 1.30

Changing paragraph alignment

PowerPoint lets you create:

• On-screen presentations
• Web presentations
• Overhead transparencies
• 35mm slides
• Audience handouts

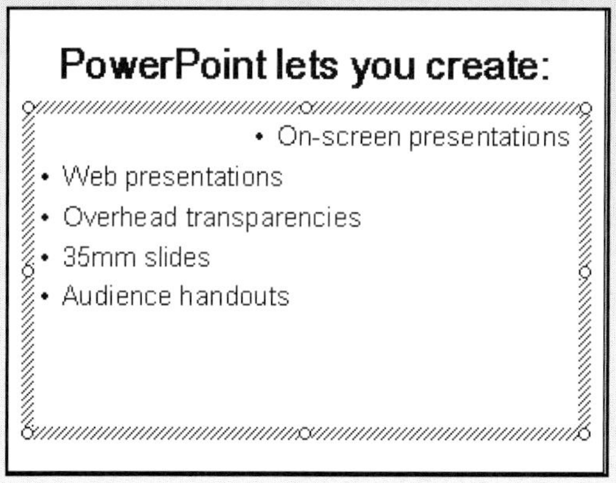

7. To move the paragraph back to its original position:
   CLICK: Align Left button (≡) on the Formatting toolbar

8. At this point, you could proceed with creating the presentation. However, to conclude this lesson, you will close the document without saving changes. From the Menu bar:
   CHOOSE: File, Close

9. In the dialog box that appears:
   CLICK: No command button
   There should be no presentations open in the application window.

1.3. What procedure would you use to change the current typeface?

1.4 Managing Files

Managing the presentations that you create is an important skill. As you create a presentation, it exists only in the computer's RAM (random access memory), which is highly volatile. In other words, if the power to your computer goes off, your presentation is lost. For safety and security, you need to save your presentation permanently to the local hard disk, a network drive, or a floppy diskette.

Saving your work to a named file on a disk is similar to placing it into a filing cabinet. For important presentations (ones that you cannot risk losing), you should save your work at least every 15 minutes. This protects against an unexpected power outage or other catastrophe. Saving a file without closing it is like placing a current copy in a filing cabinet. When naming your presentation files, you can use up to 255 characters, including spaces, but it's wise to keep the length under 20 characters. Furthermore, because they are special reserved characters, you cannot use any of the following characters in naming your presentations:

\ / : ; * ? " < > |

In the following lessons, you practice several file management procedures, including saving, closing, opening, and printing presentations.

Important: *In this guide, we refer to the files that have been created for you as the* ***student data files.*** *Depending on your computer or lab setup, these files may be located on a floppy diskette, in a folder on your hard disk, or on a network server. If necessary, ask your instructor or lab assistant exactly where to find these data files. To download the Advantage Series' student data files from the Internet, visit our Web sites at:*

http://www.mhhe.com

http://www.advantageseries.com

You will also need to identify a personal storage location like a floppy diskette or hard-drive subdirectory for the files that you create, modify, and save.

1.4.1 Saving and Closing a Presentation

feature →

You can save the currently displayed presentation by updating an existing file on the disk, by creating a new file, or by selecting a new storage location. The File, Save command and the Save button (💾) on the toolbar allow you to overwrite a disk file with the latest version of a presentation. The File, Save As command enables you to save a presentation to a new filename or storage location. When you are finished working with a presentation, ensure that you close the file to free up the valuable RAM on your computer.

method →

To save an opened presentation:

- CLICK: Save button (💾)

or

- CHOOSE: File, Save,

or

- CHOOSE: File, Save As

To close an opened presentation:

- CLICK: its Close button (☒)

or

- CHOOSE: File, Close

practice →

You will now practice saving and closing an opened presentation. Ensure that PowerPoint is loaded and that you have identified a storage location for your personal document files. If you want to use a diskette, place it into the diskette drive now.

1. So that we have a presentation to save, create a quick AutoContent presentation.
   CHOOSE: File, New
   CLICK: "From AutoContent Wizard" link in the task pane
   CLICK: Finish command button
   A presentation should now appear in the application window.

2. When working on a presentation that you have not saved yet, Word displays the Save As dialog box (Figure 1.28), regardless of the method you choose to save the file. To demonstrate:
CLICK: Save button
(*Note:* The filenames and directories that appear in your Save As dialog box may differ from those shown in Figure 1.31.) The **Places bar,** located along the left border of the dialog box, provides convenient access to commonly used storage locations.

Save As dialog box

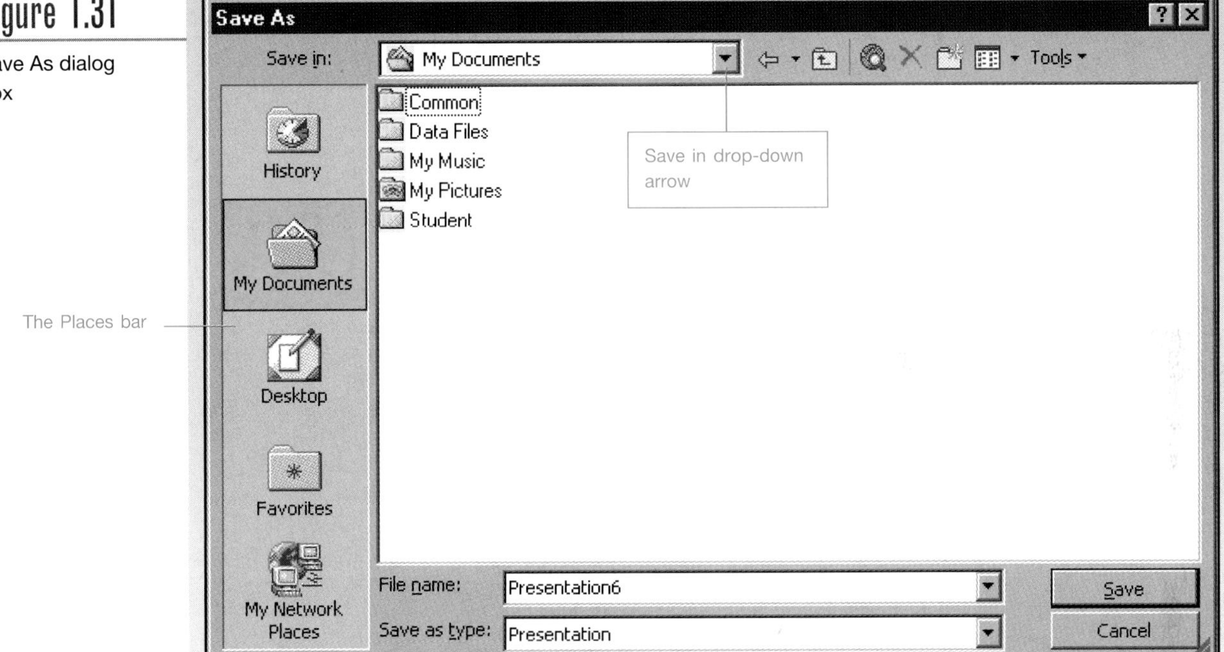

3. Before continuing, browse the local hard disk:
CLICK: down arrow attached to the *Save in* drop-down list box
SELECT: Local Disk C:
(*Note:* Your hard drive may have a different name.) The list area displays the folders and files stored in the root directory of your local hard disk.

4. To drill down into one of the folders:
DOUBLE-CLICK: Program Files folder
(*Note:* If the Program Files folder is not located on your local hard disk, select an alternate folder to open.) This folder contains the program files for several applications.

5. Continue to drill down one step further:
DOUBLE-CLICK: Microsoft Office folder
This folder contains the Microsoft Office program files. Your screen may now appear similar, but not identical, to Figure 1.32.

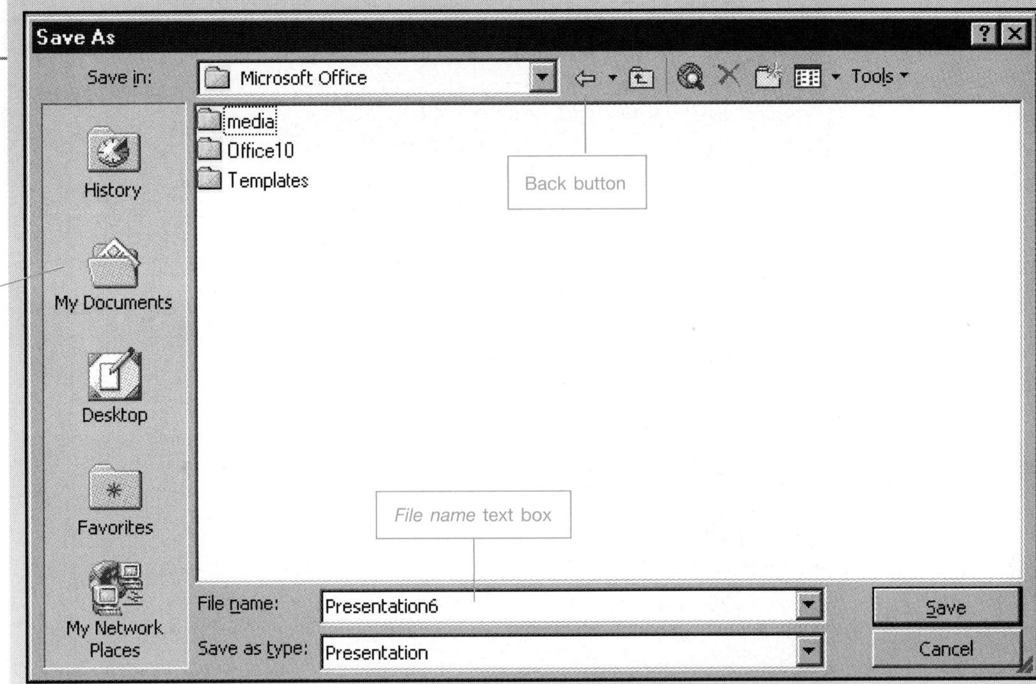

Figure 1.32

Displaying the contents of the Microsoft Office folder

6. To return to the previous display:
   CLICK: Back button ( ) in the dialog box
   (*Note:* The button is renamed "Program Files," since that is where you will end up once the button is clicked.)
7. To return to the "My Documents" display:
   CLICK: My Documents button in the Places bar
8. It is now that you need to know where (on a diskette or in a hard-disk subdirectory) you will be saving your files. Again, if necessary, ask your instructor or lab assistant for the exact location. Now, using either the Places bar or the *Save in* drop-down list box:
   SELECT: *a storage location for your personal files*
   (*Note:* In this guide, we save files to the Student folder, located on the hard disk in the My Documents folder.)
9. Next, you need to give the document file a unique name. Let's replace the existing name with one that is more descriptive. Do the following:
   DOUBLE-CLICK: the presentation name appearing in the File name text box to select it
   TYPE: **Practice Presentation**
10. To save your work:
    CLICK: Save command button
    Note that the presentation's name now appears in the Title bar (Figure 1.33).

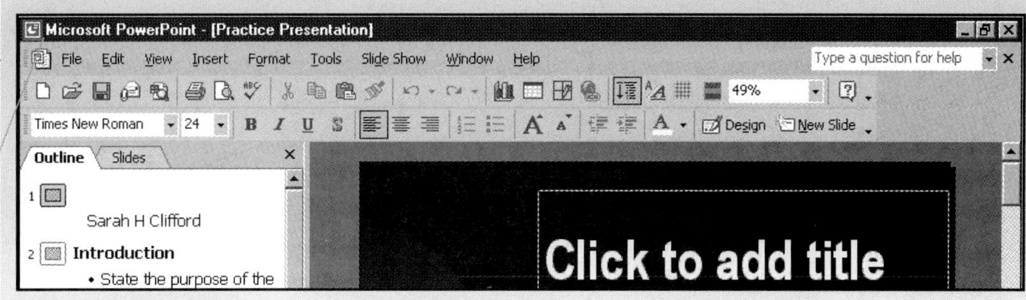

Figure 1.33

The filename now appears in the Title bar

11. In this step, insert a title on the first slide.
CLICK: the title placeholder
TYPE: **Outdoor Vacations**

12. To save the revised presentation:
CLICK: Save button ( )
There are times when you may want to save an existing presentation under a different filename. For example, you may want to keep different versions of the same presentation on your disk. Or, you may want to use one presentation as a template for future presentations that are similar in style and format. To do this, you can retrieve the original presentation file, edit the information, and then save it again under a different name using the File, Save As command.

13. Let's close the presentation:
CHOOSE: File, Close

1.4.2 Opening an Existing Presentation

feature →

You use the Open dialog box to search for and retrieve existing presentations that are stored on your local hard disk, a floppy diskette, a network server, or on the Web. If you want to load PowerPoint and an existing presentation at the same time, you can use the Open Office Document command on the Start menu. Or, if you have recently used the presentation, you can try the Start, Documents command, which lists up to 15 most recently used Office files.

method →

To open an existing presentation:

- CLICK: Open button ( )

or

- CHOOSE: File, Open

practice →

You will now open an existing file that addresses the topic of buying a personal computer. Ensure that you have completed the previous lesson and that no presentations are displayed. Also, you should know the storage location for the student data files.

1. To display the Open dialog box:
CLICK: Open button ( )
The Open dialog box should now appear similar, but not identical, to Figure 1.34. The contents of your data files folder should be displaying.

Figure 1.34

Open dialog box

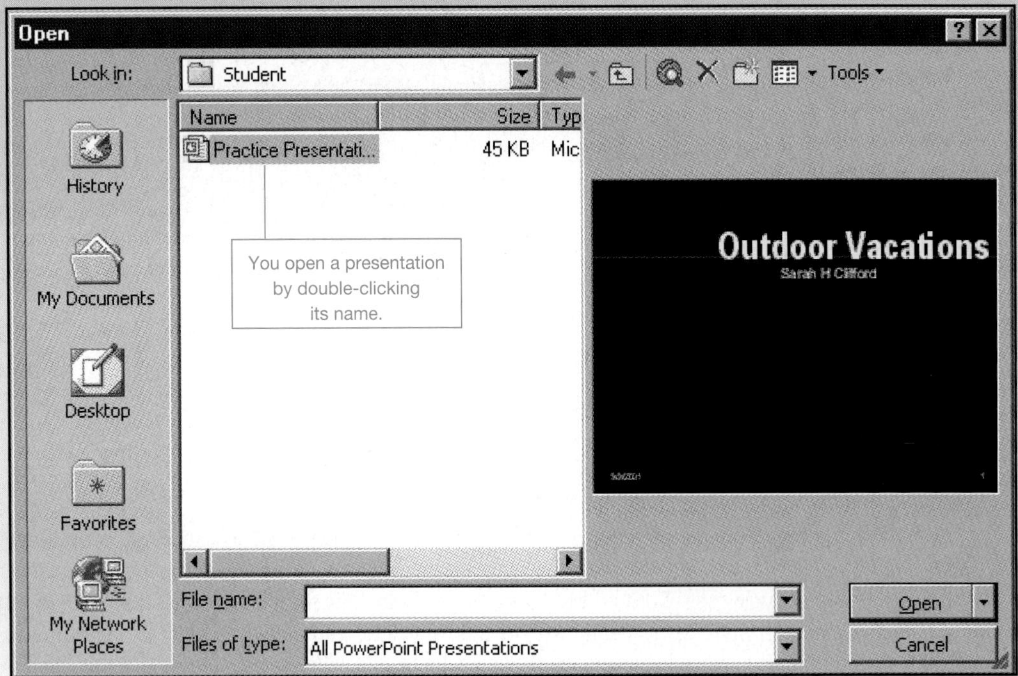

2. To open the "Practice Presentation" presentation, do the following:
DOUBLE-CLICK: "Practice Presentation"
The dialog box disappears and the presentation is loaded into the application window.

3. Proceed to the next lesson.

1.4.3 Printing a Presentation

feature

Whereas clicking the Print button (🖨) sends your presentation directly to the printer, choosing File, Print displays the Print dialog box for customizing one or more print options. You can select what to print (audience handouts, notes pages, or your presentation's outline). You can select whether to print your presentation using shades of gray or black. And you can specify how many copies to print.

method

To send a presentation directly to the printer:

- CLICK: Print button (🖨)

To customize one or more print settings:

- CHOOSE: File, Print

practice

You will now send a presentation to the printer. Ensure that the "Practice Presentation" presentation is displaying. (*Note:* If you don't have a printer installed, review the following steps without performing them.)

1. Let's send the "Practice Presentation" presentation to the printer. Do the following:
CHOOSE: File, Print
The dialog box displayed in Figure 1.35 appears. (*Note:* The quickest method for sending the current presentation to the printer directly would be to click the Print button (🖨) on the Standard toolbar.)

Figure 1.35

Print dialog box

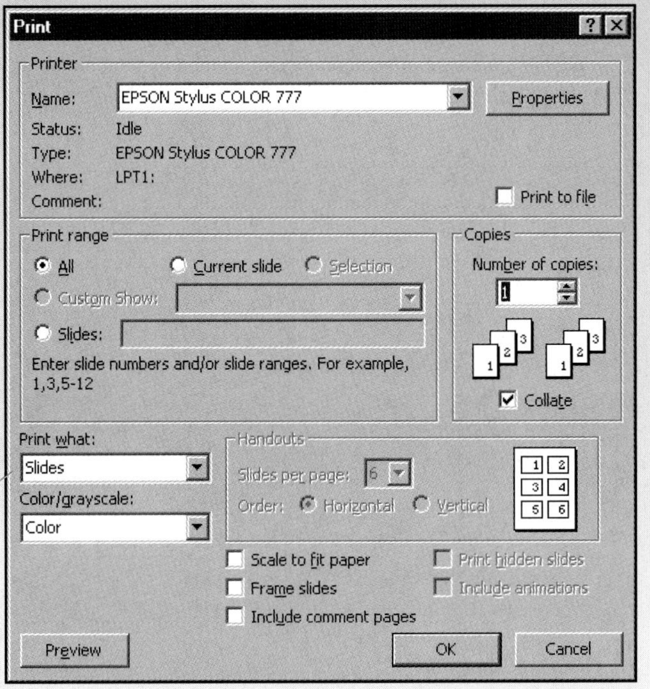

This is where you select what to print.

2. Note that "Slides" is the current selection in the *Print what* drop-down list. Let's see what the other options are:
CLICK: *Print what* drop-down arrow
Notice the additional options of Handouts, Notes Pages, and Outline View.

3. To remove the drop-down list:
PRESS: ESC

4. If you do not have access to a printer, click the Cancel button. If you have a printer connected to your computer and want to print the presentation, do the following:
CLICK: OK command button
After a few moments, the presentation will appear at the printer.

5. Continue to the next lesson, keeping the current document open.

1.4.4 Creating a New File Folder

feature

As more and more files accumulate on your computer, you may want to create folders to help you better organize your work. For example, you may have one folder for your presentations and another for your reports and memos. In PowerPoint, you create folders directly within the Open and Save As dialog boxes. Microsoft PowerPoint uses the Folder icon (📁) to identify folders.

method

To create a new folder:

- In the Open or Save As dialog box, navigate to the disk or folder where you want to create the new folder.
- RIGHT-CLICK: *an empty part of the dialog box*
- CHOOSE: New, Folder from the right-click menu
- TYPE: **a folder name**

To delete a folder:

- In the Open or Save As dialog box:
  RIGHT-CLICK: a folder
- CHOOSE: Delete from the right-click menu

practice

In this lesson, you create a folder named "My Presentations" in the My Documents folder. You then save the open file into the new folder.

1. To display the Save As dialog box:
   CHOOSE: File, Save As
2. To open the My Documents folder:
   CLICK: My Documents button in the Places bar
3. To create a new folder called My Presentations in the My Documents folder:
   RIGHT-CLICK: *an empty part of the window*
   CHOOSE: New from the right-click menu
   The New menu is shown in Figure 1.36.

Figure 1.36

Creating a new folder

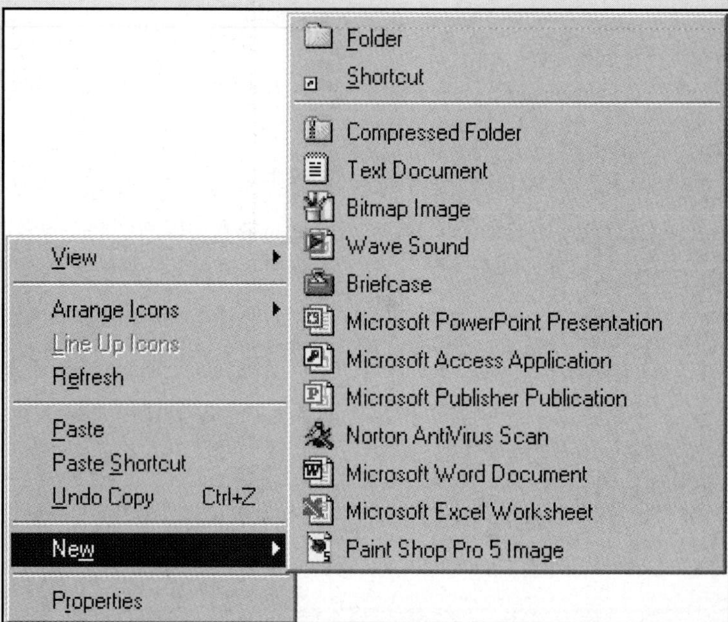

4. To proceed with creating the new folder:
   CHOOSE: Folder
   A folder entitled New Folder appears in the window.

5. Since the folder's title is already highlighted, you can simply type over the name to name your new folder. Do the following:
TYPE: **My Presentations**
PRESS: ENTER
A new folder named My Presentations should appear in the file listing. The Folder icon identifies the new item as a folder.

6. To open the new folder:
DOUBLE-CLICK: My Presentations folder
The Save As dialog box should now appear similar to Figure 1.37. Note that the folder is empty.

Figure 1.37

My Presentations folder

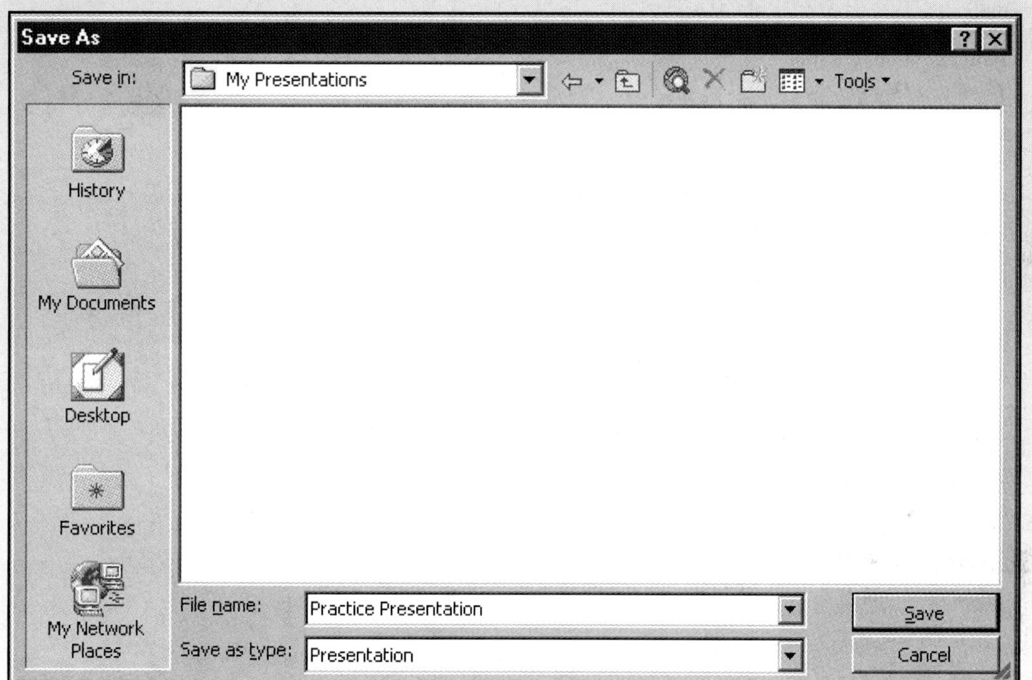

7. To save the open file to the new folder, using the same filename:
CLICK: Save command button
It's that easy to keep your files organized!

8. Close any documents that remain open.

1.4. Under what circumstances might you want to save a file under a different filename?

Chapter summary

You have several options when starting a new presentation. For content and design suggestions, consider starting a presentation using the AutoContent Wizard. For design (and no content) suggestions, consider starting a presentation from a design template. You can also choose to begin a blank presentation, in which you ignore PowerPoint's content and design suggestions altogether.

PowerPoint

After inserting a new slide, you can add text to it by clicking a text placeholder or by typing in the *Outline* tab. Besides creating presentations, it is important to know how to execute common file management procedures including saving, opening, closing, and printing presentations.

Command Summary

Many of the commands and procedures appearing in this chapter are summarized in the following table.

Skill Set	To Perform This Task	Do the Following
Creating Presentations	Launch the AutoContent wizard	CHOOSE: File, New CLICK: "From AutoContent Wizard" link in the New Presentation task pane
	Choose a design template	CHOOSE: File, New CLICK: "From Design Template" link in the New Presentation task pane DOUBLE CLICK: a design thumbnail
	Begin a blank presentation	CLICK: New button ( )
	Insert slides	CLICK: New Slide button ( )
	Delete a selected slide	CHOOSE: Edit, Delete Slide
Inserting and Modifying Text	Add text to the Slide pane	CLICK: in a text placeholder and then type
	Add text to the *Outline* tab	PRESS: ENTER to insert a new slide or continue typing at the same level PRESS: TAB to begin typing at a demoted (lower) level PRESS: SHIFT + TAB to begin typing at a promoted (higher) level
	Make text bold, italic, or underlined	CLICK: Bold ( ), Italic ( ), or Underline ( ) buttons
	Change the current font	CLICK: down arrow beside the Font drop-down list ( )
	Change font size	CLICK: down arrow beside the Font Size drop-down list ( )
	Change paragraph alignment	CLICK: Align Left button ( ) CLICK: Center button ( ) CLICK: Align Right button ( )
Managing Files	Save a presentation	CLICK: Save button ( )
	Save as a new presentation	CHOOSE: File, Save As
	Close a presentation	CLICK: Close button ( ), or CHOOSE: File, Close
	Open an existing presentation	CLICK: Open button ( ), or CHOOSE: File, Open

Skill Set	To Perform This Task	Do the Following
	Create a new file folder	RIGHT-CLICK: an empty part of the Open or Save As dialog box CHOOSE: File, New TYPE: **a folder name**
Printing Presentations	Print a presentation	CLICK: Print button ( ), or CHOOSE: File, Print
	Print slides in a variety of formats	CHOOSE: File, Print SELECT: an option from the *Print what* drop-down list

Key Terms

This section specifies page references for the key terms identified in this chapter. For a complete list of definitions, refer to the Glossary provided at the end of this learning guide.

application window, *p. 4*
AutoContent Wizard, *p. 9*
AutoFit feature, *p. 18*
design template, *p. 9*
hyperlink, *p. 9*
justification, *p. 23*
Normal view, *p. 12*
placeholder, *p. 16*
Places bar, *p. 27*
task pane, *p. 6*

Chapter quiz

Short Answer

1. Describe the procedure for changing a text selection from a size of 10 points to 16 points.
2. Describe the procedure for inserting a new slide in a presentation.
3. What is the task pane used for?
4. How would you go about deleting the current slide?
5. What are the characteristics of Normal view?
6. What is a slide layout?
7. What advantage does Word's AutoFit feature provide?
8. What is the difference between choosing File, Print and clicking the Print button ( )?
9. How would you go about applying a different layout to the current slide?
10. What happens when you click the New button ( )?

True/False

1. ____ In Normal view, the *Outline* tab is larger than the Slide pane.
2. ____ Placeholders are inserted on slides when you choose a slide layout.

3. ____ Clicking the New button (□) starts a presentation from a design template.
4. ____ Character formatting involves selecting typefaces, font sizes, and attributes for text.
5. ____ To create a blank presentation, choose File, New.
6. ____ You edit a text placeholder by clicking once in the placeholder.
7. ____ You can delete the current slide using the Menu bar or the *Outline* tab.
8. ____ PowerPoint's AutoFit feature automatically resizes placeholders to accommodate typed text.
9. ____ You can add text in both the *Outline* tab and Slide pane.
10. ____ Inserted slides are placed before the current slide.

Multiple Choice

1. Text that you realign is repositioned within the current ______________.
   a. slide
   b. presentation
   c. placeholder
   d. None of the above

2. To change the overall look of a presentation, you should apply an alternate ______________.
   a. AutoLayout
   b. placeholder
   c. design template
   d. All of the above

3. To save a presentation using a different name, choose ______________.
   a. File, Save
   b. File, Save As
   c. File, Print
   d. All of the above

4. Which of the following provides design and content suggestions?
   a. design template
   b. AutoContent Wizard
   c. blank presentation
   d. Slide Show view

5. Which of the following can you use to organize your files?
   a. *Outline* tab
   b. Slide pane
   c. folders
   d. All of the above

6. Which of the following marks the location of slide objects?
   a. folders
   b. placeholders
   c. hyperlinks
   d. fonts

7. Which of the following procedures displays the Print dialog box?
   a. CLICK: Print button (🖨)
   b. CHOOSE: File, Print
   c. CLICK: New button (□)
   d. All of the above

8. In Normal view, which of the following panes would you use to type in reminder notes?
   a. Slide pane
   b. Outline pane
   c. Notes pane
   d. None of the above

9. The Places bar is useful when ______________.
   a. saving and opening
   b. formatting text
   c. inserting slides
   d. All of the above

10. Which of the following buttons lets you select an alternate typeface?
   a. B
   b. ≡
   c. 10 ▾
   d. Times Roman ▾

exercises

1. Whiting Tours: Editing a Presentation

Whiting Tours specializes in organizing outdoor adventure trips. As president of Whiting Tours, Ralph Whiting is preparing for an upcoming presentation. Assume the role of Ralph in opening, editing, saving, and printing an existing presentation.

1. Open the PP01HE01 presentation.
2. Save the presentation as "Whiting Tours" to your personal storage location. (*Hint:* Choose File, Save As.) Your screen should now appear similar to Figure 1.38.

Figure 1.38

"Whiting Tours" presentation

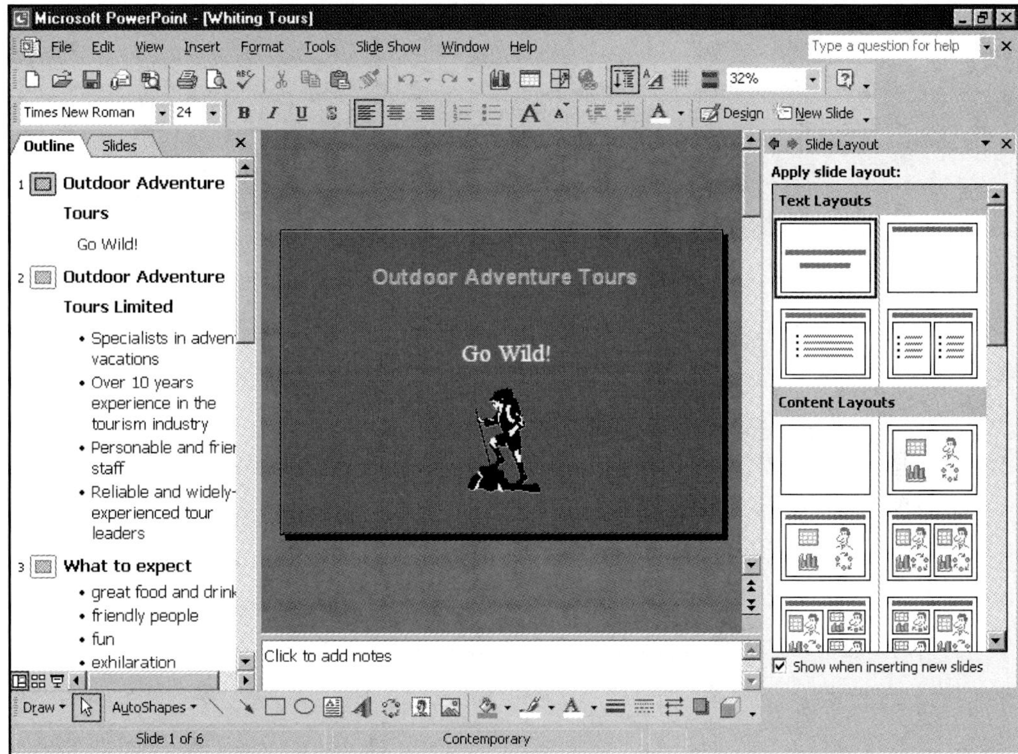

3. To view the slides in the presentation:
   CLICK: Next Slide button (▼) on the vertical scroll bar to advance to the next slide
4. Continue with step 3 until you've viewed all the slides in the presentation.
5. CLICK: Previous Slide button (▲) on the vertical scroll bar until slide 1 appears in the Slide pane
6. Using the *Outline* tab, change the text from "Go Wild!" to "Join Us on the Wild Side!"
   SELECT: the text "Go Wild!" on the first slide
   TYPE: **Join Us on the Wild Side!**

PowerPoint

7. Using the Slide pane, edit the text on the second slide.
   CLICK: Next Slide button (▾) to display slide 2
   SELECT: the word "adventure" in the first bulleted point
   TYPE: **outdoor**
   The item should now read "Specialists in outdoor vacations", as shown in Figure 1.39.

Figure 1.39

Edited slide

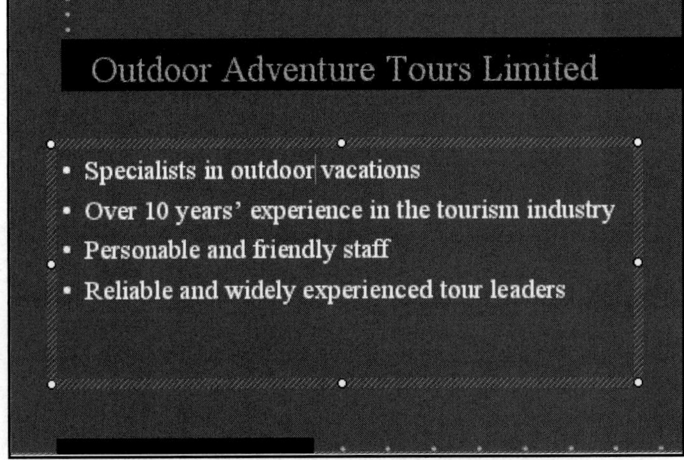

8. Let's delete the slide entitled "Special Group Rates".
   CLICK: Next Slide button (▾) on the vertical scroll bar until the fifth slide appears
   CHOOSE: Edit, Delete Slide
9. Save and then print the revised presentation.
10. Close the "Whiting Tours" presentation.

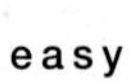

2. Glorietta Community College: Creating a Presentation

Rachel Graham works in the admissions office at Glorietta Community College. She must create a short presentation describing an upcoming open house. In this exercise, assume the role of Rachel to create a new presentation from a design template and add new slides.

1. To start a new presentation based on the "Artsy" design template, do the following:
   CHOOSE: File, New command
   CLICK: "From Design Template" link in the New Presentation task pane on the right side of your screen
2. CLICK: "Blends" thumbnail in the Slide Design task pane
   (*Note:* Select another suitable design template if "Blends" isn't available.)
3. To add text to the Title slide:
   TYPE: **Computer Open House** in the title placeholder
   CLICK: in the subtitle placeholder
   TYPE: **Glorietta Community College**
   The Title slide should appear similar to Figure 1.40.

Figure 1.40

Title slide

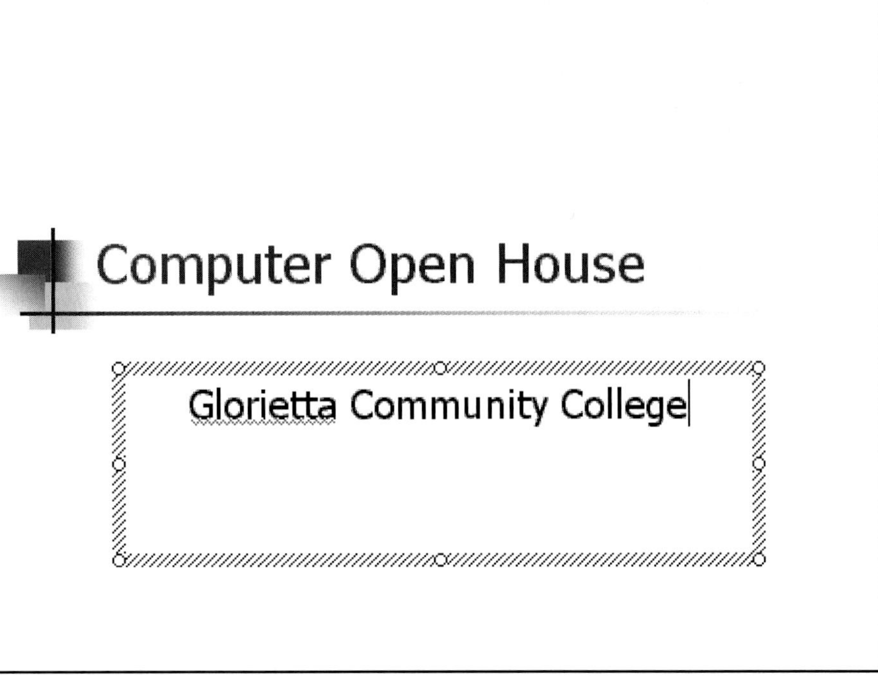

4. To insert a new slide for creating a bulleted list of items:
   CLICK: New Slide button (▣) on the Formatting toolbar
   The Title and Text layout was automatically applied. This layout is suitable for creating a bulleted list.

5. To insert a title on the second slide:
   TYPE: **When?** in the title placeholder

6. Type the following two items in the bulleted list:
   8:00 am – 6:00 pm
   Saturday, September 29, 2001

7. To insert another new slide for creating a bulleted list:
   CLICK: New Slide button (▣) on the Formatting toolbar

8. TYPE: **Where?** in the title placeholder

9. Type the following three items in the bulleted list:
   Monashee Community College
   100 College Way
   Spokane, Washington

10. Insert another new slide for creating a bulleted list and then type **Why?** in the title placeholder.

11. Type the following four items in the bulleted list:
    Visit our new computer labs
    Hourly information sessions
    Computer course registration
    Free refreshments
    The slide should appear similar to Figure 1.41. (*Note:* The graphic used for bullets may appear different on your computer.)

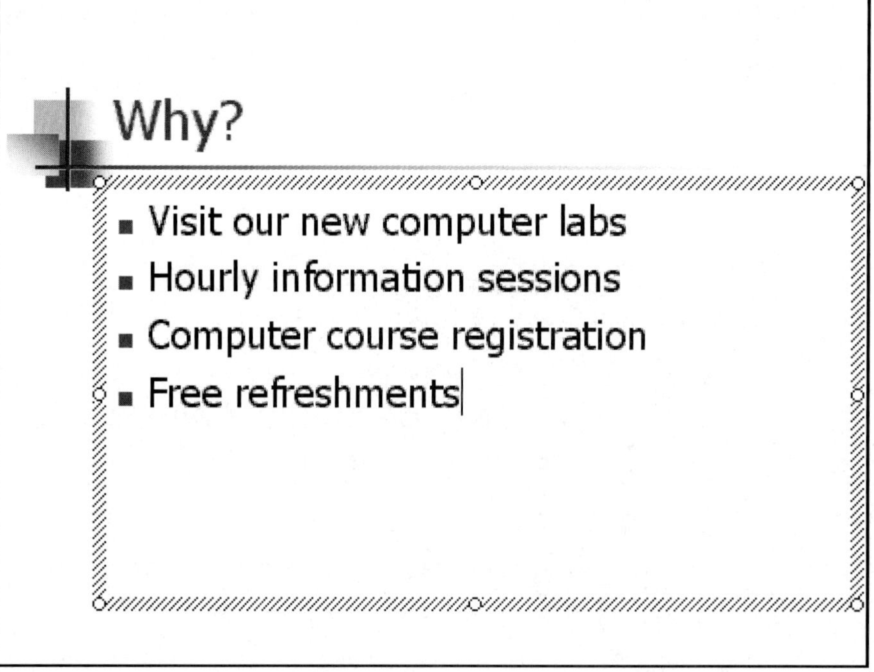
Why?
Visit our new computer labs
Hourly information sessions
Computer course registration
Free refreshments

Figure 1.41
Bulleted list

12. To save the presentation as "Open House" to your personal storage location (such as your floppy diskette), use the File, Save As command.
13. Close the presentation.

moderate

3. Catalina Marketing: Editing an AutoContent Presentation

Catalina Marketing specializes in providing strategic marketing solutions to retailers. John Chua is new to the company and has been asked to create a short presentation for an upcoming information session. In this exercise, assume the role of John and perform the steps listed below.

1. Launch the AutoContent Wizard and then make the following choices when prompted:
   - Select the "Selling a Product or Service" presentation from the "Sales/Marketing" category.
   - Select "On-screen presentation" as the output option.
   - Type **Catalina Marketing** in the *Presentation title* text box.
   - Insert **General Information** in the *Footer* text box and then click the Finish command button to compile the presentation.
2. Delete the existing text from the subtitle placeholder on the first slide and then type the following, inserting your actual name where indicated: **Prepared by:** followed by **your name**.
3. Using the *Outline* tab, delete slide 4. Then, delete the newly positioned slide 6. (*Note:* Click the OK command button if prompted.)
4. Using the *Outline* tab, edit the bulleted list on slide 2 to include the following bulleted items:
   Promote your business
   Expand your reach
   Improve customer satisfaction

5. Insert a slide that uses the Title and Text layout after slide 2.
6. Edit the new slide by typing **New Ways to Promote Business** in the title placeholder and **Web-based services**, **Local advertising**, and **Door-to-door sales** as the three new bulleted items in the bulleted list placeholder. The slide should appear similar to Figure 1.42.

Figure 1.42

Bulleted list

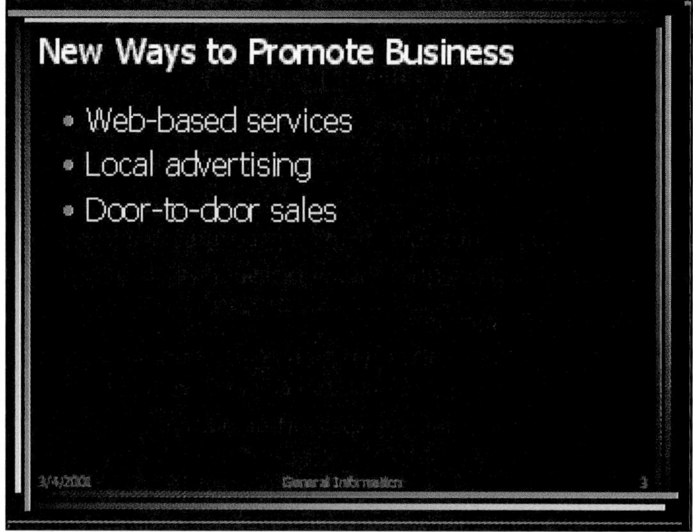

7. John decides to change the font used in the title placeholder on the first slide. Display the first slide and then do the following:
   • Increase the title's point size to 54 points
   • Apply the bold and italic attributes to the title

   The title should now appear similar to Figure 1.43.

Figure 1.43

Title with new format

Catalina Marketing

8. John has run out of time and will finish editing the presentation later. Save the presentation as "Catalina Overview" to your personal storage location.
9. Print and then close the presentation.

moderate 

4. AddIn Tennis: Adding and Editing Slides

Located in Seattle, Washington, AddIn Tennis provides tennis instruction to all levels and ages. Luke Evanisko, the company's founder, is busy in the office today working on a PowerPoint presentation that he will eventually publish on the Web. In this exercise, assume the role of Luke in creating and editing a presentation.

1. Start a new presentation based on the "Network" design template. (*Note:* If this template isn't available on your computer, select an alternate one.)
2. Save the new presentation as "AddIn Overview" to your personal storage location.

3. Create the following four slides:

Slide 1: Title Slide layout

Title: **AddIn Tennis**

Subtitle: **Giving you the tennis advantage!**

Slide 2: Title and Text layout

Title: **Why play tennis?**

- **Get out of the rain!**
- **Learn tennis from the pros!**
- **Make friends!**
- **Have fun!**

Slide 3: Title and Text layout

Title: **What we do**

- **Private lessons**
- **Tennis clinics**
- **Weekend camps**

Slide 4: Title and Text layout

Title: **Our philosophy**

- **We take the best in your game, and make it better!**
- **We show you that winning isn't everything. Having a good time is much more important.**

Figure 1.44 shows the completed fourth slide. (*Note:* The graphic used for bullets may appear different on your computer.)

Figure 1.44

Bulleted list

Our philosophy

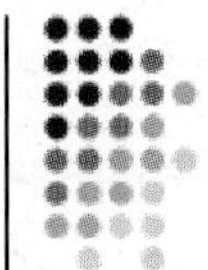

- We take the best in your game, and make it better!
- We show you that winning isn't everything. Having a good time is much more important.

4. Insert a new bulleted item containing the text **Day camps** between the second and third bullets on slide 3.

5. Display the second slide and then increase the point size of the title to 44 points. Make the same change to slides 3 and 4.

6. Save, print, and then close the revised presentation.

difficult 

5. On Your Own: Presenting "My Hobby"

Using one of PowerPoint's design templates, create a new PowerPoint presentation on a topic or hobby that interests you. Your presentation should consist of a Title slide followed by three slides containing bulleted lists. The first slide should include the name of your hobby and your name. Suggestions for the following slides are (a) Why I like my hobby, (b) How to do my hobby, and (c) What my hobby involves. Save your presentation as "My Hobby" to your personal storage location. Print and then close the presentation.

difficult 

6. On Your Own: Presenting "I Need a Vacation"

Start a blank presentation and then insert four slides (for a total of five slides) that tries to convince your audience—a relative, business associate, or other individual—why you need a vacation. Use your experience with PowerPoint to make the most compelling case possible. When you're finished, save the presentation as "Vacation" to your personal storage location and then print the presentation. Close the presentation.

Case Problems

Cushman Communications

Now that Zach has used Microsoft PowerPoint, he is eager to view his nephew's presentation and provide him with some feedback. He also plans to create a new presentation for his client, *United Pipeline Limited.* In the following case problems, assume the role of Zach and perform the same steps he identifies. You may want to re-read the chapter opening before proceeding.

1. Zach opens his nephew's PowerPoint presentation entitled PP01CS01 and then saves it as "Budgies" to his personal storage location. At this point, his screen looks similar to Figure 1.45.

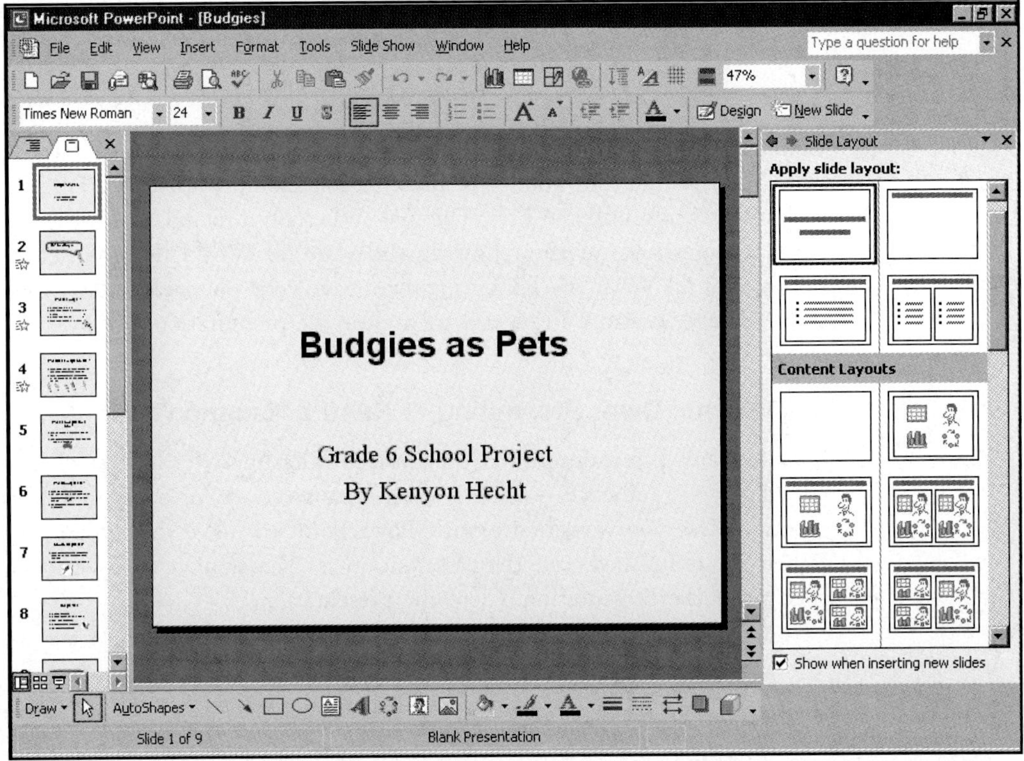

Figure 1.45

"Budgies" presentation

Zach views each of the slides in the presentation and feels ready to respond to Kenyon's e-mail. Zach closes the presentation.

2. Zach decides to use Kenyon's presentation for practice with adding and modifying slides. After opening the presentation, he saves a copy of it as "Kenyon" to his personal storage location. After the first slide, Zach adds a new slide with a Title Slide layout. He enters **Approved by Zach Reynolds** in the title placeholder, **Public Relations Coordinator** on the first line of the subtitle placeholder, and **Cushman Communications** on the second line. Zach saves the revised presentation.

3. Zach continues practicing his skills using the "Kenyon" presentation. He adds a new slide before the final slide of the presentation. After typing **Keep your budgie away from:** in the title placeholder, he inserts the following bulleted items:

   - **Hungry cats**
   - **Open windows**
   - **Hot stoves**
   - **Curious alligators**

   After deleting slide 8 ("How do budgies eat?") from the presentation, he saves it as "Kenyon Update" to his personal storage location. Next he prints and then closes the presentation.

4. With an afternoon deadline quickly approaching, Zach begins working on a PowerPoint on-screen presentation for his client, *United Pipeline Limited.* Using the AutoContent Wizard, he selects "Reporting Progress or Status" from the "Projects" category. He enters **United Pipeline Limited** in the title placeholder and then generates the presentation.

Zach edits the subtitle on the first slide and deletes any text that may already be there. He then types **Jonathan C. Edwards** on the first line and **President and CEO** on the second line. Zach then edits the bulleted items on slides 2 and 3 so that they include only the bulleted items listed below:

Slide 2

- **Project schedule**
- **Final delivery date**
- **Final cost estimates**

Slide 3

- **Schedule implications**
- **What works**

Slide 3 appears in Figure 1.46. Zach saves the presentation as "United Status" and then prints the presentation's outline for Jonathan's review. (*Hint:* Choose File, Print and then select Outline View from the *Print what* drop-down list.) As a final step, Zach closes the presentation.

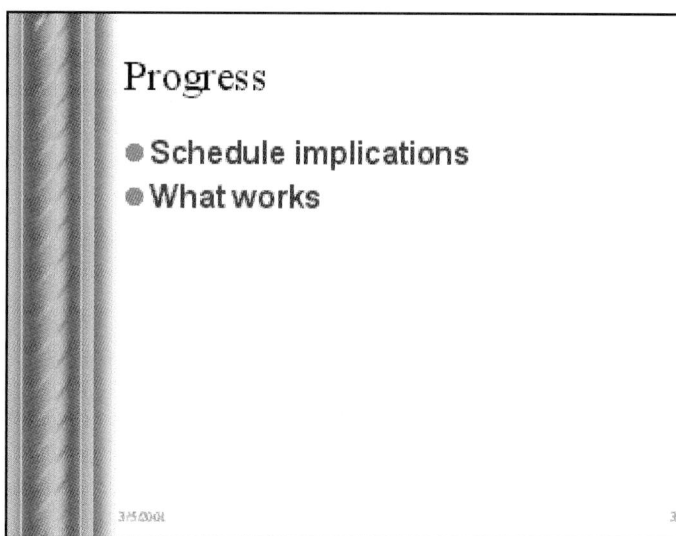

Figure 1.46

"United Status" presentation

NOTES

Microsoft® PowerPoint® 2002

CHAPTER 2

Modifying and Running Presentations

CHAPTER OUTLINE

Case Study

2.1 Editing Slides

2.2 Changing a Presentation's Design

2.3 Running a Slide Show

Chapter Summary

Chapter Quiz

Hands-On Exercises

Case Problems

PREREQUISITES

To successfully complete this chapter, you must be able to create new presentations, insert slides, and insert and format slide text. You will also be asked to open, save, and close presentations, and use PowerPoint's toolbars, Menu bar, and right-click menus.

LEARNING OBJECTIVES

After completing this chapter, you will be able to:

- Apply slide layouts and change slide order
- Add footer text to every slide
- Customize slide templates
- Start and run slide shows

CaseStudy **HOLLY HOLDMAN** Holly Holdman is a graduate student who is preparing to defend her master's thesis. Her topic, snowmelt hydrology research, involves data that she has collected from the Arctic region. Holly has created text-based presentations before but has limited experience editing them. She also has limited experience presenting them in front of a live audience.

In this chapter, you and Holly apply and customize slide layouts and templates, add footer text to every slide, and start and run slide shows.

2.1 Editing Slides

The look of your presentation is determined by several factors including the current design template and slide layouts. In this module, we focus on changing and customizing slide layouts. We also lead you through changing the order of slides in your presentation.

2.1.1 Applying an Alternate Layout

feature

You may find that an existing slide layout does not meet your needs. For example, in addition to your bulleted list placeholder, you may decide that you need a graph placeholder. In this case, you will want to change the existing slide layout to meet your new requirements.

method

- CHOOSE: Format, Slide Layout
- In the *Slides* tab:
  CLICK: the slides you want to apply the layout to (press and hold down CTRL when selecting multiple slides)
- In the Slide Layout task pane:
  CLICK: the layout you want

practice

You will now begin a new presentation and then practice changing slide layouts. Ensure that no presentations are open in the application window.

1. To create a new presentation based on the "Pixel" design template:
   CHOOSE: File, New
   CLICK: "From Design Template" link in the New Presentation task pane
2. Navigate to the "Pixel" template in the Slide Design task pane and then:
   CLICK: "Pixel" template
3. To insert text in the title placeholder:
   CLICK: the title placeholder (in the Slide pane)
   TYPE: **Current Trends**

4. To insert text in the subtitle placeholder:
CLICK: the subtitle placeholder
TYPE: **By**
PRESS: ENTER
TYPE: **Your Name**
Your screen should now appear similar to Figure 2.1, with your name displaying instead of the words "Your Name."

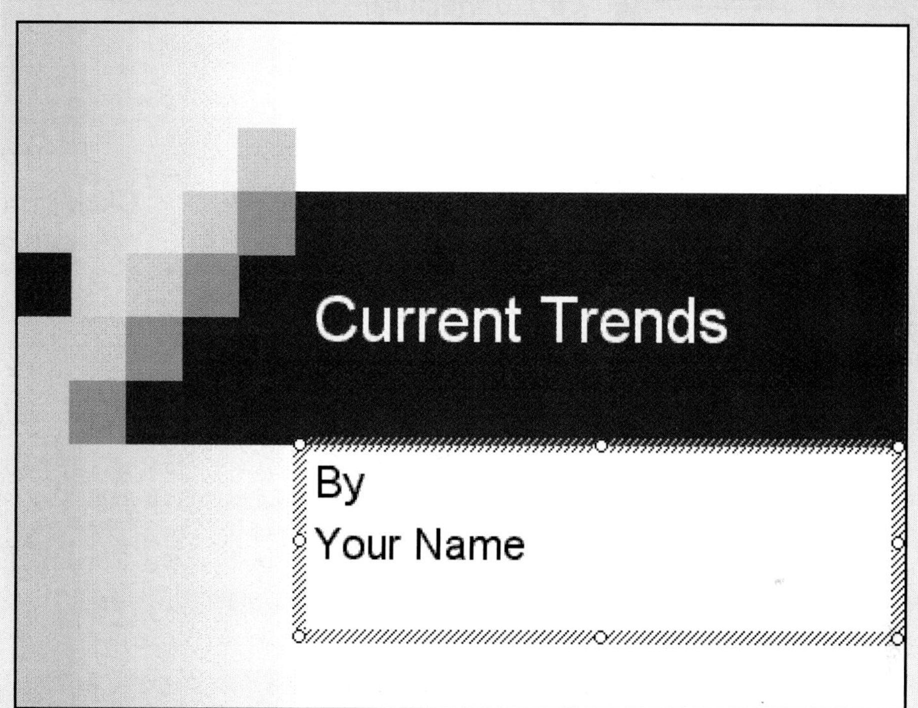

Figure 2.1

This slide uses the Title Slide layout

5. Add a second slide to the presentation.
CLICK: New Slide button ( ) on the Formatting toolbar
The new slide is currently conforming to the Title and Text layout.

6. Let's change the layout of this slide to the "Title, Text, and Content" layout. In the Slide Layout task pane, drag the vertical scroll bar downward and then:
CLICK: "Title, Text, and Content" thumbnail
The slide now includes placeholders for a title, bulleted list, and graph.

7. To add a title to the slide:
CLICK: title placeholder
TYPE: **The Leading Trends**

8. To add content to the slide:
CLICK: bulleted list placeholder (located on the left side of the slide)
TYPE: **Connectivity**
PRESS: ENTER
TYPE: **Interactivity**
PRESS: ENTER
TYPE: **Online access**
Your screen should now appear similar to Figure 2.2. (*Note:* The graphic used for the bulleted items may appear different on your computer.)

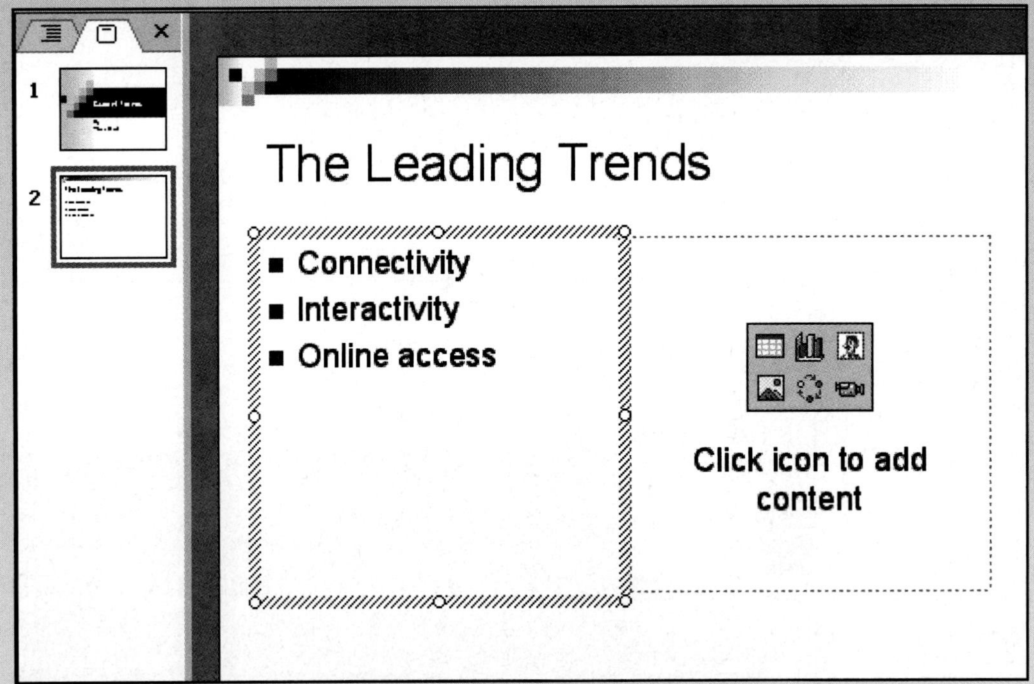

Figure 2.2

This slide uses the "Title, Text, and Content" layout

9. Change the layout of the second slide to the "Title and Text" layout.
CLICK: "Title and Text" thumbnail in the Slide Layout pane
The slide was changed to conform to the "Title and Text" layout. The text in the bulleted list appears larger and the graph placeholder no longer appears (Figure 2.3).

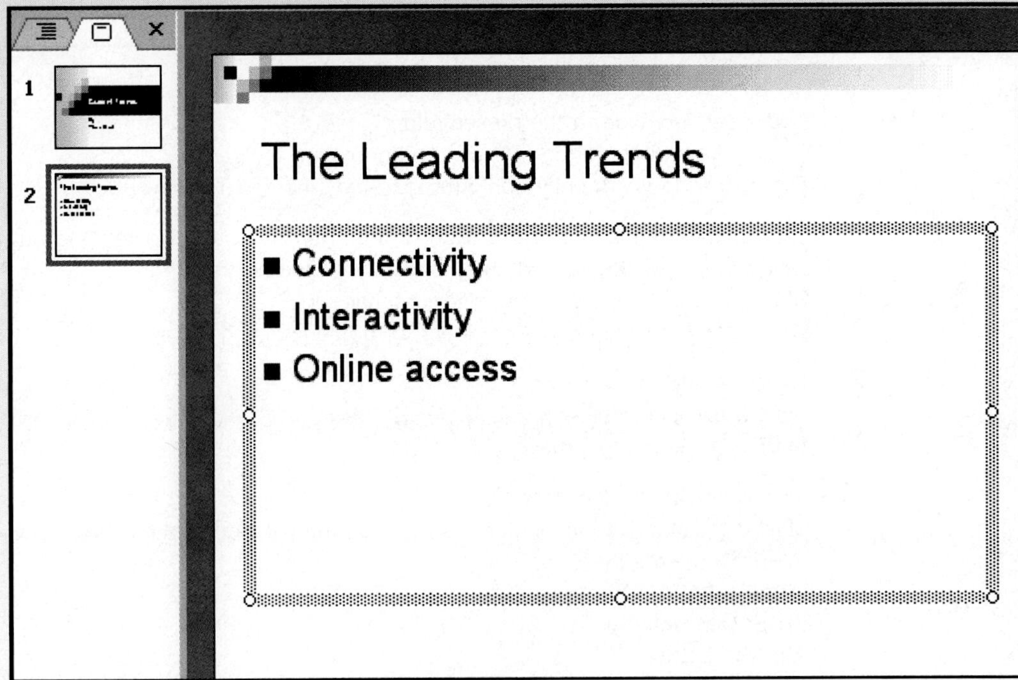

Figure 2.3

Reapplying the "Title and Text" layout

10. Save the presentation as "Current Trends" to your personal storage location.

11. Continue to the next lesson.

2.1.2 Customizing Placeholders

feature

As you know, when you choose a layout for a new or existing slide, PowerPoint inserts an arranged group of placeholders on the slide. You can move, resize, and delete object placeholders to suit your needs.

method

- Select a placeholder by clicking it.
- Move a placeholder by dragging it.
- Resize a placeholder by dragging its sizing handles.
- Delete a placeholder by pressing DELETE.

practice

You will now practice customizing the current slide layout. Ensure that you have completed the previous lesson in this module and that slide 2 in the "Current Trends" presentation is displaying in the application window.

1. On the second slide of the "Current Trends" presentation, the bulleted items appear to be positioned too close to the left edge of the slide. Let us practice resizing the bulleted list placeholder and moving it to the right. To select the placeholder:
CLICK: in the bulleted list placeholder
As shown in Figure 2.4, the placeholder is surrounded with **sizing handles** (tiny circles surrounding the object).

Figure 2.4

Selecting a slide object

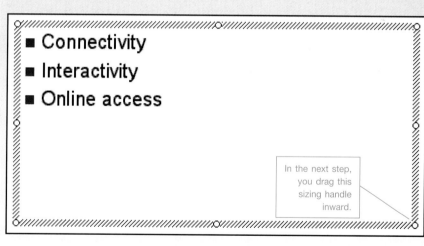

2. When you position the mouse pointer over a sizing handle, the pointer will change to a double-headed arrow. To resize the placeholder:
DRAG: the sizing handle in the bottom-right corner (see Figure 2.4) inward until the placeholder looks like Figure 2.5

Figure 2.5

Resizing a slide object

■ Connectivity
■ Interactivity
■ Online access

3. To move the placeholder to the right, position the mouse pointer over one of the placeholder borders until a four-headed arrow (✥) appears.

4. While referring to Figure 2.6:
DRAG: the placeholder to the right
Your screen should now appear similar to Figure 2.6.

Figure 2.6

The bulleted list placeholder was moved to the right

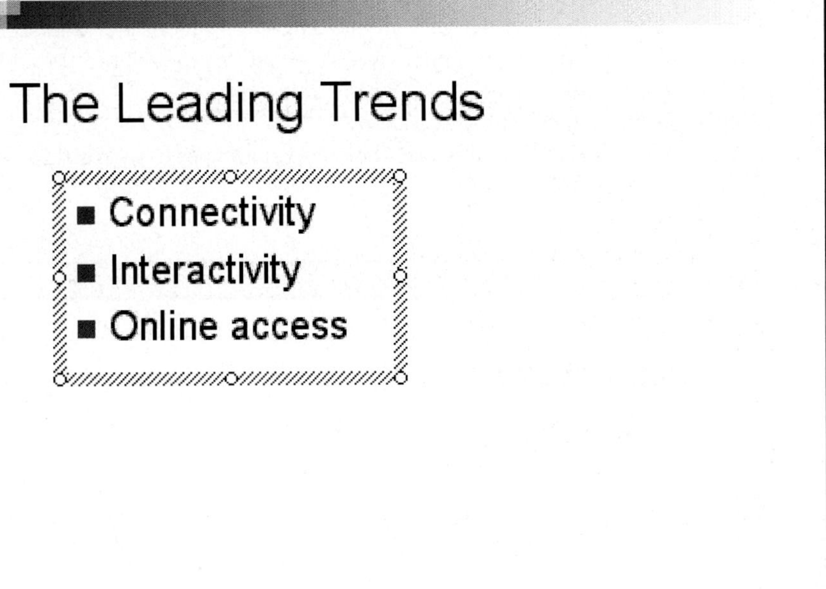

5. You can also delete selected placeholders. To practice deleting the placeholder:
PRESS: DELETE
The contents of the placeholder are now deleted. To delete the placeholder itself:
PRESS: DELETE again

6. To undo the two previous deletions:
PRESS: the curved part of the Undo button (↶) twice

7. Save the revised presentation.

8. Continue with the next lesson.

2.1.3 Changing Slide Order

feature →

Once slides are inserted in a presentation, it is easy to reorder them using either the *Outline* or *Slides* tab. The operation is a simple drag and drop.

method →

- DRAG: slide icon or slide thumbnail up or down in the slide list

practice →

You will now practice reordering slides in the *Outline* and *Slides* tabs. Ensure that you have completed the previous lesson and that the "Current Trends" presentation is displaying in Normal view. You can check whether your presentation is displaying in Normal view by choosing View, Normal from the menu.

1. To display the contents of the *Outline* tab, located on the left side of your screen:
   CLICK: *Outline* tab

2. To move slide 2 so that it is positioned before slide 1, do the following:
   CLICK: slide 2 icon
   Notice that the slide's title and bulleted items are highlighted in reverse video (Figure 2.7).

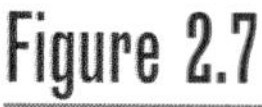

Figure 2.7

Selecting a slide in the *Outline* tab

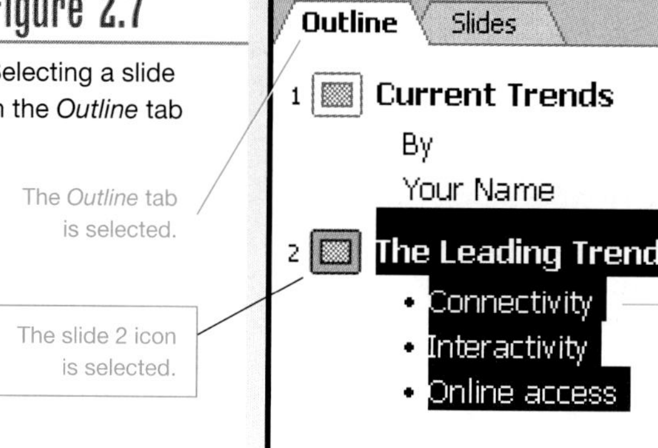
Outline
Slides
1 Current Trends
By
Your Name
2 The Leading Trends
Connectivity
Interactivity
Online access
The *Outline* tab is selected.
The slide 2 icon is selected.
The selected information is highlighted in reverse video.

3. Your current objective is to drag the slide 2 icon upward in the *Outline* tab so that it is positioned above slide 1. As you drag the icon, the slide's title and bulleted items will move with it. A narrow horizontal bar will mark where the slide will be inserted when you release the mouse button.
   DRAG: the slide 2 icon upward until the horizontal bar is one line above the slide 1 icon
   The *Outline* tab, located on the left side of your screen, should now appear similar to Figure 2.8.

Figure 2.8

Reordering slides in the *Outline* tab

4. Now we will try reordering slides using the *Slides* tab. Using the *Slides* tab, move slide 1 below slide 2.
   CLICK: *Slides* tab
5. DRAG: the slide 1 thumbnail below the slide 2 thumbnail
   The presentation has now been returned to its original order.
6. Save the revised presentation, keeping it open for use in the next lesson.

2.1.4 Adding Footer Text

feature

When you want to make a change to your presentation that affects every slide, such as inserting the current date on every slide, you don't have to edit each slide individually. Instead, you can edit the **Slide Master,** which controls the formatting of text in the footer area of your slide, as well as in title and text placeholders. Any objects or text that you insert on the Slide Master will appear on all slides. The Header and Footer command provides an easy way to insert the date and time, slide number, or optional footer text on every slide in a presentation. The Slide Master determines where this information appears on a slide.

method

- CHOOSE: View, Header and Footer
- CLICK: *Slides* tab to add information to slides
- SELECT: desired options
- CLICK: Apply (to add information to only the current slide)

or

- CLICK: Apply to All (to add information to all slides)

In this lesson, you use the Headers and Footers command. Ensure that the "Current Trends" presentation is displaying.

1. View the first slide of the "Current Trends" presentation, if it isn't displaying already.
2. CHOOSE: View, Header and Footer
   CLICK: *Slide* tab in the Header and Footer dialog box
   Your screen should now appear similar to Figure 2.9.

Figure 2.9

Header and Footer dialog box: *Slide* tab

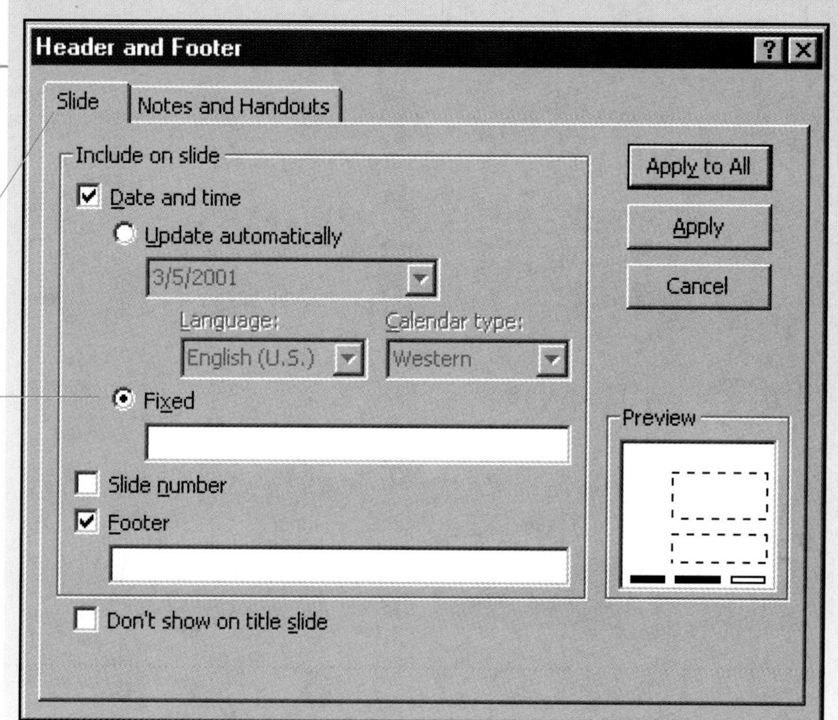

Slide tab

With this option selected, the same date will be inserted on each slide. That is, the date will not update automatically each time you open this presentation.

3. To insert the same date on every slide, ensure that the *Fixed* option button is selected and then do the following:
   CLICK: in the text box located below the *Fixed* option button
   TYPE: **4/15/2002**
4. To insert the current slide number on the slide:
   SELECT: *Slide number* check box
5. To insert footer text:
   CLICK: in the text box located below the *Footer* check box
   TYPE: **Prepared by Your Name** (substitute your actual name here)
   The Header and Footer dialog box should now appear similar to Figure 2.10.

PowerPoint

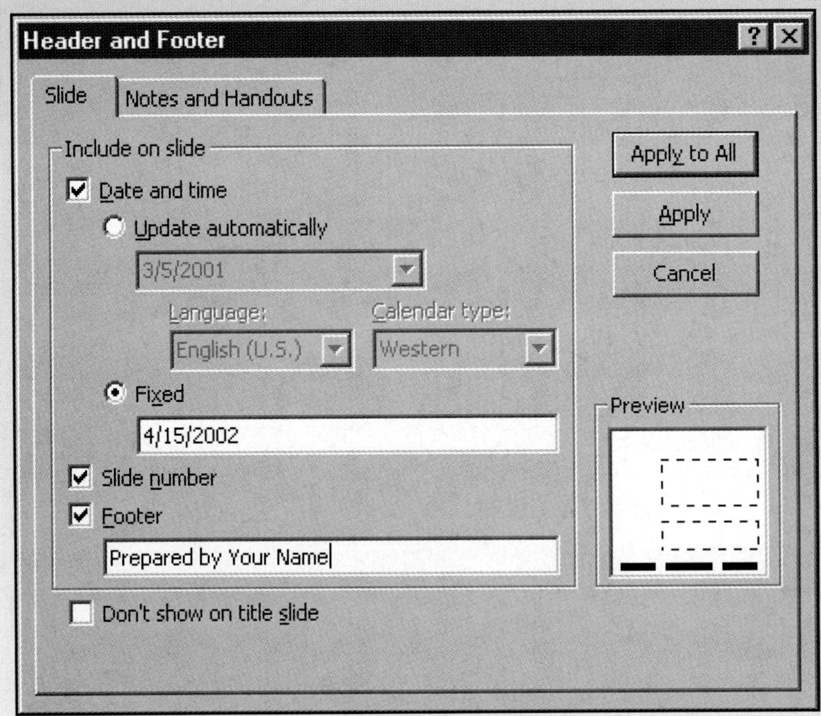

Figure 2.10

Making selections in the Header and Footer dialog box

6. To insert this information on every slide:
   CLICK: Apply to All command button
   The inserted information now appears on every slide. Figure 2.11 shows the footer on the bottom of slide 1.

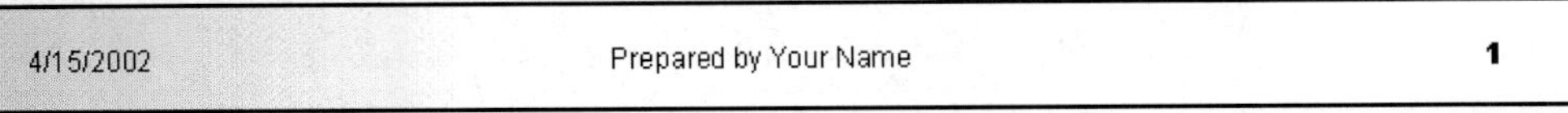

Figure 2.11

Inserted footer

7. Save and then close the revised presentation.

2.1. What is the procedure for moving and resizing object placeholders?

2.2 Changing a Presentation's Design

You learned how to create a new presentation from a design template in Chapter 1. Design templates determine what colors and text fonts are used in a presentation and the position of placeholders and other objects. By applying a design template to your presentation, you help give your presentation's slides a consistent look. In this module, you learn about applying design templates to presentations. You will also learn how to customize an existing design template.

2.2.1 Applying an Alternate Design Template

feature

Applying an alternate design template to a presentation involves selecting the design's thumbnail in the Slide Design task pane.

method

- CHOOSE: Format, Slide Design
- CLICK: a design thumbnail in the Slide Design task pane

practice

You will now practice applying design templates. Ensure that no presentations are currently open.

1. Open the PP0220 student file.
2. Save it to your personal storage location as "Santos Soups." The first slide should look like Figure 2.12.

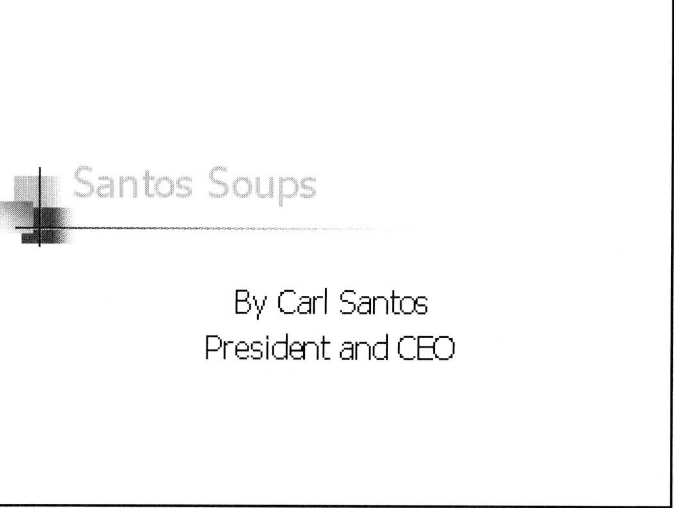

Santos Soups
By Carl Santos
President and CEO

Figure 2.12

"Santos Soups" title slide

3. Apply one of PowerPoint's design templates to the presentation.
   CHOOSE: Format, Slide Design
4. Locate the "Cascade" thumbnail in your template list, located on the right side of your screen. (*Note:* If this template isn't available, select an alternate template.)
5. CLICK: "Cascade" thumbnail in the template list
   The presentation's title slide should now appear similar to Figure 2.13. It is that easy to change the look of a presentation!

Santos Soups
By Carl Santos
President and CEO

Figure 2.13
Applying an alternate design template

6. Save the revised presentation and keep it open for use in the next lesson.

2.2.2 Applying Multiple Design Templates

feature →

You may decide to vary the design of your presentation using multiple design templates. For example, you may want to start your presentation with a colorful title slide and then follow it up with text-based slides on a white background.

method →

- CHOOSE: Format, Slide Design
- PRESS: CTRL and hold it down while clicking in the *Outline* or *Slides* tab to select slides to redesign
- RIGHT-CLICK: a design thumbnail in the Slide Design task pane
- CHOOSE: Apply to Selected Slides from the right-click menu

practice →

You will now apply a different design template to slides 2, 3, and 4 of "Santos Soups" presentation.

1. To begin, display the *Slides* tab, if it isn't selected already.
2. Do the following to select only slides 2, 3, and 4:
PRESS: CTRL and hold it down
CLICK: slides 2, 3, and 4
Slides 2, 3, and 4 should appear with a thick border in the *Slide* tab.
3. To apply the "Blends" design template to the selected slides, do the following:
RIGHT-CLICK: "Blends" template in the Slide Design task pane
CHOOSE: Apply to Selected Slides from the right-click menu
Your screen should now appear similar to Figure 2.14.

Figure 2.14

Applying more than one design template to a presentation

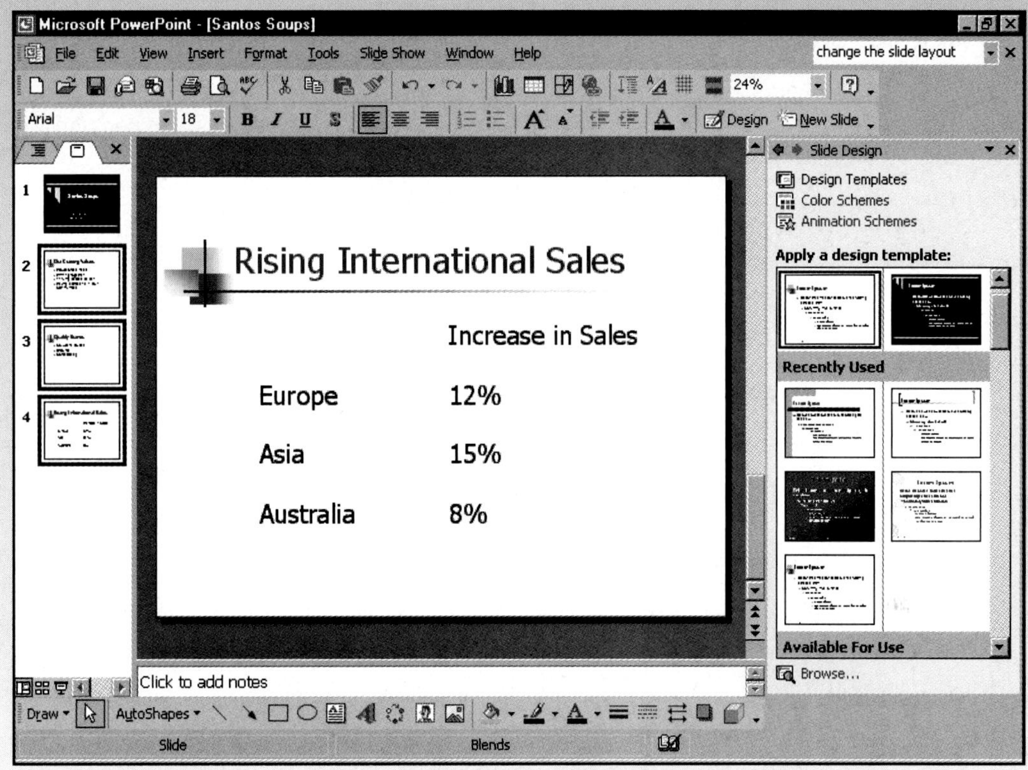

4. Before proceeding to the next lesson, let's also apply the "Blends" template to the first slide of the presentation. In the *Slides* tab:
   CLICK: the first slide
   CHOOSE: Format, Slide Design
   RIGHT-CLICK: "Blends" thumbnail (conveniently located in the "Used in This Presentation" area of the task pane)
   CHOOSE: Apply to Selected Slides from the right-click menu
5. Save the revised presentation, keeping it open for use in the next lesson.

2.2.3 Editing a Design Template

feature

Not only do design templates make it possible for beginners to create professional-looking presentations with ease, but also they help ensure a consistent look across multiple presentations. If one of PowerPoint's existing design templates works nicely for you, except for a few alterations, consider creating a new template from the existing template. You can also create a new design template from an existing presentation or create a design template entirely from scratch by starting with a blank presentation.

method

- Open an existing presentation or design template, or start a blank presentation.
- Edit the presentation or template to suit your needs.
- CHOOSE: File, Save As
- TYPE: **a name** for the new template in the *File name* text box
- SELECT: Design Template from the *Save as type* drop-down list
- Specify a storage location for the new template.

practice

In this lesson, you create a new design template from an existing presentation. Ensure that the "Santos Soups" presentation is displaying.

1. Let's create a new design template from the "Santos Soups" presentation. First we'll change the template slightly.
   CHOOSE: Format, Background
   The dialog box in Figure 2.15 appears.

Figure 2.15

Selecting an alternate background color

2. To select an alternate background color for the presentation:
   CLICK: drop-down arrow beneath the graphic
   CLICK: green from the color palette
3. To apply the revised background color to the entire presentation:
   CLICK: Apply to All command button
   Your screen should now appear similar to Figure 2.16.

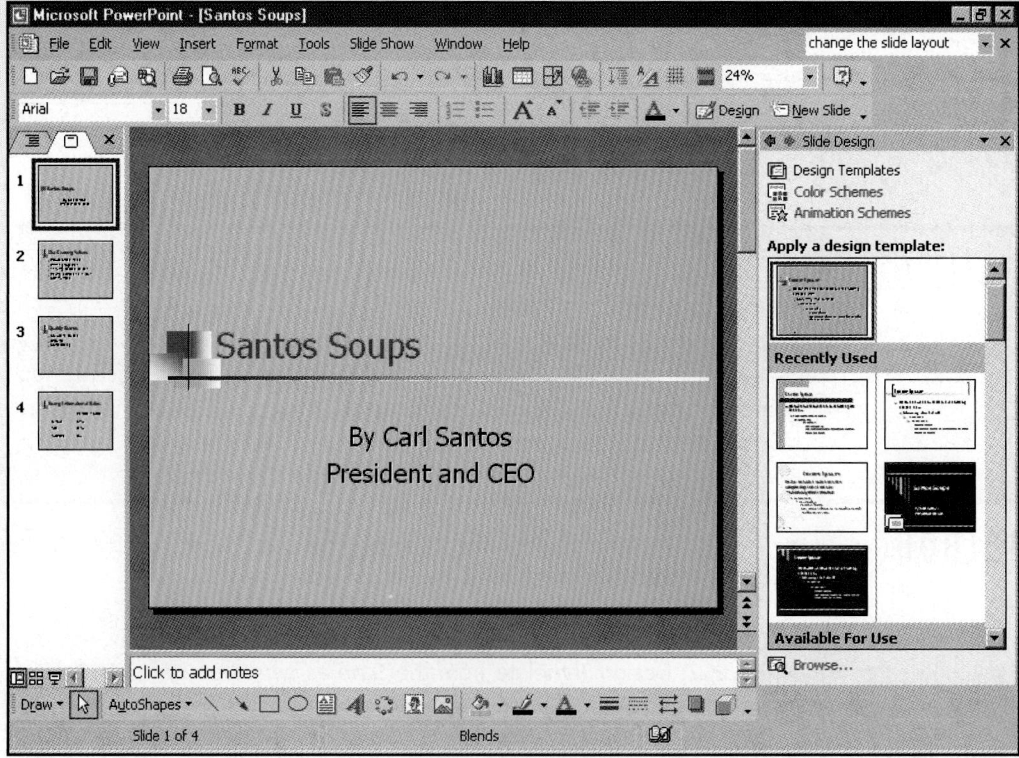

Figure 2.16

A green background has been applied to the presentation

4. To create a new design template from this presentation:
CHOOSE: File, Save As

5. Edit the name in the *File name* text box to be **Santos Soups Design**.

6. To save the file as a template:
SELECT: Design Template from the *Save as type* drop-down list
The Save As dialog box should now appear similar to Figure 2.17.

Figure 2.17

Saving a file as a design template

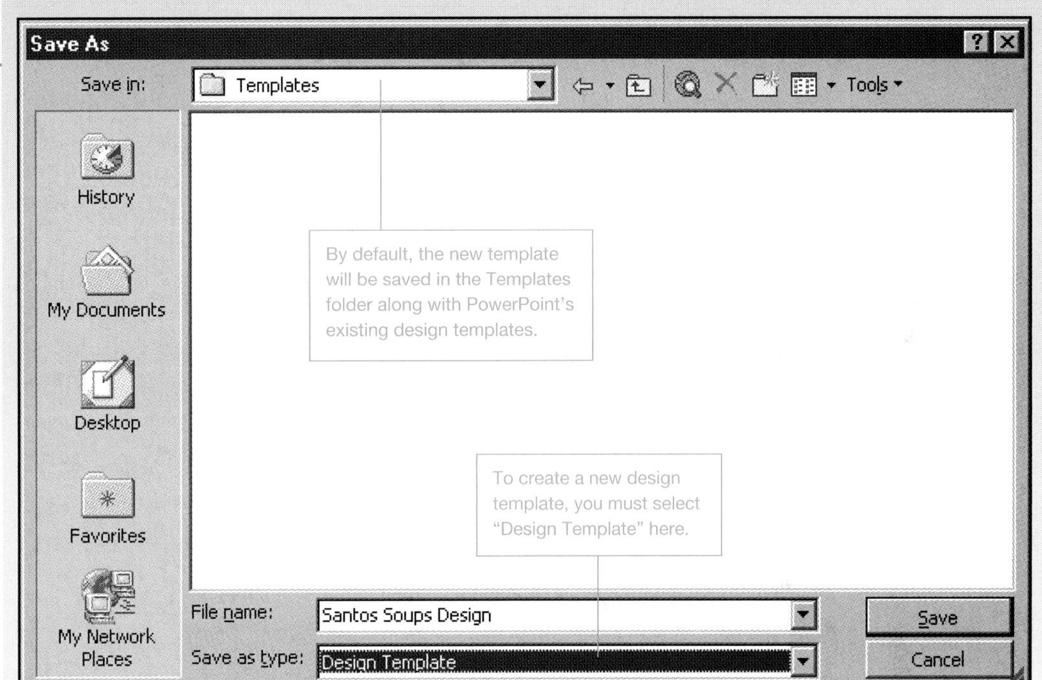

7. CLICK: Save command button

8. Close the "Santos Soups Design" template.

9. Start a blank presentation and then apply the "Santos Soups Design" template.
CLICK: New button () on the Standard toolbar

10. To apply the "Santos Soups Design" template to the presentation:
CHOOSE: Format, Slide Design

11. Locate the "Browse" link at the bottom of the Slide Design task pane, and then:
CLICK: Browse link
The Apply Design Template dialog box should now appear similar to Figure 2.18. Note that PowerPoint automatically displayed the contents of the Templates folder.

Figure 2.18

The template you created appears in the templates list

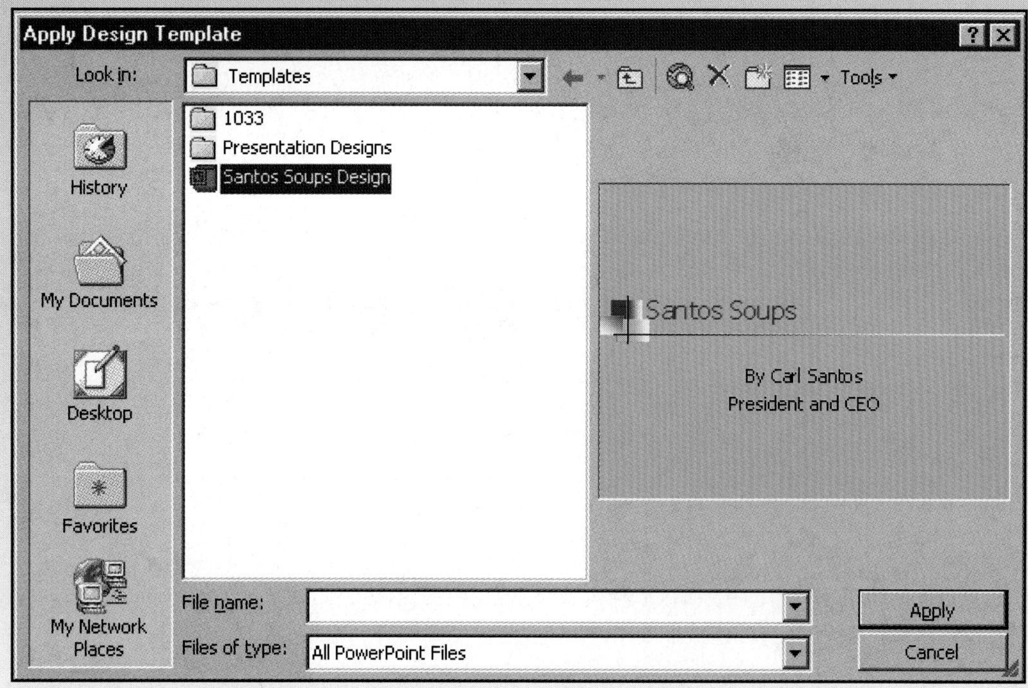

12. To apply the "Santos Soups Design" template to the blank presentation:
CLICK: "Santos Soups Design" template, if it isn't selected already
CLICK: Apply command button
13. Close the current presentation without saving.

2.2. How do you select more than one slide in the *Outline* or *Slides* tab?

2.3 Running a Slide Show

It's show time! PowerPoint provides several ways to deliver a presentation. Whereas handouts, overhead transparencies, and 35mm slides constitute static delivery approaches, online presentations are more dynamic, often incorporating special multimedia effects that help maintain an audience's attention. In this module, our focus is on starting and delivering online presentations.

2.3.1 Starting Slide Shows

PowerPoint provides several ways to start slide shows. In this lesson, we describe how to start a slide show from within PowerPoint and from the Windows desktop.

method

To start a slide show from within PowerPoint:

- CLICK: the slide you want to start on in the *Outline* or *Slides* tab
- CHOOSE: View, Slide Show (or click [icon])

To start a slide show from the Windows desktop:

- RIGHT-CLICK: the presentation filename in My Computer or Windows Explorer
- CHOOSE: Show from the right-click menu

practice

You will now open an existing presentation from within PowerPoint.

1. Open the PP0230 data file. (*Note:* You may need to use the Open dialog box to navigate to where your student files are stored, such as to your floppy diskette.)
2. Save this four-slide presentation as "Getting to Know" to your personal storage location.
3. At this point, slide 1 is the current slide.
   CHOOSE: View, Slide Show
   Note the animated ball that moves through the slide. (*Note:* The ball bounces very quickly once and then disappears.) The first slide should be displaying in Slide Show view (Figure 2.19).

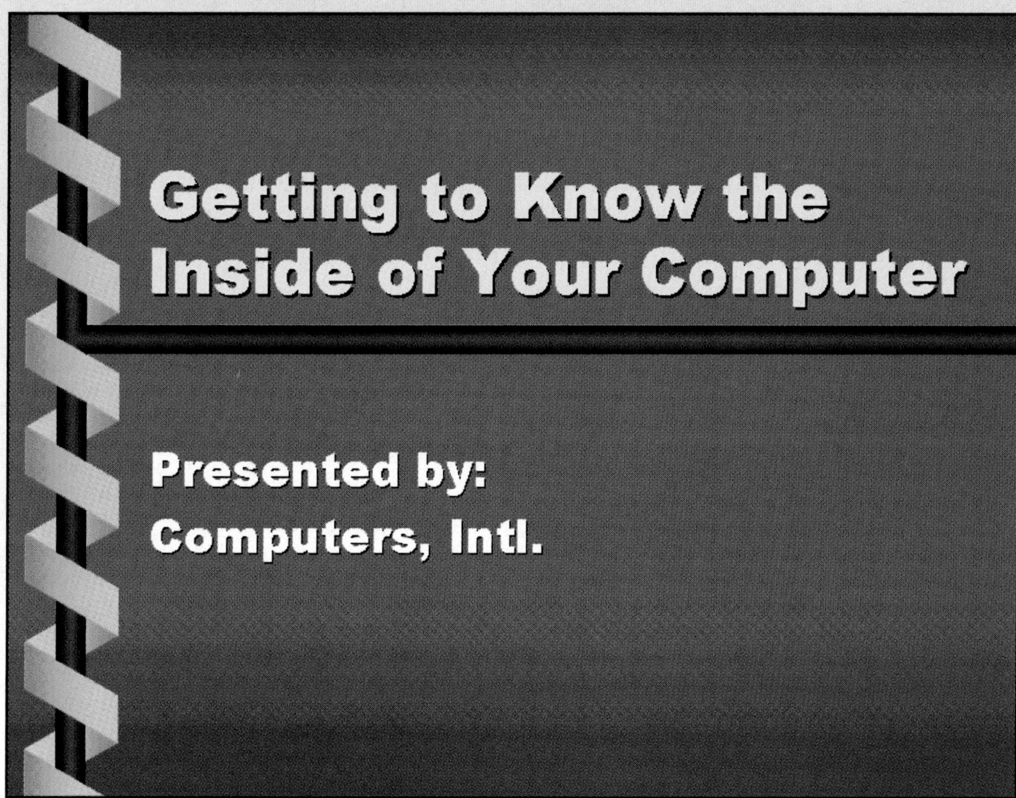

Figure 2.19

Viewing the first slide

4. To illustrate that you can start a presentation on any slide, let's exit Slide Show view, display slide 2, and then switch back to Slide Show view.
PRESS: ESC to exit Slide Show view
CLICK: Next Slide button on the vertical scroll bar to display slide 2

5. You can also start shows using the Slide Show button located beneath the *Outline* and *Slides* tabs.
CLICK: Slide Show button
The second slide is now displaying in Slide Show view.

6. Before continuing:
PRESS: ESC to exit Slide Show view
The presentation is displaying in Normal view.

7. Display the first slide of the presentation in the Slide pane.

2.3.2 Navigating Slide Shows

feature

In Slide Show view, you can navigate a presentation using the keyboard or mouse. To navigate a presentation using the mouse, you must display a right-click menu in Slide Show view. Among the available commands on the right-click menu are options for navigating the slide show, changing the characteristics of the mouse pointer, and ending the slide show.

method

To navigate a slide show using the keyboard or mouse, use any of the following options:

- PRESS: Space Bar PgDn *or* ↓ to display the next slide
- PRESS: PgUp *or* ↑ twice to display the previous slide
- CLICK: anywhere to display the next slide

or

- RIGHT-CLICK: to display a navigational right-click menu

practice

You will now practice navigating a running slide show. Ensure that the first slide of the "Getting to Know" presentation is displaying in Normal view.

1. To practice navigating the presentation using the keyboard, do the following:
CHOOSE: View, Slide Show
PRESS: Space Bar to view the next slide
PRESS: PgDn to display the next slide
PRESS: PgUp twice to display the previous slide
PRESS: ↑ twice to display the first slide

2. Explore some additional options that become available when you right-click a slide.
RIGHT-CLICK: anywhere on the current slide
The right-click menu shown in Figure 2.20 should now appear.

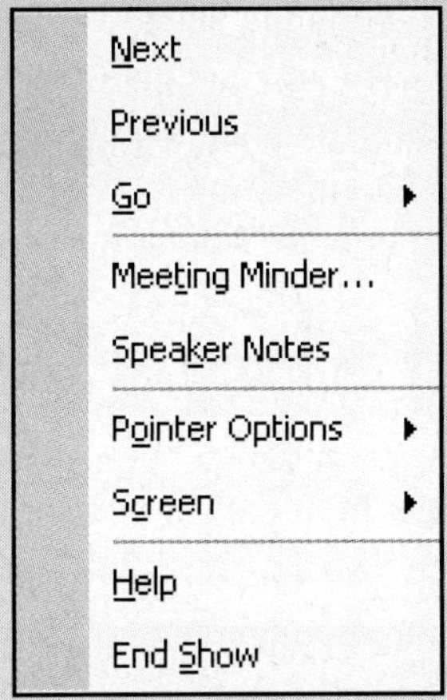

Figure 2.20

Viewing the first slide

3. To move to the next slide using the right-click menu:
   CHOOSE: Next
   Slide 2 should now appear.

4. To see a list of the slides in your presentation and then move to a specific slide:
   RIGHT-CLICK: anywhere on the current slide
   CHOOSE: Go, Slide Navigator
   The Slide Navigator dialog box should now appear (Figure 2.21).

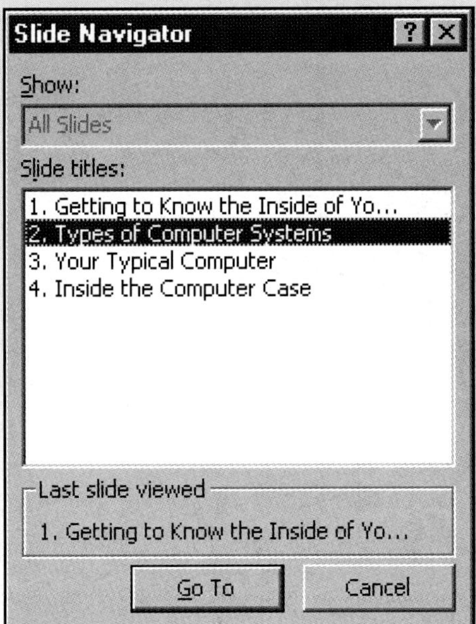

Figure 2.21

Slide Navigator dialog box

5. To display the third slide:
   CLICK: "Your Typical Computer" title in the list box
   CLICK: Go To command button
   Slide 3 should now appear in Slide Show view.

6. To return to the previously viewed slide:
   RIGHT-CLICK: anywhere on the current slide
   CHOOSE: Go, Previously Viewed
   Slide 2 should reappear in the window.

7. To change the pointer to a pen that you can write with on the screen:
RIGHT-CLICK: anywhere on the current slide
CHOOSE: Pointer Options
CHOOSE: Pen
The pen mouse pointer is now activated. You can draw on the screen by dragging the pen mouse pointer.

8. Let's emphasize the "Mainframe" bullet by drawing a line under it with the pen mouse pointer.
DRAG: with the mouse under "Mainframe"
Your screen may now appear similar, but not identical, to Figure 2.22. (*Note:* You can change the pen color by choosing Pointer Options, Pen Color from the right-click menu.)

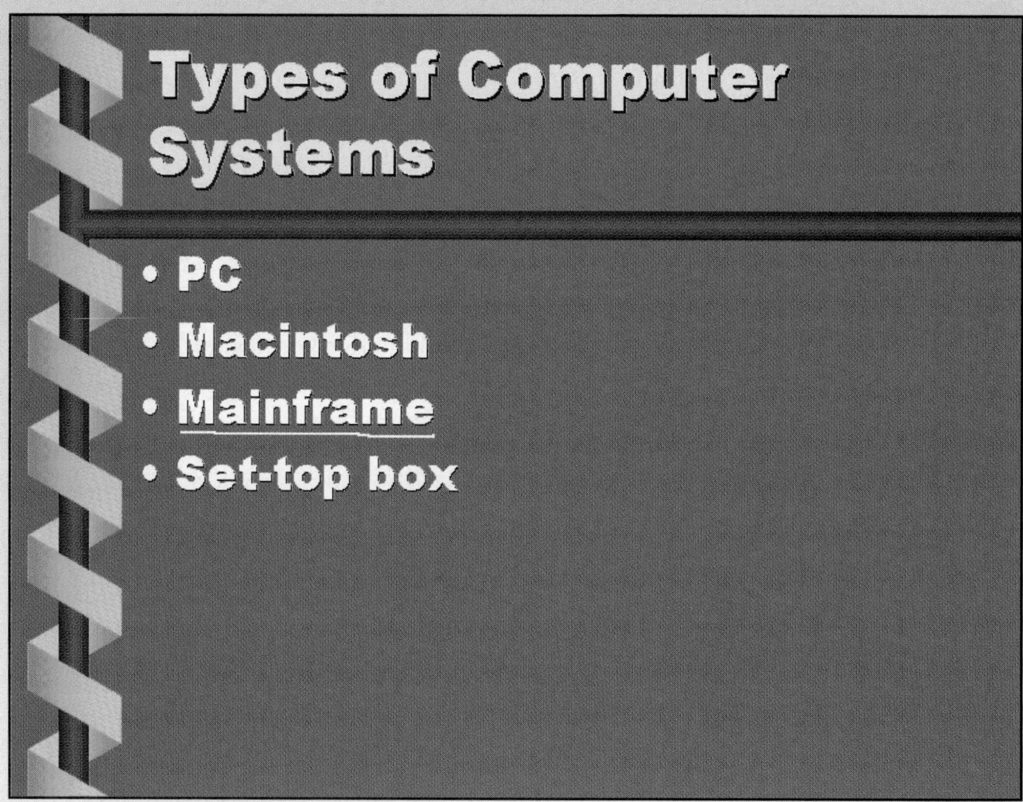

Figure 2.22

A line was drawn on this slide with the pen mouse pointer

9. To erase the inserted line:
RIGHT-CLICK: anywhere on the screen
CHOOSE: Screen, Erase Pen

10. In some presentations, a faint arrow will appear in the bottom-left corner of the screen. If you click this, the right-click menu will appear.
CLICK: arrow in the bottom-left corner of the window

11. To hide the arrow:
CHOOSE: Pointer Options, Hidden
The arrow should no longer appear in the left-hand corner.

12. To end the slide show using the right-click menu:
RIGHT-CLICK: anywhere on the screen
CHOOSE: End Show

13. Close the presentation.

2.3. How can you go to a specific slide in Slide Show view?

Chapter summary

Once created, your presentation can be changed with ease. You can apply alternate layouts to slides and modify existing layouts by manipulating the slide's placeholders. You can also modify the entire look of your slides by applying an alternate design template or customizing an existing template. When your presentation is complete, you view the presentation in Slide Show view. In this view mode, you navigate the show using the keyboard or mouse.

Command Summary

Many of the commands and procedures appearing in this chapter are summarized in the following table.

Skill Set	To Perform This Task	Do the Following
Creating Presentations	Add footer text	CHOOSE: View, Header and Footer CLICK: *Slides* tab
Modifying Presentation Formats	Apply a different layout	CHOOSE: Format, Slide Layout SELECT: the slides you want to format CLICK: a layout in the task pane
	Select a placeholder	CLICK: the placeholder
	Move a selected placeholder	POINT: to the placeholder until a double-headed arrow appears DRAG: the placeholder to a new location
	Resize a selected placeholder	DRAG: the placeholder's sizing handles
	Delete a selected placeholder	PRESS: DELETE
	Change slide order in the *Outline* or *Slides* tab	DRAG: the selected slide up or down
	Apply an alternate design template	CHOOSE: Format, Slide Design CLICK: thumbnail in the task pane
	Apply multiple design templates	CHOOSE: Format, Slide Design PRESS: CTRL and hold it down while clicking slides in the *Outline* or *Slides* tab RIGHT-CLICK: thumbnail in the task pane CHOOSE: Apply to Selected Slides
	Save a modified template	CHOOSE: File, Save As TYPE: **a name** for the new template SELECT: Design Template from the *Save as type* drop-down list

PowerPoint

Skill Set	To Perform This Task	Do the Following
Managing and Delivering Presentations	Start a slide show	CHOOSE: View, Slide Show, or CLICK: Slide Show button
	Use the keyboard to navigate a presentation	In Slide Show view: PRESS: Space Bar, PgDn, or ↓ to display the next slide, or PRESS: PgUp or ↑ twice to display the previous slide
	Use on-screen navigation tools	In Slide Show view: CLICK: to advance to the next slide RIGHT-CLICK: to display slide navigation options

Key Terms

This section specifies page references for the key terms identified in this chapter. For a complete list of definitions, refer to the Glossary provided at the end of this learning guide.

sizing handles, *p. 51*

Slide Master, *p. 54*

Chapter quiz

Short Answer

1. In Slide Show view, how do you proceed to the next slide using the keyboard?
2. What is the procedure for starting a slide show in PowerPoint?
3. What view mode must PowerPoint be in before you can use the pen mouse pointer?
4. What is the procedure for applying an alternate layout to a slide?
5. What must you know how to do before using an additional design template in a presentation?
6. What is the Slide Navigator tool used for?
7. What is the procedure for starting a slide show on the fourth slide in a presentation?
8. What is the procedure for reordering slides in the *Outline* tab?
9. When should you save a presentation as a template?
10. By default, where does PowerPoint store the templates you create?

True/False

1. ____ It is possible to resize, but not move, slide placeholders.
2. ____ In PowerPoint, you can create a new design template from an existing presentation.
3. ____ To add footer text to a presentation, choose View, Header and Footer.
4. ____ It's possible to apply multiple design templates to a single presentation.

5. ____ You resize objects by dragging their sizing handles.

6. ____ You can start a presentation by right-clicking its name in Windows Explorer or My Computer.

7. ____ To apply one of PowerPoint's design templates, choose Format, Slide Design from the Menu bar.

8. ____ It's possible to change a slide's layout in Slide Show view.

9. ____ Changing an existing slide layout may involve moving and resizing object placeholders.

10. ____ In Slide Show view, you can only navigate a presentation using the keyboard.

Multiple Choice

1. Which of the following enables you to exit Slide Show view?
   a. View, Exit
   b. File, Close
   c. File, Exit
   d. ESC

2. In Slide Show view, which of the following displays the previous slide?
   a. PgUp
   b. ↑
   c. Both a and b
   d. None of the above

3. In ______________, your presentation displays with transitions and special effects.
   a. Normal view
   b. Slide Show view
   c. the Slide Navigator
   d. All of the above

4. You can reorder slides in ______________.
   a. *Slides* tab
   b. *Outline* tab
   c. Normal view
   d. All of the above

5. What key lets you select multiple slides in the *Outline* or *Slides* tab?
   a. SHIFT
   b. ALT
   c. CTRL
   d. TAB

6. Which of the following determines where placeholders appear by default on every slide?
   a. Slide Navigator
   b. Slide Master
   c. *Outline* tab
   d. *Slides* tab

7. Which of the following can you include on every slide in a footer?
   a. date and time
   b. current slide number
   c. footer text
   d. All of the above

8. To save a presentation as a template, choose:
   a. File, New
   b. File, Save As
   c. View, Slide Master
   d. None of the above

9. To change the overall look of a presentation, you should apply an alternate ______________.
   a. AutoLayout
   b. placeholder
   c. design template
   d. All of the above

10. To delete an existing placeholder:
   a. double-click the image
   b. select the image and press DELETE
   c. drag the image out of the Slide pane
   d. All of the above

Hands-On exercises

easy 

1. Whiting Tours: Starting and Navigating a Slide Show

With an audience before him, Ralph Whiting prepares to run a slide show describing an upcoming hiking trip. In this exercise, assume the role of Ralph and get on with the show!

1. Open the PP02HE01 data file and then save it as "Whiting Hikes" to your personal storage location. Your screen should now appear similar to Figure 2.23.

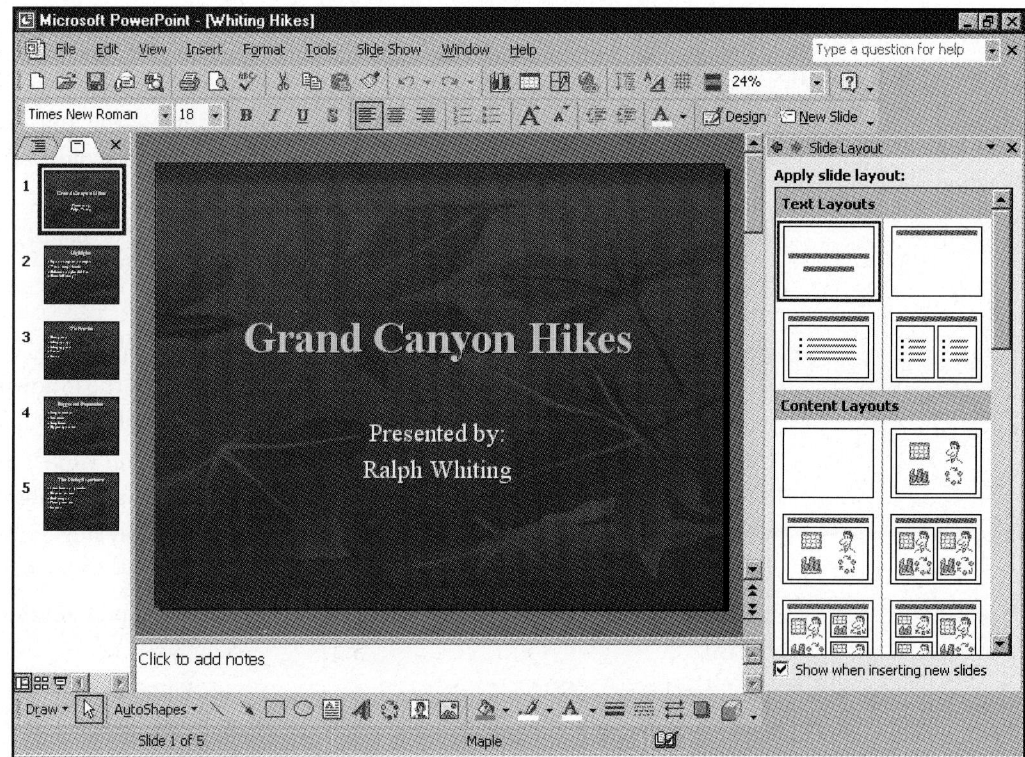

Figure 2.23
"Whiting Hikes" presentation

2. To start the presentation:
   CHOOSE: View, Slide Show
3. Do the following to progress through the slide show:
   PRESS: Space Bar to display the next slide
   PRESS: Space Bar again and again to display the entire presentation
   PRESS: Space Bar until the presentation displays in Normal view
4. Some audience members have questions about a few of your slides. Go to Slide Show view again and do the following to display the Slide Navigator dialog box:
   RIGHT-CLICK: the first slide
   CHOOSE: Go, Slide Navigator
   Your screen should appear similar to Figure 2.24.

Figure 2.24

Using the Slide Navigator

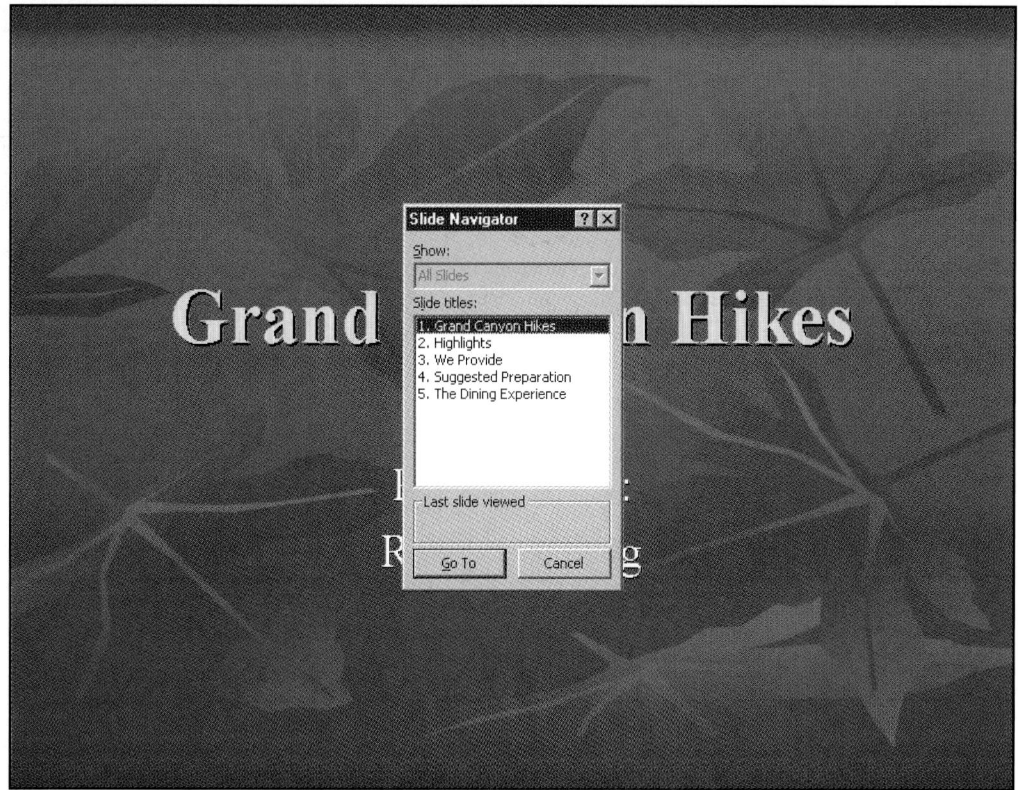

5. To go directly to the "Suggested Preparation" slide:
   CLICK: slide 4
   CLICK: Go To command button
6. On your own, use the Slide Navigator to display slide 3.
7. CLICK: the left mouse button to progress again through the entire presentation
   The presentation should now be displaying in Normal view.
8. Save and then close the presentation.

easy

2. Glorietta Community College: Modifying a Presentation

After receiving feedback from her boss, Rachel Graham, an employee in the admissions office at Glorietta Community College, must reorder slides and insert footer information in an existing presentation. In this exercise, assume the role of Rachel and perform the same steps that she identifies.

1. Open the PP02HE02 data file and then save it as "Glorietta Admissions" to your personal storage location. Your screen should appear similar to Figure 2.25.

PowerPoint

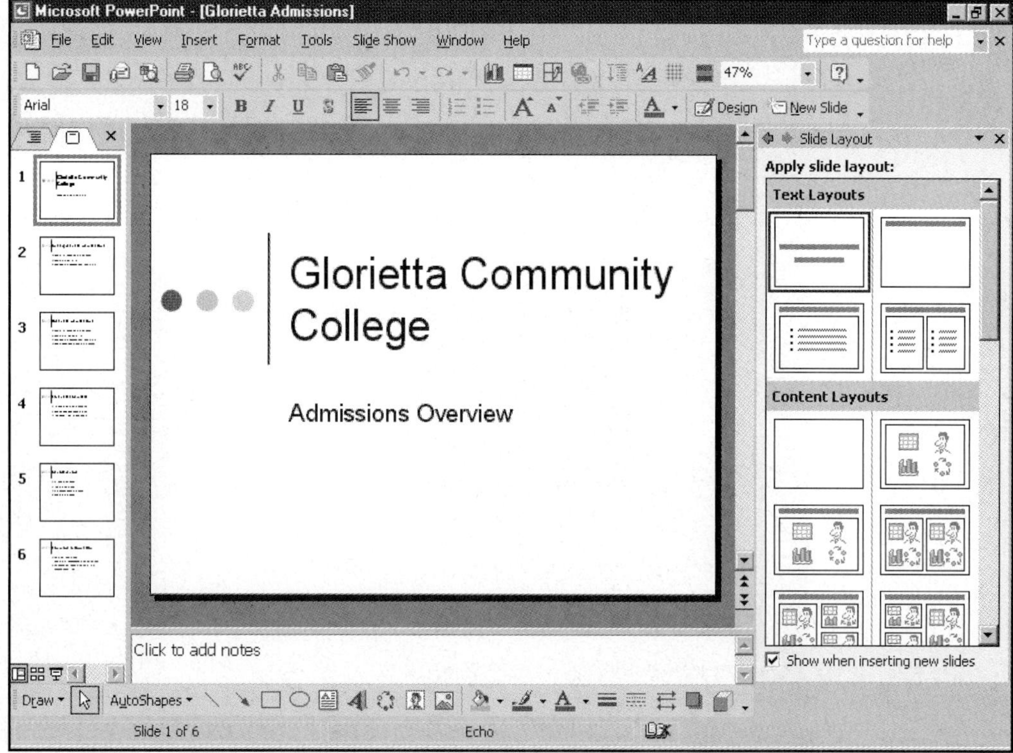

Figure 2.25

"Glorietta Admissions" presentation

2. Using the *Outline* tab, reorder the slides so they appear in the following order:
   - Glorietta Community College
   - Undergraduate Admissions
   - Graduate Admissions
   - Financial Services
   - Scholarships
   - For more information

3. To display footer information on every slide, do the following:
   CHOOSE: View, Header and Footer
   TYPE: **March 14** in the *Fixed* text box
   SELECT: *Slide number* check box
   TYPE: **Glorietta Community College** in the Footer text box
   CLICK: Apply to All command button
   The footer should appear similar to Figure 2.26.

Figure 2.26

Inserted footer

3 Glorietta Community College March 14

4. Display the entire presentation in Slide Show view.

5. Save, print, and then close the revised presentation.

moderate

3. Catalina Marketing: Changing Slide Layout and Design

John Chua, a Catalina Marketing employee, has decided to customize an existing presentation that he has been working on. Specifically he has decided to modify a few of the layouts and apply an alternate design template. In this exercise, assume the role of John and perform the steps listed below.

1. Open the PP02HE03 data file and then save it as "Catalina PR" to your personal storage location. Your screen should now appear similar to Figure 2.27.

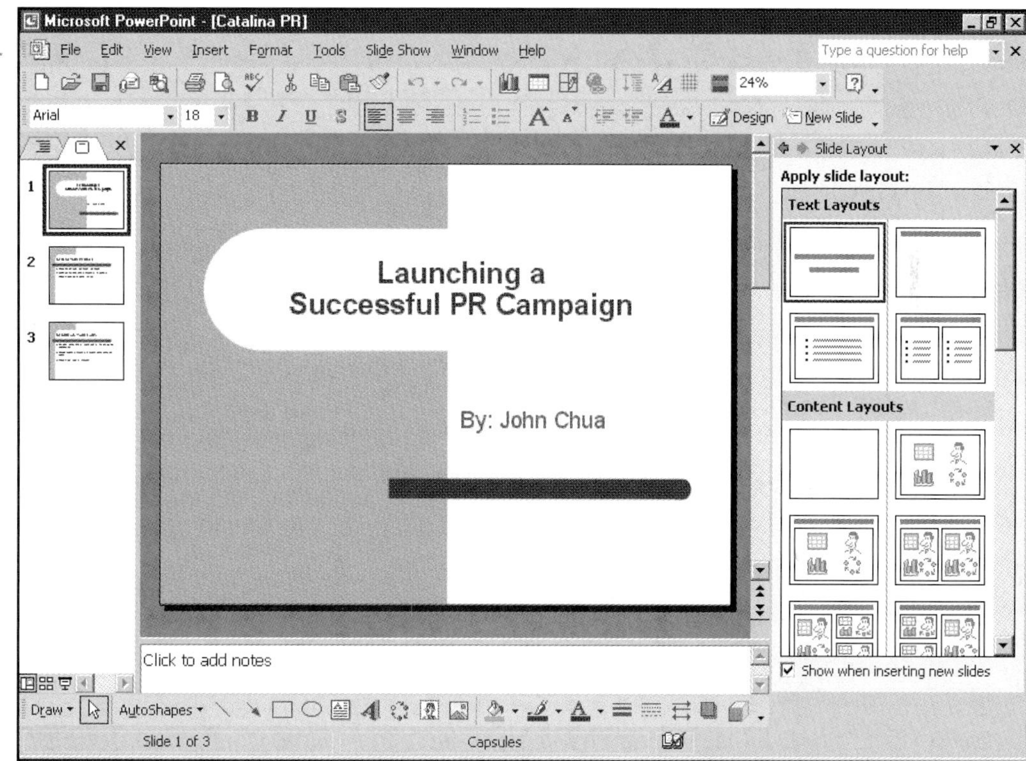

Figure 2.27

"Catalina PR" presentation

2. Apply the "Level" design template to the presentation. (*Note:* If this template isn't available on your computer, select an alternate one.) Your screen should now appear similar to Figure 2.28.

Figure 2.28

Applying an alternate design template

3. Display slide 2 and then edit its bulleted list placeholder to look like Figure 2.29.

Figure 2.29

Modifying the bulleted list placeholder

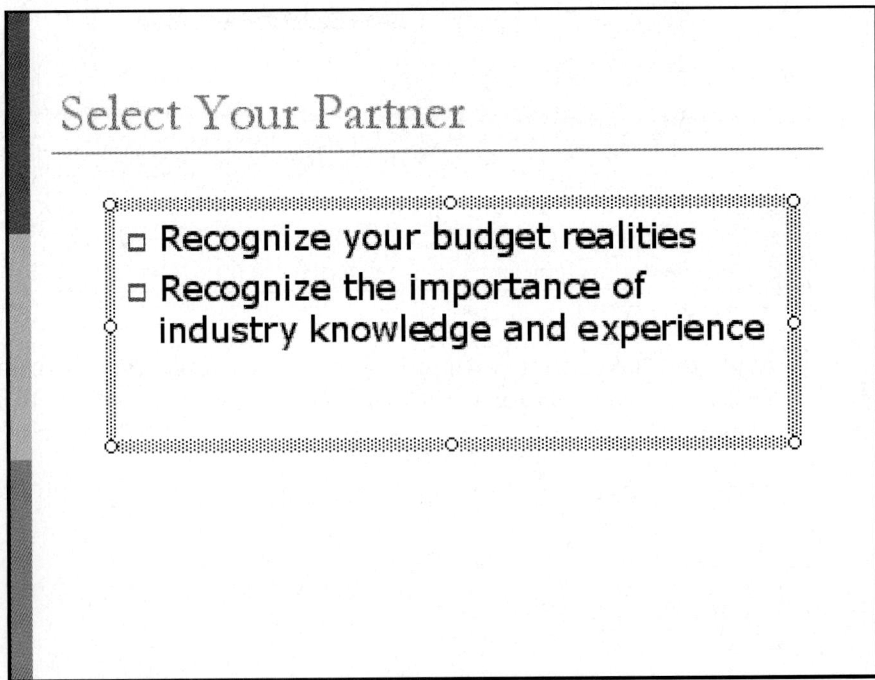

4. Edit the third slide so that its bulleted list placeholder looks like Figure 2.30.

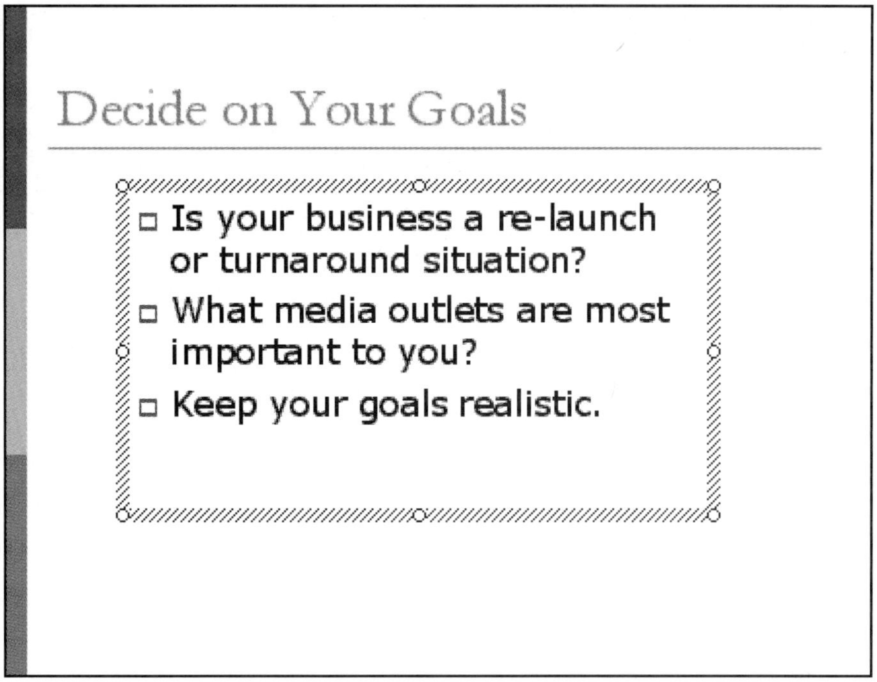

Figure 2.30
Modifying the third slide

Decide on Your Goals
- Is your business a re-launch or turnaround situation?
- What media outlets are most important to you?
- Keep your goals realistic.

5. Add the text **Catalina Marketing** as well as the current slide number to the footer.
6. Display the presentation in Slide Show view.
7. Save, print, and then close the revised presentation.

moderate 

4. AddIn Tennis: Modifying an AutoContent Presentation

Luke Evanisko, the founder of AddIn Tennis, has decided to customize one of PowerPoint's AutoContent presentations and then use it as the basis for future presentations. He likes most of what he sees in the template, but wants to change a few things. In this exercise, assume the role of Luke and perform the same steps he identifies.

1. Start a new presentation from the "From AutoContent Wizard" link in the task pane. Make the following selections as you advance through the wizard's steps:

   - Select the "Recommending a Strategy" presentation in the General category.
   - Ensure that the *On-screen presentation* option button is selected.

   After you click the Finish command button, your screen should appear similar to Figure 2.31.

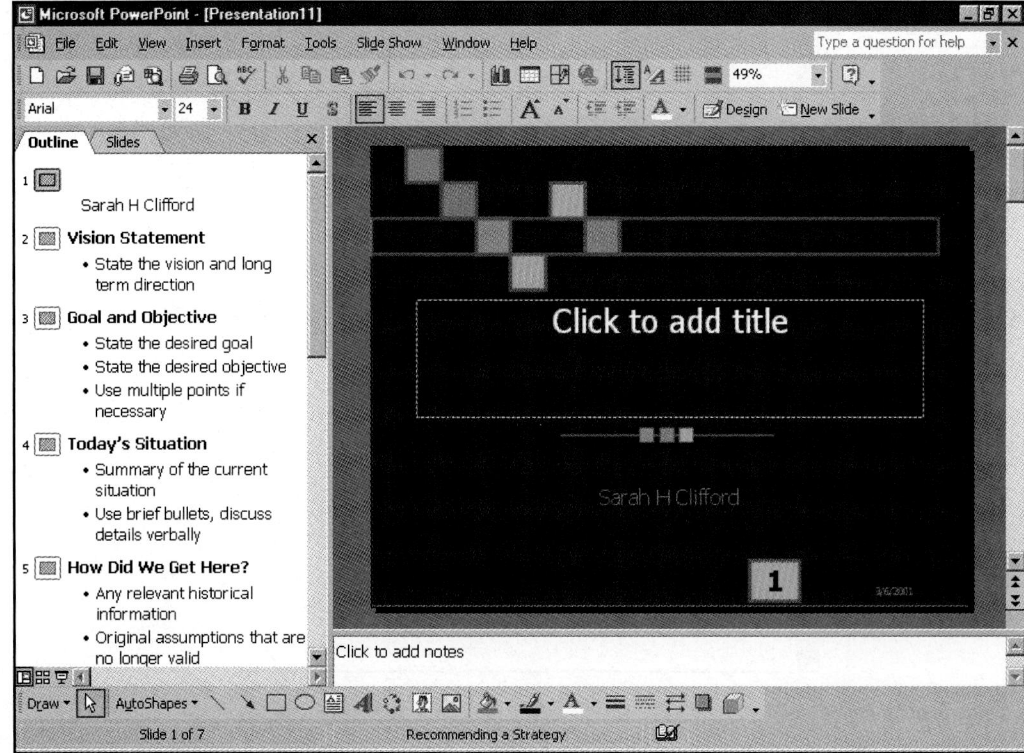

Figure 2.31 Generating an AutoContent presentation

2. Type **AddIn Tennis** in the title placeholder and then delete any text that currently appears in the subtitle placeholder. Then, type **Where tennis isn't the only racket...** in the subtitle placeholder.
3. Delete slides 3–7 from the presentation. You should now have only two slides.
4. Apply the "Balloons" design template to the presentation.
5. By referring to Figure 2.32, move and resize the title placeholder on the first slide.

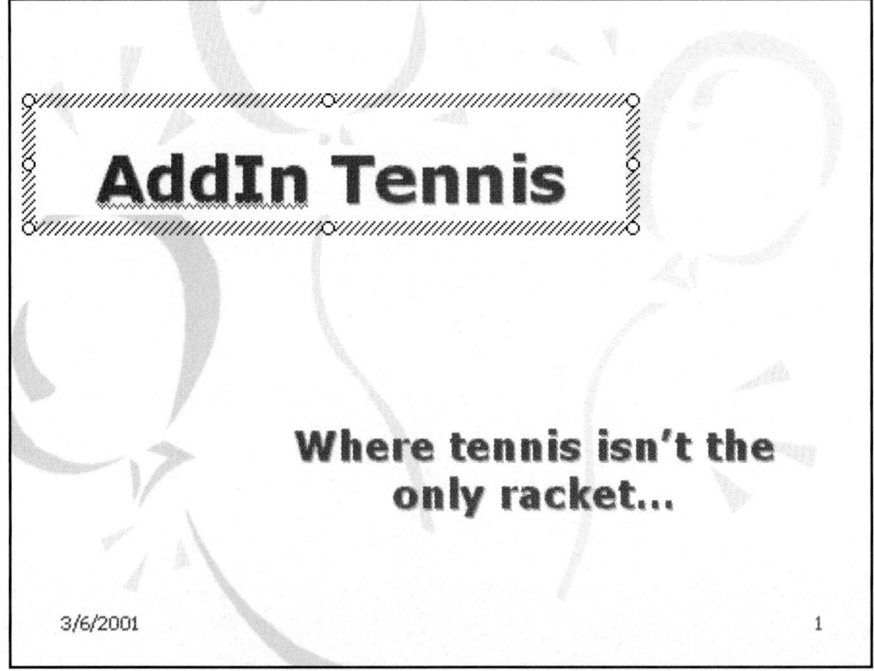

Figure 2.32 Modifying the title placeholder

6. Edit the footer area so that the current date no longer appears.
7. Change the background of the presentation to light green.
8. Save the presentation as "AddIn Racket" to your personal storage location and then print the presentation.
9. Save the presentation as a template named "AddIn Design" to the Templates folder. (*Hint:* Choose File, Save As and then select "Design Template" from the *Save as type* drop-down list.)
10. Start a new presentation and then apply the "AddIn Design" template.
11. Close any presentations that remain open.

difficult 

5. On Your Own: Presenting "Wally's Widgets"

Create a slide show that describes a fictitious company called "Wally's Widgets." The presentation should include five slides. We provide guidelines for the five slides below, but you must come up with the details. Be creative!

- Wally's Widgets

Presented by: ***Your Name***

- Contact information (address, phone number)
- What is a Widget? (features and benefits)
- Where to purchase
- Summary slide

Apply an appropriate design template to the presentation. Save your presentation as "Wally's Widgets" to your personal storage location and then run the slide show. Print and then close the presentation.

difficult 

6. On Your Own: Presenting "My Life as a Student"

Create a true or fictitious presentation that describes your life as a student. Your presentation should include at least five slides. Ideas include describing your course timetable in the form of a bulleted list, how you typically spend your time, where you like to dine, and what you would show someone who is considering attending your school. Apply a design template that is appropriate for your message. (*Note:* Remember to keep your message professional.) Save your presentation as "Student" to your personal storage location. Print and then close the presentation.

Case Problems

Holly Holdman

As you know, Holly is preparing to present her thesis on snowmelt hydrology research. Now that she has completed Chapter 2, she is ready to create and apply a new design template to her existing presentations. She also plans to change a few slide layouts and apply footers. In the following case problems, assume the role of Holly and perform the same steps that she identifies. You may want to re-read the chapter opening before proceeding.

1. Holly opens a presentation she created previously, entitled PP02CS01. Before making changes to it, she saves it as "Hydrological Research" to her personal storage location. Her screen appears similar to Figure 2.33.

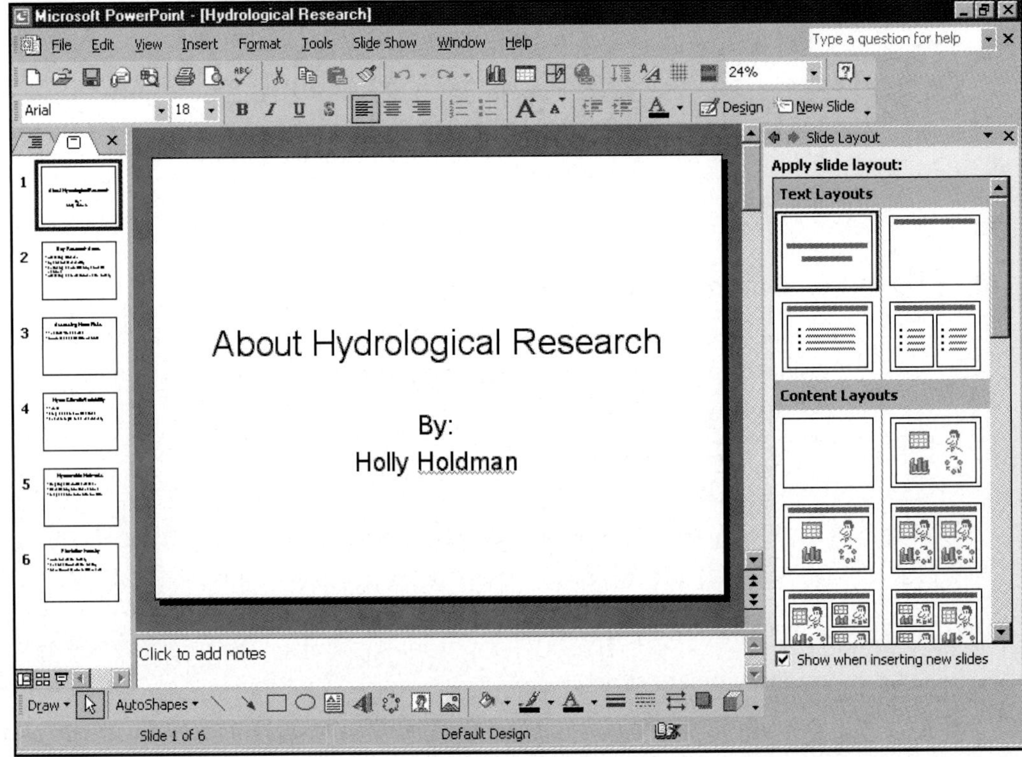

Figure 2.33

First slide of the "Hydrological Research" presentation

Holly applies the "Edge" design template to the presentation. (*Note:* If this template isn't available on your computer, choose another template that has a white background.) She then views each of the slides in Slide Show view. The second slide appears in Figure 2.34.

Figure 2.34

Second slide after applying a template

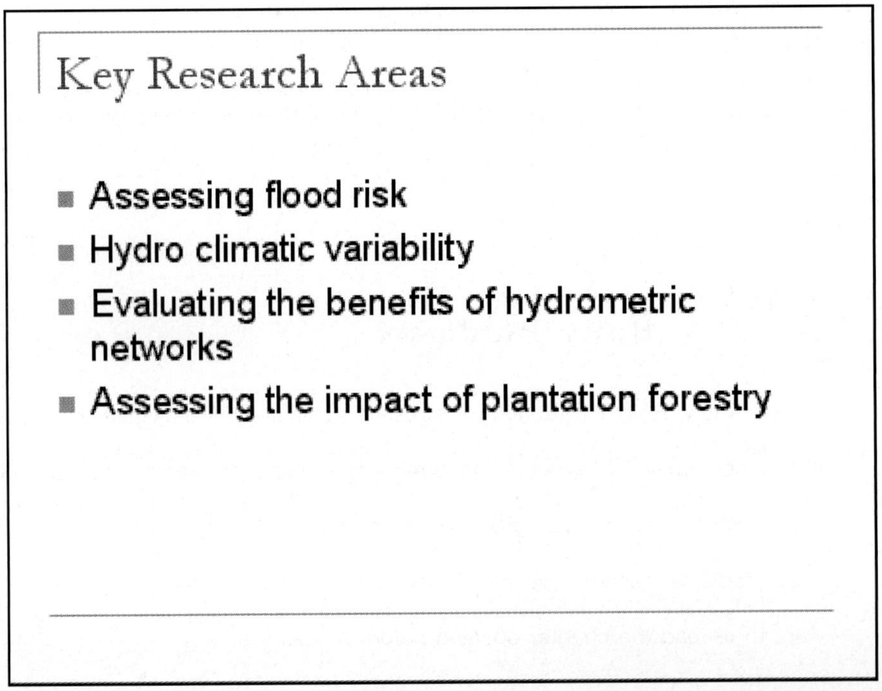

Key Research Areas

- Assessing flood risk
- Hydro climatic variability
- Evaluating the benefits of hydrometric networks
- Assessing the impact of plantation forestry

Holly decides to apply a different template to the first slide of the presentation. She displays the first slide in the Slide pane and then applies the "Ocean" template to just the selected slide. Holly saves the revised presentation and keeps it open.

2. Holly decides to edit the second slide of the "Hydrological Research" presentation. She changes the bulleted items to match the order shown in Figure 2.35. (*Tip:* You can move a bullet and its associated text using the *Outline* tab, by dragging the bullet symbol to the desired location.)

Figure 2.35

Editing the second slide

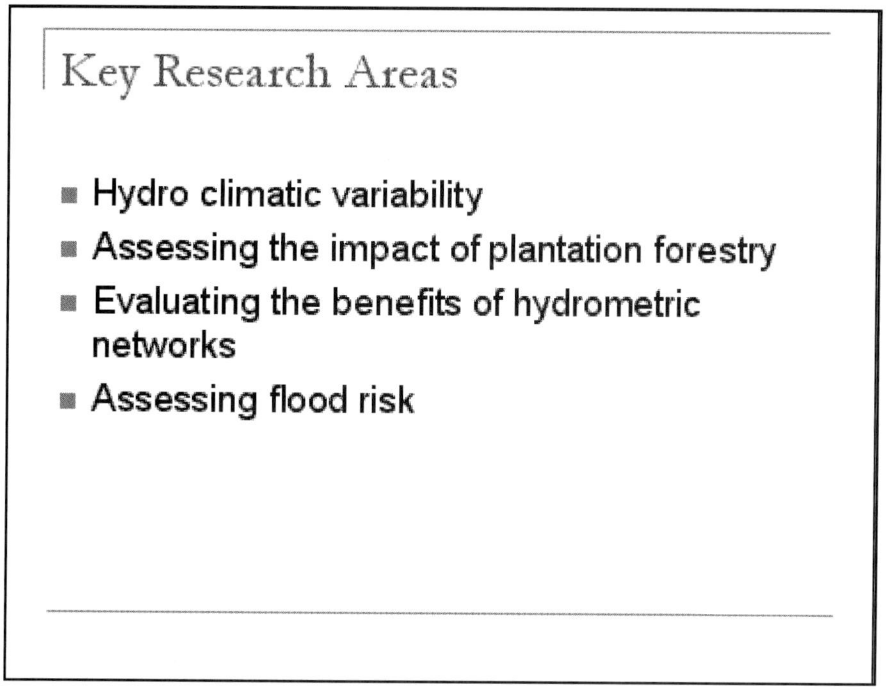

Key Research Areas

- Hydro climatic variability
- Assessing the impact of plantation forestry
- Evaluating the benefits of hydrometric networks
- Assessing flood risk

Next, she carefully reorders the next four slides to match the order of the bulleted list. Holly saves the presentation as "Hydrological Research-Revised" to her personal storage location.

3. Holly decides to run the "Hydrological Research-Revised" presentation in Slide Show view. She begins by using the keyboard to advance the presentation. Using the right-click menu, she practices moving to specific slides and using the pen pointer to underline important points. Feeling comfortable with running presentations, she closes the presentation.

4. Holly opens the PP02CS04 presentation and then saves it to her personal storage location as "Snowmelt Hydrology". The first slide looks like Figure 2.36.

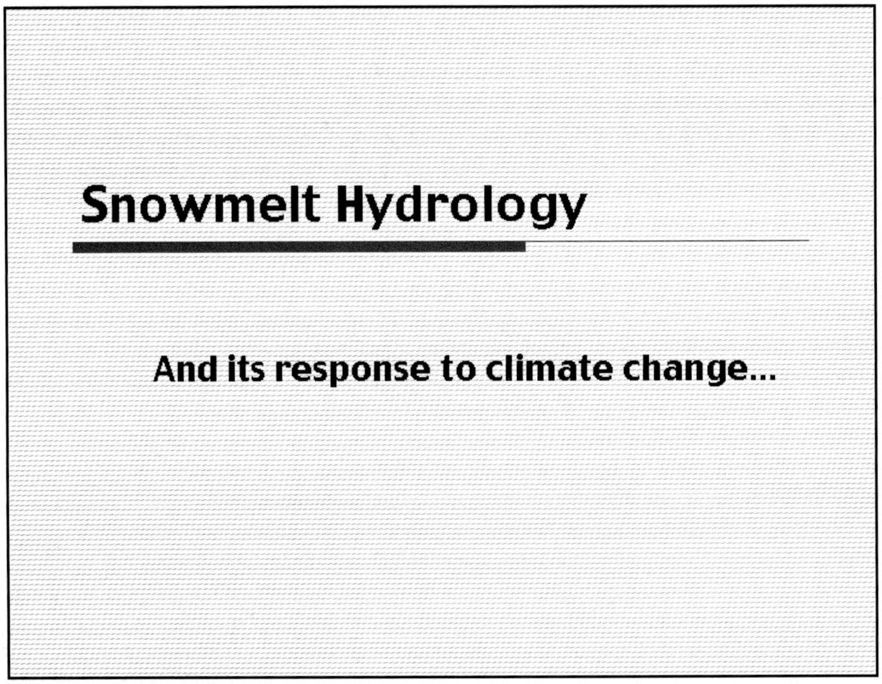

Figure 2.36

"Snowmelt Hydrology" document

Snowmelt Hydrology

And its response to climate change...

Before adding additional slides to the presentation, Holly decides to replace the background stripes with white. To accomplish this, she chooses Format, Background from the Menu bar and then clicks the drop-down arrow beneath the graphic. Next, she chooses White from the drop-down list and clicks the Apply to All command button. The first slide now appears similar to Figure 2.37.

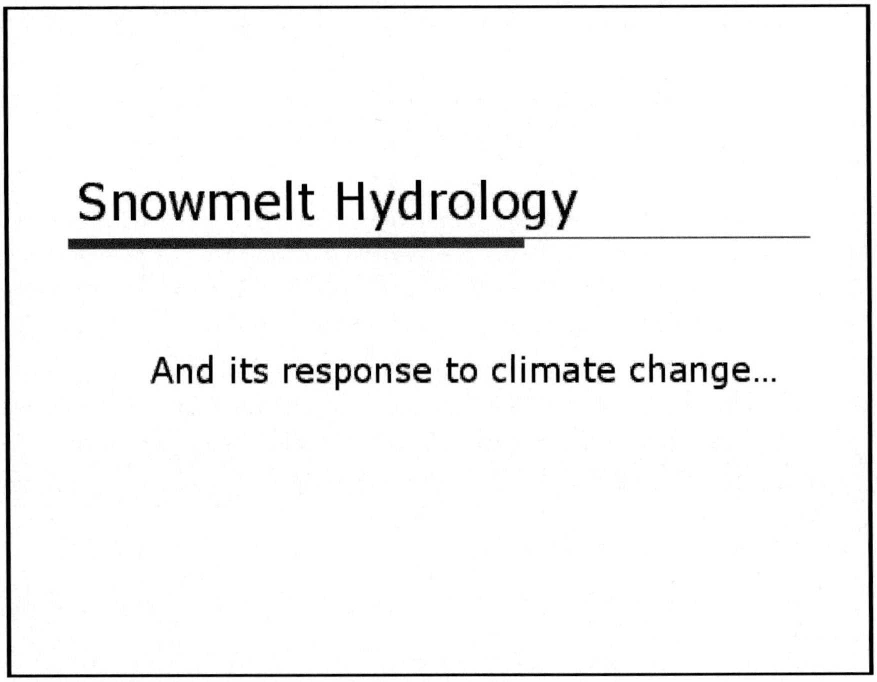

Figure 2.37

Applying a white background

Snowmelt Hydrology

And its response to climate change...

Holly likes the looks of the presentation so much that she decides to save its design as a template for future presentations. She saves the template as "Snowmelt" to the Templates folder. She then saves and closes the revised "Snowmelt Hydrology" presentation.

Microsoft® **PowerPoint®** 2002

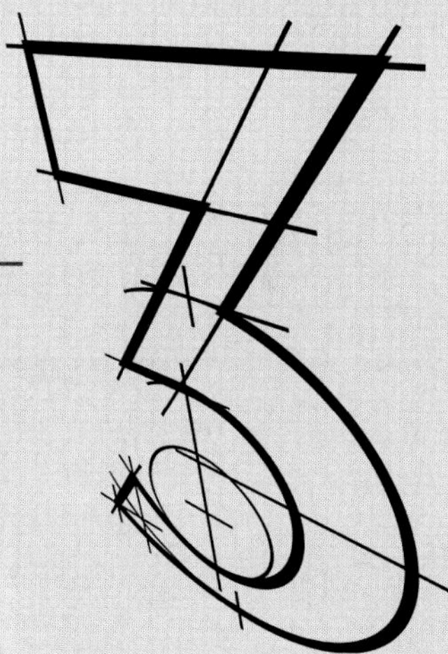

CHAPTER 3

Adding Graphics

CHAPTER OUTLINE

Case Study

3.1 Inserting Clip Art, Pictures, and More

3.2 Inserting Draw Objects

3.3 Inserting Text Labels

Chapter Summary

Chapter Quiz

Hands-On Exercises

Case Problems

PREREQUISITES

To successfully complete this chapter, you must be able to start new presentations, apply alternate layouts, and move and resize object placeholders. We also assume you know how to use toolbars, the Menu bar, right-click menus, and manage your files.

LEARNING OBJECTIVES

After completing this chapter, you will be able to:

- Insert clip art, pictures, graphs, and organization charts
- Create and modify objects using the Drawing toolbar
- Label AutoShapes and other parts of a slide

 **CaseStudy** FANTASY MOTORS Karl Walters recently purchased Lucky Lou's Car Dealership. After gaining ownership, Karl changed the name of his new business to Fantasy Motors and immediately built a new showroom to display the latest models of import cars. Karl is eager to promote his new business using PowerPoint at an upcoming car show. Karl has discovered one of Lucky Lou's previously created PowerPoint presentations; however, he would like to insert some graphics in the presentation.

In this chapter, you and Karl learn how to embellish a presentation with clip art, graphs, pictures, and organization charts. You also learn how to create, manipulate, and format graphics using the Drawing toolbar.

3.1 Inserting Clip Art, Pictures, and More

A picture is worth a thousand words! Although that phrase may be overused, its truth is undeniable. Graphics add personality to your presentations and often convey information more efficiently than text alone. In this module, you learn how to embellish your presentations with clip art and pictures, graphs, and organization charts.

3.1.1 Inserting Clip Art

feature

In PowerPoint, you can insert drawings, pictures, photographs, charts, sounds, movies, and other types of media files in your presentation. PowerPoint refers to these files as media *clips.* In this lesson, we focus on inserting clip art, one type of media clip, in your presentations. A **clip art** image is a computer graphic or picture that you can insert in your presentation, usually without having to pay royalties or licensing fees to the artist or designer. PowerPoint provides several methods for inserting clip art in your presentations. You can go directly to a selection of images, search for the right image using a typed keyword, or display a categorical listing of the clips that accompany all Microsoft Office applications.

method

To go directly to a selection of clip art images:

- CLICK: a content placeholder
- CLICK: Insert Clip Art button ( )

To search for a clip using the Clip Art task pane:

- CHOOSE: Insert, Picture, Clip Art (or click the Insert Clip Art button ( ) on the Drawing toolbar)
- TYPE: a search keyword in the *Search text* text box
- CLICK: Search command button in the task pane

To display a categorical listing of Microsoft Office clip art:

- CHOOSE: Insert, Picture, Clip Art (or click the Insert Clip Art button ( ) on the Drawing toolbar)
- CLICK: "Clip Organizer" link in the task pane
- DOUBLE-CLICK: Office Collections in the Collection List pane

You will now open a short presentation that currently contains three slides. Your objective will be to locate clip art for slides 1 and 3 of the presentation. Ensure that no presentations are open in the application window.

1. Open the PP0311 data file.
2. Save the presentation as "PC Seminar" to your personal storage location. Your screen should now appear similar to Figure 3.1. If the task pane is displaying on the right side of your screen, close it now by clicking its Close button (☒).

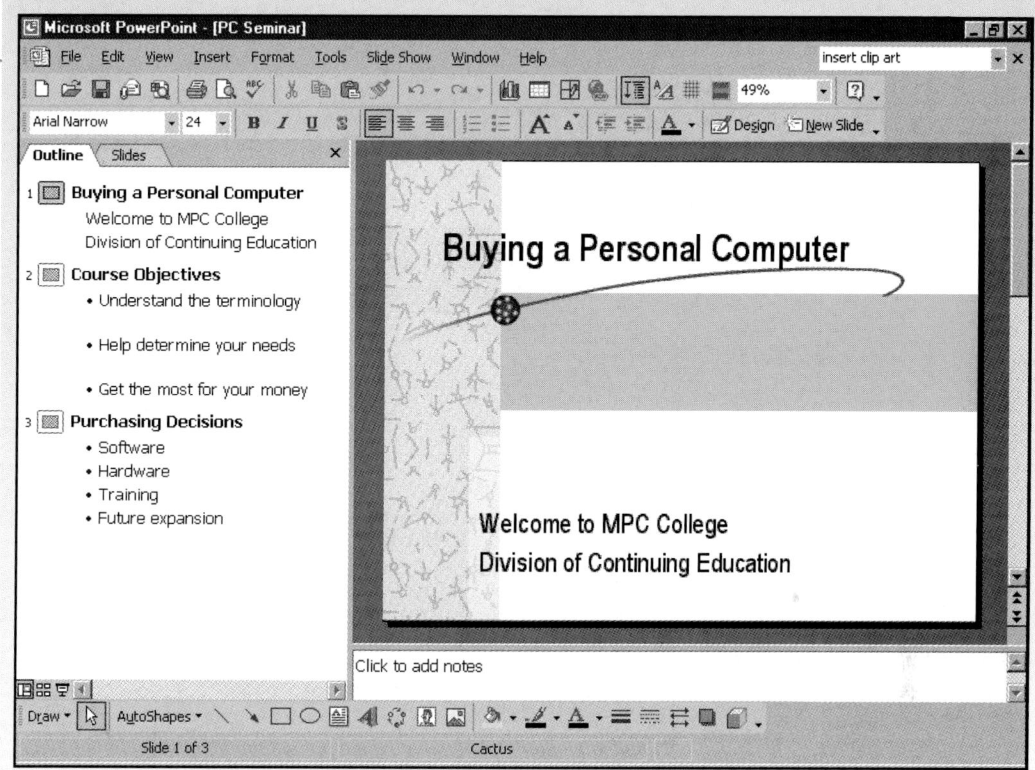

Figure 3.1

"PC Seminar" presentation

3. To search for an image that would be appropriate for the first slide:
   CHOOSE: Insert, Picture, Clip Art
   The Insert Clip Art task pane should now appear, as shown in Figure 3.2.
4. Since this presentation is about computers, let's search for a computer-related image for the first slide:
   TYPE: **computer** in the *Search text* text box
   Your screen should now appear similar to Figure 3.2.

PowerPoint

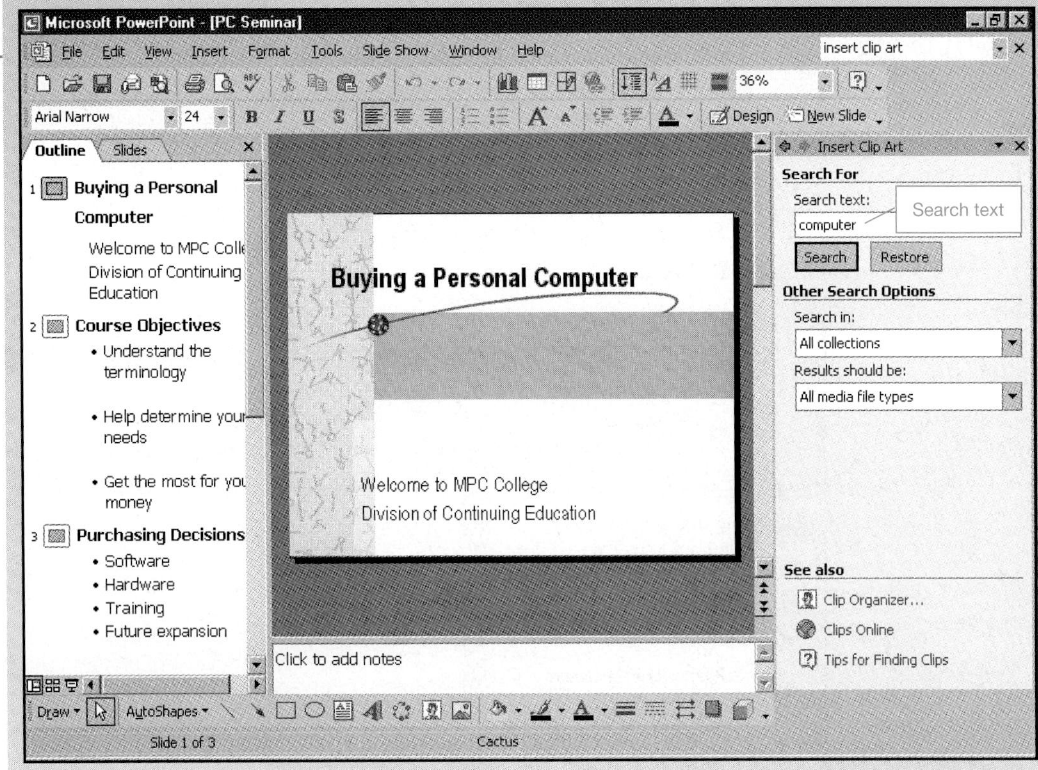

Figure 3.2

Searching for images using the task pane Insert Clip Art

5. To proceed with the search:
CLICK: Search command button in the task pane
The Insert Clip Art task pane should now appear similar to Figure 3.3.

Figure 3.3

Search results for computer-related clips

6. Practice pointing with the mouse at the different clips in the task pane. Note that for each clip a yellow pop-up description appears, detailing the associated keywords, dimensions, and file type of the image.

7. When you click an image, it will be inserted on the current slide. In the task pane, locate the image shown in Figure 3.4 and then do the following:
CLICK: the image shown in Figure 3.4
The image was inserted in the middle of the current slide, and the Picture toolbar appears also. The image appears surrounded with sizing handles. The green dot above is used for rotating an image, and will not be used in this exercise.

   After you insert clip art and other graphics objects, you will often need to move, resize, or otherwise format them to fit the specific needs of your presentation. The methods for moving and resizing graphics objects are the same as for manipulating placeholders, a topic we discussed in Chapter 2 (lesson 2.1.2). The current slide appears in Figure 3.4.

Figure 3.4

Computer clip

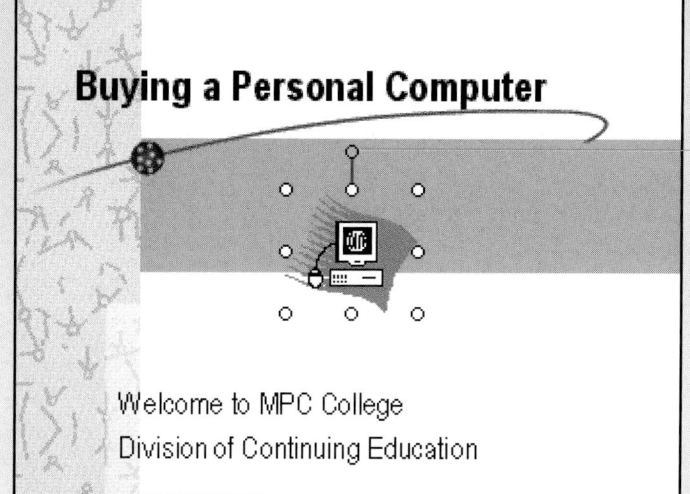

8. The floating Picture toolbar should also be displaying. Since we are not going to use the Picture toolbar in this module, close it.
CLICK: the Picture toolbar's Close button (☒)

9. On your own, resize and move the image so that your slide appears similar to Figure 3.5.

Figure 3.5

Moving and resizing a clip art image

PowerPoint

10. Insert another image on slide 3 of this presentation, but this time use a content placeholder. To display slide 3:
PRESS: Next Slide button (▼) twice slowly
The content placeholder on slide 3 appears in Figure 3.6.

Figure 3.6
Content placeholder

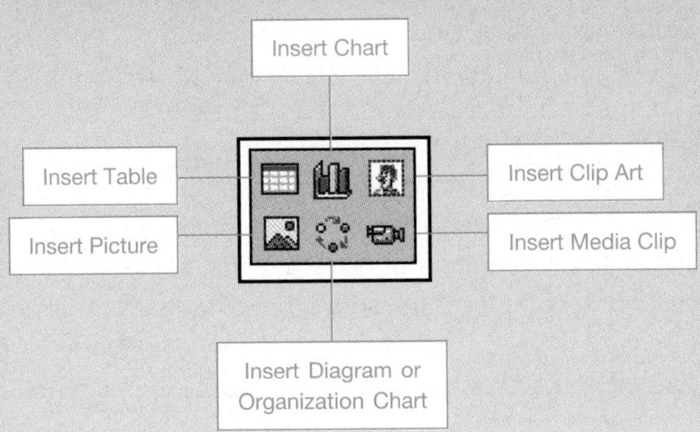

11. To insert a clip art image:
CLICK: Insert Clip Art button in the content placeholder

12. To search for the clip:
TYPE: **computer** in the *Search text* text box
CLICK: Search command button

13. Locate the clip shown in Figure 3.7 and then do the following:
CLICK: the clip
CLICK: OK command button
(*Note:* If the clip pictured in Figure 3.7 isn't available, search for an alternate clip.)

14. While referring to Figure 3.7, move and resize the image as necessary.

Figure 3.7
Using the clip art placeholder

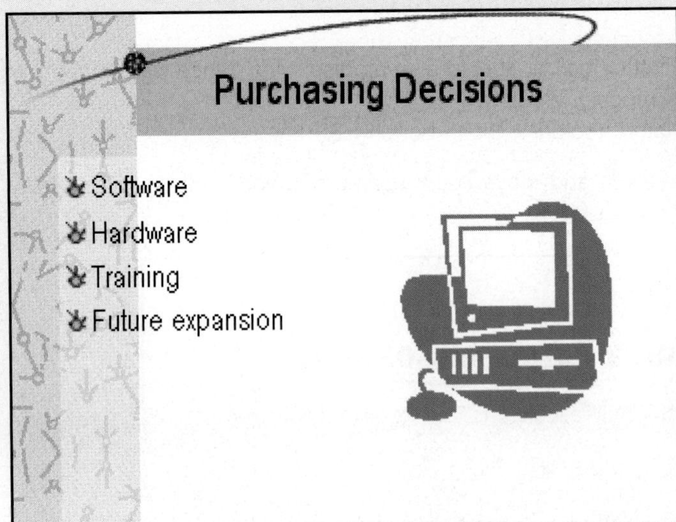

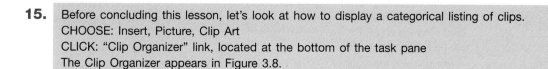

15. Before concluding this lesson, let's look at how to display a categorical listing of clips.
CHOOSE: Insert, Picture, Clip Art
CLICK: "Clip Organizer" link, located at the bottom of the task pane
The Clip Organizer appears in Figure 3.8.

Figure 3.8

Microsoft Clip Organizer

The Collection List on your computer will appear similar, but probably not identical, to the listing you see here.

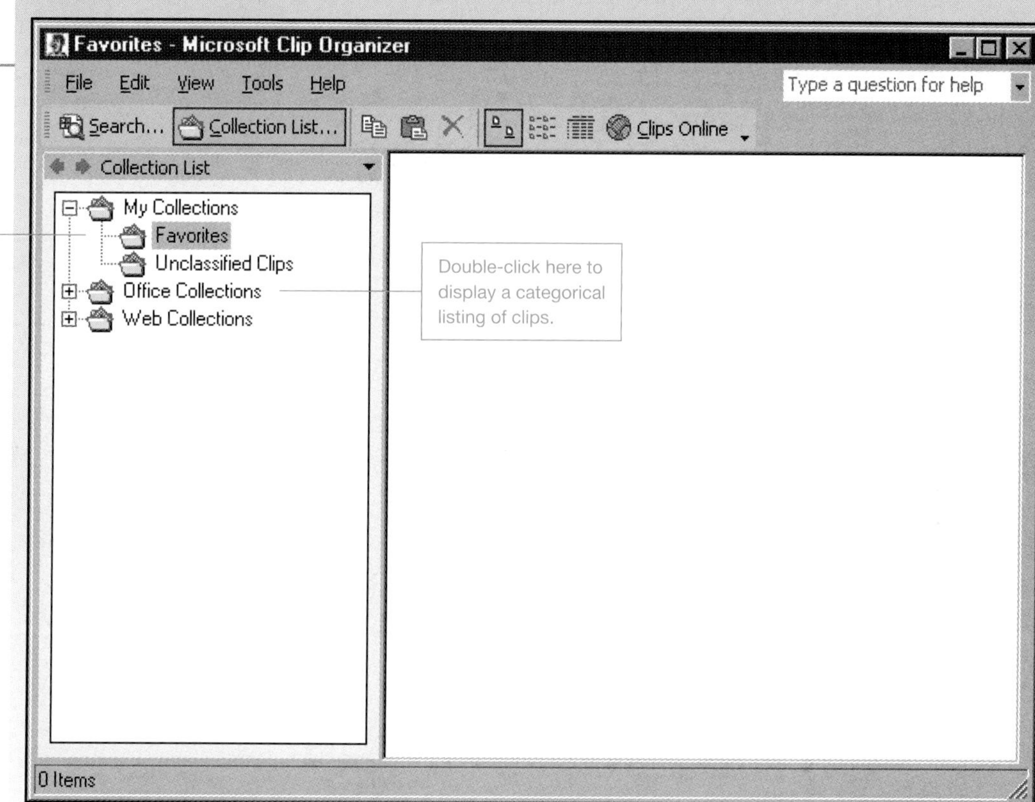

16. To display a categorical listing of Microsoft Office clips:
DOUBLE-CLICK: Office Collections folder in the left pane
A list of categories should appear in the left pane.

17. To display the contents of a category in the right pane, simply click a category. To illustrate:
CLICK: Academic category in the left pane
The dialog box should now appear similar to Figure 3.9.

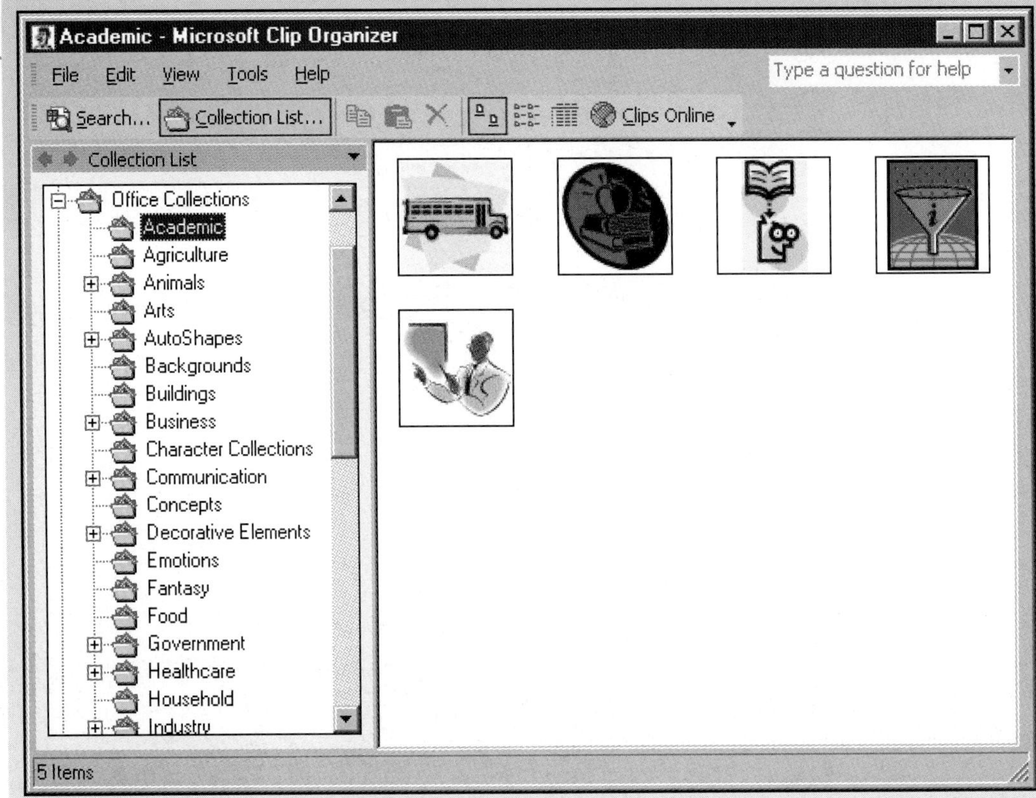

Figure 3.9

Categorical clip art listing

18. To insert a clip from the Clip Organizer on a slide, you must copy it to the clipboard and then paste it on your slide. To illustrate, point to the school bus clip, pictured in Figure 3.9. Note that a drop-down arrow appears.

19. CLICK: drop-down arrow associated with the school bus clip
CHOOSE: Copy from the menu

20. Minimize the Clip Organizer dialog box by clicking its Minimize button (▭).

21. CLICK: Paste button
The bus graphic should now appear on the current slide. (*Note:* If the Paste button isn't available to you, skip to step 23.)

22. To undo the paste procedure:
CHOOSE: Edit, Undo Paste

23. To close the Clip Organizer:
RIGHT-CLICK: its button on the taskbar (located on the bottom of your screen)
CHOOSE: Close from the right-click menu

24. Save and then close the revised presentation.

3.1.2 Inserting Pictures

Once an image has been scanned into a computer, it can easily be inserted in a PowerPoint presentation. Once it is inserted, you may choose to move or resize it to meet your particular needs.

method

- CHOOSE: Insert, Picture, From File
- SELECT: the desired disk drive and filename
- CLICK: Insert command button

practice

You will now practice inserting a picture object from a file. Ensure that no presentations are open in the application window.

1. To begin a blank presentation and then select the Title Only layout in the task pane:
CLICK: New button (□)
CLICK: Title Only layout in the task pane

2. Let's edit the title placeholder:
CLICK: in the title placeholder
TYPE: **Halloween 2000**

3. To insert a photograph that we've provided for you:
CHOOSE: Insert, Picture, From File
The Insert Picture dialog box should appear similar, but not identical, to Figure 3.10.

Figure 3.10

Insert Picture dialog box

4. To insert a file named PP0312 from the student files location:
SELECT: *the location of your student files*
SELECT: PP0312 from the list box
CLICK: Insert command button
The picture is inserted on the slide and appears selected (Figure 3.11). Also, the picture toolbar appears.

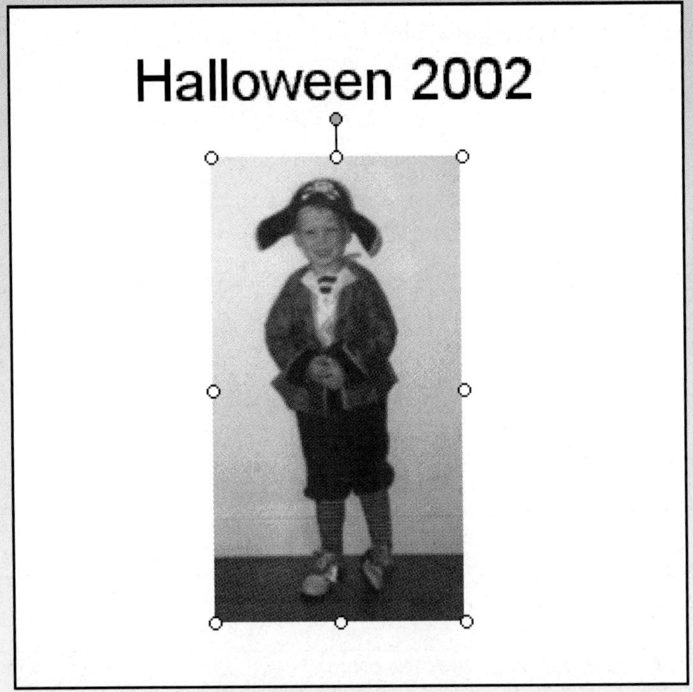

Figure 3.11

Inserting a picture from a file

5. If the Picture toolbar is displaying, click its Close button (☒).
6. Save the presentation as "Halloween" to your personal storage location.
7. Close the presentation.

3.1.3 Inserting Graphs

feature

The **Microsoft Graph** mini-application helps you produce great-looking charts and graphs from within PowerPoint! Graph does not replace a full-featured spreadsheet application like Microsoft Excel, but it does provide a more convenient tool for embedding simple charts into presentations.

method

The following methods can each be used to launch Microsoft Graph:

- CLICK: Insert Chart button (▥) on the Standard toolbar
- CLICK: Insert Chart button (▥) in a content placeholder
- CHOOSE: Insert, Chart from the menu
- CHOOSE: Insert, Object and then select Microsoft Graph Chart

To edit an inserted graph:

- DOUBLE-CLICK: the graph object

You will now insert a graph on a slide by editing a graph placeholder. Ensure that no presentations are open in the application window.

1. To begin a blank presentation and apply the Title and Content layout:
   CLICK: New button
   CLICK: Title and Content layout
   Your screen should now appear similar to Figure 3.12.

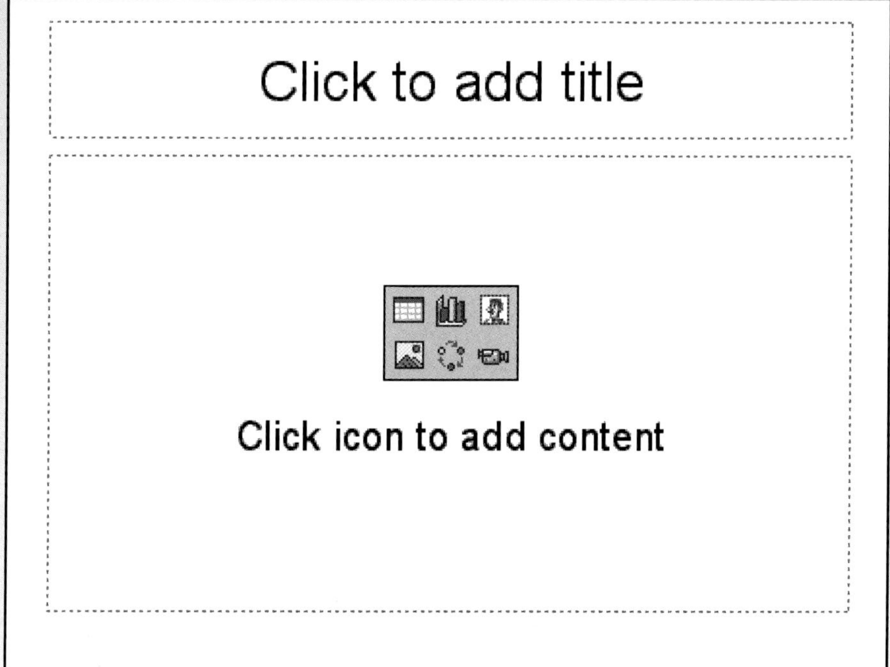

Figure 3.12

Title and Content layout

2. CLICK: in the title placeholder
   TYPE: **Grading Formula**

3. To insert a graph:
   CLICK: Insert Chart button in the content placeholder
   Your screen should appear similar to Figure 3.13.

The Graph datasheet appears in a separate window with sample information. As when using an electronic spreadsheet, you add and edit data in the datasheet that you want to plot on a graph. Figure 3.14 shows the datasheet as it first appears and how it will look after you edit it.

Figure 3.13

Inserting a chart

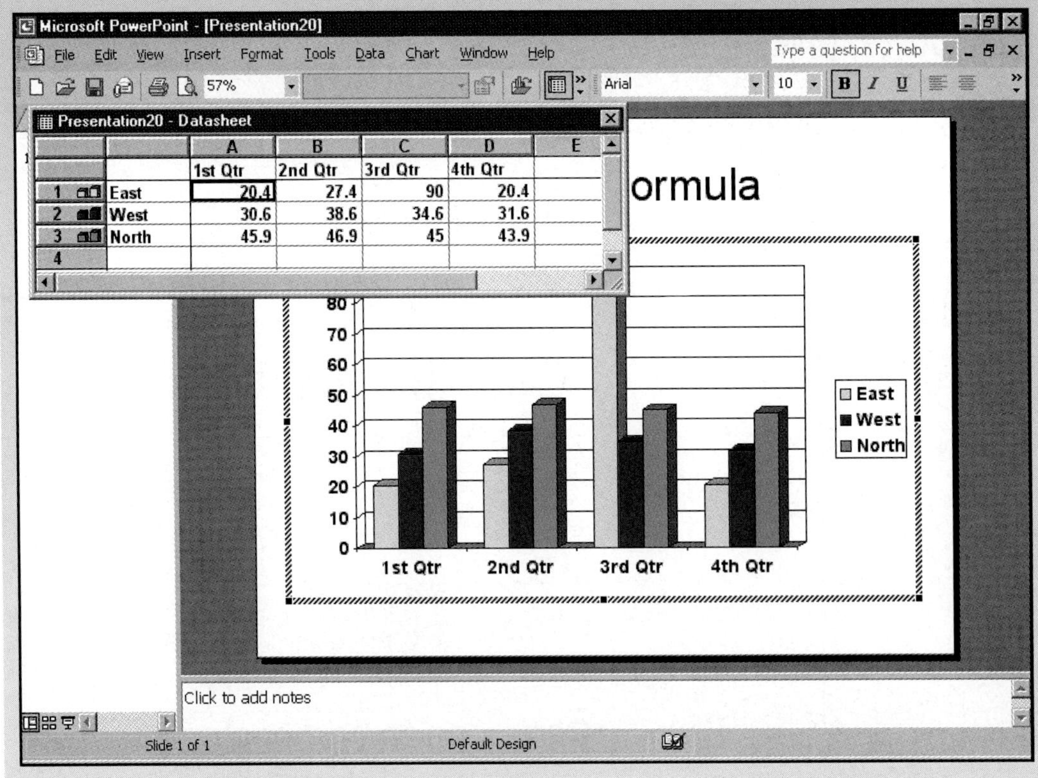

Figure 3.14

Editing the datasheet

Before

Click here to select the entire datasheet.

Presentation20 - Datasheet

		A	B	C	D	E
		1st Qtr	2nd Qtr	3rd Qtr	4th Qtr	
1	East	20.4	27.4	90	20.4	
2	West	30.6	38.6	34.6	31.6	
3	North	45.9	46.9	45	43.9	
4						

After

Double-click here to widen the first column to accommodate the headings.

Presentation1 - Datasheet

		A	B	C	D	E
1	Word	25				
2	Excel	25				
3	Access	20				
4	PowerPoint	15				
5	Integrating	15				

4. In this step, you delete all the data that currently appears in the datasheet. To do this, you first select the entire datasheet by clicking the upper-left corner of the datasheet, directly below the Title bar. You then press the DELETE key.
CLICK: the upper-left corner of the datasheet (refer to the "Before" image in Figure 3.14)
PRESS: DELETE
The datasheet should be empty.

5. To enter data into the datasheet, you click the crosshair mouse pointer on the appropriate *cell* (the intersection of a row and a column) in the datasheet. In this step, you enter the titles.
CLICK: in the cell to the right of the number 1
TYPE: **Word**
PRESS: ENTER
The insertion point automatically moved to the cell below.
TYPE: **Excel**
PRESS: ENTER
TYPE: **Access**
PRESS: ENTER
TYPE: **PowerPoint**
PRESS: ENTER
TYPE: **Integrating**
PRESS: ENTER

6. Now you prepare to enter the data. (*Note:* Be sure that the NUM LOCK key has been pressed.)
PRESS: CTRL + HOME
The insertion point automatically moved to where you will type in the first value (25).

7. To enter the data:
TYPE: **25**
PRESS: ENTER
TYPE: **25**
PRESS: ENTER
TYPE: **20**
PRESS: ENTER
TYPE: **15**
PRESS: ENTER
TYPE: **15**
PRESS: ENTER

8. If you press CTRL + HOME and then drag the bottom border of the datasheet window downward, the datasheet should appear similar to the completed datasheet in Figure 3.14. (*Note:* To widen the first column to accommodate the text, double-click where indicated in Figure 3.14.)

9. To hide the datasheet and view the inserted graph:
CLICK: anywhere in the background of your slide
The graph is inserted automatically into your presentation. Your screen should now appear similar to Figure 3.15.

Figure 3.15

Inserted graph

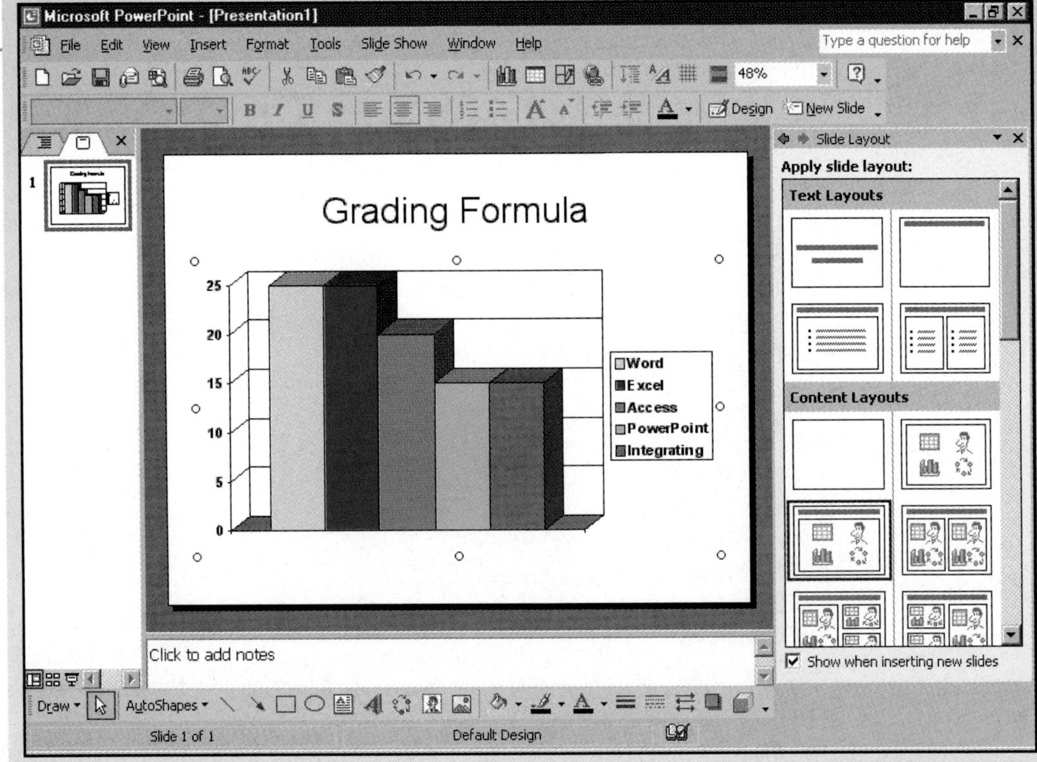

10. Once you have inserted a graph on a slide, you can edit it at any time by double-clicking the graph object. To illustrate, let's create a different type of chart:
DOUBLE-CLICK: the graph object
CHOOSE: Chart, Chart Type from the Menu bar
The Chart Type dialog box should appear (Figure 3.16).

Figure 3.16

Inserted graph

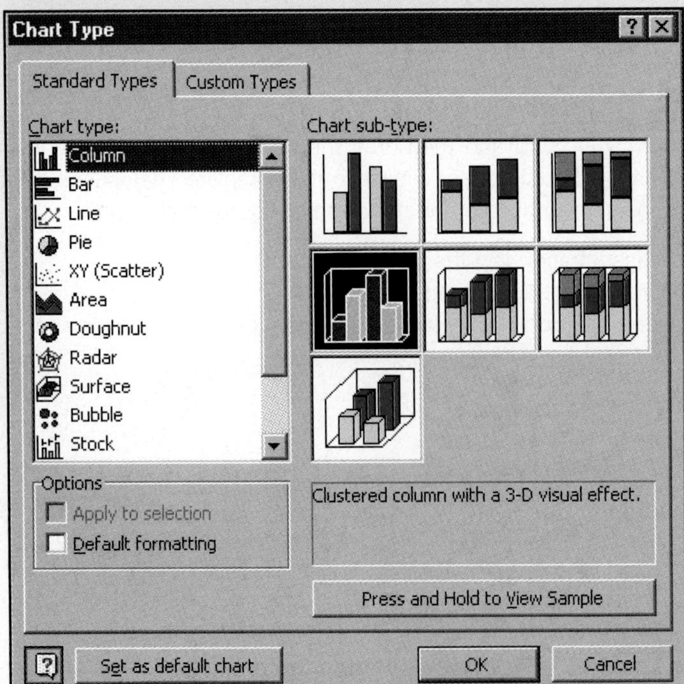

11. SELECT: Bar in the *Chart type* list box

12. Note that the first chart in the *Chart sub-type* area is selected. To modify our chart to look like this one:
CLICK: OK command button

13. To view your slide:
CLICK: anywhere in the background of your slide
Your screen should now appear similar to Figure 3.17.

Figure 3.17

Displaying an alternate chart type

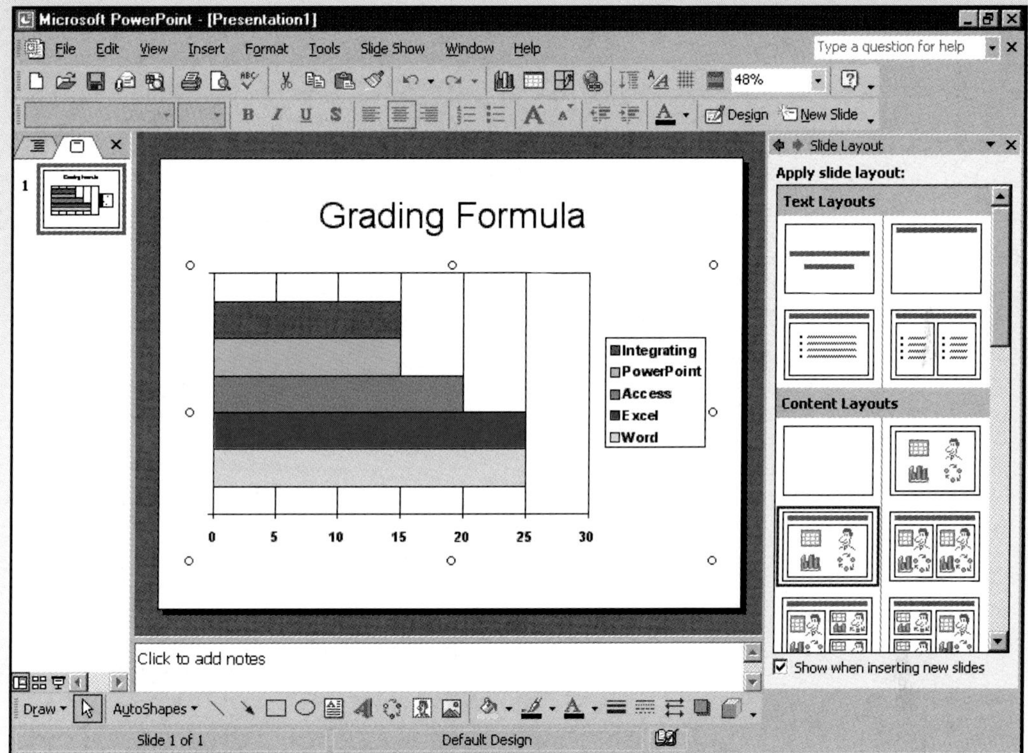

14. Save the presentation as "Practice Chart" to your personal storage location.

15. Close the presentation.

3.1.4 Inserting Organization Charts

feature

An **organization chart** is a schematic drawing showing a hierarchy of formal relationships, such as the relationships among an organization's employees. PowerPoint provides several methods for inserting organization charts in your presentations. If an organization chart doesn't meet your business need, you can select from other diagram formats using PowerPoint's **Diagram Gallery**. Alternate business formats include cycle, radial, pyramid, Venn, and target diagrams.

method

- CLICK: Insert Diagram or Organization Chart button (icon) in a content placeholder

or

- CHOOSE: Insert, Picture, Organization Chart from the menu

practice

You will now insert an organization chart on a slide by editing an organization chart placeholder. Ensure that no presentations are open in the application window.

1. To begin a blank presentation and apply the Title and Content layout:
   CLICK: New button (icon)
   CLICK: Title and Content layout
2. CLICK: in the title placeholder
   TYPE: **Practice Org Chart**
3. CLICK: Insert Diagram or Organization Chart button (icon) in a content placeholder
   The Diagram Gallery dialog box should now appear, as shown in Figure 3.18.

Figure 3.18

Diagram Gallery

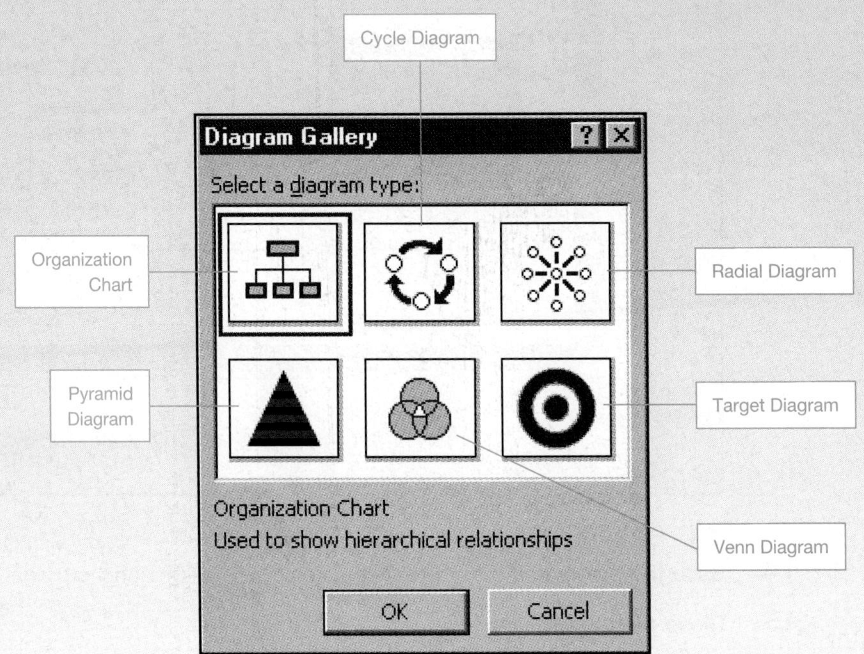

4. To create an organization chart, the currently selected option:
   CLICK: OK command button
   Your screen should now appear similar to Figure 3.19. Note that the Organization Chart toolbar is currently floating in the window. (*Note:* You can move a toolbar by dragging it by its Title bar.) You should see four boxes in the chart area. The topmost box should already be selected.

Figure 3.19

Microsoft Organization Chart application window

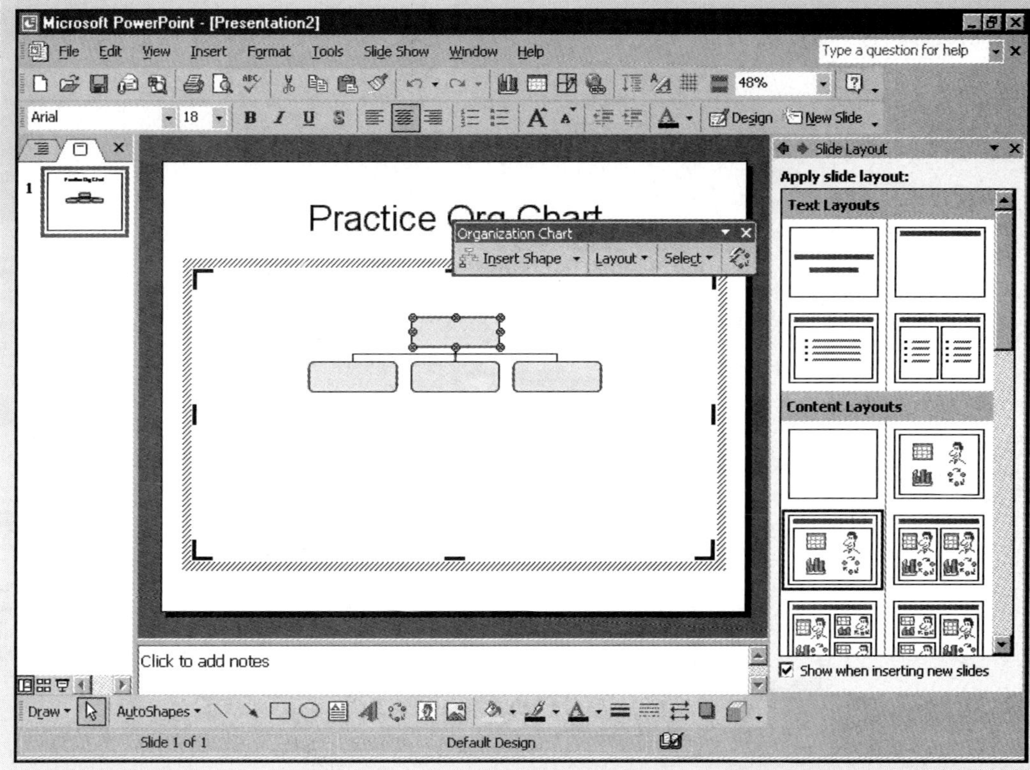

5. In the next few steps, you edit the content of the organization chart boxes. Note that the boxes automatically resize themselves to accommodate their text.
   CLICK: in the topmost chart box
   TYPE: **Your Name**
   PRESS: ENTER
   TYPE: **Lead Instructor**

6. CLICK: the far left box, located in the second row of the chart
   TYPE: **Feliberto Reyes**
   PRESS: ENTER
   TYPE: **Assistant Instructor**

7. CLICK: the box in the center of the second row
   TYPE: **Frank Rogers**
   PRESS: ENTER
   TYPE: **Lab Assistant**

8. CLICK: the box on the right of the second row
   TYPE: **Maritza James**
   PRESS: ENTER
   TYPE: **Lab Assistant**
   The organization chart should now appear on the slide, as shown in Figure 3.20.

Figure 3.20

Embedded organization chart

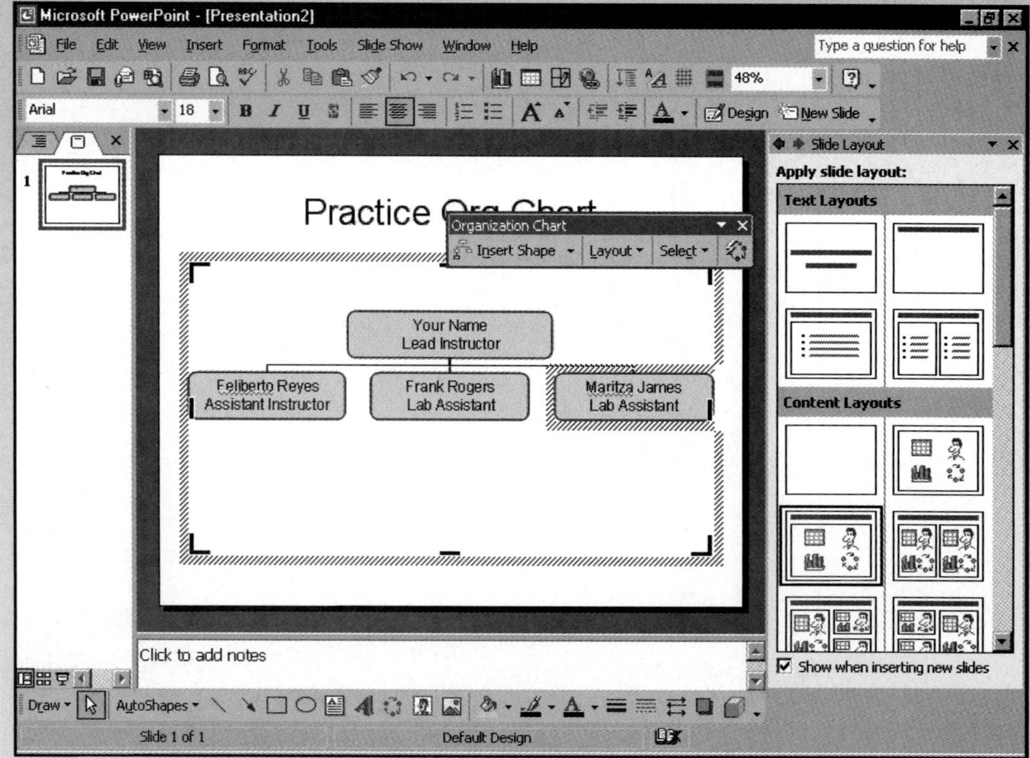

9. Edit the organization chart to include a new box below Feliberto Reyes's box.
CLICK: Feliberto Reyes's chart box
CLICK: Insert Shape drop-down arrow on the Organization Chart toolbar
The toolbar and associated drop-down menu appear in Figure 3.21.

Figure 3.21

Organization Chart toolbar

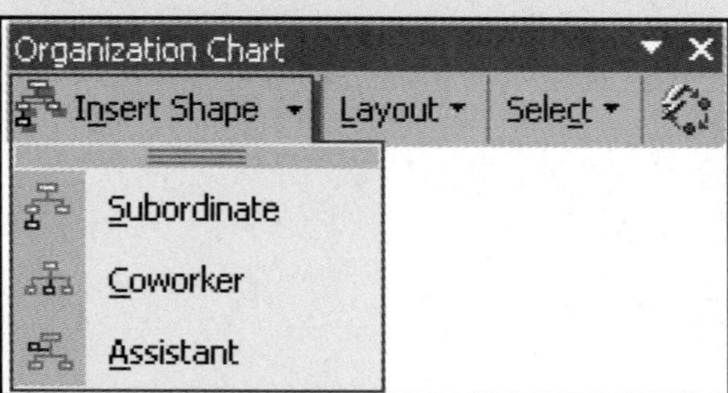

10. To add a new box to the chart:
CHOOSE: Subordinate from the drop-down menu

11. CLICK: in the newly inserted box
TYPE: **Roxanna Adams**
PRESS: ENTER
TYPE: **Student Tutor**

12. CLICK: outside the organization chart, near the upper-left corner of the slide
The organization chart should now appear similar to Figure 3.22.

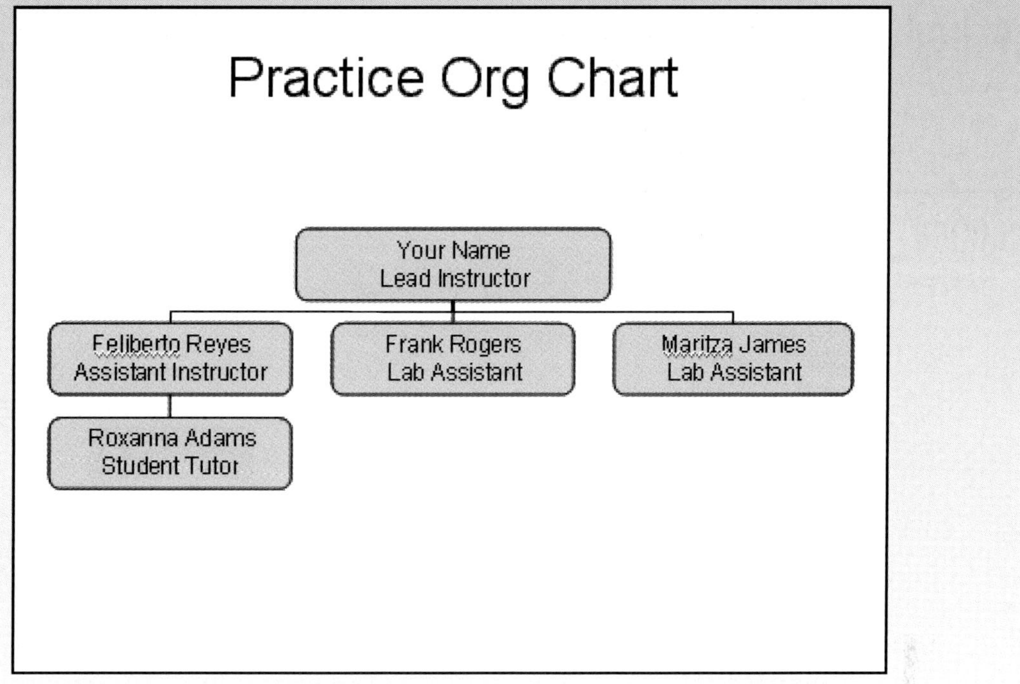

Figure 3.22
Completed organization chart

13. Save the presentation as "Practice Org Chart" to your personal storage location.
14. Close the presentation.

3.1. What are organization charts used for?

3.2 Inserting Draw Objects

Think of a slide as being composed of two layers. On the first layer, called the *slide layer,* you enter, edit, and format the text of your presentation. The second layer, known as the **draw layer,** exists as an invisible surface floating above (and mostly independent of) the slide layer. This transparent layer holds *objects,* such as lines, arrows, and text boxes. You can size, move, and delete objects on the draw layer without affecting the data stored on the underlying slide.

In this module, you learn how to insert and manipulate a variety of graphic objects on a presentation's draw layer.

3.2.1 Inserting Objects on the Draw Layer

feature →

You place lines, arrows, rectangles, ovals, and other shapes (collectively known as **AutoShapes**) on a slide's draw layer. AutoShapes can serve to draw the viewer's attention to specific areas or to simply enhance a presentation's visual appearance.

PowerPoint

method

- CLICK: an object button on the Drawing toolbar
- CLICK: on a slide to insert the object
- DRAG: the object's sizing handles to size the object
- DRAG: the center of the object to move it

practice

You now insert and manipulate AutoShape objects on the slide's draw layer. Ensure that no documents are open in the application window.

1. Open the PP0320 data file.
2. Save the document as "Metro" to your personal storage location. The presentation should now appear similar to Figure 3.23. In the next few steps, you are going to embellish this presentation with a few AutoShapes.

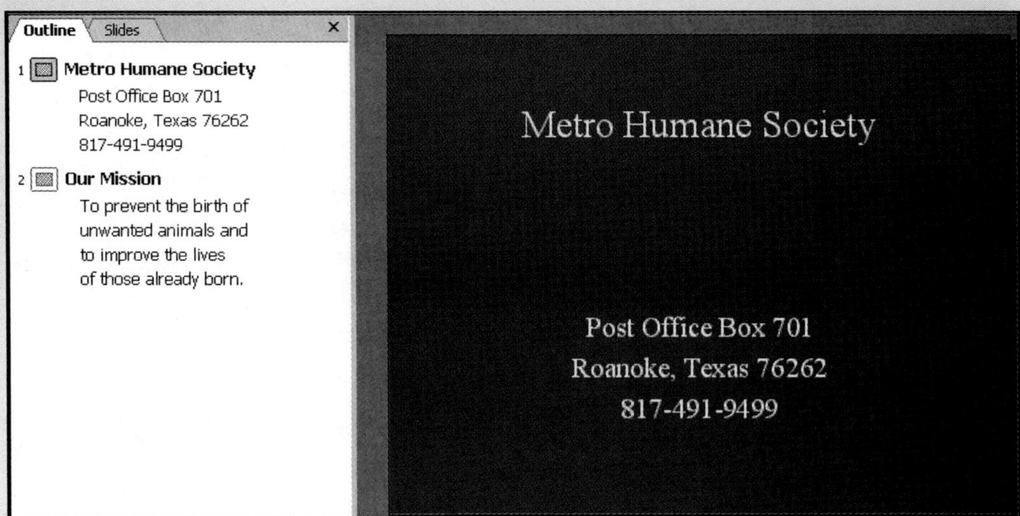

Figure 3.23
"Metro" presentation

3. To add graphics to the draw layer, you must use the Drawing toolbar. By default, this toolbar is positioned along the bottom of the application window. (*Note:* If this toolbar is not displaying, right-click an existing toolbar and then choose Drawing.) Insert the Sun AutoShape in the area between the main title and the subtitle. To begin:
   CLICK: AutoShapes button (AutoShapes ▾) on the Drawing toolbar
   CHOOSE: Basic Shapes
4. On the Basic Shapes submenu:
   CHOOSE: Sun ( )
   The pop-up menu disappears and your mouse pointer changes to a small crosshair as you move it over the slide area.
5. There are two methods for placing an object on the draw layer. For most objects, you simply click the crosshair mouse pointer anywhere on the slide to create a default-sized graphic. For more precision, you drag the mouse pointer and size the object as you place it. To insert a default-sized Sun graphic object:
   CLICK: beneath the main title

6. The Sun object appears surrounded by eight white boxes, as shown to the right. These boxes are sizing handles, similar to the circles surrounding clip art that you saw in lesson 3.1.1. The sizing handles only appear when the object is selected (Figure 3.24). As you know, you use these handles to modify the height and width of the object using the mouse. The yellow diamond is an **adjustment handle** that lets you change the appearance, not the size, of most AutoShapes. For example, by dragging the adjustment handle on the Sun graphic, you can make the circle larger or smaller. To deselect the AutoShape object:
CLICK: in the title placeholder (*or anywhere else on the slide*)
The sizing handles disappear when the graphic is no longer selected.

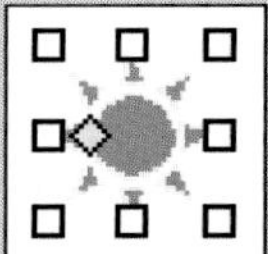

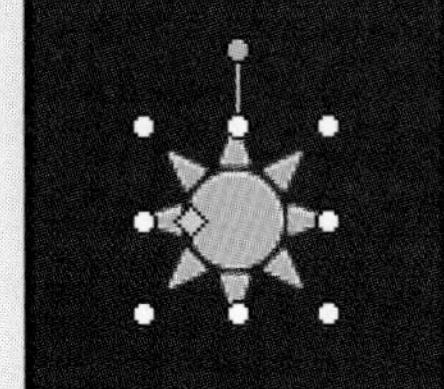

Figure 3.24

Sun object

7. Position the mouse pointer over the Sun object until the mouse pointer changes shape to a four-headed arrow. To move a graphic, position the mouse pointer in the center of the graphic and then drag it to a new location. To size a graphic, select the object and then drag its sizing handles. To size a graphic while keeping its proportions intact, hold the SHIFT key down while dragging a corner-sizing handle. To begin:
CLICK: Sun graphic once to select it
Note that the sizing handles are displayed.

8. On your own, practice moving and resizing the Sun object. Before proceeding, your screen should appear similar to Figure 3.25.

Figure 3.25

Moving and resizing the AutoShape object

9. Save the presentation and keep it open for use in the next lesson.

PowerPoint

3.2.2 Manipulating and Formatting Draw Objects

feature

Besides sizing an object, you can enhance an AutoShape's appearance and visibility by selecting line styles and fill colors. You can also move and copy objects using standard drag and drop techniques or the Clipboard. To remove an object from the draw layer, select the object and then press the DELETE key.

method

To display the Format AutoShape dialog box:

- DOUBLE-CLICK: an AutoShape object

or

- RIGHT-CLICK: an AutoShape object
- CHOOSE: Format AutoShape

practice

You now practice inserting, copying, and removing draw objects. You also apply formatting to objects using the Drawing toolbar and Format AutoShape dialog box. Ensure that you have completed the previous lesson and that the "Metro" presentation is displaying.

1. Using the Drawing toolbar, let us format the Sun object by selecting a new background fill color:
SELECT: Sun object by clicking the object once
CLICK: down arrow attached to the Fill Color button ( ) on the Drawing toolbar
SELECT: a color that resembles gray from the color palette
Note how the object has been filled with the new color (Figure 3.26).

Figure 3.26

Applying an alternate fill color

2. Insert another draw object to create a border beneath the phone number in the subtitle. Do the following:
CLICK: Line button ( ) on the Drawing toolbar

3. Rather than clicking on the slide to place a default-sized line, position the mouse pointer below the first digit (8) in the telephone number. Then, by referring to Figure 3.27, click the mouse button and drag the crosshair pointer to the right so that the line extends to just below the last digit of the phone number. To complete the operation, release the mouse button. (*Note:* Be sure to drag the mouse horizontally left to right. Dragging slightly upward or downward will create a slanted line. Holding the SHIFT key down while dragging will help constrain the angle of the line, making it easier to draw a straight line.)

Figure 3.27

Inserting a line using the Drawing toolbar

Post Office Box 701
Roanoke, Texas 76262
817-491-9499

4. Change the line's format. With the line still selected:
CHOOSE: Format, AutoShape from the menu
CLICK: *Colors and Lines* tab
The Format AutoShape dialog box appears, as shown in Figure 3.28. (*Hint:* You can also double-click the object to display the dialog box in Figure 3.28.)

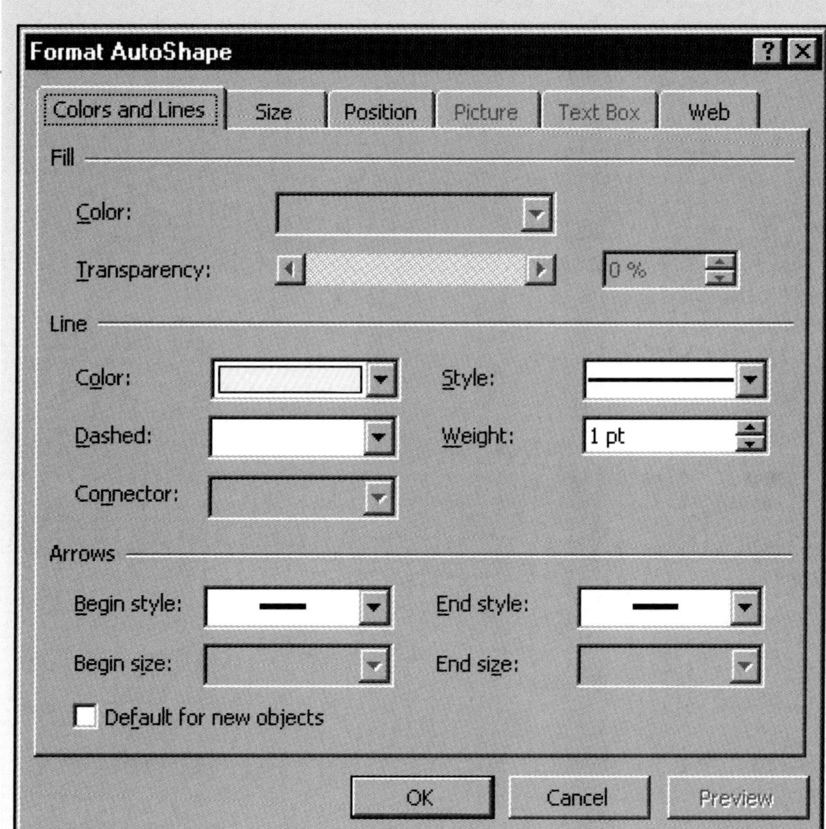

Figure 3.28

Format AutoShape dialog box: *Colors and Lines* tab

5. To change the color of the line from light yellow to light gray:
SELECT: a color that resembles light gray from the *Color* drop-down list in the *Line* area

6. To change the weight of the line to 6 points:
SELECT: 6 pt from the *Style* drop-down list
CLICK: OK command button
The slide should now appear similar to Figure 3.29.

PowerPoint

Figure 3.29

Formatting draw objects

7. Let's practice using the *Size* tab of the Format AutoShape dialog box. Using this tab, you can enter exact size dimensions and change an object's rotation. With the object still selected:
RIGHT-CLICK: Line object
CHOOSE: Format AutoShape from the right-click menu
CLICK: *Size* tab from the tab choices across the top
The dialog box should now appear similar to Figure 3.30.

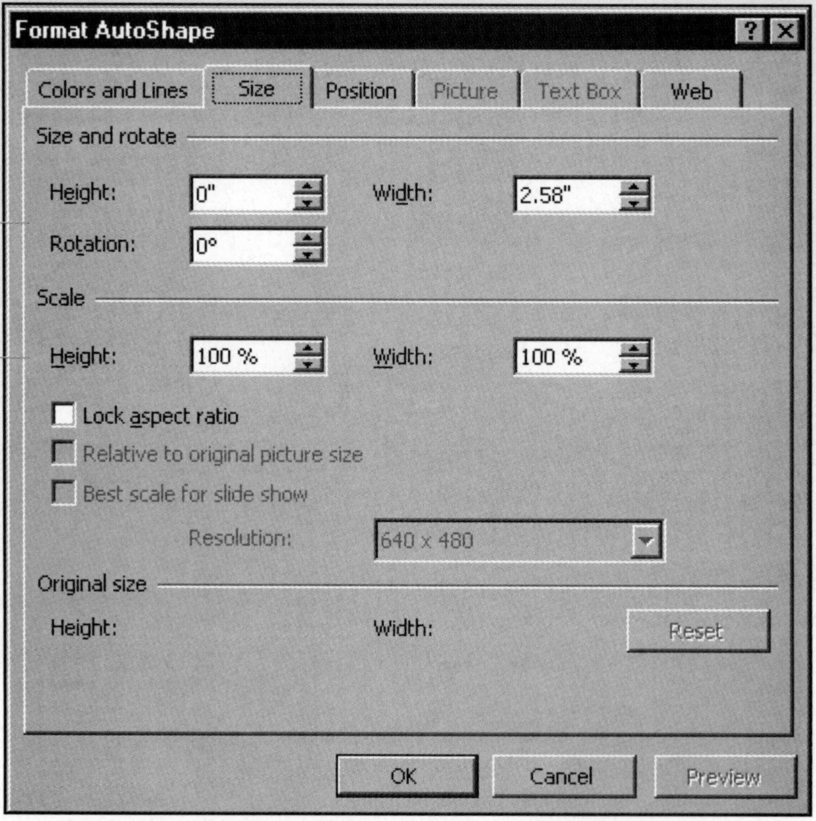

Figure 3.30

Format AutoShape dialog box: *Size* tab

Use the *Size and rotate* area to enter specific size dimensions and to change an object's rotation.

Scale an object to size using the *Height* and *Width* spin boxes.

8. Change the length of the object. In the *Size and rotate* area:
SELECT: the contents of the *Width* spin box
TYPE: **3**
The line will be 3 inches long.

9. Before closing this dialog box:
CLICK: *Position* tab to view options for positioning the object
CLICK: *Web* tab to specify the text property of a Web graphic
CLICK: *Colors and Lines* tab to return to the first tab
CLICK: OK command button

10. To undo the modification you made to the line width:
CLICK: Undo button ( )

11. In addition to sizing and moving objects, you can also use the Clipboard to copy and delete objects that you place on a slide. You will now place a copy of the Sun object to the right.
CLICK: Sun object to select it
CLICK: Copy button ( ) on the Standard toolbar
CLICK: Paste button ( ) on the Standard toolbar

12. DRAG: the copied Sun object, which is currently selected, to the right
The slide should now appear similar to Figure 3.31.

Figure 3.31

Using the Clipboard

13. To delete the second Sun object, ensure that it is selected and then do the following:
PRESS: DELETE

14. Save the revised presentation and keep it open for use in the next lesson.

3.2.3 Ordering and Grouping Objects

feature

In PowerPoint, you have control over how objects are layered on a slide. That is, you can control whether an object is positioned in front of or behind another object, or in front of or behind text. When an image is composed of multiple objects, you might want to group them together before moving, copying, or resizing the image.

method

To change where an object appears in relation to other objects and text:

- SELECT: an object
- CLICK: Draw button (Draw) on the Drawing toolbar
- CHOOSE: Order
- CHOOSE: an option from the Order menu

To create a single object out of a group of objects:

- CLICK: one of the objects
- PRESS: SHIFT and hold it down while clicking on the other objects to group
- CLICK: Draw button on the Drawing toolbar
- CHOOSE: Group

practice

You will now add an object to the first slide of the "Metro" presentation. Then, you will position the object behind the existing Sun object and then group the two objects to form a single object.

1. CLICK: Oval button on the Drawing toolbar
POINT: to the upper-left corner of the Sun graphic
DRAG: with the mouse to the right and down until a circle covers the Sun graphic (refer to Figure 3.32)
Your screen should now appear similar to Figure 3.32.

Figure 3.32

A circle appears in front of the Sun graphic

2. With the circle object still selected, let's move it to behind the Sun graphic:
CLICK: Draw button on the Drawing toolbar
CHOOSE: Order, Send to Back

3. To deselect the oval object:
CLICK: away from the object
Your screen should now appear similar to Figure 3.33.

Figure 3.33

The circle object is now in back of the Sun graphic

4. To create a single object out of the Sun and Oval objects, you must first select both objects. To do this, you must click them while holding down the SHIFT key.
CLICK: the Oval object
PRESS: SHIFT and hold it down
CLICK: the Sun object
Note that both objects are now selected, as indicated by the two sets of sizing handles (Figure 3.34).

Figure 3.34

Both objects are selected

5. To group the selected objects together:
CLICK: Draw button on the Drawing toolbar
CHOOSE: Group
The graphic should now be selected as a single group. As mentioned previously, once objects are grouped together, you manipulate them as a single object for greater ease when moving, copying, and resizing.

6. Save and then close the revised presentation.

3.2. When is it useful to group objects?

PowerPoint

3.3 Inserting Text Labels

When building presentations in PowerPoint, you will most often insert text in a slide's existing title, subtitle, and bulleted-list placeholders. However, when you want to label a draw object, picture, or chart, you will need greater control over where text is positioned. In this module, you learn how to add labels to draw objects and position text using text boxes.

3.3.1 Labeling Draw Objects

feature

When used appropriately, AutoShapes help attract your audience's attention. As such, they serve as the perfect backdrop for the words and phrases that need special emphasis.

method

To add text to an AutoShape:

- RIGHT-CLICK: the AutoShape
- CHOOSE: Add Text
- TYPE: **the text you want to insert**

To invoke text wrapping inside the AutoShape:

- RIGHT-CLICK: the AutoShape
- CHOOSE: Format AutoShape
- CLICK: *Text Box* tab
- SELECT: *Word wrap text in AutoShape* check box
- CLICK: OK command button

practice

In this lesson, you insert text inside an AutoShape and control text wrapping. Ensure that PowerPoint is loaded and that no presentations are displaying.

1. Open the PP0330 data file.
2. Save the presentation as "Laptop World" to your personal storage location. Your screen should now appear similar to Figure 3.35.

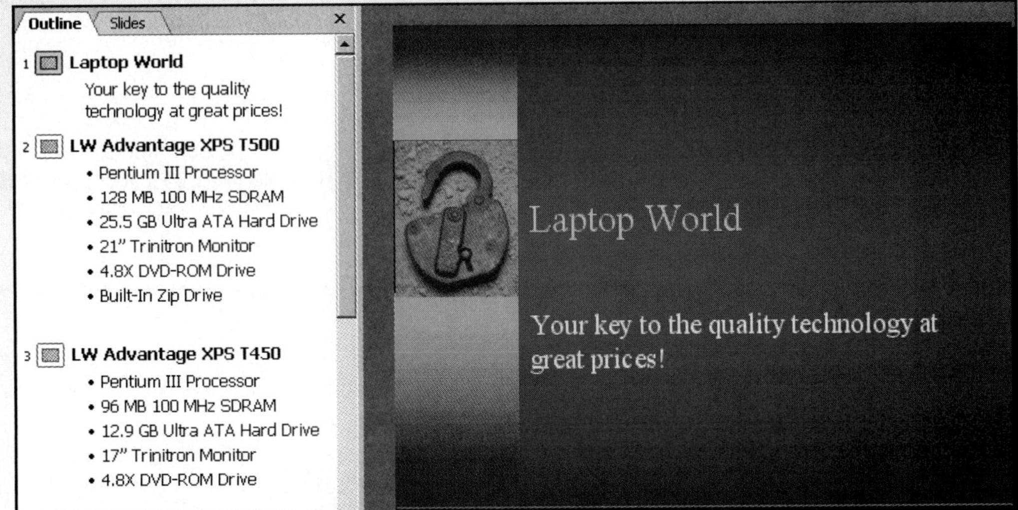

Figure 3.35

"Laptop World" presentation

3. Review each of the slides in this presentation. Before continuing, display the second slide.
4. Add the Explosion 2 AutoShape to the bottom-right corner of the current slide.
   CLICK: AutoShapes button (AutoShapes ▾) on the Drawing toolbar
   CHOOSE: Stars and Banners
   CHOOSE: Explosion 2 from the Stars and Banners submenu
5. Now insert a default-sized Explosion graphic object:
   CLICK: near the bottom-right corner of the slide
6. While referring to Figure 3.36, move and resize the Explosion object.

Figure 3.36

Moving and resizing the Explosion object

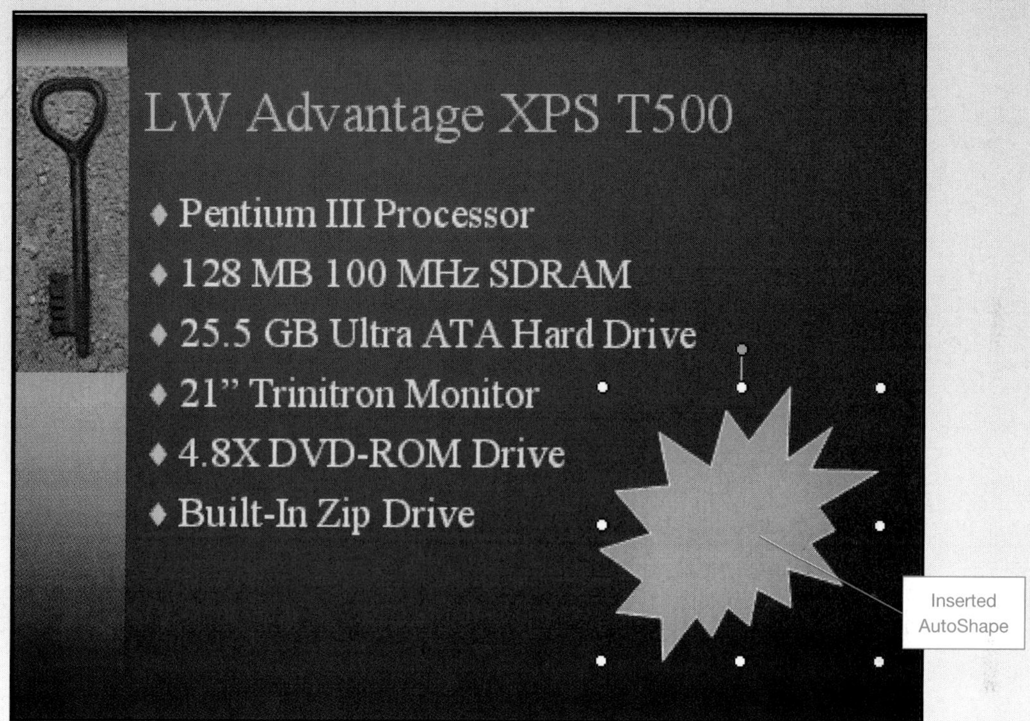

7. To add text to the Explosion object:
   RIGHT-CLICK: the object
   CHOOSE: Add Text
   The insertion point is now blinking inside the object.
8. TYPE: **Available now for $1000!**
   CLICK: outside the object to deselect it
   Note how the text remained on one line and extends outside the AutoShape.
9. Next, turn on the text-wrapping feature so that the text will fit within the AutoShape.
   RIGHT-CLICK: Explosion object
   CHOOSE: Format AutoShape from the right-click menu
   CLICK: *Text Box* tab
   The Format AutoShape dialog box should now appear similar to Figure 3.37.

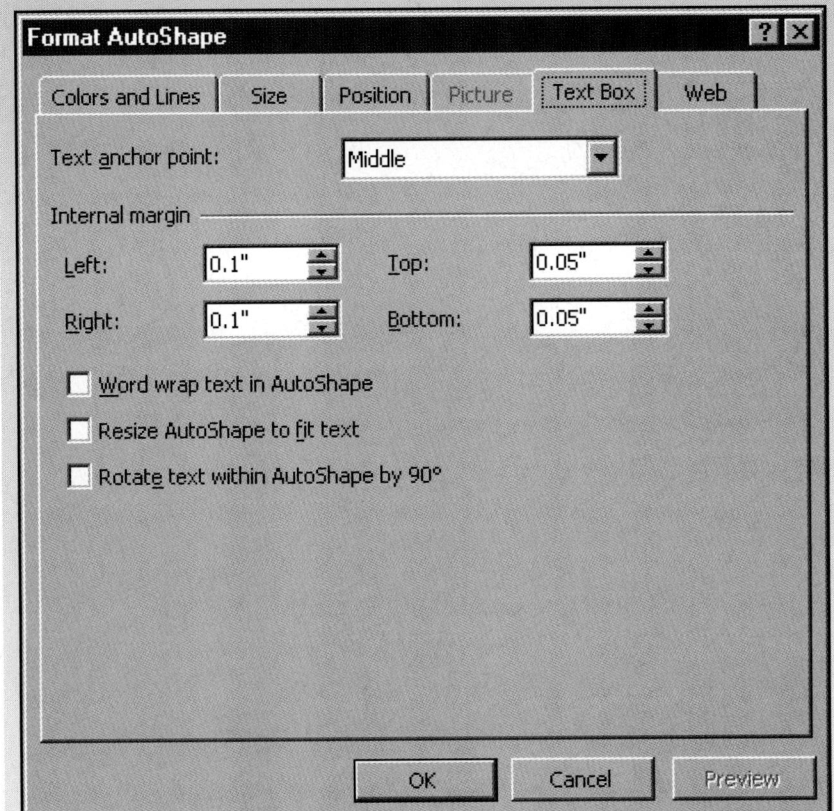

Figure 3.37

Format AutoShape dialog box: *Text Box* tab

10. SELECT: *Word wrap text in AutoShape* check box
CLICK: OK command button

11. If the text still wraps incorrectly, enlarge the AutoShape slightly by dragging one of its corner sizing handles.

12. Change the formatting of the text so that it is easier to read.
SELECT: the text inside the Explosion object
CLICK: Font Color button (A) on the Drawing toolbar
CHOOSE: dark purple from the color palette
CLICK: Bold button (B) on the Formatting toolbar

13. CLICK: outside the Explosion object to deselect it
Your screen should now appear similar to Figure 3.38.

Figure 3.38

Wrapping text inside the AutoShape

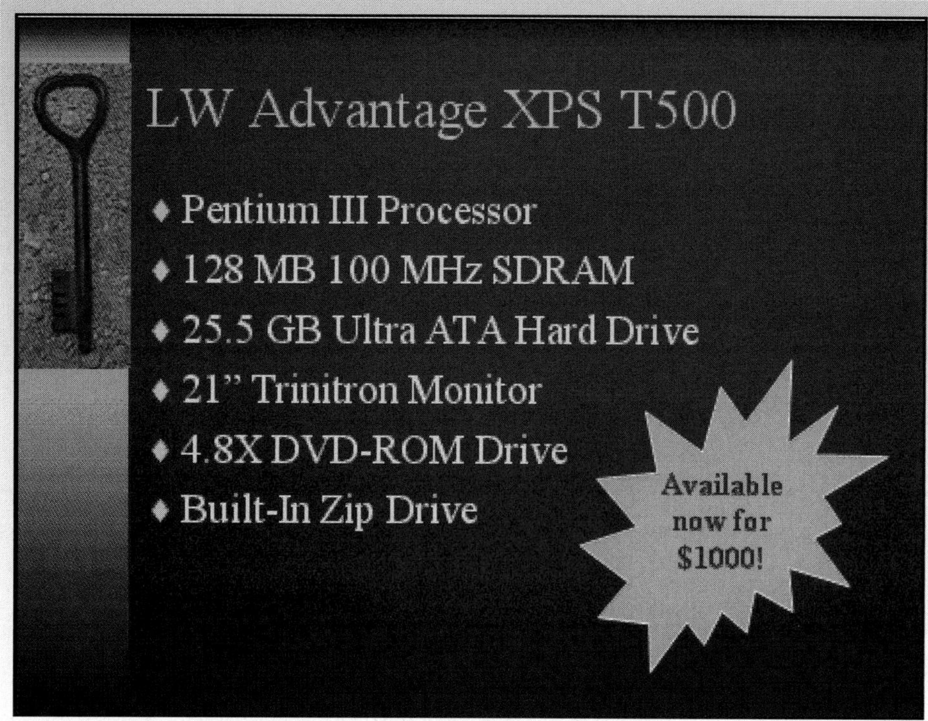

14. Save the revised presentation and keep it open for the next lesson.

3.3.2 Inserting Text Outside Placeholders

feature

Text boxes are used to position text anywhere on a slide. They act as containers for text and can contain more than one paragraph. They can also be formatted with their own unique character and paragraph formatting commands.

method

- CLICK: Text Box button ( ) on the Drawing toolbar
- CLICK: in your document to create a text box that enlarges as you type

or

- DRAG: with the mouse to establish the size of the text box

practice

You will now practice inserting a text box. Ensure that you've completed the previous lesson and that slide 2 of the "Laptop World" presentation is displaying.

1. Use the Text Box tool to insert some additional text at the bottom of slide 2:
CLICK: Text Box button ( ) on the Drawing toolbar

2. To insert a text box in the bottom left-hand corner of the slide that will enlarge as you type:
CLICK: near the bottom left-hand corner of the slide
(*Note:* You'll have an opportunity to move the text box later.) The insertion point should be blinking inside a text box, as shown below:

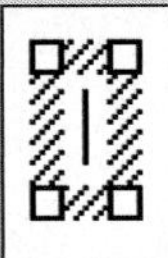

3. TYPE: **Business Lease: $59/Mo.**
4. On your own, refer to Figure 3.39 while dragging the text box into position.

Figure 3.39

Inserting a text box

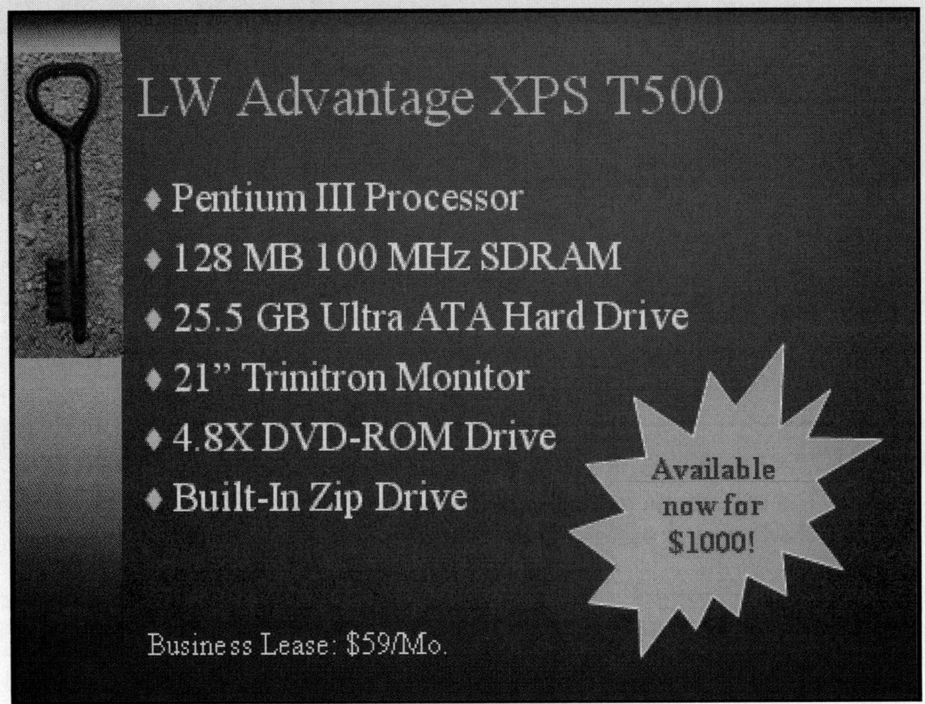

5. Save and then close the "Laptop World" presentation.

3.3. When would it be preferable to use a text box instead of a text placeholder?

Chapter summary

Most people recognize the benefit of using graphics to improve the effectiveness of their presentations. PowerPoint makes it possible to insert several types of graphic objects on your slides including clip art, pictures, graphs, organization charts, and other types of diagrams. These objects are often more effective at conveying information than text by itself, and help keep your audience's attention. The Drawing toolbar provides additional tools for creating original graphics such as company logos, and for adding labels to objects.

Command Summary

Many of the commands and procedures appearing in this chapter are summarized in the following table.

Skill Set	To Perform This Task	Do the Following
Inserting Clip Art, Pictures, Charts, and Organization Charts	Go directly to a selection of clip art images	CLICK: a content placeholder CLICK: Insert Clip Art button ( )
	Search for a clip using the Clip Art task pane	CHOOSE: Insert, Picture, Clip Art (or click the Insert Clip Art button ( ) on the Drawing toolbar) TYPE: a search keyword in the *Search text* text box CLICK: Search command button in the task pane
	Display a categorical listing of Microsoft Office clip art	CHOOSE: Insert, Picture, Clip Art (or click the Insert Clip Art button ( ) on the Drawing toolbar) CLICK: "Clip Organizer" link in the task pane DOUBLE-CLICK: Office Collections in the Collection List pane
	Insert a picture	CHOOSE: Insert, Picture, From File
	Insert a graph	CLICK: Insert Chart button ( ) on the Standard toolbar, or CLICK: Insert Chart button ( ) in a content placeholder, or CHOOSE: Insert, Chart from the menu, or CHOOSE: Insert, Object and then select Microsoft Graph Chart
	Modify a graph	DOUBLE-CLICK: graph object
	Insert an organization chart	CLICK: Insert Diagram or Organization Chart button ( ) in a content placeholder, or CHOOSE: Insert, Picture, Organization Chart
	Modify an organization chart	DOUBLE-CLICK: organization chart object
Inserting and Modifying Draw Objects	Insert a draw object	CLICK: an object button on the Drawing toolbar CLICK: on the slide to insert the object

Skill Set	To Perform This Task	Do the Following
	Size and move objects	SELECT: object DRAG: object's handles to size it, and DRAG: center of object to move it
	Delete an object on the draw layer	SELECT: an object PRESS: DELETE
	Format an AutoShape object	RIGHT-CLICK: an AutoShape object CHOOSE: Format AutoShape command
	Fill a selected AutoShape	CLICK: Fill Color button
	Scale and rotate an AutoShape	RIGHT-CLICK: an AutoShape object CHOOSE: Format AutoShape command CLICK: *Size* tab
	Change the order of a selected object	CLICK: Draw button (Draw) CHOOSE: Order
	Group objects	SELECT: two or more objects while holding down SHIFT CLICK: Draw button (Draw) CHOOSE: Group
Inserting and Modifying Text Objects	Create a text box	CLICK: Text Box button CLICK: on the slide to create a text box object
	Add text to an AutoShape	RIGHT-CLICK: the AutoShape CHOOSE: Add Text
	Wrap text within AutoShape	RIGHT-CLICK: the AutoShape CHOOSE: Format AutoShape CLICK: *Text Box* tab SELECT: *Word wrap text in AutoShape* check box

Key Terms

This section specifies page references for the key terms identified in this chapter. For a complete list of definitions, refer to the Glossary at the end of this learning guide.

adjustment handle, ***p. 101***
AutoShape, ***p. 99***
clip art, ***p. 82***
Diagram Gallery, ***p. 95***
draw layer, ***p. 99***
Microsoft Graph, ***p. 90***
organization chart, ***p. 95***
text box, ***p. 111***

Chapter quiz

Short Answer

1. In the Insert Clip Art task pane, what information displays in a pop-up window when you click an image?
2. What is Microsoft Graph used for?
3. Describe the process of inserting a picture from a file into your presentation.
4. What is the procedure for inserting a rectangle on a slide?
5. What tool would you use to insert text in the upper-right corner of a slide?
6. What is an AutoShapes adjustment handle used for?
7. What is the procedure for making a duplicate copy of an AutoShape on a slide?
8. What are text boxes used for?
9. How do you add text to AutoShapes?
10. Describe two methods for inserting an organization chart on a slide.

True/False

1. ____ You edit a graph placeholder by double-clicking.
2. ____ Organization charts are often used to represent spreadsheet data.
3. ____ Text boxes can be formatted with unique character and paragraph formatting.
4. ____ It's possible to insert an AutoShape on a slide by clicking once on the slide.
5. ____ Adjustment handles are used for sizing AutoShapes.
6. ____ It's possible to add labels to AutoShapes.
7. ____ To move an object, drag the object's sizing handles.
8. ____ To scale and rotate an object, use the *Size* tab in the Format AutoShape dialog box.
9. ____ To draw AutoShape objects, click the Draw button (Draw ▾) on the Drawing toolbar.
10. ____ To change the order of objects, click the Draw button (Draw ▾) and then choose the Order option.

Multiple Choice

1. To insert a picture file in your presentation:
   a. CHOOSE: Insert, Picture, From File
   b. CLICK: Insert Picture button
   c. CHOOSE: File, Insert
   d. All of the above

2. To control whether an object displays in front of or behind another, use the ______________ command.
   a. Group
   b. Ungroup
   c. Order
   d. Rotate

3. Which of the following should you use to enter free-form text on a slide?
   a. Text Box tool
   b. design template
   c. text placeholder
   d. Slide Master

4. To edit an organization chart on an AutoLayout slide, ______________ the placeholder.
   a. click
   b. double-click
   c. drag
   d. None of the above

5. Which of the following must you use to create lines and shapes?
   a. *Paste* option
   b. Diagram Gallery
   c. Drawing toolbar
   d. title placeholder

6. By default, lines are:
   a. white
   b. thin and dashed
   c. thin and solid
   d. None of the above

7. To delete an existing clip art image:
   a. double-click the image
   b. select the image and press DELETE
   c. drag the image outside the Slide pane
   d. All of the above

8. Which of the following can you use to change the shape, not the size, of an object?
   a. Slide Master
   b. adjustment handle
   c. sizing handle
   d. All of the above

9. Which of the following must you use to delete an object?
   a. Format AutoShape dialog box
   b. adjustment handle
   c. DELETE key
   d. All of the above

10. To display the Format AutoShape dialog box, ______________ the AutoShape.
   a. click
   b. double-click
   c. right-click
   d. Both b. and c.

Hands-On exercises

easy

1. Whiting Tours: Inserting and Moving Draw Objects

Ralph Whiting wants to embellish an existing slide with some draw objects. In this exercise, assume the role of Ralph to insert and manipulate draw objects.

1. Open the PP03HE01 presentation and save it as "Whiting Cycling" to your personal storage location.

2. Create a bicycle wheel using the Donut AutoShape. To begin:
   CLICK: AutoShapes button on the Drawing toolbar
   CHOOSE: Basic Shapes

3. On the Basic Shapes submenu:
   CHOOSE: Donut (◎)
   The pop-up menu disappears and your mouse pointer changes to a small crosshair as you move it over the slide area.
4. Now place a default-sized Donut object on the draw layer:
   CLICK: to the left of the subtitle "Cycling Vacation"
5. On your own, create a second Donut to the left of the first Donut repeating steps 2–4.
6. While referring to Figure 3.40, move the Donuts so that they are positioned side by side.

Figure 3.40

Inserting Autoshapes

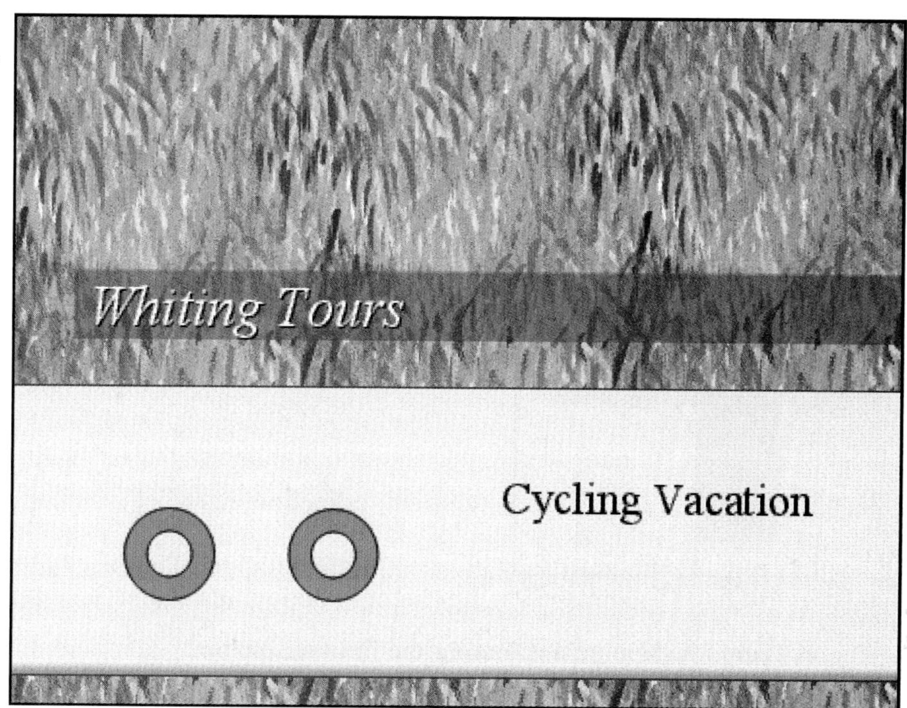

7. Then insert a line between the bicycle tires.
   CLICK: Line button (\) on the Drawing toolbar
8. Rather than clicking on the slide to place a default-sized line, position the mouse pointer in the center of the first bicycle wheel. Then, click the mouse button and drag the crosshair pointer to the right so that the line extends to the center of the second bicycle wheel. When you finish dragging the pointer, release the mouse button. (*Note:* Be sure to drag the mouse horizontally in order to create a straight line.)
9. Finally, while the line is still selected, let's change the line's formatting characteristics:
   CHOOSE: Format, AutoShape
10. To change the color of the line to pink:
    SELECT: a color that resembles pink from the *Color* drop-down list in the *Line* area
11. To change the weight of the line to 4.5 points:
    SELECT: 4½ pt from the *Style* drop-down list
    CLICK: OK command button
    The inserted AutoShapes should now appear similar to Figure 3.41.

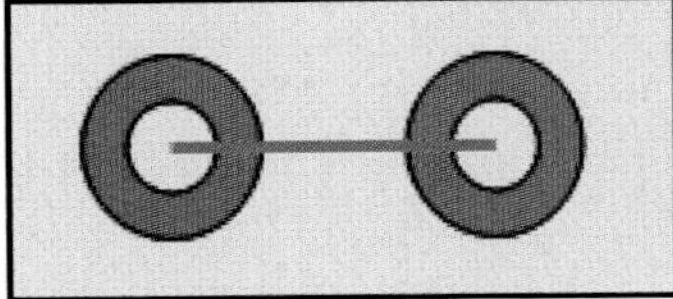

Figure 3.41
Drawing

12. Save, print and then close the "Whiting Cycling" presentation.

2. Glorietta Community College: Formatting and Manipulating Draw Objects

Impressed with the last presentation Rachel Graham created, the president of Glorietta Community College asked her to design a new logo for the school. In this exercise, assume the role of Rachel and perform the same steps that she identifies.

1. Begin a new presentation and select the Title Only layout for the first slide. Save the presentation as "Glorietta Logo" to your personal storage location.
2. Type **Glorietta Community College** in the title placeholder. In the following steps, you will create the logo shown in Figure 3.42.

Figure 3.42
Logo

3. Create the blue rectangle using the Drawing toolbar.
   CLICK: Rectangle button () on the Drawing toolbar
   CLICK: in the area below the title
4. While referring to Figure 3.42, resize the rectangle so that it is taller than it is wide.
5. To change the rectangle's color from light blue to dark blue, with the rectangle still selected:
   CLICK: Fill Color drop-down arrow () on the Drawing toolbar
   CLICK: dark blue in the color palette
6. To insert a red text box on the right side of the rectangle:
   CLICK: Text Box button () on the Drawing toolbar
   CLICK: on a blank area of the slide
   CLICK: Fill Color drop-down arrow ()
   CHOOSE: More Fill Colors
   CLICK: *Standard* tab
   CLICK: red in the color palette
   CLICK: OK command button
7. The insertion point should be blinking inside the text box.
   TYPE: **GCC** in the text box

8. Select the text "GCC" and apply Times New Roman, a 48-point font size, and the bold attribute. The text box should now appear similar to Figure 3.43.

Figure 3.43

Text box

9. While referring to Figure 3.42:
   DRAG: the text box so that it is positioned to the right of the rectangle
10. Then group the logo objects:
    CLICK: the rectangle object
    PRESS: SHIFT and hold it down
    CLICK: the text box object
    CLICK: Draw button (Draw) on the Drawing toolbar
    CHOOSE: Group
11. To finalize the current slide, drag the logo so that it is centered beneath the title and between the margins.
12. Save, print, and close the "Glorietta Logo" document.

PowerPoint

moderate 

3. Catalina Marketing: Creating an Organization Chart

With a growing knowledge of PowerPoint, John Chua has decided to diagram the relationships among Catalina Marketing's executives using an organization chart. In this exercise, assume the role of John and perform the steps he identifies.

1. Start a new presentation and select the Title Slide layout.
2. Save the new presentation as "Catalina Executives" to your personal storage location.
3. Type **Catalina Marketing** for the title and **Executive Committee** for the subtitle.
4. Insert another new slide and apply the Title and Content layout.
5. Type **Executive Committee Members** in the title placeholder.
6. Using the content placeholder, select the organization chart object type.
7. Create the organization chart pictured in Figure 3.44.

Figure 3.44

Organization chart

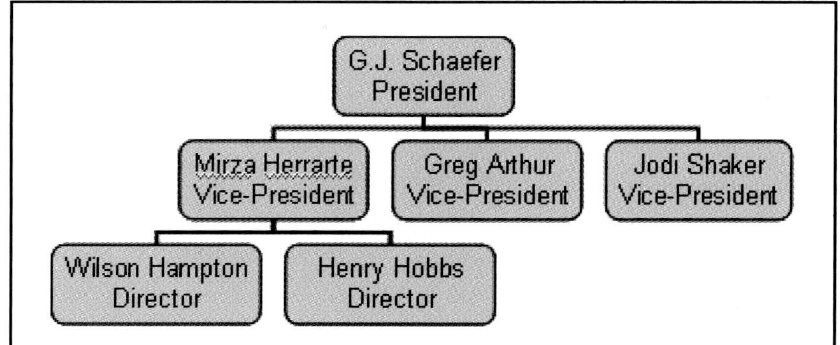

8. Apply bold formatting to the text in each of the chart's boxes.
9. Apply the "Cascade" design template, or one that is available on your computer, to the presentation.
10. Move the organization chart object so that it is centered between the margins. Your screen should now appear similar to Figure 3.45.

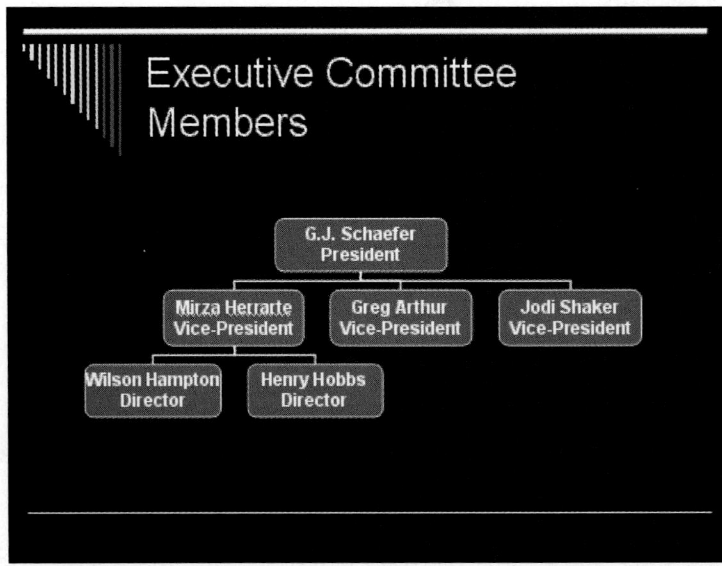

Figure 3.45
Completed slide

11. Save your changes and then close the presentation.

moderate 

4. AddIn Tennis: Inserting Graphics Objects

Luke Evanisko is preparing for an upcoming party for new members of his club. He wants to create a slide show that is visually, rather than textually, oriented. In this exercise, assume the role of Luke and perform the same steps that he identifies.

1. Open the PP03HE04 presentation and then save it as "Add-In Graphics" to your personal storage location.
2. On the second slide, insert the photograph named PP03HE04. Move the picture so your slide appears similar to Figure 3.46.

Figure 3.46

Inserting a photograph

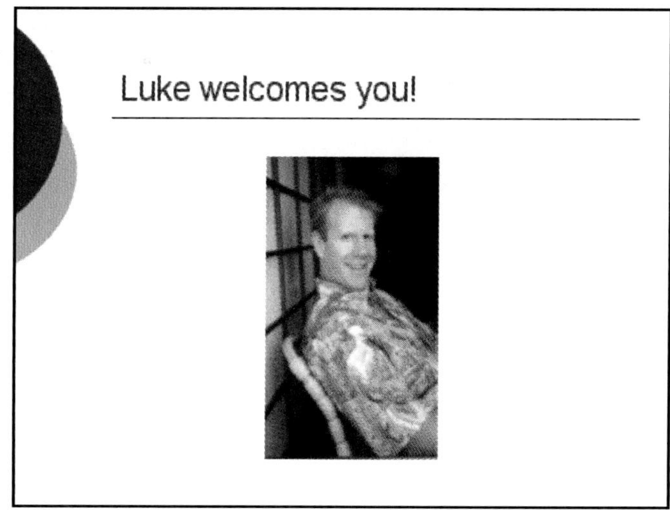

3. Insert a chart on the third slide. Edit the chart's datasheet to look like Figure 3.47.

3.47

Edited datasheet

		A	B	C	D	E
		1999	2000	2001		
1	Wins	13	15	17		
2	Losses	11	9	7		
3						
4						

4. Display the bar chart on the slide (Figure 3.48).

Figure 3.48

Inserting a graph

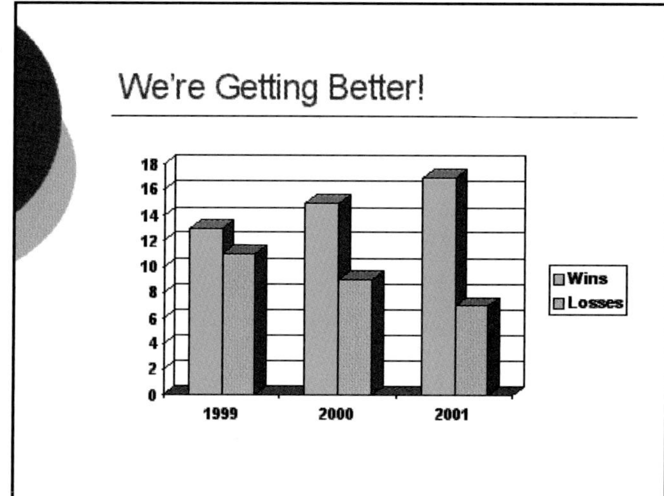

5. Edit the first slide to look like Figure 3.49. (*Hint:* Insert, resize, and move a clip art image.)

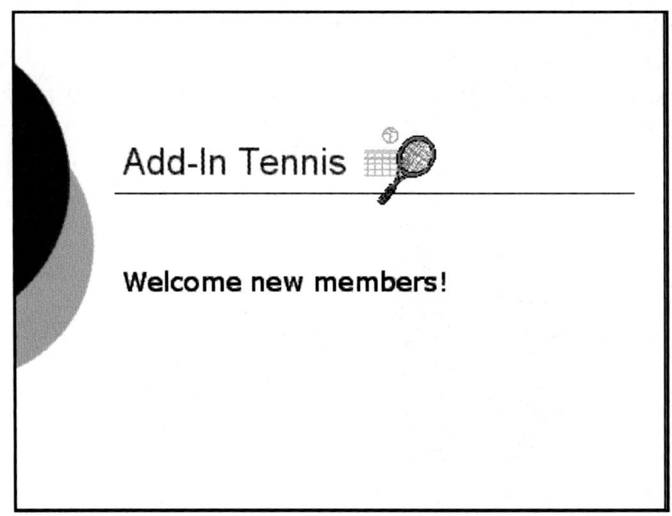

Figure 3.49
Inserting a clip art image

6. Save, print, and then close the "Add-In Graphics" presentation.

difficult 

5. On Your Own: Creating a Fictional Character

Start a new presentation and then apply the "Echo" design template. Using a variety of draw objects, produce a slide that depicts a fictional character. Use lines, arrows, labels, AutoShapes, and colors on your slide. Once your drawing is completed, group the draw objects together so they form a single object.

Save your presentation as "Fictional Character" to your personal storage location. Print and then close the presentation.

difficult 

6. On Your Own: Presenting "Clip Art World"

Open the PP03HE06 data file and then save it as "Clip Art World" to your personal storage location. Insert appropriate clips on slides 2–7 by referring to the slides' titles. Resize the bulleted placeholder on slide 8 so that the bullets line up beneath the first letter of the title. Save the revised presentation. Print and then close the presentation.

Case Problems
Fantasy Motors

After completing Chapter 3, Karl Walters is ready to modify an existing presentation for the upcoming car show. The previous owner of his car dealership created the presentation, and with a few embellishments, Karl thinks the presentation will work nicely. In the following case problems, assume the role of Karl Walters and perform the same steps that he identifies. You may want to re-read the chapter opening before proceeding.

1. Karl opens the PP03CS01 presentation and saves it as "Fantasy Motors" to his personal storage location. After viewing the presentation in Slide Show view, he decides that this

presentation calls for an alternate design template. Karl decides to apply the "Capsules" design template. Next he deletes the cloverleaf object, because it's obscuring some of the text on the first slide. Figure 3.50 provides before-and-after snapshots of the first slide. Karl saves the revised presentation.

Figure 3.50

"Fantasy Motors" presentation

Before

After

Have we got a deal for you!

Lucky Lou's Car Dealership

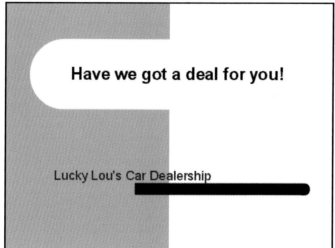

2. To acknowledge the change in ownership, Karl edits slides 1, 2, and 3 of the presentation to include the text "Fantasy Motors" rather than "Lucky Lou's Car Dealership." On the third slide, he selects the title text and then uses the Font dialog box to deselect the *Emboss* check box. Next, Walter deletes the existing clip art image and then inserts a flashier sports car. He then saves the revised presentation as "Fantasy Motors-Version 2" to his personal storage location. Figure 3.51 provides an example of slide 3 once it has been edited.

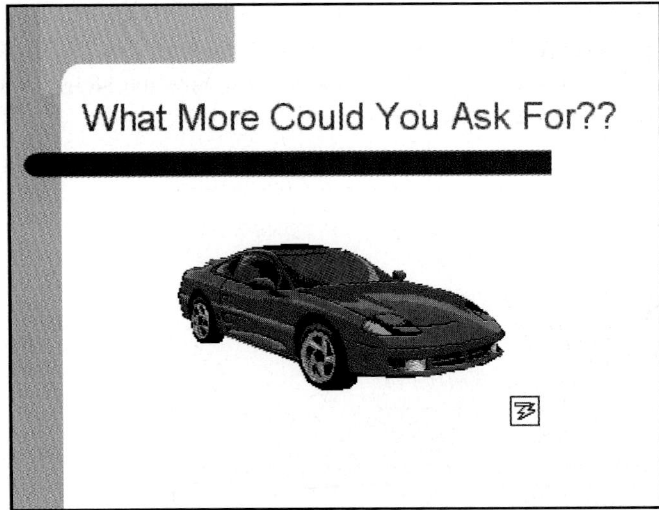

Figure 3.51
Slide 3

3. Karl edits slide 3 once again to include the text "Visit our new showroom!" beneath the clip art object. He uses the Text Box tool to accomplish this. He formats the text using the Arial 32-point font, and changes the font color to red (Figure 3.52). He saves the revised presentation as "Fantasy Motors-Version 3".

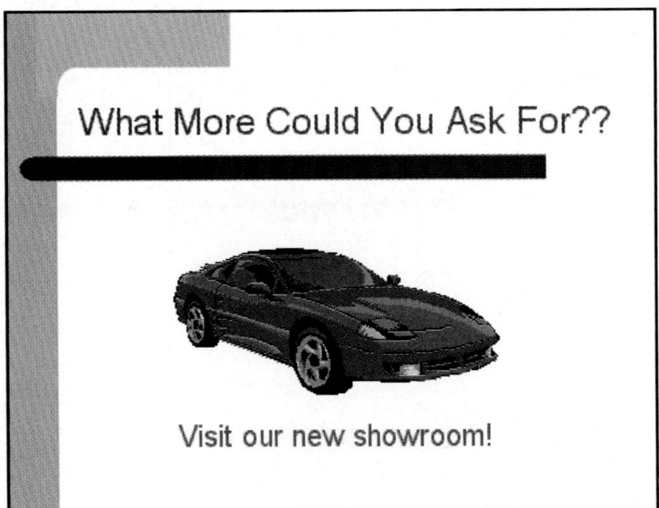

Figure 3.52
Inserted text box

4. Karl decides to add another slide to the presentation and then insert graphics on it using the Drawing toolbar. He begins by adding a new slide with a Blank layout at the end of the presentation. He omits the background graphic by choosing Format, Background and then selecting the *Omit background graphics from master* check box. He finishes this operation by clicking the Apply command button.

   Next, he selects the Explosion 1 AutoShape from the Callouts submenu and inserts it on the top right corner of the slide. He increases the size of the graphic proportionally by holding down the SHIFT key while dragging a corner-sizing handle. He then moves the object so it is centered on the slide (refer to Figure 3.53). Finally, Karl changes the background color of the object to dark blue.

Next, Karl inserts the text "Formerly Lucky Lou's Car Dealership" in the explosion object. After ensuring that the word wrap feature inside the AutoShape is selected, he changes the font color to white, the font size to 28 points, and adds the bold attribute. The completed slide appears in Figure 3.53.

Figure 3.53

Inserting graphics from the Drawing toolbar

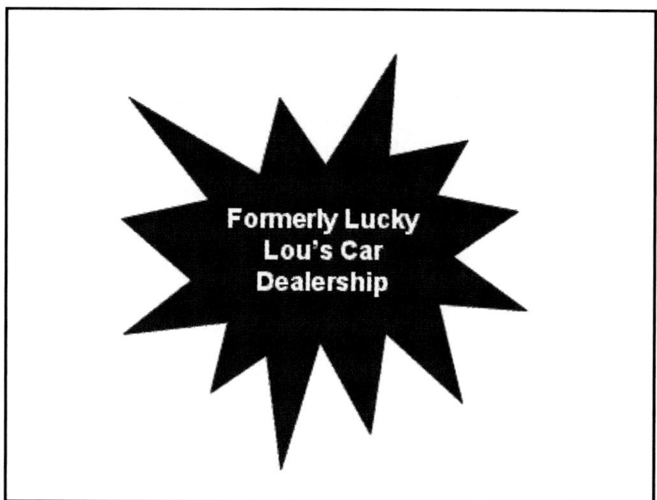

Ready for the upcoming car show, Karl saves the revised presentation as "Fantasy Motors-Version 4" to his personal storage location. He then prints and closes the presentation.

NOTES

NOTES

NOTES

Microsoft® Access® 2002

CHAPTER 1

Working with Access

CHAPTER OUTLINE

Case Study

1.1 Getting Started with Access

1.2 Viewing and Printing Your Data

1.3 Manipulating Table Data

Chapter Summary

Chapter Quiz

Hands-On Exercises

Case Problems

PREREQUISITES

Although this chapter assumes no previous experience using Microsoft Access, you should be comfortable working with the mouse in the Microsoft Windows environment. You should also be able to launch and exit programs and perform basic Windows file management operations, such as opening and closing documents.

LEARNING OBJECTIVES

After completing this chapter, you will be able to:

- Understand basic database terminology
- Describe the different components of the Access application window and the Database window
- Select commands and perform actions using the keyboard and mouse
- Open various database objects, including tables, queries, forms, and reports, for display
- View, edit, and print data in a datasheet
- Insert and delete records in a datasheet
- Open and close a database

CaseStudy LIFELONG LEARNING ACADEMY

Joanna Walsh just started a new job with the Lifelong Learning Academy, a company that specializes in career and life skills training. As an administrative assistant, Joanna knows that she is expected to answer phones, write and edit letters, and organize meetings. However, on her first day, Karen Chase, the office director, informs her of some additional expectations: "You will also be using Microsoft Access to manage our basic seminar information. Our instructors will call you if they have a problem or need to modify the database for any reason. For instance, you may be asked to look up student phone numbers and inform them when a seminar is canceled." Fortunately, Joanna knows there is a course in Microsoft Access starting next week at the local community college, so she is not overly concerned by this new job requirement.

In this chapter, you and Joanna learn about managing information in desktop databases, how to use the different components and features of Microsoft Access, and how to display, edit, and print the information stored in a database.

1.1 Getting Started with Access

Microsoft Access is a desktop database program that enables you to enter, store, analyze, and present data. For end users, power users, and software developers alike, Access provides easy-to-use yet powerful tools most often associated with higher-end **database management systems (DBMS).** In fact, Access offers scalability never before seen in desktop database software to meet needs ranging from simple to complex. At the desktop or local area network level, Access can help you manage your personal information or collect data for a research study. At the corporate and enterprise level, Access can retrieve and summarize data stored on servers located throughout the world. Access also enables you to create and publish dynamic Web-based forms and reports for delivery over the Internet.

Although this is not a database theory course, a familiarity with some basic terms will help you become more productive using Microsoft Access. The word **database**, for example, refers to a collection of related information, such as a company's accounting data. The primary object in a database for collecting and storing data is called a **table**. As shown in Figure 1.1, tables are organized into rows and columns similar to an electronic spreadsheet. An individual entry in a table (for example, a person's name and address) is called a **record** and is stored as a horizontal row. Each record in a table is composed of one or more fields. A **field** holds a single piece of data. For example, the table in Figure 1.1 divides each person's record into vertical columns or fields for ID, Surname, Given, Address, City, and State.

Figure 1.1

An Access table in Datasheet view

Contacts : Table

ID	Surname	Given	Address	City	State
1	Adams	Jake	4901 101st St.	Hampton	VA
2	Arguello	Ahmad	7279 Ridge Dr.	New York	NY
3	Bannister	Rod	1432 Lafayette	Samson	KY
4	Bingham	Wendy	341 Stockton	Redding	CA
5	Chabot	Rosalie	4 Chestnut Dr.	Bellevue	WA
(AutoNumber)					

Record: 1 of 5

Each column represents a field

Each row represents a record

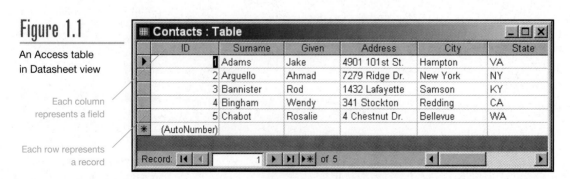

1.1.1 Loading and Exiting Access

feature

To launch Access, begin at the Windows Start menu and click the Start button (Start) on the taskbar. Then, choose the Programs menu option and, finally, click Microsoft Access. After a few moments, the Access application window appears.

When you are finished doing your work, you should exit Access so that the system's memory is freed for use by other Windows applications. To do so, choose the File, Exit command or click on the Close button (X) in the top right-hand corner. These methods close most Microsoft Windows applications.

method

To load Access:

- CLICK: Start button (Start)
- CHOOSE: Programs, Microsoft Access

To exit Access:

- CHOOSE: File, Exit from the Access Menu bar

practice

After loading Microsoft Access using the Windows Start menu, you open an existing database file in this lesson. Ensure that you have turned on your computer and that the Windows desktop appears.

1. Position the mouse pointer over the Start button (Start) appearing in the bottom left-hand corner of the Windows taskbar and then click the left mouse button once. The Start pop-up menu appears as shown here.

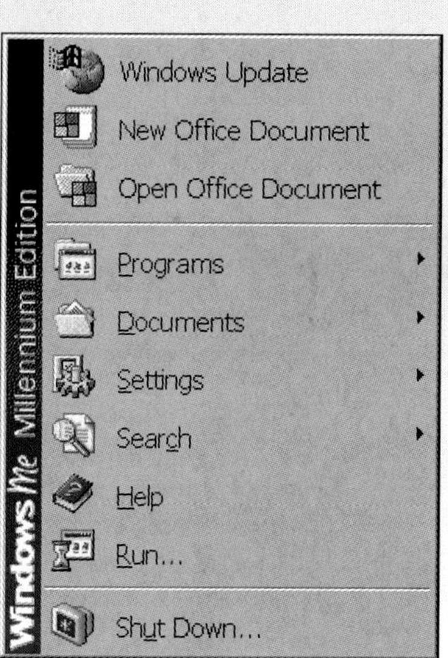

2. Position the mouse pointer over the Programs menu option. Notice that you do not need to click the left mouse button to display the list of programs in the fly-out or cascading menu.
3. Move the mouse pointer horizontally to the right until it highlights an option in the Programs menu. You can now move the mouse pointer vertically within the menu to select an application.
4. Position the mouse pointer over the Microsoft Access menu option and then click the left mouse button once. After a few seconds, the Access application window appears (Figure 1.2). Notice that a new button also appears on the taskbar at the bottom of your screen.
5. To exit Access:
   CLICK: its Close button (X) in the top right-hand corner
   Assuming that no other applications are running and displayed, you are returned to the Windows desktop.

Figure 1.2

Access application window

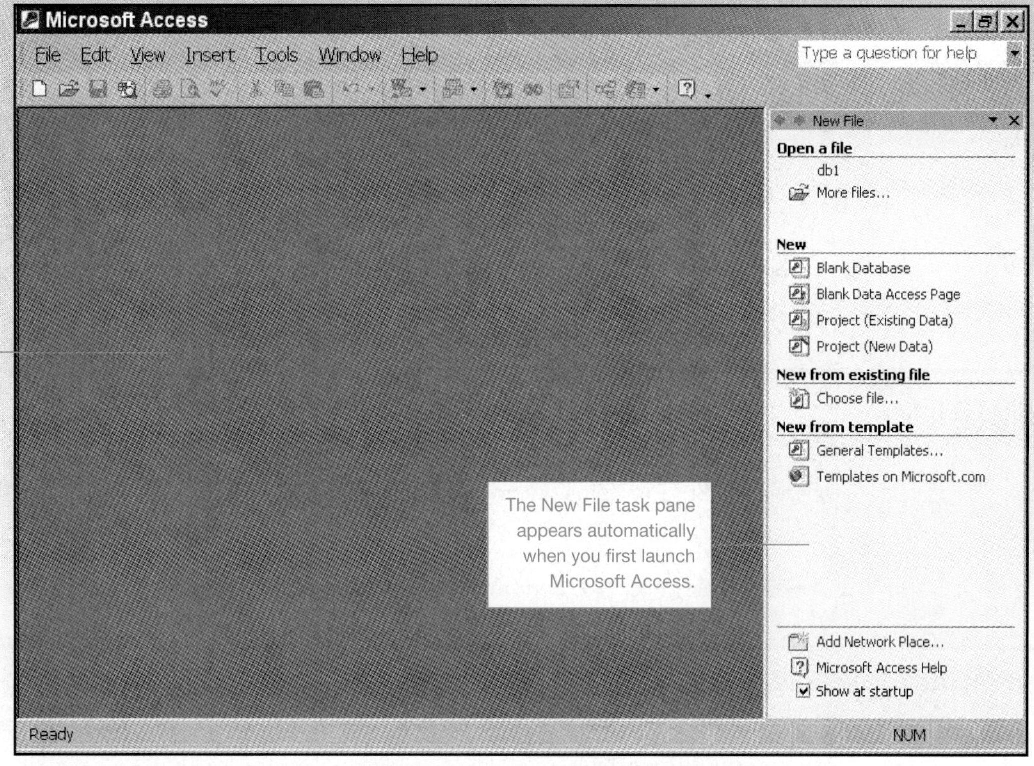

In Addition SWITCHING AMONG APPLICATIONS

A button appears on the Windows taskbar for each "running" application or open Microsoft Office document. Switching among open applications is as easy as clicking the appropriate taskbar button, like switching channels on a television set.

1.1.2 Opening a Database File at Startup

feature→

If you want to launch Access and open an existing database at the same time, choose the Open Office Document command on the Start menu. Or you can launch Access and then, in the *New File task pane,* click the filename of a database used recently. A **task pane** (see Figure 1.2) is the window area that appears docked at the right side of your screen. The New File task pane is displayed automatically when you first start Microsoft Access, or when you click the New button (□) on the toolbar. To open a database file using the task pane, click the "More files . . ." option under the *Open a file* heading. Access then displays the Open dialog box as it would if you had then clicked the Open button (📂) on the toolbar. Use the Open dialog box to search for and retrieve existing database files that are stored on your local hard disk, a floppy diskette, a network server, or on the Web.

method→

To display the Open dialog box:

- CLICK: "More files . . ." option under the *Open a file* heading in the New File task pane

or

- CHOOSE: File, Open from the Menu bar

or

- CLICK: Open button (icon) on the toolbar

To retrieve a database file using the Open dialog box:

- SELECT: *the desired folder* from the Places bar, located along the left border of the dialog box, or from the *Look in* drop-down list box
- DOUBLE-CLICK: *the desired file* from the list area

practice

You now practice navigating your computer's storage areas using the Open dialog box. Ensure that the Windows desktop appears.

1. Launch Microsoft Access, referring to the previous lesson if necessary.
2. To open an existing database:
   CLICK: Open button (icon) on the toolbar
   The Open dialog box appears, as shown in Figure 1.3.

Figure 1.3

Open dialog box

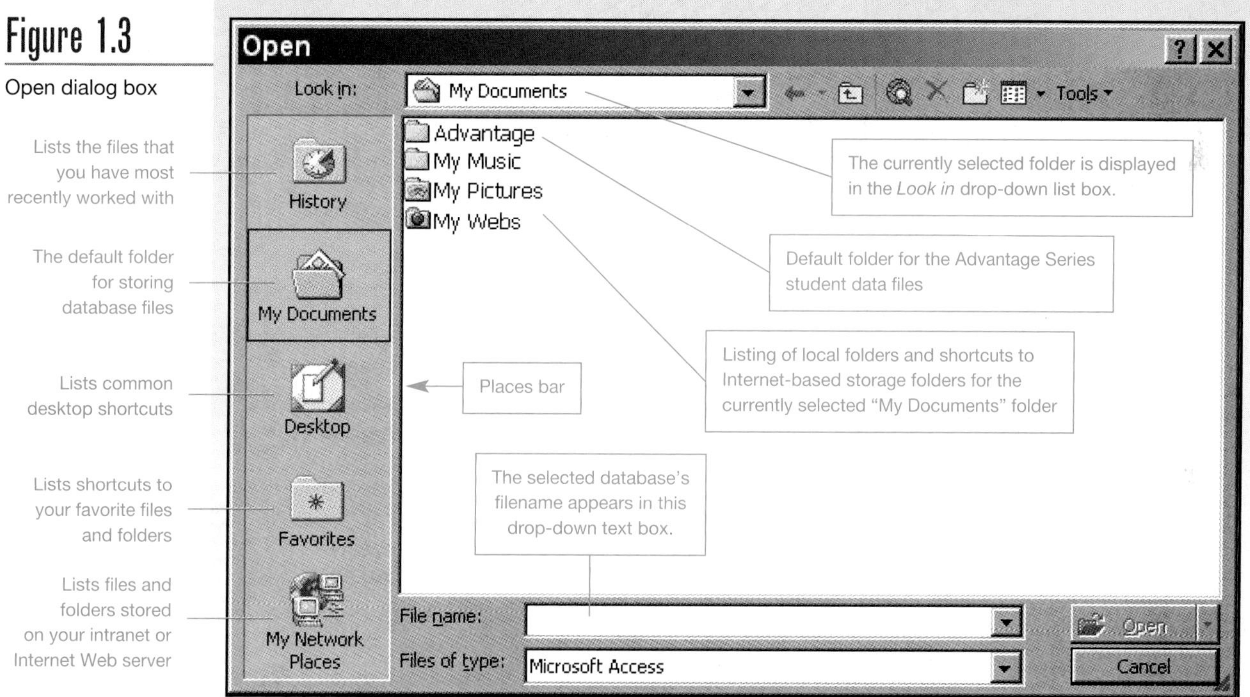
Lists the files that you have most recently worked with
The default folder for storing database files
Lists common desktop shortcuts
Lists shortcuts to your favorite files and folders
Lists files and folders stored on your intranet or Internet Web server
Open
Look in:
My Documents
Tools
Advantage
My Music
My Pictures
My Webs
History
My Documents
Desktop
Favorites
My Network Places
The currently selected folder is displayed in the Look in drop-down list box.
Default folder for the Advantage Series student data files
Listing of local folders and shortcuts to Internet-based storage folders for the currently selected "My Documents" folder
Places bar
The selected database's filename appears in this drop-down text box.
File name:
Files of type:
Microsoft Access
Open
Cancel

Important: *In this guide, we refer to the files that have been created for you as the* ***student data files.*** *Depending on your computer or lab setup, these files may be located on a floppy diskette, in a folder on your hard disk, or on a network server. If necessary, ask your instructor or lab assistant where to find these data files. You will also need to identify a storage location for the files that you create, modify, and save. To download the Advantage Series' student data files from the Internet, visit our Web sites at:*

http://www.mhhe.com/it

http://www.advantageseries.com

3. The **Places bar** provides convenient access to commonly used storage locations. To illustrate, let's view the contents of some folders:
CLICK: History folder button
A list of recently opened Office documents appears.

4. For practice, let's browse the local hard disk:
CLICK: down arrow attached to the *Look in* drop-down list box
Your screen should appear similar, but not identical, to Figure 1.4.

Figure 1.4

Navigating storage areas in the Open dialog box

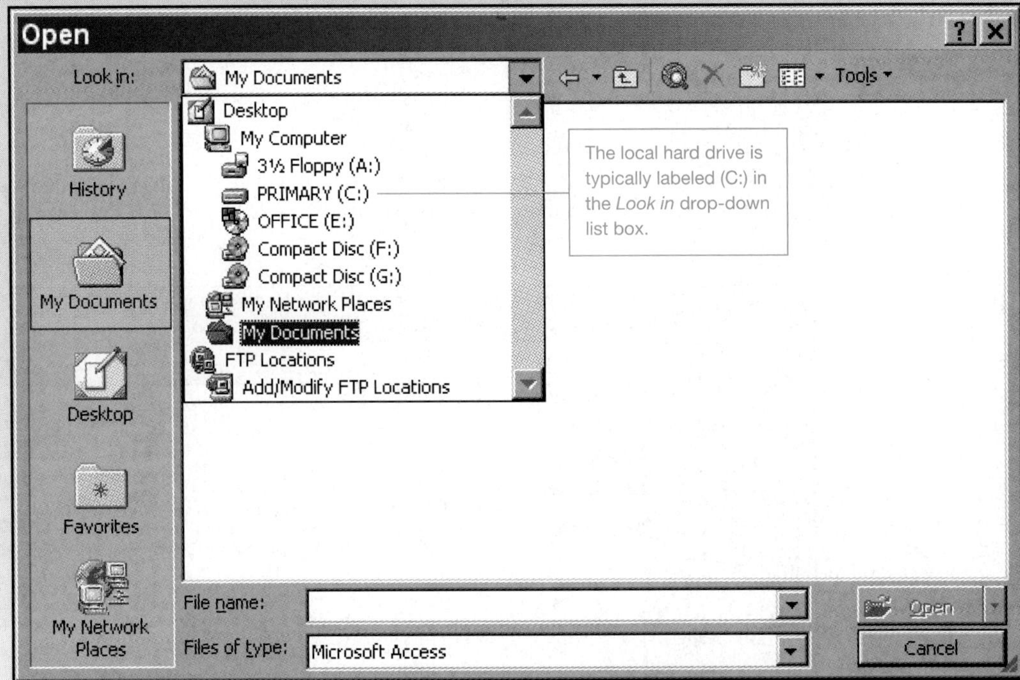

5. SELECT: Hard Disk (C:)
The list area displays the folders and files stored in the root directory of your local hard disk.

6. To view the contents of the My Documents folder:
CLICK: My Documents button

7. Using the Places bar, *Look in* drop-down list box, and the list area, locate the folder containing the student data files. (*Note*: In this guide, we retrieve the student data files from a folder named "Advantage.")

8. To view additional information about each file:
CLICK: down arrow beside the Views button
The drop-down list shown here appears.

9. CHOOSE: Details
Each database file is presented on a single line with additional file information, such as its size, type, and date. (*Hint:* You can sort the filenames in this list area by clicking on one of the column heading buttons.)

10. To display the files using large icons:
CLICK: down arrow beside the Views button (▦▾)
CHOOSE: Large Icons
Your screen should now appear similar to Figure 1.5.

Figure 1.5

Displaying the student data files

11. On your own, return the display to the List view.

12. Keep the Open dialog box open and proceed to the next lesson.

1.1.3 Touring Access

feature→

The Access **application window** acts as a container for the *Database window* and for displaying the database objects that you create and use in Access. It also contains several key interface components, including the *Windows icons, Menu bar, toolbars,* and *Status bar.* Figure 1.6 identifies several of these components.

method→

To control windows, choose from the following options:

- CLICK: Close button (☒) to close a window
- CLICK: Maximize button (☐) to maximize a window
- CLICK: Minimize button (_) to minimize a window
- CLICK: Restore button (⧉) to restore a maximized window

practice

In a guided tour, you now explore some of the interface features of the Access application window. Ensure that you have completed the previous lesson and that the Open dialog box is displayed in the application window.

1. Let's open one of the database files:
   DOUBLE-CLICK: AC0100
   The dialog box disappears and the database is loaded into the application window, as shown in Figure 1.6. (*Note:* The "AC0100" filename reflects that this workbook is used in Chapter 1 of the Microsoft Access learning guide.)

Figure 1.6

Access application and Database windows

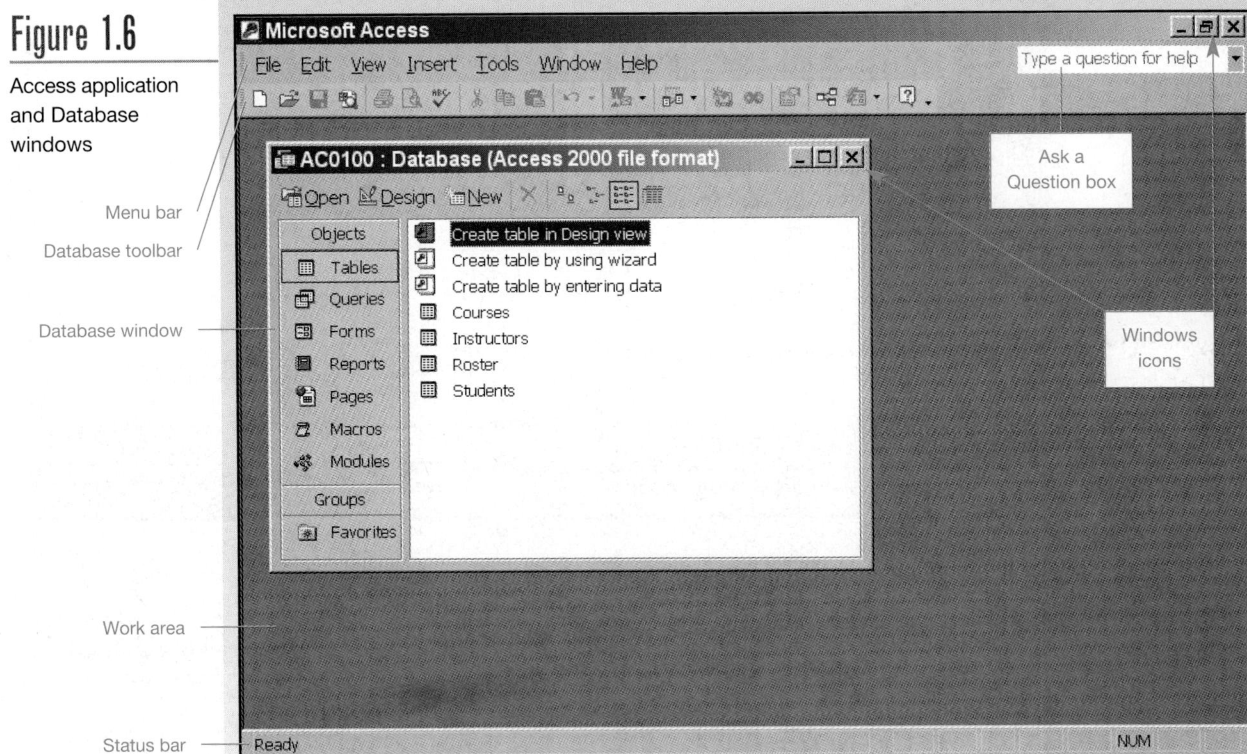

2. The Database window is best displayed as a floating window in the work area, although it may be maximized to fill the entire application window. You control the display of the application and Database windows by clicking their Title bar or Windows icons—Minimize (▁), Maximize (□), Restore (🗗), and Close (✕).

3. The Menu bar contains the Access menu commands. To execute a command, click once on the desired Menu bar option and then click again on the command. Commands that appear dimmed are not available for selection. Commands that are followed by an ellipsis (. . .) display a dialog box when selected.
   To practice using the menu:
   CHOOSE: Help

This instruction tells you to click the left mouse button once on the Help option appearing in the Menu bar. The Help menu appears, as shown here. (*Note:* All menu commands that you execute in this guide begin with the instruction "CHOOSE.")

Help
Microsoft Access Help F1
Show the Office Assistant
What's This?
Office on the Web
Activate Product...
Sample Databases...
Detect and Repair...
About Microsoft Access

4. To display other pull-down menus, move the mouse to the left over other options in the Menu bar. As each option is highlighted, a pull-down menu appears with its associated commands.

5. To leave the Menu bar without making a command selection:
CLICK: in a blank portion of the Access work area

6. Access provides context-sensitive *right-click menus* for quick access to menu commands. Rather than searching for a command in the Menu bar, position the mouse pointer on a database object and right-click to display a list of commands applicable to that object.
To display the right-click menu for a table:
RIGHT-CLICK: Students in the list area of the Database window
Your screen should now appear similar to Figure 1.7.

Figure 1.7

Right-click menu for a table object

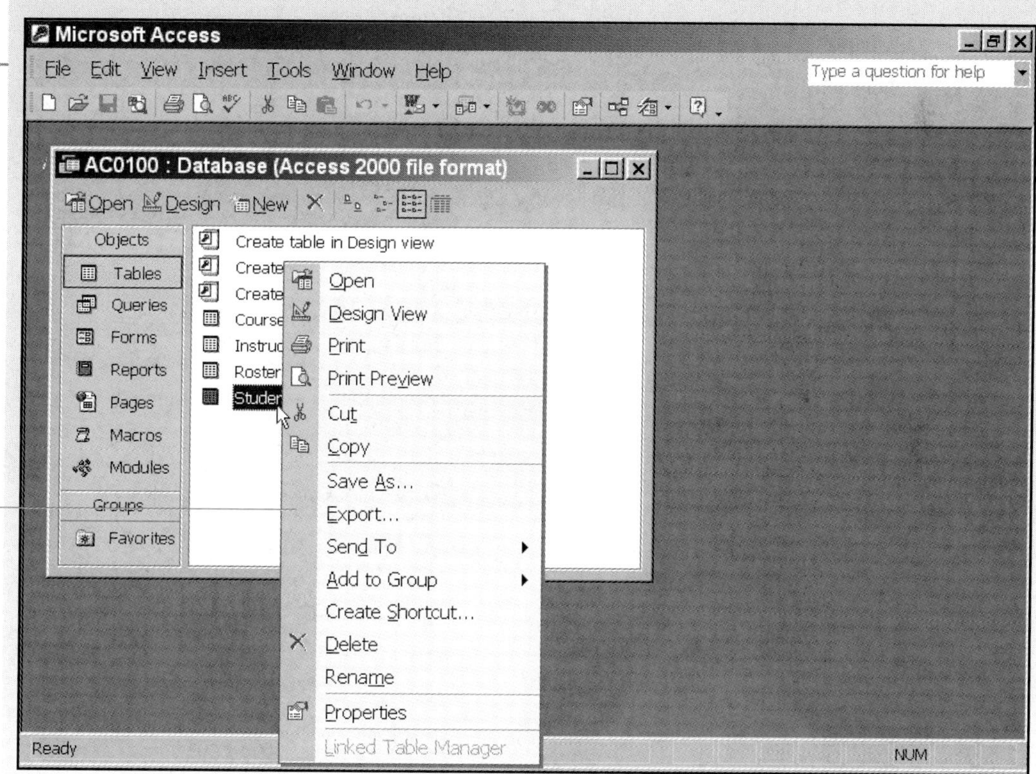

This pop-up menu appears when you right-click the Students table object.

7. To remove the right-click menu without making a selection:
PRESS: ESC
(*Hint:* You can also hide the menu by clicking a blank portion of the work area.)

8. If an Office Assistant character (as shown here) appears on your screen when proceeding through any part of this tutorial, do the following to hide it from view:
RIGHT-CLICK: *the character*
CHOOSE: Hide from the right-click menu
(*Note:* The character's name may appear in the command, such as "Hide Clippit.")

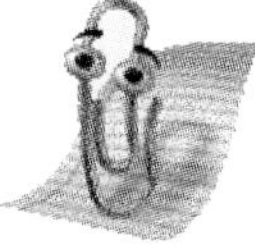

1.1.4 Working in the Database Window

feature

The Access **Database window** is your command control center; it provides the interface to your database. The **Objects bar,** located along the left border, organizes the available database objects into seven categories named *Tables, Queries, Forms, Reports, Pages, Macros,* and *Modules.* Most of your time is spent working with objects in the Database window. To organize the database objects you create, you can define your own groups to appear along with the Favorites folder in the **Groups bar.**

method

To peruse the objects in a database:

- CLICK: *the category buttons* in the Objects bar

practice

In this lesson, you practice selecting objects for display in the Database window. Ensure that the AC0100 Database window is displayed.

1. To begin, let's practice manipulating the Database window in the work area. Using the mouse, drag the Title bar of the Database window to move the window. Do the following: DRAG: the Database window to the center of the work area

2. Now, place the mouse pointer over the bottom right-hand corner of the Database window. The mouse pointer changes shape to a diagonal double-headed sizing arrow. To decrease the size of the window: DRAG: the sizing corner inward as shown in Figure 1.8

Figure 1.8

Sizing the Database window

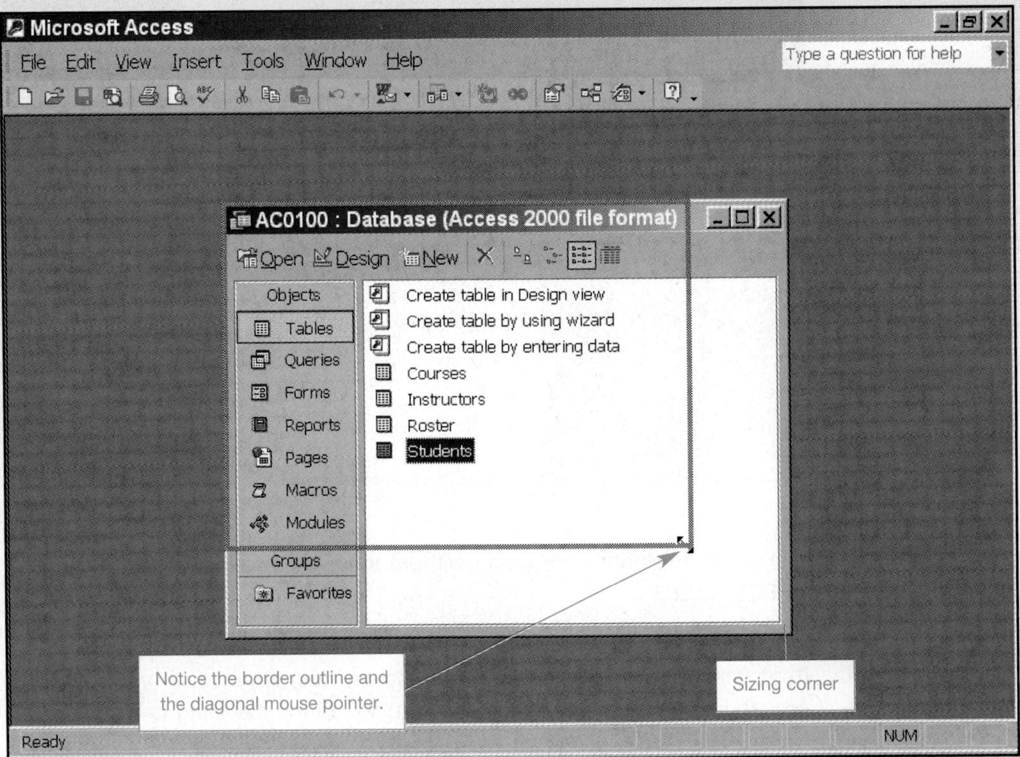

3. When you are satisfied with the size of the window, release the mouse button to complete the operation. (*Hint:* Because your system's resolution and font selections may differ from the author's, these mouse techniques may be necessary to adjust the windows in your work area to look similar to the screen figures in this tutorial.)

4. On your own, return the Database window to its original size and location, so that it appears similar to Figure 1.9. Familiarize yourself with the features labeled in the figure.

Figure 1.9

Access Database window

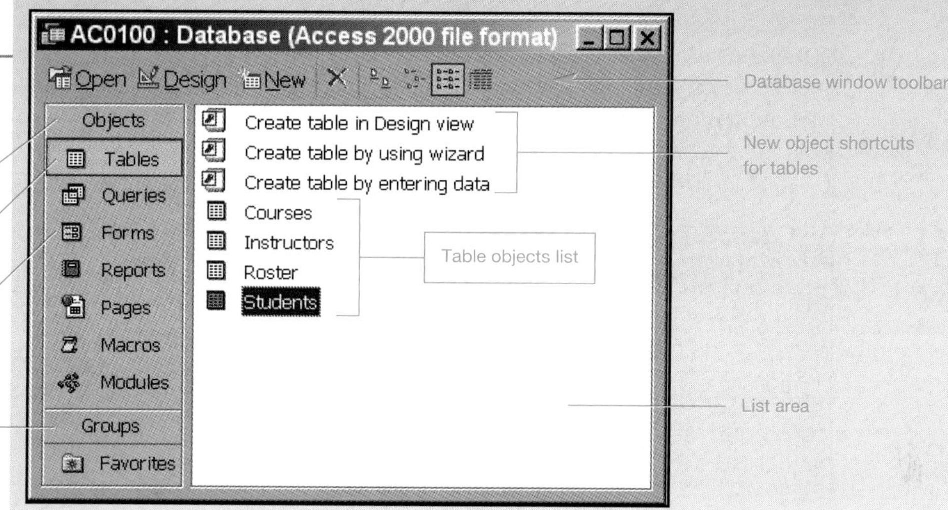

5. Table objects are the primary element of a database and are used to store and manipulate data. A single database file may contain several tables. To display the contents of a table object, ensure that the *Tables* button in the Objects bar is selected and then do the following:
DOUBLE-CLICK: Students in the list area
The Students table appears in a row-and-column layout called a *datasheet,* as shown in Figure 1.10. You will learn how to navigate and manipulate the contents of a datasheet in the next module.

Figure 1.10

Datasheet window for the Students table object

Students : Table

StudentID	LastName	FirstName	Major	Address	City	Zip
1	Stedman	Alan	Business	3710 Bush St.	Seattle	99900
2	Hernandez	Pete	Business	1485 Sonama V	Redmond	99780
3	Mohr	Judy	Arts	100 Bosley Lan	Redmond	99780
4	Buggey	Diana	Science	20 Cactus Lane	Redmond	99804
5	Seinfeld	Casey	Arts	17 Windy Way	Bellevue	98180
6	Alomar	Sandra	Business	PO Box 1465	Kirkland	97080
7	Fernandez	Rosa	Science	151 Greer Rd.	Seattle	99890
8	Peters	Bob	Arts	200 Union St.	Seattle	99850
9	Rinaldo	Sandy	Arts	1871 Orrinton R	Redmond	99704
10	Finklestein	Sue	Business	888 Burrard St.	Seattle	99904
11	Mortimer	Bruce	Science	235 Johnston S	Redmond	99704
12	Jung	Chris	Science	1005 West 9th /	Redmond	99780
13	Abu-Alba	Benji	Arts	122 Cordova Av	Bellevue	98200
14	Stockton	Gretta	Arts	4210 Bush St.	Seattle	99900
15	Sakic	Eric	Arts	875 Cordova Av	Bellevue	98180
16	Modano	Joey	Science	36 Primore St.	Kirkland	97780
17	Francis	Mike	Business	875 Broadway	Maryland	92250
18	Hillman	Frances	Business	29 Redmond Rc	Redmond	99850
19	Brewski	Randy	Science	190 Greer Rd.	Seattle	99890
20	Walsh	Moira	Arts	909 West 18th /	Seattle	99900

Record: 1 of 65

6. To close the Students datasheet:
CLICK: its Close button (☒) in the top right-hand corner

7. A **query** is a question you ask of your database. The answer, which may draw data from more than one table in the database, typically displays a datasheet of records. To see a list of the stored queries:
CLICK: *Queries* button

8. The stored query in this database links and extracts data from the Courses and Instructors tables. To display the results of the query:
DOUBLE-CLICK: Courses Query in the list area
Your screen should now appear similar to Figure 1.11. Notice that the first two columns display information from the Courses table and the remaining columns extract information from the Instructors table.

Figure 1.11

Datasheet window for the Courses Query object

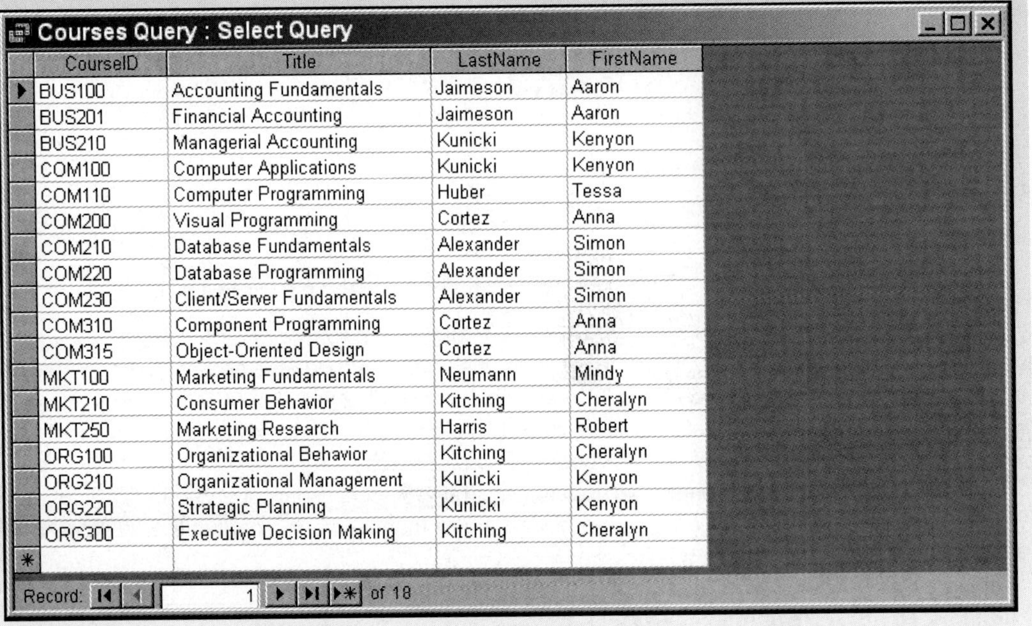

Courses Query : Select Query

CourseID	Title	LastName	FirstName
BUS100	Accounting Fundamentals	Jaimeson	Aaron
BUS201	Financial Accounting	Jaimeson	Aaron
BUS210	Managerial Accounting	Kunicki	Kenyon
COM100	Computer Applications	Kunicki	Kenyon
COM110	Computer Programming	Huber	Tessa
COM200	Visual Programming	Cortez	Anna
COM210	Database Fundamentals	Alexander	Simon
COM220	Database Programming	Alexander	Simon
COM230	Client/Server Fundamentals	Alexander	Simon
COM310	Component Programming	Cortez	Anna
COM315	Object-Oriented Design	Cortez	Anna
MKT100	Marketing Fundamentals	Neumann	Mindy
MKT210	Consumer Behavior	Kitching	Cheralyn
MKT250	Marketing Research	Harris	Robert
ORG100	Organizational Behavior	Kitching	Cheralyn
ORG210	Organizational Management	Kunicki	Kenyon
ORG220	Strategic Planning	Kunicki	Kenyon
ORG300	Executive Decision Making	Kitching	Cheralyn
*			

Record: 1 of 18

9. After reviewing the query, close the displayed datasheet:
CLICK: its Close button (☒)

10. Unlike a table's column and row layout, a **form** generally displays one record at a time. To see a list of the stored forms:
CLICK: *Forms* button

11. To display a form:
DOUBLE-CLICK: Student Input Form in the list area
Your screen should now appear similar to Figure 1.12.

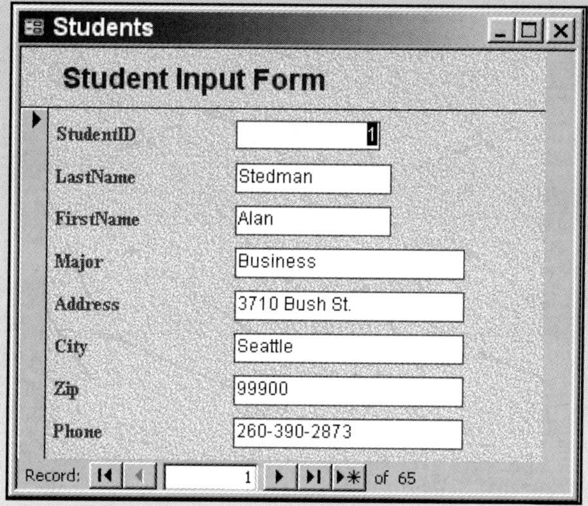

Figure 1.12

Form window for the Student Input Form object

12. To close the Student Input Form:
    CLICK: its Close button (![X])

13. Whereas datasheets and forms are used to input and modify data, you create **reports** to present, summarize, and print data. To see a list of the stored reports in the database:
    CLICK: *Reports* button

14. To view a report as it will appear when printed:
    DOUBLE-CLICK: Students by Major in the list area
    The report appears in the Print Preview window, as shown in Figure 1.13.

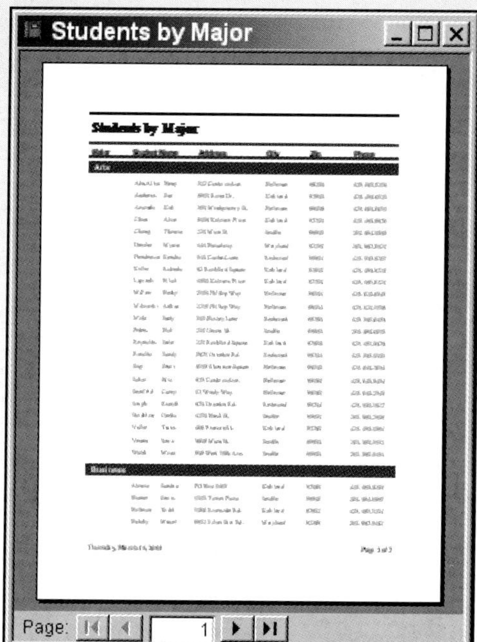

Figure 1.13

Print Preview window for the Students by Major report object

15. To close the Print Preview window:
CLICK: its Close button (☒)

16. To return to displaying the table objects:
CLICK: *Tables* button
(*Note:* If you are proceeding to the next module, keep the database open for use in the next lesson.)

In Addition ADDITIONAL DATABASE OBJECTS

The Objects bar lets you access a variety of database objects. Besides *Tables, Queries, Forms,* and *Reports,* it offers the *Pages* category to link to external Internet-ready database objects called *data access pages.* The *Macro* category stores objects that you use to automate frequently performed procedures. And for greater control, you can write code *modules* using Visual Basic for Applications (VBA), a subset of the Microsoft Visual Basic programming language.

1.1. How do you close a window that appears in the Access work area?

1.2 Viewing and Printing Your Data

Much like an electronic worksheet, a table object stores data in rows and columns called a **datasheet.** Each row represents an individual record and each column represents a field. The intersection of a row and a column is called a **cell.** This **Datasheet view** mode lets you display and work with many records at once. In this module, you learn how to navigate, customize, and print datasheets.

1.2.1 Moving Around a Datasheet

Table 1.1

Keyboard Methods for Navigating a Datasheet

Keystroke	Task Description
↑, ↓	Moves to the previous or next record
←, →	Moves cursor to the left or to the right
CTRL + ↓	Moves to the bottom of a field column
CTRL + ↑	Moves to the top of a field column
PgUp, PgDn	Moves up or down one screen
HOME	Moves to the first (leftmost) field in a record
END	Moves to the last (rightmost) field in a record
CTRL + HOME	Moves to the top (first record and first field)
CTRL + END	Moves to the bottom (last record and last field)

feature

To properly manage the data stored in a table object, you must know how to efficiently move the selection cursor to view all parts of a table. As with most Access features, both mouse and keyboard methods are available for moving the cursor. Try both methods and then select the one that appeals to you most.

method

See Table 1.1 for a list of keyboard methods.

practice

Using the Students table, you practice moving the cursor around a datasheet. Ensure that the AC0100 Database window is displayed. If not, open the AC0100 database from your student data files location.

1. Ensure that the *Tables* button in the Objects bar is selected. To display the Students datasheet, do the following:
   DOUBLE-CLICK: Students in the list area
   The Students data table is loaded into the computer's memory and displayed in Datasheet view. Depending on your screen size, you may see more or fewer records than shown in Figure 1.10.
2. A flashing cursor appears in the leftmost field of the first record. To move to the last field in the current record:
   PRESS: END
   The cursor is positioned in the "Phone" column.
3. To move one field to the left and down to the fourth record:
   PRESS: ← once
   PRESS: ↓ three times
   Your screen should appear similar to Figure 1.14. (*CAUTION:* If pressing a cursor movement key does not yield the expected result, you may have activated Edit mode accidentally. To begin navigating between records and fields again, press F2 or ENTER to end Edit mode.)

Figure 1.14

Datasheet window

The table name is displayed in the Datasheet window's Title bar.

This triangular symbol marks the current or active record.

The navigation area displays the current record number (4) and the total number of records (65).

Field cursor

Students : Table

LastName	FirstName	Major	Address	City	Zip	Phone
Stedman	Alan	Business	3710 Bush St.	Seattle	99900	260-390-2873
Hernandez	Pete	Business	1485 Sonama V	Redmond	99780	425-535-1209
Mohr	Judy	Arts	100 Bosley Lan	Redmond	99780	425-531-6453
Buggey	Diana	Science	20 Cactus Lane	Redmond	99804	425-531-1177
Seinfeld	Casey	Arts	17 Windy Way	Bellevue	98180	425-640-2543
Alomar	Sandra	Business	PO Box 1465	Kirkland	97080	425-493-3233
Fernandez	Rosa	Science	151 Greer Rd.	Seattle	99890	260-394-7645
Peters	Bob	Arts	200 Union St.	Seattle	99850	260-390-6611
Rinaldo	Sandy	Arts	1871 Orrinton R	Redmond	99704	425-535-0001
Finklestein	Sue	Business	888 Burrard St.	Seattle	99904	260-390-9273
Mortimer	Bruce	Science	235 Johnston S	Redmond	99704	425-531-9309
Jung	Chris	Science	1005 West 9th ,	Redmond	99780	425-531-8100
Abu-Alba	Benji	Arts	122 Cordova Av	Bellevue	98200	425-660-1216
Stockton	Gretta	Arts	4210 Bush St.	Seattle	99900	260-390-2909
Sakic	Eric	Arts	875 Cordova Av	Bellevue	98180	425-640-9454
Modano	Joey	Science	36 Primore St.	Kirkland	97780	425-491-1256
Francis	Mike	Business	875 Broadway	Maryland	92250	260-887-9872
Hillman	Frances	Business	29 Redmond Rc	Redmond	99850	425-531-1998
Brewski	Randy	Science	190 Greer Rd.	Seattle	99890	260-394-0778
Walsh	Moira	Arts	909 West 18th ,	Seattle	99900	260-390-5454

Record: 4 of 65

Access

4. To move the cursor down by one screen at a time:
PRESS: PgDn twice

5. To move to the top of the datasheet:
PRESS: CTRL + HOME

6. Position the mouse pointer over the scroll box on the vertical scroll bar and then drag the scroll box downward. Notice that a yellow Scroll Tip appears, identifying the current record number. Release the mouse button when you see "Record: 25 of 65" in the Scroll Tip, as shown here. (*Note:* Although the window pans downward, this method does not move the cursor. Looking in the navigation area, you will see that the first record, 1, remains the active or current record.)

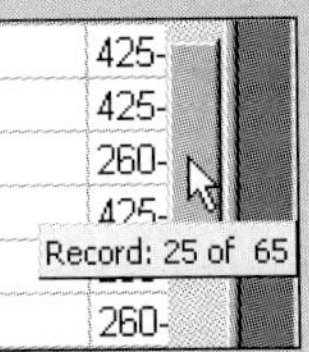

7. As illustrated in Figure 1.14, Access provides a navigation area in the bottom left-hand corner of the Datasheet window. To use this area to navigate the records in a datasheet:
CLICK: Last Record button (▶|) to move to the bottom of the datasheet
CLICK: First Record button (|◀) to move to the top of the datasheet

8. Access allows you to open a number of Datasheet windows at the same time. To display another table, first make the Database window active by clicking on it or by using the menu:
CHOOSE: Window, AC0100 : Database (Access 2000 file format)

9. To display the Roster table:
DOUBLE-CLICK: Roster in the list area
The Roster Datasheet window appears overlapping the other two windows, as shown in Figure 1.15. Like the Students table, the Roster table contains a field named StudentID. This common field enables a link to be established between the two tables.

Figure 1.15

Opening the Roster Datasheet window

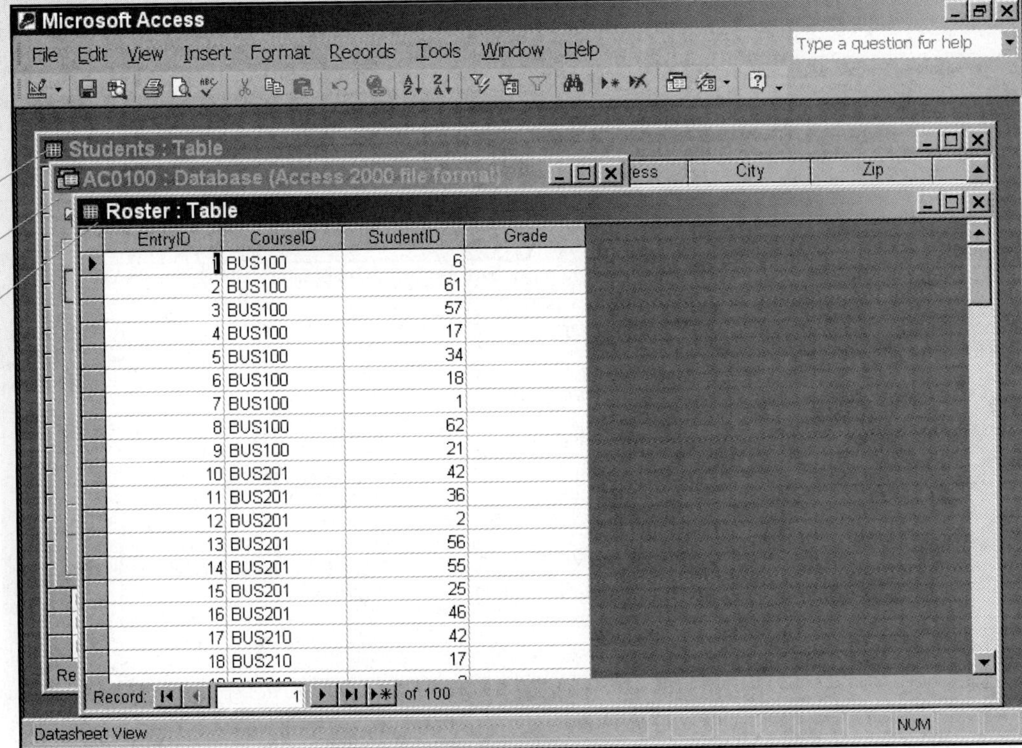

10. To display the Students datasheet once again:
CHOOSE: Window, Students : Table
(*Hint:* You can also click the "Students : Table" button that appears on the Windows taskbar at the bottom of the screen.)

11. Within the Students Datasheet window, you can display course and grade information from the Roster table using subdatasheets. A **subdatasheet** allows you to browse hierarchical and related data for a particular record. In a sense, a subdatasheet provides a picture-in-picture view of your data. To demonstrate, let's drill down and display the courses and grades for Rosa Fernandez:
CLICK: Expand button (⊞) in the left-hand column of StudentID 7
Your screen should now appear similar to Figure 1.16.

Figure 1.16

Displaying a subdatasheet

Students : Table

StudentID	LastName	FirstName	Major	Address	City	Zip	
1	Stedman	Alan	Business	3710 Bush St.	Seattle	99900	260-
2	Hernandez	Pete	Business	1485 Sonama V	Redmond	99780	425-
3	Mohr	Judy	Arts	100 Bosley Lan	Redmond	99780	425-
4	Buggey	Diana	Science	20 Cactus Lane	Redmond	99804	425-
5	Seinfeld	Casey	Arts	17 Windy Way	Bellevue	98180	425-
6	Alomar	Sandra	Business	PO Box 1465	Kirkland	97080	425-
7	Fernandez	Rosa	Science	151 Greer Rd.	Seattle	99890	260-

Displaying related records from the Roster table in a subdatasheet

EntryID	CourseID	Grade
55	COM200	86.00
66	COM210	74.00
(AutoNumber)		0.00

StudentID	LastName	FirstName	Major	Address	City	Zip	
8	Peters	Bob	Arts	200 Union St.	Seattle	99850	260-
9	Rinaldo	Sandy	Arts	1871 Orrinton R	Redmond	99704	425-
10	Finklestein	Sue	Business	888 Burrard St.	Seattle	99904	260-
11	Mortimer	Bruce	Science	235 Johnston S	Redmond	99704	425-
12	Jung	Chris	Science	1005 West 9th	Redmond	99780	425-
13	Abu-Alba	Benji	Arts	122 Cordova Av	Bellevue	98200	425-
14	Stockton	Gretta	Arts	4210 Bush St.	Seattle	99900	260-
15	Sakic	Eric	Arts	875 Cordova Av	Bellevue	98180	425-
16	Modano	Joey	Science	36 Primore St.	Kirkland	97780	425-

Record: 1 of 65

12. Using the mouse, do the following:
CLICK: a cell in the first row of the subdatasheet
Notice that the record navigation area in the Datasheet window shows Record 1 of 2. Clicking the First Record (⏮) or Last Record (⏭) buttons will move the cursor in this subdatasheet only.

13. To collapse the subdatasheet:
CLICK: Collapse button (⊟) for StudentID 7
The record navigation area shows Record 1 of 65 once again.

14. On your own, expand the subdatasheets for three records in the Students Datasheet window. When finished, collapse all of the subdatasheets and then return to the top of the Students datasheet by pressing CTRL+HOME.

15. To clean up the work area, let's close the Roster Datasheet window:
CHOOSE: Window, Roster : Table
CLICK: its Close button (☒)
(*Note:* The display of a subdatasheet does not depend on both datasheets being open in the work area, as they were in this exercise.)

16. Keep the Students Datasheet window open for use in the next lesson.

In Addition MOVING TO A SPECIFIC RECORD NUMBER

Access displays the current record number alongside the navigation buttons in the bottom left-hand corner of a Datasheet window. To move to a specific record in the datasheet or subdatasheet, double-click the mouse pointer in this text box, type a record number, and then press ENTER. The cursor immediately moves to the desired record.

1.2.2 Adjusting Column Widths and Row Heights

feature

By adjusting the column widths and row heights in a datasheet, you can enhance its appearance for both viewing and printing—much like using double-spacing in a document to make text easier to read. To change the width of a column in Datasheet view, use the sizing mouse pointer (✢) to drag its borderline in the **field header area.** You can also have Access scan the contents of the column and recommend the best width. Rows behave somewhat differently. When you adjust a single row's height in the *record selection area,* Access updates all of the rows in a datasheet. Figure 1.17 labels the field header and record selection areas for a datasheet.

method

To change a column's width using the mouse:

- DRAG: its right borderline in the field header area

To change a column's width using the menu:

- SELECT: a cell in the column that you want to format
- CHOOSE: Format, Column Width
- TYPE: the desired width

To change the default row height using the mouse:

- DRAG: its bottom borderline in the record selection area

To change the default row height using the menu:

- CHOOSE: Format, Row Height
- TYPE: the desired height

practice

In this lesson, you adjust column widths and row heights in a datasheet. Ensure that the Students datasheet is displayed.

1. To select a cell in the Zip column:
PRESS: END
PRESS: ←

2. To begin, let's reduce the width of the Zip column using the menu:
CHOOSE: Format, Column Width
The Column Width dialog box appears, as shown here.

3. Although you can type the desired width, let's have Access calculate the best width for the column:
CLICK: Best Fit command button
The column's width is decreased automatically.

4. Now let's adjust the width of the Address column. In the field header area, position the mouse pointer over the borderline between the Address and City fields. The mouse pointer changes shape (✥) when positioned correctly, as shown below.

5. CLICK: the borderline and hold down the mouse button
DRAG: the mouse pointer to the right to increase the width (to approximately the beginning of the word "City")

6. You can also set the best-fit width for a column using the mouse. To adjust the width of the Major column:
DOUBLE-CLICK: the borderline between Major and Address
The Major column is sized automatically to its best-fit width.

7. To reposition the cursor:
PRESS: CTRL+HOME

8. On your own, size the StudentID, LastName, and FirstName columns to their best-fit width.

9. Now let's change the row height setting in the Datasheet window:
CHOOSE: Format, Row Height
The Row Height dialog box appears, as shown here.

Row Height
Row Height: 12.75 OK
☑ Standard Height Cancel

10. To spread out the contents in the Datasheet window:
TYPE: **18**
CLICK: OK
All of the rows in the datasheet are updated to reflect the formatting change. Your worksheet should now appear similar to Figure 1.17.

Column *field header area* contains the field names.

Figure 1.17

Formatting the Datasheet window

The *record selection area* contains row selector buttons.

Students : Table

StudentID	LastName	FirstName	Major	Address	City	Zip	Phone
1	Stedman	Alan	Business	3710 Bush St.	Seattle	99900	260-390-2873
2	Hernandez	Pete	Business	1485 Sonama Way	Redmond	99780	425-535-1209
3	Mohr	Judy	Arts	100 Bosley Lane	Redmond	99780	425-531-6453
4	Buggey	Diana	Science	20 Cactus Lane	Redmond	99804	425-531-1177
5	Seinfeld	Casey	Arts	17 Windy Way	Bellevue	98180	425-640-2543
6	Alomar	Sandra	Business	PO Box 1465	Kirkland	97080	425-493-3233
7	Fernandez	Rosa	Science	151 Greer Rd.	Seattle	99890	260-394-7645
8	Peters	Bob	Arts	200 Union St.	Seattle	99850	260-390-6611
9	Rinaldo	Sandy	Arts	1871 Orrinton Rd.	Redmond	99704	425-535-0001
10	Finklestein	Sue	Business	888 Burrard St.	Seattle	99904	260-390-9273
11	Mortimer	Bruce	Science	235 Johnston St.	Redmond	99704	425-531-9309
12	Jung	Chris	Science	1005 West 9th Ave.	Redmond	99780	425-531-8100
13	Abu-Alba	Benji	Arts	122 Cordova Ave.	Bellevue	98200	425-660-1216
14	Stockton	Gretta	Arts	4210 Bush St.	Seattle	99900	260-390-2909
15	Sakic	Eric	Arts	875 Cordova Ave.	Bellevue	98180	425-640-9454

Record: 1 of 65

Access

1.2.3 Previewing and Printing

feature

Before sending a datasheet to the printer, you can preview it using a full-page display that resembles the printed output. In Print Preview mode, you can move back and forth through the pages, zoom in and out on desired areas, and modify page layout options such as print margins and page orientation. Once you are satisfied with its appearance, send it to the printer with a single mouse click.

method

To preview the current Datasheet window:

- CLICK: Print Preview button ( )

or

- CHOOSE: File, Print Preview

To print the current Datasheet window:

- CLICK: Print button ( )

or

- CHOOSE: File, Print

practice

You now use the Print Preview mode to display the Students datasheet. Ensure that you have completed the previous lesson and that the Students datasheet is displayed.

1. To preview how the datasheet will appear when printed:
CLICK: Print Preview button ( ) on the toolbar
The Datasheet window becomes the Print Preview window, as shown in Figure 1.18.

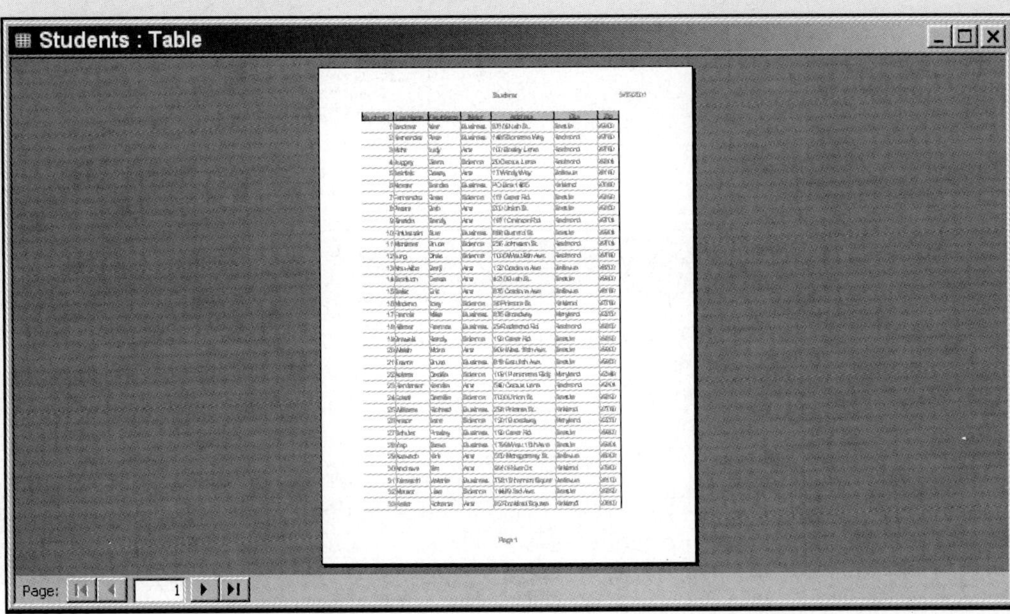

Figure 1.18

Displaying the Students datasheet in Print Preview

2. To move through the pages to print, click the navigation buttons at the bottom of the window. Let's practice:
CLICK: Next Page button (▶)
CLICK: Last Page button (▶|)
CLICK: First Page button (|◀)

3. To zoom in or magnify the Print Preview window, move the magnifying glass mouse pointer over the column headings, centered between the margins, and then click once. Your screen should now appear similar to Figure 1.19.

Figure 1.19

Zooming in on the Students datasheet

Print Preview toolbar replaces the Database toolbar.

Navigation buttons for moving among the preview pages.

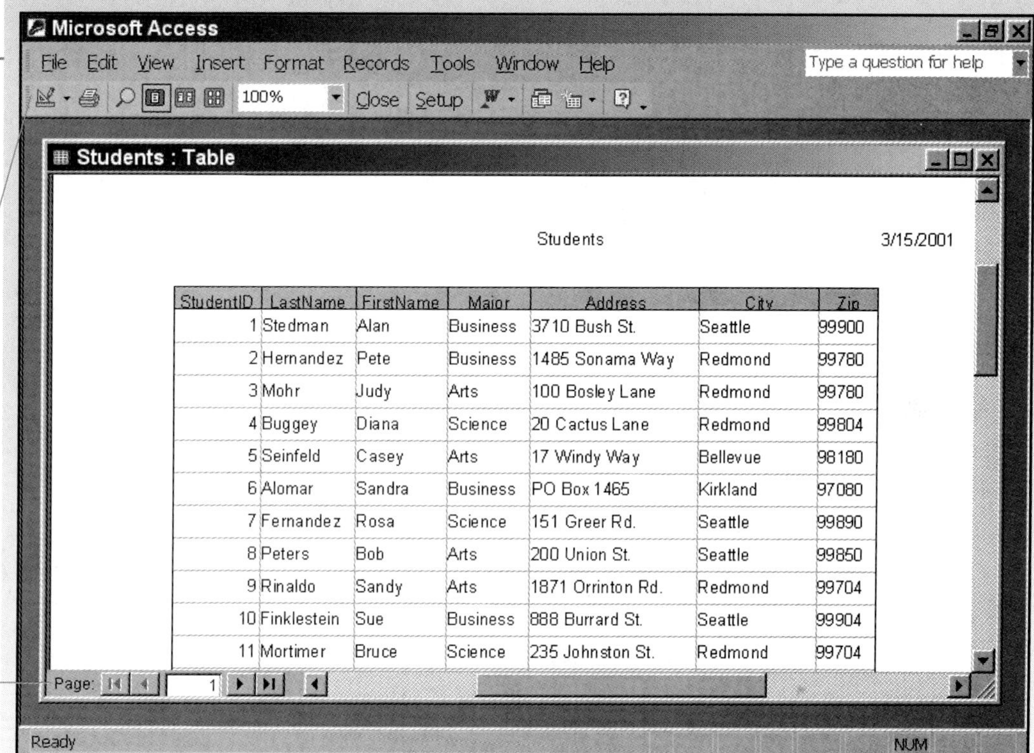

StudentID	LastName	FirstName	Major	Address	City	Zip
1	Stedman	Alan	Business	3710 Bush St.	Seattle	99900
2	Hernandez	Pete	Business	1485 Sonama Way	Redmond	99780
3	Mohr	Judy	Arts	100 Bosley Lane	Redmond	99780
4	Buggey	Diana	Science	20 Cactus Lane	Redmond	99804
5	Seinfeld	Casey	Arts	17 Windy Way	Bellevue	98180
6	Alomar	Sandra	Business	PO Box 1465	Kirkland	97080
7	Fernandez	Rosa	Science	151 Greer Rd.	Seattle	99890
8	Peters	Bob	Arts	200 Union St.	Seattle	99850
9	Rinaldo	Sandy	Arts	1871 Orrinton Rd.	Redmond	99704
10	Finklestein	Sue	Business	888 Burrard St.	Seattle	99904
11	Mortimer	Bruce	Science	235 Johnston St.	Redmond	99704

4. To zoom back out on the page:
CLICK: anywhere on the page in the Print Preview window

5. You can change the page setup to landscape orientation in order to print more columns of data on each page. Do the following:
CHOOSE: File, Page Setup
CLICK: *Page* tab
The Page Setup dialog box appears as shown in Figure 1.20. (*Note:* You can also click the Setup command button on the Print Preview toolbar.)

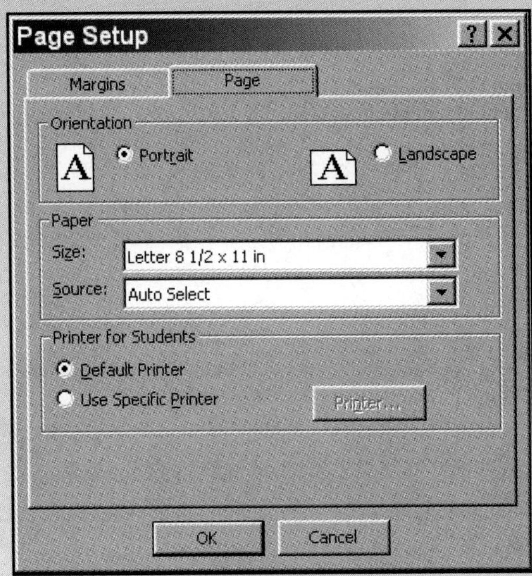

Figure 1.20

Page Setup dialog box: *Page* tab

6. In the *Orientation* area of the Page Setup dialog box:
   SELECT: *Landscape* option button
   CLICK: OK command button
   Notice that the Print Preview window is dynamically updated.
7. On your own, zoom in and out on the Print Preview window using the magnifying glass mouse pointer. All the field columns should appear on a single page.
8. There are two ways to close the Print Preview window. First, you can click the Close button (☒), which closes both the Print Preview window and the Students Datasheet window. Second, you can click the Close button (Close) in the Print Preview toolbar, which returns you to the Datasheet window. To return to the Students datasheet:
   CLICK: Close button (Close) in the toolbar
9. Now let's close the Students Datasheet window:
   CLICK: its Close button (☒)
   The following dialog box appears.

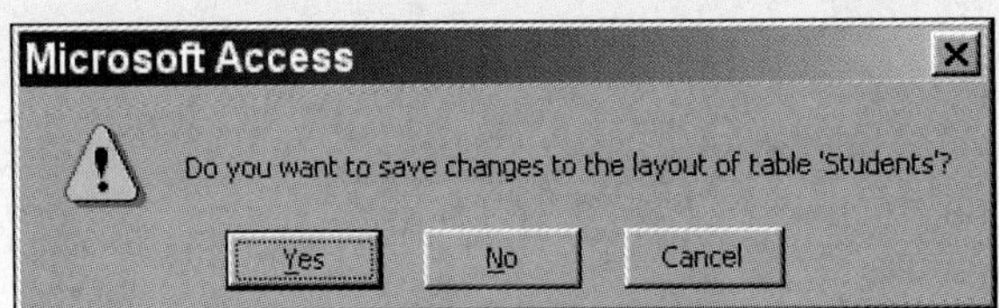

10. Since you have made changes to the layout of the Datasheet window, Access asks you to either save or discard the formatting changes. Let's discard the changes for now:
    CLICK: No command button
    You should now see the AC0100 Database window.

11. Now let's use a shortcut from the Database window for printing and previewing a datasheet. Do the following:
RIGHT-CLICK: Courses in the list area
CHOOSE: Print Preview
The Courses table object is displayed in a Print Preview window. (*Note:* To send the datasheet to the printer directly, choose the Print command from the right-click menu. It is a good idea, however, to preview a page first to ensure that it will print as expected.)

12. To close the Print Preview window:
CLICK: its Close button (☒)

1.2. Describe two methods to quickly move the cursor to the last record in a large datasheet.

1.3 Manipulating Table Data

Maintaining a database is difficult work. Updating the contents of a table, adding and deleting records, and fixing mistakes can take a tremendous amount of time. Fortunately, Access provides some tools and features that can help you manipulate data productively. In this module, you learn to enter, edit, and delete data in Datasheet view.

1.3.1 Selecting and Editing Data

feature

You can edit information either as you type or after you have entered data into a table. In Datasheet view, changes are made by selecting the data or cell and then issuing a command or typing. The editing changes are saved automatically when you move the cursor to another record.

method

Some points to keep in mind when editing in Datasheet view:

- You can press F2 to enter and end Edit mode for the current cell.
- If you start typing while data is selected, what you type replaces the entire selection.
- If the flashing insertion point is positioned in a cell but no data is selected, what you type will be inserted in the field.
- With the insertion point positioned in a cell, press BACKSPACE to remove the character to the left of the insertion point and press DELETE to remove the character to the right.

practice

In this lesson, you practice editing data in a table's datasheet. Ensure that the AC0100 Database window is displayed. If not, open the AC0100 database from your student data files location.

1. In the Database window, ensure that the *Tables* button in the Objects bar is selected. Then do the following:
DOUBLE-CLICK: Instructors in the list area
The Instructors Datasheet window is displayed, as shown in Figure 1.21.

Access

Figure 1.21

Displaying the Instructors datasheet

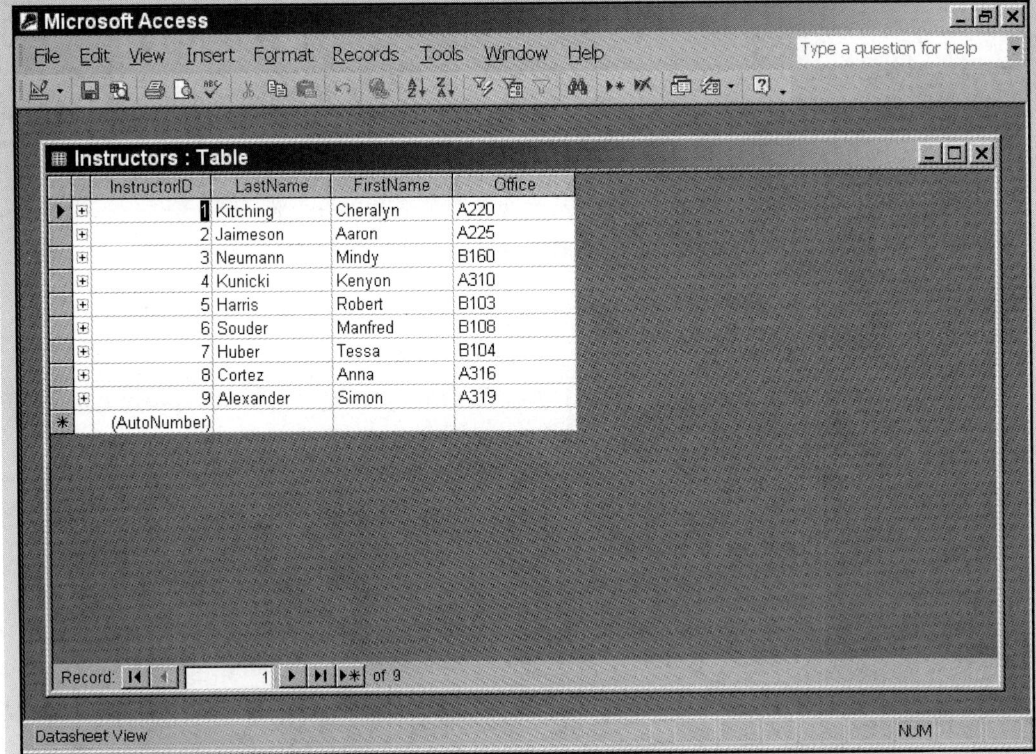

InstructorID	LastName	FirstName	Office
1	Kitching	Cheralyn	A220
2	Jaimeson	Aaron	A225
3	Neumann	Mindy	B160
4	Kunicki	Kenyon	A310
5	Harris	Robert	B103
6	Souder	Manfred	B108
7	Huber	Tessa	B104
8	Cortez	Anna	A316
9	Alexander	Simon	A319
(AutoNumber)			

2. To position the cursor in the Office column of the first record:
PRESS: → three times
Notice that the entire cell entry "A220" is selected.

3. To update the Office number:
TYPE: **B**
Notice that a pencil icon ( ) appears in the row's selector button. This icon indicates that you are now editing the data and have not yet saved the changes.

4. To complete the entry:
TYPE: **113**
PRESS: ENTER
The new office number replaces the selection. When you press ENTER, the cursor moves to the first field of the next record. Also notice that the pencil icon is no longer visible in the row's selector button.

5. Rather than retyping an entire cell's contents, you can modify the individual characters in a cell. To illustrate, let's edit the record data for InstructorID 4. First, position the I-beam mouse pointer to the right of the last name "Kunicki" and then click once. A flashing insertion point (shown below) appears to the right of the trailing letter "i," which means that you are ready to edit the cell's contents. (*Hint:* You can also position the insertion point by first selecting the cell using the cursor keys and then pressing F2 to enter Edit mode. Pressing F2 a second time will toggle the in-cell Edit mode off.)

The triangle tells you that this is the active record in the datasheet.

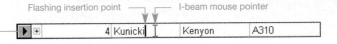

Flashing insertion point — I-beam mouse pointer

4	Kunicki	Kenyon	A310

6. To replace the final "i" in Kunicki with a "y," do the following:
PRESS: BACKSPACE
TYPE: **y**
The pencil icon (✎) appears in the row selector button, warning you that the changes have not yet been saved.

7. To complete the in-cell editing for the LastName field:
PRESS: ENTER
The cursor moves to the next field, but the pencil icon remains displayed in the row selector button as shown below.

The pencil icon tells you that the record's changes have not yet been saved.

8. To save the changes, you must move the cursor to another record:
PRESS: ↓
The pencil icon disappears. (*Note:* When working in Edit mode, pressing HOME, END, ←, and → moves the insertion point within the cell. Press F2 to toggle out of Edit mode in order to use these keys for cursor navigation around the datasheet.)

9. When you move the mouse pointer over a cell, it changes shape to an I-beam so that you may easily position the insertion point between characters. In order to select an entire cell for editing, you position the mouse pointer over the top or left grid line of a cell and click once. You know the mouse pointer is properly positioned when it changes shape to a cross (✚). To select the contents of the LastName field for InstructorID 7, position the mouse pointer as shown below.

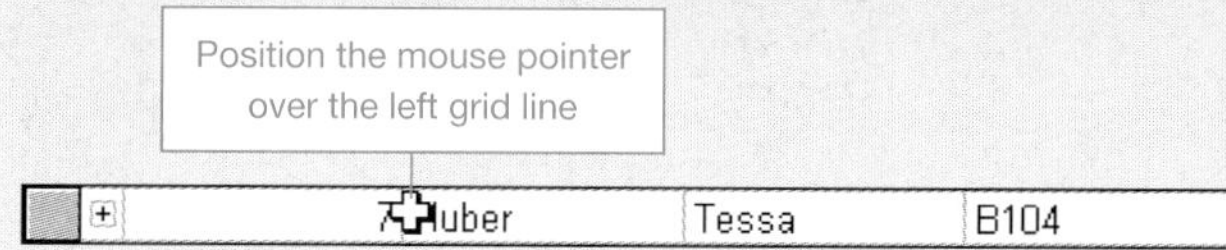

10. To select the cell:
CLICK: left mouse button once
The entire "Huber" cell is highlighted in reverse video, as shown in Figure 1.22.

Figure 1.22

Selecting a cell in a datasheet

Active record

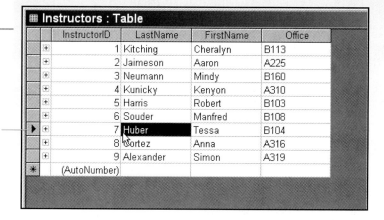

Instructors : Table

InstructorID	LastName	FirstName	Office
1	Kitching	Cheralyn	B113
2	Jaimeson	Aaron	A225
3	Neumann	Mindy	B160
4	Kunicky	Kenyon	A310
5	Harris	Robert	B103
6	Souder	Manfred	B108
7	Huber	Tessa	B104
8	Cortez	Anna	A316
9	Alexander	Simon	A319
(AutoNumber)			

Access

11. Let's assume that Tessa got married recently and has decided to change her name. Do the following:
TYPE: **Moss**
The pencil icon appears in the row's selector button.

12. To save the changes:
PRESS: ↓ to move to the next record

In Addition SAVING YOUR CHANGES

Rather than moving to another row, you can save the changes you make to the current record by pressing SHIFT+ENTER. This keyboard shortcut allows you to write the changes permanently to the disk without having to move to another record.

1.3.2 Using the Undo Command

feature →

The **Undo command** allows you to reverse mistakes during editing. Unlike other Office products, Access does not offer a multiple undo capability when editing in Datasheet view. Therefore, you must remember to choose the command immediately after making a mistake.

method →

To reverse the last action performed, do any one of the following:

- CHOOSE: Edit, Undo
- CLICK: Undo button ( )
- PRESS: CTRL+z

(*Note:* The command's name changes to reflect the action that may be reversed. For example, on the Edit pull-down menu, the command may read Undo Current Field/Record, Undo Delete, or Undo Saved Record.)

practice →

Using the Undo command, you now practice reversing common editing procedures. Ensure that you have completed the previous lesson and that the Instructors datasheet is displayed.

1. You've just been informed that "Robert Harris" prefers to go by the name "Bobby." Let's edit the table:
SELECT: the FirstName cell for InstructorID 5
(*Hint:* This instruction asks you to click the top or left grid line of the FirstName cell. When done correctly, the cell containing "Robert" is highlighted, as shown below.)

2. TYPE: **Bobby**
PRESS: ENTER
The cursor moves to the next field in the current record.

3. To undo the last edit using the Menu bar:
CHOOSE: Edit, Undo Current Field/Record
The contents revert back to "Robert," yet the cursor remains in the Office column.

4. To practice deleting a cell entry, let's remove the Office assignment for Anna Cortez:
SELECT: the Office cell for InstructorID 8, as shown below

	InstructorID	LastName	FirstName	Office
▶ ⊞	8	Cortez	Anna	A316

5. To remove the entry:
PRESS: DELETE

6. To save the changes and move to the next record:
PRESS: ↓
Your screen should appear similar to Figure 1.23.

Figure 1.23

Deleting an entire cell's contents

Instructors : Table

	InstructorID	LastName	FirstName	Office
⊞	1	Kitching	Cheralyn	B113
⊞	2	Jaimeson	Aaron	A225
⊞	3	Neumann	Mindy	B160
⊞	4	Kunicky	Kenyon	A310
⊞	5	Harris	Robert	B103
⊞	6	Souder	Manfred	B108
⊞	7	Moss	Tessa	B104
⊞	8	Cortez	Anna	
▶ ⊞	9	Alexander	Simon	A319
*	(AutoNumber)			

7. Even though this change has been saved and recorded to disk, Access lets you reverse the deletion. Do the following:
CLICK: Undo button
The Office assignment is restored for Anna Cortez. (*Note:* In this step, clicking the toolbar button executes the Edit, Undo Saved Record command.)

In Addition USING ESC TO UNDO CHANGES

Instead of choosing the Undo command from the menu, you can undo changes in the current field by pressing ESC once. Pressing ESC a second time will undo all of the unsaved changes made to the current record.

1.3.3 Adding Records

In Datasheet view, you typically add new records to the blank row appearing at the bottom of a datasheet. If the text "(AutoNumber)" appears in a cell, press ENTER, TAB, or → to bypass the cell and move to the next field. Any cell containing an *AutoNumber* field is incremented automatically by Access when a new record is added to the table.

Access

method

To position the cursor in a blank row at the bottom of the datasheet, ready for inserting a new record, use any one of the following methods:

- CLICK: New Record button (▶*) on the toolbar
- CLICK: New Record button (▶*) in the navigation bar
- CHOOSE: Insert, New Record from the Menu bar

practice

In this lesson, you insert two records into the Instructors datasheet. Ensure that the Instructors datasheet is displayed.

1. To position the cursor at the bottom of the datasheet:
CLICK: New Record button (▶*) on the toolbar
The AutoNumber entry in the first field of the new record is selected, as shown below.

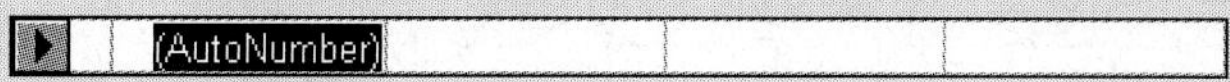

2. To let Access handle the entry for the InstructorID column, do the following:
PRESS: TAB to move to the next field
(*Note:* You can also press ENTER to move to the next field. The convention in this guide, however, is to use TAB to move the cursor forward and SHIFT+TAB to move the cursor backward. The ENTER key is sometimes used to complete in-cell editing.)

3. Let's enter the new record information:
TYPE: **Joyce**
PRESS: TAB
Notice that the AutoNumber entry for the InstructorID column is calculated and entered automatically.

4. To complete the entry:
TYPE: **James**
PRESS: TAB
TYPE: **C230**
Your screen should now appear similar to Figure 1.24. Notice that the pencil icon appears in the current row's selector button and that a new row was added, as denoted with an asterisk in its selector button.

Adding a new record

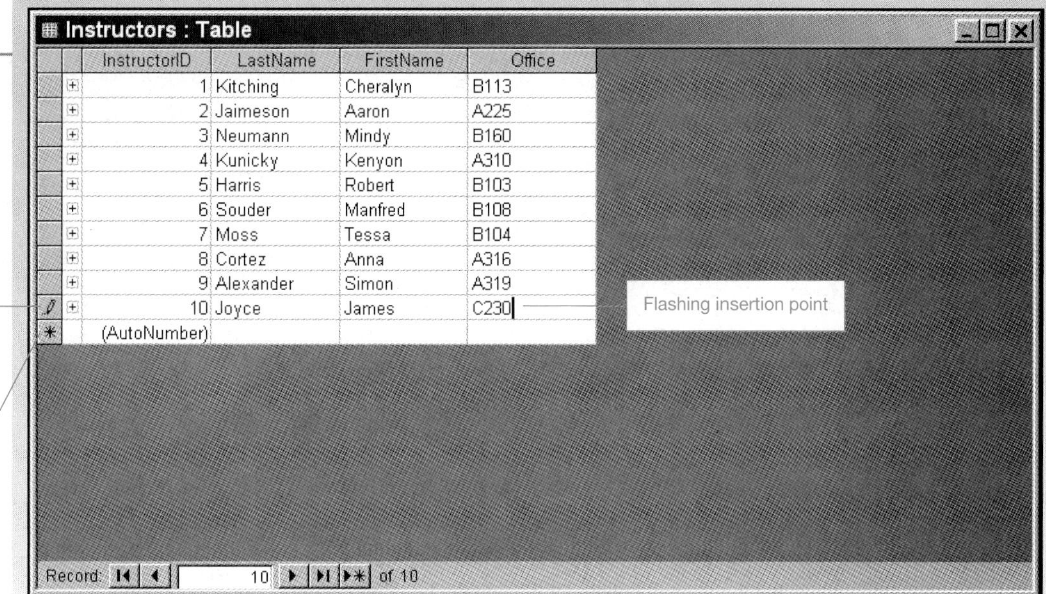

InstructorID	LastName	FirstName	Office
1	Kitching	Cheralyn	B113
2	Jaimeson	Aaron	A225
3	Neumann	Mindy	B160
4	Kunicky	Kenyon	A310
5	Harris	Robert	B103
6	Souder	Manfred	B108
7	Moss	Tessa	B104
8	Cortez	Anna	A316
9	Alexander	Simon	A319
10	Joyce	James	C230
(AutoNumber)			

The pencil icon appears because the new record has not yet been saved.

The asterisk indicates that this row provides a new blank record.

5. To save the record and move to the next row:
   PRESS: TAB
   (*Note:* Again, you can also press ENTER to move the cursor.)

6. Remembering to allow Access to complete the AutoNumber cell, add the following two records to the datasheet:

   InstructorID: **11**
   LastName: **Melville**
   FirstName: **Herman**
   Office: **C240**

   InstructorID: **12**
   LastName: **Conrad**
   FirstName: **Joseph**
   Office: **C220**

7. Move the cursor to the next blank row to ensure that the last record is saved.

8. To return to the top of the datasheet:
   PRESS: CTRL + HOME
   Your datasheet should now appear similar to Figure 1.25.

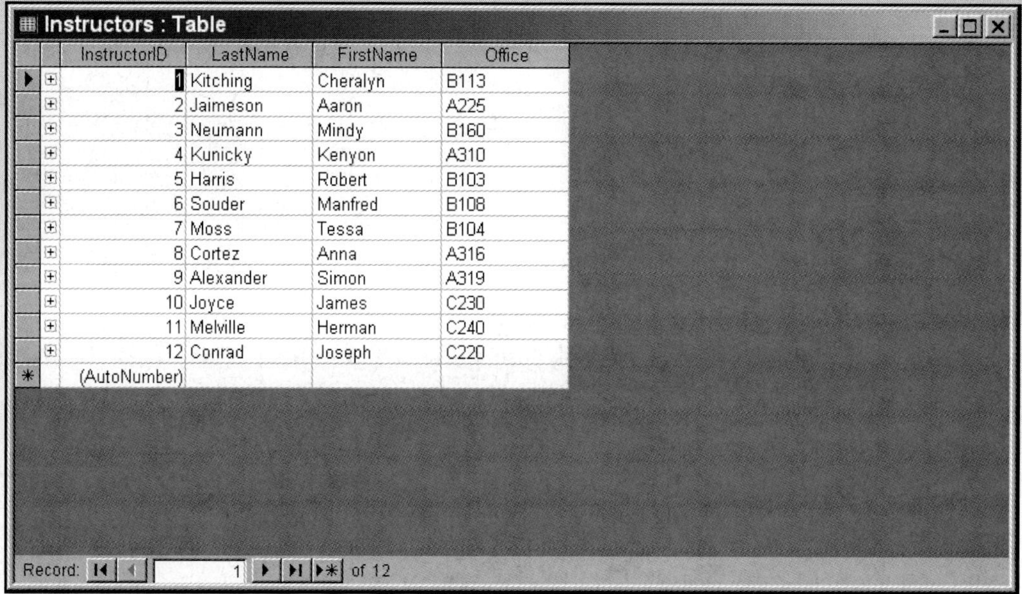

Instructors : Table

	InstructorID	LastName	FirstName	Office
▶	1	Kitching	Cheralyn	B113
	2	Jaimeson	Aaron	A225
	3	Neumann	Mindy	B160
	4	Kunicky	Kenyon	A310
	5	Harris	Robert	B103
	6	Souder	Manfred	B108
	7	Moss	Tessa	B104
	8	Cortez	Anna	A316
	9	Alexander	Simon	A319
	10	Joyce	James	C230
	11	Melville	Herman	C240
	12	Conrad	Joseph	C220
*	(AutoNumber)			

Record: 1 of 12

Figure 1.25

Adding records to the Instructors datasheet

1.3.4 Deleting Records

feature

In Datasheet view, Access provides several methods for removing records from a table. To do so efficiently, however, you must learn how to select one or more records in a datasheet. In this lesson, you learn to use the mouse to click and drag the pointer in the **record selection area,** sometimes called the *row selector buttons.* Refer to the diagram below for clarification on the parts of a Datasheet window.

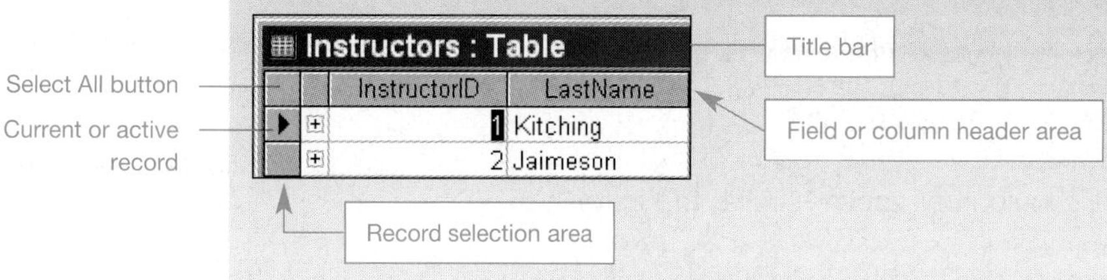

method

- SELECT: a record or group of records
- CLICK: Delete Record button

or

- PRESS: DELETE

or

- CHOOSE: Edit, Delete Record

practice →

You now practice selecting and removing records from a datasheet. Ensure that the Instructors datasheet is displayed.

1. To begin, let's practice selecting records in the datasheet. To select all of the records, do the following:
   CLICK: Select All button (▭) in the upper left-hand corner
   All of the records should now appear in reverse video (white on black), as shown in Figure 1.26.

Figure 1.26

Selecting all of the records in a datasheet

Select All button

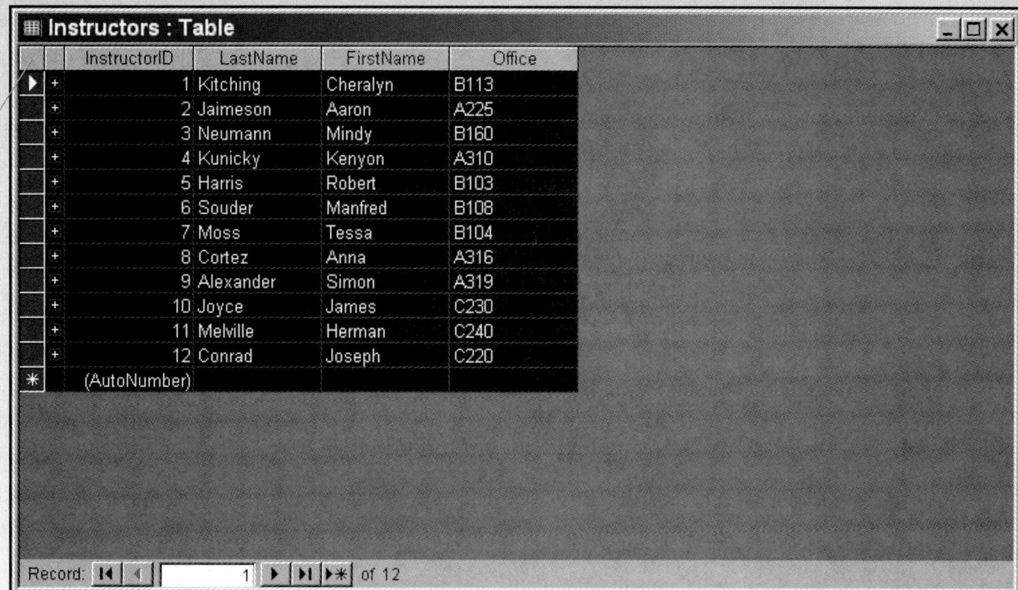
Instructors : Table

InstructorID	LastName	FirstName	Office
1	Kitching	Cheralyn	B113
2	Jaimeson	Aaron	A225
3	Neumann	Mindy	B160
4	Kunicky	Kenyon	A310
5	Harris	Robert	B103
6	Souder	Manfred	B108
7	Moss	Tessa	B104
8	Cortez	Anna	A316
9	Alexander	Simon	A319
10	Joyce	James	C230
11	Melville	Herman	C240
12	Conrad	Joseph	C220
(AutoNumber)			

Record: 1 of 12

2. To remove the highlighting:
   PRESS: HOME

3. To select the record for InstructorID 3, position the mouse pointer to the left of the desired record in the record selection area. The mouse pointer changes shape to a black horizontal right-pointing arrow (➡). When the pointer is positioned over the row selector button properly, click the left mouse button once to select the entire row. It should now appear highlighted, as shown below.

2	Jaimeson	Aaron	A225
3	Neumann	Mindy	B160
4	Kunicky	Kenyon	A310

4. Let's remove the selected record from the table:
   CLICK: Delete Record button (▣) on the toolbar
   A confirmation dialog box appears, as shown in Figure 1.27. (*CAUTION:* Access displays this dialog box whenever you delete records. Clicking the Yes command button permanently removes the record. Clicking the No button returns the datasheet to its previous state.)

Access

Figure 1.27

Removing a record from the datasheet

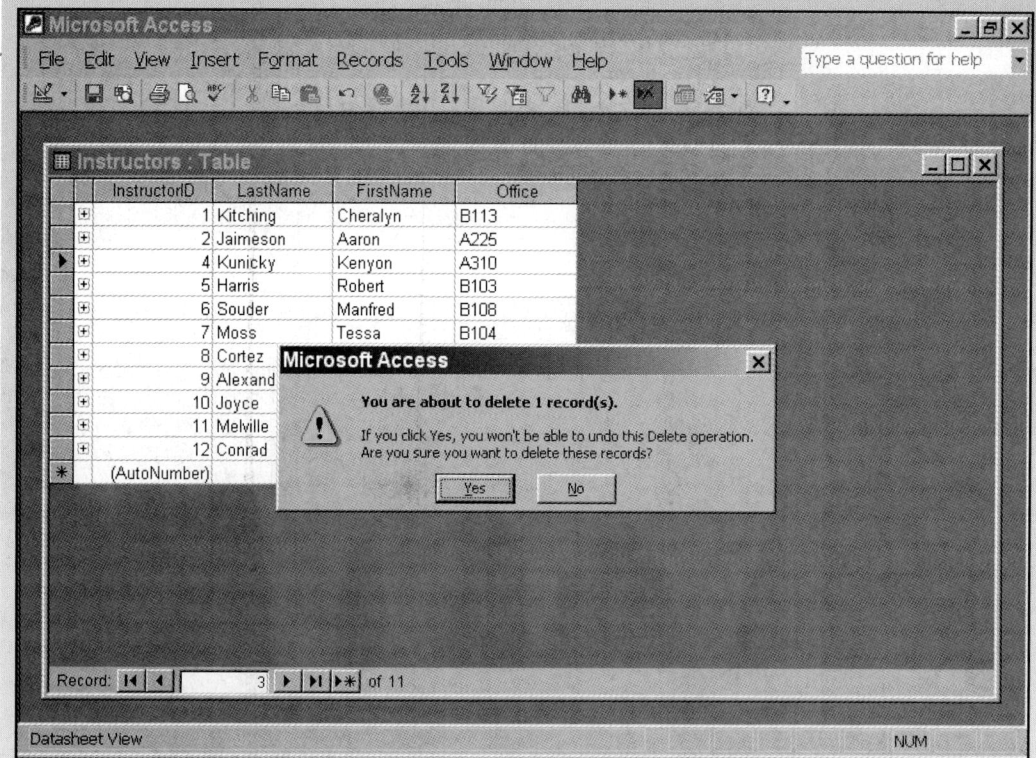

5. To confirm the deletion:
   CLICK: Yes command button
   Notice that the InstructorID column is not a dynamic record count. In other words, the remaining records are not renumbered automatically to fill the gap left by deleting InstructorID 3.

6. You can also delete numerous records with a single command. To illustrate, click once in the record selection area for Manfred Souder's entry (InstructorID 6) and hold down the left mouse button. Then drag the mouse pointer downward to Anna Cortez's record (InstructorID 8). Release the mouse button to display the selected records, as seen here.

5	Harris	Robert	B103
6	Souder	Manfred	B108
7	Moss	Tessa	B104
8	Cortez	Anna	A316
9	Alexander	Simon	A319

Mouse pointer

7. To delete the selected records:
   PRESS: DELETE
   CLICK: Yes to confirm
   Your screen should now appear similar to Figure 1.28.

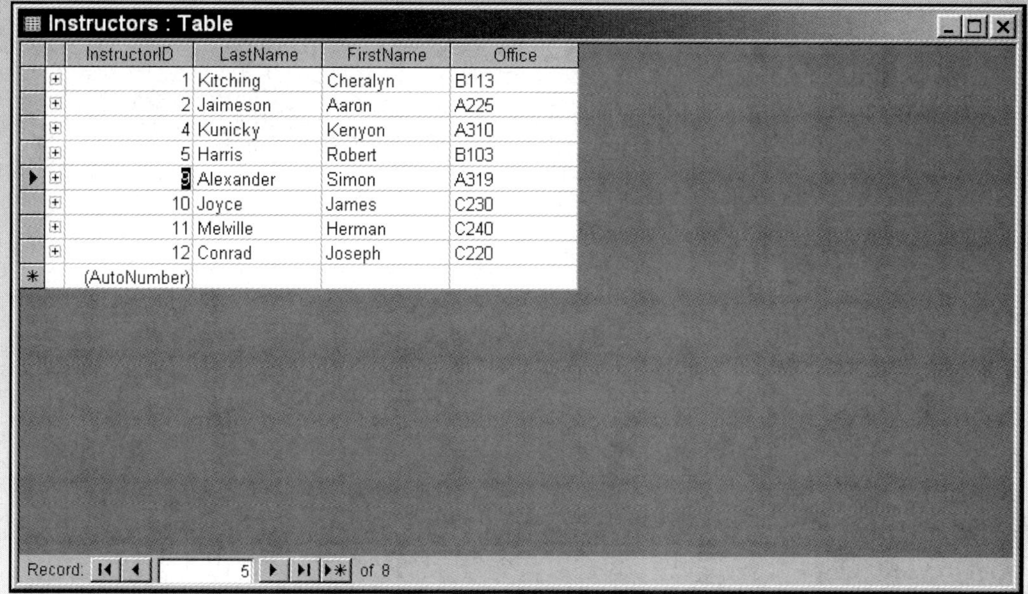

Figure 1.28

Deleting multiple records from the datasheet

8. To close the Instructors datasheet:
CLICK: the Close button (☒) on the Datasheet window
You should now see the Database window for the AC0100 database.

9. To close the AC0100 database:
CLICK: the Close button (☒) on the Database window

10. To exit Access:
CHOOSE: File, Exit

1.3. When does Access save the editing changes that you've made to a record?

Access

Chapter summary

Microsoft Access is a full-featured database management application for desktop computers. Database software enables you to store and manipulate large amounts of data such as customer mailing lists. When you first open a database using Access, you are presented with a control center called the Database window. From this one window, you can create and display a variety of objects, including tables, forms, queries, and reports. The main type of object used is tables, or datasheets. In a Datasheet window you can enter, edit, or delete data. With the Undo command you can immediately reverse your last action.

Command Summary

Many of the commands and procedures appearing in this chapter are summarized in the following table.

Skill Set	To Perform This Task	Do the Following
Using Access	Launch Microsoft Access	CLICK: Start button (Start) CHOOSE: Programs, Microsoft Access
	Exit Microsoft Access	CLICK: its Close button (X), or CHOOSE: File, Exit
	Open a database	CLICK: Open button () SELECT: the desired folder DOUBLE-CLICK: a database file
	Close a database	CLICK: its Close button (X), or CHOOSE: File, Close
Creating and Using Databases	Select and open database objects using the Objects bar	CLICK: the desired object category DOUBLE-CLICK: the desired object
	Navigate to a specific record	DOUBLE-CLICK: in the navigation text box TYPE: the desired record number PRESS: ENTER
	Adjust a column's width in a datasheet	DRAG: a column's right borderline in the field header area, or CHOOSE: Format, Column Width
	Adjust the height of all rows in a datasheet	DRAG: a row's bottom borderline in the record selection area, or CHOOSE: Format, Row Height
	Expand/collapse subdatasheets in a Datasheet window	CLICK: Expand button (+) CLICK: Collapse button (−)
	Preview a datasheet for printing	CLICK: Print Preview button (), or CHOOSE: File, Print Preview
	Print a datasheet	CLICK: Print button (), or CHOOSE: File, Print
	Change the page orientation for a printed document	CHOOSE: File, Page Setup CLICK: *Page* tab SELECT: *Portrait* or *Landscape*
Viewing and Organizing Information	Toggle Edit mode on and off for editing a datasheet cell	PRESS: F2 (Edit key)
	Reverse or undo the most recent change or mistake	CLICK: Undo button (), or CHOOSE: Edit, Undo
	Save the editing changes to the current record	PRESS: SHIFT+ENTER, or Move the cursor to the next record.
	Add a new record to a datasheet	CLICK: New Record buttons (or), or CHOOSE: Insert, New Record
	Delete selected record(s) from a datasheet	CLICK: Delete Record button (), or PRESS: DELETE, or CHOOSE: Edit, Delete Record

Key Terms

This section specifies page references for the key terms identified in this chapter. For a complete list of definitions, refer to the Glossary at the end of this learning guide.

application window, *p. 7*
cell, *p. 14*
database, *p. 2*
database management system (DBMS), *p. 2*
Database window, *p. 10*
datasheet, *p. 14*
Datasheet view, *p. 14*
field, *p. 2*
field header area, *p. 18*
form, *p. 12*
Groups bar, *p. 10*
Objects bar, *p. 10*
Places bar, *p. 6*
query, *p. 12*
record, *p. 2*
record selection area, *p. 30*
report(s), *p. 13*
subdatasheet, *p. 17*
table, *p. 2*
task pane, *p. 4*
Undo command, *p. 26*

Chapter quiz

Short Answer

1. Provide examples of when you might use a database.
2. Define the following terms: *table*, *record*, and *field*.
3. What is an *object* in Microsoft Access? Provide examples.
4. Which database object is used to collect and store data?
5. Which database object displays in Print Preview mode when opened?
6. Why is the Database window referred to as a *control center*?
7. How do you select the entire contents of a cell in a datasheet?
8. How do you select all of the records displayed in a datasheet?
9. What is the procedure for adding a record in Datasheet view?
10. What is the procedure for deleting records in Datasheet view?

True/False

1. ____ DBMS stands for database backup management system.
2. ____ When you first launch Access, the New File task pane appears.
3. ____ A *form* is a database object that displays multiple records in a column and row layout.

4. ____ A *query* allows you to ask questions of your data and to combine information from more than one table.

5. ____ The column widths of a datasheet cannot be adjusted once information has been entered into the cells.

6. ____ Changing the height of one row in a datasheet affects the height of every row.

7. ____ If you want to fit more field columns on a single page, you can select landscape orientation for printing.

8. ____ If you make a mistake while editing a field, you can press ESC to undo the error.

9. ____ In a datasheet, the *record selection area* is the gray area at the top of each column.

10. ____ Access allows you to delete several records at once.

Multiple Choice

1. Which of the following buttons does not appear in the Objects bar?
   a. Programs
   b. Modules
   c. Reports
   d. Forms

2. Which database object do you use to display information for one record at a time?
   a. table
   b. report
   c. form
   d. query

3. In a datasheet, the intersection of a row and a column is called a:
   a. cell
   b. cursor
   c. form
   d. record

4. In a datasheet, what does each column represent?
   a. database
   b. table
   c. record
   d. field

5. In a datasheet, which mouse pointer do you use to select a cell by clicking on its gridline?
   a.
   b.
   c.
   d. I

6. In a datasheet, which icon appears at the left side of a record while it is being edited?
   a. pencil ( )
   b. asterisk ( )
   c. pointer ( )
   d. selector ( )

7. When editing a record, which keystroke allows you to save the changes without leaving the current record?
   a. CTRL + ENTER
   b. CTRL + ALT
   c. ALT + ENTER
   d. SHIFT + ENTER

8. Which of the following will not reverse the last action performed?
   a. CHOOSE: Edit, Undo
   b. CLICK: Undo button ( )
   c. PRESS: CTRL +x
   d. PRESS: ESC

9. Any cell containing this type of field is incremented automatically by Access when a new record is added.
   a. AutoElevate
   b. AutoIncrement
   c. AutoNumber
   d. AutoValue

10. The row selector buttons in a datasheet are located in the:
    a. row selection area
    b. record selection area
    c. field selection area
    d. table selection area

Hands-On exercises

easy 

1. AmeriSales International: Sales Representatives

In this exercise, you practice fundamental database skills, such as opening a database, displaying a table, and navigating a datasheet. Ensure that you have turned on your computer and that the Windows desktop appears.

1. Load Microsoft Access using the Windows Start menu.
2. To open an existing database using the open dialog box:
   CLICK: Open button ( ) on the toolbar
3. Using either the Places bar or the *Look in* drop-down list box:
   SELECT: *the folder location* of your Advantage student data files
   DOUBLE-CLICK: AC01HE in the list area
   The Database window appears, as shown in Figure 1.29. (*Note:* The "HE" in the database file name stands for Hands-On Exercises.)

Figure 1.29

Opening the AC01HE database

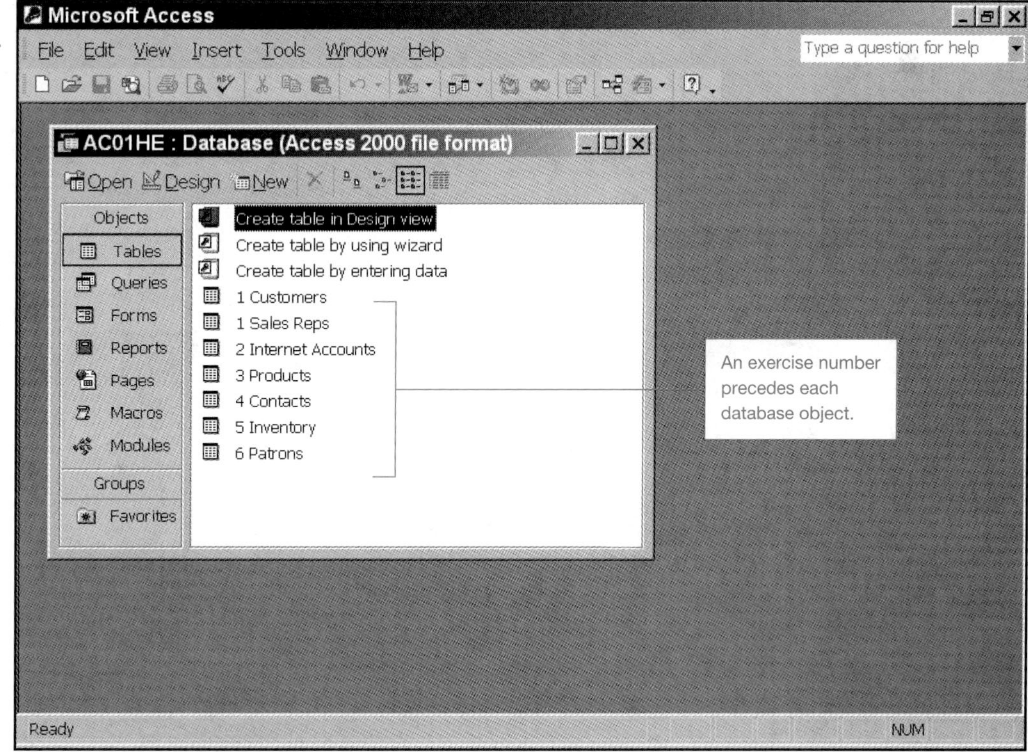

4. Ensure that the *Tables* button in the Objects bar is selected. Then do the following to display the Sales Reps table:
   DOUBLE-CLICK: 1 Sales Reps in the list area
   A table with 12 records and five field columns is displayed.
5. To move to the second field of the third record:
   PRESS: ↓ two times
   PRESS: → once
   The cursor should now highlight the name "Louis."

Access

6. Now move to the last record using the mouse:
   CLICK: Last Record button (▶|)
   Notice that the cursor moves to the last record in the same column.

7. To quickly move to the top of the datasheet using the keyboard:
   PRESS: CTRL + HOME

8. Each sales rep at AmeriSales International is responsible for servicing specific customer accounts. You can display the customer accounts for each sales rep in a *subdatasheet*. To do so, let's drill down and display the customers assigned to Peter Fink (SalesRep A14):
   CLICK: Expand button (⊞) in the left-hand column of record 5
   Your screen should now appear similar to Figure 1.30.

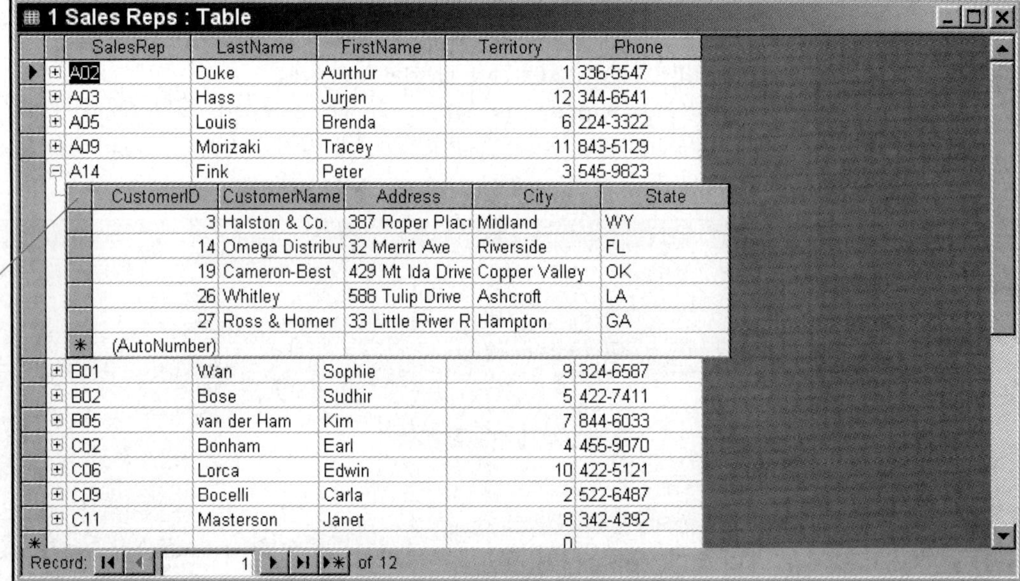

Figure 1.30

Expanding a datasheet to display a sales rep's customers

This subdatasheet displays data from the "1 Customers" table.

9. On your own, practice opening a few more subdatasheets. When you are finished, hide each subdatasheet by clicking the Collapse button (⊟) in the left-hand column.

10. To close the 1 Sales Reps Datasheet window:
    CLICK: its Close button (☒)

2. Iway Internet Group: Internet Accounts

In this exercise, you practice adjusting a datasheet's column widths and row heights before previewing it for printing. Ensure that the AC01HE Database window is displayed.

1. Let's view the Datasheet window for the Iway Internet Group:
   SELECT: *Tables* button in the Objects bar
   DOUBLE-CLICK: 2 Internet Accounts
   Your screen should now appear similar to Figure 1.31.

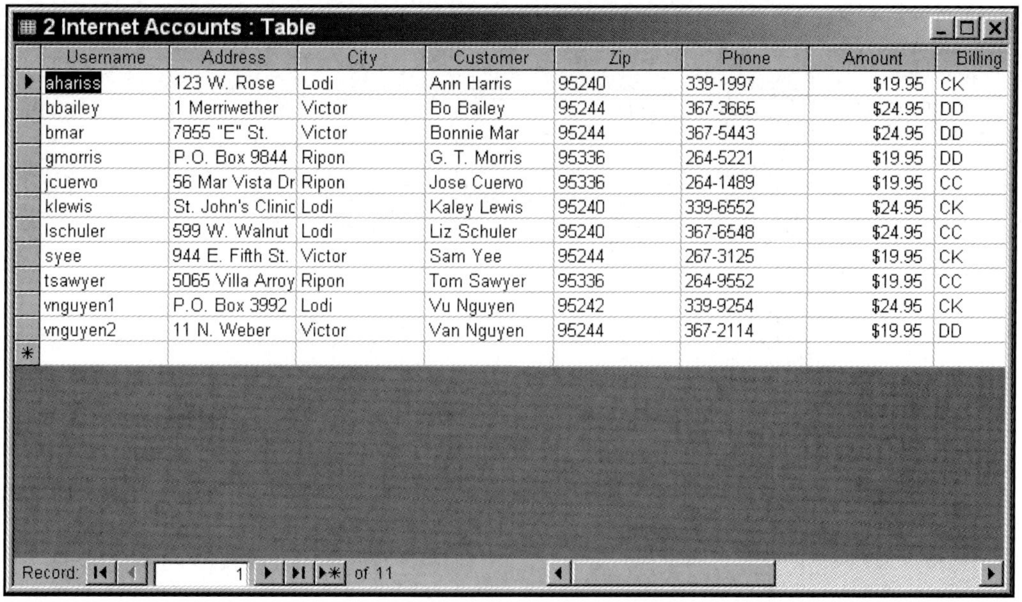

Figure 1.31

Displaying the "2 Internet Accounts" datasheet

2 Internet Accounts : Table

Username	Address	City	Customer	Zip	Phone	Amount	Billing
ahariss	123 W. Rose	Lodi	Ann Harris	95240	339-1997	$19.95	CK
bbailey	1 Merriwether	Victor	Bo Bailey	95244	367-3665	$24.95	DD
bmar	7855 "E" St.	Victor	Bonnie Mar	95244	367-5443	$24.95	DD
gmorris	P.O. Box 9844	Ripon	G. T. Morris	95336	264-5221	$19.95	DD
jcuervo	56 Mar Vista Dr	Ripon	Jose Cuervo	95336	264-1489	$19.95	CC
klewis	St. John's Clinic	Lodi	Kaley Lewis	95240	339-6552	$24.95	CK
lschuler	599 W. Walnut	Lodi	Liz Schuler	95240	367-6548	$24.95	CC
syee	944 E. Fifth St.	Victor	Sam Yee	95244	267-3125	$19.95	CK
tsawyer	5065 Villa Arroy	Ripon	Tom Sawyer	95336	264-9552	$19.95	CC
vnguyen1	P.O. Box 3992	Lodi	Vu Nguyen	95242	339-9254	$24.95	CK
vnguyen2	11 N. Weber	Victor	Van Nguyen	95244	367-2114	$19.95	DD

Record: 1 of 11

2. Let's adjust the width of the Address field column by having Access calculate its best width:
   SELECT: any cell in the Address column
   CHOOSE: Format, Column Width
   CLICK: Best Fit command button
3. Now use the mouse to adjust the width of the Phone column. In the field header area, position the mouse pointer (↔) over the borderline between the Phone and Amount fields.
   CLICK: the borderline and hold down the mouse button
   DRAG: the mouse pointer to the left to decrease the width (to approximately the end of the word "Phone")
4. To set the best-fit width for the Zip column using the mouse:
   DOUBLE-CLICK: the borderline between Zip and Phone in the field header area
5. On your own, adjust the width of the City column so that it is narrower.
6. To change the row height setting for all the rows in the datasheet:
   CHOOSE: Format, Row Height
   TYPE: **15**
   PRESS: ENTER or CLICK: OK
   Your screen should now appear similar to Figure 1.32.

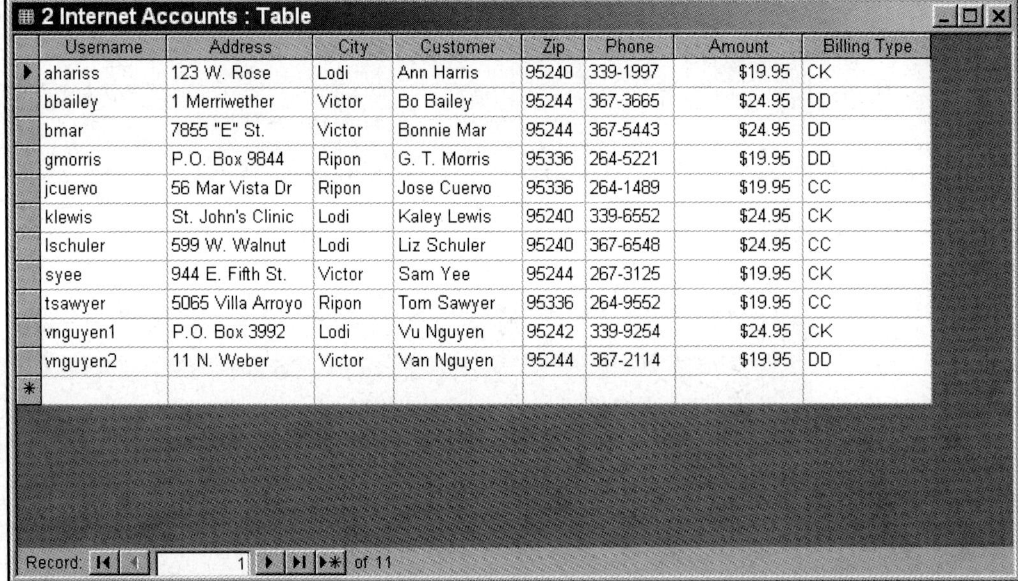

Username	Address	City	Customer	Zip	Phone	Amount	Billing Type
ahariss	123 W. Rose	Lodi	Ann Harris	95240	339-1997	$19.95	CK
bbailey	1 Merriwether	Victor	Bo Bailey	95244	367-3665	$24.95	DD
bmar	7855 "E" St.	Victor	Bonnie Mar	95244	367-5443	$24.95	DD
gmorris	P.O. Box 9844	Ripon	G. T. Morris	95336	264-5221	$19.95	DD
jcuervo	56 Mar Vista Dr	Ripon	Jose Cuervo	95336	264-1489	$19.95	CC
klewis	St. John's Clinic	Lodi	Kaley Lewis	95240	339-6552	$24.95	CK
lschuler	599 W. Walnut	Lodi	Liz Schuler	95240	367-6548	$24.95	CC
syee	944 E. Fifth St.	Victor	Sam Yee	95244	267-3125	$19.95	CK
tsawyer	5065 Villa Arroyo	Ripon	Tom Sawyer	95336	264-9552	$19.95	CC
vnguyen1	P.O. Box 3992	Lodi	Vu Nguyen	95242	339-9254	$24.95	CK
vnguyen2	11 N. Weber	Victor	Van Nguyen	95244	367-2114	$19.95	DD

Figure 1.32

Sizing rows and columns in a datasheet

7. Now let's see what the datasheet would look like if it was printed:
   CLICK: Print Preview button (🔍) on the toolbar
8. On your own, zoom in and out on the Print Preview window using the magnifying glass mouse pointer.
9. If you have a printer connected to your computer, print the datasheet using the following instruction. Otherwise, proceed to step 10.
   CLICK: Print button (🖨) on the toolbar
10. To close the Print Preview window so that the 2 Internet Accounts datasheet remains displayed:
    CLICK: Close button (Close) in the toolbar
11. To close the datasheet:
    CLICK: its Close button (☒)
    The following dialog box appears.

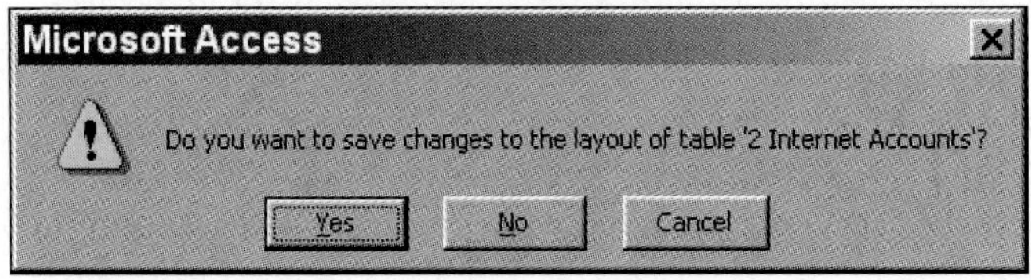

12. You can save the layout changes, so that the datasheet displays using the new column and row settings next time it is opened. To do so:
    CLICK: Yes command button

moderate 

3. Western Lumber Sales: Forest Products

In this exercise, you edit data in an existing datasheet and practice using the Undo command. Ensure that the AC01HE Database window is displayed.

1. SELECT: *Tables* button in the Objects bar
   DOUBLE-CLICK: 3 Products
   The datasheet shown in Figure 1.33 is displayed.

Figure 1.33

Displaying the "3 Products" datasheet

3 Products : Table

ProductCode	Species	Size	Grade	Finish	Category
B12	BIRCH	0.5	Cab.	G2S	Plywood
DF14	DFIR	1 X 4	Ungraded	RGH	Board
DF16	D.FIR	1 X 6	Ungraded	RGH	Board
DF210S	DFIR	2 X 10	Standard	S4S	Dim.
DF242	DFIR	2 X 4	2+	S4S	Dim.
DF24S	DFIR	2 X 4	Standard	S4S	Dim.
DF24U	DFIR	2 X 4	Utility	S4S	Dim.
DF26	DFIR	2 X 6	Standard	S4S	Dim.
DF28	DFIR	2 X 8	Standard	S4S	Dim.
O12	ROAK	0.5	Cab.	G2S	Plywood
O38	ROAK	0.375	Cab.	G2S	Plywood
P12	SPF	0.50	Constr.	G1S	Plywood
P12U	SPF	0.5	Utility	RGH	Plywood
P14	SPF	0.25	Constr.	G1S	Plywood
P34	SPF	0.75	Constr.	G1S	Plywood
P34T	SPF	0.75	Constr.	T&G	Plywood
P38	SPF	0.375	Constr.	G1S	Plywood
P58	SPF	0.625	Constr.	G1S	Plywood
P58T	SPF	0.675	Constr.	T&G	Plywood
P58U	SPF	0.625	Utility	RGH	Plywood

Record: 1 of 49

2. To position the cursor in the Species column of the third record:
   PRESS: ⬇ two times
   PRESS: ➡ once
3. Let's change this cell value to match the standard abbreviation. With the entry selected, enter the new data:
   TYPE: **DFIR**
4. To save the changes, move the cursor to the next record:
   PRESS: ⬇
   The pencil icon disappears.
5. Now let's edit the product code of record number 4. (*Hint:* Glance at the navigation bar in the Datasheet window to see the current record number.) Position the I-beam mouse pointer to the right of the product code "DF210S," as shown here. [DF210S | DFIR] Then, click once to position the flashing insertion point to the right of the letter "S."
6. To delete the final "S" in DF210S and save the change:
   PRESS: BACKSPACE
   PRESS: ⬇

Access

7. SELECT: Grade cell for record 1 using the mouse
   (*Hint:* Position the mouse pointer over the cell's left gridline so that the pointer changes to a cross shape (✚). Then click the left mouse button once to select the entire cell.)

8. Replace the cell's contents with the new Grade code "Utility" and then save the changes using the SHIFT + ENTER key combination.

9. To end the in-cell Edit mode:
   PRESS: F2

10. To delete the entry in the last field column of the first row:
    PRESS: END to move to the last field
    PRESS: DELETE
    PRESS: ⬇
    Your screen should now appear similar to Figure 1.34.

Figure 1.34

Editing cells in the "3 Products" datasheet

3 Products : Table

ProductCode	Species	Size	Grade	Finish	Category
B12	BIRCH	0.5	Utility	G2S	
DF14	DFIR	1 X 4	Ungraded	RGH	Board
DF16	DFIR	1 X 6	Ungraded	RGH	Board
DF210	DFIR	2 X 10	Standard	S4S	Dim.
DF242	DFIR	2 X 4	2+	S4S	Dim.
DF24S	DFIR	2 X 4	Standard	S4S	Dim.
DF24U	DFIR	2 X 4	Utility	S4S	Dim.
DF26	DFIR	2 X 6	Standard	S4S	Dim.
DF28	DFIR	2 X 8	Standard	S4S	Dim.
O12	ROAK	0.5	Cab.	G2S	Plywood
O38	ROAK	0.375	Cab.	G2S	Plywood
P12	SPF	0.50	Constr.	G1S	Plywood
P12U	SPF	0.5	Utility	RGH	Plywood
P14	SPF	0.25	Constr.	G1S	Plywood
P34	SPF	0.75	Constr.	G1S	Plywood
P34T	SPF	0.75	Constr.	T&G	Plywood
P38	SPF	0.375	Constr.	G1S	Plywood
P58	SPF	0.625	Constr.	G1S	Plywood
P58T	SPF	0.675	Constr.	T&G	Plywood
P58U	SPF	0.625	Utility	RGH	Plywood

Record: 2 of 49

11. To reverse the previous field cell deletion using the Menu bar:
    CHOOSE: Edit, Undo Saved Record
    (*Note:* Instead of using the menu, you can also click the Undo button (↶) to achieve the same result.)

12. Close the Datasheet window.

moderate 

4. Spring County Carnival: Contact List

You will now practice adding and deleting records in an existing table. Ensure the AC01HE Database window is displayed.

1. Display the 4 Contacts table object in Datasheet view.

2. To position the cursor at the bottom of the datasheet, ready for inserting a new record:
   CLICK: New Record button (▶*) on the toolbar

3. The first column contains an AutoNumber entry, so we can immediately move to the next field:
   PRESS: TAB

4. Let's start entering the new record information:
   TYPE: **Silverdale Search and Rescue**
   PRESS: TAB
   Notice that the AutoNumber entry for the ID column is calculated and entered automatically, as shown in Figure 1.35.

Figure 1.35

Adding a new record to the "4 Contacts" datasheet

4 Contacts : Table

	ID	Volunteer Group	Contact	Address	City	Phone 1	P
	49	Annunciation Youth Group	Susie Rainwater	530 W. Rose St.	Silverdale	464-9594	
	50	Silverdale Community Pow-Wo	Alberta Snyder	P.O. Box 4531	Silverdale	953-4017	953-4
	51	Boy Scout Troop 16	Anelise Krause	4590 Pine Valley Circle	Silverdale	476-0637	
	52	Boy Scout Troop 425	Mike Lehr	680 Aurora Ct	Manteca	823-7634	823-0
	53	S.J. Co. Sheriff Aux.	Lt Fred Meyer	7000 Michael N. Cannily B	French Camp	473-8005	468-4
	54	North Silverdale Rotary	James Hulstrom	555 W. Benjamin Holt Dr.	Silverdale	952-5850	951-7
	55	Silverdale Metropolitan Kiwis	Steve Shelby	P.O. Box 1002	Silverdale	464-4505	477-8
	56	St. Joseph's Spirit Club	Brad Singer/P.Halligan	3240 Angel Dr.	Silverdale	467-6374	474-8
	57	Beta Sigma Phi/Xi Omicron	Patty Tealdi	2251 Piccardo Circle	Silverdale	951-3553	948-6
	58	Blind Center	Mimi Eberhardt		Silverdale	951-3554	948-6
	59	Alan Short Gallery	Yvonne Sotto	1004 N. Grant St.	Silverdale	948-5759	462-5
	60	Julie Mulligan/Cathi Schuler	Julie Mulligan	9119 Casterbridge Dr	Silverdale	952-2460	946-5
	61	Julie Mulligan/Cathi Schuler	Julie Mulligan	9119 Casterbridge Dr	Silverdale	952-2460	946-5
	62	Volunteer Center	Peggy Hazlip	265 W. Knolls Way	Silverdale	943-0870	944-0
	63	Delta Valley Twins Group	Debbie Hunt	P.O. Box 691316	Silverdale	474-0662	948-6
	64	Library & Literacy Foundation	Dr. Mary Ann Cox	605 N. El Dorado St.	Silverdale	937-8384	
	65	Hospice Of San Joaquin	Sherry A. Burns	2609 E. Hammer Lane	Silverdale	957-3888	474-0
	66	National Restaurant Assn. Sch	Peter T. Valets	9617 Enchantment Lane	Silverdale	483-3548	951-3
✎	67	Silverdale Search and Rescue					
*	ber)						

Record: 67 of 67

5. To continue filling out the record:
   TYPE: **Amy McTell**
   PRESS: TAB
   TYPE: **P.O. Box 1359**
   PRESS: TAB
   TYPE: **Silverdale**
   PRESS: TAB
   TYPE: **474-9636**
   PRESS: TAB two times

6. On your own, add the following record to the datasheet:
   Volunteer Group: **Historical Society**
   Contact: **Craig Burns**
   Address: **3528 Pacific Ave.**
   City: **Silverdale**
   Phone 1: **945-6621**

7. To delete a record that was inadvertently entered twice, select ID 61 (which is also record number 61) using the record selection area. (*Hint:* The mouse pointer changes shape to a black horizontal right-pointing arrow (➡) when positioned properly.)

8. Let's remove the selected record from the table:
CLICK: Delete Record button (![]) on the toolbar
Your screen should now appear similar to Figure 1.36.

Figure 1.36

Deleting a record from the "4 Contacts" datasheet

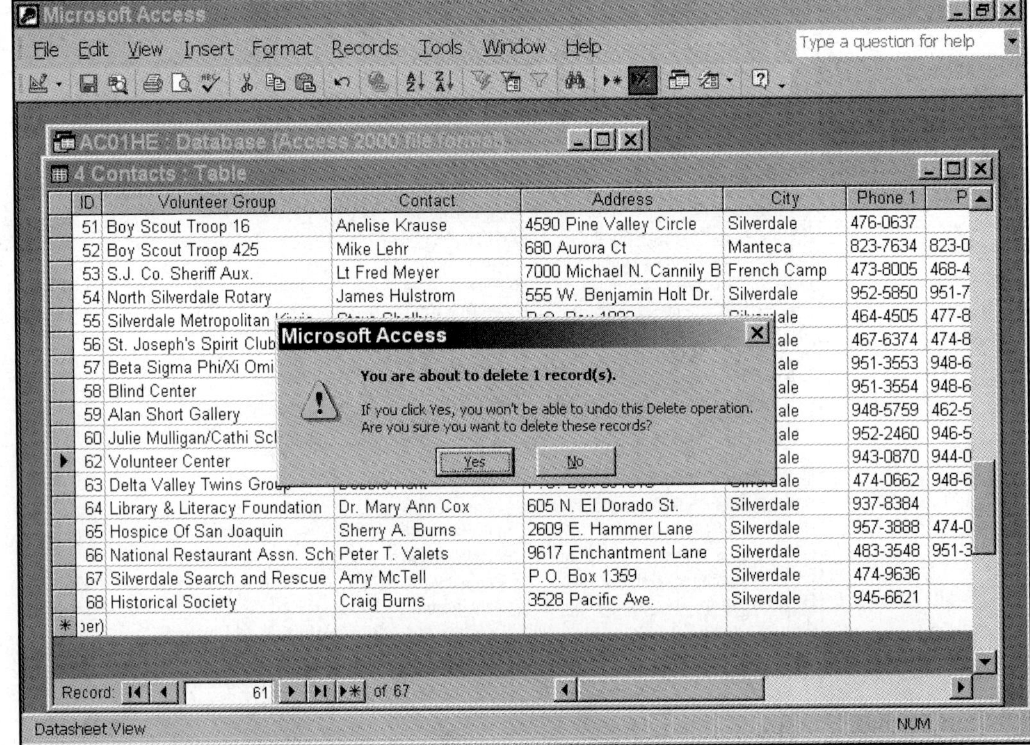

9. To confirm the deletion:
CLICK: Yes command button
Notice that the values in the ID column now jump from 60 to 62. As you can see, an AutoNumber field, such as a record ID number, is just another table value; it does not have to match a record's number.

10. Close the Datasheet window.

5. On Your Own: Benson's Office Supplies

To practice navigating and formatting a table's datasheet, open the table object named 5 Inventory in the AC01HE database. Experiment with the various mouse and keyboard methods for moving the cursor in the datasheet. After you have familiarized yourself with the table, use the keyboard to reposition the cursor to the first field of the first record.

Resize the ProductID, Description, and Suggested Retail columns to their best fit. Adjust the OnHand and Cost columns to 12 characters. Change the height of all the rows to 14 points. Now, use Print Preview to see how the datasheet will look when it's printed. Change the page setup to landscape orientation so that all the columns fit on a single page, as shown in Figure 1.37. If they do not, adjust the widths of the remaining columns until they do. When you are satisfied with the appearance of the page, print a copy. Then, close the Datasheet window and save the layout changes.

Figure 1.37

Previewing a datasheet with a landscape print orientation

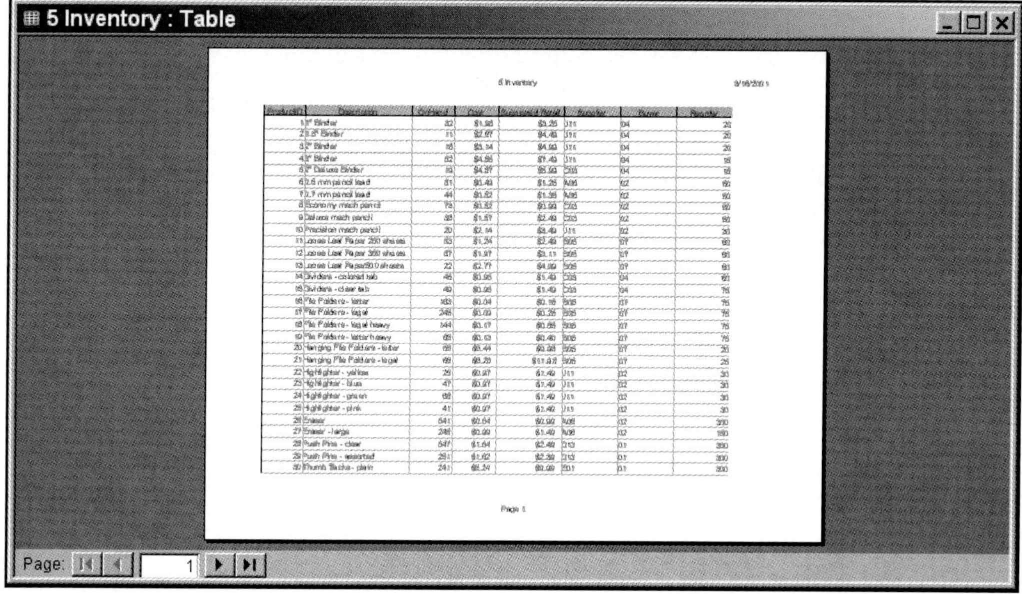

difficult 

6. On Your Own: Coldstream Valley Resorts

To practice manipulating table data, open the table object named 6 Patrons in the AC01HE database.

Make the following editing changes:

- Change the spelling of guest ID 2 from "Neely" to "Neally"
- Change the Interest of guest ID 6 from "Tennis" to "Golf"
- Change the Hometown of guest ID 8 from "Clonkurry" to "Mount Isa"
- Change the Best Time of guest ID 22 to "11:30 AM"

Make the following addition:

Guest: **Ric Fernando**
Hometown: **Manila**
State: *(leave blank)*
Co: **PHI**
Interest: **Golf**
Room#: **B311**
#Stay: **1**
Best Time: **1:00 PM**

Finally, delete the record for guest ID 15 and then move the cursor to the top of the datasheet. Your screen should appear similar to Figure 1.38. Once finished, close the Datasheet window, close the AC01HE database, and exit Microsoft Access.

Figure 1.38

Editing the "6 Patrons" datasheet

6 Patrons : Table

ID	Guest	Hometown	State	Co	Interest	Room#	#Stay	Best Time
1	John & Becky Reusche	Miami	FL	US	Tennis	A304	1	1:00 PM
2	Jan Neally & Laurie Berg	Houston	TX	US	Fishing	B222	1	9:00 AM
3	Roger Turnbeaugh	Sioux City	IA	US	Golf	A419	1	1:00 PM
5	Penny & Paul Knapp	Boulder	CO	US	Sightseeing	D126	1	9:00 AM
6	Gary Giovanetti	Miami	FL	US	Golf	B245	2	1:00 PM
7	Patti & Guissepi Gulick	Billings	MT	US	Shopping	A130	1	11:00 AM
8	Mitchell & Houston Ruggles	Mount Isa	QS	AUS	Fishing	C342	1	3:00 PM
9	Hector & Ingrid Stringer	Zurich		SW	Golf	C262	1	11:00 AM
11	Julie & Royce Mulligan	Webster	FL	US	Tennis	B142	3	3:00 PM
12	Coleman & Beatriz Sholl	Saltillo	COA	MX	Tennis	A333	1	1:00 PM
13	Putsy Hong	Cedar Rapids	IA	US	Beach	D216	3	1:00 PM
14	Jeff & Helga Wentworth	Central Falls	RI	US	Golf	C210	1	11:00 AM
17	Teresa & Harry Perry	Gainesville	FL	US	Tennis	B341	3	3:00 PM
18	Jeff Valverde	Madrid		SP	Golf	C333	1	11:00 AM
19	Judi Boone & May Heath	Shreveport	LA	US	Beach	A103	2	9:00 AM
20	Brett & Mona Henry	Solvang	CA	US	Fishing	A129	2	11:00 AM
21	Ho and Vinh Tran	El Paso	TX	US	Tennis	C239	1	9:00 AM
22	Ann & Felix Paoletti	Sao Paulo		BRA	Golf	B327	1	11:30 AM
23	Archie & Edith Bunker	Hoboken	NJ	US	Beach	D272	1	9:00 AM
24	Ric Fernando	Manila		PHI	Golf	B311	1	1:00 PM

Record: 1 of 20

Case Problems

Lifelong Learning Academy

Joanna has been working at the Lifelong Learning Academy for several days now and is becoming quite comfortable in her new job. In addition to her regular administrative duties, she is responsible for managing an Access database. Having never used database software before, she enrolled in an evening course on Microsoft Access at the local community college. Now she feels ready to open and view the contents of the company's database.

In the following case problems, assume the role of Joanna and perform the same steps that she identifies. You may want to re-read the chapter opening before proceeding.

1. Midway through the morning, Joanna receives a phone call from an agitated instructor. "Hello, Joanna? My name is Mary Sterba and I teach the 'Safety in the Workplace' seminars. Due to a family emergency, I can't make my TR145 seminar this Tuesday. Please call the students and ask if they can transfer into TR146 the following week."

To start, Joanna loads the AC01CP database located in her Advantage student data files folder. From the Database window, she opens the Trainers table and locates Mary Sterba's record. She expands the subdatasheet for Mary's record and verifies that she is indeed scheduled to teach both the TR145 and TR146 seminars. Next she expands the subdatasheet for TR146, as shown in Figure 1.39, to ensure that it does not have more than 10 students registered. After collapsing the subdatasheet for TR146, she expands the TR145 subdatasheet in order to list the names and phone numbers of all students registered in the canceled class. She will use the list to call the students and reschedule them into the next seminar. Having completed her first task using Access, Joanna closes the Trainers table.

Figure 1.39

Drilling down into a table's data using subdatasheets

Trainers : Table

Trainer ID	Trainer Last Name	Trainer First Name	Traner Phone	Classification
1	Rafat	Marcel	321-5848	C-7
2	Barnes	James	344-6521	C-2
3	Brown	Ibrahim	227-6654	C-7
4	Anderson	Victoria	345-6653	C-2
5	Azavedo	Jane	228-4512	C-6
6	Chang	Thomas	322-4151	C-2
7	Sterba	Mary	233-5784	C-2
8	Hargrove	Elliot	345-7524	C-6
9	Leopold	May	554-3363	C-7
10	Rolston	Nina	555-6488	C-2
11	Bari	Aldo	322-6855	C-6
12	DaSilva	Connie	335-6459	C-7

Data from the Seminars table

Seminar ID	Description	Date	Time	Hours	Place	Cost
TR145	Safety in the W	12/5/2001	9:00 AM	7	B203	$155.00
TR146	Safety in the W	12/12/2001	9:00 AM	7	B203	$155.00
				0		$0.00

Data from the Enrollment table

Student Numbe	Last Name	First Name	Student Phone
144	Friesen	Larry	664-8701
243	Zorn	Dolan	334-6015
0			

Record: 1 of 2

2. Later that day, Karen Chase, the office director, asks Joanna to produce a printout of the currently scheduled seminars. Joanna opens the Seminars table in the AC01CP database and adjusts the column width of the Description field so that the entire title is visible. To provide some additional white space in the printout, she adjusts the height of all the rows to 16 points. Using Print Preview to view the datasheet, Joanna notices that not all columns fit on a single page. To compensate, she changes the page setup to use landscape orientation and adjusts the datasheet's column widths as necessary. When she is satisfied with the appearance of the datasheet (Figure 1.40), Joanna prints a copy for Karen. Then she closes the Seminars table, saving the formatting changes she has made.

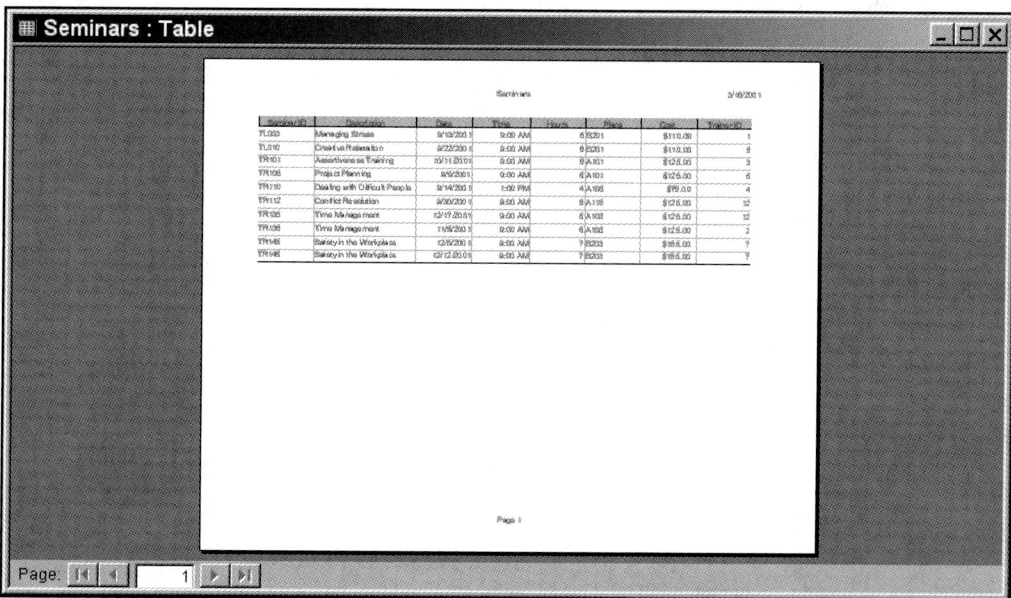

Figure 1.40

Previewing the Seminars datasheet

3. Joanna phones the five students whose phone numbers she wrote down earlier that day and determines that they are all indeed able to switch to the later "Safety in the Workplace" seminar. To update the database, Joanna begins by opening the Enrollment table. She locates the five students' records and changes the Seminar ID for each record from TR145 to TR146. She then switches to the Database window, without closing the datasheet, and opens the Seminars table. To finish the task, Joanna ensures that no students are registered in seminar TR145 and then deletes the record. Finally, she closes both Datasheet windows.

4. Toward the end of the day, Joanna receives two phone calls from people wishing to register for seminars. After writing down the information, Joanna is ready to update the database. She opens the Enrollment table and adds two new records, as shown in Figure 1.41.

   Student Number: **501**
   Last Name: **Haldane**
   First Name: **Chris**
   Student Phone: **577-9685**
   Seminar ID: **TR135**

   Student Number: **502**
   Last Name: **Zhou**
   First Name: **Shih-Chang**
   Student Phone: **345-6087**
   Seminar ID: **TR146**

   She saves the records and closes the datasheet. Then she closes the Database window and exits Microsoft Access.

Figure 1.41

Adding students to the Enrollment table

Enrollment : Table

Student Number	Last Name	First Name	Student Phone	Seminar ID
264	Jung	Han	445-3122	TR146
277	Bartok	Nick	557-3306	TR105
280	Inkster	Marla	655-4035	TR146
281	Saul	Luis	554-7088	TR136
283	Quinn	Dwayne	224-3581	TR101
288	Inglis	Diane	545-7712	TR136
291	Kowalski	Byron	255-3177	TR101
299	Jaeger	Hans	314-5858	TR112
303	Phillips	Tyler	355-8064	TR110
308	Mahal	Balinder	337-8541	TR101
311	Malone	Sean	544-6637	TL010
325	Nadeau	Pierre	441-5511	TR101
330	McMahon	Lavon	225-6634	TR101
331	Norgaard	Max	554-7787	TL010
344	Cameron	Verne	442-3080	TR135
455	Pittman	Dale	332-6674	TR101
501	Haldane	Chris	577-9685	TR135
502	Zhou	Shih-Chang	345-6087	TR146

Record: 58 of 58

Microsoft® **Access®** 2002

CHAPTER 2

Creating a Database

CHAPTER OUTLINE

2.1 Designing Your First Database

2.2 Creating a Simple Table

2.3 Using the Table Design View

2.4 Modifying a Table

Chapter Summary

Chapter Quiz

Hands-On Exercises

Case Problems

PREREQUISITES

To successfully complete this chapter, you must know how to open database objects appearing in the Database window. Most importantly, you must be able to display and navigate a table's datasheet using the mouse and keyboard. You should also be able to perform basic editing in a datasheet, including adding and deleting records.

LEARNING OBJECTIVES

After completing this chapter, you will be able to:

- Create a new database from scratch
- Create a new database using a wizard
- Define table objects for storing data
- Specify a primary key and indexes
- Rename, delete, and move fields
- Print a table's structure

Case Study: NORTH STAR FREIGHT

North Star Freight operates a fleet of trucks in the Pacific Northwest. Last week, North Star Freight's management team asked their controller, Mike Lambert, to locate and summarize a variety of information about the business. After spending three days reviewing reports and searching through filing cabinets, Mike came to the realization that he needs a better information management system. He evaluates the leading database software programs and decides to use Microsoft Access to create a company database. Mike starts the process by laying out his design ideas on paper. He wants to ensure that all of the company's relevant business information is collected, stored, and readied for processing.

In this chapter, you and Mike learn about creating databases and tables using Microsoft Access. You also learn how to modify a table's design by adding and removing fields. Finally, you use a special Access program called the Documenter to produce a printout of a table's structure.

2.1 Designing Your First Database

Desktop database software has existed since the first personal computer was introduced by IBM in the early 1980s. Since that time many database programs and applications have been developed for both personal and business use. Whatever your particular data management needs, rarely will you require a truly unique application. Refining or customizing an existing database application is a more common practice. Microsoft Access 2002 allows you to take advantage of what others before you have learned and accomplished. Using the Access wizards, you can develop an entire database application in less time than it takes to read this module!

2.1.1 Planning a Database

feature

Many people who have worked with computer databases can attest to the 90/10 rule of database design. Place 90 percent of your effort into designing a database properly in order to spend only 10 percent of your time maintaining it. As you can probably infer from this rule, many problems arising in database management are traceable to a faulty design. In this lesson, you learn some strategies for planning a well-designed database.

method

Here are five steps to designing a better database:

1. *Determine your output requirements.* State your expectations in terms of the queries and reports desired from the application. It's often helpful to write out questions, such as "How many customers live in Kansas City?", and to sketch out reports on a blank piece of paper.
2. *Determine your input requirements.* From the output requirements, identify the data that must be collected, stored, and calculated. You should also review any existing paper-based forms used for data collection in order to get a better idea of what data are available.

3. *Determine your table structures.* Divide and group data into separate tables and fields for flexibility in searching, sorting, and manipulating data. Review the following example to see what fields can be separated out of a simple address:

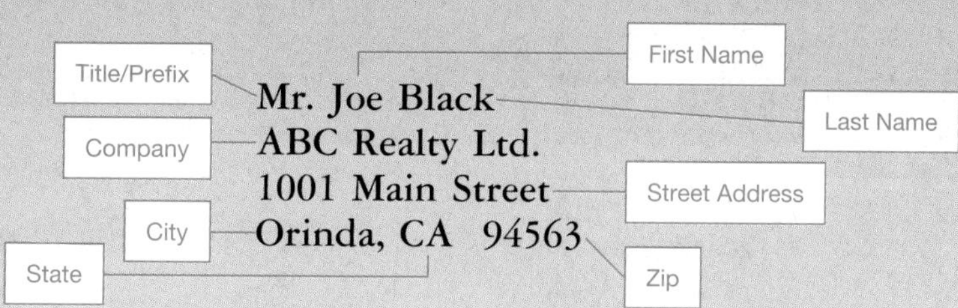

Also ensure that each record can be identified using a unique code or field, such as Order Number or Customer ID. This code need not contain information related to the subject—a numeric field that is automatically incremented works fine.

4. *Determine your table relationships.* Rather than entering or storing the same information repeatedly, strive to separate data into multiple tables and then relate the tables using a common field. For example, in a table containing book information (Books), an AuthorID field would contain a unique code that could be used to look up the author's personal data in a separate table (Authors). Without such a design, you would need to type an author's name and address each time you added one of his or her works to the Books table.

By incorporating common fields into your table structures, you can establish relationships among the tables for sharing data. This process, called *normalizing* your data, enhances your efficiency and reduces potential data redundancy and entry errors.

5. *Test your database application.* Add sample records to the table using both datasheets and forms, and then run queries and produce reports to test whether the application is robust and accurate. In addition to ensuring the validity and integrity of data, you want the information to be readily accessible.

2.1.2 Starting a New Database

Access provides two main options for creating a new database. First, you can choose to create a blank structure and then add the database objects appropriate for your specific application. Creating an empty database structure is the focus of this lesson. The second option, discussed in the next lesson, is to select a starting point from a group of professionally designed database templates. Unlike other Office XP applications, such as Word and Excel, Access allows you to work with only one database at a time. Therefore, before starting a new database, you must ensure that there is no active database displayed in the application window's work area.

method

- CLICK: New button (▯),

or

- CHOOSE: File, New
- CLICK: "Blank Database" option under the *New* area in the New File task pane

practice

In this lesson, you create a new database file for storing table objects. Load Microsoft Access, if it is not already running.

1. To create a new database application, start by ensuring that the New File task pane (shown in Figure 2.1) is displayed:
CLICK: New button (▯) on the toolbar

Figure 2.1

New File task pane

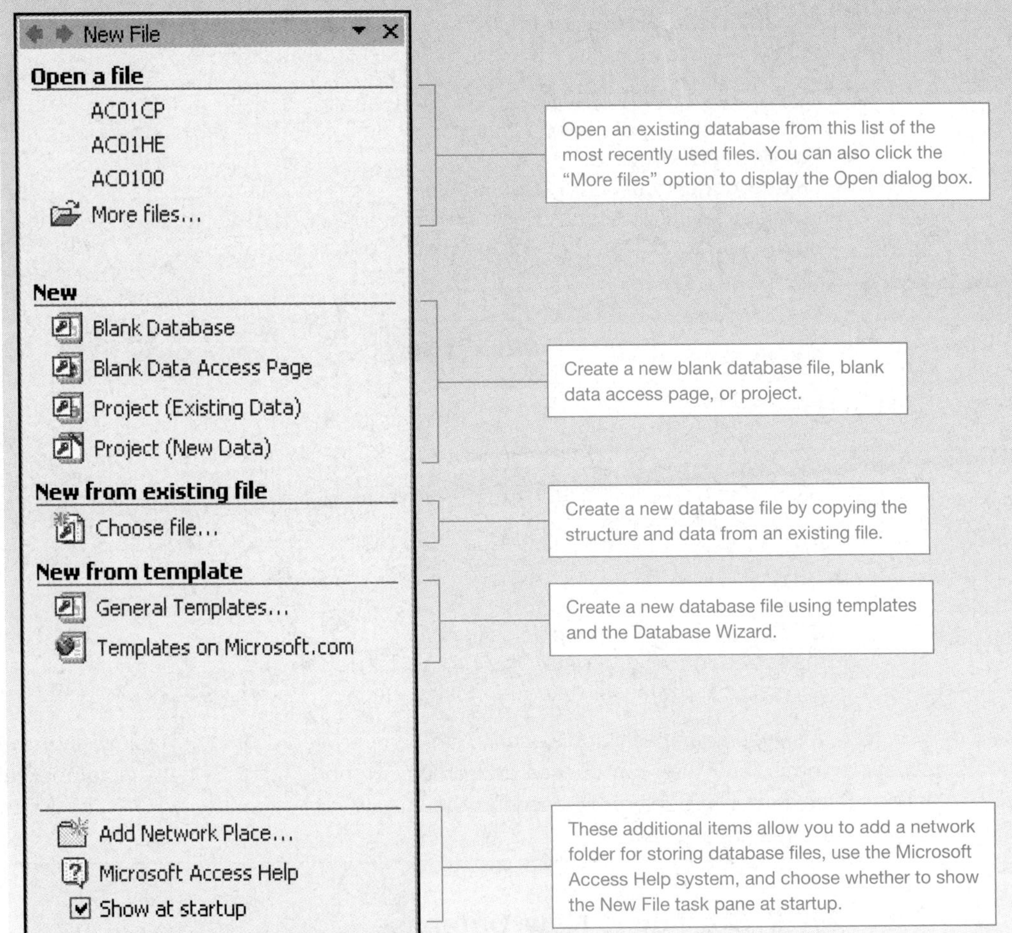

2. Using the hand mouse pointer (☝):
CLICK: Blank Database, located under the *New* heading

3. You use the File New Database dialog box (Figure 2.2) to select a storage location and filename for permanently saving the database structure. Using the Places bar or the *Save in* drop-down dialog box, select your personal storage location.

Figure 2.2

File New Database dialog box

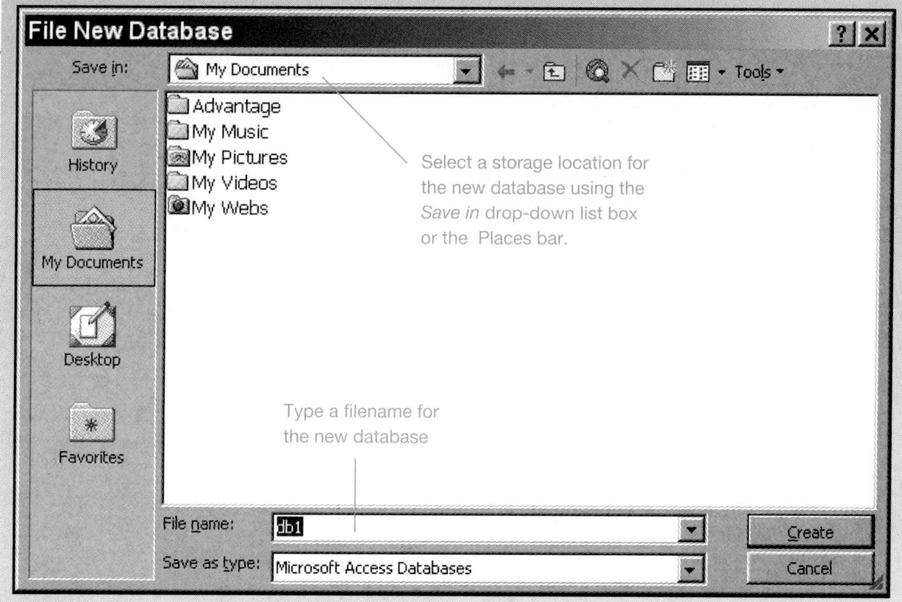

4. On your own, select the existing filename (by default, "db1") that appears in the *File name* text box using the mouse. (*Hint:* Double-click or drag over the filename using the I-beam mouse pointer.)

5. To create the new database file:
TYPE: **My Phone Book** to replace the existing filename
CLICK: Create command button
A new Database window appears in the work area, as shown in Figure 2.3. Notice that the Title bar reads "My Phone Book : Database (Access 2000 file format)." Nothing more than an empty shell at this point, the Database window contains no objects except the default New Object shortcuts. (*Note:* To facilitate information sharing among users of legacy applications, Access 2002 defaults to creating database files using the Access 2000 file format.)

Figure 2.3

Creating a blank database

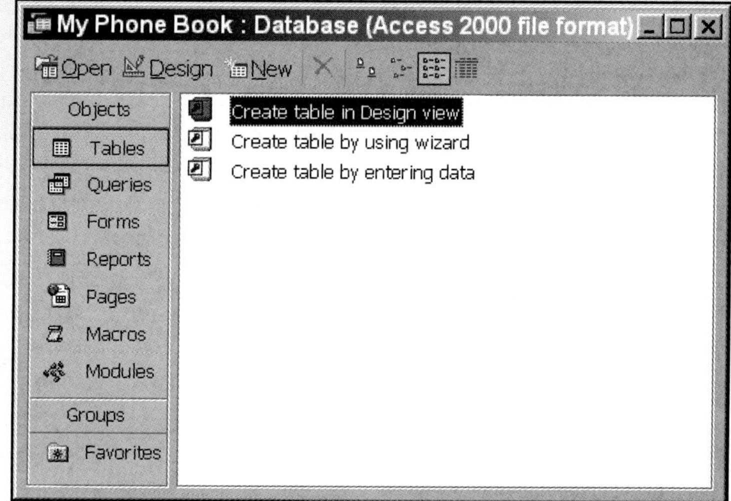

Access

6. You learn how to add table objects to an empty database in the next module. For now, close the Database window and proceed to the next lesson:
CLICK: its Close button (☒)

2.1.3 Employing the Database Wizard

feature

Besides creating an empty database structure and then populating it with objects, Access can lead you step-by-step in generating a new database using the **Database Wizard.** This wizard provides access to professionally designed templates for creating complete database applications. Each template contains tables, queries, forms, reports, and a main menu called a *switchboard* that makes the application's features easier to access.

method

- CLICK: New button (🗋),

or

- CHOOSE: File, New
- CLICK: "General Templates" option under the *New from template* area in the New File task pane
- CLICK: *Databases* tab in the Templates dialog box
- DOUBLE-CLICK: a database wizard (icon)

practice

Using the Access Database Wizard, you now create an inventory control application from scratch. Ensure that Access is loaded and that no Database window is displayed.

1. Let's begin by ensuring that the New File task pane is displayed:
CLICK: New button (🗋) on the toolbar

2. Using the hand pointer (hand icon) of the mouse
CLICK: General Templates, located under the *New from template* heading

3. The "Blank Database" template icon appears selected on the *General* tab of the Templates dialog box. This is the template used by Access when you click the "Blank Database" option under the *New* heading. To list the Database Wizard templates that are available:
CLICK: *Databases* tab
Your screen should now appear similar to Figure 2.4. (*Note:* Depending on how Access was installed and configured on your system, different template options may appear in your dialog box. If you haven't installed any database templates, you cannot perform the steps in this lesson.)

Figure 2.4

Templates dialog box: *Databases* tab

By default, Access provides the *General* and *Databases* tabs for organizing database templates.

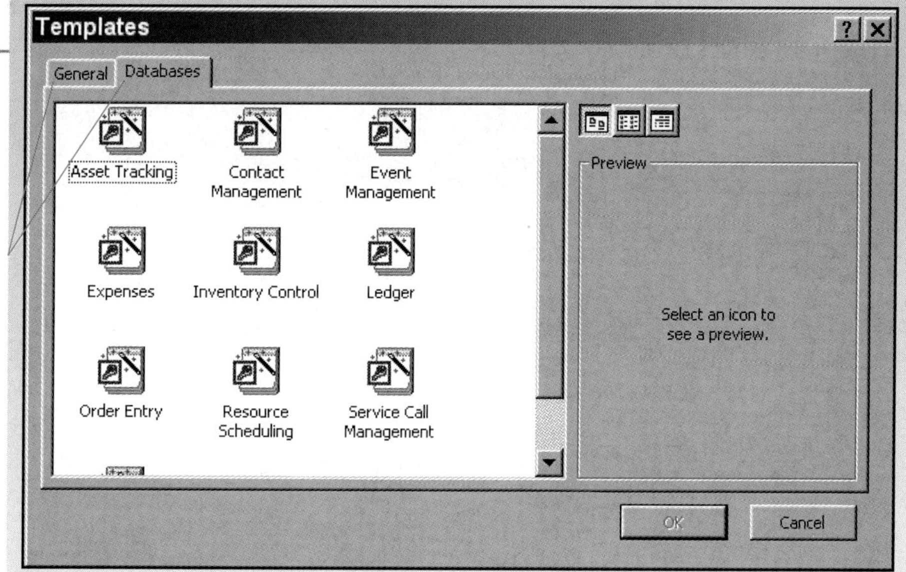

4. Using the appropriate Database Wizard template, let's create an inventory database application: DOUBLE-CLICK: Inventory Control wizard ( )

5. In the File New Database dialog box that appears, use the Places bar or the *Save in* drop-down list box to select your personal storage location. Then, select the name that appears in the *File name* text box using the mouse.

6. Now select the name (usually "Inventory Control" with the number "1" appended) that appears in the *File name* text box and do the following:
   TYPE: **My Inventory** to replace the existing filename
   CLICK: Create command button
   Wait momentarily as Access displays your new Database window and prepares the Database Wizard dialog box, shown in Figure 2.5.

Figure 2.5

Database Wizard dialog box for creating an Inventory Control database

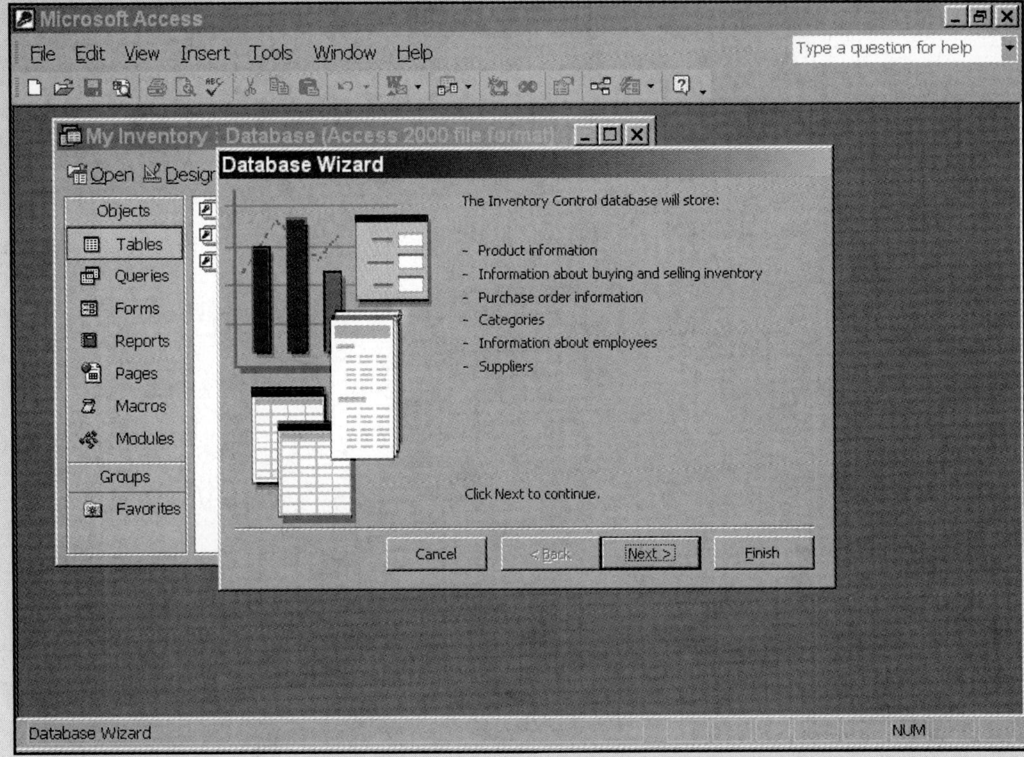

7. The opening screen of the Database Wizard dialog box provides information about the Inventory Control wizard. After reading its contents, proceed to the next step:
CLICK: Next >

8. Your first task in the Database Wizard, as shown in Figure 2.6, is to select fields for collecting and storing information in the database. Optional fields appear in italic. On your own, click on the names listed in the *Tables in the database* list box. The field names for the selected table appear in the *Fields in the table* list box. To proceed:
CLICK: Next >

Figure 2.6

Inventory Control Database Wizard: select fields

Database Wizard

The database you've chosen requires certain fields. Possible additional fields are shown italic below, and may be in more than one table.

Do you want to add any optional fields?

Tables in the database:

My Company Information
Product information
Information about buying and selling inv
Purchase order information
Categories
Information about employees
Shipping Methods
Suppliers

Fields in the table:

SetupID
Company Name
Address
City
State/Province
Postal Code
Country/Region
Phone Number
Fax Number

Cancel | < Back | Next > | Finish

9. To select a screen appearance for your forms, click on each option in the dialog box to see a preview and then:
SELECT: Sumi Painting, as shown in Figure 2.7
CLICK: Next >

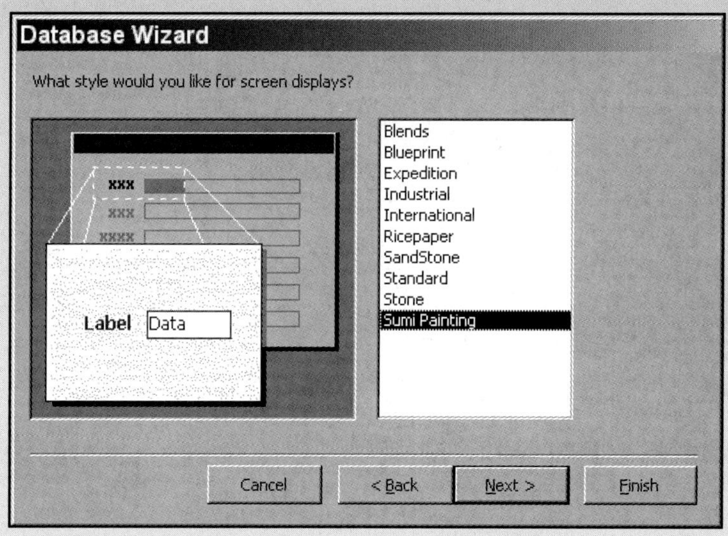

Figure 2.7
Inventory Control Database Wizard: select screen appearance

10. To select a page layout for your printed reports, click on each option in the dialog box to see a preview and then:
SELECT: Soft Gray, as shown in Figure 2.8
CLICK: Next >

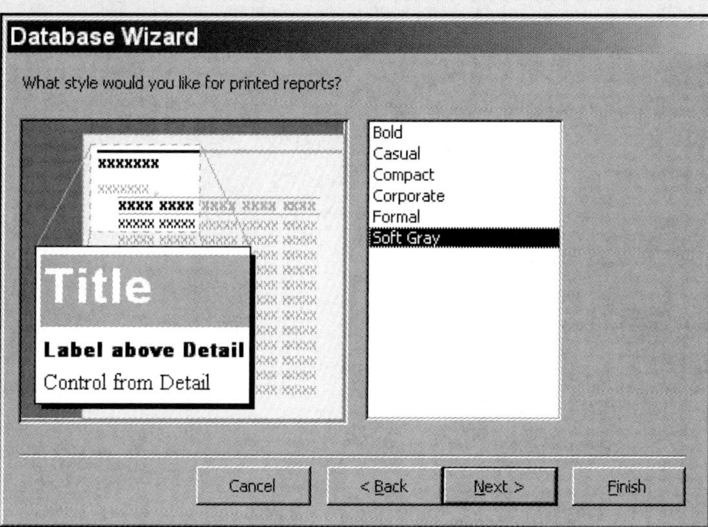

Figure 2.8
Inventory Control Database Wizard: select report appearance

11. You can also specify the title of the database and whether to include a logo or picture. To accept the defaults ("Inventory Control"):
CLICK: Next >

12. At the finish line, you tell Access to create and display the database. Ensure that the *Yes, start the database* check box is selected and then do the following:
CLICK: Finish
The Database Wizard creates the database based on your selections. Depending on the power of your system, this process can take a few minutes.

13. In this particular wizard, Access displays a dialog box asking you to furnish some company data. Click the OK command button to continue. Then, using the TAB key to move forward through the text boxes, type the information shown in Figure 2.9. When you are ready to proceed:
CLICK: its Close button (☒)

Figure 2.9

Furnishing the wizard with company information

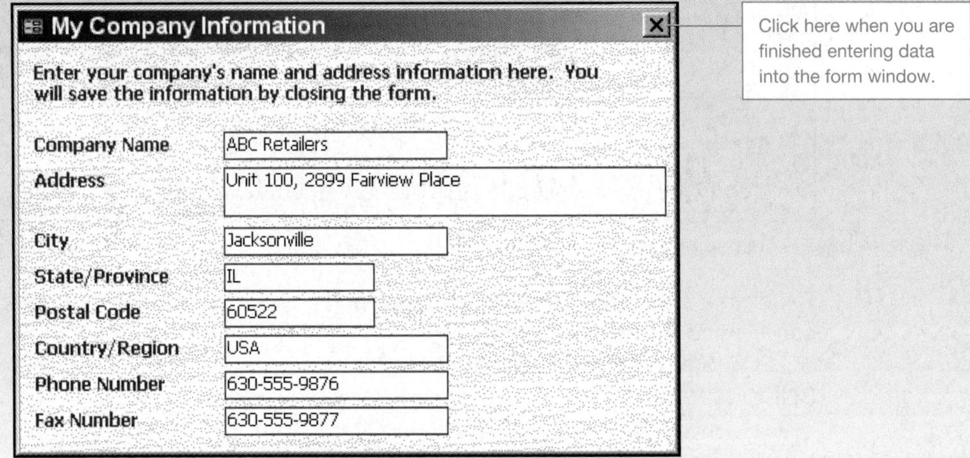

14. The Main Switchboard (Figure 2.10) for the Inventory Control application is displayed. On your own, click on the menu buttons to access and display the forms and reports created by the Database Wizard. Before proceeding, close the Print Preview windows that appear for a form or a report by clicking their Close buttons (☒).

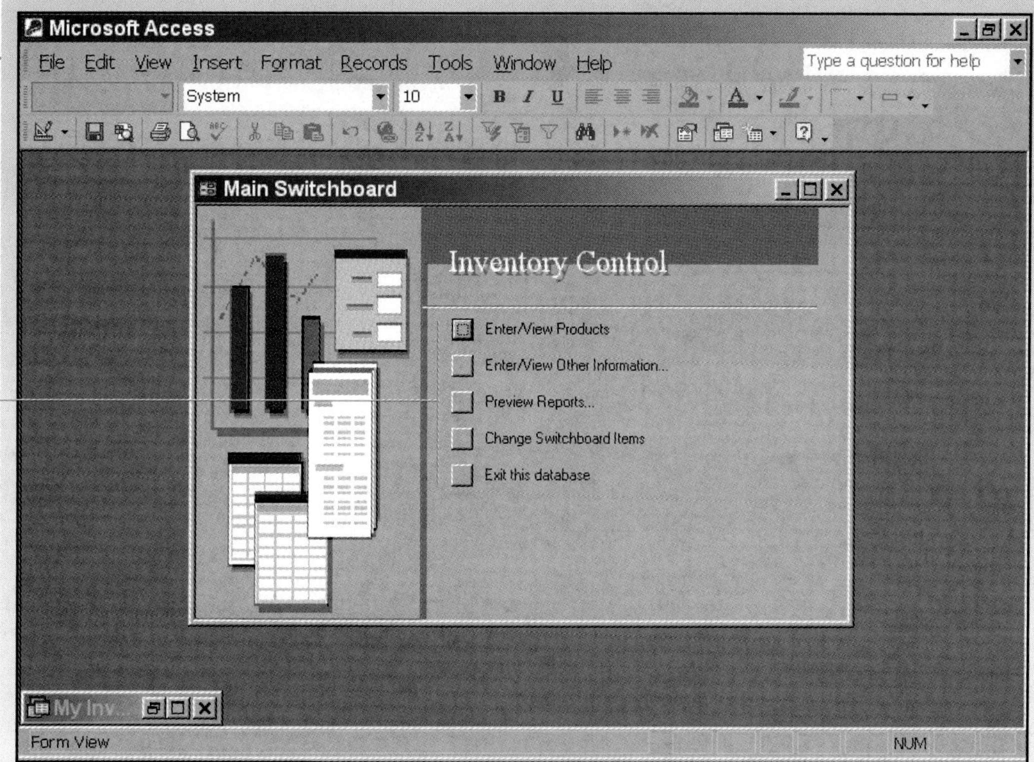

Figure 2.10

Main Switchboard for the Inventory Control application

Menu buttons on the Main Switchboard

15. Let's examine the database objects that were created by the Database Wizard for this application. From the Menu bar:
CHOOSE: Window, My Inventory : Database (Access 2000 file format)

16. In the Database window, click on the various buttons in the Objects bar to view the table, query, form, and report objects. You may need to scroll the list area or adjust the size of the Database window to see all of the object names. When you are finished, close the application:
CLICK: the Close button (☒) for the Database window
Notice that the Main Switchboard, which appears as a form object, also disappears when you close the Database window.

In Addition ACCESSING OTHER DATABASE TEMPLATES

Besides the templates that ship with Microsoft Office XP, additional templates are available for free on the Internet. For example, in the New File task pane, clicking the *Templates on Microsoft.com* option launches a Microsoft Web page in your default browser. Before creating a new database from scratch, you can peruse these templates to search for a possible starting point and save yourself some time.

2.1. What two objects are most closely associated with the output of a database application?

Access

2.2 Creating a Simple Table

An Access database file is simply a container for storing database objects. After creating an empty database structure, the next step is to define the table objects for storing data. Each table in your database should contain information about a single topic or subject. In an automobile industry database, for example, one table may contain a list of car dealerships while another table contains a list of manufacturers. Although these tables deal with different subjects, they are both related to the automobile industry. In this module, you learn two methods for quickly populating a database structure with table objects. What these methods may lack in power and flexibility, they make up for in ease of use and speed.

2.2.1 Creating a Table Using the Table Wizard

feature

Access provides the **Table Wizard** to help you create a table structure, much like you created a complete application using the Database Wizard. Rather than defining a new table from scratch, you compile it by picking and choosing fields from existing personal and business tables. This method lets you quickly populate an empty database structure with reliable and usable table objects.

method

In the Database window, select the *Tables* button and then:

- DOUBLE-CLICK: Create table by using wizard,

or

- CLICK: New button (New) on the Database window toolbar
- DOUBLE-CLICK: Table Wizard in the New Table dialog box

practice

After displaying a new database, you create a table object using the Table Wizard. Ensure that no Database window is displayed.

1. To create a new database using the New File task pane:
CLICK: New button () on the toolbar
CLICK: Blank Database, under the *New* heading in the task pane

2. In the File New Database dialog box that appears, use the Places bar or the *Save in* drop-down list box to select your personal storage location. Then, select the name that appears in the *File name* text box using the mouse.

3. TYPE: **My Business** into the *File name* text box to replace the existing filename
CLICK: Create command button
The My Business Database window will appear.

4. Your next step is to add table objects to the empty database structure. To use the Table Wizard, ensure that the *Tables* button is selected in the Objects bar and then do the following:
DOUBLE-CLICK: Create table by using wizard
The Table Wizard dialog box appears, as shown in Figure 2.11.

Figure 2.11

Table Wizard dialog box

Select a category in order to display tables appropriate for your needs.

Select one of the prebuilt tables to display the fields that are available.

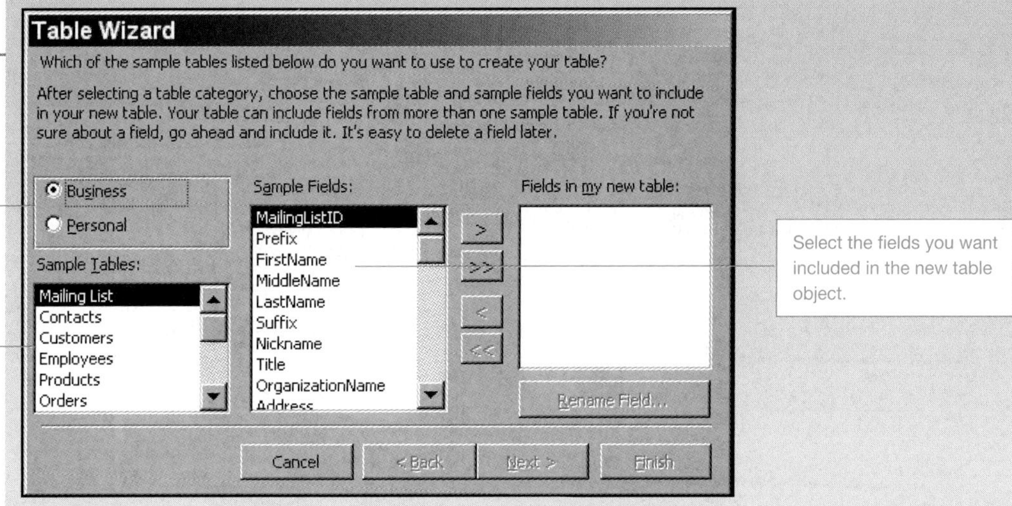

Select the fields you want included in the new table object.

5. By default, the *Business* option button is chosen in the Table Wizard dialog box. As a result, only business-related table structures appear in the *Sample Tables* list box. To view the Personal tables:
CLICK: *Personal* option button

6. On your own, scroll the *Sample Tables* list box to view the available table structures.

7. Let's create a new table to store the company's product information.
CLICK: *Business* option button
SELECT: Products in the *Sample Tables* list box
Notice that the fields for this table structure now appear in the *Sample Fields* list box, as shown here.

8. To specify fields for your new table, select individual field names in the *Sample Fields* list box and then click › to move them to the *Fields in my new table* list box. You can also select all fields by clicking ». For this step, let's include all of the suggested fields:
CLICK: Include All button (»)

9. To proceed to the next step:
CLICK: Next >
Your screen should now appear similar to Figure 2.12.

Access

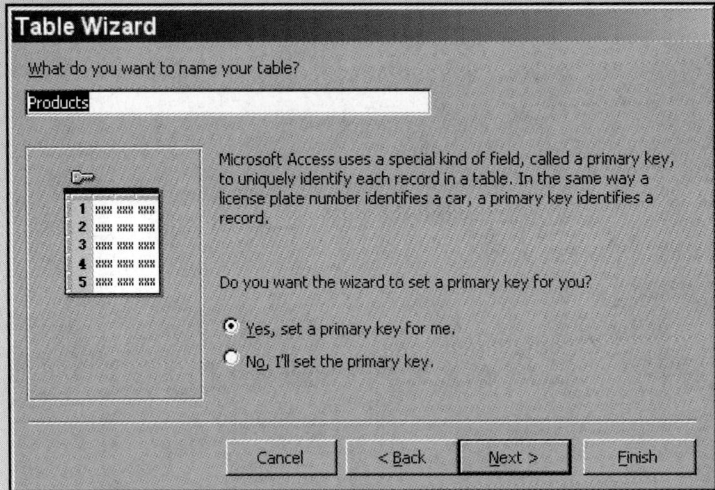

Figure 2.12

Specifying a table name in the Table Wizard dialog box

10. Let's accept the default selections in this dialog box and proceed to the next step:
CLICK: Next >

11. Ensure that the *Enter data directly into the table* option button is selected in the final dialog box and then do the following:
CLICK: Finish
The new table, called "Products," appears in a Datasheet window ready to accept data, as shown in Figure 2.13.

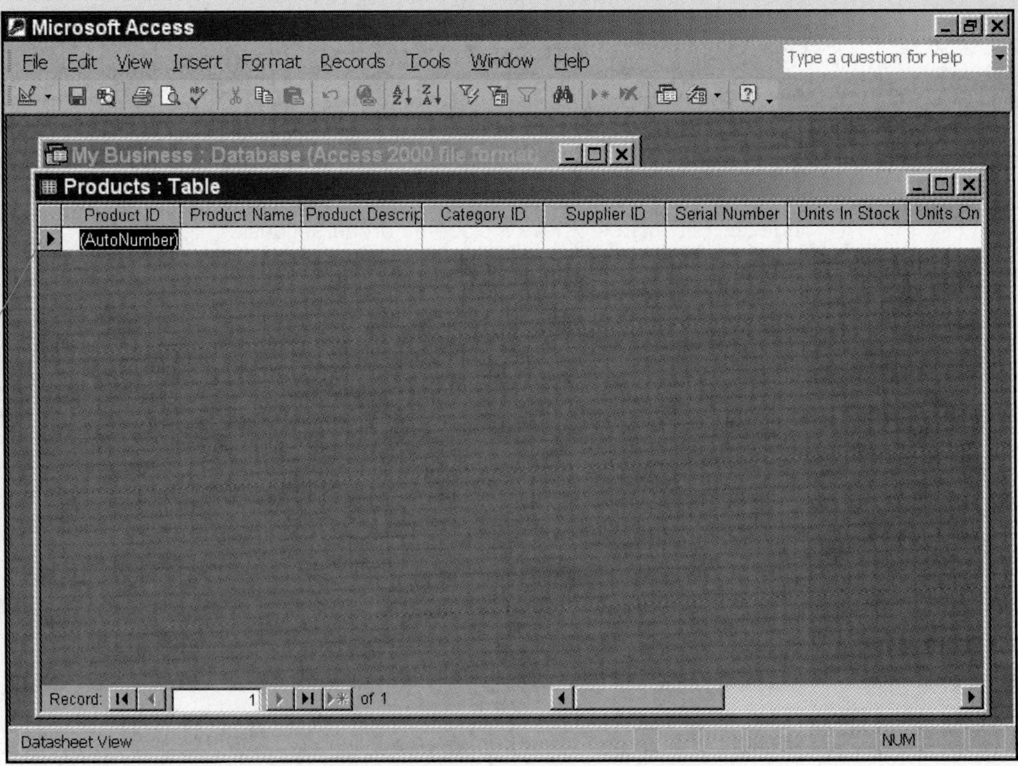

Figure 2.13

Products Datasheet window

The new Products table is displayed in Datasheet view so that you can begin entering data.

12. Close the Products Datasheet window. You should now see the Products table object in the Database window.

2.2.2 Creating a Table in Datasheet View

feature

Using Datasheet view, you create a table by typing information into a blank datasheet, just as you would when entering data into an Excel worksheet. When you save the table, Access creates the table structure and assigns the proper data types to each field based on the information you've entered. This method lets novice users create tables without an in-depth understanding of table structures and data types.

method

In the Database window, select the *Tables* button and then:

- DOUBLE-CLICK: Create table by entering data,

or

- CLICK: New button (New) on the Database window toolbar
- DOUBLE-CLICK: Datasheet View in the New Table dialog box

practice

In this lesson, you create a new table in Datasheet view for storing supplier information. Ensure that you have completed the previous lesson and that the My Business Database window is displayed.

1. To create a table using Datasheet view, ensure that the *Tables* button is selected in the Objects bar and then do the following:
   DOUBLE-CLICK: Create table by entering data
   A blank Datasheet window appears with several field columns and blank records.

2. Let's begin by renaming the column headings in the field header area. Using the column select pointer of the mouse (⬇):
   DOUBLE-CLICK: Field1
   The field or column name appears selected in the field header row, as shown here.

   Table1 : Table
   Field1 | Field2

3. Now type the new field name:
   TYPE: **SupplierID**
   PRESS: ENTER
   The new field name, SupplierID, appears in the field header area.

4. To continue renaming fields in the Datasheet window:
   DOUBLE-CLICK: Field2
   TYPE: **Company**
   DOUBLE-CLICK: Field3
   TYPE: **Contact**
   DOUBLE-CLICK: Field4
   TYPE: **Phone**
   PRESS: ENTER
   The cursor should now appear in the first field of the first record.

5. On your own, enter the two records appearing in Figure 2.14.

Figure 2.14

Entering records in Datasheet view

Table1 : Table

SupplierID	Company	Contact	Phone	Field5	Field6	Field7	F
ABCM	ABC Metals	Jane Hillman	555-9645				
ROSI	Rosie's Café	Jean Arnston	555-7750				

6. To save and name the new table structure:
CLICK: Save button (💾) on the toolbar
TYPE: **Suppliers** into the Save As dialog box
PRESS: ENTER or CLICK: OK
An Alert dialog box appears, as shown in Figure 2.15.

Figure 2.15

Defining a new table based on the contents of a datasheet

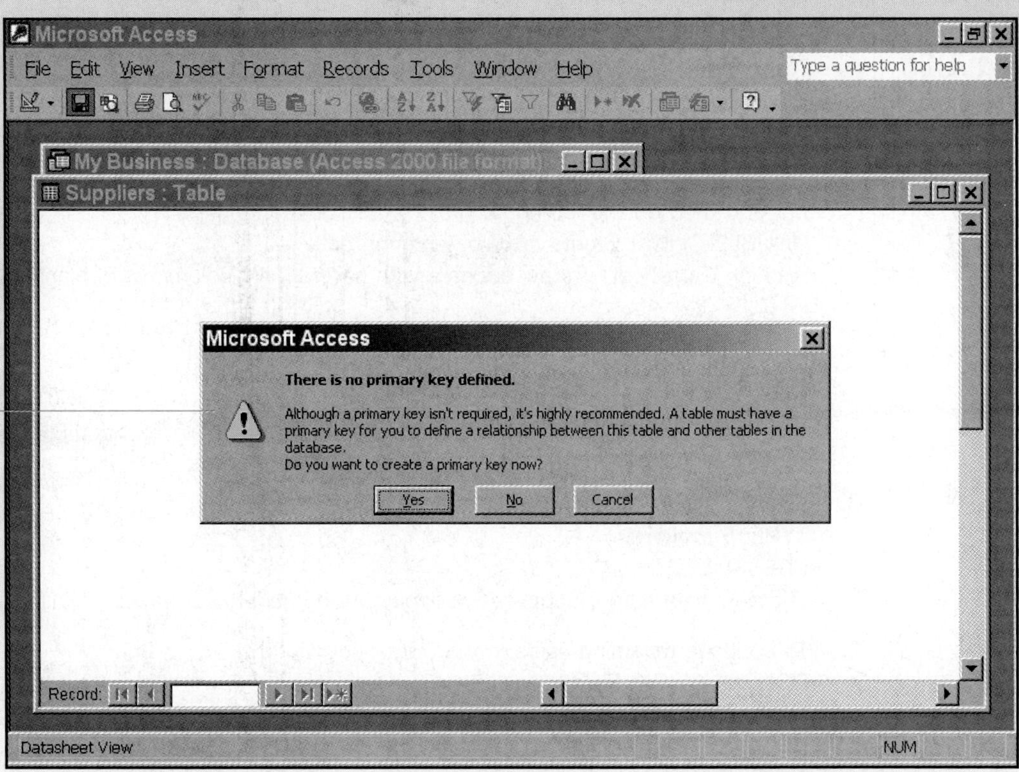

Access offers to define a primary key for the table. A primary key holds a unique value for identifying, locating, and sorting records in a table.

7. In response to the Alert dialog box, let's allow Access to define a primary key for the table. Do the following:
CLICK: Yes command button
After a few moments, Access displays the datasheet for the Suppliers table, complete with a new AutoNumber primary key field in the left-hand column.

8. Close the Suppliers Datasheet window. You should now see the Suppliers table object in the Database window.
9. Close the Database window.

2.2. How do you specify the name of a field when creating a table in Datasheet view?

2.3 Using the Table Design View

If all of your database needs are satisfied by the templates found in the Database and Table Wizards, you are already on your way to developing desktop database applications that are robust. To unlock the real power behind Access, however, you must delve into the inner workings of an Access table structure. Using Design view, you create a table by specifying its properties, characteristics, and behaviors down to the field level. Although this method requires the greatest understanding of database design, it is well worth the effort in terms of creating efficient custom table structures.

2.3.1 Creating a Table in Design View

feature

Table Design view allows you to get down to the nuts and bolts of designing and constructing a table. In Design view, you create the table structure manually, specifying the field names, data types, and indexes. After some practice, you will find that this method affords the greatest power and flexibility in designing and modifying table objects.

method

In the Database window, select the *Tables* button and then:

- DOUBLE-CLICK: Create table in Design view,

or

- CLICK: New button (New) on the Database window toolbar
- DOUBLE-CLICK: Design View in the New Table dialog box

practice

In Design view, you create a new table structure in this lesson. Ensure that no Database window is displayed.

1. To create a new database using the New File task pane:
   CLICK: New button () on the toolbar
   CLICK: Blank Database, under the *New* heading in the task pane
2. In the File New Database dialog box that appears, use the Places bar or the *Save in* drop-down list box to select your personal storage location. Then, select the name that appears in the *File name* text box using the mouse.

Access

3. TYPE: **My Library** into the *File name text box* to replace the existing filename
CLICK: Create command button
The My Library Database window will appear.

4. Because tables are the foundation for all your queries, forms, and reports, you need to create at least one table before creating any other database object. To add a new table to the database:
CLICK: New button (New) on the Database window toolbar
The New Table dialog box (Figure 2.16) offers an alternative to selecting a New Object shortcut in the list area of the Database window.

Figure 2.16

New Table dialog box

5. DOUBLE-CLICK: Design View
The table Design window (Figure 2.17), which is divided into a **Field Grid pane** and a **Field Properties pane,** appears in **Design view.** This window is used to add, delete, and rename fields for the table structure; set a field's data type; specify a field's properties or characteristics; and choose a primary key for organizing and sorting a table.

6. To define the first field in the table, ensure that the insertion point appears in the *Field Name* column and then do the following:
TYPE: **BookID**
PRESS: TAB to move to the *Data Type* column
Your screen should now appear similar to Figure 2.17. (*Note:* Access provides specific rules for naming fields in a table. First, names cannot exceed 64 characters in length. Second, names should not contain special symbols or punctuation, such as a period or exclamation point. And third, names cannot begin with a space and, in our opinion, should not contain spaces. Descriptive single-word names are best.)

Figure 2.17

Table Design window

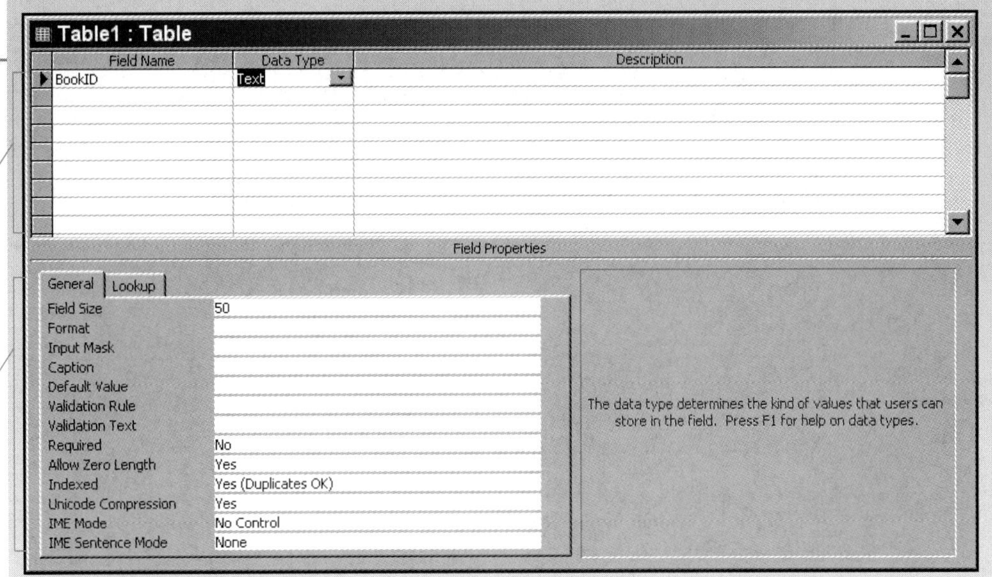

Use the Field Grid pane to define the fields that you want in the table.

When a field is selected in the Field Grid pane, the Field Properties pane is used to display and set its characteristics, such as size and display format.

7. By default, Access inserts "Text" as the data type for the BookID field. The data type you select determines the kind of values that you will be able to enter into the field. To view the other data type options, described further in Table 2.1, do the following:
CLICK: down arrow attached to the field
The drop-down list shown here is displayed.

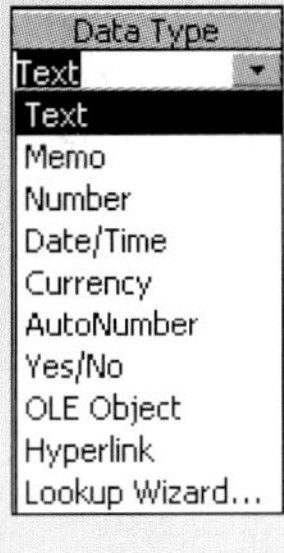

8. For the BookID field's data type:
SELECT: AutoNumber
PRESS: TAB

Table 2.1

Data Types

Type	Description
Text	Alphanumeric data, up to 255 characters. Used for entering text and numbers that are not required for calculation, such as zip codes and phone numbers.
Memo	Alphanumeric data, up to 65,535 characters. Used to store notes, comments, or lengthy descriptions.
Number	Numeric data that are used to perform mathematical calculations.
Date/Time	Dates and times, in various formats.
Currency	Numeric data with a leading dollar sign. Used to store and calculate monetary values up to four decimal places.
AutoNumber	Numeric value that increments automatically. Used for assigning a unique value to a record, which makes it an ideal *primary key* field.
Yes/No	Logical or Boolean values for toggling (turning on and off) yes/no or true/false results.

Access

OLE Object	Object Linking and Embedding (OLE) field for storing objects (Excel worksheets and Word documents), graphics, or other binary data up to one gigabyte (GB) in size.
Hyperlink	Text or numbers stored as a hyperlink address. Used to store Web site addresses, also called URLs, such as http://www.advantageseries.com/.
Lookup Wizard	A link to another table or to a static list of values for inserting data into the current table. Selecting this option launches the Lookup Wizard.

9. The *Description* column allows you to store a helpful comment describing the contents of the field. This comment will also appear in the Status bar when you select the field in Datasheet view. To proceed:
   TYPE: **Unique code generated by Access**
   PRESS: ENTER to move to the next row

10. On your own, complete the Field Grid pane as displayed in Figure 2.18. Notice that the longer field names, such as AuthorSurname, contain mixed case letters to enhance their readability. When finished, keep the table Design window displayed and proceed to the next lesson.

Figure 2.18

Completing the Field Grid pane

Row selection area of the Field Grid pane

Table1 : Table

Field Name	Data Type	Description
BookID	AutoNumber	Unique code generated by Access
ISBN	Text	International Standard Book Number
Title	Text	Main cover title
AuthorSurname	Text	Author's last name
AuthorGiven	Text	Author's first name
Publisher	Text	Publisher's name
PubYear	Number	Year published (e.g., 2002)
PageCount	Number	Total number of pages

In Addition FIELD NAMING CONVENTIONS

Besides the Access rules for naming fields, some naming conventions are used by programmers to convey specific information about fields and database objects. For example, the prefix "str" is often used to denote a string data type (such as strName) and the prefix "bln" is used to name a Boolean Yes/No field (such as blnMailingList). Furthermore, a group of database objects may be named tblBooks (table), qryBooks (query), frmBooks (form), and rptBooks (report) to describe the different types of objects related to a single subject. The important concept here is to remain consistent in whatever naming scheme you select.

2.3.2 Assigning a Primary Key

feature

As part of creating a table structure, you need to specify a field (or fields) that will uniquely identify each and every record in the table. This field, called the **primary key,** is used by Access in searching for data and in establishing relationships between tables. Once a field is defined as the primary key, its datasheet is automatically indexed, or sorted, into order by that field. Access also prevents you from entering a duplicate value or a **null value** (nothing) into a primary key field. An **AutoNumber** data type automatically increments sequentially as each new record is added to a table, making this data type one of the best choices for a primary key.

method

In table Design view:

- SELECT: the desired field using the row selection area
- CLICK: Primary Key button (🔑) on the toolbar,

or

- CHOOSE: Edit, Primary Key

practice

You now assign a primary key field for the table created in the last lesson. Ensure that you've completed the previous lesson and that the table Design window is displayed.

1. To select a field for the primary key:
   CLICK: row selector button for BookID
   (*Hint:* Position the mouse pointer in the row selection area of the Field Grid pane and click the row selector button next to the BookID field.)

2. To assign a primary key:
   CLICK: Primary Key button (🔑)
   Your screen should now appear similar to Figure 2.19.

Figure 2.19

Setting the primary key

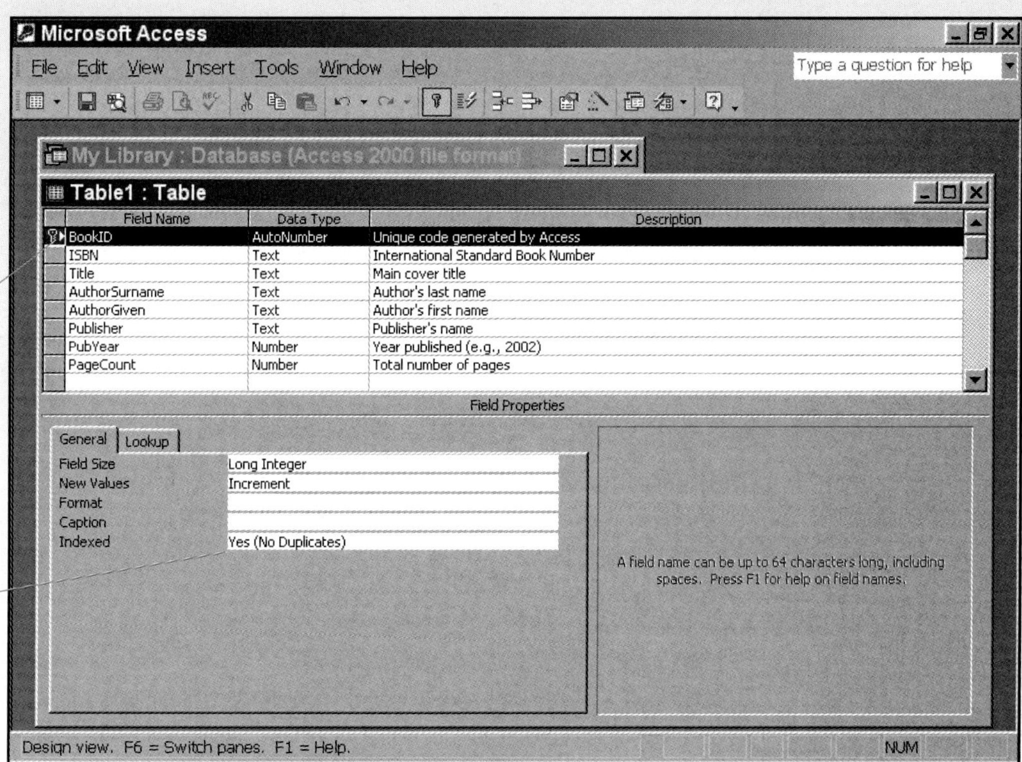

Selecting a field in the Field Grid pane and then making it the primary key field for the table.

Notice that the field is indexed (sorted) and does not allow duplicate entries.

3. Now that you've assigned the primary key, you can save the table structure. Do the following:
CLICK: Save button ()

4. In the Save As dialog box that appears:
TYPE: **Books**
PRESS: ENTER or CLICK: OK
Keep the table Design window displayed for use in the next lesson.

2.3.3 Defining and Removing Indexes

feature

An **index,** like the primary key, is a special mechanism for dynamically organizing and ordering the data stored in a table. By defining indexes, you can speed up the search and sort operations for running queries and reports. However, you do not want to create indexes for all fields, as this would slow down the common activities of adding and editing records. As a rule, just index the fields that you use frequently in searching for and sorting data, such as a Surname or Company Name field.

method

To define an index in table Design view:

- SELECT: the desired field using the row selection area
- SELECT: *Indexed* text box in the Field Properties pane
- CLICK: down arrow attached to the *Indexed* text box
- SELECT: an indexing option

To remove an index in table Design view:

- CLICK: Indexes button () on the toolbar
- RIGHT-CLICK: the desired field's row selector button
- CHOOSE: Delete Rows

practice

In this lesson, you create two indexes to complement the primary key and remove an existing index that was created by Access. Ensure that you've completed the previous lessons and that the Design window for the Books table is displayed.

1. Most people search for a book based on its title or author. Therefore, let's create indexes for these fields in the Books table. To begin:
SELECT: Title row selector button in the Field Grid pane

2. Using the I-beam mouse pointer:
CLICK: in the *Indexed* text box in the Field Properties pane
You should now see a drop-down arrow attached to the text box.

3. With the flashing insertion point in the *Indexed* text box, you may select an indexing option from the drop-down list box. To proceed:
CLICK: down arrow attached to the *Indexed* text box
Your screen should now appear similar to Figure 2.20.

Setting an index

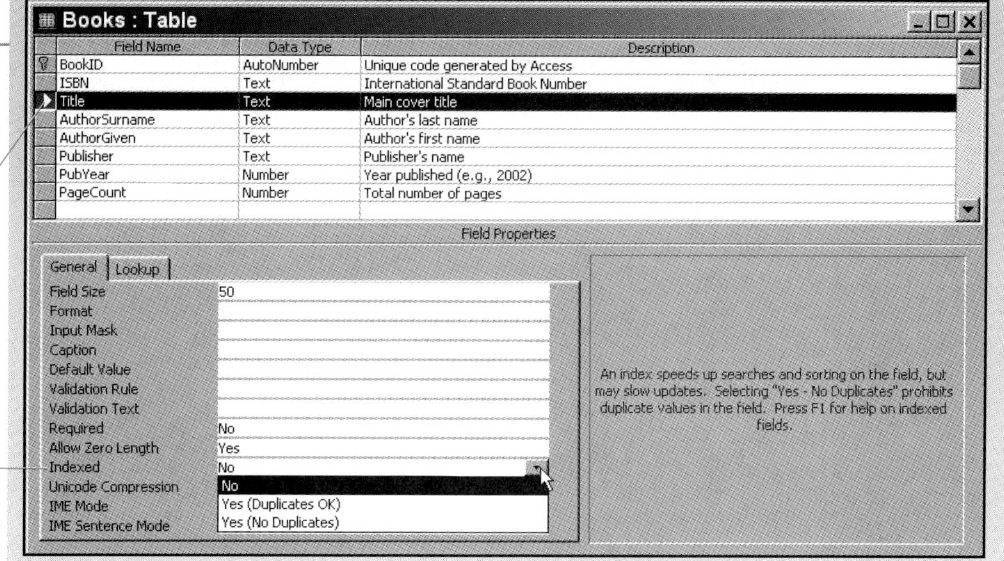

4. Because you do not want to limit the possibility of duplicate entries (different authors may have written books with the same title):
SELECT: Yes (Duplicates OK)

5. Let's define another index for the table:
SELECT: AuthorSurname in the Field Grid pane
CLICK: in the *Indexed* text box in the Field Properties pane

6. From the drop-down list attached to the *Indexed* text box:
SELECT: Yes (Duplicates OK)

7. Save the table structure:
CLICK: Save button ( )
(*Note:* It's a good habit to save the table after each major change.)

8. To display the associated indexes for the Books table:
CLICK: Indexes button ( )
The Indexes window appears as shown in Figure 2.21.

Indexes window for the Books table

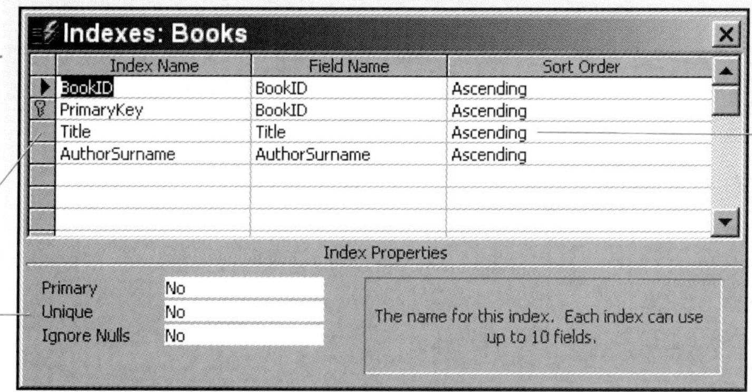

Access

9. As illustrated in Figure 2.21, Access automatically creates indexes for fields that contain the letters "ID" in their names. The BookID field, for example, is the primary key but also the name of an index. To remove the BookID index using the row select mouse pointer (➡):
RIGHT-CLICK: BookID row selector button

10. In the right-click menu that appears:
CHOOSE: Delete Rows
The BookID index is removed but the BookID primary key remains.

11. Close the Indexes window.

12. To clean up the Access work area, save and then close the table Design window. Finally, close the My Library Database window.

In Addition **SETTING FIELD PROPERTIES**

Every field in a table has a set of properties. A field property is a specific characteristic of a field or data type that enables you to provide greater control over how your data is entered, stored, displayed, and printed. Some common properties include *Field Size, Format, Decimal Places, Input Mask, Default Value, Required,* and *Indexed.* You set a field's properties using the Field Properties pane in the table Design window.

2.3. What is an AutoNumber field? Why is it useful as a primary key?

2.4 Modifying a Table

A database is a dynamic entity. It is not uncommon for the initial design requirements to change once a database is set in front of users. Fortunately, Access enables you to modify a table's structure quickly and efficiently. Adding, deleting, and changing field specifications in table Design view are similar to editing records in a datasheet. Nonetheless, you should not perform structural changes hastily. When you modify a table's structure, you also affect any forms and reports that are based on the table.

2.4.1 Inserting and Deleting Fields

feature

After displaying a table structure in Design view, you can easily add and remove fields. Adding a field is as simple as entering a field name and data type on a blank row in the Field Grid pane. Removing a field deletes the field from the Field Grid pane, but also deletes all the data stored in the field.

method

To insert a field in table Design view:

- SELECT: an empty row in the Field Grid pane
- Type a field name, select a data type, and enter a description.

To delete a field in table Design view:

- RIGHT-CLICK: row selector of the field you want to remove
- CHOOSE: Delete Rows

In this lesson, you insert and remove fields in an existing table structure. Ensure that no Database window is displayed.

1. Open the database named AC0240, located in your Advantage student data files location.
2. This database contains a single table object, named Books, that is based on the table structure you created in the last module. To display the table in Datasheet view:
   DOUBLE-CLICK: Books
   Your screen should now appear similar to Figure 2.22.

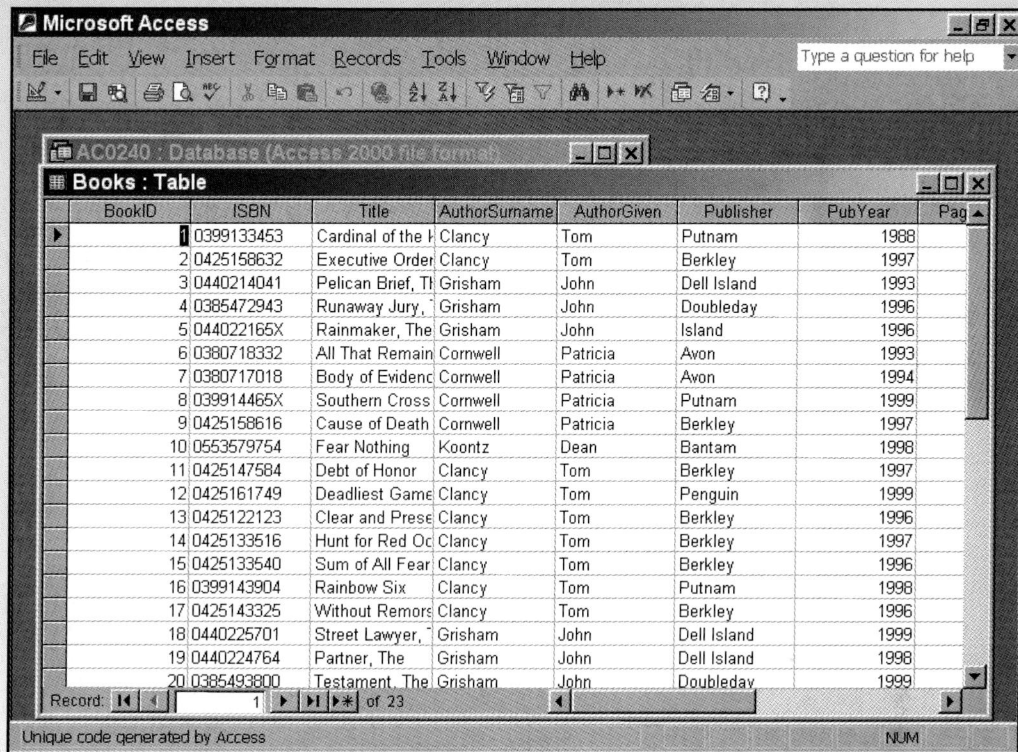

BookID	ISBN	Title	AuthorSurname	AuthorGiven	Publisher	PubYear	Pag
1	0399133453	Cardinal of the I	Clancy	Tom	Putnam	1988	
2	0425158632	Executive Order	Clancy	Tom	Berkley	1997	
3	0440214041	Pelican Brief, Th	Grisham	John	Dell Island	1993	
4	0385472943	Runaway Jury,	Grisham	John	Doubleday	1996	
5	044022165X	Rainmaker, The	Grisham	John	Island	1996	
6	0380718332	All That Remain	Cornwell	Patricia	Avon	1993	
7	0380717018	Body of Evidenc	Cornwell	Patricia	Avon	1994	
8	039914465X	Southern Cross	Cornwell	Patricia	Putnam	1999	
9	0425158616	Cause of Death	Cornwell	Patricia	Berkley	1997	
10	0553579754	Fear Nothing	Koontz	Dean	Bantam	1998	
11	0425147584	Debt of Honor	Clancy	Tom	Berkley	1997	
12	0425161749	Deadliest Game	Clancy	Tom	Penguin	1999	
13	0425122123	Clear and Prese	Clancy	Tom	Berkley	1996	
14	0425133516	Hunt for Red Oc	Clancy	Tom	Berkley	1997	
15	0425133540	Sum of All Fear	Clancy	Tom	Berkley	1996	
16	0399143904	Rainbow Six	Clancy	Tom	Putnam	1998	
17	0425143325	Without Remors	Clancy	Tom	Berkley	1996	
18	0440225701	Street Lawyer,	Grisham	John	Dell Island	1999	
19	0440224764	Partner, The	Grisham	John	Dell Island	1998	
20	0385493800	Testament, The	Grisham	John	Doubleday	1999	

Figure 2.22

Displaying the Books datasheet

3. With the Datasheet window displayed:
   CLICK: View—Design button on the toolbar
   (*Note:* Although the toolbar button is named View, we include the mode name "—Design" for clarity.)
4. Let's add a new field to the table structure that will store a reviewer's synopsis for each book. In the Field Grid pane:
   CLICK: in the *Field Name* column of the next empty row, so that the insertion point appears as shown here

   PageCount

5. Now enter the new field name:
   TYPE: **Synopsis**
   PRESS: TAB
6. Since the contents of the field will be entered mostly in paragraph form, select Memo as the field's data type:
   CLICK: down arrow attached to the *Data Type* cell
   SELECT: Memo
   PRESS: TAB

7. In the *Description* column:
TYPE: **Reviewer's synopsis or abstract**
PRESS: ENTER
The field information should appear as shown below.

8. You can insert a new field between two existing fields by right-clicking the desired row selector button and choosing the Insert Rows command. Similarly, you can delete an existing field using the right-click menu. To demonstrate, let's remove the PageCount field:
RIGHT-CLICK: row selector button for PageCount
Your screen should now appear similar to Figure 2.23.

Figure 2.23

Displaying a field's right-click menu

Right-click menu for the PageCount field

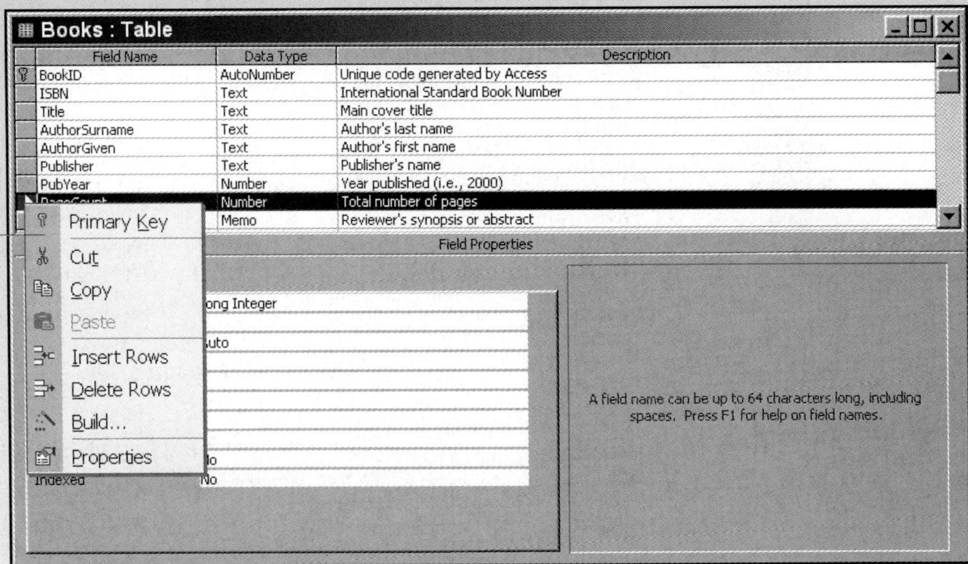

9. From the right-click menu:
CHOOSE: Delete Rows
An Alert confirmation dialog box appears, as shown below.

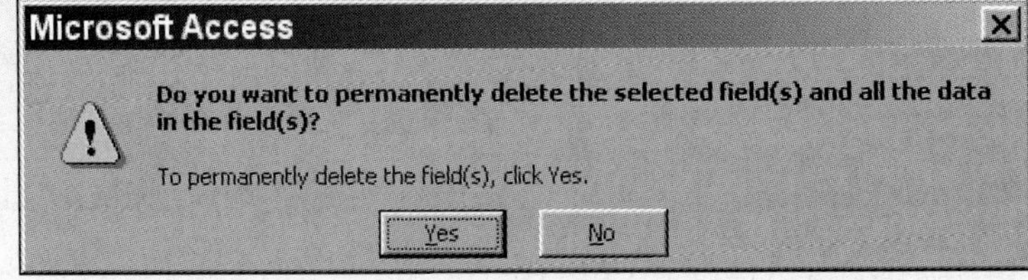

10. To confirm that the deletion will also remove all the data in the field:
CLICK: Yes command button

11. Let's save the table before proceeding:
CLICK: Save button ( )

12. Now switch back to the Datasheet window:
CLICK: View - Datasheet button

13. To enter a brief synopsis for the first record:

PRESS: END to move to the last field column
PRESS: SHIFT+F2 to zoom the window
Your screen should now appear similar to Figure 2.24.

Figure 2.24

Using the Zoom window to enter data into a memo field

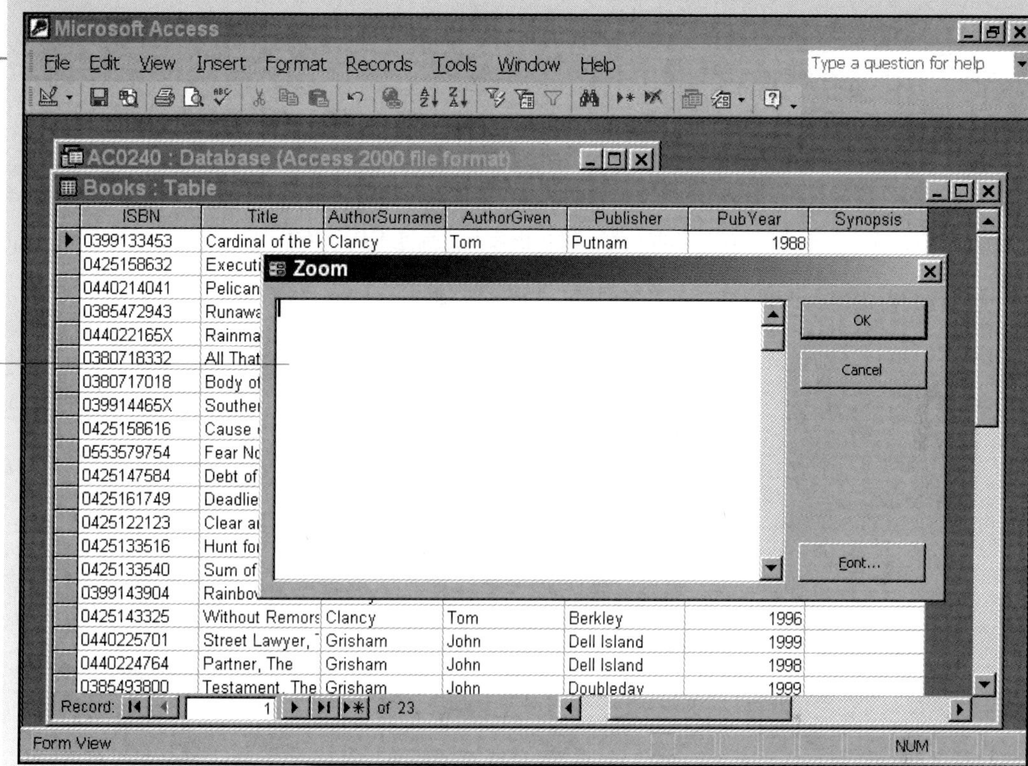

Entering a memo using the Zoom window, accessed by pressing SHIFT + F2

14. TYPE: **Another thrilling novel about Soviet and American attempts to develop a Strategic Defense Initiative (SDI). A CIA undercover confidant named the Cardinal provides a steady stream of Soviet secrets. Once compromised, however, the Cardinal must be pulled to safety, a task assigned to Jack Ryan and John Clark, an ex-Navy SEAL.**

15. To complete the entry and save the record:
CLICK: OK command button
PRESS: ↓ to move to the next record

16. Close the Datasheet window.

2.4.2 Renaming and Moving Fields

feature

In addition to modifying a table's structure, renaming and moving fields in Design view affects the display of a datasheet. You may have noticed that the columns in Datasheet view follow the field names and display order appearing in Design view. More importantly, however, you can speed up most database operations by moving frequently used fields (those used as primary keys or in indexes) to the top of a table structure.

method 

- To rename a field, edit the contents of the *Field Name* column as you would modify a cell entry in a datasheet.
- To move a field, click the field's row selector button and then drag it to the target location.

practice

You now practice renaming and moving fields in table Design view. Ensure that the AC0240 Database window is displayed.

1. To display the Books table object in Design view:
   SELECT: Books in the list area, if it is not already selected
   CLICK: Design button (Design) on the Database window toolbar
2. Let's rename the Author fields. Using the I-beam mouse pointer:
   CLICK: to the right of "AuthorSurname" in the *Field Name* column
   The flashing insertion point should appear to the right of the name.
3. To remove the "Surname" portion of the cell entry:
   PRESS: BACKSPACE seven times
4. TYPE: **Last**
   The cell entry should now read "AuthorLast," as shown here with the insertion point.
   AuthorLast
5. To complete the entry:
   PRESS: ↓
6. To remove the "Given" portion of the "AuthorGiven" field name:
   PRESS: F2 (Edit mode)
   PRESS: BACKSPACE five times
   TYPE: **First**
   The cell entry now reads "AuthorFirst."
   AuthorFirst
7. To complete the entry:
   PRESS: ↓
   Your screen should now appear similar to Figure 2.25.

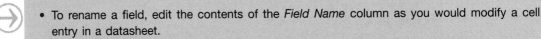

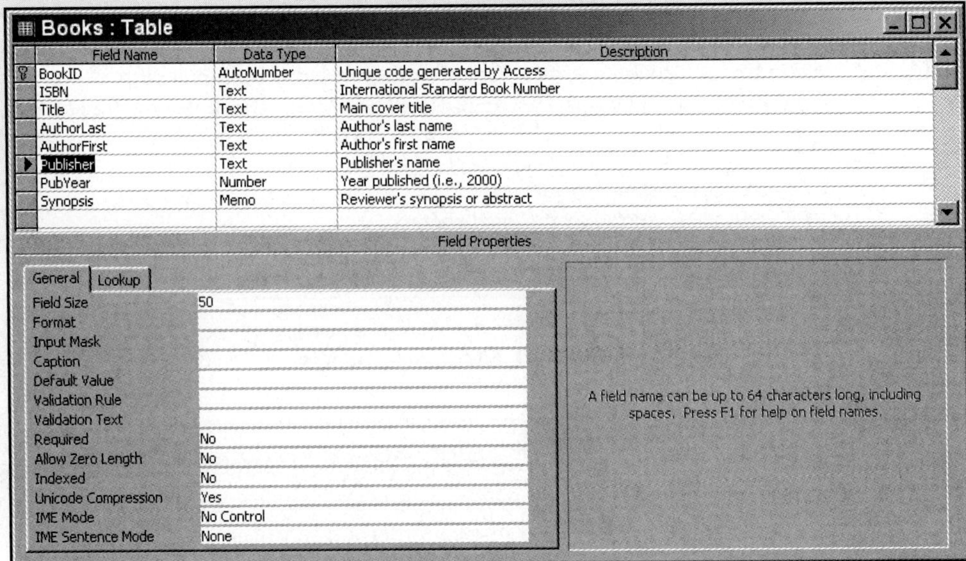

Figure 2.25

Renaming fields in the Field Grid pane

8. Let's move the ISBN field below the AuthorFirst field. To begin:
CLICK: row selector button for ISBN

9. Using the arrow mouse pointer:
DRAG: row selector button for ISBN downward until a bold gridline appears below the AuthorFirst field

10. Release the mouse button. Your screen should now appear similar to Figure 2.26.

Figure 2.26

Moving the ISBN field in the Field Grid pane

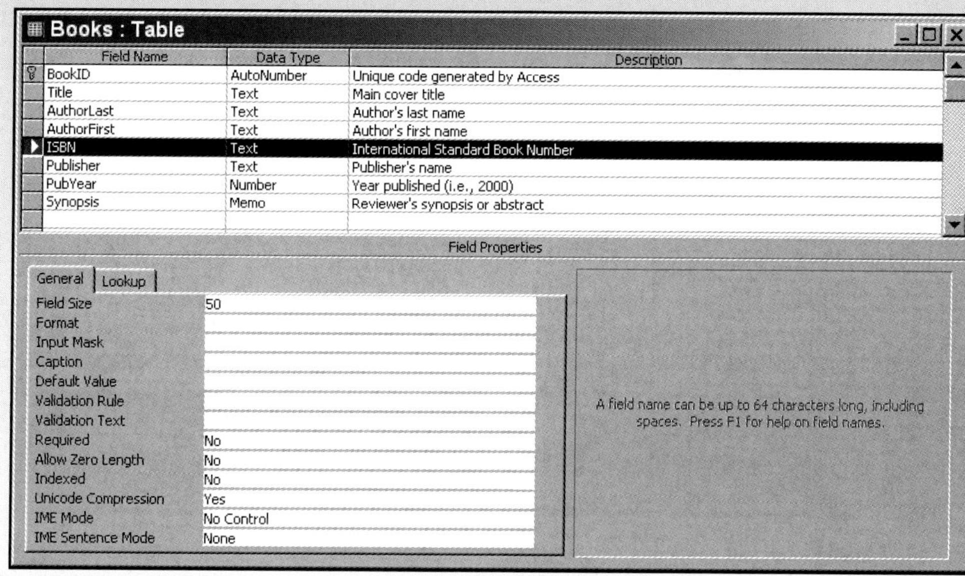

11. To save and then view the changes in Datasheet view:
CLICK: Save button (💾)
CLICK: View - Datasheet button (▦)
Notice that the field header area displays the new field names in the modified field order.

12. Close the Datasheet window.

2.4.3 Printing a Table's Design Structure

feature

Access provides a special tool called the **Documenter** that allows you to preview and print various design characteristics of your database objects, including a table's structure and field properties. This tool is especially useful when you are planning or revising a table's field specifications.

method

- CHOOSE: Tools, Analyze, Documenter
- CLICK: *Tables* tab
- SELECT: the desired object or objects
- CLICK: Options command button
- SELECT: the desired options
- CLICK: OK command button to preview the report
- CLICK: Print button (🖨) on the toolbar.

practice →

In this lesson, you prepare a documentation printout of the Books table. Ensure that the AC0240 Database window is displayed.

1. Before launching the Access Documenter, ensure that the Books table appears selected in the Database window. Then, do the following:
CHOOSE: Tools, Analyze, Documenter
The Documenter window appears as shown in Figure 2.27.

Figure 2.27

Documenter window

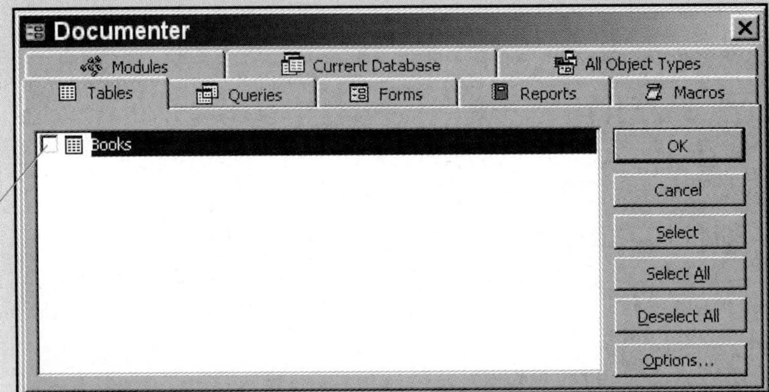

Click the check box to include an object in the Documenter's report.

2. To print the design structure for the Books table object, ensure that the *Tables* tab is selected and then:
SELECT: Books check box so that a ✓ appears

3. To specify the report options for the Documenter:
CLICK: Options command button
The Print Table Definition dialog box appears, as shown in Figure 2.28.

Figure 2.28

Print Table Definition dialog box

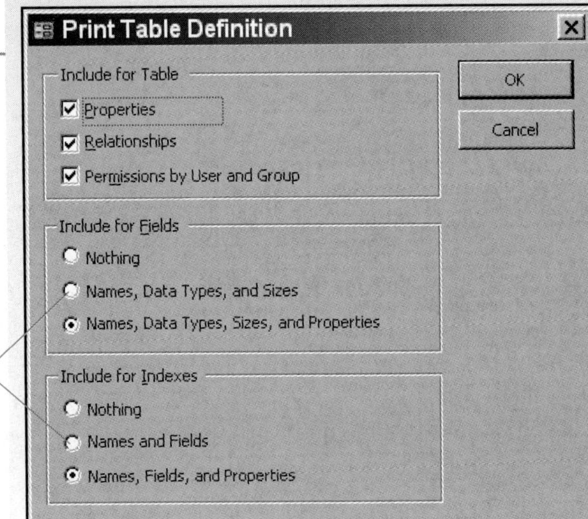

These items will be selected in the next few steps.

4. For this example, let's specify that only the table structure is printed. In the *Include for Table* area, remove all the selections so that no ✓ appears in any of the check boxes.

5. In the *Include for Fields* area:
SELECT: *Names, Data Types, and Sizes* option button

6. In the *Include for Indexes* area:
SELECT: *Names and Fields* option button
CLICK: OK command button

7. To preview the report printout:
CLICK: OK command button

8. To maximize the report's Object Definition window:
CLICK: its Maximize button (□)

9. On your own, move, size, and scroll the Object Definition window to make it appear similar to Figure 2.29.

Figure 2.29

The maximized Object Definition window

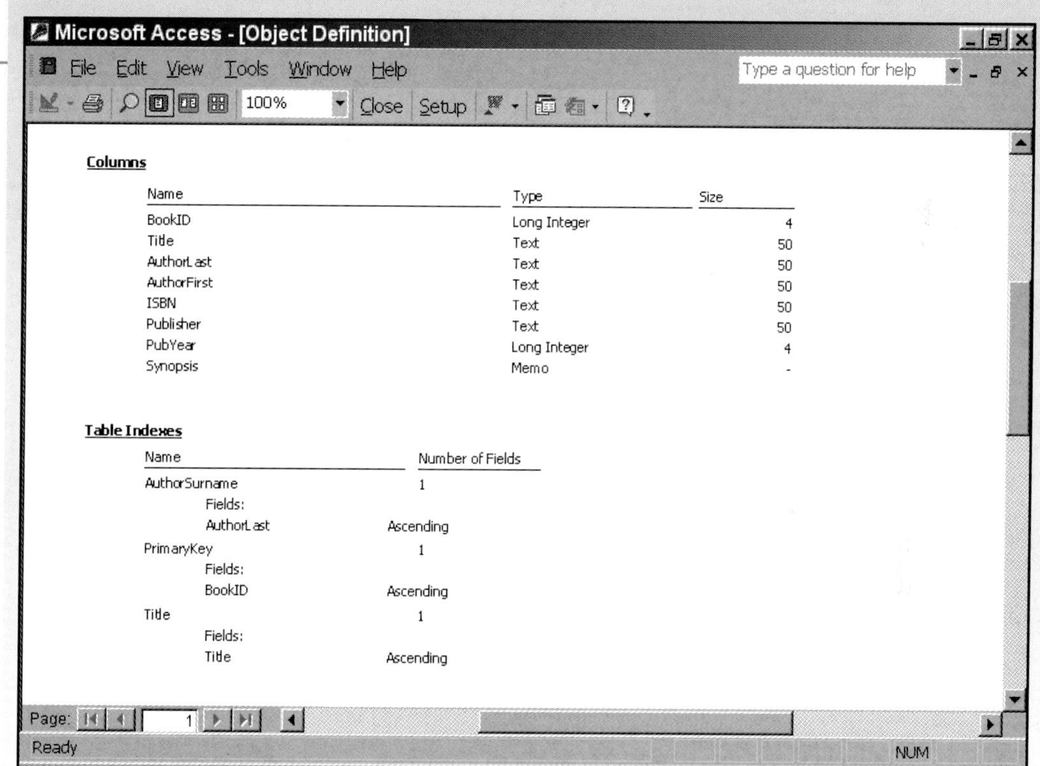

10. To print the documentation report:
CLICK: Print button (🖨) on the toolbar

11. To restore the Object Definition window to the smaller size:
CLICK: its Restore button (🗗)

12. Close the Object Definition window. Then, close the AC0240 Database window.

2.4. What happens to your table's data if you delete a field in table Design view?

Chapter summary

Microsoft Access 2002 provides several tools to help novice users create new database applications. The Database Wizard offers a variety of professionally designed template solutions for common database problems. After you proceed through a few simple steps in the wizard, Access creates a comprehensive set of database objects, including tables, forms, and reports, that you can put to use immediately. If you prefer having more control, you can opt to create an empty database and then populate it with standard tables using the Table Wizard. Another straightforward method involves designing a table simply by entering data into a Datasheet window. Or you can use Design view in order to develop a custom table object. In the table Design window, you add, delete, rename, move, and manipulate fields and indexes individually, in addition to specifying each field's properties and characteristics. The Documenter helps you quickly document the design of database objects.

Command Summary

Many of the commands and procedures appearing in this chapter are summarized in the following table.

Skill Set	To Perform This Task	Do the Following. . .
Creating and Using Databases	Create a new empty database.	CLICK: New button ( ) CLICK: Blank Database option, under the *New* heading in the New File task pane
	Create a comprehensive application using the Database Wizard	CLICK: New button ( ) CLICK: General Templates option, under the *New from template* heading in the New File task pane CLICK: *Databases* tab in the Templates dialog box DOUBLE-CLICK: a database wizard ( )
	Switch from Datasheet view to Design view	CLICK: View—Design button ( )
	Switch from Design view to Datasheet view	CLICK: View—Datasheet button ( )
	Launch the Documenter utility	CHOOSE: Tools, Analyze, Documenter
Creating and Modifying Tables	Create a table using the Table Wizard	SELECT: *Tables* object button DOUBLE-CLICK: Create table by using wizard
	Create a table in Datasheet view	SELECT: *Tables* object button DOUBLE-CLICK: Create table by entering data
	Create a table in Design view	SELECT: *Tables* object button DOUBLE-CLICK: Create table in Design view

Skill Set	To Perform This Task	Do the Following. . .
	Save the table structure in Design view	CLICK: Save button ( )
	Assign a primary key in Design view	SELECT: the desired field CLICK: Primary Key button ( )
	Add a new field in Design view	SELECT: an empty row in the Field Grid pane TYPE: field name
	Remove a field in Design view	RIGHT-CLICK: row selector for the desired field CHOOSE: Delete Rows
	Move a field in Design view	DRAG: a field's row selector button to its new location
	Define an index in Design view	SELECT: the desired field SELECT: an indexing option in the *Indexed* property text box
	Display the Indexes window	CLICK: Indexes button ( )
	Remove an index displayed in the Indexes window	RIGHT-CLICK: row selector for the desired Index field CHOOSE: Delete Rows

Key Terms

This section specifies page references for the key terms identified in this chapter. For a complete list of definitions, refer to the Glossary at the end of this learning guide.

AutoNumber, *p. 69*
Database Wizard, *p. 54*
Design view, *p. 66*
Documenter, *p. 77*
Field Grid pane, *p. 66*
Field Properties pane, *p. 66*
index, *p. 70*
null value, *p. 68*
primary key, *p. 68*
Table Wizard, *p. 60*

Access

Chapter Quiz

Short Answer

1. Name four Database Wizard templates that are available on your computer.
2. What is a switchboard?
3. Name the five steps to designing a better database.
4. Name three methods for creating a table in an Access database.
5. What are the two categories of Table Wizards?

6.. What data storage types can be defined in a table structure?

7. What is the difference between the Text and Memo data types?

8. How does a primary key differ from an index?

9. When would you want to insert a row in a table structure?

10. Why must you be careful when changing a field's data type?

True/False

1. ____ In creating a new database using a template, you select either the *General* or *Wizards* tab in the Templates dialog box.

2. ____ In the Database Wizard, the optional fields that you may select for inclusion appear in italic.

3. ____ The process of dividing related data into separate tables in order to reduce data redundancy is called *normalizing* your data.

4. ____ Like Word and Excel, you can open multiple Database windows in the Access work area.

5. ____ After selecting a sample table in the Table Wizard, you can specify only the fields that you want included in your new table.

6. ____ In table Design view, you define the names of fields in the Field Grid pane and select data types in the Field Properties pane.

7. ____ Field names cannot exceed 64 characters in length.

8. ____ What you type into the *Description* column of the Field Grid pane appears in the Title bar of a table's Datasheet window.

9. ____ Access prevents you from entering duplicate values into a primary key field.

10. ____ You print a table's structure using the Documenter tool.

Multiple Choice

1. In an application created using the Database Wizard, the main menu is presented as a ____________.
   a. form, called a *switchboard*
   b. report, called a *menu*
   c. table, called a *switchboard*
   d. query, called a *menu*

2. Which of the following is not a step presented in this chapter for designing a better database?
   a. Determine your input requirements.
   b. Test your database application.
   c. Create your tables using wizards.
   d. Determine your table structures.

3. You have the choice of either creating a table structure from scratch or using a(n) ____________ to lead you through the process.
   a. assistant
   b. coach
   c. relation
   d. wizard

4. Which data type would you use to store the price of an item within an inventory table?
   a. AutoNumber
   b. Currency
   c. Number
   d. Text

5. Which data type would you use to store a phone number?
   a. Currency
   b. Memo
   c. Number
   d. Text

6. What determines a table's sort order in a datasheet?
   a. AutoNumber field
   b. field order
   c. index field
   d. primary key

7. To display a window showing the table's primary key and indexes:
   a. CLICK: Indexes button ( )
   b. CLICK: Primary Key button ( )
   c. CLICK: View—Datasheet button ( )
   d. CLICK: View—Design button ( )

8. To delete a field in Design view, right-click the field's selector button and choose the following command:
   a. Delete Field
   b. Delete Rows
   c. Remove Field
   d. Remove Rows

9. You use this tool to generate a printout of a table's structure.
   a. Analyzer
   b. Designator
   c. Documenter
   d. Generator

10. When printing a table's structure, you use this dialog box to specify the desired options.
   a. Print Object Definition
   b. Print Table Definition
   c. Print Table Setup
   d. Print Setup Definition

Hands-On Exercises

1. AmeriSales International: New Employee Database

This exercise lets you practice creating a new database and adding a table using the Table Wizard.

1. Load Microsoft Access using the Windows Start menu.
2. To create a new database using the New File task pane:
   CLICK: New button ( ) to display the New File task pane
   CLICK: Blank Database option, under the *New* heading
3. In the File New Database dialog box:
   TYPE: **AmeriSales Payroll** into the *File name* text box
4. Using the Places bar or the *Save in* drop-down dialog box, select your personal storage location. Then, do the following:
   CLICK: Create command button
5. To use the Table Wizard, ensure that the *Tables* button is selected in the Objects bar and then do the following:
   DOUBLE-CLICK: Create table by using wizard

6. You will now create a new table to store AmeriSales's employee records. Do the following:
   SELECT: *Business* option button, if it is not already selected
   SELECT: Employees in the *Sample Tables* list box

7. Begin by including all of the suggested fields:
   CLICK: Include All button (»)
   Your screen should now appear similar to Figure 2.30.

Figure 2.30

Creating a new table using the Table Wizard

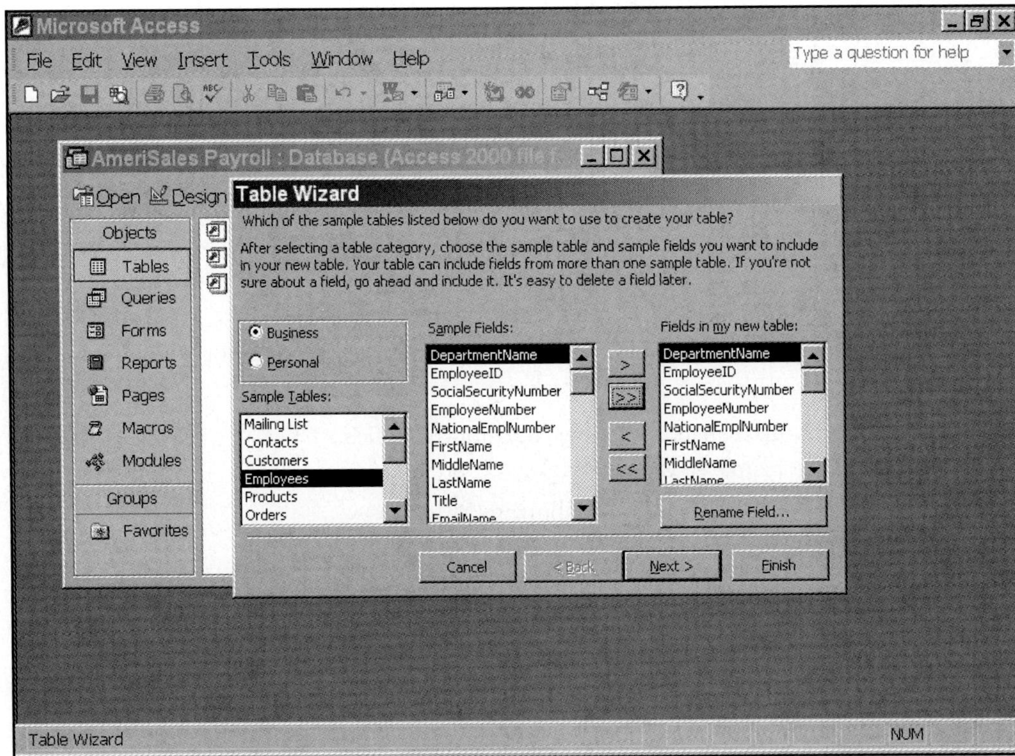

8. Now let's remove an unnecessary field. First scroll to the end of the *Fields in my new table* list. Then do the following:
   SELECT: Photograph
   CLICK: Remove button (‹)

9. On your own, remove the Notes and OfficeLocation fields.

10. To complete the wizard and open the "Employees" table in Datasheet view:
    CLICK: Finish

11. Close the Datasheet window.

12. Close the Database window.

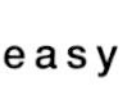 

2. Iway Internet Group: Internet Accounts

In this exercise, you practice creating two new tables in an existing database.

1. Open the database file named AC02HE. Ensure that the *Tables* button in the Objects bar is selected. Your screen should appear similar to Figure 2.31.

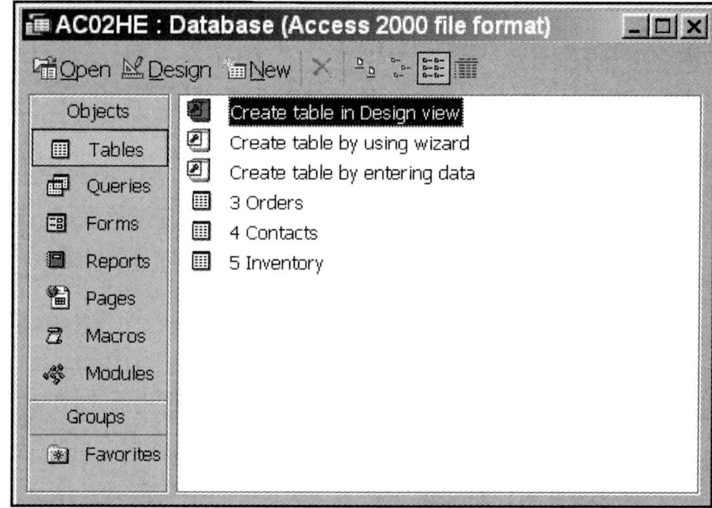

Figure 2.31

Opening the AC02HE database

2. To create a new table in Datasheet view:
   DOUBLE-CLICK: Create table by entering data
3. To start, rename the column headings in the field header area:
   DOUBLE-CLICK: Field1
   TYPE: **City**
   DOUBLE-CLICK: Field2
   TYPE: **AreaCode**
   DOUBLE-CLICK: Field3
   TYPE: **DialUp**
   PRESS: ENTER
4. Now let's enter one record before saving the table:
   TYPE: **Arjuna**
   PRESS: TAB
   TYPE: **555**
   PRESS: TAB
   TYPE: **533-1525**
5. PRESS: SHIFT+ENTER to save the record
   Your screen should now appear similar to Figure 2.32.

Access

Figure 2.32

Creating a table by entering data

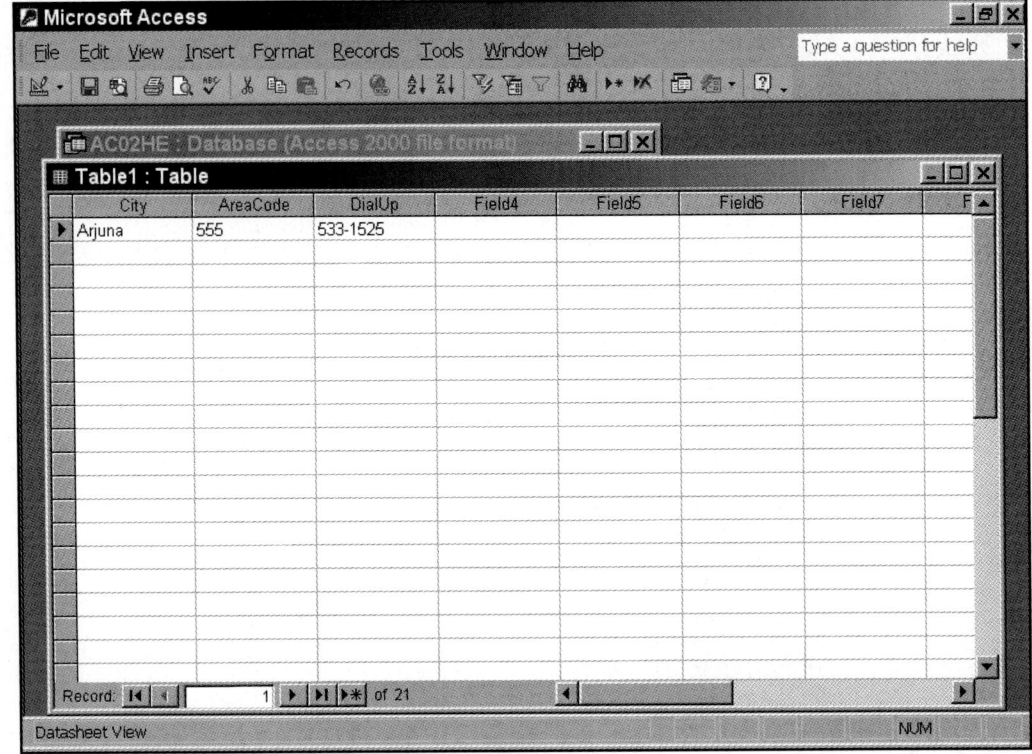

6. To save and name the new table structure:
   CLICK: Save button ( ) on the toolbar
   TYPE: **Cities** into the Save As dialog box
   PRESS: ENTER or CLICK: OK
7. Access warns you that you have not yet defined a primary key. To have Access take care of this for you:
   CLICK: Yes command button
8. Close the Datasheet window.
9. Now let's create a second table:
   DOUBLE-CLICK: Create table in Design view
10. To define a table that will store information about the company's technical support personnel:
    TYPE: **SupportID**
    PRESS: TAB to move to the *Data Type* column
    SELECT: AutoNumber
    PRESS: TAB
    TYPE: **Code to identify Tech Support**
    PRESS: ENTER to move to the next row
11. Add two more fields to the table, as shown in Figure 2.33. First add a Name field with a Text data type and the description "First and last name." Then add a Local field with a Number data type and the description "4-digit phone local."

Figure 2.33

Creating a table in table Design view

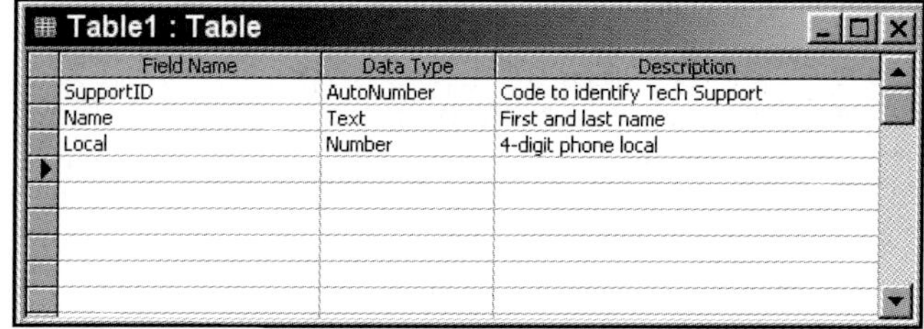

12. To save the table structure, do the following:
    CLICK: Save button (▣)
13. Enter a name for the new table:
    TYPE: **TechSupport**
    CLICK: OK command button
14. When Access offers to create a primary key:
    CLICK: Yes command button
15. Close the Datasheet window.

moderate 

3. Western Lumber Sales: Forest Products

In this exercise, you add a primary key to an existing table and then modify its indexes. Ensure that the AC02HE Database window is displayed.

1. Make sure that the *Tables* button in the Objects bar is selected.
2. To display a table in Datasheet view:
   DOUBLE-CLICK: 3 Orders in the list area
   The Datasheet window in Figure 2.34 is displayed.

Figure 2.34

Displaying the 3 Orders datasheet

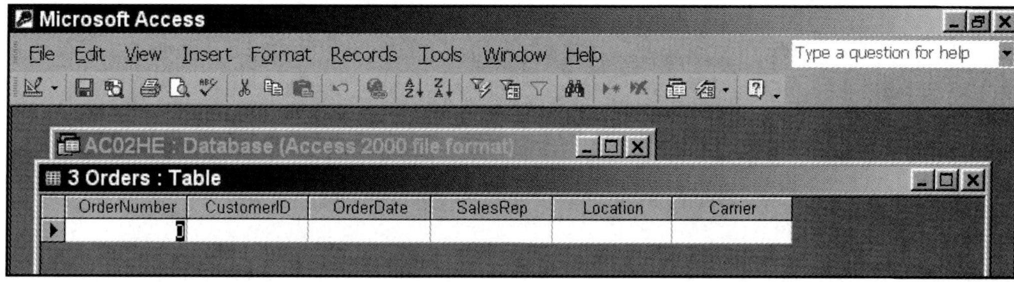

3. To display the table in Design view:
   CLICK: View—Design button (▣)
4. First, let's make the OrderNumber field the primary key of the table:
   CLICK: row selector button for OrderNumber
   CLICK: Primary Key button (▣)
   Notice that a key icon appears in the row selector button.
5. To speed up search operations for looking up a particular salesperson, let's create an index. To begin:
   SELECT: SalesRep in the Field Grid pane

6. Using the I-beam mouse pointer:
   SELECT: *Indexed* text box in the Field Properties pane
   CLICK: down arrow attached to the *Indexed* text box

7. From the drop-down list attached to the *Indexed* text box:
   SELECT: Yes (Duplicates OK)
   Your screen should now appear similar to Figure 2.35.

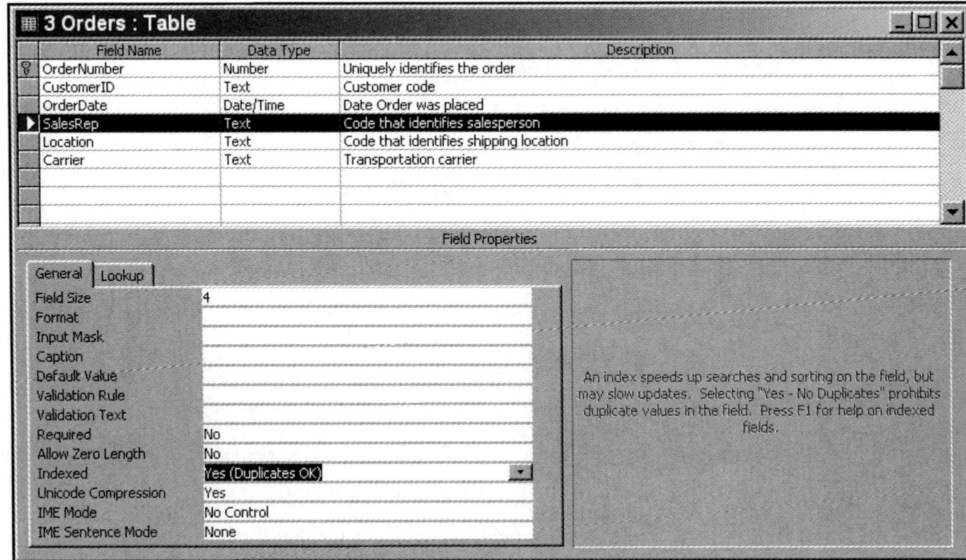

Figure 2.35
Setting a primary key and creating an index

8. To display all the indexes for the table:
   CLICK: Indexes button

9. Let's remove the OrderDate index:
   RIGHT-CLICK: row selector button for OrderDate
   CHOOSE: Delete Rows
   The Indexes window now displays three entries, as shown in Figure 2.36.

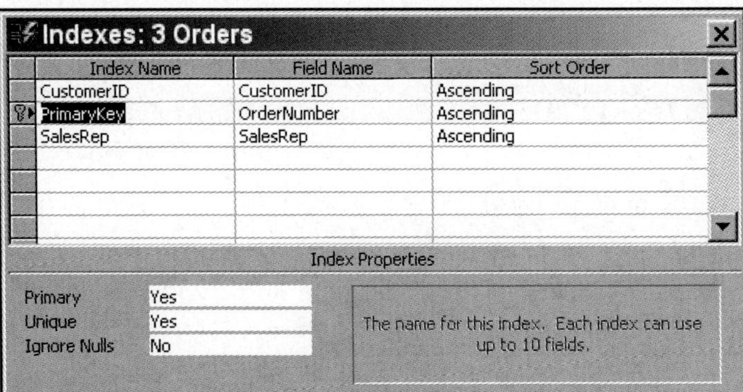

Figure 2.36
Viewing the indexes for a table

10. Close the Indexes window.

11. To save the table structure:
    CLICK: Save button

12. Close the table Design window.

moderate 

4. Spring County Carnival: Contact List

In this exercise, you practice modifying the field structure of an existing table. Ensure the AC02HE Database window is displayed.

1. To open the 4 Contacts table in Design view:
   SELECT: 4 Contacts in the list area
   CLICK: Design button (Design) on the Database window toolbar
2. First, let's rename one of the fields. Using the I-beam mouse pointer:
   CLICK: to the right of "Contact" in the *Field Name* column
3. TYPE: **Name**
   PRESS: ⬇
   The cell entry should now read "ContactName."
4. You need to add a field that stores the contact's e-mail address. In the Field Grid pane:
   CLICK: in the *Field Name* column of the next empty row
   TYPE: **Email**
   PRESS: ⬇
   Notice that the *Data Type* field accepted the Text data type by default, as shown in Figure 2.37.

Figure 2.37

Editing and adding fields to the Field Grid pane

4 Contacts : Table

Field Name	Data Type
ID	AutoNumber
Volunteer Group	Text
ContactName	Text
Address	Text
City	Text
Phone 1	Text
Phone 2	Text
Email	Text

5. To delete a field using the right-click menu:
   RIGHT-CLICK: row selector button for Phone 2
   CHOOSE: Delete Rows
6. To confirm that the deletion will remove all of the data in the field:
   CLICK: Yes command button
7. Let's move the Phone 1 field below the Email field. To begin:
   CLICK: row selector button for Phone 1
8. Using the arrow mouse pointer:
   DRAG: row selector button for Phone 1 downward so that a bold gridline appears below the last field
   (*Note:* Remember to release the mouse button to drop the field.)
9. To save and then view the changes in Datasheet view:
   CLICK: Save button (💾)
   CLICK: View—Datasheet button (▦▾)
   Your screen should now appear similar to Figure 2.38.
10. Close the Datasheet window.

Figure 2.38

Viewing the changes made to a table in Datasheet view

4 Contacts : Table

ID	Volunteer Group	ContactName	Address	City	Email
1	Downtown Rotary	John Reusche	6717 Cherokee Rd.	Silverdale	
2	Silverdale Arts Commission	Jan Neely & Laurie Berg	425 N. El Dorado St.	Silverdale	
3	Sierra Middle Sch. Ptsa	Michelle Turnbeaugh	777 Elaine Dr.	Silverdale	
4	Lady Bugs	Rachael Pappas	1660 W.Sonora St.	Silverdale	
5	American Diabetes Assn.	Penny Knapp	9883 Weeping Willow	Silverdale	
6	Delta Rotary	Gary Giovanetti	318 E. Vine Street	Silverdale	
7	Silverdale Chamber Of Comm.	Patti Glico	445 W. Weber Ave. #220	Silverdale	
8	Assistance League	Teresa Perry	137 Mc Kelley	Silverdale	
9	National Council	Janice Colombini	18543 E. Front St.	Centerville	
10	Convey, Bill	Bill Convey	3014 Country Club Blvd.	Silverdale	
11	Annunciation 5th Grade	Julie Mulligan	9119 Casterbridge Dr	Silverdale	
12	Silverdale Police Youth Activ.	Connie Wyman	22 E. Market St.	Silverdale	
13	Commodore Sktn Skills	Shirley Lopez	112 E. Sonoma St.	Silverdale	
14	Matsuya, Susie & Mike	Susie Matsuya	2828 Appling Circle	Silverdale	
15	St. Lukes Parent Club	Maria J. Castellanos	437 Cordoba Lane	Silverdale	
16	El Dorado Kiwis Club	John Monte	5334 Rivera Court	Silverdale	
17	Pinawa B.P.W.	Jackie Soupe	P.O. Box 2324	Pinawa	
18	Silverdale Chorale	Maxine Garrison	7707 N. Pershing Ave.	Silverdale	
19	Alder Market	Kitty Rustler	151 W. Alder St.	Silverdale	
20	SJ Co 4-H Club Council	Sharon Ross	420 S. Wilson Way	Silverdale	

Record: 1 of 66

difficult 

5. On Your Own: Benson's Office Supplies

To practice making changes to a table's structure, open the 5 Inventory table in the AC02HE database. After changing to Design view, add a new field named Category between the existing Description and OnHand fields. Assign a data type of Number to the new field. Next, move the Reorder field so that it appears immediately after the OnHand field and then remove the SuggestedRetail field. To speed up your table search and sort operations, create an index for the Buyer field that allows duplicate entries. Finally, in the Indexes window, remove the extraneous index on ProductID, as shown in Figure 2.39. Make sure that you do not remove the primary key for this field. When you are finished, close the Indexes window. Then, save the table changes and close the table Design window.

Figure 2.39

Adding, moving, deleting, and indexing fields

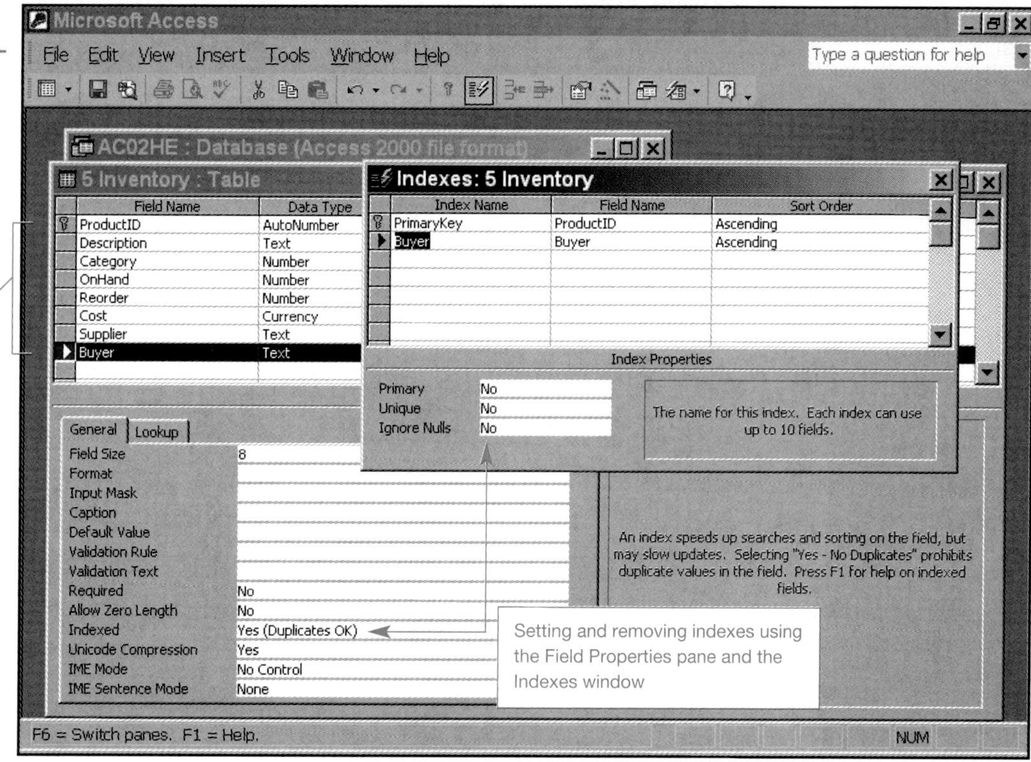

difficult 

6. On Your Own: Coldstream Valley Resorts

In this exercise, use the table Design view to create a new table in the AC02HE database. If the Database window does not appear in the work area, open it now. Your new table should contain the following fields, complete with data types and descriptions.

- *PackageID:* This field, which automatically increments by one each time a new record is added, contains a unique code that identifies each promotional package.
- *Description:* This text field stores the name of each package.
- *Price:* This field stores the suggested price in dollars for each package.
- *Nights:* This field stores the number of nights for accommodations.

Save the table as "Valley Packages" to the database and let Access create a primary key. Now use the Documenter tool to preview (Figure 2.40) and print out the table's design structure. Then, close all windows.

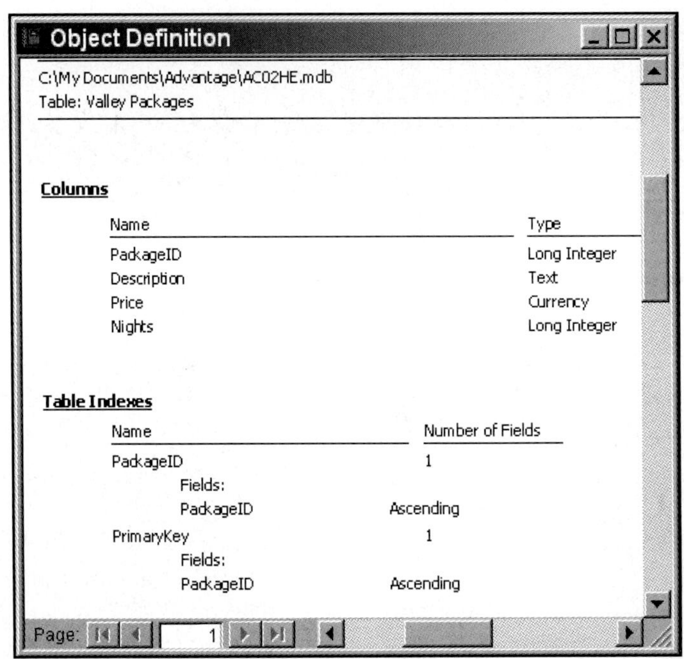

Figure 2.40

Previewing the Documenter's design report

Case Problems: North Star Freight

Having selected Microsoft Access 2002, Mike Lambert, North Star Freight's controller, focuses his attention on planning and designing a database. In order to reduce data redundancies, Mike splits the company information into three tables. The first table stores operational data for each truck in the fleet. The second table stores personnel data for each driver. The third and final table stores a detailed log of each delivery. Now Mike must launch Access, create a database structure, and initialize these tables.

In the following case problems, assume the role of Mike and perform the same steps that he identifies. You may want to re-read the chapter opening before proceeding.

1. To begin, Mike creates a new database from scratch. He names the database "North Star Freight" and then saves it to his *personal storage location.* Once the Database window appears, he proceeds to create the first table using the Table Wizard. After launching the wizard, Mike ensures that the *Business* option button is selected. He then scrolls the list of sample tables to find a suitable structure. From the list, Mike selects a table named "Assets" and then includes all of the fields for his new table. After proceeding to the next screen in the wizard's dialog box, he names the new table "Trucks" and lets Access set the primary key. In the final step, Mike opens the table in Design view in order to rename three of the fields. As shown in Figure 2.41, he changes "AssetID" to "TruckID," "AssetDescription" to "TruckDescription," and "AssetCategoryID" to "TruckCategoryID." He saves the changes to the table structure and closes the Trucks table.

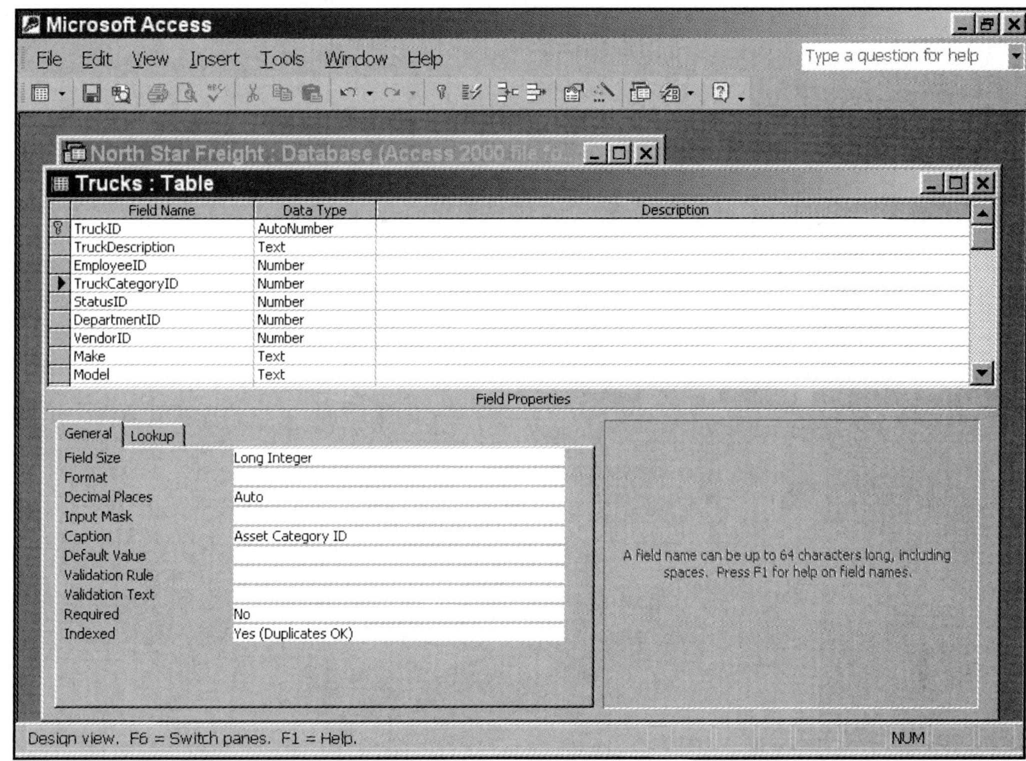

Figure 2.41

Creating and then modifying the Trucks table

2. Mike decides to create the second table in Datasheet view. After double-clicking the appropriate New Object shortcut, he renames the column headings in the empty datasheet to create the following fields:

- Name
- Address
- Phone
- Classification

Mike saves the new table object as "Drivers" and allows Access to define a primary key. Looking at the results in Figure 2.42, Mike decides to switch to Design view and rename the ID field "DriverID." He then saves the table structure and closes the table Design window.

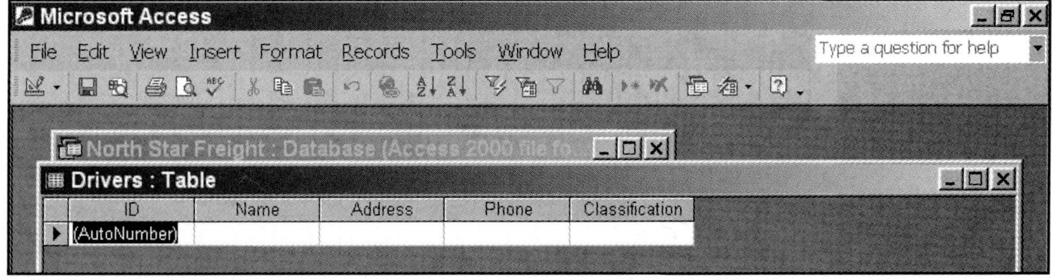

Figure 2.42

Creating the Drivers table structure in Datasheet view

3. For the third table, Mike uses Design view to create the structure displayed in Figure 2.43. As shown in the screen graphic, Mike makes the TripID field the primary key. He then saves the table as "Trips" and closes the table Design window. Using the Access Documenter tool, he prints out the Trips table structure for later review.

Figure 2.43

Creating the Trips table structure in Design view

Table1 : Table

Field Name	Data Type	Description
TripID	AutoNumber	Identifies the delivery
TruckID	Number	Identifies the truck
Date	Date/Time	Date of the trip
Destination	Text	Delivery destination
Miles	Number	Round trip mileage
DriverID	Number	Identifies the driver
LoadWeight	Number	Weight in pounds

4. Later the same day, Mike realizes he needs to make a few structural changes to some of the tables. He begins by opening the Trips table in Design view and creating an index for the Destination field. Using the Indexes window, he removes the extra index on the TripID field that Access automatically created and then closes the window. In the Field Grid pane, Mike adds a new text field named "Pickup" between the Date and Destination fields. He then moves the DriverID field to appear immediately below the TruckID field, as shown in Figure 2.44. He saves the changes and closes the table Design window.

Figure 2.44

Modifying the Trips table structure

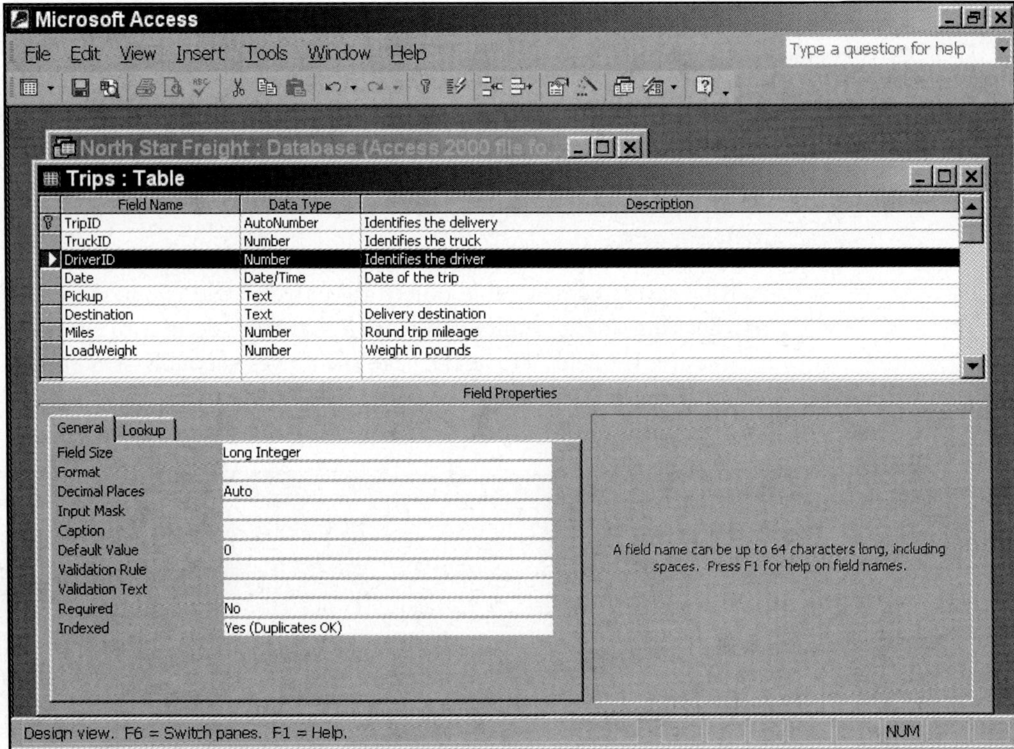

For the Trucks table, Mike opens the table in Design view and deletes the DepartmentID and BarcodeNumber fields. He then moves the Make and Model fields to be the third and fourth fields respectively. Satisfied with the progress he has made in setting up North Star Freight's new database, Mike saves his changes and exits Microsoft Access.

NOTES

Microsoft® **Access**® 2002

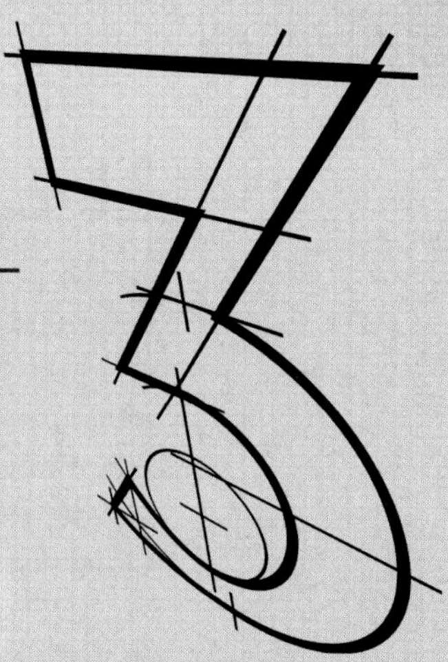

CHAPTER 3

Organizing and Retrieving Data

CHAPTER OUTLINE

Case Study

3.1 Customizing Datasheet View

3.2 Sorting, Finding, and Maintaining Data

3.3 Using Filters

3.4 Creating a Simple Query

Chapter Summary

Chapter Quiz

Hands-On Exercises

Case Problems

PREREQUISITES

To successfully complete this chapter, you must be comfortable performing basic data entry and editing tasks in the Datasheet window. You will be asked to modify the appearance of a datasheet using toolbar buttons, Menu commands, and right-click shortcut menus. You should also know how to view and print objects from the Database window.

LEARNING OBJECTIVES

After completing this chapter, you will be able to:

- Enhance the display and printing of a datasheet using fonts and special effects
- Sort the contents of a datasheet into ascending and descending order
- Find a record by entering search criteria and using wildcard characters
- Filter the records displayed in a datasheet using Filter For Input, Filter By Selection, and Filter By Form
- Create a query using the Simple Query Wizard

CaseStudy ROUNDHOUSE RENTALS Ellie Floyd is the office supervisor for Roundhouse Rentals, a rental and lease company that specializes in landscaping and gardening equipment. As well as managing the administrative and inside sales staff, Ellie's responsibilities have been expanded recently to cover the company's record-keeping. The owner and manager of Roundhouse Rentals, Sal Witherspoon, knows that Ellie just completed a course in Microsoft Access. Because much of the record-keeping data is already stored in a database, Sal asks Ellie to open the company's database using Access and peruse its contents. Sal wants Ellie to become well versed in its operation so that she can eventually take over the day-to-day management of the database.

In this session, you and Ellie learn how to enhance a Datasheet window, organize and sort records in a datasheet, filter information for display, and develop a simple query. All of these techniques enable you to better organize and retrieve information using Microsoft Access 2002.

3.1 Customizing Datasheet View

Access provides numerous options for customizing the appearance, or layout, of a datasheet. Because a datasheet is only a tool for viewing data from the underlying table, you can manipulate the datasheet's column widths, row heights, and field order without affecting the table structure itself. Exceptions to this rule are when you rename or delete a column. These changes flow through to the structural level of the table. Once the table is customized to your satisfaction, remember to save the layout changes by clicking the Save button (💾) on the toolbar. Otherwise, the modifications are discarded when you close the Datasheet window.

3.1.1 Formatting a Datasheet

feature →

To enhance the readability of a datasheet, select fonts and apply special effects for onscreen display and printing. Any changes that you make affect the entire datasheet but do not affect other database objects such as forms and reports. After formatting the datasheet to suit your needs, save the layout changes for subsequent use.

method →

To format a datasheet, choose from the following options:

- CHOOSE: Format, Font to select font characteristics
- CHOOSE: Format, Datasheet to apply special visual effects

To save the format changes:

- CLICK: Save button (💾) on the toolbar

or

- CHOOSE: File, Save from the menu

In this lesson, you format and then save an existing datasheet to appear with a custom font, color, and background. Load Microsoft Access, if it is not already running.

1. Open the database file named AC0300, located in the Advantage student data files folder.

2. To display the Courses table in Datasheet view:
DOUBLE-CLICK: Courses in the list area
The Courses Datasheet window appears in the work area, as shown in Figure 3.1.

Figure 3.1

Displaying the Courses datasheet

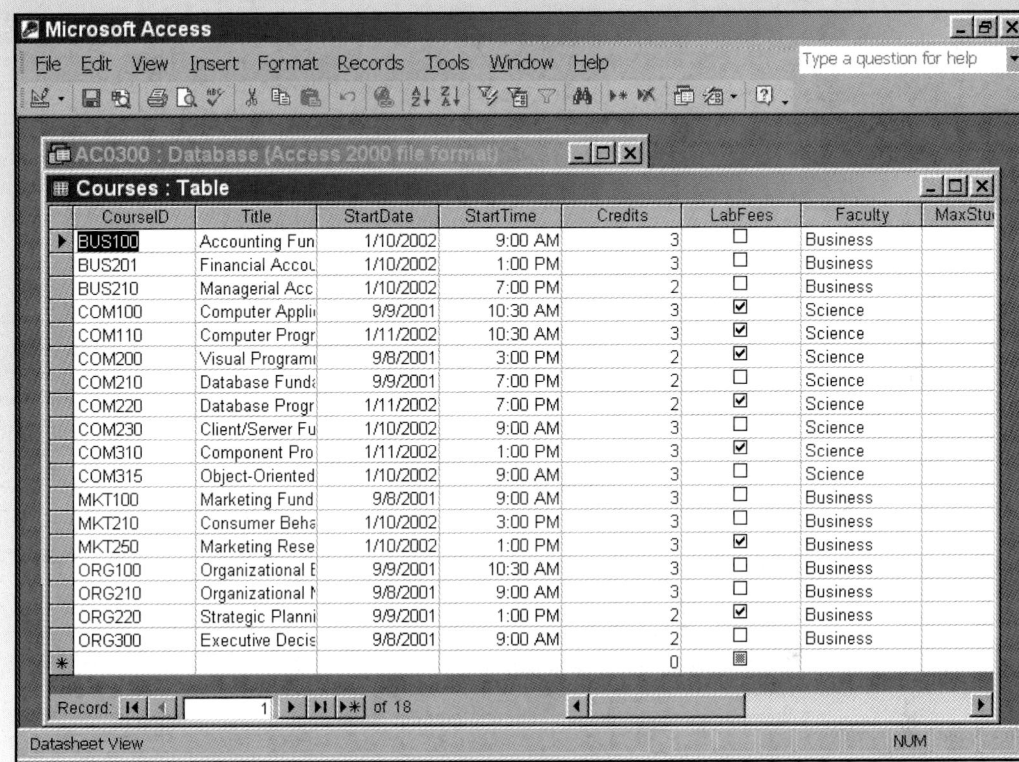

CourseID	Title	StartDate	StartTime	Credits	LabFees	Faculty	MaxStu
BUS100	Accounting Fun	1/10/2002	9:00 AM	3	☐	Business	
BUS201	Financial Accou	1/10/2002	1:00 PM	3	☐	Business	
BUS210	Managerial Acc	1/10/2002	7:00 PM	2	☐	Business	
COM100	Computer Appli	9/9/2001	10:30 AM	3	☑	Science	
COM110	Computer Progr	1/11/2002	10:30 AM	3	☑	Science	
COM200	Visual Program	9/8/2001	3:00 PM	2	☑	Science	
COM210	Database Fund	9/9/2001	7:00 PM	2	☐	Science	
COM220	Database Progr	1/11/2002	7:00 PM	2	☑	Science	
COM230	Client/Server Fu	1/10/2002	9:00 AM	3	☐	Science	
COM310	Component Pro	1/11/2002	1:00 PM	3	☑	Science	
COM315	Object-Oriented	1/10/2002	9:00 AM	3	☐	Science	
MKT100	Marketing Fund	9/8/2001	9:00 AM	3	☐	Business	
MKT210	Consumer Beh	1/10/2002	3:00 PM	3	☐	Business	
MKT250	Marketing Rese	1/10/2002	1:00 PM	3	☑	Business	
ORG100	Organizational	9/9/2001	10:30 AM	3	☐	Business	
ORG210	Organizational	9/8/2001	9:00 AM	3	☐	Business	
ORG220	Strategic Planni	9/9/2001	1:00 PM	2	☑	Business	
ORG300	Executive Decis	9/8/2001	9:00 AM	2	☐	Business	
*				0			

3. You can change the font characteristics of text displayed in a datasheet without affecting any other Datasheet window. To customize the Courses datasheet, do the following:
CHOOSE: Format, Font
The Font dialog box appears, similar but not identical to Figure 3.2. In this one dialog box, you can change the font **typeface,** style, size, and text color.

4. Make the following selections in the Font dialog box:
SELECT: Times New Roman in the *Font* list box
SELECT: Regular in the *Font style* list box
SELECT: 12 in the *Size* list box
SELECT: Navy in the *Color* drop-down list box
Notice that the *Sample* area, as shown in Figure 3.2, displays an example of the current selections.

Access

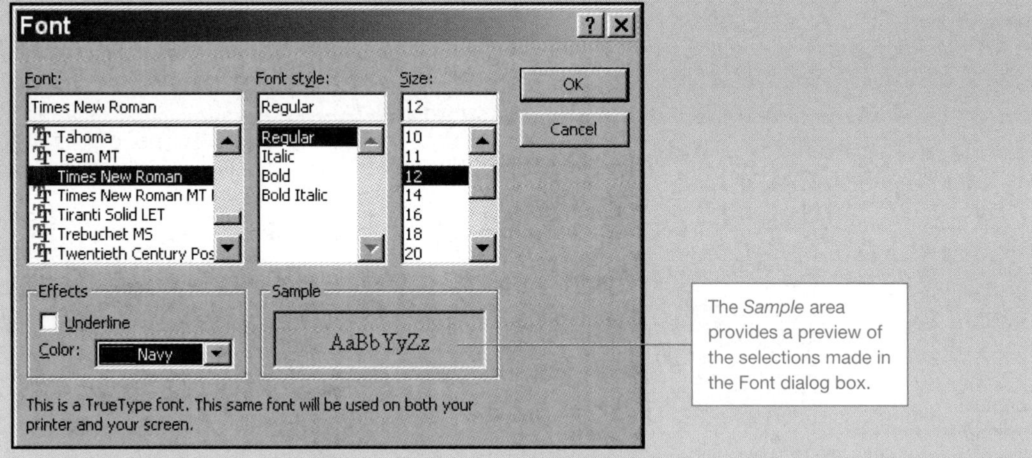

Figure 3.2

Font dialog box

5. To accept the changes:
CLICK: OK command button
The Datasheet window is updated to display the font selections.

6. You can also enhance a datasheet by formatting the window characteristics such as gridlines and background matting. To begin:
CHOOSE: Format, Datasheet
The Datasheet Formatting dialog box in Figure 3.3 is displayed. Notice that the options selected in the screen graphic are the default settings for a Datasheet window.

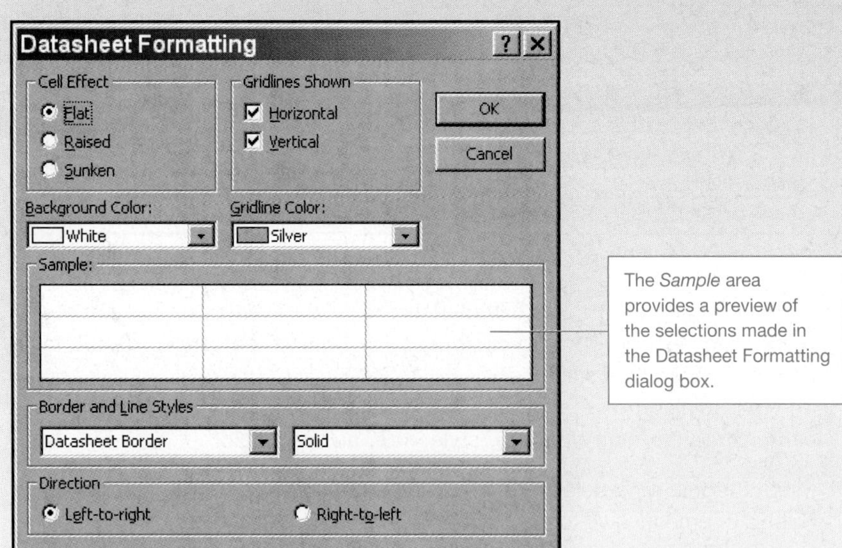

Figure 3.3

Datasheet Formatting dialog box

7. After selecting a few options, you can better appreciate the resulting changes by viewing the *Sample* area of the dialog box. To begin:
SELECT: *Raised* option button in the *Cell Effect* area
Notice that this selection nullifies the other options in the dialog box—they are no longer available for selection.

8. Let's select a different formatting enhancement. Do the following:
SELECT: *Flat* option button in the *Cell Effect* area
SELECT: *Vertical* check box so that no ✓ appears
SELECT: Teal in the *Gridline Color* drop-down list box

9. In the *Border and Line Styles* area of the dialog box:
SELECT: Horizontal Gridline in the left-hand drop-down list box
SELECT: Dots in the right-hand drop-down list box
CLICK: OK command button
The Datasheet window now appears with teal dots separating records in the datasheet as horizontal gridlines, as shown in Figure 3.4.

Figure 3.4

Formatting the Courses datasheet

Courses : Table

CourseID	Title	StartDate	StartTime	Credits	LabFees	Faculty	Max
BUS100	Accounting Fu	1/10/2002	9:00 AM	3	☐	Business	
BUS201	Financial Acco	1/10/2002	1:00 PM	3	☐	Business	
BUS210	Managerial Ac	1/10/2002	7:00 PM	2	☐	Business	
COM100	Computer App	9/9/2001	10:30 AM	3	☑	Science	
COM110	Computer Prog	1/11/2002	10:30 AM	3	☑	Science	
COM200	Visual Progran	9/8/2001	3:00 PM	2	☑	Science	
COM210	Database Fund	9/9/2001	7:00 PM	2	☐	Science	
COM220	Database Prog	1/11/2002	7:00 PM	2	☑	Science	
COM230	Client/Server F	1/10/2002	9:00 AM	3	☐	Science	
COM310	Component Pr	1/11/2002	1:00 PM	3	☑	Science	
COM315	Object-Oriente	1/10/2002	9:00 AM	3	☐	Science	
MKT100	Marketing Fun	9/8/2001	9:00 AM	3	☐	Business	
MKT210	Consumer Beh	1/10/2002	3:00 PM	3	☐	Business	
MKT250	Marketing Res	1/10/2002	1:00 PM	3	☑	Business	
ORG100	Organizational	9/9/2001	10:30 AM	3	☐	Business	
ORG210	Organizational	9/8/2001	9:00 AM	3	☐	Business	

Record: 1 of 18

10. To save the formatting changes to the datasheet:
CLICK: Save button (💾) on the toolbar

3.1.2 Changing the Field Column Order

feature

Access determines the column order displayed in a Datasheet window from the field order in the underlying table structure. You may want to modify the column order in order to display fields side by side or to perform a multiple-field sort operation. One way to change the column order is to modify the field order in table Design view. An easier and less drastic method is to move fields by dragging their column headings in Datasheet view. This method does not affect the underlying table structure. Once the columns are positioned, you can save the field column order in the datasheet along with other customizing options.

method

- SELECT: the desired column in the field header area
- DRAG: the column heading to its new location

You now practice selecting and moving columns in a datasheet. Ensure that you've completed the previous lesson and that the Courses Datasheet window is displayed.

Access

1. Before moving fields in the datasheet, let's practice selecting columns and changing column widths. Do the following:
   CLICK: CourseID in the field header area
   Notice that the mouse pointer becomes a downward pointing arrow (⬇) when positioned properly on the column heading. The entire column should now appear highlighted.
2. Using the horizontal scroll bar, scroll the window so that the last field column is visible:
   CLICK: right scroll button (▶) until InstructorID appears
3. To select all of the columns in the datasheet at once:
   PRESS: SHIFT and hold it down
   CLICK: InstructorID in the field header area
   All of the columns should now appear highlighted. (*Note:* Although it's not explicitly stated, you should release the SHIFT key after clicking on the InstructorID column heading.)
4. You can now update the columns to their best-fit widths. To do so:
   CHOOSE: Format, Column Width
   CLICK: Best Fit command button
   PRESS: HOME to remove the highlighting
   The datasheet should now appear similar to Figure 3.5.

Figure 3.5

Adjusting all columns to their best-fit width

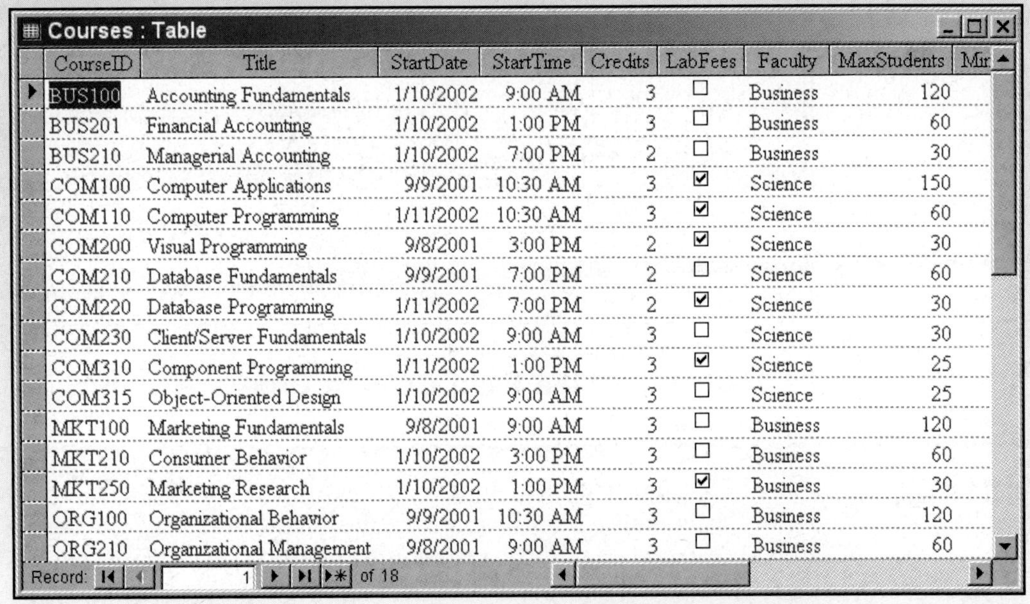

Courses : Table

CourseID	Title	StartDate	StartTime	Credits	LabFees	Faculty	MaxStudents	Mir
BUS100	Accounting Fundamentals	1/10/2002	9:00 AM	3	☐	Business	120	
BUS201	Financial Accounting	1/10/2002	1:00 PM	3	☐	Business	60	
BUS210	Managerial Accounting	1/10/2002	7:00 PM	2	☐	Business	30	
COM100	Computer Applications	9/9/2001	10:30 AM	3	☑	Science	150	
COM110	Computer Programming	1/11/2002	10:30 AM	3	☑	Science	60	
COM200	Visual Programming	9/8/2001	3:00 PM	2	☑	Science	30	
COM210	Database Fundamentals	9/9/2001	7:00 PM	2	☐	Science	60	
COM220	Database Programming	1/11/2002	7:00 PM	2	☑	Science	30	
COM230	Client/Server Fundamentals	1/10/2002	9:00 AM	3	☐	Science	30	
COM310	Component Programming	1/11/2002	1:00 PM	3	☑	Science	25	
COM315	Object-Oriented Design	1/10/2002	9:00 AM	3	☐	Science	25	
MKT100	Marketing Fundamentals	9/8/2001	9:00 AM	3	☐	Business	120	
MKT210	Consumer Behavior	1/10/2002	3:00 PM	3	☐	Business	60	
MKT250	Marketing Research	1/10/2002	1:00 PM	3	☑	Business	30	
ORG100	Organizational Behavior	9/9/2001	10:30 AM	3	☐	Business	120	
ORG210	Organizational Management	9/8/2001	9:00 AM	3	☐	Business	60	

Record: 1 of 18

5. Let's practice moving columns in the datasheet. Using the horizontal scroll bar, scroll the window so that both the Faculty and DeptHead field columns are visible.
6. CLICK: DeptHead in the field header area
7. Position the white arrow mouse pointer (↖) over the field name. Then:
   DRAG: DeptHead to the left so that the bold vertical gridline appears between the Faculty and MaxStudents field columns, as shown in Figure 3.6

Figure 3.6

Moving a field column

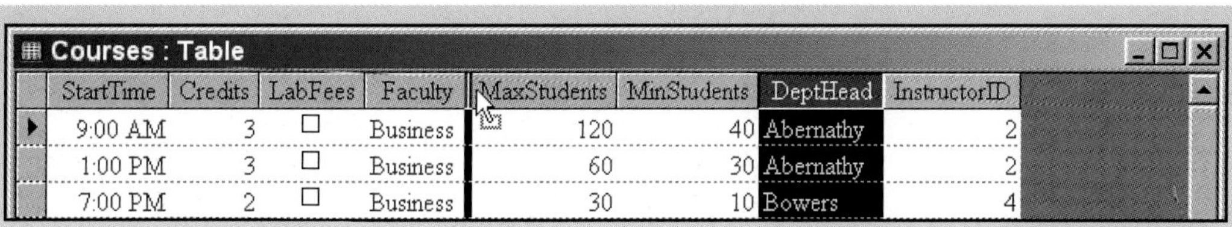

	StartTime	Credits	LabFees	Faculty	MaxStudents	MinStudents	DeptHead	InstructorID
▶	9:00 AM	3	☐	Business	120	40	Abernathy	2
	1:00 PM	3	☐	Business	60	30	Abernathy	2
	7:00 PM	2	☐	Business	30	10	Bowers	4

8. Release the mouse button to complete the move operation.

9. To move two fields at the same time:
CLICK: Faculty in the field header area
PRESS: SHIFT and hold it down
CLICK: DeptHead in the field header area
Both columns should now appear highlighted.

10. You will now reposition the two field columns. Position the mouse pointer on one of the selected column headings. Then:
DRAG: Faculty (or DeptHead) to the left so that the bold vertical gridline appears between Title and StartDate

11. After releasing the mouse button:
PRESS: HOME to remove the highlighting
Your Datasheet window should now appear similar to Figure 3.7.

Figure 3.7

Changing the field column order

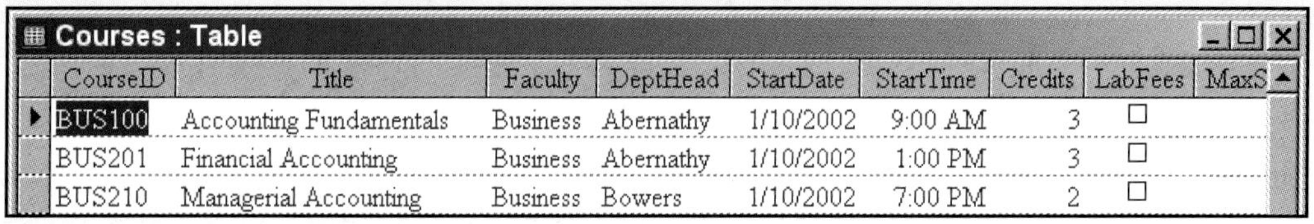

	CourseID	Title	Faculty	DeptHead	StartDate	StartTime	Credits	LabFees	MaxS
▶	BUS100	Accounting Fundamentals	Business	Abernathy	1/10/2002	9:00 AM	3	☐	
	BUS201	Financial Accounting	Business	Abernathy	1/10/2002	1:00 PM	3	☐	
	BUS210	Managerial Accounting	Business	Bowers	1/10/2002	7:00 PM	2	☐	

12. Save the layout changes by clicking the Save button ( ).

3.1.3 Hiding and Unhiding Columns

feature

Hiding columns in a datasheet is useful for temporarily restricting the display of sensitive data, such as salaries or commissions. You can also hide columns that you do not want displayed in a printout or that you are thinking about deleting permanently. Whatever your reasons, Access makes it easy to hide and unhide field columns in the Datasheet window.

method

To hide a field column using the menu:

- SELECT: the desired column in the field header area
- CHOOSE: Format, Hide Columns

To hide a field column using the right-click menu:

- RIGHT-CLICK: the desired column in the field header area
- CHOOSE: Hide Columns

To unhide a field column:

- CHOOSE: Format, Unhide Columns
- SELECT: the desired columns in the Unhide Columns dialog box
- CLICK: Close command button

practice

In this lesson, you hide and unhide columns in the active datasheet. Ensure that you've completed the previous lessons and that the Courses Datasheet window is displayed.

1. Let's assume that you've been asked to print out the Courses datasheet. However, the last three columns in this datasheet are for administrative eyes only and should not be included. Therefore, you must hide the last three field columns before printing. To begin:
PRESS: END to move the cursor to the last field column

2. Fortunately, the three columns, MaxStudents, MinStudents, and InstructorID, appear next to one another in the datasheet. To select the three columns:
CLICK: MaxStudents in the field header area
PRESS: SHIFT and hold it down
CLICK: InstructorID in the field header area
Remember to release the SHIFT key after you click InstructorID.

3. To hide the selected columns:
CHOOSE: Format, Hide Columns
The columns disappear from the Datasheet window display (Figure 3.8), although the data remain safe in the table object. (*Note:* You could also right-click a column in the field header area and choose the Hide Columns command.)

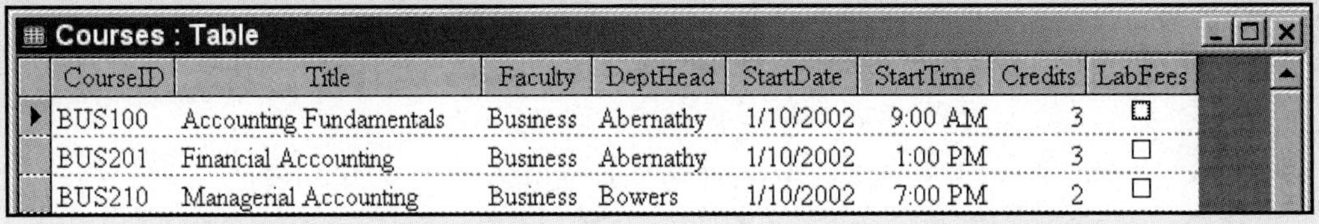

Figure 3.8

Hiding columns in Datasheet view

Courses : Table

CourseID	Title	Faculty	DeptHead	StartDate	StartTime	Credits	LabFees
BUS100	Accounting Fundamentals	Business	Abernathy	1/10/2002	9:00 AM	3	☐
BUS201	Financial Accounting	Business	Abernathy	1/10/2002	1:00 PM	3	☐
BUS210	Managerial Accounting	Business	Bowers	1/10/2002	7:00 PM	2	☐

4. To specify how the datasheet will now print:
CHOOSE: File, Page Setup
CLICK: *Page* tab
SELECT: *Landscape* option button
CLICK: OK command button

5. To preview the datasheet:
CLICK: Print Preview button ( ) on the toolbar

6. Using the magnifying glass mouse pointer, zoom in and out on the page. Notice that the hidden columns are not displayed in the Print Preview window, as shown in Figure 3.9.

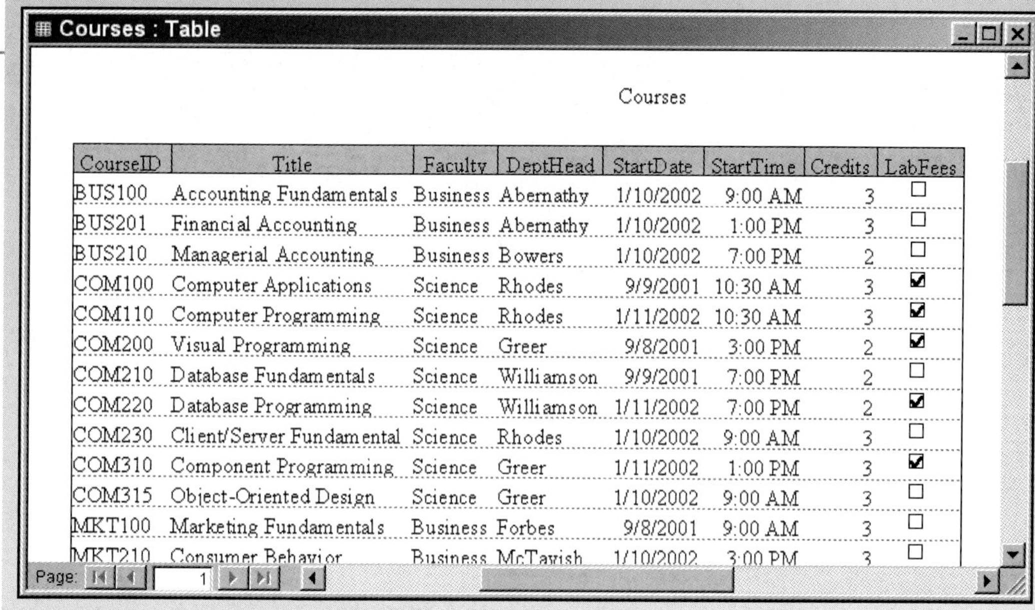

CourseID	Title	Faculty	DeptHead	StartDate	StartTime	Credits	LabFees
BUS100	Accounting Fundamentals	Business	Abernathy	1/10/2002	9:00 AM	3	☐
BUS201	Financial Accounting	Business	Abernathy	1/10/2002	1:00 PM	3	☐
BUS210	Managerial Accounting	Business	Bowers	1/10/2002	7:00 PM	2	☐
COM100	Computer Applications	Science	Rhodes	9/9/2001	10:30 AM	3	☑
COM110	Computer Programming	Science	Rhodes	1/11/2002	10:30 AM	3	☑
COM200	Visual Programming	Science	Greer	9/8/2001	3:00 PM	2	☑
COM210	Database Fundamentals	Science	Williamson	9/9/2001	7:00 PM	2	☐
COM220	Database Programming	Science	Williamson	1/11/2002	7:00 PM	2	☑
COM230	Client/Server Fundamental	Science	Rhodes	1/10/2002	9:00 AM	3	☐
COM310	Component Programming	Science	Greer	1/11/2002	1:00 PM	3	☑
COM315	Object-Oriented Design	Science	Greer	1/10/2002	9:00 AM	3	☐
MKT100	Marketing Fundamentals	Business	Forbes	9/8/2001	9:00 AM	3	☐
MKT210	Consumer Behavior	Business	McTavish	1/10/2002	3:00 PM	3	☐

Figure 3.9

Zooming in the Print Preview window

7. To return to the Datasheet window:
   CLICK: Close button (Close) on the toolbar
8. To unhide the columns:
   CHOOSE: Format, Unhide Columns
   The dialog box in Figure 3.10 appears.

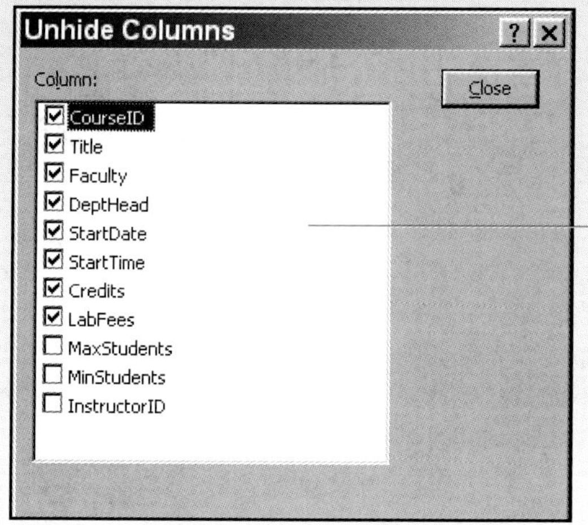

Field columns that are currently displayed in the datasheet appear in this list area with a selected check box.

Figure 3.10

Unhide Columns dialog box

9. In the Unhide Columns dialog box:
   SELECT: *MaxStudents* check box
   SELECT: *MinStudents* check box
   SELECT: *InstructorID* check box
   CLICK: Close command button
   Notice that the field columns are displayed once again.
10. Save the layout changes before proceeding.

Access

3.1.4 Freezing and Unfreezing Columns

feature

When you navigate a large table with many columns, the Datasheet window scrolls automatically to accommodate your cursor movements. The farther right you move the cursor, the more the columns scroll away from view at the left. To more easily identify the current record, Access lets you freeze or lock in place one or more columns, such as a company name or product number, along the left edge of the Datasheet window.

method

To freeze a field column using the menu:

- SELECT: the desired column(s) in the field header area
- CHOOSE: Format, Freeze Columns

To freeze a field column using the right-click menu:

- RIGHT-CLICK: the desired column in the field header area
- CHOOSE: Freeze Columns

To unfreeze columns in a datasheet:

- CHOOSE: Format, Unfreeze All Columns

practice

In this lesson, you freeze and unfreeze columns in the active datasheet. Ensure that you've completed the previous lessons and that the Courses Datasheet window is displayed.

1. Let's use the right-click menu to freeze the CourseID field column from scrolling off the screen. Do the following:
   RIGHT-CLICK: CourseID in the field header
   A shortcut menu appears, as displayed in Figure 3.11.

Figure 3.11

Displaying the right-click shortcut menu for a column

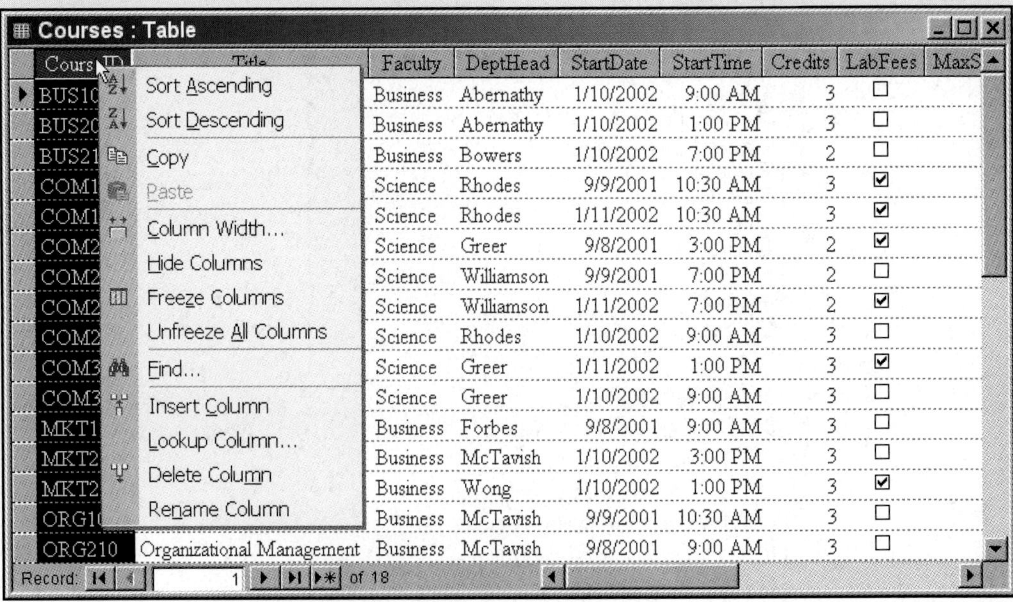

2. To freeze the column in the Datasheet window:
CHOOSE: Freeze Columns
(*Note:* Nothing appears to have happened to the column, but the effects are illustrated in the next few steps.)

3. Remove the column highlighting:
PRESS: HOME
Notice that a vertical gridline appears between the CourseID and Title field columns.

4. To demonstrate the frozen column feature:
PRESS: END to move to the last field column
The CourseID column remains displayed at the left side of the window, as shown in Figure 3.12. This command is especially useful for displaying datasheets that contain many fields.

Figure 3.12

Freezing a column in a datasheet

Courses : Table

CourseID	DeptHead	StartDate	StartTime	Credits	LabFees	MaxStudents	MinStudents	InstructorID
BUS100	Abernathy	1/10/2002	9:00 AM	3	☐	120	40	2
BUS201	Abernathy	1/10/2002	1:00 PM	3	☐	60	30	2
BUS210	Bowers	1/10/2002	7:00 PM	2	☐	30	10	4

5. To unfreeze the CourseID column:
CHOOSE: Format, Unfreeze All Columns

6. PRESS: HOME

7. Save the layout changes and then close the Datasheet window.

8. To prove that the formatting changes were indeed saved:
DOUBLE-CLICK: Courses in the list area
The Datasheet window appears with the same text and window formatting and field column order.

9. Close the Datasheet window.

3.1. Name two reasons for changing the field column order in a datasheet.

3.2 Sorting, Finding, and Maintaining Data

Information is *processed data.* This processing can take several forms, from analyzing, organizing, and summarizing data to presenting data in charts and reports. In this module, you learn how to sort and arrange records into a precise and logical order. You also find and replace data stored in a table. Finally, you learn how to spell-check the contents of a table as you would a document in Microsoft Word or a worksheet in Microsoft Excel.

3.2.1 Sorting Records in a Datasheet

feature

Records are displayed in the order that they are originally entered into a table, unless a primary key has been assigned. With a primary key, records are arranged and displayed according to the contents of the primary key field. Even so, Access allows you to rearrange the records appearing in a datasheet into ascending (0 to 9; A to Z) or descending (Z to A; 9 to 0) order by the contents of any field. A field chosen to sort by is referred to as a **sort key**. Sorting is often your first step in extracting information from raw data. It allows you to better organize records and makes it easier to scan a datasheet for specific information.

method

To sort data using the toolbar:

- SELECT: the desired column(s) in Datasheet view
- CLICK: Sort Ascending button (A↓Z) to sort in ascending order

or

- CLICK: Sort Descending button (Z↓A) to sort in descending order

To sort data using the right-click menu:

- RIGHT-CLICK: the desired column in the field header area
- CHOOSE: Sort Ascending to sort in ascending order

or

- CHOOSE: Sort Descending to sort in descending order

practice

You now practice sorting a table into ascending and descending order. Ensure that the AC0300 Database window is displayed.

1. To open the Students table in Datasheet view:
   DOUBLE-CLICK: Students in the list area
   Figure 3.13 shows the datasheet displayed in order by StudentID, the primary key field.

Figure 3.13

Displaying the Students datasheet (partial view)

Microsoft Access

File Edit View Insert Format Records Tools Window Help

Type a question for help

AC0300 : Database (Access 2000 file format)

Students : Table

StudentID	LastName	FirstName	Major	Address	City	Zip	P
1	Stedman	Alan	Business	3710 Bush St.	Seattle	99900	260-39
2	Hernandez	Pete	Business	1485 Sonama V	Redmond	99780	425-53
3	Mohr	Judy	Arts	100 Bosley Lan	Redmond	99780	425-53
4	Buggey	Diana	Science	20 Cactus Lane	Redmond	99804	425-53
5	Seinfeld	Casey	Arts	17 Windy Way	Bellevue	98180	425-64
6	Alomar	Sandra	Business	PO Box 1465	Kirkland	97080	425-49
7	Fernandez	Rosa	Science	151 Greer Rd.	Seattle	99890	260-39
8	Peters	Bob	Arts	200 Union St.	Seattle	99850	260-39
9	Rinaldo	Sandy	Arts	1871 Orrinton R	Redmond	99704	425-53
10	Finklestein	Sue	Business	888 Burrard St.	Seattle	99904	260-39
11	Mortimer	Bruce	Science	235 Johnston S	Redmond	99704	425-53
12	Jung	Chris	Science	1005 West 9th	Redmond	99780	425-53
13	Abu-Alba	Benji	Arts	122 Cordova Av	Bellevue	98200	425-66
14	Stockton	Gretta	Arts	4210 Bush St.	Seattle	99900	260-39
15	Sakic	Eric	Arts	875 Cordova Av	Bellevue	98180	425-64
16	Modano	Joey	Science	36 Primore St.	Kirkland	97780	425-49
17	Francis	Mike	Business	875 Broadway	Maryland	92250	260-88

This field column is the primary key.

2. To sort the records into order by surname:
CLICK: LastName in the field header area
CLICK: Sort Ascending button (A↓Z) on the toolbar
The contents of the datasheet are sorted immediately.

3. Instead of selecting the entire field column, you can position the cursor in any cell within the desired column for sorting. To illustrate:
CLICK: in any cell within the Zip field column
CLICK: Sort Descending button (Z↓A)

4. You can also sort a table by the contents of more than one column, if the columns are adjacent to one another. Access sorts a table starting with the values in the leftmost selected column and then, for identical values, the records are sorted further by the values appearing in the next column. For example, to sort the datasheet into order by Major and then surname, you must move the first or primary sort key, Major, to the left of the secondary sort key, LastName. To begin:
CLICK: Major in the field header area
DRAG: Major to the left of LastName
When you release the mouse button, the Major column appears between the StudentID and LastName columns.

5. Now you must select both columns. Since the Major column is already highlighted, do the following:
PRESS: SHIFT and hold it down
CLICK: LastName in the field header area
The datasheet should appear similar to Figure 3.14.

Figure 3.14

Moving and selecting columns for sorting

Students : Table

StudentID	Major	LastName	FirstName	Address	City	Zip	P
49	Science	Robinson	Red	89 Bush St.	Seattle	99950	260-39
21	Business	Towne	Bruce	818 East 8th Av	Seattle	99950	260-30
42	Business	Barnes	James	1010 Tower Pla:	Seattle	99906	260-39
28	Business	Yap	Steve	1799 West 16th	Seattle	99904	260-39
10	Business	Finklestein	Sue	888 Burrard St.	Seattle	99904	260-39
34	Business	Heurrera	Ricardo	101 West 6th A	Seattle	99904	260-39
47	Science	Garros	Roland	3109 East 5th A	Seattle	99900	260-39
35	Arts	Chang	Thomas	220 Main St.	Seattle	99900	260-39
45	Arts	Veiner	Sima	3809 Main St.	Seattle	99900	260-39
27	Business	Schuler	Presley	190 Greer Rd.	Seattle	99900	260-39
20	Arts	Walsh	Moira	909 West 18th /	Seattle	99900	260-39
14	Arts	Stockton	Gretta	4210 Bush St.	Seattle	99900	260-39
64	Science	Kaplanoff	Mitch	1234 West 23rd	Seattle	99900	260-39
1	Business	Stedman	Alan	3710 Bush St.	Seattle	99900	260-39
24	Science	Edsell	Camilla	7000 Union St.	Seattle	99890	260-39
32	Science	Matson	Lisa	14489 3rd Ave.	Seattle	99890	260-39
19	Science	Brewski	Randy	190 Greer Rd.	Seattle	99890	260-39
40	Science	Brown	Ibrahim	100 Greer Rd.	Seattle	99890	260-39
41	Science	Stevens	Patricia	1789 East 17th	Seattle	99890	260-39
7	Science	Fernandez	Rosa	151 Greer Rd.	Seattle	99890	260-39

Record: 1 of 65

6. To sort the datasheet by the contents of these columns:
CLICK: Sort Ascending button (A↓Z)

7. Using the vertical scroll bar, scroll the window down to where the values in the Major column change from Arts to Business. Notice that the student records appear sorted by surname within each major.

8. Close the Datasheet window without saving the changes.

3.2.2 Performing a Simple Search

feature

The Find command in Access lets you search an entire table for the existence of a few characters, a word, or a phrase. With large tables, this command is especially useful for moving the cursor to a particular record for editing. Most commonly, the Find command is used to locate a single record. Filters and query objects, discussed later in this chapter, are best used to locate groups of records meeting a specific criteria.

method

- SELECT: a cell in the field column you want to search
- CLICK: Find button (🔍) on the toolbar

or

- CHOOSE: Edit, Find
- SELECT: desired search options

practice

In this lesson, you attempt to find data appearing in a datasheet. Ensure that the AC0300 Database window is displayed.

1. Open the Students table in Datasheet view.

2. Finding data is much easier when the datasheet is sorted by the field in which you want to perform a search. To begin:
   RIGHT-CLICK: LastName in the field header area
   CHOOSE: Sort Ascending from the menu

3. Now find the record for Jimmy Kazo:
   CLICK: Find button (🔍) on the toolbar

4. In the Find and Replace dialog box that appears:
   TYPE: **Kazo** in the *Find What* combo box
   Notice that the LastName field already appears selected in the *Look In* drop-down list box, as shown in Figure 3.15.

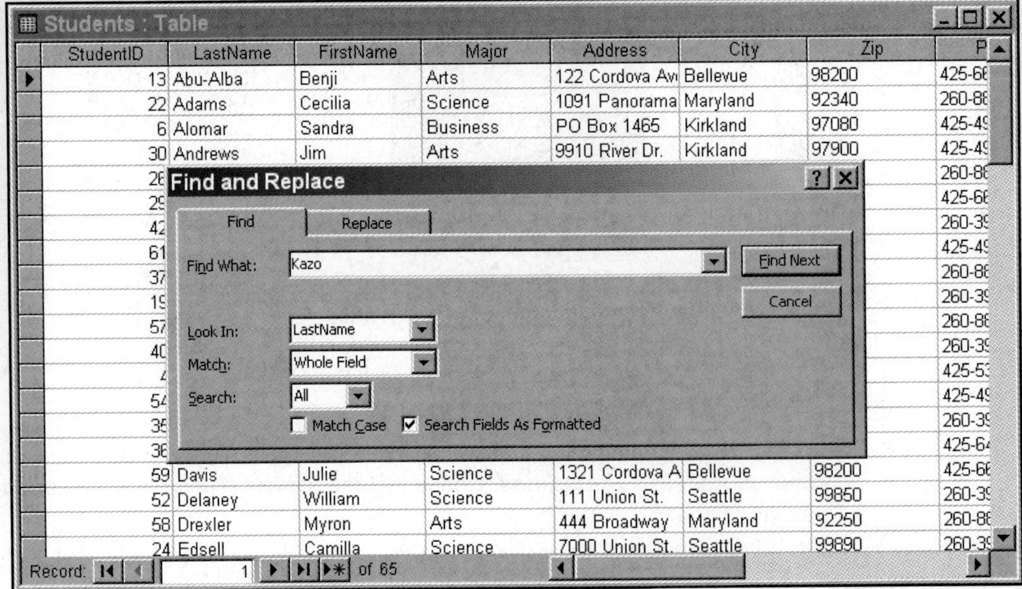

Figure 3.15

Find and Replace dialog box: *Find* tab

5. To proceed with the search:
CLICK: Find Next
The cursor moves down the column and stops on the first occurrence of "Kazo" in record 31. (*Note:* The Find and Replace dialog box does not disappear. Therefore, it may be necessary to drag it out of the way by its Title bar in order to view the selected record.)

6. You can continue the search for more entries for Kazo:
CLICK: Find Next
The following dialog box appears, informing you that no more matches were found.

Microsoft Access
Microsoft Access finished searching the records. The search item was not found.
OK

7. To dismiss the message box:
CLICK: OK command button
You are returned to the Find and Replace dialog box.

8. To end the search:
CLICK: Cancel command button

9. Close the Datasheet window without saving the changes.

3.2.3 Specifying Search Patterns

feature

Using the Find command, you can specify several options to control how a search is performed. You can also use **wildcard characters** to help locate words for which you are unsure of the spelling. These wildcards are also useful in defining search criteria for filters and queries.

method

- Use the question mark (?) in place of a single character. For example, the search pattern "??S?" matches ROSI and DISC.
- Use the number symbol (#) in place of a single number. For example, the search pattern "##9" matches 349 and 109.
- Use the asterisk (*) to represent a group of characters. For example, the search pattern "Sm*" yields entries beginning with the letters "Sm," such as Smith, Smythe, and Smallwood. You can also use the asterisk in the middle of a search pattern.

practice

You now practice using wildcards in building search criteria. Ensure that the AC0300 Database window is displayed.

1. Open the Students table in Datasheet view.

2. Your objective now is to find all the students who live on Shannon Square. To begin, select the Address column:
CLICK: Address in the field header area

Access

3. Let's change the width of the Address field column:
CHOOSE: Format, Column Width
TYPE: **25**
PRESS: ENTER or CLICK: OK

4. CLICK: Find button ()

5. In the Find and Replace dialog box:
TYPE: ***Shannon***
Notice that the existing value, Kazo, in the combo box is replaced by the new entry (Figure 3.16). Using asterisks in this search criteria tells Access to find all occurrences of the word *Shannon* anywhere within a cell entry.

Figure 3.16

Searching for data using wildcards

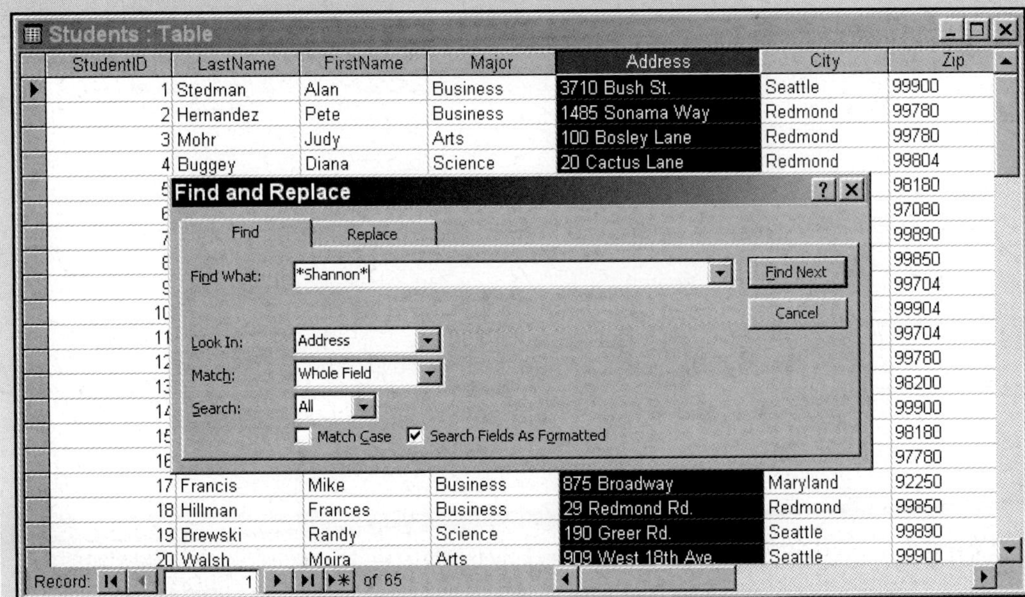

6. To begin the search:
CLICK: Find Next
The cursor moves to Valerie Trimarchi's record, number 31.

7. To continue the search:
CLICK: Find Next to move to Janos Sagi's record, number 43
CLICK: Find Next to move to Mary Timerson's record, number 62
CLICK: Find Next
A dialog box appears stating that the search item was not found.

8. To accept the dialog box and proceed:
CLICK: OK command button

9. To cancel the search:
CLICK: Cancel

10. To return to the top of the datasheet:
PRESS: CTRL + HOME

3.2.4 Performing a Find and Replace

feature

The Replace command in Access lets you perform a global find and replace operation to update the contents of an entire table. Using the same process as Find, you enter an additional value to replace all occurrences of the successful match. Replace is an excellent tool for correcting spelling mistakes and updating standard fields, such as telephone area codes.

method

- SELECT: a cell in the field column you want to search
- CHOOSE: Edit, Replace
- SELECT: desired search and replace options

practice

You now practice using the Find and Replace feature. Ensure that you've completed the previous lesson and that the Students datasheet is displayed.

1. In the next few steps, you will replace the word "Science" in the Major field column with the word "CompSci." To begin:
   CLICK: Major in the field header area
2. To proceed with the find and replace operation:
   CHOOSE: Edit, Replace
3. On the *Replace* tab of the Find and Replace dialog box:
   TYPE: **Science** in the *Find What* combo box
   PRESS: TAB
   TYPE: **CompSci** in the *Replace With* combo box
   Your dialog box should now appear similar to Figure 3.17.

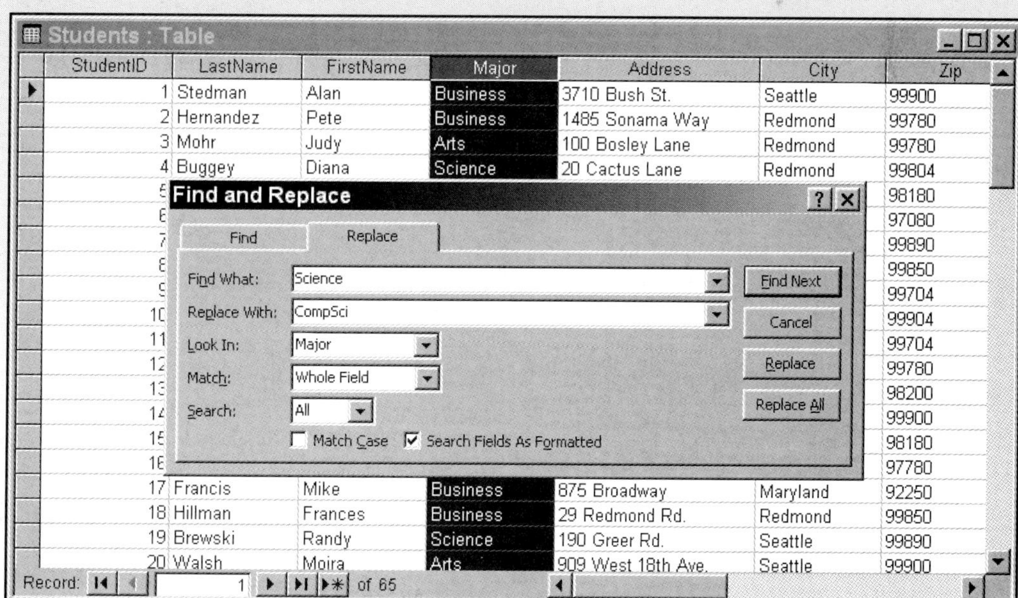

Figure 3.17

Find and Replace dialog box: *Replace* tab

4. If you want to check the values you are about to replace, click the Replace command button to proceed one change at a time. If, however, you want to change all of the values in a single step, do the following:
CLICK: Replace All command button
The following confirmation dialog box appears.

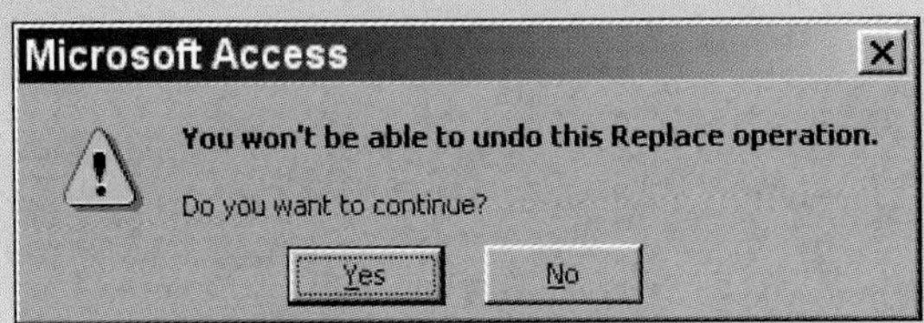

5. CLICK: Yes to accept and to remove the dialog box

6. To remove the Find and Replace dialog box:
CLICK: Cancel command button
Your datasheet should now contain "CompSci" in the Major field column, as shown in Figure 3.18.

Figure 3.18

Replacing a matching value in a datasheet

Students : Table

StudentID	LastName	FirstName	Major	Address	City	Zip
1	Stedman	Alan	Business	3710 Bush St.	Seattle	99900
2	Hernandez	Pete	Business	1485 Sonama Way	Redmond	99780
3	Mohr	Judy	Arts	100 Bosley Lane	Redmond	99780
4	Buggey	Diana	CompSci	20 Cactus Lane	Redmond	99804
5	Seinfeld	Casey	Arts	17 Windy Way	Bellevue	98180
6	Alomar	Sandra	Business	PO Box 1465	Kirkland	97080
7	Fernandez	Rosa	CompSci	151 Greer Rd.	Seattle	99890
8	Peters	Bob	Arts	200 Union St.	Seattle	99850
9	Rinaldo	Sandy	Arts	1871 Orrinton Rd.	Redmond	99704
10	Finklestein	Sue	Business	888 Burrard St.	Seattle	99904
11	Mortimer	Bruce	CompSci	235 Johnston St.	Redmond	99704
12	Jung	Chris	CompSci	1005 West 9th Ave.	Redmond	99780
13	Abu-Alba	Benji	Arts	122 Cordova Ave.	Bellevue	98200
14	Stockton	Gretta	Arts	4210 Bush St.	Seattle	99900
15	Sakic	Eric	Arts	875 Cordova Ave.	Bellevue	98180
16	Modano	Joey	CompSci	36 Primore St.	Kirkland	97780
17	Francis	Mike	Business	875 Broadway	Maryland	92250
18	Hillman	Frances	Business	29 Redmond Rd.	Redmond	99850
19	Brewski	Randy	CompSci	190 Greer Rd.	Seattle	99890
20	Walsh	Moira	Arts	909 West 18th Ave.	Seattle	99900

Record: 1 of 65

7. Keep the datasheet open for use in the next lesson.

3.2.5 Spell-Checking a Datasheet

feature

You can check the spelling of entries in a datasheet in the same way that you spell-check a word processing document. With the Datasheet window displayed, click the Spelling button (icon) on the toolbar. A dialog box appears for each word that the Spelling Checker does not recognize or believes to be misspelled. You can correct the spelling, ignore the entry, or add the word to a custom dictionary.

method

- CLICK: Spelling button (⍰) on the toolbar

or

- CHOOSE: Tools, Spelling from the menu

practice

You now practice spell-checking a datasheet. Ensure that you've completed the previous lesson and that the Students datasheet is displayed.

1. PRESS: CTRL + HOME to move to the top corner of the datasheet
2. To begin spell-checking the table contents:
   CLICK: Spelling button (⍰)
   The Spelling Checker reads through the contents of the fields and stops at the first word that it does not recognize, as shown in Figure 3.19.

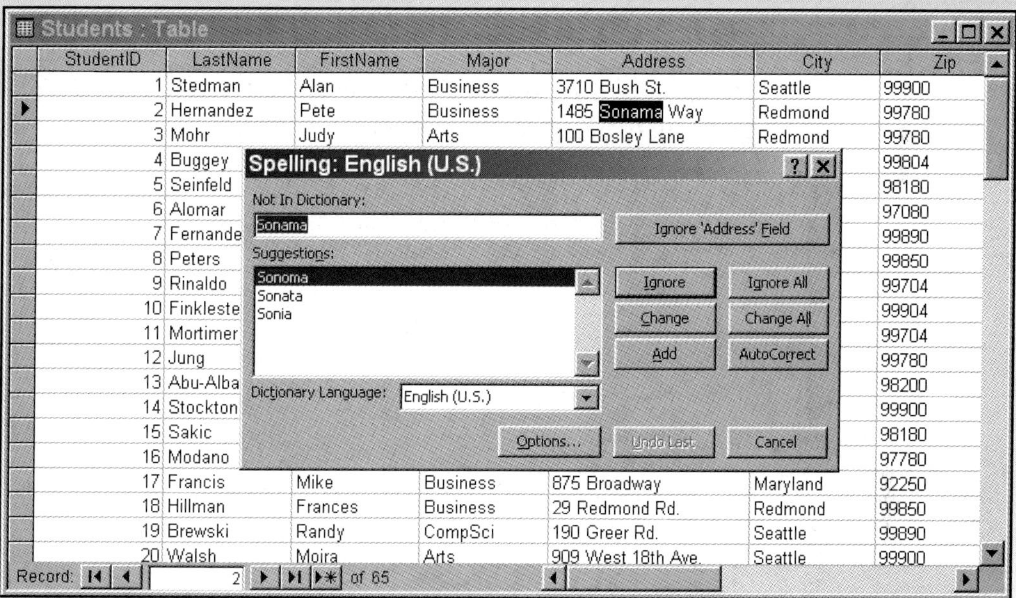

Figure 3.19

Spell-checking a datasheet

3. Because the Address field contains many names that will not likely appear in the spelling dictionary, let's tell the Spelling Checker to refrain from checking the contents of this field. Do the following:
   CLICK: Ignore 'Address' Field command button
4. Similarly, the LastName field contains proper names not typically found in a dictionary. To ignore the word "Buggey" and other names in the field column:
   CLICK: Ignore 'LastName' Field command button
5. The Spelling Checker now stops on the word "CompSci." Rather than ignore the entire field, let's ignore all the occurrences of this word only, since it is spelled correctly. Do the following:
   CLICK: Ignore All command button

6. Now ignore checking the contents of the FirstName field:
CLICK: Ignore 'FirstName' Field command button
After proceeding through the remaining cells, the Spelling Checker displays the following dialog box.

7. To dismiss the dialog box:
CLICK: OK command button

8. Close the Datasheet window and save the layout changes.

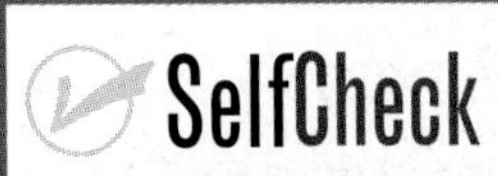

3.2. How do you perform a sort operation using more than one field column?

3.3 Using Filters

A **filter** is a technique that limits the display of records in a table using a simple matching criterion. Similar to a pasta strainer that lets water through but not the pasta, a filter allows only some records to pass through for display. Filtering is an excellent way to find a subset of records to work with that match a particular value or range of values. Several methods are available for filtering records in a table: Filter For Input, Filter By Selection, Filter Excluding Selection, and Filter By Form. These are all accessed using the Records, Filter command. In this module, you learn how to define, apply, and remove filters.

3.3.1 Filtering for Input

feature

Filtering displays a subset of records from a table. The **Filter For Input** method allows you to specify which records are let through. To apply this filter, you display a field's right-click menu and then type a value into the "Filter For:" text box. Finding the matches to this value in the current field filters the datasheet. You may return to viewing all of the records by clicking the Apply/Remove Filter button (▽) at any time.

method

- RIGHT-CLICK: any cell in the desired field column
- CHOOSE: Filter For:
- TYPE: **filter criteria**

practice

In this lesson, you use the Filter For Input method to apply a filter. Ensure that the AC0300 Database window is displayed.

1. Open the Students table in Datasheet view.
2. Let's apply a filter to the datasheet that displays only those students with a last name beginning with the letter "S." Do the following:
RIGHT-CLICK: Stedman in the LastName field column
Your screen should now appear similar to Figure 3.20.

Figure 3.20

Choosing the Filter For Input command

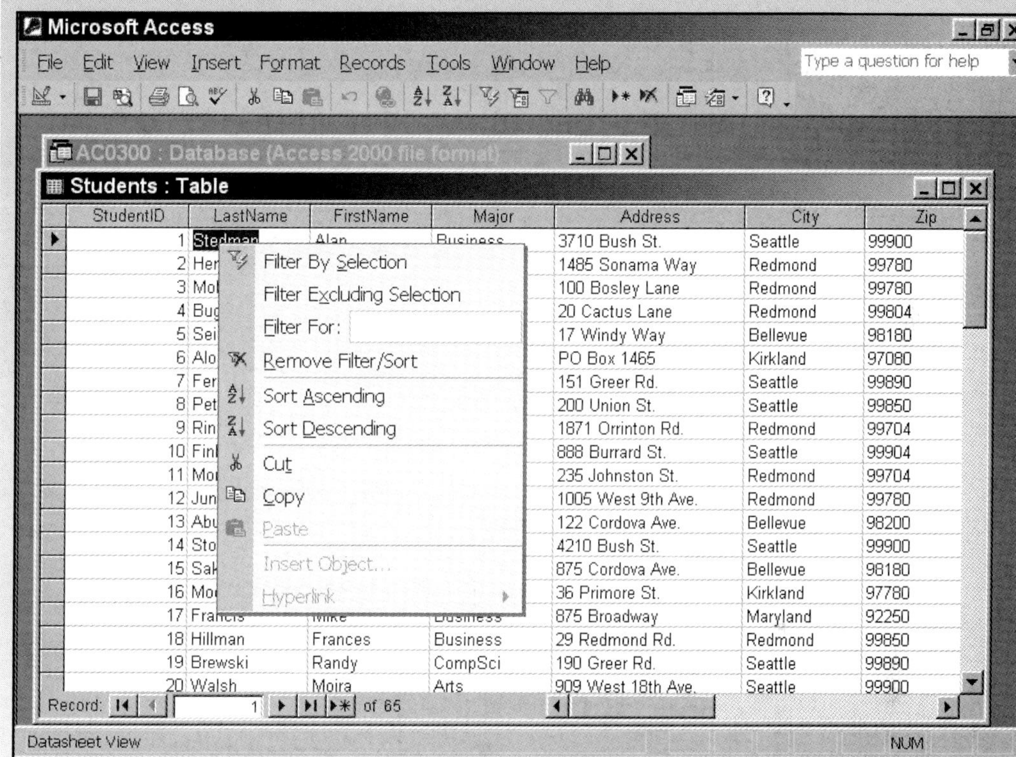

3. CHOOSE: Filter For:
A flashing insertion point should appear in the adjacent text box, as shown below.

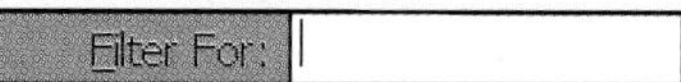

4. In the Filter For: text box:
TYPE: **s***
PRESS: ENTER
The datasheet (Figure 3.21) displays 8 of the original 65 records.

Access

Figure 3.21

A filtered datasheet

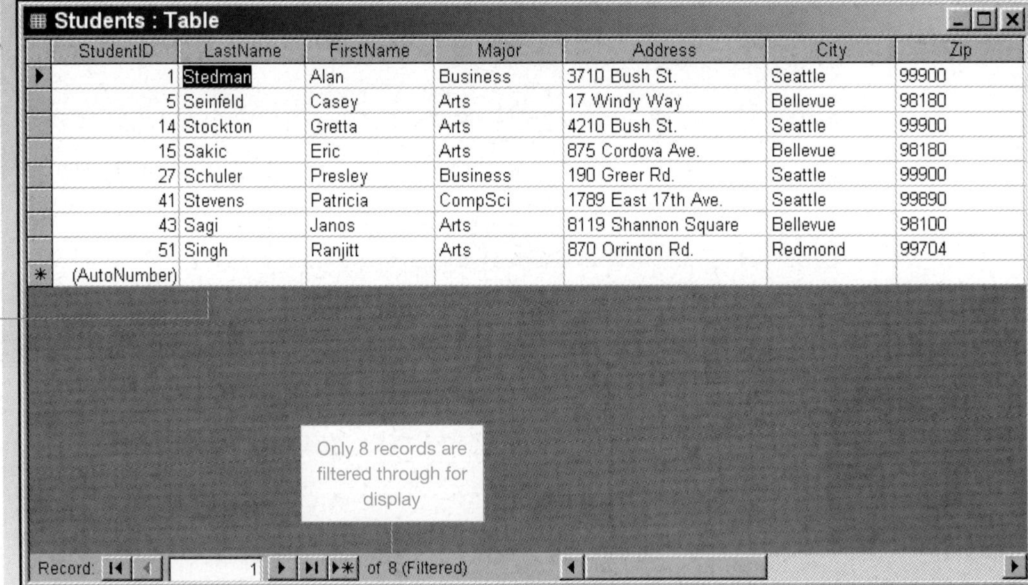

Students : Table

	StudentID	LastName	FirstName	Major	Address	City	Zip
▶	1	Stedman	Alan	Business	3710 Bush St.	Seattle	99900
	5	Seinfeld	Casey	Arts	17 Windy Way	Bellevue	98180
	14	Stockton	Gretta	Arts	4210 Bush St.	Seattle	99900
	15	Sakic	Eric	Arts	875 Cordova Ave.	Bellevue	98180
	27	Schuler	Presley	Business	190 Greer Rd.	Seattle	99900
	41	Stevens	Patricia	CompSci	1789 East 17th Ave.	Seattle	99890
	43	Sagi	Janos	Arts	8119 Shannon Square	Bellevue	98100
	51	Singh	Ranjitt	Arts	870 Orrinton Rd.	Redmond	99704
*	(AutoNumber)						

Record: 1 of 8 (Filtered)

Displays only those students with a last name beginning with "s"
Only 8 records are filtered through for display

5. Once the datasheet is filtered, you can sort the resulting subset of records using the appropriate toolbar buttons. To sort the filtered records:
   CLICK: Sort Ascending button ( )
   The datasheet now appears sorted by surname.

6. The Apply/Remove Filter button ( ) on the toolbar acts as a toggle to turn on and off the current or active filter. To illustrate:
   CLICK: Remove Filter button ( )
   Notice that the datasheet remains sorted in ascending order.

7. To reapply the last filter:
   CLICK: Apply Filter button ( )
   Notice that the toolbar button changes names depending on its toggle status.

8. Close the Datasheet window without saving the changes.

3.3.2 Filtering by Selection

feature →

Using the **Filter By Selection** method, you apply a filter based on a selected value from the datasheet. The selection may be an entire cell's contents or only a portion of the entry. Likewise, you use the **Filter Excluding Selection** method to display only those records that do not match the selected value.

method →

To apply a Filter By Selection:

- SELECT: all or part of an existing field entry
- CLICK: Filter By Selection button ( )

or

- CHOOSE: Records, Filter, Filter By Selection

To apply a Filter Excluding Selection:

- SELECT: all or part of an existing field entry
- CHOOSE: Records, Filter, Filter Excluding Selection

practice

In this lesson, you use the Filter By Selection method to apply a filter. Ensure that the AC0300 Database window is displayed.

1. Open the Students table in Datasheet view.
2. To display only those students living in the city of Redmond:
   DOUBLE-CLICK: "Redmond" in the City field column of the second record
3. To create a filter based on the selected text:
   CLICK: Filter By Selection button ( )
   A subset of 10 records is displayed in the Datasheet window, as shown in Figure 3.22.

Figure 3.22

Filtering a datasheet by selection

Students : Table

StudentID	LastName	FirstName	Major	Address	City	Zip
2	Hernandez	Pete	Business	1485 Sonama Way	Redmond	99780
3	Mohr	Judy	Arts	100 Bosley Lane	Redmond	99780
4	Buggey	Diana	CompSci	20 Cactus Lane	Redmond	99804
9	Rinaldo	Sandy	Arts	1871 Orrinton Rd.	Redmond	99704
11	Mortimer	Bruce	CompSci	235 Johnston St.	Redmond	99704
12	Jung	Chris	CompSci	1005 West 9th Ave.	Redmond	99780
18	Hillman	Frances	Business	29 Redmond Rd.	Redmond	99850
23	Henderson	Kendra	Arts	540 Cactus Lane	Redmond	99804
50	Maynard	Elaine	Business	15201 Johnston Rd.	Redmond	99702
51	Singh	Ranjitt	Arts	870 Orrinton Rd.	Redmond	99704
(AutoNumber)						

Record: 1 of 10 (Filtered)

Displays only those records containing the selected text "Redmond"

4. To remove the filter:
   CLICK: Remove Filter button ( )
5. To display only those students who are *not* taking Arts as their major:
   DOUBLE-CLICK: "Arts" in any cell of the Major field column
   CHOOSE: Records, Filter
   The following menu appears. Except for the Filter For Input option, you can access all other Filter commands using this menu.

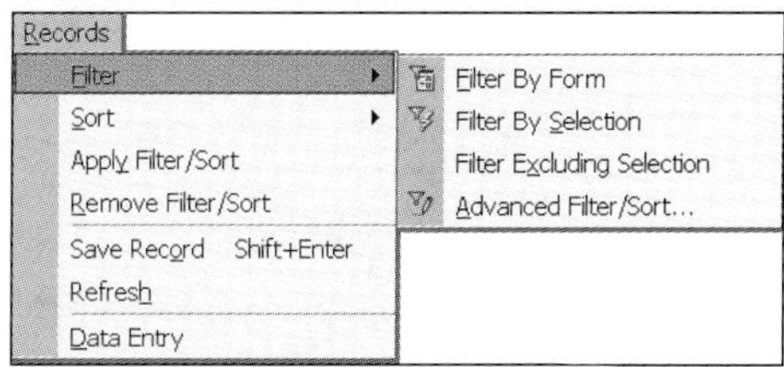

Access

6. CHOOSE: Filter Excluding Selection
A subset of 42 records is displayed in the Datasheet window.

7. To remove the filter:
CLICK: Remove Filter button ()

8. To display only those students living in Seattle and taking CompSci as their major, you need to apply two filters to the datasheet. To begin:
DOUBLE-CLICK: "CompSci" in any cell of the Major field column
CLICK: Filter By Selection button ()
A subset of 20 records is displayed.

9. Without removing the filter:
DOUBLE-CLICK: "Seattle" in any cell of the City field column
CLICK: Filter By Selection button ()
Now a subset of 11 records is displayed, as shown in Figure 3.23. These records match the criteria specified in the previous two filter selections.

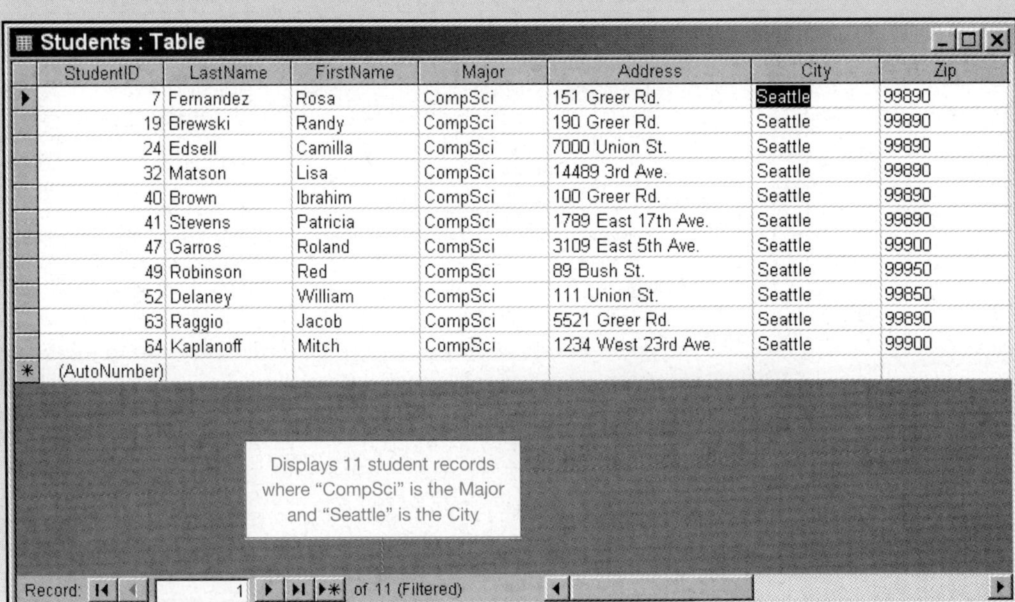

Students : Table

StudentID	LastName	FirstName	Major	Address	City	Zip
7	Fernandez	Rosa	CompSci	151 Greer Rd.	Seattle	99890
19	Brewski	Randy	CompSci	190 Greer Rd.	Seattle	99890
24	Edsell	Camilla	CompSci	7000 Union St.	Seattle	99890
32	Matson	Lisa	CompSci	14489 3rd Ave.	Seattle	99890
40	Brown	Ibrahim	CompSci	100 Greer Rd.	Seattle	99890
41	Stevens	Patricia	CompSci	1789 East 17th Ave.	Seattle	99890
47	Garros	Roland	CompSci	3109 East 5th Ave.	Seattle	99900
49	Robinson	Red	CompSci	89 Bush St.	Seattle	99950
52	Delaney	William	CompSci	111 Union St.	Seattle	99850
63	Raggio	Jacob	CompSci	5521 Greer Rd.	Seattle	99890
64	Kaplanoff	Mitch	CompSci	1234 West 23rd Ave.	Seattle	99900
(AutoNumber)						

Record: 1 of 11 (Filtered)

Figure 3.23

Filtering a datasheet using two filter specifications

10. To continue, let's filter to find those students who live on Greer Road:
DOUBLE-CLICK: "Greer" in any cell of the Address field column
CLICK: Filter By Selection button ()
Four students who live on Greer Road in Seattle are taking CompSci as their major.

11. To display all of the records once again:
CLICK: Remove Filter button ()

12. Close the Datasheet window without saving the changes.

3.3.3 Filtering by Form

feature

For more detailed filtering operations, use the **Filter By Form** method to set multiple criteria. Unlike Filter For Input or Filter By Selection, a blank datasheet row appears in which you can enter or select the desired criteria. Once you have defined a filter, Access enables you to save it as a query object in the Database window.

method

To apply a Filter By Form:

- CLICK: Filter By Form button ( )

or

- CHOOSE: Records, Filter, Filter By Form
- Enter the desired filtering criteria.
- CLICK: Apply/Remove Filter button ( )

To save a Filter By Form as a Query:

- Display the Filter By Form window.
- CLICK: Save As Query button ( )

practice

In this lesson, you use the Filter By Form method to apply a filter. Ensure that the AC0300 Database window is displayed.

1. Open the Students table in Datasheet view.
2. To use the Filter By Form method for filtering a datasheet:
CLICK: Filter By Form button ( ) on the toolbar
Your screen should now appear similar to Figure 3.24.

Figure 3.24

Creating a filter using Filter By Form

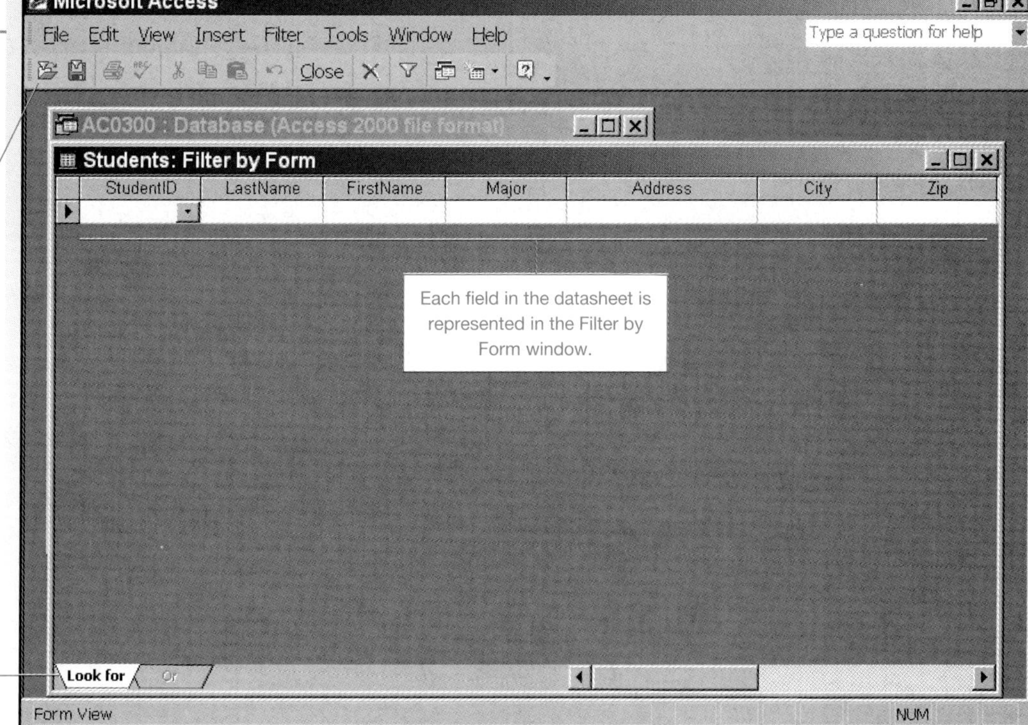

3. Let's display only those students living in Kirkland who are taking Arts as their major. To begin:
CLICK: Major cell once, immediately below the field header area
Notice that a down arrow appears next to the cell. You use this arrow to access a drop-down list of unique values taken from the datasheet.

4. CLICK: down arrow attached to the Major field
The following list appears.

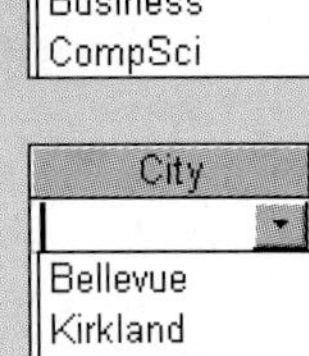

5. SELECT: Arts from the list of three values
The search criteria "Arts" is entered into the cell.

6. To specify the city criteria:
CLICK: City cell once
CLICK: down arrow attached to the City field
The following list appears.

7. SELECT: Kirkland from the list of five values
The search criteria "Kirkland" is entered into the cell.

8. To apply the filter and display the results:
CLICK: Apply Filter button ( )
A subset of 6 records is displayed, as shown in Figure 3.25.

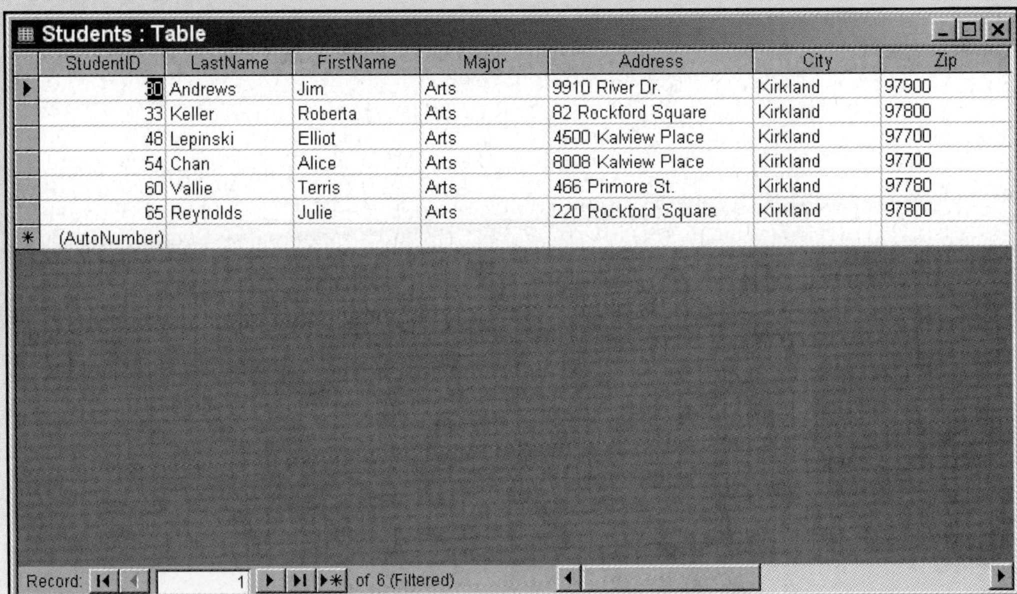
Students : Table

StudentID	LastName	FirstName	Major	Address	City	Zip
30	Andrews	Jim	Arts	9910 River Dr.	Kirkland	97900
33	Keller	Roberta	Arts	82 Rockford Square	Kirkland	97800
48	Lepinski	Elliot	Arts	4500 Kalview Place	Kirkland	97700
54	Chan	Alice	Arts	8008 Kalview Place	Kirkland	97700
60	Vallie	Terris	Arts	466 Primore St.	Kirkland	97780
65	Reynolds	Julie	Arts	220 Rockford Square	Kirkland	97800
(AutoNumber)						

Record: 1 of 6 (Filtered)

Figure 3.25

Filtering a datasheet using Filter By Form

9. Let's return to the Filter By Form window:
CLICK: Filter By Form button ( )

10. To save this filter as a query object:
CLICK: Save As Query button ( )
TYPE: **Kirkland Arts Students**
The dialog box should appear as shown to the right.

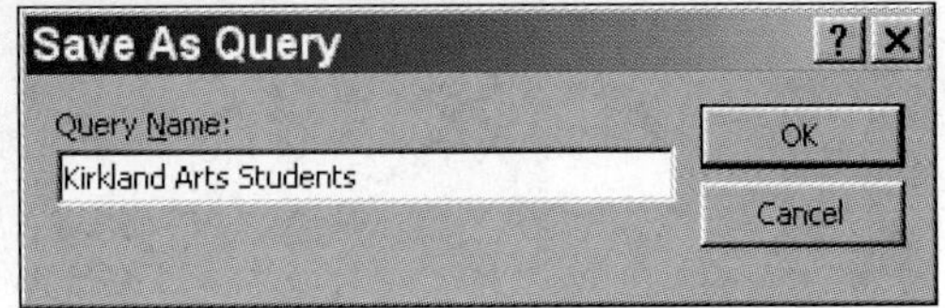

11. PRESS: ENTER or CLICK: OK

12. To specify a new filter:
CLICK: Clear Grid button ( )
The existing filter criteria are removed from the window.

13. In addition to selecting values from the drop-down list, you can type values into the Filter By Form window. To illustrate, let's display only those students with a last name starting with the letter "m":
CLICK: LastName cell once
TYPE: **m***

14. CLICK: Apply Filter button ( )
A subset of 7 records is displayed, as shown in Figure 3.26.

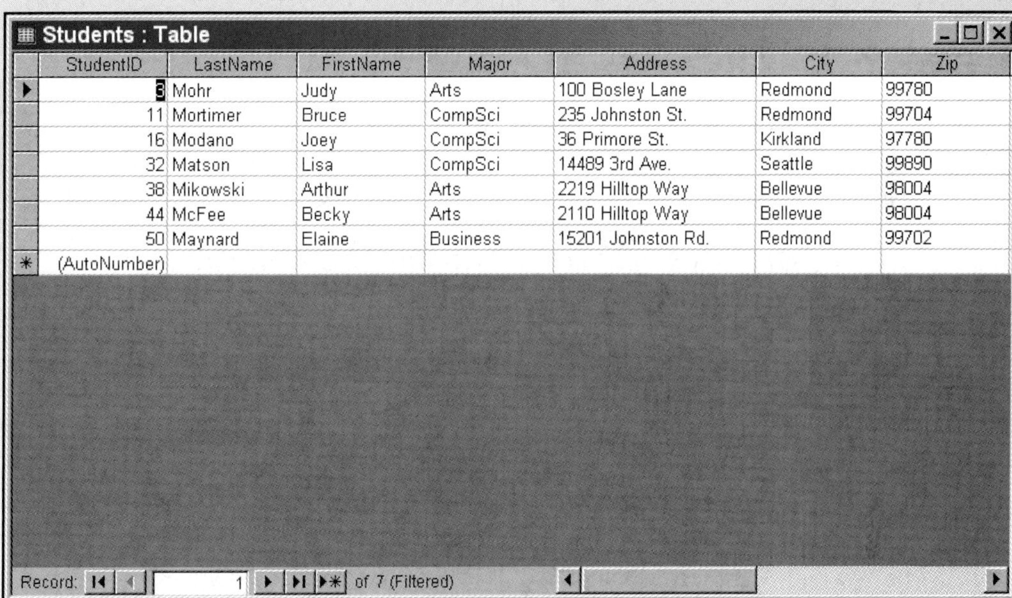

Students : Table

StudentID	LastName	FirstName	Major	Address	City	Zip
3	Mohr	Judy	Arts	100 Bosley Lane	Redmond	99780
11	Mortimer	Bruce	CompSci	235 Johnston St.	Redmond	99704
16	Modano	Joey	CompSci	36 Primore St.	Kirkland	97780
32	Matson	Lisa	CompSci	14489 3rd Ave.	Seattle	99890
38	Mikowski	Arthur	Arts	2219 Hilltop Way	Bellevue	98004
44	McFee	Becky	Arts	2110 Hilltop Way	Bellevue	98004
50	Maynard	Elaine	Business	15201 Johnston Rd.	Redmond	99702
(AutoNumber)						

Record: 1 of 7 (Filtered)

Figure 3.26

Filtering the datasheet by the LastName field

15. Close the Datasheet window without saving the changes.

16. Let's use the Filter By Form query you saved in step 10. To run this query from the Database window, first:
CLICK: *Queries* button in the Objects bar
You should see the "Kirkland Arts Students" query in the Database window.

17. DOUBLE-CLICK: Kirkland Arts Students in the list area
A datasheet displaying the filtered results appears, similar to the datasheet shown in Figure 3.25.

18. Close the Datasheet window.

3.3. In a personnel table, how would you display a subset of those employees working in the accounting department?

Access

3.4 Creating a Simple Query

A query is a question that you ask of your database, such as "How many customers live in Chicago?" or "What is the average age of employees in XYZ Corporation?" Using queries, you can prepare, view, analyze, and summarize your data. The results of a query may also be used when presenting data in forms and reports. You can also use special queries to perform advanced updating routines in your database.

Although similar to filters, queries differ in several significant areas. Both filters and queries allow you to retrieve and display a subset of records. However, queries also allow you to display data from multiple tables, to control which fields display and in what order they appear, and to perform calculations on selected field values. In addition, whereas filters provide a temporary view of a subset of records, queries are saved as independent database objects. Use the following statement as your guideline: *find* a record, *filter* a table, and *query* a database.

3.4.1 Creating a Query Using the Query Wizard

feature

The **Simple Query Wizard** is a step-by-step tool that helps you retrieve data from one or more tables in a database. Unfortunately, the wizard does not allow you to specify search criteria or sort parameters. The type of query object created by the wizard is known as a **select query,** since you use it to select data for display. The results of the query are listed in a Datasheet window, sometimes referred to as a **dynaset.** Other types of queries include action queries for updating, adding, and deleting records in a database and parameter queries for accepting input from users.

method

In the Database window, select the *Queries* button and then:

- DOUBLE-CLICK: Create query by using wizard

or

- CLICK: New button (New) on the Database window toolbar
- DOUBLE-CLICK: Simple Query Wizard in the New Query dialog box

practice

You now use the Simple Query Wizard to extract data from two tables for display in a single Datasheet window. Ensure that the AC0300 Database window is displayed.

1. The options for creating a new query object are similar to the options for creating a new table object. You can start from scratch in query Design view or get helpful guidance from wizards. In the next few steps, you use the Simple Query Wizard to create a query. To begin:
   CLICK: *Queries* button in the Objects bar, if it isn't already selected

2. To launch the Simple Query Wizard:
   DOUBLE-CLICK: Create query by using wizard
   The dialog box in Figure 3.27 appears.

Figure 3.27

Simple Query Wizard dialog box

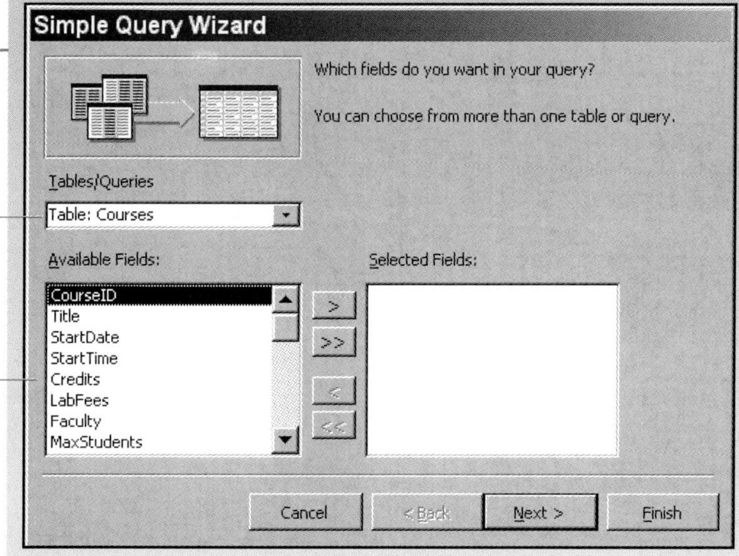

Selecting a table or query updates the fields displayed in the list box below.

Select fields for display in the resulting query.

3. In order to display a listing of courses along with the instructor's name, you must select fields from two tables. To begin, ensure that "Table: Courses" is selected in the *Tables/Queries* drop-down list box.

4. In the *Available Fields* list box:
SELECT: CourseID
CLICK: Include button (>)
SELECT: Title
CLICK: Include button (>)

5. Now select a new table:
SELECT: Table: Instructors in the *Tables/Queries* drop-down list box
Notice that new fields are displayed in the associated list box.

6. In the *Available Fields* list box:
SELECT: LastName
CLICK: Include button (>)
SELECT: FirstName
CLICK: Include button (>)
Your screen should now appear similar to Figure 3.28.

Figure 3.28

Selecting fields for display in the Simple Query Wizard

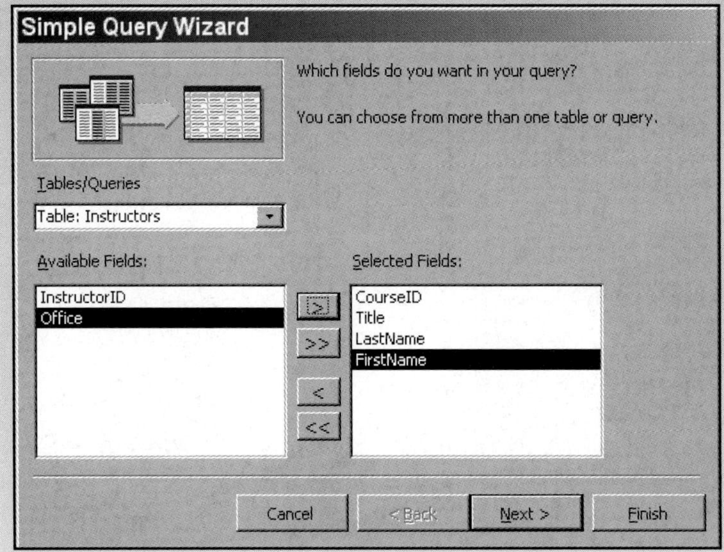

7. To proceed to the next step in the wizard:
CLICK: Next >

8. Now let's name the query:
TYPE: **Course Listing Query**

9. Ensure that the *Open the query to view information* option button is selected in the dialog box and then do the following:
CLICK: Finish
Your screen should appear similar to Figure 3.29. Data in the first two columns is taken from the Courses table and data in the last two columns is taken from the Instructors table.

Figure 3.29

Displaying dynaset results for a query

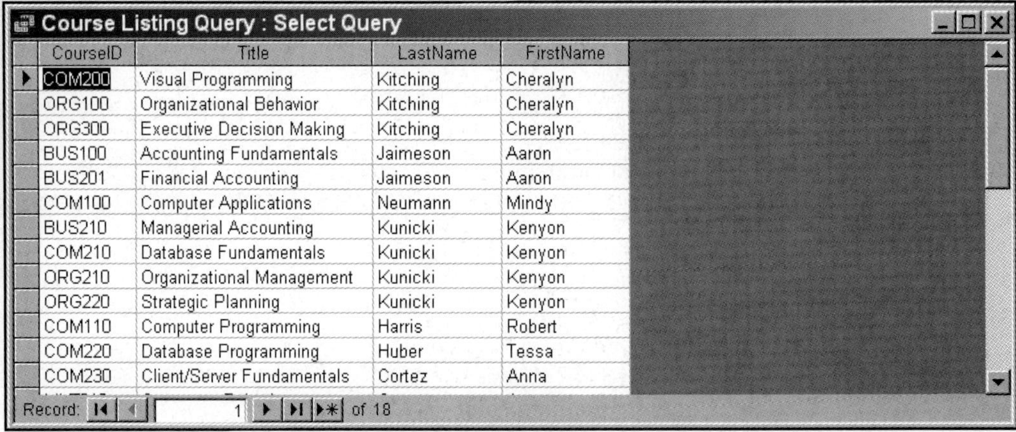

CourseID	Title	LastName	FirstName
COM200	Visual Programming	Kitching	Cheralyn
ORG100	Organizational Behavior	Kitching	Cheralyn
ORG300	Executive Decision Making	Kitching	Cheralyn
BUS100	Accounting Fundamentals	Jaimeson	Aaron
BUS201	Financial Accounting	Jaimeson	Aaron
COM100	Computer Applications	Neumann	Mindy
BUS210	Managerial Accounting	Kunicki	Kenyon
COM210	Database Fundamentals	Kunicki	Kenyon
ORG210	Organizational Management	Kunicki	Kenyon
ORG220	Strategic Planning	Kunicki	Kenyon
COM110	Computer Programming	Harris	Robert
COM220	Database Programming	Huber	Tessa
COM230	Client/Server Fundamentals	Cortez	Anna

10. Keep the Datasheet window open and proceed to the next lesson.

3.4.2 Displaying the Query Design Window

feature

The Simple Query Wizard makes it easy to get started creating queries. Modifying an existing query, however, requires that you use the query Design window. Discussed in Chapter 6 of our Introductory and Complete editions, the Design view is also used to create complex queries from scratch. In this lesson, you learn some basic techniques for displaying and editing an existing query.

method

If the query's Datasheet window is displayed:

- CLICK: View—Design button () on the toolbar

In the Database window, select the *Queries* button and then:

- SELECT: the query object that you want to modify
- CLICK: Design button (Design) on the Database window toolbar

or

- RIGHT-CLICK: the query object that you want to modify
- CHOOSE: Design View

practice

Using the query Design window, you modify the query created in the last lesson. Ensure that you've completed the previous lesson and that the Course Listing Query Datasheet window is displayed.

1. Let's change the view mode for the Course Listing Query to Design view. Do the following:
CLICK: View—Design button ()
Your screen should appear similar to Figure 3.30 before proceeding.

Figure 3.30

Query Design window for the Course Listing Query object

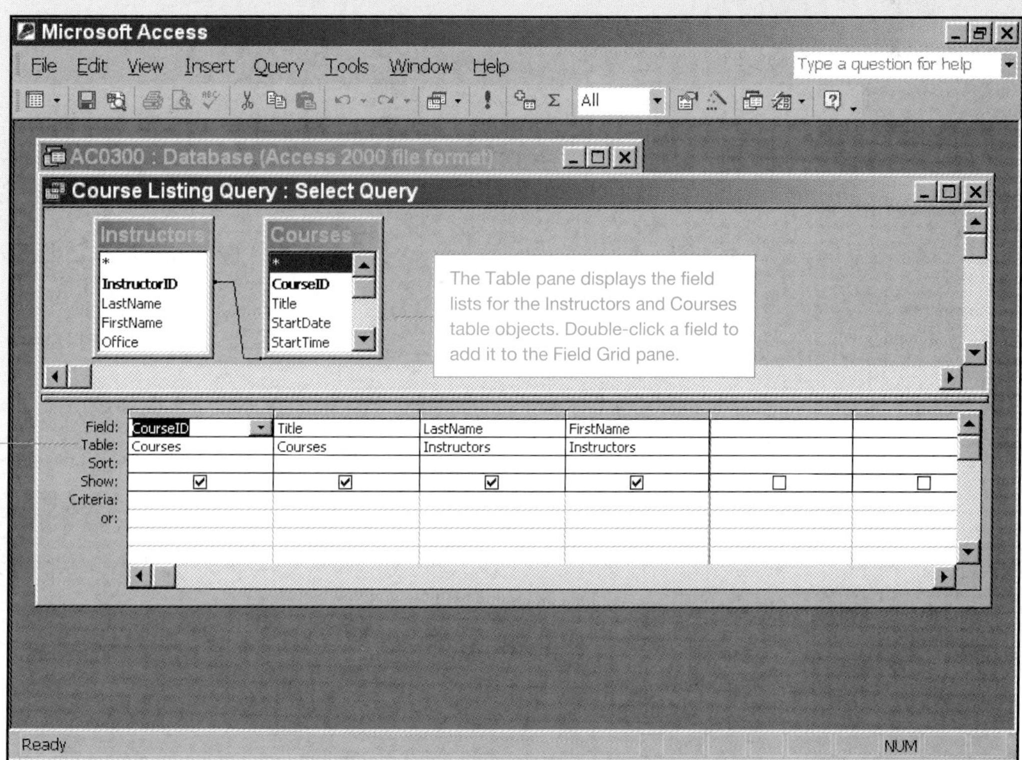

The query Design grid, in the lower portion of the Design window, displays the fields, criteria, and sort specifications for the query.

Access

2. To add a field to the query:
DOUBLE-CLICK: Office in the Instructors table object
The field "Office" is added immediately to the next empty column in the query Design grid.

3. To display the resulting dynaset:
CLICK: View—Datasheet button () on the toolbar
Notice that the Office column is now displayed in the datasheet.

4. To return to Design view:
CLICK: View—Design button ()

5. Let's limit the display of courses to only those taught by instructors with offices in the "B" wing. To do so:
CLICK: in the *Criteria* text box of the Office column
TYPE: **B***
PRESS: ⬇ to complete the entry
Notice that the criteria specification is changed to *Like "B*"* automatically by Access. Your screen should now appear similar to Figure 3.31.

Figure 3.31

Entering a criteria specification in the query Design window

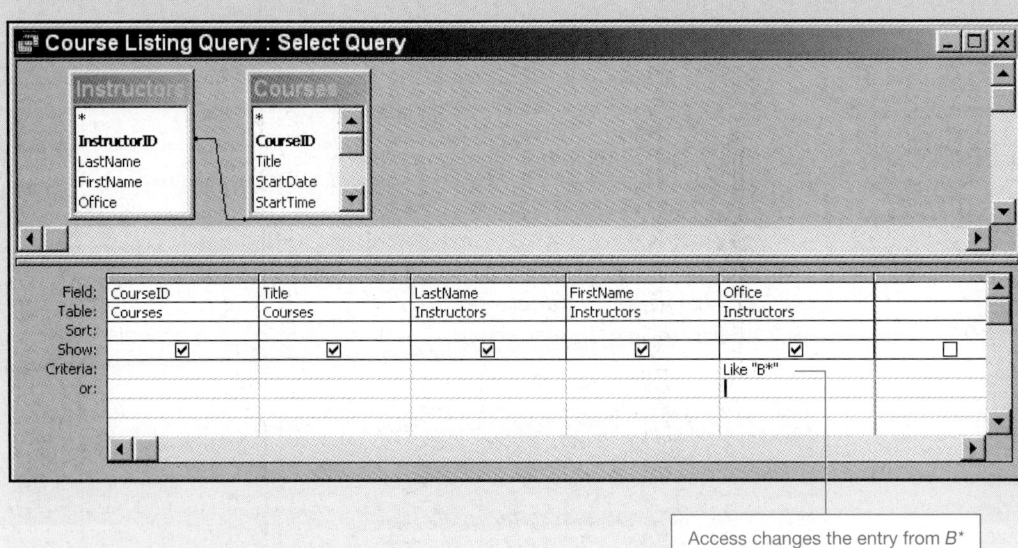

6. Let's save the query object:
CLICK: Save button ()

7. To view the resulting dynaset:
CLICK: View—Datasheet button ()
Only three records are displayed in the datasheet, as shown in Figure 3.32.

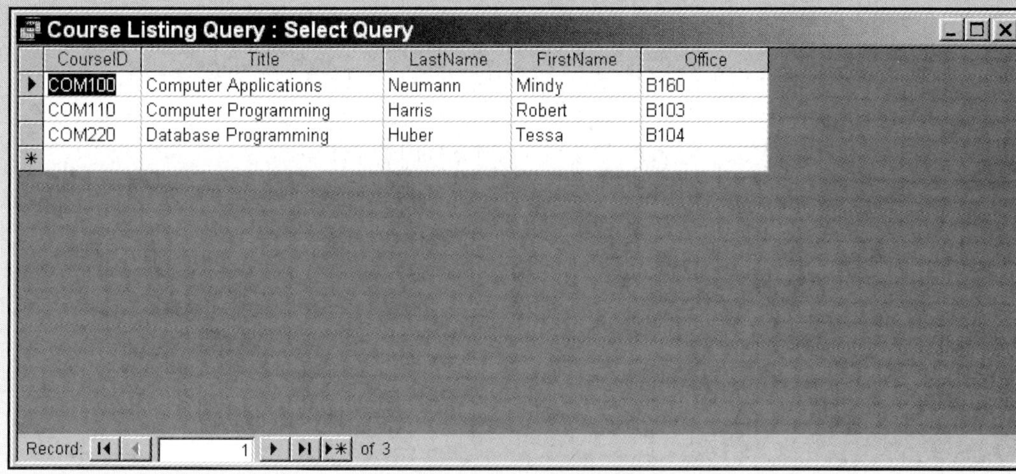

Figure 3.32

Displaying the results of a modified query object

8. Close the Datasheet window for the Course Listing Query.
9. Close the AC0300 Database window.

In Addition SPECIFYING SEARCH CRITERIA IN QUERIES

Querying a database involves more than limiting its display to specific fields. Using query Design view, you can create and modify queries to extract records from tables that meet a given criteria. You can also adjust the sorting order and perform calculations.

3.4. Name one way that a query's dynaset may differ from a table's datasheet.

Chapter summary

One of the primary advantages of using a computerized database is the ability to manipulate, retrieve, and display information quickly and easily. But making your information pleasing to read requires the ability to format and customize the results. Fortunately, you can spice up your datasheets by applying fonts, styles, and special effects. You can also improve your efficiency in working with a datasheet by moving, hiding, and freezing field columns in Datasheet view.

To help you turn raw data into information, the Sort, Find, and Filter commands enable you to organize, locate, and highlight records in a table. You can also use filters to limit the display of records in a table and queries to ask questions of your database. In addition to being able to draw data from multiple tables, queries enable you to specify complex search criteria and sort parameters. Queries are powerful database objects and the sole subject of more advanced chapters.

Command Summary

Many of the commands and procedures appearing in this chapter are summarized in the following table.

Skill Set	To Perform This Task	Do the Following
Creating and Using Databases	Enhance the text displayed in a datasheet using fonts and colors	CHOOSE: Format, Font
	Enhance the background and appearance of a Datasheet window	CHOOSE: Format, Datasheet
	Select a field column	CLICK: in the column's field header area
	Change the field column order in a datasheet	SELECT: the desired column DRAG: its column heading into position
	Hide a field column in a datasheet	SELECT: the desired column CHOOSE: Format, Hide Columns
	Unhide field columns in a datasheet	CHOOSE: Format, Unhide Columns SELECT: the columns to unhide
	Freeze or lock a field column into place in a datasheet	SELECT: the desired column CHOOSE: Format, Freeze Columns
	Unfreeze all of the locked columns in a datasheet	CHOOSE: Format, Unfreeze All Columns
	Save modifications and layout changes made to a datasheet	CLICK: Save button ( ), or CHOOSE: File, Save
Viewing and Organizing Information	Sort a field column in a datasheet into ascending order	SELECT: the desired column CLICK: Sort Ascending button ( )
	Sort a field column in a datasheet into descending order	SELECT: the desired column CLICK: Sort Descending button ( )
	Find or locate a value or record in a datasheet	CLICK: Find button ( ), or CHOOSE: Edit, Find
	Replace an existing value in a datasheet with a new value	CHOOSE: Edit, Replace
	Filter a datasheet using the Filter For Input method	RIGHT-CLICK: a cell in the desired column CHOOSE: Filter For: TYPE: **a filter criterion**
	Filter a datasheet using the Filter By Selection method	SELECT: a datasheet entry CLICK: Filter By Selection button ( )
	Filter a datasheet using the Filter Excluding Selection method	SELECT: a datasheet entry CHOOSE: Records, Filter, Filter Excluding Selection
	Filter a datasheet using the Filter By Form method	CLICK: Filter By Form button ( ) SELECT: the desired criteria

Skill Set	To Perform This Task	Do the Following
	Toggle a filter on or off	CLICK: Apply/Remove Filter button ( )
	Save the criteria entered using Filter By Form as a query object	CLICK: Save As Query button ( )
	Create a query using the Simple Query Wizard	SELECT: *Queries* object button DOUBLE-CLICK: Create query by using wizard
	Toggle between query Design view and Datasheet view	CLICK: View—Design button ( ) CLICK: View—Datasheet button ( )

Key Terms

This section specifies page references for the key terms identified in this chapter. For a complete list of definitions, refer to the Glossary at the end of this learning guide.

dynaset, *p. 124*
filter, *p. 116*
Filter By Form, *p. 120*
Filter By Selection, *p. 118*
Filter Excluding Selection, *p. 118*
Filter For Input, *p. 116*
select query, *p. 124*
Simple Query Wizard, *p. 124*
sort key, *p. 108*
typeface, *p. 99*
wildcard characters, *p. 111*

Chapter quiz

Short Answer

1. Name the three *Cell Effect* options for formatting a datasheet.
2. What command allows you to lock one or more columns of a datasheet in place? Name two ways to execute this command.
3. What are the two primary options for sorting a list?
4. What are wildcards? Provide an example of how they are used.
5. Name four methods for filtering records in a table.
6. When would you use the Find command rather than applying a filter?
7. How do the Filter For Input and Filter By Selection methods differ?
8. When would you apply a filter rather than creating a query?
9. What are two limitations of the Simple Query Wizard?
10. What type of query does the Simple Query Wizard create? What are two additional types of queries?

True/False

1. ____ You can change the color of a datasheet's background.
2. ____ In Datasheet view, click Save (💾) to save your editing changes and click Save Layout (💾) to save your formatting changes.
3. ____ To sort a datasheet by more than one column, you must first ensure that the columns are positioned next to one another.
4. ____ Once you have filtered a datasheet, you can then sort the results using the appropriate toolbar buttons.
5. ____ The search criteria ***osf*** would match "Microsoft."
6. ____ The search criteria **?crosof?** would match "Microsoft."
7. ____ You invoke the Filter Excluding Selection method by selecting text in a datasheet and then clicking a toolbar button.
8. ____ When viewing a table's data in Datasheet view, you can use a filter to limit the display of records in the active datasheet.
9. ____ When viewing a table's data in Datasheet view, you can use a query to limit the display of records in the active datasheet.
10. ____ You find a record, filter a table, and query a database.

Multiple Choice

1. In the Datasheet Formatting dialog box, which of the following is not an option in the *Border and Line Styles* drop-down list box?
   a. Datasheet Border
   b. Datasheet Underline
   c. Horizontal Gridline
   d. Vertical Gridline
2. Which of the following is not an option for customizing a Datasheet window?
   a. Freeze one column
   b. Hide one column
   c. Change one row's height
   d. Change one column's width
3. Which of the following is not a command that is selectable from a field column's right-click menu?
   a. Hide Columns
   b. Unhide Columns
   c. Freeze Columns
   d. Sort Descending
4. The process of restricting the display of records in a table to those matching a particular criterion is called:
   a. filtering
   b. restricting
   c. sifting
   d. sorting
5. Which of the following is not a type of filter method described in this chapter?
   a. Filter By Example
   b. Filter By Form
   c. Filter By Selection
   d. Filter For Input
6. What is the name of the Access tool that simplifies the process of creating a query object?
   a. Database Wizard
   b. Simple Filter Wizard
   c. Simple Query Wizard
   d. Table Wizard

7. A collection of records matching the parameters of a query is sometimes called a:

a. dynaset
b. field
c. table
d. grid

8. Which of the following criteria returns only those cities beginning with the letter "B"?

a. =B
b. B*
c. B?
d. B#

9. Which of the following criteria returns the name "Jones" as a match?

a. *ne*
b. J??nes
c. J#s
d. ?ne*

10. Which of the following statements is false?

a. A filter operation limits records displayed in a datasheet.
b. A query operation returns a Datasheet window of results.
c. A sort operation modifies the natural order of data in a table.
d. A find operation that is successful moves the cursor to the record.

Hands-On exercises

easy

1. AmeriSales International: Customer Table

In this exercise, you enhance the appearance of a datasheet by applying fonts and specifying background special effects.

1. Load Microsoft Access 2002 using the Windows Start menu.
2. Open the database file named AC03HE. Ensure that the *Tables* button in the Objects bar is selected, as shown in Figure 3.33.

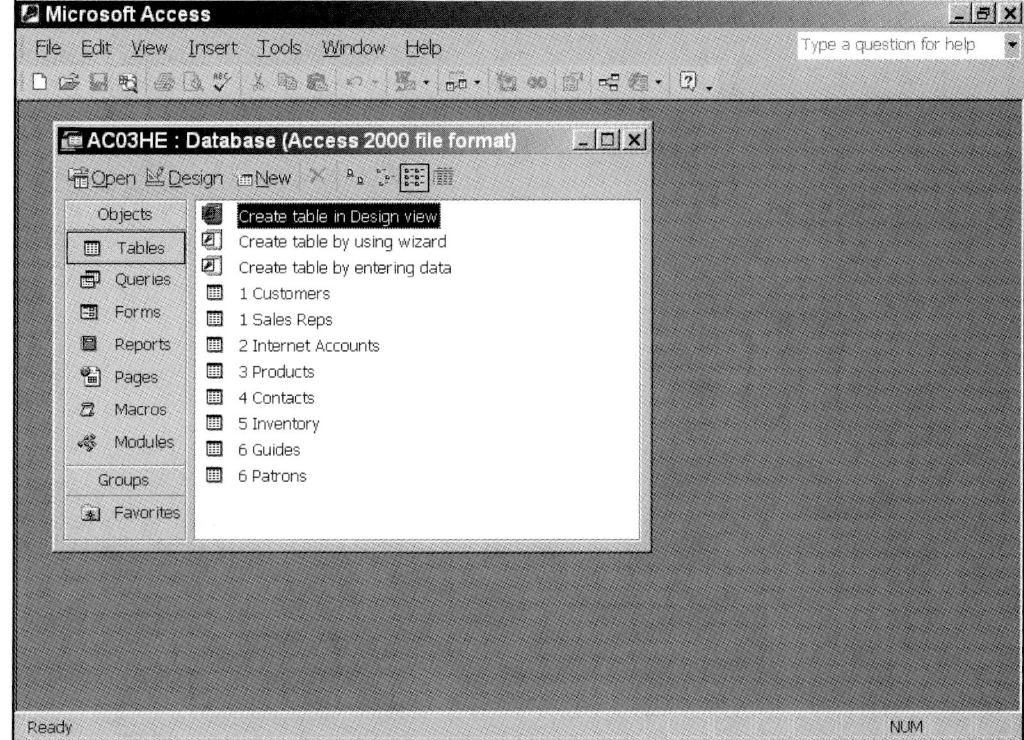

Figure 3.33

Opening the AC03HE database

Access

3. To open a table in Datasheet view:
   DOUBLE-CLICK: 1 Customers in the list area

4. Let's change the font that is used to display the data. First, open the Font dialog box using the menu:
   CHOOSE: Format, Font

5. In the Font dialog box, make the following selections:
   SELECT: Courier New in the *Font* list box
   SELECT: Bold in the *Font style* list box
   SELECT: 11 in the *Size* list box
   SELECT: Maroon in the *Color* drop-down list box
   CLICK: OK command button
   The Datasheet window is modified to display using the new settings.

6. Now let's change the appearance of the datasheet's background:
   CHOOSE: Format, Datasheet

7. In the Datasheet Formatting dialog box:
   SELECT: *Raised* option button in the *Cell Effect* area
   CLICK: OK command button
   Your screen should now appear similar to Figure 3.34.

Figure 3.34

Formatting the 1 Customers datasheet

1 Customers : Table

CustomerID	CustomerNa	Address	City	State	SalesRep
1	Segal	#11 - Hwy	Bonneville	PA	B02
2	Fair Weath	345 Wiltsh	New Surrey	MA	C06
3	Halston &	387 Roper	Midland	WY	A14
4	MMB Holdin	4090 Lethb	Creston	CA	C11
5	WardCo	35-9087 14	Munro	OR	C11
6	Bakertime	759 East 3	Trenton	AL	A02
7	Classic Ac	324 Main S	Coldwater	WA	C11
8	Summit Sup	Ridgeway C	Stoney Blu	CO	B01
9	Harper & R	288 Landsd	Sandy Row	AZ	A03
10	Profession	7241 South	Sunnyvale	NM	A03
11	Silver Clo	111 Rand A	El Rio	CA	C09
12	Ryssell Br	1255 Vollr	South Glen	VE	A03
13	DesJardins	808 Seymou	Nicola	CT	C02
14	Omega Dist	32 Merrit	Riverside	FL	A14
15	J&J Ltd.	675 Cinnam	Warrendale	MS	A05
16	Dalhousie	2233 South	Southgate	KY	B05
17	Larkspur C	4949 Dougl	Princeton	NY	A09
18	De Palma S	988 Laval	Westwood	WI	C02
19	Cameron-Be	429 Mt Ida	Copper Val	OK	A14

Record: 1 of 30

8. To move the SalesRep column so that it appears beside the CustomerID field:
   CLICK: SalesRep in the field header area

9. Position the white arrow mouse pointer ( ) over the field name. Then:
   DRAG: SalesRep to the left so that the bold vertical gridline appears between the CustomerID and CustomerName field columns
   (*Hint:* Remember to release the mouse button to drop the column into place.)

10. Finally, let's adjust some of the column widths:
    CLICK: CustomerName in the field header area
    PRESS: SHIFT and hold it down
    CLICK: City in the field header area
    Three columns should now appear selected.

11. To resize the three selected columns to their best-fit widths:
CHOOSE: Format, Column Width
CLICK: Best Fit command button

12. PRESS: HOME to remove the highlighting

13. Let's prepare the datasheet for printing:
CHOOSE: File, Page Setup
CLICK: *Page* tab in the Page Setup dialog box
SELECT: *Landscape* option button in the *Orientation* area
CLICK: OK command button

14. To preview the datasheet:
CLICK: Print Preview button ()

15. Zoom in on the Print Preview window, as shown in Figure 3.35. Practice using the horizontal and vertical scroll bars to move around the window.

Figure 3.35

Previewing a formatted datasheet (partial view)

1 Customers : Table

1 Customers

CustomerID	SalesRep	CustomerName	Address	City
1	B02	Segal	#11 - Hwy 16	Bonneville
2	C06	Fair Weather Enterprises	345 Wiltshire Ave	New Surrey
3	A14	Halston & Co.	387 Roper Place	Midland
4	C11	MMB Holdings	4090 Lethbridge	Creston
5	C11	WardCo	35-9087 14 Street	Munro
6	A02	Bakertime Mobile	759 East 31 Ave	Trenton
7	C11	Classic Accents	324 Main Street	Coldwater
8	B01	Summit Supply	Ridgeway Connector	Stoney Blu
9	A03	Harper & Ronick	288 Landsdowne	Sandy Row
10	A03	Professional Supply	7241 South Drive	Sunnyvale
11	C09	Silver Cloud	111 Rand Avenue	El Rio
12	A03	Ryssell Bros.	1255 Vollrath St	South Glen
13	C02	DesJardins	808 Seymour	Nicola

16. If you have a printer, print the datasheet by clicking the Print button (). Last, click the Close button (Close) in the toolbar.

17. Save the layout changes by clicking the Save button ().

18. Close the Datasheet window.

2. Iway Internet Group: Internet Accounts

You now practice customizing a datasheet using the Freeze, Hide, and Sort commands. Ensure that the AC03HE Database window is displayed.

1. With the *Tables* button selected in the Objects bar, do the following:
DOUBLE-CLICK: 2 Internet Accounts in the list area

2. First, let's freeze a column in the datasheet so that it is always visible when you scroll the window. Do the following:
CLICK: Username in the field header
CHOOSE: Format, Freeze Columns
Notice that the column is moved to the far left of the Datasheet window.

Access

3. To demonstrate the effect of freezing the Username column:
   PRESS: END to move to the last field column
   Notice that the Username column remains visible, as shown in Figure 3.36.

Figure 3.36

Freezing the Username column

2 Internet Accounts : Table

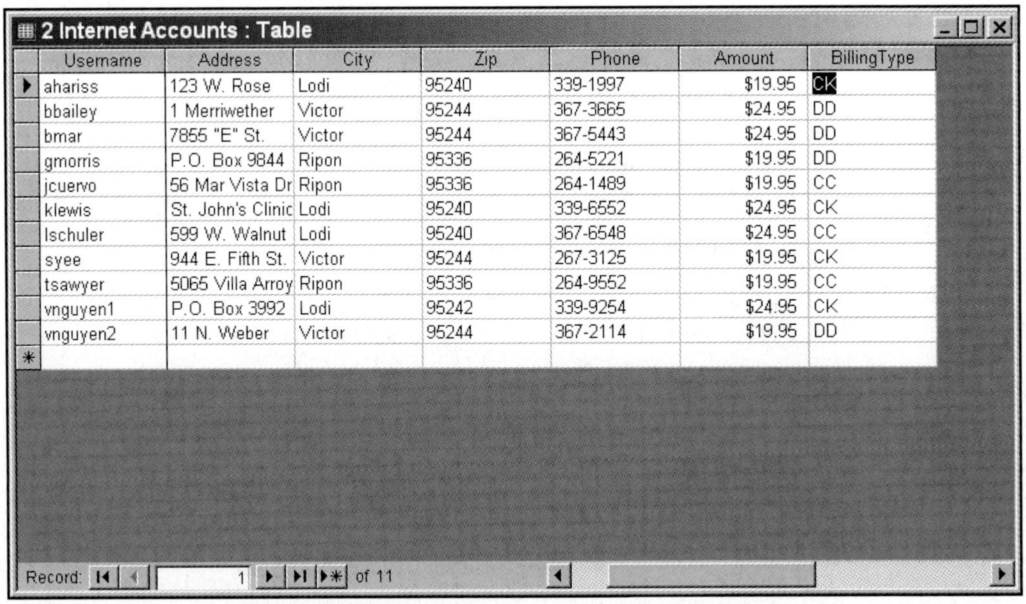

Username	Address	City	Zip	Phone	Amount	BillingType
ahariss	123 W. Rose	Lodi	95240	339-1997	$19.95	CK
bbailey	1 Merriwether	Victor	95244	367-3665	$24.95	DD
bmar	7855 "E" St.	Victor	95244	367-5443	$24.95	DD
gmorris	P.O. Box 9844	Ripon	95336	264-5221	$19.95	DD
jcuervo	56 Mar Vista Dr	Ripon	95336	264-1489	$19.95	CC
klewis	St. John's Clinic	Lodi	95240	339-6552	$24.95	CK
lschuler	599 W. Walnut	Lodi	95240	367-6548	$24.95	CC
syee	944 E. Fifth St.	Victor	95244	267-3125	$19.95	CK
tsawyer	5065 Villa Arroy	Ripon	95336	264-9552	$19.95	CC
vnguyen1	P.O. Box 3992	Lodi	95242	339-9254	$24.95	CK
vnguyen2	11 N. Weber	Victor	95244	367-2114	$19.95	DD

Record: 1 of 11

4. To unfreeze the column:
   PRESS: HOME to move to the first column
   CHOOSE: Format, Unfreeze All Columns

5. PRESS: END to move the cursor to the last field column
   Notice that the column is no longer locked into position.

6. In order to hide the last two columns, you must first select them:
   CLICK: Amount in the field header area
   PRESS: SHIFT and hold it down
   CLICK: BillingType in the field header area

7. To hide the selected columns:
   CHOOSE: Format, Hide Columns
   The Amount and BillingType columns are hidden from view but are not removed from the table.

8. Now sort the records by the contents of the City field column:
   RIGHT-CLICK: City in the field header area
   CHOOSE: Sort Ascending
   The records are grouped together into sorted order by the value appearing in the City field.

9. Adjust the width of the Address column to its best-fit width by double-clicking the borderline between the Address and City columns.

10. To preview what the datasheet looks like when sent to the printer:
    CLICK: Print Preview button () on the toolbar

11. On your own, use the magnifying glass mouse pointer to zoom in on the Print Preview window, as shown in Figure 3.37.

Figure 3.37

Previewing the 2 Internet Accounts datasheet

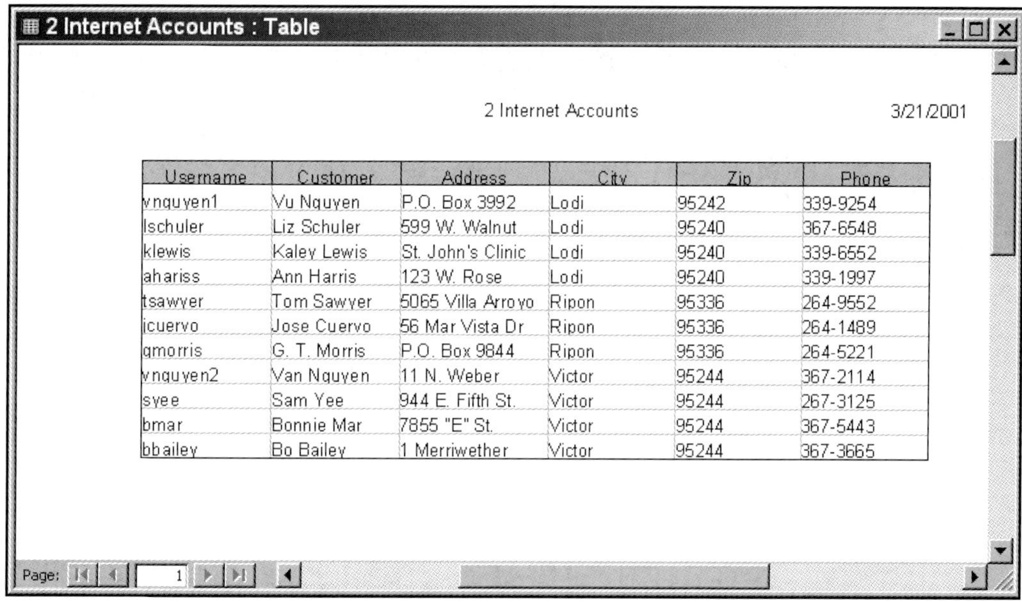

2 Internet Accounts : Table

2 Internet Accounts 3/21/2001

Username	Customer	Address	City	Zip	Phone
vnguyen1	Vu Nguyen	P.O. Box 3992	Lodi	95242	339-9254
lschuler	Liz Schuler	599 W. Walnut	Lodi	95240	367-6548
klewis	Kaley Lewis	St. John's Clinic	Lodi	95240	339-6552
ahariss	Ann Harris	123 W. Rose	Lodi	95240	339-1997
tsawyer	Tom Sawyer	5065 Villa Arroyo	Ripon	95336	264-9552
jcuervo	Jose Cuervo	56 Mar Vista Dr	Ripon	95336	264-1489
gmorris	G. T. Morris	P.O. Box 9844	Ripon	95336	264-5221
vnguyen2	Van Nguyen	11 N. Weber	Victor	95244	367-2114
syee	Sam Yee	944 E. Fifth St.	Victor	95244	267-3125
bmar	Bonnie Mar	7855 "E" St.	Victor	95244	367-5443
bbailey	Bo Bailey	1 Merriwether	Victor	95244	367-3665

Page: 1

12. If you have a printer, print the datasheet by clicking the Print button ().
13. CLICK: the Close button (Close) in the toolbar
14. To unhide the columns:
    CHOOSE: Format, Unhide Columns
15. In the Unhide Columns dialog box:
    SELECT: *Amount* check box
    SELECT: *BillingType* check box
    CLICK: Close command button
16. Save the layout changes by clicking the Save () button.
17. Close the Datasheet window.

moderate 

3. Western Lumber Sales: Forest Products

In this exercise, you sort data using more than one column and practice using the Find and Replace commands. Ensure that the AC03HE Database window is displayed.

1. Open the 3 Products table for display in Datasheet view.
2. You now perform a sort operation that orders the table by Category and then by ProductCode within each category. To begin:
   CLICK: Category in the field header area
   DRAG: Category field column to the left of ProductCode
3. To sort by category and then by product code:
   SELECT: Category and ProductCode field columns
   CLICK: Sort Ascending button () on the toolbar
   Your screen should now appear similar to Figure 3.38.

Access

Figure 3.38

Sorting a datasheet by two field columns

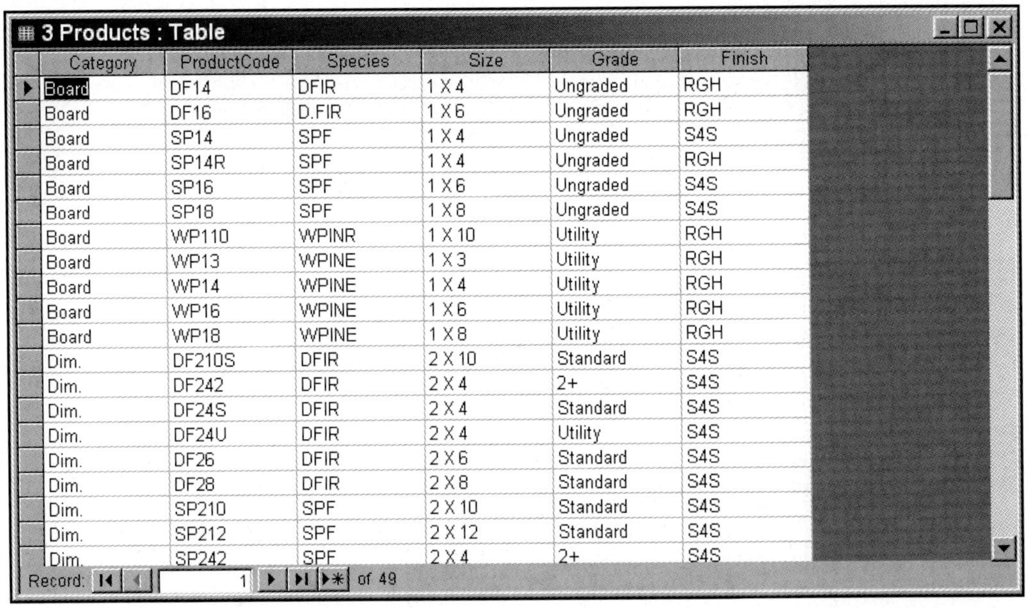

3 Products : Table

Category	ProductCode	Species	Size	Grade	Finish
Board	DF14	DFIR	1 X 4	Ungraded	RGH
Board	DF16	D.FIR	1 X 6	Ungraded	RGH
Board	SP14	SPF	1 X 4	Ungraded	S4S
Board	SP14R	SPF	1 X 4	Ungraded	RGH
Board	SP16	SPF	1 X 6	Ungraded	S4S
Board	SP18	SPF	1 X 8	Ungraded	S4S
Board	WP110	WPINR	1 X 10	Utility	RGH
Board	WP13	WPINE	1 X 3	Utility	RGH
Board	WP14	WPINE	1 X 4	Utility	RGH
Board	WP16	WPINE	1 X 6	Utility	RGH
Board	WP18	WPINE	1 X 8	Utility	RGH
Dim.	DF210S	DFIR	2 X 10	Standard	S4S
Dim.	DF242	DFIR	2 X 4	2+	S4S
Dim.	DF24S	DFIR	2 X 4	Standard	S4S
Dim.	DF24U	DFIR	2 X 4	Utility	S4S
Dim.	DF26	DFIR	2 X 6	Standard	S4S
Dim.	DF28	DFIR	2 X 8	Standard	S4S
Dim.	SP210	SPF	2 X 10	Standard	S4S
Dim.	SP212	SPF	2 X 12	Standard	S4S
Dim.	SP242	SPF	2 X 4	2+	S4S

Record: 1 of 49

4. Now let's find all of the products made from birch wood:
   PRESS: ➔ two times to move to the Species field column
   CLICK: Find button (🔍) on the toolbar

5. In the Find and Replace dialog box that appears:
   TYPE: **birch** in the *Find What* combo box
   CLICK: Find Next command button
   (*Note:* By default, the Find command is not case sensitive.) What product category does the cursor stop on first?

6. Use the Find Next command button to determine if any of the other products are made from birch. When you are finished, close the Find and Replace dialog box.

7. You now use the Replace command to replace all occurrences of the code "Dim." in the Category column with the word "Dimension":
   PRESS: CTRL + HOME to move to the first field in the table
   CHOOSE: Edit, Replace

8. On the *Replace* tab of the Find and Replace dialog box:
   TYPE: **Dim.** in the *Find What* combo box
   PRESS: TAB
   TYPE: **Dimension** in the *Replace With* combo box
   The Find and Replace dialog box appears in Figure 3.39.

Figure 3.39

Find and Replace dialog box

Find and Replace

Find | Replace

Find What: Dim.

Replace With: Dimension

Look In: Category

Match: Whole Field

Search: All

☐ Match Case ☑ Search Fields As Formatted

Find Next | Cancel | Replace | Replace All

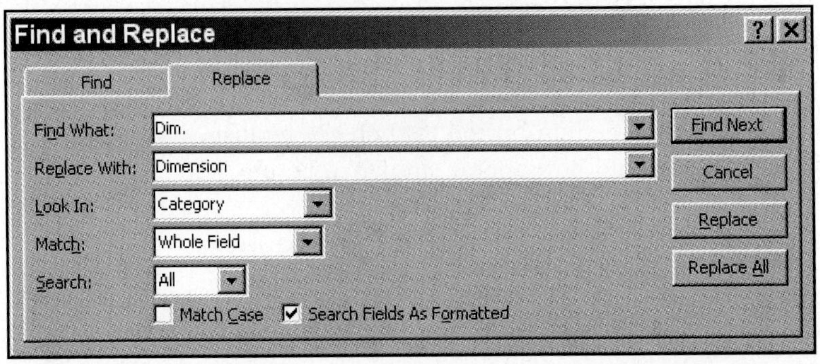

9. To complete the operation:
CLICK: Replace All command button

10. When Access asks you to confirm the replacement:
CLICK: Yes command button

11. CLICK: Cancel to remove the Find and Replace dialog box

12. Close the Datasheet window without saving your layout changes. (*Note:* The Find and Replace changes are saved, but the repositioning of the Category column and the sort order are not saved.)

moderate 

4. Spring County Carnival: Contact List

You now use the Filter For Input and Filter By Selection methods to display only those records that match a specific criterion. Ensure that the AC03HE Database window is displayed.

1. Open the 4 Contacts table for display in Datasheet view.

2. To begin, let's apply a filter so that only the records containing the word "Club" in the VolunteerGroup field column are displayed. Using the I-beam mouse pointer:
RIGHT-CLICK: the first cell in the VolunteerGroup field column
CHOOSE: Filter For:

3. In the menu command's text box:
TYPE: ***club*** in the Filter For: text box, as shown here
PRESS: ENTER
How many groups have "Club" as part of their name?

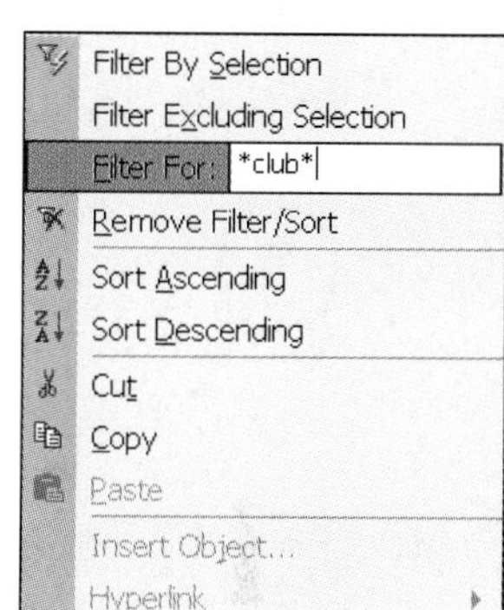

4. To remove the *club* filter:
CLICK: Remove Filter button ( )

5. To display only those groups based in the city of Pinawa:
DOUBLE-CLICK: "Pinawa" in any cell of the City field column
CLICK: Filter By Selection button ( )
How many groups contain "Pinawa" in the City field column?

6. On your own, remove the current filter and use the Filter By Selection method to display only those groups from the city of Centerville. How many groups contain "Centerville" in the City field column? Then remove the filter so that all records are displayed.

7. Now let's use the Filter Excluding Selection method to view all groups from outside the city of Silverdale. First, select the value to exclude:
DOUBLE-CLICK: "Silverdale" in any cell of the City field column

8. To exclude all the records containing Silverdale in the city column:
CHOOSE: Records, Filter, Filter Excluding Selection
Your screen should now appear similar to Figure 3.40.

Access

Figure 3.40

Using the Filter Excluding Selection method

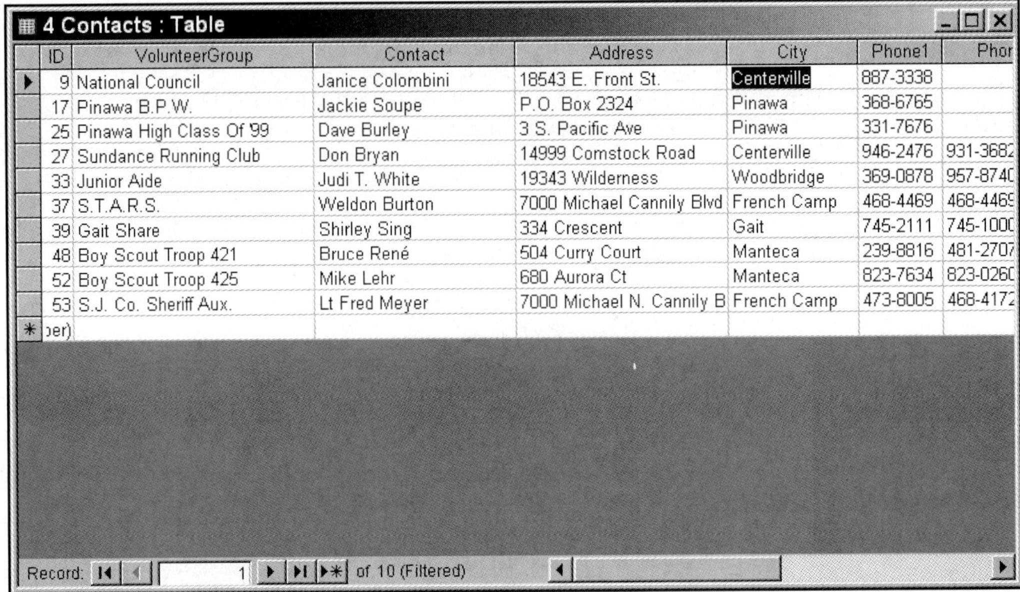

4 Contacts : Table

ID	VolunteerGroup	Contact	Address	City	Phone1	Phor
9	National Council	Janice Colombini	18543 E. Front St.	Centerville	887-3338	
17	Pinawa B.P.W.	Jackie Soupe	P.O. Box 2324	Pinawa	368-6765	
25	Pinawa High Class Of '99	Dave Burley	3 S. Pacific Ave	Pinawa	331-7676	
27	Sundance Running Club	Don Bryan	14999 Comstock Road	Centerville	946-2476	931-3682
33	Junior Aide	Judi T. White	19343 Wilderness	Woodbridge	369-0878	957-8740
37	S.T.A.R.S.	Weldon Burton	7000 Michael Cannily Blvd	French Camp	468-4469	468-4469
39	Gait Share	Shirley Sing	334 Crescent	Gait	745-2111	745-1000
48	Boy Scout Troop 421	Bruce René	504 Curry Court	Manteca	239-8816	481-2707
52	Boy Scout Troop 425	Mike Lehr	680 Aurora Ct	Manteca	823-7634	823-0260
53	S.J. Co. Sheriff Aux.	Lt Fred Meyer	7000 Michael N. Cannily B	French Camp	473-8005	468-4172

Record: 1 of 10 (Filtered)

9. To remove the filter:
   CLICK: Remove Filter button ( )

10. Close the Datasheet window without saving your changes.

5. On Your Own: Benson's Office Supplies

You now practice organizing, retrieving, and manipulating data in the Datasheet window. Open the 5 Inventory table in the AC03HE database. Perform the following database tasks:

- Using the Find and Replace command, change all records with a Supplier code of "G06" to a "J11" code.
- Use the Filter By Form method to display only those records with a Supplier "J11" code and a Buyer "02" code.
- Format the Datasheet window to display using a new and larger font.
- Hide the Reorder column.
- Adjust the widths of the remaining columns so that no data is truncated.
- Move the Supplier column so that it appears as the first field.
- Sort the datasheet by the OnHand amount so that the record with the largest amount is at the top of the datasheet.

When you are finished (Figure 3.41), preview and then print a copy of the Datasheet window. Lastly, close the Datasheet window and save your changes.

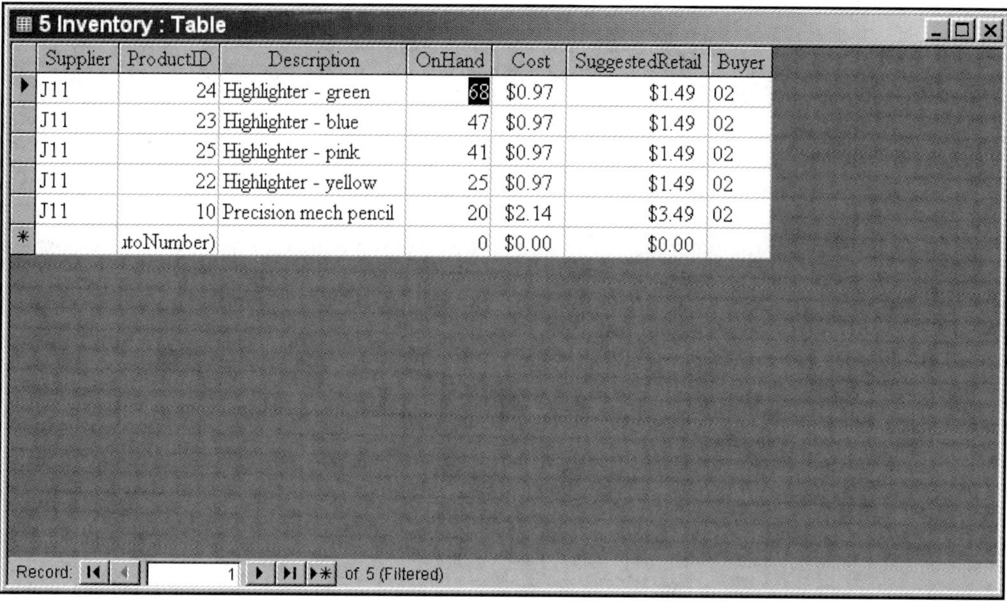

5 Inventory : Table

Supplier	ProductID	Description	OnHand	Cost	SuggestedRetail	Buyer
J11	24	Highlighter - green	68	$0.97	$1.49	02
J11	23	Highlighter - blue	47	$0.97	$1.49	02
J11	25	Highlighter - pink	41	$0.97	$1.49	02
J11	22	Highlighter - yellow	25	$0.97	$1.49	02
J11	10	Precision mech pencil	20	$2.14	$3.49	02
*	ıtoNumber)		0	$0.00	$0.00	

Record: 1 of 5 (Filtered)

Figure 3.41

Filtering and formatting the 5 Inventory datasheet

difficult 

6. On Your Own: Coldstream Valley Resorts

You now create a query object using the Simple Query Wizard. The objective of using a query in this exercise is to display data from two tables in the database. To begin, select the *Queries* button in the Objects bar and then launch the Simple Query Wizard. From the 6 Guides table, include the GuideNumber and Guide fields. From the 6 Patrons table, include the Guest, Hometown, and State fields. In the next step of the wizard, save the query as "Guides and Guests Query" and then open the query to view the results (Figure 3.42).

Guides and Guests Query : Select Query

GuideNumber	Guide	Guest	Hometown	State
13	Allison Delacroix	John & Becky Reusche	Miami	FL
13	Allison Delacroix	Gary Giovanetti	Miami	FL
13	Allison Delacroix	Julie & Royce Mulligan	Webster	FL
13	Allison Delacroix	Coleman & Beatriz Sholl	Saltillo	COA
13	Allison Delacroix	Tom & Cookie Raya	Peoria	IL
13	Allison Delacroix	Teresa & Harry Perry	Gainesville	FL
13	Allison Delacroix	Ho and Vinh Tran	El Paso	TX
16	Binky Binkleton	Patti & Guissepi Gulick	Billings	MT
19	Ned Nedry	Roger Turnbeaugh	Sioux City	IA
19	Ned Nedry	Hector & Ingrid Stringer	Zurich	
19	Ned Nedry	Jeff & Helga Wentworth	Central Falls	RI
19	Ned Nedry	Jeff Valverde	Madrid	
19	Ned Nedry	Ann & Felix Paoletti	Sao Paulo	

Record: 1 of 20

Figure 3.42

Displaying the results of a select query

Before printing the dynaset, enhance the datasheet by applying formatting commands and preview the contents of the Datasheet window. Then, save the layout changes and close the datasheet. Finally, close the Database window.

Access

Case Problems

Roundhouse Rentals

For the past week or so, Ellie Floyd, the office supervisor at Roundhouse Rentals, has been familiarizing herself with the table objects in the company's Access database. Feeling confident that she now understands the nature of the table structures, she informs the owner, Sal Witherspoon, that she is ready to begin. Glad for the opportunity to escape the office, Sal provides Ellie with some afternoon work.

In the following case problems, assume the role of Ellie and perform the same steps that she identifies. You may want to re-read the chapter opening before proceeding.

1. To begin, Sal informs Ellie that he needs a formatted printout of Roundhouse's equipment inventory. The data is stored in a table object named Equipment in the AC03CP database. While Sal thinks up other tasks for Ellie, she jots down a note to herself that Sal prefers all of his business correspondence and reports to appear using a 12-point Times New Roman font. She plans on opening the table in Datasheet view, applying the new font choice, and then removing the vertical gridlines from the Datasheet window. Just then Sal added to his requests. In addition to hiding the DataPurchased field column, Sal wants the Cost column to be positioned as the last column in the datasheet. Ellie makes an additional note to preview the datasheet, as shown in Figure 3.43, to ensure that the proper fields are hidden and positioned correctly. After printing the datasheet for Sal's review, Ellie saves the layout changes and closes the Datasheet window.

Figure 3.43

Formatting the Equipment datasheet

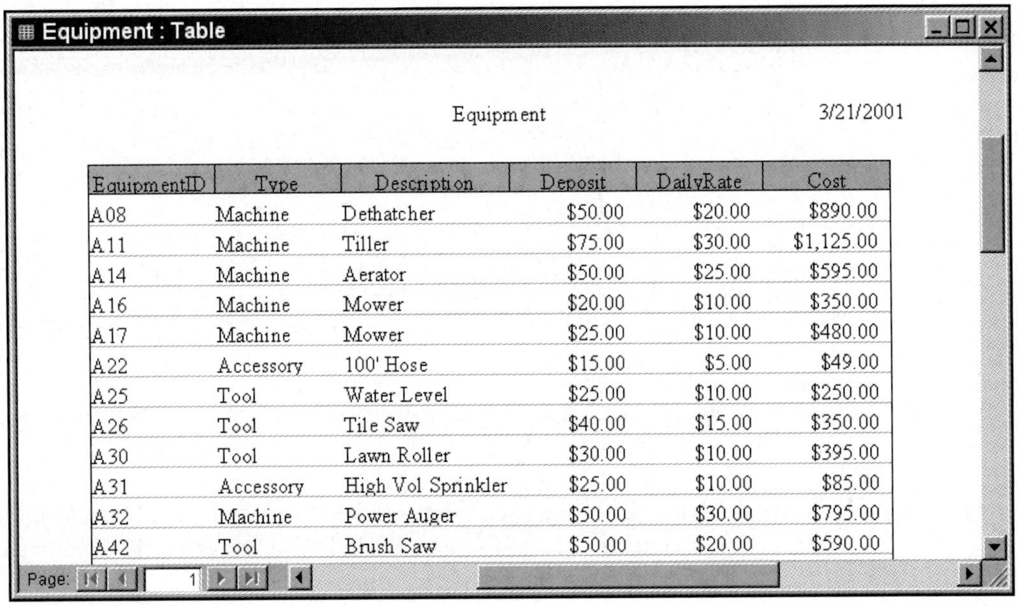

Equipment : Table

Equipment 3/21/2001

EquipmentID	Type	Description	Deposit	DailyRate	Cost
A08	Machine	Dethatcher	$50.00	$20.00	$890.00
A11	Machine	Tiller	$75.00	$30.00	$1,125.00
A14	Machine	Aerator	$50.00	$25.00	$595.00
A16	Machine	Mower	$20.00	$10.00	$350.00
A17	Machine	Mower	$25.00	$10.00	$480.00
A22	Accessory	100' Hose	$15.00	$5.00	$49.00
A25	Tool	Water Level	$25.00	$10.00	$250.00
A26	Tool	Tile Saw	$40.00	$15.00	$350.00
A30	Tool	Lawn Roller	$30.00	$10.00	$395.00
A31	Accessory	High Vol Sprinkler	$25.00	$10.00	$85.00
A32	Machine	Power Auger	$50.00	$30.00	$795.00
A42	Tool	Brush Saw	$50.00	$20.00	$590.00

Page: 1

2. Next on his list, Sal asks Ellie to make some corrections to data stored in the Rentals table. She opens the datasheet and then sorts it into CustomerID sequence. Using the Find command, she locates the record for CustomerID 41. She changes the rental start date to 5/23/01 and the number of rental days to three. After returning to the top of the datasheet, Ellie moves to the Days column and then uses the Find and Replace command to change any records that have a value of zero in the Days field to the minimum rental of one day. Then Ellie uses the Filter By Selection method to display and print only the records that have a status of "Active," as shown in Figure 3.44. She closes the Datasheet window and saves the changes.

Figure 3.44

Editing and filtering the Rentals datasheet

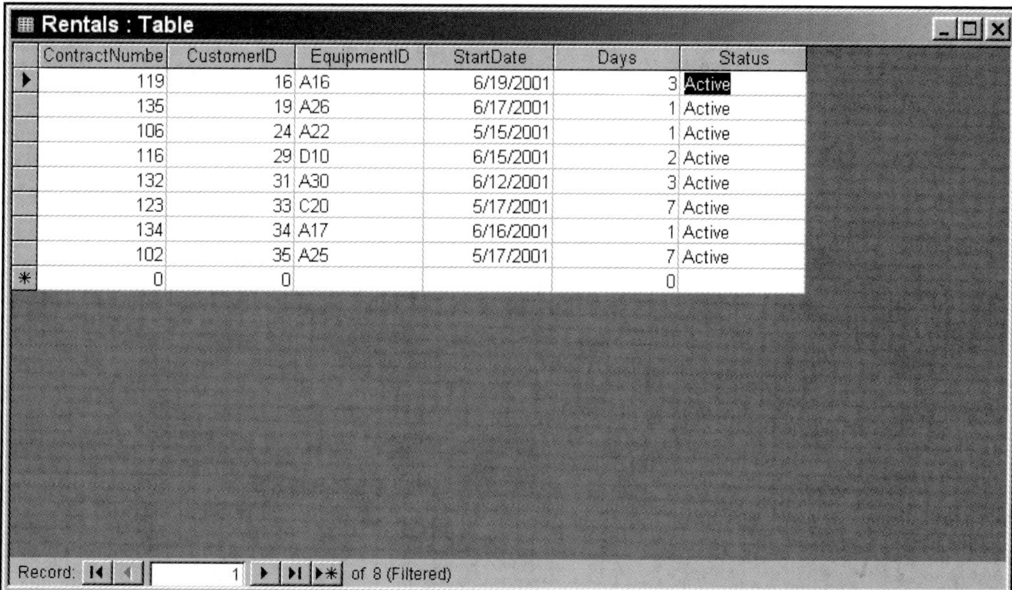

Rentals : Table

ContractNumbe	CustomerID	EquipmentID	StartDate	Days	Status
119	16	A16	6/19/2001	3	Active
135	19	A26	6/17/2001	1	Active
106	24	A22	5/15/2001	1	Active
116	29	D10	6/15/2001	2	Active
132	31	A30	6/12/2001	3	Active
123	33	C20	5/17/2001	7	Active
134	34	A17	6/16/2001	1	Active
102	35	A25	5/17/2001	7	Active
0	0			0	

Record: 1 of 8 (Filtered)

3. Before he leaves for the afternoon, Sal provides a list of questions for Ellie about Roundhouse's customer base. To answer the questions, she must find, filter, and/or query the database. Using these methods, Ellie answers the following questions:

- Which customers are not eligible for a discount, as determined by a zero value in the Discount field?
- How many customers living in Pike Mountain have an account?
- Which customer accounts are eligible for a discount of 10% on their rentals?
- How many customers are from outside the city of Kelly?

4. Finally, Ellie uses the Simple Query Wizard to create a "details" query that displays data from all three tables. She includes the following fields in the query and then saves it as "Customer Rentals Query."

Table	*Field*
Customers	Name
Rentals	StartDate
Rentals	Days
Rentals	Status
Equipment	Description

When the results are displayed (Figure 3.45), Ellie applies some formatting options, adjusts the column widths, saves the layout, and then prints the Datasheet window. She then closes all of the open windows, including AC03CP, and exits Microsoft Access.

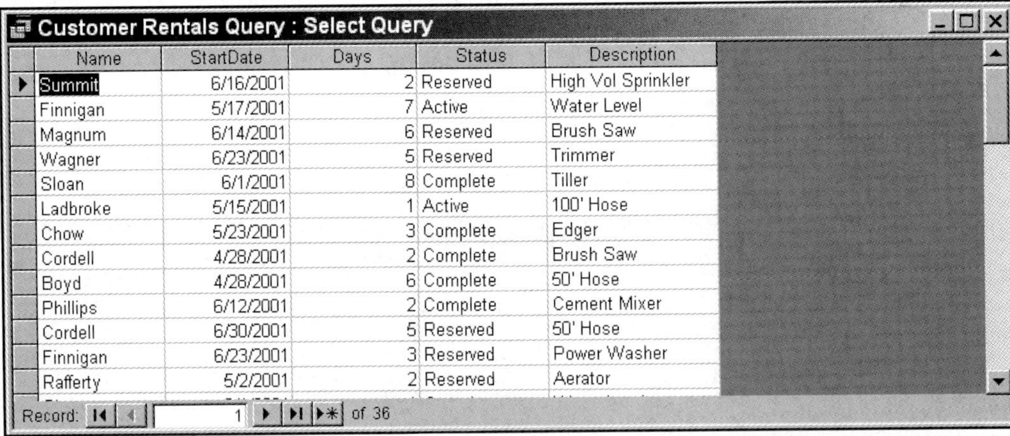
Customer Rentals Query : Select Query

Name	StartDate	Days	Status	Description
Summit	6/16/2001	2	Reserved	High Vol Sprinkler
Finnigan	5/17/2001	7	Active	Water Level
Magnum	6/14/2001	6	Reserved	Brush Saw
Wagner	6/23/2001	5	Reserved	Trimmer
Sloan	6/1/2001	8	Complete	Tiller
Ladbroke	5/15/2001	1	Active	100' Hose
Chow	5/23/2001	3	Complete	Edger
Cordell	4/28/2001	2	Complete	Brush Saw
Boyd	4/28/2001	6	Complete	50' Hose
Phillips	6/12/2001	2	Complete	Cement Mixer
Cordell	6/30/2001	5	Reserved	50' Hose
Finnigan	6/23/2001	3	Reserved	Power Washer
Rafferty	5/2/2001	2	Reserved	Aerator

Record: 1 of 36

Figure 3.45

Resulting dynaset from a multitable query

Ellie reflects on the work that she has already completed. Thankful for her excellent computer skills, Ellie looks forward to learning even more.

Microsoft® **Access**® 2002

CHAPTER 4

Presenting and Managing Data

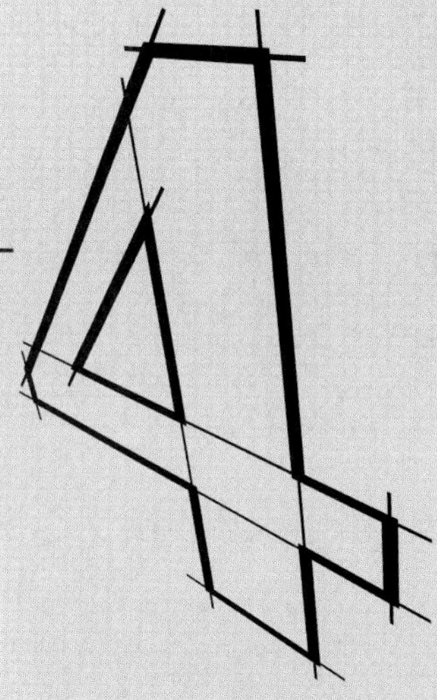

CHAPTER OUTLINE

Case Study

4.1 Creating a Simple Form

4.2 Creating a Simple Report

4.3 Generating a Mailing Labels Report

4.4 Managing Database Objects

Chapter Summary

Chapter Quiz

Hands-On Exercises

Case Problems

PREREQUISITES

This chapter assumes that you are familiar with creating, displaying, and editing table objects in Datasheet view. You should also know how Microsoft Access organizes and presents a database file's objects, including tables, queries, forms, and reports, in the Database window. Also, ensure that you are familiar with the basic steps for printing and previewing a Datasheet window.

LEARNING OBJECTIVES

After completing this chapter, you will be able to:

- Create new forms and reports using the AutoForm and AutoReport Wizards
- Create new forms and reports using the Form and Report Wizards
- Navigate and edit data using a form
- Preview and print reports from the Database window
- Create a mailing labels report using the Label Wizard
- Rename, copy, and delete database objects
- Compact, repair, and convert a database file

Case Study PORTERAI, INC.

Janice Marchant is the western regional sales representative for Porterai, Inc., a New Orleans manufacturer of stylish travel gear. Although she has only worked for the company a short time, she enjoys the job and the challenges it presents. Janice works from her home in San Francisco with a notebook computer and fax machine, but meets once a month with the national sales manager, John Lucci. Like all of the sales representatives at Porterai, Janice is responsible for tracking sales to the company's preferred clientele using Microsoft Access. Now that she's getting the hang of entering data in Datasheet view, Janice wants to add a few form objects to facilitate data entry and enable her to focus on one customer at a time. She must also create and submit monthly reports listing the items that were sold and who purchased them. This information helps Porterai's management team forecast demand levels and predict next season's sale figures.

In this chapter, you and Janice learn to create forms to help you input data and to use reports to produce professional-looking printouts and Web pages. In addition to creating forms and reports using the AutoForm and AutoReport Wizards, you employ the Form and Report Wizards for better controlling the layout of information. You also save a report as an HTML document and print out standard mailing labels. Last, you learn how to manage the database objects you create and how to compact an Access database file to improve performance and efficiency.

4.1 Creating a Simple Form

An alternative to working with a screen full of records in a datasheet is to focus your attention on a single record at a time using a form. Forms can also be customized to display multiple records and to link with data stored in other tables. Some forms that you may find useful include data entry forms that resemble their paper counterparts, switchboard forms that provide menus of choices, and custom dialog boxes that gather input from users. Forms serve many purposes in Access and can enhance the productivity of both novice and expert users. In this module, you learn to create forms using the Access **form wizards.**

4.1.1 Creating a Form Using the AutoForm Wizards

feature

An **AutoForm Wizard** provides the fastest and easiest way to create a new form. Requiring minimal information from the user, the wizard analyzes a table's field structure, designs and builds the form, and then displays it in a **Form window.** There are actually five wizards from which to choose. First, the Columnar AutoForm Wizard displays data from one record in a single column, with each field appearing on a row. The Tabular AutoForm Wizard arranges data in a table format, with field labels as column headings and each row representing a record. Similarly, the Datasheet AutoForm Wizard creates a form of rows and columns resembling a datasheet. You can also choose from the PivotTable and PivotChart AutoForm Wizards for further options. If you choose to create an AutoForm by clicking the New Object button ( ), Access creates a columnar form based on the open or selected table or query.

method

To create a columnar form quickly:

- SELECT: a table or query object in the Database window
- CLICK: New Object: AutoForm button ( )

To create a form using an AutoForm Wizard:

- SELECT: *Forms* button in the Objects bar
- CLICK: New button (New) on the Database window toolbar
- SELECT: a table or query from the drop-down list box
- DOUBLE-CLICK: an AutoForm Wizard

practice

In this lesson, you create forms using the New Object button and the Tabular AutoForm Wizard. Load Microsoft Access 2002, if it is not already running.

1. Open the database file named AC0400, located in the Advantage student data files folder. The Database window in Figure 4.1 is displayed.

Figure 4.1

AC0400 Database window

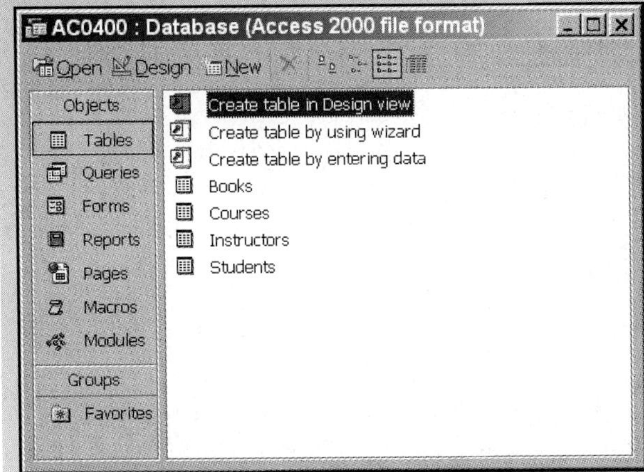

2. To have Access create a form automatically, ensure that the *Tables* button is selected in the Objects bar and then:
SELECT: Books in the table list area
(*Note:* You do not need to open the Books table. Click once on the table object so that it appears highlighted.)

3. Once a table (or query) is selected:
CLICK: New Object: AutoForm button ( )
(*Hint:* The New Object button contains a list of wizards used in creating database objects. If the AutoForm image is not currently displayed on the face of the New Object button, click the attached down arrow to show the drop-down list appearing here. Then select the AutoForm command.)

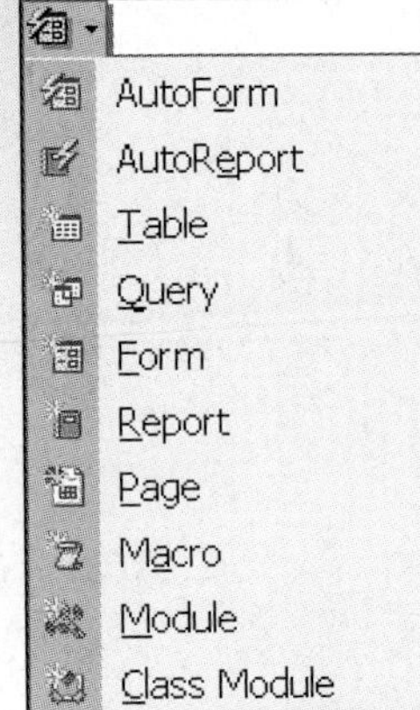

4. After a few seconds, Access displays the columnar form shown in Figure 4.2. Notice that each field appears on a separate row in the Form window. You learn how to navigate and manipulate data in a form later in this module.

Figure 4.2

A columnar form displays data for a single record

Formatting toolbar for forms and reports

Form View toolbar

Form window

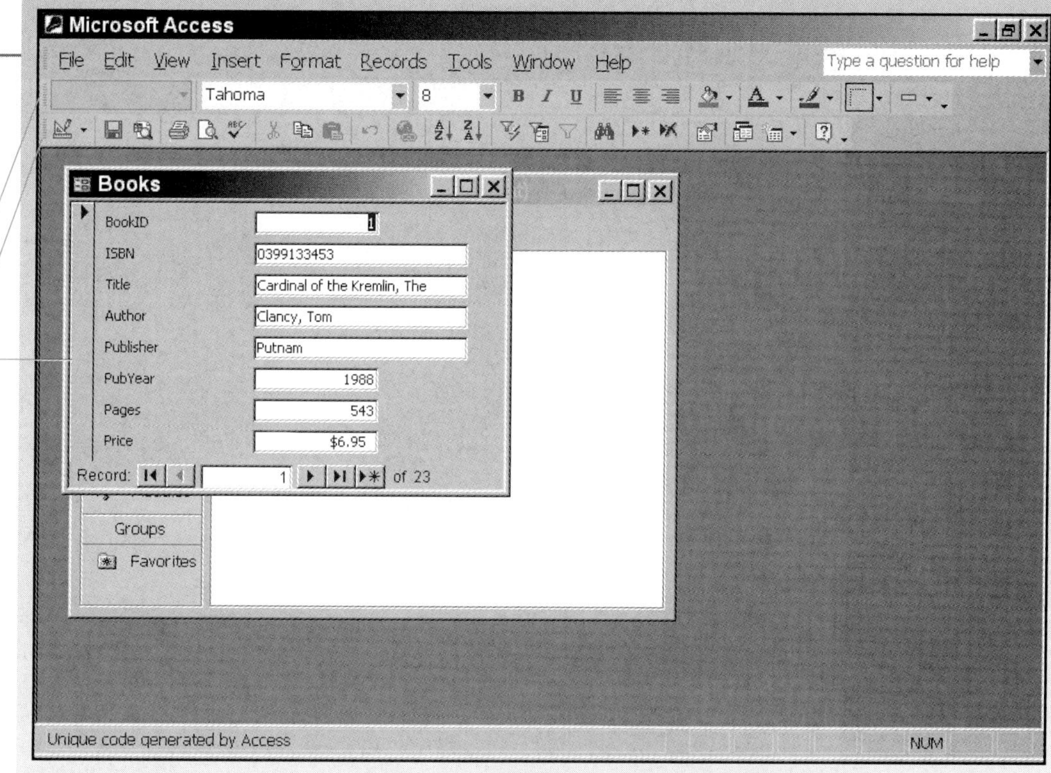

5. To close the form:
CLICK: its Close button (☒)
The following Alert dialog box appears to inform you that the form object has not yet been saved.

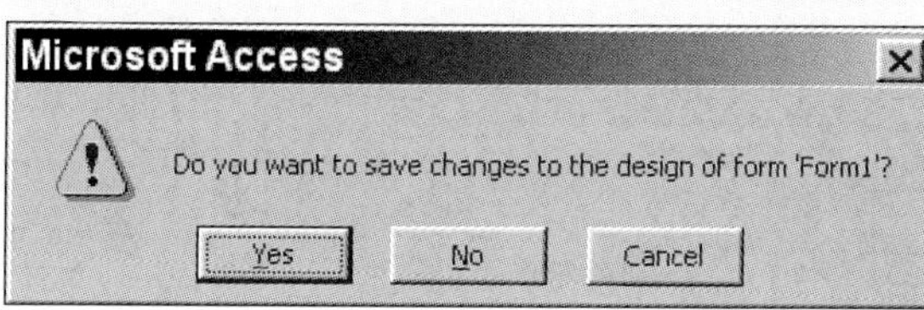

6. To proceed with saving and naming the form:
CLICK: Yes command button
TYPE: **Books - Columnar** into the *Form name* text box
PRESS: ENTER or CLICK: OK

7. The new form object is stored in the *Forms* category of the Database window. To view the object:
CLICK: *Forms* button in the Objects bar
DOUBLE-CLICK: Books - Columnar in the list area
The Form window appears as displayed previously.

8. Close the Form window.

9. To create a new form using a tabular layout, first:
CLICK: *Tables* button in the Objects bar
SELECT: Books in the list area

10. To access the other AutoForm Wizards:
CLICK: down arrow attached to the New Object button ( )
CHOOSE: Form
The New Form dialog box appears, as shown in Figure 4.3.

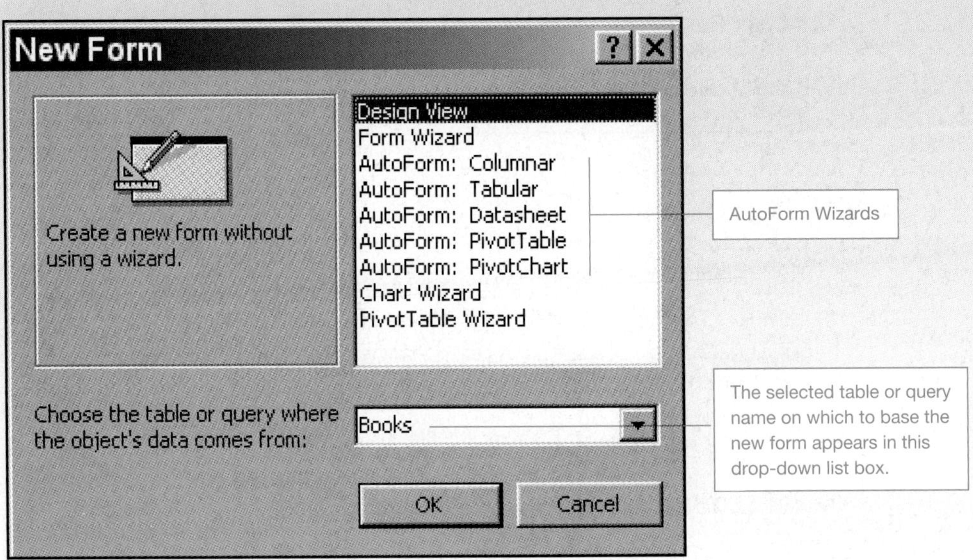

Figure 4.3

New Form dialog box

11. To create a new form using the Tabular AutoForm Wizard:
SELECT: AutoForm: Tabular
CLICK: OK command button

12. After a few moments, a tabular form similar to the one shown in Figure 4.4 is displayed. Close the Form window without saving the changes.

Figure 4.4

A tabular form displays numerous records at the same time

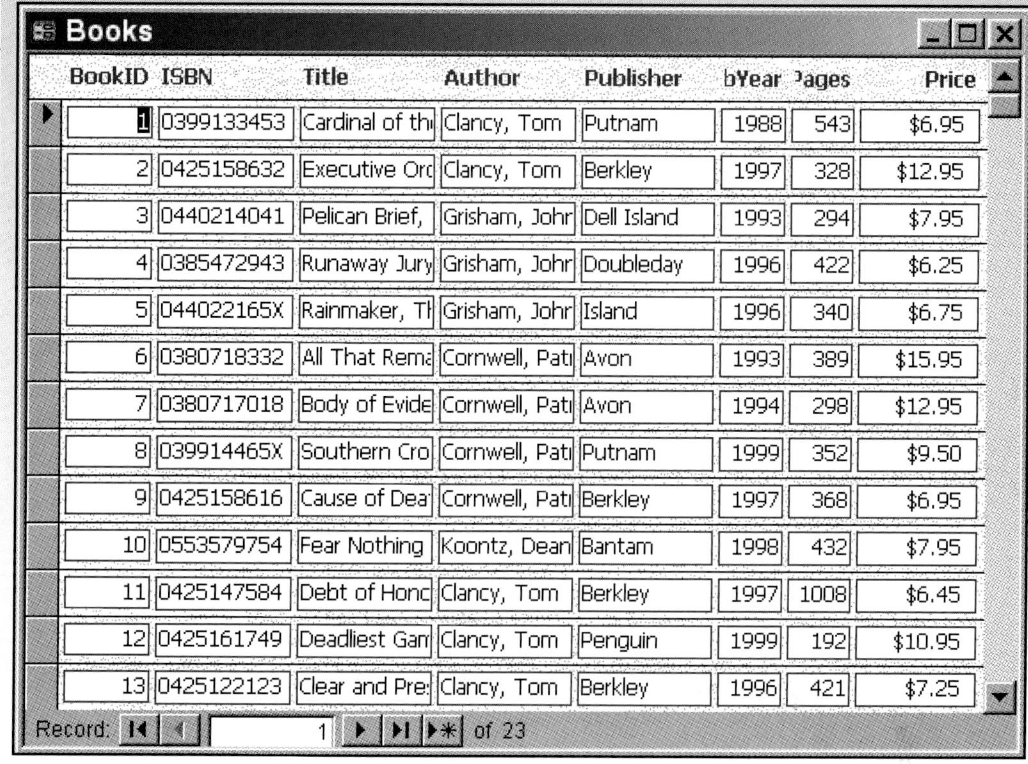

Books

BookID	ISBN	Title	Author	Publisher	bYear	›ages	Price
1	0399133453	Cardinal of thı	Clancy, Tom	Putnam	1988	543	$6.95
2	0425158632	Executive Orc	Clancy, Tom	Berkley	1997	328	$12.95
3	0440214041	Pelican Brief,	Grisham, Johr	Dell Island	1993	294	$7.95
4	0385472943	Runaway Jury	Grisham, Johr	Doubleday	1996	422	$6.25
5	044022165X	Rainmaker, Tl	Grisham, Johr	Island	1996	340	$6.75
6	0380718332	All That Remι	Cornwell, Patı	Avon	1993	389	$15.95
7	0380717018	Body of Evide	Cornwell, Patı	Avon	1994	298	$12.95
8	039914465X	Southern Cro	Cornwell, Patı	Putnam	1999	352	$9.50
9	0425158616	Cause of Dea	Cornwell, Patı	Berkley	1997	368	$6.95
10	0553579754	Fear Nothing	Koontz, Dean	Bantam	1998	432	$7.95
11	0425147584	Debt of Honc	Clancy, Tom	Berkley	1997	1008	$6.45
12	0425161749	Deadliest Garr	Clancy, Tom	Penguin	1999	192	$10.95
13	0425122123	Clear and Pre:	Clancy, Tom	Berkley	1996	421	$7.25

Record: 1 of 23

4.1.2 Creating a Form Using the Form Wizard

feature

The Form Wizard provides a step-by-step approach to creating a form from scratch. Even experienced users find using the Form Wizard a handy way to get started building a new form. Whereas an AutoForm Wizard generates a complete form using a set of default values, the Form Wizard allows you to pick and choose options from a series of dialog boxes. Using the Form Wizard, you specify what fields to display on the form and how you want it to look. The layout options include Columnar, Tabular, Datasheet, Justified, PivotTable, and PivotChart. The columnar and justified layouts are suited to viewing a single record at a time and work especially well for tables with few fields. The tabular and datasheet layouts are best used to display numerous records at a time.

method

In the Database window, select the *Forms* button and then:

- DOUBLE-CLICK: Create form by using wizard

or

- CLICK: New button (New) on the Database window toolbar
- SELECT: a table or query from the drop-down list box
- DOUBLE-CLICK: Form Wizard

practice

You now use the Form Wizard to create a standard form object. Ensure that the AC0400 Database window is displayed.

1. As with other database objects, you may create a form from scratch in Design view or get helpful guidance from the Access wizards. You access the Form Wizard using the New Form dialog box or by double-clicking a shortcut in the Database window. To begin:
CLICK: *Forms* button in the Objects bar

2. To launch the Form Wizard:
DOUBLE-CLICK: Create form by using wizard
The dialog box in Figure 4.5 appears.

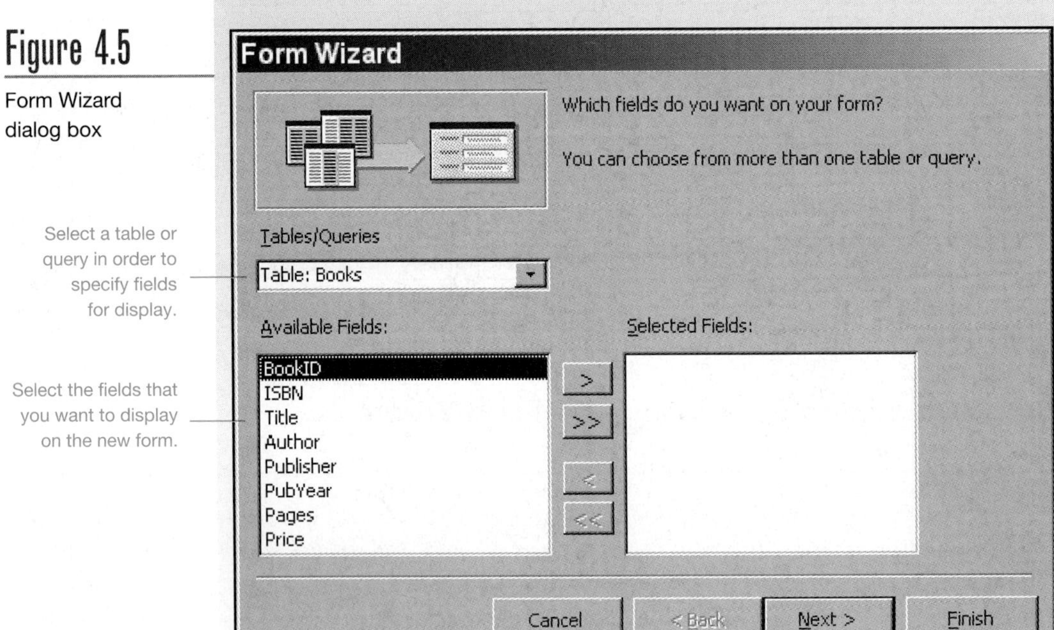

Figure 4.5
Form Wizard dialog box

3. Let's create a form that displays the data from the Courses table:
SELECT: Table: Courses from the *Tables/Queries* drop-down list box
Notice that the table's fields are displayed in the associated list box.

4. In the *Available Fields* list box:
SELECT: Title
CLICK: Include button (>)
Notice that the Title field is no longer displayed in the *Available Fields* list box. (*Hint:* You can also double-click a field name to move it between the list boxes.)

5. Using the same process, add the Faculty, DeptHead, StartDate, and StartTime fields to the *Selected Fields* list box, in the order specified.

6. To proceed to the next step (Figure 4.6) in the wizard:
CLICK: Next >

Figure 4.6

Selecting a form layout

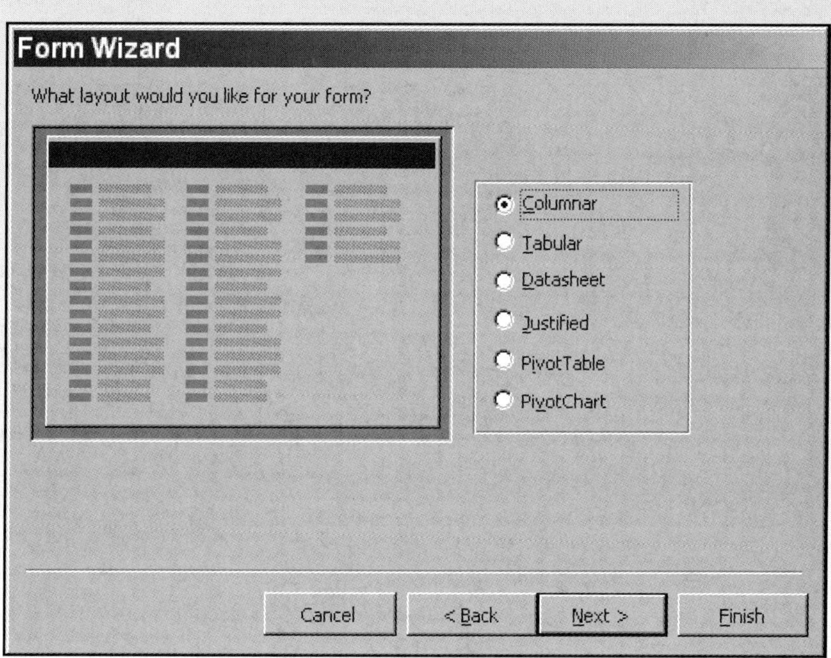

7. In this step, you specify how to arrange the selected fields in the Form window. Notice that five of the six options (Columnar, Tabular, Datasheet, PivotTable, and PivotChart) mirror the AutoForm wizards. On your own, click the layout options one at a time to view their formats in the Preview area. When you are ready to proceed:
SELECT: *Justified* option button
CLICK: Next >

8. This step (Figure 4.7) allows you to specify a formatting style for the form. On your own, click the style names appearing in the list box in order to preview their formats. When you are ready to proceed:
SELECT: Sumi Painting
CLICK: Next >
(*Note:* The next time you use the Form Wizard, the options selected here become the default selections.)

Figure 4.7

Selecting a form style

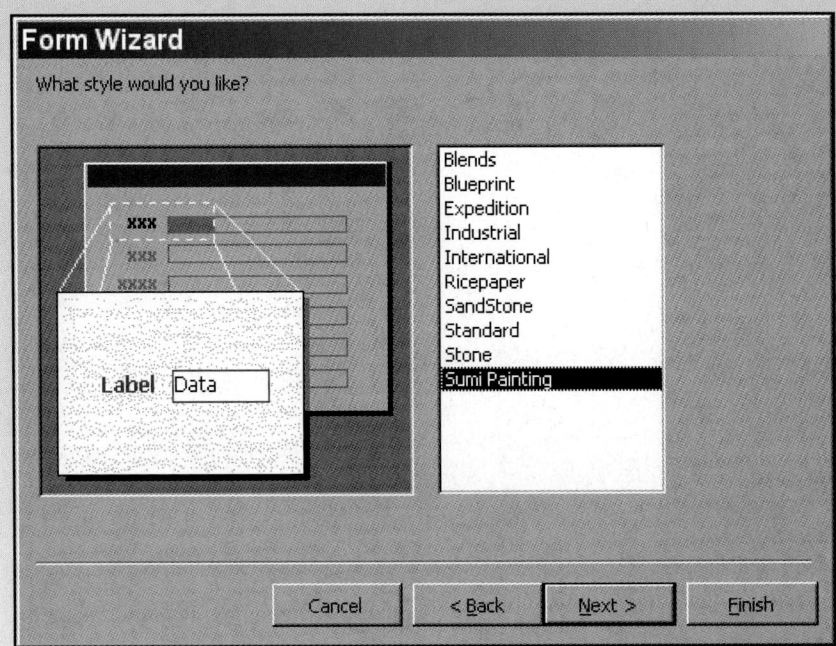

9. In the final step, you name and then choose whether to display or modify the form. Do the following:
TYPE: **Courses - Form Wizard** in the text box
SELECT: *Open the form to view or enter information* option button, if it is not already selected
CLICK: Finish
The Form window displays only the fields selected in the Form Wizard using a justified (wrapping) layout, as shown in Figure 4.8.

10. Close the Form window. Notice that the form name appears in the Database window.

Figure 4.8

A justified form created using the Form Wizard

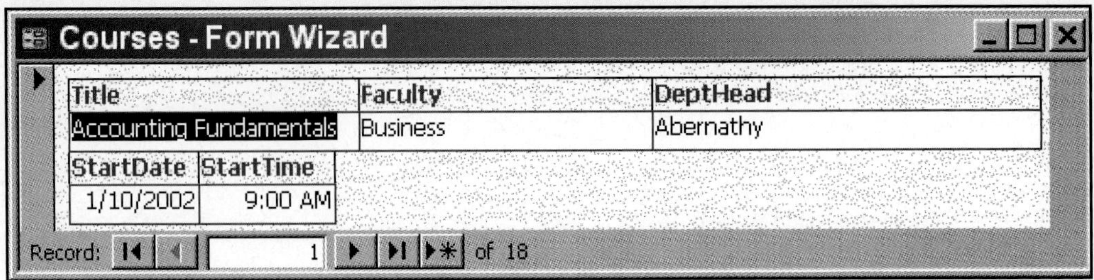

4.1.3 Navigating Data Using a Form

Table 4.1

Buttons and Keys for Navigating a Form

Button	Keystroke	Description
⏮	CTRL + HOME	Moves to the first field of the first record
◀	PgUp	Moves to the previous record
▶	PgDn	Moves to the next record
⏭	CTRL + END	Moves to the last field of the last record

feature →

An Access form provides the same navigational buttons that you find at the bottom of a Datasheet window. Use these buttons, along with the arrow keys (described further below), to move through the records in a table. To move among the fields on a form, press the arrow keys (↑ and ↓) or use TAB to move forward and SHIFT + TAB to move backward. You can also move quickly to the top of a form using HOME and to the last field on a form using END.

method →

See Table 4.1 for a list of navigational buttons and keyboard methods for navigating forms.

practice →

In this lesson, you use the AutoForm Wizard to create a form and practice navigating records in the Form window. Ensure that the AC0400 Database window is displayed.

1. Let's begin by creating a new columnar form for the Courses table:
   CLICK: *Tables* button in the Objects bar
   SELECT: Courses in the list area

2. To launch the AutoForm Wizard:
   CLICK: down arrow attached to the New Object button ()
   Notice that the New Object: Form icon appears on the face of the AutoForm button, since it was the last selection made.

3. From the drop-down menu:
   CHOOSE: AutoForm
   The Courses Form window appears, as shown in Figure 4.9.

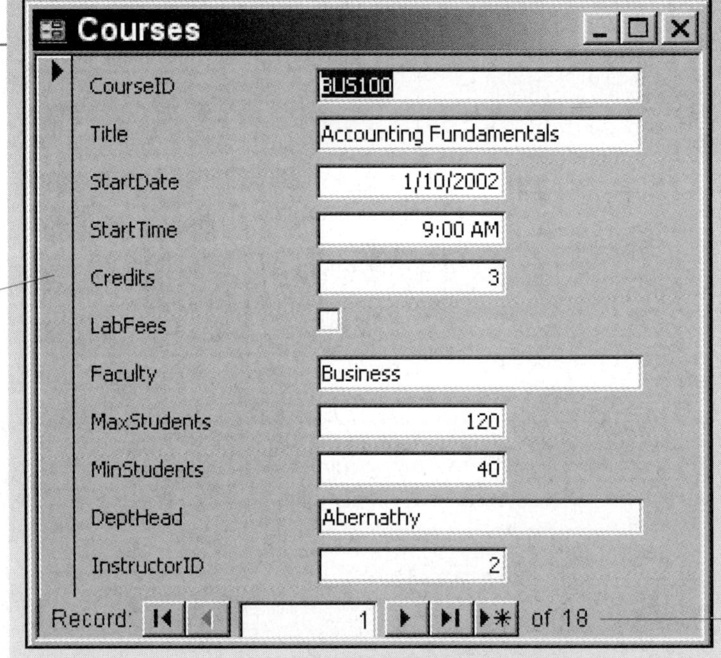

Figure 4.9

Creating a columnar AutoForm for the Courses table

4. To save the new form:
   CLICK: Save button (![save])
   TYPE: **Courses – AutoForm**
   PRESS: ENTER or CLICK: OK

5. Using the form, let's display the last record in the table:
   CLICK: Last Record button (▶|) at the bottom of the Form window
   Notice that the record navigation area displays Record 18 of 18.

6. To move to record 15:
   PRESS: PgUp three times

7. To move to the first field in the first record:
   PRESS: CTRL + HOME

8. To move the cursor into the Title field:
   PRESS: TAB

9. Like working in Datasheet view, you can use the Find, Replace, and Sort commands in Form view. Let's use the Find command to locate all courses containing the word "database." Do the following:
CLICK: Find button (🔍)
TYPE: **database** in the *Find What* combo box
SELECT: Any Part of Field in the *Match* drop-down list box
Your screen should now appear similar to Figure 4.10.

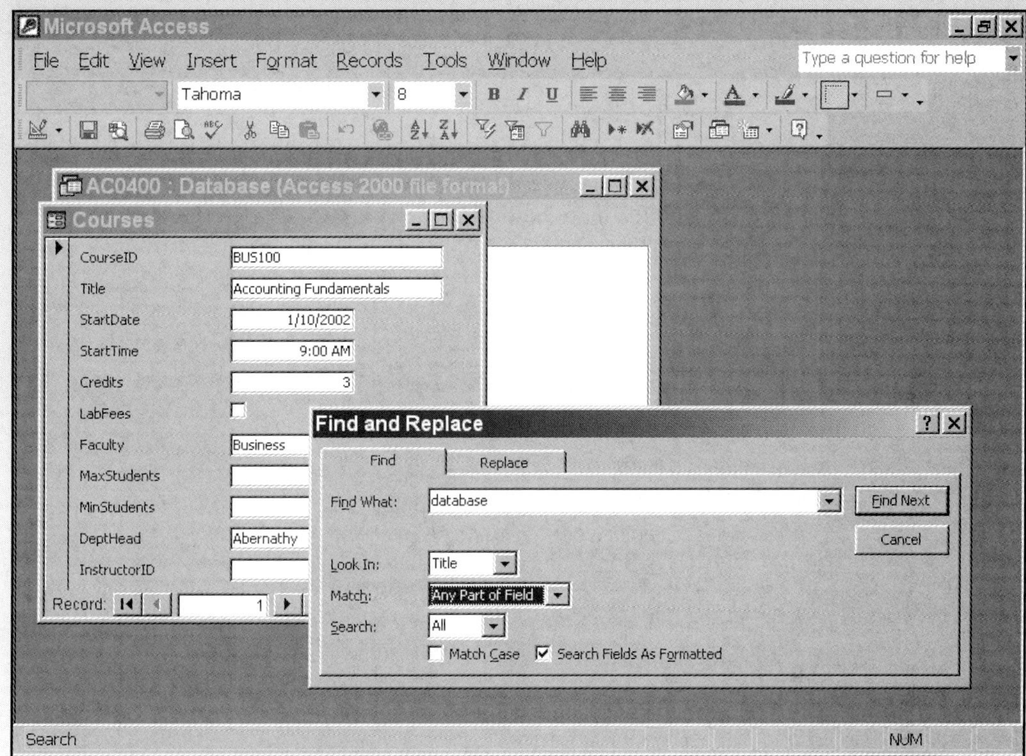

Figure 4.10
Using the Find command in Form view

10. To proceed with the search procedure:
CLICK: Find Next command button

11. Access moves the cursor to the first matching record, "Database Fundamentals" in Record 7. (*Note:* If the Find and Replace dialog box is covering the form, move the window by dragging its Title bar.)

12. In the Find and Replace dialog box, continue the search:
CLICK: Find Next command button
The next record, "Database Programming" in Record 8, is displayed.

13. Close the Find and Replace dialog box.

14. Close the Form window.

4.1.4 Working with a Form

feature

The methods for editing data in Form view are nearly identical to editing in Datasheet view. Nevertheless, many people find it easier to edit field data using a form, preferring the less cluttered interface and the ability to focus attention on a single record. After this lesson, you may also find it easier to add, delete, sort, and filter a table's records using a form.

method

Toolbar buttons available for working with forms include the following:

- CLICK: New Record button ( ) to add a new record
- CLICK: Delete Record button ( ) to remove a record
- CLICK: Sort Ascending button ( ) to sort into ascending order
- CLICK: Sort Descending button ( ) to sort into descending order
- CLICK: Print Preview button ( ) to preview a form
- CLICK: Print button ( ) to print a form

practice

You now practice sorting, adding, and deleting records, and previewing how a form will appear when printed. Ensure that you've completed the previous lesson and that the AC0400 Database window is displayed.

1. Let's start by displaying the form that you created in the last lesson:
   CLICK: *Forms* button in the Objects bar
   DOUBLE-CLICK: Courses - AutoForm in the list area

2. Using PgDn and PgUp, navigate through the records and take notice of the ascending Course ID sort order. Now let's sort the table's records into ascending order by course title. To begin:
   PRESS: CTRL + HOME to move to the first field in the first record
   PRESS: TAB to position the cursor in the Title field
   CLICK: Sort Ascending button ( )

3. While the first record, "Accounting Fundamentals," remains displayed, press the PgDn and PgUp keys to see that the table is now sorted alphabetically by course title.

4. Let's add a new record to the table:
   CLICK: New Record button ( ) on the toolbar
   An empty form appears, as shown in Figure 4.11, with "Record 19" in the record navigation area.

Figure 4.11

Adding a new record using a blank form

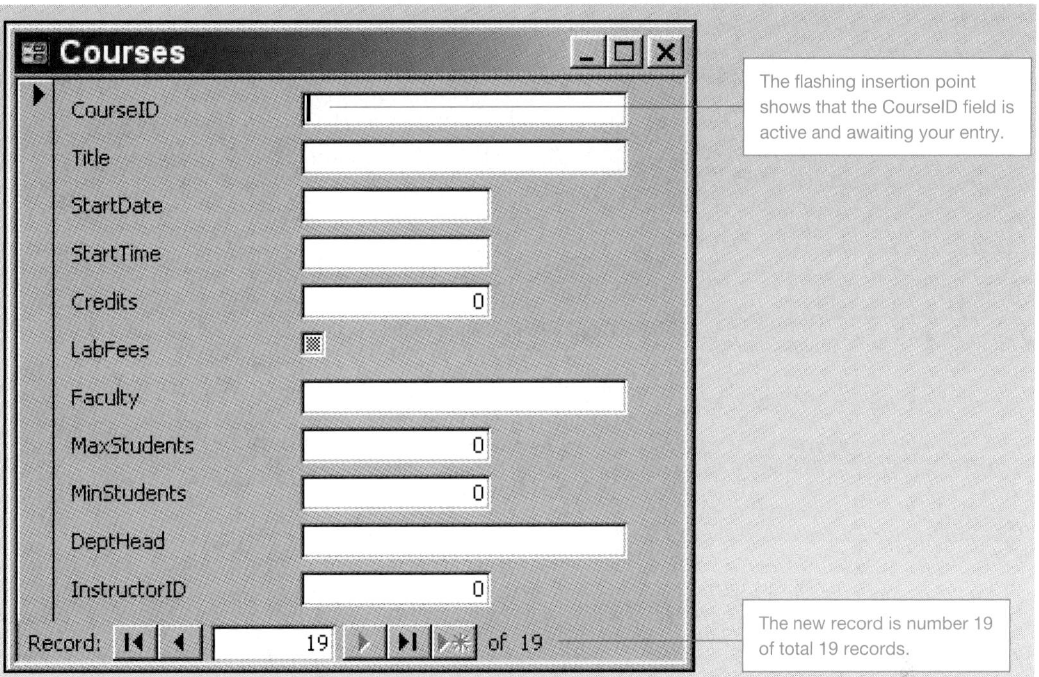

5. Enter the information appearing in Figure 4.12. Use the TAB key to move forward and SHIFT + TAB to move backward, if necessary. As you type, notice the pencil icon ( ) that appears in the record selection area of the form. When you reach the LabFees field, press the Spacebar to toggle the check box to "Yes." For the last field, InstructorID, enter the value but do not press TAB or ENTER. In other words, leave the insertion point in the InstructorID field.

Figure 4.12

Entering data into a new record

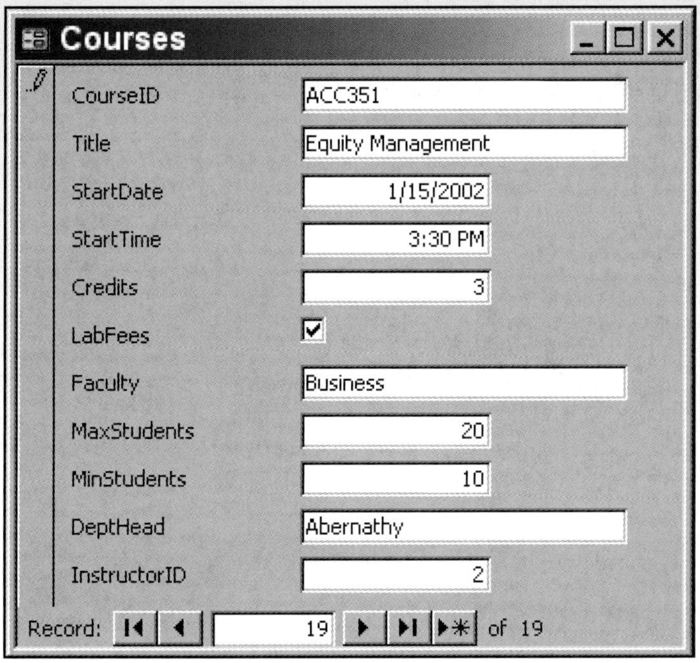

Access

6. To save the record:
PRESS: SHIFT + ENTER
Notice that the pencil icon (✎) disappears from the record selection area.

7. Now let's remove a record from the table:
PRESS: PgUp until you reach "Object-Oriented Design" in Record 14
CLICK: Delete Record button (✕)
The following dialog box appears.

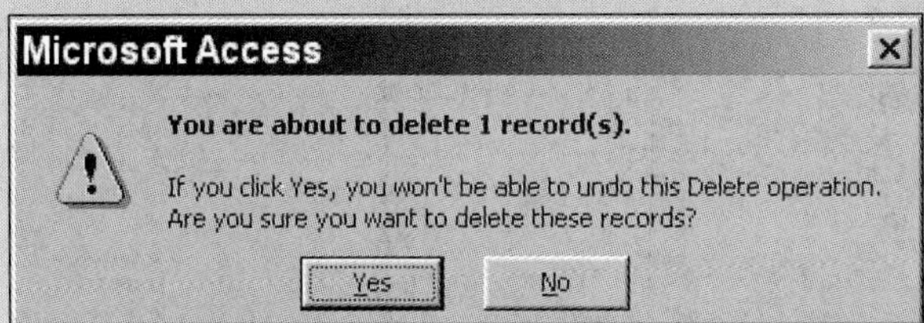

8. To confirm the deletion:
CLICK: Yes command button
Notice that the record navigation area now shows 18 as the total number of records.

9. To preview how a form will print:
CLICK: Print Preview button (🔍)

10. On your own, enlarge the Print Preview window and then use the magnifying glass mouse pointer to zoom in on the image. Your screen should appear similar to Figure 4.13.

Figure 4.13

Previewing a form

Each printed page contains as many records as possible, limited only by the number of fields and form design.

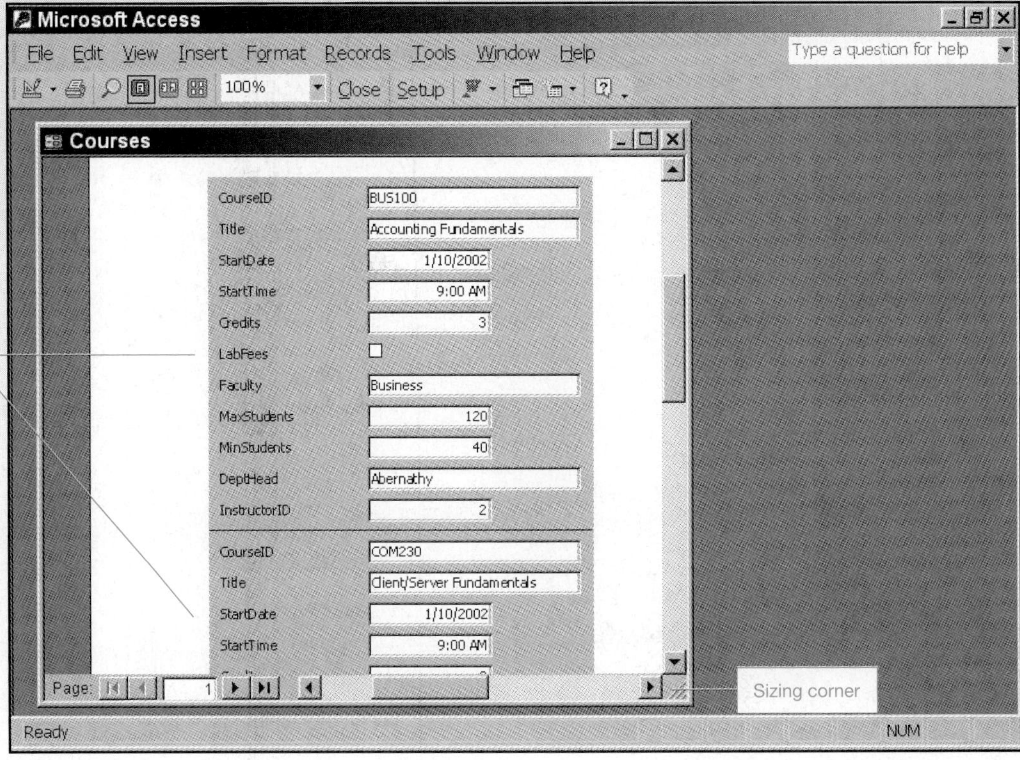

11. If you have a printer, print the form by clicking the Print button (🖨).

12. To return to the Form window:
CLICK: Close button (Close) in the toolbar
Notice that the Form window maintains the same size as the Print Preview window.

13. On your own, practice resizing the Courses Form window to appear similar to the window's size and shape shown in Figure 4.12.

14. Close the Form window.

4.1. Name the layout options for designing a form using the Form Wizard.

4.2 Creating a Simple Report

A report provides a structured display format for presenting a table's data or a query's results. Although most reports are designed for printing, you can also save reports as graphic snapshots or as Web pages. To capture and retain the attention of readers, each report may contain a variety of design elements such as fonts, lines, borders, colors, graphics, and white space. In addition to jazzing up reports, these elements combine with powerful features for summarizing data to present information clearly and concisely. Each day, people make important decisions using reports obtained from database management systems. Potential uses for reports in a typical business database application include invoices, mailing labels, address books, product catalogs, and inventory listings. In this module, you learn to create reports using the Access report wizards.

4.2.1 Creating a Report Using the AutoReport Wizards

feature

What AutoForm Wizards do for forms, AutoReport Wizards do for reports. Using an **AutoReport Wizard,** you can create a professionally designed report with the click of a button. Access provides two types of AutoReport wizards, Columnar and Tabular. Clicking the New Object button for a report (📝) generates a relatively unattractive columnar report that presents data down a single column. The Tabular option, selected from the New Report dialog box, prepares a much nicer-looking report.

method

To create a columnar report quickly:

- SELECT: a table or query object in the Database window
- CLICK: New Object: AutoReport button (📝)

To create a report using an AutoReport Wizard:

- SELECT: *Reports* button in the Objects bar
- CLICK: New button (New) on the Database window toolbar
- SELECT: a table or query from the drop-down list box
- DOUBLE-CLICK: an AutoReport Wizard

Access

practice

In this lesson, you create a columnar report using the AutoReport Wizard. Ensure that the AC0400 Database window is displayed.

1. The first step is to select a table or query for which you want to produce a report. To begin:
   CLICK: *Tables* button in the Objects bar
   SELECT: Instructors in the list area
   (*Hint:* You do not need to open the Instructors table. Click once on the table object so that it appears highlighted.)

2. To generate a report using the AutoReport Wizard:
   CLICK: New Object: AutoReport button ( )
   (*Hint:* The New Object button contains a list of wizards used in creating database objects. To access the AutoReport button ( ), click the attached down arrow and then select the command from the drop-down menu.)

3. Access opens a columnar report in the Print Preview window. Each field from the Instructors table appears on a separate row in the report. On your own, use the magnifying glass mouse pointer to zoom in and out on the report (Figure 4.14).

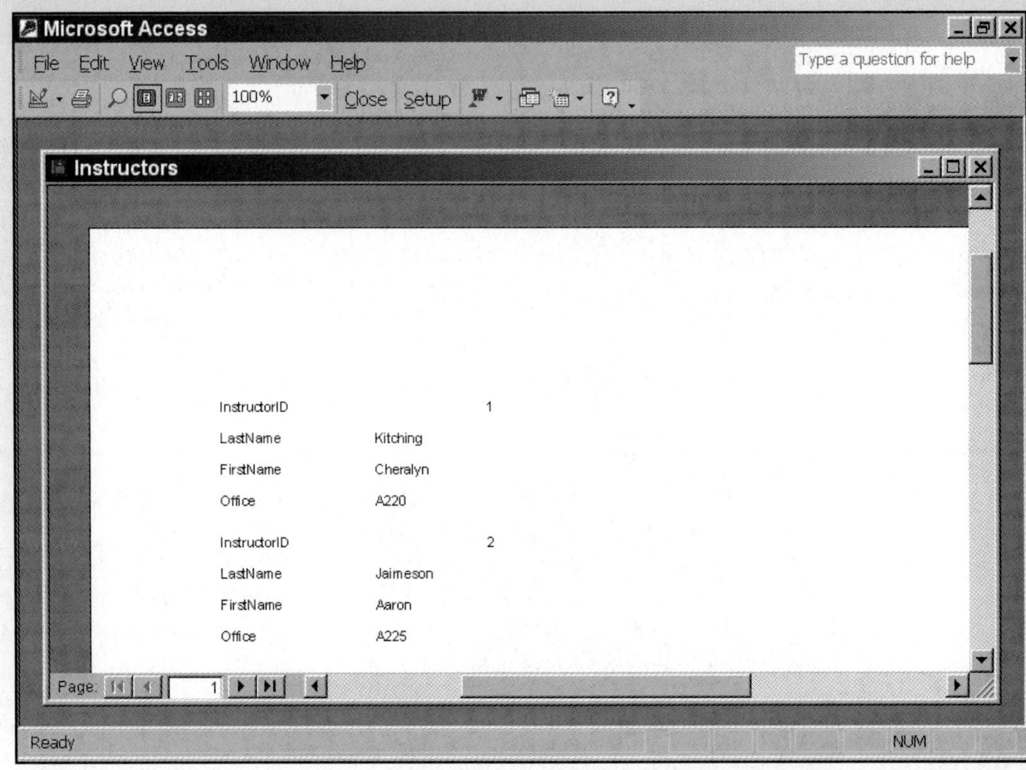

Figure 4.14

A columnar report created using the AutoReport Wizard

4. To close the report:
CLICK: its Close button (☒)
The following dialog box appears, asking whether you want to save the new report.

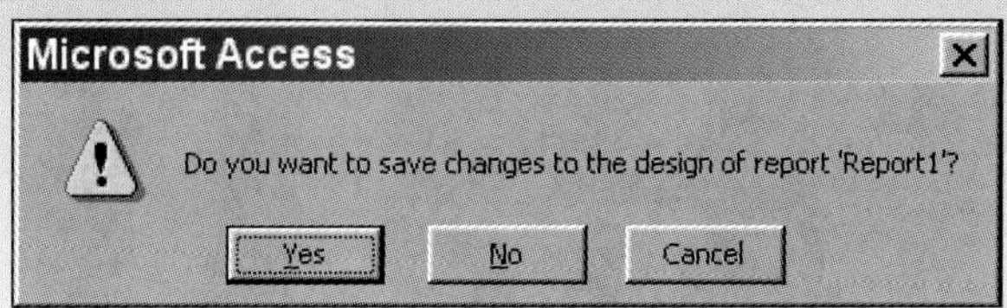

5. To save the report:
CLICK: Yes command button
TYPE: **Instructors - Columnar**
PRESS: ENTER or CLICK: OK

6. To view the new object in the Database window:
CLICK: *Reports* button in the Objects bar
DOUBLE-CLICK: Instructors - Columnar in the list area
The report opens up into the Print Preview window.

7. Close the Print Preview window by clicking its Close button (☒).

4.2.2 Creating a Report Using the Report Wizard

feature

The Report Wizard lets you select options from a series of dialog boxes when constructing a new report. After selecting the fields to display, you determine the grouping and subtotal levels, sorting options, and presentation styles. Once a report has been created and saved, you can preview and print the report at any time.

method

In the Database window, select the *Reports* button and then:

- DOUBLE-CLICK: Create report by using wizard

or

- CLICK: New button (New) on the Database window toolbar
- SELECT: a table or query from the drop-down list box
- DOUBLE-CLICK: Report Wizard

practice

You now use the Report Wizard to create a tabular report. Ensure that the AC0400 Database window is displayed.

1. To launch the Report Wizard, ensure that the *Reports* button is selected in the Database window and then:
DOUBLE-CLICK: Create report by using wizard
The first dialog box of the Report Wizard appears. Notice the similarity between this dialog box and the Form Wizard in Figure 4.5.

2. To create a report that displays data from the Students table:
SELECT: Table: Students from the *Tables/Queries* drop-down list box

3. In the *Available Fields* list box, you select the fields to include:
DOUBLE-CLICK: LastName
DOUBLE-CLICK: FirstName
DOUBLE-CLICK: Major
DOUBLE-CLICK: GradYear
DOUBLE-CLICK: GPA

4. To proceed to the next step in the wizard:
CLICK: Next >

5. In the second step of the wizard, Access lets you specify grouping levels so that you may better organize your data and perform subtotal calculations. To group the student records by the students' selected major:
DOUBLE-CLICK: Major in the list box
As shown in Figure 4.15, the layout preview area is updated to help you visualize the grouping options selected.

Figure 4.15

Report Wizard dialog box: Grouping Levels

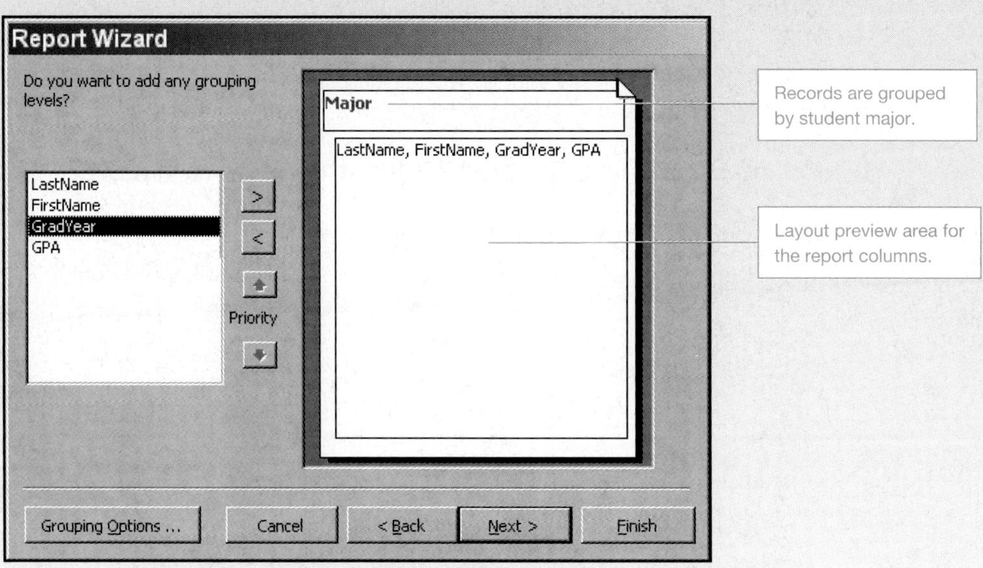

6. To proceed to the next step:
CLICK: Next >

7. In this step, you specify sorting options for the report. Since the report is already grouped (and thus sorted) by major, let's sort the report alphabetically by name. Do the following:
CLICK: down arrow attached to the first drop-down list box
SELECT: LastName
CLICK: down arrow attached to the second drop-down list box
SELECT: FirstName
The wizard's dialog box should now look like Figure 4.16. (*Hint:* If necessary, you can click the Sort Ascending button that appears to the right of each drop-down list box in order to toggle between ascending and descending order.)

Figure 4.16

Report Wizard dialog box: Sorting

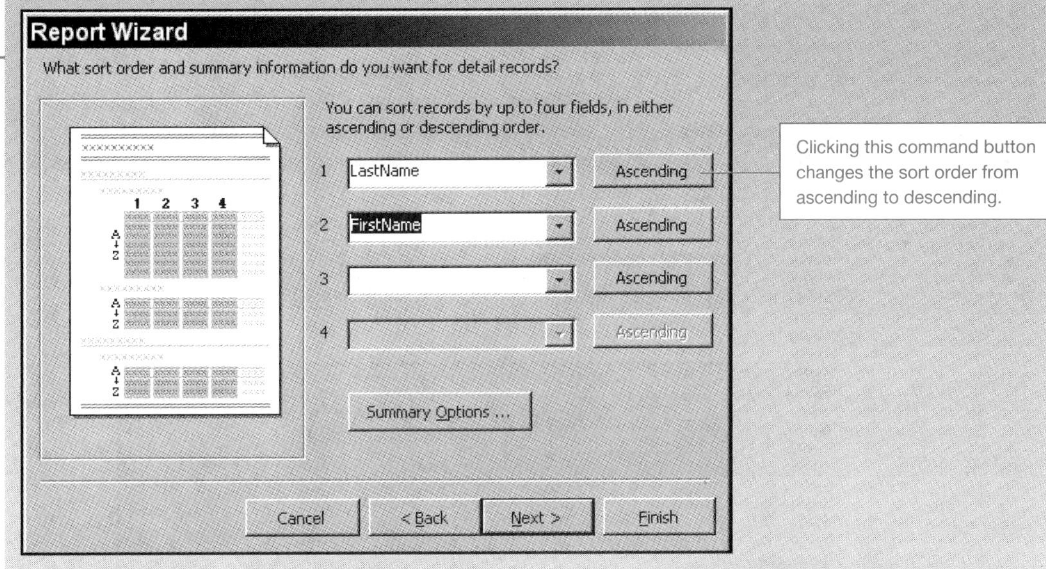

8. If the selected table or query contains numeric or currency fields, you can also use this step in the Report Wizard dialog box to include summary calculations in the report. To illustrate:
   CLICK: Summary Options command button
   The Summary Options dialog box (Figure 4.17) is displayed showing the fields that are eligible for performing calculations.

9. There are four summary calculations from which to choose. The Sum option totals record values stored in a field, and the Avg option calculates the arithmetic mean or average. The Min and Max options find the minimum and maximum values in a field, respectively. For those fields you sum, you can also calculate each record's percent share of the total value.

   In the Students table, these calculations provide no real benefit toward better understanding the GradYear field. However, summarizing the student grade point averages might provide useful information. To proceed, complete the Summary Options dialog box to match the selections shown in Figure 4.17.

Figure 4.17

Report Wizard dialog box: Summary Options

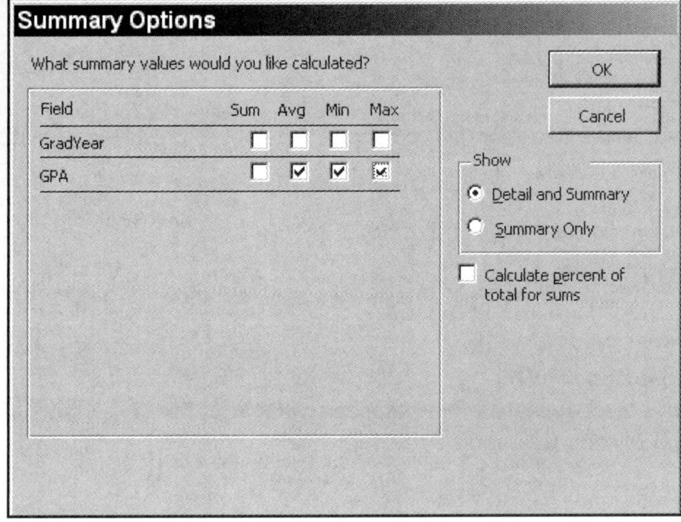

Access

10. To accept the choices made in the Summary Options dialog box and proceed to the next step:
CLICK: OK command button
CLICK: Next >

11. You now specify the desired layout and page orientation settings for the report. For grouping data, the Report Wizard provides nice formats for separating and organizing the information. Do the following:
SELECT: *Outline 1* option button in the *Layout* area
SELECT: *Portrait* option button in the *Orientation* area
Your screen should appear similar to Figure 4.18.

Figure 4.18

Report Wizard dialog box: layout options and orientation

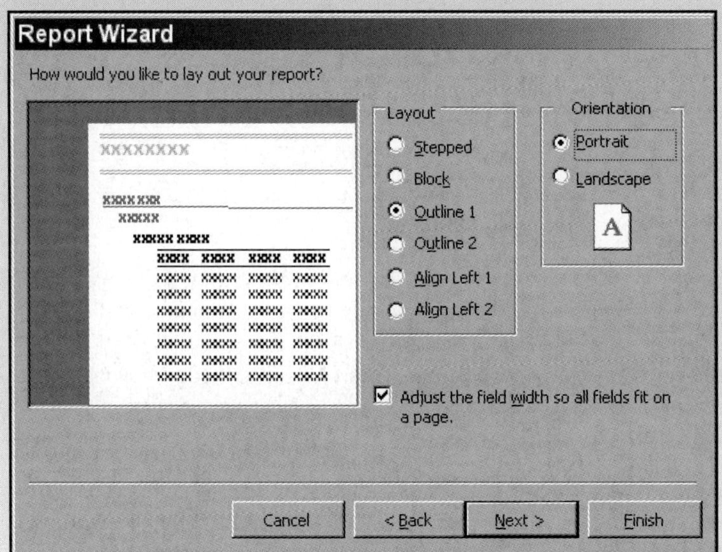

12. CLICK: Next > to proceed to the next step

13. As in the Form Wizard dialog box shown in Figure 4.7, you are now asked to select a style for your report. A style is a formatting template that Access applies to change the look and feel of a report. On your own, click on the style options in the list box to preview their formats. When you are ready to proceed:
SELECT: Corporate
CLICK: Next >

14. In the final step, name the report and determine whether to preview it or perform additional modifications. Do the following:
TYPE: **Students - By Major**
SELECT: *Preview the report* option button
CLICK: Finish
The report is displayed in the Print Preview window, as shown in Figure 4.19.

15. To close the Print Preview window:
CLICK: its Close button (☒)
The new report object appears in the Database window. In the next lesson, you learn more about previewing and printing the report.

Figure 4.19

Previewing the report Students - By Major

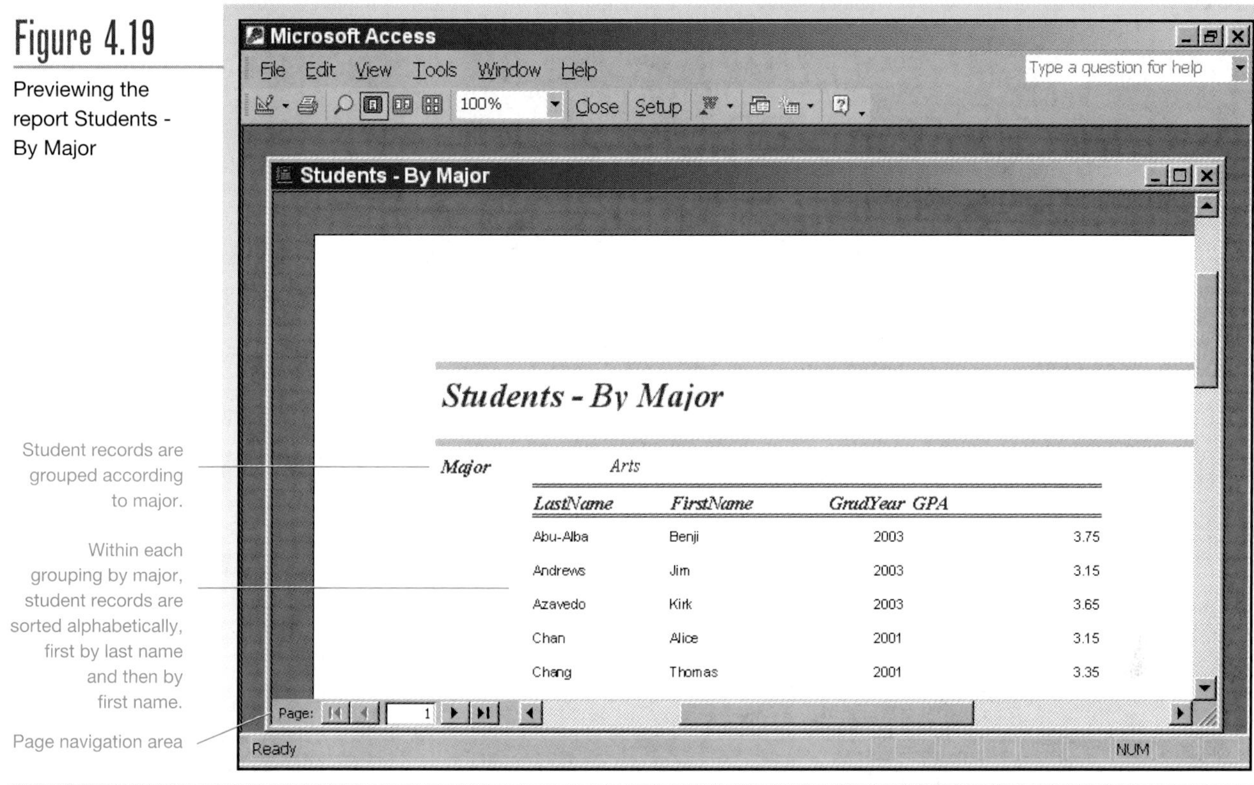

In Addition USING FORM AND REPORT DESIGN VIEWS

Although the form and report wizards let you immediately create usable objects, you may want to create a form or report from scratch or modify an existing object. Although the specifics are not covered in this chapter, you can further customize forms and reports in Design view.

4.2.3 Previewing and Printing a Report

feature→

Whereas you open tables, queries, and forms, you **preview** and print reports. Double-clicking a report object in the Database window opens the report for display in a Print Preview window. In this mode, you can navigate pages, zoom in and out, and modify page setup options.

method→

To preview the report after selecting the report object in the Database window:

- CLICK: Print Preview button ( )

or

- CHOOSE: File, Print Preview

To print the selected report:

- CLICK: Print button ( )

or

- CHOOSE: File, Print

To specify print options for the selected report:

- CHOOSE: File, Page Setup

practice

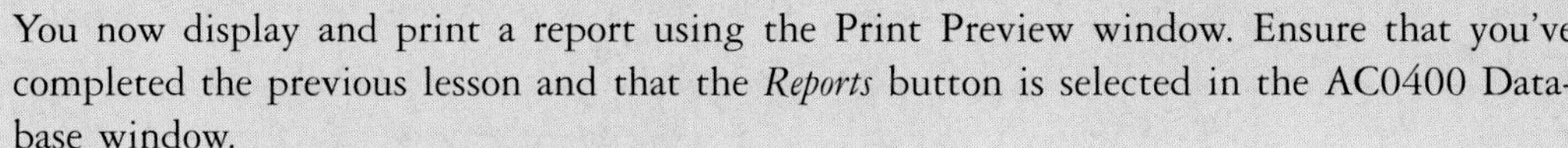

You now display and print a report using the Print Preview window. Ensure that you've completed the previous lesson and that the *Reports* button is selected in the AC0400 Database window.

1. To display a report in Print Preview mode:
   DOUBLE-CLICK: Students - By Major in the list area

2. Let's maximize the Print Preview window for a better view:
   CLICK: its Maximize button (□)
   Your screen should now appear similar to Figure 4.20. (*Hint:* If your Print Preview window does not appear as shown, ensure that the "Fit" option is selected in the Zoom button (Fit ▾) on the toolbar. You can also click the One Page button (□) to yield the same effect.)

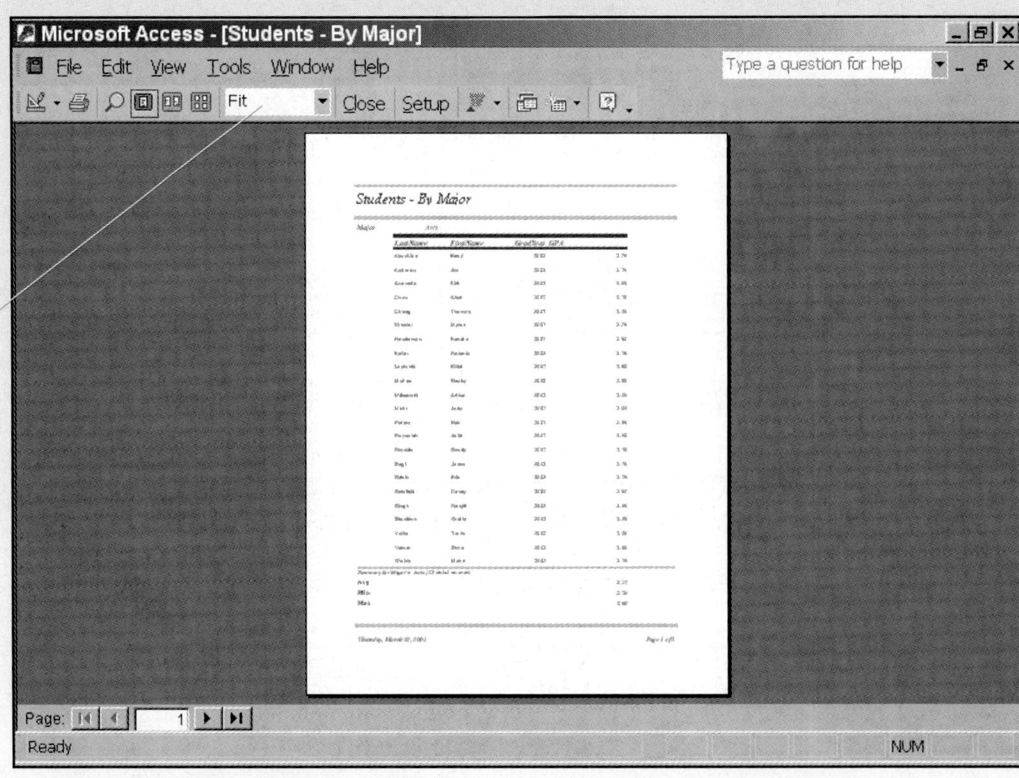

Figure 4.20
Maximized Print Preview window

The Zoom button displays "Fit" in order to shrink the report page to fit in a single screen

3. On your own, move among the pages using the navigation buttons appearing at the bottom of the Print Preview window. When you are ready to proceed, return to Page 1 of the report.

4. To view two pages of the report side by side:
   CLICK: Two Pages button (□)
   (*Hint:* For more options, choose the View, Pages command.)

5. On your own, zoom in and out on different areas of the preview. Take special note of the summary calculations appearing at the end of a category grouping, as shown in Figure 4.21.

Figure 4.21

Zooming in on the summary calculations

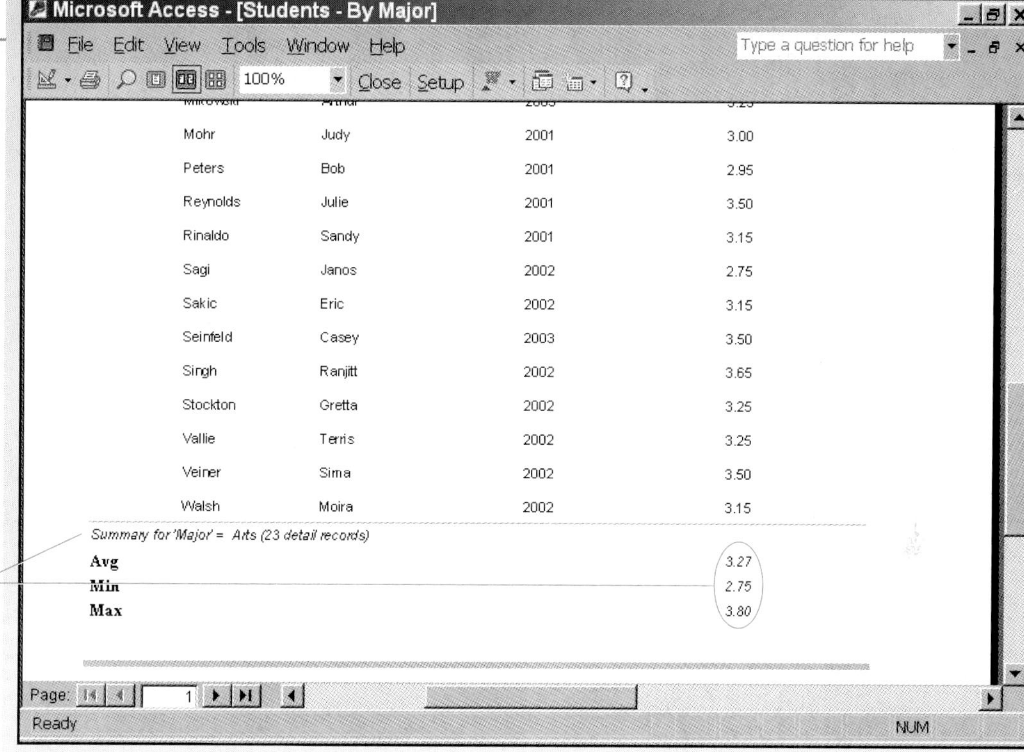

6. To view multiple pages:
CLICK: Multiple Pages button
SELECT: 1x3 Pages in the drop-down menu that appears, as shown here

1x3 Pages

7. To return to viewing a single page:
CLICK: One Page button

8. Now let's practice using the Zoom feature:
CLICK: down arrow attached to the Zoom button (100%)
SELECT: 150%
(*Hint:* You can also choose the View, Zoom command to change the magnification.)

9. Navigate the report pages and scroll the window so that you are viewing the top left-hand corner of the first page.

10. To restore the Print Preview window to a window:
CLICK: its Restore button
Your screen should now appear similar to Figure 4.22.

Figure 4.22

Manipulating the Print Preview window

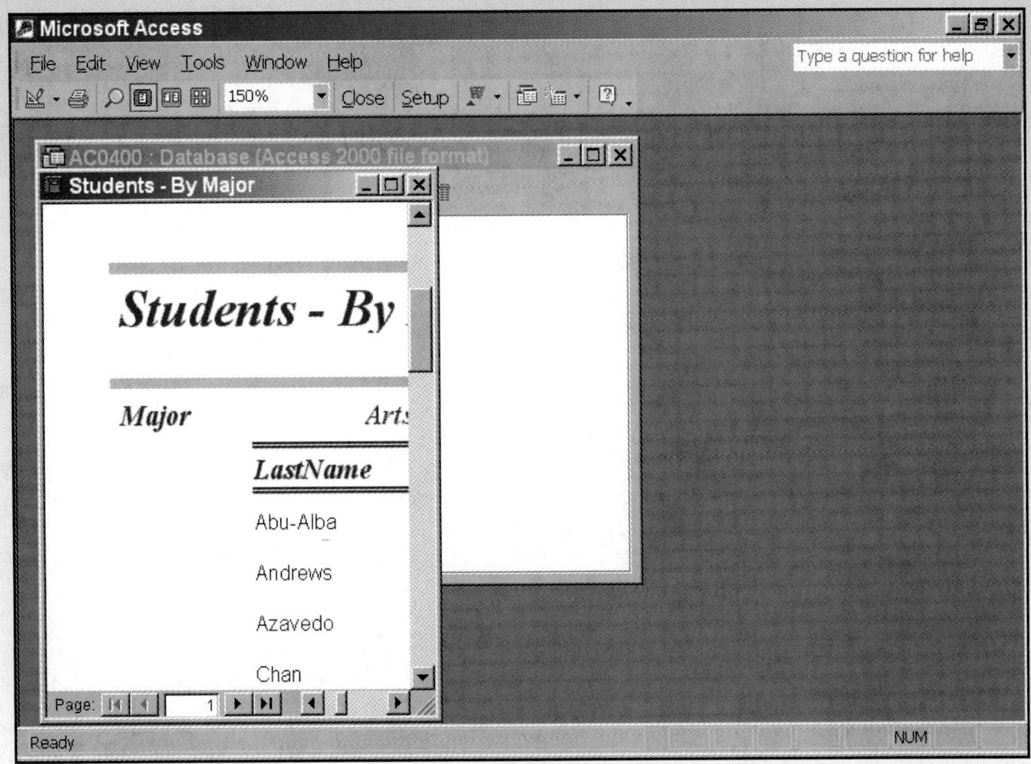

11. If you have a printer, print the report by clicking the Print button ().
12. Close the Print Preview window by clicking its Close button (). You are returned to the Database window.

In Addition PRINTING A REPORT FROM THE DATABASE WINDOW

You can also preview or print a datasheet, query, form, or report by right-clicking the desired object in the Database window and then choosing a command. From the right-click shortcut menu that appears, choose Print Preview to open the object in a Print Preview window or choose the Print command to send it directly to the printer.

4.2.4 Publishing a Static Report to the Web

feature

The **World Wide Web** is an exciting medium for exchanging data. Using **Internet** technologies, the Web provides an easy-to-use multimedia interface for finding information stored on a Web server anywhere on the planet. Microsoft Access makes it simple for you to tap the power of the Web. Once you've created a database object such as a table or report, you can export the object in **HTML** (Hypertext Markup Language) format, the standardized markup language of the Web. Such a document provides only a static representation or snapshot of a database, so Access also provides several advanced tools for creating dynamic real-time Web applications.

method

After selecting an object in the Database window:

- CHOOSE: File, Export
- TYPE: **filename** for the Web document
- SELECT: HTML documents in the *Save as type* drop-down list box
- CLICK: Export command button

practice

In this lesson, you export a report object as an HTML document. Ensure that you've completed the previous lessons and that the Reports button is selected in the AC0400 Database window.

1. To export a report for publishing to the Web:
   SELECT: Students - By Major
   The object name must appear highlighted in the list area.

2. CHOOSE: File, Export
   The Export Report dialog box appears, similar to the one shown in Figure 4.23.

Figure 4.23

Export dialog box

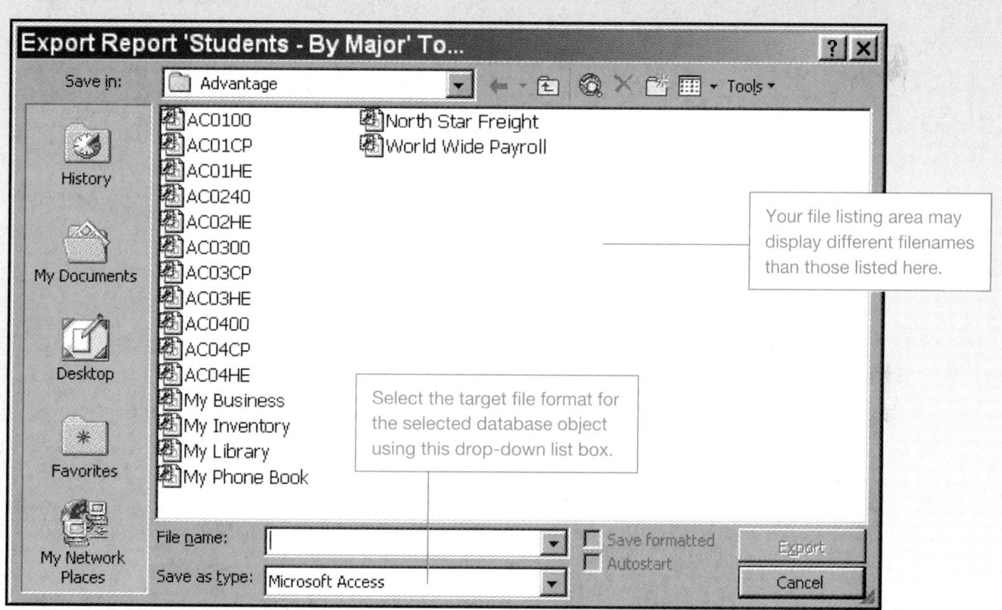

3. In the *File name* text box:
   TYPE: **Students - Web Page**

Access

4. In the Places bar or the *Save in* drop-down list box:
   SELECT: *your personal storage location*

5. In the *Save as type* drop-down list box
   SELECT: HTML Documents
   (*Note:* The listing area will display only the existing HTML documents in the target folder.)

6. To proceed with the export:
   CLICK: Export command button
   The HTML Output Options dialog box appears, as shown in Figure 4.24. This dialog box allows you to specify a template for enhancing the report's appearance, navigation, and formatting.

Figure 4.24

HTML Output Options dialog box

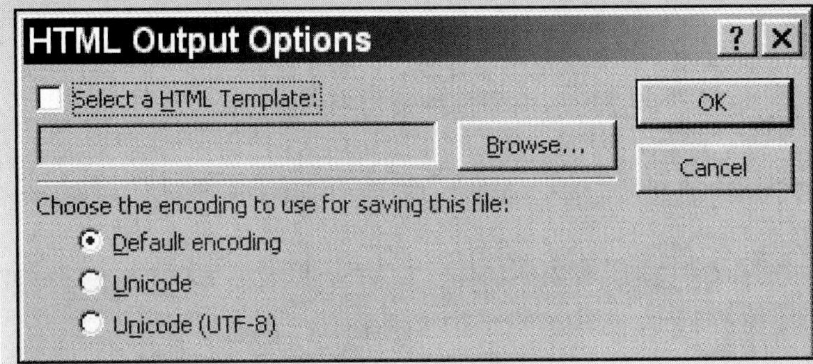

7. To continue without specifying an HTML template:
   CLICK: OK command button

8. The export process creates one HTML document for each page of the report. You are then returned to the Database window.

9. If you have access to Web browser software, open one of the pages for viewing. Click the hyperlinks appearing at the bottom of the page to navigate the report pages. Figure 4.25 provides an example of how the first page of the report is displayed using Internet Explorer. (*Note:* You can import the HTML pages into a Web application, such as Microsoft FrontPage 2002, in order to enhance their formatting or correct errors.)

10. When you are ready to proceed, close the Internet Explorer application window and return to the AC0400 Database window.

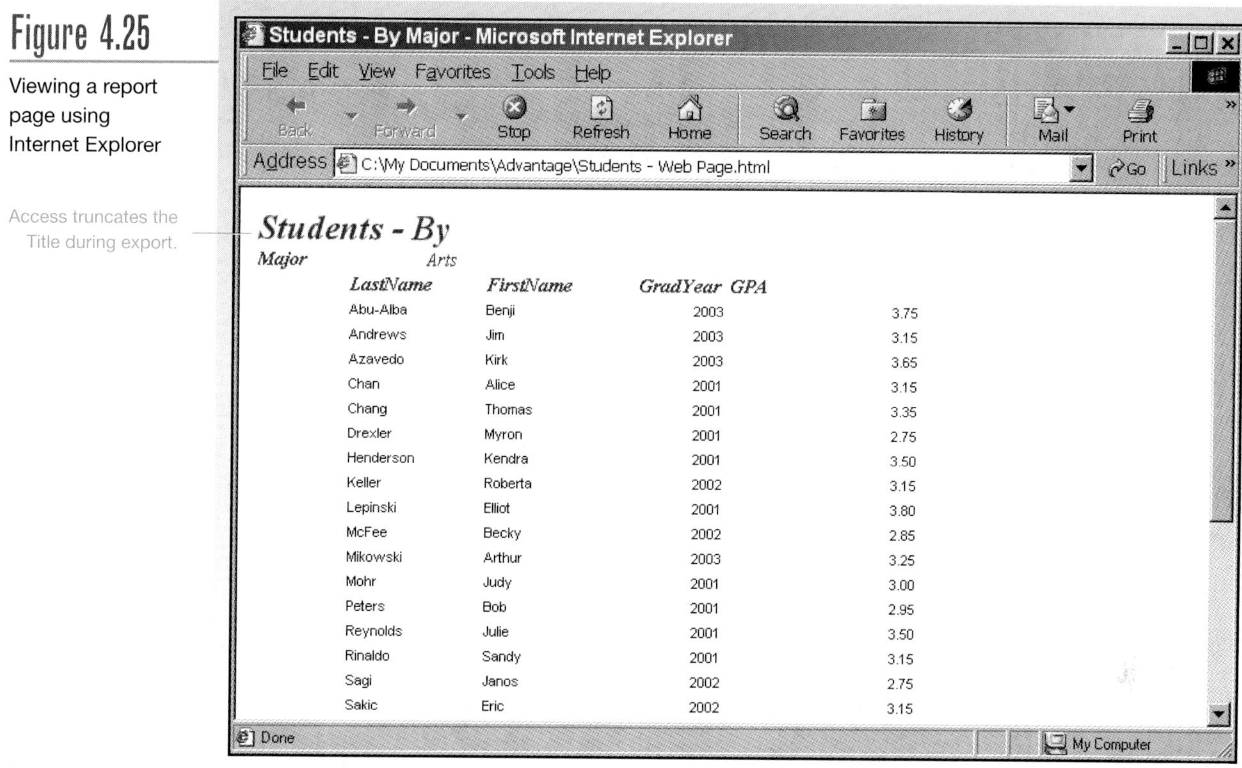

Figure 4.25

Viewing a report page using Internet Explorer

Access truncates the Title during export.

In Addition SAVING A REPORT AS A SNAPSHOT

If you regularly need to print, photocopy, and distribute Access reports, consider sending a **report snapshot** instead. A snapshot, which is stored as a graphic metafile on a disk, contains a static image of each page in a report. To create a snapshot, select the desired report in the Database window and then choose the File, Export command. After specifying a name and storage location, select "Snapshot Format" as the file type. Once the snapshot file is saved, you can distribute it via electronic mail or post it to your Web site.

4.2. What does the term "grouping data" refer to in a report?

4.3 Generating a Mailing Labels Report

Using your database to print mailing labels can save you a lot of time in preparing envelopes for greeting cards, birth announcements, or other special mailings. You can even keep track of your computer disks and files in a database and then prepare diskette labels (Avery Product Number 5296) using a report object. In this module, you learn to create, format, and print mailing labels using the Label Wizard.

4.3.1 Creating a Report Using the Label Wizard

feature →

The Access **Label Wizard** provides an easy way for you to create a mailing labels report and print standard labels that fit on envelopes, packages, and diskettes.

method →

In the Database window, select the *Reports* button and then:

- CLICK: New button (New) on the Database window toolbar
- SELECT: a table or query from the drop-down list box
- DOUBLE-CLICK: Label Wizard

practice →

You now create a mailing labels report for the Students table. Ensure that the AC0400 Database window is displayed.

1. Let's generate mailing labels for the Students table. Begin by displaying the New Report dialog box (Figure 4.26):
SELECT: *Reports* button in the Objects bar
CLICK: New button (New) on the Database window toolbar

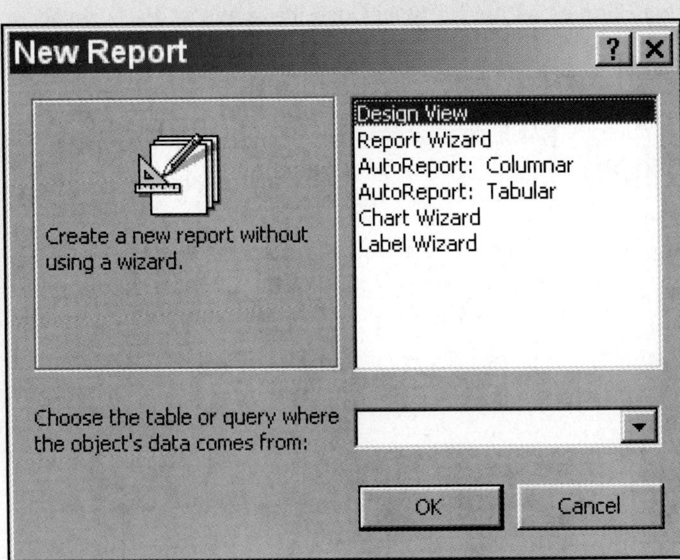

Figure 4.26

New Report dialog box

2. Now launch the Label Wizard for the Students table:
SELECT: Label Wizard in the list area
SELECT: Students in the *Choose the table* . . . drop-down list box
CLICK: OK command button
The first dialog box for the Label Wizard appears, as shown in Figure 4.27. You use this dialog box to specify the label size and format.

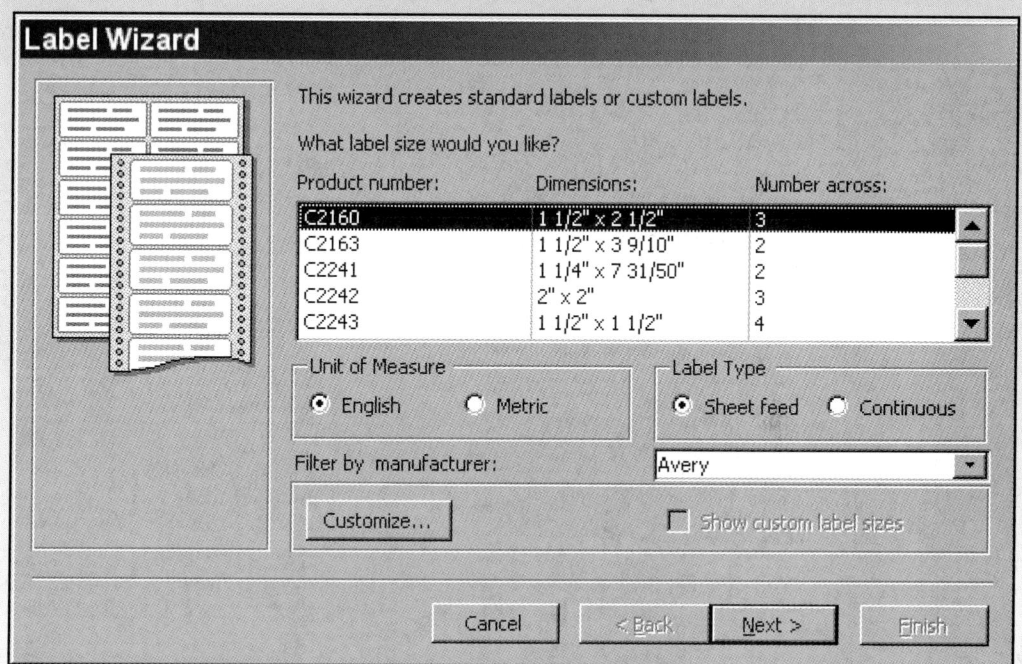

Figure 4.27

Label Wizard dialog box: type of label

3. For a standard mailing labels report, let's confirm a few settings:
SELECT: English option button in the *Unit of Measure* area
SELECT: Sheet feed option button in the *Label Type* area
SELECT: Avery in the *Filter by manufacturer* drop-down list box
SELECT: 5160 in the *Product number* column
CLICK: Next >

4. In this step, you select the font used for the labels. Do the following:
SELECT: Times New Roman from the *Font name* drop-down list box
SELECT: 10 from the *Font size* drop-down list box
Your screen should now appear similar to Figure 4.28.

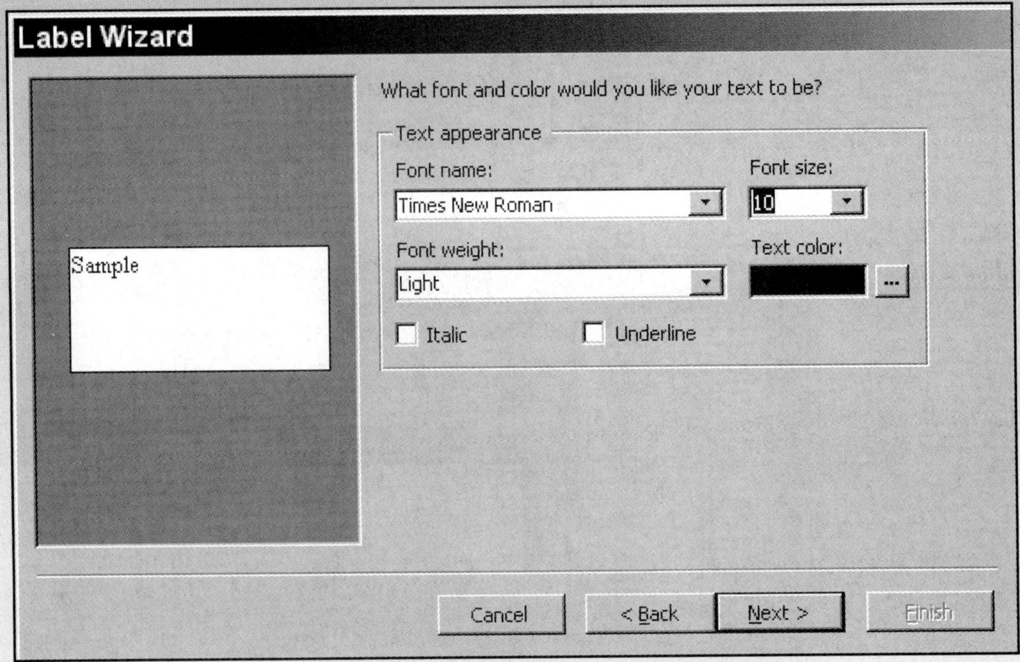

Figure 4.28

Label Wizard dialog box: font selection

5. To proceed:
CLICK: Next >

6. You now build the appearance of the label by entering text or selecting fields. In the *Available fields* list box:
DOUBLE-CLICK: FirstName
PRESS: Space Bar
DOUBLE-CLICK: LastName
PRESS: ENTER
Notice how you must enter spaces between fields and break the label into lines.

7. To finish creating the label:
DOUBLE-CLICK: Address
PRESS: ENTER
DOUBLE-CLICK: City
TYPE: **,** (a single comma)
PRESS: Space Bar
DOUBLE-CLICK: State
PRESS: Space Bar
DOUBLE-CLICK: Zip
Your label should now appear similar to Figure 4.29.

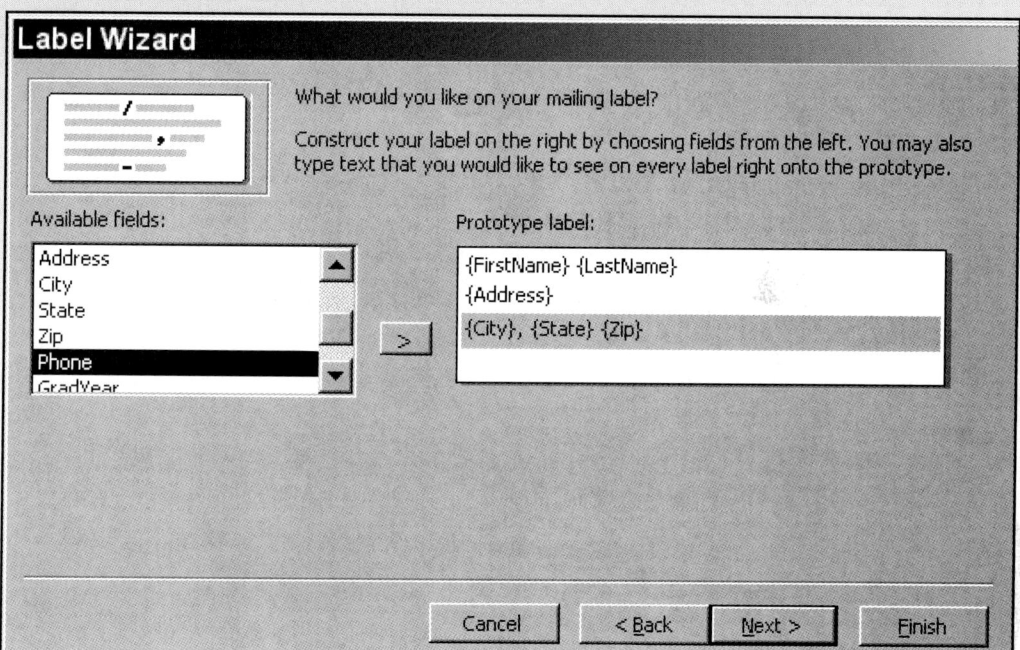

Figure 4.29

Label Wizard dialog box: adding fields

8. To proceed to the next step:
CLICK: Next >

9. You are now asked to specify a sort order for the mailing labels. Common sort orders for mailing labels include by zip code and by alphabetical last name. To sort the labels by student name:
DOUBLE-CLICK: LastName in the *Available fields* list box
DOUBLE-CLICK: FirstName in the *Available fields* list box
CLICK: Next >

10. In the final step, you name the mailing label report and specify whether to display or modify the label design. To accept the default selections:
CLICK: Finish

11. If the following dialog box appears, you can ignore the warning and continue by clicking the OK command button.

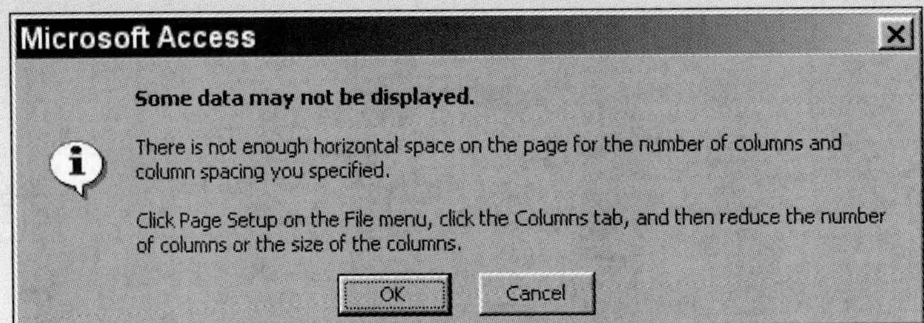

12. After a few moments, the mailing label report appears in the Print Preview window (Figure 4.30). On your own, zoom in and out on pages in the Print Preview window.

13. If you have a printer, print the report by clicking the Print button (🖨).

14. Close the Print Preview window by clicking its Close button (☒). You are returned to the Database window.

Figure 4.30

Label report generated by the Label Wizard

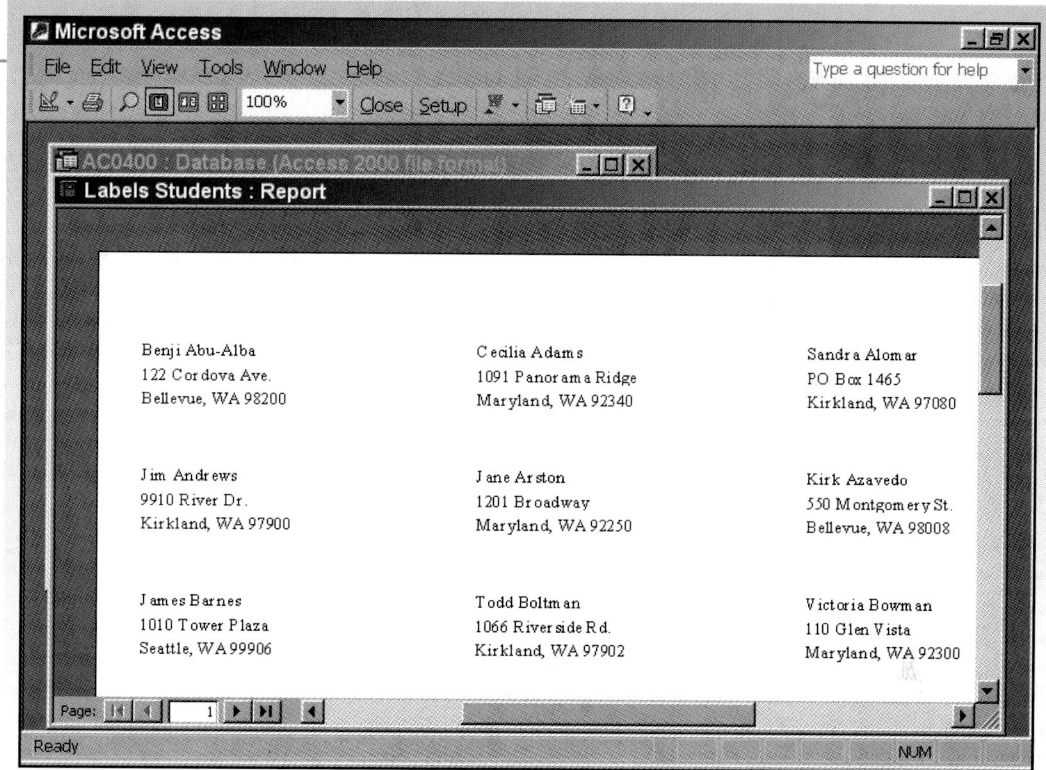

4.3. How could you use table and report objects to print diskette labels?

4.4 Managing Database Objects

As you continue to use Access, you will create many databases and many database objects, and it is important that you know how to manage them properly. In this module, you learn to rename, copy, and delete database objects and to compact and repair a database file.

4.4.1 Renaming, Copying, and Deleting Objects

feature

Similar to performing routine file management procedures using Windows Explorer, it's simple to rename, copy, and delete the individual objects stored in a database. In a sense, the Access wizards make it too easy to create database objects. Especially for novice users, it is common to find Database windows overflowing with trial editions of objects. Users quickly create a form or report using a wizard only to find that they need to make a few improvements. Because creating a new wizard-generated object is often easier than editing the existing one, the Database window can become overpopulated quickly. To avoid capacity and performance issues, these trial objects should be deleted immediately.

method

After right-clicking the desired database object, choose from the following options:

- CHOOSE: Rename to rename an object
- CHOOSE: Cut to move an object, or CLICK: Cut button ( )
- CHOOSE: Copy to copy an object, or CLICK: Copy button ( )
- CHOOSE: Paste to paste an object, or CLICK: Paste button ( )
- CHOOSE: Delete to remove an object, or CLICK: Delete button ( )

practice

You now practice managing objects in the AC0400 database. Ensure that the AC0400 Database window is displayed.

1. To begin, let's display the table objects:
   CLICK: *Tables* button in the Objects bar
2. Let's practice adjusting the view options in the list area:
   CLICK: Large Icons button ( ) on the Database window toolbar
   Your Database window should resemble the one in Figure 4.31.

Figure 4.31

Adjusting view options in the Database window

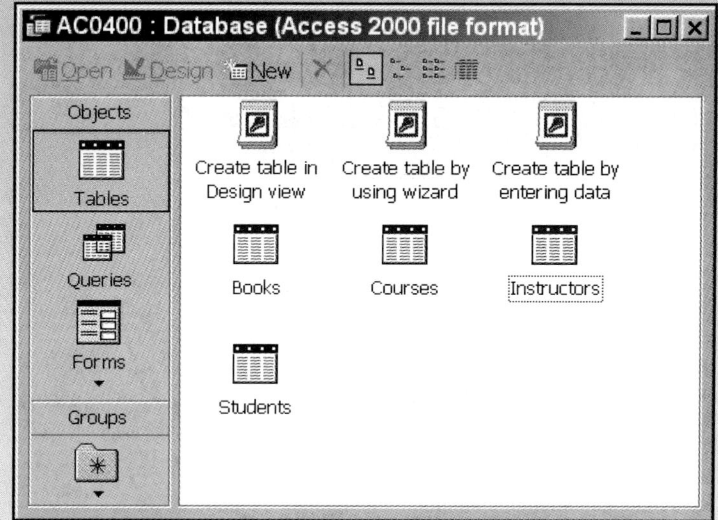

3. CLICK: Small icons button ( ) to view smaller icons
CLICK: Details button ( ) to view additional information
CLICK: List button ( ) to return to the standard view
(*Hint:* You can change the appearance and order in which the objects are displayed by choosing the View and the View, Arrange Icons commands.)

4. To rename the Books table object to Fiction:
CLICK: the name "Books" once so that it appears highlighted
CLICK: the name "Books" again to enter Edit mode, as shown here
(*Hint:* You can also select an object and press F2 to enter Edit mode. Notice that you click the name and not the icon to rename an object.)

5. To rename the table object:
TYPE: **Fiction**
PRESS: ENTER

6. Let's create a copy of the Fiction object and name it Non-Fiction:
SELECT: Fiction, if it isn't already selected
CLICK: Copy button ( ) on the toolbar
CLICK: Paste button ( ) on the toolbar
The Paste Table As dialog box appears, as shown in Figure 4.32.

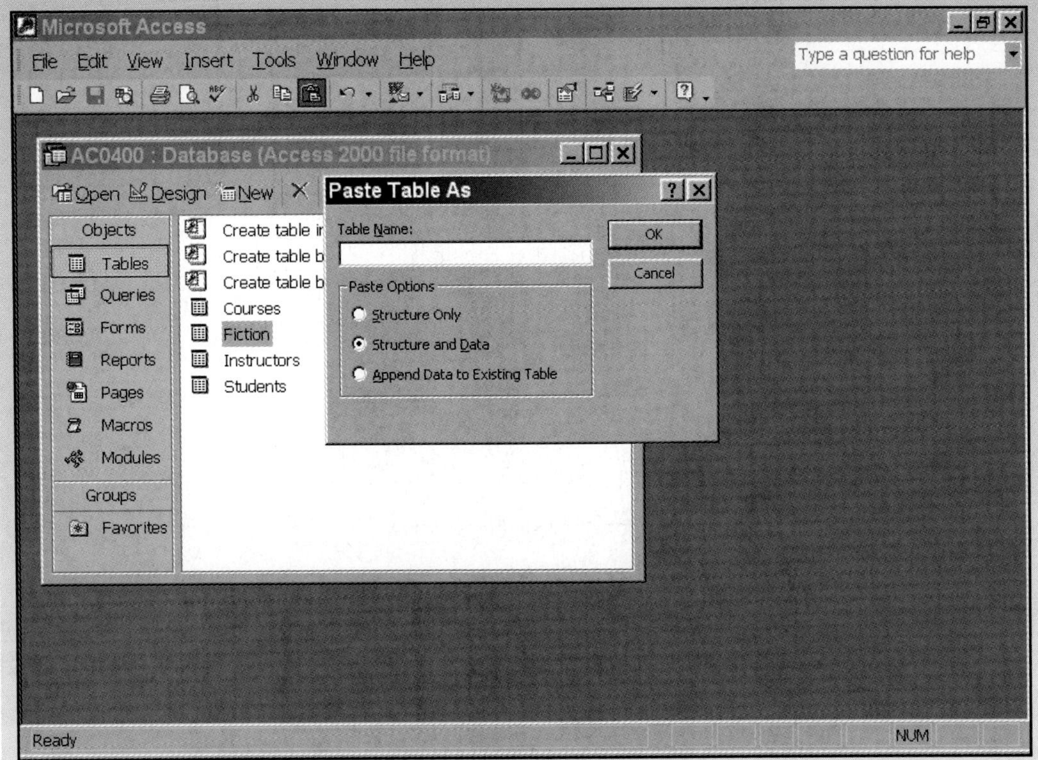

Figure 4.32

Paste Table As dialog box

7. To complete the paste operation:
TYPE: **Non-Fiction** in the *Table Name* text box
SELECT: *Structure Only* check box
CLICK: OK command button
(*Note:* You copy only the structure, since the data stored in the Fiction table is not required for the Non-Fiction table.)

8. To delete an object using the right-click menu:
RIGHT-CLICK: Non-Fiction
CHOOSE: Delete
The following dialog box appears.

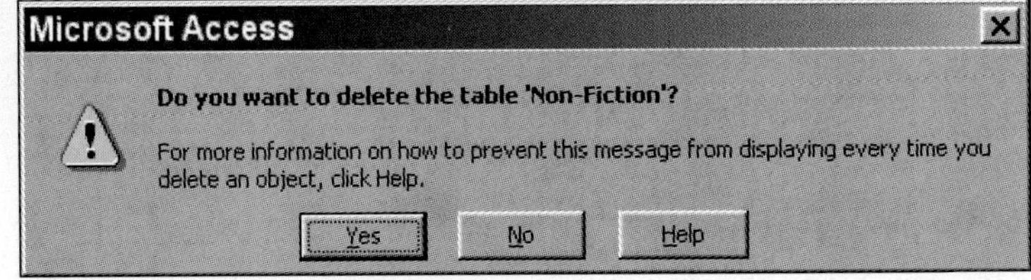

9. To confirm the deletion of the table object:
CLICK: Yes command button
The table object is removed from the Database window.

4.4.2 Compacting, Repairing, and Converting a Database

feature

An Access database file is stored on the disk with the file extension .mdb. When you make several changes to a database, such as copying and deleting objects, the file may become fragmented. Compacting a database reorganizes and packs the file more closely together, and repairing a database verifies the reliability of objects. An added benefit for those tables that contain AutoNumber fields, and where records have been deleted from the end of the table, is that compacting resets the field to the next sequential value. As a result, the next record added to the table will have an AutoNumber value that is one more than the last record in the table. In addition to saving disk space and resetting AutoNumber fields, compacting a database improves a database's performance.

Before sharing a database with another user or using a database in another application, you may need to first convert the file to another version of Access. For example, an associate using Microsoft Access 97 will not be able to work with your database files unless you first convert them to the Access 97 file format. Both the Access 2000 and Access 2002 file formats, however, are native to Microsoft Access 2002. Perhaps surprisingly, Microsoft Access 2002 defaults to creating databases in the Access 2000 file format, although this can be changed using the Tools, Options command. Before compacting or converting a database, remember to use the Windows Explorer or another utility to back up your database file.

method

To compact and repair a database:

- CHOOSE: Tools, Database Utilities, Compact and Repair Database

To convert a database to another version:

- CHOOSE: Tools, Database Utilities, Convert Database

practice

In this lesson, you compact and then convert the AC0400 database file. Ensure that the AC0400 Database window is displayed.

1. To compact and repair the AC0400 database:
   CHOOSE: Tools, Database Utilities
   The menu commands for converting, compressing, repairing, and maintaining a database appears, as shown here.

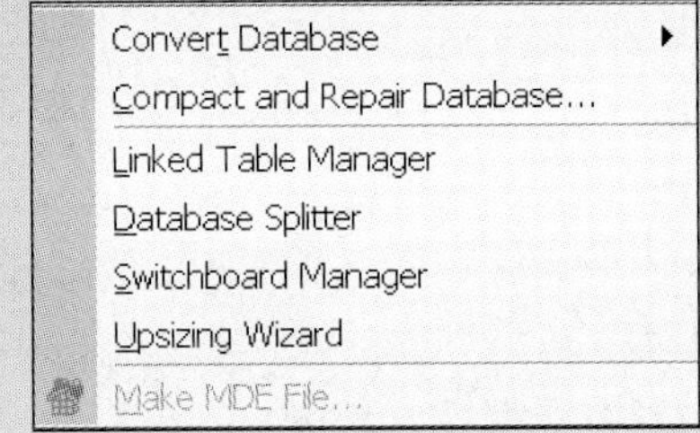

2. CHOOSE: Compact and Repair Database
   The automated process begins, processes the database objects, and then ends rather quietly. You can witness its processing status by looking in the Status bar.
3. Let's update the AC0400 database to the Access 2002 file format. Do the following:
   CHOOSE: Tools, Database Utilities
4. CHOOSE: Convert Database, To Access 2002 File Format
   The Convert Database Into dialog box appears, as shown in Figure 4.33, with a default name of "db1" for the new database.

Figure 4.33

Converting an Access database file

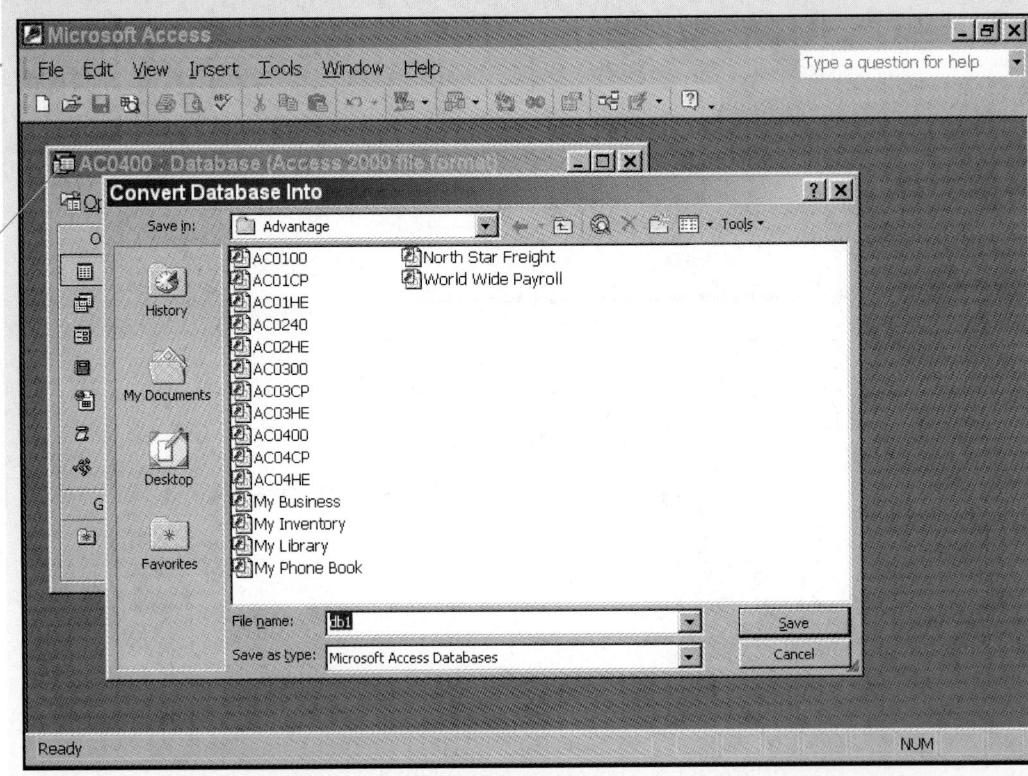

Notice that the Database window's Title bar displays the current file format version.

5. In the *File name* text box:
   TYPE: **AC02-0400**

6. In the Places bar or the *Save in* drop-down list box:
SELECT: *your personal storage location*

7. To proceed with the conversion:
CLICK: Save command button
After a few moments, you will see the following dialog box.

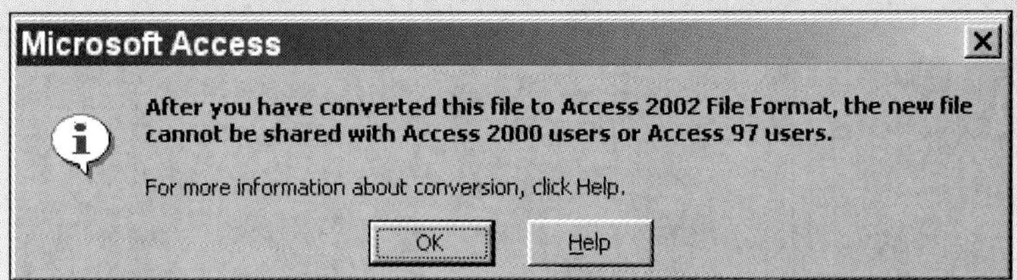

8. To accept the warning dialog box:
CLICK: OK command button

9. Before you can open the new Access 2002 database file, you must first close the AC0400 Database window.

10. On your own, open the AC02-0400 database from your personal storage location. The Database window should appear similar to Figure 4.34.

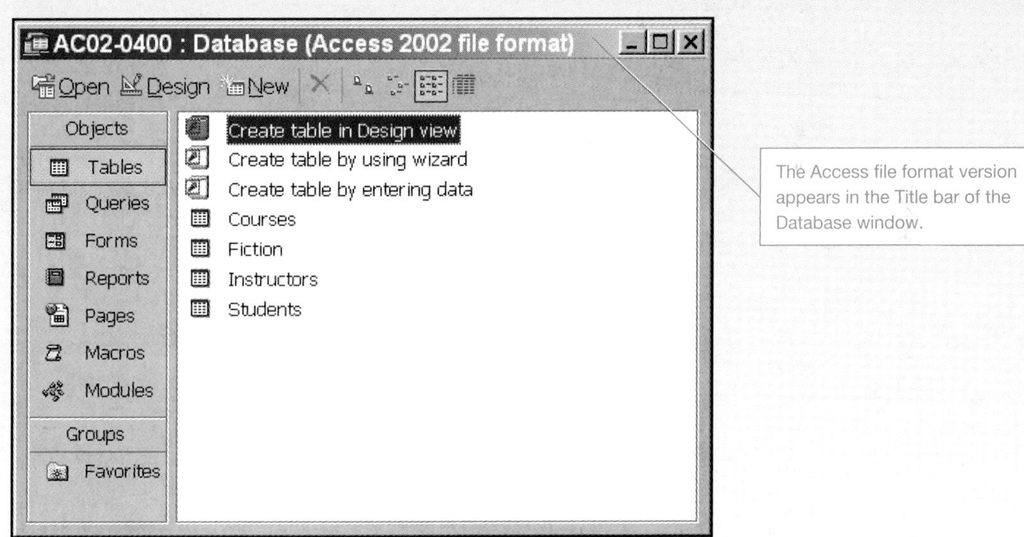

Figure 4.34
Opening an Access 2002 database file

11. Open a datasheet or report object for viewing. Notice that the conversion to the Access 2002 file format is relatively seamless to the end user. In fact, without the notification in the Title bar, you would be hard pressed to determine which version you were using.

12. Close all of the open windows, including the AC02-0400 Database window.

In Addition BACKING UP THE DATABASE

One of the most important tasks you can perform after creating and adding data to a database is to make a backup copy of it to another storage location. Most people back up a database, along with their other important data files, using "My Computer," Windows Explorer, or a specialized backup program. An Access database is stored in a file ending with the extension .mdb or .mde. You can search for this file type using the Find, Files or Folders command on the Start (Start) menu.

4.4. Name two operating system tools that you can use to back up a database.

Chapter summary

The users of a database application are most familiar with its form and report objects. Forms are used in entering and editing data, whereas reports are used for presenting and displaying information. Besides offering a more attractive interface than datasheets, forms can help focus your attention on a single record at a time. Reports, which also offer a variety of attractive layouts, are primarily meant for printing. It's uncommon to limit a report to previewing on-screen. Therefore, you must learn to match your printer's capabilities (color versus black-and-white, inkjet versus laser) with the report design and formatting options that are available. Access provides wizards that make it easier to create forms, reports, and mailing labels. For easier database management, Access also has commands for renaming, copying, and deleting objects, and compacting, repairing, and converting a database.

Command Summary

Many of the commands and procedures appearing in this chapter are summarized in the following table.

Skill Set	To Perform This Task	Do the Following
Creating and Modifying Forms	Create a new form using the AutoForm Wizard	SELECT: the desired table or query CLICK: New Object: AutoForm button
	Create a new form using the Form Wizard	CLICK: *Forms* button in the Objects bar DOUBLE-CLICK: Create form by using wizard
Producing Reports	Create a new report using the AutoReport Wizard	SELECT: the desired table or query CLICK: New Object: AutoReport button
	Create a new report using the Report Wizard	CLICK: *Reports* button in the Object bar DOUBLE-CLICK: Create report by using wizard

Skill Set	To Perform This Task	Do the Following
	Create a new mailing labels report using the Label Wizard	CLICK: *Reports* button in the Object bar CLICK: New button (New) SELECT: a table or query object from the drop-down list box DOUBLE-CLICK: Label Wizard
	Preview a report for printing	DOUBLE-CLICK: the report object, or CLICK: Print Preview button ( ), or CHOOSE: File, Print Preview
	Print a report	CLICK: Print button ( ), or CHOOSE: File, Print
Integrating with Other Applications	Export a report to HTML format for Web publishing	SELECT: the desired object CHOOSE: File, Export TYPE: **filename** for this version SELECT: HTML Documents in the *Save as type* drop-down list box CLICK: Save command button
	Export a report as a snapshot file for e-mail and Web distribution	SELECT: the desired object CHOOSE: File, Export TYPE: **filename** for this version SELECT: Snapshot Format in the *Save as type* drop-down list box CLICK: Save command button
Creating and Using Databases	Rename a database object	RIGHT-CLICK: the desired object CHOOSE: Rename
	Copy a selected database object	CLICK: Copy button ( ) CLICK: Paste button ( ) SELECT: a paste option
	Delete a database object	RIGHT-CLICK: the desired object CHOOSE: Delete
Using Access Tools	Compact and repair a database	CHOOSE: Tools, Database Utilities CHOOSE: Compact and Repair Database
	Back up and restore a database	Use Windows Explorer or "My Computer" to perform copy, backup, and restore operations for an Access database file (extension .mdb)
	Convert a database file to another file format version	CHOOSE: Tools, Database Utilities CHOOSE: Convert Database

Key Terms

This section specifies page references for the key terms identified in this chapter. For a complete list of definitions, refer to the Glossary at the end of this learning guide.

AutoForm Wizard, *p. 147*
AutoReport Wizard, *p. 161*
Form window, *p. 147*
form wizards, *p. 146*
HTML, *p. 170*
Internet, *p. 170*
Label Wizard, *p. 174*
preview, *p. 167*
report snapshot, *p. 173*
report wizards, *p. 161*
World Wide Web, *p. 170*

Chapter quiz

Short Answer

1. Why create forms for use in a database application?
2. Name five types of AutoForm Wizards.
3. List the form options available in the New Form dialog box.
4. When would you choose a columnar or justified form layout?
5. When would you choose a tabular or datasheet form layout?
6. Why create reports for use in a database application?
7. Describe two types of AutoReport Wizards.
8. List the report options available in the New Report dialog box.
9. How do you create an Access report ready to publish to the Web?
10. Describe two ways to remove objects in the Database window.

True/False

1. ___ The default AutoForm Wizard is the AutoForm: Columnar Wizard.
2. ___ The Form Wizard allows you to specify a sorting order.
3. ___ You can display data from more than one table in a form.
4. ___ In the Form window, pressing CTRL+END moves the cursor to the last field in the current record.
5. ___ The default AutoReport Wizard is the AutoReport: Tabular Wizard.

6. ___ The Report Wizard allows you to specify a sorting order.

7. ___ The information that you want summarized in a report can be extracted from either a table or a query.

8. ___ A tabular report prints several columns of information, with the field labels appearing down the left margin of the page.

9. ___ In the Database window, you can copy a table object's structure without duplicating the data stored in the table.

10. ___ You should regularly compact a database using Windows Explorer.

Multiple Choice

1. A form is used to display data from which of the following objects?
   a. tables and/or queries
   b. tables and/or reports
   c. queries and/or reports
   d. tables only

2. Which form layout is produced by default when selecting the AutoForm option from the New Object button?
   a. Circular
   b. Columnar
   c. Singular
   d. Tabular

3. Which of the following best describes a tabular form layout?
   a. data from a single record presented in a single column
   b. data from numerous records presented in a single column
   c. data from a single record presented in rows and columns
   d. data from numerous records presented in rows and columns

4. Which of the following best describes a justified form layout?
   a. data from a single record presented with stacked fields
   b. data from numerous records presented with stacked fields
   c. data from a single record presented in a single column
   d. data from numerous records presented in rows and columns

5. Which of the following performs the same action as pressing PgUp in the Form window?
   a. CLICK: |◀
   b. CLICK: ◀
   c. CLICK: ▶
   d. CLICK: ▶|

6. The Report Wizard provides the following options that are not available in the Form Wizard:
   a. Grouping and Filtering
   b. Outlining and Sorting
   c. Grouping and Sorting
   d. Outlining and Filtering

7. Which of the following is not a summary calculation available in the Summary Options dialog box of the Report Wizard?
   a. Avg
   b. Count
   c. Max
   d. Sum

8. This chapter presents which two options for exporting a static report page for publishing to the Web?
   a. ASP and HTML
   b. HTML and Java
   c. MDB and MDE
   d. HTML and Snapshot

9. The Label Wizard enables you to create a report format using standard label sizes from this vendor.

a. Avery
b. Linux
c. Microsoft
d. Sun

10. Which of the following is *not* a paste option when copying a table object?

a. Structure Only
b. Structure and Data
c. Structure, Forms, and Reports
d. Append Data to Existing Table

Hands-On exercises

easy

1. AmeriSales International: Forms and Reports

In this exercise, you create two new database objects for AmeriSales International. First, using the AutoForm Wizard, you create a columnar data entry form for the Customers table. Then, you create a tabular report using an AutoReport Wizard.

1. Load Microsoft Access using the Windows Start menu.

2. Open the database file named AC04HE. Ensure that the *Tables* button in the Objects bar is selected. Your screen should appear similar to Figure 4.35.

Figure 4.35

Opening the AC04HE database

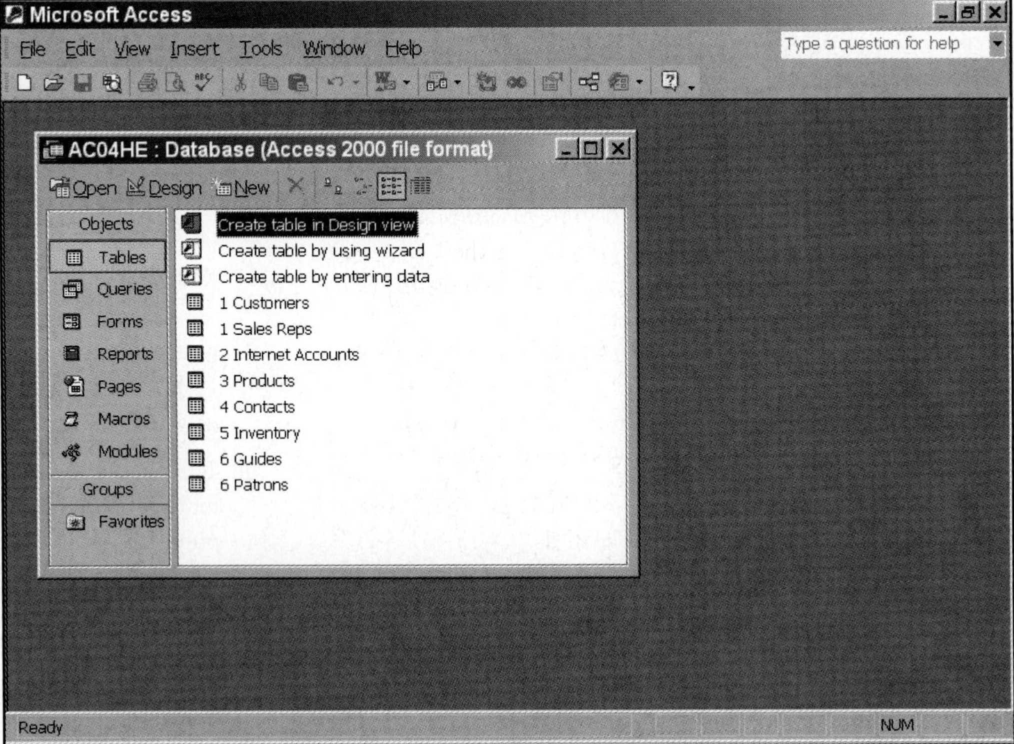

3. To create a data entry form for the Customers table:
SELECT: 1 Customers in the list area
(*Hint:* Click once on the name of the table. Do not double-click.)

4. To have Access create a new columnar form:
CLICK: New Object: AutoForm button ( )
(*Hint:* If the AutoForm image is not displayed on the button face, click the attached down arrow and choose the AutoForm command.)

5. Let's save the new form shown in Figure 4.36:
CLICK: Save button ( )
TYPE: **Customer Data Entry Form**
PRESS: ENTER or CLICK: OK

Figure 4.36

Customer Data Entry Form window

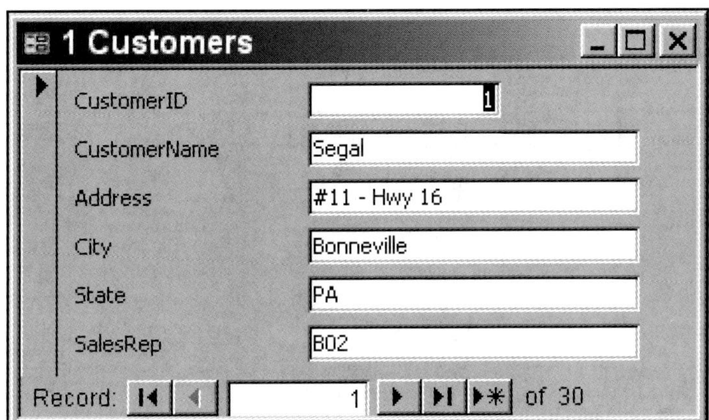

6. To close the new form:
CLICK: its Close button ( )

7. Now let's create a tabular report for the Customers table. To begin:
CLICK: *Reports* button in the Objects bar
CLICK: New button ( ) on the Database window toolbar

8. In the New Report dialog box:
SELECT: 1 Customers from the *Choose the table . . .* drop-down list box
DOUBLE-CLICK: AutoReport: Tabular
A new report is displayed in the Print Preview window, as shown in Figure 4.37.

Figure 4.37

Tabular AutoReport displayed in Print Preview

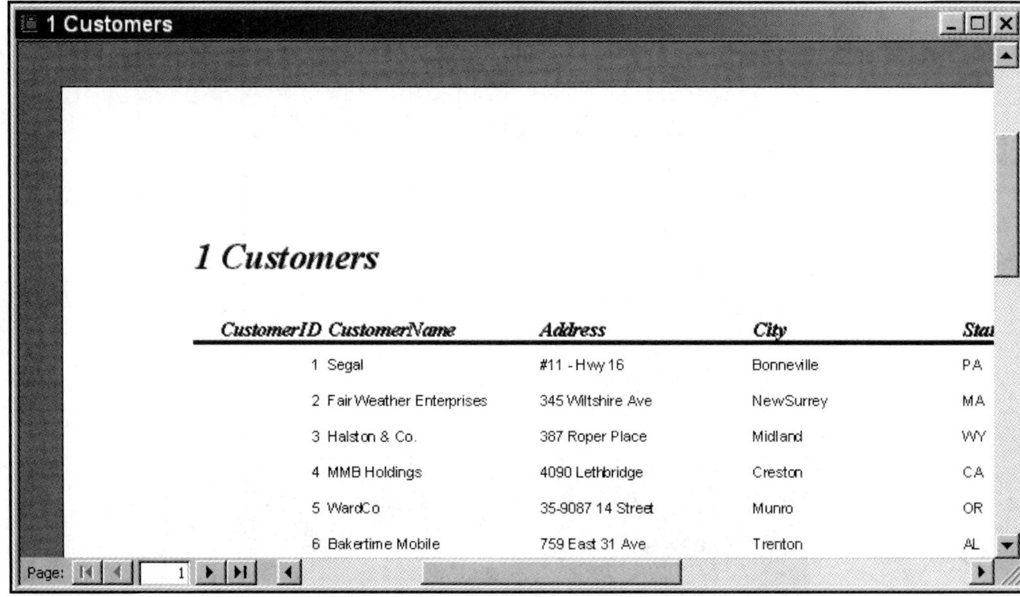

9. On your own, use the magnifying glass mouse pointer to zoom in and out on the report page.
10. To close the report's Print Preview window:
    CLICK: its Close button (☒)
11. In the confirmation dialog box that appears:
    CLICK: Yes command button
12. To name and save the new report:
    TYPE: **Customer AutoReport**
    PRESS: ENTER or CLICK: OK
    The new report object should appear in the Database window.

easy

2. Iway Internet Group: Internet Accounts

The 2 Internet Accounts table contains a listing of current user accounts for an Internet service provider (ISP). In this exercise, you create a report that groups and summarizes users according to where they live. Ensure that the AC04HE Database window is displayed.

1. With the *Reports* button in the Objects bar still selected:
   DOUBLE-CLICK: Create report by using wizard

2. In the first step of the Report Wizard dialog box:
   SELECT: Table: 2 Internet Accounts from the *Tables/Queries* drop-down list box

3. Specify the fields that you want included in the report:
   DOUBLE-CLICK: Customer
   DOUBLE-CLICK: Username
   DOUBLE-CLICK: City
   DOUBLE-CLICK: Phone
   DOUBLE-CLICK: Amount
   CLICK: Next >

4. Specify a grouping level by city, as shown in Figure 4.38:
   DOUBLE-CLICK: City
   CLICK: Next >

Figure 4.38

Specifying a grouping level

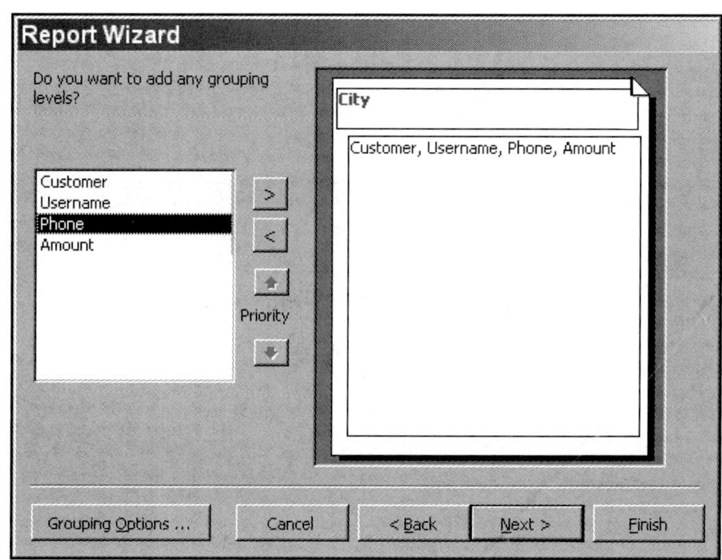

5. Specify an alphabetical sort order by the account's username:
   SELECT: Username from the first drop-down list box

6. Now let's select a summary calculation to perform:
   CLICK: Summary Options command button

7. In the Summary Options dialog box:
   SELECT: *Sum* check box for the Amount field
   CLICK: OK command button

8. To proceed to the next step:
   CLICK: Next >

9. To specify a report layout:
   SELECT: *Align Left 1* option button in the *Layout* area
   SELECT: *Landscape* option button in the *Orientation* area
   CLICK: Next >

10. To specify a report style:
    SELECT: Soft Gray in the *Style* list box
    CLICK: Next >

11. In the last step of the wizard, ensure that the *Preview the report* option button is selected and then name the report object:
    TYPE: **Internet Accounts By City**
    CLICK: Finish

12. Maximize the report's Print Preview window and then:
    SELECT: 75% from the Zoom button (100%)
    Your screen should appear similar to Figure 4.39.

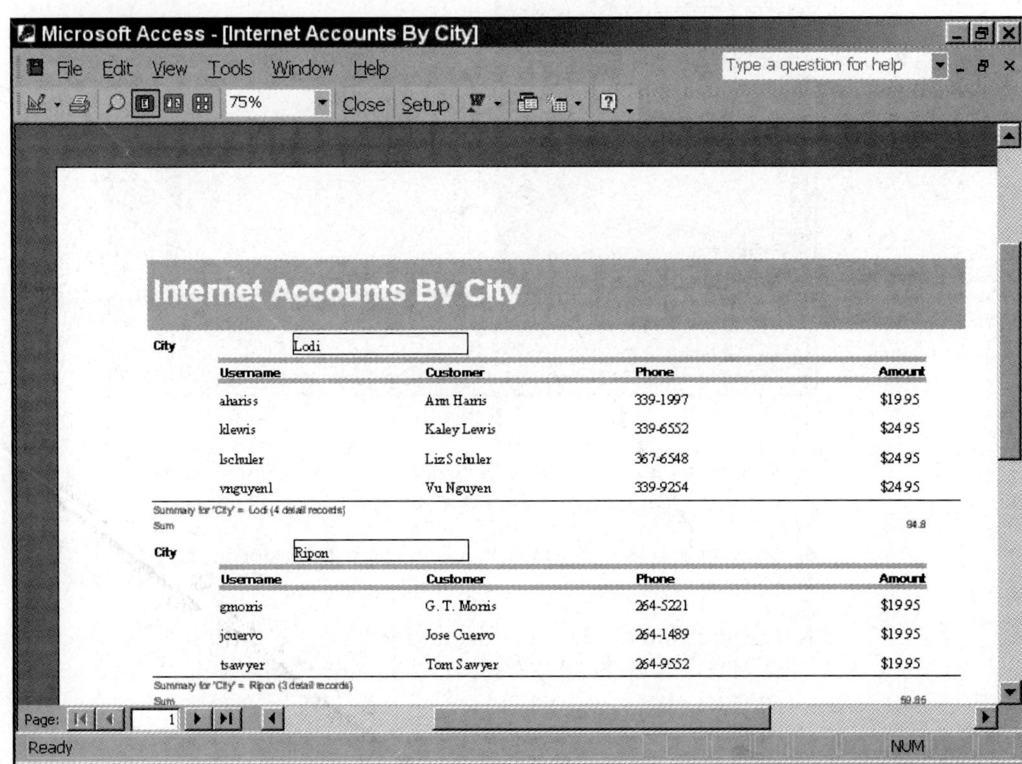

Figure 4.39

Previewing the report Internet Accounts By City

13. If you have a printer, print the report by clicking the Print button.

14. Restore the Print Preview window by clicking its Restore button.

15. Close the Print Preview window by clicking its Close button. You are returned to the Database window.

3. Western Lumber Sales: Forest Products

In this exercise, you practice creating and then working with a tabular form using the Form Wizard. Ensure that the AC04HE Database window is displayed.

1. Display the form objects in the database using the Objects bar.
2. Launch the Form Wizard using the shortcut appearing in the list area.
3. In the Form Wizard dialog box:
   SELECT: Table: 3 Products in the *Tables/Queries* drop-down list box
   CLICK: Include All button (>>) to display all of the fields
4. In the next two steps of the Form Wizard, select a *Tabular* layout and an Expedition style for the form.
5. In the last step of the wizard, enter the name "Products Tabular Form" and then open the form in Form view, as shown in Figure 4.40.

Figure 4.40

Displaying the Products Tabular Form

Products Tabular Form

ProductCode	Species	Size	Grade	Finish	Category
B12	BIRCH	0.5	Cab.	G2S	Plywood
DF14	DFIR	1 X 4	Ungraded	RGH	Board
DF16	D.FIR	1 X 6	Ungraded	RGH	Board
DF210S	DFIR	2 X 10	Standard	S4S	Dim.
DF242	DFIR	2 X 4	2+	S4S	Dim.
DF24S	DFIR	2 X 4	Standard	S4S	Dim.
DF24U	DFIR	2 X 4	Utility	S4S	Dim.
DF26	DFIR	2 X 6	Standard	S4S	Dim.
DF28	DFIR	2 X 8	Standard	S4S	Dim.
O12	ROAK	0.5	Cab.	G2S	Plywood
O38	ROAK	0.375	Cab.	G2S	Plywood
P12	SPF	0.50	Constr.	G1S	Plywood

Record: 1 of 49

6. Enter the following data after clicking the New Record button ( ):
   ProductCode: **DF99**
   Species: **DFIR**
   Size: **2 X 8**
   Grade: **Ungraded**
   Finish: **RGH**
   Category: **Dim.**

Access

7. PRESS: SHIFT+ENTER to save the new record
8. Move to the first field in the first record. Then:
   PRESS: TAB to move to the Species field column
9. Using the Sort Descending button ( ) on the toolbar, sort the table into descending order by the Species column.
10. To filter the information displayed in the form:
    DOUBLE-CLICK: SYP in the Species field column
    CLICK: Filter By Selection button ( )
    Only records of the SYP species now appear in the new form.
11. If you have a printer, print the form by clicking the Print button ( ).
12. Close the form by clicking its Close button ( ).

4. Spring County Carnival: Contact List

In this exercise, you create a mailing labels report for all the records stored in the 4 Contacts table object. Ensure that the AC04HE Database window is displayed.

1. Display the report objects in the database using the Objects bar.
2. To begin creating the mailing labels report:
   CLICK: New button (New) on the Database window toolbar
   SELECT: 4 Contacts in the *Choose the table . . .* drop-down list box
   DOUBLE-CLICK: Label Wizard
   The first step of the wizard is displayed.
3. To use standard mailing labels for printing on a laser printer:
   SELECT: *English* option button in the *Unit of Measure* area
   SELECT: *Sheet feed* option button in the *Label Type* area
   SELECT: Avery 5160 in the *Product number* column
   CLICK: Next >
4. To adjust the typeface and font style:
   SELECT: Arial in the *Font name* drop-down list box
   SELECT: 10 in the *Font size* drop-down list box
   SELECT: Normal in the *Font weight* drop-down list box
   CLICK: Next >
5. You build the label by adding fields from the *Available Fields* list box to the *Prototype label* area and by entering text. Do the following:
   DOUBLE-CLICK: Volunteer Group
   PRESS: ENTER
   TYPE: **Attn:**
   PRESS: Space Bar once
   DOUBLE-CLICK: Contact
   PRESS: ENTER
   Notice that you can input text directly onto the label.

6. Finish the label as it appears in Figure 4.41. (*Note:* The state and zip code text, "MN 56300," is used to demonstrate your ability to enter static text into a mailing label report. In a real-world application, this data would be stored in a table object and then extracted from fields for inclusion in the report.)

Figure 4.41

Designing mailing labels

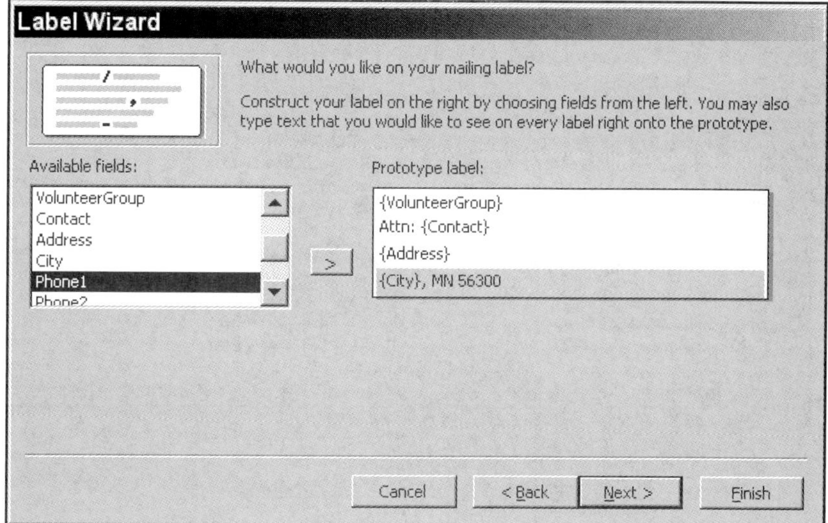

7. To proceed to the next step:
   CLICK: Next >

8. To sort the labels into order by city:
   DOUBLE-CLICK: City in the *Available fields* list box
   CLICK: Next >

9. In the last step of the wizard, enter the name "Volunteer Mailing Labels" and then display the report using the Print Preview window. (*Note:* If the following dialog box appears, you can ignore the warning and continue by clicking the OK command button.)

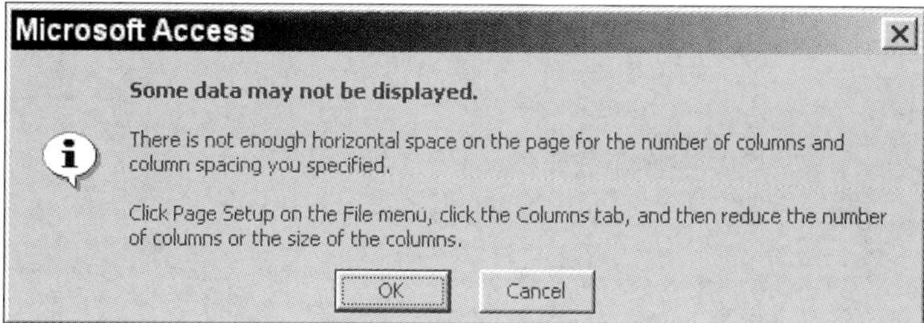

10. After a few moments, the mailing label report appears in the Print Preview window (Figure 4.42). On your own, zoom in and out on pages in the Print Preview window.

11. If you have a printer, print the report by clicking the Print button ( ).

12. Close the Print Preview window by clicking its Close button ( ). You are returned to the Database window.

Figure 4.42

Previewing the mailing labels report

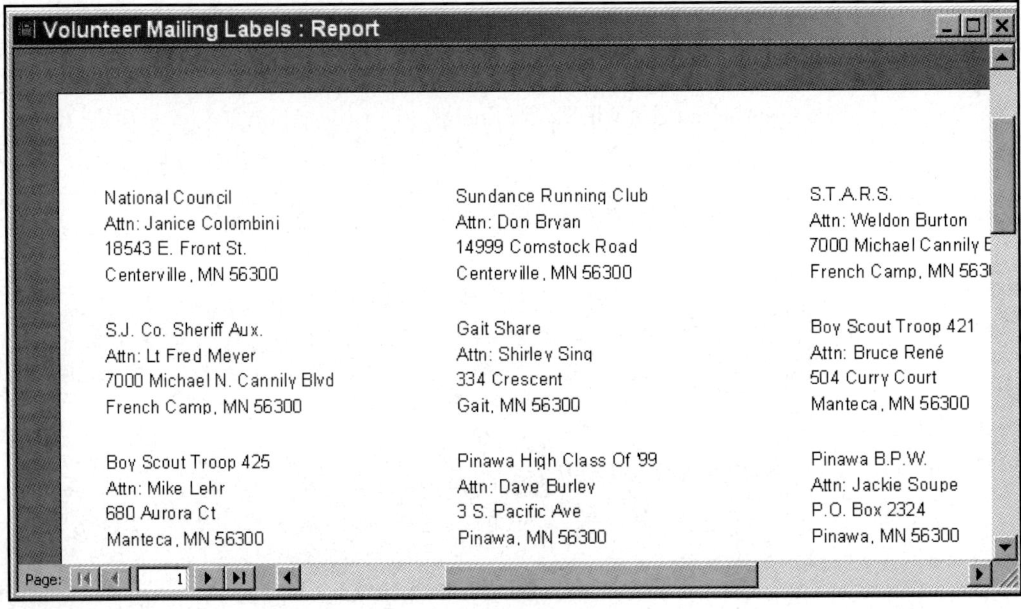

difficult 

5. On Your Own: Benson's Office Supplies

The 5 Inventory table for Benson's Office Supplies contains product information, including current stock levels, reorder quantities, costs, and suggested retail prices. Using the Form Wizard, create a justified form using the Blends style, as shown in Figure 4.43. Name the form "Inventory Input" for use in entering and editing data.

Figure 4.43

Displaying the Inventory Input form

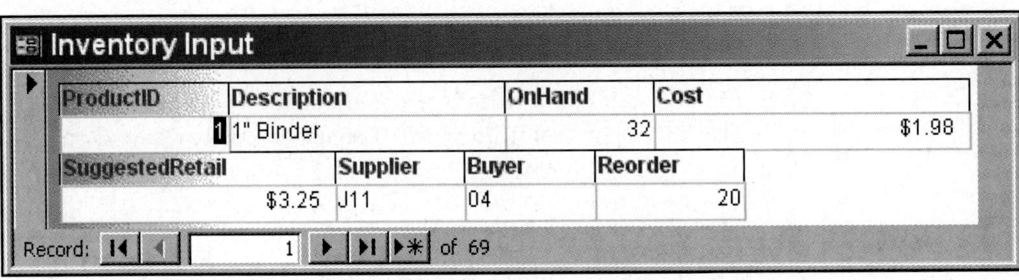

To practice working with the form, enter the following two records. (*Hint:* Access automatically adds the dollar signs to the Cost and SuggestedRetail values.) When you are finished, remember to save the last record by pressing SHIFT+ENTER and then close the Form window.

ProductID: *(Autonumber)*	ProductID: *(Autonumber)*
Description: **Push Pins**	Description: **Project Folders**
OnHand: **45**	OnHand: **112**
Cost: **$2.00**	Cost: **$9.00**
SuggestedRetail: **$4.00**	SuggestedRetail: **$13.00**
Supplier: **E01**	Supplier: **B05**
Buyer: **01**	Buyer: **07**
Reorder: **20**	Reorder: **40**

Using the Report Wizard, create a report that is grouped by supplier and sorted by product description. Then, calculate for display the minimum and maximum values for the Cost and SuggestedRetail fields. For presentation, select a Block layout with a Casual style. Name the report "Supplier Summary" and then view the report in a maximized Print Preview window with a 100% zoom factor, as shown in Figure 4.44. If you have a printer, send a copy of the report to the printer. Then restore and close the Print Preview window.

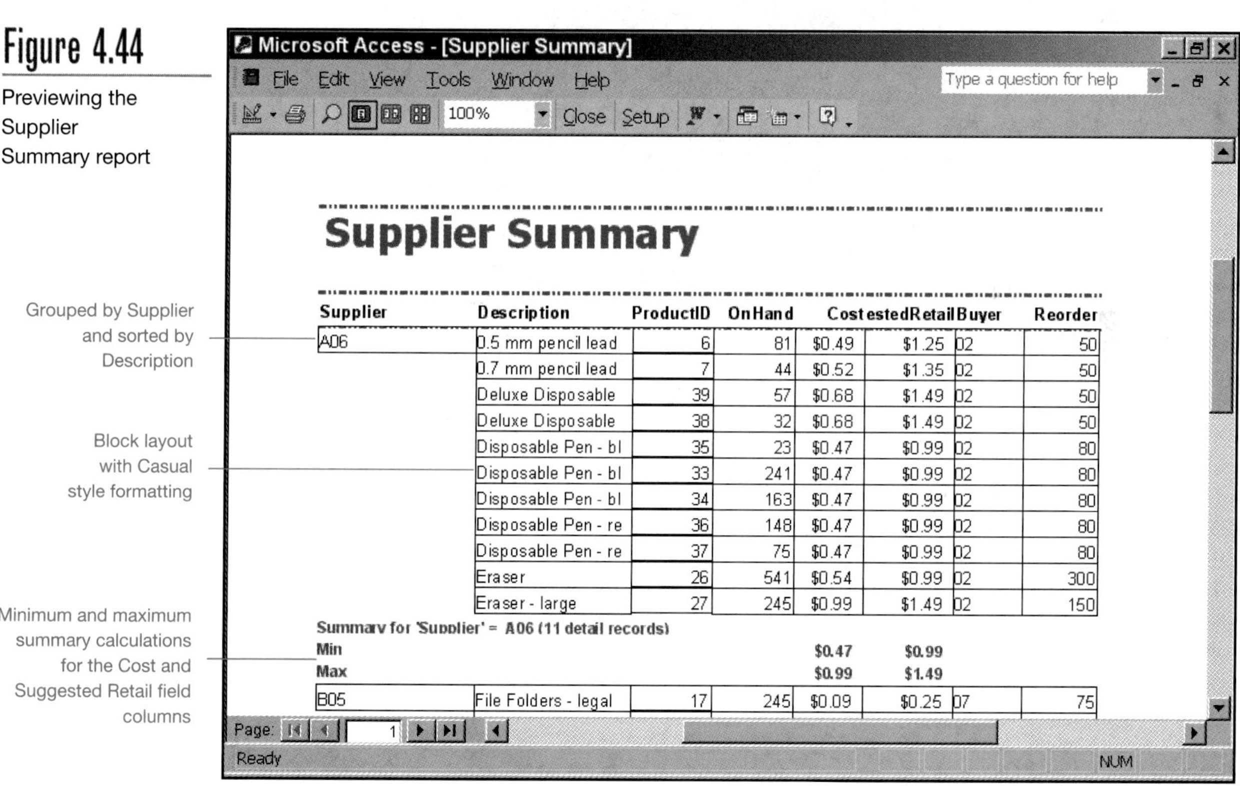

Figure 4.44 Previewing the Supplier Summary report

difficult 

6. On Your Own: Coldstream Valley Resorts

Coldstream Valley Resorts wants to make life easier for the front-counter clerks. To this end, they've asked you to create two data entry forms. Since the 6 Guides table contains only a few fields, create a tabular form using the International style and named "Guides Data Entry," as shown in Figure 4.45. Then, for the 6 Patrons table, create a columnar form using the International style and named "Patrons Data Entry." To test the usability of the forms, practice selecting records and editing data.

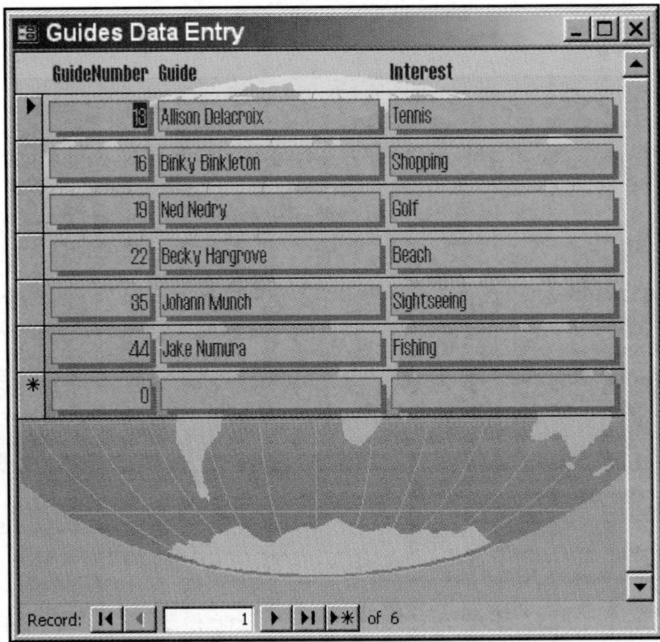

Figure 4.45
Displaying the Guides Data Entry form

You've also been asked to create a report that includes all of the fields from the Patrons table and that groups the patrons according to interest. The report is to be sorted in order by the BestTime field. After specifying a layout and style, save the report as "Patrons By Interest." Then preview the report in the Print Preview window before sending it to the printer. When finished, close the AC04HE Database window.

Case Problems

Porterai, Inc.

Porterai, Inc. manufactures and sells a limited line of travel luggage through boutiques in Seattle, San Francisco, Chicago, Boston, and New York. As the western regional sales representative, Janice is primarily responsible for servicing the repeat purchasers in San Francisco and Seattle. To keep in touch with the markets, her boss, John Lucci, has asked that Janice fax him monthly status reports. Since she must create these reports from scratch anyway, Janice decides to take this opportunity to also create form objects for her database.

In the following case problems, assume the role of Janice and perform the same steps that she identifies. You may want to re-read the chapter opening before proceeding.

1. After launching Access, Janice opens the AC04CP database that is stored in her data files folder. Wanting to get a better feel for the forms Access can create, she uses the AutoForm Wizard to generate a columnar form for the Customers table. She saves the form as "Customers - AutoForm" and then practices moving through the records using the navigation buttons in the Form window. Feeling comfortable with her creation, she closes the Form window.

   Since the AutoForm Wizard did such a nice job with the form, Janice decides to create a new report. She selects the Customers table and launches the AutoReport Wizard using the toolbar. After perusing the report, she closes the window by clicking its Close button (☒) and then saves the report as "Customers - AutoReport." After letting the report sink in for a few moments, Janice concedes that it's not quite what she had hoped for. After displaying the stored report objects, she uses the right-click menu (Figure 4.46) to delete the AutoReport object from the Database window.

Figure 4.46

Deleting a report object

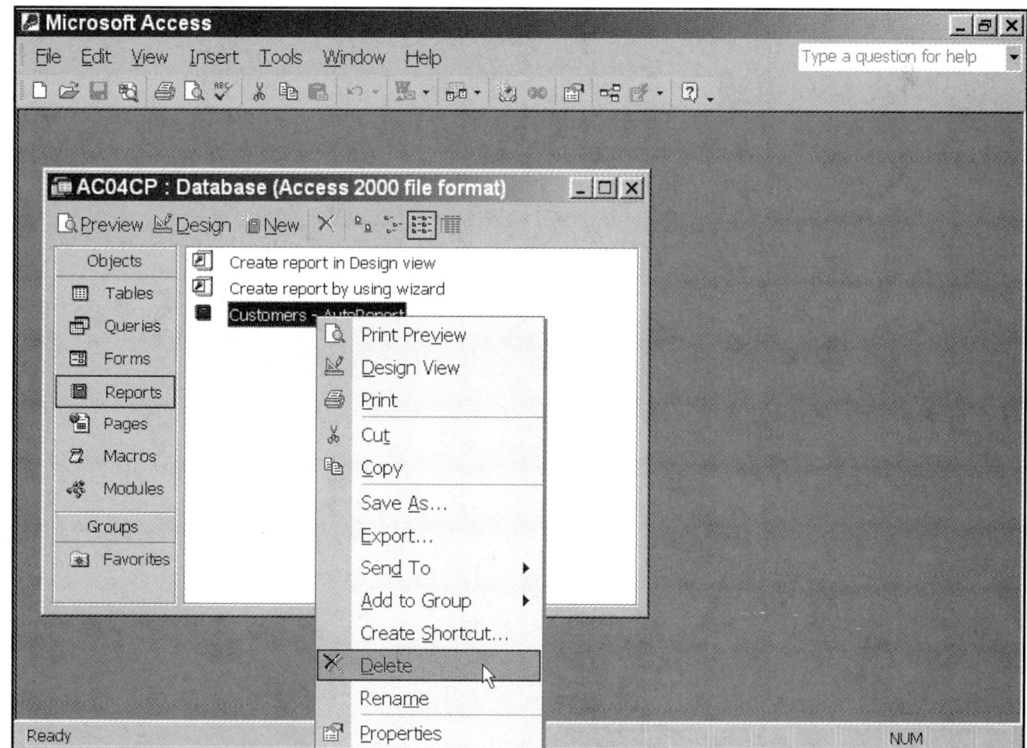

2. Being the adventurous type, Janice wants to create a new form layout for the Products table. To begin, she displays the form objects in the Database window and then double-

clicks the "Create form by using wizard" shortcut. In the first step of the wizard, she selects the Products table and includes all of the fields. Then she specifies a columnar layout and the Stone style for the form. Janice names the new form "Products - Input Form" and opens it for display (Figure 4.47). After viewing the new form, she closes it by clicking its Close button (☒).

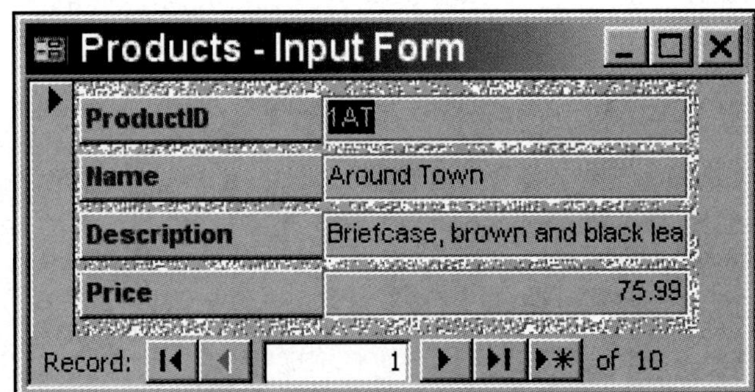

Figure 4.47

Displaying the form Products - Input Form

3. Janice wants to send out a mailing to all her preferred customers. Using the Customers table, she prepares a standard Avery 5160 mailing label. The font selected is Times New Roman with a 10-point font size. After specifying that the labels be sorted into ascending order by last name, she saves the report as "Customer Mailing." Figure 4.48 displays the results of the mailing labels report. Janice displays two pages in the Print Preview window and then sends the report to the printer. Then she closes the Print Preview window to return to the Database window.

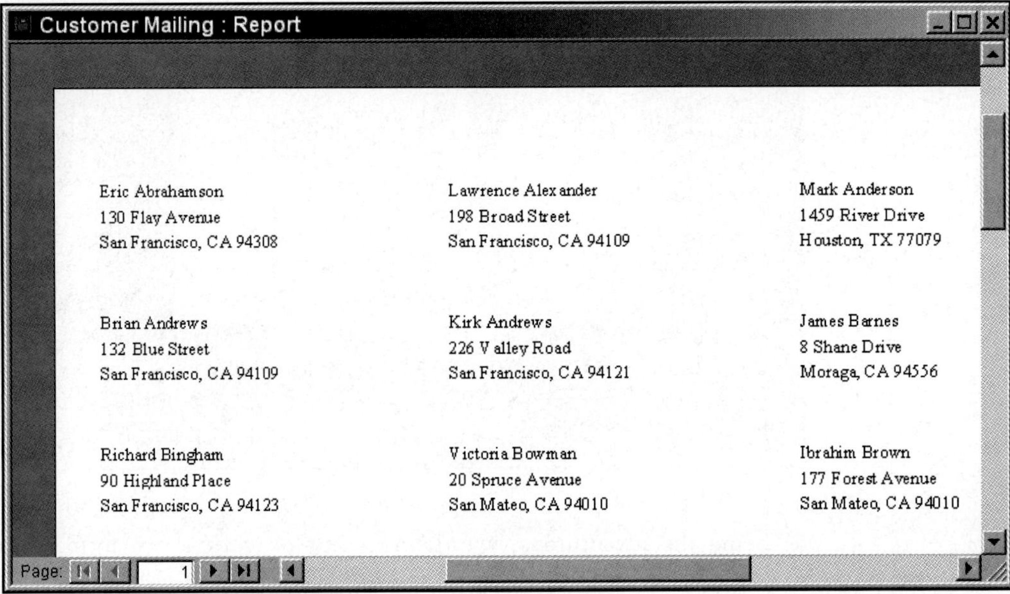

Figure 4.48

Previewing a mailing labels report

4. Janice's boss, John, commends her for the new reports, but would like to see her customers grouped by the product that they purchased. Janice knows that the Report Wizard can help her produce this report. After launching the wizard, she selects the Customers table and includes all its fields for display in the report. Janice selects the ProductID field for grouping the contents of the report and the LastName field for sorting the report. She then selects a layout, page orientation, and style. In the last step of the Report Wizard, Janice names the report "Customers - By ProductID" and then opens it for display in the Print Preview window (Figure 4.49). Satisfied with the results, Janice prints and then closes the report.

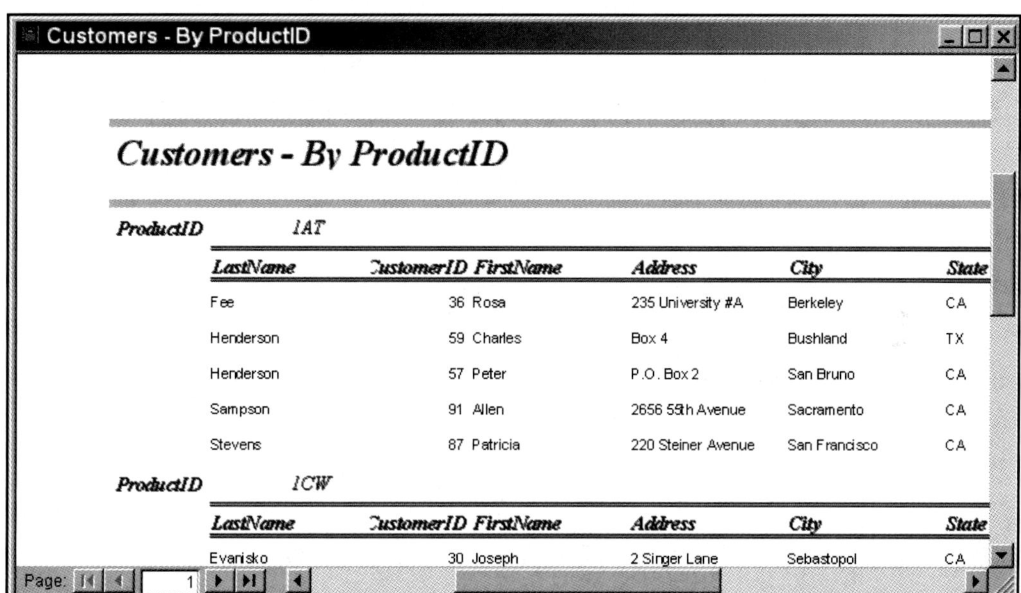

Customers - By ProductID

ProductID IAT

LastName	CustomerID	FirstName	Address	City	State
Fee	36	Rosa	235 University #A	Berkeley	CA
Henderson	59	Charles	Box 4	Bushland	TX
Henderson	57	Peter	P.O. Box 2	San Bruno	CA
Sampson	91	Allen	2656 58th Avenue	Sacramento	CA
Stevens	87	Patricia	220 Steiner Avenue	San Francisco	CA

ProductID ICW

LastName	CustomerID	FirstName	Address	City	State
Evanisko	30	Joseph	2 Singer Lane	Sebastopol	CA

Figure 4.49

A possible solution for the Customers - By Product ID report

5. "Janice, your report looks great!" John exclaims on the answering machine. "I'd like you to show Jose and Wendy how you produced it so quickly. They typically spend the last three days of each month compiling their information." Janice is pleased that the report has gone over so well. Rather than faxing the pages to Jose and Wendy, she decides to export the report as an HTML document. In the Database window, Janice selects the "Customers - By ProductID" report object and chooses the File, Export command. After locating her personal storage folder and selecting the "HTML Documents" format, she clicks the Export command button and bypasses the dialog box asking for an HTML template. She opens the first page of the report in her Web browser (Figure 4.50) to view the results. Janice will inform her associates that they can preview the report after she finishes uploading it to her personal Web site. Then she closes the AC04CP Database window and exits Microsoft Access.

Figure 4.50

Displaying a static report using Internet Explorer

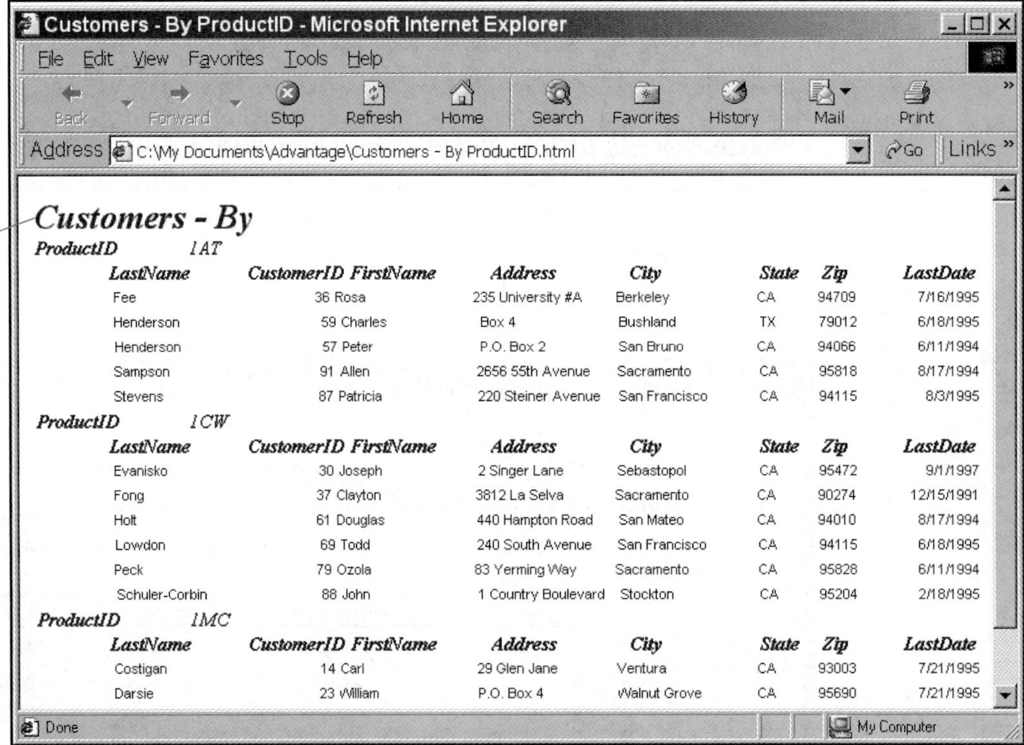

Unfortunately the Title is truncated during export.

Janice is pleased by her incredible progress with Microsoft Access 2002. She now understands how rewarding her job can be, including working from home. Janice looks forward to learning more computer skills in the future.

NOTES

NOTES

NOTES

NOTES

Integrating & Extending Microsoft® Office® XP

CHAPTER 1

Integrating Word and Excel

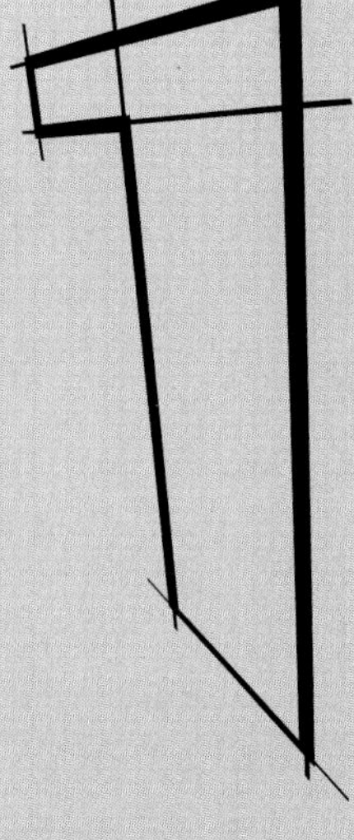

CHAPTER OUTLINE

Case Study

1.1 Using the Office Clipboard

1.2 Pasting, Linking, and Embedding

1.3 Manipulating Shared Objects

1.4 Inserting New Worksheets and Charts in Word

Chapter Summary

Chapter Quiz

Hands-On Exercises

Case Problems

PREREQUISITES

This chapter assumes you know how to create, save, edit, and print Word documents and Excel worksheets. You should also know how to select text in Word and cell ranges in Excel.

LEARNING OBJECTIVES

After completing this chapter, you will be able to:

- Use the Office Clipboard to assemble a report
- Link Excel data to a Word document
- Embed Excel data in a Word document
- Move, resize, delete, and edit shared objects
- Enhance Word documents with new Excel worksheets and charts

CaseStudy ARBOR FORESTRY Sam Houghton is the manager of the electrical division of a major lumber company called Arbor Forestry. He has worked there for several years, during which time he has become proficient using Word for creating memos, and Excel for tracking production levels. Sam would like to embellish his memos with supporting data from his Excel worksheets; however, he doesn't want to have to retype any of the Excel data. Ideally, he would like to copy existing Excel data into his Word memos. Forever cautious, Sam does not want to attempt any sharing of information between Word and Excel without first learning more about the process.

In this chapter, you and Sam learn to use the Office Clipboard to copy Microsoft Office XP objects, and then paste, link, and embed them into different programs. You will manipulate the inserted objects, and then insert new Excel worksheets and charts in Word without launching Excel.

1.1 Using the Office Clipboard

In Microsoft Office applications, the Windows and Office Clipboards enable you to copy items from one location to another. Whereas the **Windows Clipboard** can store only a single item at once, the enhanced **Office Clipboard** can store up to 24 items. The Office Clipboard is ideal for assembling reports that require excerpts from multiple documents. For example, you can copy an Excel chart, an Access table, and a PowerPoint slide to the Office Clipboard, and then paste the entire collection of items into a single Word document.

1.1.1 Activating the Office Clipboard

feature

The Clipboard task pane is used for displaying and managing the contents of the Office Clipboard. This task pane automatically displays when you copy two items to the Clipboard without an intervening paste. The Clipboard task pane uses icons to represent copied items. Note that the Windows Clipboard continues to work once the Office Clipboard is activated. The last item that was copied to the Office Clipboard will always be the one located in the Windows Clipboard.

method

To display the Clipboard task pane:

- Copy two items in sequence without an intervening paste

or

- CHOOSE: Edit, Office Clipboard

In this lesson, you copy a range of worksheet cells and a chart from an existing Excel document to the Office Clipboard. Ensure that Word and Excel are installed on your computer.

1. Start Word and then do the following:
   CHOOSE: File, Open
2. Navigate to where your student data files are stored so they are listed in the Open dialog box. Your screen should now appear similar to Figure 1.1. Note that several different icons are used to represent files. This is because each of the files shown was created using a different Microsoft Office XP application. For example, notice that IM03CS04 is a file with an Excel icon near it.

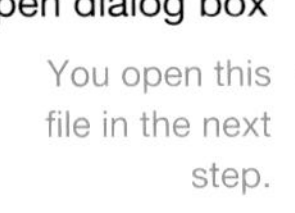

Figure 1.1

Open dialog box

You open this file in the next step.

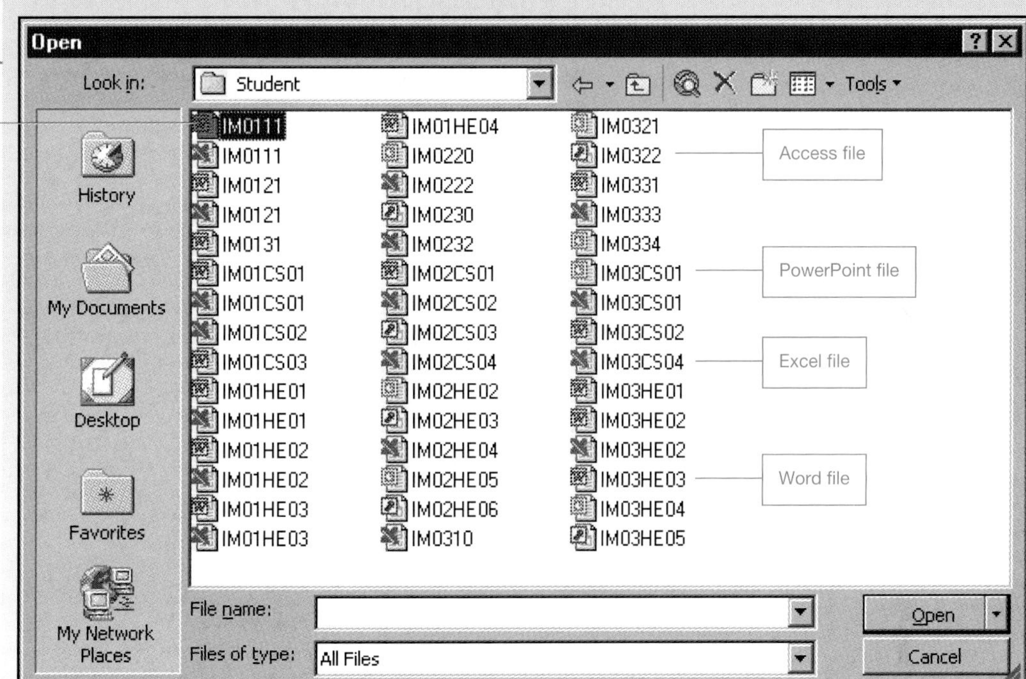

3. Open the IM0111 Word file.
4. Save the document as “Summary Memo” to your personal storage location. Your screen should now appear similar to Figure 1.2. (*Note:* The date shown in the memo will probably be different on your computer.)

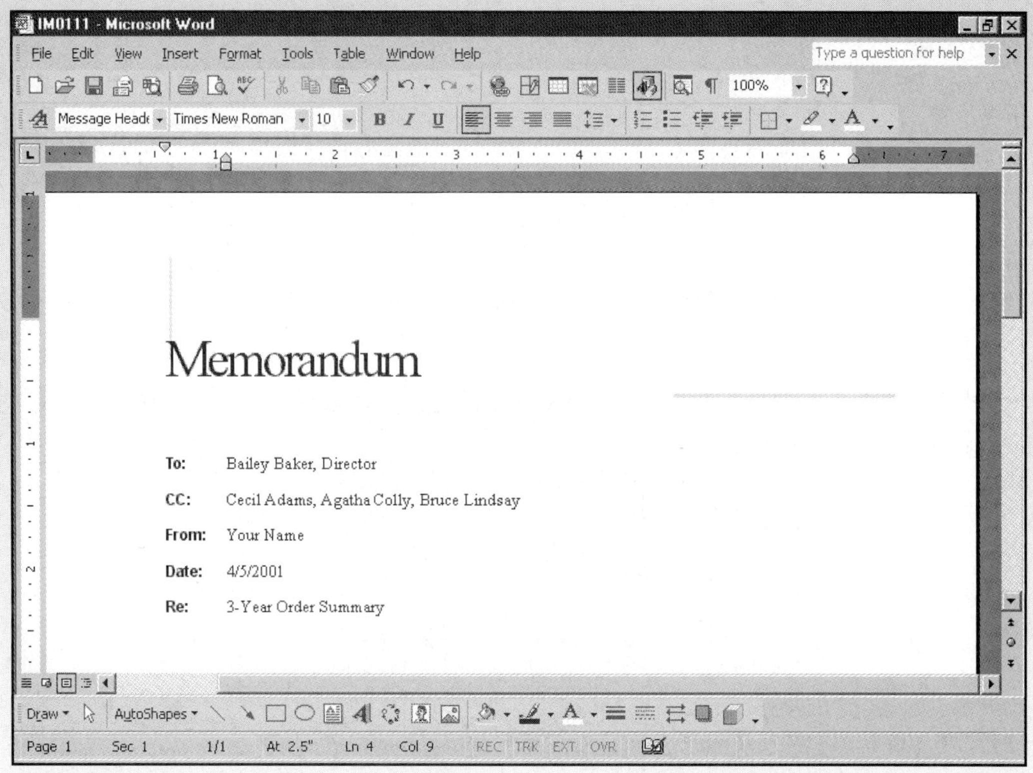

Figure 1.2

"Summary Memo" document

5. Launch Excel.
6. Open the IM0111 Excel file and then maximize the worksheet window.
7. Save the worksheet as "Orders Summary" to your personal storage location. Your screen should now appear similar to Figure 1.3.

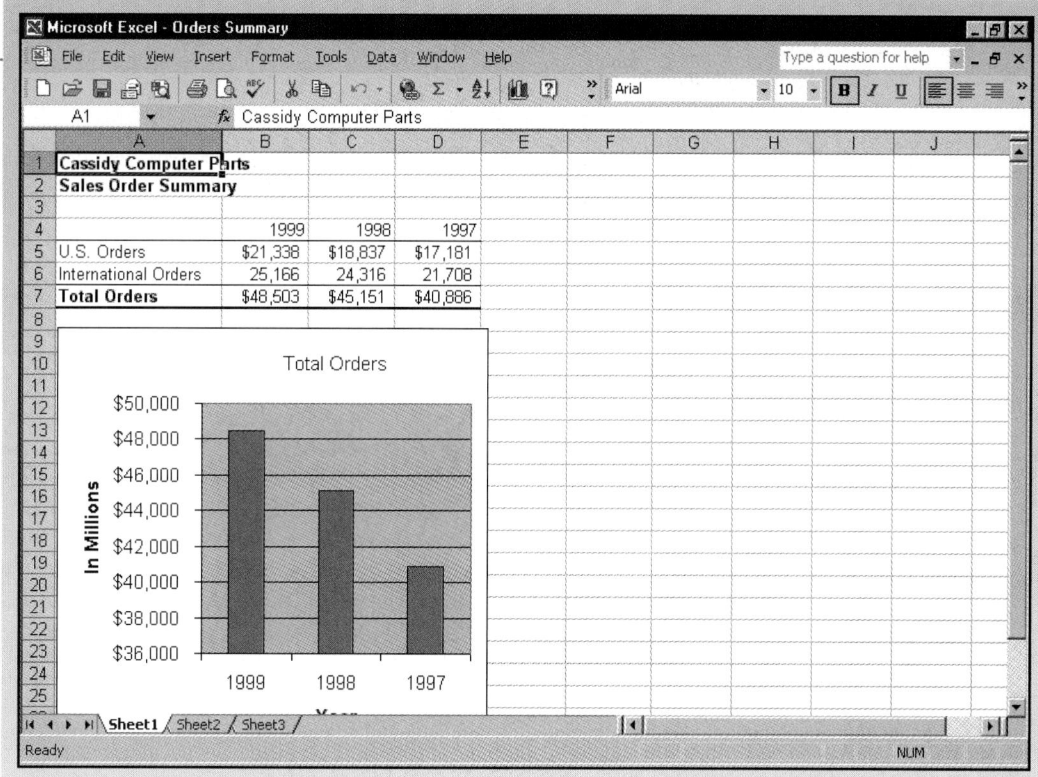

Figure 1.3

"Orders Summary" document

8. To display the Office Clipboard:
CHOOSE: Edit, Office Clipboard
The Clipboard task pane should now appear (Figure 1.4).

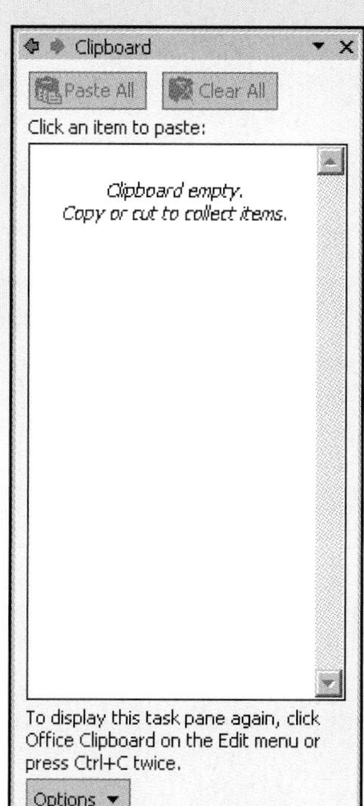

Figure 1.4

Clipboard task pane

9. When the Office Clipboard is empty, the buttons near the top of the task pane won't be available for selection. If your Clipboard isn't empty, do the following to clear the contents of Office Clipboard now:
CLICK: Clear All command button in the Clipboard task pane
The Clipboard task pane should now appear similar to Figure 1.4.

10. To copy the worksheet data to the Office Clipboard:
SELECT: cell range from A4 to D7
CLICK: Copy button () on the Standard toolbar
An icon representing the Excel data now appears in the Clipboard task pane, along with a preview of the copied data (Figure 1.5, lower item). You should also see a moving border around the cell range.

11. To select the chart:
CLICK: near the upper-left corner of the chart
(*Note:* You can actually click anywhere in the chart as long as the ScreenTip indicates "Chart Area.") The chart object should be surrounded with **sizing handles**, which are tiny boxes or circles that surround the object. Later, you learn how to use these handles to resize an object.

12. To copy the chart to the Office Clipboard:
CLICK: Copy button () on the Standard toolbar
Figure 1.5 shows the contents of the Office Clipboard.

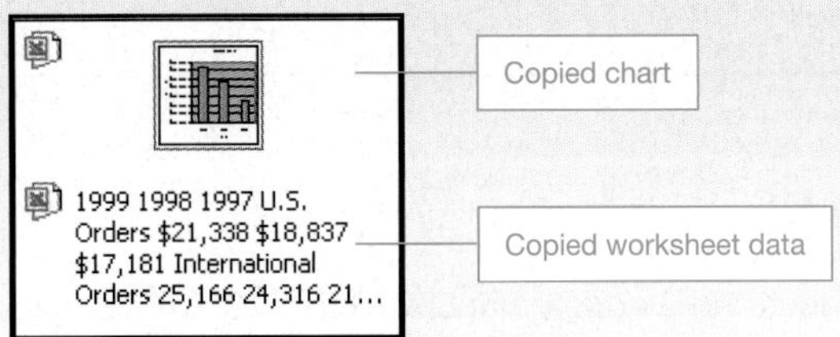

Figure 1.5

Two items have been copied to the Office Clipboard

13. Continue to the next section.

1.1.2 Pasting and Clearing Clipboard Items

feature →

Whereas the contents of the Windows Clipboard are pasted by clicking the Paste button () on the Standard toolbar, the contents of the Office Clipboard are pasted using buttons in the Clipboard task pane. You can paste the items into any one of the Office applications individually or as a group. You can also clear an individual item from the Office Clipboard or clear the entire contents at once.

method →

Options in the Clipboard task pane include the following:

- CLICK: an item in the Clipboard task pane to paste an individual item
- CLICK: Paste All command button in the Clipboard task pane to paste all items at once
- CLICK: Clear All command button in the Clipboard task pane to clear all items from the Clipboard
- CLICK: an item's drop-down arrow and then choose Delete to clear an individual item from the Clipboard

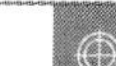

practice

You will now paste the contents of the Office Clipboard into a Word briefing memo, and then clear the contents of the Office Clipboard. Ensure that you've completed the previous lesson. The "Summary Memo" should be open in Word, and the "Orders Summary" worksheet should be open in Excel. The Excel window is the active window.

1. You can easily switch among applications using the Windows taskbar. A portion of the Windows taskbar appears in Figure 1.6. The taskbar on your computer may contain different icons to the right of the Start button. To display the "Summary Memo" document, do the following:
   CLICK: "Summary Memo" Word button on the taskbar (refer to Figure 1.6)
   The Word memo should now be displaying.

Figure 1.6

Windows taskbar

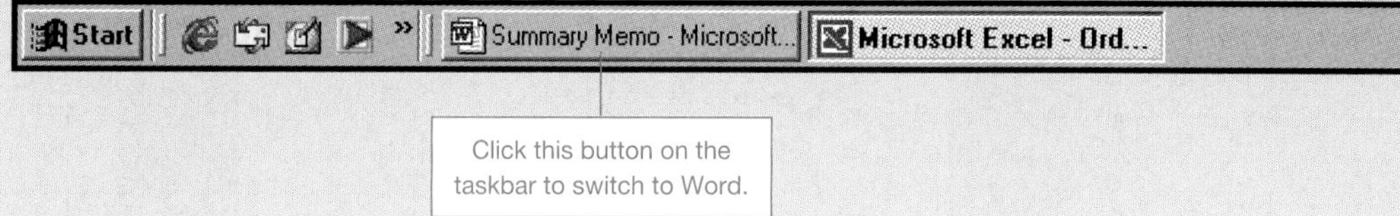

2. To position the insertion point at the end of the memo:
   PRESS: CTRL+END
3. Let's paste the entire contents of the Office Clipboard into the Word document. We must first display the Clipboard task pane.
   CHOOSE: Edit, Office Clipboard
4. In the Clipboard task pane:
   CLICK: Paste All command button, located near the top
5. To view the results of the paste, move the insertion point to the top of the document and then zoom the screen to 50%:
   PRESS: CTRL+HOME
   CLICK: Zoom arrow (100% ▾) on the Standard toolbar
   SELECT: 50%
   Your screen should now appear similar to Figure 1.7. You will often want to move or resize pasted items to improve the look of your document. For example, the document in Figure 1.7 would look better if we moved the table to the right and reduced the size of the chart. For now, however, leave the document as is. You practice manipulating shared objects in module 1.3.

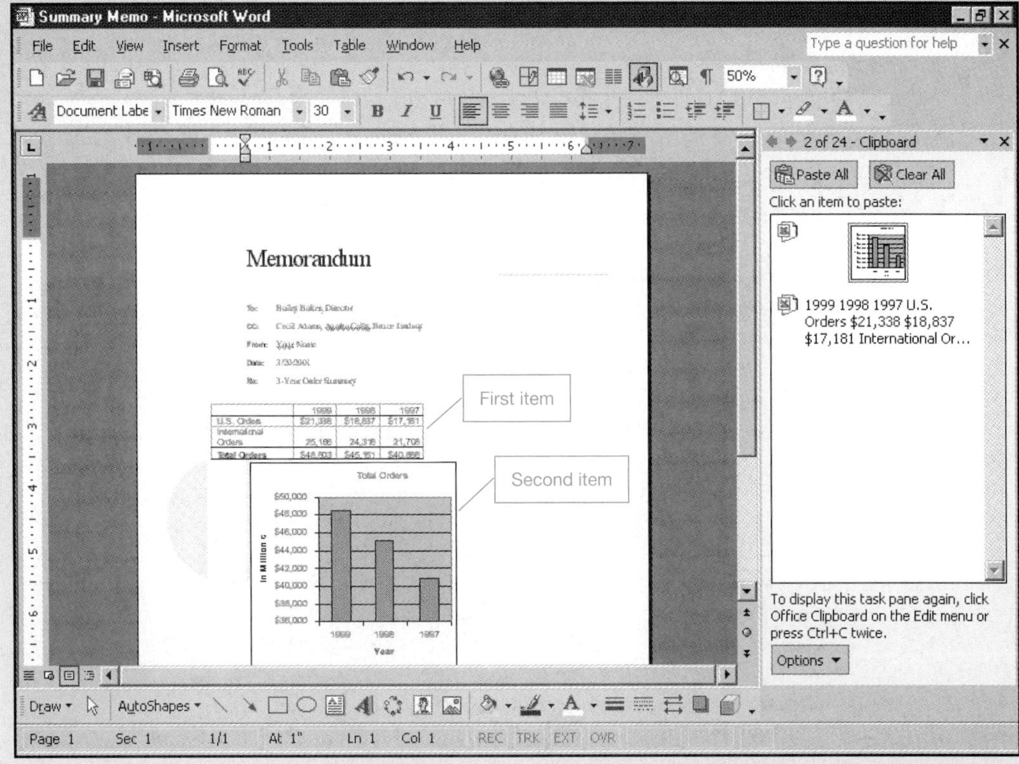

Figure 1.7

Two Excel items have been pasted into a Word document

6. Before continuing, increase the zoom factor to 100%.
   CLICK: Zoom arrow (100%) on the Standard toolbar
   SELECT: 100%
7. Save and then close the "Summary Memo" document. Note that the Clipboard task pane remains on the screen.
8. Let's practice clearing items from the Office Clipboard. You can clear an individual item from the Clipboard or clear all items at once. To illustrate how to clear an individual item, point to the chart item in the Clipboard task pane. An arrow should now appear next to the item, as shown in Figure 1.8.

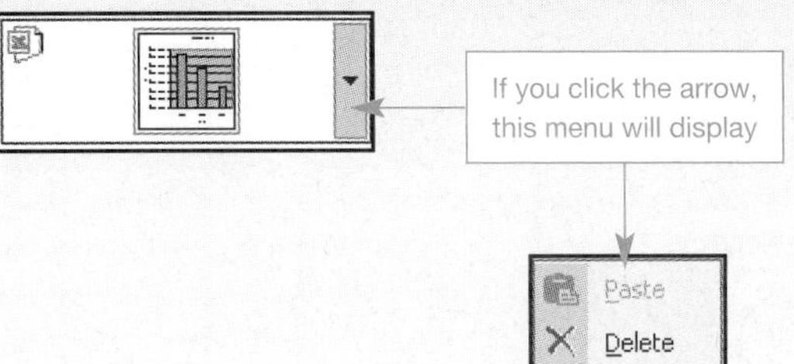

Figure 1.8

Pointing to an item in the Clipboard task pane

9. CLICK: the drop-down arrow for the chart item
   CHOOSE: Delete
10. On your own, remove the remaining worksheet item from the Office Clipboard.

11. Close the Clipboard task pane:
CLICK: Close button (☒) in the Clipboard task pane

12. Close Word and Excel.

1.1. What typically happens when you copy two items in sequence without an intervening paste?

1.2 Pasting, Linking, and Embedding

When you "paste" information from the Windows or Office Clipboards into a document, Office uses **HTML** (Hypertext Markup Language) as its default data format. HTML, as you may already know, is the language of the World Wide Web. Microsoft selected HTML as the default data format so that your text formatting, tables, and other formats will remain unchanged when you copy items among different Office applications. There may be times, however, when you do not want to use HTML as the data format, such as when you do not want to retain your original formatting. In this case, you can use the "Paste Special" command and then select an alternate data format.

When sharing data among applications, you have to consider not only the format of the shared data, but also how you want the source data (what you are copying) and the copied data to be related. Table 1.1 describes three ways to share data among Office applications. Each method involves copying the desired data from the **source document** (the document in which the data was first entered) into the **destination document** (the document that receives the data).

Table 1.1

Three Methods for Sharing Data Among Office Applications

Method	Description
Pasting	The simplest method for sharing information is to copy the desired data from the source document and then paste it into the destination document. **Pasting** data involves inserting a static representation of the source data into the destination document.
Linking	In **linking**, you not only paste the data but also establish a dynamic link between the source and destination documents. Thereafter, making changes in the source document updates the destination document automatically.
Embedding	**Embedding** data involves inserting a source document into a destination document as an object. Unlike pasted data, an embedded object is fully editable within the client application. Unlike linked data, an embedded object does not retain a connection to its source document; everything is contained in the destination document.

In the following lessons, we explore all three methods: pasting, linking, and embedding data between applications.

1.2.1 Pasting Data from Word to Excel

feature

Pasting is used to transfer data from one application to another. There is no linking of documents or embedding of objects when you paste data. The data is simply copied from the source document to the Clipboard and then inserted into the destination document.

method

- Copy data from a Word source document to the Clipboard.
- Select the target location in the Excel worksheet.
- CHOOSE: Edit, Paste

or

- CLICK: Paste button ()

practice

You now practice pasting data from an existing Word document into an Excel worksheet. Ensure that Word and Excel are installed on your computer.

1. Start Word and then open the IM0121 Word file.
2. Save the file as "Student Memo" to your personal storage location. The memo should appear similar to Figure 1.9.

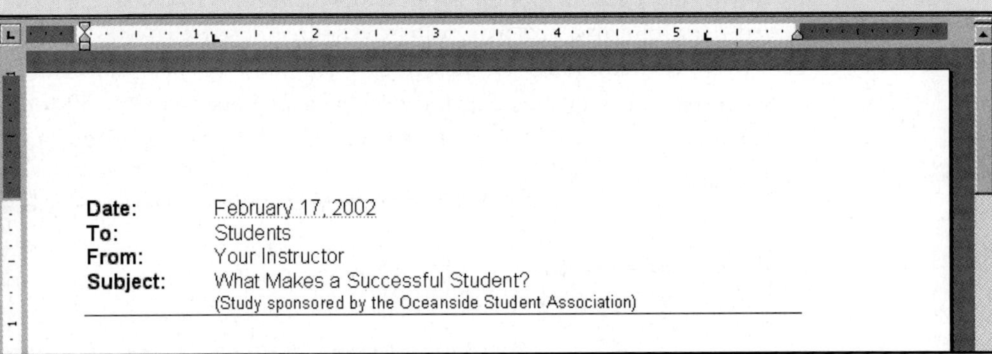

Figure 1.9
"Student Memo" document

3. Launch Excel and open the IM0121 Excel file.
4. Save the file as "Survey Results" to your personal storage location.
5. To switch back to Word:
   CLICK: "Student Memo" Word button on the taskbar
6. The insertion point is currently blinking at the top of the document. To copy all the information located at the top of the document to the Clipboard, first:
   SELECT: the five lines of information located at the top of the document
   (*Hint:* Position the mouse pointer to the left of the first line. Then, press down and hold the left mouse button as you drag the mouse pointer downward over the five lines of information.)
   The information at the top of the memo should be selected, as shown in Figure 1.10.

Figure 1.10

Selecting text in the memo

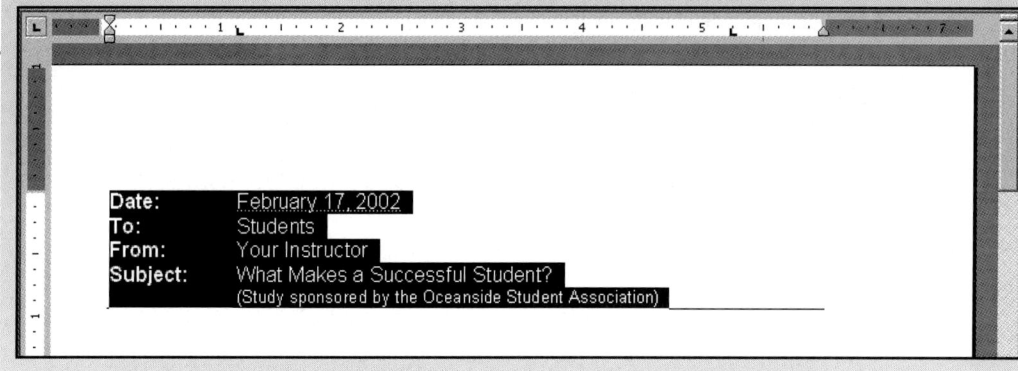

7. To copy the selected text:
CLICK: Copy button () on the Standard toolbar

8. To make the Excel application window active:
CLICK: Microsoft Excel button on the Windows taskbar

9. To insert the Word text into the worksheet:
CLICK: cell A1
CLICK: Paste button ()
As shown in Figure 1.11, the data is automatically divided into separate cells. Also note that, because the default data format for pasted data is HTML, the formatting of the Word text is retained in the Excel worksheet.

Figure 1.11

Pasting data from a Word document into an Excel worksheet

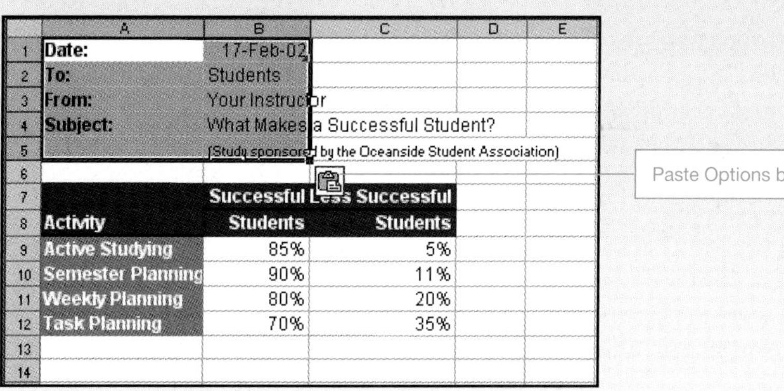

10. Note that the Paste Options button () is displaying near the bottom-right corner of the copied text. See what happens when we click this button.
CLICK: Paste Options button ()
The Paste Options menu appears in Figure 1.12. Note that the *Keep Source Formatting* option button is selected.

Figure 1.12

Paste Options menu

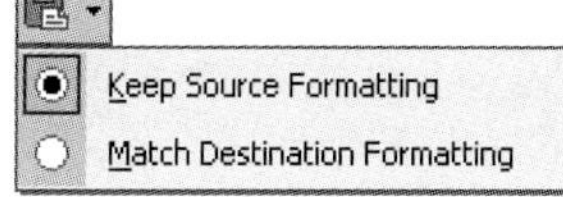

11. To close the Paste Options menu:
CLICK: Paste Options button () again

12. Save the revised worksheet and then continue to the next lesson.

1.2.2 Linking Excel Data to a Word Document

feature

You link files when the information you need from a source document is either maintained by other users or needs to be incorporated into multiple documents but may change. Because Excel is largely an analysis tool for calculating and summarizing data, worksheets typically provide the source data for use in other documents. For successful linking to occur, the source documents must always be accessible, whether stored on the same computer as the destination document or available via a network connection.

method

- Copy data from the Excel source document to the Clipboard.
- In the Word destination document, position the insertion point where you want to insert the data.
- CHOOSE: Edit, Paste Special
- SELECT: *Paste link* option button
- SELECT: a data format in the *As* list box
- CLICK: OK command button

practice

Your objective in this lesson is to copy and link an Excel table into a Word document. Ensure that you have completed the previous lesson in this module. The "Student Memo" document should be open in Word, and the "Survey Results" worksheet should be open in Excel. The Excel window is the active window.

1. Copy the "Activity" table to the Clipboard:
SELECT: cell range from A7 to C12
CLICK: Copy button ()

2. To display the Word "Student Memo" document:
CLICK: "Student Memo" Word button on the Windows taskbar

3. To position the insertion point at the bottom of the document:
PRESS: CTRL + END

4. You will now paste the table into the memo document and establish a dynamic link between the source document, "Survey Results.xls," and the destination document, "Student Memo.doc." To begin:
CHOOSE: Edit, Paste Special from the Word menu
Microsoft Word's Paste Special dialog box appears, as shown in Figure 1.13. You can select the desired format for pasting the Clipboard contents from the *As* list box. Table 1.2 describes the formats listed in the *As* list box. (Note that "HTML Format" is the currently selected option.)

1.3 Manipulating Shared Objects

Upon inserting an object in an Office document, you will most likely have to manipulate it to meet specific needs in the new document. The lessons in this module explore several techniques for manipulating shared objects.

1.3.1 Moving, Resizing, and Deleting Shared Objects

feature

Once a linked or embedded object is inserted in an Office document, the object will appear surrounded with ***sizing handles,*** which appear as tiny boxes or circles. You can also select an object that is not currently selected by clicking the object once. Once a shared object is selected, you can move and resize it to fit the dimensions and layout of your document. You can also delete selected objects.

method

To select a shared object:

- Position the mouse pointer over the object's placeholder until a four-headed arrow (✥) appears and then click.

Once the object is selected, the following options are available:

- Move a selected object by dragging.
- Resize a selected object by dragging its sizing handles.
- Delete a selected object by pressing DELETE.

practice

You now practice selecting, moving, resizing, and deleting an embedded object. Ensure that Word and Excel are installed on your computer.

1. Launch Word and open the IM0131 data file.
2. Save the file as "Cruises" to your personal storage location. The document should now appear similar to Figure 1.18.

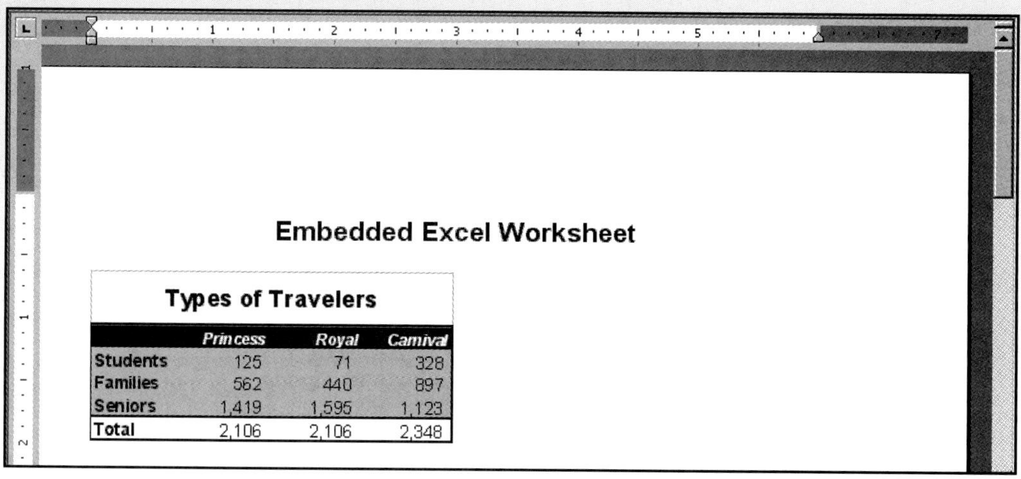

Figure 1.18

This Word document contains an embedded Excel worksheet

3. To practice resizing the embedded object and then centering it beneath the "Embedded Excel Worksheet" title:
CLICK: the Excel object
The object should be surrounded with sizing handles (Figure 1.19).

Figure 1.19

Sizing handles surround the selected object

Types of Travelers

	Princess	Royal	Carnival
Students	125	71	328
Families	562	440	897
Seniors	1,419	1,595	1,123
Total	2,106	2,106	2,348

Corner sizing handle

4. When you position the mouse pointer over a sizing handle, the pointer will change to a double-headed arrow. To resize the embedded object in Figure 1.19, point to the sizing handle located in the bottom-right corner until a double-headed arrow (↔), not a four-headed arrow, appears.

5. DRAG: the sizing handle (see Figure 1.19) outward about an inch
(*Hint:* Use the Ruler as your guide.)

6. To move the object to the right, position the mouse pointer over the embedded object until a four-headed arrow (✥) appears.

7. DRAG: the object to the right until it is centered beneath the title
Your document should now appear similar to Figure 1.20.

Figure 1.20

The object as resized and moved

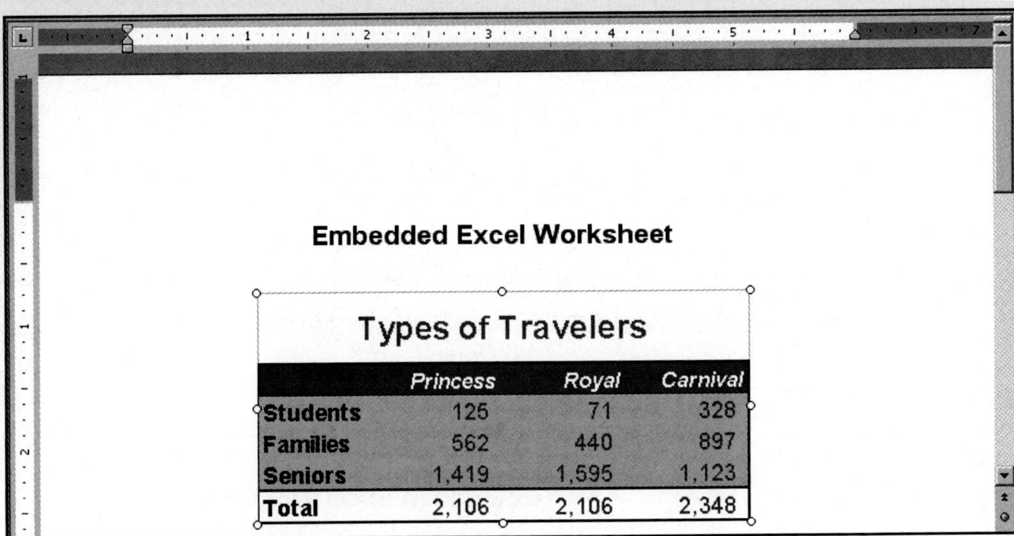

8. The object should still be selected. To practice deleting the object:
PRESS: DELETE
The object is now deleted.

9. To undo the previous action:
CLICK: Undo button ( ) once (not the drop-down arrow)
The object should again be displaying in the document.

10. Save the revised document.

1.3.2 Editing Shared Objects

feature

A feature called *Visual Editing* makes it easy to update an embedded object in place. To edit an embedded object, such as an Excel table in Word, you simply double-click the object. Rather than being taken to the server application (Excel) to perform the changes, you remain where you are (Word) and the current application's menus and toolbars are replaced with those of the server application. In other words, you do not have to exit the current application to change the embedded object. In contrast, to edit a linked object, you must switch to the server application and then make your changes. By default, linked objects are updated automatically when the destination document is opened.

method

To edit an embedded object:

- DOUBLE-CLICK: the object and then make any necessary changes
- CLICK: outside the object when you are finished making changes

To edit a linked object, switch to the server application and source document and then make any necessary changes.

practice

You now practice editing an embedded object. (*Note:* You practiced editing a linked object in lesson 1.2.2.) Ensure that you have completed the previous lesson in this module and that the "Cruises" document is open in Word.

1. To modify the embedded worksheet that's located in the "Cruises" document:
DOUBLE-CLICK: the object
Your screen should now appear similar to Figure 1.21. Note that Word's Menu bar and toolbars are replaced by the Excel Menu bar. Also, the embedded object itself is bounded by row and column frames, scroll bars, and sheet tabs.

Figure 1.21

Editing an embedded Excel object in Word

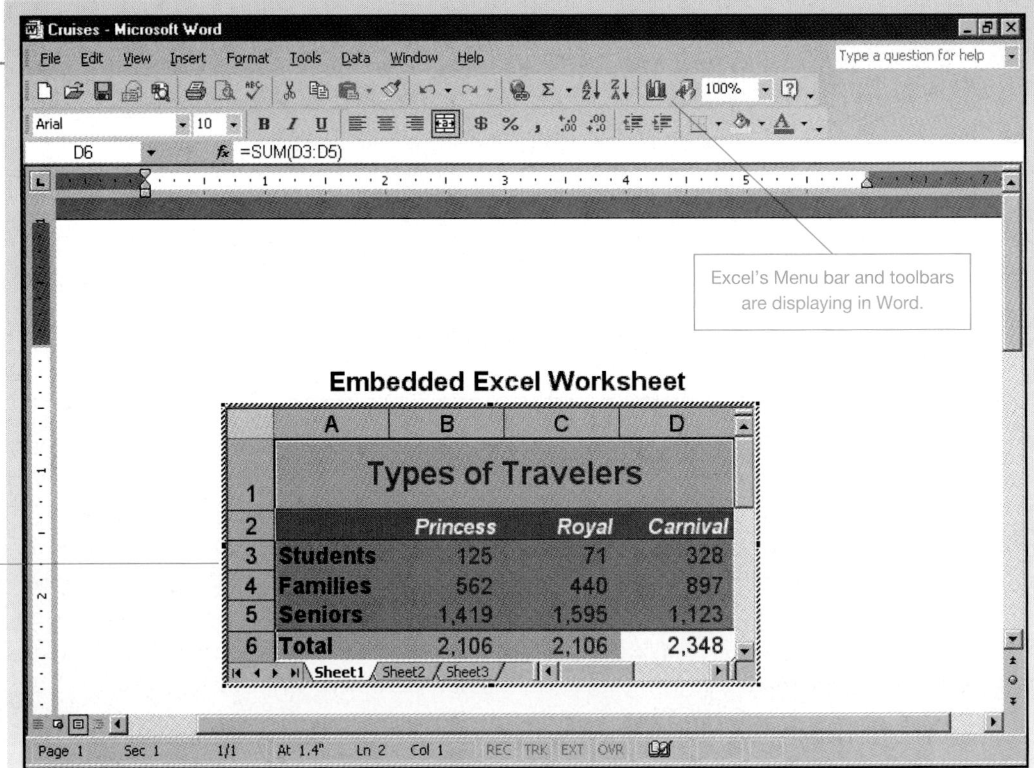

2. To practice editing an embedded object, you will now calculate a new total in the Princess column.
   CLICK: cell B3
   TYPE: **150**
   PRESS: ENTER
   Note that the worksheet area recalculates as expected.
3. To finish editing the embedded object:
   CLICK: the mouse pointer outside the object to deselect the object
   The object's hashed border disappears, and you may now size and move it as before.
4. Save the revised document and then close Word.

1.3. How would you go about resizing a shared object?

1.4 Inserting New Worksheets and Charts in Word

You can not only insert existing objects in an Office document but also create new objects. To do this, you must choose Insert, Object and then select the type of object you want to insert. Office lets you create many different types of shared objects from scratch, including (but not limited to) Excel charts, Excel worksheets, PowerPoint slides, PowerPoint presentations, and several types of Word objects. New objects are automatically embedded in the destination document. In this module, we explore inserting new worksheets and charts in a Word document.

1.4.1 Inserting a New Worksheet in Word

feature

Although Word's table features are powerful, you may prefer to build your tables in Excel, especially if your tables require extensive calculations. You can easily insert a new Excel worksheet into Word without starting Excel.

method

- Position the insertion point in the destination document.
- CHOOSE: Insert, Object
- DOUBLE-CLICK: Microsoft Excel Worksheet in the *Object type* list box
- Without leaving Word, edit the object using the menus and tools of the object's source application.
- CLICK: outside the embedded object to return to Word

practice

You will now embed a new worksheet in a Word document. Ensure that Word and Excel are installed on your computer.

1. Start Word to display a new document in the application window.
2. CHOOSE: Insert, Object
   CLICK: *Create New* tab
3. Do the following:
   DRAG: the vertical scroll bar downward slightly in the *Object type* list box
   CLICK: Microsoft Excel Worksheet in the *Object type* list box
   The Object dialog box should now appear similar to Figure 1.22.

Figure 1.22

The Object dialog box

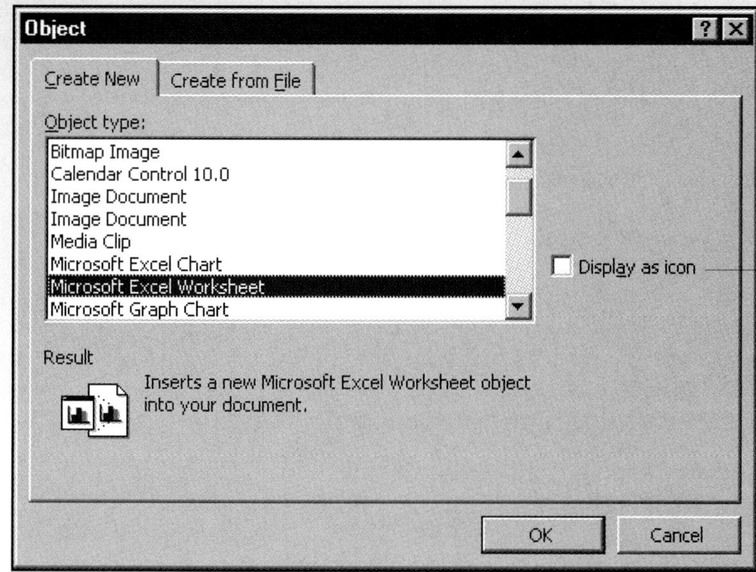

If you are concerned about file size, you may want to insert the new object as an icon that users can double-click in order to display the object. The icon takes up very little space in the document.

4. To proceed with embedding the new object:
CLICK: OK command button
Your screen should now appear similar to Figure 1.23. Note that Excel's Menu bar and Standard and Formatting toolbars have replaced those of Word.

Figure 1.23

Embedding a new worksheet

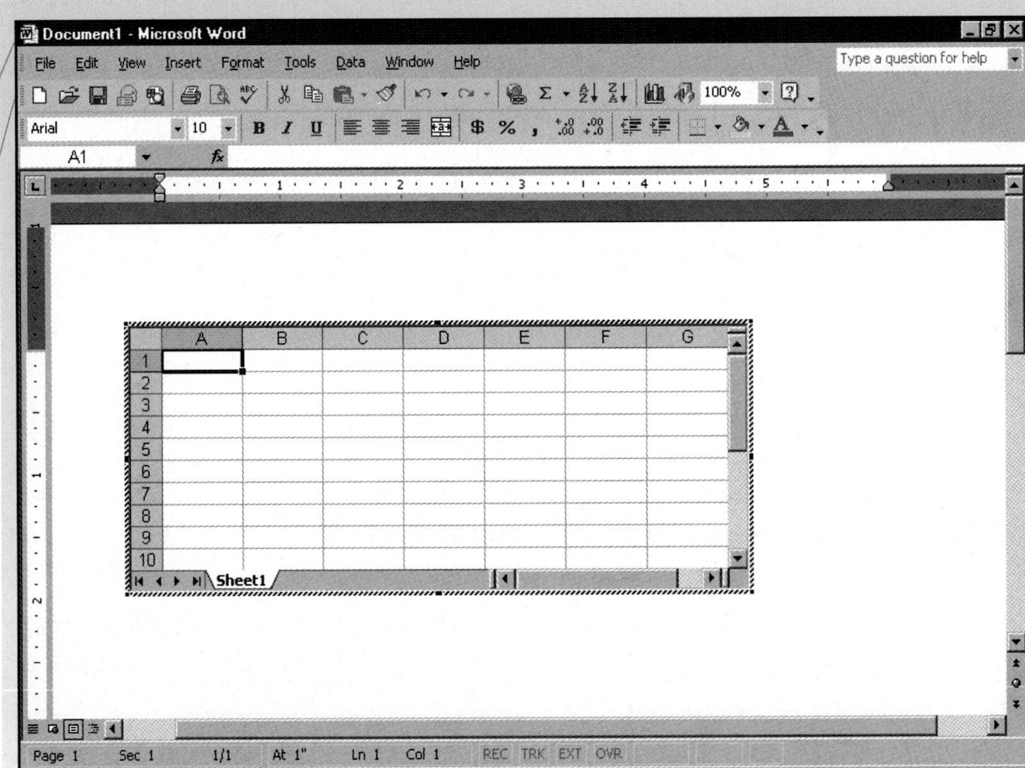

Note that Word is the active window.

Note that Excel's Menu bar and toolbars are displaying.

5. At this point, you would type your data into the worksheet and use Excel's commands to complete the worksheet. Because this isn't a lesson in building Excel worksheets, proceed with the next step.

6. To return to Word:
CLICK: outside the embedded object
An empty table grid should have been inserted in the document.

7. Pretend that you now want to edit the Excel table. Since the object is embedded, you edit it by double-clicking.
DOUBLE-CLICK: the table grid
Note that Excel's toolbars are again activated.

8. Close the document window without saving.

1.4.2 Inserting a New Chart in Word

feature

If you already know how to create charts in Excel and have access to it on your computer, you will want to use Excel to create new charts instead of Microsoft Graph. Microsoft Graph, a charting and graphing tool, is one of several mini-applications, called *applets*, that are available. Microsoft Excel, however, provides a more "robust" graphing environment.

- Position the insertion point in the destination document.
- CHOOSE: Insert, Object
- DOUBLE-CLICK: Microsoft Excel Chart in the *Object type* list box
- Without leaving Word, edit the object using the menus and tools of the object's source application.
- CLICK: outside the embedded object to return to Word

practice

You will now embed a new chart in a Word document. Ensure that you have completed the previous lesson in this module.

1. Display a new document in Word.
2. CHOOSE: Insert, Object
   CLICK: *Create New* tab
3. SELECT: Microsoft Excel Chart in the *Object type* list box
4. To proceed with embedding the new object:
   CLICK: OK command button
   Your screen should now appear similar to Figure 1.24. (*Note:* The Chart toolbar may appear on top of your chart. If necessary, drag it out of the way of the chart.)

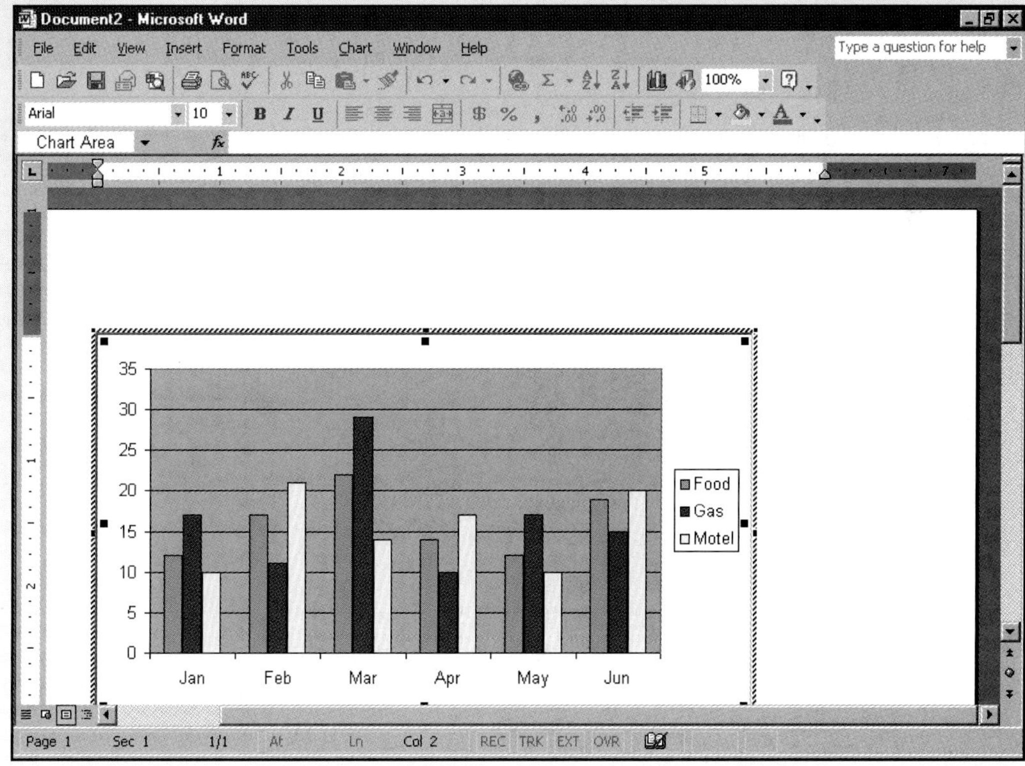

Figure 1.24
Embedding a new chart

5. At this point, you would use Excel's Menu bar and Standard and Formatting toolbars to edit the chart according to your needs. Because this is not a lesson in building Excel charts, proceed with the next step.

6. To return to Word:
CLICK: outside the embedded object
The default chart should have been inserted in the document.

7. Close Word, without saving the revised document.

1.4. What is the procedure for editing embedded objects?

Chapter summary

The Office Clipboard is an enhanced Windows Clipboard that can store up to 24 items at once. The items can be pasted into any one of the Microsoft Office applications individually or as a group. By default, pasted data is stored in an HTML data format, although you can change this setting using the Paste Special dialog box.

In Office, you share information through pasting, linking, and embedding. These three methods differ in how the source data and copied data are related. Shared objects can be moved, resized, edited, and deleted.

Command Summary

Many of the commands and procedures appearing in this chapter are summarized in the following table.

Skill Set	To Perform This Task	Do the Following
Using the Office Clipboard	Display the Office Clipboard	CHOOSE: Edit, Office Clipboard
	Paste the contents of the Office Clipboard as a group	CLICK: Paste All command button in the Clipboard task pane
	Clear the contents of the Office Clipboard	CLICK: Clear All command button in the Clipboard task pane
Pasting Data	Paste data from Word into Excel, once the data appears on the Clipboard	CHOOSE: Edit, Paste, or CLICK: Paste button ( )
Linking Data	Insert links to existing Microsoft Office data	SELECT: source information CLICK: Copy button ( ) and then position the insertion point in the destination document CHOOSE: Edit, Paste Special SELECT: *Paste link* option button SELECT: a data format in the *As* list box CLICK: OK command button
	Edit linked data that appears in the destination document	Switch to the server application and update the source document

Skill Set	To Perform This Task	Do the Following
Embedding Data	Embed Excel data in Word, once the data appears on the Clipboard	CHOOSE: Edit, Paste Special SELECT: Microsoft Excel Worksheet Object in the *As* list box CLICK: OK command button
	Embed new Microsoft Office objects, without using the Clipboard	CHOOSE: Insert, Object CLICK: *Create New* tab DOUBLE-CLICK: the desired object in the *Object type* list box
Modifying Shared Objects	Edit embedded data that appears in a destination document	DOUBLE-CLICK: the object and make your changes CLICK: outside the object, when completed
	Resize an object	SELECT: the object DRAG: the object's sizing handles
	Move an object	SELECT: the object DRAG: the object to a new location
	Delete an object	SELECT: the object PRESS: DELETE

Key Terms

This section specifies page references for the key terms identified in this chapter. For a complete list of definitions, refer to the Glossary at the end of this learning guide.

destination document, *p. 9*
embedding, *p. 9*
HTML, *p. 9*
linking, *p. 9*
Office Clipboard, *p. 2*
pasting, *p. 9*
server application, *p. 15*
sizing handles, *p. 6*
source document, *p. 9*
Windows Clipboard, *p. 2*

Chapter quiz

Short Answer

1. What is linking? Under what circumstances would you create links between documents?
2. How do embedded objects and linked objects differ?
3. Describe the general procedure for embedding a new Excel chart in a Word document.
4. What is the main difference between the Windows Clipboard and the Office Clipboard?
5. What are the three methods for sharing data among applications?
6. How would you go about deleting an embedded object?

7. How would you go about pasting the contents of the Office Clipboard as a group?
8. What is the procedure for clearing the contents of the Office Clipboard?
9. What is the procedure for editing a linked object?
10. How do you select linked and embedded objects?

True/False

1. ____ The destination document is the document that receives the data from another application.
2. ____ An embedded object is automatically updated when information in its source document changes.
3. ____ It's best to embed an object when the information needs to be updated by different people on a network.
4. ____ It is possible to embed either a new or an existing object into a document.
5. ____ The Office Clipboard can store up to 24 items of information.
6. ____ By default, linked objects are updated automatically when the destination document is opened.
7. ____ Microsoft Graph provides charting capabilities superior to Microsoft Excel.
8. ____ The last item you copy to the Office Clipboard will always be located in the Windows Clipboard.
9. ____ Objects that you insert by choosing Insert, Object are automatically linked in the destination document.
10. ____ Using a method called *pasting*, a static representation of the source data is inserted in the destination document.

Multiple Choice

1. When sharing data in Microsoft Office, the ____________ document is the document in which the data was first entered.
   a. source
   b. destination
   c. original
   d. primary
2. To establish a link between a source document and a destination document, use the ____________ command.
   a. Tools, Link, Documents
   b. Tools, Link
   c. Edit, Link
   d. Edit, Paste Special
3. ____________ is a Microsoft Office feature that makes it easy to update embedded objects.
   a. Pasting
   b. Visual Editing
   c. Edit, Links
   d. Tools, Update, Links
4. Which of the following would be the most helpful when you are assembling the different components of a large document?
   a. Windows Clipboard
   b. Office Clipboard
   c. Visual Editing
   d. links

5. To enable automatic updates in destination documents, you must establish ______________ between the source and destination documents.
   a. embedding
   b. objects
   c. relationships
   d. links

6. When you insert an Excel chart into a Word document:
   a. Word is the destination document.
   b. Excel is the destination document.
   c. The chart is the destination document.
   d. The document is the source document.

7. When you want to update the data in a linked worksheet range:
   a. DOUBLE-CLICK: the worksheet range object
   b. RIGHT-CLICK: the worksheet range and choose Edit Object
   c. Edit the data in the destination document.
   d. Edit the data in the source document.

8. When you want to update the data in an embedded worksheet range:
   a. DOUBLE-CLICK: the worksheet range object
   b. RIGHT-CLICK: the worksheet range and choose Edit Object
   c. Edit the data in the destination document.
   d. Edit the data in the source document.

9. It's possible to ______________ embedded objects.
   a. move
   b. resize
   c. delete
   d. all of the above

10. By default, data is pasted in a(n) ______________ format.
   a. RTF
   b. Enhanced Metafile
   c. Picture
   d. HTML

Hands-On exercises

1. Sweet Dreams: Pasting and Clearing Clipboard Items

Sweet Dreams is a small store specializing in toys and clothing for children. In this exercise, Hudson, a longtime employee, is preparing a short document for his boss's review. Assume the role of Hudson in copying two Excel items to the Office Clipboard, pasting them into a Word document, and then clearing the Clipboard contents.

1. Start Word and then open the IM01HE01 Word file.
2. Save the document as "Toy Sales Letter" to your personal storage location. The document should appear similar to Figure 1.25.

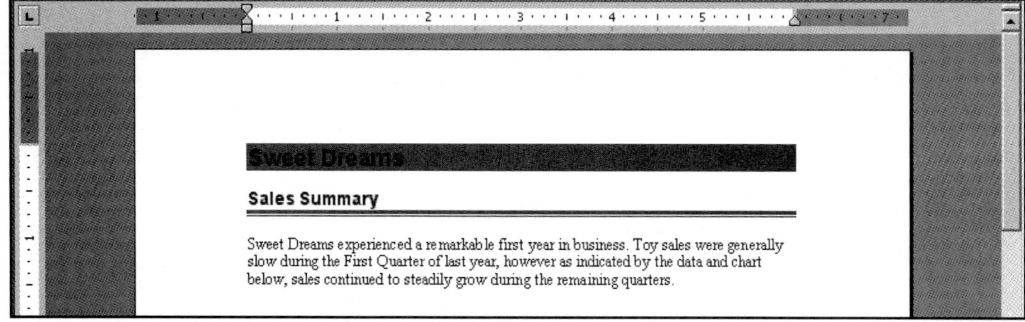

Sweet Dreams

Sales Summary

Sweet Dreams experienced a remarkable first year in business. Toy sales were generally slow during the First Quarter of last year, however as indicated by the data and chart below, sales continued to steadily grow during the remaining quarters.

Figure 1.25

"Toy Sales Letter" document

3. Start Excel and then open the IM01HE01 Excel file.
4. Save the worksheet as "Toy Sales Data" to your personal storage location. The worksheet and chart should appear similar to Figure 1.26.

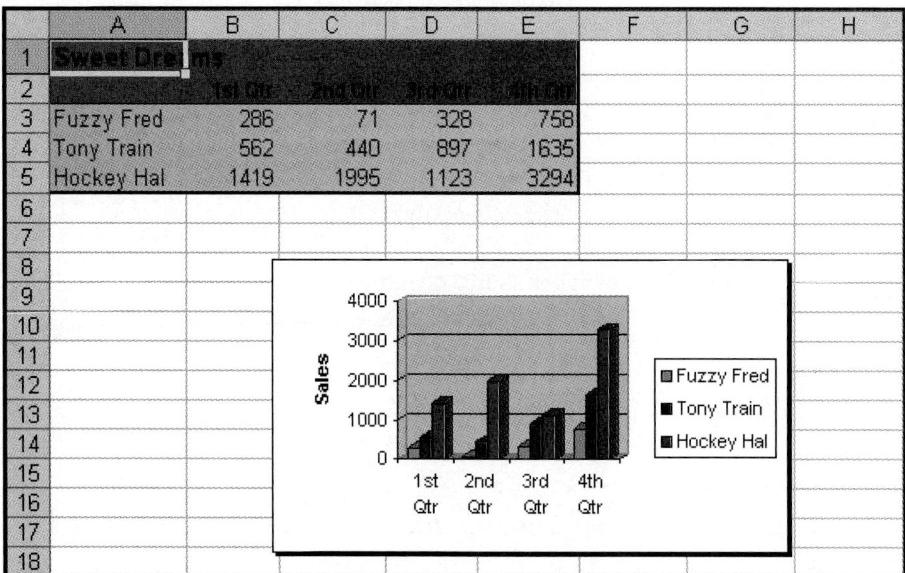

Sweet Dreams				
	1st Qtr	2nd Qtr	3rd Qtr	4th Qtr
Fuzzy Fred	286	71	328	758
Tony Train	562	440	897	1635
Hockey Hal	1419	1995	1123	3294

Figure 1.26

"Toy Sales Data" worksheet

5. To display the Clipboard task pane:
   CHOOSE: Edit, Office Clipboard
   The Clipboard task pane should now appear.
6. Clear any items in the Clipboard task pane:
   CLICK: Clear All command button in the Clipboard task pane
7. To copy a range of worksheet cells to the Office Clipboard:
   SELECT: cell range from A1 to E5
   CLICK: Copy button (📋) on the Standard toolbar
   A partial view of the copied Excel data should now appear in the Clipboard task pane, and a moving border should appear around the cell range.
8. Select and copy the Excel chart to the Office Clipboard:
   CLICK: near the upper-right corner of the chart to select it
   CLICK: Copy button (📋) on the Standard toolbar
   Both copied items should now appear in the Clipboard task pane.

9. To paste the contents of the Office Clipboard at the bottom of the Word "Toy Sales Letter" document:
   CLICK: "Toy Sales Letter" Word button on the taskbar, to display the Word document
   PRESS: CTRL+END to position the insertion point at the end of the document
   CHOOSE: Edit, Office Clipboard to display the Clipboard task pane
   CLICK: Paste All command button in the Clipboard task pane, to paste both items at once
   Your document should now appear similar to Figure 1.27.

Figure 1.27

Pasting Excel objects in a Word document

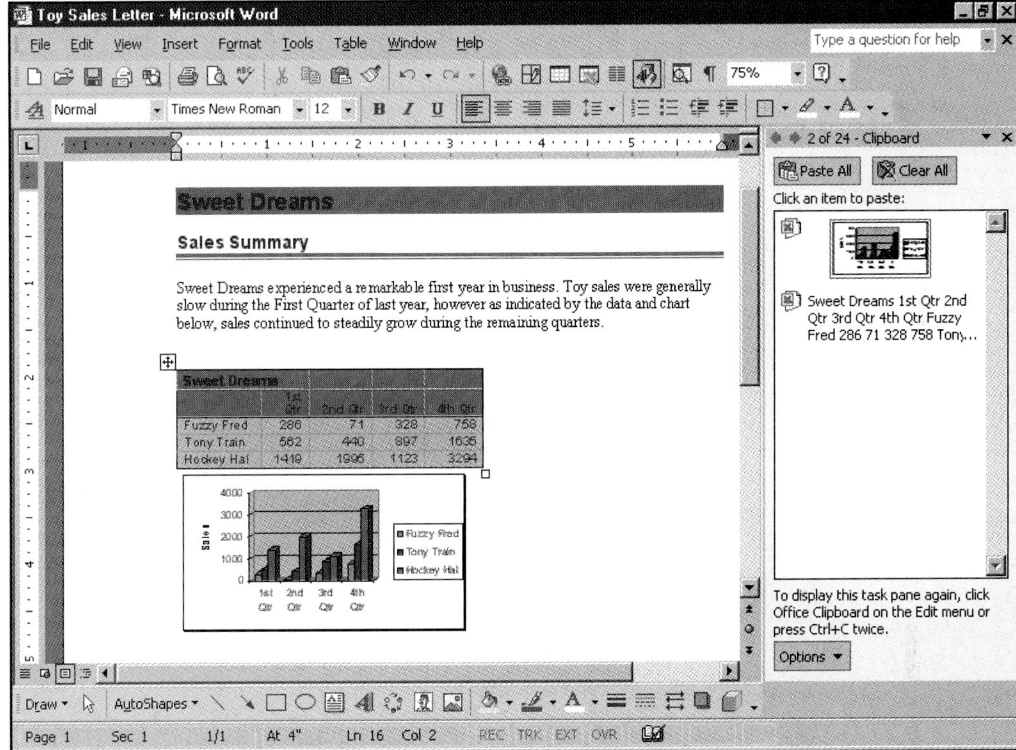

10. To clear the contents of the Office Clipboard and then close the Clipboard toolbar:
    CLICK: Clear All command button in the Clipboard task pane
    CLICK: Close button (☒) in the Clipboard task pane

11. Save, print, and close the "Toy Sales Letter" document. Close the "Toy Sales Data" worksheet.

12. Close Word and Excel.

easy 

2. Outback Exports: Inserting a Linked Chart in Word

Richard Brackton, the chairman of Outback Exports, is preparing a document for review by his team of analysts. Assume the role of Richard, who must insert and link an Excel chart to a Word document, and edit the Excel source data.

1. Start Word and then open the IM01HE02 Word file.

2. Save the document as "Chairman Letter" to your personal storage location. The document should appear similar to Figure 1.28.

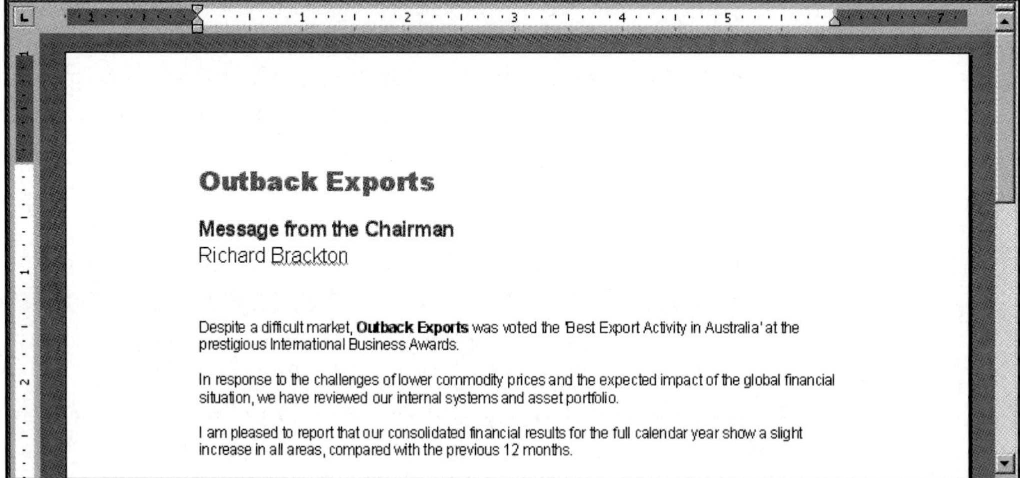

Outback Exports
Message from the Chairman
Richard Brackton
Despite a difficult market, Outback Exports was voted the 'Best Export Activity in Australia' at the prestigious International Business Awards.
In response to the challenges of lower commodity prices and the expected impact of the global financial situation, we have reviewed our internal systems and asset portfolio.
I am pleased to report that our consolidated financial results for the full calendar year show a slight increase in all areas, compared with the previous 12 months.

Figure 1.28

"Chairman Letter" document

3. Start Excel and then open the IM01HE02 worksheet.
4. Save the worksheet as "Export Data" to your personal storage location. The worksheet should appear similar to Figure 1.29.

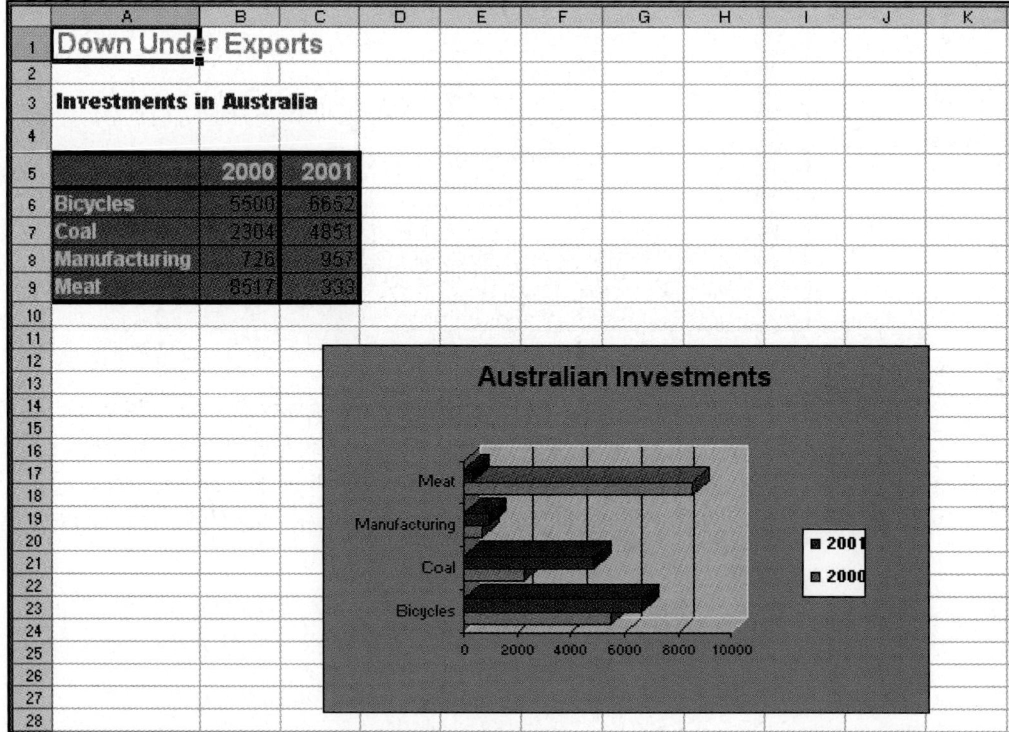

Figure 1.29

"Export Data" worksheet

5. To copy the "Australian Investments" chart to the Clipboard:
   CLICK: anywhere in the chart area of the blue chart to select it
   CLICK: Copy button (📋) on the Standard toolbar

6. To indicate where to insert the object, return to Word and position the insertion point at the bottom of the "Chairman Letter" document:
CLICK: "Chairman Letter" Word button on the Windows taskbar
PRESS: CTRL+END

7. To paste the Excel chart into the Word document and establish a dynamic link between the source document "Export Data.xls" and the destination document, "Chairman Letter.doc":
CHOOSE: Edit, Paste Special from the Word menu
SELECT: *Paste link* option button

8. "Microsoft Excel Chart Object" should be selected in the *As* list box. To proceed:
CLICK: OK command button
Observe the inserted linked chart at the bottom of the destination document (Figure 1.30).

Figure 1.30

The Excel chart was copied to the Word document

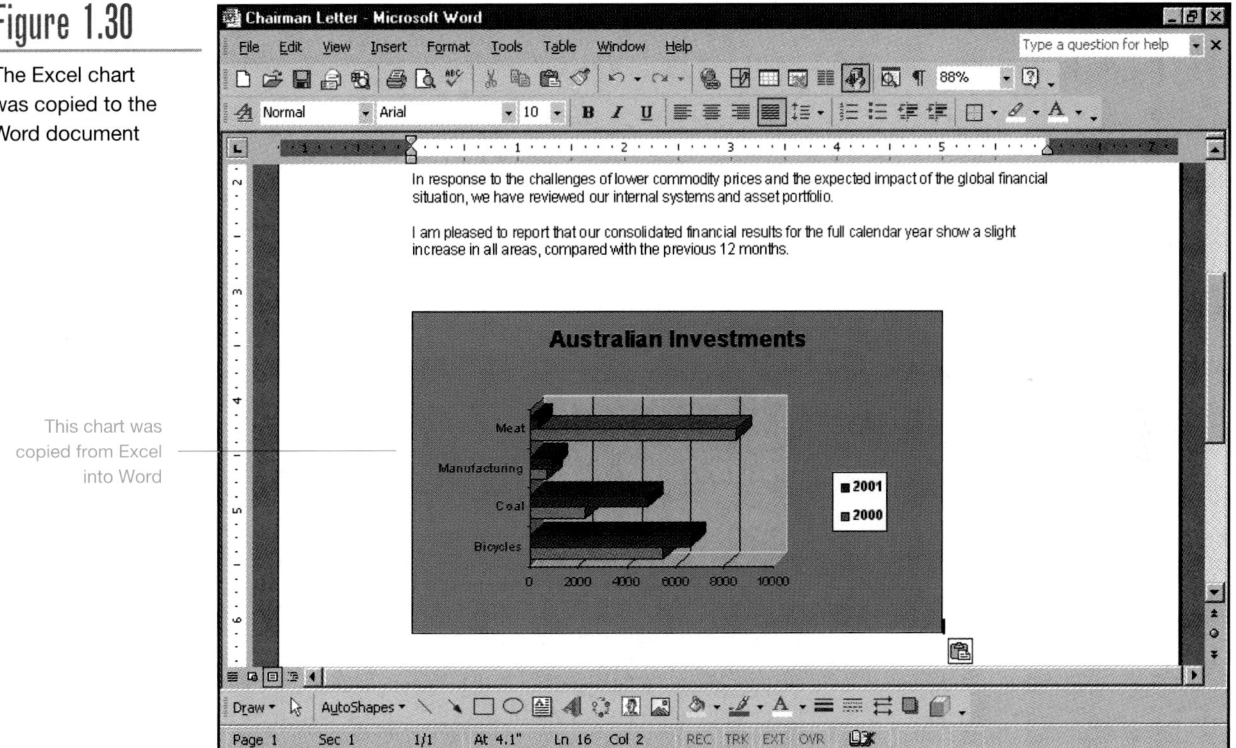
Chairman Letter - Microsoft Word
File Edit View Insert Format Tools Table Window Help
Type a question for help
Normal
Arial
10
88%
In response to the challenges of lower commodity prices and the expected impact of the global financial situation, we have reviewed our internal systems and asset portfolio.
I am pleased to report that our consolidated financial results for the full calendar year show a slight increase in all areas, compared with the previous 12 months.
Australian Investments
Meat
Manufacturing
Coal
Bicycles
0 2000 4000 6000 8000 10000
2001
2000
Draw AutoShapes
Page 1 Sec 1 1/1 At 4.1" Ln 16 Col 2 REC TRK EXT OVR

This chart was copied from Excel into Word

9. Make some alterations to the source document to demonstrate dynamic linking. To switch to Excel:
CLICK: Excel button on the Windows taskbar

10. With the worksheet displayed on the screen, change the 2001 Meat value from 333 to 9999 in the brown table:
SELECT: cell C9
TYPE: **9999**
PRESS: ENTER
You have now updated the worksheet source document as well.

11. Save your changes to the "Export Data" file, replacing the previous version, and exit Excel.

12. The linked chart should reflect the updated changes in the Excel source document. Print, save and close the revised document, and then exit Word.

moderate 

3. Bud's Parlor of Flavors: Inserting and Manipulating Shared Objects

Bud Simpson is the owner of Bud's Parlor of Flavors, an ice cream parlor in the center of town. Bud wants to practice embedding and linking Excel objects in a Word document. In this exercise, assume the role of Bud, who must insert and manipulate shared objects.

1. Start Word and open the IM01HE03 Word file.
2. Save the document as "Flavors" to your personal storage location.
3. Start Excel and open the IM01HE03 Excel file.
4. Save the worksheet as "Ice Cream" to your personal storage location. The worksheet should appear similar to Figure 1.31.

Figure 1.31

"Ice Cream" worksheet

	A	B	C
1	Bud's Parlor of Flavors		
2			
3			
4	Flavors:		
5	Chocolate Decadence	527	
6	Mud Pie	638	
7	Creamy Coconut	284	
8	Strawberry Truffle	961	
9			

5. Select, copy, and embed the pink Excel table one line below the first heading of the Word document. (*Hint:* Choose Edit, Paste Special and then select "Microsoft Excel Worksheet Object" in the *As* list box.)

6. Select, copy, and link the pink Excel table one line below the second heading of the Word document. (*Hint:* Choose Edit, Paste Special and select the *Paste link* option button. Also, select "Microsoft Excel Worksheet Object" in the *As* list box.)

7. Resize both shared objects by dragging their bottom-right sizing handles outward about one inch.

8. Edit the embedded object by changing the Chocolate Decadence value from "527" to "1000." The document should appear similar to Figure 1.32. (Remember, Bud is using this document just for practice. He does not plan to use this document in running his business.)

Figure 1.32

"Flavors" document

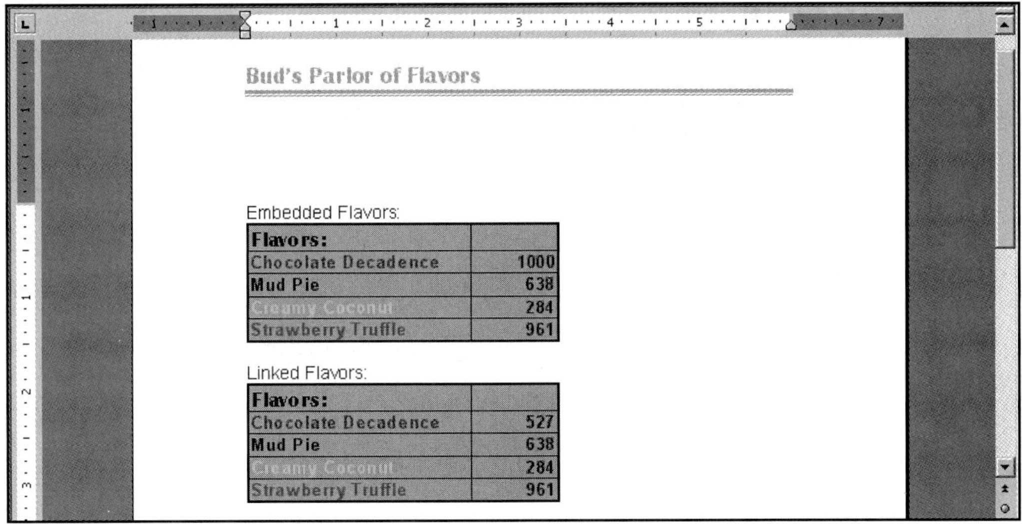

9. Save, print, and then close the revised document.
10. Close Word and Excel.

moderate

4. The Software Edge: Embedding New Excel Objects

Mary is an employee at The Software Edge, an online software retailer. She is preparing a document for her coworkers. In this exercise, assume the role of Mary, who must insert a new worksheet and a new chart in a Word document, and then edit the embedded worksheet.

1. Start Word. A blank document should be displaying.
2. Type the heading **Number of Software Edge Conventions** at the top of the document followed by five blank lines.
3. Move your insertion point up two lines by pressing ⬆ twice.
4. Using the Insert, Object command, insert a new Microsoft Excel Worksheet object at the current insertion point location.
5. Insert the following data into the Excel worksheet, beginning with cell A1.

New York	15
Chicago	10
Dallas	10
Phoenix	10

6. Return to Word by clicking outside the embedded object. Move the insertion point to the bottom of the document. The document should now appear similar to Figure 1.33.

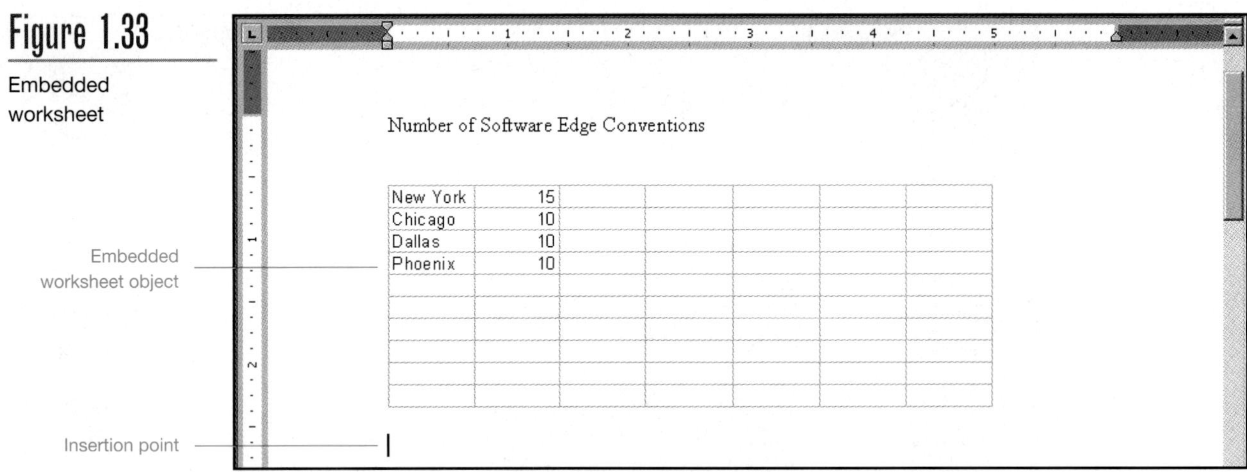

Figure 1.33

Embedded worksheet

7. Insert a second heading, "Software Edge Convention Expenses" at the insertion point, followed by two blank lines.
8. Using the Insert, Object menu command, insert a new Microsoft Excel Chart object two lines below the second heading.
9. Leaving the chart unchanged, return to Word by clicking outside the embedded chart. The document should now appear similar to Figure 1.34.

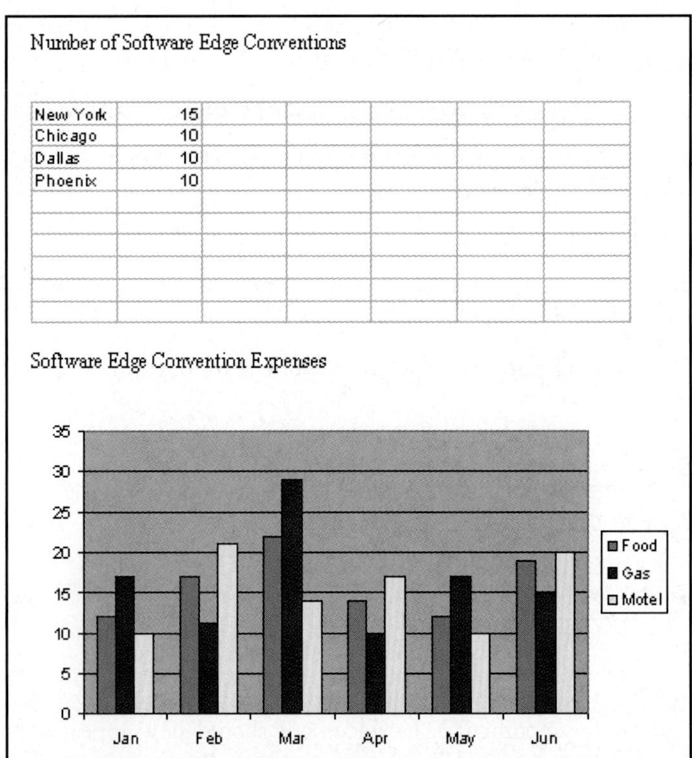

Figure 1.34

Embedded worksheet

10. Save your document as "Software Edge" to your personal storage location and then preview and print the document.
11. Close Word.

difficult 

5. On Your Own: Pasting Between Word and Excel

In this exercise, you create and copy two Word items to the Office Clipboard and then insert them all at once into a new Excel worksheet. To begin, create a new Word document entitled "Favorites" that lists your three favorite animals, followed by several blank lines, and then your three favorite colors. After clearing the Office Clipboard of all items, copy the first three items (your favorite animals) to the Office Clipboard. Next, copy the last three items (your favorite colors) to the Office Clipboard. Launch Excel and paste both objects at once into a new worksheet. Save your Excel worksheet as "Favorites" to your personal storage location, and then print it.

difficult 

6. On Your Own: Pasting, Linking, and Embedding

To practice pasting, linking, embedding, and manipulating objects in Word, this exercise practices copying an Excel table to a Word document three times. To begin, create a simple table in Excel entitled "Cities" that lists three fictional cities and their corresponding populations. Create a new Word document and insert the title "Population." Copy the Excel table and paste it in the Word document. Below the pasted table in Word, copy and link the same Excel table. Then copy and embed the same table at the bottom of the document. Change a value in the source document and observe that only the linked object changes.

At the bottom of the Word document, type the title "Average Yearly Temperatures." Then, insert a new Excel worksheet below the title using the Insert, Object menu command. In the new Excel worksheet, list the same three cities you referenced earlier and their corresponding average yearly temperatures. Save the Word document as "Statistics" and then preview and print your document.

Case Problems

Arbor Forestry

Now that Sam has learned several techniques for integrating Word and Excel, he is ready to practice embedding and linking Excel objects in his Word memos. In the following case problems, assume the role of Sam and perform the same steps that he identifies. You may want to re-read the chapter opening before proceeding.

1. Sam opens the Word file IM01CS01, a memo to the production general manager that explains the company's productivity over the past three months. He saves the memo as "Productivity" to his personal storage location. Sam decides to copy and paste data from an existing Excel worksheet into the memo. He starts Excel and opens the IM01CS01 worksheet and saves it as "Jan-Mar" to his personal storage location. Next, Sam displays the Office Clipboard and ensures that it is empty.

   Sam individually selects and copies the January, February, and March tables to the Office Clipboard. He returns to Word and moves the insertion point to the bottom of the document. After displaying the Clipboard task pane, he pastes the January table followed by a blank line, pastes the February table followed by a blank line, and then pastes the March table. After clearing the contents of the Office Clipboard, Sam prints and saves the revised memo (Figure 1.35). As a final step, he closes Word and Excel.

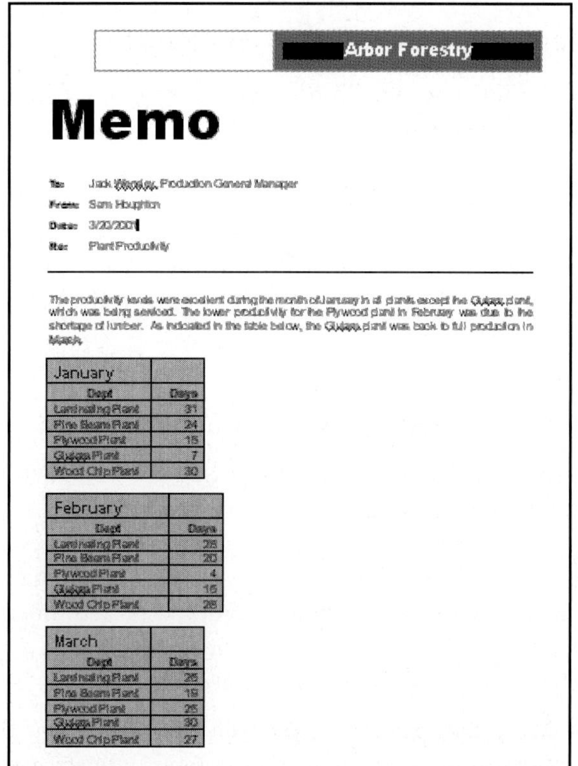

Arbor Forestry

Memo

To: Jack [illegible], Production General Manager
From: Sam Houghton
Date: 3/20/2001
Re: Plant Productivity

The productivity levels were excellent during the month of January in all plants except the [illegible] plant, which was being serviced. The lower productivity for the Plywood plant in February was due to the shortage of lumber. As indicated in the table below, the [illegible] plant was back to full production in March.

January	
Dept	Days
Laminating Plant	31
Pine Beam Plant	24
Plywood Plant	15
[illegible] Plant	7
Wood Chip Plant	30

February	
Dept	Days
Laminating Plant	28
Pine Beam Plant	20
Plywood Plant	4
[illegible] Plant	16
Wood Chip Plant	28

March	
Dept	Days
Laminating Plant	25
Pine Beam Plant	19
Plywood Plant	25
[illegible] Plant	30
Wood Chip Plant	27

Figure 1.35
"Productivity" document

2. Each month, Sam must also send the personnel manager, Harold Brock, a memo indicating the production days for each of Riverdale's plants. Sam opens a new document in Word and enters and formats the text pictured in Figure 1.36. He then saves the document as "Personnel Memo" to his personal storage location.

Figure 1.36
"Personnel Memo" document

Memo

To:	**Harold Brock**
From:	**Sam Houghton**
Subject:	**April Productivity**

Sam opens the IM01CS02 Excel document and saves it as "April" to his personal storage location. Since several of the numbers may change, Sam decides to establish a link between the April table and the Word document. He successfully copies the April table to the bottom of the Word document, establishing a link. Sam's memo now appears similar to Figure 1.37.

Figure 1.37

Memo to Harold Brock

Memo

To: Harold Brock
From: Sam Houghton
Subject: April Productivity

April	
Dept	Days
Laminating Plant	28
Pine Beam Plant	20
Plywood Plant	17
Glulam Plant	25
Wood Chip Plant	9

Prior to printing Harold's memo, Sam receives an e-mail message from the wood chip plant indicating that their April production days totaled "29" rather than "9." Sam returns to the source document to make the correction, and then previews the destination document to ensure the change has been made. Sam saves the revised "Personnel Memo" and prints a copy. Next, he closes Word, saves the revised Excel worksheet, and then exits Excel.

3. Sam is ready to edit, delete, resize, and move shared objects in a Word document. He retrieves the IM01CS03 Word document and saves it as "Conversions" to his personal storage location. Next, he edits the embedded table to read "800/900" in the first row of the PLF column, rather than "600/900." After clicking outside the worksheet object, he increases the size of the table and moves it so that it is centered between the margins. The document's contents should now appear similar to Figure 1.38. He saves, prints, and then closes the Word document.

Figure 1.38

"Conversions" document

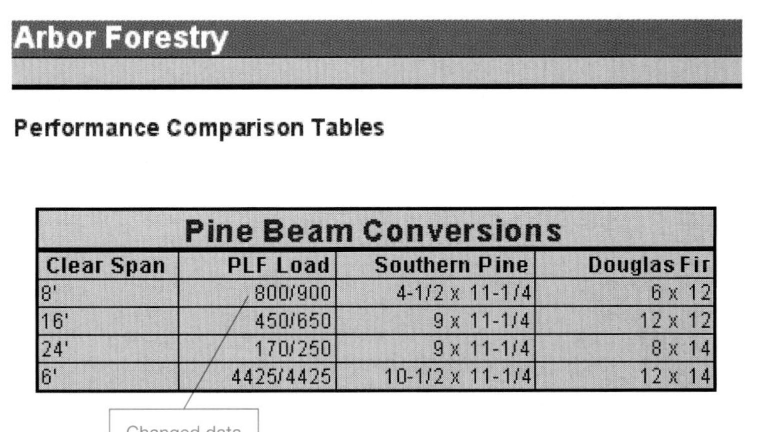

Arbor Forestry

Performance Comparison Tables

Pine Beam Conversions			
Clear Span	PLF Load	Southern Pine	Douglas Fir
8'	800/900	4-1/2 x 11-1/4	6 x 12
16'	450/650	9 x 11-1/4	12 x 12
24'	170/250	9 x 11-1/4	8 x 14
6'	4425/4425	10-1/2 x 11-1/4	12 x 14

4. Sam must complete a memo to the purchasing department to order electrical wire for an upcoming sawmill installation. Sam opens the IM01HE04 document that has already been started, and saves it as "Purchasing" to his personal storage location.

Rather than launching Excel to create a worksheet, Sam uses the Insert, Object command to insert an Excel worksheet at the bottom of the Word document. He adds the following data to the worksheet.

Number	Size	Stranding
SD18	18	16/30
SD19	19	16/30
SD20	20	30/40

At this point, Sam clicks outside the worksheet object, returning to his Word document. Upon further review, Sam notices an important omission and edits the worksheet object to include the following fourth column:

Amount
40 yds
20 yds
100 yds

He then saves and prints the memo (Figure 1.39), and then closes Word. On his way to the coffee machine, he smiles when thinking about how much time Office XP's integration capabilities will save him in the future.

Figure 1.39

"Purchasing" document

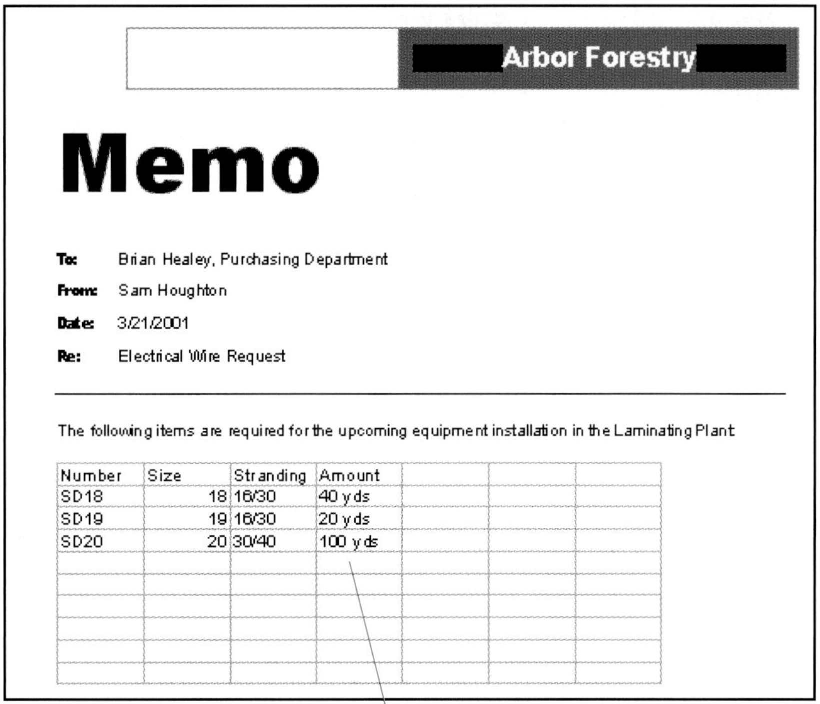

Arbor Forestry

Memo

To: Brian Healey, Purchasing Department

From: Sam Houghton

Date: 3/21/2001

Re: Electrical Wire Request

The following items are required for the upcoming equipment installation in the Laminating Plant.

Number	Size	Stranding	Amount			
SD18	18	16/30	40 yds			
SD19	19	16/30	20 yds			
SD20	20	30/40	100 yds			

Notice the additional fourth column.

NOTES

Integrating & Extending Microsoft® Office® XP

CHAPTER 2

Performing More Integration Tasks

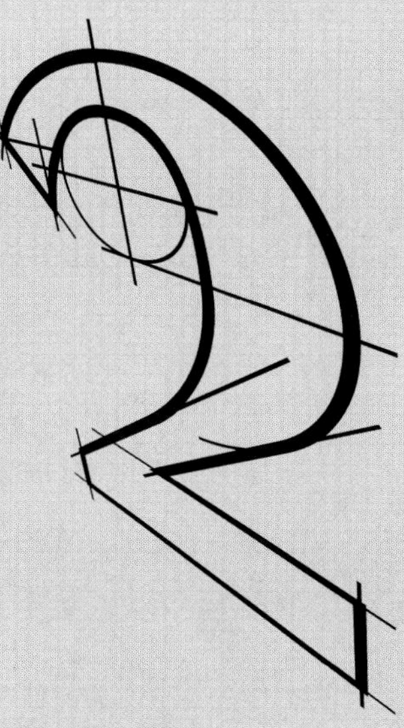

CHAPTER OUTLINE

Case Study

2.1 Creating a Presentation from a Word Document

2.2 Integrating PowerPoint with Word and Excel

2.3 Integrating Access with Word and Excel

Chapter Summary

Chapter Quiz

Hands-On Exercises

Case Problems

PREREQUISITES

This chapter assumes you know how to create, save, edit, and print Word documents, Excel worksheets, and PowerPoint presentations. You should also know how to view and print table data in Access.

LEARNING OBJECTIVES

After completing this chapter, you will be able to:

- Create an outline in Word and then convert the outline to a PowerPoint presentation
- Copy PowerPoint slides to Word
- Copy an Excel chart to PowerPoint
- Export Access reports to Word
- Transfer an Excel list to Access

CaseStudy **DEL'S DELICIOUS COOKIES** Del Paul is the owner of a successful cookie company. One of his marketing techniques is making presentations at culinary trade shows. In the past, Del created his presentations from scratch, even though much of their content already existed in Word documents. After a recent presentation, Del and a few other people began talking about Microsoft Office's integration capabilities. Since this is a topic that Del knew nothing about, he was the one asking the questions. "You mean, you can convert an existing Word document to a PowerPoint presentation? You can copy Excel charts into PowerPoint? You can convert an Excel list into Access?" After hearing a string of "yes" responses, Del could think of many reasons he wanted to know how to perform these useful operations.

In this chapter, you and Del learn how to convert a Word outline to a PowerPoint presentation. You also learn how to embed PowerPoint slides and presentations in Word, and embed an Excel chart in PowerPoint. Finally, you will export Access reports to Word, and transfer an Excel list to Access.

2.1 Creating a Presentation from a Word Document

When you need to create a long document such as a report, a term paper, or a book like this one, Word's Outline view can help you organize your thoughts. To switch to Outline view in Word, you choose View, Outline from the Menu bar or click the Outline View button (▣) located to the left of the horizontal scroll bar. A Word outline also provides a nice starting point for a PowerPoint presentation.

2.1.1 Creating an Outline in Word

feature

Many writers like to begin the writing process by creating an outline. When you create a document from scratch in Outline view, Word automatically applies its default heading styles to the different levels in the outline. (*Note:* A *style* in Word is a collection of formatting commands that, when applied to text, change its appearance.)

method

To switch to Outline view in Word:

- CHOOSE: View, Outline

or

- CLICK: Outline View button (▣) located to the left of the horizontal scroll bar

To create an outline in Word:

- PRESS: ENTER to insert a new heading at the same level
- CLICK: Demote button (➡) to begin typing at a demoted (lower) level
- CLICK: Promote button (⬅) to begin typing at a promoted (higher) level

practice

You will now create an outline in Word. Make sure that Word and PowerPoint are installed on your computer.

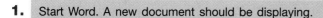

1. Start Word. A new document should be displaying.
2. To switch to Outline view:
   CHOOSE: View, Outline
   The insertion point is blinking on the first line of the outline (Figure 2.1). Note that "Heading 1" appears in the Style box on the Formatting toolbar. Also note that a new toolbar, the Outlining toolbar, appears. (The position of this toolbar may be different on your computer.)

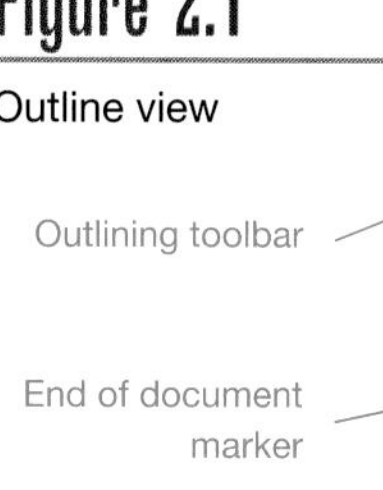

Figure 2.1
Outline view

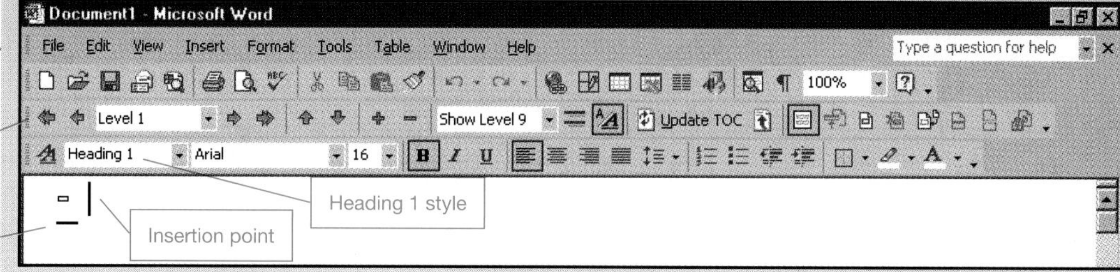

3. To begin typing your outline:
   TYPE: **Exploring the Internet**
   PRESS: ENTER to insert another heading
4. TYPE: **Popular Internet Search Tools**
   PRESS: ENTER to insert another heading
5. To type at a "demoted" level:
   CLICK: Demote button (➡) on the Outlining toolbar
   Note that "Heading 2" now appears in the Style box on the Formatting toolbar. The document should now appear similar to Figure 2.2.

Figure 2.2
Typing at a demoted level

Heading 2 style

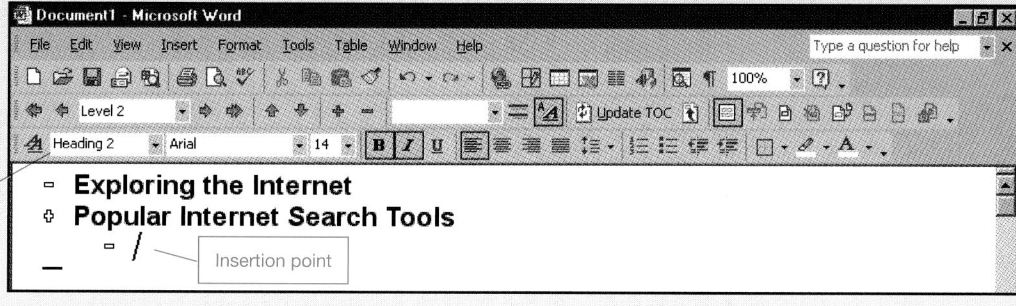

6. TYPE: **Yahoo!**
   PRESS: ENTER to insert another heading
   TYPE: **Infoseek**
   PRESS: ENTER to insert another heading
   TYPE: **AltaVista**
   PRESS: ENTER to insert another heading
   TYPE: **Excite**
   PRESS: ENTER to insert another heading
7. To type at a "promoted" level:
   CLICK: Promote button (⬅) on the Outlining toolbar
   TYPE: **About Downloading Files**
   Your document should now appear similar to Figure 2.3.

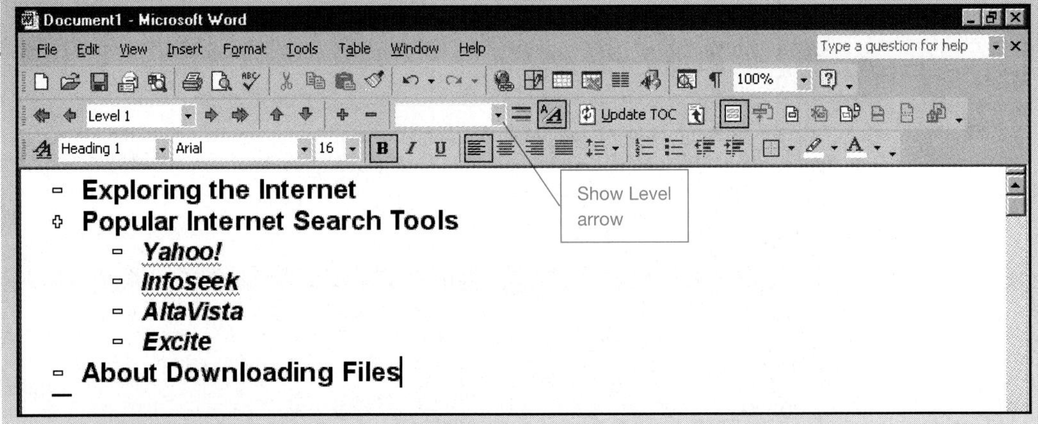

Figure 2.3

Sample Word outline

8. To view just the main headings in the outline:
CLICK: Show Level drop-down arrow (refer to Figure 2.3)
CHOOSE: Show Level 1 from the drop-down list
Your document should now appear similar to Figure 2.4.

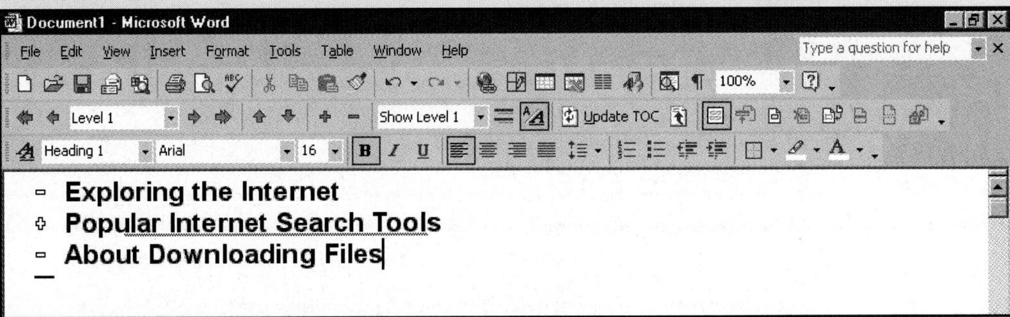

Figure 2.4

Showing the level 1 headings

9. To redisplay the entire outline:
CLICK: Show Level arrow (refer to Figure 2.3)
CHOOSE: Show All Levels from the drop-down list
The outline should again look like the outline in Figure 2.3.

10. Save the document as "Internet Outline" to your personal storage location.

2.1.2 Converting a Word Outline to PowerPoint

feature → If you have already created an outline in Word, you can transform it into a PowerPoint slide presentation in a very short time.

method →

- The headings in the Word document must be formatted with heading styles.
- CHOOSE: File, Send To, Microsoft PowerPoint
- Use PowerPoint to embellish the presentation.

This exercise practices converting a Word outline to a PowerPoint presentation. After you have completed the previous lesson, make sure that Word is the active application. The "Internet Outline" document should be displaying in Outline view.

1. To convert the Word outline to a PowerPoint presentation:
   CHOOSE: File, Send To, Microsoft PowerPoint
   After a few moments, the outline and presentation will appear in PowerPoint (Figure 2.5). (*Note:* If grids are displaying on your screen, choose View, Grid and Guides from the Menu bar and then click on the *Display grid on screen* check box to deselect the option.)

Figure 2.5

Viewing the Word outline in PowerPoint

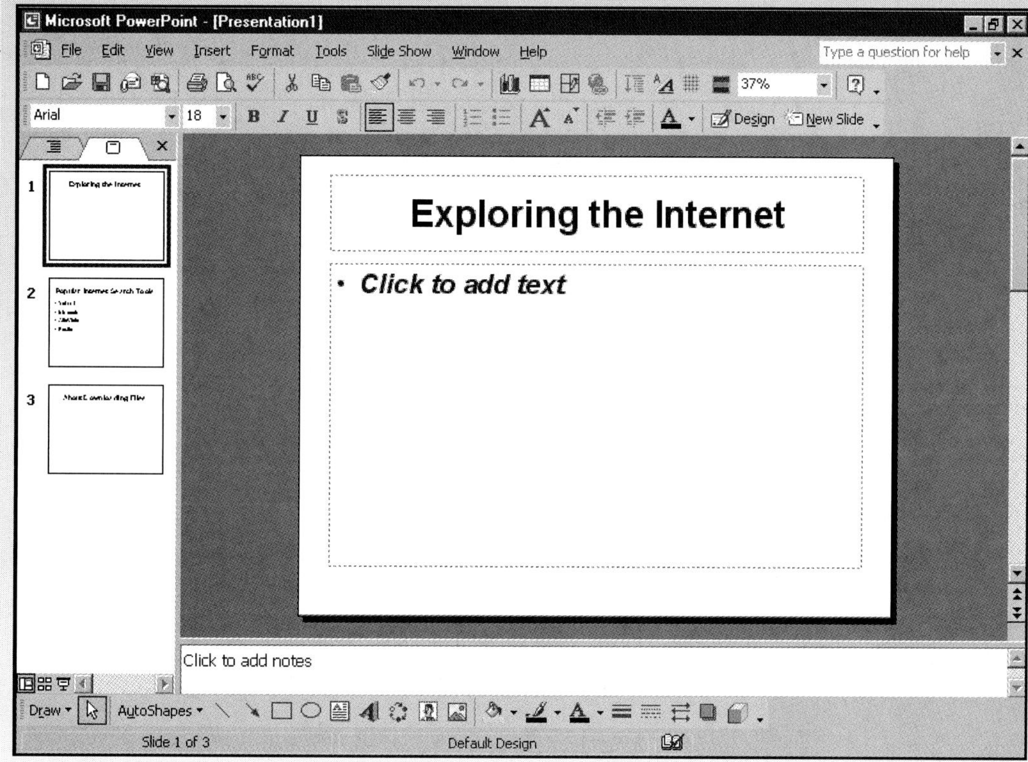

2. Now apply one of PowerPoint's design templates to the presentation.
   CHOOSE: Format, Slide Design
   The Slide Design task pane should appear.

3. Locate the "Blends" thumbnail in the Slide Design task pane. (*Note:* If this template is not available, select an alternate template or consult your instructor.)

4. CLICK: "Blends" thumbnail
   The presentation's title slide should now appear similar to Figure 2.6.

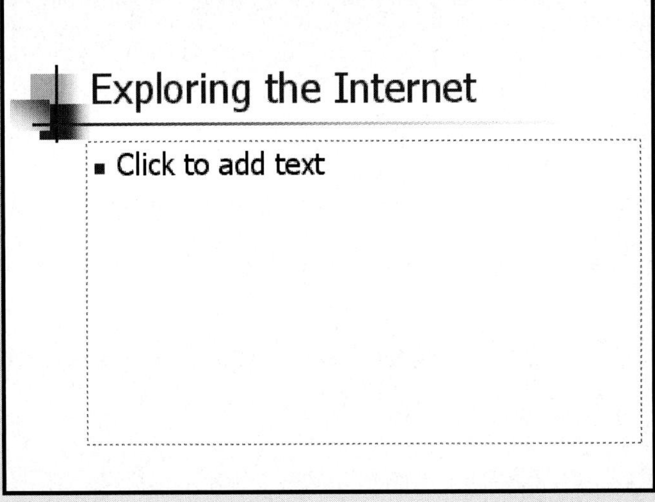

Figure 2.6

Applying an alternate design template

5. To display the short presentation as it will be seen by your audience:
   CHOOSE: View, Slide Show
   CLICK: with the mouse to proceed through the presentation
6. After you have viewed the three slides, a black screen will appear.
7. With the black screen visible:
   CLICK: once more to exit Slide Show view
8. Save the presentation as "Internet Presentation" to your personal storage location.
9. Close PowerPoint and Word.

2.1. Describe the procedure for converting a Word outline to a PowerPoint presentation.

2.2 Integrating PowerPoint with Word and Excel

In this module, we describe how to copy PowerPoint slides to a Word document and how to embellish a PowerPoint presentation with a chart created in Excel.

2.2.1 Copying PowerPoint Slides to Word

feature

PowerPoint slides can be inserted in your Word documents to add visual interest.

method

- In PowerPoint, select a slide in the Outline pane and then copy it to the Clipboard.
- Switch to Word.
- Position the insertion point where you want the object to be inserted.
- CHOOSE: Edit, Paste Special
- SELECT: a data type in the *As* list box

- SELECT: *Paste* option button (the default selection) to embed the object

or

- SELECT: *Paste link* option button to link the object
- CLICK: OK command button

practice

You now open a four-slide presentation that addresses the topic of PC operating systems. You practice inserting a slide from this presentation in a Word document. Ensure that Word and PowerPoint are installed on your computer.

1. Start Word. A new Word document should be displaying.
2. Start PowerPoint and ensure that the application window is maximized.
3. Open the IM0220 student data file.
4. Save a copy of the presentation as "OS" to your personal storage location. Your screen should now appear similar to Figure 2.7.

Figure 2.7

"OS" presentation

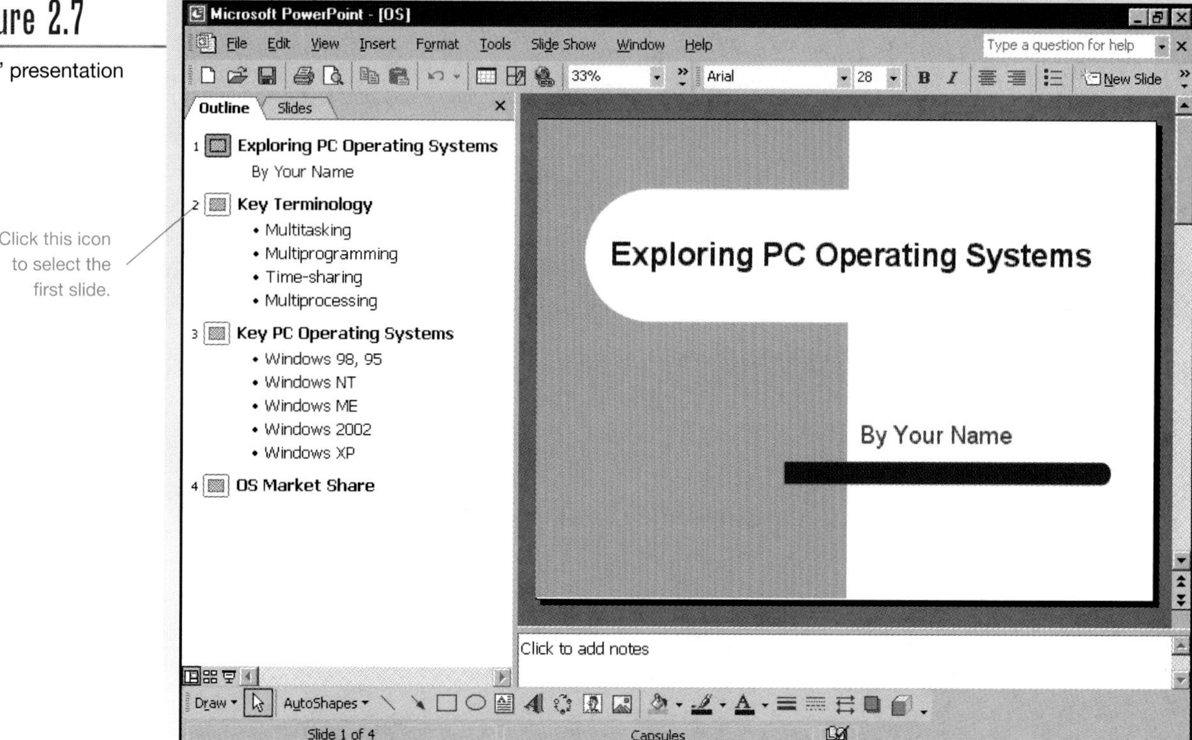

5. Copy the first slide into Word. To select the first slide, you must click its icon in the Outline pane.
   CLICK: icon for the first slide (refer to Figure 2.7)
   The first slide should appear selected in the Outline pane.
6. To copy this slide to the Clipboard:
   CLICK: Copy button () on the Standard toolbar
   (*Note:* To select a group of consecutive slides in the Outline pane, hold down the SHIFT key while selecting the first and last slide.)

Integrating

7. To switch to Word:
CLICK: its button on the Windows taskbar

8. To embed the slide in the Word document:
CHOOSE: Edit, Paste Special
SELECT: "Microsoft PowerPoint Slide Object" in the *As* list box. The Paste Special dialog box should now appear similar to Figure 2.8.

Figure 2.8

Paste Special dialog box

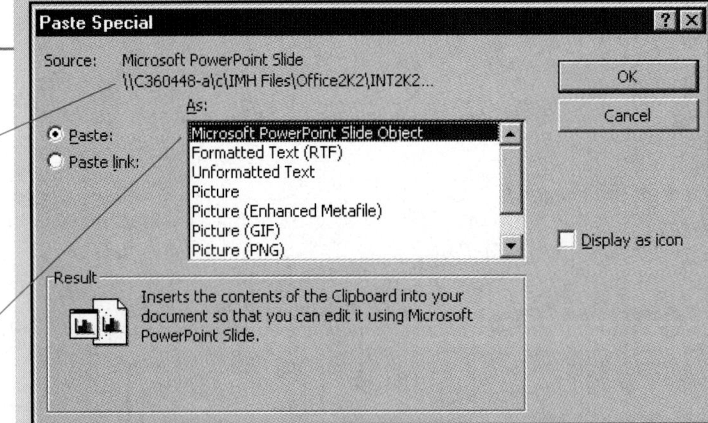

9. To proceed:
CLICK: OK
The slide is embedded in the document (Figure 2.9). As with all embedded objects, you can edit the embedded slide by double-clicking. You can also move and resize the object as desired.

Figure 2.9

Embedding a slide in a Word document

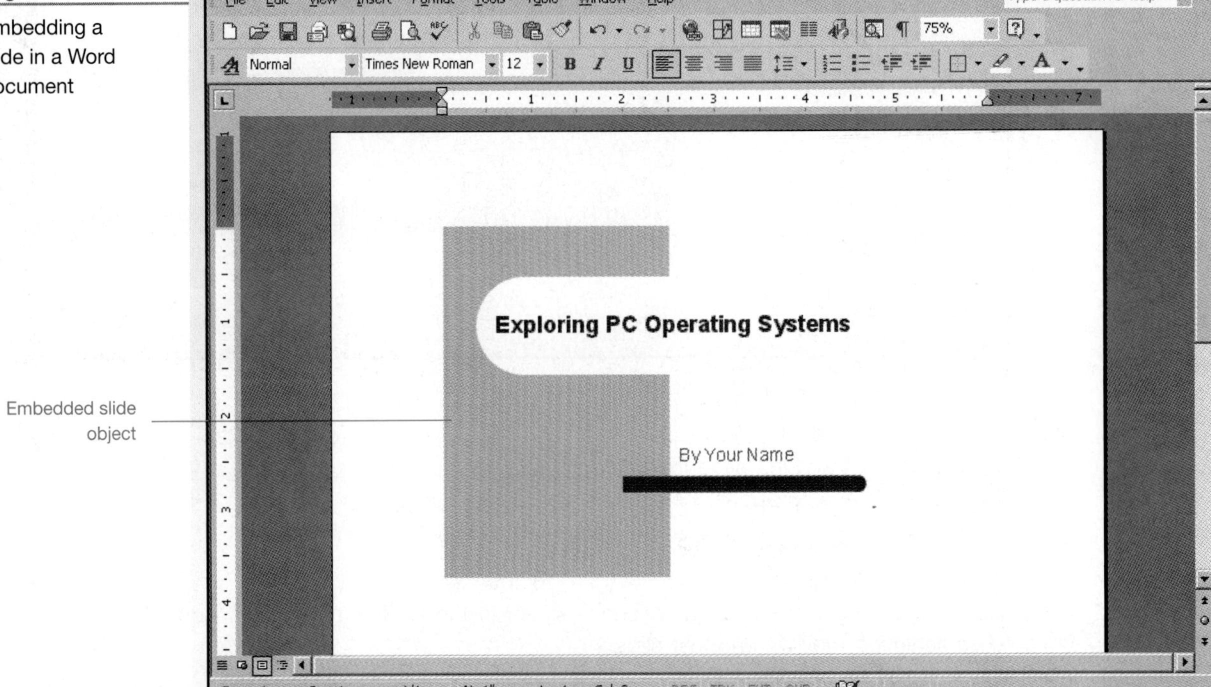

10. Close Word, without saving the current document.

2.2.2 Copying an Excel Chart to PowerPoint

feature

As in Word, in a PowerPoint presentation it is possible to link or embed any part of an Excel workbook. The source data from Excel is incorporated into the destination document.

method

- In Excel, copy the selected chart to the Clipboard.
- Switch to PowerPoint.
- Position the insertion point on the destination slide.
- CHOOSE: Edit, Paste Special
- SELECT: a data type in the *As* list box
- SELECT: *Paste* option button to embed the object

or

- SELECT: *Paste link* option button to link the object
- CLICK: OK command button

practice

You will now embed an existing Excel chart on the last slide in the "OS" presentation. Ensure that PowerPoint and Excel are installed on your computer. The "OS" presentation should be displaying in Normal view in the PowerPoint application window.

1. In PowerPoint, let's display the fourth slide in the "OS" presentation. First, locate the icon for the fourth slide in the Outline pane (Figure 2.10).

Figure 2.10

"OS" presentation

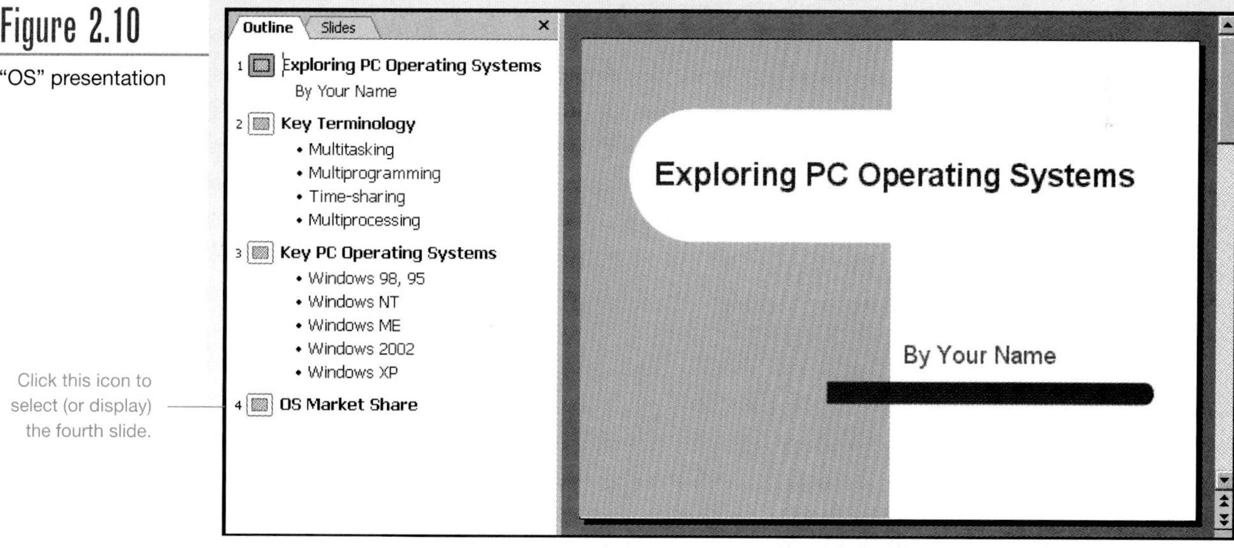

Click this icon to select (or display) the fourth slide.

2. While referring to Figure 2.10:
CLICK: slide 4 icon
The fourth slide should be displaying in the Slide pane (Figure 2.11).

Integrating

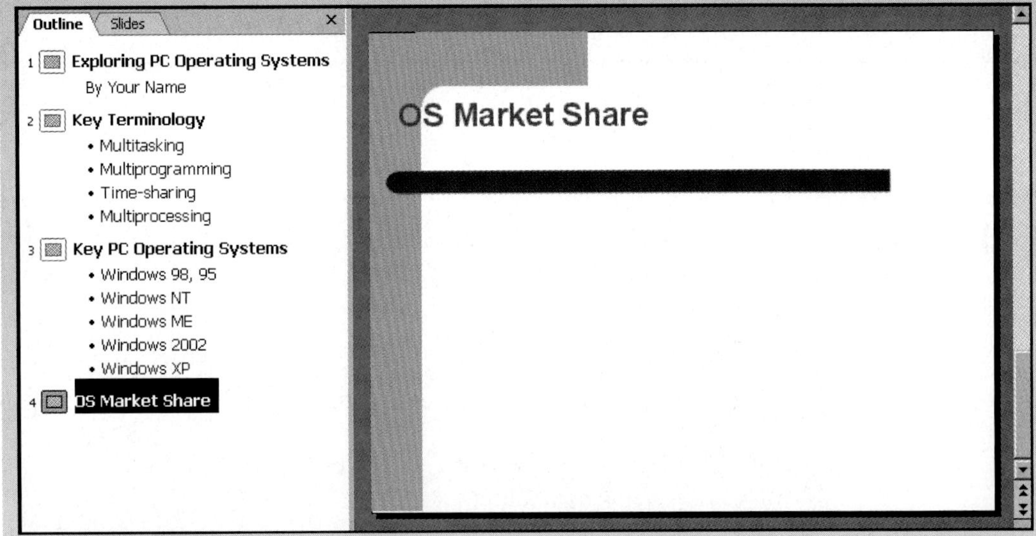

Figure 2.11

"OS" presentation

3. Start Excel and then open the IM0222 workbook. (*Note:* If necessary, maximize the Excel window and the worksheet window before continuing.)
4. Save the worksheet as "Market Share" to your personal storage location. The worksheet area should appear similar to Figure 2.12. Note that the chart is already selected.

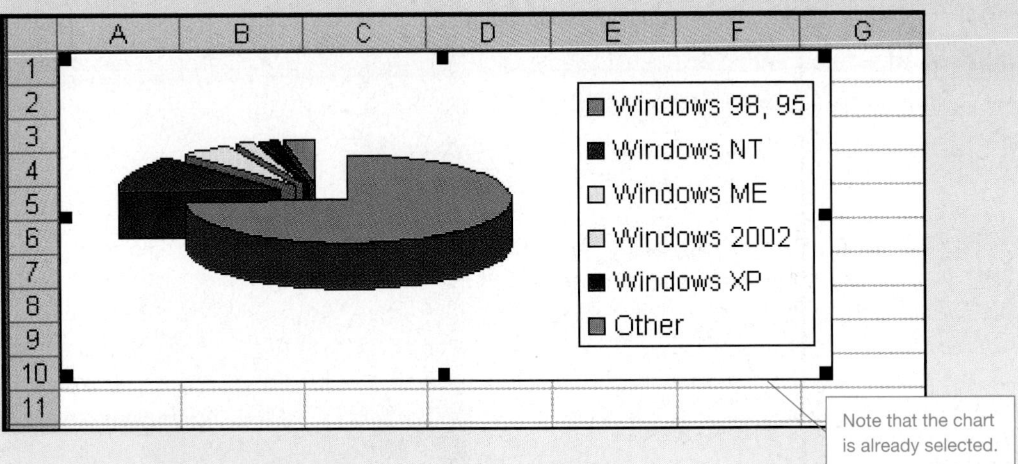

Figure 2.12

Selected chart

5. To copy the selected chart to the Clipboard:
   CLICK: Copy button ( )
6. To switch to PowerPoint:
   CLICK: its button on the Windows taskbar
7. The destination slide (slide 4) should be displaying in the Slide pane. To paste the Excel chart onto the slide:
   CHOOSE: Edit, Paste Special
8. Note that "Microsoft Excel Chart Object" is already selected in the *As* list box.
   CLICK: OK command button
9. On your own, resize and move the chart object until your slide appears similar to Figure 2.13.

Figure 2.13

Embedded Excel chart

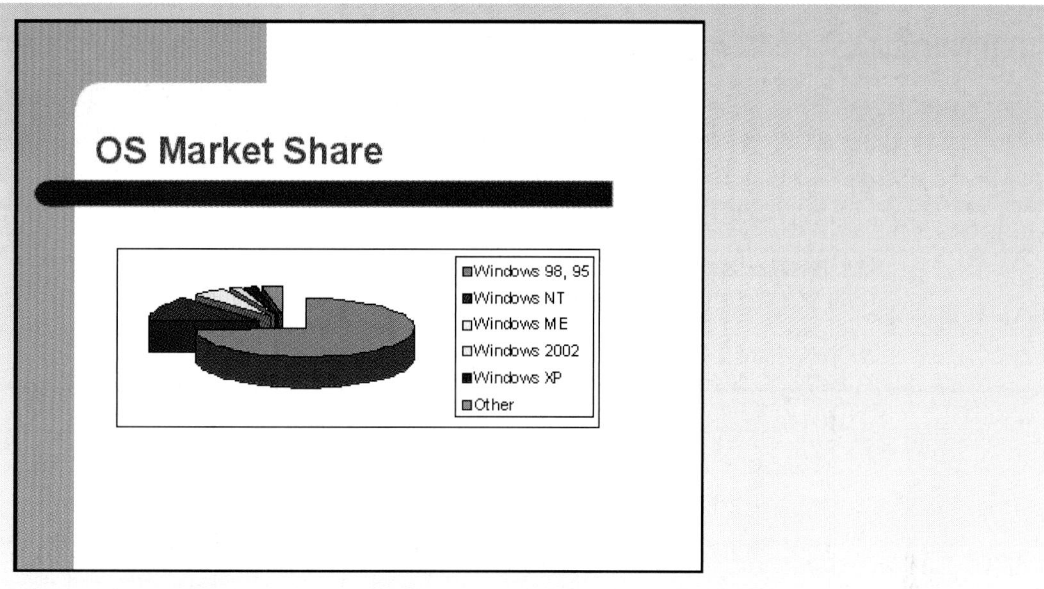

10. Save the presentation and then close PowerPoint.
11. Save the "Market Share" workbook and then close Excel.

2.2. How would you go about editing an embedded PowerPoint slide?

2.3 Integrating Access with Word and Excel

Although Excel can successfully manage simple worksheet lists, it is not the best choice for managing large databases, performing complicated queries, and generating database-style reports. If you need the power of a database application to manage your worksheet list, consider transferring your Excel data into Access. Also, if you need more flexibility in terms of how your Access reports are formatted, consider converting them into a Word format for final polishing. In this module we discuss both of these procedures.

2.3.1 Exporting Access Reports to Word

feature

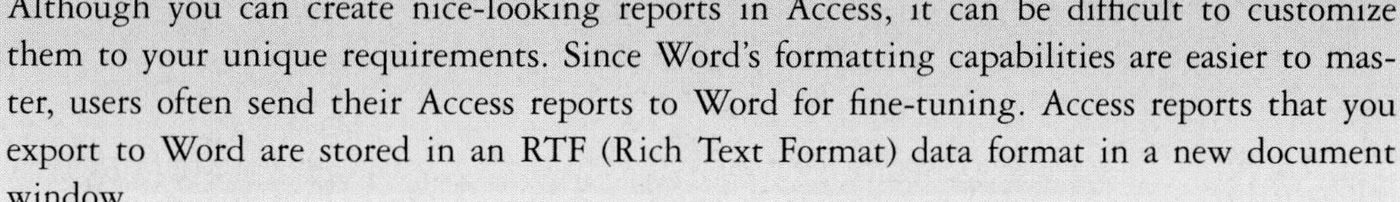

Although you can create nice-looking reports in Access, it can be difficult to customize them to your unique requirements. Since Word's formatting capabilities are easier to master, users often send their Access reports to Word for fine-tuning. Access reports that you export to Word are stored in an RTF (Rich Text Format) data format in a new document window.

method

- In Access, preview the report that you want to export to Word.
- CLICK: OfficeLinks arrow (W) on the Print Preview toolbar
- SELECT: Publish It with Microsoft Word

Integrating

practice →

This lesson practices sending an Access report to Word. In Word, you will increase the font size of the report data. Ensure that Access and Word are installed on your computer.

1. Start Access and open the IM0230 database.
2. To display the "First Year Students" report, do the following:
   CLICK: Reports button in the Objects bar
3. To preview the "First Year Students" report:
   DOUBLE-CLICK: "First Year Students" report in the list area
4. To view more of the report at once:
   CHOOSE: 75% from the Zoom drop-down list (100% ▾) on the Print Preview toolbar
5. Maximize the report window. Your screen should now appear similar to Figure 2.14. Although the report looks fairly nice as is, let's send it to Word to increase the font size of the data.

Figure 2.14

"First Year Students" report in Access

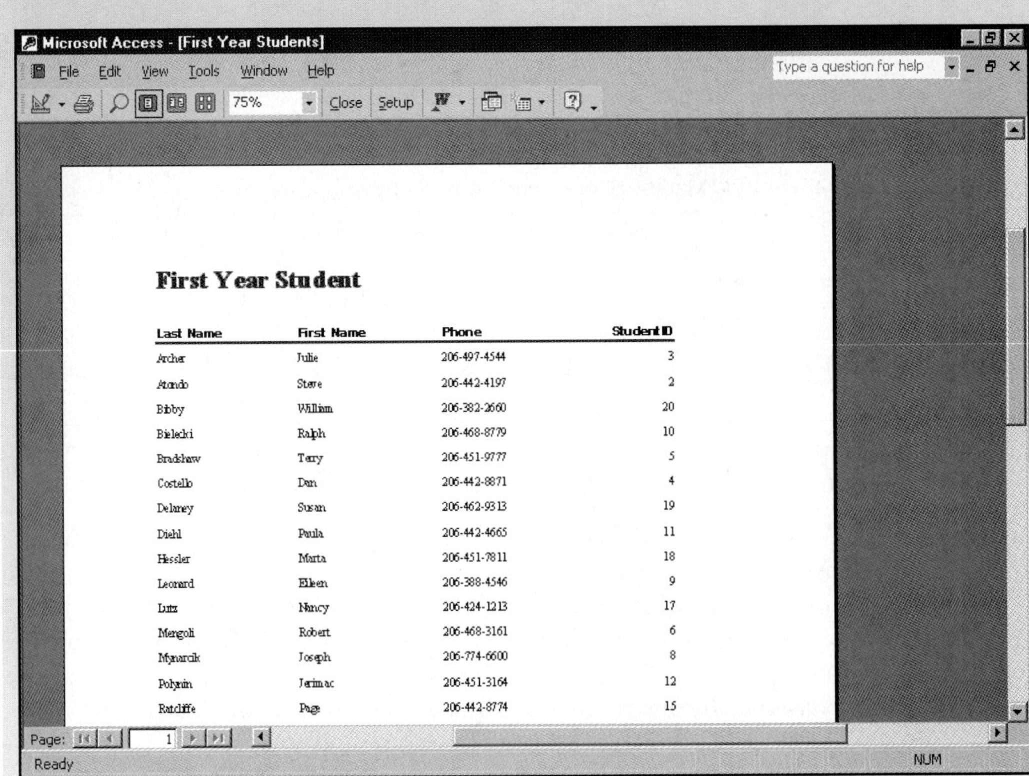

6. To send the "First Year Students" report to Word, do the following:
   CLICK: OfficeLinks arrow (W ▾) (refer to Figure 2.15)
   Your screen should now appear similar to Figure 2.15.

Figure 2.15

OfficeLinks drop-down menu

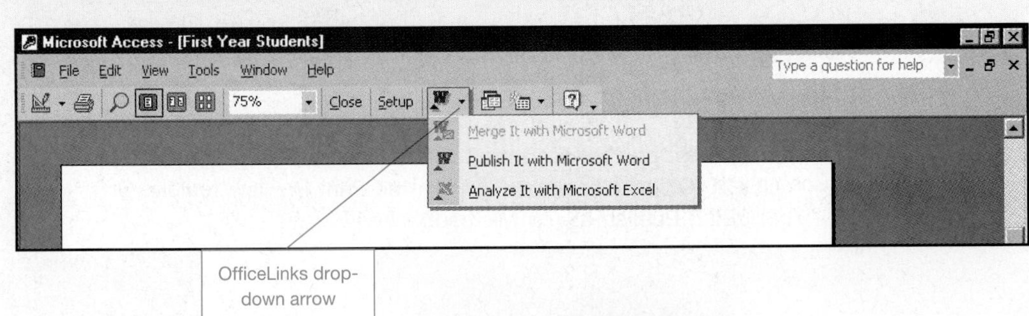

7. CHOOSE: Publish It with Microsoft Word from the drop-down menu
After a few moments, the report will display in Word, looking very much as it did in Access. Note that Word assigned the "First Year Students" filename to the report.

8. A portion of the title at the top of the Word document *may* have been truncated in the conversion to Word. If necessary, edit the title to read "First Year Students" rather than "First Year."

9. To increase the font size of all the columnar data, excluding the column headings:
SELECT: all the data beneath the headings in the Last Name, First Name, Phone, and StudentID columns

10. To enlarge the point size of the selected information:
CHOOSE: 12 from the Font Size drop-down list (10) on the Formatting toolbar

11. Move the insertion point to the top of the document. With your screen zoomed to 100%, the report should appear similar to Figure 2.16.

Figure 2.16

Access report converted to Word

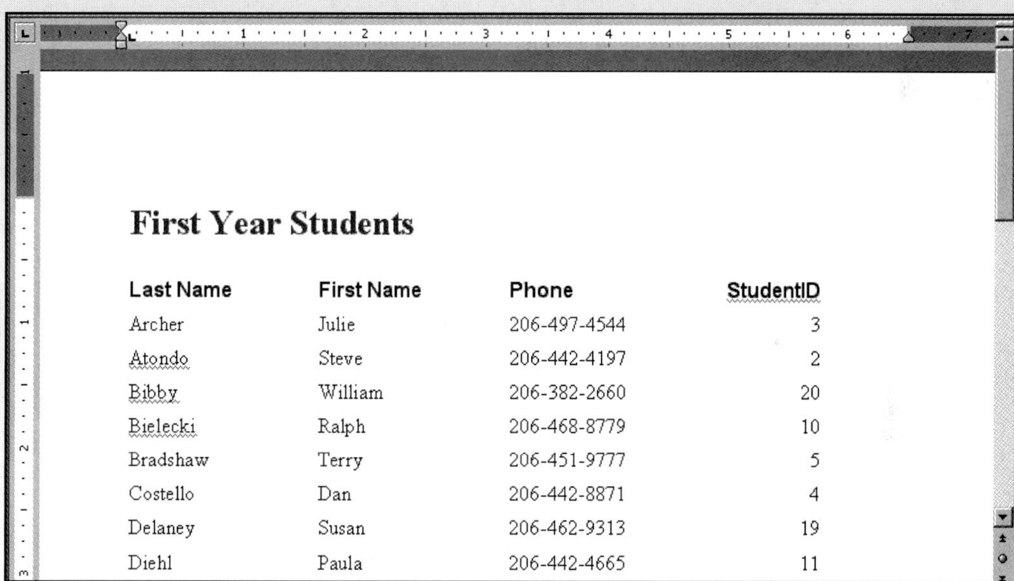

First Year Students

Last Name	First Name	Phone	StudentID
Archer	Julie	206-497-4544	3
Atondo	Steve	206-442-4197	2
Bibby	William	206-382-2660	20
Bielecki	Ralph	206-468-8779	10
Bradshaw	Terry	206-451-9777	5
Costello	Dan	206-442-8871	4
Delaney	Susan	206-462-9313	19
Diehl	Paula	206-442-4665	11

12. Save and then close the "First Year Students" document.

13. Close Word.

14. In Access, the report should be displaying in Print Preview mode. Before proceeding:
CLICK: Close button on the Print Preview toolbar

15. Continue to the next lesson.

In Addition MAIL MERGING IN WORD WITH AN ACCESS DATA SOURCE

One of the most powerful features of word processing software is the ability to combine (merge) names and addresses with a standard document for printing. This process, called *mail merge,* can be a huge time-saver, because it allows you to use a single document in printing personalized letters to many recipients. The merge process requires two files: the "main document" and the "data source." The *main document* contains the standard text, graphics, and other objects that will stay the same from document to document. The *data source* contains the variable (or "changing") data, such as names and addresses, that will be merged into the main document. A data source is essentially a table composed of a *header row, records,* and *fields.*

Access databases work nicely as data sources because their data is stored in columns and rows. Although the process of mail merge may at first sound complicated, you can master it quickly, thanks in large part to the careful prompts of Word's Mail Merge Helper. The *Mail Merge Helper* assists you in your ultimate objective of producing form letters, envelopes, mailing labels, lists, or other types of merge documents.

2.3.2 Exporting a Worksheet List to Access

feature

When a worksheet list becomes too large or complex for Excel to manage efficiently, consider importing it into Access.

method

- CHOOSE: File, Get External Data from the Access menu
- CHOOSE: Import
- Complete the steps in Access's Import Spreadsheet Wizard.

practice

You now practice converting an Excel worksheet list into an Access database. After you have completed the previous lesson, ensure that the IM0230 database is open in Access.

1. Launch Excel and then open the IM0232 worksheet. If necessary, maximize Excel's application window.

2. Save the worksheet as "Counselors" to your personal storage location. Since Access offers more powerful database management features than Excel, let's convert the "Counselors" worksheet into an Access table stored in the IM0230 database. The "Counselors" worksheet appears in Figure 2.17.

Figure 2.17

"Counselors" worksheet

	A	B	C	D	E	F	G
1	Surname	Given	Office	Building	Campus	Phone	
2	Adams	Sammy	D452	ADMIN	Redmond	Ext. 6452	
3	Ali	Rebecca	B121	ARTS	Redmond	Ext. 5121	
4	Allenby	Marylin	D325	ADMIN	Bellevue	Ext. 4325	
5	Benischek	Glenn	E110	ARTS	Bellevue	Ext. 2110	
6	Brett	Gordon	C460	CSCI	Bellevue	Ext. 7460	
7	Christian	Homer	G472	GEOG	Redmond	Ext. 5472	
8	Fanning	Rhonda	D451	ADMIN	Redmond	Ext. 6451	
9	Granz	Larry	B126	ARTS	Redmond	Ext. 5126	
10	Grelson	Ingrid	E120	ARTS	Bellevue	Ext. 2120	
11	Jackson	Ronald	PS90	PYSC	Redmond	Ext. 8090	
12	Jorgenson	Gwenyth	D320	ADMIN	Bellevue	Ext. 4320	
13	Ranz	Torrie	G940	GEOG	Bellevue	Ext. 2940	
14	Williams	Richard	C450	CSCI	Bellevue	Ext. 7450	
15	Yip	Jake	D330	ADMIN	Bellevue	Ext. 4330	
16	Zimmerman	Alan	E190	ARTS	Redmond	Ext. 5190	
17							

3. To bring the Excel worksheet into the Access database, you must first close the Excel worksheet. You will then use an Access command to import the external Excel data into Access. In Excel:
CHOOSE: File, Close to close the "Counselors" worksheet

4. Switch to Access using the Windows taskbar.

5. To bring the "Counselors" worksheet into the IM0230 database, do the following:
CHOOSE: File, Get External Data from the Access menu
CHOOSE: Import

6. Using the Import dialog box, navigate to your personal storage location and then do the following:
SELECT: Microsoft Excel from the *Files of type* drop-down list

7. DOUBLE-CLICK: "Counselors" worksheet file
The Import Spreadsheet Wizard dialog box should appear (Figure 2.18).

Figure 2.18

Import Spreadsheet Wizard dialog box

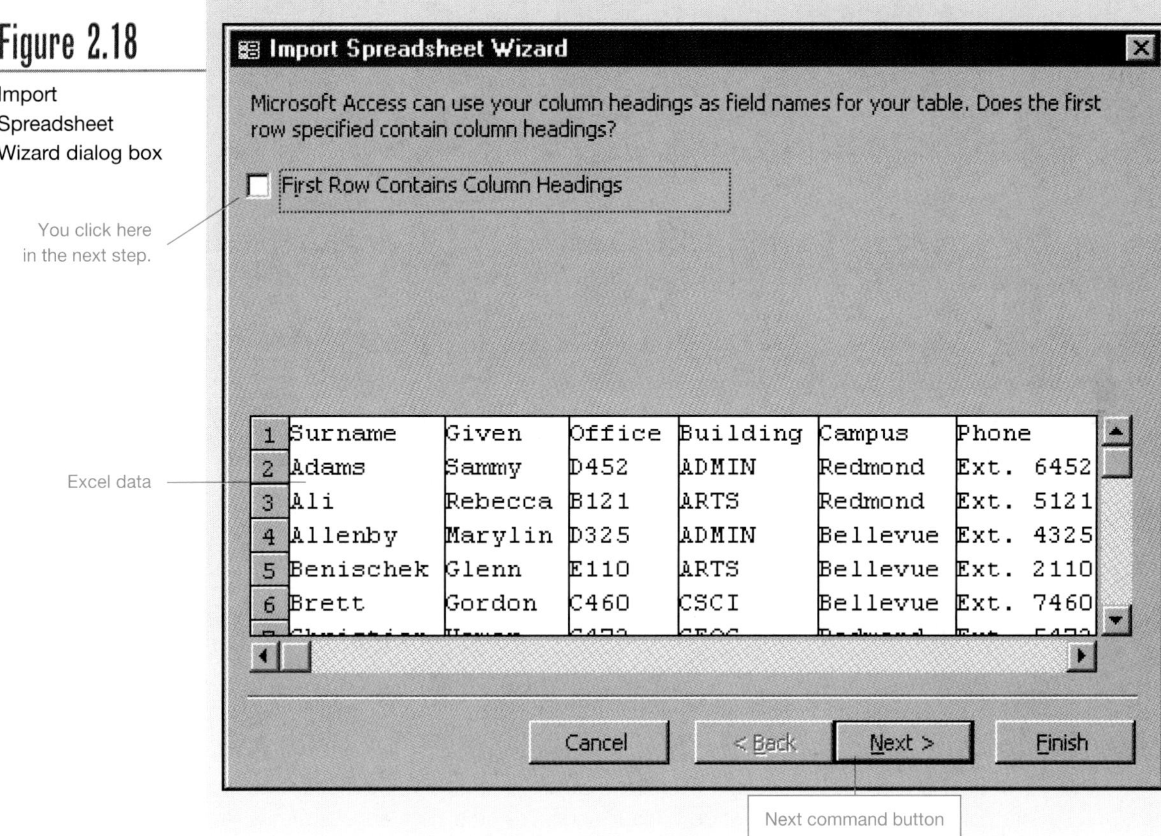

8. SELECT: *First Row Contains Column Headings* check box
Note that the headings now appear differently at the top of each column in the dialog box.

9. CLICK: Next command button

10. In this dialog box, you specify where to store your data. Do the following:
SELECT: *In a New Table* option button (the default selection)
CLICK: Next command button
You can now select which columns to import (Figure 2.19). By default, all columns will be imported into the Access database.

Integrating

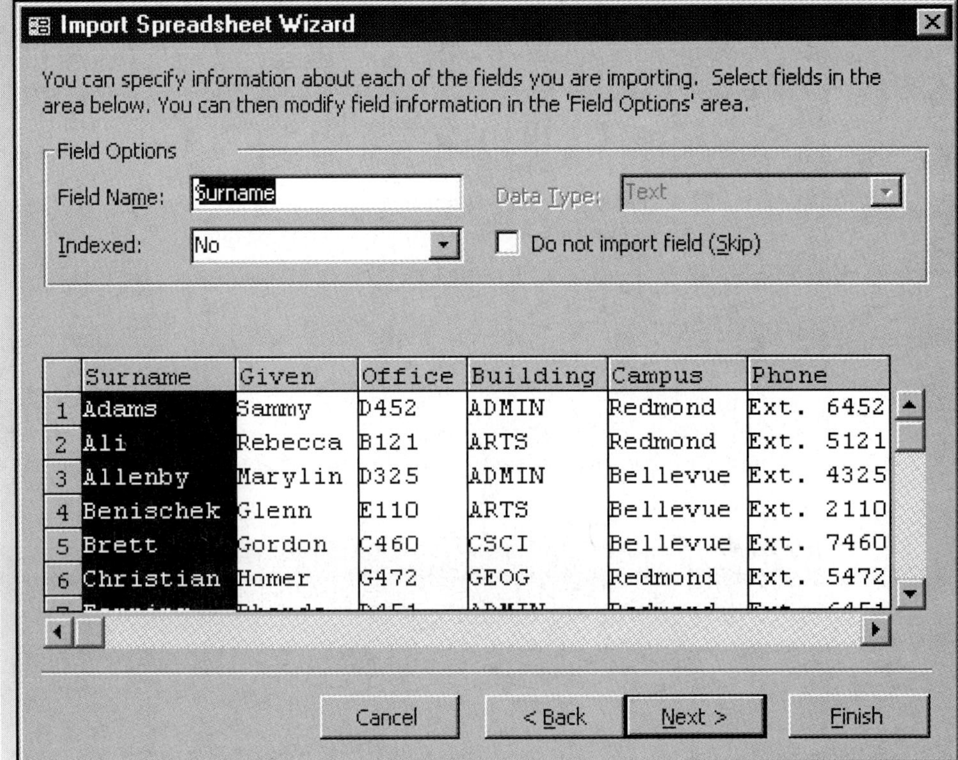

Figure 2.19

Import Spreadsheet Wizard dialog box

11. For our purposes, you will import all the data:
    CLICK: Next command button
12. To improve performance and data reliability, you can have Access create a primary key for your new table. Recall that a primary key is the field that will be used to uniquely identify and organize your records. To do so:
    SELECT: *Let Access add primary key* option button (the default selection)
    CLICK: Next command button
13. In this step, you name the table. To replace the current name, which is already selected:
    TYPE: **Counselors**
    CLICK: Finish command button
14. A dialog box will appear after the importing process has completed.
    CLICK: OK command button
15. When you are returned to the Database window, open the Counselors table by double-clicking its name in the Database window. Your screen should now appear similar to Figure 2.20.

Figure 2.20

An Excel worksheet converted to an Access table

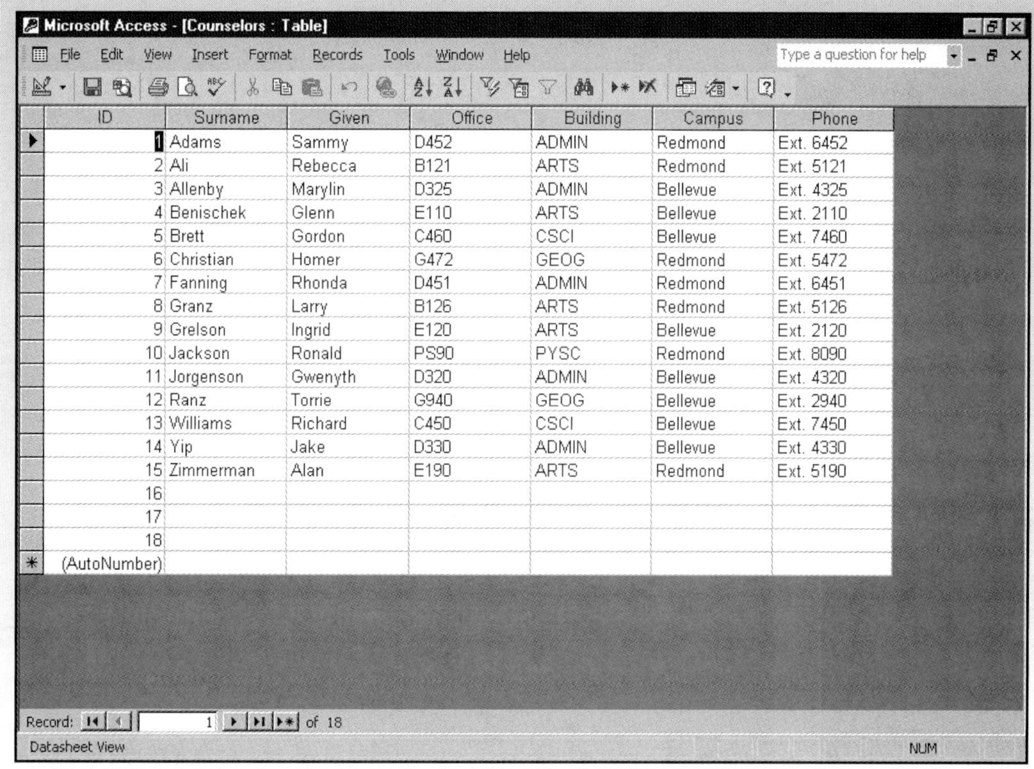

Microsoft Access - [Counselors : Table]

ID	Surname	Given	Office	Building	Campus	Phone
1	Adams	Sammy	D452	ADMIN	Redmond	Ext. 6452
2	Ali	Rebecca	B121	ARTS	Redmond	Ext. 5121
3	Allenby	Marylin	D325	ADMIN	Bellevue	Ext. 4325
4	Benischek	Glenn	E110	ARTS	Bellevue	Ext. 2110
5	Brett	Gordon	C460	CSCI	Bellevue	Ext. 7460
6	Christian	Homer	G472	GEOG	Redmond	Ext. 5472
7	Fanning	Rhonda	D451	ADMIN	Redmond	Ext. 6451
8	Granz	Larry	B126	ARTS	Redmond	Ext. 5126
9	Grelson	Ingrid	E120	ARTS	Bellevue	Ext. 2120
10	Jackson	Ronald	PS90	PYSC	Redmond	Ext. 8090
11	Jorgenson	Gwenyth	D320	ADMIN	Bellevue	Ext. 4320
12	Ranz	Torrie	G940	GEOG	Bellevue	Ext. 2940
13	Williams	Richard	C450	CSCI	Bellevue	Ext. 7450
14	Yip	Jake	D330	ADMIN	Bellevue	Ext. 4330
15	Zimmerman	Alan	E190	ARTS	Redmond	Ext. 5190
16						
17						
18						
(AutoNumber)						

Record: 1 of 18

Datasheet View NUM

16. Close Access and Excel.

2.3. When might you want to export a report created in Access to Word?

Chapter summary

PowerPoint integrates nicely with Word and Excel. Word outlines provide a good starting point for PowerPoint presentations. Also, using the techniques of linking and embedding, you can copy PowerPoint slides into Word and copy Excel charts into PowerPoint. Access also integrates well with Word and Excel. You can export an Access report to Word for final polishing, and also import Excel worksheets into Access.

Command Summary

Many of the commands and procedures appearing in this chapter are summarized in the following table.

Skill Set	To Perform This Task	Do the Following
Converting a Word Outline to a PowerPoint Presentation	Switch to Outline view in Word	CHOOSE: View, Outline, or CLICK: Outline View button
	Create an outline in Word's Outline view	PRESS: ENTER to insert a new heading at the same level, or CLICK: Demote button to begin typing at a demoted (lower) level, or CLICK: Promote button to begin typing at a promoted (higher) level
	Send a Word outline to PowerPoint	CHOOSE: File, Send To, Microsoft PowerPoint from Word's Menu bar
Integrating PowerPoint with Word and Excel	Copy a slide to Word	SELECT: a slide in PowerPoint's Outline pane CLICK: Copy button and then switch to the destination location in Word CHOOSE: Edit, Paste Special from Word's Menu bar SELECT: a data type in the *As* list box SELECT: *Paste* or *Paste Link* option button CLICK: OK command button
	Copy an Excel chart to PowerPoint	SELECT: a chart in Excel CLICK: Copy button and then switch to the destination slide in PowerPoint CHOOSE: Edit, Paste Special from Word's Menu bar SELECT: a data type in the *As* list box SELECT: *Paste* or *Paste Link* option button CLICK: OK command button
Integrating Access with Word and Excel	Export an Access report to Word	DOUBLE-CLICK: the Access report in Access's Database window to preview the report CLICK: OfficeLinks arrow on the Print Preview toolbar SELECT: Publish It with Microsoft Word
	Importing an Excel worksheet into Access	CHOOSE: File, Get External Data from the Access menu CHOOSE: Import and then complete the steps in Access's Import Spreadsheet Wizard

Chapter quiz

Short Answer

1. How must a Word document be formatted for successful conversion to PowerPoint?
2. What advantages does Word's Outline view provide?
3. How do you select a group of consecutive slides in PowerPoint's Outline pane?
4. What is the procedure for exporting an Access report to Word?
5. When might you want to import an Excel list into Access?
6. When might you want to copy a PowerPoint slide to Word?
7. What is the procedure for editing a chart that you've embedded in a PowerPoint slide?
8. After exporting an Access report to Word, what data format is used for the report in Word?
9. What command enables you to paste an Excel worksheet into Word as a Microsoft Excel Worksheet Object?
10. What command in Excel enables you to copy a chart object to the Clipboard?

True/False

1. ____ You may embed only entire PowerPoint presentations in Word, not individual slides.
2. ____ To copy a worksheet range to the Clipboard, use the Edit, Paste Special command.
3. ____ When importing an Excel list into Access, you cannot specify a primary key.
4. ____ In Word's Outline view, you can promote or demote a heading with the click of a button.
5. ____ After converting a Word outline to PowerPoint, you may apply a design template.
6. ____ It is possible to move and resize an Excel chart that you have inserted in a PowerPoint slide.
7. ____ In Word, it is possible to "collapse" a document's outline so that just the main headings appear.
8. ____ In Outline view, Word automatically applies its own heading styles to the different levels in the outline.
9. ____ To link a PowerPoint slide to a Word document, choose Edit, Paste Special.
10. ____ No matter whether you are copying an Excel chart to PowerPoint or to Word, the procedure is basically the same.

Multiple Choice

1. To convert a Word outline to a PowerPoint presentation, choose:
   a. File, Send To, PowerPoint from the Word Menu bar
   b. Insert, Object, PowerPoint from the Word Menu bar
   c. Edit, Paste Special, PowerPoint slide presentation
   d. none of the above

2. For PowerPoint to easily convert a Word outline into representative slides, the Word document must be formatted using ____________.
   a. macros
   b. OLE objects
   c. fonts
   d. styles

3. To select a slide in PowerPoint to copy to Word, you must ____________ in PowerPoint.
   a. click the slide's icon in the Outline pane
   b. double-click the slide's icon in the Outline pane
   c. display the slide in Slide Show view
   d. none of the above

4. When you place an Excel worksheet range into a PowerPoint slide:
   a. the workbook is the destination document
   b. the presentation is the destination document
   c. the presentation is the source document
   d. none of the above

5. When importing Excel data into Access, you must first ____________.
   a. close the worksheet in Excel
   b. open the worksheet in Excel
   c. display a blank worksheet in Excel
   d. none of the above

6. To import an Excel worksheet into Access, you should choose:
   a. File, Search
   b. File, Get External Data
   c. View, External Data
   d. none of the above

7. To create an outline in Word, you must choose:
   a. File, Send To, Outline
   b. File, New, Outline
   c. View, Outline
   d. b. or c.

8. To embed an existing Excel chart in a PowerPoint presentation, you should choose:
   a. Edit, Paste Special
   b. View, Slide Sorter
   c. View, Outline
   d. Insert, Object

9. To export an Access report to Word:
   a. CHOOSE: File, Send To, Microsoft Word
   b. CHOOSE: Data, Publish It with Microsoft Word
   c. CLICK: OfficeLinks drop-down arrow CHOOSE: Publish It with Microsoft Word
   d. all of the above

10. When importing an Excel list into Access, you are able to:
    a. select which columns to import
    b. name the imported table
    c. specify a primary key for the imported table
    d. all of the above

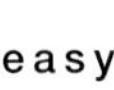

Hands-On exercises

easy

1. Sweet Dreams: Sending a Word Outline to PowerPoint

Hudson is feeling confident with newly attained Office integration skills. In this exercise, assume the role of Hudson to create a Word outline similar to Figure 2.21 and then convert the outline to a PowerPoint presentation.

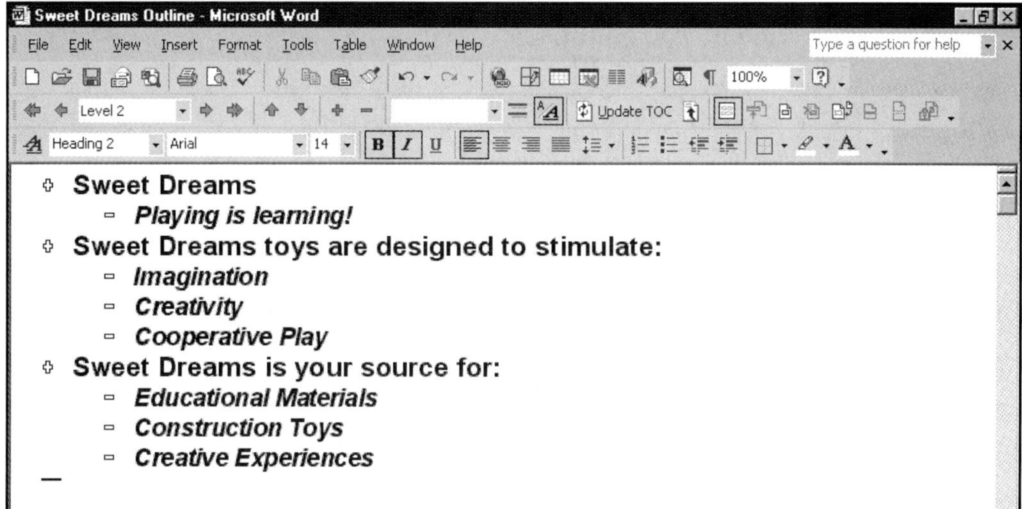

Figure 2.21

"Sweet Dreams Outline" document in Outline view

1. Start Word. A new document should be displaying.
2. To switch to Outline view:
   CHOOSE: View, Outline
3. To begin typing your outline:
   TYPE: **Sweet Dreams**
   PRESS: ENTER to insert another heading
4. To type at a demoted level:
   CLICK: Demote button (➡) on the Outlining toolbar
   TYPE: **Playing is learning!**
   PRESS: ENTER to insert another heading
5. To type at a promoted level:
   CLICK: Promote button (⬅) on the Outlining toolbar
   TYPE: **Sweet Dreams toys are designed to stimulate:**
   PRESS: ENTER to insert another heading

6. To enter some items at a demoted level:
   CLICK: Demote button (➡) on the Outlining toolbar
   TYPE: **Imagination**
   PRESS: ENTER to insert another heading
   TYPE: **Creativity**
   PRESS: ENTER to insert another heading
   TYPE: **Cooperative Play**
   PRESS: ENTER to insert another heading
7. To type text at a promoted level:
   CLICK: Promote button (⬅) on the Outlining toolbar
   TYPE: **Sweet Dreams is your source for:**
   PRESS: ENTER to insert another heading
8. To enter some items at a demoted level:
   CLICK: Demote button (➡) on the Outlining toolbar
   TYPE: **Educational Materials**
   PRESS: ENTER to insert another heading
   TYPE: **Construction Toys**
   PRESS: ENTER to insert another heading
   TYPE: **Creative Experiences**
9. Save the outline as "Sweet Dreams Outline" to your personal storage location.
10. To convert the Word outline to a PowerPoint presentation:
    CHOOSE: File, Send To, Microsoft PowerPoint
    The Word outline should now be displaying in PowerPoint.
11. Now change the layout of the first slide from the Title and Text layout to the Title Slide layout. To do this:
    CHOOSE: Format, Slide Layout
    CLICK: Title Slide layout in the Slide Layout task pane
12. Then apply one of PowerPoint's design templates to the presentation.
    CHOOSE: Format, Slide Design
    CLICK: "Crayons" thumbnail in the Slide Design task pane
    The presentation's title slide should now appear similar to Figure 2.22.

Figure 2.22

PowerPoint presentation created from a Word outline

13. Save the PowerPoint presentation as "Sweet Dreams Presentation" to your personal storage location.
14. Exit both PowerPoint and Word.

easy 

2. Outback Exports: Embedding a PowerPoint Slide in Word

Richard Brackton, the chairman of Outback Exports, is busy preparing documents for an upcoming meeting. In this exercise, assume the role of Richard and copy and embed a PowerPoint slide in a Word document.

1. Start Word. A new document should be displaying.
2. Start PowerPoint and then open the IM02HE02 presentation.
3. Save a copy of the presentation as "Coal Presentation" to your personal storage location.
4. In the Outline pane:
   CLICK: the second slide's icon to select it
   The second slide should appear selected in the Outline pane (Figure 2.23).

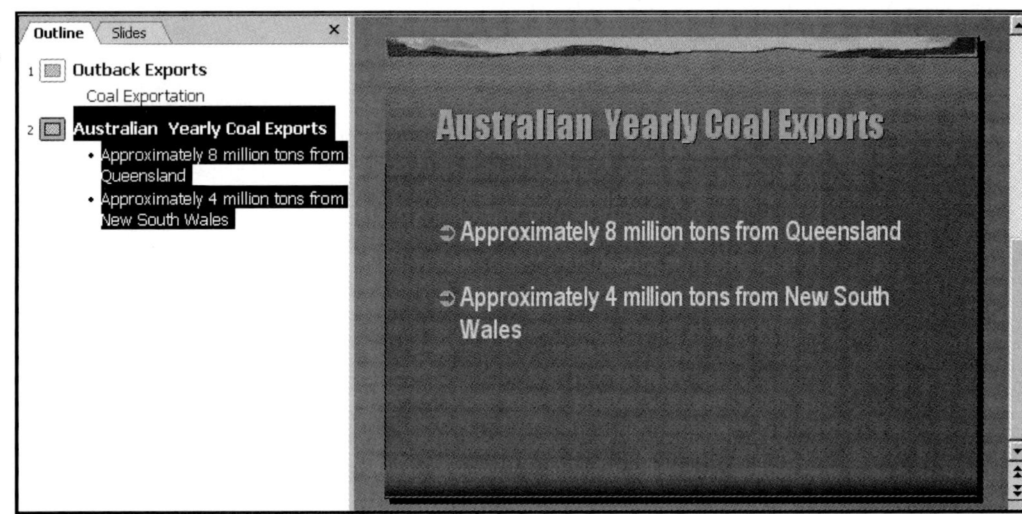

Figure 2.23
"Coal Presentation" presentation

5. To copy the second slide to the Clipboard:
   CLICK: Copy button ( ) on Standard toolbar
6. To switch to Word:
   CLICK: Word button on the Windows taskbar
7. To embed the slide in the Word document:
   CHOOSE: Edit, Paste Special
8. SELECT: "Microsoft PowerPoint Slide Object" in the *As* list box
   CLICK: OK command button
   The slide is embedded in the document.
9. To try editing the embedded slide:
   DOUBLE-CLICK: the slide object
   Note how Word's toolbars have been replaced by PowerPoint's.
10. Change "8" to "10" in the first bulleted item.

11. Click outside the embedded slide to return to Word.
12. Save the Word document as "Coal Slide" and then print it.
13. Exit Word and PowerPoint.

moderate 

3. Bud's Parlor of Flavors: Exporting an Access Report to Word

Bud Simpson, the owner of Bud's Parlor of Flavors, would rather be sitting down to enjoy a hot fudge sundae right now, but unfortunately he has work to do. In this exercise, assume the role of Bud and export an Access report to Word. Once the report has been converted to Word, you will change its formatting.

1. Start Access and open the IM02HE03 database.
2. Click the Reports button in the Objects bar and double-click "Restaurant Report" in the list area to preview it.
3. View the report, adjusting the zoom size if necessary. The report appears in Figure 2.24.

Figure 2.24

Access report

Restaurant Report

Name	*Address*	*City*	*State*	*ID*
Joseph's Added Touch	44 Joseph Street	Carson City	Nevada	1
Town and Country Delights	Box 340	Flagstaff	Arizona	2
The Greek House	745 Windsor Way	Salt Lake City	Utah	3
Christophers by the Bay	Box 45	Eureka	California	4
Santa Fe Inn	19 Main Street	Santa Fe	NewMexico	5
White Mountain Inn	9 Glacier Way	Boulder	Colorado	6
Cumberland Inn	45 Cumberland Way	NewOrleans	Louisiana	7
Asiagos Italian Restaurant	Box 3386	Rapid City	South Dakota	8

4. Send the Access report to Word using the OfficeLinks drop-down arrow.
5. The Access report should open in Word.
6. Increase the font size of the column headings to 16 point and remove the italic formatting.
7. Select the data beneath the headings and increase the font size to 10 point. The modified report appears in Figure 2.25.

Figure 2.25

Access report in Word

Restaurant Report

Name	Address	City	State	ID
Joseph's Added Touch	44 Joseph Street	Carson City	Nevada	1
Town and Country Delights	Box 340	Flagstaff	Arizona	2
The Greek House	745 Windsor Way	Salt Lake City	Utah	3
Christophers by the Bay	Box 45	Eureka	California	4
Santa Fe Inn	19 Main Street	Santa Fe	New Mexico	5
White Mountain Inn	9 Glacier Way	Boulder	Colorado	6
Cumberland Inn	45 Cumberland Way	New Orleans	Louisiana	7
Asiagos Italian Restaurant	Box 3386	Rapid City	South Dakota	8

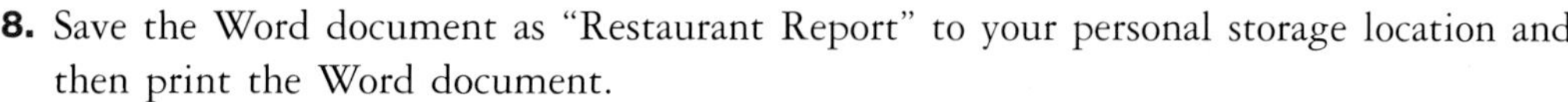

8. Save the Word document as "Restaurant Report" to your personal storage location and then print the Word document.

9. Close Word and Access.

moderate

4. The Software Edge: Importing Excel Data to Access

Mary, a Software Edge employee, is preparing for an upcoming meeting. In this exercise, assume the role of Mary and transfer an Excel worksheet list to a new Access database. Then, print the resulting table.

1. Start Excel and open the IM02HE04 worksheet.
2. Save the worksheet as "Development Teams" to your personal storage location. The worksheet appears in Figure 2.26.

Figure 2.26

"Development Teams" worksheet

	A	B	C	D	E
1	Software	Captain	Due Date	Production Date	Team Members
2	Games	D. Miller	3-Feb	29-Mar	7
3	Financial	G. Barnes	17-Jan	3-Mar	4
4	Simulation	J. Mendez	16-Apr	15-May	12
5	Translation	P.G. Smith	28-Jun	5-Aug	24
6	CAD	R. Swarez	19-Sep	7-Oct	6
7	Scientific	B. Rio	30-Mar	30-Apr	9
8	Voice Recognition	T. Golanski	22-Nov	5-Dec	19
9					

3. Close the "Development Teams" worksheet and then close Excel.
4. Start Access and create a blank database named "Software Edge."
5. Import the "Development Teams" worksheet into Access. (*Note:* In the Import dialog box, you *may* have to choose "Microsoft Excel" from the *Files of type* drop-down list.) The Import Spreadsheet Wizard should display (Figure 2.27).

Figure 2.27

Importing the "Development Teams" worksheet

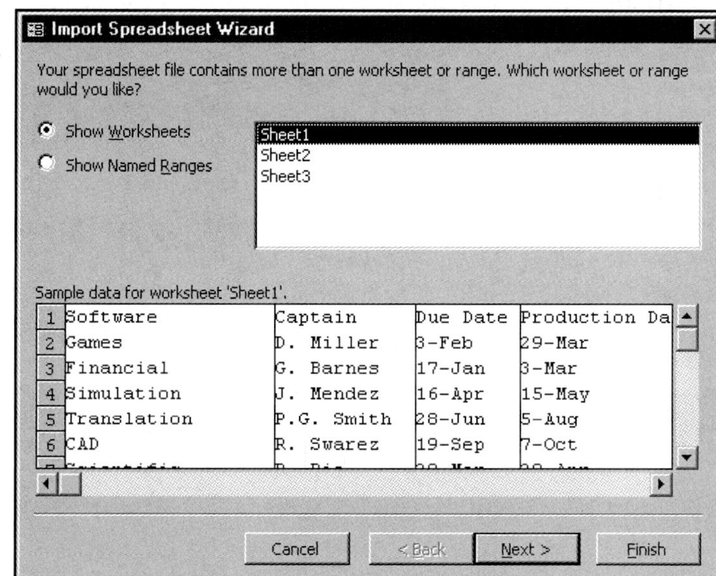

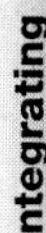

6. To accept the wizard's default assumptions:
   CLICK: Finish command button
   CLICK: OK command button

7. The table should be selected in the Access dialog box. To rename the table, do the following:
   RIGHT-CLICK: the "Sheet1" table
   CHOOSE: Rename from the right-click menu
   TYPE: **Development**
   PRESS: ENTER

8. Open the Development table in Datasheet view and then print the table.

9. Close Access.

5. On Your Own: Embedding an Entire Presentation in Word

In this exercise, you embed an entire PowerPoint presentation on the topic of Web-based training in a Word document. First, start Word. Then, start PowerPoint and open the IM02HE05 file. Save this presentation as "Web Training" to your personal storage location. In the Outline pane, select the presentation's three slides. (*Hint:* Press and hold down the SHIFT key while clicking slide 1 and then slide 3.) Your screen should appear similar to Figure 2.28.

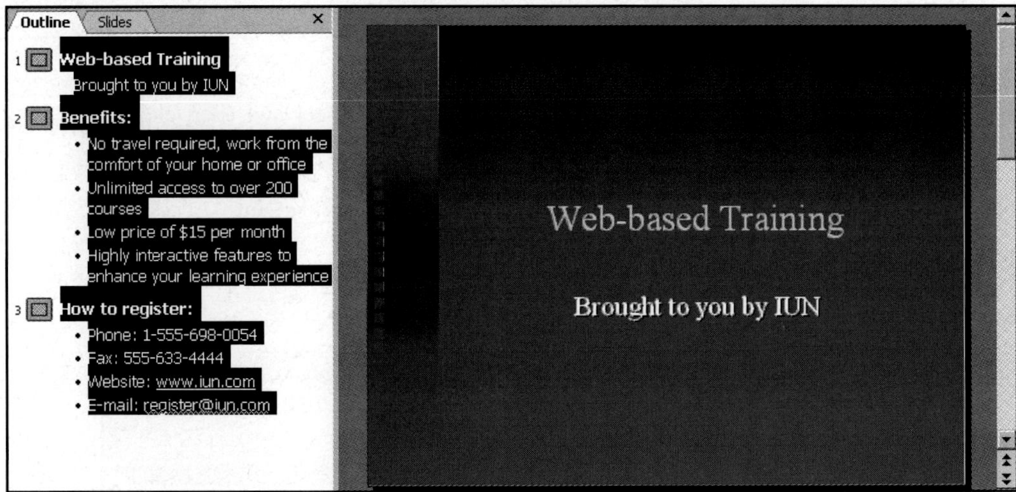

Figure 2.28

"Web Training" presentation

Copy the selected slides to the Clipboard and then switch to Word. In the Paste Special dialog box, select "Microsoft PowerPoint Presentation Object" in the *As* list box and the *Display as icon* check box. Once embedded, you can double-click the slide icon (Figure 2.29) to view the entire slide show while in Word. Save the Word document as "Web Presentation" to your personal storage location. Exit Word and PowerPoint.

Figure 2.29

PowerPoint icon embedded in Word

difficult

6. On Your Own: Embellishing an Access Report in Word

Ed, founder of Ed's Exotic Animal Emporium, has asked you to assist him in exporting an Access report to Word. Open the IM02HE06 Access database and preview the report entitled "Animal Report." This report appears in Figure 2.30.

Figure 2.30

Access report

Animal Report

ID1	Animal	Name	DOB	Gender	Offspring
1	Llama	Lizzie	2/16/1996	Female	4
2	Llama	Larry	9/23/1997	Male	
3	Llama	Melodie	0/31/1998	Female	
4	Llama	Marvin	0/31/1998	Male	
5	Alpaca	Alvin	12/5/1995	Male	
6	Alpaca	Annette	3/13/1997	Female	3
7	Yak	Yvonne	6/6/1994	Female	1
8	Yak	Ivan	2/28/1993	Male	
9	Ostrich	Olivia	6/6/1997	Female	15
10	Ostrich	Oliver	1/1/1997	Male	
11	Porcupine	Peter	4/15/1998	Male	
12	Porcupine	Paula	5/30/1998	Female	5

Send the report to Word and save the file as "Animal Report" to your personal storage location. Add the title "Ed's Inventory Report" to the top of the document. Increase the point size of the title to 22 point and then change the formatting of the rest of the document, particularly the headings and data, to your preferences. Save and print the Word document. Close Word and Access.

Case Problems

Del's Delicious Cookies

Now that Del has completed Chapter 2, he is ready to begin integrating data among Word, Excel, PowerPoint, and Access. He is confident that his new understanding about integrating Office applications will assist him in creating a new presentation, a formatted report, and an inventory list. In the following case problems, assume the role of Del and perform the same steps that he identifies. You may want to re-read the chapter opening before proceeding.

1. Del must prepare a presentation for an upcoming trade show. Rather than retyping the information, he decides to convert an existing Word outline into a PowerPoint presentation. Del opens the Word IM02CS01 file and saves it as "Cookies" to his personal storage location.

   While in Outline View, Del decides to demote the second heading entitled "We're more than good taste." After converting the outline to PowerPoint, he applies the Title Slide layout to the first slide. Next, he applies the "Edge" design template (or another appropriate design) to the presentation. After viewing the presentation, he saves it as "Delicious Cookies" to his personal storage location. He saves and then closes the Word document, but leaves the PowerPoint presentation open for the next step.

2. Del would like to insert an Excel chart on the final slide of the "Delicious Cookies" presentation. He inserts a new slide at the end of the presentation and applies the Title Only layout. He then types **Del's Ingredients** in the Title placeholder.

   Del proceeds by retrieving a previously created Excel chart. He starts Excel, opens the IM02CS02 workbook, and then saves it as "Ingredients" to his personal storage location. Next, he copies the Excel chart to the Clipboard and then switches to the final slide of the PowerPoint presentation. After Del embeds the chart object on the slide, he moves and resizes the object so that the slide looks like Figure 2.31.

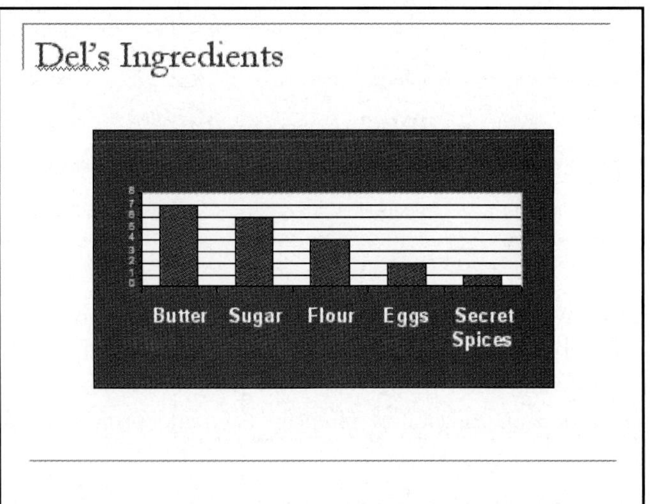

Figure 2.31

Embedded Excel chart in PowerPoint

   Del saves the revised presentation as "Delicious Cookies-Revised" to his personal storage location. He then closes both PowerPoint and Excel.

3. Del has created a report in Access; however, he is not pleased with the formatting. He decides to convert the report to Word and then make the necessary changes. Del starts Access and opens the IM02CS03 database. He previews the "Machine Ingredients" report and then publishes it in Microsoft Word.

   Once the Access report has been converted to Word, Del increases the size of the "Machine Ingredients" heading to a 22-point, Times New Roman font. He adds italic formatting to the column headings and then changes the data under the headings to a 12-point, Times New Roman font. As a final step, Del deletes the stray "6" from the bottom of the report. The completed report appears in Figure 2.32.

Figure 2.32

Access report in Word

Machine Ingredients

ID	Ingredient	Machine 1	Machine 2	Machine 3	Machine 4
1	Butter	9815	6200	4000	3200
2	Sugar	6000	3000	3750	1900
3	Flour	4000	1500	3000	1200
4	Eggs	1000	750	1000	100
5	Secret Spices	250	150	500	75

Pleased with the report's appearance, Del saves the report as "Machine Ingredients" and prints it. He then closes Word and Access.

4. Del has started a list in Excel, but now realizes it would be more usable in Access. He opens the IM02CS04 workbook and saves it as "Bowl Inventory" to his personal storage location. The worksheet appears in Figure 2.33. Del then closes Excel.

Figure 2.33

"Bowl Inventory" worksheet

	A	B	C	D
1	Del's Delicious Cookies			
2				
3	Machinery Overview			
4				
5	Mixers	Technician	Serial #	Capacity
6	Unibowl 1	P. Brett	765409	2,500
7	Unibowl 2	Z. Smedley	765825	2,500
8	Unibowl 3	P. Brett	766327	3,500
9	Aging Bowl 1	P. Brett	385	3,000
10	Aging Bowl 2	Z. Smedley	391	3,000
11	Aging Bowl 3	Z. Smedley	392	3,000
12	Aging Bowl 4	P. Brett	393	3,000
13	Aging Bowl 5	P. Brett	394	3,000
14	Aging Tank 6	Z. Smedley	395	3,000
15				
16				
17				
18				

Next, Del starts Access and creates a blank database named "Delicious Cookies." He imports the "Bowl Inventory" worksheet into Access. (*Note:* In the Import dialog box, you may have to choose "Microsoft Excel" from the *Files of type* drop-down list.) The Import Spreadsheet Wizard should display (see Figure 2.27, shown earlier). To accept the wizard's default assumptions, Del clicks the Finish command button and then the OK command button.

He renames the new table by right-clicking its name in the database window and choosing Rename. He types in the name **Bowl Inventory** and then presses ENTER. As a final step, he displays the table in Datasheet view (Figure 2.34).

Figure 2.34

"Bowl Inventory" Access table

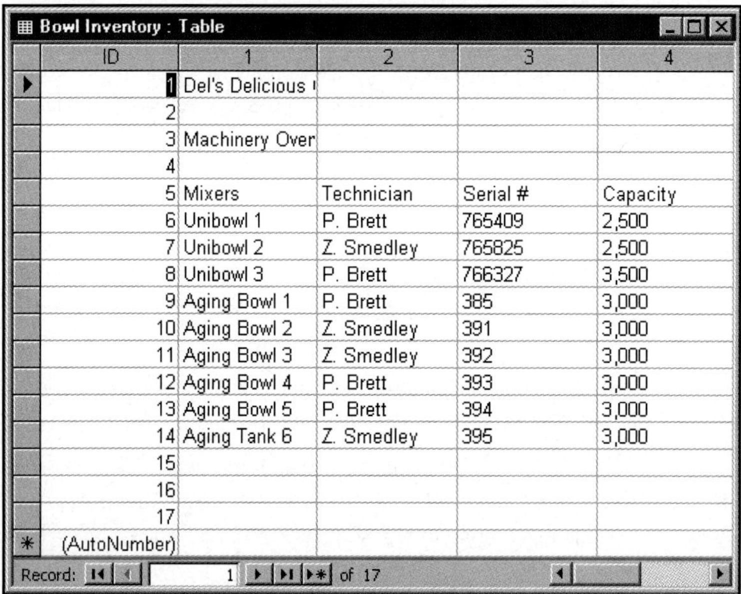

Bowl Inventory : Table

ID	1	2	3	4
1	Del's Delicious			
2				
3	Machinery Over			
4				
5	Mixers	Technician	Serial #	Capacity
6	Unibowl 1	P. Brett	765409	2,500
7	Unibowl 2	Z. Smedley	765825	2,500
8	Unibowl 3	P. Brett	766327	3,500
9	Aging Bowl 1	P. Brett	385	3,000
10	Aging Bowl 2	Z. Smedley	391	3,000
11	Aging Bowl 3	Z. Smedley	392	3,000
12	Aging Bowl 4	P. Brett	393	3,000
13	Aging Bowl 5	P. Brett	394	3,000
14	Aging Tank 6	Z. Smedley	395	3,000
15				
16				
17				
(AutoNumber)				

Record: 1 of 17

As a final step, Del prints a copy of the Access table and then closes Access. Time to enjoy cookies and coffee!

Integrating & Extending Microsoft® Office® XP

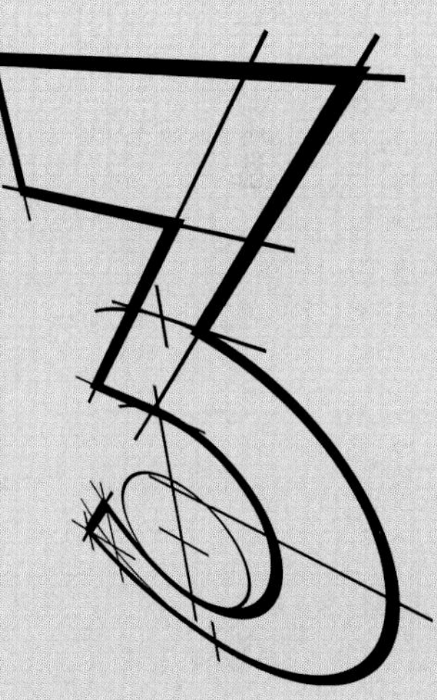

CHAPTER 3

Extending Microsoft Office to the Web

CHAPTER OUTLINE

Case Study

3.1 Using Hyperlinks

3.2 Saving Existing Documents to HTML

3.3 Preparing Web Pages Using Office

Chapter Summary

Chapter Quiz

Hands-On Exercises

Case Problems

PREREQUISITES

This chapter assumes you know how to create, save, edit, and print Word documents, Excel worksheets, and PowerPoint presentations. You should also know how to view and print table data in Access.

LEARNING OBJECTIVES

After completing this chapter, you will be able to:

- Insert hyperlinks in Office documents and browse with the Web toolbar
- Create HTML files of existing documents, worksheets, presentations, and databases
- Apply a Web theme and create a frames page in Word
- Create an interactive worksheet page and customize a presentation

CaseStudy MANFRED'S GARDEN CENTER Manfred Schickering is the owner of Manfred's Garden Center, a gardening supply store with franchises in Texas and Oklahoma. Unfortunately, Manfred has been slow to acknowledge the existence of the Internet and the World Wide Web. Finally realizing the Internet's exciting marketing potential, he has asked Cynthia, his marketing director, to create a business presence for Manfred's Garden Center on the Web. Although Cynthia is comfortable using Internet search tools, she has never created Web pages.

In this chapter, you and Cynthia learn how to insert hyperlinks in Office documents, and browse with the Web toolbar. You will also save existing Office documents to HTML and apply special formatting to them.

3.1 Using Hyperlinks

The Internet, which is often referred to as the "mother of all networks," consists of thousands of smaller networks that link computers at academic, scientific, and commercial institutions around the world. The World Wide Web provides a visual interface for the Internet and lets you search for information by simply clicking on highlighted words and images, known as *hyperlinks.* Many features of the Web have been incorporated into Microsoft Office, including the ability to insert hyperlinks in your Office documents and create Web pages. The focus of this module is on inserting hyperlinks to other Office documents, locations on the Internet, and e-mail addresses.

3.1.1 Inserting Hyperlinks in Office Documents

feature

In an Office document, to insert a hyperlink to a Web page or e-mail address, simply type the address and then press the Space Bar or ENTER key. (*Note:* The address of a Web page is frequently called a *URL,* for uniform resource locator.) For example, when you type **www.microsoft.com** into a document and then press ENTER, Word will automatically format it as a hyperlink. If you click the link, your Web browser software will open, and Microsoft's Home page will display. To insert a hyperlink to an existing Office file, you must use the Insert Hyperlink button ( ). Once the hyperlink is inserted, you can easily edit it to meet your particular needs.

method

To enter a hyperlink:

- TYPE: a valid URL or e-mail address and press the Space Bar or ENTER key

To insert a hyperlink to an existing file:

- CLICK: Insert Hyperlink button ( ) and then browse to the file using the *Look in* drop-down list
- DOUBLE-CLICK: filename
- CLICK: OK command button

To edit a hyperlink:

- RIGHT-CLICK: hyperlink
- CHOOSE: Hyperlink, Edit Hyperlink

practice

You will now practice inserting and editing hyperlinks in a Word document. Ensure that Microsoft Office is installed on your computer and that no applications are currently open.

1. Start Word. A new document should be displaying.
2. Type in a URL to the Advantage Series Web site.
TYPE: **www.advantageseries.com**
PRESS: ENTER twice
By default, Word formats hyperlinks using the Times New Roman font and the underline and blue attributes. Your hyperlink should appear similar to Figure 3.1.

Figure 3.1

Inserted hyperlink

www.advantageseries.com

3. Point with the mouse to the inserted hyperlink. Note that a description of the hyperlink, called a *ScreenTip,* appears above the pointer (Figure 3.2). As the ScreenTip indicates, to follow or travel the link, you must press and hold down the CTRL key and then click the link.

Figure 3.2

Pointing with the mouse to the hyperlink

4. You can turn off automatic hyperlink formatting using the AutoCorrect Options button, which appears labeled in Figure 3.2. To illustrate, point to the hollow underline appearing beneath the "w" of "www." The AutoCorrect Options button ( ) should appear.
5. CLICK: AutoCorrect Options button ( )
The menu in Figure 3.3 should now appear. Using this menu, you can undo the formatting applied to the current hyperlink or stop Word from creating hyperlinks altogether.

Figure 3.3

AutoCorrect Options menu

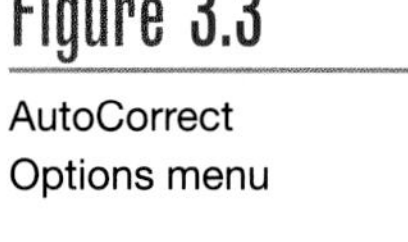

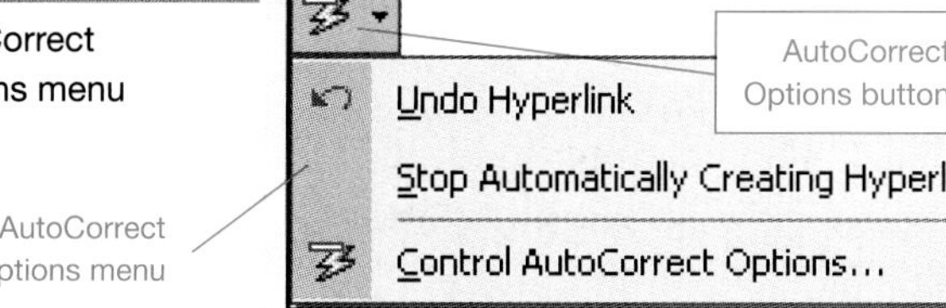

6. To undo the formatting applied to the current hyperlink:
CHOOSE: Undo Hyperlink from the drop-down menu
Your document should now appear similar to Figure 3.4.

Integrating

Figure 3.4

Undoing hyperlink formatting

www.advantageseries.com

AutoCorrect Options button

7. To reapply hyperlink formatting:
   CLICK: AutoCorrect Options button ( )
   CHOOSE: Redo Hyperlink
   PRESS: CTRL + END to prepare for the next step
   Your screen should now appear similar to Figure 3.1.

8. To insert a hyperlink to an existing Excel worksheet:
   CLICK: Insert Hyperlink button ( ) on the Standard toolbar
   The Insert Hyperlink dialog box should now appear (Figure 3.5). By default, the *Existing File or Web Page* button is selected on the *Link* to bar on the left side of the dialog box.

Figure 3.5

Insert Hyperlink dialog box

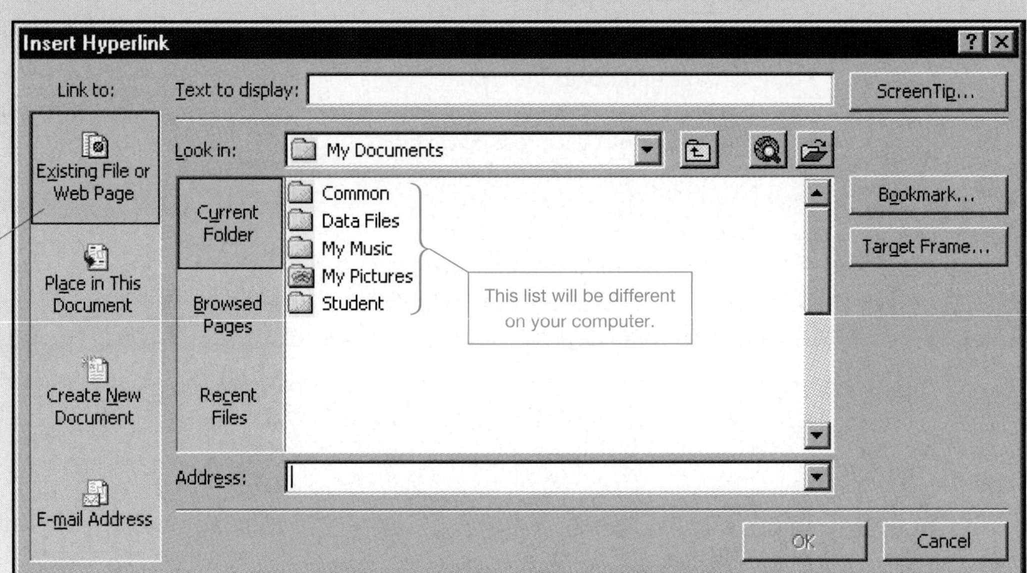

9. Use the *Look in* drop-down list to browse for the IM0310 Excel file.

10. To insert the hyperlink:
    DOUBLE-CLICK: IM0310
    The hyperlink, showing current path and filename, should appear in your document (Figure 3.6). (*Note:* The directory path may be different on your computer.)

Figure 3.6

Inserted hyperlink to a file

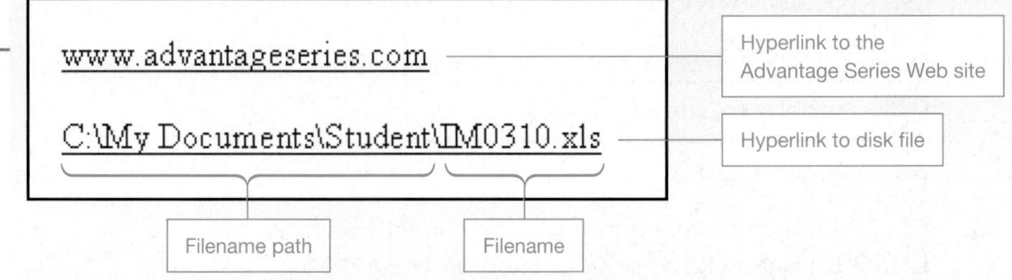

11. Now rename the hyperlink text so that it doesn't include the directory path. Do the following:
RIGHT-CLICK: the IM0310 hyperlink
CHOOSE: Edit Hyperlink
SELECT: the text in the *Text to display* text box at the top of the dialog box
TYPE: **IM0310 Student File**
CLICK: OK command button
Your document should now appear similar to Figure 3.7.

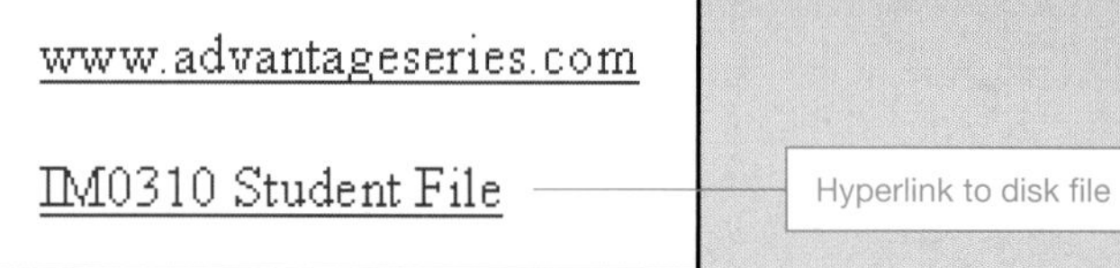

Figure 3.7
Renamed hyperlink

12. Save the current document as "Practice Web" to your personal storage location.

13. Let's see what happens when we follow the "IM0310 Student File" link.
PRESS: CTRL and hold it down

14. With the CTRL key pressed, point with the mouse to the "IM0310 Student File" link. Note that the mouse pointer has changed to a selection hand.

15. With the CTRL key still pressed:
CLICK: "IM0310 Student File" link
The IM0310 worksheet should have opened into Excel's application window. The Web toolbar should also appear (Figure 3.8). In the next lesson, you use the Web toolbar to help navigate among hyperlinks.

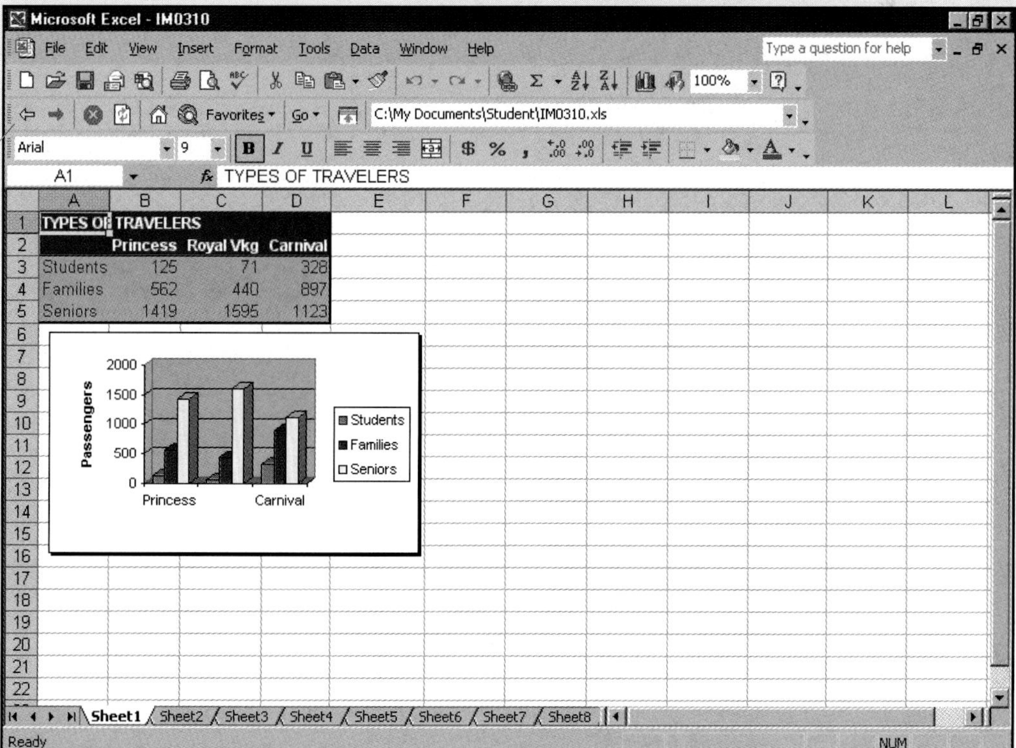

Figure 3.8
Following the IM0310 hyperlink

16. With the Excel worksheet displaying, continue to the next lesson.

3.1.2 Browsing with the Web Toolbar

feature

The **Web toolbar** helps you to navigate hyperlinks locally and on the World Wide Web. In addition to the frequently used Back (⇐) and Start Page (⌂) buttons, this toolbar stores a history of links that you have visited. You can also use the toolbar to open, search, and keep track of your favorite Office and Web documents. The Web toolbar appears automatically when you activate a hyperlink, but you can also display it manually by right-clicking an existing toolbar and choosing the Web option.

method

To browse the Web, choose among the following options on the Web toolbar:

- CLICK: Back button (⇐) to display the previously viewed document
- CLICK: Forward button (⇒) to display the next document
- CLICK: Start Page button (⌂) to display your Home page

To open a Web site:

- CLICK: in the *Address* text box
- TYPE: **Web address**
- PRESS: ENTER

practice

You now practice using the Web toolbar to browse backward and forward and to open a Web site. Ensure that you have completed the previous lesson. Excel should be the active application, and the IM0310 worksheet should be displaying. To perform all the steps in this section, your computer must be able to connect to the Internet and have browser software installed.

1. On your computer, locate the Web toolbar. This toolbar appears labeled in Figure 3.9.

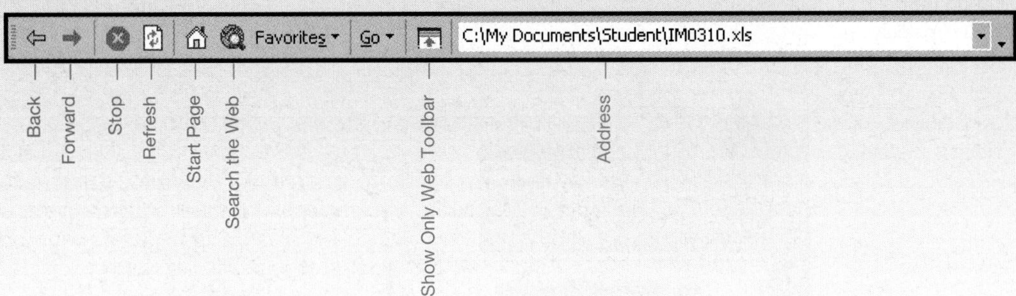

Figure 3.9
Web toolbar

2. Now return to the "Practice Web" document:
CLICK: Back button (⇐) on the Web toolbar
Note that the "IM0310 Student File" link now appears in a different color (Figure 3.10). This is Office's way of reminding you that you've already visited that hyperlink.

Figure 3.10

Hyperlinks

www.advantageseries.com
IM0310 Student File
This link now appears in a different color to remind you that you've traveled the link.

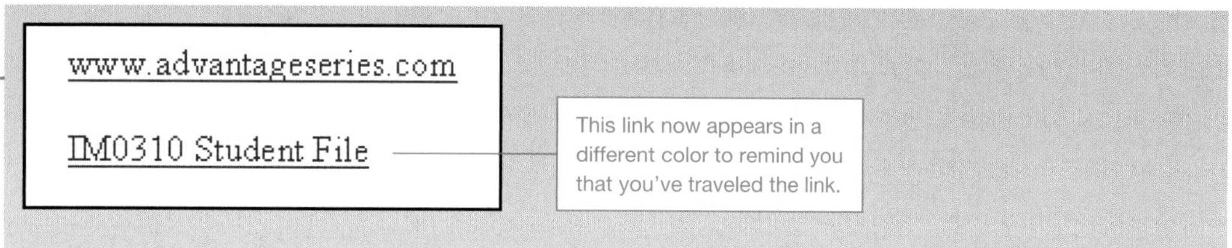

3. If the Web toolbar does not currently appear in the "Practice Web" document, do the following:
   RIGHT-CLICK: an existing toolbar
   CHOOSE: Web from the right-click menu
4. To practice opening a Web site using the Web toolbar:
   CLICK: Address text box (refer to Figure 3.9)
   By clicking in the Address text box, you've selected its entire contents. In the next step, you type a new address to replace the selected address.
5. Since the topic of "cruise ships" is relevant to the IM0310 worksheet, let's open a Web site dedicated to finding low rates on cruise ships. (*Note:* To successfully perform this step, your computer must be able to connect to the Internet.)
   TYPE: **www.cruise.com**
   PRESS: ENTER
   After connecting to the Internet, the "cruise.com" Web site should open in your browser window.
6. To browse back to your Word document:
   CLICK: Back button in your browser window
7. So that your screen will match the figures in this learning guide, hide the Web toolbar in Word.
   RIGHT-CLICK: an existing toolbar
   CHOOSE: Web
8. Close any documents that are currently open in Word and then close Word.
9. Switch back to Excel and then close the application.
10. If your computer is still actively connected to the Web, close that connection now. (*Note:* If necessary, ask your instructor for help.)

In Addition SEARCHING THE WEB

To display a search page where you can enter keywords for locating information on the Web, click the Search the Web button (🔍) on the Web toolbar. The Microsoft Network search page will open and the insertion point will be positioned in the *Search the Web for* text box. To proceed, enter your search criteria in the text box and then press ENTER.

3.1. Provide an example of when you might use a hyperlink in an Office document to access information on the Web.

Integrating

3.2 Saving Existing Documents to HTML

For most of us, knowing how to browse the Web and search for information are all the skills we require for effectively using the World Wide Web. We may have little interest in learning the "ins and outs" of programming in HTML. Fortunately, with Microsoft Office you can create Web pages from your existing Office documents without knowing anything about HTML, and most, if not all, of your document's original formatting will be retained. Nicer yet, the HTML file can be returned to its original file format without losing its unique features and formatting. In this module, we explore creating Web pages from some existing Office documents.

3.2.1 Saving Word, Excel, and PowerPoint Documents to HTML

feature →

Using Microsoft Office, publishing to the Web could hardly be easier. Simply choose File, Save as Web Page to convert your work to HTML. With very few exceptions, all the features of your Word, Excel, and PowerPoint documents will be retained in the HTML version. Note that in the process of saving to HTML, you are given the opportunity to change the title of the Web page. The importance of this title is that it will display in the browser software's Title bar when you view the Web page.

method →

To preview how a document or a worksheet will appear as a Web page:

- CHOOSE: File, Web Page Preview

To save a document, worksheet, or presentation to HTML and change the title of the resulting Web page:

- CHOOSE: File, Save as Web Page
- CLICK: Change Title command button
- TYPE: **the new title**
- CLICK: OK command button
- CLICK: Save command button

practice →

You will now save an existing PowerPoint presentation to HTML and then change the title of the Web page. Ensure that Microsoft Office is installed on your computer.

1. Start PowerPoint and then open the IM0321 data file.
2. Save the file as "Travel" to your personal storage location. Your screen should appear similar to Figure 3.11.

Figure 3.11

"Travel" presentation

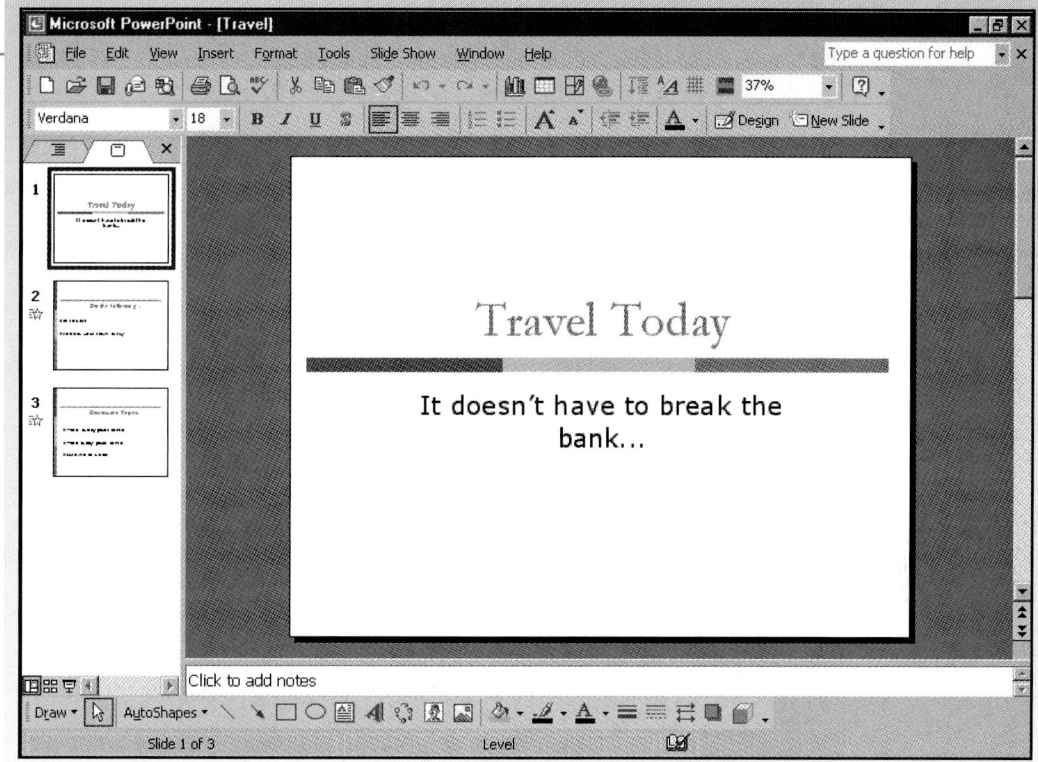

3. To preview how the presentation will appear in a Web browser:
CHOOSE: File, Web Page Preview
After a few moments, the presentation will appear in your Web browser.

4. If necessary, maximize the browser window. Figure 3.12 shows the presentation displayed using Internet Explorer. Note that "Travel" appears in the Title bar of the browser window. Shortly, you will edit the Title bar text.

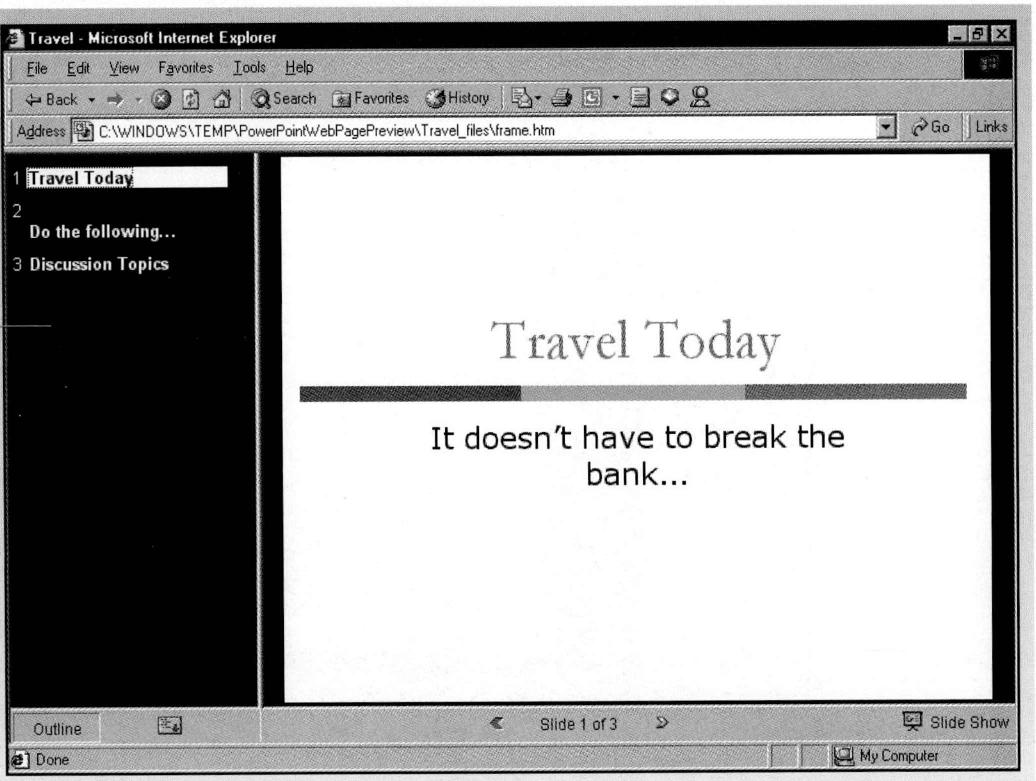

Figure 3.12

Viewing a presentation as a Web page

Navigation frame

5. To view the slides, click their titles in the navigation frame, located on the left side of your screen (see Figure 3.12).

6. To switch back to PowerPoint:
   CLICK: its button on the Windows taskbar

7. To save the current presentation as a Web page:
   CHOOSE: File, Save as Web Page
   The Save As dialog box appears with some additional options, as shown in Figure 3.13. Note that "Web Page" appears as the file type in the *Save as type* drop-down list box.

Figure 3.13

Save As dialog box for a Web page

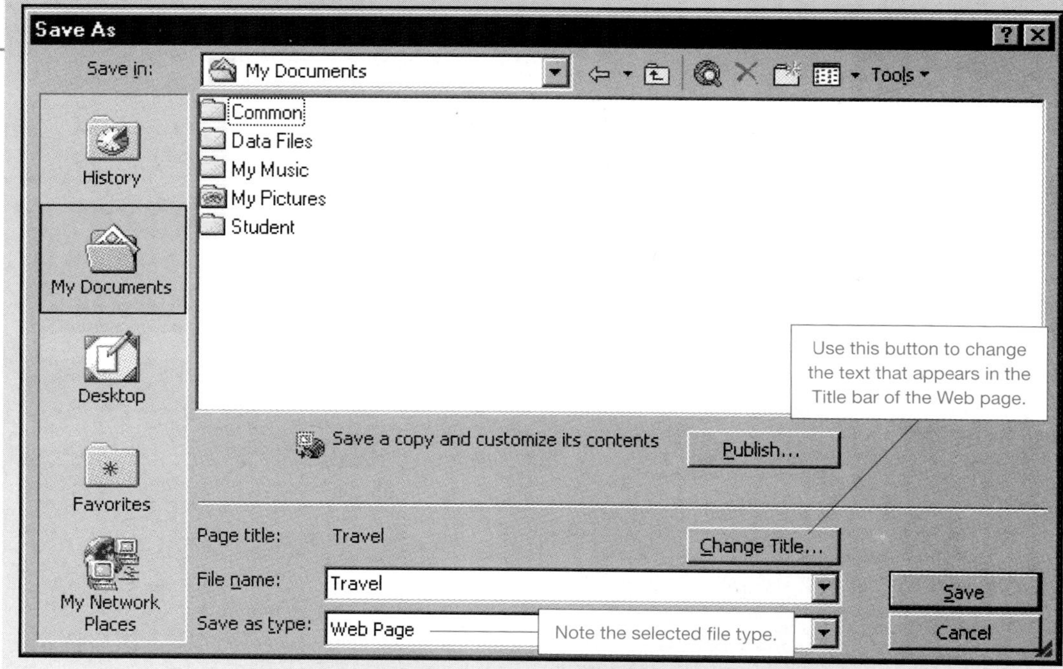

8. To change the title of the Web page:
CLICK: Change Title command button
The Set Page Title dialog box should now appear (Figure 3.14).

Figure 3.14

Save As dialog box for a Web page

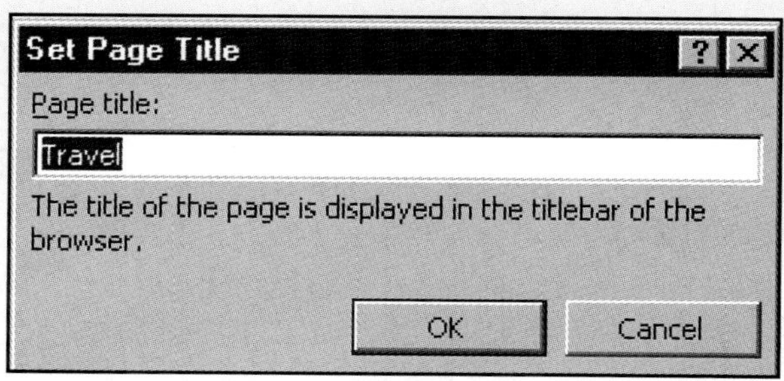

9. In the Set Page Title dialog box:
TYPE: **Travel Tips by Rosalyn Peters**
CLICK: OK command button

10. Using the *Save in* drop-down list box or the Places bar:
SELECT: *your storage location,* if not already selected

11. To proceed with the conversion to HTML:
CLICK: Save command button
The document is saved as "Travel.htm" to your personal storage location.

12. To preview the presentation again to see if the Web title appears in the Title bar:
CHOOSE: File, Web Page Preview
The text "Travel Tips by Rosalyn Peters" should appear in the Title bar, as shown in Figure 3.15.

Figure 3.15

The Title bar text has been changed

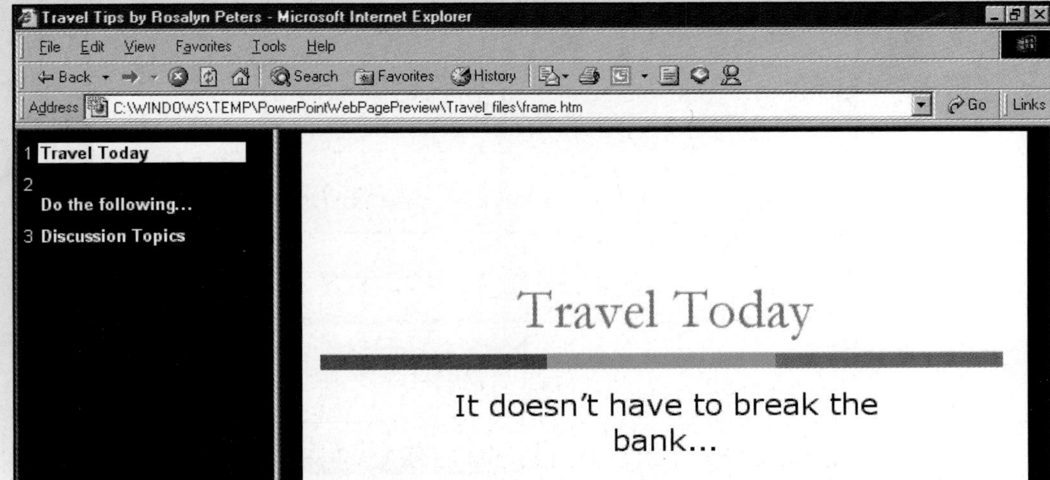

13. Close the browser window by clicking its Close button (☒).

14. Close Microsoft PowerPoint.

In Addition WEB EDITING

If you are using Internet Explorer 5.0 or later, you can easily edit an HTML document that you created in Office XP by choosing "Edit with Microsoft *Application* for Windows" from Explorer's File menu. The HMTL document will then open in its source application (Word, Excel, or PowerPoint). After editing the HTML file and then saving your changes, close the source application. Then, click the Refresh button (or press F5) in the Explorer window to view the revised page.

3.2.2 Displaying an Access Table on the Web

feature

In Microsoft Office, publishing a database to the Web involves a different procedure from publishing a document, worksheet, or presentation. To view an Access database on the Web, you must use a database object called a data access page. **Data access pages** are interactive Web pages that enable you to view and edit data managed in an Access database. Because these pages are stored in HTML files that are separate from the database files, they can be stored locally, on a network server, or on a Web server. (Note that you must be using Internet Explorer 5.0 or later to edit data displayed on a data access page. Otherwise, you will be able only to view, not change, the Access data.)

method

To create a data access page using Access's Data Access Page Wizard:

- CLICK: Pages button in the Objects bar
- DOUBLE-CLICK: "Create data access page by using wizard" object in the list area
- SELECT: a table from the *Tables/Queries* drop-down list
- CLICK: Finish command button after completing all the steps presented by the wizard

To preview the data access page in your browser:

- CLICK: Pages button in the Objects bar
- DOUBLE-CLICK: the page object in the list area
- CHOOSE: File, Web Page Preview

practice

You will now use a wizard to create a data access page for an existing database table and then preview the page in your browser. Ensure that you've completed the previous lessons in this module and that Access and Internet Explorer 5 (or later) are installed on your computer.

1. Start Access and then open the IM0322 database.
2. CLICK: Pages button in the Object bar
   Your screen should now appear similar to Figure 3.16.

Figure 3.16

IM0322 database

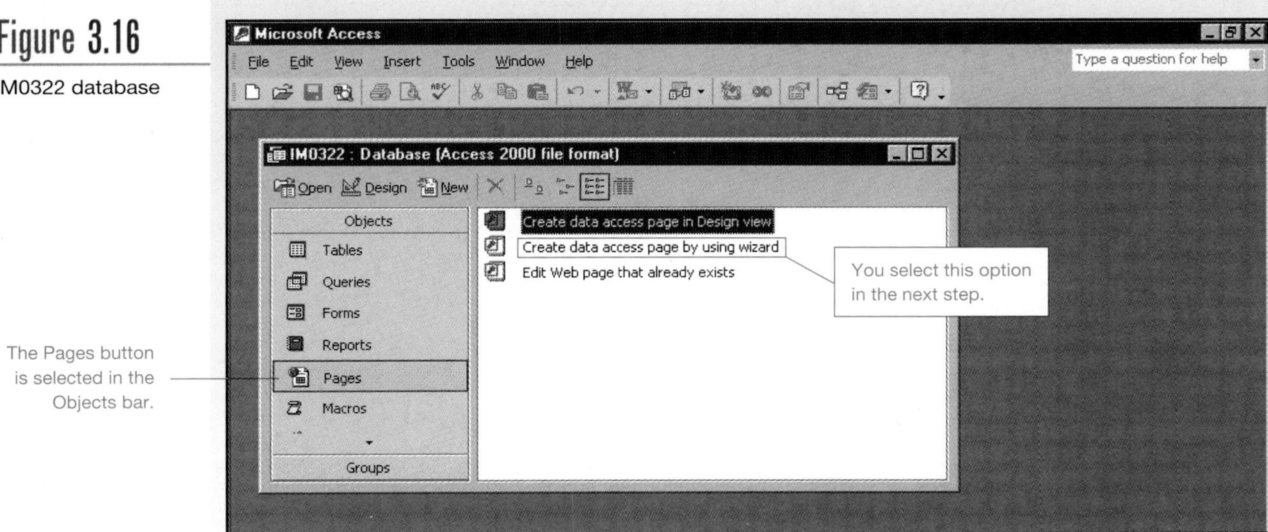

3. To start the Data Access Page Wizard:
   DOUBLE-CLICK: "Create data access page by using wizard" object in the list area
   The initial wizard screen should appear (Figure 3.17).

Integrating

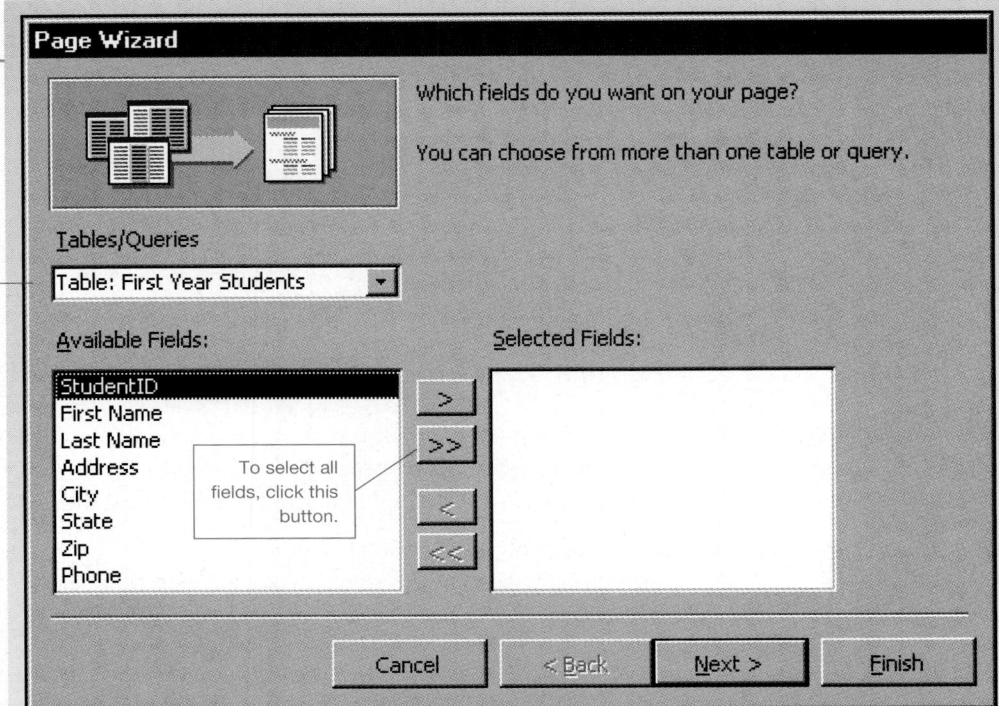

Figure 3.17

Page Wizard dialog box

If the current database contains more than one table, you will have to select the table that contains the data you want to display on the Web page.

4. Since this database contains only one table, you don't have to select a table from the *Tables/Queries* drop-down list. To incorporate all the fields from the selected table on the data access page:
   CLICK: >> in the dialog box
   All of the fields should now be displaying to the right in the *Selected Fields* list box.
5. To proceed:
   CLICK: Next command button
6. You can now specify a grouping level for the data displayed on the data access page. To leave the settings unchanged:
   CLICK: Next command button
7. You can now specify a sorting order for the table data. To leave the settings unchanged:
   CLICK: Next command button
   The wizard dialog box should now appear similar to Figure 3.18.

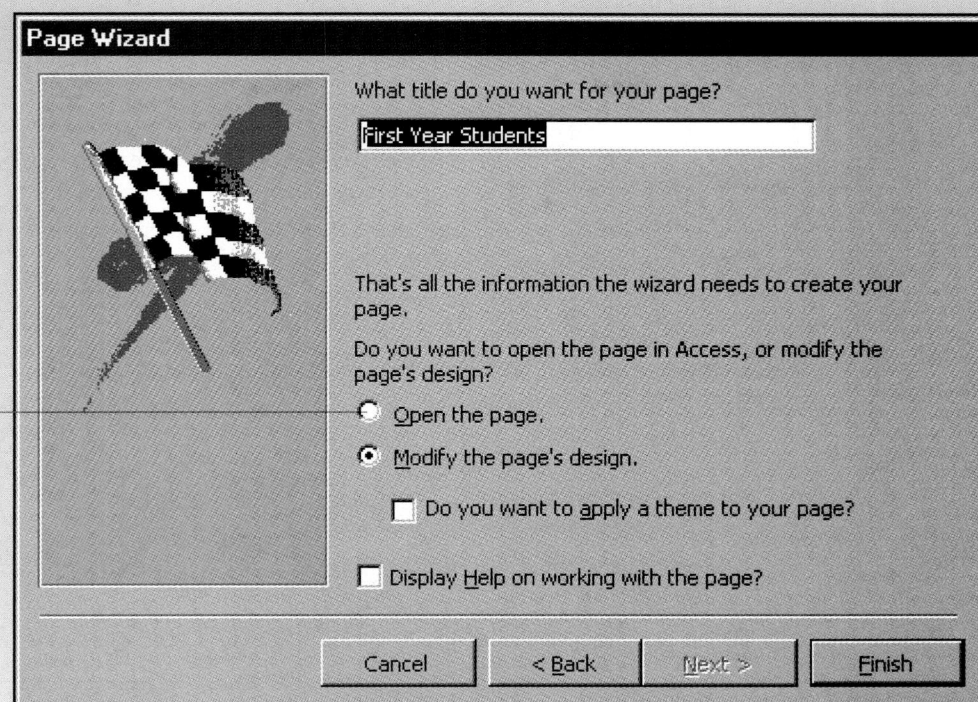

Figure 3.18

Page Wizard dialog box

If you select this option, the data access page will display in your browser when you click the Finish command button.

8. Specify a title for the data access page. Since the current title is already selected, you can replace the current title by typing a new one.
TYPE: **Student Listing**

9. To open, rather than modify, the data access page:
SELECT: *Open the page* option button
CLICK: Finish command button
The data access page should now appear similar to Figure 3.19. This is similar to how the data access page will appear in your browser. To navigate the table, you can use the navigation bar that appears beneath each record.

Figure 3.19

Data access page

Student Listing

StudentID: 1
First Name: Craig
Last Name: Sawchuk
Address: 3501 Maple Valley Dr.
City: Bellevue
State: WA
Zip: 98004
Phone: 206-451-1919

First Year Students 1 of 31

Integrating

10. To save the data access page:
CLICK: Save button (💾) on the toolbar

11. Navigate to your personal storage location.

12. To complete the Save operation:
CLICK: Save command button

13. Another dialog box may now display asking whether you want to save all future data access pages to this same location. Do the following:
CLICK: No command button
(*Note:* If "No" isn't an option on your computer, click the OK command button.)

14. To preview the data access page in your browser.
CHOOSE: File, Web Page Preview
Figure 3.20 shows the data access page in Internet Explorer. Any changes you make to the data will automatically be reflected in the underlying "First Year Students" table in the IM0322 database.

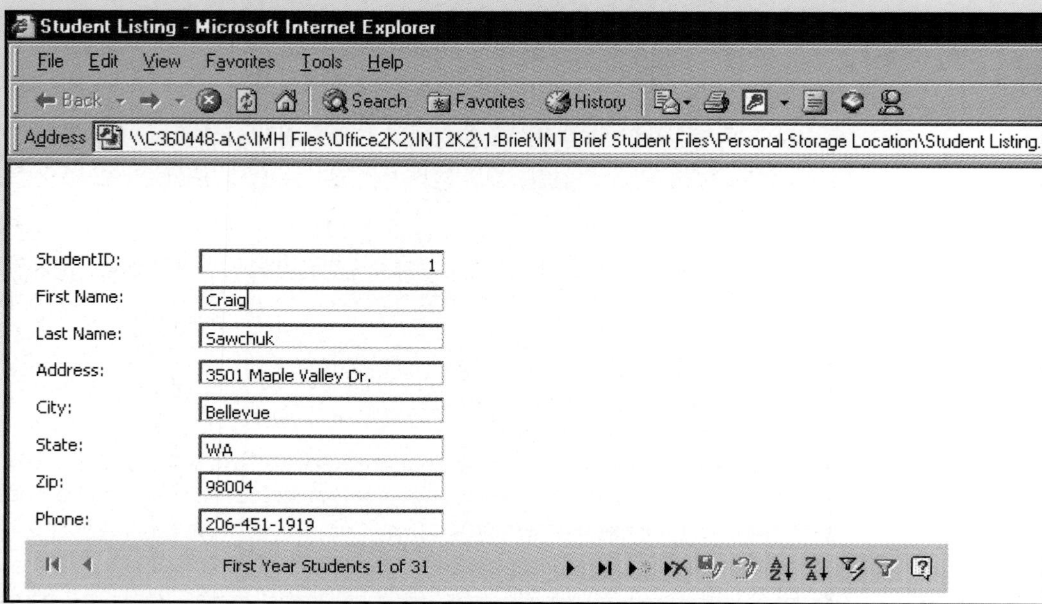

Figure 3.20
Previewing the data access page in Internet Explorer

15. Close the browser window.

16. Close Access.

3.2. What procedure must you use to convert a document, worksheet, or presentation to HTML?

3.3 Preparing Web Pages Using Office

Office provides several features for customizing Web pages. For example, you can apply Web themes to your Microsoft Word documents and divide a document into frames for easy navigation. You can add interactivity to an Excel worksheet so that others can edit it online and customize the appearance and location of the navigation buttons that appear during a Web presentation. In the following lessons, you prepare and customize a Word document, an Excel worksheet, and a PowerPoint presentation for publication on the Web.

3.3.1 Applying Web Themes to Word Documents

feature

Office includes more than 30 themes for optimizing the look of your documents in Word and on the Web. A theme determines what colors and text fonts are used in a document, as well as the appearance of other graphical elements such as bullets and horizontal lines.

method

- CHOOSE: Format, Theme from Word's Menu bar
- SELECT: a theme in the *Choose a Theme* list box
- CLICK: OK command button

practice

You will now apply a Web theme to an existing Word document.

1. Start Word and then open the IM0331 data file.
2. Save the file as "Office and the Web" to your personal storage location and then scroll down through the document to become familiar with its contents. A portion of the document appears in Figure 3.21.

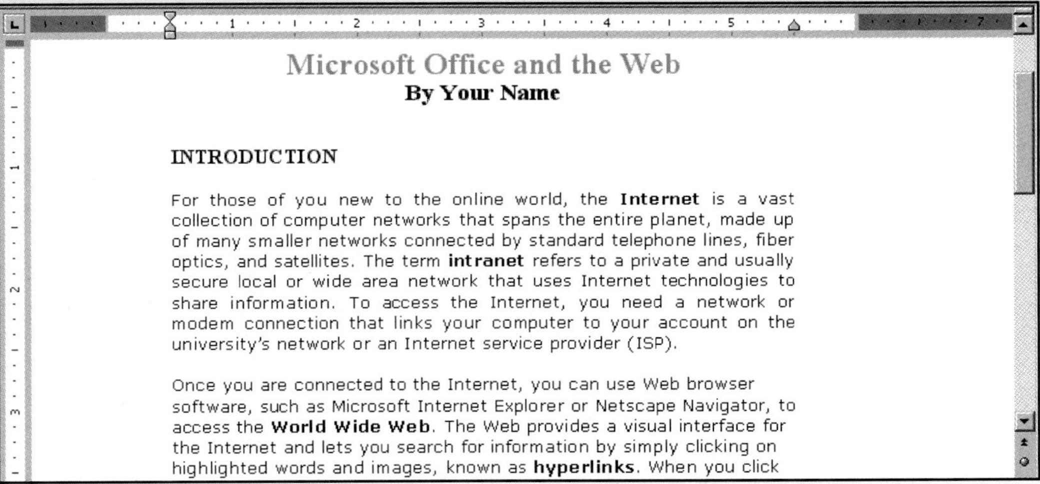

Microsoft Office and the Web
By Your Name
INTRODUCTION
For those of you new to the online world, the Internet is a vast collection of computer networks that spans the entire planet, made up of many smaller networks connected by standard telephone lines, fiber optics, and satellites. The term intranet refers to a private and usually secure local or wide area network that uses Internet technologies to share information. To access the Internet, you need a network or modem connection that links your computer to your account on the university's network or an Internet service provider (ISP).
Once you are connected to the Internet, you can use Web browser software, such as Microsoft Internet Explorer or Netscape Navigator, to access the World Wide Web. The Web provides a visual interface for the Internet and lets you search for information by simply clicking on highlighted words and images, known as hyperlinks. When you click

Figure 3.21

"Office and the Web" document

3. To apply a Web theme to this document:
   CHOOSE: Format, Theme from Word's Menu bar
4. To view some of the different themes, click their names in the *Choose a Theme* list box. (*Note:* Some of the themes will need to be installed before you can view them. Click alternate themes instead.) Before continuing:
   CLICK: Artsy in the *Choose a Theme* list box
   The Theme dialog box should now appear similar to Figure 3.22.

Integrating

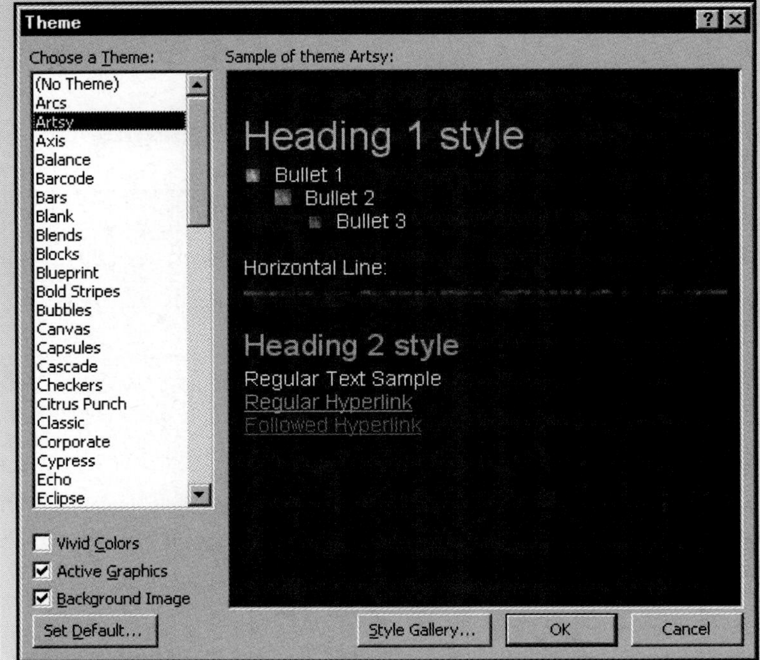

Figure 3.22

Theme dialog box

5. To apply this theme to the document:
CLICK: OK command button
With the insertion point at the top of the document, your screen should now appear similar to Figure 3.23.

Figure 3.23

Applying a Web theme

6. Save the revised document.

7. To prepare for the next lesson, check to make sure that the insertion point is at the top of the document.

3.3.2 Creating a Framed Table of Contents in Word

feature

Using Microsoft Word, it is possible to create a separate area on a Web page to show a document's table of contents or hyperlinks to other pages on a Web site. These areas are called **frames,** and a page that holds one or more frames is called a **frames page.** If the headings in your document are formatted with Word's heading styles, you can easily create a framed table of contents for a document. Most often, a frames page includes a narrow frame on the left and a larger frame to its right. In this case, when you click a hyperlink in the left frame, the information you're interested in will appear in the right frame.

method

- CHOOSE: Format, Frames, Table of Contents in Frame
- Edit the hyperlinks in the table-of-contents frame, as necessary.
- Save the frames page.

practice

You will now create a new frames page that includes a table-of-contents frame on the left side of the screen and the "Office and the Web" document on the right. Ensure that Word is the active application, and that the insertion point is positioned at the top of the "Office and the Web" document.

1. To create a table-of-contents frame for this current document:
CHOOSE: Format, Frames, Table of Contents in Frame
Your screen should now appear similar to Figure 3.24. The hyperlinks in the newly added frame correspond to the document's three main headings. Since these hyperlinks appear to be running together, we're going to insert blank lines between them shortly. Also note that the Frames toolbar is now displaying. This toolbar provides another means for inserting and deleting frames. Since we won't be using this toolbar, we'll close it in the next step.

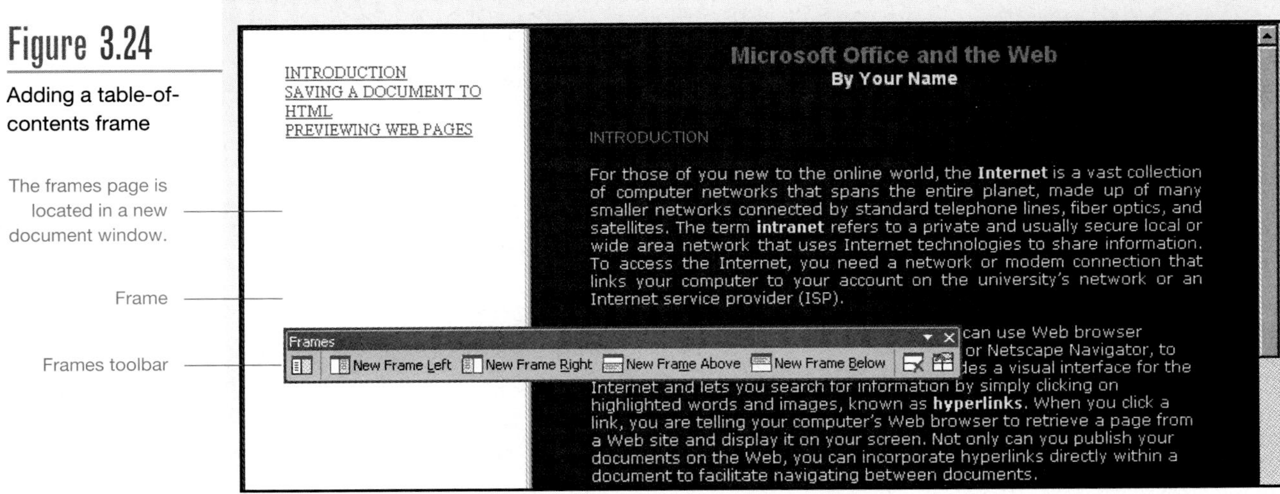

Figure 3.24

Adding a table-of-contents frame

2. To close the Frames toolbar:
CLICK: its Close button (☒)

Integrating

3. Insert a space between the three hyperlinks in the left frame. To do this, you will need to click to the right of each heading. To begin:
CLICK: to the right of the "INTRODUCTION" hyperlink
Figure 3.25 shows the current position of the insertion point.

Figure 3.25
Positioning the insertion point

INTRODUCTION
SAVING A DOCUMENT TO HTML
PREVIEWING WEB PAGES

Position the insertion point here.

4. PRESS: ENTER to insert a blank line
A blank line should have been inserted after the "INTRODUCTION" hyperlink.

5. To insert a blank line after the next heading:
CLICK: to the right of the "SAVING A DOCUMENT TO HTML" hyperlink
PRESS: ENTER to insert a blank line
The frames page should now appear similar to Figure 3.26.

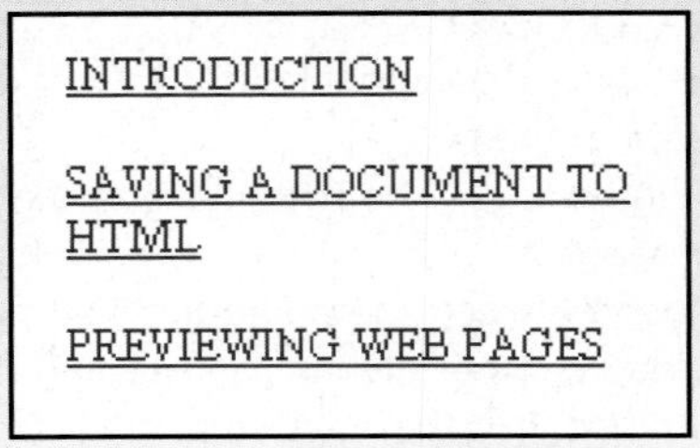

Figure 3.26
The frames page with blank lines

INTRODUCTION

SAVING A DOCUMENT TO HTML

PREVIEWING WEB PAGES

6. Save the frames page as "Frames Page" to your personal storage location.

7. Practice navigating the "Frames Page" document using the table-of-contents frame. (*Note:* Remember that to travel a link, you must press CTRL at the same time you click the link.)

8. Close Word.

3.3.3 Creating an Interactive Worksheet Page

feature

Using Microsoft Office, the Excel worksheets, charts, and PivotTables that you publish to the Web can be much more than static snapshots. Microsoft Office employs three components, called *Web components,* for publishing interactive spreadsheets, charts, and PivotTables to the Web. This lesson focuses on the **Spreadsheet component,** which makes it possible for anyone to update a worksheet through a familiar browser, much as if it were being viewed in Excel. This capability is valuable when corporate data must be made available to many people for updating. To return a worksheet that has been updated in a browser to Excel, you must export the data to a new Excel worksheet.

To create an interactive worksheet page:

- CHOOSE: File, Save as Web Page
- SELECT: *Selection: Sheet* option button in the *Save* area
- SELECT: *Add interactivity* check box
- CLICK: Publish command button and then customize the current settings
- CLICK: Publish command button again to accept the current selections

To export the changed worksheet from the browser window back to Excel:

- CLICK: Export to Excel button () on the worksheet object's toolbar

practice

You will now add interactivity to an Excel worksheet.

1. Launch Excel and then open the IM0333 worksheet.
2. Save the worksheet as "Highlights" to your personal storage location. This worksheet appears in Figure 3.27.

Figure 3.27

"Highlights" worksheet

	A	B	C	D
1	Mary's All-Natural Candies: Financial Highlights			
2				
3				
4				Increase
5		2001	2000	(Decrease)
6	**Total orders**	**$46,504**	$43,153	8%
7	**Net revenue**	**$47,061**	$42,895	10%
8	**Earnings from operations**	**$3,841**	$4,339	-11%
9	**Net earnings**	**$2,945**	$3,119	-6%
10	**Net earnings per share-Diluted**	**$2.77**	$2.95	-6%
11	**Return on assets**	**8.77%**	9.80%	
12	**Return on average equity**	**17.40%**	21.10%	
13				
14	(Amounts expressed in millions)			

3. Save this worksheet as a Web page and enable interactivity.
CHOOSE: File, Save as Web Page

4. Do the following to enable interactivity:
SELECT: *Selection: Sheet* option button
SELECT: *Add interactivity* check box
The Save As dialog box should now appear similar to Figure 3.28.

Figure 3.28

Save As dialog box

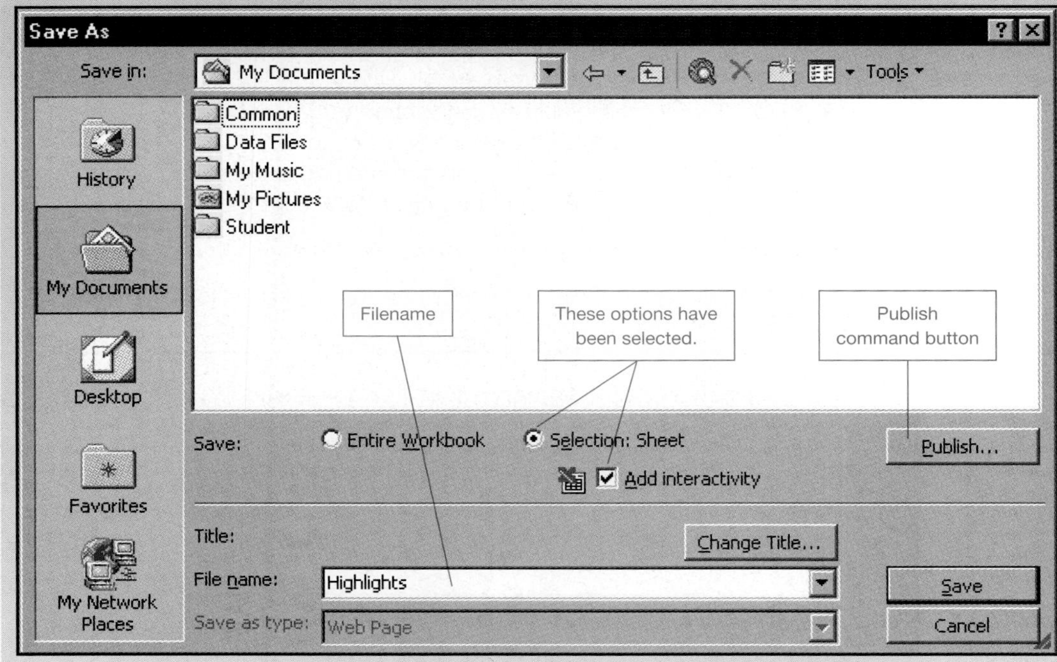

5. Using the *Save in* drop-down list or the Places bar, navigate to your personal storage location.

6. To see how the Web page will appear in your browser, do the following:
CLICK: Publish command button (refer to Figure 3.28)
The Publish as Web Page dialog box should now appear (Figure 3.29).

Figure 3.29

Publish as Web Page dialog box

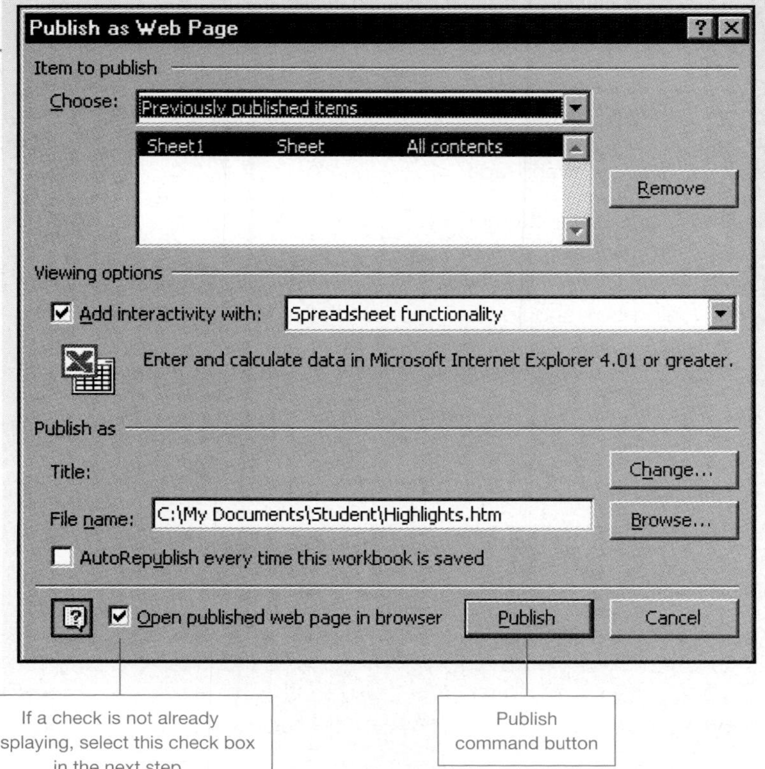

7. Leave all the settings in this dialog box unchanged. However, if a check isn't currently displaying in the *Open published web page in browser* check box, do the following:
SELECT: *Open published web page in browser* check box
A checkmark (✓) should now be displaying in the check box.

8. To see how the worksheet will look in your browser upon saving the worksheet:
CLICK: Publish command button
Figure 3.30 shows the "Highlights" document in Internet Explorer. You may need to maximize the browser window.

Figure 3.30

Viewing the interactive worksheet in Internet Explorer (partial view)

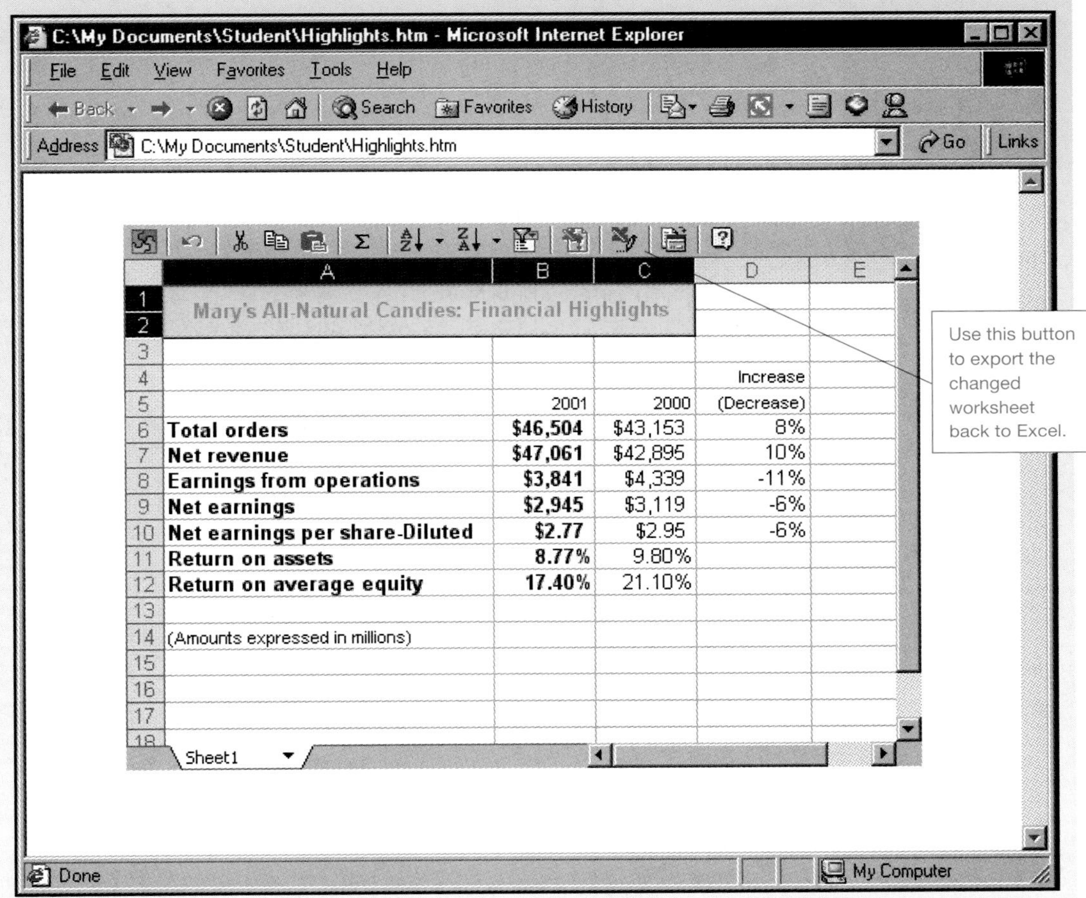

9. Suppose that the Total orders amount in the year 2001 column is incorrect. To change this amount:
CLICK: cell B6
TYPE: 52000
PRESS: ENTER and note that the worksheet recalculated

10. To export this changed worksheet back to Excel, you can use the Export to Microsoft Excel button, located on the top border of the worksheet object (refer to Figure 3.30). To illustrate:
CLICK: Export to Microsoft Excel button
Another copy of Excel was opened and the updated spreadsheet should be displaying. Note that $52,000 appears in cell B6. Note also the non-user-friendly filename in the Title bar and the designation "Read-Only." Because of the file's read-only status, if your intent were to save this file right now, you would need to specify an alternate filename or location.

11. Let's proceed without saving the exported worksheet. Close the current copy of Excel and your browser window. Then, close the remaining copy of Excel, without saving changes.

3.3.4 Customizing a Web Presentation

feature

When you save a presentation to HTML, PowerPoint automatically creates a frame for navigating the presentation and a frame for viewing any associated notes pages. You have control over several features of your published presentation including whether to display the notes frame, what colors are used in the navigation pane, and whether animated effects should be visible in the browser window.

method

To save a presentation to HTML so it can be customized:

- CHOOSE: File, Save as Web Page

To customize the presentation:

- CLICK: Publish command button
- SELECT: options in the Publish as Web Page dialog box
- CLICK: Web Options command button, and then customize the current selections on the *General* tab
- CLICK: OK command button

To save the customized presentation to HTML:

- CLICK: Publish command button

practice

You will now practice customizing an existing presentation for publishing on the Web.

1. Start PowerPoint and then open the IM0334 presentation.
2. Save the presentation as "RCMelon Clothing" to your personal storage location.
3. Preview the presentation in your browser.
   CHOOSE: File, Web Page Preview
   Figure 3.31 shows how the presentation will appear using Microsoft Internet Explorer 5. (*Note:* You may need to maximize the browser window.)

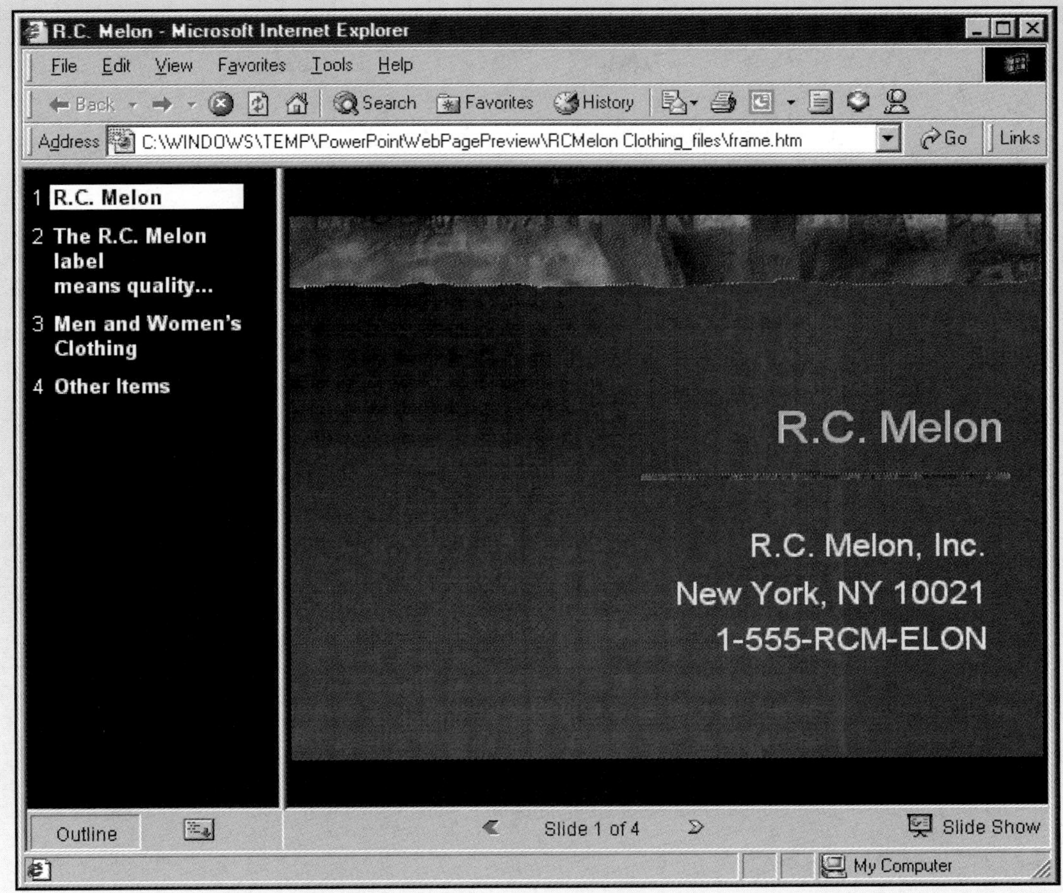

Figure 3.31

Previewing a PowerPoint presentation in Internet Explorer

4. Now customize the presentation so that a white background appears in the left frame. To return to PowerPoint:
   CLICK: PowerPoint button on the Windows taskbar

5. To initiate the "Save as Web page" command:
   CHOOSE: File, Save as Web Page
   The Save As dialog box should now appear.

6. To customize the contents of the presentation:
   CLICK: Publish command button
   The Publish as Web Page dialog box should open, as shown in Figure 3.32.

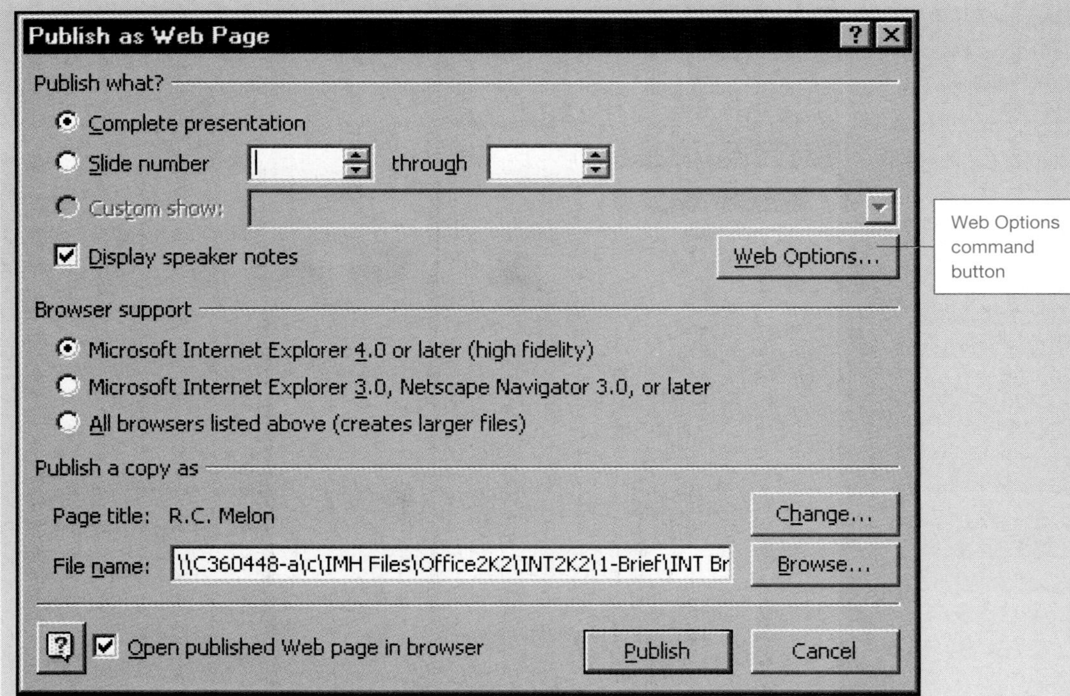

Figure 3.32

Publish as Web Page dialog box

7. To change the look of the navigation bar:
CLICK: Web Options command button
The Web Options dialog box should now appear (Figure 3.33).

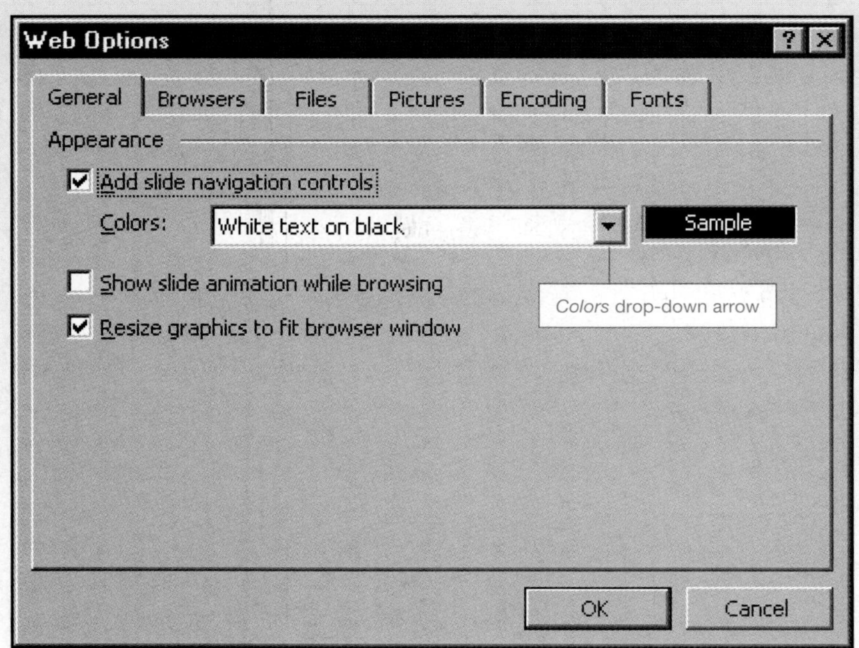

Figure 3.33

Web Options dialog box

8. CLICK: Colors arrow (see Figure 3.33)
CHOOSE: "Black text on white" from the drop-down list
CLICK: OK command button

9. To view the modified presentation in your browser:
CLICK: Publish command button
The presentation should immediately display in the browser window. Figure 3.34 shows the presentation in Internet Explorer. Note that a white background now appears in the navigation and presentation frames.

Figure 3.34

Viewing the customized PowerPoint presentation in Internet Explorer

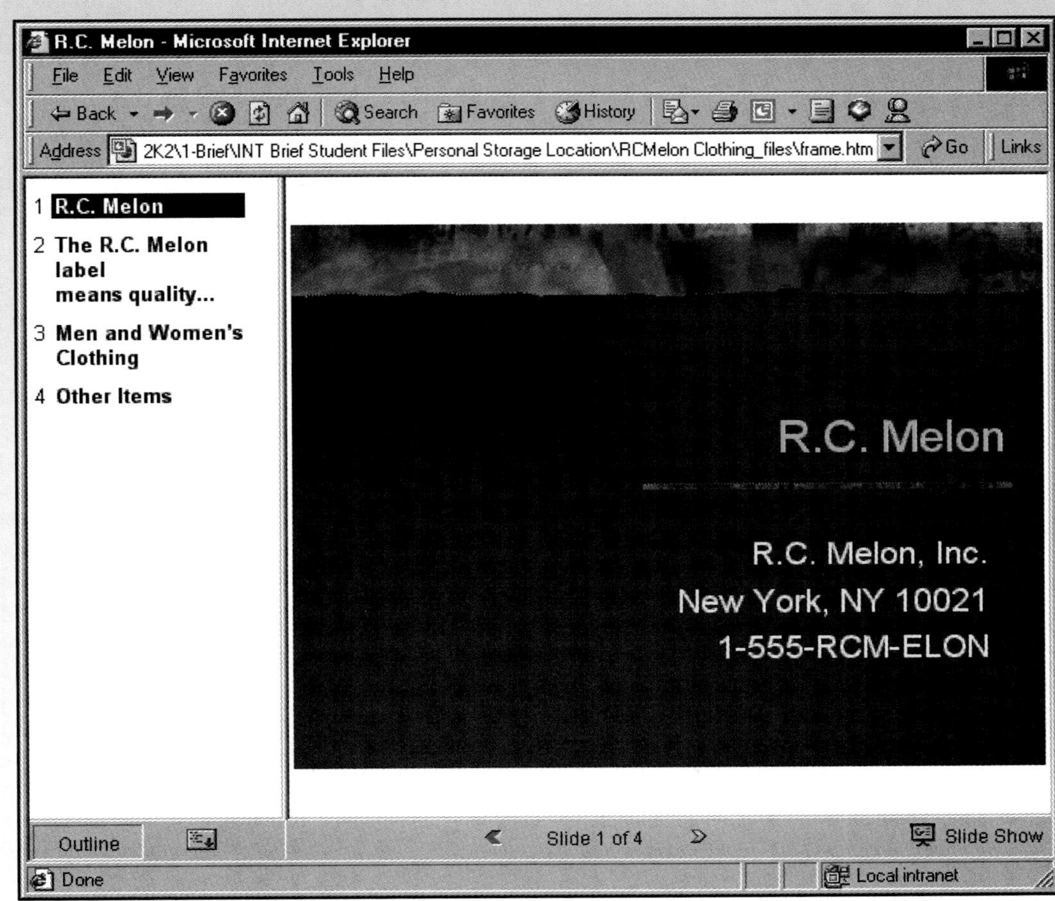

10. Close the browser window and then close PowerPoint, without saving changes.

In Addition POSTING FILES TO WEB SERVERS

To make your Microsoft Office Web pages available for others to see using their browsers, you can use the Save As dialog box to post (or copy) them to a special computer, called a **Web server.** The server computer must support **Web folders,** a Windows system extension that enables users to browse Web servers using the familiar Explorer windows and Open and Save As dialog boxes. Before you can post files to a Web server, you must locate a Web server that supports Web folder extensions and determine what your user name and password are. To perform both of these activities, talk to your system administrator or *Internet service provider (ISP),* which is a company that rents Web space. Your Office application's Help system also provides more information on this topic.

3.3. On Web pages, what are frames used for?

Chapter summary

Microsoft Office XP was developed to allow nontechnical users to take advantage of all that the Web has to offer. By most accounts, Microsoft has succeeded in delivering a software suite that is truly Web-enabled. For example, you can easily create hyperlinks in existing Office documents that lead to other Office documents, or even to locations on the Web. You can save your existing Office documents to HTML without losing the look and features of your original documents. Further, you can customize your Word pages with themes and frames, add interactivity to Excel worksheets, and customize the appearance of the navigation pane in PowerPoint.

Command Summary

Many of the commands and procedures appearing in this chapter are summarized in the following table.

Skill Set	To Perform This Task	Do the Following
Working with Hyperlinks	Insert a hyperlink to a Web or an e-mail address	TYPE: **Web or e-mail address** PRESS: ENTER (or the Space Bar)
	Insert a hyperlink to an existing file	CLICK: Insert Hyperlink button ( ) and browse to the file location DOUBLE-CLICK: filename CLICK: OK command button
	Edit a hyperlink	RIGHT-CLICK: hyperlink CHOOSE: Edit Hyperlink
	Browse using the Web toolbar	CLICK: Back button ( ) to display the previously viewed document CLICK: Forward button ( ) to display the next document CLICK: Start Page button ( ) to display your chosen Home page
Working with Word	Save a Word document to HTML	CHOOSE: File, Save as Web Page
	Apply a theme	CHOOSE: Format, Theme
	Create a table-of-contents frames page	CHOOSE: Format, Frames, Table of Contents in Frame
Working with Excel	Save an Excel worksheet to HTML	CHOOSE: File, Save as Web Page
	Create an interactive worksheet	CHOOSE: File, Save as Web Page SELECT: *Selection: Sheet* option button SELECT: *Add interactivity* check box CLICK: Publish command button CLICK: Publish command button
Working with PowerPoint	Save a PowerPoint presentation to HTML	CHOOSE: File, Save as Web Page
	Customize a Web presentation	CHOOSE: File, Save as Web Page CLICK: Publish command button CLICK: Web Options command button

Skill Set	To Perform This Task	Do the Following
Working with Access	Create a data access page	CLICK: Pages button in the Objects bar DOUBLE-CLICK: "Create data access page by using wizard" object in the list area and then follow the wizard prompts
	Preview a data access page in your browser	CLICK: Pages button in the Objects bar DOUBLE-CLICK: the page object in the list area CHOOSE: File, Web Page Preview

Key Terms

This section specifies page references for the key terms identified in this chapter. For a complete list of definitions, refer to the Glossary at the end of this learning guide.

data access page, *p. 82*

frames, *p. 89*

frames page, *p. 89*

Spreadsheet component, *p. 90*

Web folder, *p. 97*

Web server, *p. 97*

Web toolbar, *p. 76*

Chapter quiz

Short Answer

1. What is the procedure for editing a hyperlink?
2. What functions do the Back (⇦) and Forward (⇨) buttons on the Web toolbar perform?
3. What is a Web folder?
4. What is a Web server?
5. When saving an Office document to HTML, what is the purpose for the Change Title command button in the Save As dialog box?
6. What is a data access page?
7. In Word, what are themes?
8. What is the procedure for creating a hyperlink to a Web address?
9. In Microsoft Office, what is the Web toolbar used for?
10. In Microsoft Office, what Web activity does the Spreadsheet component enable?

True/False

1. ____ The File, Web Page Preview command is available in Word, Excel, Access, and PowerPoint.

2. ____ When you save a PowerPoint presentation to HTML, PowerPoint automatically creates a frame for navigating the presentation.

3. ____ To create a hyperlink to an existing filename, simply type the filename path and filename into your Office document.

4. ____ A data access page is an Excel feature for displaying worksheet data.

5. ____ A page that holds frames is called a *frames page.*

6. ____ Once you add a frame to a Word document, it's impossible to change the contents of the frame.

7. ____ Office's Spreadsheet component enables you to share data between Word and Excel.

8. ____ A Web folder is essentially a shortcut to a location on a Web server.

9. ____ Using Microsoft Office, there's no way to rename an inserted hyperlink.

10. ____ A data access page is stored in a file that's separate from its underlying database.

Multiple Choice

1. To convert a Word document to HTML, choose:

a. File, Convert
b. File, Export
c. File, Format
d. File, Save as Web Page

2. Which of the following procedures inserts a hyperlink to an existing filename?

a. CHOOSE: Hyperlink, Edit Hyperlink
b. CHOOSE: Hyperlink, Format Hyperlink
c. CLICK: Insert Hyperlink button ( )
d. all of the above

3. Which of the following can you use to navigate documents?

a. frames
b. hyperlinks
c. Web toolbar
d. all of the above

4. Which of the following enables you to view Access data on a Web page?

a. data access page
b. frames
c. Web toolbar
d. hyperlinks

5. Office's Spreadsheet component enables you to:

a. change a worksheet when viewing it in your browser
b. publish interactive worksheets
c. copy a worksheet into Word
d. both a. and b.

6. Which of the following applications can you use to create a data access page?

a. Word
b. Excel
c. Access
d. all of the above

7. In Word, which of the following changes the overall look of a document?

a. frame
b. theme
c. table of contents
d. none of the above

8. Which of the following can you use to divide a Web page into areas?

a. frame
b. theme
c. table of contents
d. none of the above

9. By selecting the ______________ in Excel's Save As dialog box, you can publish interactive worksheets.
   a. *Selection: Sheet* option button
   b. *Add interactivity* check box
   c. *Spreadsheet component* check box
   d. none of the above

10. When publishing PowerPoint presentations to the Web, you have control over:
    a. whether a frames page displays
    b. what colors are used in the navigation frame
    c. whether animated effects should be visible in the browser window
    d. all of the above

Hands-On exercises

1. Sweet Dreams: Inserting Hyperlinks

Hudson is eager to practice inserting hyperlinks in a Word document. In this exercise, assume the role of Hudson and perform the same steps he identifies.

1. Start Word.
2. Save the blank document as "Toys Hyperlinks" to your personal storage location.
3. Type a URL to the Fisher-Price Toys home page:
   TYPE: **www.fisher-price.com**
   PRESS: ENTER
4. To move the insertion point down a few more lines:
   PRESS: ENTER twice
5. Now insert a hyperlink to an existing Word document.
   CLICK: Insert Hyperlink button ( ) on the Standard toolbar and then browse to the file using the *Look in* drop-down list
6. To browse for the IM03HE01 Word document:
   DOUBLE-CLICK: IM03HE01 file name
   The hyperlink, containing the file's path and name, should be displaying in your document.
7. Then rename the hyperlink text.
   RIGHT-CLICK: the IM03HE01 hyperlink
   CHOOSE: Edit Hyperlink
   SELECT: the text in the *Text to display* text box at the top of the dialog box
   TYPE: **Career Opportunities**
   CLICK: OK command button
   Your document should now appear similar to Figure 3.35.

Integrating

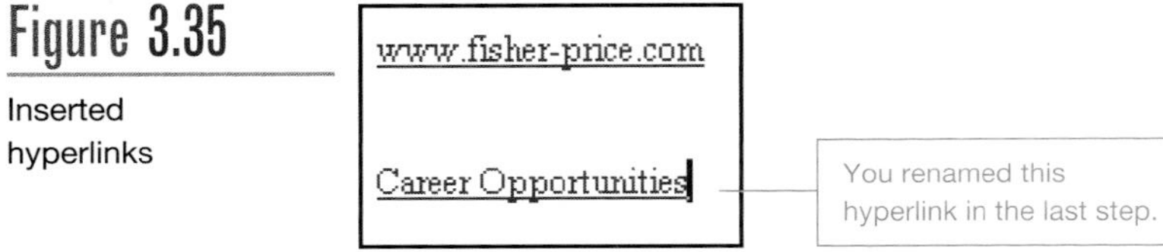

Figure 3.35
Inserted hyperlinks

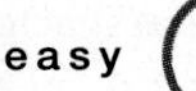

8. Save the revised document.
9. Close Word.

easy

2. Outback Exports: Inserting Hyperlinks and Browsing

Richard Brackton, the chairman of Outback Exports, continues to prepare documents for an upcoming meeting. In this exercise, assume the role of Richard and perform the same steps that he identifies.

1. Start Word and open the IM03HE02 file.
2. Save the document as "Browsing" to your personal storage location. The document appears in Figure 3.36.

Figure 3.36

Inserted hyperlinks

3. Now replace the text "Investments in Australia" with a hyperlink to an Excel worksheet.
   SELECT: the text "Investments in Australia"
   CLICK: Insert Hyperlink button ( ) on the Standard toolbar
4. Use the *Look in* drop-down list to browse for the IM03HE02 Excel worksheet.
5. To proceed with inserting the hyperlink:
   DOUBLE-CLICK: IM03HE02 in the file list
   The text "Investments in Australia" is now formatted as a hyperlink (Figure 3.37).

Figure 3.37

Inserted hyperlinks

Outback Exports
Important Australian Hyperlinks
Investments in Australia
www.tasmania.com
This is now a link to the IM03HE02 Excel student file.

6. Now try the new hyperlink.
   PRESS: CTRL and hold it down
   CLICK: "Investments in Australia" hyperlink
   The IM03HE02 Excel worksheet should have opened into Excel's application window, and the Web toolbar should be displaying (Figure 3.38).

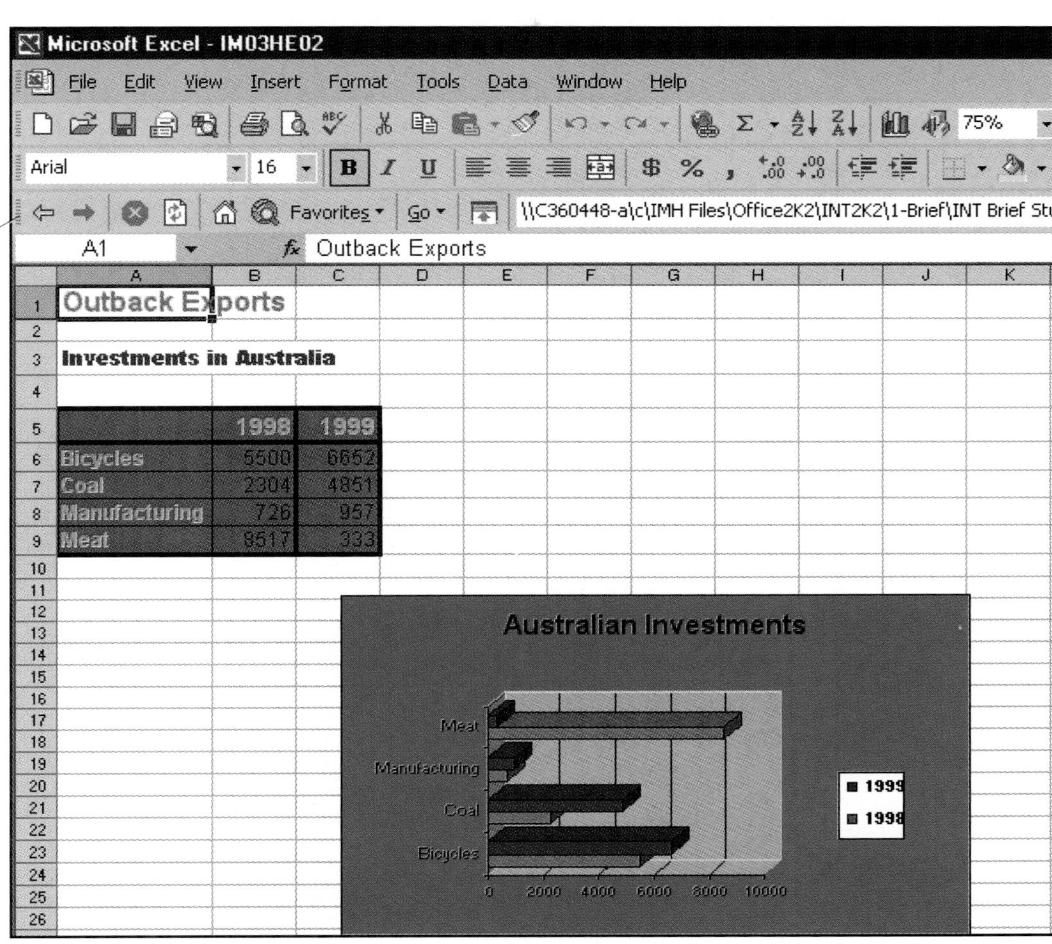

Figure 3.38
IM03HE02 worksheet

7. To return to the "Browsing" document in Word:
   CLICK: Back button (⇦) on the Web toolbar in Excel
8. Let's visit the "www.tasmania.com" Web site:
   PRESS: CTRL and hold it down
   CLICK: "www.tasmania.com" hyperlink in the "Browsing" document
9. To return to the "Browsing" document:
   CLICK: Back button (⇦)
10. Save the revised Word document, and then close Word and Excel. (*Note:* If your Internet connection is still active, close it now.)

moderate 

3. Bud's Parlor of Flavors: Preparing a Word Document for the Web

Bud is still working hard, but not at scooping ice cream. Instead, he's preparing a Word document for display on the Web. In this exercise, assume the role of Bud and perform the same steps that he identifies.

1. Open the IM03HE03 Word document and then save it as "History" to your personal storage location.
2. Preview how the document will appear in a Web browser using the File, Web Page Preview menu command. Your screen should now appear similar to Figure 3.39.

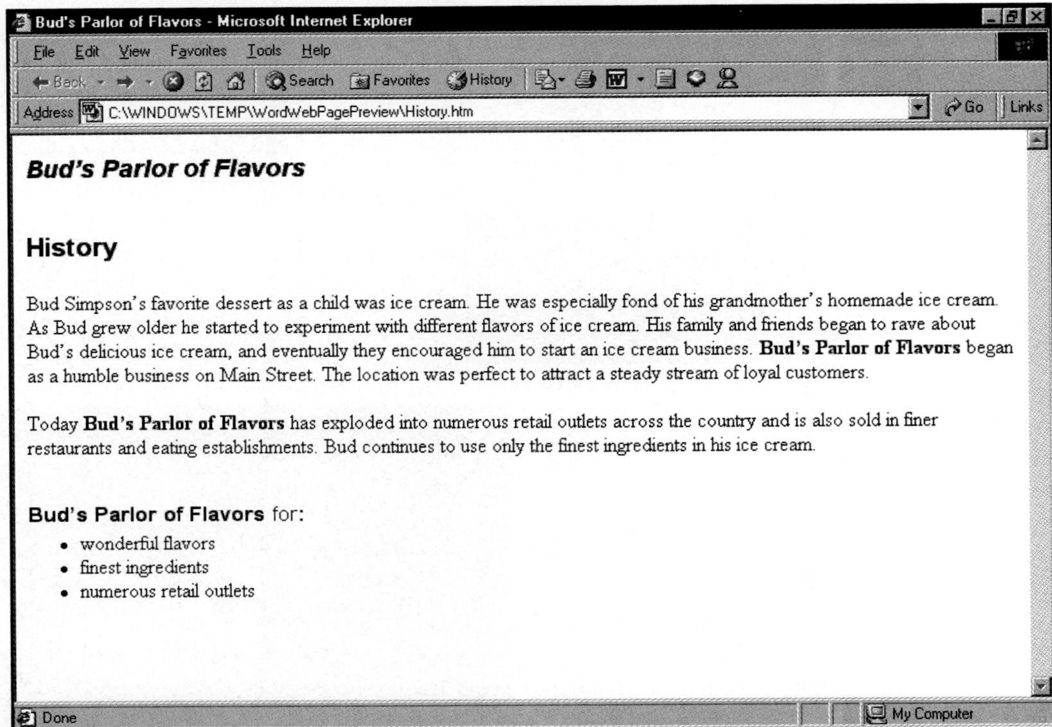

Figure 3.39

Viewing the "History" document in a Web browser

3. Close the browser window. The "History" document should be displaying.
4. Apply an appropriate Web theme to this document.
5. Save the document as a Web page named "History," making sure to change the title of the Web page to **How We Started.**
6. Preview the Web page once more to confirm that the specified text displays in the Title bar.
7. Close the browser window.
8. Print the Word document and then close Word.

moderate

4. The Software Edge: Customizing a Web Presentation

Mary is very focused on the task at hand. In this exercise, Mary publishes a PowerPoint presentation to the Web and then customizes it so that a white background appears in the navigation bar and in the slide area.

1. Start PowerPoint and then open the IM03HE04 presentation.
2. Save the presentation as "Orientation" to your personal storage location.
3. Use the Web Page Preview command to view the presentation in your Web browser. View each of the presentation's slides by clicking their corresponding heading in the left frame.
4. Close the browser window, returning to PowerPoint.
5. In the process of saving the presentation as a Web page to your personal storage location, change the look of the navigation bar so that white text appears on a black background.
6. Save the presentation, viewing it directly in the Web browser by clicking the *Open published Web page in browser* check box in the Publish as Web Page dialog box. In the browser window, your presentation should appear similar to Figure 3.40.

Figure 3.40

Viewing the "History" document in a Web browser

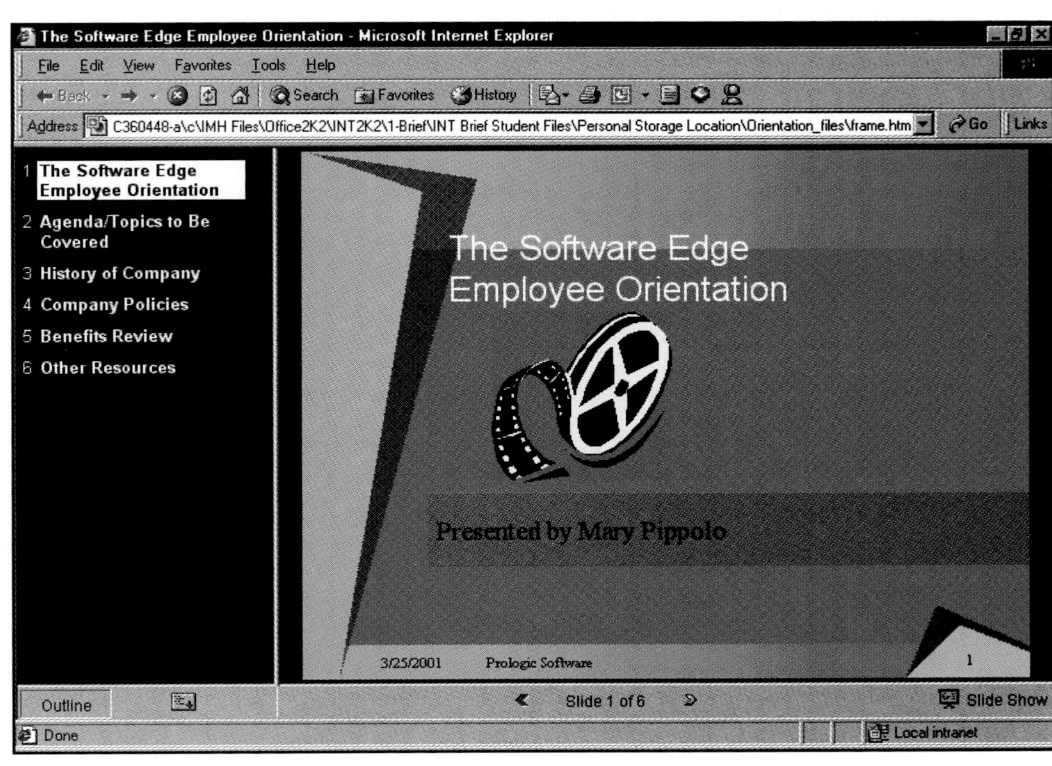

7. Close any windows that remain open.

Integrating

difficult 

5. On Your Own: Publishing an Access Database to the Web

In this exercise, you publish an Access database to the Web using the Data Access Page Wizard. Start Access and open the IM03HE05 database. Create a data access page for the "Used Cars" table. In your browser, the completed data access page should look like Figure 3.41.

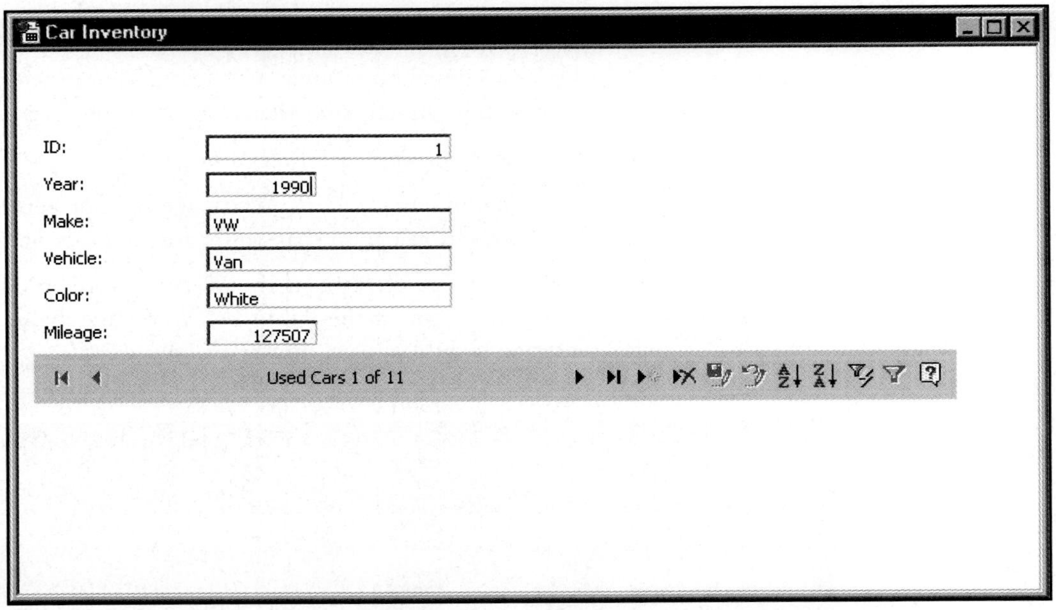

Figure 3.41

Data access page

Car Inventory

ID: 1
Year: 1990
Make: VW
Vehicle: Van
Color: White
Mileage: 127507
Used Cars 1 of 11

Print a copy of the data access page and then close the open database without saving changes. Close Access and any other windows that remain open.

difficult 

6. On Your Own: Creating an Online Resume

In this exercise, you create an online resume in Word. Use what you know about enhancing Word documents for the Web to create the most attractive online resume possible. If you don't yet have work experience, use fictitious data in your resume. Save the resume as a Web page named "My Resume" to your personal storage location and then close Word.

Case Problems

Manfred's Garden Center

Now that Cynthia has completed Chapter 3, she is ready to tackle the World Wide Web. She has numerous Office documents that she would like to publish to the Web. In the following case problems, assume the role of Cynthia and perform the same steps that she identifies. You may want to re-read the chapter opening before proceeding.

1. Cynthia would like her marketing staff to have instant access to several Office documents and Web sites. The obvious solution would be the creation of a Word document that contains these important links. Cynthia creates a new document in Word and saves it as "Manfred's Links" to her personal storage location. At the top of the document she types the heading "Manfred's Favorite Links," applies the formatting of her choice to the title, and then inserts three blank lines.

   Cynthia starts Excel and opens the IM03CS01 worksheet. She then saves it as "Campaigns" to her personal storage location and closes Excel. Next, she starts PowerPoint and opens the IM03CS01 presentation. She then saves it as "Marketing Plan" to her personal storage location and then closes PowerPoint. The Word document should again be displaying.

   At the insertion point, Cynthia creates a hyperlink to the "Campaigns" worksheet file and then inserts three blank lines. She then creates a hyperlink to the "Marketing Plan" presentation file. Finally, she types the URL "www.gardening.com" a few lines below the previous hyperlink.

   Cynthia decides to change the Excel hyperlink name to "Marketing Campaigns" and the PowerPoint hyperlink name to "Manfred's Marketing Plan." Finally, she returns to the "Manfred's Links" Word document and prints it. The completed document appears in Figure 3.42. As a final step, she closes all the other files and windows.

Figure 3.42

"Manfred's Links" document

2. Cynthia is ready to publish an existing Word document to the Web. She opens the IM03CS02 Word document and saves it as "Plants" to her personal storage location. Cynthia applies a theme to the document that supports the document's message. She then saves the document as a Web page named "Plants."

   Cynthia returns to the Save As Web Page dialog box to change the title of the Web page from "Plants" to "Manfred's Plant Varieties." She saves the Web page once more, and then previews it in her Web browser to ensure the title has changed. After closing her Web browser, she returns to Word and then prints the "Plants" file. She leaves the "Plants" file open for use in the next exercise.

3. Since the headings of the previously created "Plants" document are already formatted with Word's heading styles, Cynthia inserts a framed table of contents on the left side of the document.

To make the table of contents easier to read, Cynthia carefully adds blank lines between the topic headings. She also selects all the headings and applies a 16-point font and the bold attribute. Next, she experiments by traveling each of the hyperlinks in the left frame. As a final step, Cynthia saves the document as "Plants TOC". She closes all documents and open applications.

4. Cynthia would like to create an interactive Excel worksheet page to be used by all of Manfred's employees. She starts Excel and opens the IM03CS04 worksheet. She saves the worksheet as "Promotions" to her personal storage location. In the process of saving the worksheet as a Web page to her personal storage location, she adds interactivity to the worksheet. She also opens the worksheet in her browser before clicking the Publish command button. The published worksheet appears in Figure 3.43.

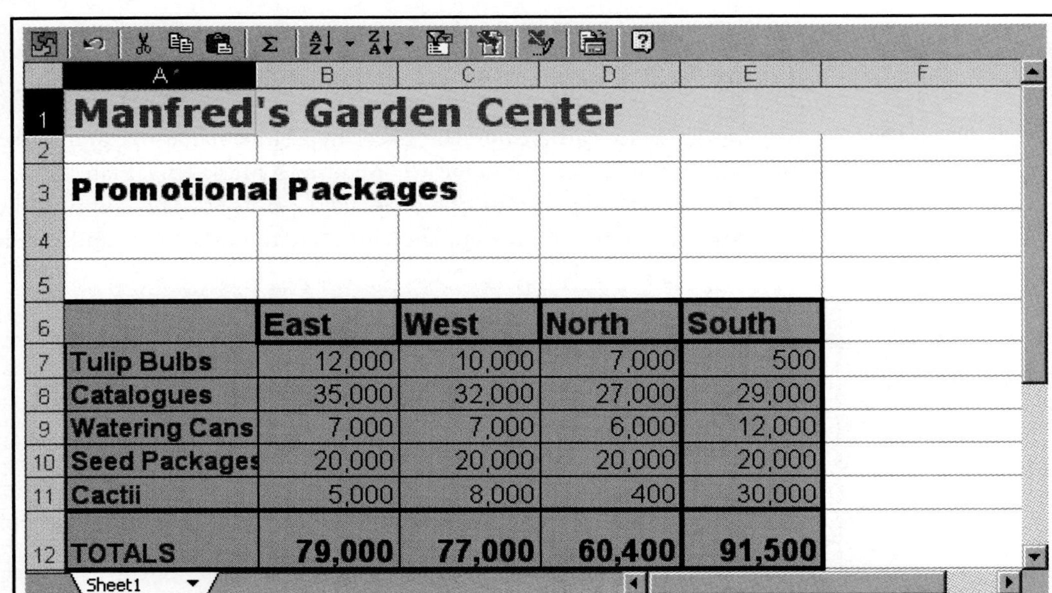

	A	B	C	D	E	F
1	Manfred's Garden Center					
2						
3	Promotional Packages					
4						
5						
6		East	West	North	South	
7	Tulip Bulbs	12,000	10,000	7,000	500	
8	Catalogues	35,000	32,000	27,000	29,000	
9	Watering Cans	7,000	7,000	6,000	12,000	
10	Seed Packages	20,000	20,000	20,000	20,000	
11	Cactii	5,000	8,000	400	30,000	
12	TOTALS	79,000	77,000	60,400	91,500	

Sheet1

Figure 3.43

Published worksheet

Cynthia prints a copy of the worksheet from the Web browser and then closes the Web browser. She saves the Excel worksheet and closes Excel. Cynthia is pleased by all of the excellent computer work she has done.

NOTES

NOTES

NOTES

NOTES

Answers to self-check questions

SelfCheck

1.1. How do you remove a right-click menu from view? Click in the blank part of the document area.

1.2. How would you insert a word in the middle of a sentence? Simply position the insertion point in the desired location and then type the desired word.

1.3. Under what circumstances might you want to save a file under a different filename? You might want to save different versions of the same document, create a backup copy, or use a document as a template for future documents.

1.4. What is the different between Normal and Print Layout view? In Normal view, your document displays without headers, footers, and columns. To view how text and graphics will appear on the printed page, use the Print Layout view.

2.1. What is the difference between the Undo and Repeat commands? The Undo command enables you to cancel the last several commands you performed in a document. The Repeat command repeats the last action you performed in the document.

2.2. What is the procedure for replacing text in a document? Choose Edit, Replace and then specify the text you are searching for and the replacement text.

2.3. How would you go about moving text to the Clipboard? Select the text you want to move and then click the Cut button ( ).

2.4. What is the procedure for adding a word to Word's custom dictionary? In the Spelling and Grammar dialog box, click the Add command button.

3.1. How would you boldface and underline existing text? Select the text and then click the Bold ( ) and Underline buttons ( ).

3.2. How do you display a document's hidden symbols? Click the Show/Hide button ( ). Clicking it again removes the symbols.

3.3. What dialog box enables you to create an outline-numbered list? The Bullets and Numbering dialog box.

3.4. What are page borders used for? Page borders extend around the perimeter of the page and are used to enhance a document's appearance.

4.1. What is the procedure for printing your work? Click the Print button ( ) to send your work directly to the printer or choose File, Print to display the Print dialog box.

4.2. In inches, how wide are the left and right margins by default? The left and right margins are 1.25 inches and the top and bottom margins are 1 inch each.

4.3. How do you insert page numbers in a document? Choose Insert, Page Numbers. Or, if the Header and Footer toolbar is displayed, click the Insert Page Number button ( ).

4.4. What are sections used for? Sections are useful for varying the formatting within a document.

4.5. Why might you want to convert a Word document to HTML? You must convert your documents to HTML before posting them to a Web site or your company's intranet.

Glossary

Adaptive menus: The dynamic menu bars and toolbars that are personalized to the way you work. Office XP watches the tasks that you perform in an application and then displays only those commands and buttons that you use most often.

Application window: In Microsoft Windows, each running application program appears in its own application window. These windows can be sized and moved anywhere on the Windows desktop.

AutoCorrect feature: Software feature that corrects common typing and spelling mistakes automatically as you type. It also enables you to enter complex symbols quickly and easily.

AutoFormat feature: Software feature that enhances your text's appearance as you type, applying special formatting to headings, bulleted and numbered lists, borders, and numbers.

AutoText feature: Software feature that makes it easy to insert frequently used text, such as the current date.

Bullets: The symbols used to set apart points in a document. Bullets are typically round dots and appear in paragraphs with a hanging indent.

Drag and drop: A software feature that allows you to copy and move information by dragging information from one location to another using the mouse.

End of Document Marker: The black horizontal bar that appears at the end of a Word document. You cannot move the insertion point beyond this marker.

Font(s): All the characters of one size in a particular typeface; includes numbers, punctuation marks, and upper- and lowercase letters.

Footer(s): Descriptive information (such as page number and date) that appears at the bottom of each page of a document.

Format Painter: Software feature that enables you to copy only the formatting attributes and styles from one location to another.

Gutter: In Word, the gutter is where pages are joined together in a bound document.

Header(s): Descriptive information (such as page number and data) that appears at the top of each page of a document.

HTML: An acronym for Hypertext Markup Language, which is the standardized markup language used in creating documents for display on the World Wide Web.

Hyperlink: In terms of Internet technologies, a text string or graphics that when clicked take you to another location, either within the same document or to a separate document stored on your computer, an intranet resource, or onto the Internet.

Insertion point: The vertical flashing bar in Word that indicates your current position in the document. The insertion point shows where the next typed characters will appear.

Internet: A worldwide network of computer networks that are interconnected by standard telephone lines, fiber optics, and satellites.

Intranet: A private local or wide area network that uses Internet protocols and technologies to share information within an institution or corporation.

Justification: Refers to how a paragraph is aligned within the left and right indent markers (left, centered, right, or justified).

Landscape orientation: Describes how a page is printed. Letter-size paper with a landscape orientation measures 11 inches wide by 8.5 inches high. Legal-size paper with a landscape orientation measures 14 inches wide by 8.5 inches high.

Leaders: The symbols, lines, dots, or dashes that fill the gap between text and tab stops.

Normal view: In this display mode, your document displays without headers, footers, and columns.

Office Clipboard: A program, in Office XP, that allows you to copy and move information within or among Office XP applications. Unlike the Windows Clipboard, the Office Clipboard can store up to 12 items and then paste them all at once.

Orphan: Single sentence that appears at the bottom of a page, separated from the rest of its paragraph on the next page.

Outline view: In this display mode, you view the main headings of a document. This view mode also provides a convenient environment for organizing a document.

Paragraph mark: The symbol (¶) at the end of a paragraph that stores all of Word's paragraph formatting information.

Places bar: The strip of icon buttons appearing in the Open and Save As dialog boxes that allow you to display the most common areas for retrieving and storing files using a single mouse click.

Portrait orientation: Describes how a page is printed. Letter-size paper with a portrait orientation measures 8.5 inches wide by 11 inches high. Legal-size paper with a landscape orientation measures 8.5 inches wide by 14 inches high.

Print Layout view: In this display mode, you see how text and graphics will appear on the printed page.

Repeat command: Repeats the last action you performed.

Section break: A nonprinting code that marks the beginning of a new document section.

Selection bar: The leftmost column of the document window. The Selection bar provides shortcut methods for selecting text in a document using the mouse.

Smart tag: Data that Word recognizes and marks with a purple dotted underline. Using an associated Smart Tag Actions menu, you can perform several different actions on the data.

Smart Tag Actions button: Button that appears when you move the mouse pointer over a smart tag.

Spelling and Grammar command: A proofing tool that analyzes your document all at once for spelling and grammar errors and reports the results.

Style: A collection of character and/or paragraph formatting commands.

Task pane: Context-sensitive toolbar in Word that provides convenient access to relevant commands and procedures.

Template: A document that has been saved to a special file and location so that it may be used again and again as a model for creating new documents.

Thesaurus: A proofing tool that provides quick access to synonyms and antonyms for a given word or phrase. A synonym is a word that has the same meaning as another word. An antonym has the opposite meaning.

Undo command: A command that makes it possible to reverse up to the last 16 commands or actions performed.

Web Layout view: In this display mode, you see how your document will look in a Web browser.

Widow: Single sentence that appears at the top of a page, separated from the rest of its paragraph on the previous page.

Windows Clipboard: A program, in Windows, that allows you to copy and move information within an application or among applications. The Windows Clipboard temporarily stores the information in memory before you paste the data in a new location.

Wizard: A program or process whereby a series of dialog boxes lead you step-by-step through performing a procedure.

Word processing: Preparation of a document using a microcomputer.

Word wrap: When the insertion point reaches the right-hand margin of a line, it automatically wraps to the left margin of the next line; the user does not have to press ENTER at the end of each line.

World Wide Web: A visual interface to the Internet based on hyperlinks. Using Web browser software, you click on hyperlinks to navigate resources on the Internet.

Index

Adaptive menus, WD-6
disabling, WD-6–7
Align Center button, WD-95–96
Align Left button, WD-95–96
Alignment of paragraphs, WD-95–96
Align Right button, WD-95–96, 148
Application window
Formatting toolbar. *See* Formatting toolbar
menus. *See* Menus
Standard toolbar. *See* Standard toolbar
Application window, components of, WD-3–4
AutoCorrect feature, WD-10
capitalization, WD-12
AutoFormat feature, WD-10
AutoText feature, WD-10
dates, WD-14–15

b

Back button, WD-24
BACKSPACE key, WD-10, 13
Blank lines
deleting, WD-12
inserting, WD-10–11
Bold button, WD-83–84
Header and Footer toolbar, WD-143–144
Bolding text, WD-83–84
Borders
page, WD-116–117
paragraphs, WD-113–115
Borders and Shading dialog box
Borders tab, WD-114
Page Border tab, WD-116
Shading tab, WD-112
Breaks
page breaks, WD-138–139
section breaks, WD-145–147
Bulleted lists, WD-102–103
Bullets and Numbering dialog box, WD-104, 106
Bullets button, WD-103
Buttons
Align Center, WD-95–96
Align Left, WD-95–96
Align Right, WD-95–96, 148
Back, WD-24
Bold, WD-83–84
Bold (Header and Footer toolbar), WD-143–144
Bullets, WD-103
Center (Header and Footer toolbar), WD-143
Close, WD-2, 4
Copy, WD-61–62
Cut, WD-61, 63
Decrease indent, WD-97–98
Find Next, WD-58–59
Font Color, WD-85
Format Painter, WD-90–91
Highlight, WD-92
History, WD-23
Increase indent, WD-97
Insert Date (Header and Footer toolbar), WD-144
Insert Page Number (Header and Footer toolbar), WD-148
Insert Time (Header and Footer toolbar), WD-144
Italic, WD-83–84
Justify, WD-95–96
Landscape (page orientation), WD-136
Maximize, WD-4
Minimize, WD-4
Multiple Pages (in Print Preview), WD-131
My Documents, WD-23
New, WD-19–20
Next (Header and Footer toolbar), WD-149
Next Page, WD-50–51
Normal view, WD-31–32
Numbering, WD-103–104
One Page (in Print Preview), WD-132
Open, WD-26
Outline, WD-31
Page Break, WD-138
Paste, WD-61, WD-62–63
Paste Options, WD-62–63
Portrait (page orientation), WD-137
Previous (Header and Footer toolbar), WD-149
Previous Page, WD-50
Print, WD-26–27, 132–133
Print Layout, WD-31
Print Preview, WD-130
Replace All, WD-60
Restore, WD-4
Save, WD-22, 24–25
Smart Tag Actions, WD-17–18
Spell and Grammar, WD-67
Start, WD-2
Style, WD-88–89
Switch Between Header and Footer, WD-150
Tab Alignment, WD-108–109
Underline, WD-83–84
Undo, WD-52–53, 56

Capitalization with AutoCorrect feature, WD-12
Case problems
Animal Care League, WD-126–128
Main Street Antiques, WD-78–80
Student Tutoring Services, WD-43–46
Yard Smart Designs, WD-168–170
"Celsius Gear, USA" exercises
Copying and Moving Information, WD-75–76
Creating a Fax from a Template, WD-41–42
Reformatting a Memo, WD-124
Varying a Report's Formatting, WD-165
Center (Header and Footer toolbar) button, WD-143
Center justification, WD-95–96
Characters. See Fonts
Click and Type, WD-35
Clipboards
Office Clipboard, WD-61, 64
Windows Clipboard, WD-61–63
"Clippit," WD-3
Close button, WD-2, 4
Closing documents, WD-25
Color
fonts, WD-85–86
highlighting, WD-92
Commands
See also Menus
dimmed, WD-4
ellipsis (...) following, WD-4
executing, WD-4

Exit, WD-2
Find, WD-57
Go To, WD-51
Help, What's This?, WD-94
New, WD-19
New, Folder, WD-28
Open, WD-26
Print, WD-132
Print Preview, WD-130
Repeat, WD-52–53
Replace, WD-59–60
Save, WD-22
Save As, WD-22
Save as Web Page, WD-156
Show/Hide (Formatting toolbar), WD-94
Start, Open Office Document, WD-25
Undo, WD-52–53
Word Count, WD-68
Context-sensitive, right-click. *See* Right-click menus
CONTROL key. *See* CTRL key
Copy button, WD-61–62
Copying formatting attributes, WD-90–91
Copying text, WD-61–62
drag and drop, WD-64–66
CTRL key
- [, WD-83
-], WD-83
- b key, WD-83–84
- c key, WD-61
- ENTER key, WD-138
- F4 key, WD-89
- HOME key, WD-12–13, 51–52, 64, 91
- i key, WD-83–84
- left mouse button click, WD-55
- selection bar click, WD-56
- SHIFT key 1 a, WD-83
- SHIFT key 1 f, WD-83
- SHIFT key 1 F3, WD-83
- SHIFT key 1 p, WD-83
- SHIFT key 1 Space Bar, WD-83
- u key, WD-83–84
- v key, WD-61
- x key, WD-61
- y key, WD-89, 113
- z key, WD-52

Customize dialog box, Options tab, WD-6
Cut button, WD-61, 63
Cutting text, WD-61, 63

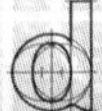

Date and Time dialog box, WD-15
Dates
AutoText feature, WD-14–15
Insert Date (Header and Footer toolbar), WD-144
inserting, WD-14–15
Decrease indent button, WD-97–98
DELETE key, WD-10
Dialog boxes
Borders and Shading dialog box. *See* Borders and Shading dialog box
Bullets and Numbering dialog box, WD-104, 106
check marks, WD-7
Customize dialog box, Options tab, WD-6
Date and Time dialog box, WD-15
Find and Replace dialog box, WD-58, 60
Go To dialog box, WD-51–52
Open dialog box, WD-26–27
Page Numbers dialog box, WD-141
Page Setup dialog box. *See* Page Setup dialog box
Paragraph dialog box. *See* Paragraph dialog box
Print dialog box, WD-133
Save As dialog box, WD-23–24
Spelling and Grammar dialog box, WD-67
Tabs dialog box, WD-110
Templates dialog box, WD-21
Theme dialog box, WD-155
Thesaurus dialog box, WD-69
Word Count dialog box, WD-68
"DigiTech Services" exercises
Creating Letterhead Stationary, WD-163–164
Designing a Memo, WD-122–124
Editing an Existing Document, WD-40–41
Editing a Report, WD-75
Dimmed commands, WD-4
Documents
closing, WD-25
creating, WD-9
naming, WD-19
navigating, WD-50–52
new document creation, WD-19–22
opening. *See* Opening documents
previewing, WD-130–132
printing, WD-27, 132–133
saving. *See* Saving documents
selecting, WD-25, 56
templates, WD-19–21
viewing. *See* Viewing documents
Dragging, WD-50
drag and drop, WD-64–66

Edit menu
Find, WD-57
Go To, WD-51
Office Clipboard, WD-61
Repeat, WD-52–53
Replace, WD-59–60
Undo, WD-52–53
END key, WD-51
CTRL key +, WD-15, 51
ENTER key, WD-10
CTRL key +, WD-138
Executing commands, WD-4
Exercises
Applying Styles, WD-126
Celsius Gear, USA. *See* "Celsius Gear, USA" exercises
Creating a Letter to a Friend, WD-43
Customizing Your Work Area, WD-43
Describing Your Hobby, WD-77
Designing a Budget Document, WD-166–167
DigiTech Services. *See* "DigiTech Services" exercises
Finalizing a Document, WD-77–78
Formatting a News Letter, WD-168
Garage Sale Notice, WD-125
Laura Howard. *See* "Laura Howard" exercises
Worldwide Conventions, Inc. *See* "Worldwide Conventions, Inc." exercises
Exit command, WD-2
Exiting Word, WD-2

F3 key 1 SHIFT key, WD-66
F4 key 1 CTRL key, WD-89
F5 key, WD-51
F7 key 1 SHIFT key, WD-69
File management, WD-18–19
folders. *See* Folders
naming files, WD-19
opening files. *See* Opening documents
saving files. *See* Saving documents
sorting files, WD-27
File menu
Exit, WD-2
New, WD-19
Open, WD-26
Page Setup, WD-134, 151–152
Print, WD-132
Print Preview, WD-130

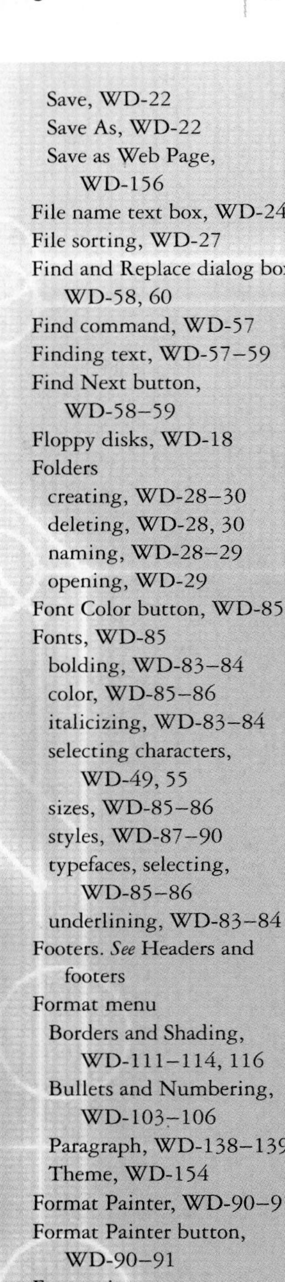

Save, WD-22
Save As, WD-22
Save as Web Page, WD-156
File name text box, WD-24
File sorting, WD-27
Find and Replace dialog box, WD-58, 60
Find command, WD-57
Finding text, WD-57–59
Find Next button, WD-58–59
Floppy disks, WD-18
Folders
creating, WD-28–30
deleting, WD-28, 30
naming, WD-28–29
opening, WD-29
Font Color button, WD-85
Fonts, WD-85
bolding, WD-83–84
color, WD-85–86
italicizing, WD-83–84
selecting characters, WD-49, 55
sizes, WD-85–86
styles, WD-87–90
typefaces, selecting, WD-85–86
underlining, WD-83–84
Footers. *See* Headers and footers
Format menu
Borders and Shading, WD-111–114, 116
Bullets and Numbering, WD-103–106
Paragraph, WD-138–139
Theme, WD-154
Format Painter, WD-90–91
Format Painter button, WD-90–91
Formatting
AutoFormat feature, WD-10
characters. *See* Fonts
paragraphs. *See* Paragraphs
sections. *See* Section formatting
shading words and paragraphs, WD-111–113
Formatting toolbar, WD-8
displaying and hiding, WD-6–7
moving, WD-9
Full justification, WD-95–96

Go To command, WD-51
Go To dialog box, WD-51–52
Grammar
checker, WD-66–68
correcting mistakes as you go, WD-53–54
Green wavy underlines, WD-53
Gutters, WD-134

Hands-on exercises. *See* Exercises
Hanging indents, WD-99
Hard disks, WD-18
Header and Footer toolbar, WD-143
Headers and footers, WD-141
creating, WD-142–145
page numbers, WD-141–142
section formatting, WD-148–151
Help, What's This?, WD-94
Highlight button, WD-92
Highlighting text for review, WD-92–93
History button, WD-23
HOME key
CTRL key 1, WD-12–13, 51–52, 64, 91
document navigation, WD-51
inserting text, WD-11
HTML (Hypertext Markup Language), WD-156
Hyperlinks, WD-19–20, 153

Increase indent button, WD-97
Indenting paragraphs, WD-97–99
Indent markers, WD-99
Independent service providers (ISPs), WD-153
Insert Date (Header and Footer toolbar) button, WD-144
Insertion point, WD-10
positioning, WD-11–12, 49–52
Insert menu
Break, WD-145–147
Date and Time, WD-14
Page Numbers, WD-141
Insert mode, WD-10, 13
Insert Page Number (Header and Footer toolbar) button, WD-148
Insert Time (Header and Footer toolbar) button, WD-144
Internet, WD-153
publishing. *See* Web publishing
Intranet, WD-153
Italic button, WD-83–84
Italicizing text, WD-83–84

Justification of paragraphs, WD-95–96
Justify button, WD-95–96

Keystrokes
BACKSPACE key, WD-10, 13
CTRL key. *See* CTRL key
DELETE key, WD-10
document navigation, WD-51
END key. *See* END key
ENTER key. *See* ENTER key
F3 key 1 SHIFT key, WD-66
F4 key 1 CTRL key, WD-89
F5 key, WD-51
F7 key 1 SHIFT key, WD-69
HOME key. *See* HOME key
SHIFT key. *See* SHIFT key
TAB key, WD-110

Landscape orientation, WD-136
Landscape (page orientation) button, WD-136
Launching Word, WD-2–3
"Laura Howard" exercises
Creating a Document, WD-39–40
Customizing a Resume, WD-162–163
Formatting a Letter, WD-121–122
Proofing a Letter, WD-73–74
Leaders, WD-108
Left justification, WD-95–96
Letters. *See* Fonts
Lines
blank. *See* Blank lines
selecting, WD-49
spacing, WD-100–102
Lists, WD-102
bulleted, WD-102–103
numbered, WD-102, 104–105
outline–numbered list, WD-105–107

Maximize button, WD-4
Menu bar, WD-4
Menus
See also Commands
adaptive. *See* Adaptive menus
customizing, WD-6–7
Edit. *See* Edit menu
ellipsis (...), WD-4
extending, WD-7
File. *See* File menu
Format. *See* Format menu
Help, WD-4
Insert. *See* Insert menu
pull-down, WD-4
right-click. *See* Right-click menus
Style, WD-88
Tools. *See* Tools menu
View. *See* View menu
Minimize button, WD-4
Mouse
dragging. *See* Dragging
insertion point. *See* Insertion point
Moving text, WD-61, 63
drag and drop, WD-64–66

Multiple Pages (in Print Preview) button, WD-131
My Documents button, WD-23

Naming documents, WD-19
Naming folders, WD-28–29
Network drives, WD-18
New, Folder command, WD-28
New button, WD-19–20
New command, WD-19
New Document task pane, WD-19–20
Next (Header and Footer toolbar) button, WD-149
Next Page button, WD-50–51
Normal view, WD-32
Normal view button, WD-31–32
Numbered lists, WD-102, 104–105
  outline–numbered list, WD-105–107
Numbered outlines, WD-105–107
Numbering button, WD-103–104
Numbering pages, WD-141–142

Office Assistant characters
"Clippit," WD-3
  right-click hiding, WD-6
Office Clipboard, WD-61, 64
One Page (in Print Preview) button, WD-132
Open button, WD-26
Open command, WD-26
Open dialog box, WD-26–27
Opening documents, WD-25–27
  web pages, WD-158
Open Office Document command, WD-25
Orphans, WD-137
Outline button, WD-31
Outlines, numbered, WD-105–107
Outline view, WD-33
Overtype mode, WD-10, 12

Page borders, WD-116–117
Page Break button, WD-138
Page breaks, WD-138–139
Page layout, WD-133–134
  headers and footers. *See* Headers and footers
  margins, WD-134–136
  page orientation, WD-136–137
  pagination, WD-137–140
  sections. *See* Section formatting
Page numbers, WD-141–142
Page Numbers dialog box, WD-141
Page orientation, WD-136–137
  section formatting, WD-153
Page Setup dialog box
  Layout tab, WD-152
  Margins tab, WD-135
Pagination, WD-137–140
Paragraph dialog box, WD-102
  Line and Page Breaks tab, WD-139–140
Paragraph mark, WD-93
Paragraphs
  alignment, WD-95–96
  borders for, WD-113–115
  displaying formatting characteristics, WD-98
  indenting, WD-97–99
  line spacing, WD-100–102
  revealing formatting, WD-93–95
  selecting, WD-49, 56
  shading, WD-111–113, 115
  styles, WD-87–90
Paste button, WD-61–63
Paste Options button, WD-62–63
Pasting text, WD-61–63
Places bar, WD-23–24
Points, WD-85
Point size, WD-85–86
Portrait orientation, WD-136
Portrait (page orientation) button, WD-137
Previewing documents, WD-130–132
Previous (Header and Footer toolbar) button, WD-149
Previous Page button, WD-50
Print button, WD-26–27, WD-132–133
Print command, WD-132
Print dialog box, WD-133
Printing documents, WD-27, 132–133
Print Layout button, WD-31
Print Layout view, WD-33
  Click and Type, WD-35
  with landscape orientation, WD-137
Print Preview button, WD-130
Print Preview command, WD-130
Purple spotted underlines, WD-16–18

Quitting Word, WD-2

RAM (Random Access Memory), WD-18
Red wavy underlines, WD-53
Repeat command, WD-52–53
Replace All button, WD-60
Replace command, WD-59–60
Replacing text, WD-59–61
Restore button, WD-4
Right-click menus, WD-5
  hiding the character, WD-6
  new folder creation, WD-28
Right justification, WD-95–96

Save As command, WD-22
Save As dialog box, WD-23–24
Save as Web Page command, WD-156
Save button, WD-22, 24–25
Save command, WD-22
Save-in drop down list box, WD-23–24
Saving documents, WD-18–19, 22–25
  as web pages, WD-156–157
Scrolling, WD-50
Section formatting, WD-145
  headers and footers, WD-148–151
  inserting section breaks, WD-145–147
  page orientation, WD-153
  page setup options, WD-151–153
Selecting text, WD-54–57
Selection bar, WD-48, 56
Sentences, selecting, WD-49, 55–56
Shading words and paragraphs, WD-111–113, 115
SHIFT key
- CTRL key 1 a, WD-83
- CTRL key 1 f, WD-83
- CTRL key 1 F3, WD-83
- CTRL key 1 p, WD-83
- CTRL key 1 Space Bar, WD-83
- F3 key, WD-66
- F7 key, WD-69

Show/Hide (Formatting toolbar), WD-94
Sizes of fonts, WD-85–86
Smart Tag Actions button, WD-17–18
Smart tags, WD-16–18
Sorting files, WD-27
Spaces
  inserting, WD-10
  line spacing, WD-100–102
Spell and Grammar button, WD-67
Spelling
  checker, WD-66–68

Word

correcting mistakes as you go, WD-53–54
Spelling and Grammar dialog box, WD-67
Standard toolbar, WD-8
displaying and hiding, WD-6–7
moving, WD-9
Start button, WD-2
Starting Word, WD-2–3
Style button, WD-88–89
Styles, WD-87–90
Switch Between Header and Footer button, WD-150

Tab Alignment button, WD-108–109
Tab leaders, WD-108
Tabs, WD-108–111
Tabs dialog box, WD-110
Tags, WD-16–18
Task pane
Formatting, WD-95
New Document, WD-19
showing and hiding, WD-6, 8
Templates, WD-19–21
Templates dialog box, WD-21
Text
AutoText feature. *See* AutoText feature
bolding, WD-83–84
changing, WD-56
color, WD-85–86
copying, WD-61–62
cutting, WD-61, 63
drag and drop, WD-64–66
finding, WD-57–59
grammar and spelling error correction, WD-53–54
highlighting for review, WD-92–93
inserting and deleting, WD-10–14
italicizing, WD-83–84
lists. *See* Lists
paragraphs. *See* Paragraphs
pasting, WD-61–63
point size, WD-85–86
replacing, WD-59–61
selecting, WD-49, 54–57
styles, WD-87–90
typefaces, WD-85–86
underlining, WD-83–84
"word wrap" feature, WD-15–16
Theme dialog box, WD-155
Thesaurus dialog box, WD-69
Time
inserting, WD-14
Insert Time (Header and Footer toolbar), WD-144
Title bar icons, WD-4
Toolbars
command, WD-6
docked, WD-9
Formatting toolbar. *See* Formatting toolbar
Header and Footer, WD-143
moving, WD-9
Standard toolbar. *See* Standard toolbar
undocked, WD-9
Tools menu, WD-6–7
Language, Thesaurus, WD-69
Spelling and Grammar, WD-67
Typefaces, selecting, WD-85–86

Underline button, WD-83–84
Underlining text, WD-83–84
Undo and repeat, WD-52–53
Undo button, WD-52–53, 56
Undo command, WD-52–53

Viewing documents
selecting a view, WD-31–33
zooming in and out, WD-33–35
View menu
Header and Footer, WD-142, 152
Normal, WD-31–32
Outline, WD-31, 33
Print Layout, WD-31, 33
task pane, WD-6, 8
Toolbars, WD-6
Web Layout, WD-31, 33
Zoom, WD-33

Web Layout view, WD-33
Click and Type, WD-35
Web publishing, WD-153
pages, WD-156–158
themes, WD-154–156
Widows, WD-137
Windows Clipboard, WD-61–63
Wizards, WD-19
Word Count command, WD-68
Word Count dialog box, WD-68
Words
selecting, WD-49, 55
shading, WD-111–113
Word Count command, WD-68
"Word wrap" feature, WD-15–16
"Worldwide Conventions, Inc." exercises
Bulletin, WD-124–125
Editing a Memo, WD-42–43
Formatting a Document for the Web, WD-165–166
Modifying a Document, WD-76–77
World Wide Web, WD-153
publishing. *See* Web publishing

Zooming in and out, WD-33–35

Answers
to self-check questions

SelfCheck

1.1. How do you turn the adaptive menus feature on or off? Choose the Tools, Customize command and then check the *Always show full menus* check box to turn the adaptive menus feature off. Remove the check to turn the feature back on.

1.2. Explain why a phone number is not considered a numeric value in an Excel worksheet. Although it contains numbers, a phone number is never used to perform mathematical calculations.

1.3. Why is worksheet editing such a valuable skill? Most worksheets in use today are revisions and updates of older worksheets. As a novice user, you often spend more time updating existing worksheets than constructing new ones.

1.4. In the Open and Save As dialog boxes, how do the List and Details views differ? Name two other views that are accessible from the Views button. The List view uses a multicolumn format. The Details view displays one file per row. Furthermore, the Details view displays other information, including the file size, type, and modification date. The other views that appear on the drop-down menu include Large Icons, Small Icons, Properties, Preview, Thumbnails, and WebView.

2.1. Which of the "Auto" features enables you to sum a range of values and display the result in the Status bar? AutoCalculate

2.2. Which method would you use to copy several nonadjacent worksheet values for placement into a single column? The Office Clipboard would provide the fastest method. After displaying the Clipboard task pane, you would clear the Clipboard and collect up to 24 items in the desired sequence. Then, you would move to the target range and paste these items into a single column.

2.3. Why must you be careful when deleting rows or columns? If you delete the entire row or column, you may inadvertently delete data that exists further down a column or across a row. Ensure that a row or column is indeed empty before deleting it.

3.1. What is the basic difference between using the Underline button ( ) and the Borders button ( )? When you apply an underline to a cell, only the words in the cell appear underlined. When you apply a border underline to a cell, the entire cell is underlined. Also, borders may be applied to each side of a cell, such as top, bottom, left, and right.

3.2. How might you ensure that related worksheets and workbooks are formatted consistently? Use the same predefined AutoFormat style to format all of the worksheets.

3.3. How does the Print Preview display mode differ from the Web Page Preview display mode? Print Preview appears in the Excel application window and displays the workbook as it will appear when printed. Web Page Preview uses the computer's default Web browser to display an HTML rendering of the current worksheet.

3.4. How would you create a custom footer that displayed your name against the left page border and your company's name against the right page border? In the Page Setup dialog box, you would click the Custom Footer command button on the *Header/Footer* tab. Then, you would enter your name into the left text box and your company's name into the right text box of the Footer dialog box.

4.1. Why is "AD2002" an unacceptable name for a cell range? You cannot name a cell range using an actual cell reference on the worksheet.

4.2. When might you use the Function Arguments dialog box or Insert Function dialog box to enter a function into the worksheet? If you need help entering the arguments in the correct order or if you cannot remember a function's name or proper syntax, you can use these tools to refresh your memory or to assist you in completing the task.

4.3. What must you do when selecting the print range for a worksheet that contains an embedded chart? Because charts do not appear in cells on a worksheet, you must be sure to select the print range to include these graphic objects. For example, select the cells that appear underneath the embedded chart that you want to print.

Glossary

Absolute cell address: Cell reference in a worksheet that does not adjust when copied to other cells. You make a cell address absolute by placing dollar signs ($) before the column letter and row number, such as $C$4.

Adaptive menus: The dynamic menu bars and toolbars that are personalized to the way you work. Office XP watches the tasks that you perform in an application and then displays only those commands and buttons that you use most often.

Application window: In Windows, each running application program appears in its own application window. These windows may be sized and moved anywhere on the Windows desktop.

Arguments: The parameters used in entering a function according to its *syntax.* Arguments may include text, numbers, formulas, functions, and cell references.

AutoCalculate: In Excel, a software feature that sums the selected range of cells and displays the result in the Status bar.

AutoComplete: In Excel, a software feature that assists you in entering data into a worksheet by filling in letters from existing entries in the column as you type.

AutoFill: In Excel, a software feature that enables you to copy and extend a formula or data series automatically in a worksheet.

AutoFit: In Excel, a software feature that calculates the optimal row height or column width based on existing data in the worksheet.

AutoFormat: A software feature that applies professionally designed formatting styles to your documents.

AutoSum: A software feature that automatically inserts a formula for adding values from a surrounding row or column of cells.

Bar chart: A chart that compares one data element to another data element using horizontal bars. Similar to a *column chart.*

Cell: The intersection of a column and a row.

Cell address: The location of a cell on a worksheet given by the intersection of a column and a row. Columns are labeled using letters. Rows are numbered. A cell address combines the column letter with the row number (for example, B9 or DF134).

Cell alignment: The positioning of data entered into a worksheet cell in relation to the cell borders.

Cell pointer: The cursor on a worksheet that points to a cell. The cell pointer is moved using the arrow keys or the mouse.

Cell range: One or more cells in a worksheet that together form a rectangle.

Chart sheet: A sheet tab or page within a workbook file that is used to create, modify, and display a chart graphic.

Chart Wizard: A linear step progression of dialog boxes that leads you through creating a chart in Excel.

Column chart: A chart that compares one data element with another data element and can show variations over a period of time.

Document window: In Excel, each open *workbook* appears in its own document window. These windows may be sized and moved anywhere within the application window.

Drag and drop: A software feature that allows you to copy and move information by dragging cell information from one location to another using the mouse.

Embedded chart: A chart that is placed on the draw layer of a worksheet.

Fill handle: The small black square that is located in the bottom right-hand corner of a cell or cell range. You use the fill handle to create a series or to copy cell information.

Font: All the characters of one size in a particular *typeface;* includes numbers, punctuation marks, and upper- and lowercase letters.

Footer: Descriptive information (such as page number and date) that appears at the bottom of each page of a document.

Format Painter: A software feature that enables you to copy only the formatting attributes and styles from one location to another.

Formula: A mathematical expression that typically defines the relationships among various cells in a worksheet or table.

Functions: Built-in shortcuts that can be used in formulas to perform calculations.

Gridlines: The lines on a worksheet that assist the user in lining up the cell pointer with a particular column letter or row number.

Header: Descriptive information (such as page number and data) that appears at the top of each page of a document.

HTML: An acronym for Hypertext Markup Language, which is the standardized markup language used in creating documents for display on the World Wide Web.

Hyperlinks: In terms of Internet technologies, a text string or graphics that when clicked take you to another location, either within the same document or to a separate document stored on your computer, an intranet resource, or onto the Internet.

In-cell editing: In Excel, the feature that enables you to revise text labels, numbers, dates, and other entries directly within a cell. To activate in-cell editing, you double-click a cell.

Internet: A worldwide network of computer networks that are interconnected by standard telephone lines, fiber optics, and satellites.

Intranet: A private local or wide area network that uses Internet protocols and technologies to share information within an institution or corporation.

Line chart: A chart that plots trends or shows changes over a period of time.

Macro virus: A malicious program that attaches itself to a document or template and performs instructions that may damage files on your computer.

Margins: Space between the edge of the paper and the top, bottom, left, and right edges of the printed document.

Mixed cell address: Cell reference in a worksheet that includes both *relative* and *absolute cell references.* For example, the address C$4 provides a "relative" column letter and an "absolute" row number.

Name box: The text box appearing at the left-hand side of the Formula bar that displays the current cell address and that enables you to navigate quickly to any cell location in the worksheet.

Natural language formula: In Excel, a type of *formula* that allows you to use the column and row labels within a worksheet in building a mathematical expression.

Normal view: In Excel, the standard view mode used for creating a workbook. You can adjust a zoom factor for viewing more or less of a worksheet in this mode.

Office Clipboard: A program, in Office XP, that allows you to copy and move information within or among Office XP applications. Unlike the Windows Clipboard, the Office Clipboard can store up to 24 items and then paste them all at once.

Page Break Preview: In Excel, the preview mode used prior to printing in order to adjust the print area and page breaks that occur in a workbook.

Pie chart: A chart that shows the proportions of individual components compared to the whole.

Places bar: The strip of icon buttons appearing in the Open and Save As dialog boxes that allow you to display the most common areas for retrieving and storing files using a single mouse click.

Print Preview: In Excel, the preview mode used to view a workbook in a full-page WYSIWYG display prior to printing. You can use Print Preview to move through pages, zoom in and out on areas of a worksheet, and adjust page margins and column widths.

Range Finder: An Excel feature that color-codes the cell or range references in a formula expression for easy reference and error-checking.

Range name: A name that is given to a range of cells in the worksheet. This name can then be used in formulas and functions to refer to the cell range.

Redo command: A command that makes it possible to reverse the effects of an Undo command.

Relative cell address: Default cell reference in a worksheet that automatically adjusts when copied to other cells.

Scatter plot diagram: A chart that shows how one or more data elements relate to another data element. Also called *XY chart.*

Series: A sequence of numbers or dates that follows a mathematical or date pattern.

Syntax: The rules, structure, and order of *arguments* used in entering a formula or function.

Task pane: A toolbar-like window providing quick access to frequently used commands. By default, the task pane appears docked to the right side of the application window, but it may be displayed and hidden using the View menu command.

Template: A workbook or document that has been saved to a special file and location so that it may be used again and again as a model for creating new documents.

Typeface: The shape and appearance of characters. There are two categories of typefaces: serif and sans serif. Serif type (for example, Times Roman) is more decorative and, some say, easier to read than sans serif type (for example, Arial).

Undo command: A command that makes it possible to reverse up to the last 16 commands or actions performed.

Windows Clipboard: A program, in Windows, that allows you to copy and move information within an application or among applications. The system, or Windows, Clipboard temporarily stores the information in memory before you paste the data in a new location.

Wizard: A program or process whereby a series of dialog boxes lead you step-by-step through performing a procedure.

Workbook: The disk file that contains the *worksheets* and *chart sheets* that you create in Excel.

Worksheet: A sheet tab or page within a workbook file that is used to create, modify, and display a worksheet grid of columns and rows.

World Wide Web: A visual interface to the Internet based on *hyperlinks.* Using Web browser software, you click on hyperlinks to navigate resources on the Internet.

XY chart: Chart that shows how one or more data elements relate to another data element. Also called scatter plot diagram.

Index

Absolute cell addresses, EX-21, 167–169
Adaptive menus, EX-8
  disabling, EX-8–9
Adding values (SUM function), EX-172–174
Align Left button, EX-117–118
Alignment
  cells, EX-117–118
  numbers, EX-16
  text, EX-16
Align Right button, EX-117–118
Application window, EX-5
  components of, EX-6
Arguments, functions, EX-171
Arrowkeys, EX-11–12
AutoCalculate, EX-62–65
AutoComplete, EX-60–62
AutoFill, EX-77–80
AutoFill Options icon, EX-78
Autofit
  column width, EX-83, 85
  row height, EX-85, 88
AutoFormat command, EX-131–132
AutoFormat dialog box, EX-131–132
AutoSum button, EX-62, 64–65
AVERAGE function, EX-174–175

Bar charts, EX-183
Bold button, EX-111–112, 126
Bolding, EX-111–113
Borders and shading, EX-120–124
Borders button, EX-120–123
Borders toolbar, EX-123–124
"Brentwood Academy" exercises, EX-42–43, 96–98, 150–151, 195–196
Buttons
  See also specific name of button on Windows taskbar, EX-5

Case problems
Citywide Insurance Agency, EX-106–108
  H. F. Charters, EX-52–54
  Hip Hop Hits, EX-158–160
  Prairie Soccer Association, EX-202–206
Cell address, EX-2
  absolute cell address, EX-21, 167–169
  mixed cell address, EX-167
  relative cell address, EX-21–167
Cell pointer, EX-7, 11
Cell ranges, EX-56
  AutoFill, EX-77–80
  copying and pasting, EX-70–71
  deleting, EX-66, 68
  dragging and dropping data, EX-75–77
  filling, EX-81–82
  inserting, EX-66–67
  naming. *See* Range names
  printing, EX-143–146
  selecting, EX-56–59
Cells, EX-2, 7
  alignment, EX-117–118
  dates in. *See* Dates
  deleting, EX-66, 68
  editing contents, EX-21, 23
  erasing contents, EX-24–26
  extending cell's contents, EX-80–82
  Format Cells dialog box. *See* Format Cells Dialog box
  formatting. *See* generally Formatting
  formulas in. *See* Formulas
  inserting, EX-66–67
  merger and center contents, EX-117–119
  numbers in. *See* Numbers
  selecting. *See* Selecting cells
  splitting merged cells, EX-119
  text in. *See* Text
Center button, EX-117–118
Character formatting, EX-111–113
Charts, EX-182–184
  See also specific name of chart
  embedded. *See* Embedded charts
Chart sheets, EX-3
Chart Wizard, EX-185–189
Chart Wizard button, EX-185–186
Clear, Formats command, EX-127–128
Clear All button (Office Clipboard), EX-73–75
Clipboards
  Office Clipboard, EX-72–75
  Windows Clipboard, EX-69–72
"Clippit," EX-5
Close button, EX-4–5
Close command, EX-34
Color
  Fill Color, EX-120, 122
  fonts, EX-111, 113
Column, AutoFit command, EX-83, 85
Column, Width command, EX-84
Column charts, EX-183
Columns, EX-2
  date headings, entering, EX-15–16
  deleting, EX-88–90
  headings, entering, EX-22
  headings, printing, EX-145
  hiding/unhiding, EX-91–92
  inserting, EX-88–90
  widths, changing, EX-83–85
Column Width dialog box, EX-84
Commands
  See also specific name of command
  dimmed, EX-7
  ellipsis (...), EX-7
  erasing cell attributes, EX-24
  erasing cell contents, EX-24–25
  executing, EX-7
  formatting. *See* generally Formatting
  saving files, EX-30–31
Context-sensitive, right-click menus. *See* Right-click menus
Copy button, EX-69–70
  Office Clipboard, EX-73
Copy command, EX-69
Copying and moving data
  drag and drop technique, EX-75–77
  Office Clipboard, EX-72–75
  Windows Clipboard, EX-69–72

COUNTA function, EX-176
COUNT function, EX-175–176
Create New Folder button, EX-36–37
CTRL-selecting, EX-58–59
Currency Style button, EX-114, 116, 126
Custom Header button, EX-141–142
Custom Header dialog box, EX-142–143
Custom headers, EX-142–143
Customize dialog box, EX-9
Cut button, EX-69
Cut command, EX-69

Dates
  entering in cells, EX-15–16
  extending headings, EX-81
  formatting, EX-116–117
  functions, EX-179–182
Decimal buttons
Decrease, EX-114
  Increase, EX-114–115
Define Name dialog box, EX-165–166
Delete command, EX-38
Deleting
  cell contents, EX-24–26
  cells and cell ranges, EX-66, 68
  files, EX-38
  rows and columns, EX-88–90
Dialog boxes. *See* specific name of dialog box
Dimmed commands, EX-7
Docked toolbars, EX-11
Documents command, on Start menu, EX-34
Document window, EX-5
  components of, EX-7–8
Double-clicking
  Autofit columns, EX-83, 85
  Autofit rows, EX-85–86
Downloading
  templates, EX-30
Dragging and dropping data, EX-75–77
Draw Borders button, EX-123
Duplicating data. *See* Copying and moving data

Editing worksheets, EX-21, 23–24
Ellipsis (...) command, EX-7
Embedded charts, EX-184–185
Chart Wizard, EX-188–189
  previewing and printing, EX-189–191
END key, EX-11–12
Erasing. *See* Deleting
Exercises
  Auto Fuel Comparison, EX-201–202
  "Brentwood Academy," EX-42–43, 96–98, 150–151, 195–196
  Magic Financial Data Table, EX-156–157
  Magic Lights Personnel, EX-104–105
  Magic Personal Expense Comparison, EX-157
  My Grade Book, EX-51
  Personal Expense Chart, EX-202
  Personal Monthly Budget, EX-50–51
  Running Diary, EX-105
  "Staples Foods," EX-46–47, 101–103, 154–155, 199–200
  "Sutton House Realty," EX-48–49, 103–104, 155–156, 200–201
  "Top Picks Video," EX-43–46, 98–101, 152–153, 197–198
Exiting Excel, EX-4–5
Extending cell's contents, EX-80–82
Extending rows, EX-78–79

F2 (EDIT) key, EX-23
F4 (ABS) key, EX-168
F9 (CALC) key, EX-181
File management, EX-28
  deleting files, EX-38
  folders, EX-36–EX-38
  naming files. *See* Naming files
  opening files. *See* Opening files
  saving files. *See* Saving files
Fill Color button, EX-120–122
Fill commands, EX-80
Fill handle, EX-78–81, 93
Filling cells, EX-80–82
Floating toolbars, EX-11
Folders, EX-36–38
Font Color button, EX-111–122, 126, 128
Font list box, EX-111–112
Fonts
  bolding, EX-111–113
  color, EX-111, 113, 122, 126, 128
  sizing, EX-111–113
  typefaces, changing, EX-111–113
  underlining, EX-111–112
Font Size list box, EX-111–112
Footers, EX-141–143
Format Cells dialog box
  character formatting, EX-113
  date formatting, EX-116
  merger and center cell contents, EX-118–119
  number formatting, EX-115
  rotating text, EX-119
Format Painter, EX-124–127
Format Painter button, EX-124–127
Formatting
  aligning cells, EX-117–118
  AutoFormat command, EX-131–132
  borders and shading, EX-120–124
  character, EX-111–113
  dates, EX-116–117
  merging and centering cell contents, EX-117–119
  numbers, EX-114–116
  page layout settings, EX-138–140
  Paste Special command, EX-129–130
  removing, EX-127–128
  rotating text, EX-119
Formatting toolbar, EX-8
  displaying, EX-8–10
Formulas
  absolute cell addresses, EX-21, 167–169
  entering in cells, EX-17–21
  extending, EX-81–82
  natural language, EX-169–171
  pointing method of entry, EX-18–19
  relative cell addresses, EX-21
Function Arguments dialog box, EX-179–180
Functions, EX-171
  See also specific name of function
  arguments, EX-171
  categories, EX-172
  syntax, EX-171

Gridlines, printing, EX-145

Hands-on exercises. *See* Exercises
Headers, EX-141–143
Help command, EX-7
Hiding/unhiding rows and columns, EX-91–92
HOME key, EX-11–12
HTML (Hypertext Markup Language), EX-136
Hyperlinks, EX-133

IF function, EX-182
Inactive sheet tab, EX-7
In-cell editing, EX-21, 23
Insert Function button, EX-171, 180–181
Insert Function dialog box, EX-171, 180
Inserting
  cells and cell ranges, EX-66–67
  rows and columns, EX-88–90

Internet, EX-133
publishing, EX-136–138
templates, downloading, EX-30
Intranets, sharing templates on, EX-30
Italic button, EX-111, 126, 128

Keystrokes
character formatting, EX-113
copying data, EX-69
cutting data, EX-69
erasing cell contents, EX-24–26
F2 (EDIT) key, EX-23
F4 (ABS) key, EX-168
F9 (CALC) key, EX-181
navigating worksheets, EX-11–12
pasting data, EX-69
Print Screen, EX-146
selecting cell ranges, EX-57, 58
Undo, EX-26

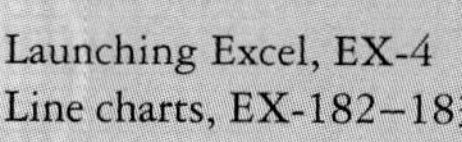

Launching Excel, EX-4
Line charts, EX-182–183

Macro virus, EX-29
Margin settings, adjusting, EX-140–141
Mathematical calculations
AutoCalculate, EX-62–65
date values, EX-15–16
Mathematical functions, EX-65
See also specific name of function
MAX function, EX-176–179
Maximize button, EX-7
Menu bar
commands. *See* Commands
using, EX-7
Menus
adaptive menus. *See* Adaptive menus
commands. *See* Commands
context-sensitive, right-click menus. *See* Right-click menus
Office Clipboard, EX-72
Programs menu, EX-4
pull-down menus, EX-4
Merge and Center button, EX-117–118
Merger and center cell contents, EX-117–119
MIN function, EX-176–177
Mixed cell address, EX-167
Mouse pointer, EX-7
dragging and dropping data, EX-75–77
Format Pointer, EX-126
formulas, entering, EX-18–19
navigating worksheets, EX-12
selecting cell ranges, EX-57–59
Moving data. *See* Copying and moving data
Moving toolbars, EX-11

Name box, EX-11–12
Naming files, EX-28, 33–34
replacing existing name, EX-33, 38
Natural language formulas, EX-169–171
New button, EX-22, 28–30
New command, EX-28
New Workbook task pane
displaying, EX-9–10
hiding, EX-9–10
templates, displaying, EX-29
Normal view, EX-133
Numbers
alignment, EX-16
entering in cells, EX-16–17
formatting, EX-114–116

Office Assistant characters, EX-5
Office Clipboard, EX-72–75
Open button, EX-34
Open command, EX-34
Open dialog box, EX-34–35
Opening files
of different formats, EX-36
workbooks, EX-34–36
Open Office Document command, EX-34
Options dialog box, EX-13, 170
Outside Borders button, EX-122

Page Break Preview, EX-133
Page layout settings, EX-138–140
Page Setup command, EX-139–140
Page Setup dialog box, EX-140, 142, 145
Paste All button (Office Clipboard), EX-74
Paste button, EX-69, 71, 129
Paste command, EX-69
Paste Options icon, EX-71, 130
Paste Special command, EX-129–130
Paste Special dialog box, EX-129–130
Percent Style button, EX-114
PgDn key, EX-11–12
PgUp key, EX-11–12
Phone numbers, EX-16
Pie charts, EX-183–184
Places bar in Save As dialog box, EX-32–33
Pointing to enter formulas, EX-18–19
Print Area command, EX-143, 190
Print button, EX-133, 135
Print command, EX-134
Printing, EX-133–136
page layout settings, EX-138–140
selected content, EX-143–146
Print Preview button, EX-133–134, 139, 141
Print Preview command, EX-133–134, 190
Print Screen key, EX-146
Programs menu, EX-4
Pull-down menus, EX-7

Range Finder, EX-18
Range names, EX-162–165
managing, EX-165–167
Ranges of cells. *See* Cell ranges
Redo button, EX-26
Redo command, EX-26
Relative cell addresses, EX-21, 167
Renaming files, EX-33, 38
Renaming folders, EX-38
Restore button, EX-6
Right-click menus, EX-8
hiding/unhiding rows and columns, EX-91
inserting/deleting rows and columns, EX-88–90
Rotating text, EX-119
Row, AutoFit command, EX-86, 88
Row, Height command, EX-86
Row height text box, EX-87
Rows, EX-2
deleting, EX-88–90
extending, EX-78–79
headings, printing, EX-145
heights, changing, EX-86–88
hiding/unhiding, EX-91–92
inserting, EX-88–90
text labels, entering, EX-13–14

Save As command, EX-30–31
files in different formats, EX-36
web page format, EX-136–137
Save As dialog box, EX-31–34
new folder creation, EX-36–37
Save button, EX-31, 33
Save-in drop-down list box, EX-32–33
Saving files, EX-28, 30–31
in different formats, EX-36

Scatter plot charts, EX-184
Scroll boxes, EX-7
Select a function, list box, EX-181
Select All button, EX-86
Selecting cells
  cell ranges, EX-56–59
  to erase information, EX-25
Series, EX-77–79, 93
Shading, borders and, EX-120–124
Shift cells down option button, EX-66
Shift cells right option button, EX-66
SHIFT-selecting, EX-58–59
Sizing corner, EX-7
Sizing fonts, EX-111–113
Social Security numbers, EX-16
Splitting merged cells, EX-119
Standard toolbar, EX-8
  displaying, EX-8–10
"Staples Foods" exercises, EX-46–47, 101–103, 154–155, 199–200
Starting Excel, EX-4
SUM function, EX-172–174
"Sutton House Realty" exercises, EX-48–49, 103–104, 155–156, 200–201
Switching applications, EX-5
Syntax, functions, EX-171

t

Tab Scrolling arrows, EX-7
Tab Slot box, EX-7
Task pane. *See* New Workbook task pane
Templates
  downloading additional templates, EX-30
  workbook, EX-28–30
Templates dialog box, EX-29
Text
  alignment, EX-16
  entering in cells, EX-13–14
  fonts. *See* Fonts
  long entries in cells, EX-120
  rotating, EX-119
Title Bar icons, EX-6
Titles, entering, EX-13
Toolbars
  See also specific name of toolbar
  docked, EX-11
  moving, EX-11
  undocked, EX-11
"Top Picks Video" exercises, EX-43–46, 98–101, 152–153, 197–198
Typefaces
  See also Fonts changing, EX-111–113

Underline button, EX-111–112, 122
Underlining, EX-111–112
Undo, EX-26–27
Undo button, EX-26–127
Undocked toolbars, EX-11
Undo command, EX-26–27

Views button, EX-35
Viruses, EX-29

Web Page Preview command, EX-136–137
Windows
  application window, EX-5–6
  document window, EX-5, 7–8
Windows Clipboard, EX-69–72
Wizards
  Chart Wizard, EX-185–189
  new workbook creation, EX-28
Workbooks, EX-3
  deleting, EX-38
  naming files. *See* Naming files
  New button, EX-22, 28–30
  opening files. *See* Opening files
  previewing, EX-134
  re-using, EX-34
  saving files. *See* Saving files
  templates, EX-28–30
  as web pages, EX-138
Worksheets
  Active sheet tab, EX-7
  cells. *See* Cells
  document window, EX-5, 7–8
  editing, EX-21, 23–24
  elements, EX-2
  formatting. *See* Formatting
  navigating, EX-11–12
  printing, EX-133–136
  rows. *See* Rows
  titles, entering, EX-13
  web publishing, EX-136–138
  zooming in and out, EX-135
World Wide Web. *See* Internet

XY charts, EX-184

Z

Zip codes, EX-16
Zooming in and out, EX-135

Answers
to self-check questions

SelfCheck

1.1. How do you remove a right-click menu from view? Click outside the right-click menu or press ESC.

1.2. How does an AutoContent presentation differ from a design template? Whereas the AutoContent Wizard provides design and content suggestions, a design template provides just design (no content) suggestions.

1.3. What procedure would you use to change the current typeface? To select an alternate typeface, click the Font drop-down list (Times Roman) on the Formatting toolbar and then select an alternate font.

1.4. Under what circumstances might you want to save a file under a different filename? You may want to keep different versions of the same presentation on your disk. Or, you may want to use one presentation as a template for future presentations that are similar in style and format.

2.1. What is the procedure for moving and resizing object placeholders? To move a placeholder, position the mouse pointer over the placeholder until a four-headed arrow appears. Then drag the placeholder to a new location. You resize placeholders by dragging the object's sizing handles.

2.2. How do you select more than one slide in the *Outline* or Slides tab? Press the CTRL key while clicking slides.

2.3. How can you go to a specific slide in Slide Show view? Right-click anywhere on the slide and then choose Go, Slide Navigator from the right-click menu. Then, click the slide you want to display and click the Go To command button.

3.1. What are organization charts used for? Organization charts are schematic drawings showing a hierarchy of formal relationships, such as the relationships among a company's different departments.

3.2. When is it useful to group objects? Once objects are grouped together, you manipulate them as a single object for greater ease when moving, copying, and resizing.

3.3. When would it be preferable to use a text box instead of a text placeholder? Text boxes are commonly used for adding slide labels. Text boxes provide greater flexibility than text placeholders.

Glossary

Adjustment handle: Tiny yellow diamond that lets you change the appearance, not the size, of most AutoShapes.

Application window: In Microsoft Windows, each running application program appears in its own application window. These windows can be sized and moved anywhere on the Windows desktop.

AutoContent Wizard: A PowerPoint feature that assists you in beginning new presentations by providing content and design suggestions.

AutoFit feature: With this feature enabled, PowerPoint automatically resizes placeholders to accommodate inserted text.

AutoShape: Ready-made shape that you can insert in your document and then move, resize, and otherwise format to meet your needs.

Clip art: Computer graphic that you can insert into your document to make it more interesting or entertaining.

Design template: A presentation whose background, color schemes, typefaces, and other formatting options can be applied to another presentation.

Diagram Gallery: PowerPoint dialog box providing a selection of business diagrams for insertion on your slides.

Draw layer: Invisible surface floating above (and mostly independent of) the slide layer. Used for holding objects, such as lines, arrows, and clip art images.

Hyperlink: In terms of Internet technologies, a text string or graphics that when clicked take you to another location, either within the same document or to a separate document stored on your computer, an intranet resource, or onto the Internet.

Justification: In PowerPoint, a description of how text and objects are aligned (left, center, right, full) in a placeholder.

Microsoft Graph: An Office mini-application that lets you create charts and graphs for insertion in the current document.

Normal view: In this view mode, the *Outline* tab, Slide pane, and Notes pane appear. This view mode provides one place for viewing the different parts of your presentation.

Organization chart: Schematic drawing showing a hierarchy of formal relationships.

Placeholder: Marks the location of a slide object and provides instructions for editing the object.

Places bar: The strip of icon buttons appearing in the Open and Save As dialog boxes that allow you to display the most common areas for retrieving and storing files using a single mouse click.

Sizing handles: Tiny circles or boxes that surround a selected object. You drag the sizing handles to resize an object.

Slide Master: This slide holds the formatting specifications for all slides in your presentation.

Task pane: Context-sensitive toolbar in PowerPoint that provides convenient access to relevant commands and procedures.

Text box: A container for text, graphics, tables, or other objects. You can position text boxes anywhere on a slide.

Index

"AddIn Tennis" exercises
adding and editing slides, PP-41–43
AutoContent presentation modification, PP-75–77
graphics, PP-120–122
Adjustment handles, PP-101
Align Left button, PP-23, 25
Alignment of paragraphs, PP-23–24
Align Right button, PP-23, 25
Application window, PP-4–5, 8, 97
Apply Design Template dialog box, PP-61–62
Arrows, draw objects. *See* Draw objects
AutoContent Wizard, PP-9–13
AutoFit, PP-18, 24
AutoFit Options button, PP-24
AutoShapes, PP 99–105, 108–111
AutoShapes button, PP-100, 109

Back button, PP-28
Blank presentations, starting with, PP-16–18
Bold button, PP-23–24, 110
Bulleted lists, PP-20, PP-22
Buttons. *See* specific name of button

Case problems
Cushman Communications, PP-43–45
Fantasy Motors, PP-122–125
Holly Holdman, PP-77–80
"Catalina Marketing" exercises
editing an AutoContent presentation, PP-40–41
organization charts, PP-119–120
slide layout and design, PP-73–75
Center button, PP-23
Chart button, PP-90
Charts, PP-90–95
organization charts, PP-95–99
text labels, PP-108–112
Chart Type dialog box, PP-94
Check marks, PP-7
Clip art, PP-82–88
Clip Art button, PP-82
Clip Art task pane, PP-82
Clipboard, PP-88, 102, 105
Clip organizer, PP-82, 87–88
Close button, PP-2, 4, 7, 26
Closing a presentation, PP-26–29
Colors, PP-102, 103
Column width, PP-92–93
Commands, PP-5
design template, PP-14
Insert, PP-89
Open Office Document, PP-29
Search, PP-84, 86
Copy button, PP-105
Copying and pasting draw objects, PP-105
Creating presentations
AutoContent Wizard, PP-9–13
design template, PP-13–16
textual presentations. *See* Textual presentations
Customize dialog box, PP-7
Cutting and pasting clip art, PP-88

Datasheets, PP-92–93
Deleting a folder, PP-32
Demoting an outline level, PP-21
Design templates, PP-9, 13–16
alternate design templates, PP-57–58
editing, PP-59–62
multiple design templates, PP-58–59
Diagram gallery, PP-95
Diagram Gallery dialog box, PP-96
Dialog boxes. *See* specific name of dialog box
Double-clicking, PP-14–15
clip art, PP-87
column width, PP-92, 93
draw objects, PP-102
folders, PP-33
graphs, PP-90, 94
saving a presentation, PP-27
Dragging and dropping data, PP-19, 51–54
draw objects, PP-100–107
text boxes, PP-111–112
Draw button, PP-106
Drawing toolbar, PP-82, 100, 102
Draw layer, PP-99
Draw objects, PP-99–107
inserting objects on the draw layer, PP-99–101
labeling, PP-108–111
manipulating and formatting, PP-102–105
ordering and grouping, PP-106–107
text labels, PP-108–112

Editing design templates, PP-59–62
Editing slide layout
adding footer text, PP-54–56
applying an alternate layout, PP-48–50
changing slide order, PP-53–54
customizing placeholders, PP-51–52
Editing text, PP-19–20
Exercises
AddIn Tennis. *See* "AddIn Tennis" exercises
Catalina Marketing. *See* "Catalina Marketing" exercises
clip art, PP-122
Glorietta Community College. *See* "Glorietta Community College" exercises
graphics, PP-122
hobbies, PP-43
presentations, PP-77
slide shows, PP-77
vacations, PP-43
Whiting Tours. *See* "Whiting Tours" exercises
Exiting, PP-2–4

File management, PP-25–33
closing a presentation, PP-26–29
folders, PP-31–33

opening an existing presentation, PP-29–30
printing a presentation, PP-30–31
saving presentations, PP-26–29
Fill Color button, PP-102
Folders, PP-31–33
Font Color button, PP-110
Font drop-down list of Formatting toolbar, PP-23–24
Font Size drop-down list of Formatting toolbar, PP-23–24
Footer text, PP-54–56
Format AutoShape dialog box, PP-102, 109–110
Formatting draw objects, PP-102–105
Formatting text, PP-23–25
Formatting toolbar, PP-5, 23
customizing, PP-6–8

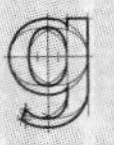

"Glorietta Community College" exercises
creating a presentation, PP-38–40
draw objects, PP-118–119
modifying a presentation, PP-71–72
Graphics
clip art, PP-82–PP-88
draw objects. *See* Draw objects
graphs, PP-90–95
labels, PP-108–112
organization charts, PP-95–99
pictures, PP-88–90, 108–112
Graphs, PP-90–95
Guided tours, PP-4–6

"Hand" pointer, PP-10
Header and Footer dialog box, PP-55–56
Hyperlinks, PP-10

Icons, PP-4–5
Insert Chart button, PP-91
Insert Clip Art button, PP-86
Insert Clip Art task pane, PP-83–84
Insert command, PP-89
Insert Diagram or Organization Chart button, PP-96
Inserting new slides, PP-20–23
Insert Picture dialog box, PP-89
Internet links, PP-10
Italic button, PP-23

Justification, PP-23

Keystrokes
bulleted lists, PP-20, 22
datasheets, PP-93
deleting slides, PP-20
demoting an outline level, PP-21
design templates, PP-58
draw objects, PP-101–102, 105–106
layouts, PP-48
navigating slide shows, PP-64
placeholders, PP-51–52
printing, PP-31
slide shows, PP-64

Labels, text, PP-108–112
Layout changes, PP-48–50
Layouts, text. *See* Text layouts
Line button, PP-102
Lines, draw objects. *See* Draw objects
Lists, bulleted, PP-20, 22
Loading, PP-2–4

Maximize button, PP-4
Memory, PP-2, 25–26
Menu bar, PP-4–5
Menus
context-sensitive, right-click menus. *See* Right-click menus
Programs menu, PP-3
Start menu, PP-2–3, 29
Microsoft Graph, PP-90
Minimize button, PP-4
Mouse double-clicking. *See* Double-clicking
Mouse pointer, PP-5
clip art, PP-85
datasheets, PP-93
design template, PP-14
draw objects, PP-100–102
launching PowerPoint, PP-3
pen mouse pointer, PP-66
placeholders, PP-51–52
Title Slide layout, PP-16
Move bar, PP-8
My Documents folder button, PP-28

Naming files, PP-25
New button, PP-9, 16, 89, 91
New Presentation task pane, PP-9–10, 14
New Slide button, PP-20, 22
New slide insertion, PP-20–23
Next Slide button, PP-13, 64
Normal view, PP-12
Notes pane, PP-12, 17

Objects, PP-99
Office Assistant, PP-4
Open button, PP-29
Open dialog box, PP-29–32
Opening an existing presentation, PP-29–30
Opening screen of, PP-4
Open Office Document command, PP-29
Order of slides, PP-53–54
Organization Chart application window, PP-97
Organization charts, PP-95–99
Organization Chart toolbar, PP-96, 98
Outline tab, PP-12, 18–23
changing slide order, PP-53–54
design templates, PP-58
Oval button, PP-106

Paragraph alignment, PP-23–24
Paste button, PP-105
Pasting clip art, PP-88
Pasting draw objects, PP-105
Pen mouse pointer, PP-66
Pictures, PP-88–90
text labels, PP-108–112
Picture toolbar, PP-85
Placeholders, PP-16, 51–52, 86, 96
inserting text outside, PP-111–112
Places bar, PP-27
Previous Slide button, PP-13
Print button, PP-30–31
Print dialog box, PP-30–31
Printing a presentation, PP-30–31
Programs menu, PP-3

Reordering slides, PP-53–54
Restore button, PP-4
Right-click menus, PP-5–6
design templates, PP-58
drawing toolbar, PP-100
draw objects, PP-102, 104, 108–109
folders, PP-32

navigating slide shows, PP-64
Office Assistant, PP-4
slide shows, PP-63
Rotation of object, PP-104

Save As dialog box, PP-27, 31–33, 61
Save button, PP-26–27
Saving presentations, PP-26–29
Search command, PP-84, 86
Searching for clip art, PP-82–84, 86
Sizing handles, PP-51, 85, 101, 107, 110
Slide Design task pane, PP-14, 57–58
Slide layer, PP-99
Slide Layout task pane, PP-17, 48
Slide Master, PP-54
Slide Navigator dialog box, PP-65
Slide pane, PP-12
Slide Show button, PP-63–64
Slide shows, PP-62–66
navigating, PP-64–66
starting, PP-62–64
Slide Show view, PP-63–64
Slides tab of Normal view, PP-12–13
Standard toolbar, PP-5
customizing, PP-6–8
Start button, PP-2
Starting slide shows, PP-62–64
Start menu, PP-2–3, 29
Status bar, PP-4–5
Subtitles, PP-19

Task pane, PP-4
customizing, PP-6–8
Templates, design. *See* Design templates
Text Box button, PP-111
Text boxes, PP-111–112
Text labels, PP-108–112
Text layouts, PP-16
Title and text layout, PP-49–50, 91
Title only layout, PP-17, 89
Title Slide layout, PP-17, 49
Textual presentations, PP-16–25
blank presentations, PP-16–18
formatting text on slides, PP-23–25
new slides, PP-20–23
Outline tab, PP-20–23
title slides, PP-18–20
Text wrapping, PP-108–110
Title and 2-column Text layout, PP-16
Title and text layout, PP-16, 49–50, 91
Title bar, PP-4–5, 28–29
Title only layout, PP-16–17, 89
Title slide creation, PP-18–20
Title Slide layout, PP-16–17, 49
Toolbars, PP-4–5, 96
See also specific name of toolbar
customizing, PP-6–8
moving, PP-8
Touring, PP-4–6

Underline button, PP-23–24
Undo button, PP-52, 105

V

View buttons, PP-4–PP-5
Views
Normal view, PP-12
Slide Show view, PP-63–64

Web links, PP-10
"Whiting Tours" exercises
draw objects, PP-116–118
editing a presentation, PP-37–38
slide shows, PP-70–71
Word wrapping, PP-108–110

Answers to self-check questions

SelfCheck

1.1. How do you close a window that appears in the Access work area? Click on its Close button (☒).

1.2. Describe two methods to quickly move the cursor to the last record in a large datasheet. Here are three methods. First, you can use the cursor movement keys CTRL+↓ or CTRL+END to move the cursor to the last record. Second, you can use the mouse to click the Last Record button (▶|). And third, you can scroll the window by dragging the vertical scroll box and then click in a field of the last record. (*Note:* You must click in the record's row in order to move the cursor. Otherwise, you simply scroll the window.)

1.3. When does Access save the editing changes that you've made to a record? Editing changes to a record are saved permanently to disk when the cursor is moved to another record or when the user presses the SHIFT+ENTER combination.

2.1. What two objects are most closely associated with the output of a database application? Query objects (the questions you ask of a database) and report objects (the structured printed output from a database).

2.2. How do you specify the name of a field when creating a table in Datasheet view? You double-click the column name in the field header area and then type the desired field name.

2.3. What is an AutoNumber field? Why is it useful as a primary key? An AutoNumber field is a data type that automatically increments a numeric value each time a new record is added to a table. It is useful as a primary key since it already supplies a unique value for each record in a table.

2.4. What happens to your table's data if you delete a field in table Design view? The table data that is stored in the field is removed along with the field definition in Design view.

3.1. Name two reasons for changing the field column order in a datasheet. Some reasons for changing the field order include customizing a datasheet's appearance for printing, displaying fields side by side in a datasheet, and arranging columns for performing multiple-field sort operations.

3.2. How do you perform a sort operation using more than one field column? You must first ensure that the columns are adjacent to one another. The leftmost column should contain the primary or first sort key. The next column(s) provides the secondary sort level(s). You must then select all of the columns involved in the sort operation and click the appropriate Sort button on the toolbar.

3.3. In a personnel table, how would you display a subset of those employees working in the accounting department? Using Filter For Input, you enter "Accounting" as the criterion. Using Filter By Selection, you select "Accounting" from the datasheet. Using Filter By Form, you select "Accounting" from the drop-down list attached to the department field. You then apply and remove the filter by clicking on the Apply/Remove Filter button (▼) on the toolbar.

3.4. Name one way that a query's dynaset may differ from a table's datasheet. A query's dynaset may display results from two or more tables in the same Datasheet window.

4.1. Name the layout options for designing a form using the Form Wizard. Columnar, Tabular, Datasheet, Justified, PivotTable, and PivotChart.

4.2. What does the term "grouping data" refer to in a report? You can arrange data so that it appears combined into categories in a report. The categories are based on field values and appear sorted into ascending order, by default. Grouping data also enables you to prepare subtotal calculations.

4.3. How could you use table and report objects to print diskette labels? You store the diskette names, titles, and other information in a table and then use a mailing labels report to print the information using the Avery 5296 diskette label.

4.4. Name two operating system tools that you can use to back up a database. Windows Explorer and "My Computer".

Glossary

Application window: In Windows, each running application program appears in its own application window. These windows may be sized and moved anywhere on the Windows desktop.

AutoForm Wizard: An Access wizard that creates a form automatically, using all of the fields from the selected table object in the Database window. There are three types of AutoForm Wizards: Columnar, Tabular, and Datasheet.

AutoNumber: A field data type that provides a unique value for each record automatically. The three types of AutoNumber fields include sequential (incremented by 1), random, and replication. You cannot delete or modify the values generated for an AutoNumber field.

AutoReport Wizard: An Access wizard that creates a columnar or tabular report automatically, using all of the fields from the selected table or query object in the Database window. There are two types of AutoReport Wizards: Columnar and Tabular.

Cell: In a datasheet, the intersection of a column (field) and a row (record).

Database: A collection of related data. In Access, a database includes a collection of objects—tables, queries, reports, forms, and other objects.

Database management system (DBMS): A software tool that lets you create and maintain an information database.

Database window: The control center for an Access database. Using the *Objects bar,* categorizes and lists the objects stored in a database.

Database Wizard: In Access, a software feature for creating a complete database application based on professionally designed database templates.

Datasheet: A window used for displaying multiple records from a table using an electronic spreadsheet layout of horizontal rows and vertical columns.

Datasheet view: The method or mode of displaying table data using a datasheet.

Design view: Each database object in Access may be opened in display mode or Design view mode. You use Design view to define table structures, construct queries, build forms, and design reports.

Documenter: In Access, a tool for documenting and printing the design characteristics of a database object.

Dynaset: In Access, the result of a query. A dynaset is displayed as a table in Datasheet view of the records matching the query parameters.

Field: A single item, or column, of information in a *record.*

Field Grid pane: In table Design view, the top portion of the window where you specify field names, data types, and descriptions.

Field header area: In an Access Datasheet window, the top frame or border area that contains the field names as column headings.

Field Properties pane: In table Design view, the bottom portion of the window where you specify field properties and characteristics.

Filter: The process or method of temporarily restricting the display of records in a table to those that match a particular search criterion or pattern.

Filter By Form: In Access, a command that searches a table and returns a subset of records matching multiple criteria.

Filter By Selection: In Access, a command that searches a table and returns a subset of records matching the selected value in a datasheet.

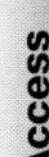

Filter Excluding Selection: In Access, a command that searches a table and returns a subset of records not matching the selected value in a datasheet.

Filter For Input: In Access, a command that searches a table and returns a subset of records matching a filter specification that you enter in a right-click menu's text box.

Form: A database object used for displaying table data one record at a time.

Form window: In Access, a window that displays a form object.

Form wizards: Access tools that simplify the process of creating a form.

Groups bar: The icon buttons appearing in the Database window that allow you to create custom groups and organize object shortcuts for managing a database.

HTML: An acronym for Hypertext Markup Language, which is the standardized markup language used in creating documents for display on the *World Wide Web.*

Index: A feature of a table object that allows you to presort a table based on key values. Indexes speed up searching, sorting, and other database operations. (*Note:* The *primary* key is indexed automatically.)

Internet: A worldwide network of computer networks that are interconnected by standard telephone lines, fiber optics, and satellites.

Label Wizard: An Access wizard that creates a mailing labels report based on the size, shape, and formatting of standard mailing labels.

Null value: Nothing; an empty or zero-length string.

Objects bar: The strip of icon buttons appearing in the Database window that allows you to choose a particular category of database objects for display.

Places bar: The strip of icon buttons appearing in the Open and Save As dialog boxes that allow you to display the most common areas for retrieving and storing files using a single mouse click.

Preview: The act of displaying on-screen a document, worksheet, or report prior to sending it to the printer. An on-screen preview window displays a *soft copy* of a document; the printer produces the *hard copy.*

Primary key: A field whose values uniquely identify each record in a table. The primary key provides the default sort order for a table and is used to establish connections to and relationships with other tables.

Query: A database object that you use to ask a question of your data. The results from a query are typically displayed using a *datasheet.*

Record: An individual entry, or row, in a *table.* A record contains one or more *fields.*

Record selection area: The row frame area located to the left of the first column in a *datasheet.* Used for selecting records.

Report snapshot: A Windows graphic metafile that stores an accurate representation, including fonts, graphics, and colors, of each page in a report. You do not need Access installed on your computer to view a report snapshot. Instead, you can use the free Microsoft Snapshot Viewer to open, view, and print snapshots.

Report wizards: Access tools that simplify the process of creating a report.

Report(s): A database object used for viewing, compiling, summarizing, and printing information.

Select query: A type of query object that lets you ask questions of your database, retrieve data from multiple tables, sort the data, and display the results in a datasheet.

Simple Query Wizard: In Access, a software feature that simplifies the process of creating a query.

Sort key: A field or column used to sort the contents of a datasheet.

Subdatasheet: An extension of a datasheet that provides a picture-in-picture display of related or hierarchical data.

Table: A database object used to collect and store data relating to a particular subject or topic.

Table Wizard: In Access, a software feature that simplifies the process of creating a table.

Task pane: A toolbar-like window providing quick access to frequently used commands. By default, the task pane appears docked at the right side of the application window, but it may be displayed and hidden using the View, Toolbars menu command.

Typeface: The shape and appearance of characters. There are two categories of typefaces: serif and sans serif. Serif type (for example, Times Roman) is more decorative and, some say, easier to read than sans serif type (for example, Arial).

Undo command: A command that makes it possible to reverse the last command or action performed.

Wildcard characters: Special symbols that are used to represent other alphanumeric characters in search, filter, and query operations. You can use the question mark (?) to represent any single character and the asterisk (*) to represent any group of characters.

World Wide Web: A visual interface to the Internet based on hyperlinks. Using Web browser software, you click on hyperlinks to navigate resources on the Internet.

Index

Active category buttons, AC-11
Alert confirmation dialog box, AC-31–32, 64, 74
Applications, AC-4, 14
Application window, AC-4, 7–8
Apply Filter button, AC-116, 122–123
Arithmetic mean, AC-165
Arrange Icons commands, AC-181
Ask a Question box, AC-8
Asterisks, AC-29, 111–112
Autofit, AC-19
AutoForm button, AC-147–148
AutoForm command, AC-148
AutoForm Wizards, AC-146–151, 153, 155–157
AutoNumber data, AC-67, 69
AutoNumber field, AC-27–29, 183
AutoReport button, AC-161
AutoReport Wizards, AC-161–163
Averages, AC-165

Backing up the database, AC-186
Best Fit command button, AC-18–19, 102
BIN, AC-68
Blank Databases, AC-52–54
Blank forms, AC-159
Business options button, AC-61
Buttons
  See also specific name of button
  active category buttons, AC-11
  applications, switching among, AC-4
  inactive category buttons, AC-11
  reports. *See* Reports
  right scroll button, AC-102
  row selector buttons, AC-30, 71
  small icons, AC-181
  tables. *See* Tables

Case problems, AC-46–48, 92–95, 142–144, 200–204
Cells, AC-14, 27–29
Charts, AC-147
Clear Grid button, AC-123
Close button, AC-3, 7–8, 22–23
Collapse button, AC-17
Color drop-down list box, AC-99
Columnar AutoForm Wizard, AC-147
Columnar AutoReport Wizards, AC-161–163
Columnar forms, AC-149, 155–156
Columnar layout, AC-151, 153
Columns, AC-2, 101–107
  Description column, AC-68
  renaming, AC-63
  width adjustment, AC-18–19, 102, 112
  zooming in or magnifying, AC-21
Commands
  See also specific name of command
  ellipsis (...), AC-7
Compacting a database, AC-183–186
Converting a database, AC-183–186
Copy button, AC-180–181
Copying objects, AC-180–183
CTRL key
- END key, AC-155
- HOME key, AC-16, 112, 115, 155, 158
- Z key, AC-26

Currency data, AC-67
Cut button, AC-180

Data access pages, AC-14
Database, AC-2
Database management systems (DBMS), AC-2
Database object management, AC-179–186
Database window, AC-7–8, 10–11, 170, 181
Datasheet AutoForm Wizard, AC-147
Datasheet button, AC-75, 77, 128
Datasheet Formatting dialog box, AC-100
Datasheet layout, AC-151, 153
Datasheets, AC-11
  column order, changing, AC-101–103
  filtering, AC-116–123
  formatting, AC-98–101
  navigating, AC-14, 18
  spell-checking, AC-114–116
Datasheet view, AC-14, 62–65, 73–74, 104
Datasheet window, AC-15–16, 62
Data types, AC-67–68
Date/time data, AC-67
Decimal Places, AC-72
Default Value, AC-72
Delete button, objects, AC-180
DELETE key, AC-30
Delete Record button, AC-30, 158, 160
Deleting objects, AC-180–183
Deleting records, AC-30–33
Description column, AC-68
Design button, AC-73, 76, 127–128
Details button, AC-181
Dialog boxes. *See* specific name of dialog box
Dictionaries, AC-114
Documenter, AC-77–79
Documenter window, AC-78
Double-clicking
  Autofit, AC-19
  AutoReport Wizard, AC-161
  Form Wizard, AC-152
  Label Wizard, AC-174
  query Design window, AC-127–128
  Report Wizard, AC-163
Dragging and dropping, AC-10, 32, 101–103, 109
Dynaset, AC-124, 126, 128

Editing data, AC-23–26
Edit mode, AC-15
Ellipsis (...) command, AC-7
END key, AC-15, 155
ENTER key, AC-15, 18, 27–28, 64
ESC key, AC-9, 27
Exercises
  AmeriSales International, AC-37–38, 83–84, 133–135, 190–192

Benson's Office Supplies, AC-44–45, 90–91, 140–141, 198–199
Coldstream Valley, AC-45–46, 91–92, 141, 200
Iway Internet Group, AC-38–40, 84–87, 135–137, 192–194
Spring County Carnival, AC-42–44, 89–90, 139–140, 196–198
Western Lumber Sales, AC-41–42, 87–88, 137–139, 195–196
Exiting Access, AC-3
Export command button, AC-171, 173
Export Report dialog box, AC-171

f

Field cursor, AC-15
Field Grid pane, AC-66–69, 72–73
  moving fields, AC-77
  query Design window, AC-127
  renaming fields, AC-76
Field header areas, AC-18–19, 63, 101–107
Field properties, setting, AC-72
Field Properties pane, AC-66–67, 70
Fields, AC-2
  column order, AC-101–103
  data types, AC-67–68
  deleting, AC-72–75
  Description column, AC-68
  hiding/unhiding, AC-103–105
  inserting, AC-72–75
  Inventory Control wizard, AC-56
  moving, AC-75–77
  naming fields, AC-66, 68, 75–77
  planning, AC-51
  primary key, AC-64, 68–70
  renaming, AC-75–77
  Simple Query Wizard, AC-125–126
  Table Wizard dialog box, AC-61
Field Size, AC-72
File management, AC-3, 5, 7
File name text box, AC-60, 65
File New Database dialog box, AC-52–53, 60, 65
Filter, AC-116
"Filter" a table, AC-124
Filter by Form button, AC-120–122
Filter by Selection button, AC-118–120
Filter Excluding Selection, AC-118–119
Filter For Input command, AC-117
"Filter For:" text box, AC-116–117
Filtering by form, AC-120–123
Filtering by selection, AC-118–120
Filtering for input, AC-116–118
Filter/Sorter toolbar, AC-121
Find and replace, AC-113–114
Find and Replace dialog box, AC-110–114, 157
"Find" a record, AC-124
Find button, AC-110, 112
Find command, AC-110–111, 157
Find Next command button, AC-157
Finish button, AC-58, 62
First Page button, AC-21
First Record button, AC-16–17
F2 key, AC-15, 23–25, 181
Font dialog box, AC-99–100
Font name drop-down list box, AC-175
Fonts, AC-98
Font size drop-down list box, AC-175
Font style list box, AC-99
Formatting, AC-72
  datasheets, AC-98–101
  Form Wizard, AC-153–154
  reports, AC-163, 165
Formatting dialog box, AC-100
Formatting toolbar, AC-149
Form layouts, AC-151, 153
Forms, AC-10, 12–13, 57, 146–161
Form View toolbar, AC-149
Form Window, AC-13, 147, 149
Form Wizard, AC-151–154
Form Wizard dialog box, AC-152
Fragmentation, AC-183
FrontPage 2002, AC-172

Gridlines, AC-100–101
Groups bar, AC-10–11

HOME key, AC-31, 102–103, 107, 155
HTML, AC-170
HTML Output Options dialog box, AC-172
Hyperlink data, AC-68

Inactive category buttons, AC-11
Include All button, AC-61
Include for Fields area, AC-79
Include for Indexes area, AC-79
Include for Table area, AC-79
Indexed text box, AC-70
Indexes, AC-70–72
Indexes button, AC-70
Indexes window, AC-71
Input Mask, AC-72
Input requirements, AC-50
Insert Rows command, AC-74
Internet, AC-59, 170–173
Internet Explorer, AC-173
Inventory Control wizard, AC-55–59

Justified layout, AC-151
Justified option button, AC-153–154

Keystrokes
  See also specific name of key
  navigating datasheets, AC-14

l

Labels, AC-174–179
Label Wizard, AC-174–179
Label Wizard dialog box, AC-175–177
Landscape printing, AC-21–22, 104
Large icons, AC-7, 180–181
Last page button, AC-21
Last Record button, AC-16–17, 155–156
Launching Access, AC-3–4
Layout preview area, AC-163–164
Line styles, AC-101
List area, AC-11
List button, AC-181
Logos, AC-57
Look in drop-down list box, AC-110
Lookup Wizard data, AC-68

Macro category, AC-10, 14
Magnifying. *See* Zooming in and out
Main Switchboard for Inventory Control application, AC-58–59
Mathematical calculations, AC-165, 169
Matting, AC-100
Maximize button, AC-7–8, 79, 168
Maximum value in a field, AC-165
Memo data, AC-67, 75
Menu bar, AC-7–8
Menus, AC-3, 9, 18, 186
  context-sensitive, right-click menus. *See* Right-click menus
Microsoft.com, AC-59
Microsoft Visual basic, AC-14

Minimize button, AC-7–8
Minimum value in a field, AC-165
Modules, AC-10, 14
Mouse double-clicking. *See* Double-clicking
Mouse pointer
 adjusting column widths and row heights, AC-18–19
 column order, AC-102
 column selection, AC-63
 deleting records, AC-31–32
 editing data, AC-24–25
 magnifying, AC-21
 navigating datasheets, AC-16–18
 new databases, AC-52, 54
 records, moving to a specific record number, AC-18
 subdatasheets, AC-17–18
Wizards, AC-54
Multiple Pages button, AC-169

Naming column headings, AC-63
Naming databases, AC-57
Naming fields, AC-66, 68, 75–77
Naming tables, AC-62
Navigating data using forms, AC-155–157
Navigation areas, AC-15–16
New button, AC-4, 52
 AutoForms, AC-147
 Database Wizard, AC-54
 Form Wizard, AC-152
 labels, AC-174
 queries, AC-124
 reports, AC-161, 163
 table creation in datasheet view, AC-63
 table creation in Design view, AC-65–66
 Table wizard, AC-60
New databases, AC-51–59
New File task pane, AC-4, 52
 Database Wizard, AC-54
 table creation in Design view, AC-65
 Table Wizard, AC-60
 templates, AC-59
New Form dialog box, AC-150, 152
New Object button, AC-147–150, 161
New Record button, AC-28, 158
New Report dialog box, AC-161, 174
New Table dialog box, AC-60, 63, 65–66
Next button, AC-56–57, 61–62
Next Page button, AC-21
No button, AC-31–32
Null value, AC-68
Number data, AC-67

Object Definition window, AC-79
Object management, AC-179–186
Objects bar, AC-10–11, 147, 150, 152, 161
Office Assistant character, AC-9
OLE object data, AC-68
One Page button, AC-168–169
Open button, AC-4–5
Open dialog box, AC-4–6
Opening files at Startup, AC-4
Open Office Document command, AC-4
Orientation of page, AC-21–22, 165–166
Output requirements, AC-50

PgDn key, AC-16, 155, 158
PgUp key, AC-155, 158
Page layout, AC-57
Page navigation area, AC-167
Pages category, AC-10, 14
Page setup, AC-21, 104
Page Setup dialog box, AC-21–22
Page tab, AC-21–22
Paste button, AC-180–181
Paste Table As dialog box, AC-182
Pencil icon, AC-24–25, 29, 159
Percentages, AC-165
Personal option button, AC-61
Pictures, AC-57
PivotChart AutoForm Wizard, AC-147
PivotChart layout, AC-151, 153
PivotTable AutoForm Wizard, AC-147
PivotTable layout, AC-151, 153
Places bar in Open dialog box, AC-6
Places bar in Save In dialog box, AC-52–53, 60, 65
Planning a database, AC-50–51
Portrait orientation, AC-165–166
Previewing, AC-13, 20–23, 57, 79
Form Wizard, AC-153
 hiding columns, AC-104–105
 reports, AC-163–164, 166–170
Primary key, AC-64, 68–70, 107–109
Print button, AC-20, 78–79, 158, 167
Printing, AC-20–23, 77–79, 104, 167–170
Print Preview button, AC-20, 104, 158–161, 167
Print previews generally. *See* Previewing
Print Preview toolbar, AC-21
Print Preview window, AC-13, 20–21, 104–105, 168, 170
Print Table definition dialog box, AC-78
Programming languages, AC-14
Programs menu, AC-3
Publishing to the Web, AC-170–173
Pull-down menus, AC-9

Queries, AC-10, 12, 50–51, 124–129
Queries button, AC-124, 127
"Query" a database, AC-124
Query Design grid, AC-127
Query Design Window, AC-127–129

Raised option button of Cell Effect area, AC-100
Record navigation area, AC-156
Records, AC-2, 15–17
 adding, AC-27–30
 deleting, AC-30–33
 filtering by form, AC-120–123
 filtering by selection, AC-118–120
 filtering for input, AC-116–118
 moving to a specific record number, AC-19
 planning, AC-51
 sorting, AC-107–109
Record selection area, AC-18–19, 30
Remove Filter button, AC-116, 119–120
Renaming columns, AC-63
Renaming fields, AC-75–77
Renaming objects, AC-180–183
Repairing a database, AC-183–186
Replace All command button, AC-114
Replace command, AC-113–114, 157
Replace With combo box of Find and Replace dialog box, AC-113
Reports, AC-13, 161–173
 AutoReport Wizards, AC-161–163
 elements, AC-161
 labels, AC-174–179
 Objects bar, AC-10
 output requirements, AC-50
 page layout, AC-57
 previewing, AC-167–170
 printing, AC-167–170
 publishing to the Web, AC-170–173
Report Wizard, AC-163–167
 testing, AC-51
 uses, AC-161
Report snapshots, AC-173

Report Wizard, AC-163–167
Restore button, AC-7–8, 79, 169
Right-click menus, AC-9, 170, 180–182
  filtering for input, AC-116
  freezing/unfreezing columns, AC-106–107
  hiding/unhiding rows and columns, AC-103–104
  inserting/deleting new fields, AC-74
  sorting data, AC-108
Right scroll button, AC-102
Rows, AC-2, 18–19
Row selector buttons, AC-30, 71

Sample area, AC-100
Samples Tables list box, AC-61
Save As dialog box, AC-64, 70
Save As Query button, AC-122
Save as type drop-down list box, AC-172
Save button, AC-64, 69, 77, 98
Save in drop-down list box, AC-52–53, 60, 65
Saving files, AC-24–26, 52
Screen appearance, AC-57
Searching, AC-110–112
Search patterns, AC-111–112
Select All button, AC-30–31
Selecting data, AC-23–26
Select query, AC-124
SHIFT key, AC-102–104
• ENTER key, AC-26
• F2 key, AC-75
• TAB key, AC-28, 155, 159
Simple Query Wizard, AC-124–126
Size list box, AC-99
Sizing, AC-10–11, 18–19
Small icons button, AC-181
Snapshots of reports, AC-173
Sort Ascending button, AC-108–109, 158, 164
Sort command, AC-157
Sort Descending button, AC-108–109, 158
Sort key, AC-108
Spell-checking, AC-114–116
Spelling button, AC-114–115
Start button, AC-3
Start menu, AC-186
Status bar, AC-7–8
Storage area navigation, AC-5, 7
STR, AC-68
Style, AC-166
Subdatasheets, AC-17
Summary Options command button, AC-165
Summary Options dialog box, AC-165

t

Table Design view, AC-65–72, 101, 167
Table design window, AC-66–67
Tables, AC-2
  creating in datasheet view, AC-63–65
  creating in design view, AC-65–72, 101, 167
  creating using Table Wizard, AC-60–63
  editing data, AC-23–26
  Filter Excluding Selection, AC-118–119
  Filtering by Form, AC-120–123
  Filtering by Selection, AC-118–120
  Filtering for Input, AC-116–118
  find and replace, AC-113–114
  indexes, AC-70–72
  naming, AC-62
  new object shortcuts, AC-11
  objects, AC-11
  Objects bar, AC-10
  PivotTable AutoForm Wizard, AC-147
  primary key, AC-64, 68–70, 107–109
  printing, AC-77–79
  records. *See* Records
  relationships, determining, AC-51
  searching, AC-110–112
  search patterns, AC-111–112
  selecting data, AC-23–26
  structure, determining, AC-51
Table Wizard, AC-60–63
Table Wizard dialog box, AC-60–62
Tabular AutoForm Wizard, AC-146–151
Tabular AutoReport Wizards, AC-161
Tabular forms, AC-151
Tabular layout, AC-151, 153
Task panes, AC-4
Templates, AC-59
Templates dialog box, AC-54–55
Testing, AC-51
Text data, AC-67
Title bar, AC-10, 15
Titles of databases, AC-57
Toolbars, AC-7–8
  See also specific name of toolbar
Two Pages button, AC-168
Typeface, AC-99

Undo button, AC-26
Undo command, AC-26–27
Unhide Columns dialog box, AC-104–105

Vertical scroll bar, AC-109
Viewing data, AC-14–19
Views button, AC-6–7, 73
Visual Basic for Applications (VBA), AC-14

Web publishing, AC-170–173
Wildcard characters, AC-111–112
Windows
  application window, AC-4, 7–8
  Database window, AC-7–8, 10–11, 170, 181
  datasheet window, AC-15–16, AC-62
  Documenter window, AC-78
  Form Window, AC-13, 147, 149
  icons, AC-7–8
  Indexes, AC-71
  New File task pane, AC-4
  Object Definition window, AC-79
  Print Preview, AC-13, 20–21, 104–105, 168, 170
  Query Design Window, AC-127–129
  sizing, AC-10–11
  table design window, AC-66–67
Wizards. See specific name of wizard
Work areas, AC-8

Yes command button, AC-31–32, 183
Yes/no data, AC-67

Z

Zoom button, AC-169
Zooming in and out, AC-21, 75
  forms, AC-160
  hiding columns, AC-104–105

Answers to self-check questions

SelfCheck

1.1. What typically happens when you copy two items in sequence without an intervening paste? The Clipboard task pane will appear.

1.2. When you paste data, what is the default data format? HTML.

1.3. How would you go about resizing a shared object? To resize an object, drag one of its sizing handles inward or outward.

1.4. What is the procedure for editing embedded objects? You edit embedded objects by double-clicking.

2.1. Describe the procedure for converting a Word outline to a PowerPoint presentation. In Word, choose File, Send To, Microsoft PowerPoint.

2.2. How would you go about editing an embedded PowerPoint slide? Double-click the embedded slide object.

2.3. When might you want to export a report created in Access to Word? Users often send their Access reports to Word in order to apply additional formatting.

3.1. Provide an example of when you might use a hyperlink in an Office document to access information on the Web. If your document will be read on-screen, hyperlinks can enhance your reader's understanding of the current topic. For example, if your topic concerns travel in Asia, include a link to a Web site that specializes in Asian tours and another that specializes in Asian history.

3.2. What procedure must you use to convert a document, worksheet, or presentation to HTML? Choose File, Save as Web Page from the Menu bar in Word, Excel, or PowerPoint.

3.3. On Web pages, what are frames used for? Frames are used to show links to a document's table of contents or other parts of a Web site.

Glossary

Data access page: Interactive Web pages that enable you to view and edit data managed in an Access database.

Destination document: An Office document that contains data copied from another application.

Embedding: A method for sharing data in Microsoft Office applications. Embedded data is fully editable within the destination document and doesn't retain a connection to its source document.

Frames: Separate area on a Web page to show hyperlinks to a document's table of contents or other pages on a Web site.

Frames page: Document or Web page that contains frames.

HTML: An acronym for Hypertext Markup Language, which is the standardized markup language used in creating documents for display on the World Wide Web.

Linking: A method for sharing data in Microsoft Office applications. In linking, you not only paste the data, you also establish a dynamic link between the source and destination documents.

Office Clipboard: A program, in Microsoft Office, that allows you to copy and move information within or among Microsoft Office applications. Unlike the Windows Clipboard, the Office Clipboard can store up to 24 items and then paste them all at once.

Pasting: A method for sharing data in Microsoft Office applications. Pasting data involves inserting a static representation of the source data into the destination document.

Server application: For data shared among Office applications, this term refers to the application that was used to create the shared data.

Sizing handles: The tiny boxes or circles that surround a selected object.

Source document: Original document in which information is created for transfer to a destination document.

Spreadsheet component: Microsoft Office Web component for publishing interactive worksheets on the Web.

Web folder: Shortcut to a Web-server location.

Web server: Computer for storing Web pages.

Web toolbar: Microsoft Office toolbar for navigating hyperlinks locally and on the World Wide Web.

Windows Clipboard: A program, in Windows, that allows you to copy and move information within an application or among applications. The Windows Clipboard temporarily stores the information in memory before you paste the data in a new location.

Index

Access
displaying tables on the Web, IMO-82–86
exporting Access reports to Word, IMO-51–54
exporting worksheet list to, IMO-54–57
Import Spreadsheet Wizard, IMO-54
integrating with Word and Excel, IMO-51–57
mail merging, IMO-53–54
Primary key, IMO-56
Applets, IMO-22
As list box, IMO-12–13
copying an Excel chart to PowerPoint, IMO-49
copying PowerPoint slides to Word, IMO-46, 48
embedding Excel data in a Word document, IMO-15
AutoCorrect Options button, IMO-73–74
AutoCorrect Options menu, IMO-73

Back button, IMO-76
Bitmaps, IMO-13
"Bud's Parlor of Flavors" exercises
exporting an Access report to Word, IMO-64–65
inserting and manipulating shared objects, IMO-32–33
preparing Word documents for the Web, IMO-104
Buttons, IMO-74
See also specific name of button

Case problems
Arbor Forestry, IMO-35–39
Del's Delicious Cookies, IMO-67–70
Manfred's Garden Center, IMO-106–108
Change Title command button, IMO-78, 81
Charts, IMO-49–50, 90
inserting new charts in Word, IMO-22–23
Chart toolbar, IMO-23
Choose a Theme list box, IMO-87
Clear All command button, IMO-6
Clearing Office Clipboard items, IMO-8–9
Clipboards
Office Clipboard activation, IMO-2–6
Office Clipboard pasting and clearing, IMO-6–9
Windows Clipboard, IMO-2, 6
Clipboard task pane, IMO-2, 5–9
Commands. *See* specific name of command
Converting outlines to PowerPoint, IMO-44–46
Copy button, IMO-6, 11, 47
Copying and moving data
dragging and dropping, IMO-17–18, 21
Excel chart to PowerPoint, IMO-49–50
Office Clipboard activation, IMO-2–6
Office Clipboard pasting and clearing, IMO-6–9
PowerPoint slides to Word, IMO-46–48
shared objects, IMO-17–19
Windows Clipboard, IMO-2, 6
Corner sizing handles, IMO-17

Data access pages, IMO-82–86
Data Access Page Wizard, IMO-83–86
Deleting shared objects, IMO-17–19
Demote button, IMO-42–43
Destination document, IMO-9
Dialog boxes. *See* specific name of dialog box
Double-clicking
Access tables on the Web, IMO-83
editing shared objects, IMO-19, 48
embedded object editing, IMO-19, 48
exporting Access reports to Word, IMO-52
exporting a worksheet list to Access, IMO-55
hyperlinks, IMO-72, 74
inserting new Excel charts in Word, IMO-23
inserting new Excel worksheets in Word, IMO-21–22
Dragging and dropping data
inserting new Excel worksheets into Word, IMO-21
shared objects, IMO-17–18

Editing shared objects, IMO-19–20, 48
Embedded object editing, IMO-19–20, 48
Embedding Excel data in a Word document, IMO-15–16
Embedding Excel data in PowerPoint, IMO-49–50
End of document marker, IMO-43
Excel
copying an Excel chart to PowerPoint, IMO-49–50
creating an interactive worksheet page, IMO-90–94
embedding Excel data in a Word document, IMO-15–16
exporting worksheet list to Access, IMO-54–57
inserting new Excel charts in Word, IMO-22–23
inserting new Excel worksheets into Word, IMO-21–22
integrating Access, IMO-51–57
integrating with PowerPoint, IMO-46–51
linking Excel data to a Word document, IMO-12–14
pasting data from Word to Excel, IMO-9–12
saving documents to HTML, IMO-78–82
Excel objects, IMO-13
Exercises
Bud's Parlor of Flavors. *See* "Bud's Parlor of Flavors" exercises

creating an online resume, IMO-106
embedding an entire presentation in Word, IMO-66
embellishing an Access report in Word, IMO-67
Outback Exports.. *See* "Outback Exports" exercises
pasting, linking and embedding, IMO-35
pasting between Word and Excel, IMO-35
publishing an Access database to the Web, IMO-106
The Software Edge. *See* "The Software edge" exercises
Sweet Dreams. *See* "Sweet Dreams" exercises
Exporting Access reports to Word, IMO-51–54
Exporting worksheet list to Access, IMO-54–57
Export to Excel button, IMO-91, 93

Font Size drop-down list on Formatting toolbar, IMO-53
Formatted text (RTF), IMO-13, 51
Formatting
hyperlinks, IMO-73–75
linking Excel data to a Word document, IMO-12–13
saving documents to HTML, IMO-78–82
Web themes, IMO-87–88
Formatting toolbar, IMO-22–23, 43
Font Size drop-down list, IMO-53
Forward button, IMO-76
Frames, IMO-89
Frames page, IMO-89, 90
Frames toolbar, IMO-89

Hashed borders, IMO-20
HTML, IMO-9, 11
customizing a Web presentation, IMO-94–97
linking Excel data to a Word document, IMO-12–13
saving documents to, IMO-78–82
Web editing, IMO-82
Hyperlinks, IMO-72–75
creating a framed table of contents in Word, IMO-89–90

Icons
copying PowerPoint slides to Word, IMO-47
inserting new objects, IMO-21
Import dialog box, IMO-55
Import Spreadsheet Wizard dialog box, IMO-55–56
Import Spreadsheet Wizard of Access, IMO-54
Insert Hyperlink button, IMO-72, 74
Insert Hyperlink dialog box, IMO-74
Interactive worksheet pages, IMO-90–94
Internet, IMO-9
See also Web
Access tables, IMO-82–86
hyperlinks, IMO-72–75
publishing. *See* Web publishing
saving document to HTML, IMO-78–82
Search the Web button, IMO-77
Internet Explorer
customizing web presentations, IMO-94–95, 97
data access pages, IMO-86
interactive worksheet pages, IMO-93
Web editing, IMO-82
Internet service provider (ISP), IMO-97

Keystrokes
copying PowerPoint slides to Word, IMO-47
hyperlinks, IMO-72–73
outlines, IMO-42–43
pasting, IMO-7
shared objects, IMO-17, 19

Linked object editing, IMO-19
Linking Excel data to a Word document, IMO-12–14
Linking Excel data to PowerPoint, IMO-49–50

Mail merging, IMO-53–54
Menu bar, IMO-22, 23
commands. *See* Commands
outlines, IMO-42
themes, IMO-87
Menus
AutoCorrect Options menu, IMO-73
commands. *See* Commands
context-sensitive, right-click menus. *See* Right-click menus
OfficeLinks drop-down menu, IMO-52
Paste Options menu, IMO-11
Microsoft Graph, IMO-22
Microsoft Network search page, IMO-77
Mouse double-clicking. *See* DOUBLE-CLICKING
Mouse pointer
hyperlinks, IMO-73, 75
shared objects, IMO-17
Moving data. *See* Copying and moving data

Object dialog box, IMO-21
Objects, shared. *See* Shared objects
Objects bar, IMO-83
Object type list box, IMO-21, 23
Office Clipboard activation, IMO-2–6
Office Clipboard pasting and clearing, IMO-6–9
OfficeLinks arrow on Print Preview toolbar, IMO-51–52
OfficeLinks drop-down menu, IMO-52
Open dialog box, IMO-3
Open the page option button, IMO-85
"Outback Exports" exercises
embedding a PowerPoint slide in Word, IMO-63–64
inserting a linked chart in Word, IMO-29–32
inserting hyperlinks and browsing, IMO-102–103
Outline pane, IMO-46–47
Outlines, IMO-42–44
converting to PowerPoint, IMO-44–46
Outline view, IMO-42–43
Outline View button, IMO-42
Outlining toolbar, IMO-43

Pages button, IMO-83
Page Wizard dialog box, IMO-84–85
Paste All command button, IMO-7
Paste button, IMO-6, 10–11
Paste link option button, IMO-12–13, 47
copying an Excel chart to PowerPoint, IMO-49
Paste options button, IMO-11, 47, 49
Paste Options menu, IMO-11
Paste Special dialog box, IMO-15–16
copying PowerPoint slides to Word, IMO-48
of Word, IMO-12–13
Pasting data from Word to Excel, IMO-9–12
Pasting Office Clipboard items, IMO-6–9
Pictures, IMO-13

PivotTables, IMO-90
Posting files to Web servers, IMO-97
PowerPoint
  converting outlines to, IMO-44–46
  copying an Excel chart to, IMO-49–50
  copying slides to Word, IMO-46–48
  customizing a Web presentation, IMO-94–97
  integrating with Word and Excel, IMO-46–51
  saving documents to HTML, IMO-78–82
Presentations created from Word documents, IMO-42–46
Previewing
  Access tables on the Web, IMO-83, 86
  customizing web presentations, IMO-94–95, 97
  interactive worksheet pages, IMO-92–93
  Web pages, IMO-79–80, 82
Primary key, IMO-56
Print Preview toolbar, IMO-51–52
Promote button, IMO-42, 43
Publish as Web Page dialog box, IMO-92, 94–96
Publish command button, IMO-91–93
  customizing a Web presentation, IMO-94–95, 97

r

Refresh button, IMO-82
Renaming hyperlinks, IMO-75
Resizing shared objects, IMO-17–19
Rich Text Format (RTF), IMO-13, 51
Right-click menus
  browsing, IMO-77
  hyperlinks, IMO-72, 75

Save As dialog box, IMO-80–81, 91–92
  customizing Web presentations, IMO-95, 97
Save button, IMO-86
ScreenTip, IMO-73
Search the Web button, IMO-77
Server application, IMO-15
Set Page Title dialog box, IMO-81
Shared objects
  editing, IMO-19–20
  moving, resizing and deleting, IMO-17–19
Sheet option button, IMO-91
Sizing handles, IMO-6, 17–18
Source document, IMO-9
Spreadsheet component, IMO-90
Standard toolbar, IMO-22–23, 74
Start Page button, IMO-76
Style box on Formatting toolbar, IMO-43
Styles, IMO-42
"Sweet Dreams" exercises
  inserting hyperlinks, IMO-101–102
  pasting and clearing clipboard items, IMO-27–29
  sending a Word outline to PowerPoint, IMO-61–63

Tables of contents on the Web, IMO-89–90
Templates, IMO-45–46
Theme dialog box, IMO-87–88
Themes, IMO-87–88
"The Software Edge" exercises
  customizing Web presentations, IMO-105
  embedding new Excel objects, IMO-33–34
  importing Excel data to Access, IMO-65–66
Toolbars. *See* specific name of toolbar

Undo button, IMO-19
Unformatted text, IMO-13
URL (uniform resource locator), IMO-72

Visual editing, IMO-19–20

Web, IMO-9
  Access tables, IMO-82–86
  hyperlinks, IMO-72–75
  saving document to HTML, IMO-78–82
  Search the Web button, IMO-77
Web components, IMO-90
Web editing, IMO-82
Web folders, IMO-97
Web Options command button, IMO-94, 96
Web Options dialog box, IMO-96
Web publishing
  Access tables, IMO-82–86
  applying Web themes to Word documents, IMO-87–88
  creating a framed table of contents in Word, IMO-89–90
  creating an interactive worksheet page, IMO-90–94
  customizing a Web presentation, IMO-94–97
  posting files to Web servers, IMO-97
  saving documents to HTML, IMO-78–82
Web servers, IMO-97
Web themes, IMO-87–88
Web toolbar, IMO-75–77
Windows Clipboard, IMO-2, 6
Windows taskbar, IMO-7
Wizards. See specific name of wizard
Word
  applying Web themes, IMO-87–88
  copying PowerPoint slides to, IMO-46–48
  creating a framed table of contents in, IMO-89–90
  embedding Excel data in a Word document, IMO-15–16
  exporting Access reports to, IMO-51–54
  inserting new Excel charts, IMO-22–23
  inserting new Excel worksheets, IMO-21–22
  integrating Access, IMO-51–57
  integrating with PowerPoint, IMO-46–51
  linking Excel data to a Word document, IMO-12–14
  mail merging, IMO-53–54
  outlines, IMO-42–46
  Paste Special dialog box, IMO-12–13
  pasting data from Word to Excel, IMO-9–12
  saving to HTML, IMO-78–82
World Wide Web. *See* Web

Z

Zooming in and out, IMO-7–8
  exporting Access reports to Word, IMO-52

Appendix

Preparing to Use Office XP

Getting Started with Windows

Microsoft Windows is an operating system intended for use on desktop and notebook computers. An *operating system* is a collection of software programs that manage, coordinate, and, in a sense, bring life to the computer hardware (the physical components of a computer). Every computer must have an operating system to control its basic input and output operations, such as receiving commands from the keyboard or mouse (input) and displaying information to the screen (output). An operating system is also responsible for managing the storage areas of the computer, namely, hard disks and diskettes, and for connecting to networks and the Internet. Without an operating system, you cannot communicate with your computer.

Starting Windows

feature

Microsoft Windows provides a graphical environment for working in your application software, such as Microsoft Office XP. In Windows, you display your work in one or more *windows* (lowercase "w") on the desktop. You interact with content in these windows using the keyboard, mouse, voice command, or other input device.

method

To start Windows:

- Turn on your computer and monitor.
- If you are attached to a network, enter your assigned user name and password.

practice

In this lesson, you start your computer and load Windows.

1. Turn on the power switches for your computer and monitor.
2. After a few seconds, a dialog box may appear asking you to enter your *User name* and *Password.* Enter this information now or ask your instructor for further instructions. (*Note:* If this dialog box doesn't display on your computer, proceed to the next step.)
3. The entire screen area is referred to as your *desktop.* If any windows are open on your desktop, do the following:
   CLICK: Close button (☒) in the top right-hand corner of each open window
   Your Windows desktop should now appear similar, but not identical, to Figure 1. Think of the Windows desktop as a virtual desktop where you view your work in progress. In addition, graphical *icons,* such as "My Computer," represent the tools on your desktop that you use most. Some icons allow you to launch applications. Other icons allow you to access and display the contents of storage areas. Since the Windows desktop represents your personal working area, it is likely that your desktop will look different from Figure 1.

Figure 1

The Windows desktop

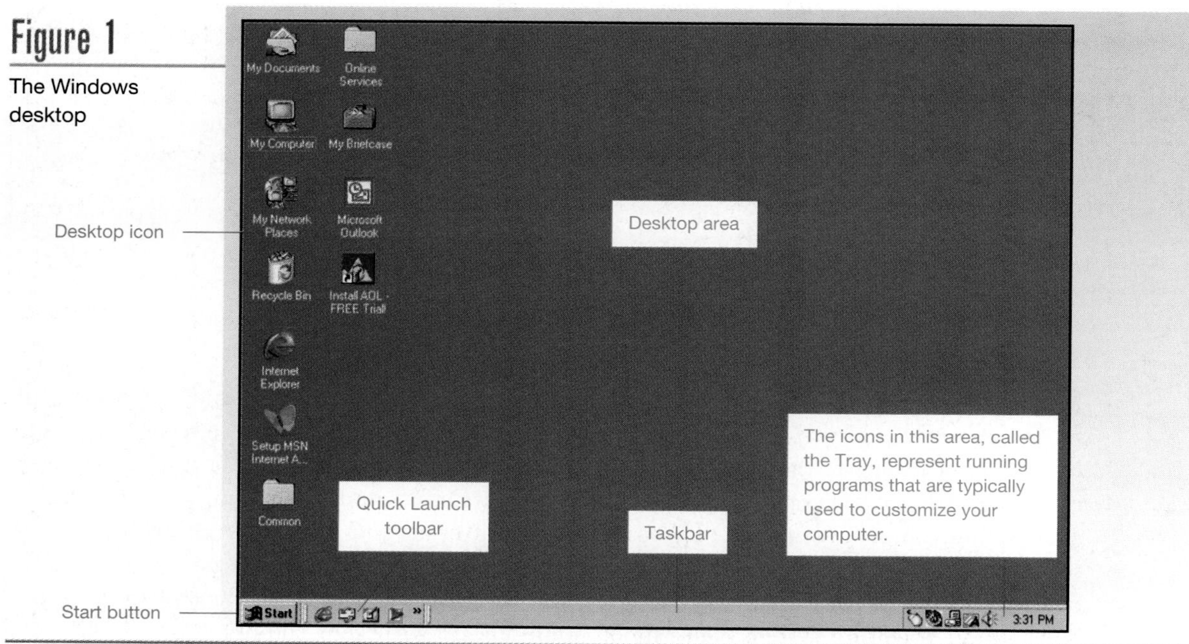

Using the Mouse

feature

A *mouse* is an input device that is rolled about on a desktop to direct a pointer on your computer's display screen. To work effectively in Windows, you must know how to use the mouse.

method

The most common mouse actions in Windows are:

Point	Slide the mouse on your desk to position the tip of the mouse pointer over the desired object on the screen.
Click	Press down and release the left mouse button quickly. This action, often referred to as *single-clicking,* is typically used for selecting items.
Right-click	Press down and release the right mouse button quickly. Right-clicking the mouse pointer on an object, such as an icon, displays a context-sensitive menu, if available.
Double-click	Press down and release the left mouse button twice in rapid succession. This action is typically used for opening items or programs.
Drag	Press down and hold the mouse button as you move the mouse pointer across the screen. When the mouse pointer reaches the desired location, release the mouse button. Dragging is used to move objects or windows or to create shortcuts for objects.

practice

In this lesson, you practice pointing, clicking, right-clicking, and double-clicking with the mouse. Having loaded Windows, ensure that your Windows desktop appears similar to Figure 1.

1. The default shape for the mouse pointer looks like a left-pointing diagonal arrow. As you work in Windows, the mouse pointer will change shape as you move it over different parts of the

screen or when an application performs a certain task. Each mouse pointer shape has its own purpose and may provide you with important information. There are four primary mouse pointer shapes you should be aware of:

	left arrow	Used to select objects, choose menu commands, and access buttons on the taskbar and application toolbars.
	hourglass	Informs you that Windows is occupied and requests that you wait.
	I-beam	Used to edit text and to position the insertion point (also called a *cursor*).
	hand	In the Help window, use the hand to select topics and definitions. When browsing your computer or the Web, use the hand to select a hyperlink that launches an application or takes you to a new document or bookmark.

2. To practice clicking with the mouse:
CLICK: "My Computer" icon ( ) on your desktop
The "My Computer" icon should now appear shaded. This shading indicates that the object is now selected.

3. To deselect the "My Computer" icon:
CLICK: on a blank area of the desktop

4. To practice right-clicking, do the following:
RIGHT-CLICK: on a blank area of the desktop
A context-sensitive menu is displayed, as shown here. In this learning guide, we refer to menus that you display by right-clicking as *right-click menus.*

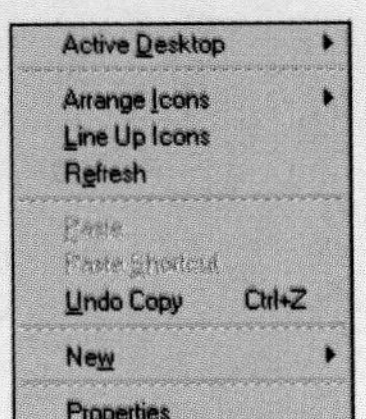

5. To remove the right-click menu:
CLICK: on a blank area of the desktop

6. To practice double-clicking, do the following:
DOUBLE-CLICK: "My Computer" icon ( ) on your desktop
A window should have opened, similar to the one shown in Figure 2.

7. Keep this window open for use in the next lesson.

Figure 2

The "My Computer" window

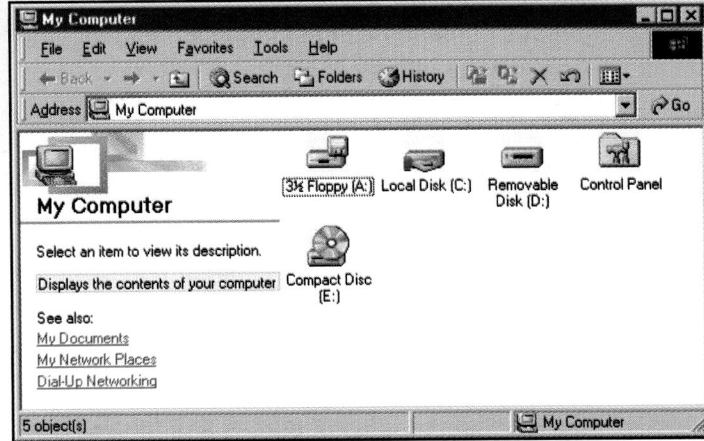

Using Dialog Boxes

feature

In Windows applications, dialog boxes are also used to display messages or to ask for the confirmation of commands. In a dialog box, you indicate the options you want to use and then click the OK command button when you're finished. Dialog boxes are sometimes composed of multiple tabs that allow you to access additional pages within the dialog box by simply clicking on the named tab.

method

A dialog box uses the following types of controls or components for collecting information:

Name	*Example*	*Action*
Check box	☑ Always ☐ Never	Click an option to turn it on or off. A check mark (✓) appears in the box when the option is turned on.
Command button	OK / Cancel	Click a command button to execute an action. Click OK to accept your selections or click Cancel to exit the dialog box.
Combo or drop-down list box	Screen Saver: None	Make a choice from the list that appears when you click the down arrow next to the box; only the currently selected option is visible.
List box	Wallpaper: (None), Arcade, Argyle	Make a choice from the scrollable list box; several choices, if not all, are always visible.
Option button	Display: Tile Center	Select an exclusive option from a group of related options.
Slide box	Desktop area: Less — More, 640 by 480 pixels	Drag the slider bar to make a selection, like using a radio's volume control.
Spin box	Wait: 6 minutes	Click the up and down arrows to the right of the text box until the number you want appears.
Tab	Contents | Index | Search	Click a named tab to access other pages in the dialog box.
Text box	File name: untitled	Click inside the text box and then type the desired information.

practice

In this lesson, you practice using a dialog box. Ensure that the "My Computer" window is open on the desktop.

1. To practice using a dialog box, let's open the Folder Options dialog box. In this step, you choose the Tools option by clicking it once in the Menu bar.
CHOOSE: Tools (as shown here)

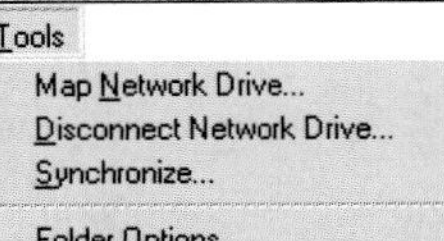

2. From the Tools menu, you will now choose the Folder Options by clicking it in the drop-down menu. Do the following:
CHOOSE: Folder Options from the Tools menu
The Folder Options dialog box appears, as shown in Figure 3. Depending on the version of Windows you are using, this dialog box displays a minimum of three tabs: *General, View,* and *File Types.* With Windows 2000, you'll see an additional tab named *Offline Files.*

Figure 3

Folder Options dialog box

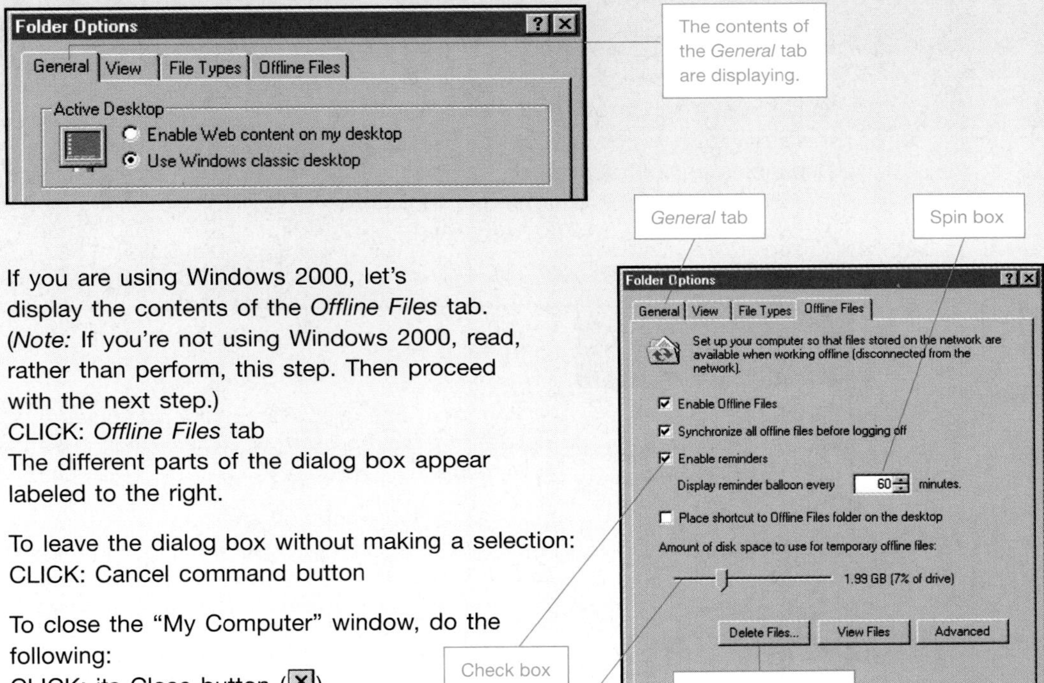

3. If you are using Windows 2000, let's display the contents of the *Offline Files* tab. (*Note:* If you're not using Windows 2000, read, rather than perform, this step. Then proceed with the next step.)
CLICK: *Offline Files* tab
The different parts of the dialog box appear labeled to the right.

4. To leave the dialog box without making a selection:
CLICK: Cancel command button

5. To close the "My Computer" window, do the following:
CLICK: its Close button (☒)

Shutting Down Windows

feature

In Windows, the task of exiting Windows is referred to as "shutting down" the computer. You should always follow the suggested steps in this lesson before turning off the computer's power. Otherwise, you run the risk of losing your data.

method

To shut down Windows:

- CLICK: Start button (Start)
- CHOOSE: Shut Down from the Start menu
- SELECT: Shut Down from the drop-down menu
- CLICK: OK command button
- Wait to turn off your computer until a message appears indicating that it is safe to do so.

practice

In this lesson, you display the Shut Down Windows dialog box.

1. CLICK: Start
   CHOOSE: Shut Down from the drop-down menu
   The Shut Down Windows dialog box should now display, as shown to the right. Depending on your version of Windows, the dialog box may appear differently on your computer.

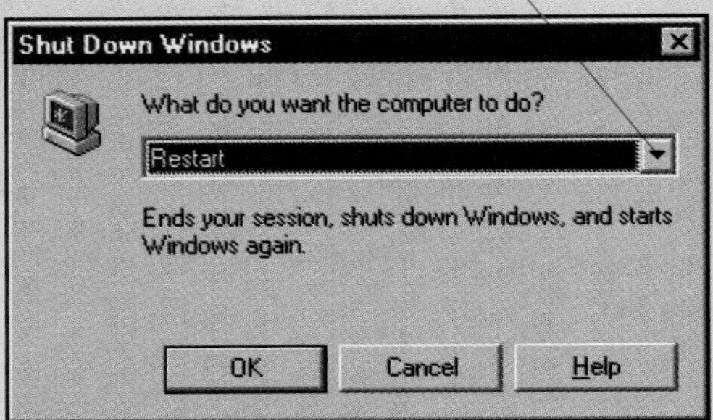

2. To display the options available in the drop-down list box, do the following:
   CLICK: the down arrow attached to the drop-down list box
   Depending on your version of Windows, four options will appear in the drop-down list. Table 1 summarizes these Shut Down options.

Table 1
Windows Shut Down options

Command	When to use
Log off	If more than one user shares your computer, this option may appear in the drop-down list. This option ends the current user's work session.
Shut down	Use this option when you are done with the current work session and want to turn off your computer. After choosing this option, wait to turn off your computer until Windows says it's all right to do so.
Restart	Use this option when you want to continue working with Windows but load a fresh copy of Windows into memory.
Stand by	In Stand By mode, your computer uses less power when it is idle. In this mode, if the power to your computer is interrupted, you lose any unsaved work that is in memory.
Hibernate	Hibernate mode shuts down your computer and saves any work currently stored in memory. When you bring the computer out of Hibernate mode, all previously open windows and documents are restored to your desktop.

3. To leave the menu without making a selection:
   CLICK: down arrow again
4. To leave the dialog box without shutting down your computer:
   CLICK: Cancel command button

Getting Help in Office XP

Microsoft Office XP provides several context-sensitive help features and a comprehensive library of online documentation. Like many developers trying to minimize the retail price of software and maximize profits, Microsoft has stopped shipping volumes of print-based documentation in favor of online and Web-based Help options. This module describes several methods for finding answers to your questions.

Using the Ask a Question Text Box

feature

The Ask a Question text box is located on the right side of the Menu bar and provides quick access to your application's Help system. This text box is a convenient starting point for finding answers to your questions. Furthermore, it is available across all of the Office XP applications.

method

To use the Ask a Question text box:

- CLICK: in the Ask a Question text box
- TYPE: **a question or topic**
- PRESS: ENTER

practice

In this lesson, you use the Ask a Question box to access an application's Help system.

1. Let's begin by loading an Office XP application. To load Microsoft Word, do the following:
CLICK: Start button (Start)
CHOOSE: Programs in the displayed menu
CHOOSE: Microsoft Word from the list of programs
The Microsoft Word application window should appear.

2. Locate the Ask a Question text box on the right side of the Menu bar (Figure 4).

Figure 4

Microsoft Word application window

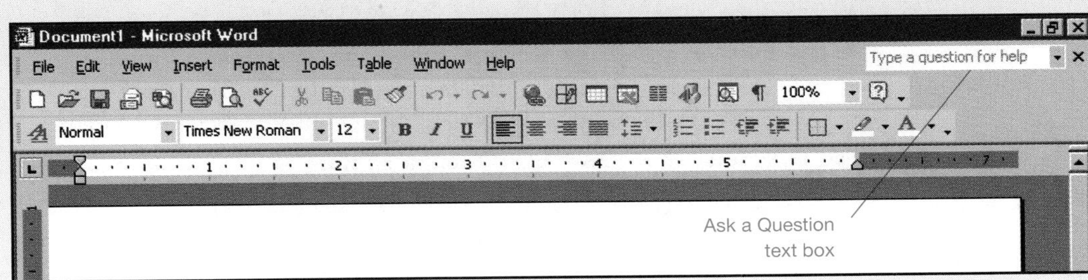

3. To find out how to write a formal letter using Word, do the following:
CLICK: in the Ask a Question text box
TYPE: **create a letter**
PRESS: ENTER
A drop-down menu should now appear beneath the text box, as shown to the right.

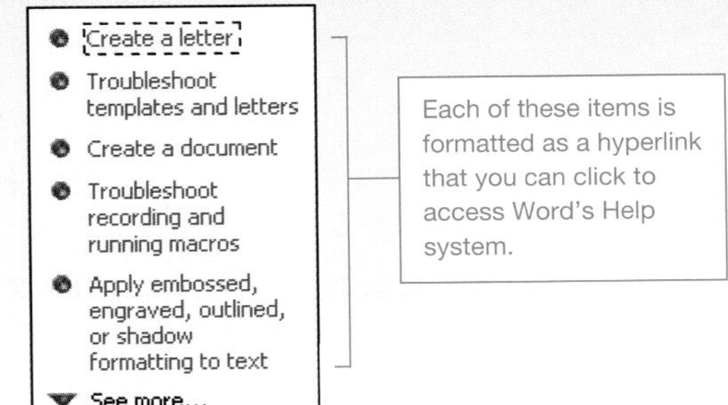

4. To display information for a specific topic:
CLICK: "Create a letter" topic

5. For easier viewing, let's maximize the Windows Help window. Do the following:
CLICK: Maximize button (□)
Your screen should now appear similar to Figure 5.

Figure 5

Help window (partial view)

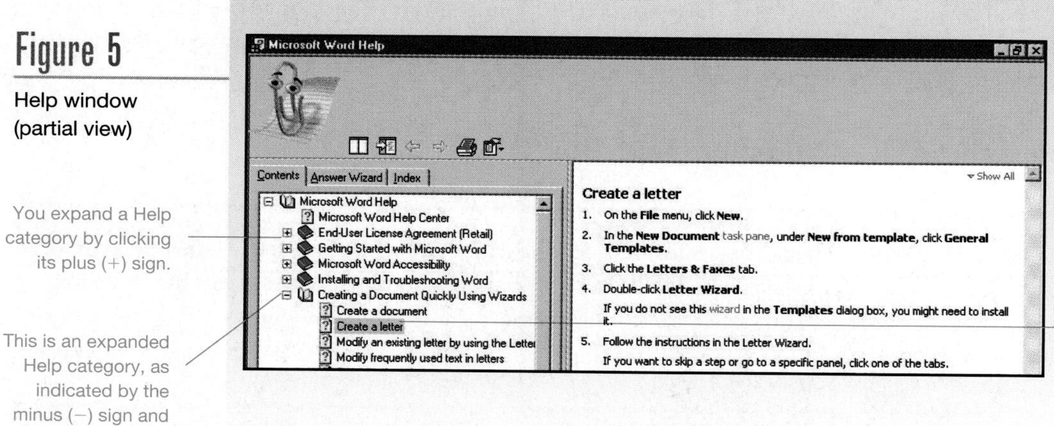

This is the selected Help topic. Its description is displaying on the right.

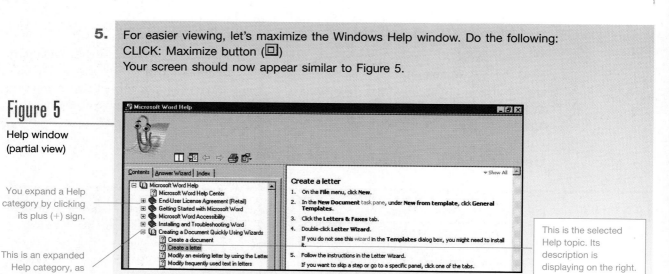

6. Keep the Help window open for use in the next lesson.

Using the Help Window

feature →

You can think of the Help window as the front door to your application's vast help resources. The Help window provides three different tools, each on its own tab, to help you find the information you need quickly and easily. The *Contents* tab displays a list of help topics organized as a hierarchy of books and pages. Think of this tab as the Table of Contents for the entire Help system. The *Answer Wizard* tab lets you obtain answers by typing in words and phrases. The Index tab displays an alphabetical list of keywords and phrases, similar to a traditional book index.

method →

To access the Help window:

- Use the Ask a Question box and then select a suggested topic.
- CHOOSE: Help, Microsoft *application* Help from the Menu bar
  (*Note:* For this command to work, you must have previously deactivated the Office Assistant, a procedure we describe in the next lesson.)

In this lesson, you use the Help window. Ensure that the Microsoft Word Help window is displaying. Your screen should appear similar to Figure 5.

1. Note that the *Contents* tab is selected and that the "Creating a Document Quickly Using Wizard" category is expanded. Let's expand a different topic.
DOUBLE-CLICK: "Getting Started with Microsoft Word" topic
A topic and a few additional categories should now be displaying.

2. To display information about what's new in Microsoft Word:
CLICK: "What's new in Microsoft Word" topic
Your screen should now appear similar to Figure 6.

Figure 6

Help window: *Contents* tab (partial view)

The *Contents* tab is currently selected. Use this tab to display the Table of Contents for the entire Help system.

The *Answer Wizard* tab enables you to obtain help information by typing in questions.

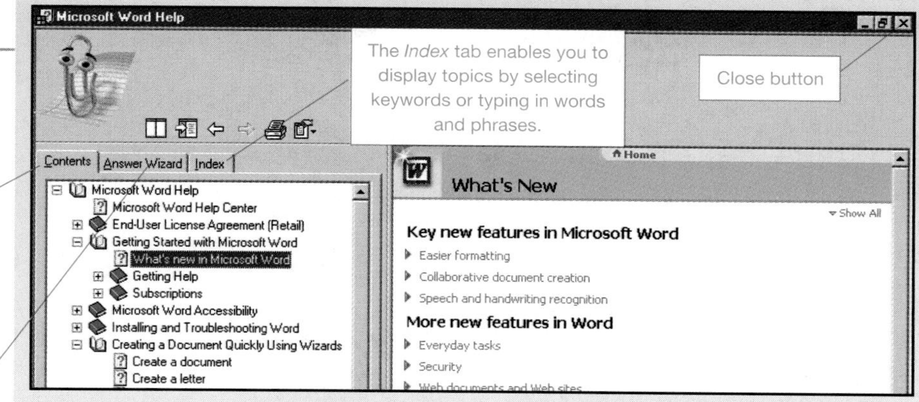

3. Now, let's practice using the *Index* tab.
   CLICK: *Index* tab

4. To retrieve help information on the Mail Merge command:
   TYPE: **merge**
   PRESS: ENTER
   In this case, there are several merge-related topics to choose from.

5. To display information about the "Create and print form letters" topic:
   CLICK: "Create and print form letters" in the topics list
   The Help window should now appear similar to Figure 7.

Figure 7

Help window: *Index* tab (partial view)

The Print button lets you print this topic for later reference.

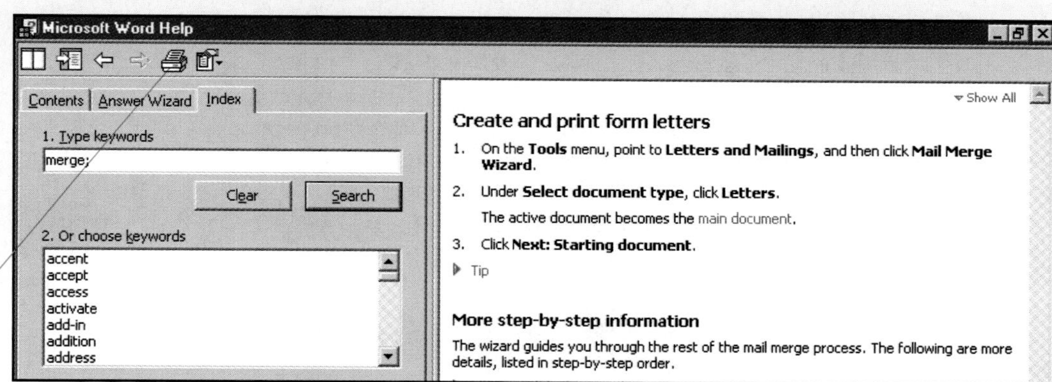

6. To close the Help window:
   CLICK: its Close button (☒)

Using the Office Assistant

feature

The Office Assistant watches your keystrokes and mouse clicks as you work and offers suggestions and shortcuts to make you more productive and efficient. For example, in Word, if the Assistant sees that you're creating a letter, it will provide a list of Help topics and tips for creating the letter. You can choose to hide or turn off the Assistant, or otherwise customize it to meet your needs.

method

To hide or show the Office Assistant:

- CHOOSE: Help, Hide the Office Assistant

or

- CHOOSE: Help, Show the Office Assistant

To obtain help from the Office Assistant:

- CLICK: the Office Assistant character to display the tip window
- CLICK: a displayed Help topic

or

- TYPE: **one or more keywords** in the text box and then press ENTER

To deactivate the Office Assistant:

- RIGHT-CLICK: the Office Assistant character
- CHOOSE: Options from the right-click menu
- SELECT: *Use the Office Assistant* check box to clear the check box

practice

In this lesson, you practice using the Office Assistant. Ensure that Microsoft Word Help is loaded.

1. If the Office Assistant character isn't displaying, do the following:
CHOOSE: Help, Show the Office Assistant
An Office Assistant character should be displaying, as shown below. Because you can select alternate Office Assistant characters, the character on your computer might not be the same as ours.

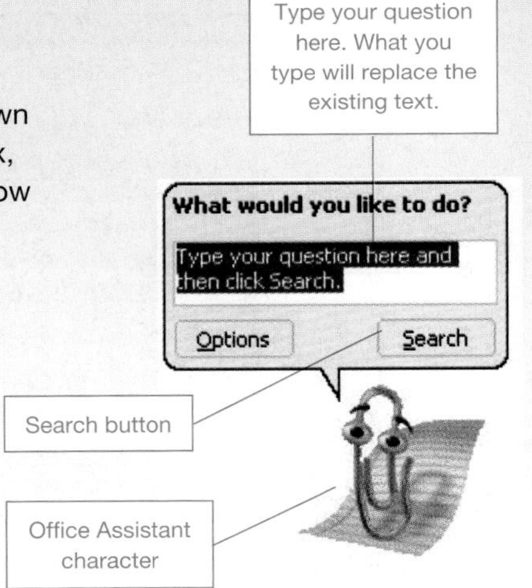

2. To display a tip window:
CLICK: the Office Assistant character
The Office Assistant and associated tip window are shown to the right. Similar to using the Ask a Question text box, described earlier, you type your question in the tip window and then press ENTER or click the Search button.
A list of suggested topics will display.

3. To remove a tip window:
CLICK: in your document
The insertion point is blinking at the very beginning of your document.

4. To close Microsoft Word:
CLICK: Close button (☒) appearing in the top right-hand corner

In Addition GETTING HELP ON THE WEB

You can obtain additional help from the Web by choosing Help, Office on the Web from your application's Menu bar.

NOTES

NOTES

NOTES

NOTES